STRATEGIES TOWARD SUSTAINABLE DEVELOPMENT:

IMPLEMENTING AGENDA 21

Nicholas A. Robinson, Editor

Gilbert & Sarah Kerlin Distinguished Professor
of Environmental Law
Pace University School of Law
and
Chair, Commission on Environmental Law
International Union for the Conservation of
Nature and Natural Resources

Oceana Publications, Inc., Dobbs Ferry, New York

Library of Congress Control Number: 2004104265

ISBN 0-379-21520-9

© 2004 by Oceana Publications, Inc.

Manufactured in the United States of America on acid-free paper.

SUMMARY TABLE OF CONTENTS

ABOUT THE EDITOR . . . . **xi**

INTRODUCTION—GLOBAL ENVIRONMENTAL STEWARDSHIP: IMPLEMENTING
AGENDA 21 AND OTHER INTERNATIONAL LEGAL INSTRUMENTS FOR
SUSTAINABLE DEVELOPMENT **1**

AGENDA 21—ANNOTATED ACTION PLAN. **47**

MILLENNIUM DECLARATION AND REPORT. **571**

MONTERREY CONSENSUS OF THE INTERNATIONAL CONFERENCE ON
FINANCING FOR DEVELOPMENT AND FOLLOW-UP REPORT **655**

JOHANNESBURG DECLARATION ON SUSTAINABLE DEVELOPMENT AND
PLAN OF IMPLEMENTATION OF THE WORLD SUMMIT ON SUSTAINABLE
DEVELOPMENT **757**

UNITED NATIONS RESOLUTIONS AND IMPLEMENTING MEASURES **839**

DOCUMENT INDEX **933**

DETAILED TABLE OF CONTENTS

ABOUT THE EDITOR, NICHOLAS A. ROBINSON xi

INTRODUCTION

GLOBAL ENVIRONMENTAL STEWARDSHIP: Implementing Agenda 21 and
Other International Legal Instruments for Sustainable Development 3

    A. Shaping International Environmental Governance Through Action Plans
    and Policy Priorities 4

    B. The Rio Consensus on International Environmental Stewardship 7

    C. Issues Regarding Environmental Governance 10

    D. The Growing Urgency of Earth's Environmental Problems 12

    E. Contemporary Intergovernmental Environmental Governance 16

    F. Whither Environmental Governance? 19

    G. Factors in Future Deliberations on Environmental Governance. 28

    H. The Prospects for Environmental Governance 39

    I. The Roadmap Forward 44

AGENDA 21
ANNOTATED ACTION PLAN

CHAPTER 1 Preamble 49

SECTION 1: SOCIAL AND ECONOMIC DIMENSIONS

CHAPTER 2   International Cooperation to Accelerate Sustainable
Development in Developing Countries and Related Domestic Policies 51

CHAPTER 3 Combating Poverty 67

CHAPTER 4 Changing Consumption Patterns 73

CHAPTER 5 Demographic Dynamics and Sustainability 81

CHAPTER 6 Protecting and Promoting Human Health 93

CHAPTER 7 Promoting Sustainable Human Settlement Development 113

CHAPTER 8 Integration of Environment and Development in Decision-Making . . 139

SECTION 2: CONSERVATION AND MANAGEMENT
OF RESOURCES FOR DEVELOPMENT

CHAPTER 9 Protection of the Atmosphere 157

CHAPTER 10 Integrated Approach to the Planning and Management of Land
Resources 169

CHAPTER 11 Combating Deforestation 177

CHAPTER 12 Managing Fragile Ecosystems: Combating Desertification and Drought. 197

CHAPTER 13 Managing Fragile Ecosystems: Sustainable Mountain Development . 219

CHAPTER 14 Promoting Sustainable Agriculture and Rural Development 229

CHAPTER 15 Conservation of Biological Diversity. 263

CHAPTER 16 Environmentally Sound Management of Biotechnology. 273

CHAPTER 17 Protection of the Oceans, All Kinds of Seas, Including Enclosed and Semi-Enclosed Seas, and Coastal Areas and the Protection, Rational Use and Development of Their Living Resources 295

CHAPTER 18 Protection of the Quality and Supply of Freshwater Resources: Application of Integrated Approaches to the Development, Management and Use of Water Resources 335

CHAPTER 19 Environmentally Sound Management of Toxic Chemicals, Including Prevention of Illegal International Traffic in Toxic and Dangerous Products 379

CHAPTER 20 Environmentally Sound Management of Hazardous Wastes Including Prevention of Illegal International Traffic in Hazardous Wastes 401

CHAPTER 21 Environmentally Sound Management of Solid Wastes and Sewage-Related Issues 419

CHAPTER 22 Safe and Environmentally Sound Management of Radioactive Wastes 439

SECTION 3: STRENGTHENING THE ROLE OF MAJOR GROUPS

CHAPTER 23 Preamble. 443

CHAPTER 24 Global Action for Women Towards Sustainable and Equitable Development 445

CHAPTER 25 Children and Youth in Sustainable Development 451

CHAPTER 26 Recognizing and Strengthening the Role of Indigenous People and Their Communities. 457

CHAPTER 27 Strengthening the Role of Non-Governmental Organizations: Partners for Sustainable Development 463

CHAPTER 28 Local Authorities Initiatives in Support of Agenda 21. 467

CHAPTER 29 Strengthening the Role of Workers and Their Trade Unions 471

CHAPTER 30 Strengthening the Role of Business and Industry 475

CHAPTER 31 Scientific and Technological Community 481

CHAPTER 32 Strengthening the Role of Farmers 487

SECTION 4. MEANS OF IMPLEMENTATION

CHAPTER 33 Financial Resources and Mechanisms 493

CHAPTER 34 Transfer of Environmentally Sound Technology, Cooperation and Capacity-Building. 499

CHAPTER 35 Science for Sustainable Development 509

CHAPTER 36 Promoting Education, Public Awareness and Training 523

CHAPTER 37 National Mechanisms and International Cooperation for Capacity-Building in Developing Countries. 535

CHAPTER 38 International Institutional Arrangements 543

CHAPTER 39 International Legal Instruments and Mechanisms. 557

CHAPTER 40 Information for Decision-Making 563

MILLENNIUM DECLARATION
AND
REPORT

MILLENNIUM DECLARATION, UN Res. 55/2 573

   I. Values and Principles 573

   II. Peace, Security and Disarmament 575

   III. Development and Poverty Eradication 576

   IV. Protecting our Common Environment 578

   V. Human Rights, Democracy and Good Governance 579

   VI. Protecting the Vulnerable 580

   VII. Meeting the Special Needs of Africa 580

   VIII. Strengthening the United Nations 581

MILLENNIUM REPORT "WE THE PEOPLES: THE ROLE OF THE UNITED NATIONS IN THE TWENTY-FIRST CENTURY", UN General Assembly Report 54/2000 583

   I. New Century, New Challenges 583

   II. Globalization and Governance 586

   III. Freedom from Want. 595

   IV. Freedom from Fear 618

   V. Sustaining Our Future 630

   VI. Renewing the United Nations 642

   For Consideration by the Summit. 650

MONTERREY CONSENSUS OF THE INTERNATIONAL CONFERENCE ON FINANCING FOR DEVELOPMENT AND FOLLOW-UP REPORT

UNITED NATIONS REPORT OF THE INTERNATIONAL CONFERENCE ON FINANCING FOR DEVELOPMENT, Monterrey, Mexico, 18-22 March 2002, UN Doc. A/CONF. 198/11 657

Chapter I. Resolutions Adopted by the Conference 657

Chapter II. Attendance and Organization of Work 676

Chapter III. Report of the High-Level Officials Segment 684

Chapter IV. Report of the Ministerial Segment 685

Chapter V. Report of the Summit Segment 709

Chapter VI. Adoption of the Monterrey Consensus 725

Chapter VII. Report of the Credentials Committee 725

Chapter VIII. Adoption of the Report of the Conference 727

Chapter IX. Closure of the Conference 727

Annex I. List of documents 728

Annex II. Opening Statements 729

   Statement by Vicente Fox Quesada, President of Mexico and President of the International Conference on Financing for Development 729

   Statement by Kofi Annan, Secretary-General of the United Nations 731

   Statement by Han Seung-soo, President of the General Assembly of the United Nations 732

   Statement by James D. Wolfensohn, President of the World Bank Group 734

   Statement by Horst Koehler, Managing Director of the International Monetary Fund 737

   Statement by Mike Moore, Director-General, World Trade Organization 740

Annex III. Parallel and Associated Activities 743

FOLLOW-UP TO THE INTERNATIONAL CONFERENCE ON FINANCING FOR DEVELOPMENT, UN General Assembly Report 58/494 747

I. Introduction 747

II. Consideration of proposals 749

III. Recommendation of the Second Committee 753

JOHANNESBURG DECLARATION ON SUSTAINABLE DEVELOPMENT
AND
PLAN OF IMPLEMENTATION OF THE
WORLD SUMMIT ON SUSTAINABLE DEVELOPMENT (WSSD)

THE JOHANNESBURG DECLARATION ON SUSTAINABLE DEVELOPMENT,   4 September 2002, UN Doc. A/CONF. 199/L-6 Rev.2 759

From our Origins to the Future 759

From Stockholm to Rio de Janeiro to Johannesburg 760

The Challenges We Face 760

Our Commitment to Sustainable Development 761

Multilateralism is the Future 762

Making it Happen! 763

PLAN OF IMPLEMENTATION OF THE WORLD SUMMIT ON SUSTAINABLE DEVELOPMENT,   4 September 2002, UN Doc. A/CONF. 199/L-6 Rev.2 765

I. Introduction 765

II. Poverty Eradication 766

III. Changing Unsustainable Patterns of Consumption and Production 771

IV. Protecting and Managing the Natural Resource Base of Economic and Social Development 779

V. Sustainable Development in a Globalizing World 799

VI. Health and Sustainable Development 800

VII. Sustainable Development of Small Island Developing States 803

VIII. Sustainable Development for Africa 806

IX. Other Regional Initiatives 811

X. Means of Implementation 814

XI. Institutional Framework for Sustainable Development 829

UNITED NATIONS RESOLUTIONS AND IMPLEMENTING MEASURES

Agenda 21

GENERAL ASSEMBLY RESOLUTION 47/190   Report of the United Nations Conference on Environment and Development 841

GENERAL ASSEMBLY RESOLUTION 47/194   Capacity-Building for Agenda 21 843

GENERAL ASSEMBLY RESOLUTION 47/191   Institutional Arrangements to Follow Up the United Nations Conference on Environment and Development . . . 845

GENERAL ASSEMBLY RESOLUTION 58/218   Implementation of Agenda 21, the Programme for the Further Implementation of Agenda 21 and the Outcomes of the World Summit on Sustainable Development 855

GENERAL ASSEMBLY RESOLUTION 58/219   United Nations Decade of Education for Sustainable Development 861

Climate

GENERAL ASSEMBLY RESOLUTION 58/243 Protection of Global Climate for
Present and Future Generations of Mankind 863

Biological Diversity

GENERAL ASSEMBLY RESOLUTION 58/212 Convention on Biological Diversity. . . 867

Desertification

GENERAL ASSEMBLY RESOLUTION 58/242 Implementation of the United
Nations Convention to Combat Desertification in Those Countries
Experiencing Serious Drought and/or Desertification, Particularly in Africa 871

Habitat

GENERAL ASSEMBLY RESOLUTION 58/226 Implementation of the outcome
of the United Nations Conference on Human Settlements (Habitat II) and
the strengthening of the United Nations Human Settlements Programme
(UN-Habitat). 875

GENERAL ASSEMBLY SECOND COMMITTEE REPORT 58/491 Implementation
of the Outcome of the United Nations Conference on Human Settlements
(Habitat II) and of the Twenty-Fifth Special Session of the General Assembly 881

Sustainable Development

GENERAL ASSEMBLY RESOLUTION 57/261 Promoting an Integrated
Management Approach to the Caribbean Sea Area in the Context of
Sustainable Development 891

GENERAL ASSEMBLY RESOLUTION 58/213 Further Implementation of
the Programme of Action for the Sustainable Development of Small Island
Developing States. 897

Ocean Resources

GENERAL ASSEMBLY RESOLUTION 57/142 Large-Scale Pelagic Drift-Net
Fishing, Unauthorized Fishing in Zones of National Jurisdiction and on the
High Seas/Illegal, Unreported and Unregulated Fishing, Fisheries By-Catch
and Discards, and Other Developments 903

GENERAL ASSEMBLY RESOLUTION 57/143 Agreement for the Implementation
of the Provisions of the United Nations Convention on the Law of the Sea of
10 December 1982 Relating to the Conservation and Management
of Straddling Fish Stocks and Highly Migratory Fish Stocks 911

GENERAL ASSEMBLY RESOLUTION 58/14 Sustainable Fisheries, Including
Through the 1995 Agreement for the Implementation of the Provisions of
the United Nations Convention on the Law of the Sea of 10 December 1982
Relating to the Conservation and Management of Straddling Fish Stocks and
Highly Migratory Fish Stocks, and Related Instruments 919

DOCUMENT INDEX

DOCUMENT INDEX 935

Nicholas A. Robinson

Gilbert & Sarah Kerlin Distinguished Professor in Environmental Law
Pace University School of Law

Prof. Nicholas A. Robinson has specialized in environmental law since his appointment in 1970 to serve on the Legal Advisory Committee to the President's Council on Environmental Quality. He founded the environmental legal studies program at Pace University School of Law in 1978, after practicing environmental law in New York City and clerking for federal Judge Morris E. Lasker. He currently holds the senior position in environmental law internationally, having been elected by the World Conservation Congress as Chair of the Commission on Environmental Law of the International Union for the Conservation of Nature and Natural Resources (IUCN). In 1992 the l'Université Libre de Bruxelles conferred on him the Elizabeth Haub Prize In Environmental Law. He has taught at the Law Faculty of the National University of Singapore and at University College (London), and has lectured by invitation at universities across Europe, Canada, South America, China and S.E. Asia, Australia, Southern Africa, and elsewhere. He is author or editor of 2 treatises, seven books, and over 150 articles; his two treatises have been translated and published in Russian and Chinese. Among his civic contributions within New York, he served as General Counsel and Deputy Commissioner of the State's Department of Environmental Conservation, chaired and organized the Greenway Heritage Conservancy for the Hudson River Valley, and chaired and organized the Freshwater Wetlands Appeals Board. He is the draftsman of New York's Tidal Wetland Act and Wild Birds Law. From 1974-92, he served under five presidents as a US delegate to the environmental law negotiations between the USA and USSR, and later served as an expert on Russian environmental law to the United Nations, the Food & Agricultural Organization, the World Bank and others. He currently serves as IUCN's Legal Advisor and is Legal Advisor to IUCN's Observer Mission to the United Nations; he previously practiced environmental law internationally with law firms in London and New York. He has served by election as the Chairman of the Board for the World Environment Center and the International Vice President of the Sierra Club, and has chaired environmental law committees for many bar associations. He is a graduate of Brown University (A.B., 1967, Phi Beta Kappa) and Columbia University School of Law (J.D., 1970, cum laude), and was an International Fellow at the Council on Foreign Relations (1977). Pace University invested him as its James Hopkins Professor of Law (1990-91) and with the Gilbert & Sarah Kerlin Chair in Environmental Law in 1999.

INTRODUCTION

Global Environmental Stewardship:

Implementing Agenda 21 and Other International Legal Instruments for Sustainable Development

Introduction
by
Nicholas A. Robinson[1]

This book sets forth the agreed action plans for governments to attain sustainable development: "development that meets the needs of the present without compromising the ability of future generations to meet their own needs."[2] The documents gathered here, for the first time, collectively set forth the strategic decisions, action plans and priorities by which the international community of nations will move toward sustainable development. Together these documents guide investment decisions of governments and direct foreign investment by the private sector in the development of water, sewage, energy, ecosystem management, agricultural production, urban settlements and housing and other infrastructure within developing nations and the nations with economies in transition from centrally planned economies to market economies.

As a road map toward sustainable development, these documents also form the foundation for the emerging world order concerning environmental governance of the Earth. There is no comprehensive United Nations or other international body with comprehensive authority for the management of Earth's biosphere. The bounty that sustains life on Earth is governed by a Balkanized and fragmented set of controls. The control of natural systems is not yet fully grounded on scientific knowledge about how to sustainably manage nature. The control often advantages the rich and leaves the growing number of poor impoverished. The irony is that the global trends show a deterioration of global

---

1   Gilbert & Sarah Kerlin Distinguished Professor of Environmental Law, Pace University School of Law, and Chair, Commission on Environmental Law, International Union for the Conservation of Nature and Natural Resources.

2   U.N. World Commission on Environment and Development, *Our Common Future,* at p. 43 (Oxford University Press, 1987).

conditions that threaten the rich and the poor alike. Within "spaceship earth" all fates are linked.

Establishing the systems to manage these links is the ultimate objective of the decisions reflected on these pages. As the recommendations set forth here are implemented, nations will decide how to cooperate further together. They are not yet ready to combine forces into a new international agency for environmental stewardship. Over time, their experience in implementing the decisions of Agenda 21 may build their confidence to the point where this becomes possible.

This introduction surveys the broader context for the often specific and incremental decisions of Agenda 21, the UN Millennium Declaration, the Johannesburg Plan of Implementation, and other related documents. These are "soft law" instruments, not treaties or statutes. As such, they provide fundamental guidance in a comprehensive way to all the sectors that help determine development policy, public and private. They have emerged in the midst of on-going diplomatic negotiations, described broadly in this introductory essay. There is a consensus among academic and professional experts that global environmental stewardship requires a new international agency. There is, however, too much anxiety among foreign ministries and governments to support establishing such a body at this time. Although the proposals for a new agency are not a part of this roadmap in the documents provided here, they are a part of the wider debate surrounding the production of these documents, and thus are referenced in this introduction.

A. Shaping International Environmental Governance Through Action Plans and Policy Priorities

Today environmental law and management are important elements of government in practically every nation. In 2002, the United Nations World Summit on Environment and Development in its Johannesburg Declaration stated that environmental protection is one of the three pillars of "sustainable development," together with the economic and social pillars. How environmental stewardship will further sustainable development has been the subject of critically important intergovernmental negotiations since 1992. The decisions resulting from these deliberations are set forth in a set of documents that have been gathered and published together here for the first time. Collectively, they provide the foundation for an emerging network of obligations that are coming to comprise international environmental governance.

It is through the implementation of these decisions, rather than in the establishment of any new environmental intergovernmental organizations, that the framework of international governance of the environment is being forged. The need for international cooperation in the field of environmental protection was not much understood before the United Nations convened the 1972 Conference on the Human Environment in Stockholm. To be sure, in 1948 France and other nations had established the International Union for the Conservation of Nature and Natural Resources (IUCN),[3] but it was only in connection with the 1972 Stockholm Conference that nations learned to build environmental ministries and work across sectors nationally. The nations at Stockholm recommended the establishment of the United Nations Environment Programme (UNEP), under the U.N. Economic & Social Council. As UNEP's small secretariat and governing council went to work, the nations built a system of multilateral environmental agreements, through which they could address global and regional environmental problems. In doing so, national governments discovered how difficult it is to reshape entrenched national practices in order to curb pollution and conserve natural resources. With growing experience and knowledge, national governments have come to realize that no one government alone can safeguard the environment, and that international cooperation needs to be enhanced.

Twenty years after Stockholm, and largely because nations by then had developed the capacity to assess environmental conditions, the international community had come to understand that environmental conditions were deteriorating more extensively than had earlier been understood. IUCN had called for "sustainable development," in its action plan, "Caring for the Earth: A Strategy for Sustainable Living," launched in 1980.[4] Subsequently, the UN World Commission on Environment and Development, chaired by Gro Harlem Brundtland, further documented the worsening environmental trends around the world. As a result of the release of the Brundtland Commission's report, *Our Common Future*, in 1987,[5] the General Assembly of the United Nations decided in 1990 to convene in 1992 the UN Conference on Environment and Development (UNCED) in Rio de Janeiro. UNCED capped two years of intense negotiation, in its Preparatory Committee, of an Action Plan to cope with environmental degradation, and to build the environmental foundations for sustainable development. This Action Plan is *Agenda 21*, the longest "soft law" instrument promulgated to date. It is a blue print for environmental, international cooperation across all sectors.

Despite, however, the clarity of UNCED's extensive recommendations in Agenda 21, and the annual oversight assessing the implementation of these recommendations through the deliberations of the UN Commission on Sustainable Development, which UN Member States had established under the UN Economic & Social Council to oversee the implementation of Agenda 21, the momentum to organize the international community to address environmental problems flagged subsequent to Rio. In the interim also, the United Nations convened a Millennium Summit on economic and social development, which also adopted priorities for sustainable development. These did not attract the same amount of global attention as had the 1992 Earth Summit, and in order to refocus, and

---

3   See Martin Holdgate, *The Green Web* (Earthscan, London; Island Press, USA, 2000).

4   IUCN, in cooperation with UNEP and the WWF (the Worldwide Fund for Nature), published *Caring for the Earth: A Strategy for Sustainable Living* (Gland, Switzerland, IUCN, 1980) reprinted in Mitchell Beazley, *Caring for the Earth* (U.K., Reed International Books, 1993).

5   UN World Commission on Environment and Development, *Our Common Future* (Oxford University Press, 1987).

re-energize efforts to advance international environmental governance toward attaining sustainable development goals, the United Nations General Assembly decided to convene the World Summit on Sustainable Development (WSSD) in Johannesburg in 2002. The WSSD was to chart a path toward attaining the Millennium Sustainable Development priorities, and this mission competed with attempts by UNEP and others to help the nations enhance their system of international environmental governance.

Despite the widely acknowledged understanding that environmental conditions world-wide have deteriorated since UNCED in 1992,[6] the WSSD proved to be capable of responding only modestly to the gathering challenges. The nations assembled in Johannesburg made modest progress in addressing sustainable energy, a subject not covered in Agenda 21, and they achieved some consensus that the supply of potable water and sewage treatment must be an urgent global priority, but they could do little more. No decisions were taken to address ways to improve the international institutional systems for managing environmental problems. This reluctance to grapple with environmental governance was all the more remarkable because it constituted a retreat from the prior consensus that enhancing international environmental governance was a priority, and should have been counted as one of the outcomes from the WSSD.[7] The WSSD simply reaffirmed the governance systems already in place as of 1992, and urged the existing bodies to do their jobs more effectively.

Why did the issue of international environmental governance stall at the WSSD, and whither will these issues now tend? While it is premature to hazard answers to these queries, what is clear is that there is a growing congruence among the national environmental management systems. These harmonized national programs make it *possible* to implement the recommendations of both the Rio Earth Summit and the WSSD. Whether competing political causes, such as concerns over terrorism or world trade, will hinder this implementation, remains to be seen. If not now, then in 2007 (15 years after Agenda 21) or 2012 (on the 20th anniversary), the nations will convene again because the integrity of many of Earth's natural systems upon which human well-being depends will have eroded faster than solutions were set in place to sustain them.

---

6   See, e.g., Paragraph 1.1 of *Agenda 21*, and the several annual reports of the World Watch Institute, *State of the World*, 1984-2004 (Washington, D.C.).

7   For instance, the Malmö Ministerial Declaration had declared, ". . . the 2002 conference should review the requirement for a greatly strengthened institutional structure for international environmental governance based on an assessment of future needs for an institutional architecture that has the capacity to effectively address wide-ranging environmental threats in a globalized world. UNEP's role in this regard should be strengthened and its financial base broadened and made more predictable." See Global Ministerial Environment Forum, U.N. Doc.UNEP/GCSS.VI/L.3 (May 31, 2000). See also Chapters 38 ("International Institutional Arrangements") and 39 ("International Legal Instruments and Mechanisms") in *Agenda 21*.

B. The Rio Consensus on
International Environmental Stewardship

The root causes for the impasse regarding international environmental governance at the WSSD are several. As scientists report increases in pollution, in desertification, in losses of habitat, and the like, it is apparent that Earth's governments are failing to respect the fundamental human right to live and work in a healthy and balanced environment. This occurs despite moral and religious injunctions to the contrary; Earth's theocratic and secular governments alike are failing to heed the religious and ethical belief common to every diverse cultural tradition, which is to respect nature.[8] It would seem that world events have conspired to distract governments from making environmental stewardship a priority.

Since the Rio "Earth Summit" in 1992, the Cold War ended. Countries once with centrally planned economies are rapidly converting to a market economy, and are not building as rapidly their own internal environmental governance system.[9] Significant governmental resources have been invested in developing liberalized trade, establishing the World Trade Organization, and in coping with the unanticipated protests against "globalization." Since 2001, governments preoccupied with immediate concerns for combating terrorism appear to be incapable of also addressing the festering problems of environmental security for their people and resources. In short, in the decade after UNCED, other priorities intruded so that there was virtually no progress in advancing environmental governance.

Considering the WSSD's impasse in this historical perspective, and the need to respond to immediate political situations, perhaps it is too much to expect that governance systems might respond rapidly to threats that grow only incrementally and gradually, as is the case with most environmental problems. There is no external enemy, for each society and economy contributes to the problems. Moreover, given that the system of nation states has a crowded tradi-

---

8   See, e.g. "Ecological Crisis: A Common Responsibility," a Message of His Holiness Pope John Paul II for the Celebration of the World Day of Peace (1990): "In our day, there is a growing awareness that world peace is threatened not only be the arms race, regional conflicts and continued injustices among peoples and nations, but also by a lack of respect for nature, by the plundering of natural resources and by a progressive decline in the quality of life. Respect for life, and above all for the dignity of the human person is the ultimate guiding norm for any sound economic, industrial or scientific progress. . . . No peaceful society can afford to neglect either respect for life or the fact that there is an integrity to creation."

9   For instance, in 1998, President Putin dismantled the independent Environment Ministry (then the State Committee on the Environment, "Goskomecologia") and merged it into the Natural Resources Ministry of the Russian Federation; at roughly the same time, China upgraded its National Environmental Protection Administration to ministerial status, in recognition the rapid economic growth has also produced vast pollution of air and water, and depletion of natural resources.

tional agenda,[10] national governments take action to address environmental threats only gradually. Throughout the post-UNCED decade, both international and national decision-makers largely assumed that the laws of nature would function "normally" to serve human society. Although fish populations collapsed in the wake of excessive fishing, entire species became extinct, the glaciers melted and other warning signs persisted, by and large governments and their leaders continued to take the bounty of nature for granted.

Between the 1972 Stockholm Conference on the Human Environment, and the 1992 UN Conference on Environment and Development in Rio de Janeiro, nations concentrated on adopting their national norms and standards needed to address environmental threats. National legislation established environmental rules, constitutions were amended to provide the right to a balanced environment, and treaties were negotiated and ratified to establish regional and international standards. The result has been enactment of an increasingly complex set of legal norms in most sectors, from the village through to the global commons.[11] A legal matrix of rules, intersecting each dimension of human activity, now operates as a continuum of environmental management to guide state conduct toward the environment, and require a stewardship of natural resources.

At the Rio "Earth Summit," in 1992, most political leaders formally acknowledged that the traditional assumptions about nature's cornucopia could no longer be made. The new consensus that emerged at Rio asserted that proactive management would be needed to sustain the air, water and other natural resources upon which the human economy depended. However, it has proved easier for nations to "agree" that such stewardship is needed, than for them to decide *how* to work together to establish either the norms or the mechanisms for that stewardship. Upon returning home from Rio, relatively few heads of state gave environmental governance the importance that they had announced in their decisions at UNCED.

Despite the gradual emergence of new national and international laws establishing norms for sustaining the environment, there was little agreement about the

---

10   The Westphalian system, taking its most recent form with the establishment of the collective security system of the United Nations after the Second World War, has been preoccupied with ensuring national security and promoting economic growth through trade. Social priorities were added with the International Labor Organization (ILO, established under the League of Nations initially, to deal with labor unrest) and then the World Health Organization (WHO), and the other specialized agencies. Since nations derive wealth from exploiting natural resources, there have been economic pressures to avoid limiting resource extraction, and while UNEP may address pollution, no comparable mandate has been extended to address ecosystem management or nature conservation. IUCN's mission has grown to fill this gap, but to date neither UNEP nor IUCN have the resources necessary to address the needs of their State Members or the international community.

11   For instance, UNEP assisted states in negotiating regional seas agreements, to integrate coastal and marine issues shared by groups of nations. The UNECE developed an extensive set of regional treaties across the Northern Hemisphere.

institutional systems by which these norms are to be applied, observed and enforced. The negotiations associated with annual meetings in April of the UN Commission on Sustainable Development produced less rather than more agreement on the need for, or the type of, environmental governance that the world needed. The individual diplomats, who under Ambassador Tommy Koh of Singapore had negotiated and understood the recommendations of Rio, had each moved on to new assignments, and their successors seemed less informed and less sure about what had been agreed in Agenda 21. National parliaments enacted domestic frameworks of environmental legislation nationally, but the diplomats meeting internationally knew little about these complicated regimes.

Although within countries the process of enacting further norms will doubtless continue, and current standards will be streamlined and enhanced, it is evident that more attention must be devoted on the international level to the design of governing institutions capable of efficiently and effectively implementing those norms. The Rio Earth Summit foresaw the need for new systems of international environmental governance, and recommended measures toward such.[12]

In the years after Rio, national priorities focused on liberal trade issues, or the AIDS/HIV pandemic, or on geo-political crises, and less on environmental issues. Environmental concerns competed for a hearing among other issues. The Commission on Environmental Cooperation was established to ensure that environmental standards were a priority in association with the North American Free Trade Agreement. More widely, however, the foreign policies favoring liberalized world trade led to instances of popular resistance against the World Trade Organization (WTO) and the efforts to build new rounds of negotiations to broaden the General Agreement on Tariffs and Trade (GATT). Debate raged against trends in economic or social "globalization," with street riots emerging for the World Trade Organization meetings in Seattle or the Group of Eight Summit Meeting in Italy. Ultimately, the terrorist assault on the World Trade Center in New York City on September 11, 2002, triggered a restructuring of the foreign policy of the United States. Both trade and environment were eclipsed by concerns for the threat and reality of terrorism less than a year before the scheduled World Summit on Sustainable Development in 2002.[13] In short, national governments relegated the Rio consensus to a low priority, or forgot it altogether.

Nonetheless, scientific reports continue to document the deterioration of the environment across the globe. The WSSD's adoption of the Johannesburg Plan of Implementation is intended to restore the consensus favoring strategic action to attain sustainable development goals. It remains to be seen whether these cooperative national actions can leverage into existence the new international

---

12   Agenda 21, Chapter 8 for domestic laws and Chapters 38 and 39 for international law.

13   Indeed, the dates of the WSSD were advanced a fortnight to avoid holding the Summit on the one year anniversary of the September 11th attacks. This reduced the time needed to prepare for Summit at a time when preparations by both the host government, South Africa, and the nations attending, were already somewhat behind their anticipated preparatory schedules.

programs to build sustainable development. It may be that a new intergovernmental institution will yet be required.

In reviewing the documents collected together in this volume, it may be useful to (a) recall the reasons why the consensus for fashioning new mechanisms of environmental governance emerged at the Earth Summit, (b) restate briefly the competing possible options for these new institutional arrangements for environmental governance, and (c) identify what further measures might be taken to improve environmental governance and rebuild the consensus, before the environmental damage becomes so acute that options are constrained.

The sequence of UN conferences on the environment—1972 Stockholm, to 1992 Rio de Janeiro, to 2002 Johannesburg—suggest that there will be calls for a further conference in 2012. It may take a score of years, and not just the decade between Rio and Johannesburg, for sound political judgment to emerge about international environmental governance.[14] Be that as it may, in the decade since Rio, the policies of the nation states evidence a fuzzy vision about just how to attain environmentally sustainable practices. The World Summit on Sustainable Development will be recalled for its modest progress, and its actions that effectively postponed decisions about environmental governance into the future.

C. Issues Regarding Environmental Governance

The need for more effective international cooperation to safeguard Earth's environment had been evident since before the UN Stockholm Conference on the Human Environment in 1992.[15] That Conference provided for the establishment of the United Nations Environment Programme (UNEP), and perhaps it was because of the success of UNEP that nations came to recognize the need for nations to take ever more effective international measures to prevent environmental degradation around the world. The need to do so, however, was not matched by a clear vision about *how* to do so.

In adopting *Agenda 21*, the nations assembled at Rio de Janeiro in 1992 agreed that the recommendations of *Agenda 21* should integrate environment and development in order "to enhance the role and functioning of the United Nations system in the field of environment and development"[16] and to "strengthen

---

14   The UN General Assembly took note of what had been accomplished since Rio in 2000. See "10-Year Review of Progress Achieved in the Implementation of the Outcome of the UN Conference on Environment and Development," UN Doc. A/55/199 (2000), available on line at www.un.org/Depts/dhl/resguide/r55all2.htm.

15   See, e.g. George Kennan, "To Prevent a World Wasteland: A Proposal," 48 Foreign Affairs 410 (1970); and Barbara Ward, *Spaceship Earth* (New York, Columbia University Pre4ss, 1966); René Dubos and Barbara Ward, *Only One Earth: The Care and Maintenance of a Small Planet,* (New York, W.W. Norton, 1972).

16   Para. 38.8(b), Agenda 21.

institutional capabilities and arrangements required for the effective implementation, follow-up and review of Agenda 21,"[17] with UNEP "retaining its role as the principal body within the United Nations system in the field of environment,"[18] and "to establish effective cooperation and exchange of information between the United Nations organs, organizations, programmes, and multilateral financial bodies, within the institutional arrangements for the follow-up of *Agenda 21*."[19] No additional financial resources, however, were allocated to UNEP or any of the UN organs to undertake this new work, other than the establishment of the UN Commission on Sustainable Development. All specialized agencies of the UN System were called upon to "consider ways of strengthening and adjusting their activities and programmes in line with Agenda 21."[20] *Agenda 21* also called for a review of international environmental law "to improve the effectiveness of institutions, mechanisms, and procedures for the administration of agreements and instruments."[21]

Despite the establishment of the Commission on Sustainable Development, and the launch of some new programs, such as those undertaken through the Convention on Biological Diversity, it was evident to many that the existing international order was inadequate either to implement the recommendations of *Agenda 21*, or meet the challenges of environmental degradation around the Earth. Both academic commentators,[22] and governmental advisory

---

17   Para. 38.8(e), Agenda 21.

18   Para 38.23, Agenda 21.

19   Para. 38.8(f), Agenda 21.

20   Para. 38.28 of Agenda 21.

21   Para. 39.3(f)

22   See, e.g. Frank Biermann, "The Case for a World Environment Organization," 42 Environment 22 (2000); Daniel C. Esty, "The Case for a Global Environmental Organization," in Peter B. Kenen (ed.,) *Managing the World Economy: Fifty Years After Bretton Woods*, (Washington, DC, Institute for International Economics,1994); Daniel C. Esty, "Toward Optimal Environmental Governance," 74 New York University Law Review 1495 (1999); Peter M. Hass, Robert O. Keohane, Marc A. Levy (Eds.), *Institutions For The Earth* (Cambridge, MIT Press, 1993) ;Peter M. Hass, "Environment: Pollution," in P.J. Simmons and Chantel de Jonge Outdraat (eds.), *Managing Global Issues: Lessons Learned* at p. 310 (2001; Lawrence David Levien, "A Structural Model for a WEO: the ILO Experience," 40 George Washington L. Rev. 464 (1972); Geoffrey Palmer, "New Ways to Make International Environmental Law," 86 American Journal of International Law 259 (1992);Wolfgang H. Reinicke, *Global Public Policy: Governing Without Government?* (Washington, DC, Brookings Institution Press, 2000); Ford Runge, "A Global Environmental Organization (GEO) and the World Trading System," 5 Environment and Development Economics 510 (2000); Oran R. Young and Gail Oshenenko, *International Cooperation: Building Regimes for Natural Resources and the Environment* (Ithaca, NY, Cornell University Press, 1993); Oran R. Young (ed.), *Global Governance: Drawing Insights from Environmental Experience* (Cambridge, MIT Press, 1997); Oran R. Young, George J. Demko, and Kilparti Ramakrishna, *Global Environmental Governance* (Boulder, Colo., Rienner, 1997); Jacob Werksman (ed.), *Greening International Institutions* (London, Earthscan, 1996). Compare Juma Calestrous, "The Perils of Centralizing Global Environmental Governance, "Environment Matters 13 (2000), available at www.esd.worldbank.org/envmat/vol00/toc.htm.

bodies,[23] made recommendations for institutional change as to how to implement *Agenda 21*'s recommendation that new governing relationships were needed if sustainable development was to be realized.

Unlike the recommendations of Chapter 38 of *Agenda 21*, to use and strengthen the existing UN systems, commentary from outside the UN system saw the need for new arrangements in view of the increasing pressure to abate worldwide trends toward environmental degradation.

D. The Growing Urgency of Earth's Environmental Problems

Scientific monitoring of environmental degradation trends should give national leaders everywhere pause. Three trends are evident. First, it is evident that the accumulation of many local actions are now producing adverse effects on a global scale. Human induced climate changes or relative rises in sea levels or the global dispersion of chemicals as "persistent organic pollutants" are such events. Second, comparable local actions in one region are causing measurable harm in other regions. Transboundary pollution of river waters, or the diminutions in the numbers of migratory species across their range, such as in birds, butterflies or fish in the seas, or the harms resulting from "acid rain" illustrate such inter-regional impact. Third, within nations the loss of natural areas, pollution of urban air, contamination of drinking water sources, or exhaustion of natural resources constitute growing problems that, over all, are increasing in intensity as human population growth and migration overwhelm once traditional environmental management systems. These are common problems recurring throughout the earth, and they require the sharing of common solutions before they exacerbate in ways that aggravate the negative environmental trends at regional and global levels.

These phenomena destabilize economic and social human conditions. Unregulated human acts of commission or omission have caused diseases, such as "West Nile virus" or alien species, such as the "Zebra Mussel," to leave one continent to infect another, causing death and pervasive economic loss in their wake. Failures to provide distributed energy systems in Africa or parts of Asia cause local communities to burn available tress and other biomass, with loss of forests, resultant soil degradation and erosion, and aggravation of desertification. Ecological refugees flee uninhabitable conditions, and their numbers will rise as increases in sea levels inundates communities on small islands or erodes low lying river deltas from the Ganges to the Mississippi. The numbers of species becoming extinct or threatened with extinction grows in all regions. Migration of humans into mega cities spawns extensive slums, where the lack of

---

23   See, e.g., German Advisory Council on Global Change, "World In Transition: New Structures for Global Environmental Policy," (2001) at www.wbgu.de; see also for Canada, Wolfgang H. Reinicke and Frances Deng, "Critical Choices: The United Nations, Networks, and the Future of Global Governance," (Ottawa, Canada: International Development Research Council, 2001).

decent infrastructure, jobs, education, parks or sanitary conditions breeds political unrest.

It is no longer deemed remarkable that such troubling trends exist. In 1985, at the urging of the Commission on Environmental Law of the International Union for the Conservation of Nature and Natural Resources (IUCN), and with the endorsement of the UN Environment Programme, the UN General Assembly had adopted the World Charter for Nature,[24] as standard by which to measure state conduct toward the environment. Tested against these norms, there was a growing awareness that nations were failing in their stewardship duties toward nature. Scientific documentation sufficiently demonstrated to have caused the United Nations General Assembly to convene the World Commission on Environment and Development, whose report, *Our Common Future*,[25] prompted the convening[26] of the world's largest summit meeting ever held, the United Nations Conference in Environment and Development (UNCED) held in Rio de Janeiro in 1992. Under the remarkable chairmanship of Prof. Tommy Koh of Singapore, the delegates to the Rio "Earth Summit" culminated a two-year negotiation with the production of an action plan to induce nations to cooperate together to combat these deteriorating environmental trends. *Agenda 21,*[27] as an action plan, was adopted by consensus at UNCED and then unanimously by the United Nations General Assembly.

In *Agenda 21*, national leaders and their negotiators challenged themselves and their peers to respond to these trends. They created the U.N. Commission on Sustainable Development to follow-up on how well nations implement the recommendations of *Agenda 21*, and stated both their fears and their aspirations in the opening paragraph[28] of this remarkable agreement, thus:

> "Humanity stands at a defining moment in its history. We are confronted with a perpetuation of disparities between and within nations, a worsening of poverty, hunger, ill health and illiteracy, and the continuing deterioration of the ecosystems on which we depend for our well-bring. However, integration of environment and development concerns, and greater attention to them will lead to the fulfillment of basic needs, improved living standards for all, better protected and managed ecosystems and a safer, more prosperous future. No nation can achieve this on its own; but together we can—in a global partnership for sustainable development."

---

24   UNGA Res. 37/7 (1982).

25   The World Commission on Environment and Development (Gro Harlem Brundtland, Chair), *Our Common Future* (Oxford University Press, 1987).

26   The UN General Assembly in UN Res. 44/228 (22 December 1989) authorized the preparation of UNCED and recognized the importance of integrating environmental and developmental concerns.

27   UN Doc. A/CONF. 151/26 (five volumes), 1992; reprinted with annotations in N.A. Robinson, *Agenda 21: Earth's Action Plan* (Dobbs Ferry, Oceana Publications, 1993).

28   Agenda 21, paragraph 1.1.

Response to this political recognition, that Earth's nations are at a defining point in history, was intended to be measured and concrete. In its Chapters 8[29] and 37,[30] *Agenda 21* called on nations to reorganize their national governance to better address their internal environmental problems. In Chapters 38[31] and 39,[32] *Agenda 21* called upon nations to cooperate together to fashion new international mechanisms to cope with inter-regional and global threats. In connection with UNCED and its immediate aftermath, the nations launched three treaties to ensure a coordinated response to certain of these phenomena. The Convention on Biological Diversity,[33] the UN Framework Convention on Climate Change,[34] and the Convention to Combat Desertification,[35] complement Part XII of the UN Convention on the Law of the Sea,[36] the Convention on Migratory and Straddling Fish Stocks,[37] or the Convention on the Protection of the Stratospheric Ozone Layer.[38] Together these, and some 200 other regional[39] and global treaties[40] provide a legal mosaic for a law of the biosphere. Properly implemented, in a coordinated way, these thoughtfully crafted treaties from different sectors could provide an effective foundation for concerted measures, undertaken by nations within each region.

International Law requires each nation to use and develop the resources in its territory or under its control so as not to cause damage to the environment of other States or of areas beyond the limits of national jurisdiction, such as the

---

29 "Integrating environment and development in decision-making."

30 "National Mechanisms and International Cooperation for Capacity-Building in Developing Countries."

31 International Institutional Arrangements."

32 "International Legal Instruments and Mechanisms."

33 — UNTS —, 31 I.L.M. 818 (1992); Treaties and International Agreements Online, CTIA 10362.000 (Oceana Publications, Inc., <www.oceanalaw.com>).

34 — UNTS —31 I.L.M. 849 (1992); Treaties and International Agreements Online, CTIA 9736.000 (Oceana Publications, Inc., <www.oceanalaw.com>).

35 — UNTS — ; Treaties and International Agreements Online, CTIA 9269.000 (Oceana Publications, Inc., <www.oceanalaw.com>).

36 Part XII sets forth the environmental rules for the marine environment. — UNTS — ; UN Doc. A/CONF. 62/122; 21 I.L.M. 1261 (1982).

37 — UNTS — ; Treaties and International Agreements Online, CTIA 10278.000 (Oceana Publications, Inc., <www.oceanalaw.com>).

38 — UNTS — ; 26 I.L.M. 1529 (1987); Treaties and International Agreements Online, CTIA 8392.000 (Oceana Publications, Inc., <www.oceanalaw.com>).

39 For instance, the UN Economic Commission for Europe has sponsored the Espoo Convention on Environmental Impact Assessment in a Transboundary Context, — UNTS —, 31 I.L.M. 800 (1991), Treaties and International Agreements Online, CTIA 9737.000 (Oceana Publications, Inc., <www.oceanalaw.com>), and the Åarhus Convention on Public Access to Information, Participation in Environmental Decision-making, and Access to Environmental Justice, — UNTS—(1998), — I.L.M. —.

40 See, for instance, the collection of such treaties in L.D. Guruswamy, G.W.R. Palmer, and B.H. Weston (Eds), *Supplement of Basic Documents to International Environmental Law & World Order* (West Pub. Co, 1994). The U.S.A. is a party to most of these conventions. See N.A. Robinson (ed.), *Environmental Law Treaties of the United States* (Dobbs Ferry, Oceana Publications, 1997).

commons of the High Seas or the atmosphere. This rule of customary international law was recodified in 1972 at the first international summit on the environment, as "Principle 21" of the Declaration of the UN Stockholm Conference on the Human Environment.[41] The body of environmental treaties, and *Agenda 21*, provide prescriptions about how to observe the responsibilities set forth in "Principle 21." Patently, however, as the evidence accumulates that each nation is causing harm abroad, or allowing activity within its territory to cause harm abroad, it is clear that national responses are inadequate to discharge their duties to each other under international law. These duties, of course, vary from region to region, depending on the geography, the concentrations of population, the level of economic development and technological innovation, and other factors. Recognizing these variations, the nations assembled at Rio both restated Stockholm's "Principle 21"[42] and also posited that nations have "common but differentiated responsibilities"[43] to cooperate together to resolve the festering environmental agenda.

Since the conclusion of UNCED in 1992, however, rather too little has been achieved to implement the recommendations in *Agenda 21*. Many nations have not yet ratified the several environmental treaties, and many developing nations or states with economies in transition from communist to market systems, may well lack the national resources to be able to implement those treaties. Levels of international assistance to build the capacity of these states to be able to observe the environmental treaties, or cooperate to implement *Agenda 21*, have declined since 1992, while direct foreign investment has induced economic development in some places faster than the pace of establishing environmental protection systems on the ground. Unintentionally, such uncoordinated economic growth has often led to exacerbating urban trends in environmental problems.

Despite the annual meetings of the Commission on Sustainable Development about the implementation of *Agenda 21*, and the initial work of the conferences of the parties for the Convention on Biological Diversity, the UNFCCC and the Convention on Desertification, there has been almost no measurable improvement in the deteriorating environmental conditions that stimulated the Bruntdland Commission Report and *Agenda 21*. For this reason, the decision to

---

41   UN Doc. A/Conf. 48/14 at 2-65, and Corr. 1 (1972); 11 I.L.M. 1416 (1972).

42   Principle 21 of the Stockholm Declaration on the Human Environment appears as Principle 2 of the Rio Declaration on Environment and Development: " States have, in accordance with the Charter of the United Nations and the principles of international law, the sovereign right to exploit their own resources pursuant to their own environmental and developmental policies, and the responsibility to ensure that activities within their jurisdiction or control do not cause damage to the environment of other States or of areas beyond the limits of national jurisdiction."

43   See, e.g. UN Framework Convention on Climate Change, 31 I.L.M. 849 (May 29, 1992), Preambular paragraph 6, and Article 3(1).

convene a United Nations World Summit on Sustainable Development (WSSD)[44] in Johannesburg, South Africa, in August of 2002, was widely expected to tackle the issues of environmental governance. The failure of the UN WSSD to advance Rio's recommendations on global environmental governance in any substantial and material way has left the challenge posed by *Agenda 21* largely intact.

Humanity, and the impact of humans within the biosphere, remains at a defining point in human history. Humans may or may not play a memorable role in the natural history of Earth over geologic time, but in terms of human evolution and recent natural history, it *is* important what human society does to address accumulated environment problems of the earth. Since human society functions collectively at national and international levels through legal institutions, how law shapes environmental governance will critically influence the path that human society takes in the coming years.

E. Contemporary Intergovernmental Environmental Governance

Chapter 38 of *Agenda 21* provides a blueprint of the current arrangements for international environmental governance under the UN Charter. Part XI of the Johannesburg Plan of Implementation recognizes that "an effective institutional framework for sustainable development at all levels is key to the full implementation of *Agenda 21*, the follow-up to the outcomes of the World Summit on Sustainable Development and meeting emerging sustainable development challenges."[45] The need for some institutional reforms were noted, for "increasing effectiveness and efficiency through limiting overlap and duplication of activities of international organizations, within and outside the United Nations system, based on their mandates and comparative advantages."[46] Notwithstanding the various proposals for change noted blow, the nations reaffirmed in 2002 as they did in 1992, the existing intergovernmental systems for environmental governance established under the UN Charter.

The UN General Assembly adopted *Agenda 21*,[47] and following the WSSD carried agenda items on its 57th session for the "Implementation of *Agenda 21* and the Programme for the Further Implementation of *Agenda 21*."[48] In 1992, the UN General Assembly expressly endorsed Chapter 38 of *Agenda 21*, and established the Commission on Sustainable Development. In 2002, the nations at the WSSD

---

44   UN GA Res. 55/199 (Dec. 20, 2000); the General Assembly emphasized that WSSD should undertake "action-oriented decisions in areas where further efforts are needed to implement Agenda 21, address, within the framework of Agenda 21, new challenges and opportunities, and result in renewed political commitment and support for sustainable development, consistent, *inter alia*, with the principle of common but differentiated responsibilities."

45   Article 137, Plan of Implementation, WSSD (Sept. 4, 2002).

46   Id., article 139(f).

47   UNGA Res. 47/190 (Dec. 22, 1992).

48   Agenda of the 57th Session of the UN General Assembly, Item 87, UN Doc. A/57/251 (Sept. 20, 2002).

also chose to reaffirm the role of the UN General Assembly to oversee the general policies, and the role of the Economic and Social Council to oversee the system-wide coordination of the specialized agencies. The General Assembly undertakes its work through committees of the whole. It delegates agenda items on environment and natural resources to the Second Committee, and issues of international law to the Sixth Committee.[49] Should an environmental matter ever become a threat to the peace, it could be raised in the UN Security Council.

The implementation of *Agenda 21* was assigned in 1992 to the Commission on Sustainable Development.[50] The WSSD re-emphasized the role and function of the Commission on Sustainable Development as the principal high level forum for integrating social, environment and economic developmental issues. Although it did not indicate how, the nations at the WSSD observed that "the Commission needs to be strengthened, taking into account the role of relevant institutions and organizations."[51]

Within the UN system, the Secretary General of the UN has fostered cooperation and coordination among specialized agencies through the United Nations System Chief Executives' Board for Coordination. There have always been problems of integrating the disparate UN specialized agencies, since they each have different budgets, different mandates that take priority over inter-agency cooperation, different numbers of nations as State Parties and limitations on their work in non-State Parties, and different levels of staff available for such cooperation. In every case, the first priority is assigned to the core work of the organization, as the governing body of each may require. The nations assign different delegations to each governing body, depending on their expertise, so that the national health ministry works with the World Health Organization, or the agricultural department with the UN Food & Agricultural Organization. This retards work on issues that cut across both such agencies, as in the case of adverse human health impacts of persistent organic pollutants from the use of agricultural pesticides. In fact, since few if any nations, effectively coordinate environmental governance issues among the sectors of their governments domestically, it should not be surprising to find this sectoralized pattern among the UN specialized agencies. The civil service in national ministries tends closely to the needs of its analogue international agency; the foreign diplomats assigned to the UN General Assembly or Commission on Sustainable Development rotate every few years, and there are very few with any seniority in service to the UN General Assembly. Thus, in terms of the experience of the government officials responsible, there

---

49 Although the Sixth Committee covers legal issues, the WSSD Johannesburg Plan of Implementation recommended that the Commission on Sustainable Development should "take into account significant legal developments in the field of sustainable development, with due regard to the role of relevant intergovernmental bodies in promoting the implementation of Agenda 21 relating to international legal instruments and mechanisms." Article 148(e), the Johannesburg Plan of Implementation (Sept. 4, 2002).

50 UNGA Res. 47/191 (Dec. 22, 1992).

51 Article 145, Johannesburg Plan of Implementation (Sept. 4, 2002).

is continuity in the sectoral work of the UN system, and discontinuity among those assigned to leadership of policy-making functions.

The disparate mandates among international bodies mirrors national experience. When newer international organizations for traditional issues, such as the World Trade Organization, have come into existence, they are matched with their respective national governmental units, such as the Office of the Trade Representative in the USA or a ministry of commerce. When the newer organizations are established to address new global environmental problems, such as climate change or biodiversity conservation, there usually is no national governmental agency analogous to the international entity; consequently, they tend to be rather weaker in both policy formulation and program implementation. A similar weakness is evident in those cross-cutting functions, such as environmental impact assessment or integrated coastal zone management, or cross-cutting issues such as acid rain or transboundary water pollution, that require inter-agency cooperation and address common environmental issues. No one sector of government is responsible for these functions or issues, and thus all tend to shun them as being of low priority.

One innovation since the 1992 UNCED in Rio de Janeiro deserves attention. The Global Environmental Facility (GEF) was established by the World Bank, the UN Environment Programme (UNEP) and the UN Development Programme (UNDP) to be a vehicle for nations to fund new projects to build sustainable development.[52] GEF has been an important new innovation in the institutional framework for international environmental governance. However, the GEF has become rather independent of its sponsoring entities, and not closely coordinated with them or with the UN specialized agencies or the MEAs in developing funding for an integrated program furthering international environmental governance. The nations at the WSSD encouraged the further use of the GEF, without addressing its relevance to issues of governance.[53]

From this brief survey, it is evident that current arrangements for environmental governance among nations remain only modestly effective. The system is neither up to the tasks of galvanizing action to reverse the trends in environmental degradation, nor capable of coordinating international cooperation to enhance environmental quality. The efforts devoted to training and building the capacity to restore and maintain the environment in many nations are too meager to make much of a difference. Moreover, these arrangements are uneven across sectors, leaving some issues addressed competently and others neglected.

---

52   The scope of the work of the GEF is at www.gef.org.

53   Article 87 of the Johannesburg Plan of Implementation (Sept. 4, 2002), provides that the WSSD welcomes "the successful and substantial third replenishment of the Global Environment Facility, which will enable it to address the funding requirements of new focal areas and existing ones and continue to be responsive to the needs and concerns of its recipient countries, in particular developing countries, and further encourage Global Environment Facility to leverage additional funds from key public and private organizations, improve the management of funds through more speedy and streamlined procedures and simplify its project cycle."

F. Whither Environmental Governance?

It was widely recognized prior to the WSSD that international cooperation to implement Agenda 21 was making but halting progress. The United Nations encouraged cooperation among its component organs.[54] In order to go beyond mere cooperation among previously authorized programs, several significant initiatives were undertaken to cultivate a new consensus about what restructured institutional systems could be established to enhance environmental governance.[55] In the end, none won the support of the nations assembled at the WSSD.

Managing the environment is a continuous activity at all levels of government. It is not exclusively either a local or national or international endeavor. Rather, it requires a coordination of roles at each level. As the nature of environmental problems becomes better understood, nations recognized the need to develop and apply environmental law to build sustainable development at national[56] as well as international levels.[57] The continued urgency of this task was underscored at the recent World Summit on Sustainable Development (WSSD) in Johannesburg, South Africa. In The Johannesburg Declaration on Sustainable Development, nations assumed "a collective responsibility to advance and strengthen the interdependent and mutually reinforcing pillars of sustainable development—economic development, social development and environmental protection—at local, national, regional and global levels."[58]

However, it is easier to recognize that environmental stewardship must be an element of every level of government than it is to determine how to establish or coordinate among such levels. Legal systems have evolved over time to manage the relationships among different levels of government, and the new environmental laws have been adopted in this framework. However, rather than being simply a new dimension of existing governance patterns, environmental laws are shaping new relationships within these frameworks. These new relationships must be understood by those who would shape new international environmental governance systems, and it may be that the contemporary reluctance of nations to establish new systems is in part because these new patterns are not well understood. The new patterns can be characterized as at once being a "continuum" and a "matrix."

---

54 See UNGA Res. 53/242 (Aug. 10, 1999), which endorsed a proposal from the UN Secretary General for creating an Environmental Management Group for inter-agency coordination in the field of the environment and human settlements. See "Report of the Secretary General on Environment and Human Settlements," UN Doc. A/53/463 (Oct. 6, 1998); on line at www.un.org/documents/ga/res/53/a53r242.pdf.

55 See, e.g. "Report of the Secretary General: International Institutional Arrangements Related to Environment and Development," UN Doc. A/54/468 (Oct. 15, 1999). The leading proposals for innovations beyond the current institutional arrangements, regarding UNEP and GEF and the Trusteeship Council, are described infra.

56 Chapter 8 in *Agenda 21* (1992).

57 Id., Chapters 37-39.

58 Article 5 of the Declaration, A/CONF.199/L.6/Rev 2.

A continuum of law and governance is essential if environmental law is to reflect the "laws of nature." The environmental law of the village and hamlet is tied to the fate of the state and nation and region, and ultimately of the biosphere, and *vice versa*. Environmental law is neither just national or municipal law, nor international law. Rather is a network of legal relationships wherever human societies are functioning. It makes transparent our interdependence on the same ecosystems and other natural systems, across borders and continents. This is a unique shift in emphasis from the laws that are seen as solely national prerogatives or international agreements. To be effective, any governance system for environmental laws must build the linkages between each level of government in this chain of stewardship for shared natural systems.

At the same time, environmental governance must function across all sectors of governance. Matrix systems permeate the field of environmental law. The same basic principles or legal tools can apply across many sectors, and many biomes or environmental regions. For instance, environmental impact assessment (EIA) procedures[59] and public participation rules[60] are essential elements of transport projects, agricultural and irrigation projects, housing projects, energy projects, and every other developmental activity. EIA applies to park and protected area management. To be effective, EIA procedures need to be used at local, state or provincial, national and international levels, and in each sector and level EIA needs to observe the same procedural elements of detailed scientific analysis, public disclosure of the information and public comment, and the identification of ways to avoid or mitigate any adverse environmental impacts. Similarly, a matrix system is evident in measures to curb carbon dioxide emissions for meeting objectives of the Kyoto Protocol,[61] or in ensuring that habits can be consistently maintained for migratory birds across several continents.[62] Systems of environmental laws aim to apply their norms and tools holistically, across sectors. Of course traditional governmental leaders of each sector do not at once have the time, resource or inclination to embrace the environmental duties thrust upon them. Indeed, one of the rationales for a new international environmental agency is to facilitate integration of environmental governance responsibilities into in each part of the matrix. Environmental law exists in every sector and level, and is not the province of an environment ministry.

---

59   E.g., the US National Environmental Policy Act (NEPA), 42 USC 4321., applies to "all" agencies of the federal government for all activities having a significant effect on the quality of the human environment. Section 102(2)(c).

60   E.g., the US Administrative Procedure Act, 5 USC 551, with its notice and comment rules and its provisions for judicial review, and the US Freedom of Information Act (FOIA), 5 USC 552, ensure that the public has the same rights of participation across all regulatory agencies. These rules, as well as the EIA provisions, have been incorporated in the Aarhus Agreement on Access to Justice, Public participation in Environmental Decision-making, etc., to apply across all sectors of the nations that have adhered to this treaty.

61   UN Framework Convention on Climate Change, 31 I.L.M. 849 (May 29, 1992, in force), Treaties and International Agreements Online, CTIA 9736.000 (Oceana Publications, Inc., <www.oceanalaw.com>)., and the Kyoto Protocol (not in force), 37 ILM 22; Treaties and International Agreements Online, CTIA 10080.000 (Oceana Publications, Inc., <www.oceanalaw.com>).

62   Bonn Convention on Migratory Species, 19 I.L.M. 11 (June 23, 1979).

Finally, those with environmental responsibilities across the continuum and within the matrix all need to understand and be guided by the same body of environmental science. This is not yet the case. Environmental governance, law and policy depends upon a scientific foundation. Environmental law is constrained by what physics, biology, ecology and the environmental sciences reveal about Earth's natural systems. Such constraints are not present in many other legal fields such as economic trade laws,[63] in which largely (if not purely)[64] human norms for conduct are agreed upon by legislatures in nations or through treaties among nations, based on a wide spread of possible choices. In the field of environmental law it is the environmental and natural scientists that set forth the description of how a natural system works. Whether it is the Intergovernmental Panel on Climate Change (IPCC) or a local hydrologist describing conditions of eutrophication in a lake, the legal response must be grounded on the best scientific estimation of the ambient environmental conditions. Environmental law is truly a partnership between law and science, far more so than many today understand.[65] At the international level, scientific subsidiary bodies have been established to guide the development of newer multilateral environmental agreements.[66] Such scientific expertise is found at national levels also, but sporadically. Today environmental catastrophes are many for those who built on a flood plains or an eroding steep slopes.[67] The goal is to bring human society's laws into accord with what earlier generations characterized as the "laws of nature," being "in harmony of nature."[68]

---

63   General Agreement on Tariffs and Trade (GATT), 55 U.N.T.S. 187 (Oct. 30, 1947) and the World Trade Organization (WTO), 33 I.L.M. 1125 (April 15, 1994).

64   Economic analysis, as a social science, is not able to prescribe the consequences of human activity with the concrete rigor that the physical and natural sciences do with respect to the environment.

65   Ralph Waldo Emerson, in his essay Nature (1830) envisioned this relationship. He observed that human stewardship of nature was constrained by the "discipline" of nature.

66   Article 25, Convention on Biological Diversity, establishes the Subsidiary Body on Scientific, Technical and Technological Advice (SBSTTA), 31 I.L.M. 818 (June 5, 1992); Treaties and International Agreements Online, CTIA 10362.000 (Oceana Publications, Inc., <www.oceanalaw.com>).

67   For instance, the devastation of Hurricane Mitch in Central America was greatly exacerbated by the unplanned development of human settlements in places of risk. Even where such advice once existed, as in the Soil Conservation Service, through which soils scientists advised local authorities and land owners, as times change governments mistakenly conclude that there is no need for such scientific advice and discontinue programs that provide it. SCS reference.

68   The need to strengthen scientific studies to provide the foundations for sound environmental stewardship as a basis for sustainable development was a major recommendation of AGENDA 21, Chapter 31. The development of an "Earth Systems Science" or a "Science of Sustainability," however, has not much advanced since 1992, despite clear and coherent descriptions of what is needed. See Board on Sustainable Development, National Research Council, "Our Common Journey: A Transition Toward Sustainability," (1999), discussed in William C. Clark, "A Transition Toward Sustainability," 27 Ecology Law Quarterly 1021 (2001). Some of the reasons why support for Environmental Science is lagging is set forth in N.A. Robinson, "Legal Systems, Decisionmaking, and the Science of Earth's Systems: Procedural Missing Links," 27 Ecology Law Quarterly 1077 (2001).

Understanding that any enhanced environmental governance institutions will necessary work within this *system* of scientists, governments at all levels, and across all sectors, it is possible to posit several functions that may be undertaken. Among these functions are the following:

1) *Provide for cooperation where no lead institution now exists*: There are some international environmental law cooperative sectors for which there is no umbrella forum, most notably the State responsibilities reflected in Part XII of the UN Convention on the Law of the Sea; these duties are now largely observed in the breach, and until oversight is provided it is likely that the environmental quality of Earth's marine areas will deteriorate further. Also, the issues of vessel pollution under the International Maritime Organization (IMO) and those for fish under the Convention on Migratory and Straddling Fish Stocks, are not coordinated with Part XII or other related provisions of multilateral environmental agreements.

2) *Facilitate the collaboration among MEAs*: Although each of the multilateral environmental organizations has its specific duties and mandates, there is no network to build on commonalities among these MEAs. The secretariats for the MEAs understand the value of working together when their roles are linked,[69] but this remains unavoidably a low priority for them. Moreover, it is increasingly difficult for all nations to send fully briefed delegations to all the many meetings of the MEAs, and a more streamlined approach to their decision-making and work could make it easier for the States Parties to the several agreements to field their treaty responsibilities.

3) *Compile and disseminate scientific data on environmental trends*: There is no one place for data collection to compile and disseminate a "state of the world" on environmental trends. No nation can assemble such an overview alone, and even the most advanced States neglect to note trends because of policy blinders such as not being members of an MEA (for instance the USA has not ratified or adhered to the Bonn Convention on Migratory Species), or because they have established priorities that defer or decline to examine certain trends, or they lack the resources to study all trends, as is the case with most developing nations or nations with economies in transition. Where no systems exist for compiling data, there is a need to build cooperative networks of nations that could undertake the monitoring and compiling of the data.

---

69   For instance, the Executive Secretary for the UNFCCC reported to the Conference of the Parties about enhancement of synergies between the UNFCCC, the UN Convention to Combat Desertification (UNCCD), and the Convention on Biological Diversity (CBD), and the UNFCCC Secretariat presented a "scoping paper on cross-cutting thematic areas" between UNFCCC, UNCCD and the CBD to the Eighth Conference of the Parties of the UNFCCC. See Earth Negotiations Bulletin, vol. 12, no. 209, "Summary of the Eighth Conference of the Parties to the UN Framework Convention on Climate Change," reports for 23 and 25 October 2002, at www.iisd.ca/linkages/climate/cop8(Nov. 4, 2002); Treaties and International Agreements Online, CTIA 9269.000 and CTIA 10362.000 (Oceana Publications, Inc., <www.oceanalaw.com>).

4) *Serve as a policy catalyst for negotiations of new international environmental agreements*: A major accomplishment of UNEP under its Executive Director Mustafa Tolba, was to bring nations together to develop new environmental treaties.[70] Notwithstanding these accomplishments, there remain many disturbing environmental trends for which there is as yet no international law, and very little national law. The need for integrated coastal zone management along all marine areas is urgent. The need for coherent land use and habitat management for migratory butterflies and other insects, as well as many bird species, is urgently needed. The need for assessments of pollutants that scientists have identified as of concern, such as polycyclic aromatic hydrocarbons, and appropriate action by nations, is largely unaddressed. Some organizations, such as IUCN and the studies of its Commission on Environmental Law on the needs for soils legislation and an international soils convention, continue their work in this field, but either UNEP should restore its work in this area, or a new environmental agency could do so. The development of agreements for cooperation remains a priority, as the lack of any soils system illustrates.[71]

5) *Facilitate, through training and capacity building, integration of environment and development*: As *Agenda 21* makes clear, the environment is a cross-sectoral theme and needs to be integrated into the mandates of every institution in every sector. Some agency is needed to build the links along the continuum of governmental environmental responsibility, and across the matrix. This is hard—if not impossible—to legislate; the integration is best accomplished by education and training. There is no international authority that can make the case for such integration, and help build the capacity in each sector to accomplish such integration. The holistic approach will not emerge on its own, it will come rather too slowly to help curb trends in environmental deterioration. What is needed is an agency that can help facilitate the integration sector by sector, as other institutions recognize the need for help in attaining such integration.

6) *Coordinate and foster cooperation for funding environmental governmental tasks*: None of the current environmental intergovernmental organizations and programmes is adequately funded to meet its agreed functions. There would be inevitable savings in consolidated core administrative support systems upon which each MEA and UNEP and other institutions now depend. While economies of scale and services may not be a sufficient rationale in themselves for consolidations, when these tangible benefits are added to the substantive rationales above, there is every reason to see why finance ministries would support establishing a consolidated and new entity that could save their national treasuries some funds.

---

70 Mustafa K. Tolba, *Global Environmental Diplomacy* (Massachusetts Institute of Technology, 1998).

71 Ian Hammon with Ben Boer, *Legal and Institutional Frameworks for Sustainable Soils* (IUCN, 2002).

7) *Provide directly environmental services, and build capacity, where they are lacking within nations:* There are many national environmental ministries, which, frankly, cannot do the job needed within their national boundaries. If there were an international organization that could undertake, on request, to provide missing national services, it would be a great benefit to all nations, since their well-being as well as the welfare of the natural systems in the biosphere, depend on these national roles being implemented. For instance, there is a need to design and install fresh water systems and sewage treatment systems in much of the world; this is not being done by many national governments now, and if the people in those areas are to enjoy their human right to have potable water, a global water effort must be undertaken. It remains to be seen how the recommendations of the WSSD on water security will be realized.

8) *Provide funding for leveraging local and national and regional resources:* The success of the Global Environment Facility suggests strongly the need to expand the funding mechanisms for enhancing environmental protection. This can be done internationally, but it would be more effective if it can integrate with the funding and human and other resources available through local authorities and national governments. Funding needs to be collaborative and tied to common over-all goals and objectives. It ultimately must build local capacities to carry on the programs that some international funding can stimulate.

There are, of course, many other functions that could be ascribed to an international environmental governance system. These eight functions are as yet imperfectly served by the existing United Nations system for advancing either environmental protection or sustainable development.

A recognition of the need to provide systems of international cooperation regarding any of these eight functions would provide ample rationales for revamping existing systems for international cooperation, or for establishing a new international environmental organization to address the apparent needs. This has occurred to a number of nations. Predictably, awareness that these needs are unmet has generated a range of proposals for reforms. The agenda for the UN World Summit on Sustainable Development anticipated that reforms would be made to enhance systems of international environmental governance. This goal exceeded the grasp of the nations at the WSSD. Although the political consensus does not yet exist behind any of these reforms, that day may come and it is important to understand the debate leading up to and, in the wake of, the UN World Summit on Sustainable Development in 2002.

The most ambitious negotiations to build a renew mandate for strong international environmental governance came from the UN Environment Programme in the lead up to Johannesburg. The UNEP Governing Council, under the chairmanship of Canada's Environment Minister, and with the diligent and able leadership of UNEP's Executive Director, Dr. Klaus Töpfer, formerly the Environment Minister of Germany, undertook a decision in 2001 to convene an "Open-ended Intergovernmental Group of Ministers or their Representatives on International Environmental Governance."[72] This Group met six times, with a final meeting in Cartegena, Colombia.[73] It produced a remarkably thorough and thoughtful body of analysis about how to improve international environmental governance.[74] However, the governments were not persuaded that the reforms were timely. At the Cartegena meeting, deep divisions were evident. Developing nations and China supported strengthening UNEP within its already existing mandate, and did not favor changes to the governance of each multilateral environmental agreement. These nations, plus the Russian Federation and United States of America opposed moving UNEP into a specialized agency structure. No consensus on any new international environmental governance had emerged. It is not surprising, therefore, that the topic made no headway in the preparations for the WSSD or its outcome.

The political declaration submitted by the President of the WSSD, entitled "The Johannesburg Declaration on Sustainable Development,"[75] repeats *Agenda 21*'s recognition "that humanity is at a crossroad,"[76] but says nothing about international environmental governance other than a commitment "to act together, united by a common determination to save our planet, promote human development and achieve universal prosperity and peace,"[77] and to support "the Johannesburg Plan of Implementation."[78] The "Plan of Implementation" adopted on September 4, 2002, in Part XI, entitled "Institutional Framework for Sustainable Development," provides no significant new or enhanced governance measures to attain these objectives. Unable to agree on improvements for environmental governance, the Plan reaffirmed the institutional agreements that had been put in place at Rio. No efforts were made to build systematically upon "synergies" that existed between the conferences of the parties and their secretariat for the several independent environmental treaty systems.

It had been evident at the Fourth Preparatory Committee meeting for the WSSD in Bali, Indonesia, that no consensus existed upon which to build new environmental governance measures. The Chair of the Preparatory Committee, Emil Salim of Indonesia, noted that the delegates at Bali could not reach agreement on such key issues as setting time-tables for implementation of the proposed

---

72   Decision 21/21 of February 9, 2001. See www.unep.org/governingbodies.

73   See the Report of the Open-Ended Intergovernmental Group of Ministers or their Representatives on International Environmental Governance, (Oct. 15, 2001), on line at www.unep.org/governingbodies/gc/specialsessions/gsss_vii/Reports.htm.

74   See, e.g. "International Environmental Governance: Report of the Executive Director of UNEP." For the Fourth Group meeting in Montreal on 30 November – 1 December 2001, UN Doc. UNEP/IGM/4/3 (Nov. 16, 2001); and the Report of the Chair, Fourth Meeting of the Intergovernmental Group of Minister, UN Doc. UNEP/IGM/4/6 (Dec. 27, 2001).

75   Agenda 21 ¶1, UN Doc. A/CONF. 199/L.6 (Rev. 2), September 4, 2002.

76   *Ibid* at Article 7.

77   Johannesburg Declaration, UN Doc. A/CONF. 199/L.6.rev. 2, at Article 35.

78   *Ibid* at Article 36.

WSSD recommendations. Salim stated, "The meeting has failed to reach a compromise on essential issues . . . due to the lack of good faith and spirit of constructive dialogue and compromise."[79] The eventual WSSD negotiations and final Plan of Implementation confirmed the fact that nations were ready to agree on only rather modest goals. Three, from among many, issues illustrate the halting negotiations leading up to the decisions of the WSSD: environmental governance, energy and ethics.

For instance, then as at the prior Preparatory Committee meetings, some delegates had promoted recommendations for enhancing the role of the Governing Council of the United Nations Environment Programme (UNEP) as a global ministerial body with universal UN Membership, to provide the focus for the coordination of environmental cooperation.[80] Others sought recommendations for new energy policies and programmes, building upon the work of the 9th Meeting of the UN Commission on Sustainable Development. Several nations, led by Colombia's Environment Minister, Juan Mayr, sought to emphasize the need for a common, fundamental ethical foundation for global environmental stewardship. After each "Prepcom" meeting, the efforts to agree on these points were set aside by the Chair and Secretariat, and the negotiations had to start again. The proposals on UNEP were deemed "important but complex" and were referred to the UN General Assembly for further consideration.[81] The recommendations of the Commission on Sustainable Development at its 9th Session in 2001, were endorsed but the WSSD failed to agree on any time tables or quantitative objectives for securing renewable energy sources and other energy innovations. The major petroleum producing nations—both developed nations, such as the USA, and developing nations, such as Saudi Arabia and Nigeria—succeeded in opposing setting measurable energy goals. On the issue of ethics, the developing nations were able to prevail and insert a single paragraph into the Plan: "We acknowledge the importance of ethics for sustainable development and, therefore, we emphasize the need to consider ethics in the implementation of Agenda 21."[82] Such a modest, albeit profound, statement is still far from the elaboration of ethics norms as set forth in the "Earth Charter,"

---

79   See Associated Press, "No Deal Reached on Indonesia Environment Gab," *The Philippine Star*, June 9, 2002, p. B-6, col. 1.

80   These proposals had been discussed at the "Open-Ended Intergovernmental Group of Ministers or their Representatives on International Environmental Governance," convened through the good offices of the Director General of UNEP. See, e.g. the UNEP paper prepared for the First Meeting, 18 April 2001, at the UN in New York, UN Doc. UNEP/IGM/1/Inf/2, summarizing various recommendations on reforms for environmental governance.

81   The Johannesburg Plan of Implementation (4 September 2002) states: "fully implement the outcomes of the decision on international environmental governance adopted by the Governing Council of the United Nations Environment Programme at its seventh special session, and invite the General Assembly at its fifty-seventh session to consider the important but complex issue of establishing universal membership for the Governing Council/Global Ministerial Environment Forum." (Article 140(e).)

82   The Johannesburg Plan of Implementation (4 September 2002) (Article 6).

as prepared by the Earth Council.[83] The delegates to the WSSD declined to make even a passing reference to the "Earth Charter," which had been developed as a "peoples' charter," in consultations and town meetings across the globe. The nations assembled in UNCED at Rio de Janeiro in 1992 had declined also to try to agree on a statement of fundamental environmental norms, and now the nations assembled at the Johannesburg WSSD again have retreated from the task.

What the WSSD did agree to regarding environmental governance was not exceptional. First, the WSSD was focused on social development, economic development, and environmental protection, which many characterized as the three "pillars" of sustainable development.[84] These three aspects are not equal in their attention to governance. For instance, governance for economic development has been a well established priority for scores of years and is now advanced in the World Trade Organization and in a range of economic development institutions. In social sectors, the International Labour Organization or World Health Organization provides significant governance. However, there is no comparable governance framework for the environmental sector; the many conferences of the parties for the environmental secretariats are independent of one another. Moreover, the governance among the three sectors are not integrated. By fostering the policy image of the three sectors each being a pillar of sustainable development, the WSSD has substituted rhetoric for reality, and largely avoided dealing with the larger environmental governance agenda.

In reaffirming the currently existing "institutional framework for sustainable development,"[85] the WSSD reaffirms the role of the UN General Assembly, as the overall decision-making body.[86] The Second Committee of the UN General Assembly will thus have the overall focus. It cites the role of the Economic and Social Council,[87] and under its umbrella the Commission on Sustainable Development.[88] By doing so, it relegates UNEP as a subsidiary organ of the UN reporting through ECOSOC, to a lower status. It also recommends that the CSD "[f]ocus on actions related to the implementation of Agenda 21, limiting negotiations in the sessions of the Commission to every two years."[89] While this diminution of CSD activity will help the nations who have had difficulty organizing

---

83   The text of the Earth Charter is at www.eathercharter.org.

84   Article 5 of the Johannesburg Declaration on Sustainable Development recites that ". . . we assume a collective responsibility to advance and strengthen the interdependent and mutually reinforcing pillars of sustainable development—economic development, social development and environmental protection—at local, national, regional and global levels." Article 139(b) of the Johannesburg Plan of Implementation states as one objective "Integration of the economic, social and environmental dimensions of sustainable development in a balanced manner."

85   Part XI of the Johannesburg Plan of Implementation.

86   Article 143 of the Plan of Implementation.

87   Article 144 of the Plan of Implementation.

88   Articles 145-150 of the Draft Plan if Implementation. UNGA Res. 47/191 was re-affirmed. Article 145.

89   Articel 147(d) of the Plan of Implementation.

their resources work with the CSD each year, it sends a signal that the oversight of the CSD in furthering environmental sustainability is less important.

The WSSD stressed the need to encourage cooperation in implementing *Agenda 21* on the part of international institutions.[90] It is curious that no mention was made of the specialized environmental treaty organizations, such as the systems set up for Climate Change or Biodiversity Conservation. Nations apparently are not yet ready to address specific ways to enhance the synergies among the Multilateral Environmental Agreements. The delegates did recommend that cooperation be strengthened between the world's financial and trade institutions, specifically the "Bretton Woods" institutions and the World Trade Organization,[91] and the environmental institutions, such as UNEP and UN specialized agencies.[92] The WSSD repeatedly promoted the use of the existing institutional mechanisms for coordination of the UN agencies,[93] and reiterated their support for the role of the Economic and Social Council (ECOSOC) for policy oversight of the implementation of Agenda 21.[94]

G. Factors in Future Deliberations on Environmental Governance

By reaffirming the use of existing institutional arrangements for the implementation of *Agenda 21*, the delegates expressly declined to address a range of imaginative proposals intended to enhance international coordination of efforts to

---

90   Articles 151-157 of the Plan of Implementation.

91   In addition to the World Bank and International Monetary Fund, there are the regional development banks (such as the Asian Development Bank, which has important environmental programs, or the European Bank for Reconstruction and Development, which has an express duty in its organic charter to advance environmental protection in the former centrally planned economies), and the UN regional economic commissions.

92   Articles 154 and 151(b). The other UN specialized agencies with important responsibilities are the World Health Organization (WHO), now headed by Gro Harlem Bruntland who had chaired the UN World Commission on Sustainable Development that produced the seminal report *Our Common Future*, the World Meteorological Organization (WMO), the UN Food and Agricultural Organization (FAO), the UN Education, Scientific and Cultural Organization (UNESCO), and the UN Industrial Development Organization (UNIDO). It is interesting that the role of the International Maritime Organization (IMO), headquartered in London, with oversight of vessel pollution of the marine environment, is not included in the WSSD Plan of Implementation in this regard.

93   Such inter-agency coordination processes include the Inter-Agency Committee on Sustainable Development (IACSD), and the UN System Chief Executives Board for Coordination (noted in Article 152). See also Article 29 of the Johannesburg Plan of Implementation in the context of renewed work for enhancing fresh water management: "Promote effective coordination among the various international and intergovernmental bodies and processes working on water-related issues, both within the United Nations system and between the United Nations and international financial institutions, drawing on the contributions of other international institutions and civil society to inform intergovernmental decision-making; closer coordination should also be promoted to elaborate and support proposals and undertake activities related to the International Year of Freshwater, 2003 and beyond."

94   Article 152, and 144.

realize the recommended actions set forth in *Agenda 21*.[95] Clearly, the delegates consciously chose to underscore their commitment to past multilateral agreements to reemphasize the need to make the extant UN systems work,[96] before trying to innovate or consolidate and reform. Before evaluating what will be needed for the present institutional system to be effective, it is useful to survey the range of proposals that were not addressed, and the one concrete proposal, which concerned the role of the United Nations Environment Programme, that the delegates declined to accept but referred to the UN General Assembly.

Several recommendations have emerged favoring establishment of a new institution, such as UN specialized agency.[97] It could be built upon the existing foundation of UNEP,[98] or it could become an umbrella organization providing support and coordination for the benefit of the several multilateral environmental organizations (MEAs).[99] The MEAs are each independent treaty organizations with small secretariats and conferences of the States that are parties to each agreement (COP): the Convention on Biological Diversity in Montreal,[100] the UN Framework Convention on Climate Change in Bonn,[101] and the UN Convention to Combat Desertification.[102] Others have stressed the argument that since there is a World Trade Organization, there should be a counter-weight for the

---

95 Such proposals can be found in several UN sponsored studies, e.g. "Renewing the United Nations: A Programme for Reform," UN Doc. A/51/950 (July 14, 1997).

96 The Declaration of Johannesburg Declaration on Sustainable Development, in Article 32, stressed that: " We reaffirm our commitment to the principles and purposes of the UN Charter and international law as well as the strengthening of multi-lateralism. We support the leadership role of the United Nations as the most universal and representative organization in the world, which is best placed to promote sustainable development." UN Doc., A/CONF. 199/L.6/Rev.2. This point is stressed again in Para. 102 of the Johannesburg Plan of Implementation, which urges States to refrain from unilateral action. In the political context of the then-current USA foreign policy of the George W. Bush Administration, this statement was an oblique rebuke of some of the Bush Administration's announced foreign policies.

97 See, e.g. Bharat H. Desai, "Revitalizing International Environmental Institutions: The UN Task Force Report and Beyond," 40 Indian J. Int'l L. 455 (July-Sept. 2000). See also John Walley and Ben Zissimos, "Making Environmental Deals: The Economic Case for a World Environmental Organization," in Daniel C. Esty and Maria H. Ivanova, *Global Environmental Governance: Options and Opportunities* (New Haven, Conn., Yale School of Environmental Science & Forestry, 2002), available at www.yale.edu/environment/publications.

98 Under the United Nations Charter, Article 22, the General Assembly can establish new subsidiary organs.

99 A study of the United Nations University presenting the options for a new World Environment Organization was presented as a "side-event" for the third meeting of the Preparatory Committee for the WSSD in New York, which was also the 10th annual session of the Commission on Sustainable Development. (25 March–5 April 2002). The delegates did not undertake to examine these recommendations during this meeting. The conclusions of the UN University ("UNU") study, undertaken by its Institute of Advanced Studies ("IAS"), are set forth in UNU/IAS Report, "International Sustainable Development Governance—The Question of Reform: Key Issues and Proposals," (Final Report, August 2002); see www.ias.unu.edu.

100 The CBD's scope of work and membership is at www.cbd.org.

101 The UNFCCC's scope of work and membership is at www.unfccc.org.

102 The UNCCD's scope of work and membership is at www.unccd.org.

environment, a new World Environment Organization, and the UN could establish a new specialized agency for the environment.[103] There has been rather shallow consideration of how this agency would relate to the Food & Agricultural Organization (FAO) in Rome,[104] the International Maritime Organization (IMO) in London,[105] the World Health Organization (WHO) in Geneva,[106] the World Meteorological Organization (WMO) in Geneva,[107] the International Labor Organization in Geneva,[108] or the UN Educational, Scientific, and Cultural Organization (UNESCO) in Paris.[109] Unlike the composition of the United Nations itself, not all nations have ratified the treaties that establish the MEAs and the specialized agencies.

Would any new agency or institution complement existing specialized agencies, or have functions transferred to be co-located into the new agency? Since the environment is cross-sectoral, how would the special treaty organizations under multilateral environmental agreements for biodiversity or climate change, for instance, be incorporated into the new agency? Logically, one new agency could consolidate the conferences of the parties, if all States agreed to so amend the conventions that establish these bodies. One could imagine one standard protocol that would be adopted by each of the constituent conferences of the parties as an amendment to each.

Some advanced the proposal[110] that a new UN world environmental organizations should follow the pattern of the World Intellectual Property Organization (WIPO), whose headquarters are in Geneva.[111] WIPO was established in 1967 in order to integrate the various intellectual property treaties into a coherent framework. This approach is rather too facile, since intellectual property is a distinct field in its own right, but it is not yet clear how the MEAs relate to each other. Environment covers many sectors, whereas the WIPO covers essentially once sector.

The establishment of such a specialized agency would parallel the evolution of national environment ministries. The national environmental agencies would

---

103　Under the United Nations Charter, Article 59, authority exists to establish a specialized agency either building on UNEP or on a new framework.

104　The FAO's scope of work and membership is at www.fao.org.

105　The IMO's scope of work and membership is at www.imo.org.

106　The WHO's scope of work and membership is at www.who.org.

107　The WMO's scope of work and membership are at www.wmo.org.

108　The ILO's scope of work and membership is at www.ilo.org. The ILO has a unique constitution, through which the 29 nations that are members of the ILO's governing body meet three times a year, and all the members meet annually, with delegations composed of individuals drawn from labor, from commerce, and from government.

109　UNESCO's scope of work and membership is at www.unesco.org. President George W. Bush announced to the UN General Assembly that the USA decided to rejoin UNESCO as a State Member in 2002.

110　UNU/IAS Report, *op. cit. supra* note 74, at p. 11.

111　The scope of work of WIPO is at www.wipo.org.

become the national focal points for this new international agency, just as the national health ministries relate to the WHO or the agricultural and forest ministries relate to the FAO.

One of the most fully elaborated analysis of how such a new environmental governance system could be developed was advanced by the German Advisory Council on Global Change in 2000.[112] It would provide for an independent scientific assessment function, would establish an "Earth Organization" as a specialized UN agency (or an internal UN entity such as the UN Conference on Trade and Development), and would have a funding function which would include levying utilization fees on natural resources taken from the global commons.

Canada advanced this idea with the following points: "In essence, the debate concerns the relative merits of further centralized governance and decision-making through the creation of a new organization—which some have identified as a World Environment Organization—versus a decentralized but strengthened system similar to that which currently exists. While much has been written about strengthening the existing United Nations system, particularly in the context of United Nations and UNEP reform, there has been no detailed analysis and assessment of alternative options like a World Environment Organization. Ideally, debates on form (i.e. institutional and financial matters) should follow discussions on function (i.e. mandate and authority). Questions about mandate and authority should precede any debate about institutional structure."[113] The United Nations General Assembly could reconstitute UNEP under the United Nations Charter.[114] While UNEP ensured that the discussions over function and form were carried on through the informal ministerial consultations, no consensus emerged. More thorough studies largely remain to be undertaken.[115]

UNEP's leadership did not itself advance this idea for a World Environment Organization, preferring the more modest proposal of an upgrade of the UNEP governing council into a ministerial council, as discussed below.[116] Other specialized agencies did not encourage this option because of a concern that it might compromise their existing mandates and scarce financial support bases. Unlike a national system, where a strong executive or legislature could merge

---

112 "World In Transition: New Structures for Global Environmental Policy: Summary for Policy Makers," German Advisory Council on Global Change (September 2000).

113 "International Environmental Institutions: Where from Here?" Canada paper for the Bergen Informal Ministerial Meeting (Bergen, Norway, September 15-17, 2000).

114 UN Charter, Article 22.

115 The United Nations University and a Japanese University did present informally in a "side event" held during the Third Preparatory Committee meeting for the UN WSSD in New York in April 2002.

116 See "International Environmental Governance: Report of the Executive Director," UN Environment Programme, (Nairobi, Kenya, UNEP 2001), available at www.unep.org/IEG/docs/working%20documents/reportfromED/GM_1_2E.doc.

national agencies into one new environmental agency,[117] the international re-gime of nation states lacks a driving political force, and requires a consensus of blocs of nations across several regions to put such a fundamental reorganization into place. Finally, the UN Secretariat opposed this option, preferring instead to promote capacity building for sustainable development, and not a strengthening of the environmental pillar itself; the leadership for the WSSD promoted the role of the UN Development Programme, not the UNEP, as the vehicle for advancing capacity building for sustainable development, including the environmental aspects.

The Global Environmental Facility (GEF) was established by the World Bank, the UN Environment Programme, and the UN Development Programme, to provide a vehicle for providing environmental assistance to nations to develop their envi-ronmental management systems. The GEF developed its own largely autono-mous secretariat, and has established a substantial record of providing effective assistance for the implementation of *Agenda 21*'s recommendations and other environmental objectives.

The need to enhance the funding to build the capacity for environmental man-agement is evident. GEF has had its financing replenished, which is an endorse-ment of the mandate given to it after UNCED in 1992. Some have seen a basis to expand that mandate.[118] For instance, the Council of the European Union in 2000 concluded as follows: "Stable, predictable and adequate funding is a prerequisite for improving governance. . . . The possibility of extending the domains of GEF, and of adapting its resources accordingly, should be examined on the occasion of the replenishment of its resources and the meeting of its Assembly in autumn 2002."[119] When in 2001 GEF proposed that nations consider an expansion to its mandate, it was rebuffed.

For the moment, while the GEF could be consolidated into a new environmental specialized agency, or could be expanded either to undertake a wider scope of capacity building beyond funding, or to effectively provide the institutional basis for such an agency, there is no consensus in this direction.

Several nations have sought to enhance the role of UNEP, chief among them ini-tially was the European Union. The Council of the EU stated: "We should consider . . . the role of UNEP and its status, with a view to giving it the resources it needs to promote better coordination. The Global Ministerial Environment Forum should further promote the enhancement of UNEP's authority by providing polit-ical impulse and direction . . . including setting up a coordination mechanism to bring together, under the aegis of UNEP, all institutions with a largely

---

117 The US Environmental Protection Agency, for instance, was established by an Executive Or-der of President Richard M. Nixon, in 1970, consolidating functions of several agencies into one new agency.

118 Charlotte Streck, "The Global Environmental Facility—A Role Model for International Gover-nance?" in 1 Global Environmental Politics 71 (2001).

119 2321st Meeting of Council, European Union, "Global Environmental Governance," Brussels, Belgium, (December 18-19, 2000).

environmental remit, in order to harmonize on a thematic basis, schedules, assessment actions and strategies. . . . "[120]

The six negotiating sessions of the Open-Ended Intergovernmental Group of Ministers or their Representatives on International Environmental Governance, organized by UNEP, refined a fairly clear proposal for enhancing UNEP's work.[121]

Since the existing UN organs have crowded agendas on which many topics compete for time and attention with the environmental agenda items, there have been proposals to combine all environmental issues under one policy-making forum. This is deemed essential if environmental stewardship and security is to be made as high a priority as military collective security, which is the domain of the UN Security Council, or economic and social issues, which are within the purview of the UN Economic and Social Council (ECOSOC). The ecological and scientific and technical aspects of environmental stewardship require more attention than diplomats in ECOSOC have time to devote. Since the colonies are now, for the most part, sovereign states and members of the UN, there is no functional need for the Trusteeship Council under the UN Charter's original architecture. Today the most profound need for a collective trusteeship is the stewardship of the natural systems in the biosphere.[122]

Although no political consensus favors such a measure, it would be logical to re-invent the Trusteeship Council as an Environmental Trusteeship Council. It could coordinate the work of the MEAs, the UN programs such as UNEP, UNDP or UNCTADS, and the work of the specialized agencies. A revision to the United Nations Charter could be designed to give effect to this idea, as provision has been made for amendment to the UN Charter.[123] This revised Council could also exercise oversight for Earth's commons, the atmosphere, the climate, the high seas, the bio-chemical cycles such as the nitrogen or carbon cycles, and the Antarctic.

What has prevented any serious consideration of this option is a fear on the part of many nations that the UN Members would not be content to amend just one article of the United Nations Charter. The fear is that one or another UN Member would put forward other amendments, unrelated to the environment. In this assessment, a range of politically unacceptable amendments could emerge that would hold the environmental amendment hostage. Rather than risk this eventuality, States have declined to seriously advance any proposals for an environmental trusteeship.

A more modest proposal to enhance the cooperation and produce synergies among the several environmental inter-governmental organizations has been to

---

120 Ibid.

121 See "Report of the Open-Ended Intergovernmental Group of Ministers or their Representatives on International Environmental Governance," UN Doc. UNEP/IGC/Decision SS.VII/1 (Feb. 15, 2002), Annex, available at www.unep.org/governingbodies.

122 UNEP's Director General took note of this proposal in his report on International Environmental Governance, UN Doc. UNEP/IGM/4/3 (Nov. 16, 2001).

123 United Nations Charter, Amendments.

co-locate them. Efforts by Switzerland, and its Canton of Geneva, to create a shared environmental headquarters in Geneva, Switzerland, were undermined when Canada secured the Secretariat of the Convention on Biological Diversity for Montreal, and Germany secured the Secretariat for the UN Framework Convention on Climate Change in its former capital of Bonn. Germany, and Bonn, would like to make Bonn a UN headquarters for environmental agencies. It already has the Desertification Secretariat and the Migratory Species Secretariat, plus the IUCN Environmental Law Centre.

It would make great sense either to consolidate these offices in Bonn, but that would mean a sacrifice on the part of either the Swiss or the Canadians. It is equally helpful to co-locate the secretariat in Geneva, but this is contrary again to the German and Canadian government interests, and thus is problematic. Since it is unlikely that the locations will be consolidated, as localized national economic interests militate against doing so, ways to integrate programs and projects should be sought. However, all these secretariats are small in size, and have modest operations, and without adequate resources it will not be possible to integrate them into a more coordinated program. There seems to be little consensus behind the option of fully integrating the MEAs, as each of the individual secretariats for the multilateral environmental agreements would need to see some material advantage in doing so. If the several nations, which, after all, comprise roughly the same membership of each MEA, were to consolidate and increase their financial support, they could facilitate such enhancements.

It may be considered troubling that none of these innovations has received priority attention by the very nations that have created the current disjointed system of environmental governance. The WSSD Plan of Implementation makes it clear that the UNCED's goal of integrating environment with development is as far ahead in the future today as it was in 1992. The WSSD emphasis on there being three pillars of sustainable development—economic viability, ecological sustainability, and social compatibility—is largely rhetorical.[124] Economic decisions, and even social decisions, are still made without regard to environmental considerations. Where environmental procedures have been established to integrate the three, such as is the case with environmental impact assessment,[125] the economic development interests have often sought to maximize their capacity to

---

124 Article 3 to the Johannesburg Declaration on Sustainable Development provides that, in order that youth and future generations will "inherit a world free of the indignity and indecency occasioned by poverty, environmental degradation and patterns of unsustainable development." "Accordingly, we assume a collective responsibility to advance and strengthen the interdependent and mutually reinforcing pillars of sustainable development—economic development, social development, and environmental protection—at local, national, regional and global levels." (Article 5).

125 Principle 17 of the Declaration of Rio de Janeiro on Environment and Development; See Article 206 of the UN Convention on the Law of the Sea, and the UN ECE Espoo Convention on Environmental Impact in a Transboundary Context, 1989 U.N.T.S. 309, 30 I.L.M. 800 (Feb. 25, 1991), and the Åarhus Convention on Access to Information, Public Participation in Decision-making, and Access to Justice in Environmental Matters, 38 I.L.M. 517 (June 15, 1998).

profit by eliminating the process altogether.[126] The emphasis in Europe today on ensuring that the public has access to environmental information in order to participate in governmental decision-making that has environmental conse-quences,[127] indicates that the preconditions do not yet fully exist for treating en-vironmental sectors as co-equal with economic and social sectors.

Given the WSSD's stalemate in considering innovations in international environmen-tal governance, how can the vision that UNCED provided in *Agenda 21* be restored?

Many governments have noted that the foundation now exists for a more effec-tive system of governance. Many, if not all, of the legal norms are in place through environmental treaties. Many nations have established implementation systems for those norms through national legislations and programs. Canada, in particular, had tabled several proposals for enhancing environmental gover-nance at the international level.[128] As Canada put it, "The current structure of in-ternational environmental institutions belongs to a different age. As we enter a new century, our approach to managing the global environment must reflect what we have learned over the past decades, and where we are going. New sci-entific knowledge is illustrating the close interconnectedness of environmental issues, calling traditional 'issue-by-issue' problem-solving into question."[129]

Over the past three decades, a great deal has been learned about the short-com-ings of environmental governance around the world. These were summarized by the Minister of the Environment of Norway at the Bergen Informal Ministerial Meeting in September of 2000. Minister Siri Bjerke summarized the key issues that emerged from the experience to date as follows:[130]

(a) A need for the four "C's": coherence, coordination, compliance and capacity-building;

(b) A lack of coordination between different environmental organizations and structures and the multilateral environmental agreements;

(c) Weak international dispute mechanisms existing for the environmental agreements;

(d) The absence of an environmental counterweight to the World Trade Organization;

---

126 See N.A. Robinson, "Legal Systems, Decisionmaking, and The Science of Earth's Systems: Pro-cedural Missing Links," 27 Ecology Law Quarterly 1077 at 1124-1131 (2001).

127 The Åarhus Convention on Access to Information, Public Participation in Decisionmaking, and Access to Justice in Environmental Matters, 38 I.L.M. 517 (June 15, 1998). See generally N.A. Robinson, "Enforcing Environmental Norms: Diplomatic and Judicial Approaches," 26 Hastings International and Comparative Law Review 387 (2003), discussing the Åarhus Con-vention and relating that to the norms of the draft "Earth Charter."

128 "International Environmental Institutions: Where from Here?" Paper by Canada for the Bergen Informal Ministerial Meeting (Bergen, Norway, September 15-17, 2000).

129 "Global Environmental Governance" Paper by Canada (January 2001).

130 Chairman's Summary of the Bergen Informal Ministerial Meeting, Bergen, Norway, Septem-ber 15-17, 2000.

(e) A need for stronger implementation of and compliance with the multilateral environmental agreements; and

(f) A need to increase environmental security

In addition to these observations, there is a widespread agreement that there are too many ad hoc environmental organizations, regionally and internationally. Most nations cannot attend all the meetings with full delegations. Even the European Union and the USA find this volume of meetings to be burdensome. As the Council of the EU has put it: "The continuous increase in the number of international bodies with environmental competence carries the risk of reduced participation of States owing to an increased workload, and makes it necessary to create or strengthen the synergies between all these bodies."[131]

It is evident that the major obstacle to enhancing environmental governance lies with the nations themselves. Within the capitals of each nation, there is a need to understand what new cooperative measures are important and what collaborative work among the MEAs or within the UN systems is in the national interest of each nation. Climate change may provide the incentive for such, since with the global changes reflected in sea level rise and changing weather patterns, nations have recognized that their environmental security is at risk. The one major new political decision that the WSSD induced was the decisions by Canada and the Russian Federation to ratify the Kyoto Protocol. Upon the receipt of these ratifications, the Kyoto Protocol will enter into force, and major reductions of carbon dioxide emission will become mandatory over many economic sectors. Multinational companies with operations in Europe and Canada will put pressure the USA to give legal recognition to their carbon dioxide emission reductions or sequestration decisions.

However flawed one may consider the current Kyoto Protocol's formulas for containing green house gas emission, it does offer the rudiments of a new system of international cooperation. Accounting for sequestration of carbon dioxide through photosynthesis can mean new emphasis on restoring and maintaining the biota found in wetlands systems, providing a stimulus to the Ramsar Convention on Wetlands of International Importance.[132] Similarly, the UN Forum on Forests would have a pressing reason to collaborate with the Convention on Biological Diversity in ensuring continued photosynthesis through restoration and maintenance of diverse forest ecosystems. It lends support to planting vegetation to combat desertification. Payments to build natural sequestration systems can infuse funding from carbon dioxide emitting companies into these treaty systems and their national implementation systems. Fees, rather than overseas development assistance or taxes, can fuel the investment in biological systems.

---

131 Council of the European Union, 2321st Council Meeting, "Global Environmental Governance—Conclusions," Brussels, Belgium (December 18-19, 2000).

132 Ramsar Convention on Wetlands of Internal Importance Especially as Waterfowl Habitat, (February 2, 1971), as amended by the Protocol of Paris (Dec. 3, 1982), 1976 U.N.T.S. 245.

There needs to be a policy forum through which such cooperation can be facilitated. The Second Committee of the UN General Assembly is the current home for this policy debate, but its agenda is too crowded to give any single matter sustained attention, and it lacks the secretariat support to follow-through on its decisions. The Commission on Sustainable Development could do so, but it too would need a secretariat capable of attending to the coordination efforts over time. ECOSOC lacks a secretariat skilled in environmental issues, and its leadership is also reconstituted annually. It too lacks the sustained focus needed to interact with the specific MEA secretariats to effect such cooperation. These bodies are reconstituted annually, and are thus ill equipped for the functions of continuous oversight.

Lacking an international focus, regional coordination will be the only effective way to build consensus and tackle the complex environmental issues, and their economic and social implications. The European Union is already doing so, and could do so more explicitly, especially as it enlarges. The Canadian and USA joint commission does much to harmonize the environmental protection for the Great Lakes Basin, and beyond, and with encouragement it could do more. The Association of South East Asian Nations (ASEAN) has moved its framework for cooperation closer to such environmental integration.[133] The Andean Pact has such a potential, as does the reconstituted African Union, or the regional Southern African Development Community (SADEC). The South Pacific Regional Environmental Programme (SPREP) can provide this framework in the Pacific region, as CARICOM could in the Caribbean. If concerned nations wanted to promote such regional measures as a means of building comparable and compatible regional frameworks for environmental cooperation, funding should be made available to strengthen these regional agreements.

With the key geographic regions of the Earth engaged in comparable measures to implement MEAs and address common environmental challenges, the likelihood of consensus among the capitals on specific questions of international environmental governance would increase.

Cooperation among comparable officials within each nation can also encourage such a common vision. Already the environmental agencies cooperate. Although not a part of the WSSD, the Global Judges' Symposium held by UNEP Johannesburg on the eve of the WSSD provided a useful way for courts to share common experiences on the application and enforcement of environmental law. This meeting was part of a series of meetings in Africa, South Asia, South East Asia, Mexico, and in October, 2002, in Kuwait for the Arab nations and in London for West European nations. Both UNEP and IUCN are providing facilitation for judges to confer and continue to exchange experience on environmental law

---

133   See Koh Kheng Lian and Nicholas A. Robinson, "Strengthening Sustainable Development in Regional Inter-Governmental Governance: Lessons from the 'ASEAN' Way," 6 Singapore Journal of International and Comparative Law 640 (2002).

issues. There is also a fledgling system of cooperation among environmental prosecutors.

IUCN could do more to promote a common perspective among capitals on the need to enhance international environmental governance. IUCN is a unique hybrid international organization, comprised of 75 sovereign states, some 120 ministries within states, and some 480 non-governmental organizations reflecting civil society at national and international levels.[134] The educational capacity of such a Union to bring about regional and even global consensus is evident. IUCN is constrained by a lack of funds, and again the same set of States that comprise the membership of IUCN also comprise the MEAs and the UN Second Committee. Since IUCN has more grassroots environmental capacity in civil society and among environmental experts, IUCN may be uniquely situated to build elements of the consensus that is now lacking.

UNEP's Governing Council could also take on these tasks, but since the many of the diplomats who attend the Governing Council are the ones posted in Nairobi, they have less capacity to galvanize the consensus back in the capitals. UNEP needs to serve as a catalyst to stimulate new cooperation among nations, as it did in the negotiation of several environmental agreements, most recently the UN Convention signed in Stockholm on Persistent Organic Pollutants. A similar basis for functional cooperation is found in the report of the World Commission on Dams.[135] Some have urged the formation of a "Global Environmental Mechanism" to serve the functional needs "to promote environmental collective action at the international scale."[136]

Building regional or national consensus in favor of enhancing international environmental governance will not be easy, but it is the only way forward. International environmental action at the international level will remain stalled until either a new ecological catastrophe motivates nations to act together, or the geographic regions strengthen their own frameworks for environmental cooperation, rendering it easier to link these into an international framework. Such regional and national efforts will have to overcome predictable opposition to reforms. Some opposition comes from vested interests, and some from conditions of poverty and a lack of resources. In many capitals, the lack of access to environmental information must be addressed. Others face competing

---

134 IUCN's Statutes, as the organic act establishing the Union, and a description of its organization and activities is at www.iucn.org.

135 World Commission on Dams, "Dams and Development: A New Framework for Decision Making: The Report of the World Commission on Dams," (London, Earthscan Pubs., 2000), available at www.dams.org/report/contents.htm; see also Navroz K. Dubash, Mairi Dupar, Smitu Kothari and Tundu Lissu, "A Watershed in Global Governance? An Independent Assessment of the World Commission on Dams" (Washington, DC, World Resources Institute, 2001), available at www.wcdassessment.org/reeport.htm

136 Daniel C. Esty and Maria H. Ivanova, "Revitalizing Global Environmental Governance: A Function-Driven Approach," in Daniel C. Esy and Maria H. Ivanova, Global Environmental Governance: Options and Opportunities 180 at p. 191 (New Haven, Yale School of Forestry and Environmental Science, 2002), available at www.yale.edu/environment/publications.

social crises, such as the pandemic of AIDS/HIV that makes the already difficult cooperation in Africa even more problematic. A few, but influential capitals are preoccupied with their ideological priorities. Organizations such as IUCN will need to work especially long and hard to cope with the ecological illiteracy that such opposing forces engender, which blinds them to the demonstrated facts of environmental deterioration.

H. The Prospects for Environmental Governance

Paths toward a clearer and shared vision on enhancing international environmental governance are charted in the documents collected in this volume. These paths will be pursued by individual nations, in bilateral and regional contexts and also through international cooperation. Steps toward future international institution-building are likely to be characterized by slow and halting progress. Nations will muddle through toward shaping new systems of international environmental governance rather than taking forthright actions.[137] Since, as *Agenda 21* emphasizes, environmental factors are found in every sector of governmental activity, it is probable that enhancements in governmental systems for environmental stewardship will come in individual sectors or across selected sectors. For instance, integrated coastal zone management is premised on such cross-sectoral cooperation,[138] and protected area management inevitably requires coordination with land use management of geographic areas adjacent to the parks or reserves. However, how and whether nations can build on such improvements in environmental governance to fashion wider regional or global governance systems are questions as yet unanswered.

Perhaps it will take a crisis to galvanize action among nations. Nations are preoccupied with the urgent crises of armed conflict, terrorism, or drug trafficking. These are seen as pressing issues, requiring priority attention. Nations tend to ignore gradual trends in environmental degradation as problems of a lower magnitude of priority; they can put them off for a later time. Action is galvanized only when the crisis reaches the breaking point, as when ecological refuges flee their homelands lacking food or water, or regional economies collapse lacking water, or epidemics threaten as diseases migrate from one land to another. The need for emergency national action with international cooperation comes too

---

137 In this regard, Article 30 of the Johannesburg Declaration on Sustainable Development ("We undertake to strengthen and improve governance at all levels, for the effective implementation of Agenda 21. . . ") stands in striking contrast to the endorsement of the status quo on governance in Part XI ("Institutional Framework for Sustainable Development") and the decisions not to act on any specific environmental governance reforms. Since deliberate decisions to strengthen and improve governance escaped the grasp of nations assembled at the WSSD, the process toward governance reform will evolve incrementally.

138 See Donna Craig, Nicholas A. Robinson, Koh Kheng-Lian (Eds), *Capacity Building for Environmental Law in the Asian and Pacific Region—Approaches and Resources,* Chapter 14, "Integrated Coastal Zone Management," pp. 175-232 (2002).

late. If environmental governance is to have a role, it must be to anticipate and organize action before the crisis point.

The WSSD treated the worsening trends in environmental degradation as a lower priority than the scientific facts would warrant. It left the "business as usual" decision-making systems to attend to these trends, while paying lip service to their seriousness. In this respect, the WSSD must be seen as but a small step toward the day when more effective environmental governance can come into being. A further reform effort will need to be re-initiated after this failure of vision at the WSSD.

Since, absent some ecological catastrophe, a consensus toward more effective environmental governance is likely to build gradually only with a functional approach, what could stimulate such gradual reform measures? While the Westphalian system of nation states, now under the collective security of the United Nations Charter, may be said to have worked for military security and trade relations, it decidedly has as yet not worked for environment protection. National borders do not coincide with environmental systems, and never will. New patterns of cross-border cooperation are required, along with global cooperation on issues affecting the biosphere as a whole. The Declaration of The Hague[139] dramatically made this observation in 1989: ". . . the conditions of life on our planet are threatened by the severe attacks to which the earth's atmosphere is subjected. . . . Because the problem is planet-wide in scope, solutions can only be devised on a global level . . . [and therefore] the signatories acknowledge and will promote the . . . the principle of developing, within the framework of the United Nations, new institutional authority. . . ." Neither UNCED nor WSSD accomplished much to give recognition to this Declaration.

Since international measures to fashion new institutions for environmental governance have not yet brought into being the needed new systems,[140] it may be that reforms will be advanced more gradually through two distinct stimuli:

First, individual states within regions can cooperate within and across regions. The cooperation on functional issues, in a pragmatic way, will necessarily build

---

139 The Declaration of The Hague (March 31, 1989), 28 I.L.M. 1308 (1989).

140 Two commentators have noted that nations have four choices: (1) to do nothing, (2) to refine the status quo governance structures, (3) to launch a new Global Environmental Organization, or (4) to develop a new governance approach as a "Global Environmental Mechanisms." Daniel C. Esy and Maria H. Ivanova, "The Road Ahead: Conclusions and Action Agenda," in Esy and Ivanova, *Global Environmental Governance: Options and Opportunities* (New Haven, Conn., Yale School of Environmental Science and Forestry, 2002), 225 at p. 226. However, nations are not doing "nothing" as they incrementally respond to environmental problems, and while the WSSD has chosen to pursue option 2 and refine existing governance systems, the nations will need to more. Nations are unlikely at once to agree to options 3 or 4, and thus the way forward is either a 5th option, that of regional cooperation and integration, with a possible 6th option based upon a more rapid recognition of environmental duties based on fundamental principles of environmental rights. These latter two options require further study and are outlined in the conclusions of this article.

the new systems for international environmental governance. The nations at the WSSD apparently recognized the importance of encouraging regional cooperation by featuring regional initiatives explicitly within the Johannesburg Plan of Implementation.[141] The progressive integration of the environmental regimes in the several nations of the European Union (EU) through the many environmental directives provides a remarkable history of governance coordination and harmonization over a large region.[142] With the enlargement of the EU by the addition of the accession states, a pan-European environmental governance system is emerging. In a different and yet equally promising way, the Association of Southeast Asian Nations (ASEAN) has gradually established a framework for cooperation toward regional environmental governance.[143] The negotiation of a treaty on combating transboundary air pollution from forest fires in the region is a recent example of ASEAN members taking concerted action.[144] In North America, the Great Lakes Water Quality Agreement is another effective illustration of such concrete regional integration of environmental protection systems.[145]

States lack experience with each other in tackling environmental problems of the biosphere. They can and do work effectively with their neighbors in each region. As they cooperate, they build both experience in coping with environmental issues and confidence in integrating their governance authorities to do so. It would be in the interests of all nations to encourage such regional cooperation as the future foundations for international environmental governance institutions.

Second, nations can decide to coordinate their actions because their national leaders conclude it is morally right to do so. This is the basis for cooperation to affirm and apply human rights and international humanitarian law. It should be also for environmental duties and laws. Nations need not wait for an ecological catastrophe before deciding to cooperate. The basis for such an ethical ap-

---

141 Part VIII, Sustainable Development in Africa, in articles 62-71, and Part IX, "Other Regional Initiatives" in articles 72-80 (September 4, 2002).

142 See Alexandre Kiss and Dinah Shelton, *Manual of European Environmental Law* (2d ed., Cambridge University Press, 1997).

143 Koh Kheng Lian and Nicholas A. Robinson, "Regional Environmental Governance: Examining the Association of Southeast Asian Nations (ASEAN) Model," in Daniel C. Esty and Maria H. Ivanova (Eds.), *Global Environmental Governance: Options and Opportunities* (New Haven, Conn., Yale School of Forestry and Environmental Studies, 2002), available at www.yale.edu/environment/publications. See also Andre Dua and Daniel C. Esty, *Sustaining the Asian Pacific Miracle: Economic Integration and Environmental Protection* (Washington, DC., Institute for International Economics, 1997).

144 See Simon Tay, "The Southeast Asian Fires and Sustainable Development: What should be Done? 3 Asia Pacific Journal of Environmental Law 205 (1998); Allan Tan, Forest Fires of Indonesia: State Responsibility and International Liability," 48 International and Comparative Law Quarterly 826 (1999); and Nicholas A. Robinson, "Forest Fires as a Common International Concern: Precedents for the Progressive Development of International Environmental Law, 18 Pace Environmental Law Review 459 (2000).

145 Great Lakes Water Quality Agreement, 30 U.S.T. 1383 (Nov. 22, 1987).

proach to fostering international environmental governance exists within international environmental law. The principles that all nations have "common but differentiated responsibilities"[146] for transnational environmental problems can be elaborated and implemented through new institutional arrangements. For instance, while all nations have a common duty to strive to stabilize green house gases in the atmosphere in order to mitigate the severity of such environmental impacts, nations with advanced capacity in industrial technology have different duties to deploy engineering means to avert growth in gaseous emissions, or nations in mountain regions have duties to share management means to avert environmental harm as glaciers melt.[147] However differentiated, these responsibilities have a common foundation: ethics.

The documents collected in this volume can guide humanity to make the shift from depletingly exploitative and environmentally unsustainable patterns into new stewardship modes of conduct. The directions charted here implicitly acknowledge the common but differentiated responsibilities of States around the Earth. Just as international order under the Charter of the United Nations is based on a sense of justice as well as force, these documents of environmental stewardship reflect ethical choices. As the Johannesburg Plan of Implementation acknowledges, "ethics is important for sustainable development"[148] and must play a role in implementing *Agenda 21*. Ethics are increasingly recognized as a necessary guide for economic decisions; ethics are the foundation for social decisions. The norms of the World Charter for Nature,[149] or the more comprehensive but yet to be adopted "Earth Charter,"[150] provide foundations for an ethics of environmental sustainability.

National policy, and international policy, is rooted ultimately in human society, and the individuals within it. The consensus of ethical instincts among individuals and nations can nurture the changes recommended in *Agenda 21* and the Johannesburg Plan of Implementation. Humaneness, which uniquely distinguishes

---

146 Cite Rio Declaration Principle and the UN FCCC article 3.1 "The Parties should protect the climate system for the benefit of present and future generations of humankind, on the basis of equity and in accordance with their common but differentiated responsibilities and respective capabilities."

147 2002 was declared by the UN General Assembly to be the Year of the Mountains and a conference held in Bistek, Kyrgystan in November 2002.

148 Johannesburg Plan of Implementation, (Sept. 4, 2002).

149 UN Res. 37/7 (Oct. 28, 1982), 22 I.L.M. 455 (1983).

150 The delegates to the UNCED could not agree on adoption of an Earth Charter in 1992, and the challenge to frame a universal set of ethical norms for stewardship of Earth was taken up by the "Earth Council," a non-governmental organization based in Costa Rica. Under the leadership of Prof. Steven Rockefeller, the Earth Council sought contributions were sought from all religions, from a review of treaties and national laws, and from an analysis of over 200 governmental and non-governmental declarations. Prof. Rockefeller held hundreds of consultations world-wide with many thousands of individuals and organizations. As the principal draftsman, Prof. Rockefeller has prepared an "Earth Charter" with particular clarity and internal integrity. See the text at www.earthcouncil.org.

homo sapiens from other living species on Earth, is grounded in ethics. The diplomatic decisions to build the roadmap to sustainable development reflect basic moral duties that are implicit in the diplomatic acknowledgement of "common but differentiated responsibilities." Absent an international organization to champion these values, they need to be elaborated and pressed in the capitals of each nation, so that national decision-makers come to agree on international measures for environmental stewardship. The precedent of Mohandas Gandhi's resort to fundamental ethics to change the colonial governance of India suggests that this approach can bear fruit. Gandhi advised the United Nations in 1946, "I learned from my illiterate but wise Mother that all rights to be deserved and preserved came from duty well done. Thus the very right to live accrues to us only when we do the duty of citizenship of the world. From this one fundamental statement, perhaps it is easy enough to define the duties of Man and Woman and correlate every right to some corresponding duty to be first performed."[151]

The duties of environmental stewardship are imperfectly performed today, and Earth's social and economic and environmental conditions are far from being sustainable. The present failures to attain elements of sustainable development jeopardize our ability to do so in the future, while currently denying the human environmental rights of people, the continuation of species and diversity of life. Ultimately, these shortcomings even threaten to compromise the natural systems upon which life on earth depends. The general principle of international law is clear: nations—and thus their leaders—"have the responsibility to ensure that activities within their jurisdiction or control do not cause damage to the environment of other States or of areas beyond the limits of national jurisdiction."[152] Today, acid rain from North Asia and South East Asia pollutes the Indian Ocean's atmosphere and is deposited on South Asia; today, acid rain from the North American mid-west pollutes the north east of that continent, and acid rain from western and central Europe pollutes northern Europe and Eurasia. It is not enough for scientists to document such affairs, and similarly it is insufficient for lawyers to observer that this national conduct is both illegal and unethical. Such observations have been made to no effect. What *is* required is for States to cooperate to shape anew systems of international environmental governance to resolve the problem of acid rain, and other environmental assaults on the fabric of life on Earth.

---

151 Mohandas Gandhi, "Letter Address to the Director General of UNESCO, 1946", quoted in Mary Ann Glendon, *A World Made New*, at p. 75. (New York: Random House, 2001).

152 Principle 21, Stockholm Declaration on the Human Environment. See also the UN Economic Commission of Europe's European Charter on Environmental Rights and Obligations, Principle 2: "Everyone has the responsibility to protect and conserve the environment for the benefit of present and future generation." (1990).

Public participation in environmental decision-making has become an internationally recognized process.[153] Public participation is the means whereby ethical duties can be invoked and produce consensus in the capitals about acting on "common but differentiated responsibilities." It is through public participation that national or local decision-makers are called upon, in the words of Aldo Leopold, to "examine each question in terms of what is ethically and esthetically right, as well as what is economically expedient."[154] If nations remain cool to their potential roles in international environmental governance, nongovernmental organizations at national and international levels are espousing more effective environmental protection measures with vigor.[155] The role of civil society and NGOs will be essential to building a new global moral consensus for establishing and observing environmental duties.[156] The popularity of the "Earth Charter" within civil society—if not yet with national governments—is a good illustration of the growing consensus that civil society brings to win support of environmental action within the democracies of the world.

Ultimately, the challenge of international environmental governance is to build acceptance of our common ethical responsibilities. A better understanding of the ecological problems that confront nations today can propel us toward the ethics of stewardship. In the wake of those acknowledged roles, the new systems for international environmental governance will be found.

I. The Roadmap Forward

The action plans collected in this volume provide the roadmap forward. They depend upon public participation for their implementation, as much as they depend upon the financial and technical aid marshaled by national governments and international organizations. These documents are a remarkable mix of practical steps forward, imbued with the ethical judgments embraced in the Johannesburg Declaration, and the earlier Rio and Stockholm Declarations.

---

153 The most extensive statement is the Åarhus Convention on Access to Information, Public Participation in Decisionmaking and Access to Justice in Environmental Matters (June 25, 1988), 38 I.L.M. 517. While this is a UN Economic Commission for Europe sponsored treaty, it is open to states elsewhere to adhere to it. It provides an explicit application to environmental stewardship within the broader context of the Universal Declaration of Human Rights (1948) and the UN Covenant on Civil and Political Rights (1976), 999 U.N.T.S. 171 (1966).

154 Aldo Leopold, *A Sand County Almanac*, Oxford University Press, 1948). This statement sets the stage for Leopold's ethical maxim: "A thing is right when it tends to preserve the integrity, stability, and beauty of the biotic community. It is wrong when it tends otherwise." *Id.* at p. 224-5.

155 Paul Wapner, "The Transnational Politics of Environmental NGOs: Government, Economic and Social Activism," in Pamela S. Chasek, *The Global Environment in the Twenty-First Century: Prospects for International Cooperation* (Tokyo, UN University, 2000), available at www.ciaonet.org/book/chasek/.

156 See Barbara Gemmell and Abimbola Bamidele-Izu, "The Role of NGOs and Civil Society in Global Environmental Governance," in Daniel C. Esty and Maria H. Ivanova (Eds.), *Global Environmental Governance Options and Opportunities* (New Haven, Conn., Yale School of Forestry and Environmental Studies, 2002), available at www.yale.edu/environment/publications.

If the Member States of the United Nations are not now prepared to fashion a new intergovernmental environmental agency to manage Earth's shared natural systems, they are at least ready to coordinate their national policies and programs to do so.

The U.N. Commission on Sustainable Development will meet in two-year cycles to assess the implementation of the Johannesburg priorities. The recommendations on water and sewage and habitat are being evaluated in 2004-5, and the recommendations on energy are to be evaluated in 2006-7. By the benchmark year of 15 years after the Rio Earth Summit, 2007, there should be enough experience with the Johannesburg Plan of Implementation to determine if the roadmap works effectively enough to continue to guide international cooperation toward sustainable development.

AGENDA 21
ANNOTATED ACTION PLAN

Chapter 1

Preamble

1.1. Humanity stands at a defining moment in its history. We are confronted with a perpetuation of disparities between and within nations, a worsening of poverty, hunger, ill health and illiteracy, and the continuing deterioration of the ecosystems on which we depend for our well-being. However, integration of environment and development concerns, and greater attention to them will lead to the fulfilment of basic needs, improved living standards for all, better protected and managed ecosystems and a safer, more prosperous future. No nation can achieve this on its own; but together we can—in a global partnership for sustainable development.

1.2. This global partnership must build on the premises of General Assembly resolution 44/228 of 22 December 1989, which was adopted when the nations of the world called for the United Nations Conference on Environment and Development, and on the acceptance of the need to take a balanced and integrated approach to environment and development questions.

1.3. Agenda 21 addresses the pressing problems of today and also aims at preparing the world for the challenges of the next century. It reflects a global consensus and[1] political commitment at the highest level on development and environment cooperation. Its successful implementation is first and foremost the responsibility of Governments.[2] National strategies, plans, policies and processes are crucial in achieving this. International cooperation should support and supplement such national efforts. In this context, the United Nations system has a key role to play. Other international, regional and sub-regional organizations are also called upon to contribute to this effort. The broadest public participation and the active involvement of the non-governmental organizations and other groups should also be encouraged.

---

1   Draft paragraph 1.3 of A/CONF. 151/4 (22 April 1992) included brackets around the words "political commitment at the highest level". The brackets were deleted by decision of the Main Committee of UNCED on 10 June 1992. See A/CONF. 151/L.3/Add. 1 (11 June 1992).

2   When the term Governments is used, it will be deemed to include the European Economic Community within the areas of its competence. Throughout Agenda 21 the term "environmentally sound" means "environmentally safe and sound", in particular when applied to the terms "energy sources", "energy supplies", "energy systems" and "technology" or "technologies." [This Footnote in A/CONF. 151/26 (vol. 1), p. 15, was set with an asterisk following the word "Preamble" above.]

1.4. The developmental and environmental objectives of Agenda 21 will require a substantial flow of new and additional financial resources to developing countries in order to cover the incremental costs for the actions they have to undertake to deal with global environmental problems and to accelerate sustainable development. Financial resources are also required for strengthening the capacity of international institutions for the implementation of Agenda 21. An indicative order-of-magnitude assessment of costs is included in each of the programme areas. This assessment will need to be examined and refined by the relevant implementing agencies and organizations.[3]

1.5. In the implementation of the relevant programme areas identified in Agenda 21, special attention should be given to the particular circumstances facing the economies in transition. It must also be recognized that these countries are facing unprecedented challenges in transforming their economies, in some cases in the midst of considerable social and political tension.[4]

1.6. The programme areas that constitute Agenda 21 are described in terms of the basis for action, objectives, activities and means of implementation. Agenda 21 is a dynamic programme. It will be carried out by the various actors according to the different situations, capacities and priorities of countries and regions in full respect of all the principles contained in the Rio Declaration on Environment and Development. It could evolve over time in the light of changing needs and circumstances. This process marks the beginning of a new global partnership for sustainable development.[5]

---

3   Draft paragraph 1.4 of A/CONF. 151/4 (22 April 1992) was amended by decision of the Main Committee of UNCED on 10 June 1992. See A/CONF. 151/L.3/Add. 1 (11 June 1992). The first sentence of paragraph 1.4 of the former draft read as follows:

   The developmental and environmental objectives of Agenda 21 will require a substantial flow of new and additional financial resources to countries in need, particularly to developing countries in order to cover the incremental costs for the actions they have to undertake to deal with global environmental problems and to accelerate sustainable development.

4   Draft A/CONF. 151/4 (22 April 1992) did not include the preceding two sentences. The sentences were added by decision of the Main Committee of UNCED on 10 June 1992. See A/CONF. 151/L. 3/Add. 1 (11 June 1992).

5   Draft paragraph 1.5 of A/CONF. 151/4 (22 April 1992) was replaced by decision of the Main Committee of UNCED on 10 June 1992. See A/CONF. 151/L. 3/Add. 1 (12 June 1992). The former draft read as follows:

   The programme areas that constitute Agenda 21 are described in terms of the Basis for Action, Objectives, Activities and Means of implementation. Agenda 21 is a dynamic programme. It will be carried out by the various actors according to the different situations, capacities and priorities of countries and regions. It could evolve over time in the light of changing needs and circumstances. This process marks the beginning of a new global partnership for sustainable development.

Section 1: Social and Economic Dimensions

Chapter 2

International Cooperation to Accelerate Sustainable Development in Developing Countries and Related Domestic Policies

INTRODUCTION

2.1. In order to meet the challenges of environment and development, States have decided to establish a new global partnership. This partnership commits all States to engage in a continuous and constructive dialogue, inspired by the need to achieve a more efficient and equitable world economy, keeping in view the increasing interdependence of the community of nations and that sustainable development should become a priority item on the agenda of the international community. It is recognized that, for the success of this new partnership, it is important to overcome confrontation and to foster a climate of genuine cooperation and solidarity. It is equally important to strengthen national and international policies and multinational cooperation to adapt to the new realities.[1]

2.2. Economic policies of individual countries and international economic relations both have great relevance to sustainable development. The reactivation and acceleration of development requires both a dynamic and a supportive international economic environment and determined policies at the national level. It will be frustrated in the absence of either of these requirements. A supportive external economic environment is crucial. The development process will not

---

1   Draft paragraph 2.1 of A/CONF.151/4 (22 April 1992) was replaced by decisi o n of the Main Committee of UNCED on 10 June 1992. See A/CONF.151/L.3/Add.2 (12 June 1992). The former draft read as follows:

  In order to confront the challenge of environment and development, States decided to establish a new partnership. This partnership commits all States to engage in a continuous and constructive dialogue inspired by the need to achieve a more efficient and equitable world economy. It is recognized that, for the success of this new partnership, it is important to overcome confrontation and to foster a climate of genuine cooperation and solidarity. It is equally important to strengthen national and international policies and multilateral cooperation to adapt to the new realities.

gather momentum if the global economy lacks dynamism and stability and is be-set with uncertainties. Neither will it gather momentum if the developing countries are weighted down by external indebtedness, if development finance is inadequate, if barriers restrict access to markets and if commodity prices and the terms of trade of developing countries remain depressed. The record of the 1980s was essentially negative on each of these counts and needs to be reversed. The policies and measures needed to create an international environment that is strongly supportive of national development efforts are thus vital. International cooperation in this area should be designed to complement and support—not to diminish or subsume—sound domestic economic policies, in both developed and developing countries, if global progress towards sustainable development is to be achieved.

2.3. The international economy should provide a supportive international climate for achieving environment and development goals by:

(a) Promoting sustainable development through trade liberalization;

(b) Making trade and environment mutually supportive;

(c) Providing adequate financial resources to developing countries and dealing with international debt;

(d) Encouraging macroeconomic policies conducive to environment and development.

2.4. Governments recognize that there is a new global effort to relate the elements of the international economic system and mankind's needs for a safe and stable natural environment. Therefore, it is the intent of Governments that consensus-building at the intersection of the environmental and trade and development areas will be ongoing in existing international forums, as well as in the domestic policy of each country.

PROGRAMME AREAS

A. Promoting sustainable development through trade

Basis for action

2.5. An open, equitable, secure, non-discriminatory and predictable multilateral trading system that is consistent with the goals of sustainable development and leads to the optimal distribution of global production in accordance with comparative advantage is of benefit to all trading partners. Moreover, improved market access for developing countries' exports in conjunction with sound macroeconomic and environmental policies would have a positive environmental impact and make therefore an important contribution towards sustainable development.

2.6. Experience has shown that sustainable development requires a commitment to sound economic policies and management, an effective and predictable public administration, the integration of environmental concern into decision-making and progress towards democratic governments, in the light of country-specific conditions, which allows for full participation of all parties concerned. These attributes are essential for the fulfilment of policy directions and objectives listed below.

2.7. The commodity sector dominates the economies of many developing countries in terms of production, employment and export earnings. An important feature of the world commodity economy in the 1980s was the prevalence of very low and declining real prices for most commodities in international markets and a resulting substantial contraction in commodity export earnings for many producing countries. The ability of those countries to mobilize, through international trade, the resources needed to finance investments required for sustainable development may be impaired by this development and by tariff and non-tariff impediments, including tariff escalation, limiting their access to export markets. The removal of existing distortions in international trade is essential. In particular, the achievement of this objective requires that there be substantial and progressive reduction in the support and protection of agriculture—covering internal regimes, market access and export subsidies—as well as of industry and other sectors, in order to avoid inflicting large losses on the more efficient producers, especially in developing countries. Thus, in agriculture and other sectors, there is scope for initiatives aimed at trade liberalisation and at policies to make production more responsive to environment and development needs. Trade liberalisation should therefore be pursued on a global basis across economic sectors so as to contribute to sustainable development.

2.8. The international trading environment has been affected by a number of developments that have created new challenges and opportunities and have made multilateral economic cooperation of even greater importance. World trade has continued to grow faster than world output in recent years. However, the expansion of world trade has been unevenly spread, and only a limited number of developing countries have been capable of achieving appreciable growth in their exports. Protectionist pressures and unilateral policy actions continue to endanger the functioning of an open multilateral trading system, affecting particularly the export interests of developing countries. Economic integration processes have intensified in recent years and should impart dynamism to global trade and enhance the trade and development possibilities for developing countries. In recent years, a growing number of these countries have adopted courageous policy reforms involving ambitious autonomous trade liberalization, while far-reaching reforms and profound restructuring processes are taking place in Central and Eastern European countries, paving the way for their integration into the world economy and the international trading system. Increased attention is being devoted to enhancing the role of enterprises and promoting competitive markets through adoption of competitive policies. The GSP [generalised system of preferences] has proved to be a useful trade policy instrument, although its objectives will have to be fulfilled, and trade facilitation strategies relating to electronic data interchange (EDI) have been effective in improving the trading efficiency of the public and private sectors. The interactions between environment policies and trade issues are manifold and have not yet been fully assessed. An early, balanced, comprehensive and successful outcome of the Uruguay Round of multilateral trade negotiations [under the General Agreement On Tariffs and Trade, GATT] would bring about further liberalization and expansion of world trade, enhance the trade and development possibilities of developing countries and provide greater security and predictability to the international trading system.

Objectives

2.9. In the years ahead, and taking into account the results of the Uruguay Round of multilateral trade negotiations, Governments should continue to strive to meet the following objectives:

(a) To promote an open non-discriminatory and equitable multilateral trading system that will enable all countries—in particular, the developing countries—to improve their economic structures and improve the standard of living of their populations through sustained economic development;

(b) To improve access to markets for exports of developing countries;

(c) To improve the functioning of commodity markets and achieve sound, compatible and consistent commodity policies at national and international levels with a view to optimizing the contribution of the commodity sector to sustainable development taking into account environmental considerations;

(d) To promote and support policies, domestic and international, which make economic growth and environmental protection mutually supportive.

Activities

(a) International and regional cooperation and coordination

Promoting an international trading system that takes account of the needs of developing countries

2.10. Accordingly, the international community should:

(a) Halt and reverse protectionism in order to bring about further liberalization and expansion of world trade, to the benefit of all countries, in particular the developing countries;

(b) Provide for an equitable, secure, non-discriminatory and predictable international trading system;

(c) Facilitate, in a timely way, the integration of all countries into the world economy and the international trading system;

(d) Ensure that environment and trade policies are mutually supportive, with a view to achieving sustainable development;

(e) Strengthen the international trade policies system through an early, balanced, comprehensive and successful outcome of the Uruguay Round of multilateral trade negotiations.

2.11. The international community should aim at finding ways and means of achieving a better functioning and enhanced transparency of commodity markets, greater diversification of the commodity sector in developing economies within a macroeconomic framework that takes into consideration a country's economic structure, resource endowments and market opportunities, and better management of natural resources that takes into account the necessities of sustainable development.

2.12. Therefore, all countries should implement previous commitments to halt and reverse protectionism and further expand market access, particularly in areas of interest to developing countries. This improvement of market access will be facilitated by appropriate structural adjustment in developed countries. Developing countries should continue the trade-policy reforms and structural adjustment they have undertaken. It is thus urgent to achieve an improvement in market access conditions for commodities, notably through the progressive removal of barriers that restrict imports, particularly from developing countries, of commodity products in primary and processed forms, as well as the substantial and progressive reduction of types of support that induce uncompetitive production, such as production and export subsidies.

(b) Management related activities

Developing domestic policies that maximize the benefits of trade liberalization for sustainable development

2.13. For developing countries to benefit from the liberalization of trading systems, they should implement the following policies, as appropriate:

(a) Create a domestic environment supportive of an optimal balance between production for the domestic and export markets and remove biases against exports and discourage inefficient import-substitution;

(b) Promote the policy framework and the infrastructure required to improve the efficiency of export and import trade as well as the functioning of domestic markets.

2.14. The following policies should be adopted by developing countries with respect to commodities consistent with market efficiency:

(a) Expand processing, distribution and improve marketing practices and the competitiveness of the commodity sector;

(b) Diversify in order to reduce dependence on commodity exports;

(c) Reflect efficient and sustainable use of factors of production in the formation of commodity prices including the reflection of environmental, social and resources costs.

(c) Data and information

Encouraging data collection and research

2.15. GATT, UNCTAD [United Nations Conference On Trade and Development] and other relevant institutions should continue to collect appropriate trade data and information. The Secretary-General of the United Nations is requested to strengthen the Trade Control Measures Information System managed by UNCTAD.

Improving international cooperation in commodity trade and the diversification of the sector

2.16. With regard to commodity trade, Governments should, directly or through appropriate international organizations, where appropriate:

(a) Seek optimal functioning of commodity markets, *inter alia,* through improved market transparency involving exchanges of views and information on investment plans, prospects and markets for individual commodities. Substantive negotiations between producers and consumers should be pursued with a view to achieving viable and more efficient international agreements, that take into account market trends, or arrangements, as well as study groups. In this regard, particular attention should be paid to the agreements on cocoa, coffee, sugar and tropical timber. The importance of international commodity agreements and arrangements is underlined. Occupational health and safety matters, technology transfer and services associated with the production, marketing and promotion of commodities, as well as environmental considerations, should be taken into account;

(b) Continue to apply compensation mechanisms for short-falls in commodity export earnings of developing countries in order to encourage diversification efforts;

(c) Provide assistance to developing countries upon request in the design and implementation of commodity policies and the gathering and utilization of information on commodity markets;

(d) Support efforts of developing countries to promote the policy framework and infrastructure required to improve the efficiency of export and import trade;

(e) Support the diversification initiatives of the developing countries at the national, regional and international levels.

Means of implementation

(a) Financing and cost evaluation

2.17. The Conference secretariat has estimated the average total annual cost (1993-2000) of implementing the activities in this programme area to be about $8.8 billion from the international community on grant or concessional terms.

These are indicative and order-of-magnitude estimates only and have not been reviewed by Governments. Actual costs and financial terms, including any that are non-concessional, will depend upon, *inter alia*, the specific strategies and programmes Governments decide upon for implementation.[2]

(b) Capacity-building

2.18. The above-mentioned technical cooperation activities aim at strengthening national capabilities for design and implementation of commodity policy, use and management of national resources and the gathering and utilization of information on commodity markets.

B. Making trade and environment mutually supportive

Basis of action

2.19. Environment and trade policies should be mutually supportive. An open, multilateral trading system makes possible a more efficient allocation and use of resources and thereby contributes to an increase in production and incomes and to lessening demands on the environment. It thus provides additional resources needed for economic growth and development and improved environmental protection. A sound environment, on the other hand, provides the ecological and other resources needed to sustain growth and underpin a continuing expansion of trade. An open, multilateral trading system, supported by the adoption of sound environmental policies, would have a positive impact on the environment and contribute to sustainable development.

2.20. International cooperation in the environmental field is growing, and in a number of cases trade provisions in multilateral environment agreements have played a role in tackling global environmental challenges. Trade measures have thus been used in certain specific instances, where considered necessary, to enhance the effectiveness of environmental regulations for the protection of the environment. Such regulations should address the root causes of environmental degradation so as not to result in unjustified restrictions on trade. The challenge

---

2   Draft paragraph 2.16 of A/CONF.151/4 (22 April 1992) was replaced by decision of the Main Committee of UNCED on 10 June 1992. See A/CONF.151/L.3/Add.2 (12 June 1992). The former draft paragraph 2.16 read as follows:

    Costs of international cooperation activities presented above would be a follows:

    a. Commodity agreements. The annual administrative expenditures of 10 existing agreements and arrangements amount to approximately US$ 22.5 million. Additional needs for cooperation on other commodities could bring this figure up to about US$ 30 million a year, an increase of about US$ 7.5 million a year.

    b. Compensation of export earnings shortfalls. Annual average commodity sector shortfalls for developing countries, which could be compensated, amounted to US$ 8.7 billion between 1985 and 1989.

    c. Technical cooperation requirements would be in the order of US$ 5 million per year.

    d. Support for infrastructure development is estimated to amount to US$ 100 million annually.

    e. Strengthening the Trade Control Measures Information System within UNCTAD would cost US$ 0.5 million annually.

is to ensure that trade and environment policies are consistent and reinforce the process of sustainable development. However, account should be taken of the fact that environmental standards valid for developed countries may have unwarranted social and economic costs in developing countries.

Objectives

2.21. Governments should strive to meet the following objectives, through relevant multilateral forums including GATT, UNCTAD and other international organizations:

(a) To make international trade and environment policies mutually supportive in favour of sustainable development;

(b) To clarify the role of GATT, UNCTAD and other international organizations in dealing with trade and environment-related issues including, where relevant, conciliation procedure and dispute settlement;

(c) To encourage international productivity and competitiveness and encourage a constructive role on the part of industry in dealing with environment and development issues.

Activities

Developing an environment/trade and development agenda

2.22. Governments should encourage GATT, UNCTAD and other relevant international and regional economic institutions to examine, in accordance with their respective mandates and competences, the following propositions and principles:

(a) Elaborate adequate studies for the better understanding of the relationship between trade and environment for the promotion of sustainable development;

(b) Promote a dialogue between trade, development and environment communities;

(c) In those cases when trade measures related to environment are used, ensure transparency and compatibility with international obligations;

(d) Deal with the root causes of environment and development problems in a manner which avoids the adoption of environmental measures resulting in unjustified restrictions on trade;

(e) Seek to avoid the use of trade restrictions or distortions as a means to offset differences in cost arising from differences in environmental standards and regulations since their application could lead to trade distortions and increase protectionist tendencies;

(f) Ensure that environment-related regulations or standards, including those related to health and safety standards, do not constitute a means of arbitrary or unjustifiable discrimination or a disguised restriction on trade;

(g) Ensure that special factors affecting environment and trade policies in the developing countries are borne in mind in the application of environmental standards as well as in the use of any trade measures. It is worth noting that standards that are valid in the most advanced countries may be inappropriate and of unwarranted social cost for the developing countries;

(h) Encourage participation of developing countries in multilateral agreements through such mechanisms such as special transitional rules;

(i) Avoid unilateral actions to deal with environmental challenges outside the jurisdiction of the importing country should be avoided. Environmental measures addressing transborder or global environmental problems should, as far as possible, be based on an international consensus. Domestic measures targeted to achieve certain environmental objectives may need trade measures to render them effective. Should trade policy measures be found necessary for the enforcement of environmental policies, certain principles and rules should apply. These could include, *inter alia*, the principle of non-discrimination; the principle that the trade measure chosen should be the least trade-restrictive necessary to achieve the objectives; an obligation to ensure transparency in the use of trade measures related to the environment and to provide adequate notification of national regulations; and the need to give consideration to the special conditions and developmental requirements of developing countries as they move towards internationally agreed environmental objectives;

(j) Develop more precision, where necessary, and clarify the relationship between GATT provisions and some of the multilateral measures adopted in the environment area;

(k) Ensure public input in the formation, negotiation and implementation of trade policies as a means of fostering increased transparency in the light of country-specific conditions;

(l) Ensure that environmental policies provide the appropriate legal and institutional framework to respond to new needs for the protection of the environment that may result from changes in production and trade specialization.

C. Providing adequate financial resources to developing countries

Basis for action

2.23. Investment is critical to the ability of developing countries to achieve needed economic growth to improve the welfare of their populations and to meet their basic needs in a sustainable manner, all without deteriorating or depleting the resource base that underpins development. Sustainable development requires increased investment, for which domestic and external financial resources are needed. Foreign private investment and the return of flight capital which depend on a healthy investment climate are an important source of financial resources. Many developing countries have experienced a decade-long situation of negative net transfer of financial resources, during which their financial receipts were exceeded by payments they had to make, in particular for debt-servicing. As a result, domestically mobilized resources had to be transferred abroad instead of being invested locally in order to promote sustainable economic development.

2.24. For many developing countries, the reactivation of development will not take place without an early and durable solution to the problems of external indebtedness, taking into account the fact that, for many developing countries, external debt burdens are a significant problem. The burden of debt-service payments on those countries has imposed severe constraints on their ability to accelerate growth and eradicate poverty and has led to a contraction in imports, investment and consumption. External indebtedness has emerged as a main factor in the economic stalemate in the developing countries. Continued vigorous implementation of the evolving international debt strategy is aimed at restoring debtor countries' external financial viability and the resumption of their growth and development would assist in achieving sustainable growth and development. In this context, additional financial resources in favour of developing countries and the efficient utilization of such resources are essential.[3]

Objectives

2.25. The specific requirements for the implementation of the sectoral and cross-sectoral programmes included in Agenda 21 are dealt with in the relevant programme areas and in chapter 33 entitled (Financial resources and mechanisms).[4]

---

3   The last sentence of this paragraph 2.24, formerly draft paragraph 2.23 of A/CONF.151/4 (22 April 1992), was revised by decision of the Main Committee of UNCED on 10 June 1992. See A/CONF.151/L.3/Add.2 (12 June 1992). The former draft included brackets and the last sentence read as follows:

   In this context, additional financial resources in favour of developing countries are essential.

4   Draft paragraph 2.24 of A/CONF.151/4 (22 April 1992) was replaced here as paragraph 2.25 by decision of the Main Committee of UNCED on 10 June 1992. See A/CONF.151/L.3/Add.2 (12 June 1992). The former draft read as follows:

   The specific requirements for the implementation of the sectoral and cross-sectoral programmes included in Agenda 21 are dealt with in the relevant programme area and in the related discussion of financial resources and mechanisms. However, in order to provide an efficient macroeconomic framework that would restore the ability of developing countries to invest for sustainable development, it is necessary to ensure substantial financial resources to developing countries. To this end, developed country donors should implement the undertakings they have made to attain the agreed international target of devoting 0.7 per cent of GNP to ODA. There should also be continued improvements in the quality of aid as well as its utilization. Furthermore, the continuation of the process of debt and debt-service reduction is required.

Activities

(a) Meeting international targets of official development assistance funding

2.26. As discussed in chapter 33, new and additional resources should be provided to support Agenda 21 programmes.[5]

(b) Addressing the debt issue

2.27. In regard to the external debt incurred with commercial banks, the progress being made under the strengthened debt strategy is recognized and a more rapid implementation of this strategy is encouraged. Some countries have already benefited from the combination of sound adjustment policies and commercial bank debt reduction or equivalent measures. The international community encourages:

(a) Other countries with heavy debts to banks to negotiate similar commercial bank debt reduction with their creditors;

(b) The parties to such a negotiation to take due account of both the medium-term debt reduction and new money requirements of the debtor country;

(c) Multilateral institutions actively engaged in the strengthened international debt strategy to continue to support debt-reduction packages related to commercial bank debt with a view to ensuring that the magnitude of such financing is consonant with the evolving debt strategy;

(d) Creditor banks to participate in debt and debt-service reduction;

(e) Strengthened policies to attract direct investment, avoid unsustainable levels of debt and foster the return of flight capital.

2.28. With regard to debt owed to official bilateral creditors, the recent measures taken by the Paris Club with regard to more generous terms of relief to the poorest most indebted countries are welcomed. Ongoing efforts to implement these "Trinidad terms" measures in a manner commensurate with the payments capacity of those countries and in a way that gives additional support to their economic reform efforts are welcomed. The substantial bilateral debt reduction undertaken by some creditor countries is also welcomed, and others which are in a position to do so are encouraged to take similar action.

---

5   Draft paragraph 2.25 of A/CONF.151/4 (22 April 1992) was replaced here as paragraph 2.26 decision of the Main Committee of UNCED on 10 June 1992. See A/CONF.151/L.3/Add.2 (12 June 1992). The former draft read as follows:

> Developed countries should implement the undertakings they have made to attain the agreed international target of devoting 0.7 per cent of gross national product to official development assistance and 0.15 per cent to the least developed countries. Developed countries should enhance the quality and the quantity of their aid (para. 27 of General Assembly Res. 18/3).

2.29. The actions of low-income countries with substantial debt burdens which continue, at great cost, to service their debt and safeguard their credit-worthiness are commended. Particular attention should be paid to their resource needs. Other debt-distressed developing countries which are making great efforts to continue to service their debt and meet their external financial obligations also deserve due attention.

2.30. In connection with multilateral debt, it is urged that serious attention should be given to continuing to work towards growth-oriented solutions to the problem of developing countries with serious debt-servicing problems, including those whose debt is mainly to official creditors or to multilateral financial institutions. Particularly in the case of low-income countries in the process of economic reform, the support of the multilateral financial institutions in the form of new disbursements and the use of their concessional funds is welcomed. The use of support groups should be continued in providing resources to clear arrears of countries embarking upon vigorous economic reform programmes supported by IMF and the World Bank. Measures by the multilateral financial institutions such as the refinancing of interest on non-concessional loans with IDA reflows—"fifth dimension"—are noted with appreciation.

Means of implementation

Financing and cost-evaluation[6]

D. Encouraging economic policies conducive to sustainable development

Basis for action

2.31. The unfavourable external environment facing developing countries makes domestic resource mobilization, and efficient allocation and utilization of do-

---

6   See chap. 33 (Financial resources and mechanisms). [This Footnote appeared as an asterisk in Agenda 21, A/CONF. 151/26, vol. I., p. 27.] The former Draft of this chapter included paragraphs which read as follows:

ODA: An increase in official development assistance to 0.7 per cent of GDP funding would amount to approximately a doubling of current levels, which are in the order of US$ 55 billion per year, to US$ 110 billion per year. Debt relief: On the basis of a study by the World Bank, it should be possible to reduce debt owed to private banks by developing countries by about US$ 200 billion for a cost of about US$ 25 billion, through coordinated action. Debt owed to bilateral official creditors by severely indebted low-income countries amounts to some US$ 40 billion. It has been suggested that most or all of this debt should be written off. Debt owed to bilateral creditors by severely indebted middle-income countries is in the order of US$ 80 billion. A reduction of some US$ 40 billion should be given consideration in order to make a substantial positive impact on the economies of debtor countries. Arrears owed to multilateral creditors suggested for clearing amount to some US$ 3.5 billion. An annual subsidy of some US$ 2 billion could be given consideration in order to substantially reduce debt service to be paid by severely indebted low and middle-income countries to multilateral creditors. In total, a one-time payment of US$ 28.5 billion, a recurrent interest rate subsidy of US$ 2 billion a year and a write-off of US$ 80 billion are suggested. The budgetary cost associated with the suggested write-off would be significantly lower than the amount of the write-off when account is taken of the actual amounts due for repayment in the medium-term, the likelihood of default and other such factors.

mestically mobilized resources all the more important for the promotion of sustainable development. In a number of countries, policies are necessary to correct misdirected public spending, large budget deficits and other macroeconomic imbalances, restrictive policies and distortions in the areas of exchange rates, investment and finance, and obstacles to entrepreneurship. In developed countries, continuing policy reform and adjustment, including appropriate savings rates, would help generate resources to support the transition to sustainable development both domestically and in developing countries.[7]

2.32. Good management that fosters the association of effective, efficient, honest, equitable and accountable public administration with individual rights and opportunities, is an essential element for sustainable, broadly based development and sound economic performance at all development levels. All countries should increase their efforts to eradicate mismanagement of public and private affairs, including corruption, taking into account the factors responsible for, and agents involved in, this phenomenon.

2.33. Many indebted developing countries are undergoing structural adjustment programmes relating to debt rescheduling or new loans. While such programmes are necessary for improving the balance in fiscal budgets and balance-of-payments accounts, in some cases they have resulted in adverse social and environmental effects, such as cuts in allocations for health care, education and environmental protection. It is important to ensure that structural adjustment programmes do not have negative impacts on the environment and social development so that such programmes can be more in line with the objectives of sustainable development.

Objectives

2.34. It is necessary to establish, in the light of the country-specific conditions, economic policy reforms that promote the efficient planning and utilization of resources for sustainable development through sound economic and social policies, fostering entrepreneurship and the incorporation of social and environmental costs in resource pricing, and removing sources of distortion in the area of trade and investment.

---

7   Draft paragraph 2.30 of A/CONF.151/4 (22 April 1992) was revised here as paragraph 2.31 by decision of the Main Committee of UNCED on 10 June 1992. See A/CONF.151/L.3/Add.2 (12 June 1992). The former draft read as follows:

In developed countries such policy reforms would help to release resources for supporting the transition to sustainable development domestically and for supporting such a transition in developing countries. An increase in domestic savings in developed countries would be a complement to policies to restrain consumption on environmental grounds.

Activities

(a) Management-related activities

Promoting sound economic policies

2.35. The industrialized countries and other countries in a position to do so should strengthen their efforts:

(a) To encourage a stable and predictable international economic environment, particularly with regard to monetary stability, real rates of interest and fluctuations in key exchange rates;

(b) To stimulate savings and reduce fiscal deficits;

(c) To ensure that the processes of policy coordination take into account the interests and concerns of the developing countries, including the need to promote positive action to support the efforts of the least developed countries to halt their marginalization from the world economy;

(d) To undertake appropriate national macroeconomic and structural policies aimed at promoting non-inflationary growth, narrowing their major external imbalances and increasing the adjustment capacity of their economies.

2.36. Developing countries should consider strengthening their efforts to implement sound economic policies:

(a) That maintain monetary and fiscal discipline required to promote price stability and external balance;

(b) That result in realistic exchange rates;

(c) That raise domestic savings and investment as well as improve returns to investment.

2.37. More specifically, all countries should develop policies that improve efficiency in the allocation of resources and take full advantage of the opportunities offered by the changing global economic environment. In particular, wherever appropriate, and taking into account national strategies and objectives, countries should:

(a) Remove the barriers to progress caused by bureaucratic inefficiencies, administrative strains, unnecessary controls and the neglect of market conditions;

(b) Promote transparency in administration and decision-making;

(c) Encourage the private sector and foster entrepreneurship by improving institutional facilities for enterprise creation and market entry. The essential objective would be to simplify or remove the restrictions, regulations and formalities that make it more complicated, costly and time-consuming to set up and operate enterprises in many developing countries;

(d) Promote and support the investment and infrastructure required for sustainable economic growth and diversification on an environmentally sound and sustainable basis;

(e) Provide scope for appropriate economic instruments, including market mechanisms, in harmony with the objectives of sustainable development and fulfilment of basic needs;

(f) Promote the operation of effective tax systems and financial sectors;

(g) Provide opportunities for small-scale enterprises, both farm and non-farm, and for the indigenous population and local communities to contribute fully to attain the objective of sustainable development;

(h) Remove biases against exports and in favour of inefficient import substitution and establish policies that allow them to benefit fully from the flows of foreign investment, within the framework of national, social, economic and developmental goals;

(i) Promote the creation of a domestic economic environment supportive of an optimal balance between production for the domestic and export markets.

(b) International and regional cooperation and coordination

2.38. Governments of developed countries and those of other countries in a position to do so should, directly or through appropriate international and regional organizations and international lending institutions, enhance their efforts to provide developing countries with increased technical assistance for the following:

(a) Capacity-building in the nation's design and implementation of economic policies, upon request;

(b) Design and operation of efficient tax systems, accounting systems and financial sectors;

(c) Promotion of entrepreneurship.

2.39. International financial and development institutions should further review their policies and programmes in the light of the objective of sustainable development.

2.40. Stronger economic cooperation among developing countries has long been accepted as an important component of efforts to promote economic growth and technological capabilities and accelerate development in the developing world. Therefore, the efforts of the developing countries to promote economic cooperation among themselves should be enhanced and continue to be supported by the international community.

Means of implementation

(a) Financing and cost-evaluation

2.41. The Conference secretariat has estimated the average total annual cost (1993-2000) of implementing the activities in this programme area to be about $50 million from the international community on grant or concessional terms. These are indicative and order of magnitude estimates only and have not been reviewed by Governments. Actual costs and financial terms, including any that are non-concessional, will depend upon, *inter alia*, the specific strategies and programmes Governments decide upon for implementation.[8]

(b) Capacity-building

2.42. The above-mentioned policy changes in developing countries involve substantial national efforts for capacity-building in the areas of public administration, central banking, tax administration, savings institutions and financial markets.[9]

2.43. Particular efforts in the implementation of the four programme areas identified in this chapter are warranted in view of the specially acute environmental and developmental problems of the least developed countries.

---

8   The preceding paragraph was inserted by the decision of the Main Committee of UNCED on 10 June 1992. See A/CONF.151/L.3/Add.2 (12 June 1992). This paragraph replaced one sentence in the draft of A/CONF.151/4 (22 April 1992). The former draft sentence read as follows:

The cost of the above mentioned technical cooperation activities would be in the order of US$ 50 million annually.

9   The draft of this paragraph previously read as follows:

In the implementation of the four programme areas identified in this chapter, special attention should be given to the special circumstances facing the economies in transition. It is also to be recognized that these countries are facing unprecedented challenges in transforming their economies, in some cases in the midst of considerable social and political tensions. See former para. 2.45, in A/CONF. 151/4 (Part I), p. 20.

Chapter 3

Combating Poverty

PROGRAMME AREA

Enabling the poor to achieve sustainable livelihoods

Basis for action

3.1. Poverty is a complex multidimensional problem with origins in both the national and international domains. No uniform solution can be found for global application. Rather, country-specific programmes to tackle poverty and international efforts supporting national efforts, as well as the parallel process of creating a supportive international environment, are crucial for a solution to this problem. The eradication of poverty and hunger, greater equity in income distribution and human resources development remain major challenges everywhere. The struggle against poverty is the shared responsibility of all countries.

3.2. While managing resources sustainably, an environmental policy that focuses mainly on the conservation and protection of resources must take due account of those who depend on the resources for their livelihoods. Otherwise it could have an adverse impact both on poverty and chances for long-term success in resource and environmental conservation. Equally, a development policy that focuses mainly on increasing the production of goods without addressing the sustainability of the resources on which production is based will sooner or later run into declining productivity, which could also have an adverse impact on poverty. A specific anti-poverty strategy is therefore one of the basic conditions for ensuring sustainable development. An effective strategy for tackling problems of poverty, development and environment simultaneously should begin by focusing on resources, production and people, and should cover demographic issues, enhanced health care and education, the rights of women, the role of youth and of indigenous people and local communities and a democratic participation process in association with improved governance.

3.3. Integral to such action is, together with international support, the promotion of economic growth in developing countries that is both sustained and sustainable and direct action in eradicating poverty by strengthening employment and income-generating programmes.

Objectives

3.4. The long-term objective of enabling all people to achieve sustainable livelihoods should provide an integrating factor that allows policies to address issues of development, sustainable resource management and poverty eradication simultaneously. The objectives of this programme area are:

(a) To provide all persons urgently with the opportunity to earn a sustainable livelihood;

(b) To implement policies and strategies which promote adequate levels of funding and focus on integrated human development policies, including income generation, increased local control of resources, local institution-strengthening and capacity-building and greater involvement of non-governmental organizations and local levels of government as delivery mechanisms;

(c) To develop for all poverty-stricken areas integrated strategies and programmes of sound and sustainable management of the environment, resource mobilization, poverty eradication and alleviation, employment and income generation;

(d) To create a focus in national development plans and budgets on investment in human capital, with special policies and programmes directed at rural areas, the urban poor, women and children.

Activities

3.5. Activities that will contribute to the integrated promotion of sustainable livelihoods and environmental protection cover a variety of sectoral interventions involving a range of actors, from local to global, and are essential at every level, especially the community and local levels. Enabling actions will be necessary at the national and international levels, taking full account of regional and subregional conditions to support a locally driven and country-specific approach. In general design, the programmes should:

(a) Focus on the empowerment of local and community groups through the principle of delegating authority, accountability and resources to the most appropriate level to ensure that the programme will be geographically and ecologically specific;

(b) Contain immediate measures to enable those groups to alleviate poverty and to develop sustainability;

(c) Contain a long-term strategy aimed at establishing the best possible conditions for sustainable local, regional and national development that would eliminate poverty and reduce the inequalities between various population groups. It should assist the most disadvantaged groups—in particular, women, children, and youth within those groups—and refugees.[1] The groups will include poor smallholders, pastoralists, artisans, fishing communities, landless people, indigenous communities, migrants and the urban informal sector.

3.6 The focus here is on specific cross-cutting measures—in particular, in the areas of basic education, primary/maternal health care, and the advancement of women.

(a) Empowering communities

3.7. Sustainable development must be achieved at every level of society. Peoples' organizations, women's groups and non-governmental organizations are important sources of innovation and action at the local level and have a strong interest and proven ability to promote sustainable livelihoods. Governments, in cooperation with appropriate international and non-governmental organizations should support a community-driven approach to sustainability, which would include, *inter alia*:

(a) Empowering women through full participation in decision-making;

(b) Respecting the cultural integrity and the rights of indigenous people and their communities;

(c) Promoting or establishing grass-roots mechanisms to allow for the sharing of experience and knowledge between communities;

(d) Giving communities a large measure of participation in the sustainable management and protection of the local natural resources in order to enhance their productive capacity;

(e) Establishing a network of community-based learning centres for capacity-building and sustainable development.

(b) Management-related activities

3.8. Governments, with the assistance of and in cooperation with appropriate international, non-governmental, and local community organizations, should establish measures which will directly or indirectly:

(a) Generate remunerative employment and productive occupational opportunities compatible with country-specific factor endowments, on a scale sufficient to take care of prospective increases in the labour force and to cover backlogs;

(b) With international support, where necessary, develop adequate infrastructure, marketing systems, technology systems, credit systems and the like and

---

1   The preceding sentence was amended by decision of the Main Committee of UNCED on 10 June 1992. See A/CONF.151/L.3/Add.3 (12 June 1992). In the former draft, A/CONF.151/4 (22 April 1992), the preceding sentence read as follows:

It should assist the most disadvantaged groups—in particular, women, children, and youth within those groups—refugees and people under occupation.

human resources needed to support the above actions and to achieve a widening of options for resource-poor people. High priority should be given to basic education and professional training;

(c) Provide substantial increases in economically efficient resource productivity and measures to ensure that the local population benefits in adequate measure from resource use;

(d) Empower community organizations and people to enable them to achieve sustainable livelihoods;

(e) Set up an effective primary health care and maternal health care system accessible to all;

(f) Consider strengthening/developing legal frameworks for land management, access to land resources and land ownership—in particular, for women—and for the protection of tenants;

(g) Rehabilitate degraded resources, to the extent practicable, and introduce policy measures to promote sustainable use of resources for basic human needs;

(h) Establish new community-based mechanisms and strengthen existing mechanisms to enable communities to gain sustained access to resources needed by the poor to overcome their poverty;

(i) Implement mechanisms for popular participation—particularly by poor people, especially women—in local community groups, to promote sustainable development;

(j) Implement, as a matter of urgency, in accordance with country specific conditions and legal systems, measures to ensure that women and men have the same right to decide freely and responsibly on the number and spacing of their children and to have access to the information, education and means, as appropriate, to enable them to exercise this right in keeping with their freedom, dignity and personally held values, taking into account ethical and cultural considerations. Governments should take active steps to implement programmes to establish and strengthen preventive and curative health facilities which include, women-centred, women-managed, safe and effective reproductive health care and affordable, accessible services, as appropriate, for the responsible planning of family size, in keeping with freedom, dignity and personally held values, taking into account ethical and cultural considerations. Programmes should focus on providing comprehensive health care, including pre-natal care, education and information on health and responsible parenthood and should provide the opportunity for all women to breast-feed fully at least during the first four months post-partum. Programmes should fully support women's productive and reproductive roles and well-being, with special attention to the need for providing equal and improved health care for all children and the need to reduce the risk of maternal and child mortality and sickness;

(k) Adopt integrated policies aiming at sustainability in the management of urban centres;

STRATEGIES TOWARD SUSTAINABLE DEVELOPMENT

(l) Undertake activities aimed at the promotion of food security and, where appropriate, food self-sufficiency within the context of sustainable agriculture;

(m) Support research on and integration of traditional methods of production which have been shown to be environmentally sustainable;

(n) Actively seek to recognize and integrate informal-sector activities into the economy by removing regulations and hindrances that discriminate against activities in those sectors;

(o) Consider making available lines of credit and other facilities for the informal sector and improved access to land for the landless poor so that they can acquire the means of production and reliable access to natural resources. In many instances special considerations for women are required. Strict feasibility appraisals are needed for borrowers to avoid debt crises;

(p) Provide the poor with access to fresh water and sanitation;

(q) Provide the poor with access to primary education.

(c) Data, information and evaluation

3.9. Governments should improve the collection of information on target groups and target areas in order to facilitate the design of focused programmes and activities, consistent with the target-group needs and aspirations. Evaluation of such programmes should be gender-specific, since women are a particularly disadvantaged group.

(d) International and regional cooperation and coordination

3.10. The United Nations system, through its relevant organs, organizations and bodies, in cooperation with Member States and with appropriate international and non-governmental organizations, should make poverty alleviation a major priority and should:

(a) Assist Governments, when requested, in the formulation and implementation of national action programmes on poverty alleviation and sustainable development. Action-oriented activities of relevance to the above objectives, such as poverty eradication, projects and programmes supplemented where relevant by food aid, and support and special emphasis to employment and income generation, should be given particular attention in this regard;

(b) Promote technical cooperation among developing countries for poverty eradication activities;

(c) Strengthen existing structures in the United Nations system for coordination of action relating to poverty eradication, including the establishment of a focal point for information exchange and the formulation and implementation of replicable pilot projects to combat poverty;

(d) In the follow-up of the implementation of Agenda 21, give high priority to the review of the progress made in eradicating poverty;

(e) Examine the international economic framework, including resource flows and structural adjustment programmes, to ensure that social and environmental concerns are addressed, and in this connection, conduct a review of the policies of international organizations, bodies and agencies, including financial institutions, to ensure the continued provision of basic services to the poor and needy;

(f) Promote international cooperation to address the root causes of poverty. The development process will not gather momentum if developing countries are weighted down by external indebtedness, if development finance is inadequate, if barriers restrict access to markets and if commodity prices and the terms of trade in developing countries remain depressed.

Means of implementation

(a) Financing and cost evaluation

3.11. The secretariat of the Conference has estimated the average total annual cost (1993-2000) of implementing the activities of this programme to be about $30 billion, including about $15 billion from the international community on grant or concessional terms. These are indicative and order-of-magnitude estimates only and have not been reviewed by Governments. This estimate overlaps estimates in other parts of Agenda 21. Actual costs and financial terms, including any that are non-concessional, will depend upon, *inter alia*, the specific strategies and programmes Governments decide upon for implementation.[2]

(b) Capacity-building

3.12. National capacity-building for implementation of the above activities is crucial and should be given high priority. It is particularly important to focus capacity-building at the local community level in order to support a community-driven approach to sustainability and to establish and strengthen mechanisms to allow sharing of experience and knowledge between community groups at national and international levels. Requirements for such activities are considerable and related to the various relevant sectors of Agenda 21 calling for requisite international, financial and technological support.

---

2   The draft of Chapter 3 in A/CONF.151/4 (Part I), p. 26, included three paragraphs that were deleted, which read as follows:

   3.11. Direct costing of the array of activities envisaged above is not possible, since specific activities would be designed to respond to the specific conditions prevailing in each case country. However, indirect costing points to an estimate in the very rough order of magnitude of US$ 30 billion, of which approximately $15 billion would be provided through external assistance if this effort is to be shared equally by recipients and donors.

   3.12. The formulation and implementation of the global action programme mentioned in paragraph 5 above would require the strengthening of the international organizations concerned. Average annual costs over the period would be in the order of $50 million.

   3.13. In many instances, these costs pertain to the implementation of activities included in various chapters of Agenda 21, so that funding for these activities would contribute to achieving both sectoral objectives and poverty alleviation.

Chapter 4

Changing Consumption Patterns

4.1. This chapter contains the following programme areas:

(a) Focusing on unsustainable patterns of production and consumption;

(b) Developing national policies and strategies to encourage changes in unsustainable consumption patterns.

4.2. Since the issue of changing consumption patterns is very broad, it is addressed in several parts of Agenda 21, notably those dealing with energy, transportation and wastes, and in the chapters on economic instruments and transfer of technology. The present chapter should also be read in conjunction with Chapter 5 (Demographic dynamics and sustainability).

PROGRAMME AREAS

A. Focusing on unsustainable patterns of production and consumption

Basis for action

4.3. Poverty and environmental degradation are closely interrelated. While poverty results in certain kinds of environmental stress, the major cause of the continued deterioration of the global environment is the unsustainable pattern of consumption and production, particularly in industrialized countries, which is a matter of grave concern, aggravating poverty and imbalances.[1]

---

1   Draft paragraph 4.3 of A/CONF.151/4 (22 April 1992) was replaced by decision of the Main Committee of UNCED on 10 June 1992. See A/CONF.151/L.3/Add.4 (12 June 1992). The former draft read as follows:

   While poverty largely results in certain kinds of environmental stress, one of the most serious problems now facing the planet is that associated with historical patterns of unsustainable consumption and production, leading to environmental degradation, aggravation of poverty and imbalances in the development of countries.

4.4. Measures to be undertaken at the international level for the protection and enhancement of the environment must take fully into account the current imbalances in the global patterns of consumption and production.

4.5. Special attention should be paid to the demand for natural resources generated by unsustainable consumption and to the efficient use of those resources consistent with the goal of minimizing depletion and reducing pollution. Although consumption patterns are very high in certain parts of the world, the basic consumer needs of a large section of humanity are not being met. This results in excessive demands and unsustainable lifestyles among the richer segments, which place immense stress on the environment. The poorer segments, meanwhile, are unable to meet food, health care, shelter and educational needs. Changing consumption patterns will require a multipronged strategy focusing on demand, meeting the basic needs of the poor, and reducing wastage and the use of finite resources in the production process.[2]

4.6 Growing recognition of the importance of addressing consumption has also not yet been matched by understanding of its implications. Some economists are questioning traditional concepts of economic growth and underlining the importance of pursuing economic objectives which take account of the full value of natural resource capital. More needs to be known about the role of consumption in relation to economic growth and population dynamics in order to formulate coherent international and national policies.

Objectives

4.7. Action is needed to meet the following broad objectives:

(a) To promote patterns of consumption and production that reduce environmental stress and will meet the basic needs of humanity;

(b) To develop of better understanding of the role of consumption and how to bring about more sustainable consumption patterns.

---

2 Draft paragraph 4.5 of A/CONF.151/4 (22 April 1992) was replaced by decision of the Main Committee of UNCED on 10 June 1992. See A/CONF.151/L.3/Add.4 (12 June 1992). The former draft read as follows:

Special attention should be paid to the demand for natural resources generated by unsustainable consumption and to efficient use of those resources consistent with the goal of minimizing depletion and reducing pollution. Although consumption patterns are very high in certain parts of the world, the basic consumer needs of a large section of humanity are not being met. This inequitable distribution of income and wealth results in excessive demands and unsustainable lifestyles among the richer segments, which place immense stress on the environment. The poorer, meanwhile, are unable to meet food, health care, shelter and educational needs. Changing consumption patterns will require a multipronged strategy focusing on demand, meeting the basic needs of the poor, and reducing wastage and the use of finite resources in the production process.

Activities

(a) Management-related activities

Adopt an international approach to achieving sustainable consumption patterns

4.8. In principle, countries should be guided by the following basic objectives in their efforts to address consumption and lifestyles in the context of environment and development:

(a) All countries should strive to promote sustainable consumption patterns;

(b) Developed countries should take the lead in achieving sustainable consumption patterns;

(c) Developing countries should seek to achieve sustainable consumption patterns in their development process, guaranteeing the provision of basic needs for the poor, while avoiding those unsustainable patterns, particularly in industrialized countries, generally recognized as unduly hazardous to the environment, inefficient and wasteful, in their development processes. This requires enhanced technological and other assistance from industrialized countries.

4.9. In the follow-up of the implementation of Agenda 21 the review of progress made in achieving sustainable consumption patterns should be given high priority.

(b) Data and information

Undertaking research on consumption

4.10. In order to support this broad strategy, Governments, and/or private research and policy institutes, with the assistance of regional and international economic and environmental organizations, should make a concerted effort to:

(a) Expand or promote databases on production and consumption and develop methodologies for analysing them;

(b) Assess the relationship between production and consumption, environment, technological adaptation and innovation, economic growth and development, and demographic factors;

(c) Examine the impact of ongoing changes in the structure of modern industrial economies away from materials intensive economic growth;

(d) Consider how economies can grow and prosper while reducing energy material use and production of harmful materials;

(e) Identify balanced patterns of consumption world wide which the Earth can support in the long term.

Developing new concepts of sustainable economic growth and prosperity

4.11. Consideration should also be given to the present concepts of economic growth, and the need for new concepts of wealth and prosperity, which allow higher standards of living through changed lifestyles and are less dependent on the Earth's finite resources and more in harmony with the Earth's carrying capacity. This should be reflected in the evolution of new systems of national accounts and other indicators of sustainable development.

(c) International cooperation and coordination

4.12. While international review processes exist for examining economic, development and demographic factors, more attention needs to be paid to issues related to consumption and production patterns and sustainable lifestyles and environment.

4.13. In the follow-up of the implementation of Agenda 21, reviewing the role and impact of unsustainable production and consumption patterns and lifestyles and their relation to sustainable development should be given high priority.

Financing and cost evaluation

4.14. The Conference secretariat has estimated that implementation of this programme is not likely to require significant new financial resources.[3]

B. Developing national policies and strategies to encourage changes in unsustainable consumption patterns

Basis for action

4.15. Achieving the goals of environmental quality and sustainable development will require efficiency in production and changes in consumption patterns in order to emphasize optimization of resource use and minimization of waste. In many instances, this will require reorientation of existing production and consumption patterns which have developed in industrial societies and are in turn emulated in much of the world.

4.16. Progress can be made by strengthening positive trends and directions which are emerging, as part of a process aimed at achieving significant changes in consumption patterns of industries, Governments, households and individuals.

---

3   Draft paragraph 4.14 of A/CONF.151/4 (22 April 1992) was replaced by decision of the Main Committee of UNCED on 10 June 1992. See A/CONF.151/L.3/Add.4 (12 June 1992). The former draft read as follows:

  Implementation of this programme is unlikely to require significant new financial resources. A research programme and an international process, once established, would require support (probably in the range of about $1 million).

Objectives

4.17. In the years ahead, Governments, working with appropriate organizations, should strive to meet the following broad objectives:

(a) To promote efficiency in production processes and reduce wasteful consumption in the process of economic growth, taking into account the development needs of developing countries;

(b) To develop a domestic policy framework which will encourage a shift to more sustainable patterns of production and consumption;

(c) To reinforce both values which encourage sustainable production and consumption patterns and policies which encourage the transfer of environmentally sound technologies to developing countries.

Activities

(a) Encouraging greater efficiency in the use of energy and resources

4.18. Reducing the amount of energy and materials used per unit in the production of goods and services can contribute both to the alleviation of environmental stress and to greater economic and industrial productivity and competitiveness. Governments, in cooperation with industry, should therefore intensify efforts to use energy and resources in an economically efficient and environmentally sound manner by:

(a) Encouraging the dissemination of existing environmentally sound technologies;

(b) Promoting research and development in environmentally sound technologies;

(c) Assisting developing countries to use these technologies efficiently and to develop technologies suited to their particular circumstances;

(d) Encouraging the environmentally sound use of new and renewable sources of energy;

(e) Encouraging the environmentally sound and sustainable use of renewable natural resources.

(b) Minimizing the generation of wastes

4.19. At the same time, society needs to develop effective ways of dealing with the problem of disposing of mounting levels of waste products and materials. Governments, together with industry, households and the public, should make a concerted effort to reduce the generation of wastes and waste products by:

(a) Encouraging recycling in industrial processes and at the consumed level;

(b) Reducing wasteful packaging of products;

(c) Encouraging the introduction of more environmentally sound products.

(c) Assisting individuals and households to make environmentally sound purchasing decisions

4.20. The recent emergence in many countries of a more environmentally conscious consumer public, combined with increased interest on the part of some industries in providing environmentally sound consumer products, is a significant development that should be encouraged. Governments and international organizations, together with the private sector, should develop criteria and methodologies for the assessment of environmental impacts and resource requirements throughout the full life cycle of products and processes. Results of those assessments should be transformed into clear indicators in order to inform consumers and decision makers.

4.21. Governments, in cooperation with industry and other relevant groups, should encourage expansion of environmental labelling and other environmentally related product information programmes designed to assist consumers to make informed choices.

4.22. They should also encourage the emergence of an informed consumer public and assist individuals and households to make environmentally informed choices by:[4]

(a) Providing information on the consequences of consumption choices and behaviour, so as to encourage demand for environmentally sound products and use of products;

(b) Making consumers aware of the health and environmental impact of products, through means such as consumer legislation and environmental labelling;

(c) Encouraging specific consumer-oriented programmes, such as recycling and deposit/refund systems.

(d) Exercising leadership through government purchasing

4.23. Governments themselves also play a role in consumption, particularly in countries where the public sector plays a large role in the economy and can have a considerable influence on both corporate decisions and public perceptions. They should therefore review the purchasing policies of their agencies and departments so that they may improve, where possible, the environmental content of government procurement policies, without prejudice to international trade principles.

---

4   In the prior draft, A/CONF. 151/4, Part I, P.32, the word "by" was used thereafter at Rio the words "in the following ways" were substituted; the original was restored in the final version.

(e) Moving towards environmentally sound pricing

4.24. Without the stimulus of prices and market signals that make clear to producers and consumers the environmental costs of the consumption of energy, materials and natural resources and the generation of wastes, significant changes in consumption and production patterns seem unlikely to occur in the near future.

4.25. Some progress has begun in the use of appropriate economic instruments to influence consumer behaviour. These instruments include environmental charges and taxes, deposit/refund systems, etc. This process should be encouraged in the light of country-specific conditions.

(f) Reinforcing values that support sustainable consumption

4.26. Governments and private-sector organizations should promote more positive attitudes towards sustainable consumption through education, public awareness programmes and other means such as positive advertising of products and services that utilize environmentally sound technologies or encourage sustainable production and consumption patterns. In the review of the implementation of Agenda 21, an assessment of the progress achieved in developing these national policies and strategies should be given due consideration.

Means of implementation

4.27. This programme is concerned primarily with changes in unsustainable patterns of consumption and production and values that encourage sustainable consumption patterns and lifestyles. It requires the combined efforts of Governments, consumers and producers. Particular attention should be paid to the significant role played by women and households as consumers and the potential impacts of their combined purchasing power on the economy.

Chapter 5

Demographic Dynamics and Sustainability

5.1. This chapter contains the following programme areas:

(a) Developing and disseminating knowledge concerning the links between demographic trends and factors and sustainable development;

(b) Formulating integrated national policies for environment and development, taking into account demographic trends and factors;

(c) Implementing integrated, environment and development programmes at the local level, taking into account demographic trends and factors.

PROGRAMME AREAS

A. Developing and disseminating knowledge concerning the links between demographic trends and factors and sustainable development

Basis for action

5.2. Demographic trends and factors and sustainable development have a synergistic relationship.

5.3. The growth of world population and production combined with unsustainable consumption patterns places increasingly severe stress on the life-supporting capacities of our planet. These interactive processes affect the use of land, water, air, energy and other resources. Rapidly growing cities, unless well-managed, face major environmental problems. The increase in both the number and size of cities calls for greater attention to issues of local government and municipal management. Human dimensions are key elements to consider in this intricate set of relationships and they should be adequately taken into consideration in comprehensive policies for sustainable development. Such policies should address the linkages of demographic trends and factors, resource use, appropriate technology dissemination, and development. Population policy should also recognize the role played by human beings in environmental and development concerns. There is a need to increase awareness of this issue among decision makers at all levels and to provide both better information on which to base national and international policies and framework against which to interpret this information.

5.4. There is a need to develop strategies to mitigate both the adverse impact on the environment of human activities as well as the adverse impact of environmental change on human populations. The world's population is expected to exceed 8 billion by the year 2020. Sixty percent of the world's population already live in coastal areas, while 65 per cent of cities with populations above 2.5 million are located along the world coasts, several of them are already at or below the present sea level.

Objectives

5.5. The following objectives should be achieved as soon as practicable:

(a) To incorporate demographic trends and factors in the global analysis of environment and development issues;

(b) To develop a better understanding of the relationships among demographic dynamics, technology, cultural behaviour, natural resources and life support systems;

(c) To assess human vulnerability in ecologically sensitive areas and centres of population to determine the priorities for action at all levels, taking full account of community defined needs.

Activities

Research on the interaction between demographic trends and factors and sustainable development

5.6. Relevant international, regional and national institutions should consider undertaking the following activities:

(a) Identifying the interactions between demographic processes, natural resources and life support systems, bearing in mind regional and subregional variations deriving from, *inter alia*, different levels of development;

(b) Integrating demographic trends and factors into the ongoing study of environmental change, using the expertise of international, regional and national research networks and of local communities, first, to study the human dimensions of environmental change and, second, to identify vulnerable areas;

(c) Identifying priority areas for action and develop strategies and programmes to mitigate the adverse impact of environmental change on human populations, and vice versa.

Means of implementation

(a) Financing and cost evaluation

5.7. The secretariat of the Conference has estimated the average total annual cost (1993-2000) of implementing the activities of this programme to be about $10 million from the international community on grant or concessional terms. These are indicative and order-of-magnitude estimates only and have not been reviewed by Governments. Actual costs and financial terms, including any that are non-concessional, will depend upon, *inter alia*, the specific strategies and programmes Governments decide upon for implementation.[1]

(b) Strengthening research programmes that integrate population, environment and development

5.8. In order to integrate demographic analysis into a broader social sciences perspective of environment and development, interdisciplinary research should be increased. International institutions and networks of experts should enhance their scientific capacity taking full account of community experience and knowledge, and disseminate the experience gained in multidisciplinary approaches and in linking theory to action.

5.9. Better modelling capabilities should be developed, identifying the range of possible outcomes of current human activities, especially the interrelated impact of demographic trends and factors, per capita resource use and wealth distribution, as well as the major migration flows which may be expected with increasing climatic events and cumulative environmental change that may destroy people's local livelihoods.

(c) Developing information and public awareness

5.10. Socio-demographic information should be developed in a suitable format for interfacing with physical, biological and socio-economic data. Compatible spatial and temporal scales, cross-country and time-series information, as well as global behavioral indicators should be developed, learning from local communities' perceptions and attitudes.

5.11. Awareness should be increased at all levels concerning the need to optimize the sustainable use of resources through efficient resource management taking into account the development needs of the populations of developing countries.

---

1   Draft paragraph 5.7 of A/CONF.151/4 (22 April 1992) was replaced by decision of the Main Committee of UNCED on 10 June 1992. See A/CONF.151/L.3/Add.5 (12 June 1992). The former draft read as follows:

Research and dissemination of results will require US$ 10 million annually from international sources. It should be adequately financed taking into account the role of existing agencies in this field.

5.12. Awareness should be increased of the fundamental linkages between improving the status of women and demographic dynamics, particularly through women's access to education, primary and reproductive health care programmes, economic independence and their effective, equitable participation in all levels of decision-making.

5.13. Results of research should be disseminated through technical reports, scientific journals, the media, workshops, forums or other means so that the information can be used by decision makers at all levels and increase public awareness.

(d) Developing and/or enhancing institutional capacity and collaboration

5.14. Collaboration and exchange of information should be increased between research institutions and international, regional and national agencies and all other sectors (including the private sector, local communities, non-governmental organizations and scientific institutions) from both the industrialized and developing countries, as appropriate.

5.15. Efforts should be intensified to enhance the capacities of national and local governments, the private sector and non-governmental organizations in developing countries to meet the growing needs for improved management of rapidly growing urban areas.

B. Formulating integrated national policies for environment and development, taking into account demographic trends and factors

Basis for action

5.16. Existing plans for sustainable development have generally recognized demographic trends and factors as elements that have a critical influence on consumption patterns, production, lifestyles and long-term sustainability. But in future, more attention will have to be given to these issues in general policy formulation and the design of development plans. To do this, all countries will have to improve their own capacities to assess the environment and development implications of their demographic trends and factors. They will also need to formulate and implement policies and action programmes where appropriate. Policies should be designed to address the consequences of population growth built into population momentum, while, at the same time incorporating measures to bring about demographic transition. They should combine environmental concerns and population issues within a holistic view of development whose primary goals include: alleviation of poverty; secure livelihoods; good health; quality of life; improvement of the status and income of women and their access to schooling and professional training, as well as fulfillment of their personal aspirations; and empowerment of individuals and communities. Recognizing that large increases in the size and number of cities will occur in developing countries under any likely population scenario, greater attention should be given to preparing for the needs, in particular of women and children, for improved municipal management and local government.

Objective

5.17. Full integration of population concerns into national planning, policy and decision-making processes should continue. Population policies and programmes should be considered, with full recognition of women's rights.

Activities

5.18. Governments and other relevant actors should, *inter alia*, undertake the following activities, with appropriate assistance of aid agencies, and report on their status of implementation to the International Conference on Population and Development to be held in 1994, especially to its committee on population and environment.

(a) Assess the implications of national demographic trends and factors

5.19. The relationships between demographic trends and factors, and environmental change and between environmental degradation and the components of demographic change should be analysed.

5.20. Research should be conducted on how environmental factors interact with socio-economic ones as a cause of migration.

5.21. Vulnerable population groups (such as rural landless workers, ethnic minorities, refugees, migrants, displaced people, women heads of household) whose changes in demographic structure may have specific impacts on sustainable development should be identified.

5.22. An assessment should be made of the implications of the age structure of the population on resource demand and dependency burdens, ranging from educational expenses for the young, to health care and support for the elderly, and household income generation.

5.23. An assessment should also be made of national population carrying capacity in the context of satisfaction of human needs and sustainable development, and special attention should be given to critical resources, such as water and land, and environmental factors, such as ecosystem health and biodiversity.

5.24. The impact of national demographic trends and factors on the traditional livelihoods of indigenous groups and local communities, including changes in traditional land use because of internal population pressures, should be studied.

(b) Building and strengthening a national information base

5.25. National databases on demographic trends and factors and environment should be built and/or strengthened, disaggregating data by ecological region (ecosystem approach) and population/environment profiles should be established by region.

5.26. Methodologies and instruments should be developed to identify areas where sustainability is, or may be, threatened by the environmental effects of demographic trends and factors, incorporating both current and projected demographic data linked to natural environmental processes.

5.27. Case-studies of local level responses by different groups to demographic dynamics should be developed, particularly in areas subject to environmental stress and deteriorating urban centres.

5.28. Population data should be disaggregated by, *inter alia*, sex and age in order to take into account the implications of the gender division of labour for the use and management of natural resources.

(c) Incorporating demographic features into policy and plans

5.29. In formulating human settlements policies, account should be taken of the resource needs, waste production and ecosystem health.

5.30. The direct and induced effects of demographic changes in environment and development programmes should, where appropriate, be integrated, and the impact on demographic features assessed.

5.31. National population policy goals and programmes that are consistent with national environment and development plans for sustainability and in keeping with the freedom, dignity and personally held values of individuals, should be established and implemented.

5.32. Appropriate socio-economic policies for the young and the elderly, both in terms of family and state support systems, should be developed.

5.33. Policies and programmes should be developed for handling the various types of migrations that result from, or induce environmental disruptions, with special attention to women and vulnerable groups.

5.34. Demographic concerns, including concerns for environmental migrants and displaced people should be incorporated in the programmes for sustainable development of relevant international and regional institutions.

5.35. National reviews should be conducted and the integration of population policies in national development and environment strategies should be monitored nationally.

Means of implementation

(a) Financing and cost evaluation

5.36. The Conference secretariat has estimated the average total annual cost (1993-2000) of implementing the activities of this programme to be about

$90 million from the international community on grant or concessional terms. These are indicative and order-of-magnitude estimates only and have not been reviewed by Governments. Actual costs and financial terms, including any that are non-concessional, will depend upon, *inter alia*, the specific strategies and programmes Governments decide upon for implementation.[2]

(b) Raising awareness of demographic and sustainable development interactions

5.37. Understanding of the interactions between demographic trends and factors and sustainable development should be increased in all sectors of society. Stress should be put on local and national action. Demographic and sustainable development education should be coordinated and integrated in both the formal and non-formal education sectors. Particular attention should be given to population literacy programmes, notably for women. Special emphasis should be placed on the linkage between these programmes, primary environmental care and the provision of primary health care and services.

(c) Strengthening institutions

5.38. The capacity of national, regional and local structures to deal with issues relating to demographic trends and factors, and sustainable development should be enhanced. This would involve strengthening the relevant bodies responsible for population issues to enable them to elaborate policies consistent with the national prospects for sustainable development. Cooperation among government, national research institutions, non-governmental organizations and local communities in assessing problems and evaluating policies should also be enhanced.

5.39. The capacity of the relevant United Nations organs, organizations and bodies, international and regional intergovernmental bodies, non-governmental organizations and local communities should, as appropriate, be enhanced to help countries develop sustainable development policies on request and, as appropriate, provide assistance to environmental migrants and displaced people.

5.40. Inter-agency support for national sustainable development policies and programmes should be improved through better coordination of population and environment activities.

(d) Promoting human resources development

5.41. The international and regional scientific institutions should assist Governments, upon request to include concerns regarding the population/environment

---

2   Draft paragraph 5.36 of A/CONF.151/4 (22 April 1992) was replaced by decision of the Main Committee of UNCED on 10 June 1992. See A/CONF.151/L.3/Add.5 (12 June 1992). The former draft read as follows:

   The implementation of these activities by Governments will require at least $90 million annually from international sources.

interactions at the global, ecosystem and micro-levels in the training of demographers, population and environment specialists. Training should include research on linkages and ways to design integrated strategies.

C. Implementing integrated environment and development programmes at the local level, taking into account demographic trends and factors

Basis for action

5.42. Population programmes are more effective when implemented together with appropriate cross-sectoral policies. To attain sustainability at the local level, a new framework is needed that integrates demographic trends and factors with such factors as ecosystem health, technology, human settlements, and with socio-economic structures and access to resources. Population programmes should be consistent with socio-economic and environmental planning. Integrated sustainable development programmes should closely correlate action on demographic trends and factors with resources management activities and development goals meeting the needs of the people concerned.

Objective

5.43. Population programmes should be implemented along with natural resources management and development programmes at the local level, that will ensure sustainable use of natural resources, improve the quality of life of the people and enhance environmental quality.

Activities

5.44. Governments, local communities including community-based women's organizations and national non-governmental organizations, consistent with national plans, objectives, strategies and priorities, could, *inter alia*, undertake the activities set out below with the assistance and cooperation of international organizations, as appropriate. Governments could share their experience in the implementation of Agenda 21 at the International Conference on Population and Development to be held in 1994, especially to its committee on population and environment.

(a) Developing a framework for action

5.45. An effective consultative process should be established and implemented with concerned groups of society where the formulation and decision-making of all components of the programmes are based on a nationwide consultative process drawing on community meetings, regional workshops and national seminars, as appropriate. This process should ensure that views of women and men on needs, perspective and constraints are equally well reflected in the design of programmes, and that solutions are rooted in specific experience. The poor and underprivileged should be priority groups in this process.

5.46. Nationally determined policies for integrated and multifaceted programmes, with special attention to women, to the poorest people living in critical areas and to other vulnerable groups should be implemented, ensuring the involvement of groups with a special potential to act as agents for change and sustainable development. Special emphasis should be placed on those programmes that achieve multiple objectives, encouraging sustainable economic development, and mitigating adverse impacts of demographic trends and factors, and avoiding long-term environmental damage. Food security, access to secure tenure, basic shelter, and essential infrastructure, education, family welfare, women's reproductive health, family credit schemes, reforestation programmes, primary environmental care, women's employment should, as appropriate, be included among other factors.

5.47. An analytical framework should be developed to identify complementary elements of sustainable development policies as well as the national mechanisms to monitor and evaluate their effects on population dynamics.

5.48. Special attention should be given to the critical role of women in population/environment programmes and in achieving sustainable development. Projects should take advantage of opportunities to link social, economic and environmental gains for women and their families. Empowerment of women is essential and should be assured through education, training and policies to accord and improve women's right and access to assets, human and civil rights, labour-saving measures, job opportunities and participation in decision-making. Population/environment programmes must enable women to mobilize themselves to alleviate their burden and improve their capacity to participate in and benefit from socio-economic development. Specific measures should be undertaken to close the gap between female and male illiteracy rates.

(b) Supporting programmes that promote changes in demographic trends and factors towards sustainability

5.49. Reproductive health programmes and services, should, as appropriate, be developed and enhanced to reduce maternal and infant mortality from all causes and enable women and men to fulfil their personal aspirations in terms of family size, in a way in keeping with their freedom and dignity and personally held values.

5.50. Governments should take active steps to implement, as a matter of urgency, in accordance with country-specific conditions and legal systems, measures to ensure that women and men have the same right to decide freely and responsibly on the number and spacing of their children, to have access to the information, education and means, as appropriate, to enable them to exercise this right in keeping with their freedom, dignity and personally held values taking into account ethical and cultural considerations.

5.51. Governments should take active steps to implement programmes to establish and strengthen preventive and curative health facilities that include women-centred, women-managed, safe and effective reproductive health care and affordable, accessible services, as appropriate, for the responsible planning of family size, in keeping with freedom, dignity and personally held values and taking into account ethical and cultural considerations. Programmes should focus on providing comprehensive health care, including pre-natal care, education and information on health and responsible parenthood and should provide the opportunity for all women to breast-feed fully at least during the first four months post-partum. Programmes should fully support women's productive and reproductive roles and well being, with special attention to the need for providing equal and improved health care for all children and the need to reduce the risk of maternal and child mortality and sickness.

5.52. Consistent with national priorities, culturally based information and education programmes that transmit reproductive health messages to men and women that are easily understood should be developed.

(c) Creating appropriate institutional conditions

5.53. Constituencies and institutional conditions to facilitate the implementation of demographic activities should, as appropriate, be fostered. This requires support and commitment from political, indigenous, religious and traditional authorities, the private sector and the national scientific community. In developing these appropriate institutional conditions, countries should closely involve established national machinery for women.

5.54. Population assistance should be coordinated with bilateral and multilateral donors to ensure that population needs and requirements of all developing countries are addressed, fully respecting the overall coordinating responsibility, and the choice and strategies of the recipient countries.

5.55. Coordination should be improved at local and international levels. Working practices should be enhanced in order to make optimum use of resources, draw on collective experience and improve the implementation of programmes. UNFPA and other relevant agencies should strengthen the coordination of international cooperation activities with recipient and donor countries in order to ensure that adequate funding is available to respond to growing needs.

5.56. Proposals should be developed for local, national and international population/environment programmes in line with specific needs for achieving sustainability. Where appropriate, institutional changes must be implemented so that old-age security does not entirely depend on input from family members.

Means of implementation

(a) Financing and cost evaluation

5.57. The Conference secretariat has estimated the average total annual cost (1993-2000) of implementing the activities of this programme to be about

$7 billion, including about $3.5 billion from the international community on grant or concessional terms. These are indicative and order-of-magnitude estimates only and have not been reviewed by Governments. Actual costs and financial terms, including any that are non-concessional, will depend upon, *inter alia*, the specific strategies and programmes Governments decide upon for implementation.[3]

(b) Research

5.58. Research should be undertaken with a view to developing specific action programmes; it will be necessary to establish priorities between proposed areas of research.

5.59. Socio-demographic research should be conducted on how populations respond to a changing environment.

5.60. Understanding of socio-cultural and political factors that can positively influence acceptance of appropriate population policy instruments should be improved.

5.61. Surveys of changes in needs for appropriate services relating to responsible planning of family size, reflecting variations among different socio-economic groups, and variations in different geographical regions should be undertaken.

(c) Human resources development and capacity-building

5.62. The areas of human resources development and capacity-building, with particular attention to education and training of women, are areas of critical importance and are a very high priority in the implementation of population programmes.

5.63. Workshops to help programme and projects managers to link population programmes to other development and environmental goals should be conducted.

5.64. Educational materials, including guides/workbooks for planners and decision makers and other actors of population/environment/development programmes, should be developed.

5.65. Cooperation should be developed between Governments, scientific institutions and non-governmental organizations within the region, and similar insti-

---

3   Draft paragraph 5.57 of A/CONF.151/4 (22 April 1992) was replaced by decision of the Main Committee of UNCED on 10 June 1992. See A/CONF.151/L.3/Add.5 (12 June 1992). The former draft read as follows:

The total resources, national as well as external, currently devoted to population activities in developing countries is estimated to be $4.5 billion a year. Of that amount, nearly 80 per cent is provided by developing countries themselves. To carry out intensified programmes, and implement integrated population/environment actions in line with the above activities, an average of $7 billion is needed annually in the 1993-2000 period, of which about half is required from international sources. The goal is to mobilize resources amounting to $9 billion a year by the turn of the century. About $6 million annually is needed to strengthen international institutions.

tutions outside the region. Cooperation with local organizations should be fostered in order to raise awareness, engage in demonstration projects and report on the experience gained.

5.66. The recommendations contained in this chapter should in no way prejudice discussions at the International Conference on Population and Development in 1994, which would be the appropriate forum for dealing with population and development issues, taking into account the recommendations of the International Conference on Population, held in Mexico City in 1984,[4] and the Forward-looking Strategies for the Advancement of Women,[5] 151/26, vol. I, p. 53 adopted by the World Conference to Review and Appraise the Achievements of the United Decade for Women; Equality, Development and Peace, held in Nairobi in 1985.

---

4   *Report of the International Conference on Population, Mexico City, -1 August 19*   (United Nations publication. Sales No. E. 84. XIII 8), Chap. I. [This footnote appears in Agenda 21 as number 1 to this Chapter. A/CONF. 151/26, vol. I, p. 53].

5   *Report of the World Conference to Review and Appraise the Achievements of the United Nations Decade for Women: E uality, Development and Peace, Nairobi,* 15-26 July 1985 (United Nations publication, Sales No. E. 84. IV. 10), Chap. I, Sect. A. [This footnote appears in Agenda 21 as number 2 to this Chapter. A/CONF. 151/26, vol. I, p. 53].

Chapter 6

Protecting and Promoting Human Health

INTRODUCTION

6.1. Health and development are intimately interconnected. Both insufficient development leading to poverty and inappropriate development resulting in over-consumption, coupled with expanding world population, can result in severe environmental health problems in both developing and developed nations. Action items under Agenda 21 must address the primary health needs of the world's population, since they are integral to the achievement of the goals of sustainable development and primary environmental care. The linkage of health, environmental and socio-economic improvements requires intersectoral efforts. Such efforts, involving education, housing, public works and community groups, including businesses, schools and universities and religious, civic and cultural organizations, are aimed at enabling people in their communities to ensure sustainable development. Particularly relevant is the inclusion of prevention programmes rather than relying solely on the remediation and treatment. Countries ought to develop plans for priority actions, drawing on the programme areas, which are based on cooperative planning by the various levels of government, non-governmental organizations and local communities. An appropriate international organization, such as WHO [the World Health Organization], should coordinate these activities.[1]

6.2. The following programme areas are contained in this chapter:

(a) Meeting primary health care needs, particularly in rural areas;

(b) Control of communicable diseases;

(c) Protecting vulnerable groups;

(d) Meeting the urban health challenge;

(e) Reducing health risks from environmental pollution and hazards.

---

1   Draft paragraph 6.1 of A/CONF.151/4 (22 April 1992) included brackets around the entire text of paragraph 6.1. The brackets were deleted by decision of the Main Committee of UNCED on 10 June 1992. See A/CONF.151/L.3/Add.6 (12 June 1992).

PROGRAMME AREAS

A. Meeting primary health care needs, particularly in rural areas

Basis for action

6.3. Health ultimately depends on the ability to successfully manage the interaction between the physical, spiritual, biological and economic/social environment. Sound development is not possible without a healthy population; yet most developmental activities affect the environment to some degree the environment which, in turn, causes or exacerbates many health problems. Conversely, it is the very lack of development that adversely affects the health condition of many people, which can be alleviated only through development. The health sector cannot meet basic needs and objectives on its own; it is dependent on social, economic, and spiritual development, while directly contributing to such development. It is also dependent on a healthy environment, including the provision of a safe water supply and sanitation, and the promotion of a safe food supply and proper nutrition. Particular attention should be directed towards food safety, with priority on the elimination of food contamination; comprehensive and sustainable water policies to ensure safe drinking water and sanitation to preclude both microbial and chemical contamination; and promotion of health education, immunization and provision of essential drugs. Education and appropriate services regarding responsible planning of family size, with respect for cultural, religious and social aspects in keeping with freedom, dignity and personally held values and taking into account ethical and cultural considerations, also contribute to these intersectoral activities.

Objectives

6.4. Within the overall strategy to achieve health for all by the year 2000, to meet basic health needs of rural, peri-urban and urban populations; to provide necessary specialized environmental health services; and to coordinate involvement of citizens, the health sector, the health related sectors, and relevant non-health sectors (business, social, educational and religious institutions) in solutions to health problems. As a matter of priority, health service coverage should be achieved for population groups in greatest need, particularly those living in rural areas.

Activities

6.5. National Governments and local authorities, with the support of relevant non-governmental organizations and international organizations, in the light of countries' specific conditions and needs, should strengthen their health sector programmes, with special attention to rural needs, to:

(a) Build basic health infrastructures, monitoring and planning systems:

(i) Develop and strengthen primary health care systems that are practical, community-based, scientifically sound, socially acceptable and appropriate to their needs and that meet basic health needs of clean water, safe food and sanitation;

(ii) Support the use and strengthening of mechanisms that improve the co-ordination between health and related sectors at all appropriate levels of government, and in communities and relevant organizations;

(iii) Develop and implement rational and affordable approaches to the establishment and maintenance of health facilities;

(iv) Ensure and, where appropriate, increase provision of social services support;

(v) Develop strategies, including reliable health indicators, to monitor the progress and evaluate the effectiveness of health programmes;

(vi) Explore ways to finance the health system based on the assessment of the resources needed and identify the various financing alternatives;

(vii) Promote health education in schools, information exchange, technical support and training;

(viii) Support initiatives for self-management of services by vulnerable groups;

(ix) Integrate traditional knowledge and experience into national health systems, as appropriate;

(x) Promote the provisions for necessary logistics for outreach activities, particularly in rural areas;

(xi) Promote and strengthen community-based rehabilitation activities for the rural handicapped.

(b) Support research and methodology development:

(i) Establish mechanisms for sustained community involvement in environmental health activities, including optimization of the appropriate use of community financial and human resources;

(ii) Conduct environmental health research, including behaviour research and research on ways to increase coverage and ensure greater utilization of services by peripheral, underserved and vulnerable populations, as appropriate to good prevention services and health care;

(iii) Conduct research into traditional knowledge of prevention and curative health practices.

Means of implementation

(a) Financing and cost evaluation

6.6. The Conference secretariat has estimated the average total annual cost (1993-2000) of implementing the activities of this programme to be about $40 billion, including about $5 billion from the international community on grant or concessional terms. These are indicative and order-of-magnitude estimates only and have not been reviewed by Governments. Actual costs and financial terms, including any that are non-concessional will depend upon, *inter alia*, the specific strategies and programmes Governments decide upon for implementation.

(b) Scientific and technological means

6.7. New approaches to planning and managing health care systems and facilities should be tested, and research on ways of integrating appropriate technologies into health infrastructures supported. The development of scientifically sound health technology should enhance adaptability to local needs and maintainability by community resources, including the maintenance and repair of equipment used in health care. Programmes to facilitate the transfer and sharing of information and expertise should be developed, including communication methods and educational materials.

(c) Human resource development

6.8. Intersectoral approaches to the reform of health personnel development should be strengthened to ensure its relevance to the "Health for All" strategies. Efforts to enhance managerial skills at the district level should be supported, with the aim of ensuring the systematic development and efficient operation of the basic health system. Intensive, short, practical training programmes with emphasis on skills in effective communication, community organization and facilitation of behaviour change should be developed in order to prepare the local personnel of all sectors involved in social development for carrying out their respective roles. In cooperation with the education sector, special health education programmes should be developed focusing on the role of women in the health care system.

(d) Capacity-building

6.9. Governments should consider adopting enabling and facilitating strategies to promote the participation of the communities in meeting its own needs in addition to providing direct support to the provision of health care services. A major focus should be the preparation of community-based health and health-related workers to assume an active role in community health education with emphasis on team work, social mobilization and the support of other development workers. National programmes should cover district health systems in urban, peri-urban and rural areas; the delivery of health programmes at the district level, and the development and support of referral services.

B. Control of communicable diseases

Basis for action

6.10. Advances in the development of vaccines and chemotherapeutic agents have brought many communicable diseases under control. However there remain many important communicable diseases for which environmental control measures are indispensable, especially in the field of water supply and sanitation such as cholera, diarrhoeal diseases, leishmaniasis, malaria and schistosomiasis. In all such instances, the environmental measures, either as an integral part of primary health care or undertaken outside the health sector, form an indispensable component of overall disease control strategies, together with health and hygiene education, and in some cases, are the only component.

6.11. With HIV infection levels estimated to increase to 30-40 million by the year 2000, the socio-economic impact of the pandemic is expected to be devastating for all countries and increasingly for women and children. While direct health costs will be substantial, they will be dwarfed by the indirect costs of the pandemic mainly costs associated with the loss of income and decreased productivity of the workforce. The pandemic will inhibit growth of the service and industrial sectors and significantly increase the costs of human capacity-building and retraining. The agricultural sector is particularly affected where production is labour-intensive.

Objectives

6.12. A number of goals have been formulated through extensive consultations in various international forums attended by virtually all Governments, relevant United Nations organizations (including WHO, UNICEF [U.N. Children's Fund], UNFPA [U.N. Population Fund], UNESCO [U.N. Educational, Scientific and Cultural Organization], UNDP [U.N. Development Programme] and the World Bank) and a number of non-governmental organizations. Goals (including but not limited to those listed below) are recommended for implementation by all countries where they are applicable, with appropriate adaptation to the specific situation of each country in terms of phasing, standards, priorities and availability of resources, with respect for cultural, religious and social aspects, in keeping with freedom, dignity and personally held values and taking into account ethical considerations. Additional goals that are particularly relevant to a country's specific situation should be added in the country's national plan of action (Plan of Action for the Implementation of the World Declaration on the Survival, Protection and

Development of Children in the 1990s).[2] Such national level action plans should be coordinated and monitored from within the public health sector. Some major goals are:

(a) By the year 2000, to eliminate Guinea worm disease (dracunculiasis);

(b) By the year 2000, eradicate polio;

(c) By the year 2000, to effectively control onchocerciasis (river blindness) and leprosy;

(d) By 1995, to reduce measles deaths by 95 per cent and reduce measles cases by 90 per cent compared with pre-immunization levels;

(e) By continued efforts, to provide health and hygiene education and to ensure universal access to safe drinking water and universal access to sanitary measures of excreta disposal, thereby markedly reducing waterborne diseases such as cholera and schistosomiasis and reducing:

(i) By the year 2000, the number of deaths from childhood diarrhoea in developing countries by between 50 to 70 per cent;

(ii) By the year 2000, the incidence of childhood diarrhoea in developing countries by at least 25 to 50 per cent;

(f) By the year 2000, to initiate comprehensive programmes to reduce mortality from acute respiratory infections in children under five years by at least one third, particularly in countries with high infant mortality;

(g) By the year 2000, to provide 95 per cent of the world's child population with access to appropriate care for acute respiratory infections within the community and at first referral level;

(h) By the year 2000, to institute anti-malaria programmes in all countries where malaria presents a significant health problem and maintain the transmission-free status of areas freed from endemic malaria;

(i) By the year 2000, to implement control programmes in countries where major human parasitic infections are endemic and achieve an overall reduction in the prevalence of schistosomiasis and of other trematode infections by 40 per cent and 25 per cent respectively, from a 1984 baseline, as well as a marked reduction in incidence, prevalence and intensity of filarial infections;

(j) To mobilize and unify national and international efforts against AIDS to prevent infection and to reduce the personal and social impact of HIV infection;

(k) To contain the resurgence of tuberculosis with particular emphasis on multiple antibiotic resistant forms;

---

2   A/45/625, annex. [This footnote appears in Agenda 21 as number 1 to this Chapter, A/CONF. 151/26, vol. I, pp 58 and 72].

(l) To accelerate research on improved vaccines and implement to the fullest extent possible the use of vaccines in the prevention of disease.

Activities

6.13. Each national Government, in accordance with national plans, for public health, priorities and objectives, should consider developing a national health action plan with appropriate international assistance and support including, at a minimum, the following components:

(a) National public health systems:

(i) Programmes to identify environmental hazards in the causation of communicable diseases;

(ii) Monitoring systems of epidemiological data to ensure adequate forecasting of the introduction, spread or aggravation of communicable diseases;

(iii) Intervention programmes, including measures consistent with the principles of the global AIDS strategy;

(iv) Vaccines for the prevention of communicable diseases;

(b) Public information and health education:

(i) Provide education and disseminate information on the risks of endemic communicable diseases and build awareness on environmental methods for control of communicable diseases to enable communities to play a role in the control of communicable diseases;

(c) Intersectoral cooperation and coordination:

(i) Second experienced health professionals to relevant sectors, such as planning, housing and agriculture;

(ii) Develop guidelines for effective coordination in the areas of professional training, assessment of risks and development of control technology;

(d) Control the environmental factors that influence the spread of communicable diseases:

(i) Apply methods for the prevention and control of communicable diseases, including water supply and sanitation control, water pollution control, food quality control, integrated vector control, garbage collection and disposal and environmentally sound irrigation practices;

(e) Primary health care system:

(i) Strengthen prevention programmes, with particular emphasis on adequate and balanced nutrition;

(ii) Strengthen early diagnostic programmes and improve capacities for early preventative/treatment action;

(iii) Reduce the vulnerability to HIV infection of women and of their offspring;

(f) Support the research and methodology development:

(i) Intensify and expand multidiscipline research, including focused efforts on the mitigation and environmental control of tropical diseases;

(ii) Carry out intervention studies to provide a solid epidemiological basis for control policies and to evaluate the efficiency of alternative approaches;

(iii) Undertake studies in the population and among health workers to determine the influence of cultural, behavioural and social factors on control policies;

(g) Development and dissemination of technology:

(i) Develop new technologies for the effective control of communicable diseases;

(ii) Promote studies to determine how to optimally disseminate results from research;

(iii) Ensure technical assistance including the sharing of knowledge and know-how.

Means of implementation

(a) Financing and cost evaluation

6.14. The Conference secretariat has estimated the average total annual cost (1993-2000) of implementing the activities of this programme to be about $4 billion, including about $900 million from the international community on grant or concessional terms. These are indicative and order-of-magnitude estimates only and have not been reviewed by Governments. Actual costs and financial terms, including any that are non-concessional, will depend upon, *inter alia*, the specific strategies and programmes Governments decide upon for implementation.[3]

---

3   Draft paragraphs 6.14 and 6.15 of A/CONF.151/4 (22 April 1992) were replaced by decision of the Main Committee of UNCED on 10 June 1992. See A/CONF.151/L.3/Add.6 (12 June 1992). The former draft read as follows:

The health sector expenditure of developing countries for the control and prevention of communicable diseases, particularly the tropical and vector-borne diseases, is estimated at $ 2 billion annually. The international financial support should contribute about one third of the health sector costs, or $ 600 million, annually. This includes $ 4 million annually for the support of international institutions. In addition, vector control services and insecticides require annual expenditures in the order of $ 1 billion annually.

The public health expenditures for the prevention of AIDS and the treatment of AIDS cases is estimated to cost the developing countries around $ 1 billion annually. The international financial support should cover about $ 300 million thereof, including global and regional institutions and programmes.

(b) Scientific and technological means

6.15. Efforts to prevent and control diseases should include investigations of the epidemiological, social and economic bases for the development of more effective national strategies for the integrated control of communicable diseases. Cost-effective methods of environmental control should be adapted to local developmental conditions.

(c) Human resources development

6.16. National and regional training institutions should promote broad intersectoral approaches to prevention and control of communicable diseases, including training in epidemiology and community prevention and control, immunology, molecular biology and the application of new vaccines. Health education materials should be developed for use by community workers and for the education of mothers for the prevention and treatment of diarrhoeal diseases in the home.

(d) Capacity-building

6.17. The health sector should develop adequate data on the distribution of communicable diseases as well as the institutional capacity to respond and collaborate with other sectors for prevention, mitigation and correction of communicable disease hazards through environmental protection. The advocacy at policy- and decision-making levels should be gained, professional and societal support mobilized, and communities organized in developing their self-reliance.

C. Protecting vulnerable groups

Basis for action

6.18. In addition to meeting basic health needs, specific emphasis has to be given to protecting and educating vulnerable groups, particularly infants, youth, women, indigenous people and the very poor as a prerequisite for sustainable development.[4] Special attention should also be paid to the health needs of the elderly and disabled population.

6.19. *Infants and children.* Approximately one third of the world's population are children under 15 years old. At least 15 million of these children die annually from such preventable causes as birth trauma, birth asphyxia, acute respiratory infections, malnutrition, communicable diseases and diarrhoea. The health of children is affected more severely than other population groups by malnutrition

---

4   Draft paragraph 6.19 of A/CONF.151/4 (22 April 1992) was replaced by decision of the Main Committee of UNCED on 10 June 1992. See A/CONF.151/L.3/Add.6 (12 June 1992). The first sentence of the former draft paragraph read as follows:

In addition to meeting basic health needs, specific emphasis has to be given to protecting and educating vulnerable groups, particularly infants, youth, women, indigenous people [, people under occupation] and the very poor as a prerequisite for sustainable development.

and adverse environmental factors, and many children risk exploitation as cheap labour or in prostitution.

6.20. *Youth*. As has been the historical experience of all countries, youth are particularly vulnerable to the problems associated with economic development, which often weakens traditional forms of social support essential for healthy development of young people. Urbanization and changes in social mores have increased substance abuse, unwanted pregnancy and sexually transmitted diseases, including AIDS. Currently more than half of all people alive are under the age of 25, and 4 of every 5 live in developing countries. Therefore it is important to ensure that historical experience is not replicated.

6.21. *Women*. In developing countries, the health status of women remains relatively low, and during the 1980s poverty, malnutrition and general ill-health in women were even rising. Most women in developing countries still do not have adequate basic educational opportunities and they lack the means of promoting their health, responsibly controlling their reproductive life and improving their socio-economic status. Particular attention should be given to the provision of pre-natal care to ensure healthy babies.

6.22. *Indigenous people and their communities*. Indigenous people had their communities make up a significant percentage of global population. The outcomes of their experience have tended to be very similar in that the basis of their relationship with traditional lands has been fundamentally changed. They tend to feature disproportionately in unemployment, lack of housing, poverty and poor health. In many countries the number of indigenous people is growing faster than the general population. Therefore it is important to target health initiatives for indigenous people.

Objectives

6.23. The general objectives of protecting vulnerable groups are to ensure that all such individuals should be allowed to develop to their full potential (including healthy physical, mental and spiritual development); to ensure that young people can develop, establish and maintain healthy lives; to allow women to perform their key role in society; and to support indigenous people through educational, economic and technical opportunities.[5]

6.24. Specific major goals for child survival, development and protection were agreed upon at the World Summit for Children and remain valid also for Agenda 21. Supporting and sectoral goals cover women's health and education, nutri-

---

5   Draft paragraph 6.24 of A/CONF.151/4 (22 April 1992) was replaced by decision of the Main Committee of UNCED on 10 June 1992. See A/CONF.151/L.3/Add.6 (12 June 1992). The former draft read as follows:

The general objectives of protecting vulnerable groups are to ensure that all such individuals should be allowed to develop to their full potential (including healthy, physical, mental and spiritual development); to ensure that young people can develop, establish and maintain healthy lives; to allow women to perform their key role in society; and to support indigenous people [and people under occupation] through educational, economic and technical opportunities.

tion, child health, water and sanitation, basic education and children in difficult circumstances.

6.25. Governments should take active steps to implement, as a matter of urgency, in accordance with country specific conditions and legal systems, measures to ensure that women and men have the same right to decide freely and responsibly on the number and spacing of their children, to have access to the information, education and means, as appropriate, to enable them to exercise this right in keeping with their freedom, dignity and personally held values taking into account ethical and cultural considerations.

6.26. Governments should take active steps to implement programmes to establish and strengthen preventive and curative health facilities which include women-centered, woman-managed, safe and effective reproductive health care and affordable, accessible services as appropriate for the responsible planning of family size, in keeping with freedom, dignity and personally held values and taking into account ethical and cultural considerations. Programmes should focus on providing comprehensive health care, including pre-natal care, education and information on health and responsible parenthood and should provide the opportunity for all women to breast-feed fully at least during the first four months post-partum. Programmes should fully support women's productive and reproductive roles and well being, with special attention to the need for providing equal and improved health care for all children and the need to reduce the risk of maternal and child mortality and sickness.

Activities

6.27. National Governments, in cooperation with local and non-governmental organizations, should initiate or enhance programmes in the following areas:

(a) Infants and children:

(i) Strengthen basic health-care services for children in the context of primary health-care delivery, including prenatal care, breast-feeding, immunization and nutrition programmes;

(ii) Undertake widespread adult education on the use of oral rehydration therapy for diarrhoea, treatment of respiratory infections and prevention of communicable diseases;

(iii) Promote the creation, amendment and enforcement of a legal framework protecting children from sexual and workplace exploitation;

(iv) Protect children from the effects of environmental and occupational toxic compounds;

(b) Youth:

Strengthen services for youth in health, education and social sectors in order to provide better information, education, counselling and treatment for specific health problems, including drug abuse;

(c) Women:

(i) Involve women's groups in decision-making at the national and community levels to identify health risks and incorporate health issues in national action programmes on women and development;

(ii) Provide concrete incentives to encourage and maintain attendance of women of all ages at school and adult education courses, including health education and training in primary, home and maternal health care;

(iii) Carry out baseline surveys and knowledge, attitude and practice studies on the health and nutrition of women throughout their life cycle, especially as related to the impact of environmental degradation and adequate resources;

(d) Indigenous people and their communities:

(i) Strengthen, through resources and self-management, preventative and curative health services;

(ii) Integrate traditional knowledge and experience into health systems.

Means of implementation

(a) Financing and cost evaluation

6.28. The Conference secretariat has estimated the average total annual cost (1993-2000) of implementing the activities of this programme to be about $3.7 billion, including about $400 billion from the international community on grant or concessional terms. These are indicative and order-of-magnitude estimates only and have not been reviewed by Governments. Actual costs and financial terms, including any that are non-concessional, will depend upon, *inter alia*, the specific strategies and programmes Governments decide upon for implementation.[6]

(b) Scientific and technological means

6.29. Educational, health and research institutions should be strengthened to provide support to improve the health of vulnerable groups. Social research on the specific problems of these groups should be expanded and methods for implementing flexible pragmatic solutions explored, with emphasis on preventive measures. Technical support should be provided to Governments, institutions

---

6   Draft paragraph 6.29 of A/CONF.151/4 (22 April 1992) was replaced by decision of the Main Committee of UNCED on 10 June 1992. See A/CONF.151/L.3/Add.6 (12 June 1992). The former draft read as follows:

The incremental cost, above the basic health needs, for activities to address the special needs of vulnerable groups is an estimated $ 3.7 billion per year to cover child health programmes, youth programmes and women's health programmes. About $ 400 million would be needed from international sources, including $ 5 million annually to strengthen international institutions.

and non-governmental organizations for youth, women and indigenous people in the health sector.[7]

(c) Human resources development

6.30. The development of human resources for the health of children, youth and women should include reinforcement of educational institutions, promotion of interactive methods of education for health and increased use of mass media in disseminating information to the target groups. This requires the training of more community health workers, nurses, midwives, physicians, social scientists and educators, the education of mothers, families and communities and the strengthening of ministries of education, health, population etc.

(d) Capacity-building

6.31. The Governments should promote where necessary (i) the organization of national, intercountry and interregional symposia and other meetings for the exchange of information among agencies and groups concerned with the health of children, youth, women and indigenous people, and (ii) women's organizations, youth groups and indigenous peoples' organizations to facilitate health and consult them on the creation, amendment and enforcement of legal frameworks to ensure a healthy environment for children, youth, women and indigenous peoples.[8]

D. Meeting the urban health challenge

Basis for action

6.32. For hundreds of millions of people, the poor living conditions in urban and peri-urban areas are destroying lives, health, and social and moral values. Urban growth has outstripped society's capacity to meet human needs, leaving hundreds of millions of people with inadequate incomes, diets, housing and services. Urban growth exposes populations to serious environmental hazards and has out-

---

7   Draft paragraph 6.30 of A/CONF.151/4 (22 April 1992) was replaced by decision of the Main Committee of UNCED on 10 June 1992. See A/CONF.151/L.3/Add.6 (12 June 1992). The last sentence of draft paragraph 6.30 read as follows:

> Educational, health and research institutions should be strengthened to provide support to improve the health of vulnerable groups. Social research on the specific problems of these groups should be expanded and methods for implementing flexible pragmatic solutions explored with emphasis on preventive measures. Technical support should be provided to Governments, institutions and youths', women's and indigenous peoples' [and people under occupation] non-governmental organizations in the health sector.

8   Draft paragraph 6.32 of A/CONF.151/4 (22 April 1992) was replaced by decision of the Main Committee of UNCED on 10 June 1992. See A/CONF.151/L.3/Add.6 (12 June 1992) and A/CONF.151/L.3/Add.6/Corr.1 (13 June 1992). The former draft read as follows:

> The Governments should promote where necessary (i) the organization of national, intercountry and interregional symposia and other meetings for the exchange of information among agencies and groups concerned with the health of children, youth, women and indigenous peoples, and (ii) women's organizations, youth groups and indigenous peoples' organizations [and various bodies and organizations under occupation] to facilitate health and consult them on the creation, amendment and enforcement of legal frameworks to ensure a healthy environment for children, youth, women and indigenous peoples [and people under occupation].

stripped the capacity of municipal and local governments to provide the environmental health services that the people need. All too often, urban development is associated with destructive effects on the physical environment and the resource base needed for sustainable development. Environmental pollution in urban areas is associated with excess morbidity and mortality. Overcrowding and inadequate housing contribute to respiratory diseases, tuberculosis, meningitis and other diseases. In urban environments, many factors that affect human health are outside the health sector. Improvements in urban health therefore will depend on coordinated action by all levels of government, health care providers, businesses, religious groups, social and educational institutions and citizens.

Objectives

6.33. To improve the health and well-being of all urban dwellers, so that they can contribute to economic and social development. The global objective is to achieve a 10 to 40 per cent improvement in health indicators by the year 2000. The same rate of improvement should be achieved for environmental, housing, and health services indicators. These include the development of quantitative objectives for: infant mortality, maternal mortality, percentage of low birth weight newborns, and specific indicators (e.g. tuberculosis as an indicator of crowded housing, diarrhoeal diseases as indicators of inadequate water and sanitation, rates of industrial and transportation accidents that indicate possible opportunities for prevention of injury, and social problems such as drug abuse, violence and crime that indicate underlying social disorders).

Activities

6.34. Local authorities, with the appropriate support of national Governments and international organizations should be encouraged to take effective measures to initiate or strengthen the following activities:

(a) Develop and implement municipal and local health plans:

(i) Establish or strengthen intersectoral committees at both the political and technical level, including active collaboration on linkages with scientific, cultural, religious, medical, business, social and other city institutions, using networking arrangements;

(ii) Adopt or strengthen municipal or local "enabling strategies" that emphasize "doing with" rather than "doing for" and create supportive environments for health;

(iii) Ensure that public health education in schools, workplace, mass media etc. is provided or strengthened;

(iv) Encourage communities to develop personal skills and awareness of primary health care;

(v) Promote and strengthen community-based rehabilitation activities for the urban and peri-urban disabled and the elderly;

(b) Survey, where necessary, the existing health, social and environmental conditions in cities including documentation of intra-urban differences;

(c) Strengthen environmental health services:

(i) Adopt health impact and environmental impact assessment procedures;

(ii) Provide basic and in-service training for new and existing personnel;

(d) Establish and maintain city networks for collaboration and exchange of models of good practice.

Means of implementation

(a) Financing and cost evaluation

6.35. The secretariat of the Conference has estimated the average total annual cost (1993-2000) of implementing the activities of this programme to be about $222 million, including about $22 million from the international community on grant or concessional terms. These are indicative and order of magnitude estimates only and have not been reviewed by Governments. Actual costs and financial terms, including any that are non-concessional, will depend upon, *inter alia*, the specific strategies and programmes Governments decide upon for implementation.[9]

(b) Scientific and technological means

6.36. Decision-making models should be further developed and more widely used to assess the costs and the health and environment impacts of alternative technologies and strategies. Improvement in urban development and management requires better national and municipal statistics based on practical, standardized indicators. Development of methods is a priority for the measurement of intra-urban and intra-district variations in health status and environmental conditions, and for the application of this information in planning and management.

(c) Human resources development

6.37. Programmes must supply the orientation and basic training of municipal staff required for the healthy city processes. Basic and in-service training of environmental health personnel will also be needed.

---

9   Draft paragraph 6.36 of A/CONF.151/4 (22 April 1992) was replaced by decision of the Main Committee of UNCED on 10 June 1992. See A/CONF.151/L.3/Add.6 (12 June 1992). The former draft read as follows:

   Most of the programme activities should be performed by the cities using local resources. For the implementation of healthy cities and other similar programmes, the local cost of activities would be in the order of $ 200 million annually. The international contributions in support of accelerated development is estimated to be about $ 20 million per year until the year 2000. Strengthening of international institutions is required to provide collaborative networks, development of assessment methods for planning purposes, design of new technologies and managerial support. International financing of labour $ 2 million is required annually for this.

(d) Capacity-building

6.38. The programme is aimed towards improved planning and management capabilities in the municipal and local government and its partners in central Government, the private sector and universities. Capacity development should be focused on obtaining sufficient information, improving coordination mechanisms linking all the key actors, and making better use of available instruments and resources for implementation.

E. Reducing health risks from environmental pollution and hazards

Basis for action

6.39. In many locations around the world the general environment (air, water and land), workplaces and even individual dwellings are so badly polluted that the health of hundreds of millions of people is adversely affected. This is, *inter alia*, due to past and present developments in consumption and production patterns and lifestyles, in energy production and use, in industry, in transportation etc., with little or no regard for environmental protection. There have been notable improvements in some countries, but deterioration of the environment continues. The ability of countries to tackle pollution and health problems is greatly restrained because of lack of resources. Pollution control and health protection measures have often not kept pace with economic development. Considerable development-related environmental health hazards exist in the newly industrializing countries. Furthermore, the recent analysis of the WHO has clearly established the interdependence among the factors of health, environment and development and has revealed that most countries are lacking such integration as would lead to an effective pollution control mechanism.[10] Without prejudice to such criteria as may be agreed upon by the international community, or to standards which will have to be determined nationally, it will be essential in all cases to consider the systems of values prevailing in each country and the extent of the applicability of standards that are valid for the most advanced countries but may be inappropriate and of unwarranted social cost for the developing countries.

Objectives

6.40. The overall objective is to minimize hazards and maintain the environment to a degree that human health and safety is not impaired or endangered and yet encourage development to proceed. Specific programme objectives are:

(a) By the year 2000, to incorporate appropriate environmental and health safeguards as part of national development programmes in all countries;

---

10   Report of the WHO Commission on Health and Environment (Geneva, forthcoming). [This footnote appears in Agenda 21 as number 2 to this Chapter, A/CONF. 151/26, vol. I, pp 68 and 72.

(b) By the year 2000, to establish, as appropriate, adequate national infrastructure and programmes for providing environmental injury, hazard surveillance and the basis for abatement in all countries;

(c) By the year 2000, to establish, as appropriate, integrated programmes for tackling pollution at source and at disposal site with a focus on abatement actions in all countries;

(d) To identify and compile, as appropriate, the necessary statistical information on health effects to support cost benefit analysis including environmental health impact assessment for pollution control, prevention, and abatement measures.

Activities

6.41. Nationally determined action programmes, with international assistance, support and coordination, where necessary, in this area should include:

(a) Urban air pollution:

(i) Develop appropriate pollution control technology on the basis of risk assessment and epidemiological research for the introduction of environmentally sound production processes and suitable safe mass transport;

(ii) Develop air pollution control capacities in large cities, emphasizing enforcement programmes using monitoring networks, as appropriate;

(b) Indoor air pollution:

(i) Support research and develop programmes for applying prevention and control methods to reducing indoor air pollution, including the provision of economic incentives for the installation of appropriate technology;

(ii) Develop and implement health education campaigns, particularly in developing countries, to reduce the health impact of domestic use of biomass and coal;

(c) Water pollution:

(i) Develop appropriate water pollution control technologies on the basis of health risk assessment;

(ii) Develop water pollution control capacities in large cities;

(d) Pesticides:

Develop mechanisms to control the distribution and use of pesticides in order to minimize the risks to human health by transportation, storage, application and residual effects of pesticides used in agriculture and preservation of wood;

(e) Solid waste:

(i) Develop appropriate solid waste disposal technologies on the basis of health risk assessment;

(ii) Develop appropriate solid waste disposal capacities in large cities;

(f) Human settlements:

Develop programmes for improving health conditions in human settlements, in particular within slums and non-tenured settlements, on the basis of health risk assessment;

(g) Noise:

Develop criteria for maximum permitted safe noise exposure levels and promote noise assessment and control as part of environmental health programmes;

(h) Ionizing and non-ionizing radiation:

Develop and implement appropriate national legislation, standards and enforcement procedures on the basis of existing international guidelines;

(i) Effects of ultraviolet radiation:

(i) Undertake, as a matter of urgency, research on the effects on human health of the increasing ultraviolet radiation reaching the earth's surface as a consequence of depletion of the stratospheric ozone layer;

(ii) On the basis of the outcome of this research, consider taking appropriate remedial measures to mitigate the above-mentioned effects on human beings;

(j) Industry and energy production:

(i) Establish environmental health impact assessment procedures for the planning and development of new industries and energy facilities;

(ii) Incorporate appropriate health risk analysis in all national programmes for pollution control and management, with particular emphasis on toxic compounds such as lead;

(iii) Establish industrial hygiene programmes in all major industries for the surveillance of workers' exposure to health hazards;

(iv) Promote the introduction of environmentally sound technologies within the industry and energy sectors;

(k) Monitoring and assessment:

Establish, as appropriate, adequate environmental monitoring capacities for the surveillance of environmental quality and the health status of populations;

(l) Injury monitoring and reduction:

(i) Support, as appropriate, the development of systems to monitor the incidence and cause of injury to allow well-targeted intervention/prevention strategies;

(ii) Develop, in accordance with national plans, strategies in all sectors (industry, traffic and others) consistent with the WHO safe cities and safe communities programmes, to reduce the frequency and severity of injury;

(iii) Emphasize preventive strategies to reduce occupationally derived diseases and diseases caused by environmental and occupational toxins to enhance worker safety;

(m) Research promotion and methodology development:

(i) Support the development of new methods for the quantitative assessment of health benefits and cost associated with different pollution control strategies;

(ii) Develop and carry out interdisciplinary research on the combined health effects of exposure to multiple environmental hazards, including epidemiological investigations of long-term exposures to low levels of pollutants and the use of biological markers capable of estimating human exposures, adverse effects and susceptibility to environmental agents.

Means of implementation

(a) Financing and cost evaluation

6.42. The Conference secretariat has estimated the average total annual cost (1993-2000) of implementing the activities of this programme to be about $3 billion, including about $115 million from the international community on grant or concessional terms. These are indicative and order-of-magnitude estimates only and have not been reviewed by Governments. Actual costs and financial terms, including any that are non-concessional, will depend upon, *inter alia*, the specific strategies and programmes Governments decide upon for implementation.[11]

(b) Scientific and technological means

6.43. Although technology to prevent or abate pollution is readily available for a large number of problems, for programme and policy development countries should undertake research within an intersectoral framework. Such efforts should include collaboration with the business sector. Cost effect analysis and environmental impact assessment methods should be developed through coop-

---

11   Draft paragraphs 6.43 and 6.44 of A/CONF.151/4 (22 April 1992) were replaced by decision of the Main Committee of UNCED on 10 June 1992. See A/CONF.151/L.3/Add.6 (12 June 1992). The former draft read as follows:

The reduction of air pollution in urban areas of the developing countries requires annual investments on the order of $ 2.5 billion, with a private sector component of about $ 2.0 billion. The public expenditure component of about $ 500 million includes an international financial contribution of about $ 50 million annually. The reduction of indoor air pollution from household biomass use is estimated at $ 500 million annually with an international financing component of about $ 50 million annually.

The establishment and strengthening of health-oriented monitoring systems for air, water and soil in developing countries and of national capacities for dealing with air pollution, indoor air quality, noise, radiation, health impact assessment and research promotion requires about $ 30 million annually with $ 15 million coming from international sources, including $ 2 million for the strengthening of international institutions.

erative international programmes and applied to the setting of priorities and strategies in relation to health and development.

6.44. In the activities listed in paragraph 6.41 (a) to (m) above, developing country efforts should be facilitated by access to and transfer of technology, know-how and information, from the repositories of such knowledge and technologies, in conformity with chapter 34.[12]

(c) Human resource development

6.45. Comprehensive national strategies should be designed to overcome the lack of qualified human resources, which is a major impediment to progress in dealing with environmental health hazards. Training should include environmental and health officials at all levels from managers to inspectors. More emphasis needs to be placed on including the subject of environmental health in the curricula of secondary schools and universities and on educating the public.

(d) Capacity-building

6.46. Each country should develop the knowledge and practical skills to foresee and identify environmental health hazards, and the capacity to reduce the risks. Basic capacity requirements must include knowledge about environmental health problems and awareness on the part of leaders, citizens and specialists; operational mechanisms for intersectoral and intergovernmental cooperation in development planning and management and in combating pollution; arrangements for involving private and community interests in dealing with social issues; delegation of authority and distribution of resources to intermediate and local levels of government to provide front-line capabilities to meet environmental health needs.[13]

---

12 Draft paragraph 6.46 of A/CONF.151/4 (22 April 1992) was replaced by decision of the Main Committee of UNCED on 10 June 1992. See A/CONF.151/L.3/Add.6 (12 June 1992). The former draft read as follows:

In the activities listed under (a) to (l) above, developing country efforts should be facilitated by access to and transfer of technology, know-how and information, from the repositories of such knowledge and technologies[, on concessional and preferential terms.]

13 Section E of Chapter 6 contained a draft footnote that was deleted by the main committee. The footnote read as follows:

These paragraphs contain matters relating to means of implementation, including cost estimates, which are indicative secretariat figures provided pursuant to decision A/CONF/151/PC/L.49. They remain in brackets as they have not been negotiated.

Chapter 7

Promoting Sustainable Human Settlement Development

INTRODUCTION

7.1. In industrialized countries, the consumption patterns of cities are severely stressing the global ecosystem, while settlements in the developing world need more raw material, energy, and economic development simply to overcome basic economic and social problems. Human settlement conditions in many parts of the world, particularly the developing countries, are deteriorating mainly as a result of the low levels of investment in the sector attributable to the overall resource constraints in these countries. In the low-income countries for which recent data are available, an average of only 5.6 per cent of central government expenditure went to housing, amenities, social security and welfare.[1] Expenditure by international support and finance organizations is equally low. For example, only 1 per cent of the United Nations system's total grant-financed expenditures in 1988 went to human settlements[2] while in 1991, loans from the World Bank and the International Development Association (IDA) for urban development and water supply and sewerage amounted to 5.5 and 5.4 per cent, respectively, of their total lending.[3]

7.2. On the other hand, available information indicates that technical cooperation activities in the human settlement sector generate considerable public and private sector investment. For example, every dollar of UNDP technical coopera-

---

1   No aggregate figures are available on internal expenditure or official development assistance on human settlements. However, data available in the *World Development Report, 1991*, for 16 low-income developing countries show that the percentage of central government expenditure on housing, amenities and social security and welfare for 1989 averaged 5.6 per cent, with a high of 15.1 per cent in the case of Sri Lanka, which has embarked on a vigorous housing programme. In OECD industrialized countries, during the same year, the percentage of central government expenditure on housing, amenities and social security and welfare ranged from a minimum of 29.3 per cent to a maximum of 49.4 per cent, with an average of 39 per cent (World Bank, *World Development Report, 1991*, World Development Indicators, table 11 (Washington, D.C., 1991)).

2   See the report of the Director-General for Development and International Economic Cooperation containing preliminary statistical data on operational activities of the United Nations system for 1988 (A/44/324-E/1989/106/Add.4, annex).

3   World Bank, *Annual Report, 1991* (Washington, D.C., 1991).

tion expenditure on human settlements in 1988 generated a follow-up invest-ment of $122, the highest of all UNDP sectors of assistance.[4]

7.3. This is the foundation of the "enabling approach" advocated for the human settlement sector. External assistance will help to generate the internal re-sources needed to improve the living and working environments of all people by the year 2000 and beyond, including the growing number of unemployed—the no-income group. At the same time the environmental implications of urban de-velopment should be recognized and addressed in an integrated fashion by all countries, with high priority being given to the needs of the urban and rural poor, the unemployed and the growing number of people without any source of income.

Human settlement objective

7.4. The overall human settlement objective is to improve the social, economic and environmental quality of human settlements and the living and working en-vironments of all people, in particular the urban and rural poor. Such improve-ment should be based on technical cooperation activities, partnerships among the public, private and community sectors and participation in the decision-making process by community groups and special interest groups such as women, indigenous people, the elderly and the disabled. These approaches should form the core principles of national settlement strategies. In developing these strategies, countries will need to set priorities among the eight pro-gramme areas in this chapter in accordance with their national plans and objectives, taking fully into account their social and cultural capabilities. Fur-thermore, countries should make appropriate provision to monitor the impact of their strategies on marginalized and disenfranchised groups, with particular reference to the needs of women.

7.5. The programme areas included in this chapter are:

(a) Providing adequate shelter for all;

(b) Improving human settlement management;

(c) Promoting sustainable land-use planning and management;

(d) Promoting the integrated provision of environmental infrastructure: wa-ter, sanitation, drainage and solid-waste management;

(e) Promoting sustainable energy and transport systems in human settlements;

(f) Promoting human settlement planning and management in disaster-prone areas;

---

4   UNDP, "Reported investment commitments related to UNDP-assisted projects, 1988", table 1, "Sectoral distribution of investment commitment in 1988-1989".

(g) Promoting sustainable construction industry activities;

(h) Promoting human resource development and capacity-building for human settlement development.

PROGRAMME AREAS

A. Providing adequate shelter for all

Basis for action

7.6. Access to safe and healthy shelter is essential to a person's physical, psychological, social and economic well-being and should be a fundamental part of national and international action. The right to adequate housing as a basic human right is enshrined in the Universal Declaration of Human Rights and the International Covenant on Economic, Social and Cultural Rights. Despite this, it is estimated that at the present time, at least 1 billion people do not have access to safe and healthy shelter and that if appropriate action is not taken, this number will increase dramatically by the end of the century and beyond.

7.7. A major global programme to address this problem is the Global Strategy for Shelter to the Year 2000, adopted by the General Assembly in December 1988 (resolution 43/181, annex). Despite its widespread endorsement, the Strategy needs a much greater level of political and financial support to enable it to reach its goal of facilitating adequate shelter for all by the end of the century and beyond.

Objective

7.8. The objective is to achieve adequate shelter for rapidly growing populations and for the currently deprived urban and rural poor through an enabling approach to shelter development and improvement that is environmentally sound.

Activities

7.9. The following activities should be undertaken:

(a) As a first step towards the goal of providing adequate shelter for all, all countries should take immediate measures to provide shelter to their homeless poor, while the international community and financial institutions should undertake actions to support the efforts of the developing countries to provide shelter to the poor;

(b) All countries should adopt and/or strengthen national shelter strategies, with targets based, as appropriate, on the principles and recommendations contained in the Global Strategy for Shelter to the Year 2000. People should be protected by law against unfair eviction from their homes or land;

(c) All countries should, as appropriate, support the shelter efforts of the urban and rural poor, the unemployed and the no-income group by adopting and/or adapting existing codes and regulations, to facilitate their access to land, finance and low-cost building materials and by actively promoting the regularization and upgrading of informal settlements and urban slums as an expedient measure and pragmatic solution to the urban shelter deficit;

(d) All countries should, as appropriate, facilitate access of urban and rural poor to shelter by adopting and utilizing housing and finance schemes and new innovative mechanisms adapted to their circumstances;

(e) All countries should support and develop environmentally compatible shelter strategies at national, state/provincial and municipal levels through partnerships among the private, public and community sectors and with the support of community-based organizations;

(f) All countries, especially developing ones, should, as appropriate, formulate and implement programmes to reduce the impact of the phenomenon of rural to urban drift by improving rural living conditions;

(g) All countries, where appropriate, should develop and implement resettlement programmes that address the specific problems of displaced populations in their respective countries;

(h) All countries should, as appropriate, document and monitor the implementation of their national shelter strategies by using, *inter alia*, the monitoring guidelines adopted by the Commission on Human Settlements and the shelter performance indicators being produced jointly by the United Nations Centre for Human Settlements (Habitat) and the World Bank;

(i) Bilateral and multilateral cooperation should be strengthened in order to support the implementation of the national shelter strategies of developing countries;

(j) Global progress reports covering national action and the support activities of international organizations and bilateral donors should be produced and disseminated on a biennial basis, as requested in the Global Strategy for Shelter to the Year 2000.

Means of implementation

(a) Financing and cost evaluation

7.10. The Conference secretariat has estimated the average total annual cost (1993-2000) of implementing the activities of this programme to be about $75 billion, including about $10 billion from the international community on grant or concessional terms. These are indicative and order of magnitude estimates only and have not been reviewed by Governments. Actual costs and financial terms, including any that are non-concessional, will depend upon,

inter alia, the specific strategies and programmes Governments decide upon for implementation.[5]

(b) Scientific and technological means

7.11. The requirements under this heading are addressed in each of the other programme areas included in the present chapter.

(c) Human resource development and capacity-building

7.12. Developed countries and funding agencies should provide specific assistance to developing countries in adopting an enabling approach to the provision of shelter for all, including the no-income group, and covering research institutions and training activities for government officials, professionals, communities and non-governmental organizations and by strengthening local capacity for the development of appropriate technologies.

B. Improving human settlement management

Basis for action

7.13. By the turn of the century, the majority of the world's population will be living in cities. While urban settlements, particularly in developing countries, are showing many of the symptoms of the global environment and development crisis, they nevertheless generate 60 per cent of gross national product and, if properly managed, can develop the capacity to sustain their productivity, improve the living conditions of their residents and manage natural resources in a sustainable way.

7.14. Some metropolitan areas extend over the boundaries of several political and/or administrative entities (counties and municipalities) even though they conform to a continuous urban system. In many cases this political heterogeneity hinders the implementation of comprehensive environmental management programmes.

Objective

7.15. The objectives are to ensure sustainable management of all urban settlements, particularly in developing countries, in order to enhance their ability to improve living conditions of residents, especially the marginalized and disen-

---

5   Draft paragraphs 7.10 and 7.11 of A/CONF.151/4 (22 April 1992) were replaced by decision of the Main Committee of UNCED on 10 June 1992. See A/CONF.151/L.3/Add.7 (12 June 1992); The previous text of paragraph 7.10-11 read as follows:

7.10 The total requirements for obtaining adequate shelter conditions for the urban and rural poor by the year 2000 are about $ 75 billion annually, to be financed primarily from household, community and national resources. About US$ 10 billion per year in external financing will be needed.

7.11 Annual support costs for strengthening international institutions in support of the Strategy's programme of action are estimated at $ 10 million per year, a portion of which will be needed by the United Nations Centre for Human Settlements (Habitat), to support its role as the agency designated by the General Assembly as the secretariat for the Strategy.

franchised, thereby contributing to the achievement of national economic development goals.

Activities

(a) Improving urban management

7.16. One existing framework for strengthening management is in the United Nations Development Programme/World Bank/United Nations Centre for Human Settlements (Habitat) Urban Management Programme (UMP), a concerted global effort to assist developing countries in addressing urban management issues. Its coverage should be extended to all interested countries during the period 1993-2000. All countries should, as appropriate and in accordance with national plans, objectives and priorities and with the assistance of non-governmental organizations and representatives of local authorities, undertake the following activities at the national, state/provincial and local levels, with the assistance of relevant programmes and support agencies:

(a) Adopting and applying urban management guidelines in the areas of land management, urban environmental management, infrastructure management and municipal finance and administration;

(b) Accelerating efforts to reduce urban poverty through a number of actions, including:

(i) Generating employment for the urban poor, particularly women, through the provision, improvement and maintenance of urban infrastructure and services and the support of economic activities in the informal sector, such as repairs, recycling, services and small commerce;

(ii) Providing specific assistance to the poorest of the urban poor through, *inter alia*, the creation of social infrastructure in order to reduce hunger and homelessness, and the provision of adequate community services;

(iii) Encouraging the establishment of indigenous community-based organizations, private voluntary organizations and other forms of non-governmental entities that can contribute to the efforts to reduce poverty and improve the quality of life for low-income families;

(c) Adopting innovative city planning strategies to address environmental and social issues by:

(i) Reducing subsidies on, and recovering full costs of, environmental and other services of high standard (e.g. water supply, sanitation, waste collection, roads, telecommunications) provided to higher income neighbourhoods;

(ii) Improving the level of infrastructure and service provision in poorer urban areas;

(d) Developing local strategies for the improvement of the quality of life and the environment, integrating decisions on land use and land management, investing in the public and private sectors and mobilizing human and material resources, thereby promoting employment generation that is environmentally sound and protective of human health.

(b) Strengthening urban data systems

7.17. During the period 1993-2000 all countries should undertake, with the active participation of the business sector as appropriate, pilot projects in selected cities for the collection, analysis and subsequent dissemination of urban data, including environmental impact analysis, at the local, state/provincial, national and international levels and the establishment of city data management capabilities.[6] United Nations organizations such as Habitat, UNEP and UNDP, could provide technical advice and model data management systems.

(c) Encouraging intermediate city development

7.18. In order to relieve pressure on large urban agglomerations of developing countries, policies and strategies should be implemented towards the development of intermediate cities which create employment opportunities for unemployed labour in the rural areas and support rural-based economic activities, although sound urban management is essential to ensure that urban sprawl does not expand resource degradation over an ever wider land area and increase pressures to convert open space and agricultural/buffer lands for development.

7.19. Therefore, all countries should, as appropriate, conduct reviews of urbanization processes and policies in order to assess environmental impacts of growth and apply urban planning and management approaches specifically suited to the needs, resource capabilities and characteristics of their growing intermediate-sized cities. As appropriate, they should also concentrate on activities aimed at facilitating the transition from rural to urban lifestyles and settlement patterns and at promoting the development of small-scale economic activities, particularly the production of food, to support local income generation and the production of intermediate goods and services for rural hinterlands.

7.20. All cities, particularly those characterized by severe sustainable development problems, should, in accordance with national laws, rules and regulations, develop and strengthen programmes aimed at addressing such problems and guiding their development along a sustainable path. Some international initiatives in support of such efforts, as in the Sustainable Cities Programme of Habi-

---

6   A pilot programme of this type, the City Data Programme (CDP), is already in operation in the United Nations Centre on Human Settlements (Habitat) aimed at the production and dissemination to participating cities of microcomputer application software designed to store, process and retrieve city data for local, national and international exchange and dissemination. [This footnote appears in Agenda 21 as number 5 to this Chapter, A/CONF. 151/26, pp. 78 and 97].

tat and the Healthy Cities Programme of WHO, should be intensified. Additional initiatives involving the World Bank, the regional development banks and bilateral agencies, as well as other interested stakeholders, particularly international and national representatives of local authorities, should be strengthened and coordinated. Individual cities should, as appropriate:

(a) Institutionalize a participatory approach to sustainable urban development, based on a continuous dialogue between the actors involved in urban development (the public sector, private sector and communities), especially women and indigenous people;

(b) Improve the urban environment by promoting social organization and environmental awareness through the participation of local communities in the identification of public services needs, the provision of urban infrastructure, the enhancement of public amenities and the protection and/or rehabilitation of older buildings, historic precincts and other cultural artifacts. In addition, "green works" programmes should be activated to create self-sustaining human development activities and both formal and informal employment opportunities for low-income urban residents;

(c) Strengthen the capacities of their local governing bodies to deal more effectively with the broad range of developmental and environmental challenges associated with rapid and sound urban growth through comprehensive approaches to planning that recognize the individual needs of cities and are based on ecologically sound urban design practices;

(d) Participate in international "sustainable city networks" to exchange experiences and mobilize national and international technical and financial support;

(e) Promote the formulation of environmentally sound and culturally sensitive tourism programmes as a strategy for sustainable development of urban and rural settlements and as a way of decentralizing urban development and reducing discrepancies among regions;

(f) Establish mechanisms, with the assistance of relevant international agencies to mobilize resources for local initiatives to improve environmental quality;

(g) Empower community groups, non-governmental organizations and individuals to assume the authority and responsibility for managing and enhancing their immediate environment through participatory tools, techniques and approaches embodied in the concept of environmental care.

7.21. Cities of all countries should reinforce cooperation among themselves and cities of the developed countries, under the aegis of non-governmental organizations active in this field, such as the International Union of Local Authorities (IULA), the International Council for Local Environmental Initiatives (ICLEI) and the World Federation of Twin Cities.

Means of implementation

(a) Financing and cost evaluation

7.22. The Conference secretariat has estimated the average total annual cost (1993-2000) of implementing the activities of this programme to be about $100 billion, including about $15 billion from the international community on grant or concessional terms. These are indicative and order of magnitude estimates only and have not been reviewed by Governments. Actual costs and financial terms, including any that are non-concessional, will depend upon, *inter alia*, the specific strategies and programmes Governments decide upon for implementation.[7]

(b) Human resource development and capacity-building

7.23. Developing countries should, with appropriate international assistance, consider focusing on training and developing a cadre of urban managers, technicians, administrators and other relevant stakeholders needed to success-fully manage environmentally sound urban development and growth and are equipped with the skills necessary to analyse and adapt innovative experiences of other cities. For this purpose, the full range of training methods—from for-mal education to the use of the mass media—should be utilized, as well as the "learning by doing" option.

7.24. Developing countries should also encourage technological training and re-search through joint efforts by donors, non-governmental organizations and pri-vate business in such areas as the reduction of waste, water quality, saving of energy, safe production of chemicals and less polluting transportation.

7.25. Capacity-building activities carried out by all countries, assisted as sug-gested above, should go beyond the training of individuals and functional groups to include institutional arrangements, administrative routines, inter-agency linkages, information flows and consultative processes.

7.26. In addition, international efforts, such as the Urban Management Pro-gramme, in cooperation with multilateral and bilateral agencies, should continue to assist the developing countries in their efforts to develop a partici-patory structure by mobilizing the human resources of the private sector, non-governmental organizations and the poor, particularly women and the disadvantaged.

---

7   Draft paragraph 7.23 of A/CONF.151/4 (22 April 1992) was replaced by decision of the Main Committee of UNCED on 10 June 1992. See A/CONF.151/L.3/Add.7 (12 June 1992). The former draft read as follows:

   Total annual requirements, primarily for infrastructure maintenance and operations for municipal services in developing countries are roughly estimated at $ 100 billion, to be financed mostly by rev-enues. The total external financial and technical assistance required is estimated at about $ 15 bil-lion per year. About $ 10 million would be needed for strengthening international institutions.

C. Promoting sustainable land use planning and management

Basis for action

7.27. Access to land resources is an essential component of sustainable low impact lifestyles. Land resources are the basis for (human) living systems and provide soil, energy, water and the opportunity for all human activity. In rapidly growing urban areas, access to land is rendered increasingly difficult by the conflicting demands of industry, housing, commerce, agriculture, land tenure structures and the need for open spaces. Furthermore, the rising costs of urban land prevent the poor from gaining access to suitable land. In rural areas, unsustainable practices, such as the exploitation of marginal lands and the encroachment on forests and ecologically fragile areas by commercial interests and landless rural populations, result in environmental degradation as well as in diminishing returns for impoverished rural settlers.

Objective

7.28. The objective is to provide for the land requirements of human settlement development through environmentally sound physical planning and land use so as to ensure access to land to all households and where appropriate, the encouragement of communally and collectively owned and managed land.[8] Particular attention should be paid to the needs of women and indigenous people for economic and cultural reasons.

Activities

7.29. All countries should consider, as appropriate, undertaking a comprehensive national inventory of their land resources in order to establish a land information system in which land resources will be classified according to their most appropriate uses and environmentally fragile or disaster-prone areas will be identified for special protection measures.

7.30. Subsequently, all countries should consider developing national land-resource management plans to guide land-resource development and utilization and, to that end, should:

(a) Establish, as appropriate, national legislation to guide the implementation of public policies for environmentally sound urban development, land utilization, housing and for the improved management of urban expansion;

(b) Create, where appropriate, efficient and accessible land markets that meet community development needs by, *inter alia*, improving land registry systems and streamlining procedures in land transactions;

---

8   This calls for integrated land-resource management policies, which are also addressed in chapter 10 of Agenda 21 (Integrated approach to planning and management of land resources. [This footnote appears in Agenda 21 as number 6 to this Chapter, A/CONF. 151/26, vol I., pp. 81 and 97.]

(c) Develop fiscal incentives and land-use control measures, including land-use planning solutions for a more rational and environmentally sound use of limited land resources;

(d) Encourage partnerships among the public, private and community sectors in managing land resources for human settlements development;

(e) Strengthen community-based land-resource protection practices in existing urban and rural settlements;

(f) Establish appropriate forms of land tenure which provide security of tenure for all land-users, especially indigenous people, women, local communities, the low-income urban dwellers and the rural poor;

(g) Accelerate efforts to promote access to land by the urban and rural poor, including credit schemes for the purchase of land and for building/acquiring or improving safe and healthy shelter and infrastructure services;

(h) Develop and support the implementation of improved land-management practices which deal comprehensively with potentially competing land requirements for agriculture, industry, transport, urban development, green spaces, preserves and other vital needs;

(i) Promote understanding among policy makers of the adverse consequences of unplanned settlements in environmentally vulnerable areas and of the appropriate national and local land-use and settlements policies required for this purpose.

7.31. At the international level, global coordination of land-resource management activities should be strengthened by the various bilateral and multilateral agencies and programmes, such as UNDP, FAO, the World Bank, the regional development banks, other interested organizations and the UNDP/World Bank/Habitat Urban Management Programme, and action should be taken to promote the transfer of applicable experience on sustainable land-management practices to and among developing countries.

Means of implementation

(a) Financing and cost evaluation

7.32. The Conference secretariat has estimated the average total annual cost (1993-2000) of implementing the activities of this programme to be about $3 billion, including about $300 million from the international community on grant or concessional terms. These are indicative and order-of-magnitude estimates only and have not been reviewed by Governments. Actual costs and financial terms, including any that are non-concessional, will depend upon,

inter alia, the specific strategies and programmes Governments decide upon for implementation.[9]

(b) Scientific and technological means

7.33. All countries, particularly developing countries, alone or in regional or subregional groupings, should be given access to modern techniques of land-resource management, such as geographical information systems, satellite photography/imagery and other remote-sensing technologies.

(c) Human resource development and capacity-building

7.34. Environmentally focused training activities in sustainable land-resources planning and management should be undertaken in all countries, with developing countries being given assistance through international support and funding agencies in order to:

(a) Strengthen the capacity of national, state/provincial and local educational research and training institutions to provide formal training of land management technicians and professionals;

(b) Facilitate the organizational review of government ministries and agencies responsible for land questions, in order to devise more efficient mechanisms of land-resource management, and carry out periodic in-service refresher courses for the managers and staff of such ministries and agencies in order to familiarize them with up-to-date land-resource management technologies;

(c) Where appropriate, provide such agencies with modern equipment, such as computer hardware and software and survey equipment;

(d) Strengthen existing programmes and promote an international and inter-regional exchange of information and experience in land management through the establishment of professional associations in land-management sciences and related activities, such as workshops and seminars.

---

9   Draft paragraph 7.33 of A/CONF.151/4 (22 April 1992) was replaced as paragraph 7.32 by decision of the Main Committee of UNCED on 10 June 1992. See A/CONF.151/L.3/Add.7 (12 June 1992). The former draft read as follows:

The overall cost is about $ 3 billion annually, including about $ 300 million from the international community. About $ 4 million will be needed for strengthening international organizations. Some aspects of this programme may be funded under the land use programmes detailed in other Agenda 21 chapters. These programmes should be funded in an integrated fashion.

D. Promoting the integrated provision of environmental infrastructure: water, sanitation, drainage and solid waste management

Basis for action

7.35. The sustainability of urban development is defined by many parameters relating to the availability of water supplies, air quality and the provision of environmental infrastructure for sanitation and waste management. As a result of the density of users, urbanization, if properly managed, offers unique opportunities for the supply of sustainable environmental infrastructure through adequate pricing policies, educational programmes and equitable access mechanisms that are economically and environmentally sound. In most developing countries, however, the inadequacy and lack of environmental infrastructure is responsible for widespread ill-health and a large number of preventable deaths each year. In those countries conditions are set to worsen due to growing needs that exceed the capacity of Governments to respond adequately.

7.36. An integrated approach to the provision of environmentally sound infrastructure in human settlements, in particular for the urban and rural poor, is an investment in sustainable development that can improve the quality of life, increase productivity, improve health and reduce the burden of investments in curative medicine and poverty alleviation.

7.37. Most of the activities whose management would be improved by an integrated approach, are covered in Agenda 21 as follows: chapters 6 (Protecting and promoting human health conditions), chapters 9 (Protecting the atmosphere), 18 (Protecting the quality and supply of freshwater resources) and 21 (Environmentally sound management of solid wastes and sewage-related issues).

Objective

7.38. The objective is to ensure the provision of adequate environmental infrastructure facilities in all settlements by the year 2025. The achievement of this objective would require that all developing countries incorporate in their national strategies programmes to build the necessary technical, financial and human resource capacity aimed at ensuring better integration of infrastructure and environmental planning by the year 2000.

Activities

7.39. All countries should assess the environmental suitability of infrastructure in human settlements, develop national goals for sustainable management of waste, and implement environmentally sound technology to ensure that the environment, human health and quality of life are protected. Settlement infrastructure and environmental programmes designed to promote an integrated human settlements approach to the planning, development, maintenance and management of environmental infrastructure (water supply, sanitation, drainage, solid waste management) should be strengthened with the assistance of bilateral and multilateral agencies. Coordination among these agencies and with collaboration from international and national representatives of local authorities, the private sector, and community groups should also be strengthened. The activities of all agencies engaged in providing environmental infrastructure should, where possible, reflect an ecosystem or metropolitan area approach to settlements and should include monitoring, applied research, capacity-building, transfer of appropriate technology and technical cooperation among the range of programme activities.

7.40. Developing countries should be assisted at the national and local levels in adopting an integrated approach to the provision of water supply, energy, sanitation, drainage and solid waste management, and external funding agencies should ensure that this approach is applied in particular to environmental infrastructure improvement in informal settlements based on regulations and standards that take into account the living conditions and resources of the communities to be served.

7.41. All countries should, as appropriate, adopt the following principles for the provision of environmental infrastructure:

(a) Adopt policies that minimize if not altogether avoid environmental damage, whenever possible;

(b) Ensure that relevant decisions are preceded by environmental impact assessments and also take into account the costs of any ecological consequences;

(c) Promote development in accordance with indigenous practices and adopt technologies appropriate to local conditions;

(d) Promote policies aimed at recovering the actual cost of infrastructure services, while at the same time recognizing the need to find suitable approaches (including subsidies) to extend basic services to all households;

(e) Seek joint solutions to environmental problems that affect several localities.

7.42. The dissemination of information from existing programmes should be facilitated and encouraged among interested countries and local institutions.

Means of implementation

(a) Financing and cost evaluation

7.43. The Conference secretariat has estimated most of the costs of implementing the activities of this programme in other chapters. The secretariat estimates the average total annual cost (1993-2000) of technical assistance from the international community on grant or concessional terms to be about $50 million. These are indicative and order-of-magnitude estimates only and have not been reviewed by Governments. Actual costs and financial terms, including any that

are non-concessional, will depend upon, *inter alia*, the specific strategies and programmes Governments decide upon for implementation.[10]

(b) Scientific and technological means

7.44. Scientific and technological means within the existing programmes should be coordinated wherever possible and should:

(a) Accelerate research in the area of integrated policies of environmental infrastructure programmes and projects based on cost benefit analysis and overall environmental impact;

(b) Promote methods of assessing "effective demand", utilizing environment and development data as criteria for selecting technology.

(c) Human resource development and capacity-building

7.45. With the assistance and support of funding agencies, all countries should, as appropriate, undertake training and popular participation programmes aimed at:

(a) Raising awareness of the means, approaches and benefits of the provision of environmental infrastructure facilities, especially among indigenous people, women, low-income groups and the poor;

(b) Developing a cadre of professionals with adequate skills in integrated infrastructural service planning and maintenance of resource efficient, environmentally sound and socially acceptable systems;

(c) Strengthening the institutional capacity of local authorities and administrators in the integrated provision of adequate infrastructure services in partnership with local communities and the private sector;

(d) Adopting appropriate legal and regulatory instruments, including cross-subsidy arrangements, to extend the benefits of adequate and affordable environmental infrastructure to unserved population groups, especially the poor.

E. Promoting sustainable energy and transport systems in human settlements

Basis for action

7.46. Most of the commercial and non-commercial energy produced today is used in and for human settlements, and a substantial percentage of it is used by

---

10   Draft paragraph 7.44 of A/CONF.151/4 (22 April 1992) was replaced by decision of the Main Committee of UNCED on 10 June 1992. See A/CONF.151/L.3/Add.7 (12 June 1992). The former draft read as follows:

Financial requirements for major development programmes are estimated in other chapters, especially those dealing with health, energy, freshwater resources, sanitation and solid wastes. Annual technical assistance requirements for the settlement infrastructure environmental programmes are estimated at about $ 50 million; $ 3 million will be needed to strengthen international institutions.

the household sector. Developing countries are at present faced with the need to increase their energy production to accelerate development and raise the living standards of their populations, while at the same time reducing energy production costs and energy-related pollution. Increasing the efficiency of energy use to reduce its polluting effects and to promote the use of renewable energies must be a priority in any action taken to protect the urban environment.

7.47. Developed countries, as the largest consumers of energy, are faced with the need for energy planning and management, promoting renewable and alternate sources of energy, and evaluating the life-cycle costs of current systems and practices as a result of which many metropolitan areas are suffering from pervasive air quality problems related to ozone, particulate matters and carbon monoxide. The causes have much to do with technological inadequacies and with an increasing fuel consumption generated by inefficiencies, high demographic and industrial concentrations and a rapid expansion in the number of motor vehicles.

7.48. Transport accounts for about 30 per cent of commercial energy consumption and for about 60 per cent of total global consumption of liquid petroleum. In developing countries, rapid motorization and insufficient investments in urban-transport planning, traffic management and infrastructure, are creating increasing problems in terms of accidents and injury, health, noise, congestion and loss of productivity similar to those occurring in many developed countries. All of these problems have a severe impact on urban populations, particularly the low-income and no-income groups.

Objectives

7.49. The objectives are to extend the provision of more energy-efficient technology and alternative/renewable energy for human settlements and to reduce negative impacts of energy production and use on human health and on the environment.

Activities

7.50. The principal activities relevant to this programme area are included in chapter 9 (Protection of the atmosphere), programme area B, subprogramme 1 (Energy development, efficiency and consumption) and subprogramme 2 (Transportation).

7.51. A comprehensive approach to human settlements development should include the promotion of sustainable energy development in all countries, as follows:

(a) Developing countries, in particular, should:

(i) Formulate national action programmes to promote and support reafforestation and national forest regeneration with a view to achieve sustained

　　　　　　　　　STRATEGIES TOWARD SUSTAINABLE DEVELOPMENT

provision of the biomass energy needs of the low-income groups in urban areas and the rural poor, in particular women and children;

(ii) Formulate national action programmes to promote integrated development of energy saving and renewable energy technologies, particularly for the use of solar, hydro, wind and biomass sources;

(iii) Promote wide dissemination and commercialization of renewable energy technologies through suitable measures, *inter alia*, fiscal and technology transfer mechanisms;

(iv) Carry out information and training programmes directed at manufacturers and users in order to promote energy saving techniques and energy-efficient appliances;

(b) International organizations and bilateral donors should:

(i) Support developing countries in implementing national energy programmes in order to achieve widespread use of energy-saving and renewable energy technologies, particularly the use of solar, wind, biomass and hydro sources;

(ii) Provide access to research and development results to increase energy-use efficiency levels in human settlements.

7.52. Promoting efficient and environmentally sound urban transport systems in all countries should be a comprehensive approach to urban-transport planning and management. To this end, all countries should:

(a) Integrate land-use and transportation planning to encourage development patterns which reduce transport demand;

(b) Adopt urban-transport programmes favouring high-occupancy public transport in countries, as appropriate;

(c) Encourage non-motorized modes of transport by providing safe cycleways and footways in urban and suburban centres in countries, as appropriate;

(d) Devote particular attention to effective traffic management, efficient operation of public transport and maintenance of transport infrastructure;

(e) Promote the exchange of information among countries and representatives of local and metropolitan areas;

(f) Re-evaluate the present consumption and production patterns in order to reduce the use of energy and national resources.

Means of implementation

(a) Financing and cost evaluation

7.53. The Conference secretariat has estimated the costs of implementing the activities of this programme in chapter 9 (Protection of the atmosphere).[11]

(b) Human resource development and capacity-building

7.54. In order to enhance the skills of energy service and transport professionals and institutions, all countries should, as appropriate:

(a) Provide on-the-job and other training of government officials, planners, traffic engineers and managers involved in the energy-service and transport section;

(b) Raise public awareness of the environmental impacts of transport and travel behaviour through mass media campaigns and support for non-governmental and community initiatives promoting the use of non-motorized transport, shared driving and improved traffic safety measures;

(c) Strengthen regional, national, state/provincial, and private sector institutions that provide education and training on energy service and urban transport planning and management.

F. Promoting human settlement planning and management in disaster-prone areas

Basis for action

7.55. Natural disasters cause loss of life, disruption of economic activities and urban productivity, particularly for highly susceptible low-income groups, and environmental damage, such as loss of fertile agricultural land and contamination of water resources, and can lead to major resettlement of populations. Over the past two decades, they are estimated to have caused some 3 million deaths and affected 800 million people. Global economic losses have been estimated by the Office of the United Nations Disaster Relief Coordinator to be in the range of $30-50 billion per year.[12]

---

11 Draft paragraph 7.54 of A/CONF.151/4 (22 April 1992) was replaced by decision of the Main Committee of UNCED on 10 June 1992. See A/CONF.151/L.3/Add.7 (12 June 1992). The former draft read as follows:

The financing for this programme area is included in the estimate for Chapter 9 of Agenda 21 (Protecting the atmosphere).

12 Estimates of the Office of the United Nations Disaster Relief Coordinator.

7.56. The General Assembly, in resolution 44/236, proclaimed the 1990s as the International Decade for Natural Disaster Reduction. The goals of the Decade[13] bear relevance to the objectives of the present programme area.

7.57. In addition, there is an urgent need to address the prevention and reduction of man-made disasters and/or disasters caused by, *inter alia*, industries, unsafe nuclear power generation and toxic wastes (see chapter 6 of Agenda 21).

Objective

7.58. The objective is to enable all countries, in particular those that are disaster-prone, to mitigate the negative impact of natural and man-made disasters on human settlements, national economies and the environment.

Activities

7.59. Three distinct areas of activity are foreseen under this programme area, namely, the development of a "culture of safety", pre-disaster planning and post-disaster reconstruction.

(a) Developing a culture of safety

7.60. To promote a "culture of safety" in all countries, especially those that are disaster-prone, the following activities should be carried out:

(a) Completing national and local studies on the nature and occurrence of natural disasters, their impact on people and economic activities, the effects of inadequate construction and land use in hazard-prone areas, and the social and economic advantages of adequate pre-disaster planning;

(b) Implementing nationwide and local awareness campaigns through all available media, translating the above knowledge into information easily

---

13   The goals of the International Decade for Natural Disaster Reduction, set out in the annex to General Assembly resolution 44/236, are as follows:

(a) To improve the capacity of each country to mitigate the effects of natural disasters expeditiously and effectively, paying special attention to assisting developing countries in the assessment of disaster damage potential and in the establishment of early warning systems and disaster-resistant structures when and where needed;

(b) To devise appropriate guidelines and strategies for applying existing scientific and technical knowledge, taking into account the cultural and economic diversity among nations;

(c) To foster scientific and engineering endeavours aimed at closing critical gaps in knowledge in order to reduce loss of life and property;

(d) To disseminate existing and new technical information related to measures for the assessment, prediction and mitigation of natural disasters;

(e) To develop measures for the assessment, prediction, prevention and mitigation of natural disasters through programmes of technical assistance and technology transfer, demonstration projects, and education and training, tailored to specific disasters and locations, and to evaluate the effectiveness of those programmes.

[This footnote appears in Agenda 21 as number 7 to Chapter 7, A/CONF. 151/26, vol. I, pp. 89 and 97-8.].

comprehensible to the general public and to the populations directly exposed to hazards;

(c) Strengthening, and/or developing global, regional, national and local early warning systems to alert populations to impending disasters;

(d) Identifying industrially based environmental disaster areas at the national and international levels and implementing strategies aimed at the rehabilitation of these areas through, *inter alia*:

(i) Restructuring of the economic activities and promoting new job opportunities in environmentally sound sectors;

(ii) Promoting close collaboration between governmental and local authorities, local communities and non-governmental organizations and private business;

(iii) Developing and enforcing strict environmental control standards.

(b) Developing pre-disaster planning

7.61. Pre-disaster planning should form an integral part of human settlement planning in all countries. The following should be included:

(a) Undertaking complete multi-hazard research into risk and vulnerability of human settlements and settlement infrastructure, including water and sewerage, communication and transportation networks, as one type of risk reduction may increase vulnerability to another (e.g., an earthquake-resistant house made of wood will be more vulnerable to wind storms);

(b) Developing methodologies for determining risk and vulnerability within specific human settlements and incorporating risk and vulnerability reduction into the human settlement planning and management process;

(c) Redirecting inappropriate new development and human settlements to areas not prone to hazards;

(d) Preparing guidelines on location, design and operation of potentially hazardous industries and activities;

(e) Developing tools (legal, economic etc.) to encourage disaster-sensitive development, including means of ensuring that limitations on development options are not punitive to owners, or incorporate alternative means of compensation;

(f) Further developing and disseminating information on disaster-resistant building materials and construction technologies for buildings and public works in general;

(g) Developing training programmes for contractors and builders on disaster-resistant construction methods. Some programmes should be directed particularly to small enterprises, which build the great majority of housing and other small buildings in the developing countries, as well as to the rural populations, which build their own houses;

(h) Developing training programmes for emergency site managers, non-governmental organizations and community groups which cover all aspects of disaster mitigation, including urban search and rescue, emergency communications, early warning techniques, and pre-disaster planning;

(i) Developing procedures and practices to enable local communities to receive information about hazardous installations or situations in these areas, and facilitate their participation in early warning and disaster abatement and response procedures and plans;

(j) Preparing action plans for the reconstruction of settlements, especially the reconstruction of community life-lines.

(c) Initiating post-disaster reconstruction and rehabilitation planning

7.62. The international community, as a major partner in post-reconstruction and rehabilitation, should ensure that the countries involved derive the greatest benefits from the funds allocated by undertaking the following activities:

(a) Carrying out research on past experiences on the social and economic aspects of post-disaster reconstruction and adopting effective strategies and guidelines for post-disaster reconstruction, with particular focus on development-focused strategies in the allocation of scarce reconstruction resources, and on the opportunities which post-disaster reconstruction provides to introduce sustainable settlement patterns;

(b) Preparing and disseminating international guidelines for adaptation to national and local needs;

(c) Support efforts of national Governments to initiate contingency planning, with participation of affected communities, for post-disaster reconstruction and rehabilitation.

Means of implementation

(a) Financing and cost evaluation

7.63. The Conference secretariat has estimated the average total annual cost (1993-2000) of implementing the activities of this programme to be about $50 million from the international community on grant or concessional terms. These are indicative and order of magnitude estimates only and have not been reviewed by Governments. Actual costs and financial terms, including any that

are non-concessional, will depend upon, *inter alia*, the specific strategies and programmes Governments decide upon for implementation.[14]

(b) Scientific and technological means

7.64. Scientists and engineers specializing in this field in both developing and developed countries should collaborate with urban and regional planners in order to provide the basic knowledge and means to mitigate losses owing to disasters as well as environmentally inappropriate development.

(c) Human resource development and capacity-building

7.65. Developing countries should conduct training programmes on disaster-resistant construction methods for contractors and builders, who build the majority of housing in the developing countries. This should focus on the small business enterprises, which build the majority of housing in the developing countries.

7.66. Training programmes should be extended to government officials and planners and community and non-governmental organizations to cover all aspects of disaster mitigation, such as early warning techniques, pre-disaster planning and construction, post-disaster construction and rehabilitation.

G. Promoting sustainable construction industry activities

Basis for action

7.67. The activities of the construction sector are vital to the achievement of the national socio-economic development goals of providing shelter, infrastructure and employment. However, they can be a major source of environmental damage through depletion of the natural resource base, degradation of fragile eco-zones, chemical pollution and the use of building materials harmful to human health.

Objectives

7.68. The objectives are, first, to adopt policies and technologies and to exchange information on them in order to enable the construction sector to meet human settlement development goals, while avoiding harmful side-effects on human health and on the biosphere, and, second, to enhance the employment-generation capacity of the construction sector. Governments should work in close collaboration with the private sector in achieving these objectives.

---

14   Draft paragraph 7.64 of A/CONF.151/4 (22 April 1992) was replaced by decision of the Main Committee of UNCED on 10 June 1992. See A/CONF.151/L.3/Add.7 (12 June 1992). The former draft read as follows:

   External assistance will continue to be required for post-disaster investments, which are roughly estimated to run at about $ 600 million annually. Technical assistance connected with this programme area could cost about $ 50 million annually; $ 2 million is suggested for strengthening international organizations.

Activities

7.69. All countries should, as appropriate and in accordance with national plans, objectives and priorities:

(a) Establish and strengthen indigenous building materials industry, based, as much as possible, on inputs of locally available natural resources;

(b) Formulate programmes to enhance the utilization of local materials by the construction sector by expanding technical support and incentive schemes for increasing the capabilities and economic viability of small-scale and informal operatives which make use of these materials and traditional construction techniques;

(c) Adopt standards and other regulatory measures which promote the increased use of energy-efficient designs and technologies and sustainable utilization of natural resources in an economically and environmentally appropriate way;

(d) Formulate appropriate land-use policies and introduce planning regulations specially aimed at the protection of eco-sensitive zones against physical disruption by construction and construction-related activities;

(e) Promote the use of labour-intensive construction and maintenance technologies which generate employment in the construction sector for the underemployed labour force found in most large cities, while at the same time promoting the development of skills in the construction sector;

(f) Develop policies and practices to reach the informal sector and self-help housing builders by adopting measures to increase the affordability of building materials on the part of the urban and rural poor, through, *inter alia*, credit schemes and bulk procurement of building materials for sale to small-scale builders and communities.

7.70. All countries should:

(a) Promote the free exchange of information on the entire range of environmental and health aspects of construction, including the development and dissemination of databases on the adverse environmental effects of building materials through the collaborative efforts of the private and public sectors;

(b) Promote the development and dissemination of databases on the adverse environmental and health effects of building materials and introduce legislation and financial incentives to promote recycling of energy-intensive materials in the construction industry and conservation of waste energy in building-materials production methods;

(c) Promote the use of economic instruments, such as product charges, to discourage the use of construction materials and products that create pollution during their life-cycle;

(d) Promote information exchange and appropriate technology transfer among all countries, with particular attention to developing countries, for resource management in construction, particularly for non-renewable resources;

(e) Promote research in construction industries and related activities, and establish and strengthen institutions in this sector.

Means of implementation

(a) Financing and cost evaluation

7.71. The Conference secretariat has estimated the average total annual cost (1993-2000) of implementing the activities of this programme to be about $40 billion, including about $4 billion from the international community on grant or concessional terms. These are indicative and order-of-magnitude estimates only and have not been reviewed by Governments. Actual costs and financial terms, including any that re non-concessional, will depend upon, *inter alia*, the specific strategies and programmes Governments decide upon for implementation.[15]

(b) Human resource development and capacity-building

7.72. Developing countries should be assisted by international support and funding agencies in upgrading the technical and managerial capacities of the small entrepreneur and the vocational skills of operatives and supervisors in the building materials industry, using a variety of training methods. These countries should also be assisted in developing programmes to encourage the use of non-waste and clean technologies through appropriate transfer of technology.

7.73. General education programmes should be developed in all countries, as appropriate, to increase builder awareness of available sustainable technologies.

7.74. Local authorities are called upon to play a pioneering role in promoting the increased use of environmentally sound building materials and construction technologies, e.g., by pursuing an innovative procurement policy.

H. Promoting human resource development and capacity-building for human settlements development

Basis for action

7.75. Most countries, in addition to shortcomings in the availability of specialized expertise in the areas of housing, settlement management, land manage-

---

15 This paragraph previously appeared as 7.72, which read as follows:

> 7.72. It is roughly estimated that the construction activities of developing countries amount to about $ 400 billion annually and will increase by about $ 20 billion annually. The stream of new investments for these levels of activity and to bring in clean technologies is estimated at $ 40 billion annually, primarily from private sources. If 10 per cent of the new investments come from the international community, this would amount to $ 40 billion annually. About $ 3 million would be needed to strengthen international organizations.

ment, infrastructure, construction, energy, transport, and pre-disaster planning and reconstruction, face three cross-sectoral human resource development and capacity-building shortfalls. First is the absence of an enabling policy environment capable of integrating the resources and activities of the public sector, the private sector and the community, or social sector; second is the weakness of specialized training and research institutions; and third is the insufficient capacity for technical training and assistance for low-income communities, both urban and rural.

Objective

7.76. The objective is to improve human resource development and capacity-building in all countries by enhancing the personal and institutional capacity of all actors, particularly indigenous people and women, involved in human settlement development. In this regard, account should be taken of traditional cultural practices of indigenous people and their relationship to the environment.

Activities

7.77. Specific human resource development and capacity-building activities have been built into each of the programme areas of this chapter. More generally, however, additional steps should be taken to reinforce those activities. In order to do so, all countries, as appropriate, should take the following action:

(a) Strengthening the development of the human resources and of capacities of public sector institutions through technical assistance and international cooperation so as to achieve by the year 2000 substantial improvement in the efficiency of governmental activities;

(b) Creating an enabling policy environment supportive of the partnership between the public, private and community sectors;

(c) Providing enhanced training and technical assistance to institutions providing training for technicians, professionals and administrators, and appointed, elected and professional members of local governments and strengthening their capacity to address priority training needs, particularly in regard to social, economic and environmental aspects of human settlements development;

(d) Providing direct assistance for human settlement development at the community level, *inter alia*, by:

(i) Strengthening and promoting programmes for social mobilization and raising awareness of the potential of women and youth in human settlements activities;

(ii) Facilitating coordination of the activities of women, youth, community groups and non-governmental organizations in human settlements development;

(iii) Promoting research on women's programmes and other groups, and evaluating progress made with a view to identifying bottlenecks and needed assistance;

(e) Promoting the inclusion of integrated environmental management into general local government activities.

7.78. Both international organizations and non-governmental organizations should support the above activities by, *inter alia*, strengthening subregional training institutions, providing updated training materials and disseminating the results of successful human resource and capacity-building activities, programmes and projects.

Means of implementation

(a) Financing and cost evaluation

7.79. The Conference secretariat has estimated the average total annual cost (1993-2000) of implementing the activities of this programme to be about $65 million from the international community on grant or concessional terms. These are indicative and order-of-magnitude estimates only and have not been reviewed by Governments. Actual costs and financial terms, including any that are non-concessional, will depend upon, *inter alia*, the specific strategies and programmes Governments decide upon for implementation.[16]

(b) Scientific and technological means

7.80. Both formal training and non-formal types of human resource development and capacity-building programmes should be combined, and use should be made of user-oriented training methods, up-to-date training materials and modern audio-visual communication systems.

---

16   Draft paragraph 7.80 of A/CONF.151/4 (22 April 1992) was replaced here as paragraph 7.79 by decision of the Main Committee of UNCED on 10 June 1992. See A/CONF.151/L.3/Add.7 (12 June 1992). The former draft read as follows:

International technical assistance to support national programmes is estimated at about $ 60 million annually; $ 5 million will be needed for strengthening international institutions.

Chapter 8

Integration of Environment and Development in Decision-Making

INTRODUCTION

8.1. The present chapter contains the following areas:

(a) Integrating environment and development at the policy, planning and management levels;

(b) Providing an effective legal and regulatory framework;

(c) Making effective use of economic instruments and market and other incentives;

(d) Establishing systems for integrated environmental and economic accounting;

PROGRAMME AREAS

A. Integrating environment and development at the policy, planning and management level

Basis for action

8.2. Prevailing systems for decision-making in many countries tend to separate economic, social and environmental factors at the policy, planning and management levels. This influences the actions of all groups in society, including Governments, industry and individuals, and has important implications for the efficiency and sustainability of development. An adjustment or even a fundamental reshaping of decision-making, in the light of country-specific conditions, may be necessary if environment and development is to be put at the centre of economic and political decision-making, in effect achieving a full integration of these factors. In recent years, some Governments have also begun to make significant changes in the institutional structures of government in order to enable more systematic consideration of the environment when decisions are made on economic, social, fiscal, energy, agricultural, transportation, trade and other policies, as well as the implications of policies in these areas for the environment. New forms of dialogue are also being developed for achieving better integration among national and local government, industry, science, environmental groups and the public in the process of developing effective approaches to environment and development. The responsibility for bringing about changes lies with Governments in partnership with the private sector and local authorities, and in collaboration with national, regional and international organizations including in particular UNEP [U.N. Environment Programme], UNDP [U.N. Development Programme] and the World Bank. Exchange of experience between countries can also be significant. National plans, goals and objectives, national rules, regulations and law, and the specific situation in which different countries are placed are the overall framework in which such integration takes place. In this context, it must be borne in mind that environmental standards may pose severe economic and social costs if they are uniformly applied in developing countries.

Objectives

8.3. The overall objective is to improve or restructure the decision-making process so that consideration of socio-economic and environmental issues is fully integrated and a broader range of public participation assured. Recognizing that countries will develop their own priorities in accordance with their prevailing conditions, needs, national plans, policies and programmes, the following objectives are proposed:

(a) To conduct a national review of economic, sectoral and environmental policies, strategies and plans to ensure the progressive integration of environmental and developmental issues;

(b) To strengthen institutional structures to allow the full integration of environmental and developmental issues, at all levels of decision-making;

(c) To develop or improve mechanisms to facilitate the involvement of concerned individuals, groups and organizations in decision-making at all levels;

(d) To establish domestically determined procedures to integrate environment and development issues in decision-making.

Activities

(a) Improving decision-making processes

8.4. The primary need is to integrate environmental and developmental decision-making processes. To do this, Governments should conduct a national review and, where appropriate, improve the processes of decision-making so as to achieve the progressive integration of economic, social and environmental issues in the pursuit of development that is economically efficient, socially equitable and responsible and environmentally sound. Countries will develop their own priorities in accordance with their national plans, policies and programmes for the following activities:

(a) Ensuring the integration of economic, social and environmental considerations in decision-making at all levels and in all ministries;

(b) Adopting a domestically formulated policy framework that reflects a long-term perspective and cross-sectoral approach as the basis for decisions, taking account of the linkages between and within the various political, economic, social and environmental issues involved in the development process;

(c) Establishing domestically determined ways and means to ensure the coherence of sectoral, economic, social and environmental policies, plans and policy instruments, including fiscal measures and the budget; these mechanisms should apply at various levels and bring together those interested in the development process;

(d) Monitoring and evaluating the development process systematically, conducting regular reviews of the state of human resources development, economic and social conditions and trends, the state of the environment and natural resources; this could be complemented by annual environment and development reviews, with a view to assessing sustainable development achievements by the various sectors and departments of government;

(e) Ensuring transparency of, and accountability for, the environmental implications of economic and sectoral policies;

(f) Ensuring access by the public to relevant information, facilitating the reception of public views and allowing for effective participation.

(b) Improving planning and management systems

8.5. To support a more integrated approach to decision-making, the data systems and analytical methods used to support such decision-making processes may need to be improved. Governments, in collaboration, where appropriate, with national and international organizations, should review the status of the planning and management system and, where necessary, modify and strengthen procedures so as to facilitate the integrated consideration of social, economic and environmental issues. Countries will develop their own priorities in accordance with their national plans, policies and programmes for the following activities:

(a) Improving the use of data and information at all stages of planning and management, making systematic and simultaneous use of social, economic, developmental, ecological and environmental data; analysis should stress interactions and synergisms; a broad range of analytical methods should be encouraged so as to provide various points of view;

(b) Adopting comprehensive analytical procedures for prior and simultaneous assessment of the impacts of decisions, including the impacts within and among the economic, social and environmental spheres; these procedures should extend beyond the project level to policies and programmes; analysis should also include assessment of costs, benefits and risks;

(c) Adopting flexible and integrative planning approaches that allow the consideration of multiple goals and enable adjustment of changing needs; integrative area approaches at the ecosystem or watershed level can assist in this approach;

(d) Adopting integrated management systems, particularly for the management of natural resources; traditional or indigenous methods should be studied and considered wherever they have proved effective; women's traditional roles should not be marginalized as a result of the introduction of new management systems;

(e) Adopting integrated approaches to sustainable development at a regional level, including transboundary areas, subject to the requirements of particular circumstances and needs;

(f) Using policy instruments (legal/regulatory and economic) as a tool for planning and management, seeking incorporation of efficiency criteria in decisions; instruments should be regularly reviewed and adapted to ensure that they continue to be effective;

(g) Delegating planning and management responsibilities to the lowest level of public authority consistent with effective action; in particular the advantages of effective and equitable opportunities for participation by women should be discussed;

(h) Establishing procedures for involving local communities in contingency planning for environmental and industrial accidents, and maintaining an open exchange of information on local hazards.

(c) Data and information

8.6. Countries could develop systems for monitoring and evaluation of progress towards achieving sustainable development by adopting indicators that measure changes across economic, social and environmental dimensions.

(d) Adopting a national strategy for sustainable development

8.7. Governments, in cooperation, where appropriate, with international organizations, should adopt a national strategy for sustainable development based on, *inter alia*, the implementation of decisions taken at the Conference, particularly in respect of Agenda 21. This strategy should build upon and harmonize the various sectoral economic, social and environmental policies and plans that are operating in the country. The experience gained through existing planning exercises such as national reports for the Conference, national conservation strategies and environment action plans should be fully used and incorporated into a country-driven sustainable development strategy. Its goals should be to ensure socially responsible economic development while protecting the resource base and the environment for the benefit of future generations. It should be developed through the widest possible participation. It should be based on a thorough assessment of the current situation and initiatives.

Means of implementation

(a) Financing and cost evaluation

8.8 The Conference secretariat has estimated the average total annual cost (1993-2000) of implementing the activities of this programme to be about $50 million from the international community on grant or concessional terms. These are indicative and order-of-magnitude estimates only and have not been reviewed by Governments. Actual costs and financial terms, including any that are non-concessional, will depend upon, *inter alia*, the specific strategies and programmes Governments decide upon for implementation.[1]

(b) Researching environment and development interactions

8.9. Governments, in collaboration with the national and international scientific community and in cooperation with international organizations, as appropriate, should intensify efforts to clarify the interactions between and within social, economic and environmental considerations. Research should be undertaken with the explicit objective of assisting policy decisions and providing recommendations on improving management practices.

(c) Enhance education and training

8.10. Countries, in cooperation, where appropriate, with national, regional or international organizations, should ensure that essential human resources exist, or be developed, to undertake the integration of environment and development at various stages of the decision-making and implementation process. To do this, they should improve education and technical training, particularly for women and girls, by including interdisciplinary approaches, as appropriate, in technical, vocational and university and other curricula. They should also undertake systematic training of government personnel, planners and managers on a regular basis, giving priority to the requisite integrative approaches and planning and management techniques that are suited to country-specific conditions.

(d) Promoting public awareness

8.11. Countries, in cooperation with national institutions and groups, the media and the international community, should promote awareness in the public at

---

1   Draft paragraph 8.8 of A/CONF.151/4 (22 April 1992) was replaced by decision of the Main Committee of UNCED on 10 June 1992. See A/CONF.151/L.3/Add.8 (12 June 1992). The former draft read as follows:

> To assist developing countries, it is suggested that the requisite technical and technological cooperation funding from international sources should be made available to developing countries at an annual cost of about $ 50 million.

large, as well as in specialized circles, of the importance of considering environment and development in an integrated manner, and should establish mechanisms for facilitating a direct exchange of information and views with the public.
Priority should be given to highlighting the responsibilities and potential contributions of different social groups.

(e) Strengthen national institutional capacity

8.12. Governments, in cooperation, where appropriate, with international organizations, should strengthen national institutional capability and capacity to integrate social, economic, developmental and environmental issues at all levels
of development decision-making and implementation. Attention should be
given to moving away from narrow sectoral approaches, progressing towards
full cross-sectoral coordination and cooperation.

B. Providing an effective legal and regulatory framework

Basis for action

8.13. Laws and regulations suited to country-specific conditions are among the
most important instruments for transforming environment and development
policies into action, not only through "command and control" methods, but also
as a normative framework for economic planning and market instruments. Yet,
although the volume of legal texts in this field is steadily increasing, much of the
law-making in many countries seems to be ad hoc and piecemeal, or has not
been endowed with the necessary institutional machinery and authority for enforcement and timely adjustment.

8.14. While there is continuous need for law improvement in all countries, many
developing countries have been affected by shortcomings of laws and regulations. To effectively integrate environment and development in the policies and
practices of each country, it is essential to develop and implement integrated,
enforceable and effective laws and regulations that are based upon sound social,
ecological, economic and scientific principles. It is equally critical to develop
workable programmes to review and enforce compliance with the laws, regulations and standards that are adopted. Technical support may be needed for
many countries to accomplish these goals. Technical cooperation requirements
in this field include legal information, advisory services and specialized training
and institutional capacity-building.

8.15. The enactment and enforcement of laws and regulations (at the regional,
national, state/provincial or local/municipal level) are also essential for the implementation of most international agreements in the field of environment and
development, as illustrated by the frequent treaty obligation to report on legislative measures. The survey of existing agreements undertaken in the context of
conference preparations has indicated problems of compliance in this respect,
and the need for improved national implementation and, where appropriate, re-

lated technical assistance. In developing their national priorities, countries should take account of their international obligations.

Objectives

8.16. The overall objective is to promote, in light of country-specific conditions, the integration of environment and development policies through appropriate legal and regulatory policies, instruments and enforcement mechanisms at the national, state, provincial and local level. Recognizing that countries will develop their own priorities in accordance with their needs and national and, where appropriate, regional plans, policies and programmes, the following objectives are proposed:

(a) To disseminate information on effective legal and regulatory innovations in the field of environment and development, including appropriate instruments and compliance incentives, with a view to encouraging their wider use and adoption at the national, state, provincial and local level;

(b) To support countries that request it in their national efforts to modernize and strengthen the policy and legal framework of governance for sustainable development, having due regard for local social values and infrastructures;

(c) To encourage the development and implementation of national, state, provincial and local programmes that assess and promote compliance and respond appropriately to non-compliance.

Activities

(a) Making laws and regulations more effective

8.17. Governments, with the support, where appropriate, of competent international organizations, where appropriate, should regularly assess the laws and regulations enacted and the related institutional/administrative machinery established at the national/state and local/municipal level in the field of environment and sustainable development, with a view to rendering them effective in practice. Programmes for this purpose could include the promotion of public awareness, preparation and distribution of guidance material, and specialized training, including workshops, seminars, education programmes and conferences, for public officials who design, implement, monitor and enforce laws and regulations.

(b) Establishing judicial and administrative procedures

8.18. Governments and legislators, with the support, where appropriate, of competent international organizations, should establish judicial and administrative procedures for legal redress and remedy of actions affecting environment and development that may be unlawful or infringe on rights under the law, and should provide access to individuals, groups and organizations with a recognized legal interest.

(c) Providing legal reference and support services

8.19. Competent intergovernmental and non-governmental organizations could cooperate to provide Governments and legislators, upon request, with an integrated programme of environment and development law (sustainable development law) services, carefully adapted to the specific requirements of the recipient legal and administrative systems. Such systems could usefully include assistance in the preparation of comprehensive inventories and reviews of national legal systems. Past experience has demonstrated the usefulness of combining specialized legal information services with legal expert advice. Within the United Nations system, closer cooperation between all agencies concerned would avoid duplication of databases and facilitate division of labour. These agencies could examine the possibility and merit of performing reviews of selected national legal systems.

(d) Establishing a cooperative training network for sustainable development law

8.20. Competent international and academic institutions could, within agreed frameworks, cooperate to provide, especially for trainees from developing countries, postgraduate programmes and in-service training facilities in environment and development law. Such training should address both the effective application and the progressive improvement of applicable laws, the related skills of negotiating, drafting and mediation, and the training of trainers. Intergovernmental and non-governmental organizations already active in this field could cooperate with related university programmes to harmonize curriculum planning and to offer an optimal range of options to interested Governments and potential sponsors.

(e) Developing effective national programmes for reviewing and enforcing compliance with national, state, provincial and local laws on environment and development

8.21. Each country should develop integrated strategies to maximize compliance with its laws and regulations relating to sustainable development, with assistance from international organizations and other countries as appropriate. The strategies could include:

(a) Enforceable, effective laws, regulations and standards that are based on sound economic, social and environmental principles and appropriate risk assessment, incorporating sanctions designed to punish violations, obtain redress, and deter future violations;

(b) Mechanisms for promoting compliance;

(c) Institutional capacity for collecting compliance data, regularly reviewing compliance, detecting violations, establishing enforcement priorities, undertaking effective enforcement, and conducting periodic evaluations of the effectiveness of compliance and enforcement programmes;

(d) Mechanisms for appropriate involvement of individuals and groups in the development and enforcement of laws and regulations on environment and development.

(f) National monitoring of legal follow-up to international instruments

8.22. Contracting parties to international agreements, in consultation with the appropriate secretariats of relevant international conventions as appropriate, should improve practices and procedures for collecting information on legal and regulatory measures taken. Contracting parties to international agreements could undertake sample surveys of domestic follow-up action subject to agreement by the sovereign States concerned.

Means of implementation

(a) Financing and cost evaluation

8.23. The Conference secretariat has estimated the average total annual cost (1993-2000) of implementing the activities of this programme to be about $6 million from the international community on grant or concessional terms. These are indicative and order of magnitude estimates only and have not been reviewed by Governments. Actual costs and financial terms, including any that are non-concessional, will depend upon, *inter alia*, the specific strategies and programmes Governments decide upon for implementation.[2]

(b) Scientific and technological means

8.24. The programme relies essentially on a continuation of ongoing work for legal data collection, translation and assessment. Closer cooperation between existing databases may be expected to lead to better division of labour (e.g., in geographical coverage of national legislative gazettes and other reference sources) and to improved standardization and compatibility of data, as appropriate.

(c) Human resources development

8.25. Participation in training is expected to benefit practitioners from developing countries and to enhance training opportunities for women. Demand for this

---

2   Draft paragraph 8.23 of A/CONF.151/4 (22 April 1992) was replaced by decision of the Main Committee of UNCED on 10 June 1992. See A/CONF.151/L.3/Add.8 (12 June 1992). The former draft read as follows:

Most of the programme activities could be carried out, with government consent, through organizations and institutions already active or competent in this field, including mechanisms of technical cooperation between developing countries.

(a) Additional technical cooperation costs for a projected series of 20 country missions per year with the consent of the sovereign States concerned (to prepare comprehensive inventories of national legal systems with regard to sustainable development), and for direct assistance to developing countries in national implementation of international instruments, are estimated at $4 million;

(b) Additional support costs to international organizations and institutions (to provide, upon request and under preferential conditions, legal reference, advisory and training services to Governments of developing countries and economies in transition) are estimated at $2 million per year.

type of postgraduate and in-service training is known to be high. The seminars, workshops and conferences on review and enforcement that have been held to date have been very successful and well attended. The purpose of these efforts is to develop resources (both human and institutional) to design and implement effective programmes to continuously review and enforce national and local laws, regulations and standards on sustainable development.

(d) Strengthening legal and institutional capacity

8.26. A major part of the programme should be oriented towards improving the legal-institutional capacities of countries to cope with national problems of governance and effective law-making and law-applying in the field of environment and sustainable development. Regional centres of excellence could be designated and supported to build up specialized databases and training facilities for linguistic/cultural groups of legal systems.

C. Making effective use of economic instruments and market and other incentives

Basis for action

8.27. Environmental law and regulation are important but cannot alone be expected to deal with the problems of environment and development. Prices, markets and governmental fiscal and economic policies also play a complementary role in shaping attitudes and behaviour towards the environment.

8.28. During the past several years, many Governments, primarily in industrialized countries but also in Central and Eastern Europe and in developing countries, have been making increasing use of economic approaches, including those that are market-oriented. Examples include the polluter-pays principle and the more recent natural-resource-user-pays concept.

8.29. Within a supportive international and national economic context and given the necessary legal and regulatory framework, economic and market-oriented approaches can in many cases enhance capacity to deal with the issues of environment and development. This would be achieved by providing cost-effective solutions, applying integrated pollution prevention control, promoting technological innovation and influencing environmental behaviour, as well as providing financial resources to meet sustainable development objectives.

8.30. What is needed is an appropriate effort to explore and make more effective and widespread use of economic and market-oriented approaches within a broad framework of development policies, law and regulation suited to country-specific conditions as part of a general transition to economic and environmental policies that are supportive and mutually reinforcing.

Objectives

8.31. Recognizing that countries will develop their own priorities in accordance with their needs and national plans, policies and programmes, the challenge is to achieve significant progress in the years ahead in meeting three fundamental objectives:

(a) To incorporate environmental costs in the decisions of producers and consumers, to reverse the tendency to treat the environment as a "free good" and to pass these costs on to other parts of society, other countries, or to future generations;

(b) To move more fully towards integration of social and environmental costs into economic activities, so that prices will appropriately reflect the relative scarcity and total value of resources and contribute towards the prevention of environmental degradation;

(c) To include, wherever appropriate, the use of market principles in the framing of economic instruments and policies to pursue sustainable development.

Activities

(a) Improving or reorienting governmental policies

8.32. In the near term, Governments should consider gradually building on experience with economic instruments and market mechanisms by undertaking to reorient their policies, keeping in mind national plans, priorities and objectives, in order to:

(a) Establish effective combinations of economic, regulatory and voluntary (self-regulatory) approaches;

(b) Remove or reduce those subsidies which do not conform with sustainable development objectives;

(c) Reform or recast existing structures of economic and fiscal incentives to meet environment and development objectives;

(d) Establish a policy framework that encourages the creation of new markets in pollution control and environmentally sounder resource management;

(e) Move towards pricing consistent with sustainable development objectives.

8.33. In particular, Governments should explore, in cooperation with business and industry, as appropriate, how effective use can be made of economic instruments and market mechanisms in the following areas:

(a) Issues related to energy, transportation, agriculture and forestry, water, wastes, health, tourism and tertiary services;

(b) Global and transboundary issues;

(c) The development and introduction of environmentally sound technology and its adaptation, diffusion and transfer to developing countries in conformity with chapter 34.[3]

(b) Taking account of the particular circumstances of developing countries and countries with economies in transition

8.34. A special effort should be made to develop applications of the use of economic instruments and market mechanisms geared to the particular needs of developing countries and countries with economies in transition, with the assistance of regional and international economic and environmental organizations and, as appropriate, non-governmental research institutes, by:

(a) Providing technical support to those countries on issues relating to the application of economic instruments and market mechanisms;

(b) Encouraging regional seminars and, possibly, the development of regional centres of expertise.

(c) Creating an inventory of effective uses of economic instruments and market mechanisms

8.35. Given the recognition that the use of economic instruments and market mechanisms is relatively recent, exchange of information about different countries' experiences with such approaches should be actively encouraged. In this regard, Governments should encourage the use of existing means of information exchange to look at effective uses of economic instruments.

(d) Increasing understanding of the role of economic instruments and market mechanisms

8.36. Governments should encourage research and analysis on effective uses of economic instruments and incentives with the assistance and support of regional and international economic and environmental organizations, as well as non-governmental research institutes, with a focus on such key issues as:

(a) The role of environmental taxation suited to national conditions;

(b) The implications of economic instruments and incentives for competitiveness and international trade, and potential needs for appropriate future international cooperation and coordination;

(c) The possible social and distributive implications of using various instruments.

---

3   Draft paragraph 8.33(c) of A/CONF.151/4 (22 April 1992) was replaced by decision of the Main Committee of UNCED on 10 June 1992. See A/CONF.151/L.3/Add.8 (12 June 1992). The former draft read as follows:

(c) The development and introduction of environmentally sound technology and its adaptation, diffusion and transfer to developing countries, [on concessional and preferential terms].

(e) Establishing a process for focusing on pricing

8.37. The theoretical advantages of using pricing policies, where appropriate, need to be better understood, and accompanied by greater understanding of what it means to take significant steps in this direction. Processes should therefore be initiated, in cooperation with business, industry, large enterprises, transnational corporations, as well as other social groups, as appropriate, at both the national and international levels, to examine:

(a) The practical implications of moving towards greater reliance on pricing that internalize environmental costs appropriate to help achieve sustainable development objectives;

(b) The implications for resource pricing in the case of resource-exporting countries, including the implications of such pricing policies for developing countries;

(c) The methodologies used in valuing environmental costs.

(f) Enhancing understanding of sustainable development economics

8.38. Increased interest in economic instruments, including market mechanisms, also requires a concerted effort to improve understanding of sustainable development economics by:

(a) Encouraging institutions of higher learning to review their curricula and strengthen studies in sustainable development economics;

(b) Encouraging regional and international economic organizations and non-governmental research institutes with expertise in this area to provide training sessions and seminars for government officials;

(c) Encouraging business and industry, including large industrial enterprises and transnational corporations with expertise in environmental matters, to organize training programmes for the private sector and other groups.

Means of implementation

8.39. This programme involves adjustments or reorientation of policies on the part of Governments. It also involves international and regional economic and environmental organizations and agencies with expertise in this area, including transnational corporations.

(a) Financing and cost evaluation

8.40. The Conference secretariat has estimated the average total annual cost (1993-2000) of implementing the activities of this programme to be about $5 million from the international community on grant or concessional terms. These are indicative and order-of-magnitude estimates only and have not been reviewed by Governments. Actual costs and financial terms, including any that

are non-concessional, will depend upon, *inter alia*, the specific strategies and programmes Governments decide upon for implementation.[4]

D. Establishing systems for integrated environmental and economic accounting

Basis for action

8.41. A first step towards the integration of sustainability into economic management is the establishment of better measurement of the crucial role of the environment as a source of natural capital and as a sink for by-products generated during the production of man-made capital and other human activities. As sustainable development encompasses social, economic and environmental dimensions, it is also important that national accounting procedures are not restricted to measuring the production of goods and services that are conventionally remunerated. A common framework needs to be developed whereby the contributions made by all sectors and activities of society, that are not included in the conventional national accounts, are included, to the extent consistent with sound theory and practicability, in satellite accounts. A programme to develop national systems of integrated environmental and economic accounting in all countries is proposed.

Objectives

8.42. The main objective is to expand existing systems of national economic accounts in order to integrate environment and social dimensions in the accounting framework, including at least satellite systems of accounts for natural resources in all member States. The resulting systems of integrated environmental and economic accounting (IEEA) to be established in all member States at the earliest date should be seen as a complement to, rather than a substitute for, traditional national accounting practices for the foreseeable future. IEEAs would be designed to play an integral part in the national development decision-making process. National accounting agencies should work in close collaboration with national environmental statistics as well as the geographic and natural resource departments. The definition of economically active could be expanded to include people performing productive but unpaid tasks in all countries. This would enable their contribution to be adequately measured and taken into account in decision-making.

---

4   Draft paragraph 8.40 of A/CONF.151/4 (22 April 1992) was replaced by decision of the Main Committee of UNCED on 10 June 1992. See A/CONF.151/L.3/Add.8 (12 June 1992). The former draft read as follows:

    Additional costs associated with implementing these activities would be minimal, in the range of not more than $5 million annually, associated with the creation of a global inventory and regional seminars. Any costs are far outweighed by the potential for additional financial resources arising from increased reliance on economic instruments and market incentives.

Activities

(a) Strengthening international cooperation

8.43. The Statistical Office of the United Nations Secretariat should:

(a) Make available to all member States the methodologies contained in the *SNA Handbook on Integrated Environmental and Economic Accounting*;

(b) In collaboration with other relevant United Nations organizations, further develop, test, refine and then standardize the provisional concepts and methods such as those proposed by the *SNA Handbook*, keeping member States informed of the status of the work throughout this process;

(c) Coordinate, in close cooperation with other international organizations, the training of national accountants, environmental statisticians and national technical staff in small groups for the establishment, adaptation and development of national IEEAs.

8.44. The Department of Economic and Social Development of the United Nations Secretariat, in close collaboration with other relevant United Nations organizations, should:

(a) Support, in all member States, the utilization of sustainable development indicators in national economic and social planning and decision-making practices, with a view to ensuring that IEEAs are usefully integrated in economic development planning at the national level;

(b) Promote improved environmental and economic and social data collection.

(b) Strengthening national accounting systems

8.45. At the national level, the programme could be adopted mainly by the agencies dealing with national accounts, in close cooperation with environmental statistics and natural resource departments with a view to assisting national economic analysts and decision makers in charge of national economic planning. National institutions should play a crucial role not only as the depositary of the system but also in its adaptation, establishment and continuous use. Unpaid productive work such as domestic work and child care should be included, where appropriate, in satellite national accounts and economic statistics. Time-use surveys could be a first step in the process of developing these satellite accounts.

(c) Establishing an assessment process

8.46. At the international level, the Statistical Commission should assemble and review experience and advise member States on technical and methodological issues related to the further development and implementation of IEEAs in member States.

8.47. Governments should seek to identify and consider measures to correct price distortions arising from environmental programmes affecting land, water, energy and other natural resources.

8.48. Governments should encourage corporations:

(a) To provide relevant environmental information through transparent reporting to shareholders, creditors, employees, governmental authorities, consumers and the public;

(b) To develop and implement methods and rules for accounting for sustainable development;

(d) Strengthening data and information collection

8.49. National Governments could consider implementing the necessary enhancement in data collection to set in place national IEEAs with a view to contributing pragmatically to sound economic management. Major efforts should be made to augment the capacity to collect and analyse environmental data and information and to integrate it with economic data, including gender disaggregated data. Efforts should also be made to develop physical environmental accounts. International donor agencies should consider financing the development of intersectoral data banks to help ensure that national planning for sustainable development is based on precise, reliable and effective information and is suited to national conditions.

(e) Strengthening technical cooperation

8.50. The Statistical Office of the United Nations Secretariat, in close collaboration with the relevant United Nations organizations, should strengthen existing mechanisms for technical cooperation among countries. This should also include exchange of experience in the establishment of IEEAs, particularly in connection with the valuation of non-marketed natural resources and standardization in data collection. The cooperation of business and industry, including large industrial enterprises and transnational corporations with experience in valuation of such resources, should also be sought.

Means of implementation

(a) Financing and cost evaluation

The Conference secretariat has estimated the average total annual cost (1993-2000) of implementing the activities of this programme to be about $2 million from the international community on grant or concessional terms. These are indicative and order of magnitude estimates only and have not been reviewed by Governments. Actual costs and financial terms, including any that are non-concessional, will depend upon, *inter alia*, the specific strategies and programmes Governments decide upon for implementation.[5]

(b) Strengthening institutions

8.52. To ensure the application of IEEAs:

(a) National institutions in developing countries could be strengthened to ensure the effective integration of environment and development at the planning and decision-making levels;

(b) The Statistical Office should provide the necessary technical support to member States in close collaboration with the assessment process to be established by the Statistical Commission; the Statistical Office should provide appropriate support for establishing IEEAs in collaboration with relevant United Nations agencies.

(c) Enhancing use of information technology

8.53. Guidelines and mechanisms could be developed and agreed upon for the adaptation and diffusion of information technologies to developing countries. State-of-the-art data management technologies should be adopted for the most efficient and widespread use of IEEAs.

(d) Strengthening national capacity

8.54. Governments, with the support of the international community, should strengthen national institutional capacity to collect, store, organize, assess and use data in decision-making. Training in all areas related to the establishment of IEEAs, and at all levels, will be required, especially in developing countries. This should include technical training of those involved in economic and environmental analysis, data collection and national accounting, as well as training decision makers to use such information in a pragmatic and appropriate way.

---

5   Draft paragraph 8.51 of A/CONF.151/4 (22 April 1992) was replaced by decision of the Main Committee of UNCED on 10 June 1992. See A/CONF.151/L.3/Add.8 (12 June 1992). The former draft read as follows:

> Financing will have to be increased, particularly for activities connected to environmental data gathering and assessment at both the national and international levels. Based on the experience and estimates by the United Nations Statistical Office, the establishment of IEEAs requires some additional international funding. However, the costs can be significantly higher if countries do not have reasonably developed national statistical systems. Cost estimates assume that national counterparts play an instrumental role in the process and that contributions in terms of human resources and infrastructure are readily available in the country. Approximately $ 2 million per year in external costs will be needed.

Section 2: Conservation and Management of Resources for Development

Chapter 9

Protection of the Atmosphere

INTRODUCTION

9.1. Protection of the atmosphere is a broad and multidimensional endeavour involving various sectors of economic activity. The options and measures described in the present chapter are recommended for consideration and, as appropriate, implementation by Governments and other bodies in their efforts to protect the atmosphere.

9.2. It is recognized that many of the issues discussed in this chapter are also addressed in such international agreements as the 1985 Vienna Convention for the Protection of the Ozone Layer, the 1987 Montreal Protocol on Substances that Deplete the Ozone Layer as amended, the 1992 United Nations Framework Convention on Climate Change and other international, including regional, instruments. In the case of activities covered by such agreements, it is understood that the recommendations contained in this chapter do not oblige any Government to take measures which exceed the provisions of these legal instruments. However, within the framework of this chapter, Governments are free to carry out additional measures which are consistent with those legal instruments.

9.3. It is also recognized that activities that may be undertaken in pursuit of the objectives of this chapter should be coordinated with social and economic development in an integrated manner with a view to avoiding adverse impacts on the latter, taking into full account the legitimate priority needs of developing countries for the achievement of sustained economic growth and the eradication of poverty.

9.4. In this context particular reference is also made to programme area A of chapter 2 of Agenda 21 (Promoting sustainable development through trade).

9.5. The present chapter includes the following four programme areas:

(a) Addressing the uncertainties: improving the scientific basis for decision-making;

(b) Promoting sustainable development:

(i) Energy development, efficiency and consumption;

(ii) Transportation;

(iii) Industrial development;

(iv) Terrestrial and marine resource development and land use;

(c) Preventing stratospheric ozone depletion;

(d) Transboundary atmospheric pollution.

PROGRAMME AREAS

A. Addressing the uncertainties: improving the scientific basis for decision-making

Basis for action

9.6. Concern about climate change and climate variability, air pollution and ozone depletion has created new demands for scientific, economic and social information to reduce the remaining uncertainties in these fields. Better understanding and prediction of the various properties of the atmosphere and of the affected ecosystems, as well as health impacts and their interactions with socio-economic factors, are needed.

Objectives

9.7. The basic objective of this programme area is to improve the understanding of processes that influence and are influenced by the Earth's atmosphere on a global, regional and local scale, including, *inter alia*, physical, chemical, geological, biological, oceanic, hydrological, economic and social processes; to build capacity and enhance international cooperation; and to improve understanding of the economic and social consequences of atmospheric changes and of mitigation and response measures addressing such changes.

Activities

9.8. Governments at the appropriate level, with the cooperation of the relevant United Nations bodies and, as appropriate, intergovernmental and non-governmental organizations, and the private sector, should:

(a) Promote research related to the natural processes affecting and being affected by the atmosphere, as well as the critical linkages between sustainable development and atmospheric changes, including impacts on human health, ecosystems, economic sectors and society;

(b) Ensure a more balanced geographical coverage of the Global Climate Observing System and its components, including the Global Atmosphere Watch, by facilitating, *inter alia*, the establishment and operation of additional systematic observation stations, and by contributing to the development, utilization and accessibility of these databases;

(c) Promote cooperation in:

(i) The development of early detection systems concerning changes and fluctuations in the atmosphere;

(ii) The establishment and improvement of capabilities to predict such changes and fluctuations and to assess the resulting environmental and socio-economic impacts;

(d) Cooperate in research to develop methodologies and identify threshold levels of atmospheric pollutants, as well as atmospheric levels of greenhouse gas concentrations, that would cause dangerous anthropogenic interference with the climate system and the environment as a whole, and the associated rates of change that would not allow ecosystems to adapt naturally.

(e) Promote, and cooperate in the building of scientific capacities, the exchange of scientific data and information, and the facilitation of the participation and training of experts and technical staff, particularly of developing countries, in the fields of research, data assembly, collection and assessment, and systematic observation related to the atmosphere.

B. Promoting sustainable development

1. Energy development, efficiency and consumption

Basis for action

9.9. Energy is essential to economic and social development and improved quality of life. Much of the world's energy, however, is currently produced and consumed in ways that could not be sustained if technology were to remain constant and if overall quantities were to increase substantially. The need to control atmospheric emissions of greenhouse and other gases and substances will increasingly need to be based on efficiency in energy production, transmission, distribution and consumption, and on growing reliance on environmentally sound energy systems, particularly new and renewable sources of energy.[1]

9.10. The existing constraints to increasing the environmentally sound energy supplies required for pursuing the path towards sustainable development, particularly in developing countries, need to be removed.

---

1   New and renewable sources are solar thermal, solar photovoltaic, wind, hydro, biomass, geothermal, ocean, animal and human power, as referred to in the reports of the Committee of the Development and Utilization of New and Renewable Sources of Energy, prepared specifically for the Conference (see A/CONF.151/PC/119 and A/AC.218/1992/5).

Objectives

9.11. The basic and ultimate objective of this programme area is to reduce adverse effects on the atmosphere from the energy sector by promoting policies or programmes, as appropriate, to increase the contribution of environmentally safe and sound and cost-effective energy systems, particularly new and renewable ones, through less polluting and more efficient energy production, transmission, distribution and use. This objective should reflect the need for equity, adequate energy supplies and increasing energy consumption in developing countries, and should take into consideration the situations of countries that are highly dependent on income generated from the production, processing and export, and/or consumption of fossil fuels and associated energy-intensive products and/or the use of fossil fuels for which countries have serious difficulties in switching to alternatives, and the situations of countries highly vulnerable to adverse effects of climate change.

Activities

9.12. Governments at the appropriate level, with the cooperation of the relevant United Nations bodies and, as appropriate, intergovernmental and non-governmental organizations, and the private sector, should:

(a) Cooperate in identifying and developing economically viable, environmentally sound energy sources to promote the availability of increased energy supplies to support sustainable development efforts, in particular in developing countries;

(b) Promote the development at the national level of appropriate methodologies for making integrated energy, environment and economic policy decisions for sustainable development, *inter alia*, through environmental impact assessments;

(c) Promote the research, development, transfer and use of improved energy-efficient technologies and practices, including endogenous technologies in all relevant sectors, giving special attention to the rehabilitation and modernization of power systems, with particular attention to developing countries;

(d) Promote the research, development, transfer and use of technologies and practices for environmentally sound energy systems, including new and renewable energy systems, with particular attention to developing countries;

(e) Promote the development of institutional, scientific, planning and management capacities, particularly in developing countries, to develop, produce and use increasingly efficient and less polluting forms of energy;

(f) Review current energy supply mixes to determine how the contribution of environmentally sound energy systems as a whole, particularly new and renewable energy systems, could be increased in an economically efficient manner, taking into account respective countries' unique social, physical, economic and political characteristics, and examining and implementing, where appropriate, measures to overcome any barriers to their development and use;

(g) Coordinate energy plans regionally and subregionally, where applicable, and study the feasibility of efficient distribution of environmentally sound energy from new and renewable energy sources;

(h) In accordance with national socio-economic development and environment priorities, evaluate and, as appropriate, promote cost-effective policies or programmes, including administrative, social and economic measures, in order to improve energy efficiency;

(i) Build capacity for energy planning and programme management in energy efficiency, as well as for the development, introduction, and promotion of new and renewable sources of energy;

(j) Promote appropriate energy efficiency and emission standards or recommendations at the national level,[2] aimed at the development and use of technologies that minimize adverse impacts on the environment;

(k) Encourage education and awareness-raising programmes at the local, national, subregional and regional levels concerning energy efficiency and environmentally sound energy systems;

(l) Establish or enhance, as appropriate, in cooperation with the private sector, labelling programmes for products to provide decision makers and consumers with information on opportunities for energy efficiency.

2. Transportation

Basis for action

9.13. The transport sector has an essential and positive role to play in economic and social development, and transportation needs will undoubtedly increase. However, since the transport sector is also a source of atmospheric emissions, there is need for a review of existing transport systems for more effective design and management of traffic and transport systems.

Objectives

9.14. The basic objective of this programme area is to develop and promote cost-effective policies or programmes, as appropriate, to limit, reduce or control, as appropriate, harmful emissions into the atmosphere and other adverse environmental effects of the transport sector, taking into account development priorities as well as the specific local and national circumstances and safety aspects.

---

2   This includes standards or recommendations promoted by regional economic integration organizations.

Activities

9.15. Governments at the appropriate level, with the cooperation of the relevant United Nations bodies and, as appropriate, intergovernmental and non-governmental organizations, and the private sector, should:

(a) Develop and promote, as appropriate, cost-effective, more efficient, less polluting and safer transport systems, particularly integrated rural and urban mass transit, as well as environmentally sound road networks, taking into account the needs for sustainable social, economic and development priorities, particularly in developing countries;

(b) Facilitate at the international, regional, subregional and national levels access to and the transfer of safe, efficient, including resource-efficient, and less polluting transport technologies, particularly to the developing countries, including the implementation of appropriate training programmes;

(c) Strengthen, as appropriate, their efforts at collecting, analysing and exchanging relevant information on the relation between environment and transport, with particular emphasis on the systematic observation of emissions and the development of a transport database;

(d) In accordance with national socio-economic development and environment priorities, evaluate and, as appropriate, promote cost-effective policies or programmes, including administrative, social and economic measures, in order to encourage use of transportation modes that minimize adverse impacts on the atmosphere;

(e) Develop or enhance, as appropriate, mechanisms to integrate transport planning strategies and urban and regional settlement planning strategies, with a view to reducing the environmental impacts of transport;

(f) Study, within the framework of the United Nations and its regional commissions, the feasibility of convening regional conferences on transport and the environment.

3. Industrial development

Basis for action

9.16. Industry is essential for the production of goods and services and is a major source of employment and income, and industrial development as such is essential for economic growth. At the same time, industry is a major resource and materials user and consequently industrial activities result in emissions into the atmosphere and the environment as a whole. Protection of the atmosphere can be enhanced, *inter alia*, by increasing resource and materials efficiency in industry, installing or improving pollution abatement technologies and replacing chlorofluorocarbons (CFCs) and other ozone-depleting substances with appropriate substitutes, as well as by reducing wastes and by-products.

Objectives

9.17. The basic objective of this programme area is to encourage industrial development in ways that minimize adverse impacts on the atmosphere by, *inter alia*, increasing efficiency in the production and consumption by industry of all resources and materials, by improving pollution-abatement technologies and by developing new environmentally sound technologies.

Activities

9.18. Governments at the appropriate level, with the cooperation of the relevant United Nations bodies and, as appropriate, intergovernmental and non-governmental organizations, and the private sector, should:

(a) In accordance with national socio-economic development and environment priorities, evaluate and, as appropriate, promote cost-effective policies or programmes, including administrative, social and economic measures, in order to minimize industrial pollution and adverse impacts on the atmosphere;

(b) Encourage industry to increase and strengthen its capacity to develop technologies, products and processes that are safe, less polluting and make more efficient use of all resources and materials, including energy;

(c) Cooperate in development and transfer of such industrial technologies and in development of capacities to manage and use such technologies, particularly with respect to developing countries;

(d) Develop, improve and apply environmental impact assessments to foster sustainable industrial development;

(e) Promote efficient use of materials and resources, taking into account the life cycles of products, in order to realize the economic and environmental benefits of using resources more efficiently and producing fewer wastes;

(f) Support the promotion of less polluting and more efficient technologies and processes in industries, taking into account area-specific accessible potentials for energy, particularly safe and renewable sources of energy, with a view to limiting industrial pollution, and adverse impacts on the atmosphere.

4. Terrestrial and marine resource development and land use

Basis for action

9.19. Land-use and resource policies will both affect and be affected by changes in the atmosphere. Certain practices related to terrestrial and marine resources and land use can decrease greenhouse gas sinks and increase atmospheric emissions. The loss of biological diversity may reduce the resilience of ecosystems to climatic variations and air pollution damage. Atmospheric changes can have important impacts on forests, biodiversity, and freshwater and marine ecosystems, as well as on economic activities, such as agriculture. Policy objectives in different sectors may often diverge and will need to be handled in an integrated manner.

Objectives

9.20. The objectives of this programme area are:

(a) To promote terrestrial and marine resource utilization and appropriate land-use practices that contribute to:

(i) The reduction of atmospheric pollution and/or the limitation of anthropogenic emissions of greenhouse gases;

(ii) The conservation, sustainable management and enhancement, where appropriate, of all sinks for greenhouse gases;

(iii) The conservation and sustainable use of natural and environmental resources;

(b) To ensure that actual and potential atmospheric changes and their socio-economic and ecological impacts are fully taken into account in planning and implementing policies and programmes concerning terrestrial and marine resources utilization and land-use practices.

Activities

9.21. Governments at the appropriate level, with the cooperation of the relevant United Nations bodies and, as appropriate, intergovernmental and non-governmental organizations, and the private sector, should:

(a) In accordance with national socio-economic development and environment priorities, evaluate and, as appropriate, promote cost-effective policies or programmes, including administrative, social and economic measures, in order to encourage environmentally sound land-use practices;

(b) Implement policies and programmes that will discourage inappropriate and polluting land-use practices and promote sustainable utilization of terrestrial and marine resources;

(c) Consider promoting the development and use of terrestrial and marine resources and land-use practices that will be more resilient to atmospheric changes and fluctuations;

(d) Promote sustainable management and cooperation in the conservation and enhancement, as appropriate, of sinks and reservoirs of greenhouse gases, including biomass, forests and oceans, as well as other terrestrial, coastal and marine ecosystems.

C. Preventing stratospheric ozone depletion

Basis for action

9.22. Analysis of recent scientific data has confirmed the growing concern about the continuing depletion of the Earth's stratospheric ozone layer by reactive chlorine and bromine from man-made CFCs, halons and related substances. While the 1985 Vienna Convention for the Protection of the Ozone Layer and the 1987 Montreal Protocol on Substances that Deplete the Ozone Layer (as amended in London in 1990) were important steps in international action, the total chlorine loading of the atmosphere of ozone-depleting substances has continued to rise. This can be changed through compliance with the control measures identified within the Protocol.

Objectives

9.23. The objectives of this programme area are:

(a) To realize the objectives defined in the Vienna Convention and the Montreal Protocol and its 1990 amendments, including the consideration in those instruments of the special needs and conditions of the developing countries and the availability to them of alternatives to substances that deplete the ozone layer. Technologies and natural products that reduce demand for these substances should be encouraged;

(b) To develop strategies aimed at mitigating the adverse effects of ultraviolet radiation reaching the Earth's surface as a consequence of depletion and modification of the stratospheric ozone layer.

Activities

9.24. Governments at the appropriate level, with the cooperation of the relevant United Nations bodies and, as appropriate, intergovernmental and non-governmental organizations, and the private sector, should:

(a) Ratify, accept or approve the Montreal Protocol and its 1990 amendments; pay their contributions towards the Vienna/Montreal trust funds and the interim multilateral ozone fund promptly; and contribute, as appropriate, towards ongoing efforts under the Montreal Protocol and its implementing mechanisms, including making available substitutes for CFCs and other ozone-depleting substances and facilitating the transfer of the corresponding technologies to developing countries in order to enable them to comply with the obligations of the Protocol;

(b) Support further expansion of the Global Ozone Observing System by facilitating—through bilateral and multilateral funding—the establishment and operation of additional systematic observation stations, especially in the tropical belt in the southern hemisphere;

(c) Participate actively in the continuous assessment of scientific information and the health and environmental effects, as well as of the technological/economic implications of stratospheric ozone depletion; and consider further actions that prove warranted and feasible on the basis of these assessments;

(d) Based on the results of research on the effects of the additional ultraviolet radiation reaching the Earth's surface, consider taking appropriate remedial measures in the fields of human health, agriculture and marine environment;

(e) Replace CFCs and other ozone-depleting substances, consistent with the Montreal Protocol, recognizing that a replacement's suitability should be evaluated holistically and not simply based on its contribution to solving one atmospheric or environmental problem.

D. Transboundary atmospheric pollution

Basis for action

9.25. Transboundary air pollution has adverse health impacts on humans and other detrimental environmental impacts, such as tree and forest loss and the acidification of water bodies. The geographical distribution of atmospheric pollution monitoring networks is uneven, with the developing countries severely underrepresented. The lack of reliable emissions data outside Europe and North America is a major constraint to measuring transboundary air pollution. There is also insufficient information on the environmental and health effects of air pollution in other regions.

9.26. The 1979 Convention on Long-range Transboundary Air Pollution, and its protocols, have established a regional regime in Europe and North America, based on a review process and cooperative programmes for systematic observation of air pollution, assessment and information exchange. These programmes need to be continued and enhanced, and their experience needs to be shared with other regions of the world.

Objectives

9.27. The objectives of this programme area are:

(a) To develop and apply pollution control and measurement technologies for stationary and mobile sources of air pollution and to develop alternative environmentally sound technologies;

(b) To observe and assess systematically the sources and extent of transboundary air pollution resulting from natural processes and anthropogenic activities;

(c) To strengthen the capabilities, particularly of developing countries, to measure, model and assess the fate and impacts of transboundary air pollution, through *inter alia*, exchange of information and training of experts;

(d) To develop capabilities to assess and mitigate transboundary air pollution resulting from industrial and nuclear accidents, natural disasters and the deliberate and/or accidental destruction of natural resources;

(e) To encourage the establishment of new and the implementation of existing regional agreements for limiting transboundary air pollution;

(f) To develop strategies aiming at the reduction of emissions causing transboundary air pollution and their effects.

Activities

9.28. Governments at the appropriate level, with the cooperation of the relevant United Nations bodies and, as appropriate, intergovernmental and non-governmental organizations, the private sector and financial institutions, should:

(a) Establish and/or strengthen regional agreements for transboundary air pollution control and cooperate, particularly with developing countries, in the areas of systematic observations and assessment, modelling and the development and exchange of emission control technologies of mobile and stationary sources of air pollution. In this context, greater emphasis should be put on addressing the extent, causes, health and socio-economic impacts of ultraviolet radiation, acidification of the environment and photo-oxidant damage to forests and other vegetation;

(b) Establish or strengthen early warning systems and response mechanisms for transboundary air pollution resulting from industrial accidents and natural disasters and the deliberate and/or accidental destruction of natural resources;

(c) Facilitate training opportunities and exchange of data, information and national and/or regional experiences;

(d) Cooperate on regional, multilateral and bilateral bases to assess transboundary air pollution, and elaborate and implement programmes identifying specific actions to reduce atmospheric emissions and to address their environmental, economic, social and other effects.

Means of implementation

International and regional cooperation

9.29. Existing legal instruments have created institutional structures which relate to the purposes of these instruments, and relevant work should primarily continue in those contexts. Governments should continue to cooperate and enhance their cooperation at the regional and global levels, including within the United Nations system. In this context reference is made to the recommendations in chapter 38 of Agenda 21 (International institutional arrangements).

Capacity-building

9.30. Countries, in cooperation with the relevant United Nations bodies, international donors and non-governmental organizations, should mobilize technical and financial resources and facilitate technical cooperation with developing countries to reinforce their technical, managerial, planning and administrative capacities to promote sustainable development and the protection of the atmosphere, in all relevant sectors.

Human resource development

9.31. Education and awareness-raising programmes concerning the promotion of sustainable development and the protection of the atmosphere need to be introduced and strengthened at the local, national and international levels in all relevant sectors.

Financial and cost evaluation

9.32. The Conference secretariat has estimated the average total annual cost (1993-2000) of implementing the activities under programme area A to be about $640 million from the international community on grant or concessional terms. These are indicative and order-of-magnitude estimates only and have not been reviewed by Governments. Actual costs and financial terms, including any that are non-concessional, will depend upon, *inter alia*, the specific strategies and programmes Governments decide upon for implementation.

9.33. The Conference secretariat has estimated the average total annual cost (1993-2000) of implementing the activities of the four-part programme under programme area B to be about $20 billion from the international community on grant or concessional terms. These are indicative and order-of-magnitude estimates only and have not been reviewed by Governments. Actual costs and financial terms, including any that are non-concessional, will depend upon, *inter alia*, the specific strategies and programmes Governments decide upon for implementation.

9.34. The Conference secretariat has estimated the average total annual cost (1993-2000) of implementing the activities under programme area C to be in the range of $160-590 million on grant or concessional terms. These are indicative and order-of-magnitude estimates only and have not been reviewed by Governments. Actual costs and financial terms, including any that re non-concessional, will depend upon, *inter alia*, the specific strategies and programmes Governments decide upon for implementation.

9.35. The Conference secretariat has included costing for technical assistance and pilot programmes under paragraphs 9.32 and 9.33.

Chapter 10

Integrated Approach to the Planning and Management of Land Resources

INTRODUCTION

10.1. Land is normally defined as a physical entity in terms of its topography and spatial nature; a broader integrative view also includes natural resources: the soils, minerals, water and biota that the land comprises. These components are organized in ecosystems which provide a variety of services essential to the maintenance of the integrity of life-support systems and the productive capacity of the environment. Land resources are used in ways that take advantage of all these characteristics. Land is a finite resource, while the natural resources it supports can vary over time and according to management conditions and uses. Expanding human requirements and economic activities are placing ever increasing pressures on land resources, creating competition and conflicts and resulting in suboptimal use of both land and land resources. If, in the future, human requirements are to be met in a sustainable manner, it is now essential to resolve these conflicts and move towards more effective and efficient use of land and its natural resources. Integrated physical and land-use planning and management is an eminently practical way to achieve this. By examining all uses of land in an integrated manner, it makes it possible to minimize conflicts, to make the most efficient trade-offs and to link social and economic development with environmental protection and enhancement, thus helping to achieve the objectives of sustainable development. The essence of the integrated approach finds expression in the coordination of the sectoral planning and management activities concerned with the various aspects of land use and land resources.

10.2. The present chapter consists of one programme area, the integrated approach to the planning and management of land resources, which deals with the reorganization and, where necessary, some strengthening of the decision-making structure, including existing policies, planning and management procedures and methods that can assist in putting in place an integrated approach to land resources. It does not deal with the operational aspects of planning and management, which are more appropriately dealt with under the relevant sectoral programmes. Since the programme deals with an important cross-sectoral aspect of decision-making for sustainable development, it is closely related to a number of other programmes that deal with that issue directly.

PROGRAMME AREA

Integrated approach to the planning and management of land resources

Basis for action

10.3. Land resources are used for a variety of purposes which interact and may compete with one another; therefore, it is desirable to plan and manage all uses in an integrated manner. Integration should take place at two levels, considering, on the one hand, all environmental, social and economic factors (including, for example, impacts of the various economic and social sectors on the environment and natural resources) and, on the other, all environmental and resource components together (i.e., air, water, biota, land, geological and natural resources). Integrated consideration facilitates appropriate choices and trade-offs, thus maximizing sustainable productivity and use. Opportunities to allocate land to different uses arise in the course of major settlement or development projects or in a sequential fashion as lands become available on the market. This in turn provides opportunities to support traditional patterns of sustainable land management or to assign protected status for conservation of biological diversity or critical ecological services.

10.4. A number of techniques, frameworks and processes can be combined to facilitate an integrated approach. They are the indispensable support for the planning and management process, at the national and local level, ecosystem or area levels and for the development of specific plans of action. Many of its elements are already in place but need to be more widely applied, further developed and strengthened. This programme area is concerned primarily with providing a framework that will coordinate decision-making; the content and operational functions are therefore not included here but are dealt with in the relevant sectoral programmes of Agenda 21.

Objectives

10.5. The broad objective is to facilitate allocation of land to the uses that provide the greatest sustainable benefits and to promote the transition to a sustainable and integrated management of land resources. In doing so, environmental, social and economic issues should be taken into consideration. Protected areas, private property rights, the rights of indigenous people and their communities and other local communities and the economic role of women in agriculture and rural development, among other issues, should be taken into account. In more specific terms, the objectives are as follows:

(a) To review and develop policies to support the best possible use of land and the sustainable management of land resources, by not later than 1996;

(b) To improve and strengthen planning, management and evaluation systems for land and land resources, by not later than 2000;

(c) To strengthen institutions and coordinating mechanisms for land and land resources, by not later than 1998;

(d) To create mechanisms to facilitate the active involvement and participation of all concerned, particularly communities and people at the local level, in decision-making on land use and management, by not later than 1996.

Activities

(a) Management-related activities

Developing supportive policies and policy instruments

10.6. Governments at the appropriate level, with the support of regional and international organizations, should ensure that policies and policy instruments support the best possible land use and sustainable management of land resources. Particular attention should be given to the role of agricultural land. To do this, they should:

(a) Develop integrated goal-setting and policy formulation at the national, regional and local levels that takes into account environmental, social, demographic and economic issues;

(b) Develop policies that encourage sustainable land use and management of land resources and take the land resource base, demographic issues and the interests of the local population into account;

(c) Review the regulatory framework, including laws, regulations and enforcement procedures, in order to identify improvements needed to support sustainable land use and management of land resources and restricts the transfer of productive arable land to other uses;

(d) Apply economic instruments and develop institutional mechanisms and incentives to encourage the best possible land use and sustainable management of land resources;

(e) Encourage the principle of delegating policy-making to the lowest level of public authority consistent with effective action and a locally driven approach.

Strengthening planning and management systems

10.7. Governments at the appropriate level, with the support of regional and international organizations, should review and, if appropriate, revise planning and management systems to facilitate an integrated approach. To do this, they should:

(a) Adopt planning and management systems that facilitate the integration of environmental components such as air, water, land and other natural resources, using landscape ecological planning (LANDEP) or other approaches that focus on, for example, an ecosystem or a watershed;

(b) Adopt strategic frameworks that allow the integration of both developmental and environmental goals; examples of these frameworks include sustainable livelihood systems, rural development, the World Conservation Strategy/Caring for the Earth,[1] primary environmental care (PEC) and others;

(c) Establish a general framework for land-use and physical planning within which specialized and more detailed sectoral plans (e.g., for protected areas, agriculture, forests, human settlements, rural development) can be developed; establish intersectoral consultative bodies to streamline project planning and implementation;

(d) Strengthen management systems for land and natural resources by including appropriate traditional and indigenous methods; examples of these practices include pastoralism, Hema reserves (traditional Islamic land reserves) and terraced agriculture;

(e) Examine and, if necessary, establish innovative and flexible approaches to programme funding;

(f) Compile detailed land capability inventories to guide sustainable land resources allocation, management and use at the national and local levels.

Promoting application of appropriate tools for planning and management

10.8. Governments at the appropriate level, with the support of national and international organizations, should promote the improvement, further development and widespread application of planning and management tools that facilitate an integrated and sustainable approach to land and resources. To do this, they should:

(a) Adopt improved systems for the interpretation and integrated analysis of data on land use and land resources;

(b) Systematically apply techniques and procedures for assessing the environmental, social and economic impacts, risks, costs and benefits of specific actions;

(c) Analyse and test methods to include land and ecosystem functions and land resources values in national accounts.

Raising awareness

10.9. Governments at the appropriate level, in collaboration with national institutions and interest groups and with the support of regional and international organizations, should launch awareness-raising campaigns to alert and educate people on the importance of integrated land and land resources management and the role that individuals and social groups can play in it. This should be ac-

---

1   *Caring for the Earth* was published by IUCN—The World Conservation Union, in cooperation with the U.N. Environment Programme and the World-wide Fund for Nature. See the Introduction to this volume by Nicholas A. Robinson for further references.

companied by provision of the means to adopt improved practices for land use and sustainable management.

Promoting public participation

10.10. Governments at the appropriate level, in collaboration with national organizations and with the support of regional and international organizations, should establish innovative procedures, programmes, projects and services that facilitate and encourage the active participation of those affected in the decision-making and implementation process, especially of groups that have, hitherto, often been excluded, such as women, youth, indigenous people and their communities and other local communities.

(b) Data and information

Strengthening information systems

10.11. Governments at the appropriate level, in collaboration with national institutions and the private sector and with the support of regional and international organizations, should strengthen the information systems necessary for making decisions and evaluating future changes on land use and management. The needs of both men and women should be taken into account. To do this, they should:

(a) Strengthen information, systematic observation and assessment systems for environmental, economic and social data related to land resources at the global, regional, national and local levels and for land capability and land-use and management patterns;

(b) Strengthen coordination between existing sectoral data systems on land and land resources and strengthen national capacity to gather and assess data;

(c) Provide the appropriate technical information necessary for informed decision-making on land use and management in an accessible form to all sectors of the population, especially to local communities and women;

(d) Support low-cost, community-managed systems for the collection of comparable information on the status and processes of change of land resources, including soils, forest cover, wildlife, climate and other elements.

(c) International and regional coordination and cooperation

Establishing regional machinery

10.12. Governments at the appropriate level, with the support of regional and international organizations, should strengthen regional cooperation and exchange of information on land resources. To do this, they should:

(a) Study and design regional policies to support programmes for land-use and physical planning;

(b) Promote the development of land-use and physical plans in the countries of the region;

(c) Design information systems and promote training;

(d) Exchange, through networks and other appropriate means, information on experiences with the process and results of integrated and participatory planning and management of land resources at the national and local levels.

Means of implementation

(a) Financing and cost evaluation

10.13. The Conference secretariat has estimated the average total annual cost (1993-2000) of implementing the activities of this programme to be about $50 million from the international community on grant or concessional terms. These are indicative and order-of-magnitude estimates only and have not been reviewed by Governments. Actual costs and financial terms, including any that are non-concessional, will depend upon, *inter alia*, the specific strategies and programmes Governments decide upon for implementation.[2]

(b) Scientific and technological means

Enhancing scientific understanding of the land resources system

10.14. Governments at the appropriate level, in collaboration with the national and international scientific community and with the support of appropriate national and international organizations, should promote and support research, tailored to local environments, on the land resources system and the implications for sustainable development and management practices. Priority should be given, as appropriate, to:

(a) Assessment of land potential capability and ecosystem functions;

(b) Ecosystemic interactions and interactions between land resources and social, economic and environmental systems;

(c) To developing indicators of sustainability for land resources, taking into account environmental, economic, social, demographic, cultural and political factors.

Testing research findings through pilot projects

10.15. Governments at the appropriate level, in collaboration with the national and international scientific community and with the support of the relevant in-

---

2   Draft paragraph 10.13 of A/CONF.151/4 (22 April 1992) was replaced by decision of the Main Committee of UNCED on 10 June 1992. See A/CONF.151/L.3/Add.10 (12 June 1992). The former draft read as follows:

      It is assumed that most costs will be borne by Governments as part of the regular planning and management process. It is suggested that technical cooperation funding from international sources be made available at an annual cost of about $ 50 million.

ternational organizations, should research and test, through pilot projects, the applicability of improved approaches to the integrated planning and management of land resources, including technical, social and institutional factors.

(c) Human resource development

Enhancing education and training

10.16. Governments at the appropriate level, in collaboration with the appropriate local authorities, non-governmental organizations and international institutions, should promote the development of the human resources that are required to plan and manage land and land resources sustainably. This should be done by providing incentives for local initiatives and by enhancing local management capacity, particularly of women, through:

(a) Emphasizing interdisciplinary and integrative approaches in the curricula of schools and technical, vocational and university training;

(b) Training all relevant sectors concerned to deal with land resources in an integrated and sustainable manner;

(c) Training communities, relevant extension services, community based groups and non-governmental organizations on land management techniques and approaches applied successfully elsewhere.

(d) Capacity-building

Strengthening technological capacity

10.17. Governments at the appropriate level, in cooperation with other Governments and with the support of relevant international organizations, should promote focused and concerted efforts for education and training and transfer of techniques and technologies that support the various aspects of the sustainable planning and management process at the national, state/provincial and local levels.

Strengthening institutions

10.18. Governments at the appropriate level, with the support of appropriate international organizations, should:

(a) Review and, where appropriate, revise the mandates of institutions that deal with land and natural resources to include explicitly the interdisciplinary integration of environmental, social and economic issues;

(b) Strengthen coordinating mechanisms between institutions that deal with land-use and resources management to facilitate integration of sectoral concerns and strategies;

(c) Strengthen local decision-making capacity and improve coordination with higher levels.

Chapter 11

Combating Deforestation

PROGRAMME AREAS

A. Sustaining the multiple roles and functions of all types of forests, forest lands and woodlands

Basis for action

11.1. There are major weaknesses in the policies, methods and mechanisms adopted to support and develop the multiple ecological, economic, social and cultural roles of trees, forests and forest lands. Many developed countries are confronted with the effects of air pollution and fire damage on their forests. More effective measures and approaches are often required at the national level to improve and harmonize policy formulation, planning and programming; legislative measures and instruments; development patterns; participation of the general public, especially women and indigenous people; involvement of youth; roles of the private sector, local organizations, non-governmental organizations and cooperatives; development of technical and multidisciplinary skills and quality of human resources; forestry extension and public education; research capability and support; administrative structures and mechanisms, including intersectoral coordination, decentralization and responsibility and incentive systems; and dissemination of information and public relations. This is especially important to ensure a rational and holistic approach to the sustainable and environmentally sound development of forests. The need for securing the multiple roles of forests and forest lands through adequate and appropriate institutional strengthening has been repeatedly emphasized in many of the reports, decisions and recommendations of FAO [Food and Agriculture Organization], ITTO [International Tropical Timber Organization], UNEP [U.N. Environment Programme], the World Bank, IUCN [International Union For The Conservation of Nature & Natural Resources, also known as the World Conservation Union] and other organizations.

Objectives

11.2. The objectives of this programme area are as follows:

(a) To strengthen forest-related national institutions, to enhance the scope and effectiveness of activities related to management, conservation and the sustainable development of forests, and to effectively ensure sustainable utilization and production of forests' goods and services in both the developed and the developing countries; by the year 2000, to strengthen the capacities and capabilities of national institutions to enable them to acquire necessary knowledge for the protection and conservation of forests, as well as to expand their scope and, correspondingly, enhance the effectiveness of programmes and activities related to the management and development of forests;

(b) To strengthen and improve human, technical and professional skills, as well as expertise and capabilities to effectively formulate and implement policies, plans, programmes, research and projects on management, conservation and sustainable development of all types of forests and forest-based resources, and forest lands inclusive, as well as other areas from which forest benefits can be derived.

Activities

(a) Management-related activities

11.3. Governments at the appropriate level, with the support of regional, subregional and international organizations, should, enhance institutional capability to promote the multiple roles and functions of all types of forests and vegetation inclusive of other related lands and forest-based resources in supporting sustainable development and environmental conservation in all sectors. This should be done wherever possible and necessary, by strengthening and/or modifying the existing structures and arrangements, and by improving cooperation and coordination of their respective roles. Some of the major activities in this regard are as follows:

(a) Rationalizing and strengthening administrative structures and mechanisms, including provision of adequate levels of staff and allocation of responsibilities, decentralization of decision-making, provision of infrastructural facilities and equipment, intersectoral coordination and an effective system of communication;

(b) Promoting participation of the private sector, labour unions, rural cooperatives, local communities, indigenous people, youth, women, user groups and non-governmental organizations in forest-related activities, and access to information and training programmes within the national context;

(c) Reviewing and, if necessary, revising measures and programmes relevant to all types of forests and vegetation, inclusive of other related lands and forest-based resources, and relating them to other land uses and development policies and legislation; promoting adequate legislation and other measures as a basis against uncontrolled conversion to other types of land uses;

(d) Developing and implementing plans and programmes, including definition of national and if necessary, regional and subregional goals, programmes and criteria for their implementation and subsequent improvement;

(e) Establishing, developing and sustaining an effective system of forest extension and public education to ensure better awareness, appreciation and management of forests with regard to the multiple roles and values of trees, forests and forest lands;

(f) Establishing and/or strengthening institutions for forest education and training as well as forestry industries, for developing an adequate cadre of trained and skilled staff at the professional, technical and vocational levels, with emphasis on youth and women;

(g) Establishing and strengthening capabilities for research related to the different aspects of forests and forest products, for example, on the sustainable management of forests, research on biodiversity, on the effects of air-borne pollutants, on traditional uses of forest resources by local populations and indigenous people, and on improving market returns and other non-market values from the management of forests.

(b) Data and information

11.4. Governments at the appropriate level, with the assistance and cooperation of international, regional, subregional and bilateral agencies, where relevant, should develop adequate databases and baseline information necessary for planning and programme evaluation. Some of the more specific activities include the following:

(a) Collecting, compiling and regularly updating and distributing information on land classification and land use, including data on forest cover, areas suitable for afforestation, endangered species, ecological values, traditional/indigenous land use values, biomass and productivity, correlating demographic, socio-economic and forest resources information at the micro- and macro-levels, and undertaking periodic analyses of forest programmes;

(b) Establishing linkages with other data systems and sources relevant to supporting forest management, conservation and development, while further developing or reinforcing existing systems such as geographic information systems, as appropriate;

(c) Creating mechanisms to ensure public access to this information.

(c) International and regional cooperation and coordination:

11.5. Governments at the appropriate level, and institutions should cooperate in the provision of expertise and other support and the promotion of international research efforts, in particular with a view to enhancing transfer of technology and specialized training and ensuring access to experiences and research results. There is need for strengthening coordination and improving the performance of existing forest-related international organizations in providing technical cooperation and support to interested countries for the management, conservation and sustainable development of forests.

Means of implementation

(a) Financial and cost evaluation

11.6. The secretariat of the Conference has estimated the average total annual cost (1993-2000) of implementing the activities of this programme to be about $2.5 billion, including about $860 million from the international community on grant or concessional terms. These are indicative and order of magnitude estimates only and have not been reviewed by Governments. Actual costs and financial terms, including any that are non-concessional, will depend upon, *inter alia*, the specific strategies and programmes Governments decide upon for implementation.[1]

(b) Scientific and technological means

11.7. The planning, research and training activities specified will form the scientific and technological means for implementing the programme, as well as its output. The systems, methodology and know-how generated by the programme will help improve efficiency. Some of the specific steps involved should include:

(a) Analysing achievements, constraints and social issues for supporting programme formulation and implementation;

(b) Analysing research problems and research needs, research planning and implementation of specific research projects;

(c) Assessing needs for human resources, skill development and training;

(d) Developing, testing and applying appropriate methodologies/approaches in implementing forest programmes and plans.

---

1   Draft paragraphs 11.8 and 11.9 of A/CONF.151/4 (22 April 1992) were replaced here as paragraph 11.6 by decision of the Main Committee of UNCED on 10 June 1992. See A/CONF.151/L.3/Add.11 (11 June 1992). The former draft read as follows:

   Annual estimated funding required to implement these activities is about $ 2,500 million for the period 1993-2000. A major part required will need to be financed from national governments, the private sector and in some cases, NGOs. The estimated amount of international financing required, annually, for developing countries has been estimated at $ 860 million, of which $ 840 million are related to accelerating development and $ 20 million for strengthening the capacity of international institutions. Accelerating development would consist of implementing management-related and data/information activities listed above.

(c) Human resource development

11.8. The specific components of forest education and training will effectively contribute to human resource development. These include:

(a) Launching of graduate and post-graduate degree, specialization and research programmes;

(b) Strengthening of pre-service, in-service and extension service training programmes at the technical and vocational levels, including training of trainers/teachers, and developing curriculum and teaching materials/methods;

(c) Special training for staff of national forest-related organizations in aspects such as project formulation, evaluation and periodical evaluations.

(d) Capacity-building

11.9. This programme area is specifically concerned with capacity-building in the forest sector and all programme activities specified contribute to that end. In building new and strengthened capacities, full advantage should be taken of the existing systems and experience.

B. Enhancing the protection, sustainable management and conservation of all forests, and the greening of degraded areas, through forest rehabilitation, afforestation, reforestation and other rehabilitative means

Basis for action

11.10. Forests world wide have been and are being threatened by uncontrolled degradation and conversion to other types of land uses, influenced by increasing human needs; agricultural expansion; and environmentally harmful mismanagement, including, for example, lack of adequate forest-fire control and anti-poaching measures, unsustainable commercial logging, overgrazing and unregulated browsing, harmful effects of airborne pollutants, economic incentives and other measures taken by other sectors of the economy. The impacts of loss and degradation of forests are in the form of soil erosion; loss of biological diversity, damage to wildlife habitats and degradation of watershed areas, deterioration of the quality of life and reduction of the options for development.

11.11. The present situation calls for urgent and consistent action for conserving and sustaining forest resources. The greening of suitable areas, in all its component activities, is an effective way of increasing public awareness and participation in protecting and managing forest resources. It should include the consideration of land use and tenure patterns and local needs and should spell out and clarify the specific objectives of the different types of greening activities.

Objectives

11.12. The objectives of this programme area are as follows:

(a) To maintain existing forests through conservation and management, and sustain and expand areas under forest and tree cover, in appropriate areas of both developed and developing countries, through the conservation of natural forests, protection, forest rehabilitation, regeneration, afforestation, reforestation, and tree planting, with a view to maintaining or restoring the ecological balance and expanding the contribution of forests to human needs and welfare;

(b) To prepare and implement, as appropriate, national forestry action programmes and/or plans for the management, conservation and sustainable development of forests. These programmes and/or plans should be integrated with other land uses. In this context, country-driven national forestry action programmes and/or plans under the Tropical Forestry Action Programme are currently being implemented in more than 80 countries, with the support of the international community;

(c) To ensure the sustainable management and, where appropriate, conservation of existing and future forest resources;

(d) To maintain and increase the ecological, biological, climatic, socio-cultural and economic contributions of forest resources;

(e) To facilitate and support effective implementation of the non-legally binding authoritative statement of principles for a global consensus on the management, conservation and sustainable development of all types of forests, adopted by the United Nations Conference on Environment and Development, and on the basis of the implementation of these principles to consider the need for and the feasibility of all kinds of appropriate internationally agreed arrangements to promote international cooperation on forest management, conservation, and sustainable development of all types of forests, including afforestation, reforestation and rehabilitation.

Activities

(a) Management-related activities

11.13. Governments should recognize the importance of categorizing forests, within the framework of long-term forest conservation and management policies, into different forest types and setting up sustainable units in every region/watershed with a view to securing the conservation of forests. Governments, with the participation of the private sector, non-governmental organizations, local community groups, indigenous people, women, local government units and the public at large, should act to maintain and expand the existing vegetative cover wherever ecologically, socially and economically feasible, through technical cooperation and other forms of support. Major activities to be considered include:

(a) Ensuring the sustainable management of all forest ecosystems and wood-lands, through improved proper planning, management and timely imple-mentation of silvicultural operations, including inventory and relevant research, as well as rehabilitation of degraded natural forests to restore productivity and environmental contributions, giving particular attention to human needs for economic and ecological services, wood-based energy, agroforestry, non-timber forest products and services, watershed and soil protection, wildlife management, and forest genetic resources;

(b) Establishing, expanding and managing, as appropriate to each national context, protected area systems, which includes systems of conservation units for their environmental, social and spiritual functions and values, in-cluding conservation of forests in representative ecological systems and landscapes, primary old-growth forests, conservation and management of wildlife, nomination of World Heritage Sites under the World Heritage Con-vention, as appropriate, conservation of genetic resources, involving *in situ* and *ex situ* measures and undertaking supportive measures to ensure sustain-able utilization of biological resources and conservation of biological diver-sity and the traditional forest habitats of indigenous people, forest dwellers and local communities.

(c) Undertaking and promoting buffer and transition zone management;

(d) Carrying out revegetation in appropriate mountain areas, highlands, bare lands, degraded farm lands, arid and semi-arid lands and coastal areas for combating desertification and preventing erosion problems and for other protective functions and national programmes for rehabilitation of degraded lands, including community forestry, social forestry, agroforestry and silvo-pasture, while also taking into account the role of forests as national carbon reservoirs and sinks;

(e) Developing industrial and non-industrial planted forests in order to support and promote national ecologically sound afforestation and reforesta-tion/regeneration programmes in suitable sites, including upgrading of exist-ing planted forests of both industrial and non-industrial and commercial purpose to increase their contribution to human needs and offset pressure on primary/old growth forests. Measures should be taken to promote and provide intermediate yields and to improve the rate of returns on invest-ments in planted forests, through interplanting and underplanting valuable crops;

(f) Developing/strengthening a national and/or master plan for planted for-ests as a priority, indicating, *inter alia*, the location, scope and species, and specifying areas of existing planted forests requiring rehabilitation, taking into account the economic aspect for future planted forest development, giv-ing emphasis to native species;

(g) Increasing the protection of forests from pollutants, fire, pests and diseases and other human-made interferences such as forest poaching, mining and unmitigated shifting cultivation, the uncontrolled introduction of exotic plant and animal species, as well as developing and accelerating research for a better understanding of problems relating to the management and regeneration of all types of forests; strengthening and/or establishing appropriate measures to assess and/or check inter-border movement of plants and related materials;

(h) Stimulating development of urban forestry for the greening of urban, peri-urban and rural human settlements for amenity, recreation and production purposes and for protecting trees and groves;

(i) Launching or improving opportunities for participation of all people, including youth, women, indigenous people and local communities in the formulation, development and implementation of forest-related programmes and other activities, taking due account of the local needs and cultural values;

(j) Limiting and aiming to halt destructive shifting cultivation by addressing the underlying social and ecological causes.

(b) Data and information

11.14. The management-related activities should involve collection, compilation and analysis of data/information, including baseline surveys. Some of the specific activities include the following:

(a) Carrying out surveys and developing and implementing land-use plans for appropriate greening/planting/afforestation/re-forestation/forest rehabilitation;

(b) Consolidating and updating land use and forest inventory and management information for management and land-use planning of wood and non-wood resources, including data on shifting cultivation and other agents of forest destruction;

(c) Consolidating information on genetic resources and related biotechnology, including surveys and studies, as necessary;

(d) Carrying out surveys and research on local/indigenous knowledge of trees and forests and their uses to improve the planning and implementation of sustainable forest management;

(e) Compiling and analysing research data on species/site interaction of species used in planted forests and assessing the potential impact on forests of climatic change, as well as effects of forests on climate, and initiating in-depth studies on the carbon cycle relating to different forest types to provide scientific advice and technical support;

(f) Establishing linkages with other data/information sources that relate to sustainable management and use of forests and improving access to data and information;

(g) Developing and intensifying research to improve knowledge and under-standing of problems and natural mechanisms related to the management and rehabilitation of forests, including research on fauna and its interrelation with forests;

(h) Consolidating information on forest conditions and site-influencing immissions and emissions.

(c) International and regional cooperation and coordination

11.15. The greening of appropriate areas is a task of global importance and impact. The international and regional community should provide technical cooperation and other means for this programme area. Specific activities of international nature, in support of national efforts, should include the following:

(a) Increasing cooperative actions to reduce pollutants and trans-boundary impacts affecting the health of trees and forests and conservation of repre-sentative ecosystems;

(b) Coordinating regional and subregional research on carbon sequestration, air pollution and other environmental issues;

(c) Documenting and exchanging information/experience for the benefit of countries with similar problems and prospects;

(d) Strengthening the coordination and improving the capacity and abil-ity of intergovernmental organizations such as FAO, ITTO, UNEP and UNESCO to provide technical support for the management, conservation and sustainable development of forests, including support for the nego-tiation of the International Tropical Timber Agreement of 1983, due in 1992/1993.

Means of implementation

(a) Financial and cost evaluation

11.16. The secretariat of the Conference has estimated the average total annual cost (1993-2000) of implementing the activities of this programme to be about $10 billion, including about $3.7 billion from the international community on grant or concessional terms. These are indicative and order-of-magnitude estimates only and have not been reviewed by Governments. Actual costs and financial terms, including any that are non-concessional, will depend upon,

inter alia, the specific strategies and programmes Governments decide upon for implementation.[2]

(b) Scientific and technological means

11.17. Data analysis, planning, research, transfer/development of technology and/or training activities form an integral part of the programme activities, providing the scientific and technological means of implementation. National institutions should:

(a) Develop feasibility studies and operational planning related to major forest activities;

(b) Develop and apply environmentally sound technology relevant to the various activities listed;

(c) Increase action related to genetic improvement and application of biotechnology for improving productivity and tolerance to environmental stress and including, for example, tree breeding, seed technology, seed procurement networks, germ-plasm banks, "in vitro" techniques, and *in situ* and *ex situ* conservation.

(c) Human resource development

11.18 Essential means for effectively implementing the activities include training and development of appropriate skills, working facilities and conditions, public motivation and awareness. Specific activities include:

(a) Providing specialized training in planning, management, environmental conservation, biotechnology etc.;

(b) Establishing demonstration areas to serve as models and training facilities;

(c) Supporting local organizations, communities, non-governmental organizations, private land owners, in particular women, youth, farmers and indigenous people/shifting cultivators, through extension and provision of inputs and training.

(d) Capacity-building

11.19. National Governments, the private sector, local organizations/communities, indigenous people, labour unions and non-governmental organizations should develop capacities, duly supported by relevant international organiza-

---

2   Paragraph 11.16, formerly 11.18 of A/CONF. 151/4 (Part II), p. 35, was revised by decision of the main committee of UNCED. The prior text read as follows:

The estimated annual financing required to implement these activities is about $ 10 billion for the period 1993-2000. Of this amount about $ 3.7 billion in international financing will be needed for developing countries. From that amount $ 3,510 million are related to accelerating development; $ 150 million are needed for global environmental issues and $ 20 million for strengthening the capacity of international institutions.

tions, to implement the programme activities. Such capacities should be developed and strengthened in harmony with the programme activities. Capacity-building activities include policy and legal frameworks, national institution building, human resource development, development of research and technology, development of infrastructure, enhancement of public awareness etc.

C. Promoting efficient utilization and assessment to recover the full valuation of the goods and services provided by forests, forest lands and woodlands

Basis for action

11.20. The vast potential of forests and forest lands as a major resource for development is not yet fully realized. The improved management of forests can increase the production of goods and services and, in particular, the yield of wood and non-wood forest products, thus helping to generate additional employment and income, additional value through processing and trade of forest products, increased contribution to foreign exchange earnings, and increased return on investment. Forest resources, being renewable, can be sustainably managed in a manner that is compatible with environmental conservation. The implications of the harvesting of forest resources for the other values of the forest should be taken fully into consideration in the development of forests policies. It is also possible to increase the value of forests through non-damaging uses such as eco-tourism and managed supply of genetic materials. Concerted action is needed in order to increase people's perception of the value of forests and of the benefits they provide. The survival of the forests and their continued contribution to human welfare depends to a great extent on succeeding in this endeavour.

Objectives

11.21. The objectives of this programme area are as follows:

(a) To improve recognition of the social, economic and ecological values of trees, forests and forest lands, including the consequences of the damage caused by the lack of forests; to promote methodologies with a view to incorporating social, economic and ecologic values of trees, forests and forest lands into the national economic accounting systems; to ensure their sustainable management in a way which is consistent with land use, environmental considerations and development needs;

(b) To promote efficient, rational and sustainable utilization of all types of forests and vegetation inclusive of other related lands and forest-based resources, through the development of efficient forest-based processing industries, value-adding secondary processing and trade in forest products, based on sustainably managed forest resources and in accordance with plans which integrate all wood and non-wood values of forests;

(c) To promote more efficient and sustainable use of forest and trees for fuelwood and energy supplies;

(d) To promote more comprehensive use and economic contributions of forest areas by incorporating eco-tourism into forest management and planning.

Activities

(a) Management-related activities

11.22. Governments, with the support of the private sector, scientific institutions, indigenous people, non-governmental organizations, cooperatives and entrepreneurs, where appropriate, should undertake the following activities, properly coordinated at the national level, with financial and technical cooperation from international organizations:

(a) Carrying out detailed investment studies, supply-demand harmonization and environmental impact analysis to rationalize and improve trees and forest utilization and to develop and establish appropriate incentive schemes and regulatory measures, including tenurial arrangements, to provide a favourable investment climate and promote better management;

(b) Formulating scientifically sound criteria and guidelines for the management, conservation and sustainable development of all types of forests;

(c) Improving environmentally sound methods and practices of forest harvesting, which are ecologically sound and economically viable, including planning and management, improved use of equipment, storage and transportation to reduce and, if possible, maximize the use of waste and improve value of both wood and non-wood forest products;

(d) Promoting the better use and development of natural forests and woodlands, including planted forests, wherever possible, through appropriate and environmentally sound and economically viable activities, including silvicultural practices and management of other plant and animal species;

(e) Promoting and supporting the downstream processing of forest products to increase retained value and other benefits;

(f) Promoting/popularizing non-wood forest products and other forms of forest resources, apart from fuelwood (e.g., medicinal plants, dyes, fibres, gums, resins, fodder, cultural products, rattan, bamboo) through programmes and social forestry/participatory forest activities, including research on their processing and uses;

(g) Developing, expanding and/or improving the effectiveness and efficiency of forest-based processing industries, both wood and non-wood based, involving such aspects as efficient conversion technology and improved sustainable utilization of harvesting and process residues; promoting underutilized species in natural forests through research, demonstration and commercialization; promoting value-adding secondary processing for improved employment, income and retained value; and promoting/improving markets for, and trade in, forest products through relevant institutions, policies and facilities.

(h) Promoting and supporting the management of wildlife, as well as eco-tourism, including farming, and encouraging and supporting the husbandry and cultivation of wild species, for improved rural income and employment, ensuring economic and social benefits without harmful ecological impacts;

(i) Promoting appropriate small-scale forest-based enterprises for supporting rural development and local entrepreneurship;

(j) Improving and promoting methodologies for a comprehensive assessment that will capture the full value of forests with a view to including that value in the market-based pricing structure of wood and non-wood based products;

(k) Harmonizing sustainable development of forests with national development needs and trade policies that are compatible with the ecologically sound use of forest resources, using, for example, the ITTO Guidelines for Sustainable Management of Tropical Forests;

(l) Developing, adopting and strengthening national programmes for accounting the economic and non-economic value of forests.

(b) Data and information

11.23. The objectives and management-related activities presuppose data and information analysis, feasibility studies, market surveys and review of technological information. Some of the relevant activities include:

(a) Undertaking analysis of supply and demand for forest products and services, to ensure efficiency in their utilization, wherever necessary;

(b) Carrying out investment analysis and feasibility studies, including environmental impact assessment, for establishing forest-based processing enterprises;

(c) Conducting research on the properties of currently underutilized species for their promotion and commercialization;

(d) Supporting market surveys of forest products for trade promotion and intelligence;

(e) Facilitating the provision of adequate technological information as a measure to promote better utilization of forest resources.

(c) International and regional cooperation and coordination

11.24. Cooperation and assistance of international agencies and the international community in technology transfer, specialization and promotion of fair terms of trade, without resorting to unilateral restrictions and/or bans on forest products contrary to GATT [General Agreement on Tariffs and Trade] and other multilateral trade agreements, the application of appropriate market mechanisms and incentives will help in addressing global environmental concerns.

Strengthening the coordination and performance of existing international organizations, in particular FAO, UNIDO [U.N. Industrial Development Organization], UNESCO [U.N. Educational, Scientific and Cultural Organization], UNEP [U.N. Environment Programme], ITC [International Tin Council]/UNCTAD [U.N. Conference on Trade and Development]/GATT, ITTO and ILO [International Labour Organisation], for providing technical assistance and guidance in this programme area is another specific activity.

Means of implementation

(a) Financial and cost evaluation

11.25. The secretariat of the Conference has estimated the average total annual cost (1993-2000) of implementing the activities of this programme to be about $18 billion, including about $880 million from the international community on grant or concessional terms. These are indicative and order-of-magnitude estimates only and have not been reviewed by Governments. Actual costs and financial terms, including any that are non-concessional, will depend upon, *inter alia*, the specific strategies and programmes Governments decide upon for implementation.[3]

(b) Scientific and technological means

11.26. The programme activities presuppose major research efforts and studies, as well as improvement of technology. This should be coordinated by national Governments in collaboration with and supported by relevant international organizations and institutions. Some of the specific components include:

(a) Research on properties of wood and non-wood products and their uses, to promote improved utilization;

(b) Development and application of environmentally sound and less-polluting technology for forest utilization;

(c) Models and techniques of outlook analysis and development planning;

(d) Scientific investigations on the development and utilization of non-timber forest products;

(e) Appropriate methodologies to comprehensively assess the value of forests.

---

3   Draft paragraphs 11.35 and 11.36 of A/CONF.151/4 (22 April 1992) were replaced by decision of the Main Committee of UNCED on 10 June 1992. See A/CONF.151/L.3/Add.11 (11 June 1992). The former draft read as follows:

Estimated annual financing required to implement the programme activities is about $ 18 billion, for the period 1993-2000. The bulk of it is expected to be invested by the private sector. Part of it will also be invested by the national governments. Smaller investments will come from cooperatives and households. International assistance will, however, act as a catalyst and stimulant to promote development.

The amount of international financing, required annually by developing countries has been estimated at $ 880 million of which $ 660 million are related to accelerated development; $ 200 million for global environmental issues and $ 20 million for strengthening the capacity of international organizations.

(c) Human resources development

11.27. The success and effectiveness of the programme depends on the availability of skilled personnel. Specialized training is an important factor in this regard. New emphasis should be given to the incorporation of women. Human resource development for programme implementation, in quantitative and qualitative terms should include:

(a) Developing the required specialized skills to implement the programme, including establishing of special training facilities at all levels;

(b) Introducing/strengthening refresher training courses, including fellowships and study tours, to update skills and technological know-how and improve productivity;

(c) Strengthening capability for research, planning, economic analysis, periodical evaluations and evaluation, relevant to improved utilization of forest resources;

(d) Promoting efficiency and capability of private and cooperative sectors through provision of facilities and incentives.

(d) Capacity-building

11.28. Capacity building, including strengthening of existing capacity, is implicit in the programme activities. Improving administration, policy and plans, national institutions, human resources, research and scientific capabilities, technology development, and periodical evaluations and evaluation are important components of capacity-building.

D. Establishing and/or strengthening capacities for the planning, assessment and systematic observations of forests and related programmes, projects and activities, including commercial trade and processes

Basis for action

11.29. Assessment and systematic observations are essential components of long-term planning, for evaluating effects, quantitatively and qualitatively, and for rectifying inadequacies. This mechanism, however, is one of the often neglected aspects of forest resources, management, conservation and development. In many cases, even the basic information related to the area and types of forests, existing potential and volume of harvest is lacking. In many developing countries, there is a lack of structures and mechanisms to carry out these functions. There is an urgent need to rectify this situation for a better understanding of the role and importance of forests and to realistically plan for their effective conservation, management, regeneration, and sustainable development.

Objectives

11.30. The objectives of this programme area are as follows:

(a) To strengthen or establish systems for the assessment and systematic observations of forest and forest lands with a view to assessing the impacts of programmes, projects and activities on the quality and extent of forest resources, land available for afforestation, and land tenure, and to integrate the systems in a continuing process of research and in-depth analysis, while ensuring necessary modifications and improvements for planning and decision-making process. Specific emphasis should be given to the participation of the rural people in these processes;

(b) To provide the economists, planners, decision makers and local communities with sound and adequate updated information on forests and forest land resources.

Activities

(a) Management-related activities

11.31. Governments and institutions, in collaboration, where necessary, with appropriate international agencies and organizations, universities and non-governmental organizations, should undertake assessments and systematic observations of forests and related programmes and processes with a view to their continuous improvement. This should be linked to related activities of research and management and, wherever possible, be built upon existing systems. Major activities to be considered are:

(a) Assessing and carrying out systematic observations of the quantitative and qualitative situation and changes of forest cover and forest resources endowments, including land classification, land use and updates of its status, at the appropriate national level, and linking this activity, as appropriate, with planning as a basis for policy and programme formulation;

(b) Establishing national assessment and systematic observation systems and evaluation of programmes and processes, including establishment of definitions, standards, norms and intercalibration methods, and the capability for initiating corrective actions as well as improving the formulation and implementation of programmes and projects;

(c) Making estimates of impacts of activities affecting forestry developments and conservation proposals, in terms of key variables such as developmental goals, benefits and costs, contributions of forests to other sectors, community welfare, environmental conditions and biological diversity and their impacts at the local, regional and global levels, where appropriate, to assess the changing technological and financial needs of countries;

(d) Developing national systems of forest resource assessment and valuation, including necessary research and data analysis, which account for, where possible, the full range of wood and non-wood forest products and services, and incorporating results in plans and strategies and, where feasible, in national systems of accounts and planning;

(e) Establishing necessary intersectoral and programme linkages, including improved access to information, in order to support a holistic approach to planning and programming.

(b) Data and information

11.32. Reliable data and information are vital to this programme. National Governments, in collaboration, where necessary, with relevant international agencies, should, as appropriate, undertake to improve data and information continuously and to ensure its exchange. Major activities to be considered are as follows:

(a) Collecting, consolidating and exchanging existing information and establishing baseline information on aspects relevant to this programme;

(b) Harmonizing the methodologies for programmes involving data and information activities to ensure accuracy and consistency;

(c) Undertaking special surveys on, for example, land capability and suitability for afforestation action;

(d) Enhancing research support and improving access to and exchange of research results.

(c) International and regional cooperation and coordination

11.33. The international community should extend to the Governments concerned necessary technical and financial support for implementing this programme area, including consideration of the following activities:

(a) Establishing conceptual framework and formulating acceptable criteria, norms and definitions for systematic observations and assessment of forest resources;

(b) Establishing and strengthening national institutional coordination mechanisms for forest assessment and systematic observation activities;

(c) Strengthening existing regional and global networks for the exchange of relevant information;

(d) Strengthening the capacity and ability and improving the performance of existing international organizations, such as the Consultative Group on International Agricultural Research (CGIAR), FAO, ITTO, UNEP, UNESCO and UNIDO, to provide technical support and guidance in this programme area.

Means of Implementation

(a) Financial and Cost Evaluation

11.34. The secretariat of the Conference has estimated the average total annual cost (1993-2000) of implementing the activities of this programme to be about $750 million, including about $230 million from the international community on grant or concessional terms. These are indicative and order-of-magnitude estimates only and have not been reviewed by Governments. Actual costs and financial terms, including any that are non-concessional, will depend upon, *inter alia*, the specific strategies and programmes Governments decide upon for implementation.[4]

11.35. Accelerating development consists of implementing the management-related and data/information activities cited above. Activities related to global environmental issues are those that will contribute to global information for assessing/evaluating/addressing environmental issues on a worldwide basis. Strengthening the capacity of international institutions consists of enhancing the technical staff and the executing capacity of several international organizations in order to meet the requirements of countries.

(b) Scientific and technological means

11.36. Assessment and systematic observation activities involve major research efforts, statistical modelling and technological innovation. These have been internalized into the management-related activities. The activities in turn will improve the technological and scientific content of assessment and periodical evaluations. Some of the specific scientific and technological components included under these activities are:

(a) Developing technical, ecological and economic methods and models related to periodical evaluations and evaluation;

(b) Developing data systems, data processing and statistical modelling;

(c) Remote sensing and ground surveys;

(d) Developing geographic information systems;

(e) Assessing and improving technology.

---

4   Paragraph 11.34, formerly paragraph 11.37 of A/CONF 151/4 (Part II), p. 43, was revised by the main committee of UNCED. The prior text read as follows:

   The estimated annual financing required to implement these activities is about $750 million for the period 1993-2000. About 70 per cent of the required financing will come from national Governments and the private sector. The amount of annual international financing required by developing countries has been estimated at $230 million, of which $180 million are related to accelerating development, $30 million are for the global environmental issues and $20 million for strengthening the capacity of international organizations.

11.37. These are to be linked and harmonized with similar activities and components in the other programme areas.

(c) Human resource development

11.38. The programme activities foresee the need and include provision for human resource development in terms of specialization (e.g., the use of remote-sensing, mapping and statistical modelling), training, technology transfer, fellowships and field demonstrations.

(d) Capacity-building

11.39. National Governments, in collaboration with appropriate international organizations and institutions, should develop the necessary capacity for implementing this programme area. This should be harmonized with capacity-building for other programme areas. Capacity-building should cover such aspects as policies, public administration, national-level institutions, human resource and skill development, research capability, technology development, information systems, programme evaluation, intersectoral coordination and international cooperation.

(e) Funding of international and regional cooperation

11.40. The secretariat of the Conference has estimated the average total annual cost (1993-2000) of implementing the activities of this programme to be about $750 million, including about $530 million from the international community on grant or concessional terms. These are indicative and order-of-magnitude estimates only and have not been reviewed by Governments. Actual costs and financial terms, including any that are non-concessional, will depend upon, *inter alia*, the specific strategies and programmes Governments decide upon for implementation.[5]

---

5   Draft paragraph 11.52 of A/CONF.151/4 (22 April 1992) was replaced here as paragraph 11.40 by decision of the Main Committee of UNCED on 10 June 1992. See A/CONF.151/L.3/Add.11 (11 June 1992). The former draft read as follows:

Funding of international and regional cooperation. The estimated investment required annually to implement international and regional cooperation is estimated at about $ 750 million, for the period 1993-2000. Nearly 70 per cent of the required financing would come from international sources. The amount of international financing required annually has been estimated to be $ 530 million of which $ 430 million are related to accelerating development; $ 80 million for global environmental issues and $ 20 million for strengthening the capacity of international organizations.

Chapter 12

Managing Fragile Ecosystems: Combating Desertification and Drought

INTRODUCTION

12.1. Fragile ecosystems are important ecosystems, with unique features and resources. Fragile ecosystems include deserts, semi-arid lands, mountains, wetlands, small islands and certain coastal areas. Most of these ecosystems are regional in scope, as they transcend national boundaries. This chapter addresses land resource issues in deserts, as well as arid, semi-arid and dry sub-humid areas. Sustainable mountain development is addressed in Chapter 13; small islands and coastal areas are discussed in Chapter 17.

12.2. Desertification is land degradation in arid, semi-arid and dry sub-humid areas resulting from various factors, including climatic variations and human activities. Desertification affects about one sixth of the world's population, 70 per cent of all drylands, amounting to 3.6 billion hectares, and one quarter of the total land area of the world. The most obvious impact of desertification, in addition to widespread poverty, is the degradation of 3.3 billion hectares of the total area of rangeland, constituting 73 per cent of the rangeland with a low potential for human and animal carrying capacity; decline in soil fertility and soil structure on about 47 per cent of the dryland areas constituting marginal rainfed cropland; and the degradation of irrigated cropland, amounting to 30 per cent of the dryland areas with a high population density and agricultural potential.

12.3. The priority in combating desertification should be the implementation of preventive measures for lands that are not yet degraded, or which are only slightly degraded. However, the severely degraded areas should not be neglected. In combating desertification and drought, the participation of local communities, rural organizations, national Governments, non-governmental organizations and international and regional organizations is essential.

12.4. The following programme areas are included in this chapter:

(a) Strengthening the knowledge base and developing information and monitoring systems for regions prone to desertification and drought, including the economic and social aspects of these ecosystems;

(b) Combating land degradation through, *inter alia*, intensified soil conservation, afforestation and reforestation activities;

(c) Developing and strengthening integrated development programmes for the eradication of poverty and promotion of alternative livelihood systems in areas prone to desertification;

(d) Developing comprehensive anti-desertification programmes and integrating them into national development plans and national environmental planning;

(e) Developing comprehensive drought preparedness and drought-relief schemes, including self-help arrangements, for drought-prone areas and designing programmes to cope with environmental refugees;

(f) Encouraging and promoting popular participation and environmental education, focusing on desertification control and management of the effects of drought.

PROGRAMME AREAS

A. Strengthening the knowledge base and developing information and monitoring systems for regions prone to desertification and drought, including the economic and social aspects of these ecosystems

Basis for action

12.5. The global assessments of the status and rate of desertification conducted by the United Nations Environment Programme (UNEP) in 1977, 1984 and 1991 have revealed insufficient basic knowledge of desertification processes. Adequate world-wide systematic observation systems are helpful for the development and implementation of effective anti-desertification programmes. The capacity of existing international, regional and national institutions, particularly in developing countries, to generate and exchange relevant information is limited. An integrated and coordinated information and systematic observation system based on appropriate technology and embracing global, regional, national and local levels is essential for understanding the dynamics of desertification and drought processes. It is also important for developing adequate measures to deal with desertification and drought and improving socio-economic conditions.

Objectives

12.6. The objectives of this programme area are:

(a) To promote establishment and/or strengthening of national environmental information coordination centres that will act as focal points within Governments for sectoral ministries and provide the necessary standardization and back-up services; to ensure also that national environmental information systems on desertification and drought are linked together through a network at subregional, regional and interregional levels;

(b) To strengthen regional and global systematic observation networks linked to the development of national systems for the observation of land degradation and desertification caused both by climate fluctuations and by human impact, and to identify priority areas for action;

(c) To establish a permanent system at both national and international levels for monitoring desertification and land degradation with the aim of improving living conditions in the affected areas.

Activities

(a) Management-related activities

12.7. Governments at the appropriate level, with the support of the relevant international and regional organizations, should:

(a) Establish and/or strengthen environmental information systems at the national level;

(b) Strengthen national, state/provincial and local assessment and ensure co-operation/networking between existing environmental information and monitoring systems, such as Earthwatch and the Sahara and Sahel Observatory;

(c) Strengthen the capacity of national institutions to analyse environmental data so that ecological change can be monitored and environmental information obtained on a continuing basis at the national level.

(b) Data and information

12.8. Governments at the appropriate level, with the support of the relevant international and regional organizations, should:

(a) Review and study the means for measuring the ecological, economic and social consequences of desertification and land degradation and introduce the results of these studies internationally into desertification and land degradation assessment practices;

(b) Review and study the interactions between the socio-economic impacts of climate, drought and desertification and utilize the results of these studies to secure concrete action.

12.9. Governments at the appropriate level, with the support of the relevant international and regional organizations, should:

(a) Support the integrated data collection and research work of programmes related to desertification and drought problems;

(b) Support national, regional and global programmes for integrated data collection and research networks carrying out assessment of soil and land degradation;

(c) Strengthen national and regional meteorological and hydrological networks and monitoring systems to ensure adequate collection of basic information and communication among national, regional and international centres.

(c) International and regional cooperation and coordination

12.10. Governments at the appropriate level, with the support of the relevant international and regional organizations, should:

(a) Strengthen regional programmes and international cooperation, such as the Permanent Inter-State Committee on Drought Control in the Sahel (CILSS), the Intergovernmental Authority for Drought and Development (IGADD), the Southern African Development Coordination Conference (SADCC), the Arab Maghreb Union and other regional organizations, as well as such organizations as the Sahara and Sahel Observatory;

(b) Establish and/or develop a comprehensive desertification, land degradation and human condition database component that incorporates both physical and socio-economic parameters. This should be based on existing and, where necessary, additional facilities, such as those of Earthwatch and other information systems of international, regional and national institutions strengthened for this purpose;

(c) Determine benchmarks and define indicators of progress that facilitate the work of local and regional organizations in tracking progress in the fight for anti-desertification. Particular attention should be paid to indicators of local participation.

Means of implementation

(a) Financing and cost evaluation

12.11 The Conference secretariat has estimated the average total annual cost (1993-2000) of implementing the activities of this programme to be about $350 million, including about $175 million from the international community on grant or concessional terms. These are indicative and order-of-magnitude estimates only and have not been reviewed by Governments. Actual costs and financial terms, including any that are non-concessional, will depend upon, *inter alia*, the specific strategies and programmes Governments decide upon for implementation.[1]

---

1   Draft paragraph 12.11 of A/CONF.151/4 (22 April 1992) was replaced by decision of the Main Committee of UNCED on 10 June 1992. See A/CONF.151/L.3/Add.12 (12 June 1992). The former draft read as follows:

> The total financing required to implement this programme area is about $350 million a year, while the average annual financing required from international sources is about $175 million. From this international figure, the average annual costs related to accelerated development would be about $165 million and the costs for strengthening the capacity of international institutions would be about $10 million a year.

(b) Scientific and technological means

12.12. Governments at the appropriate level, with the support of the relevant international and regional organizations working on the issue of desertification and drought, should:

(a) Undertake and update existing inventories of natural resources, such as energy, water, soil, minerals, plant and animal access to food, as well as other resources, such as housing, employment, health, education and demographic distribution in time and space;

(b) Develop integrated information systems for environmental monitoring, accounting and impact assessment;

(c) International bodies should cooperate with national Governments to facilitate the acquisition and development of appropriate technology for monitoring and combating drought and desertification.

(c) Human resource development

12.13. Governments at the appropriate level, with the support of the relevant international and regional organizations working on the issue of desertification and drought, should develop the technical and professional skills of people engaged in monitoring and assessing the issue of desertification and drought.

(d) Capacity-building

12.14. Governments at the appropriate level, with the support of the relevant international and regional organizations working on the issue of desertification and drought, should:

(a) Strengthen national and local institutions by providing adequate staff equipment and finance for assessing desertification;

(b) Promote the involvement of the local population, particularly women and youth, in the collection and utilization of environmental information through education and awareness-building.

B. Combating land degradation through, *inter alia*, intensified soil conservation, afforestation and reforestation activities

Basis for action

12.15. Desertification affects about 3.6 billion hectares, which is about 70 per cent of the total area of the world's drylands or nearly one quarter of the global land area. In combating desertification on rangeland, rainfed cropland and irrigated land, preventative measures should be launched in areas which are not yet affected or are only slightly affected by desertification; corrective measures should be implemented to sustain the productivity of moderately desertified land; and rehabilitative measures should be taken to recover severely or very severely desertified drylands.

12.16. An increasing vegetation cover would promote and stabilize the hydrological balance in the dryland areas and maintain land quality and land productivity. Prevention of not yet degraded land and application of corrective measures and rehabilitation of moderate and severely degraded drylands, including areas affected by sand dune movements, through the introduction of environmentally sound, socially acceptable, fair and economically feasible land-use systems. This will enhance the land carrying capacity and maintenance of biotic resources in fragile ecosystems.

Objectives

12.17. The objectives of this programme area are:

(a) As regards areas not yet affected or only slightly affected by desertification, to ensure appropriate management of existing natural formations (including forests) for the conservation of biodiversity, watershed protection, sustainability of their production and agricultural development, and other purposes, with the full participation of indigenous people;

(b) To rehabilitate moderately to severely desertified drylands for productive utilization and sustain their productivity for agropastoral/agroforestry development through, *inter alia*, soil and water conservation;

(c) To increase the vegetation cover and support management of biotic resources in regions affected or prone to desertification and drought, notably through such activities as afforestation/reforestation, agroforestry, community forestry and vegetation retention schemes;

(d) To improve management of forest resources, including woodfuel, and to reduce woodfuel consumption through more efficient utilization, conservation and the enhancement, development and use of other sources of energy, including alternative sources of energy.

Activities

(a) Management-related activities

12.18. Governments at the appropriate level, and with the support of the relevant international and regional organizations, should:

(a) Implement urgent direct preventive measures in drylands that are vulnerable but not yet affected, or only slightly desertified drylands, by introducing (i) improved land-use policies and practices for more sustainable land productivity; (ii) appropriate, environmentally sound and economically feasible agricultural and pastoral technologies; and (iii) improved management of soil and water resources;

(b) Carry out accelerated afforestation and reforestation programmes, using drought-resistant, fast-growing species, in particular native ones, including legumes and other species, combined with community-based agroforestry schemes. In this regard, creation of large-scale reforestation and afforestation schemes, particularly through the establishment of green belts, should be considered, bearing in mind the multiple benefits of such measures.

(c) Implement urgent direct corrective measures in moderately to severely desertified drylands, in addition to the measures listed in paragraph 19 (a) above, with a view to restoring and sustaining their productivity;

(d) Promote improved land/water/crop-management systems, making it possible to combat salinization in existing irrigated croplands; and to stabilize rainfed croplands and introduce improved soil/crop-management systems into land-use practice;

(e) Promote participatory management of natural resources, including rangeland, to meet both the needs of rural populations and conservation purposes, based on innovative or adapted indigenous technologies;

(f) Promote *in situ* protection and conservation of special ecological areas through legislation and other means for the purpose of combating desertification while ensuring the protection of biodiversity;

(g) Promote and encourage investment in forestry development in drylands through various incentives, including legislative measures;

(h) Promote the development and use of sources of energy which will lessen pressure on ligneous resources, including alternative sources of energy and improved stoves.

(b) Data and information

12.19. Governments at the appropriate level, with the support of the relevant international and regional organizations, should:

(a) Develop land-use models based on local practices for the improvement of such practices, with a focus on preventing land degradation. The models should give a better understanding of the variety of natural and human-induced factors that may contribute to desertification. Models should incorporate the interaction of both new and traditional practices to prevent land degradation and reflect the resilience of the whole ecological and social system;

(b) Develop, test and introduce, with due regard to environmental security considerations, drought resistant, fast-growing and productive plant species appropriate to the environment of the regions concerned.

(c) International and regional cooperation and coordination

12.20. The appropriate United Nations agencies, international and regional organizations, non-governmental organizations and bilateral agencies should:

(a) Coordinate their roles in combating land degradation and promoting reforestation, agroforestry and land-management systems in affected countries;

(b) Support regional and subregional activities in technology development and dissemination, training and programme implementation to arrest dryland degradation.

12.21. The national Governments concerned, the appropriate United Nations agencies and bilateral agencies should strengthen the coordinating role in dryland degradation of subregional intergovernmental organizations set up to cover these activities, such as CILSS, IGADD, SADCC and the Arab Maghreb Union.

Means of implementation

(a) Financing and cost-evaluation

12.22. The Conference secretariat has estimated the average total annual cost (1993-2000) of implementing the activities of this programme to be about $6 billion, including about $3 billion from the international community on grant or concessional terms. These are indicative and order-of-magnitude estimates only and have not been reviewed by Governments. Actual costs and financial terms, including any that are non-concessional, will depend upon, *inter alia*, the specific strategies and programmes Governments decide upon for implementation. From this international figure, costs related to accelerated development would be about $2.6 billion a year, the requirements for global environmental issues would be about $370 million a year, and the amount for strengthening the capacity of international institutions would be about $30 million a year.[2]

(b) Scientific and technological means

12.23. Governments at the appropriate level and local communities, with the support of the relevant international and regional organizations, should:

(a) Integrate indigenous knowledge related to forests, forest lands, rangeland and natural vegetation into research activities on desertification and drought;

(b) Promote integrated research programmes on the protection, restoration and conservation of water and land resources and land-use management based on traditional approaches, where feasible.

---

2   Draft paragraph 12.22 of A/CONF.151/4 (22 April 1992) was replaced by decision of the Main Committee of UNCED on 10 June 1992. See A/CONF.151/L.3/Add.12 (12 June 1992). The former draft read as follows:

    The total financing required to implement this programme area in developing countries is about $6 billion a year, while the average annual financing required from international sources is about $3 billion.

(c) Human resource development

12.24. Governments at the appropriate level and local communities, with the support of the relevant international and regional organizations, should:

(a) Establish mechanisms to ensure that land users, particularly women, are the main actors in implementing improved land use, including agroforestry systems, in combating land degradation;

(b) Promote efficient extension-service facilities in areas prone to desertification and drought, particularly for training farmers and pastoralists in the improved management of land and water resources in drylands.

(d) Capacity-building

12.25. Governments at the appropriate level and local communities, with the support of the relevant international and regional organizations, should:

(a) Develop and adopt, through appropriate national legislation, and introduce institutionally, new and environmentally sound development-oriented land-use policies;

(b) Support community-based people's organizations, especially farmers and pastoralists.

C. Developing and strengthening integrated development programmes for the eradication of poverty and promotion of alternative livelihood systems in areas prone to desertification

Basis for action

12.26. In areas prone to desertification and drought, current livelihood and resource-use systems are not able to maintain living standards. In most of the arid and semi-arid areas, the traditional livelihood systems based on agropastoral systems are often inadequate and unsustainable, particularly in view of the effects of drought and increasing demographic pressure. Poverty is a major factor in accelerating the rate of degradation and desertification. Action is therefore needed to rehabilitate and improve the agropastoral systems for sustainable management of rangelands, as well as alternative livelihood systems.

Objectives

12.27. The objectives of this programme area are:

(a) To create the capacity of village communities and pastoral groups to take charge of their development and the management of their land resources on a socially equitable and ecologically sound basis;

(b) To improve production systems in order to achieve greater productivity within approved programmes for conservation of national resources and in the framework of an integrated approach to rural development;

(c) To provide opportunities for alternative livelihoods as a basis for reducing pressure on land resources while at the same time providing additional sources of income, particularly for rural populations, thereby improving their standard of living.

Activities

(a) Management-related activities

12.28. Governments at the appropriate level, with the support of the relevant international and regional organizations, should:

(a) Adopt policies at the national level regarding a decentralized approach to land-resource management, delegating responsibility to rural organizations;

(b) Create or strengthen rural organizations in charge of village and pastoral land management;

(c) Establish and develop local, national and intersectoral mechanisms to handle environmental and developmental consequences of land tenure expressed in terms of land use and land ownership. Particular attention should be given to protecting the property rights of women and pastoral and nomadic groups living in rural areas;

(d) Create or strengthen village associations focused on economic activities of common pastoral interest (market gardening, transformation of agricultural products, livestock, herding, etc.);

(e) Promote rural credit and mobilization of rural savings through the establishment of rural banking systems;

(f) Develop infrastructure, as well as local production and marketing capacity, by involving the local people to promote alternative livelihood systems and alleviate poverty;

(g) Establish a revolving fund for credit to rural entrepreneurs and local groups to facilitate the establishment of cottage industries/business ventures and credit for input to agropastoral activities.

(b) Data and information

12.29. Governments at the appropriate level, with the support of the relevant international and regional organizations, should:

(a) Conduct socio-economic baseline studies in order to have a good understanding of the situation in the programme area regarding, particularly, resource and land tenure issues, traditional land-management practices and characteristics of production systems;

(b) Conduct inventory of natural resources (soil, water and vegetation) and their state of degradation, based primarily on the knowledge of the local population (e.g., rapid rural appraisal);

(c) Disseminate information on technical packages adapted to the social, economic and ecological conditions of each;

(d) Promote exchange and sharing of information concerning the development of alternative livelihoods with other agro-ecological regions.

(c) International and regional cooperation and coordination

12.30. Governments at the appropriate level and with the support of the relevant international and regional organizations should:

(a) Promote cooperation and exchange of information among the arid and semi-arid land research institutions concerning techniques and technologies to improve land and labour productivity, as well as viable production systems;

(b) Coordinate and harmonize the implementation of programmes and projects funded by the international organization communities and non-governmental organizations that are directed towards the alleviation of poverty and promotion of an alternative livelihood system.

Means of implementation

(a) Financing and cost evaluation

12.31. The Conference secretariat has estimated the costs for this programme area in chapter 3 (Combatting poverty) and chapter 14 (Promoting sustainable agricultural and rural development).[3]

(b) Scientific and technological means

12.32. Governments at the appropriate level, and with the support of the relevant international and regional organizations, should:

(a) Undertake applied research in land use with the support of local research institutions;

(b) Facilitate regular national, regional and interregional communication on and exchange of information and experience between extension officers and researchers;

(c) Support and encourage the introduction and use of technologies for the generation of alternative sources of incomes.

---

3   Draft paragraph 12.31 of A/CONF.151/4 (22 April 1992) was replaced by decision of the Main Committee of UNCED on 10 June 1992. See A/CONF.151/L.3/Add.12 (12 June 1992). The former draft read as follows:

The total financing required for these programme areas is about $3 billion a year, while the average annual financing required from international sources is about $1.5 billion.

(c) Human resource development

12.33. Governments at the appropriate level, with the support of the relevant international and regional organizations, should:

(a) Train members of rural organizations in management skills and train agropastoralists in such special techniques as soil and water conservation, water harvesting, agroforestry and small-scale irrigation;

(b) Train extension agents and officers in the participatory approach to integrated land management.

(d) Capacity-building

12.34. Governments at the appropriate level, with the support of the relevant international and regional organizations, should establish and maintain mechanisms to ensure the integration into sectoral and national development plans and programmes of strategies for poverty alleviation among the inhabitants of lands prone to desertification.

D. Developing comprehensive anti-desertification programmes and integrating them into national development plans and national environmental planning

Basis for action

12.35. In a number of developing countries affected by desertification, the natural resource base is the main resource upon which the development process must rely. The social systems interacting with land resources make the problem much more complex, requiring an integrated approach to the planning and management of land resources. Action plans to combat desertification and drought should include management aspects of the environment and development, thus conforming with the approach of integrating national development plans and national environmental action plans.

Objectives

12.36. The objectives of this programme area are:

(a) To strengthen national institutional capabilities to develop appropriate anti-desertification programmes and to integrate them into national development planning;

(b) To develop and integrate strategic planning frameworks for the development, protection and management of natural resources in dryland areas into national development plans, including national plans to combat desertification, and environmental action plans in countries most prone to desertification;

(c) To initiate a long-term process for implementing and monitoring strategies related to natural resources management;

(d) To strengthen regional and international cooperation for combating desertification through, *inter alia*, the adoption of legal and other instruments.[4]

Activities

(a) Management-related activities

12.37. Governments at the appropriate level and with the support of the relevant international and regional organizations should:

(a) Establish or strengthen, national and local anti-desertification authorities within government and local executive bodies, as well as local committees/associations of land users, in all rural communities affected, with a view to organizing working cooperation between all actors concerned, from the grass-roots level (farmers and pastoralists) to the higher levels of government;

(b) Develop national plans of action to combat desertification and as appropriate, make them integral parts of national development plans and national environmental action plans;

(c) Implement policies directed towards improving land use, managing common lands appropriately, providing incentives to small farmers and pastoralists, involving women and encouraging private investment in the development of drylands;

(d) Ensure coordination among ministries and institutions working on anti-desertification programmes at national and local levels.

(b) Data and information

12.38. Governments at the appropriate level, with the support of the relevant international and regional organizations, should promote information exchange and cooperation with respect to national planning and programming among affected countries, *inter alia*, through networking.

(c) International and regional cooperation and coordination

12.39. The relevant international organizations, multilateral financial institutions, non-governmental organizations and bilateral agencies should strengthen their cooperation in assisting with the preparation of desertification control programmes and their integration into national planning strategies, with the establishment of national coordinating and systematic observation mechanisms and with the regional and global networking of these plans and mechanisms.

---

4   Draft paragraph 12.36(d) of A/CONF.151/4 (22 April 1992) included brackets around the words "through, *inter alia*, the adoption of legal and other instruments." The brackets were deleted by decision of the Main Committee of UNCED on 10 June 1992. See A/CONF.151/L.3/Add.12 (12 June 1992).

12.40. The General Assembly, at its forty-seventh session, should be requested to establish, under the aegis of the General Assembly, an intergovernmental negotiating committee for the elaboration of an international convention to combat desertification, in in those countries experiencing serious drought and/or desertification, particularly in Africa, with a view to finalizing such a convention by June 1994.[5]

Means of implementation

(a) Financing and cost evaluation

12.41. The Conference secretariat has estimated the average total annual cost (1993-2000) of implementing the activities of this programme to be about $180 million, including about $90 million from the international community on grant or concessional terms. These are indicative and order-of-magnitude estimates only and have not been reviewed by Governments. Actual costs and financial terms, including any that are non-concessional, will depend upon, *inter alia*, the specific strategies and programmes Governments decide upon for implementation.[6]

(b) Scientific and technological means

12.42. Governments at the appropriate level, with the support of the relevant international and regional organizations, should:

(a) Develop and introduce appropriate improved sustainable agricultural and pastoral technologies that are socially and environmentally acceptable and economically feasible;

(b) Undertake applied study on the integration of environmental and developmental activities into national development plans.

---

5   Draft paragraph 12.40 of A/CONF.151/4 (22 April 1992) was replaced by decision of the Main Committee of UNCED on 10 June 1992. See A/CONF.151/L.3/Add.12 (12 June 1992). The former draft read as follows:

    Governments, intergovernmental organizations, relevant non-governmental organizations, and the scientific community should improve and strengthen international cooperation and solidarity in the fight against desertification through the preparation and adoption of an international convention to combat desertification in all affected areas of the world, particularly in Africa. This convention should contain concrete and specific commitments from the participating parties (both the countries affected by desertification and other countries parties to the convention) and should take into account the needs of Governments as well as of populations affected by desertification. It is proposed that the servicing of the mechanism that will be set up for the preparation of that convention could be entrusted to the United Nations Sudano-Sahelian Office, thereby benefiting from the experience gained by that organization in desertification control activities.

6   Draft paragraph 12.41 of A/CONF.151/4 (22 April 1992) was replaced by decision of the Main Committee of UNCED on 10 June 1992. See A/CONF.151/L.3/Add.12 (12 June 1992). The former draft read as follows:

    The total financing required to implement this programme area is about $180 million a year, while the average annual financing required from international sources is about $90 million. Of this latter figure, costs related to accelerated development would amount to about $80 million a year, and costs for strengthening the capacity of international institutions would be about $10 million a year.

(c) Human resource development

12.43. Governments at the appropriate level, with the support of the relevant international and regional organizations, should undertake nationwide major anti-desertification awareness/training campaigns within countries affected through existing national mass media facilities, educational networks and newly created or strengthened extension services. This should ensure people's access to knowledge of desertification and drought and to national plans of action to combat desertification.

(d) Capacity-building

12.44. Governments at the appropriate level, with the support of the relevant international and regional organizations, should establish and maintain mechanisms to ensure coordination of sectoral ministries and institutions, including local-level institutions and appropriate non-governmental organizations, in integrating anti-desertification programmes into national development plans and national environmental action plans.

E. Developing comprehensive drought preparedness and drought-relief schemes, including self-help arrangements, for drought-prone areas and designing programmes to cope with environmental refugees

Basis for action

12.45. Drought, in differing degrees of frequency and severity, is a recurring phenomenon throughout much of the developing world, especially Africa. Apart from the human toll—an estimated 3 million people died in the mid-1980s because of drought in sub-Saharan Africa—the economic costs of drought-related disasters are also high in terms of lost production, misused inputs and diversion of development resources.

12.46. Early-warning systems to forecast drought will make possible the implementation of drought-preparedness schemes. Integrated packages at the farm and watershed level, such as alternative cropping strategies, soil and water conservation and promotion of water harvesting techniques, could enhance the capacity of land to cope with drought and provide basic necessities, thereby minimizing the number of environmental refugees and the need for emergency drought relief. At the same time, contingency arrangements for relief are needed for periods of acute scarcity.

Objectives

12.47. The objectives of this programme area are:

(a) To develop national strategies for drought preparedness in both the short and long term, aimed at reducing the vulnerability of production systems to drought;

(b) To strengthen the flow of early-warning information to decision makers and land users to enable nations to implement strategies for drought intervention;

(c) To develop and integrate drought-relief schemes and means of coping with environmental refugees into national and regional development planning.

Activities

(a) Management-related activities

12.48. In drought-prone areas, Governments at the appropriate level, with the support of the relevant international and regional organizations, should:

(a) Design strategies to deal with national food deficiencies in periods of production shortfall. These strategies should deal with issues of storage and stocks, imports, port facilities, food storage, transport and distribution;

(b) Improve national and regional capacity for agrometeorology and contingency crop planning. Agrometeorology links the frequency, content and regional coverage of weather forecasts with the requirements of crop planning and agricultural extension;

(c) Prepare rural projects for providing short-term rural employment to drought-affected households. The loss of income and entitlement to food is a common source of distress in times of drought. Rural works help to generate the income required to buy food for poor households;

(d) Establish contingency arrangements, where necessary, for food and fodder distribution and water supply;

(e) Establish budgetary mechanisms for providing, at short notice, resources for drought relief;

(f) Establish safety nets for the most vulnerable households.

(b) Data and information

12.49. Governments of affected countries, at the appropriate level, with the support of the relevant international and regional organizations, should:

(a) Implement research on seasonal forecasts to improve contingency planning and relief operations and allow preventive measures to be taken at the farm level, such as the selection of appropriate varieties and farming practices, in times of drought;

(b) Support applied research on ways of reducing water loss from soils, on ways of increasing the water absorption capacities of soils and on water harvesting techniques in drought-prone areas;

(c) Strengthen national early-warning systems, with particular emphasis on the area of risk-mapping, remote-sensing, agrometeorological modelling, integrated multidisciplinary crop-forecasting techniques and computerized food supply/demand analysis.

(c) International and regional cooperation and coordination

12.50. Governments at the appropriate level, with the support of the relevant international and regional organizations, should:

(a) Establish a system of stand-by capacities in terms of foodstock, logistical support, personnel and finance for a speedy international response to drought-related emergencies;

(b) Support programmes of the World Meteorological Organization (WMO) on agrohydrology and agrometeorology, the Programme of the Regional Training Centre for Agrometeorology and Operational Hydrology and their Applications (AGRHYMET), drought-monitoring centres and the African Centre of Meteorological Applications for Development (ACMAD), as well as the efforts of the Permanent Inter-State Committee on Drought Control in the Sahel (CILSS) and the Intergovernmental Authority for Drought and Development (IGADD);

(c) Support FAO [Food and Agricultural Organization] programmes and other programmes for the development of national early-warning systems and food security assistance schemes;

(d) Strengthen and expand the scope of existing regional programmes and the activities of appropriate United Nations organs and organizations, such as the World Food Programme (WFP), the Office of the United Nations Disaster Relief Coordinator (UNDRO) and the United Nations Sudano-Sahelian Office as well as of non-governmental organizations, aimed at mitigating the effects of drought and emergencies.

Means of implementation

(a) Financing and cost evaluation

12.51. The Conference secretariat has estimated the average total annual cost (1993-2000) of implementing the activities of this programme to be about $1.2 billion, including about $1.1 billion from the international community on grant or concessional terms. These are indicative and order-of-magnitude estimates only and have not been reviewed by Governments. Actual costs and financial terms, including any that are non-concessional, will depend upon,

inter alia, the specific strategies and programmes Governments decide upon for implementation.[7]

(b) Scientific and technological means

12.52. Governments at the appropriate level and drought-prone communities, with the support of the relevant international and regional organizations, should:

(a) Use traditional mechanisms to cope with hunger as a means of channelling relief and development assistance;

(b) Strengthen and develop national, regional and local interdisciplinary research and training capabilities for drought-prevention strategies.

(c) Human resource development

12.53. Governments at the appropriate level, with the support of the relevant international and regional organizations, should:

(a) Promote the training of decision makers and land users in the effective utilization of information from early-warning systems;

(b) Strengthen research and national training capabilities to assess the impact of drought and to develop methodologies to forecast drought.

(d) Capacity-building

12.54. Governments at the appropriate level, with the support of the relevant international and regional organizations, should:

(a) Improve and maintain mechanisms with adequate staff, equipment and finances for monitoring drought parameters to take preventive measures at regional, national and local levels;

(b) Establish interministerial linkages and coordinating units for drought monitoring, impact assessment and management of drought-relief schemes.

---

7   Draft paragraph 12.51 of A/CONF.151/4 (22 April 1992) was replaced by decision of the Main Committee of UNCED on 10 June 1992. See A/CONF.151/L.3/Add.12 (12 June 1992). The former draft read as follows:

This programme area requires two sets of cost-evaluations. The first set deals with developing drought-preparedness and drought-relief schemes, the total cost of which is about $200 million a year, the average annual financing required from international sources amounting to about $100 million. From this international figure, costs related to accelerated development would be about $90 million a year and the amount for strengthening the capacity of international institutions would be about $10 million a year. The second set deals with the cost required to cope with environmental refugees displaced from their homes by emergencies such as drought, among other natural disasters. The international financing required to cope with such emergencies is about $1 billion a year.

F. Encouraging and promoting popular participation and environmental education, focusing on desertification control and management of the effects of drought

Basis for action

12.55. The experience to date on the successes and failures of programmes and projects points to the need for popular support to sustain activities related to desertification and drought control. But it is necessary to go beyond the theoretical ideal of popular participation and to focus on obtaining actual active popular involvement, rooted in the concept of partnership. This implies the sharing of responsibilities and the mutual involvement of all parties. In this context, this programme area should be considered an essential supporting component of all desertification-control and drought-related activities.

Objectives

12.56. The objectives of this programme area are:

(a) To develop and increase public awareness and knowledge concerning desertification and drought, including the integration of environmental education in the curriculum of primary and secondary schools;

(b) To establish and promote true partnership between government authorities, at both the national and local levels, other executing agencies, non-governmental organizations and land users stricken by drought and desertification, giving land users a responsible role in the planning and execution processes in order to benefit fully from development projects;

(c) To ensure that the partners understand one another's needs, objectives and points of view by providing a variety of means such as training, public awareness and open dialogue;

(d) To support local communities in their own efforts in combating desertification, and to draw on the knowledge and experience of the populations concerned, ensuring the full participation of women and indigenous populations.

Activities

(a) Management-related activities

12.57. Governments at the appropriate level, with the support of the relevant international and regional organizations, should:

(a) Adopt policies and establish administrative structures for more decentralized decision-making and implementation;

(b) Establish and utilize mechanisms for the consultation and involvement of land users and for enhancing capability at the grass-roots level to identify and/or contribute to the identification and planning of action;

(c) Define specific programme/project objectives in cooperation with local communities; design local management plans to include such measures of progress, thereby providing a means of altering project design or changing management practices, as appropriate;

(d) Introduce legislative, institutional/organizational and financial measures to secure user involvement and access to land resources;

(e) Establish and/or expand favourable conditions for the provision of services, such as credit facilities and marketing outlets for rural populations;

(f) Develop training programmes to increase the level of education and participation of people, particularly women and indigenous groups, through, inter alia, literacy and the development of technical skills;

(g) Create rural banking systems to facilitate access to credit for rural populations, particularly women and indigenous groups, and to promote rural savings;

(h) Adopt appropriate policies to stimulate private and public investment.

(b) Data and information

12.58. Governments at the appropriate level, with the support of the relevant international and regional organizations, should:

(a) Review, develop and disseminate gender-disaggregated information, skills and know-how at all levels on ways of organizing and promoting popular participation;

(b) Accelerate the development of technological know-how, focusing on appropriate and intermediate technology;

(c) Disseminate knowledge about applied research results on soil and water issues, appropriate species, agricultural techniques and technological know-how.

(c) International and regional cooperation and coordination

12.59. Governments at the appropriate level, with the support of the relevant international and regional organizations, should:

(a) Develop programmes of support to regional organizations such as CILSS, IGADD, SADCC and the Arab Maghreb Union and other intergovernmental organizations in Africa and other parts of the world, to strengthen outreach programmes and increase the participation of non-governmental organizations together with rural populations;

(b) Develop mechanisms for facilitating cooperation in technology and promote such cooperation as an element of all external assistance and activities related to technical assistance projects in the public or private sector;

(c) Promote collaboration among different actors in environment and development programmes;

(d) Encourage the emergence of representative organizational structures to foster and sustain interorganizational cooperation.

Means of implementation

(a) Financing and cost evaluation

12.60. The Conference secretariat has estimated the average total annual cost (1993-2000) of implementing the activities of this programme to be about $1.0 billion, including about $500 million from the international community on grant or concessional terms. These are indicative and order-of-magnitude estimates only and have not been reviewed by Governments. Actual costs and financial terms, including any that are non-concessional, will depend upon, *inter alia*, the specific strategies and programmes Governments decide upon for implementation.

(b) Scientific and technological means

12.61. Governments, at the appropriate level, with the support of the relevant international and regional organizations, should promote the development of indigenous know-how and technology transfer.

(c) Human resource development

12.62. Governments, at the appropriate level, with the support of the relevant international and regional organizations, should:

(a) Support and/or strengthen institutions involved in public education, including the local media, schools and community groups;

(b) Increase the level of public education.

(d) Capacity-building

12.63. Governments at the appropriate level, with the support of the relevant international and regional organizations, should promote members of local rural organizations and train and appoint more extension officers working at the local level.[8]

---

8   A prior paragraph was present in the draft considered at UNCED, but deleted at the end of the UNCED as shown in the final text of Agenda 21, A/CONF. 151/26, vol. II, p. 61. Where two asterisks appeared in the draft, it indicated that those paragraphs contained matters relating to means of implementation, including cost estimates, which are indicative secretariat figures provided pursuant to decision A/CONF.151/PC/L.49**. Such texts remained in brackets until the end of UNCED as they had not been negotiated before.

Chapter 13

Managing Fragile Ecosystems: Sustainable Mountain Development

INTRODUCTION

13.1. Mountains are an important source of water, energy and biological diversity. Furthermore, they are a source of such key resources such as minerals, forest products and agricultural products and of recreation. As a major ecosystem representing the complex and interrelated ecology of our planet, mountain environments are essential to the survival of the global ecosystem. Mountain ecosystems are, however, rapidly changing. They are susceptible to accelerated soil erosion, landslides and rapid loss of habitat and genetic diversity. On the human side, there is widespread poverty among mountain inhabitants and loss of indigenous knowledge. As a result, most global mountain areas are experiencing environmental degradation. Hence, the proper management of mountain resources and socio-economic development of the people deserves immediate action.

13.2. About 10 per cent of the world's population depends on mountain resources. A much larger percentage draws on other mountain resources, including and especially water. Mountains are a storehouse of biological diversity and endangered species.

13.3. Two programme areas are included in this chapter to further elaborate the problem of fragile ecosystems with regard to all mountains of the world. These are:

(a) Generating and strengthening knowledge about the ecology and sustainable development of mountain ecosystems;

(b) Promoting integrated watershed development and alternative livelihood opportunities.

PROGRAMME AREAS

A. Generating and strengthening knowledge about the ecology and sustainable development of mountain ecosystems

Basis for action

13.4. Mountains are highly vulnerable to human and natural ecological imbalance. Mountains are the most sensitive areas to all climatic changes in the atmosphere. Specific information on ecology, natural resource potential and socio-economic activities is essential. Mountain and hillside areas hold a rich variety of ecological systems. Because of their vertical dimensions, mountains create gradients of temperature, precipitation and insolation. A given mountain slope may include several climatic systems—such as tropical, subtropical, temperate and alpine—each of which represents a microcosm of a larger habitat diversity. There is, however, a lack of knowledge of mountain ecosystems. The creation of a global mountain database is therefore vital for launching programmes that contribute to the sustainable development of mountain ecosystems.

Objectives

13.5. The objectives of this programme area are:

(a) To undertake a survey of the different forms of soils, forest, water use, crop, plant and animal resources of mountain ecosystems, taking into account the work of existing international and regional organizations;

(b) To maintain and generate database and information systems to facilitate the integrated management and environmental assessment of mountain ecosystems, taking into account the work of existing international and regional organizations;

(c) To improve and build the existing land/water ecological knowledge base regarding technologies and agricultural and conservation practices in the mountain regions of the world with the participation of local communities;

(d) To create and strengthen the communications network and information clearing-house for existing organizations concerned with mountain issues;

(e) To improve coordination of regional efforts to protect fragile mountain ecosystems through the consideration of appropriate mechanisms, including regional legal and other instruments;

(f) To generate information to establish database and information systems to facilitate an evaluation of environmental risks and natural disasters in mountain ecosystems.

Activities

(a) Management-related activities

13.6 Governments at the appropriate level, with the support of the relevant international and regional organizations, should:

(a) Strengthen existing institutions or establish new ones at local, national and regional levels to generate a multidisciplinary land/water ecological knowledge base on mountain ecosystems;

(b) Promote national policies that would provide incentives to local people for the use and transfer of environment-friendly technologies and farming and conservation practices;

(c) Build up the knowledge base and understanding by creating mechanisms for cooperation and information exchange among national and regional institutions working on fragile ecosystems;

(d) Encourage policies that would provide incentives to farmers and local people to undertake conservation and regenerative measures;

(e) Diversify mountain economies, *inter alia*, by creating and/or strengthening tourism, in accordance with integrated management of mountain areas;

(f) Integrate all forest, rangelands and wildlife activities in such a way that specific mountain ecosystems are maintained;

(g) Establish appropriate natural reserves in representative species-rich sites and areas.

(b) Data and information

13.7. Governments at the appropriate level, with the support of the relevant international and regional organizations, should:

(a) Maintain and establish meteorological, hydrological and physical monitoring analysis and capabilities that would encompass the climatic diversity as well as water distribution of various mountain regions of the world;

(b) Build an inventory of different forms of soils, forests, water use and crop, plant and animal genetic resources, giving priority to those under threat of extinction. Genetic resources should be protected *in situ* by maintaining and establishing protected areas and improving traditional farming and animal husbandry activities and establishing programmes for evaluating the potential value of the resources;

(c) Identify hazardous areas that are most vulnerable to erosion, floods, landslides, earthquakes, snow avalanches and other natural hazards;

(d) Identify mountain areas threatened by air pollution from neighbouring industrial and urban areas.

(c) International and regional cooperation

13.8. National Governments and international organizations should:

(a) Coordinate regional and international cooperation and facilitate an exchange of information and experience among the specialized agencies, the World Bank, IFAD [International Fund For Agricultural Development] and other international and regional organizations, national Governments, research institutions and non-governmental organizations working on mountain development;

(b) Encourage regional, national and international networking of people's initiatives and the activities of international, regional and local non-governmental organizations working on mountain development, such as the United Nations University (UNU), the Woodland Mountain Institutes (WMI), the International Center for Integrated Mountain Development (ICIMOD), the International Mountain Society (IMS), the African Mountain Association and the Andean Mountain Association, besides supporting those organizations in exchange of information and experience;

(c) Protect Fragile Mountain Ecosystem through the consideration of appropriate mechanisms including regional legal and other instruments.

Means of implementation

(a) Financing and cost evaluation

13.9. The Conference secretariat has estimated the average total annual cost (1993-2000) of implementing the activities of this programme to be about $50 million from the international community on grant or concessional terms. These are indicative and order-of-magnitude estimates only and have not been reviewed by Governments. Actual costs and financial terms, including any that are non-concessional, will depend upon, *inter alia*, the specific strategies and programmes Governments decide upon for implementation.[1]

(b) Scientific and technological means

13.10. Governments at the appropriate level, with the support of the relevant international and regional organizations, should strengthen scientific research and technological development programmes, including diffusion through national

---

1   Draft paragraph 13.9 of A/CONF.151/4 (22 April 1992) was replaced by decision of the Main Committee of UNCED on 10 June 1992. See A/CONF.151/L.3/Add.13 (13 June 1992). The former draft read as follows:

The total cost required to implement this programme area is about US$ 330 million a year, while the average annual financing required from international sources is about US$ 50 million. This includes US$ 40 million for technical cooperation and US$ 10 million for the strengthening of international institutions, particularly the United Nations Educational, Scientific and Cultural Organization, the United Nations University, the World Conservation Union (IUCN), the International Mountain Society (IMS), the Woodland Mountain Institutes (WMI) and the International Center for Integrated Mountain Development (ICIMOD), as well as the African Mountain Association and the Andean Mountain Association.

and regional institutions, particularly in meteorology, hydrology, forestry, soil sciences and plant sciences.

(c) Human resource development

13.11. Governments at the appropriate level, and with the support of the relevant international and regional organizations, should:

(a) Launch training and extension programmes in environmentally appropriate technologies and practices that would be suitable to mountain ecosystems;

(b) Support higher education through fellowships and research grants for environmental studies in mountains and hill areas, particularly for candidates from indigenous mountain populations;

(c) Undertake environmental education for farmers, in particular for women, to help the rural population better understand the ecological issues regarding the sustainable development of mountain ecosystems.

(d) Capacity-building

13.12. Governments at the appropriate level, with the support of the relevant international and regional organizations, should build up national and regional institutional bases that could carry research, training and dissemination of information on the sustainable development of the economies of fragile ecosystems.

B. Promoting integrated watershed development and alternative livelihood opportunities

Basis for action

13.13. Nearly half of the world's population is affected in various ways by mountain ecology and the degradation of watershed areas. About 10 per cent of the Earth's population lives in mountain areas with higher slopes, while about 40 per cent occupies the adjacent medium- and lower-watershed areas. There are serious problems of ecological deterioration in these watershed areas. For example, in the hillside areas of the Andean countries of South America a large portion of the farming population is now faced with a rapid deterioration of land resources. Similarly, the mountain and upland areas of the Himalayas, South-East Asia and East and Central Africa, which make vital contributions to agricultural production, are threatened by cultivation of marginal lands due to expanding population. In many areas this is accompanied by excessive livestock grazing, deforestation and loss of biomass cover.

13.14. Soil erosion can have a devastating impact on the vast numbers of rural people who depend on rainfed agriculture in the mountain and hillside areas. Poverty, unemployment, poor health and bad sanitation are widespread. Promoting integrated watershed development programmes through effective participation of local people is a key to preventing further ecological imbalance. An integrated approach is needed for conserving, upgrading and using the natural resource base of land, water, plant, animal and human resources. In addition, promoting alternative livelihood opportunities, particularly through development of employment schemes that increase the productive base, will have a significant role in improving the standard of living among the large rural population living in mountain ecosystems.

Objectives

13.15. The objectives of this programme area are:

(a) By the year 2000, to develop appropriate land-use planning and management for both arable and non-arable land in mountain-fed watershed areas to prevent soil erosion, increase biomass production and maintain the ecological balance;

(b) To promote income-generating activities, such as sustainable tourism, fisheries and environmentally sound mining, and to improve infrastructure and social services, in particular to protect the livelihoods of local communities and indigenous people;

(c) To develop technical and institutional arrangements for affected countries to mitigate the effects of natural disasters through hazard-prevention measures, risk zoning, early-warning systems, evacuation plans and emergency supplies.

Activities

(a) Management-related activities

13.16. Governments at the appropriate level, with the support of the relevant international and regional organizations, should:

(a) Undertake measures to prevent soil erosion and promote erosion-control activities in all sectors;

(b) Establish task forces or watershed development committees, complementing existing institutions, to coordinate integrated services to support local initiatives in animal husbandry, forestry, horticulture and rural development at all administrative levels;

(c) Enhance popular participation in the management of local resources through appropriate legislation;

(d) Support non-governmental organizations and other private groups assisting local organizations and communities in the preparation of projects that would enhance participatory development of local people;

(e) Provide mechanisms to preserve threatened areas that could protect wildlife, conserve biological diversity or serve as national parks;

(f) Develop national policies that would provide incentives to farmers and local people to undertake conservation measures and to use environment-friendly technologies;

(g) Undertake income-generating activities in cottage and agro-processing industries, such as the cultivation and processing of medicinal and aromatic plants;

(h) Undertake the above activities, taking into account the need for full participation of women, including indigenous people and local communities, in development.

(b) Data and information

13.17. Governments at the appropriate level, with the support of the relevant international and regional organizations, should:

(a) Maintain and establish systematic observation and evaluation capacities at the national, state or provincial level to generate information for daily operations and to assess the environmental and socio-economic impacts of projects;

(b) Generate data on alternative livelihoods and diversified production systems at the village level on annual and tree crops, livestock, poultry, beekeeping, fisheries, village industries, markets, transport and income-earning opportunities, taking fully into account the role of women and integrating them into the planning and implementation process.

(c) International and regional cooperation

13.18. Governments at the appropriate level, with the support of the relevant international and regional organizations, should:

(a) Strengthen the role of appropriate international research and training institutes such as the Consultative Group on International Agricultural Research Centers (CGIAR) and the International Board for Soil Research and Management (IBSRAM) as well as regional research centers, such as the Woodland Mountain Institutes and the International Center for Integrated Mountain Development, in undertaking applied research relevant to watershed development;

(b) Promote regional cooperation and exchange of data and information among countries sharing the same mountain ranges and river basins, particularly those affected by mountain disasters and floods;

(c) Maintain and establish partnerships with non-governmental organizations and other private groups working in watershed development.

Means of implementation

(a) Financial and cost evaluation

13.19. The Conference secretariat has estimated the average total annual cost (1993-2000) of implementing the activities of this programme to be about $13 billion, including about $1.9 billion from the international community on grant or concessional terms. These are indicative and order-of-magnitude estimates only and have not been reviewed by Governments. Actual costs and financial terms, including any that are non-concessional, will depend upon, *inter alia*, the specific strategies and programmes Governments decide upon for implementation.[2]

13.20. Financing for the promotion of alternative livelihoods in mountain ecosystems should be viewed as part of a country's anti-poverty or alternative livelihoods programme, which is also discussed in chapter 3 (Combating Poverty) and chapter 14 (Promoting sustainable agriculture and rural development) of Agenda 21.

(b) Scientific and technical means

13.21. Governments at the appropriate level, with the support of the relevant international and regional organizations, should:

(a) Consider undertaking pilot projects that combine environmental protection and development functions with particular emphasis on some of the traditional environmental management practices or systems that have a good impact on the environment;

(b) Generate technologies for specific watershed and farm conditions through a participatory approach involving local men and women, researchers and extension agents who will carry out experiments and trials on farm conditions;

(c) Promote technologies of vegetative conservation measures for erosion prevention, *in situ* moisture management, improved cropping technology, fodder production and agroforestry that are low-cost, simple and easily adopted by local people.

---

2   Draft paragraph 13.19 of A/CONF.151/4 (22 April 1992) was replaced by decision of the Main Committee of UNCED on 10 June 1992. See A/CONF.151/L.3/Add.13 (13 June 1992). The former draft read as follows:

       Total funding required to implement this programme area is about US$ 13 billion a year, mostly from national local and private sources. Of the US$ 13 billion about US$ 1.9 billion would be needed from international sources. About US$ 1.7 billion would be related to development and about US$ 1.7 billion could be ascribed to global environmental issues. About US$ 30 million is needed for strengthening the capacity of international institutions, in particular those involved in watershed development such as the United Nations Development Programme, the Food and Agriculture Organization of the United Nations and the World Bank.

(c) Human resource development

13.22. Governments at the appropriate level, with the support of the relevant international and regional organizations, should:

(a) Promote a multidisciplinary and cross-sectoral approach in training and the dissemination of knowledge to local people on a wide range of issues, such as household production systems, conservation and utilization of arable and non-arable land, treatment of drainage lines and recharging of groundwater, livestock management, fisheries, agroforestry and horticulture;

(b) Develop human resources by providing access to education, health, energy and infrastructure;

(c) Promote local awareness and preparedness for disaster prevention and mitigation combined with the latest available technology for early warning and forecasting.

(d) Capacity-building

13.23. Governments at the appropriate level, with the support of the relevant international and regional organizations, should develop and strengthen national centers for watershed management to encourage a comprehensive approach to the environmental, socio-economic, technological, legislative, financial and administrative aspects and provide support to policy makers, administrators, field staff and farmers for watershed development.

13.24. The private sector and local communities, in cooperation with national Governments, should promote local infrastructure development, including communication networks, mini- or micro-hydro development to support cottage industries, and access to markets.

Chapter 14

Promoting Sustainable Agriculture and Rural Development

INTRODUCTION

14.1. By the year 2025, 83 per cent of the expected global population of 8.5 billion will be living in developing countries. Yet the capacity of available resources and technologies to satisfy the demands of this growing population for food and other agricultural commodities remains uncertain. Agriculture has to meet this challenge, mainly by increasing production on land already in use and by avoiding further encroachment on land that is only marginally suitable for cultivation.

14.2. Major adjustments are needed in agricultural, environmental and macro-economic policy, at both national and international levels, in developed as well as developing countries, to create the conditions for sustainable agriculture and rural development (SARD). The major objective of SARD is to increase food production in a sustainable way and enhance food security. This will involve education initiatives, utilization of economic incentives and the development of appropriate and new technologies, thus ensuring stable supplies of nutritionally adequate food, access to those supplies by vulnerable groups and production for markets; employment and income generation to alleviate poverty; and natural resource management and environmental protection.

14.3 The priority must be on maintaining and improving the capacity of the higher potential agricultural lands to support an expanding population. However, conserving and rehabilitating the natural resources on lower potential lands in order to maintain sustainable man/land ratios is also necessary. The main tools of SARD are policy and agrarian reform, participation, income diversification, land conservation and improved management of inputs. The success of SARD will depend largely on the support and participation of rural people, national Governments, the private sector and international cooperation, including technical and scientific cooperation.

14.4. The following programme areas are included in this chapter:

(a) Agricultural policy review, planning and integrated programming in light of the multifunctional aspect of agriculture, particularly with regard to food security and sustainable development;

(b) Ensuring people's participation and promoting human resources development for sustainable agriculture;

(c) Improving farm production and farming systems through diversification of farm and non-farm employment and infrastructure development;

(d) Land resource planning information and education for agriculture;

(e) Land conservation and rehabilitation;

(f) Water for sustainable food production and sustainable rural development;

(g) Conservation and sustainable utilization of plant genetic resources for food and sustainable agriculture;

(h) Conservation and sustainable utilization of animal genetic resources for sustainable agriculture;

(i) Integrated pest management and control in agriculture;

(j) Sustainable plant nutrition to increase food production;

(k) Rural energy transition to enhance productivity;

(l) Evaluation of the effects of ultraviolet radiation on plants and animals caused by the depletion of stratospheric ozone layer.

PROGRAMME AREAS

A. Agricultural policy review, planning and integrated programmes in the light of the multifunctional aspect of agriculture, particularly with regard to food security and sustainable development

Basis for action

14.5. There is a need to integrate sustainable development considerations with agricultural policy analysis and planning in all countries, particularly in developing countries. The recommendations should contribute directly to development of realistic and operational medium- to long-term plans and programmes, and thus to concrete actions. Support to and monitoring of implementation should follow.

14.6. The absence of a coherent national policy framework for sustainable agriculture and rural development (SARD) is widespread and is not limited to the developing countries. In particular the economies in transition from planned to market-oriented systems need such a framework to incorporate environmental considerations into economic activities, including agriculture. All countries need to assess comprehensively the impacts of such policies on food and agriculture sector performance, food security, rural welfare and international trading relations as a means for identifying appropriate offsetting measures. The major thrust of food security in this case is to bring about a significant increase in agricultural production in a sustainable way and to achieve a substantial improvement in people's entitlement to adequate food and culturally appropriate food supplies.

14.7. Sound policy decisions pertaining to international trade and capital flows also necessitate action to overcome: (a) a lack of awareness of the environmental costs incurred by sectoral and macroeconomic policies and hence their threat to sustainability; (b) insufficient skills and experience in incorporating issues of sustainability into policies and programmes; and (c) inadequacy of tools of analysis and monitoring.[1]

Objectives

14.8. The objectives of this Programme area are:

(a) By 1995, to review and, where appropriate, establish a programme to integrate environmental and sustainable development with policy analysis for the food and agriculture sector and relevant macroeconomic policy analysis, formulation and implementation;

(b) To maintain and develop, as appropriate, operational multisectoral plans, programmes and policy measures, including programmes and measures to enhance sustainable food production and food security within the framework of sustainable development, not later than 1998;

(c) To maintain and enhance the ability of developing countries, particularly the least developed ones, to themselves manage policy, programming and planning activities, not later than 2005.

Activities

(a) Management-related activities

14.9. Governments at the appropriate level, with the support of the relevant international and regional organizations, should:

(a) Carry out national policy reviews related to food security, including adequate levels and stability of food supply and access to food by all households;

(b) Review national and regional agricultural policy in relation, *inter alia*, to foreign trade, price policy, exchange rate policies, agricultural subsidies and taxes, as well as organization for regional economic integration;

(c) Implement policies to influence land tenure and property rights positively with due recognition of the minimum size of land-holding to maintain production and check further fragmentation;

---

1   Some of the issues in this programme areas are presented in chapter 3 of Agenda 21 "Combating Poverty".

(d) Consider demographic trends and population movements and identify critical areas for agricultural production;

(e) Formulate, introduce and monitor policies, laws and regulations and incentives, leading to sustainable agricultural and rural development and improved food security and to the development and transfer of appropriate farm technologies, including, where appropriate, low-input sustainable agricultural (LISA) systems;

(f) Support national and regional early warning systems through food-security assistance schemes that monitor food supply and demand and factors affecting household access to food;

(g) Review policies with respect to improving harvesting, storage, processing, distribution and marketing of products at the local, national and regional levels;

(h) Formulate and implement integrated agricultural projects that include other natural resources activities, such as management of rangelands, forests, and wildlife, as appropriate;

(i) Promote social and economic research and policies that encourage sustainable agriculture development, particularly in fragile ecosystems and densely populated areas;

(j) Identify storage and distribution problems affecting food availability; support research, where necessary, to overcome these problems and cooperate with producers and distributors to implement improved practices and systems.

(b) Data and information

14.10. Governments at the appropriate level, with the support of the relevant international and regional organizations, should:

(a) Cooperate actively to expand and improve the information on early warning system on food and agriculture at both regional and national levels;

(b) Examine and undertake surveys and research to establish baseline information on the status of natural resources relating to food and agriculture production and planning in order to assess the impacts of various uses on these resources, and develop methodologies and tools of analysis, such as environmental accounting.

(c) International and regional cooperation and coordination

14.11. United Nations agencies, such as FAO [Food and Agriculture Organization], the World Bank, IFAD [International Fund for Agricultural Development] and GATT [General Agreement On Tariffs and Trade], and regional organizations, bilateral donor agencies and other bodies should, within their respective mandates, assume a role in working with national Governments in the following activities:

(a) Implement integrated and sustainable agricultural development and food security strategies at the subregional level that use regional production and trade potentials, including organizations for regional economic integration, to promote food security;

(b) Encourage, in the context of achieving sustainable agricultural development and consistent with relevant internationally agreed principles on trade and environment, a more open and non-discriminatory trading system and the avoidance of unjustifiable trade barriers which together with other policies will facilitate the further integration of agricultural and environmental policies so as to make them mutually supportive;

(c) Strengthen and establish national, regional and international systems and networks to increase the understanding of the interaction between agriculture and the state of the environment, identify ecologically sound technologies and facilitate the exchange information on data sources, policies, and techniques and tools of analysis.

Means of implementation

(a) Financing and cost evaluation

14.12. The Conference secretariat has estimated the average total annual cost (1993-2000) of implementing the activities of this programme to be about $3 billion, including about $450 million from the international community on grant or concessional terms. These are indicative and order-of-magnitude estimates only and have not been reviewed by Governments. Actual costs and financial terms, including any that are non-concessional, will depend upon, *inter alia*, the specific strategies and programmes Governments decide upon for implementation.[2]

(b) Scientific and technological means

14.13. Governments at the appropriate level and with the support of the relevant international and regional organizations should assist farming households and communities to apply technologies related to improved food production and security, including storage, monitoring of production and distribution.

---

2   Paragraph 14.12 of Agenda 21 was revised by the main committee of UNCED. The prior text in A/CONF. 151/4 (Part II), p. 81, read as follows:

  The total financing required to implement this programme area is about US$ 3 billion per year, including international concessional financing of about US$ 450 million. This includes about US$ 430 million for accelerated development and US$ 20 million for strengthening the capacity of international institutions.

(c) Human resource development

14.14. Governments at the appropriate level, with the support of the relevant international and regional organizations, should:

(a) Involve and train local economists, planners and analysts to initiate national and international policy reviews and develop frameworks for sustainable agriculture;

(b) Establish legal measures to promote access of women to land and remove biases in their involvement in rural development.

(d) Capacity-building

14.15. Governments at the appropriate level, with the support of the relevant international and regional organizations, should strengthen ministries for agriculture, natural resources and planning.

B. Ensuring people's participation and promoting human resource development for sustainable agriculture

Basis for action

14.16. This component bridges policy and integrated resource management. The greater the degree of community control over the resources on which it relies, the greater will be the incentive for economic and human resources development. At the same time, policy instruments to reconcile long-run and short-run requirements must be set by the national Governments. The approaches focus on fostering self-reliance and cooperation, providing information and supporting user-based organizations. Emphasis should be on management practices, building agreements for changes in resource utilization, the rights and duties associated with use of land, water and forests, the functioning of markets, prices, and the access to information, capital and inputs. This would require training and capacity-building to assume greater responsibilities in sustainable development efforts.[3]

Objectives

14.17. The objectives of this programme area are:

(a) To promote greater public awareness of the role of people's participation and people's organizations, especially women's groups, youth, indigenous people, local communities and small farmers, in sustainable agriculture and rural development;

---

3   Some of the issues in this programme area are discussed in chapter 8 of Agenda 21 (Integrating environment and development in decision-making) and in chapter 37 of Agenda 21 (National mechanisms and international cooperation for capacity building in developing countries). [This footnote appears in Agenda 21 as number 5 to Chapter 14, A/CONF. 151/26, vol. II, pp. 76 and 102.]

(b) To ensure equitable access of rural people, particularly women, small farmers, landless and indigenous people, to land, water and forest resources and to technologies, financing, marketing, processing and distribution;[4]

(c) To strengthen and develop the management and the internal capacities of rural people's organizations and extension services and to decentralize decision-making at the lowest community level.

Activities

(a) Management-related activities

14.18. Governments at the appropriate level, with the support of the relevant international and regional organizations, should:

(a) Develop and improve integrated agricultural extension services and facilities and rural organizations and undertake natural resource management and food security activities, taking into account the different needs of subsistence agriculture as well as market-oriented crops;

(b) Review and refocus existing measures to achieve wider access to land, water and forest resources and ensure equal rights of women and other disadvantaged groups, with particular emphasis on rural populations, indigenous peoples and local communities;[5]

(c) Assign clear titles, rights and responsibilities for land and for individuals or communities to encourage investment in land resources;

(d) Develop guidelines for decentralization policies for rural development through reorganization and strengthening of rural institutions;

(e) Develop policies in extension, training, pricing, input distribution, credit and taxation to ensure necessary incentives and equitable access by the poor to production-support services;

(f) Provide support services and training, recognizing the variation in agricultural circumstances and practices by location; the optimal use of on-farm inputs and the minimal use of external inputs; optimal use of local natural

---

4   Draft paragraphs 14.17(a) and 14.17(b) of A/CONF.151/4 (22 April 1992) were revised by decision of the Main Committee of UNCED on 10 June 1992. See A/CONF.151/L.3/Add.14 (12 June 1992). The former draft read in A/CONF. 151/4 (Part II), p. 82, as follows:

    Review and refocus existing measures to achieve wider access to land, water and forest resources and ensure equal rights of women and other disadvantaged groups, with particular emphasis on rural populations, indigenous people, [people under occupation] and local communities.

5   Draft paragraph 14.18(b) of A/CONF.151/4 (22 April 1992) was revised by decision of the Main Committee of UNCED on 10 June 1992. See A/CONF.151/L.3/Add.14 (12 June 1992). The former draft read as follows:

    Review and refocus existing measures to achieve wider access to land, water and forest resources and ensure equal rights of women and other disadvantages groups, with particular emphasis on rural populations, indigenous peoples [and people under occupation] and local communities;

resources and management of renewable energy sources; and the establishment of networks that deal with the exchange of information on alternative forms of agriculture.

(b) Data and information

14.19. Governments at the appropriate level, and with the support of the relevant international and regional organizations, should collect, analyse, and disseminate information on human resources, the role of Governments, local communities and non-governmental organizations in social innovation and strategies for rural development.

(c) International and regional cooperation and coordination

14.20. Appropriate international and regional agencies should:

(a) Reinforce their work with non-governmental organizations in collecting and disseminating information on people's participation and people's organizations, testing participatory development methods, training and education for human resource development and strengthening the management structures of rural organizations;[6]

(b) Help develop information available through non-governmental organizations and promote an international ecological agricultural network to accelerate the development and implementation of ecological agriculture practices.

Means of implementation

(a) Financing and cost evaluation

14.21. The Conference secretariat has estimated the average total annual cost (1993-2000) of implementing the activities of this programme to be about $4.4 billion, including about $650 million from the international community on grant or concessional terms. These are indicative and order-of-magnitude estimates only and have not been reviewed by Governments. Actual costs and financial terms, including any that are non-concessional, will depend upon,

---

6   Draft paragraph 14.20(a) of A/CONF.151/4 (22 April 1992) was revised by decision of the Main Committee of UNCED on 10 June 1992. See A/CONF.151/L.3/Add.14 (12 June 1992). The former draft read as follows:

Reinforce their work with NGOs in collecting and disseminating information on people's participation and people's organizations, [and people under occupation] testing participatory development methods, training and education for human resource development and strengthening management structures of rural organizations.

inter alia, the specific strategies and programmes Governments decide upon for implementation.[7]

(b) Scientific and technological means

14.22. Governments at the appropriate level, with the support of the relevant international and regional organizations, should:

(a) Encourage people's participation on farm technology development and transfer, incorporating indigenous ecological knowledge and practices;

(b) Launch applied research on participatory methodologies, management strategies and local organizations.

(c) Human resource development

14.23. Governments at the appropriate level, with the support of the relevant international and regional organizations, should provide management and technical training to government administrators and members of resource user groups in the principles, practice and benefits of people's participation in rural development.

(d) Capacity-building

14.24. Governments at the appropriate level, with the support of the relevant international and regional organizations should introduce management strategies and mechanisms, such as accounting and audit services for rural people's organizations and institutions for human resource development, and delegate administrative and financial responsibilities to local levels for decision-making, revenue-raising and expenditure.

C. Improving farm production and farming systems through diversification of farm and non-farm employment and infrastructure development

Basis for action

14.25. Agriculture needs to be intensified to meet future demands for commodities and to avoid further expansion onto marginal lands and encroachment on fragile ecosystems. Increased use of external inputs and development of specialized production and farming systems tend to increase vulnerability to environmental stresses and market fluctuations. There is, therefore, a need to intensify agriculture by diversifying the production systems for maximum efficiency in

---

7   Draft paragraph 14.21 of A/CONF.151/4 (22 April 1992) was replaced by decision of the Main Committee of UNCED on 10 June 1992. See A/CONF.151/L.3/Add.14 (12 June 1992). The former draft read as follows:

The total financing required to implement this programme area is about US$ 4,400 million per year, including international concessional financing of about US$ 650 million. This includes US$ 640 million for accelerated development and US$ 10 million for strengthening international institutions.

the utilization of local resources, while minimizing environmental and economic risks. Where intensification of farming systems is not possible, other on-farm and off-farm employment opportunities should be identified and developed, such as cottage industries, wildlife utilization, aquaculture and fisheries, non-farm activities, such as light village-based manufacturing, farm commodity processing, agribusiness, recreation and tourism, etc.

Objectives

14.26. The objectives of this programme are:

(a) To improve farm productivity in a sustainable manner, as well as to increase diversification, efficiency, food security and rural incomes, while ensuring that risks to the ecosystem are minimized;

(b) To enhance the self-reliance of farmers in developing and improving rural infrastructure, and to facilitate the transfer of environmentally sound technologies for integrated production and farming systems, including indigenous technologies and the sustainable use of biological and ecological processes, including agroforestry, sustainable wildlife conservation and management, aquaculture, inland fisheries and animal husbandry;

(c) To create farm and non-farm employment opportunities, particularly among the poor and those living in marginal areas, taking into account the alternative livelihood proposal *inter alia* on dryland areas.

Activities

(a) Management-related activities

14.27. Governments at the appropriate level, with the support of the relevant international and regional organizations, should:

(a) Develop and disseminate to farming households integrated farm management technologies, such as crop rotation, organic manuring and other techniques involving reduced use of agricultural chemicals, multiple techniques for sources of nutrients and the efficient utilization of external inputs, while enhancing techniques for waste and by-product utilization and prevention of pre- and post-harvest losses, taking particular note of the role of women;

(b) Create non-farm employment opportunities through private small-scale agro-processing units, rural service centres and related infrastructural improvements;

(c) Promote and improve rural financial networks that utilize investment capital resources raised locally;

(d) Provide the essential rural infrastructure for access to agricultural inputs and services, as well as to national and local markets, and reduce food losses;

(e) Initiate and maintain farm surveys, on-farm testing of appropriate technologies and dialogue with rural communities to identify constraints and bottlenecks and find solutions;

(f) Analyse and identify possibilities for economic integration of agricultural and forestry activities, as well as water and fisheries, and to take effective measures to encourage forest management and growing of trees by farmers (farm forestry) as an option for resource development.

(b) Data and information

14.28. Governments at the appropriate level, with the support of the relevant international and regional organizations, should:

(a) Analyse the effects of technical innovations and incentives on farm-household income and well-being;

(b) Initiate and maintain on-farm and off-farm programmes to collect and record indigenous knowledge;

(c) International and regional cooperation and coordination.

14.29. International institutions, such as FAO and IFAD, international agricultural research centers, such as CGIAR [Consultative Group On International Agricultural Research], and regional centres should diagnose the world's major agro-ecosystems, their extension, ecological and socio-economic characteristics, their susceptibility to deterioration and their productive potential. This could form the basis for technology development and exchange and for regional research collaboration.

Means of implementation

(a) Financing and cost evaluation

14.30. The Conference secretariat has estimated the average total annual cost (1993-2000) of implementing the activities of this programme to be about $10 billion, including about $1.5 billion from the international community on grant or concessional terms. These are indicative and order-of-magnitude estimates only and have not been reviewed by Governments. Actual costs and financial terms, including any that are non-concessional, will depend upon, *inter alia*, the specific strategies and programmes Governments decide upon for implementation.[8]

---

8   Draft paragraph 14.30 of A/CONF.151/4 (22 April 1992) was replaced by decision of the Main Committee of UNCED on 10 June 1992. See A/CONF.151/L.3/Add.14 (12 June 1992). The former draft read as follows:

The total financing required to implement this programme area is about US$ 10,000 million per year, including international concessional financing of about US$ 1,500 million. This includes US$ 10 million for strengthening international institutions. The remaining amount is for development.

(b) Scientific and technological means

14.31. Governments at the appropriate level, with the support of the relevant international and regional organizations, should strengthen research on agricultural production systems in areas with different endowments and agroecological zones, including comparative analysis between intensification, diversification and different levels of external and internal inputs.

(c) Human resource development

14.32. Governments at the appropriate level, with the support of the relevant international and regional organizations, should:

(a) Promote educational and vocational training for farmers and rural communities through formal and non-formal education;

(b) Launch awareness and training programmes for entrepreneurs, managers, bankers and traders in rural servicing and small-scale agro-processing techniques.

(d) Capacity-building

14.34. Governments at the appropriate level, with the support of the relevant international and regional organizations, should:

(a) Improve their organizational capacity to deal with issues related to off-farm activities and rural industry development;

(b) Expand credit facilities and rural infrastructure related to processing, transportation and marketing.

D. Land-resources planning, information and education for agriculture

Basis for action

14.34. Inappropriate and uncontrolled land uses are a major cause of degradation and depletion of land resources. Present land use often disregards the actual potentials, carrying capacities and limitations of land resources, as well as their diversity in space. It is estimated that the world's population, now at 5.4 billion, will be 6.25 billion by the turn of the century. The need to increase food production to meet the expanding needs of the population will put enormous pressure on all natural resources, including land.

14.35. Poverty and malnutrition are already endemic in many regions. The destruction and degradation of agricultural and environmental resources is a major issue. Techniques for increasing production and conserving soil and water resources are already available but are not widely or systematically applied. A systematic approach is needed for identifying land uses and production systems that are sustainable in each land and climate zone, including the economic, social and institutional mechanisms necessary for their implementation.[9]

Objectives

14.36. The objectives of this programme area are:

(a) To harmonize planning procedures, involve farmers in the planning process, collect land-resource data, design and establish databases, define land areas of similar capability, identify resource problems and values that need to be taken into account to establish mechanisms to encourage efficient and environmentally sound use of resources;

(b) To establish agricultural planning bodies at national and local levels to decide priorities, channel resources and implement programmes.

Activities

(a) Management-related activities

14.37. Governments at the appropriate level, with the support of the relevant international and regional organizations, should:

(a) Establish and strengthen agricultural land-use and land-resource planning, management, education and information, at national and local levels;

(b) Initiate and maintain district and village agricultural land-resources planning, management and conservation groups to assist in problem identification, development of technical and management solutions, and project implementation.

(b) Data and information

14.38. Governments at the appropriate level, with the support of the relevant international and regional organizations, should:

(a) Collect, continuously monitor, update and disseminate information, whenever possible, on the utilization of natural resources and living conditions, climate, water and soil factors, and on land use, distribution of vegetation cover and animal species, utilization of wild plants, production systems and yields, costs and prices, and social and cultural considerations that affect agricultural and adjacent land use;

(b) Establish programmes to provide information, promote discussion and encourage the formation of management groups.

---

9   Some of the issues are presented in chapter 10 of Agenda 21 (Integrated approach to planning and management of land resources). [This footnote appears in Agenda 21 as number 3 to Chapter 14, A/CONF. 151/26, vol. II, pp. 82 and 102.]

(c) International and regional cooperation and coordination

14.39. The appropriate United Nations agencies and regional organizations should:

(a) Strengthen or establish international, regional and subregional technical working groups with specific terms of reference and budgets to promote integrated use of land resources for agriculture, planning, data collection and diffusion of simulation models of production and information dissemination;

(b) Develop internationally acceptable methodologies for the establishment of databases, description of land uses and multiple goal optimization.

Means of implementation

(a) Financing and cost evaluation

14.40. The Conference secretariat has estimated the average total annual cost (1993-2000) of implementing the activities of this programme to be about $1.7 billion, including about $250 million from the international community on grant or concessional terms. These are indicative and order-of-magnitude estimates only and have not been reviewed by Governments. Actual costs and financial terms, including any that are non-concessional, will depend upon, *inter alia*, the specific strategies and programmes Governments decide upon for implementation.[10]

(b) Scientific and technological means

14.41. Governments at the appropriate level, with the support of the relevant international and regional organizations, should:

(a) Develop databases and geographical information systems to store and display physical, social and economic information pertaining to agriculture, and the definition of ecological zones and development areas;

(b) Select combinations of land uses and production systems appropriate to land units through multiple goal optimization procedures, and strengthen delivery systems and local community participation;

(c) Encourage integrated planning at the watershed and landscape level to reduce soil loss and protect surface and groundwater resources from chemical pollution.

---

10   Draft paragraph 14.40 of A/CONF.151/4 (22 April 1992) was replaced by decision of the Main Committee of UNCED on 10 June 1992. See A/CONF.151/L.3/Add.14 (12 June 1992). The former draft read as follows:

The total financing required to implement this programme area is about US$ 1,700 million per year, including international concessional financing of about US$ 250 million. This includes US$ 2 million for strengthening international institutions. The remaining amount is for development.

(c) Human resource development

14.42. Governments at the appropriate level, with the support of the relevant international and regional organizations, should:

(a) Train professionals and planning groups at national, district and village levels through formal and informal instructional courses, travel and interaction;

(b) Generate discussion at all levels on policy, development and environmental issues related to agricultural land use and management, through media programmes, conferences and seminars.

(d) Capacity-building

14.43. Governments at the appropriate level, with the support of the relevant international and regional organizations, should:

(a) Establish land resources mapping and planning units at national, district and village levels to act as focal points and links between institutions and disciplines, and between Governments and people;

(b) Establish or strengthen Governments and international institutions with responsibility for agricultural resource survey, management and development; rationalize and strengthen legal frameworks; and provide equipment and technical assistance.

E. Land conservation and rehabilitation

Basis for action

14.44. Land degradation is the most important environmental problem affecting extensive areas of land in both developed and developing countries. The problem of soil erosion is particularly acute in developing countries, while problems of salinization, waterlogging, soil pollution and loss of soil fertility are increasing in all countries. Land degradation is serious because the productivity of huge areas of land is declining just when populations are increasing rapidly and the demand on the land is growing to produce more food, fibre and fuel. Efforts to control land degradation, particularly in developing countries, have had limited success to date. Well planned, long-term national and regional land conservation and rehabilitation programmes, with strong political support and adequate funding, are now needed. While land use planning and land zoning, combined with better land management, should provide long-term solutions, it is urgent to arrest land degradation and launch conservation and rehabilitation programmes in the most critically affected and vulnerable areas.

Objectives

14.45. The objectives of this programme area:

(a) By the year 2000, to review and initiate, as appropriate, national land-resource surveys, detailing the location, extent and severity of land degradation;

(b) To prepare and implement comprehensive policies and programmes leading to the reclamation of degraded lands and the conservation of areas at risk, as well as improve the general planning, management and utilization of land resources and preserve soil fertility for sustainable agricultural development.

Activities

(a) Management-related activities

14.46. Governments at the appropriate level, with the support of the relevant international and regional organizations, should:

(a) Develop and implement programmes to remove and resolve the physical, social and economic causes of land degradation, such as land tenure, appropriate trading systems and agricultural pricing structures, which lead to inappropriate land use management;

(b) Provide incentives and, where appropriate and possible, resources for the participation of local communities in the planning, implementation and maintenance of their own conservation and reclamation programmes;

(c) Develop and implement programmes for the rehabilitation of land degraded by water-logging and salinity;

(d) Develop and implement programmes for the progressive use of non-cultivated land with agricultural potential in a sustainable way.

(b) Data and information

14.47. Governments, at the appropriate level, with the support of the relevant international and regional organizations, should:

(a) Conduct periodic surveys to assess the extent and state of its land resources;

(b) Strengthen and establish national land-resource data banks, including identification of the location, extent and severity of existing land degradation, as well as areas at risk and evaluate the progress of the conservation and rehabilitation programmes launched in this regard;

(c) Collect and record information on indigenous conservation and rehabilitation practices and farming systems as a basis for research and extension programmes.

(c) International and regional cooperation and coordination

14.48. The appropriate United Nations agencies, regional organizations and non-governmental organizations should:

(a) Develop priority conservation and rehabilitation programmes with advisory services to Governments and regional organizations;

(b) Establish regional and subregional networks for scientists and technicians to exchange experiences, develop joint programmes and spread successful technologies on land conservation and rehabilitation.

Means of implementation

(a) Financing and cost evaluation

14.49. The Conference secretariat has estimated the average total annual cost (1993-2000) of implementing the activities of this programme to be about $5 billion, including about $800 million from the international community on grant or concessional terms. These are indicative and order-of-magnitude estimates only and have not been reviewed by Governments. Actual costs and financial terms, including any that are non-concessional, will depend upon, *inter alia*, the specific strategies and programmes Governments decide upon for implementation.[11]

(b) Scientific and technological means

14.50. Governments at the appropriate level, with the support of the relevant international and regional organizations, should assist farming household communities to investigate and promote site-specific technologies and farming systems that conserve and rehabilitate land, while increasing agricultural production, including conservation tillage agroforestry, terracing and mixed cropping.

(c) Human resource development

14.51. Governments at the appropriate level, with the support of the relevant international and regional organizations, should train field staff and land users in indigenous and modern techniques of conservation and rehabilitation and should establish training facilities for extension staff and land users.

---

11 Draft paragraph 14.49 of A/CONF.151/4 (22 April 1992) was replaced by decision of the Main Committee of UNCED on 10 June 1992. See A/CONF.151/L.3/Add.14 (12 June 1992). The former draft read as follows:

The total financing required to implement this programme area is about US$ 5,000 million per year, including international concessional financing of about US$ 800 million. This includes US$ 10 million for strengthening international institutions. The remaining amount is for development.

(d) Capacity-building

14.52. Governments at the appropriate level, with the support of the relevant international and regional organizations, should:

(a) Develop and strengthen national research institutional capacity to identify and implement effective conservation and rehabilitation practices that are appropriate to the existing socio-economic physical conditions of the land users;

(b) Coordinate all land conservation and rehabilitation policies, strategies and programmes with related ongoing programmes, such as national environment action plans, the Tropical Forestry Action Plan and national development programmes.

F. Water for sustainable food production and sustainable rural development

14.53. This programme area is included in chapter 18 (Protection of the quality and supply of freshwater resources), programme area F.[12]

G. Conservation and sustainable utilization of plant genetic resources for food and sustainable agriculture

Basis for action

14.54. Plant genetic resources for agriculture are an essential resource to meet future needs for food. Threats to the security of these resources are growing, and efforts to conserve, develop and use genetic diversity are underfunded and understaffed. Many existing gene banks provide inadequate security and, in some instances, the loss of plant genetic diversity in gene banks is as great as it is in the field.

14.55. The primary objective is to safeguard the world's genetic resources while preserving them to use sustainably. This includes the development of measures to facilitate the conservation and use of plant genetic resources, networks of *in situ* conservation areas and use of tools such as *ex situ* collections and germ plasma banks. Special emphasis could be placed on the building of endogenous capacity for characterization, evaluation and utilization of PGRFA, particularly for the minor crops and other underutilized or non-utilized species of food and agriculture, including tree species for agro-forestry. Subsequent action could be aimed at consolidation and efficient management of networks of *in situ* conservation areas and use of tools such as *ex situ* collections and germ plasma banks.

---

12 Presented in chapter 18 of Agenda 21, "Protection of the Quality and the Supply of Freshwater Resources: Application of Integrated Approaches to the Development Management and use of Water Resources." [This footnote appeared in the draft of Agenda 21, but not in the final version.]

14.56. Major gaps and weaknesses exist in the capacity of existing national and international mechanisms to assess, study, monitor and use plant genetic resources to increase food production. Existing institutional capacity, structures and programmes are generally inadequate and largely underfunded. There is genetic erosion of invaluable crop species. Existing diversity in crop species is not used to the extent possible for increased food production in a sustainable way.[13]

Objectives

14.57. The objectives of this programme area are:

(a) To complete the first regeneration and safe duplication of existing *ex situ* collections on a world-wide basis as soon as possible;

(b) To collect and study plants useful for increasing food production through joint activities, including training, within the framework of networks of collaborating institutions;

(c) Not later than the year 2000, to adopt policies and strengthen or establish programmes for *in situ* on-farm and *ex situ* conservation and sustainable use of plant genetic resources for food and agriculture, integrated into strategies and programmes for sustainable agriculture;

(d) To take appropriate measures for the fair and equitable sharing of benefits and results of research and development in plant breeding between the sources and users of plant genetic resources.[14]

Activities

(a) Management-related activities

14.58. Governments at the appropriate level, with the support of the relevant international and regional organizations, should:

(a) Develop and strengthen institutional capacity, structures and programmes for conservation and use of PGRFA [Plant genetic resources for agriculture];

(b) Strengthen and establish research in the public domain on PGRFA evaluation and utilization, with the objectives of sustainable agriculture and rural development in view;

(c) Develop multiplication/propagation, exchange and dissemination facilities for PGRFAs (seeds and planting materials), particularly in developing countries and monitor, control and evaluate plant introductions;

---

13   The activities of this programme are related to some of the activities in chapter 15 of Agenda 21 Conservation of biological diversity). [This footnote appears in Agenda 21 as number 4 to Chapter 14, A/CONF. 151/26, vol. II, pp. 87 and 102.]

14   Draft paragraph 14.57(d) of A/CONF.151/4 (22 April 1992), included brackets around the words "the fair and equitable." The brackets were deleted by decision of the Main Committee of UNCED on 10 June 1992. See A/CONF.151/L.3/Add.14 (12 June 1992).

(d) Prepare plans or programmes of priority action on conservation and sustainable use of PGRFA, based, as appropriate, on country studies on PGRFA;

(e) Promote crop diversification in agricultural systems where appropriate, including new plants with potential value as food crops;

(f) Promote utilization as well as research on poorly known, but potentially useful, plants and crops, where appropriate;

(g) Strengthen national capabilities for utilization of PGRFA, plant breeding and seed production capabilities, both by specialized institutions and farming communities.

(b) Data and information

14.59. Governments at the appropriate level, with the support of the relevant international and regional organizations, should:

(a) Develop strategies for networks of *in situ* conservation areas and use of tools such as on-farm *ex situ* collections, germplasm banks and related technologies;

(b) Establish *ex situ* base collection networks;

(c) Review periodically and report on the situation on PGRFA, using existing systems and procedures;

(d) Characterize and evaluate PGRFA material collected, disseminate information to facilitate the use of PGRFA collections and assess genetic variation in collections.

(c) International and regional cooperation and coordination

14.60. The appropriate United Nations agencies and regional organizations should:

(a) Strengthen the Global System on the Conservation and Sustainable Use of PGRFA by, *inter alia*, accelerating the development of the Global Information and Early Warning System to facilitate the exchange of information; developing ways to promote the transfer of environmentally sound technologies, in particular to developing countries; and taking further steps to realize farmers' rights;

(b) Develop subregional, regional and global networks of PGRFA *in situ* in protected areas;

(c) Prepare periodic state of the world reports on PGRFA;

(d) Prepare a rolling global cooperative plan of action on PGRFA;

(e) Promote, for 1994, the Fourth International Technical Conference on the Conservation and Sustainable Use of PGRFA, which is to adopt the first state of the world report and the first global plan of action on the conservation and sustainable use of PGRFA;

(f) Adjust the Global System for the Conservation and Sustainable Use of PGRFA in line with the outcome of the negotiations of a convention on biological diversity.

Means of implementation

(a) Financing and cost evaluation

14.61. The Conference secretariat has estimated the average total annual cost (1993-2000) of implementing the activities of this programme to be about $600 million, including about $300 million from the international community on grant or concessional terms. These are indicative and order-of-magnitude estimates only and have not been reviewed by Governments. Actual costs and financial terms, including any that are non-concessional, will depend upon, *inter alia*, the specific strategies and programmes Governments decide upon for implementation.[15]

(b) Scientific and technological means

14.62. Governments, at the appropriate level, with the support of the relevant international and regional organizations, should:

(a) Develop basic science research in such areas as plant taxonomy and phytogeography, utilizing recent developments, such as computer sciences, molecular genetics and *in vitro* cryopreservation;

(b) Develop major collaborative projects between research programmes in developed and developing countries, particularly for the enhancement of poorly known or neglected crops;

(c) Promote cost-effective technologies for keeping duplicate sets of *ex situ* collections (which can also be used by local communities);

(d) Develop further conservation sciences in relation to *in situ* conservation and technical means to link it with *ex situ* conservation efforts.

(c) Human resource development

14.63. Governments at the appropriate level and with the support of the relevant international and regional organizations should:

(a) Promote training programmes at both undergraduate and post-graduate levels in conservation sciences for running PGRFA facilities and for the design and implementation of national programmes in PGRFA;

---

15   Draft paragraph 14.61 of A/CONF.151/4 (22 April 1992) was replaced by decision of the Main Committee of UNCED on 10 June 1992. See A/CONF.151/L.3/Add.14 (12 June 1992). The former draft read as follows:

The total financing required to implement this programme area is about US$ 600 million per year, including international concessional financing of about US$ 300 million. This includes about US$ 10 million for strengthening international institutions, the remaining US$ 290 million to be divided between development and global environmental issues.

(b) Raise the awareness of agricultural extension services in order to link PGRFA activities with user communities;

(c) Develop training materials to promote conservation and utilization of PGRFA at the local level.

(d) Capacity-building

14.64. Governments at the appropriate level, with the support of the relevant international and regional organizations, should establish national policies to provide legal status for and strengthen legal aspects of PGRFA, including long-term financial commitment for germplasm collections and implementation of activities in PGRFA.

H. Conservation and utilization of animal genetic resources for sustainable agriculture

Basis for action

14.65. The need for increased quantity and quality of animal products and for draught animals calls for conservation of the existing diversity of animal breeds to meet future requirements, including those for use in biotechnology. Some local animal breeds, in addition to their socio-cultural value, have unique attributes for adaptation, disease resistance and specific uses and should be preserved. These local breeds are threatened by extinction as a result of the introduction of exotic breeds and of changes in livestock production systems.

Objectives

14.66. The objectives of this programme area are:

(a) To enumerate and describe all breeds of livestock used in animal agriculture in as broad a way as possible and begin a 10-year programme of action;

(b) To establish and implement action programmes to identify breeds at risk, together with the nature of the risk and appropriate preservation measures;

(c) To establish and implement development programmes for indigenous breeds in order to guarantee their survival, avoiding the risk of their being replaced by breed substitution or cross-breeding programmes.

Activities

(a) Management-related activities

14.67. Governments at the appropriate level, with the support of the relevant international and regional organizations, should:

(a) Draw up breed preservation plans, for endangered populations, including semen/embryo collection and storage, farm-based conservation of indigenous stock or *in situ* preservation;

(b) Plan and initiate breed development strategies;

(c) Select indigenous populations on the basis of regional importance and genetic uniqueness, for a 10-year programme, followed by selection of an additional cohort of indigenous breeds for development.

(b) Data and information

14.68. Governments at the appropriate level, with the support of the relevant international and regional organizations, should prepare and complete national inventories of available animal genetic resources. Cryogenic storage could be given priority over characterization and evaluation. Training of nationals in conservation and assessment techniques would be given special attention.

(c) International and regional cooperation and coordination

14.69. The appropriate United Nations and other international and regional agencies should:

(a) Promote the establishment of regional gene banks to the extent that they are justified, based on principles of technical cooperation among developing countries;

(b) Process, store and analyse animal genetic data at the global level, including the establishment of a world watch list and an early warning system for endangered breeds; global assessment of scientific and intergovernmental guidance of the programme and review of regional and national activities; development of methodologies, norms and standards (including international agreements), monitoring of their implementation; and related technical and financial assistance;

(c) Prepare and publish a comprehensive database of animal genetic resources, describing each breed, its derivation, its relationship with other breeds, effective population size and a concise set of biological and production characteristics;

(d) Prepare and publish a world watch list on farm animal species at risk to enable national Governments to take action to preserve endangered breeds and to seek technical assistance, where necessary.

Means of implementation

(a) Financing and cost evaluation

14.70. The Conference secretariat has estimated the average total annual cost (1993-2000) of implementing the activities of this programme to be about $200 million, including about $100 million from the international community on grant or concessional terms. These are indicative and order-of-magnitude estimates only and have not been reviewed by Governments. Actual costs and financial terms, including any that are non-concessional, will depend upon, *inter alia*, the specific strategies and programmes Governments decide upon for implementation.[16]

(b) Scientific and technological means

14.71. Governments at the appropriate level, with the support of the relevant international and regional organizations, should:

(a) Use computer-based data banks and questionnaires to prepare a global inventory/world watch list;

(b) Using cryogenic storage of germplasm, preserve breeds at serious risk and other material from which genes can be reconstructed.

(c) Human resource development

14.72. Governments at the appropriate level, with the support of the relevant international and regional organizations, should:

(a) Sponsor training courses for nationals to obtain the necessary expertise for data collection and handling and for the sampling of genetic material;

(b) Enable scientists and managers to establish an information base for indigenous livestock breeds and promote programmes to develop and conserve essential livestock genetic material.

(d) Capacity-building

14.73. Governments at the appropriate level, with the support of the relevant international and regional organizations, should:

(a) Establish in-country facilities for artificial insemination centres and *in situ* breeding farms;

(b) Promote in-country programmes and related physical infrastructure for animal livestock conservation and breed development, as well as for strengthening national capacities to take preventive action when breeds are endangered.

I. Integrated pest management and control in agriculture

Basis for action

14.74. World food demand projections indicate an increase of 50 per cent by the year 2000; which will more than double again by 2050. Conservative estimates

---

16   Draft paragraph 14.70 of A/CONF.151/4 (22 April 1992) was replaced by decision of the Main Committee of UNCED on 10 June 1992. See A/CONF.151/L.3/Add.14 (12 June 1992). The former draft read as follows:

The total financing required to implement this programme area is about US$ 200 million per year, including international concessional financing of about US$ 100 million. This includes about US$ 10 million for strengthening international institutions, the remaining US$ 80 million to be divided between development and global environmental issues.

put pre-harvest and post-harvest losses caused by pests between 25 and 50 per cent. Pests affecting animal health also cause heavy losses and in many areas prevent livestock development. Chemical control of agricultural pests has dominated the scene, but its overuse has adverse effects on farm budgets, human health and the environment, as well as on international trade. New pest problems continue to develop. Integrated pest management, which combines biological control, host plant resistance and appropriate farming practices and minimizes the use of pesticides, is the best option for the future, as it guarantees yields, reduces costs, is environmentally friendly and contributes to the sustainability of agriculture. Integrated pest management should go hand in hand with appropriate pesticide management to allow for pesticide regulation and control, including trade, and for the safe handling and disposal of pesticides, particularly those that are toxic and persistent.

Objectives

14.75. The objectives of this programme area are:

(a) No later than the year 2000, to improve and implement plant protection and animal health services, including mechanisms to control the distribution and use of pesticides, and to implement the International Code of Conduct on the Distribution and Use of Pesticides;

(b) To improve and implement programmes to put integrated pest-management practices within the reach of the farmers through farmer networks, extension services and research institutions;

(c) No later than the year 1998, to establish operational and interactive networks among farmers, researchers and extension services to promote and develop integrated pest management.

Activities

(a) Management-related activities

14.76. Governments at the appropriate level, with the support of the relevant international and regional organizations, should:

(a) Review and reform national policies and the mechanisms that would ensure the safe and appropriate use of pesticides—for example, pesticide pricing, pest control brigades, price-structure of inputs and outputs and integrated pest-management policies and action plans;

(b) Develop and adopt efficient management systems to control and monitor the incidence of pests and disease in agriculture and the distribution and use of pesticides at the country level;

(c) Encourage research and development into pesticides that are target specific and readily degrade into harmless constituent parts after use;

(d) Ensure that pesticide labels provide farmers with understandable information about safe handling, application and disposal.

(b) Data and information

14.77. Governments at the appropriate level, with the support of the relevant international and regional organizations, should:

(a) Consolidate and harmonize existing information and programmes on the use of pesticides that have been banned or severely restricted in different countries;

(b) Consolidate, document and disseminate information on biological control agents and organic pesticides, as well as on traditional and other relevant knowledge and skills regarding alternative non-chemical ways of controlling pests;

(c) Undertake national surveys to establish baseline information on the use of pesticides in each country and the side-effects on human health and environment, and also undertake appropriate education.

(c) International and regional cooperation and coordination

14.78. Appropriate United Nations agencies and regional organizations should:

(a) Establish a system for collecting, analysing and disseminating data on the quantity and quality of pesticides used every year and their impact on human health and the environment;

(b) Strengthen regional interdisciplinary projects and establish integrated pest management networks to demonstrate the social, economic and environmental benefits of IPM for food and cash crops in agriculture;

(c) Develop proper IPM, comprising the selection of the variety of biological, physical and cultural control, as well as chemical controls, taking into account specific regional conditions.

Means of implementation

(a) Financing and cost evaluation

14.79. The Conference secretariat has estimated the average total annual cost (1993-2000) of implementing the activities of this programme to be about $1.9 billion, including about $285 million from the international community on grant or concessional terms. These are indicative and order-of-magnitude estimates only and have not been reviewed by Governments. Actual costs and financial terms, including any that are non-concessional, will depend upon,

inter alia, the specific strategies and programmes Governments decide upon for implementation.[17]

(b) Scientific and technological means

14.80. Governments at the appropriate level, with the support of the relevant international and regional organizations, should launch on-farm research in the development of non-chemical alternative pest management technologies.

(c) Human resource development

14.81. Governments at the appropriate level, with the support of the relevant international and regional organizations, should:

(a) Prepare and conduct training programmes on approaches and techniques for integrated pest management and control of pesticide use, to inform policy makers, researchers, non-governmental organizations and farmers;

(b) Train extension agents and involve farmers and women's groups in crop health and alternative non-chemical ways of controlling pests in agriculture.

(d) Capacity-building

14.82. Governments at the appropriate level, with the support of the relevant international and regional organizations, should strengthen national public administrations and regulatory bodies in the control of pesticides and the transfer of technology for integrated pest management.

J. Sustainable plant nutrition to increase food production

Basis for action

14.83. Plant nutrient depletion is a serious problem resulting in loss of soil fertility, particularly in developing countries. To maintain soil productivity, the FAO sustainable plant nutrition programmes could be helpful. In sub-Saharan Africa, nutrient output from all sources currently exceeds inputs by a factor of three or four, the net loss being estimated at some 10 million metric tons per year. As a result, more marginal lands and fragile natural ecosystems are put under agricultural use, thus creating further land degradation and other environmental problems. The integrated plant nutrition approach aims at ensuring a sustainable supply of plant nutrients to increase future yields without harming the environment and soil productivity.

---

17   Draft paragraph 14.79 of A/CONF.151/4 (22 April 1992) was replaced by decision of the Main Committee of UNCED on 10 June 1992. See A/CONF.151/L.3/Add.14 (12 June 1992). The former draft read as follows:

The total financing required to implement this programme area is about US$ 1,900 million per year, including international concessional financing of about US$ 285 million. This includes US$ 275 million for accelerated development, US$ 7 million for global environmental issues and US$ 3 million for strengthening the capacity of international institutions.

14.84. In many developing countries, population growth rates exceed 3 per cent a year, and national agricultural production has fallen behind food demand. In these countries the goal should be to increase agricultural production by at least 4 per cent a year, without destroying the soil fertility. This will require increasing agricultural production in high-potential areas through efficiency in the use of inputs. Trained labour, energy supply, adapted tools and technologies, plant nutrients and soil enrichment will all be essential.

Objectives

14.85. The objectives of this programme area are:

(a) Not later than the year 2000, to develop and maintain in all countries the integrated plant nutrition approach, and to optimize availability of fertilizer and other plant nutrient sources;

(b) Not later than the year 2000, to establish and maintain institutional and human infrastructure to enhance effective decision-making on soil productivity;

(c) To develop and make available national and international know-how to farmers, extension agents, planners and policy makers on environmentally sound new and existing technologies and soil-fertility management strategies for application in promoting sustainable agriculture.

Activities

(a) Management-related activities

14.86. Governments at the appropriate level, with the support of the relevant international and regional organizations, should:

(a) Formulate and apply strategies that will enhance soil fertility maintenance to meet sustainable agricultural production and adjust the relevant agricultural policy instruments accordingly;

(b) Integrate organic and inorganic sources of plant nutrients in a system to sustain soil fertility and determine mineral fertilizer needs;

(c) Determine plant nutrients requirements and supply strategies and optimize the use of both organic and inorganic sources, as appropriate, to increase farming efficiency and production;

(d) Develop and encourage processes for the recycling of organic and inorganic waste into the soil structure, without harming the environment, plant growth and human health.

(b) Data and information

14.87. Governments at the appropriate level, with the support of the relevant international and regional organizations should:

(a) Assess "national accounts" for plant nutrients, including supplies (inputs) and losses (outputs), and prepare balance sheets and projections by cropping systems;

(b) Review technical and economic potentials of plant nutrient sources, including national deposits, improved organic supplies, recycling, wastes, topsoil produced from discarded organic matter and biological nitrogen fixation.

(c) International and regional cooperation and coordination

14.88. The appropriate United Nations agencies, such as FAO, the international agricultural research institutes, and non-governmental organizations should collaborate in carrying out information and publicity campaigns about the integrated plant nutrients approach, efficiency of soil productivity and their relationship to the environment.

Means of implementation

(a) Financing and cost evaluation

14.89. The Conference secretariat has estimated the average total annual cost (1993-2000) of implementing the activities of this programme to be about $3.2 billion, including about $475 million from the international community on grant or concessional terms. These are indicative and order-of-magnitude estimates only and have not been reviewed by Governments. Actual costs and financial terms, including any that are non-concessional, will depend upon, *inter alia*, the specific strategies and programmes Governments decide upon for implementation.[18]

(b) Scientific and technological means

14.90. Governments at the appropriate level, with the support of the relevant international and regional organizations, should:

(a) Develop site-specific technologies at benchmark sites and farmers' fields that fit prevailing socio-economic and ecological conditions through research that involves the full collaboration of local populations;

---

18   Draft paragraph 14.89 of A/CONF.151/4 (22 April 1992) was replaced by decision of the Main Committee of UNCED on 10 June 1992. See A/CONF.151/L.3/Add.14 (12 June 1992). The former draft read as follows:

    The total financing required to implement this programme area is about US$ 3,200 million per year, including international concessional financing of about US$ 475 million. This includes US$ 460 million for accelerated development, US$ 10 million for global environmental issues and US$ 5 million for strengthening the capacity of international institutions.

(b) Reinforce interdisciplinary international research and transfer of technology in cropping and farming systems research, improved *in situ* biomass production techniques, organic residue management and agroforestry technologies.

(c) Human resource development

14.91. Governments at the appropriate level, with the support of the relevant international and regional organizations, should:

(a) Train extension officers and researchers in plant nutrient management, cropping systems and farming systems, and in economic evaluation of plant nutrient impact;

(b) Train farmers and women's groups in plant nutrition management, with special emphasis on topsoil conservation and production.

(d) Capacity-building

14.92. Governments at the appropriate level, with the support of the relevant international and regional organizations, should:

(a) Develop suitable institutional mechanisms for policy formulation to monitor and guide the implementation of integrated plant nutrition programmes through an interactive process involving farmers, research, extension services and other sectors of society;

(b) Where appropriate, strengthen advisory services and train staff, develop and test new technologies and facilitate the adoption of practices to upgrade and maintain full productivity of the land.

K. Rural energy transition to enhance productivity

Basis for action

14.93. Energy supplies in many countries are not commensurate with their development needs and are highly priced and unstable. In rural areas of the developing countries, the chief sources of energy are fuelwood, crop residues and manure, together with animal and human energy. More intensive energy inputs are required for increased productivity of human labour and for income-generation. To this end, rural energy policies and technologies should promote a mix of cost-effective fossil and renewable energy sources that is itself sustainable and ensures sustainable agricultural development. Rural areas provide energy supplies in the form of wood. The full potential of agriculture and agroforestry, as well as common property resources, as sources of renewable energy, is far from being realized. The attainment of sustainable rural development is intimately linked with energy demand and supply patterns.[19]

Objectives

14.94. The objectives of this programme area are:

(a) Not later than the year 2000, to initiate and encourage a process of environmentally sound energy transition in rural communities, from unsustainable energy sources, to structured and diversified energy sources by making available alternative new and renewable sources of energy;

(b) To increase the energy inputs available for rural household and agro-industrial needs through planning and appropriate technology transfer and development;

(c) To implement self-reliant rural programmes favouring sustainable development of renewable energy sources and improved energy efficiency.

Activities

(a) Management-related activities

14.95. Governments at the appropriate level, with the support of the relevant international and regional organizations, should:

(a) Promote pilot plans and projects consisting of electrical, mechanical and thermal power (gasifiers, biomass, solar driers, wind-pumps and combustion systems) that are appropriate and likely to be adequately maintained;

(b) Initiate and promote rural energy programmes supported by technical training, banking and related infrastructure;

(c) Intensify research and the development, diversification and conservation of energy, taking into account the need for efficient use and environmentally sound technology.

(b) Data and information

14.96. Governments at the appropriate level, with the support of the relevant international and regional organizations, should:

(a) Collect and disseminate data on rural energy supply and demand patterns related to energy needs for households, agriculture and agro-industry;

(b) Analyse sectoral energy and production data in order to identify rural energy requirements.

---

19   The activities of this programme area are related to some of the activities in chapter 9 of Agenda 21, (Protection of the atmosphere). [This footnote appears in Agenda 21 as number 5 to Chapter 14, A/CONF. 151/26, vol. III, p. 99 and 102.]

(c) International and regional cooperation and coordination

14.97. The appropriate United Nations agencies and regional organizations should, drawing on the experience and available information of non-governmental organizations in this field, exchange country and regional experience on rural energy planning methodologies in order to promote efficient planning and select cost-effective technologies.

Means of implementation

(a) Financing and cost evaluation

14.98. The Conference secretariat has estimated the average total annual cost (1993-2000) of implementing the activities of this programme to be about $1.8 billion, including about $265 million from the international community on grant or concessional terms. These are indicative and order-of-magnitude estimates only and have not been reviewed by Governments. Actual costs and financial terms, including any that are non-concessional, will depend upon, *inter alia*, the specific strategies and programmes Governments decide upon for implementation.[20]

(b) Scientific and technological means

14.99. Governments at the appropriate level, with the support of the relevant international and regional organizations, should:

(a) Intensify public and private sector research in developing and industrialized countries on renewable sources of energy for agriculture;

(b) Undertake research and transfer of energy technologies in biomass and solar energy to agricultural production and post-harvest activities.

(c) Human resource development

14.100. Governments at the appropriate level, with the support of the relevant international and regional organizations, should enhance public awareness of rural energy problems, stressing the economic and environmental advantages of renewable energy sources.

---

20 Draft paragraph 14.98 of A/CONF.151/4 (22 April 1992) was replaced by decision of the Main Committee of UNCED on 10 June 1992. See A/CONF.151/L.3/Add.14 (12 June 1992). The former draft read as follows:

The total financing required to implement this programme area is about US$ 1,800 million per year, including international concessional financing of about US$ 265 million. This includes US$ 230 million for accelerated development, US$ 30 million for global environmental issues and US$ 5 million for strengthening the capacity of international institutions.

(d) Capacity-building

14.101. Governments at the appropriate level, with the support of the relevant international and regional organizations, should:

(a) Establish national institutional mechanisms for rural energy planning and management that would improve efficiency in agricultural productivity and reaching village and household level;

(b) Strengthen extension services and local organizations to implement plans and programmes for new and renewable sources of energy at village level.

L. Evaluation of the effects of ultraviolet radiation on plants and animals caused by the depletion of stratospheric ozone layer

Basis for action

14.102. The increase of ultraviolet radiation as a consequence of the depletion of the stratospheric ozone layer is a phenomenon that has been recorded in different regions of the world, particularly in the southern hemisphere. Consequently, it is important to evaluate its effects on plant and animal life, as well as on sustainable agricultural development.

Objective

14.103. The objective of this programme is to undertake research to determine the effects of increased ultraviolet radiation resulting from stratospheric ozone layer depletion on the Earth's surface, and on plant and animal life in affected regions, as well as its impact on agriculture, and to develop, as appropriate, strategies aimed at mitigating its adverse effects.

Activities

(a) Management-related activities

14.104. In affected regions, Governments at the appropriate level, with the support of the relevant international and regional organizations, should take the necessary measures, through institutional cooperation, to facilitate the implementation of research and evaluation regarding the effects of enhanced ultraviolet radiation on plant and animal life, as well as on agricultural activities, and consider taking appropriate remedial measures.

Chapter 15

Conservation of Biological Diversity

INTRODUCTION

15.1. The objectives and activities in this chapter of Agenda 21 are intended to improve the conservation of biological diversity and the sustainable use of biological resources, as well as to support the Convention on Biological Diversity.[1]

15.2. Our planet's essential goods and services depend on the variety and variability of genes, species, populations and ecosystems. Biological resources feed and clothe us and provide housing, medicines and spiritual nourishment. The natural ecosystems of forests, savannahs, pastures and rangelands, deserts, tundras, rivers, lakes and seas contain most of the Earth's biodiversity. Farmers' fields and gardens are also of great importance as repositories, while gene banks, botanical gardens, zoos and other germplasm repositories make a small but significant contribution. The current decline in biodiversity is largely the result of human activity and represents a serious threat to human development.

PROGRAMME AREA

Conservation of biological diversity

Basis for action

15.3. Despite mounting efforts over the past 20 years, the loss of the world's biological diversity, mainly from habitat destruction, over-harvesting, pollution and the inappropriate introduction of foreign plants and animals, has continued. Biological resources constitute a capital asset with great potential for yielding

---

1   Draft paragraph 15.1 of A/CONF.151/4 (22 April 1992) was replaced by decision of the Main Committee of UNCED on 10 June 1992. See A/CONF.151/L.3/Add.15 (12 June 1992). The former draft read as follows:

The objectives and activities in this chapter of Agenda 21 are intended to improve the conservation of biological diversity and the sustainable use of biological resources, as well as to support the draft Convention on Biological Diversity. As negotiations are continuing on that instrument, these objectives and activities, where they relate directly to the draft Convention, are without prejudice to those negotiations.

sustainable benefits. Urgent and decisive action is needed to conserve and maintain genes, species and ecosystems, with a view to the sustainable management and use of biological resources. Capacities for the assessment, study and systematic observation and evaluation of biodiversity need to be reinforced at national and international levels. Effective national action and international cooperation is required for the *in situ* protection of ecosystems, for the *ex situ* conservation of biological and genetic resources and for the enhancement of ecosystem functions. The participation and support of local communities are elements essential to the success of such an approach. Recent advances in biotechnology have pointed up the likely potential for agriculture, health and welfare and for the environmental purposes of the genetic material contained in plants, animals and micro-organisms. At the same time, it is particularly important in this context to stress that States have the sovereign right to exploit their own biological resources pursuant to their environmental policies, as well as the responsibility to conserve their biodiversity and use their biological resources sustainably, and to ensure that activities within their jurisdiction or control do not cause damage to the biological diversity of other States or of areas beyond the limits of national jurisdiction.

Objectives

15.4. Governments at the appropriate level, with the cooperation of the relevant United Nations bodies and regional, intergovernmental and non-governmental organizations, the private sector and financial institutions, and taking into consideration indigenous people and their communities, as well as social and economic factors, should:[2]

(a) Press for the early entry into force of the Convention on Biological Diversity with the widest possible participation;

(b) Develop national strategies for the conservation of biological diversity and the sustainable use of biological resources;

(c) Integrate strategies for the conservation of biological diversity and the sustainable use of biological resources into national development strategies and/or plans;

(d) Take appropriate measures for the fair and equitable sharing of benefits derived from research and development and use of biological and genetic re-

---

2   The introductory phrase of draft paragraph 15.4 of A/CONF.151/4 (22 April 1992) was replaced by decision of the Main Committee of UNCED on 10 June 1992. See A/CONF.151/L.3/Add.15 (12 June 1992). The former draft read as follows:

"Governments at the appropriate levels, with the cooperation of the relevant United Nations bodies and [where necessary] regional, intergovernmental and non-governmental organizations, the private sector and financial institutions, and taking into consideration indigenous people and their communities, as well as social and economic factors, should:".

sources, including biotechnology, between the sources of those resources and those who use them;[3]

(e) Carry out country studies, as appropriate, on the conservation of biological diversity and the sustainable use of biological resources, including analyses of relevant costs and benefits, with particular reference to socio-economic aspects;

(f) Produce regularly updated world reports on biodiversity based upon national assessments;

(g) Recognize and foster the traditional methods and the knowledge of indigenous people and their communities, emphasizing the particular role of women, relevant to the conservation of biological diversity and the sustainable use of biological resources, and ensure the opportunity for the participation of those groups in the economic and commercial benefits derived from the use of such traditional methods and knowledge;[4]

(h) Implement mechanisms for the improvement, generation, development and sustainable use of biotechnology and its safe transfer, particularly to developing countries, taking account the potential contribution of biotechnology to the conservation of biological diversity and the sustainable use of biological resources;[5]

(i) Promote broader international and regional cooperation in furthering scientific and economic understanding of the importance of biodiversity and its functions in ecosystems;

(j) Develop measures and arrangements to implement the rights of countries of origin of genetic resources or countries providing genetic resources, as defined in the Convention on Biological Diversity, particularly developing countries, to benefit from the biotechnological development and the com-

---

3   Draft paragraph 15.4(d) of A/CONF.151/4 (22 April 1992) included brackets around the words "fair and equitable." The brackets were deleted by decision of the Main Committee of UNCED on 10 June 1992. See A/CONF.151/L.3/Add.15 (12 June 1992).

4   See chap. 26 (Recognizing and strengthening the role of indigenous people and their communities), and chap. 24 (Global action for women towards sustainable and equitable development). [This footnote appears in Agenda 21 as number 1 to Chapter 15, A/CONF. 151/26, vol. II, pp. 104 and 110.]

5   See chap. 16 (Environmentally sound management of biotechnology). [This footnote in Agenda 21 appears as number 2 to Chapter 15, A/CONF. 151/26, vol. II, pp. 109 and 110. Note 2 appears twice, after (h) and (j) in paragraph 15.4.]

mercial utilization of products derived from such resources. See chap. 16 (Environmentally sound management of biotechnology).[6,7,8]

Activities

(a) Management-related activities

15.5. Governments at the appropriate levels, consistent with national policies and practices, with the cooperation of the relevant United Nations bodies and, as appropriate, intergovernmental organizations and, with the support of indigenous people and their communities, non-governmental organizations and other groups, including the business and scientific communities, and consistent with the requirements of international law, should, as appropriate:[9]

(a) Develop new or strengthen existing strategies, plans or programmes of action for the conservation of biological diversity and the sustainable use of biological resources, taking account of education and training needs;[10]

(b) Integrate strategies for the conservation of biological diversity and the sustainable use of biological and genetic resources into relevant sectoral or cross-sectoral plans, programmes and policies, with particular reference to

---

6   Article 2 (Use of terms) of the Convention on Biological Diversity includes the following definitions:

"Country of origin of genetic resources" means the country which possesses those genetic resources in in-situ conditions.

"Country providing genetic resources" means the country supplying genetic resources collected from in-situ sources, including populations of both wild and domesticated species, or taken from ex-situ sources, which may or may not have originated in that country.

[This footnote in Agenda 21 appears as number 3 to Chapter 15, A/CONF. 151/26, vol. II, pp. 105 and 110.]

7   Draft paragraph 15.4(j) of A/CONF.151/4 (22 April 1992) was replaced by decision of the Main Committee of UNCED on 10 June 1992. See A/CONF.151/L.3/Add.4 (12 June 1992). The former draft read as follows:

Develop measures and arrangements to implement the rights of countries of origin—areas of origin and/or natural diversification—of genetic resources, particularly developing countries, to benefit from the biotechnological development and the commercial utilization of products derived from such resources.

8   See Chapter 16 "Environmentally Sound Management of Biotechnology." [This note appeared in the draft of Agenda 21, but was deleted from the final version.]

9   The introductory phrase of draft paragraph 15.5 of A/CONF.151/4 (22 April 1992) was replaced by decision of the Main Committee of UNCED on 10 June 1992. See A/CONF.151/L.3/Add.15 (12 June 1992). The former draft read as follows:

Governments at the appropriate levels, consistent with national policies and practices, with the co-operation of the relevant United Nations bodies and, as appropriate, intergovernmental organizations[, where necessary,] and with the support of indigenous people and their communities, non-governmental organizations and other groups, including the business and scientific communities, and consistent with the requirements of international law, should, as appropriate:.

10   See chap. 36 (Promoting education, public awareness and training). [This footnote in Agenda 21 appears as number 4 in Chapter 15, A/CONF. 151/26, vol. II, pp. 105 and 110.]

the special importance of terrestrial and aquatic biological and genetic resources for food and agriculture;[11]

(c) Undertake country studies or use other methods to identify components of biological diversity important for its conservation and for the sustainable use of biological resources, ascribe values to biological and genetic resources, identify processes and activities with significant impacts upon biological diversity, evaluate the potential economic implications of the conservation of biological diversity and the sustainable use of biological and genetic resources, and suggest priority action;

(d) Take effective economic, social and other appropriate incentive measures to encourage the conservation of biological diversity and the sustainable use of biological resources, including the promotion of sustainable production systems, such as traditional methods of agriculture, agroforestry, forestry, range and wildlife management, which use, maintain or increase biodiversity;[12]

(e) Subject to national legislation, take action to respect, record, protect and promote the wider application of the knowledge, innovations and practices of indigenous and local communities embodying traditional lifestyles for the conservation of biological diversity and the sustainable use of biological resources, with a view to the fair and equitable[13] sharing of the benefits arising, and promote mechanisms to involve those communities, including women, in the conservation and management of ecosystems;[14]

(f) Undertake long-term research into the importance of biodiversity for the functioning of ecosystems and the role of ecosystems in producing goods, environmental services and other values supporting sustainable development, with particular reference to the biology and reproductive capacities of key terrestrial and aquatic species, including native, cultivated and cultured species; new observation and inventory techniques; ecological conditions necessary for biodiversity conservation and continued evolution; and social behaviour and nutrition habits dependent on natural ecosystems, where women play key roles. The work should be undertaken with the widest possi-

---

11   See chap. 14 (Promoting sustainable agriculture and rural development) and chap. 11 (Combating deforestation). [This footnote appears in Agenda 21 as number 5 in Chapter 15, A/CONF. 151/26, vol. II, pp. 105 and 110. It appears twice, after (b) and (d) to paragraph 15.5.]

12   See chap. 14 (Promoting sustainable agriculture and rural development) and chap. 11 (Combatting deforestation).

13   Footnote 1 to Chapter 15 of Agenda 21 is repeated here (see note 4, *supra*). Draft paragraph 15.5(e) of A/CONF.151/4 (22 April 1992) included brackets around the words "fair and equitable." The brackets were deleted by decision of the Main Committee of UNCED on 10 June 1992. See A/CONF.151/L.3/Add.15 (12 June 1992).

14   See chap. 26 (Recognizing and strengthening the role of indigenous people and their communities) and chap. 24 (Global action for women towards sustainable and equitable development).

ble participation, especially of indigenous people and their communities, including women;[15]

(g) Take action where necessary for the conservation of biological diversity through the *in situ* conservation of ecosystems and natural habitats, as well as primitive cultivars and their wild relatives, and the maintenance and recovery of viable populations of species in their natural surroundings, and implement *ex situ* measures, preferably in the source country. *In situ* measures should include the reinforcement of terrestrial, marine and aquatic protected area systems to embrace, *inter alia*, vulnerable freshwater and other wetlands and coastal ecosystems, such as estuaries, coral reefs and mangroves;[16]

(h) Promote the rehabilitation and restoration of damaged ecosystems and the recovery of threatened and endangered species;

(i) Develop policies to encourage the conservation of biodiversity and the sustainable use of biological and genetic resources on private lands;

(j) Promote environmentally sound and sustainable development in areas adjacent to protected areas with a view to furthering protection of these areas;

(k) Introduce appropriate environmental impact assessment procedures for proposed projects likely to have significant impacts upon biological diversity, providing for suitable information to be made widely available and for public participation, where appropriate and encourage the assessment of the impacts of relevant policies and programmes on biological diversity;

(l) Promote, where appropriate, the establishment and strengthening of national inventory, regulation or management and control systems related to biological resources, at the appropriate level;[17]

(m) Take measures to encourage a greater understanding and appreciation of the value of biological diversity, as manifested both in its component parts and in the ecosystem services provided.

(b) Data and information

15.6. Governments at the appropriate levels, consistent with national policies and practices, with the cooperation of the relevant United Nations bodies and,

---

15   This note appears in Agenda 21 as note 1 to Chapter 15, as follows:

      See chap. 26 (Recognizing and strengthening the role of indigenous people and their communities) and chap. 24 (Global action for women towards sustainable and equitable development).

16   See chap. 17 (Protection of the oceans, all kinds of seas, including enclosed and semi-enclosed seas, and coastal areas and the protection, rational use and development of their living resources). [This note appears in Agenda 21 as note 6 to Chapter 15, A/CONF. 151/26, vol. II, pp. 106 and 110.]

17   Draft paragraph 15.5(l) of A/CONF.151/4 (22 April 1992) was revised by decision of the Main Committee of UNCED on 10 June 1992. See A/CONF.151/L.3/Add.15 (12 June 1992). The former draft read as follows:

      Promote, where appropriate, the establishment and strengthening of [national registration], regulation or management and control systems at the appropriate level related to biological resources.

as appropriate, intergovernmental organizations, and with the support of indigenous people and their communities, non-governmental organizations and other groups, including the business and scientific communities, and consistent with the requirements of international law, should, as appropriate:[18]

(a) Regularly collate, evaluate and exchange information on the conservation of biological diversity and the sustainable use of biological resources;

(b) Develop methodologies with a view to undertaking systematic sampling and evaluation on a national basis of the components of biological diversity identified by means of country studies;

(c) Initiate or further develop methodologies and begin or continue work on surveys at the appropriate level on the status of ecosystems and establish baseline information on biological and genetic resources, including those in terrestrial, aquatic, coastal and marine ecosystems, as well as inventories undertaken with the participation of local and indigenous people and their communities;

(d) Identify and evaluate the potential economic and social implications and benefits of the conservation and sustainable use of terrestrial and aquatic species in each country, building upon the results of country studies;

(e) Undertake the updating, analysis and interpretation of data derived from the identification, sampling and evaluation activities described above;

(f) Collect, assess and make available relevant and reliable information in a timely manner and in a form suitable for decision-making at all levels, with the full support and participation of local and indigenous people and their communities.

(c) International and regional cooperation and coordination

15.7. Governments at the appropriate level, with the cooperation of the relevant United Nations bodies and, as appropriate, intergovernmental organizations, and, with the support of indigenous people and their communities, non-governmental organizations and other groups, including the business and

---

18   See chap. 40 (Information for decision-making). [This note appears as number 7 to Chapter 15 in Agenda 21, A/CONF. 151/26, vol. II, pp. 107 and 110. To this note, a further annotation had originally provided as follows:

The introductory phrase to draft paragraph 15.6 of A/CONF.151/4 (22 April 1992) was revised by decision of the Main Committee of UNCED on 10 June 1992. See A/CONF.151/L.3/Add.15 (12 June 1992).

The former draft read as follows:

"Governments at the appropriate levels, consistent with national policies and practices, with the cooperation of the relevant United Nations bodies and, as appropriate, intergovernmental organizations and [, where necessary,] with the support of indigenous people and their communities, non-governmental organizations and other groups, including the business and scientific communities, and consistent with the requirements of international law, should, as appropriate:"]

scientific communities, and consistent with the requirements of international law, should, as appropriate:[19]

(a) Consider the establishment or strengthening of national or international capabilities and networks for the exchange of data and information of relevance to the conservation of biological diversity and the sustainable use of biological and genetic resources;[20]

(b) Produce regularly updated world reports on biodiversity based upon national assessments in all countries;

(c) Promote technical and scientific cooperation in the field of conservation of biological diversity and the sustainable use of biological and genetic resources. Special attention should be given to the development and strengthening of national capabilities by means of human resource development and institution-building, including the transfer of technology and/or development of research and management facilities, such as herbaria, museums, gene banks, and laboratories, related to the conservation of biodiversity;[21]

(d) Without prejudice to the relevant provisions of the Convention on Biological Diversity, facilitate for this chapter the transfer of technologies relevant to the conservation of biological diversity and the sustainable use of biological resources or technologies that make use of genetic resources and cause no significant damage to the environment, in conformity with chapter 34, and recognizing that technology includes biotechnology;[22]

---

19   The introductory phrase to draft paragraph 15.7 of A/CONF.151/4 (22 April 1992) was revised by decision of the Main Committee of UNCED on 10 June 1992. See A/CONF.151/L.3/Add.15 (12 June 1992). The former draft read as follows:

"Governments at the appropriate levels, with the cooperation of the relevant United Nations bodies and, as appropriate, intergovernmental organizations, and [, where necessary,] with the support of indigenous people and their communities, non-governmental organizations and other groups, including the business and scientific communities, and consistent with the requirements of international law, should, as appropriate:".

20   See chap. 40 (Information for decision-making). [This is note 7 to Chapter 15 of Agenda 21. It appears twice, with paragraphs 15.6 and 15.7(a).]

21   See chap. 34 (Transfer of environmentally sound technology, cooperation and capacity-building). [This footnote appears as number 8 to Chapter 15 of Agenda 21. It appears twice, with paragraph 15.7(c) and (d). A/CONF. 151/26, vol. II, pp. 108 and 110.]

22   The note in Agenda 21 repeats notes 2 and 8 to Chapter 15 of Agenda 21, which provide as follows:

See chap. 16 (Environmentally sound management of biotechnology). See chap. 34 (Transfer of environmentally sound technology, coooperation and capacity-building).

To this note, a further annotation had originally provided as follows:

Draft paragraph 15.7(d) of A/CONF.151/4 (22 April 1992) was replaced by decision of the Main Committee of UNCED on 10 June 1992. See A/CONF.151/L.3/Add.15 (12 June 1992).

The former draft read as follows:

Provide and/or facilitate the transfer of and cooperation on technologies relevant to the conservation of biological diversity and the sustainable use of biological resources or that make use of genetic resources and cause no significant damage to the environment, recognizing that technology includes biotechnology.

(e) Promote cooperation between the parties to relevant international conventions and action plans with the aim of strengthening and coordinating efforts to conserve biological diversity and the sustainable use of biological resources;

(f) Strengthen support for international and regional instruments, programmes and action plans concerned with the conservation of biological diversity and the sustainable use of biological resources;

(g) Promote improved international coordination of measures for the effective conservation and management of endangered/non-pest migratory species, including appropriate levels of support for the establishment and management of protected areas in transboundary locations;

(h) Promote national efforts with respect to surveys, data collection, sampling and evaluation, and the maintenance of gene banks.

Means of implementation

(a) Financing and cost-evaluation

15.8. The Conference secretariat has estimated the average total annual cost (1993-2000) of implementing the activities of this chapter to be about $3.5 billion, including about $1.75 billion from the international community on grant or concessional terms. These are indicative and order-of-magnitude estimates only and have not been reviewed by Governments. Actual costs and financial terms, including any that are non-concessional, will depend upon, *inter alia*, the specific strategies and programmes Governments decide upon for implementation.[23]

(b) Scientific and technological means

15.9. Specific aspects to be addressed include the need to develop:

(a) Efficient methodologies for baseline surveys and inventories, as well as for the systematic sampling and evaluation of biological resources;

---

23   Draft paragraph 15.8 of A/CONF.151/4 (22 April 1992) was replaced by decision of the Main Committee of UNCED on 10 June 1992. See A/CONF.151/L.3/Add.15 (12 June 1992). The former draft read as follows:

   The estimated average annual cost of the programme area in this chapter during the period 1993-2000 is expected to be about $3.5 billion. The estimated average annual cost of strengthening international organizations to assist countries to conduct programmes is expected to be about $24 million. Pending the outcome of the work of the Intergovernmental Negotiating Committee for a Convention on Biological Diversity, these estimated costs have been arbitrarily divided equally between national Governments—supported as appropriate by non-governmental organizations, local communities and others—and the international community.

   To this note, a further annotation had originally provided as follows:

   This paragraph contains matters relating to means of implementation, including cost estimates, which are indicative secretariat figures provided pursuant to decision A/CONF.151/PC/L.49*. They remain in brackets as they have not been negotiated, but they have been adjusted by the Secretariat to reflect the orientation and content of A/CONF.151/PC/WG.I/L.44.

(b) Methods and technologies for the conservation of biological diversity and the sustainable use of biological resources;

(c) Improved and diversified methods for *ex situ* conservation with a view to the long-term conservation of genetic resources of importance for research and development.

(c) Human resource development

15.10. There is a need, where appropriate, to:

(a) Increase the number and/or make more efficient use of trained personnel in scientific and technological fields relevant to the conservation of biological diversity and the sustainable use of biological resources;

(b) Maintain or establish programmes for scientific and technical education and training of managers and professionals, especially in developing countries, on measures for the identification, conservation of biological diversity and the sustainable use of biological resources;

(c) Promote and encourage understanding of the importance of the measures required for the conservation of biological diversity and the sustainable use of biological resources at all policy-making and decision-making levels in Governments, business enterprises and lending institutions, and promote and encourage the inclusion of these topics in educational programmes.

(d) Capacity-building

15.11. There is a need, where appropriate, to:

(a) Strengthen existing institutions and/or establish new ones responsible for the conservation of biological diversity and to consider the development of mechanisms such as national biodiversity institutes or centres;

(b) Continue to build capacity for the conservation of biological diversity and the sustainable use of biological resources in all relevant sectors;

(c) Build capacity, especially within Governments, business enterprises and bilateral and multilateral development agencies, for integrating biodiversity concerns, potential benefits and opportunity cost calculations into project design, implementation and evaluation processes, as well as for evaluating the impact on biological diversity of proposed development projects;

(d) Enhance the capacity of governmental and private institutions, at the appropriate level, responsible for protected area planning and management to undertake intersectoral coordination and planning with other governmental institutions, non-governmental organizations and, where appropriate, indigenous people and their communities.

Chapter 16

Environmentally Sound Management of Biotechnology

INTRODUCTION

16.1. Biotechnology is the integration of the new techniques emerging from modern biotechnology with the well-established approaches of traditional biotechnology. Biotechnology, an emerging knowledge-intensive field, is a set of enabling techniques for bringing about specific man-made changes in deoxyribonucleic acid (DNA), or genetic material, in plants, animals and microbial systems, leading to useful products and technologies. By itself, biotechnology cannot resolve all the fundamental problems of environment and development, so expectations need to be tempered by realism. Nevertheless, it promises to make a significant contribution in enabling the development of, for example, better health care, enhanced food security through sustainable agricultural practices, improved supplies of potable water, more efficient industrial development processes for transforming raw materials, support for sustainable methods of afforestation and reforestation, and detoxification of hazardous wastes. Biotechnology also offers new opportunities for global partnerships, especially between the countries rich in biological resources (which include genetic resources) but lacking the expertise and investments needed to apply such resources through biotechnology and the countries that have developed the technological expertise to transform biological resources so that they serve the needs of sustainable development.[1] Biotechnology can assist in the conservation of those resources through, for example, *ex situ* techniques. The programme areas set out below seek to foster internationally agreed principles to be applied to ensure the environmentally sound management of biotechnology, to engender public trust and confidence, to promote the development of sustainable applications of biotechnology and to establish appropriate enabling mechanisms, especially within developing countries, through the following activities:

(a) Increasing availability of food, feed and renewable raw materials;

(b) Improving human health;

(c) Enhancing protection of the environment;

---

1   See chap. 15 (Conservation of biological diversity.)

(d) Enhancing safety and developing international mechanisms for cooperation;

(e) Establishing enabling mechanisms for the environmentally sound application of biotechnology.

PROGRAMME AREAS

A. Increasing the availability of food, feed and renewable raw materials

Basis for action

16.2. To meet the growing consumption needs of the global population, the challenge is not only to increase food supply, but also to improve food distribution significantly while simultaneously developing more sustainable agricultural systems. Much of this increased productivity will need to take place in developing countries. It will require the successful and environmentally safe application of biotechnology in agriculture, in the environment and in human health care. Most of the investment in modern biotechnology has been in the industrialized world. Significant new investments and human resource development will be required in biotechnology, especially in the developing world.

Objectives

16.3. The following objectives are proposed, keeping in mind the need to promote the use of appropriate safety measures based on programme area D:

(a) To increase to the optimum possible extent the yield of major crops, livestock, and aquaculture species, by using the combined resources of modern biotechnology and conventional plant/animal/micro-organism improvement, including the more diverse use of genetic material resources, both hybrid and original.[2] Forest product yields should similarly be increased, to ensure the sustainable use of forests;[3]

(b) To reduce the need for volume increases of food, feed and raw materials by improving the nutritional value (composition) of the source crops, animals and micro-organisms, and to reduce post-harvest losses of plant and animal products;

(c) To increase the use of integrated pest, disease and crop management techniques to eliminate overdependence on agrochemicals, thereby encouraging environmentally sustainable agricultural practices;

---

2   See chap. 14 (Promoting sustainable agriculture and rural development).
3   See chap. 11 (Combatting deforestation).

(d) To evaluate the agricultural potential of marginal lands in comparison with other potential uses to develop where appropriate systems allowing for sustainable productivity increases;

(e) To expand the applications of biotechnology in forestry, both for increasing yields and more efficient utilization of forest products and for improving afforestation and reforestation techniques. Efforts should be concentrated on species and products that are grown in and are of value particularly for developing countries;

(f) To increase the efficiency of nitrogen fixation and mineral absorption by the symbiosis of higher plants with micro-organisms;

(g) To improve capabilities in basic and applied sciences and in the management of complex interdisciplinary research projects.

Activities

(a) Management-related activities

16.4. Governments at the appropriate level, with the assistance of international and regional organizations and with the support of non-governmental organizations, the private sector, and academic and scientific institutions, should improve both plant and animal breeding and micro-organisms through the use of traditional and modern biotechnologies, to enhance sustainable agricultural output to achieve food security, particularly in developing countries, with due regard to the prior identification of desired characteristics before modification, taking into account the needs of farmers, the socio-economic, cultural and environmental impacts of modifications and the need to promote sustainable social and economic development, paying particular attention to how the use of biotechnology will impact on the maintenance of environmental integrity.[4]

16.5. More specifically, these entities should:

(a) Improve productivity, nutritional quality and shelf-life of food and animal feed products, with efforts including work on pre- and post-harvest losses;

(b) Further develop resistance to diseases and pests;

---

4   Draft paragraph 16.4 of A/CONF.151/4 (22 April 1992) was replaced by decision of the Main Committee of UNCED on 10 June 1992. See A/CONF.151/L.3/Add.16 (11 June 1992). The former draft read as follows:

Governments at the appropriate level, with the assistance of international and regional organizations and [,where necessary,] with the support of non-governmental organizations, the private sector, and academic and scientific institutions, should improve both plant and animal breeding and micro-organisms through the use of traditional and modern biotechnologies, to enhance sustainable agricultural output to achieve food security, particularly in developing countries, with due regard to the prior identification of desired characteristics before modification, taking into account the needs of farmers, the socio-economic, cultural and environmental impacts of modifications and the need to promote sustainable social and economic development and paying particular attention to how the use of biotechnology will impact on the maintenance of environmental integrity.

(c) Develop plant cultivars tolerant and/or resistant to stress from factors such as pests and diseases and from abiotic causes;

(d) Promote the use of underutilized crops of possible future importance for human nutrition and industrial supply of raw materials;

(e) Increase the efficiency of symbiotic processes that assist sustainable agricultural production;

(f) Facilitate the conservation and safe exchange of plant, animal and microbial germ plasm by applying risk assessment and management procedures, including improved diagnostic techniques for detection of pests and diseases by better methods of rapid propagation;

(g) Develop improved diagnostic techniques and vaccines for the prevention and spread of diseases and for rapid assessment of toxins or infectious organisms in products for human use or livestock feed;

(h) Identify more productive strains of fast-growing trees, especially for fuel wood, and develop rapid propagation methods to aid their wider dissemination and use;

(i) Evaluate the use of various biotechnology techniques to improve the yields of fish, algal and other aquatic species;

(j) Promote sustainable agricultural output by strengthening and broadening the capacity and scope of existing research centres to achieve the necessary critical mass through encouragement and monitoring of research into the development of biological products and processes of productive and environmental value that are economically and socially feasible, while taking safety considerations into account;

(k) Promote the integration of appropriate and traditional biotechnologies for the purposes of cultivating genetically modified plants, rearing healthy animals and protecting forest genetic resources;

(l) Develop processes to increase the availability of materials derived from biotechnology for use in food, feed and renewable raw materials production.

(b) Data and information

16.6. The following activities should be undertaken:

(a) Consideration of comparative assessments of the potential of the different technologies for food production, together with a system for assessing the possible effects of biotechnologies on international trade in agricultural products;

(b) Examination of the implications of the withdrawal of subsidies and the possible use of other economic instruments to reflect the environmental costs associated with the unsustainable use of agrochemicals;

(c) Maintenance and development of data banks of information on environmental and health impacts of organisms to facilitate risk assessment;

(d) Acceleration of technology acquisition, transfer and adaptation by developing countries to support national activities that promote food security.

(c) International and regional cooperation and coordination

16.7. Governments at the appropriate level, with the support of relevant international and regional organizations, should promote the following activities in conformity with international agreements or arrangements on biological diversity, as appropriate:

(a) Cooperation on issues related to conservation of, access to and exchange of germ plasm; rights associated with intellectual property and informal innovations including farmers' and breeders' rights; access to the benefits of biotechnology; and bio-safety;

(b) Promotion of collaborative research programmes, especially in developing countries, to support activities outlined in this programme area, with particular reference to cooperation with local and indigenous people and their communities in the conservation of biological diversity and sustainable use of biological resources, as well as the fostering of traditional methods and knowledge of such groups in connection with these activities;

(c) Acceleration of technology acquisition, transfer and adaptation by developing countries to support national activities that promote food security, through the development of systems for substantial and sustainable productivity increases that do not damage or endanger local ecosystems;[5]

(d) Development of appropriate safety procedures based on programme area D, taking account of ethical considerations.

Means of implementation

(a) Financing and cost evaluation

16.8. The Conference secretariat has estimated the average total annual cost (1993-2000) of implementing the activities of this programme to be about $5 billion, including about $50 million from the international community on grant or concessional terms. These are indicative and order-of-magnitude estimates only and have not been reviewed by Governments. Actual costs and financial terms, including any that are non-concessional, will depend upon,

---

5   See chap. 34 (Transfer of environmentally sound technology, cooperation and capacity-building). [This footnote appears in Agenda 21 as number 9 to Chapter 16, A/CONF. 151/26, vol. II, pp. 115 and 129.]

inter alia, the specific strategies and programmes Governments decide upon for implementation.[6]

(b) Scientific and technological means[7]

(c) Human resource development

16.9. Training of competent professionals in the basic and applied sciences at all levels (including scientific personnel, technical staff and extension workers) is one of the most essential components of any programme of this kind. Creating awareness of the benefits and risks of biotechnology is essential. Given the importance of good management of research resources for the successful completion of large multidisciplinary projects, continuing programmes of formal training for scientists should include managerial training. Training programmes should also be developed, within the context of specific projects, to meet regional or national needs for comprehensively trained personnel capable of using advanced technology to reduce the "brain drain" from developing to developed countries. Emphasis should be given to encouraging collaboration between and training of scientists, extension workers and users to produce integrated systems. Additionally, special consideration should be given to the execution of programmes for training and exchange of knowledge on traditional biotechnologies and for training on safety procedures.

(d) Capacity-building

16.10. Institutional upgrading or other appropriate measures will be needed to build up technical, managerial, planning and administrative capacities at the national level to support the activities in this programme area. Such measures should be backed up by international, scientific, technical and financial assistance adequate to facilitate technical cooperation and raise the capacities of the developing countries. Programme area E contains further details.[8]

---

6   Draft paragraph 16.8 of A/CONF.151/4 (22 April 1992) was replaced by decision of the Main Committee of UNCED on 10 June 1992. See A/CONF.151/L.3/Add.16 (11 June 1992). The former draft read as follows:

   The estimated average annual cost of this programme area for the period 1993-2000 could be upwards of $5 billion, of which it is estimated that about $50 million would come from international financing sources. Most of the amount for this programme area is included in the cost evaluation of other chapters. Both the total amount and the proportion of global investments currently being made by developing countries in biotechnology research and development need to be increased significantly over the period 1993-2000 and beyond to enable them to take advantage of the increasing opportunities offered by biotechnology for accelerated development.

7   See paras. 16.6 and 16.7. [This footnote appears as an asterisk to subheading (b) under means of implementation, "Management Related Activities," p. 115 to A/CONF. 151/26, vol. II, p. 115.]

8   Draft paragraph 16.11 of A/CONF.151/4 (22 April 1992) included brackets around the entire text of paragraph 16.11. The brackets were deleted by decision of the Main Committee of UNCED on 10 June 1992. See A/CONF.151/L.3/Add.16 (11 June 1992).

B. Improving human health

Basis for action

16.11. The improvement of human health is one of the most important objectives of development. The deterioration of environmental quality, notably air, water and soil pollution owing to toxic chemicals, hazardous wastes, radiation and other sources, is a matter of growing concern. This degradation of the environment resulting from inadequate or inappropriate development has a direct negative effect on human health. Malnutrition, poverty, poor human settlements, lack of good-quality potable water and inadequate sanitation facilities add to the problems of communicable and non-communicable diseases. As a consequence, the health and well-being of people are exposed to increasing pressures.

Objectives

16.12. The main objective of this programme area is to contribute, through the environmentally sound application of biotechnology to an overall health programme to:[9]

(a) Reinforce or inaugurate (as a matter of urgency) programmes to help combat major communicable diseases;

(b) Promote good general health among people of all ages;

(c) Develop and improve programmes to assist in specific treatment of and protection from major non-communicable diseases;

(d) Develop and strengthen appropriate safety procedures based on programme area D, taking account of ethical considerations;

(e) Create enhanced capabilities for carrying out basic and applied research and for managing interdisciplinary research.

Activities

(a) Management-related activities

16.13. Governments at the appropriate level, with the assistance of international and regional organizations, academic and scientific institutions, and the pharmaceutical industry, should, taking into account appropriate safety and ethical considerations:

(a) Develop national and international programmes for identifying and targeting those populations of the world most in need of improvement in general health and protection from diseases;

---

9   See chap. 6 (Protection and promotion of human health conditions). [This footnote appears as number 5 to Chapter 16 in Agenda 21, A/CONF. 151/26, vol. II, pp. 116 and 129.]

(b) Develop criteria for evaluating the effectiveness and the benefits and risks of the proposed activities;

(c) Establish and enforce screening, systematic sampling and evaluation procedures for drugs and medical technologies with a view to barring the use of those which are unsafe for the purposes of experimentation; ensure that drugs and technologies relating to reproductive health are safe and effective and take account of ethical considerations;[10]

(d) Improve, systematically sample and evaluate drinking-water quality by introducing appropriate specific measures, including diagnosis of water-borne pathogens and pollutants;

(e) Develop and make widely available new and improved vaccines against major communicable diseases that are efficient and safe and offer protection with a minimum number of doses, including intensifying efforts directed at the vaccines needed to combat common diseases of children;

(f) Develop biodegradable delivery systems for vaccines that eliminate the need for present multiple-dose schedules, facilitate better coverage of the population and reduce the costs of immunization;

(g) Develop effective biological control agents against disease-transmitting vectors, such as mosquitoes and resistant variants, taking account of environmental protection considerations;

(h) Using the tools provided by modern biotechnology, develop, *inter alia,* improved diagnostics, new drugs and improved treatments and delivery systems;

(i) Develop the improvement and more effective utilization of medicinal plants and other related sources;

(j) Develop processes to increase the availability of materials derived from biotechnology, for use in improving human health.

(b) Data and information

16.14. The following activities should be undertaken:

(a) Research to assess the comparative social, environmental and financial costs and benefits of different technologies for basic and reproductive health care within a framework of universal safety and ethical considerations;

(b) Development of public education programmes directed at decision makers and the general public to encourage awareness and understanding of the relative benefits and risks of modern biotechnology, according to ethical and cultural considerations.

---

10   Draft paragraph 16.14(c) of A/CONF.151/4 (22 April 1992) included brackets around the words "and take account of ethical considerations." The brackets were deleted by decision of the Main Committee of UNCED on 10 June 1992. See A/CONF.151/L.3/Add.16 (11 June 1992).

(c) International and regional cooperation and coordination

16.15. Governments at the appropriate levels, with the support of relevant international and regional organizations, should:

(a) Develop and strengthen appropriate safety procedures based on programme area D, taking account of ethical considerations;

(b) Support the development of national programmes, particularly in developing countries, for improvements in general health, especially protection from major communicable diseases, common diseases of children and disease-transmitting factors.

Means of implementation

16.16. To achieve the above goals, the activities need to be implemented with urgency if progress towards the control of major communicable diseases is to be achieved by the beginning of the next century. The spread of some diseases to all regions of the world calls for global measures. For more localized diseases, regional or national policies will be more appropriate. The achievement of goals calls for:

(a) Continuous international commitment;

(b) National priorities with a defined time-frame;

(c) Scientific and financial input at global and national levels.[11]

(a) Financing and cost evaluation

16.17. The Conference secretariat has estimated the average total annual cost (1993-2000) of implementing the activities of this programme to be about $4 billion, including about $130 million from the international community on grant or concessional terms. These are indicative and order-of-magnitude estimates only and have not been reviewed by Governments. Actual costs and financial terms, including any that are non-concessional, will depend upon, *inter alia*, the specific strategies and programmes Governments decide upon for implementation.[12]

(b) Scientific and technological means

16.18. Well-coordinated multidisciplinary efforts involving cooperation between scientists, financial institutions and industries will be required. At the global

---

11 Draft paragraph 16.17 of A/CONF.151/4 (22 April 1992) included brackets around the entire text of paragraph 16.17. The brackets were deleted by decision of the Main Committee of UNCED on 10 June 1992. See A/CONF.151/L.3/Add.16 (11 June 1992).

12 Draft paragraph 16.18 of A/CONF.151/4 (22 April 1992) was replaced by decision of the Main Committee of UNCED on 10 June 1992. See A/CONF.151/L.3/Add.16 (11 June 1992). The former draft read as follows:

The estimated average annual cost of this programme area could be upwards of $14 billion, of which it is estimated that about $130 million would come from international financing sources.

level, this may mean collaboration between research institutions in different countries, with funding at the intergovernmental level, possibly supported by similar collaboration at the national level. Research and development support will also need to be strengthened, together with the mechanisms for providing the transfer of relevant technology.

(c) Human resource development

16.19. Training and technology transfer is needed at the global level, with regions and countries having access to, and participation in exchange of, information and expertise, particularly indigenous or traditional knowledge and related biotechnology. It is essential to create or enhance endogenous capabilities in developing countries to enable them to participate actively in the processes of biotechnology production. The training of personnel could be undertaken at three levels:

(a) That of scientists required for basic and product-oriented research;

(b) That of health personnel (to be trained in the safe use of new products) and of science managers required for complex intermultidisciplinary research;

(c) That of tertiary-level technical workers required for delivery in the field.

(d) Capacity-building[13]

C. Enhancing protection of the environment

Basis for action

16.20. Environmental protection is an integral component of sustainable development. The environment is threatened in all its biotic and abiotic components: animals, plants, microbes and ecosystems comprising biological diversity; water, soil and air, which form the physical components of habitats and ecosystems; and all the interactions between the components of biodiversity and their sustaining habitats and ecosystems.[14] With the continued increase in the use of chemicals, energy and non-renewable resources by an expanding global population, associated environmental problems will also increase. Despite increasing efforts to prevent waste accumulation and to promote recycling, the amount of environmental damage caused by overconsumption, the quantities of waste generated and the degree of unsustainable land use appear likely to continue growing.

16.21. The need for a diverse genetic pool of plant, animal and microbial germ plasm for sustainable development is well established. Biotechnology is one of

---

13   See programme area E. [This footnote appears as an asterisk to the subheading in Agenda 21. A/CONF. 151/26, vol. II, p. 119.]

14   Draft paragraph 16.22 of A/CONF.151/4 (22 April 1992) was revised by decision of the Main Committee of UNCED on 10 June 1992. See A/CONF.151/L.3/Add. 16 (11 June 1992). The word "soil" in the second sentence read "oil" in the former draft.

many tools that can play an important role in supporting the rehabilitation of degraded ecosystems and landscapes. This may be done through the development of new techniques for reforestation and afforestation, germ plasm conservation, and cultivation of new plant varieties. Biotechnology can also contribute to the study of the effects exerted on the remaining organisms and on other organisms by organisms introduced into ecosystems.

Objectives

16.22. The aim of this programme is to prevent, halt and reverse environmental degradation through the appropriate use of biotechnology in conjunction with other technologies, while supporting safety procedures as an integral component of the programme. Specific objectives include the inauguration as soon as possible of specific programmes with specific targets:

(a) To adopt production processes making optimal use of natural resources, by recycling biomass, recovering energy and minimizing waste generation;[15]

(b) To promote the use of biotechnologies, with emphasis on bio-remediation of land and water, waste treatment, soil conservation, reforestation, afforestation and land rehabilitation;[16]

(c) To apply biotechnologies and their products to protect environmental integrity with a view to long-term ecological security.

Activities

(a) Management-related activities

16.23. Governments at the appropriate level, with the support of relevant international and regional organizations, the private sector, non-governmental organizations and academic and scientific institutions should:[17]

(a) Develop environmentally sound alternatives and improvements for environmentally damaging production processes;

---

15   See chap. 21 (Environmentally sound management of solid wastes and sewage-related issues). [This footnote appears as number 6 to Chapter 16 in Agenda 21, A/CONF. 151/26, vol. II, pp. 120 and 129.]

16   See chap. 10 (Integrated approach to planning and management of land resources). See chap. 18 (Protection of the quality and supply of freshwater resources: application of integrated approaches to the development, management and use of water resources). [This footnote appears as numbers 7 and 8, both at the end of paragraph 16.22(b) to Agenda 21, A/CONF. A/CONF. 15/26, vol II, pp 120 and 129.]

17   The introductory phrase to draft paragraph 16.25 of A/CONF.151/4 (22 April 1992) was revised by decision of the Main Committee of UNCED on 10 June 1992. See A/CONF.151/L.3/Add.16 (11 June 1992). The former draft read as follows:

"Governments at the appropriate levels and[, where necessary,] with the support of relevant international and regional organizations, the private sector, non-governmental organizations and academic and scientific institutions should:".

(b) Develop applications to minimize the requirement for unsustainable synthetic chemical input and to maximize the use of environmentally appropriate products, including natural products (see programme area A);

(c) Develop processes to reduce waste generation, treat waste before disposal and make use of biodegradable materials;

(d) Develop processes to recover energy and provide renewable energy sources, animal feed and raw materials from recycling organic waste and biomass;

(e) Develop processes to remove pollutants from the environment, including accidental oil spills, where conventional techniques are not available or are expensive, inefficient or inadequate;

(f) Develop processes to increase the availability of planting materials, particularly indigenous varieties, for use in afforestation and reforestation and to improve sustainable yields from forests;

(g) Develop applications to increase the availability of stress-tolerant planting material for land rehabilitation and soil conservation;

(h) Promote the use of integrated pest management based on the judicious use of bio-control agents;

(i) Promote the appropriate use of bio-fertilizers within national fertilizer programmes;

(j) Promote the use of biotechnologies relevant to the conservation and scientific study of biological diversity and the sustainable use of biological resources;

(k) Develop easily applicable technologies for the treatment of sewage and organic waste;

(l) Develop new technologies for rapid screening of organisms for useful biological properties;

(m) Promote new biotechnologies for tapping mineral resources in an environmentally sustainable manner.

(b) Data and information

16.24. Steps should be taken to increase access both to existing information about biotechnology and to facilities based on global databases.

(c) International and regional cooperation and coordination

16.25. Governments at the appropriate levels, with the support of relevant international and regional organizations, should:

(a) Strengthen research, training and development capabilities, particularly in developing countries, to support the activities outlined in this programme area;

(b) Develop mechanisms for scaling up and disseminating environmentally sound biotechnologies of high environmental importance, especially in the short term, even though those biotechnologies may have limited commercial potential;

(c) Enhance cooperation, including transfer of biotechnology, between participating countries for capacity-building;

(d) Develop appropriate safety procedures based on programme area D, taking account of ethical considerations.

Means of implementation

(a) Financing and cost evaluation

16.26. The Conference secretariat has estimated the average total annual cost (1993-2000) of implementing the activities of this programme to be about $1 billion, including about $10 million from the international community on grant or concessional terms. These are indicative and order-of-magnitude estimates only and have not been reviewed by Governments. Actual costs and financial terms, including any that are non-concessional, will depend upon, *inter alia*, the specific strategies and programmes Governments decide upon for implementation.[18]

(b) Scientific and technological means[19]

(c) Human resource development

16.27. The activities for this programme area will increase the demand for trained personnel. Support for existing training programmes needs to be increased, for example, at the university and technical institute level, as well as the exchange of trained personnel between countries and regions. New and additional training programmes also need to be developed, for example, for technical and support personnel. There is also an urgent need to improve the level of understanding of biological principles and their policy implications among decision makers in Governments, and financial and other institutions.

Capacity-building

16.28. Relevant institutions will need to have the responsibility for undertaking, and the capacity (political, financial and workforce) to undertake, the above-mentioned activities and to be dynamic in response to new biotechnological developments (see programme area E).

---

18 Draft paragraph 16.28 of A/CONF.151/4 (22 April 1992) was replaced by decision of the Main Committee of UNCED on 10 June 1992. See A/CONF.151/L.3/Add.16 (11 June 1992). The former draft read as follows:

> The estimated average annual cost of this programme area could be upwards of $1 billion, of which it is estimated that about $10 million would come from international financing sources.

19 See paras. 16.23-16.25 above. [This footnote appears as an asterisk following subheading (b), under Means of Implementation for "Enhancing Protection of the Environment" in Chapter 16.]

D. Enhancing safety and developing international mechanisms for cooperation

Basis for action

16.29. There is a need for further development of internationally agreed principles on risk assessment and management of all aspects of biotechnology, which should build upon those developed at the national level. Only when adequate and transparent safety and border-control procedures are in place will the community at large be able to derive maximum benefit from, and be in a much better position to accept the potential benefits and risks of, biotechnology. Several fundamental principles could underlie many of these safety procedures, including primary consideration of the organism, building on the principle of familiarity, applied in a flexible framework, taking into account national requirements and recognizing that the logical progression is to start with a step-by-step and case-by-case approach, but also recognizing that experience has shown that in many instances a more comprehensive approach should be used, based on the experiences of the first period, leading, *inter alia*, to streamlining and categorizing; complementary consideration of risk assessment and risk management; and classification into contained use or release to the environment.[20]

Objectives

16.30. The aim of this programme area is to ensure safety in biotechnology development, application, exchange and transfer through international agreement on principles to be applied on risk assessment and management,[21] with particular reference to health and environmental considerations, including the widest possible public participation and taking account of ethical considerations.

Activities

16.31. The proposed activities for this programme area call for close international cooperation. They should build upon planned or existing activities to ac-

---

20   Draft paragraph 16.32 of A/CONF.151/4 (22 April 1992) was replaced by decision of the Main Committee of UNCED on 10 June 1992. See A/CONF.151/L.3/Add.16 (11 June 1992). The former draft read as follows:

     Several fundamental principles could underlie many of these safety procedures, including: [primary consideration of the organism, building on the principle of familiarity applied in a flexible framework and, as appropriate, step-by-step and case-by-case]; complementary consideration of risk assessment and risk management, and classification into contained use or release to the environment.

21   See research paper No. 55, entitled "Environmentally sound management of biotechnology: safety in biotechnology—assessment and management of risk" (February 1992), prepared by the United Nations Conference on Environment and Development secretariat to take account of comments made at the third session of the Preparatory Committee for the United Nations Conference on Environment and Development on part II of document A/CONF.151/PC/67, which incorporated the findings of the ad hoc workshop of Senior-level Experts on Assessing and Managing Biotechnology Risks, held in London in June 1991. [This note, deleted from the final version of Agenda 21, was inserted in a corrigendum. See A/CONF. 151/26, vol. II,/Corr. 1 (21 October 1992). The note also appears after para. 16.31.]

celerate the environmentally sound application of biotechnology, especially in developing countries.[22]

(a) Management-related activities

16.32. Governments at the appropriate level, with the support of relevant international and regional organizations, the private sector, non-governmental organizations, academic and scientific institutions, should:[23]

(a) Make the existing safety procedures widely available by collecting the existing information and adapting it to the specific needs of different countries and regions;

(b) Further develop, as necessary, the existing safety procedures to promote scientific development and categorization in the areas of risk assessment and risk management (information requirements; databases; procedures for assessing risks and conditions of release; establishment of safety conditions; monitoring and inspections, taking account of ongoing national, regional and international initiatives and avoiding duplication wherever possible);

(c) Compile, update and develop compatible safety procedures into a framework of internationally agreed principles as a basis for guidelines to be applied on safety in biotechnology, including consideration of the need for and feasibility of an international agreement, and promote information exchange as a basis for further development, drawing on the work already undertaken by international or other expert bodies;[24]

---

22 See research paper No. 55, entitled "Environmentally sound management of biotechnology: safety in biotechnology—assessment and management of risk" (February 1992), prepared by the United Nations Conference on Environment and Development secretariat to take account of comments made at the third session of the Preparatory Committee for the United Nations Conference on Environment and Development on part II of document A/CONF.151/PC/67, which incorporated the findings of the ad hoc workshop of Senior-level Experts on Assessing and Managing Biotechnology Risks, held in London in June 1991. [This note, deleted from the final version of Agenda 21, was inserted in a corrigendum. See A/CONF. 151/26, vol. II,/Corr. 1 (21 October 1992).]

23 The introductory phrase to draft paragraph 16.35 of A/CONF.151/4 (22 April 1992) was replaced by decision of the Main Committee of UNCED on 10 June 1992. See A/CONF.151/L.3/Add.16 (11 June 1992). The former draft read as follows:

"Governments at the appropriate levels and [, where necessary], with the support of relevant international and regional organizations, the private sector, non-governmental organizations, academic and scientific institutions, should:".

24 Draft paragraph 16.35(c) of A/CONF.151/4 (22 April 1992) was replaced by decision of the Main Committee of UNCED on 10 June 1992. See A/CONF.151/L.3/Add.16 (11 June 1992). The former draft read as follows:

Compile, update and develop compatible safety procedures into a framework of internationally agreed principles to be applied on safety in biotechnology [as a basis for the development of an international agreement [legal instrument/code of conduct], taking into account decision 1/17 adopted by the Preparatory Committee at its first session], and promote information exchange as a basis for further development, drawing on the work already undertaken by international or other expert bodies.

(d) Undertake training programmes at national and regional levels on the application of the proposed technical guidelines;

(e) Assist in exchanging information about the procedures required for safe handling and risk management and about the conditions of release of the products of biotechnology, and cooperate in providing immediate assistance in cases of emergencies that may arise in conjunction with the use of biotechnology products.

(b) Data and information[25]

(c) International and regional cooperation and coordination

16.33. Governments at the appropriate level, with the support of the relevant international and regional organizations, should raise awareness of the relative benefits and risks of biotechnology.

16.34. Further activities should include the following (see also para. 16.32):

(a) Organizing one or more regional meetings between countries to identify further practical steps to facilitate international cooperation in bio-safety;

(b) Establishing an international network incorporating national, regional and global contact points;

(c) Providing direct assistance upon request through the international network, using information networks, databases and information procedures;

(d) Considering the need for and feasibility of internationally agreed guidelines on safety in biotechnology releases, including risk assessment and risk management, and considering studying the feasibility of guidelines which could facilitate national legislation on liability and compensation.[26]

Means of implementation

(a) Financing and cost evaluation

16.35. The UNCED secretariat has estimated the average total annual cost (1993-2000) of implementing the activities of this programme to be about $2 million from the international community on grant or concessional terms. These are indicative and order of magnitude estimates only and have not been reviewed by Governments. Actual costs and financial terms, including any that

---

25 See paras. 16.32 and 16.33. [This note appears as an asterisk to subheading b, to Activities for "Enhancing Safety and developing international mechanisms for cooperation" in Agenda 21, A/CONF. 151/26, vol. II, p. 124.]

26 Draft paragraph 16.38(d) of A/CONF.151/4 (22 April 1992) was replaced by decision of the Main Committee of UNCED on 10 June 1992. See A/CONF.151/L.3/Add.16 (11 June 1992). The former draft read as follows:

Preparing internationally agreed guidelines on safety in biotechnology releases, including risk assessment and risk management, liability and compensation.

are non-concessional, will depend upon, *inter alia*, the specific strategies and programmes Governments decide upon for implementation.[27]

(b) Scientific and technological means[28]

(c) Human resource development[29]

(d) Capacity-building

16.36. Adequate international technical and financial assistance should be provided and technical cooperation to developing countries facilitated in order to build up technical, managerial, planning and administrative capacities at the national level to support the activities in this programme area (see also programme area E).[30]

E. Establishing enabling mechanisms for the development and the environmentally sound application of biotechnology

Basis for action

16.37. The accelerated development and application of biotechnologies, particularly in developing countries, will require a major effort to build up institutional capacities at the national and regional levels. In developing countries, enabling factors such as training capacity, know-how, research and development facilities and funds, industrial building capacity, capital (including venture capital) protection of intellectual property rights, and expertise in areas including marketing research, technology assessment, socio-economic assessment and safety assessment are frequently inadequate. Efforts will therefore need to be made to build up capacities in these and other areas and to match such efforts with appropriate levels of financial support. There is therefore a need to strengthen the endogenous capacities of developing countries by means of new international initiatives to support research in order to speed up the development and application of both new and conventional biotechnologies to serve the needs of sustainable development at local, national and regional levels. National mechanisms to allow for informed comment by the public with regard to biotechnology research and application should be part of the process.

---

27   Draft paragraph 16.39 of A/CONF.151/4 (22 April 1992) was replaced by decision of the Main Committee of UNCED on 10 June 1992. See A/CONF.151/L.3/Add.16 (11 June 1992). The former draft read as follows:

The estimated average annual cost of this programme area for the period 1993-2000 could be about $2 million, all of which would come from international sources.

28   See para. 16.32. [This note appears in Agenda 21 as an asterisk on p. 125, A/CONF. 151/26, vol. II. It also appears after subheading e.]

29   See para. 16.32.

30   Draft paragraph 16.42 of A/CONF.151/4 (22 April 1992) included brackets around the entire text of paragraph 16.42. The brackets were deleted by decision of the Main Committee of UNCED on 10 June 1992. See A/CONF.151/L.3/Add.16 (11 June 1992).

16.38. Some activities at the national, regional and global levels already address the issues outlined in programme areas A, B, C and D, as well as the provision [sic] of advice to individual countries on the development of national guidelines and systems for the implementation of those guidelines.[31] These activities are generally uncoordinated, however, involving many different organizations, priorities, constituencies, time-scales, funding sources and resource constraints. There is a need for a much more cohesive and coordinated approach to harness available resources in the most effective manner. As with most new technologies, research in biotechnology and the applications of its findings could have significant positive and negative socio-economic as well as cultural impacts. These impacts should be carefully identified in the earliest phases of the development of biotechnology in order to enable appropriate management of the consequences of transferring biotechnology.[32]

Objectives

16.39. The objectives are as follows:

(a) To promote the development and application of biotechnologies, with special emphasis on developing countries, by:

(i) Enhancing existing efforts at national, regional and global levels;

(ii) Providing the necessary support for biotechnology, particularly research and product development, at the national, regional and international levels;

(iii) Raising public awareness regarding the relative beneficial aspects of and risks related to biotechnology, to contribute to sustainable development;

(iv) Helping to create a favourable climate for investments, industrial capacity-building and distribution/marketing;

(v) Encouraging the exchange of scientists among all countries and discouraging the "brain drain";

(vi) Recognizing and fostering the traditional methods and the knowledge of indigenous peoples and their communities and ensuring the opportu-

---

31 The first sentence of draft paragraph 16.44 of A/CONF.151/4 (22 April 1992) was replaced by decision of the Main Committee of UNCED on 10 June 1992. See A/CONF.151/L.3/Add.16 (11 June 1992). The former draft read as follows:

Some activities at the national, regional and global levels already address the issues outlined in programme areas A, B and C.

32 The final sentence of draft paragraph 16.44 of A/CONF.151/4 (22 April 1992) was replaced by decision of the Main Committee of UNCED on 10 June 1992. See A/CONF.151/L.3/Add.16 (11 June 1992). The former draft read as follows:

Research in biotechnology and the applications of its findings could have significant positive and negative socio-economic as well as cultural impacts and should therefore be carefully considered in the earliest phases of the development of biotechnology.

nity for their participation in the economic and commercial benefits arising from developments in biotechnology.[33]

(b) To identify ways and means of enhancing current efforts, building wherever possible on existing enabling mechanisms, particularly regional, to determine the precise nature of the needs for additional initiatives, particularly in respect of developing countries, and develop appropriate response strategies, including proposals for any new international mechanisms;[34]

(c) To establish or adapt appropriate mechanisms for safety appraisal and risk assessment at the local, regional and international levels, as appropriate.[35]

Activities

(a) Management-related activities

16.40. Governments at the appropriate level, with the support of international and regional organizations, the private sector, non-governmental organizations and academic and scientific institutions, should:[36]

(a) Develop policies and mobilize additional resources to facilitate greater access to the new biotechnologies, particularly by and among developing countries;

---

33 See chap. 26 (Recognizing and strengthening the role of indigenous people and their communities). To this note, a further annotation had originally provided as follows:

> Draft paragraph 16.45(a)(vi) of A/CONF.151/4 (22 April 1992) was replaced by decision of the Main Committee of UNCED on 10 June 1992. See A/CONF.151/L.3/Add.16 (11 June 1992). The former draft read as follows: Recognize and protect the traditional methods and knowledge of indigenous people and their communities and ensure their participation in the economic and commercial benefits arising from developments in biotechnology;

34 This following text was present in the draft considered at UNCED, but deleted at the end of the UNCED as shown in the final text of A/CONF. 151/26, vol. II, p. 126, distributed at the UN during the 47th General Assembly:

> Note: To be consistent with the agreed negotiated language of Chapter 15.4 (g) ("Conservation of Biological Diversity"), this would need to be expressed as: "Recognise and foster the traditional methods and the knowledge of indigenous people and their communities and ensure the opportunity for their participation in the economic and commercial benefits arising from developments in biotechnology."

35 This following text was present in the draft considered at UNCED, but deleted at the end of of UNCED as shown in the final text of A/CONF. 151/26, vol. II, p. 127, distributed at the UN during the 47th General Assembly:

> (d) [Consider extending legislation to include liability and compensation for damage resulting from applications of biotechnology.]

36 The introductory phrase to 16.46 of A/CONF.151/4 (22 April 1992) was revised by decision of the Main Committee of UNCED on 10 June 1992. See A/CONF.151/L.3/Add.16 (11 June 1992). The former draft read as follows:

> "Governments at the appropriate levels, [where necessary] with the support of international and regional organizations, the private sector, non-governmental organizations and academic and scientific institutions should:".

(b) Implement programmes to create greater awareness of the potential and relative benefits and risks of the environmentally sound application of bio-technology among the public and key decision makers;

(c) Undertake an urgent review of existing enabling mechanisms, pro-grammes and activities at the national, regional and global levels to identify strengths, weaknesses and gaps, and to assess the priority needs of develop-ing countries;[37]

(d) Undertake an urgent follow-up and critical review to identify ways and means of strengthening endogenous capacities within and among developing countries for the environmentally sound application of bio-technology, including, as a first step, ways to improve existing mecha-nisms, particularly at the regional level, and, as a subsequent step, the consideration of possible new international mechanisms, such as regional biotechnology centres;

(e) Develop strategic plans for overcoming targeted constraints by means of appropriate research, product development and marketing;

(f) Establish additional quality-assurance standards for biotechnology applica-tions and products where necessary.

(b) Data and information

16.41. The following activities should be undertaken: facilitation of access to ex-isting information dissemination systems, especially among developing coun-tries; improvement of such access where appropriate; and consideration of the development of a directory of information.

(c) International and regional cooperation and coordination

16.42. Governments at the appropriate level, with the assistance of interna-tional and regional organizations, should develop appropriate new initiatives to identify priority areas for research based on specific problems and facilitate ac-cess to new biotechnologies, particularly by and among developing countries, among relevant undertakings within those countries, in order to strengthen en-dogenous capacities and to support the building of research and institutional capacity in those countries.

---

37 This following text was present in the draft considered at UNCED, but deleted at the end of of UNCED as shown in the final text of A/CONF. 151/26, vol. II, p. 127, distributed at the UN during the 47th General Assembly:

    (d) Define and implement strategies to overcome constraints identified in the areas of food, feed and renewable raw materials; human health; and environmental protection, building upon existing strengths.

Means of implementation

(a) Financing and cost evaluation

16.43. The Conference secretariat has estimated the average total annual cost (1993-2000) of implementing the activities of this programme to be about $5 million from the international community on grant or concessional terms. These are indicative and order-of-magnitude estimates only and have not been reviewed by Governments. Actual costs and financial terms, including any that are non-concessional, will depend upon, *inter alia*, the specific strategies and programmes Governments decide upon for implementation.[38]

(b) Scientific and technological means

16.44. Workshops, symposia, seminars and other exchanges among the scientific community at the regional and global levels, on specific priority themes, will need to be organized, making full use of the existing scientific and technological manpower in each country for bringing about such exchanges.

(c) Human resource development

16.45. Personnel development needs will need to be identified and additional training programmes developed at the national, regional and global levels, especially in developing countries. These should be supported by increased training at all levels, graduate, postgraduate and post-doctoral, as well as by the training of technicians and support staff, with particular reference to the generation of trained manpower in consultant services, design, engineering and marketing research. Training programmes for lecturers training scientists and technologists in advanced research institutions in different countries throughout the world will also need to be developed, and systems giving appropriate rewards, incentives and recognition to scientists and technologists will need to be instituted (see para. 16.44). Conditions of service will also need to be improved at the national level in developing countries to encourage and nurture trained manpower with a view to retaining that manpower locally. Society should be informed of the social and cultural impact of the development and application of biotechnology.

(d) Capacity-building

16.46. Biotechnology research and development is undertaken both under highly sophisticated conditions and at the practical level in many coun-

---

38   Draft paragraph 16.49 of A/CONF.151/4 (22 April 1992) was replaced by decision of the Main Committee of UNCED on 10 June 1992. See A/CONF.151/L.3/Add.16 (11 June 1992). The former draft read as follows:

    The estimated average annual cost of this programme area for the period 1993-2000 could be about $5 million, all of which would come from international financing sources. This does not include the costs of any innovative mechanisms arising from the implementation of this programme area. Mobilise additional financial resources and institute innovative financing mechanisms, as necessary for selected priorities, to address the specific needs of different regions or socio-economic conditions.

tries. Efforts will be needed to ensure that the necessary infrastructure facilities for research, extension and technology activities are available on a decentralized basis. Global and regional collaboration for basic and applied research and development will also need to be further enhanced and every effort should be made to ensure that existing national and regional facilities are fully utilized. Such institutions already exist in some countries and it should be possible to make use of them for training purposes and joint research projects. Strengthening of universities, technical schools and local research institutions for the development of biotechnologies and extension services for their application will need to be developed, especially in developing countries.[39]

---

39   This following text was present in the draft considered at UNCED, but deleted at the end of of UNCED as shown in the final text of A/CONF. 151/26, vol II, p 129. distributed at the UN during the 47th General Assembly the former note read as follows:

  These paragraphs contain matters relating to means of implementation, including cost estimates, which are indicative secretariat figures provided pursuant to decision A/CONF.151/PC/L.49. They remain in brackets as they have not been negotiated.

Chapter 17

Protection of the Oceans, All Kinds of Seas, Including Enclosed and Semi-Enclosed Seas, and Coastal Areas and the Protection, Rational Use and Development of Their Living Resources

INTRODUCTION

17.1. The marine environment—including the oceans and all seas and adjacent coastal areas—forms an integrated whole that is an essential component of the global life-support system, and a positive asset that presents opportunities for sustainable development. International law, as reflected in the provisions of the United Nations Convention on the Law of the Sea[1,2] referred to in this chapter of Agenda 21, sets forth rights and obligations of States and provides the international basis upon which to pursue the protection and sustainable development of the marine and coastal environment and its resources. This requires new approaches to marine and coastal area management and development, at the national, subregional, regional and global levels, approaches that are integrated in content and are precautionary and anticipatory in ambit, as reflected in the following programme areas:[3]

(a) Integrated management and sustainable development of coastal areas, including exclusive economic zones;

(b) Marine environmental protection;

(c) Sustainable use and conservation of marine living resources of the high seas;

---

1   References to the United Nations Convention on the Law of the Sea in this chapter of Agenda 21 do not prejudice the position of any State with respect to signature, ratification of or accession to the Convention.

2   References to the United Nations Convention on the Law of the Sea in this chapter of Agenda 21 do not prejudice the position of States which view the Convention as having a unified character.

3   Nothing in the programme areas of this chapter should be interpreted as prejudicing the rights of the States involved in a dispute of sovereignty or in the delimitation of the maritime areas concerned.

(d) Sustainable use and conservation of marine living resources under national jurisdiction;

(e) Addressing critical uncertainties for the management of marine environment and climate change;

(f) Strengthening international, including regional cooperation and coordination;

(g) Sustainable development of islands.

17.2. The implementation by developing countries of the activities set forth below shall be commensurate with their individual technological and financial capacities and priorities in allocating resources for development needs and ultimately depends on the technology and financial resources required and made available to them.

PROGRAMME AREAS

A. Integrated management and sustainable development of coastal and marine areas, including exclusive economic zones

Basis for action

17.3. The coastal area contains diverse and productive habitats important for human settlements, development and local subsistence. More than half the world's population lives within 60 km of the shoreline, and this could rise to three quarters by the year 2020. Many of the world's poor are crowded in coastal areas. Coastal resources are vital for many local communities and indigenous people. The Exclusive Economic Zone (EEZ) is also an important marine area where the States manage the development and conservation of natural resources for the benefit of their people. For small island States or countries, these are the areas most available for development activities.

17.4. Despite national, subregional, regional and global efforts, current approaches to the management of marine and coastal resources have not always proved capable of achieving sustainable development and coastal resources and the coastal environment are being rapidly degraded and eroded in many parts of the world.

Objectives

17.5. Coastal States commit themselves to integrated management and sustainable development of coastal areas and the marine environment under their national jurisdiction. To this end, it is necessary to, *inter alia*:

(a) Provide for an integrated policy and decision-making process, including all involved sectors, to promote compatibility and balance of uses;

(b) Identify existing and projected uses of coastal areas and their interactions;

(c) Concentrate on well-defined coastal management related issues;

(d) Apply preventive and precautionary approaches in project planning and implementation, including prior assessment and systematic observation of the impacts of major projects;

(e) Promote the development and application of methods, such as national resource and environmental accounting, that reflect changes in value resulting from uses of coastal and marine areas, including pollution, marine erosion, loss of resources and habitat destruction;

(f) Provide access, as far as possible, for concerned individuals, groups and organizations to relevant information and opportunities for consultation and participation in planning and decision-making at appropriate levels.

Activities

(a) Management-related activities

17.6. Each coastal State should consider establishing, or where necessary strengthening, appropriate coordinating mechanisms (such as a high-level policy planning body) for integrated management and sustainable development of coastal and marine areas and their resources, at both the local and national levels. Such mechanisms should include consultation, as appropriate, with the academic and private sectors, non-governmental organizations, local communities, resource user groups, and indigenous people. Such national coordinating mechanisms could provide, *inter alia*, for:

(a) Preparation and implementation of land and water use and siting policies;

(b) Implementation of integrated coastal and marine management and sustainable development plans and programmes at appropriate levels;

(c) Preparation of coastal profiles identifying critical areas, including eroded zones, physical processes, development patterns, user conflicts and specific priorities for management;

(d) Prior environmental impact assessment, systematic observation and follow-up of major projects including the systematic incorporation of results in decision-making;

(e) Contingency plans for human induced and natural disasters, including likely effects of potential climate change and sea level rise, as well as contingency plans for degradation and pollution from anthropogenic origin, including spills of oil and other materials;

(f) Improvement of coastal human settlements, especially in housing, drinking water and treatment and disposal of sewage, solid wastes and industrial effluents;

(g) Periodic assessment of the impacts of external factors and phenomena to ensure that the objectives of integrated management and sustainable development of coastal areas and the marine environment are met;

(h) Conservation and restoration of altered critical habitats;

(i) Integration of sectoral programmes on sustainable development for settlements, agriculture, tourism, fishing, ports and industries affecting the coastal area;

(j) Infrastructure adaptation and alternative employment;

(k) Human resource development and training;

(l) Public education, awareness and information programmes;

(m) Promoting environmentally sound technology and sustainable practices;

(n) Development and simultaneous implementation of environmental quality criteria.

17.7. Coastal States, with the support of international organizations, upon request, should undertake measures to maintain biological diversity and productivity of marine species and habitats under national jurisdiction. *Inter alia*, these measures might include: surveys of marine biodiversity, inventories of endangered species and critical coastal and marine habitats; establishment and management of protected areas; and support of scientific research and dissemination of its results.

(b) Data and information

17.8. Coastal States, where necessary, should improve their capacity to collect, analyse, assess and use information for sustainable use of resources, including environmental impacts of activities affecting the coastal and marine areas. Information for management purposes should receive priority support in view of the intensity and magnitude of the changes occurring in the coastal and marine areas. To this end, it is necessary to, *inter alia*:

(a) Develop and maintain databases for assessment and management of coastal areas and all seas and their resources;

(b) Develop socio-economic and environmental indicators;

(c) Conduct regular environmental assessment of the state of the environment of coastal and marine areas;

(d) Prepare and maintain profiles of coastal area resources, activities, uses, habitats and protected areas based on the criteria of sustainable development;

(e) Exchange information and data.

17.9. Cooperation with developing countries, and, where applicable, subregional and regional mechanisms, should be strengthened to improve their capacities to achieve the above.

(c) International and regional cooperation and coordination

17.10. The role of international cooperation and coordination on a bilateral basis and, where applicable, within a subregional, interregional, regional or global framework, is to support and supplement national efforts of coastal States to promote integrated management and sustainable development of coastal and marine areas.

17.11. States should cooperate, as appropriate, in the preparation of national guidelines for integrated coastal zone management and development, drawing on existing experience. A global conference to exchange experience in the field could be held before 1994.

Means of implementation

(a) Financing and cost evaluation

17.12. The Conference secretariat has estimated the average total annual cost (1993-2000) of implementing the activities of this programme to be about $6 billion including about $50 million from the international community on grant or concessional terms. These are indicative and order-of-magnitude estimates only and have not been reviewed by Governments. Actual costs and financial terms, including any that are non-concessional, will depend upon, *inter alia*, the specific strategies and programmes Governments decide upon for implementation.[4]

(b) Scientific and technological means

17.13. States should cooperate in the development of necessary coastal systematic observation, research and information management systems. They should provide access to and transfer environmentally safe technologies and methodologies for sustainable development of coastal and marine areas to developing countries. They should also develop technologies and endogenous scientific and technological capacities.

---

4   Draft paragraphs 17.12 and 17.13 of A/CONF.151/4 (22 April 1992) were replaced by decision of the Main Committee of UNCED on 10 June 1992. See A/CONF.151/L.3/Add.17 (12 June 1992). The former draft read as follows:

> 17.12 The total cost estimate for all countries to implement integrated management and sustainable development of coastal areas and exclusive economic zones is approximately $85 billion through the year 2000. The cost estimate for developing countries would be approximately $50 billion, or about $6/billion per year for 1993-2000.

> 17.13 Of the $6 billion annual estimated costs about $50 million per year between 1993-2000 in catalytic funding is proposed to support programmes for integrated management and sustainable development of coastal areas. Of this, $36 million is proposed to assist developing countries with technical cooperation and training for institutional strengthening, improvement of databases, upgrading of research and management capacity, implementation of pilot demonstration projects and production of detailed operational guidelines, plus $6 million to address global issues. The sum of $8/million is proposed to help strengthen global and regional organizations in this field.

17.14. International organizations, whether subregional, regional or global, as appropriate, should support coastal States, upon request, in these efforts, as indicated above, devoting special attention to developing countries.

(c) Human resource development

17.15. Coastal States should promote and facilitate the organization of education and training in integrated coastal and marine management and sustainable development for scientists, technologists, managers, including community-based managers and users, leaders, indigenous peoples, fisherfolk, women and youth among others. Management and development, as well as environmental protection concerns and local planning issues should be incorporated in educational curricula and public awareness campaigns, with due regard to traditional ecological knowledge and socio-cultural values.

17.16. International organizations, whether subregional, regional or global, as appropriate, should support coastal States, upon request, in the areas indicated above, devoting special attention to developing countries.

(d) Capacity-building

17.17. Full cooperation should be extended, upon request, to coastal States in their capacity-building efforts and, where appropriate, capacity-building should be included in bilateral and multilateral development cooperation. Coastal States may consider, *inter alia*:

(a) Ensuring capacity-building at the local level;

(b) Consulting on coastal and marine issues with local administrations, the business community, the academic sector, resource user groups and the general public;

(c) Coordinating sectoral programmes while building capacity;

(d) Identifying existing and potential capabilities, facilities and needs for human resources development and scientific and technological infrastructure;

(e) Developing scientific and technological means and research;

(f) Promoting and facilitating human resource development and education;

(g) Supporting "centres of excellence" in integrated coastal and marine resource management;

(h) Supporting pilot demonstration programmes and projects in integrated coastal and marine management.

B. Marine environmental protection

Basis for action

17.18. Degradation of the marine environment can result from a wide range of sources. Land-based sources contribute 70 per cent of marine pollution, while maritime transport and dumping-at-sea activities contribute 10 per cent each. The contaminants that pose the greatest threat to the marine environment are in variable order of importance and depending on differing national or regional situations, sewage, nutrients, synthetic organic compounds, sediments, litter and plastics, metals, radionuclides, oil/hydrocarbons, and polycyclic aromatic hydrocarbons (PAHs). Many of the polluting substances originating from land-based sources are of particular concern to the marine environment since they exhibit at the same time toxicity, persistence and bioaccumulation in the food chain. There is currently no global scheme to address marine pollution from land-based sources.

17.19. Degradation of the marine environment can also result from a wide range of activities on land. Human settlements, land use, construction of coastal infrastructure, agriculture, forestry, urban development, tourism and industry can affect the marine environment. Coastal erosion and siltation are of particular concern.

17.20. Marine pollution is also caused by shipping and sea-based activities. Approximately 600,000 tons of oil enter the oceans each year, as a result of normal shipping operations, accidents and illegal discharges. With respect to offshore oil and gas activities, currently machinery space discharges are regulated internationally and six regional conventions to control platform discharges have been under consideration. The nature and extent of environmental impacts from offshore oil exploration and production activities generally account for a very small proportion of marine pollution.

17.21. A precautionary and anticipatory rather than a reactive approach is necessary to prevent the degradation of the marine environment. This requires, *inter alia*, the adoption of precautionary measures, environmental impact assessments, clean production techniques, recycling, waste audits and minimization, construction and/or improvement of sewage treatment facilities, quality management criteria for the proper handling of hazardous substances, and a comprehensive approach to damaging impacts from air, land and water. Any management framework must include the improvement of coastal human settlements and the integrated management and development of coastal areas.

Objectives

17.22. States, in accordance with the provisions of the United Nations Convention on the Law of the Sea on protection and preservation of the marine environment, commit themselves, in accordance with their policies, priorities and resources, to prevent, reduce and control degradation of the marine environment so as to maintain and improve its life-support and productive capacities. To this end, it is necessary to:

(a) Apply preventive, precautionary and anticipatory approaches so as to avoid degradation of the marine environment, as well as to reduce the risk of long-term or irreversible adverse effects upon it;

(b) Ensure prior assessment of activities that may have significant adverse impacts upon the marine environment;

(c) Integrate protection of the marine environment into relevant general environmental, social and economic development policies;

(d) Develop economic incentives, where appropriate, to apply clean technologies and other means consistent with the internalization of environmental costs, such as the polluter pays principle, so as to avoid degradation of the marine environment;

(e) Improve the living standards of coastal populations, particularly in developing countries, so as to contribute to reducing the degradation of the coastal and marine environment.

17.23. States agree that provision of additional financial resources, through appropriate international mechanisms, as well as access to cleaner technologies and relevant research, would be necessary to support action by developing countries to implement this commitment.

Activities

(a) Management-related activities

Prevention, reduction and control of degradation of the marine environment from land-based activities

17.24. In carrying out their commitment to deal with degradation of the marine environment from land-based activities, States should take action at the national level and, where appropriate, at the regional and subregional levels, in concert with action to implement programme area A, and take account of the Montreal Guidelines for the Protection of the Marine Environment from Land-Based Sources.

17.25. To this end, States, with the support of the relevant international environmental, scientific, technical and financial organizations, should cooperate, *inter alia*, to:

(a) Consider updating, strengthening and extending the Montreal Guidelines, as appropriate;

(b) Assess the effectiveness of existing regional agreements and action plans, where appropriate, with a view to identifying means of strengthening action, where necessary, to prevent, reduce and control marine degradation caused by land-based activities;

(c) Initiate and promote the development of new regional agreements, where appropriate;

(d) Develop means of providing guidance on technologies to deal with the major types of pollution of the marine environment from land-based sources, according to the best scientific evidence;

(e) Develop policy guidance to relevant global funding mechanisms;

(f) Identify additional steps requiring international cooperation.

17.26. The UNEP Governing Council is invited to convene, as soon as practicable, an intergovernmental meeting on protection of the marine environment from land-based activities.

17.27. As concerns sewage, priority actions to be considered by States may include:

(a) Incorporating sewage concerns when formulating or reviewing coastal development plans, including human settlement plans;

(b) Building and maintaining sewage treatment facilities in accordance with national policies and capacities and international cooperation available;

(c) Locating coastal outfalls so as to maintain an acceptable level of environmental quality and to avoid exposing shell fisheries, water intakes and bathing areas to pathogens;

(d) Promoting environmentally sound co-treatments of domestic and compatible industrial effluents, with the introduction, where practicable, of controls on the entry of effluents that are not compatible with the system;

(e) Promoting primary treatment of municipal sewage discharged to rivers, estuaries and the sea, or other solutions appropriate to specific sites;

(f) Establishing and improving local, national, subregional and regional, as necessary, regulatory and monitoring programmes to control effluent discharge using minimum sewage effluent guidelines and water quality criteria giving due consideration to the characteristics of receiving bodies and the volume and type of pollutants.

17.28. As concerns other sources of pollution, priority actions to be considered by States may include:

(a) Establishing or improving, as necessary, regulatory and monitoring programmes to control effluent discharges and emissions including the development and application of control and recycling technologies;

(b) Promoting risk and environmental impact assessments to help ensure an acceptable level of environmental quality;

(c) Promoting assessment and cooperation at the regional level, where appropriate, with respect to the input of point source pollutants from new installations;

(d) Eliminating the emission or discharge of organohalogen compounds which threaten to accumulate to dangerous levels in the marine environment;

(e) Reducing the emission or discharge of other synthetic organic compounds which threaten to accumulate to dangerous levels in the marine environment;

(f) Promoting controls over anthropogenic inputs of nitrogen and phosphorus which enter coastal waters where such problems as eutrophication threaten the marine environment or its resources;

(g) Cooperating with developing countries, through financial and technological support, to maximize best practicable control and reduction of substances and wastes that are toxic, persistent or liable to bio-accumulate, and to establish environmentally sound land-based waste disposal alternatives to sea dumping;

(h) Cooperating in the development and implementation of environmentally sound land-use techniques and practices to reduce run-off to water-courses and estuaries which would cause pollution or degradation of the marine environment;

(i) Promoting the use of environmentally less harmful pesticides and fertilizers and alternative methods for pest control, and considering prohibition of those found to be environmentally unsound;

(j) Adopting new initiatives at national, subregional and regional levels for controlling the input of non-point source pollutants, which require broad changes in sewage and waste management, agricultural practices, mining, construction and transportation.

17.29. As concerns physical destruction of coastal and marine areas causing degradation of the marine environment, priority actions should include control and prevention of coastal erosion and siltation due to anthropogenic factors related to, *inter alia*, land-use and construction techniques and practices. Watershed management practices should be promoted so as to prevent, control and reduce degradation of the marine environment.

Prevention, reduction and control of degradation of the marine environment from sea-based activities

17.30. States, acting individually, bilaterally, regionally or multilaterally and within the framework of IMO and other relevant international organizations, whether subregional, regional or global, as appropriate, should assess the need for additional measures to address degradation of the marine environment:

(a) From shipping, by:

(i) Supporting wider ratification and implementation of relevant shipping conventions and protocols;

(ii) Facilitating the processes in (i), providing support to individual States upon request to help them overcome the obstacles identified by them;

(iii) Cooperating in monitoring marine pollution from ships, especially from illegal discharges (e.g., aerial surveillance) and enforcing MARPOL discharge, provisions more rigorously;

(iv) Assessing the state of pollution caused by ships in particularly sensitive areas identified by IMO and taking action to implement applicable measures, where necessary, within such areas to ensure compliance with generally accepted international regulations;

(v) Taking action to ensure respect of areas designated by coastal States, within their exclusive economic zones, consistent with international law, in order to protect and preserve rare or fragile ecosystems, such as coral reefs and mangroves;

(vi) Considering adoption of appropriate rules on ballast water discharge to prevent the spread of non-indigenous organisms;

(vii) Promoting navigational safety by adequate charting of coasts and ship-routing, as appropriate;

(viii) Assessing the need for stricter international regulations to further reduce the risk of accidents and pollution from cargo ships (including bulk carriers);

(ix) Encouraging IMO and IAEA to work together to complete consideration of a code on the carriage of irradiated nuclear fuel in flasks on board ships;

(x) Revising and updating the IMO Code of Safety for Nuclear Merchant Ships and considering how best to implement a revised code;

(xi) Supporting the ongoing activity within IMO regarding development of appropriate measures for reducing air pollution from ships;

(xii) Supporting the ongoing activity within IMO regarding the development of an international regime governing the transportation of hazardous and noxious substances carried by ships and further considering whether the compensation funds similar to the ones established under the Fund Convention would be appropriate in respect of pollution damage caused by substances other than oil;

(b) From dumping, by:

(i) Supporting wider ratification, implementation and participation in relevant Conventions on dumping at sea including early conclusion of a future strategy for the London Dumping Convention;

(ii) Encouraging the London Dumping Convention parties to take appropriate steps to stop ocean dumping and incineration of hazardous substances;

(c) From offshore oil and gas platforms, by assessing existing regulatory measures to address discharges, emissions, and safety and the need for additional measures;

(d) From ports, by facilitating establishment of port reception facilities for the collection of oily and chemical residues and garbage from ships, especially in MARPOL special areas, and promoting the establishment of smaller scale facilities in marinas and fishing harbours.

17.31. IMO and as appropriate, other competent United Nations organizations, when requested by the States concerned, should assess, where appropriate, the state of marine pollution in areas of congested shipping, such as heavily used international straits, with a view to ensuring compliance with generally accepted international regulations, particularly those related to illegal discharges from ships, in accordance with the provisions of Part III of the United Nations Convention on the Law of the Sea.

17.32. States should take measures to reduce water pollution caused by organotin compounds used in anti-fouling paints.

17.33. States should consider ratifying the Convention on Oil Pollution Preparedness, Response and Cooperation, which addresses, *inter alia*, the development of contingency plans on the national and international level, as appropriate, including provision of oil-spill response material and training of personnel, including its possible extension to chemical spill response.

17.34. States should intensify international cooperation to strengthen or establish, where necessary, regional oil/chemical-spill response centres and/or, as appropriate, mechanisms in cooperation with relevant subregional, regional or global intergovernmental organizations and, where appropriate, industry-based organizations.

(b) Data and information

17.35. States should, as appropriate, and in accordance with the means at their disposal and with due regard for their technical and scientific capacity and resources, make systematic observations on the state of the marine environment. To this end, States should, as appropriate, consider:

(a) Establishing systematic observation systems to measure marine environmental quality, including causes and effects of marine degradation, as a basis for management;

(b) Regularly exchanging information on marine degradation caused by land-based and sea-based activities and on actions to prevent, control and reduce such degradation;

(c) Supporting and expanding international programmes for systematic observations such as the mussel watch programme, building on existing facilities with special attention to developing countries;

(d) Establishing a clearing-house on marine pollution control information, including processes and technologies to address marine pollution control and to support their transfer to developing countries and other countries with demonstrated needs;

(e) Establishing a global profile and database providing information on the sources, types, amounts and effects of pollutants reaching the marine environment from land-based activities in coastal areas and sea-based sources;

(f) Allocating adequate funding for capacity-building and training programmes to ensure the full participation of developing countries, in particular in any international scheme under the organs and organizations of the United Nations system for the collection, analysis and use of data and information.

Means of implementation

(a) Financing and cost evaluation

17.36. The Conference secretariat has estimated the average total annual cost (1993-2000) of implementing the activities of this programme to be about $200 million from the international community on grant or concessional terms. These are indicative and order-of-magnitude estimates only and have not been reviewed by Governments. Actual costs and financial terms, including any that are non-concessional, will depend upon, *inter alia*, the specific strategies and programmes Governments decide upon for implementation.[5]

---

5   Draft paragraphs 17.37, 17.38 and 17.39 of A/CONF.151/4 (22 April 1992) were replaced by decision of the Main Committee of UNCED on 10 June 1992. See A/CONF.151/L.3/Add.17 (12 June 1992). The former draft read as follows:

17.37 Since many activities on land have impacts on the marine environment, the cost estimates to control the major sources of pollution and other impacts are very high. A crude extrapolation based on a few regional studies in semi-enclosed seas gives figures ranging from $5-20 billion per year over 20/years for the necessary investments. On the other hand, the benefits gained from protecting major economic activities in marine and coastal areas far outweigh the costs in the regions studied. Mechanisms such as user fees and charges for pollution violations are needed to raise the necessary sums from those most directly concerned and best able to bear the costs, and to channel the revenues into construction and operation of the necessary facilities. For technical cooperation with developing countries to implement Agenda 21 activities, the following amounts are proposed: $14 million in direct assistance, $4 million to address global issues and $2 million to strengthen international organizations, for a total of $20 million per year. This amount needs to be complemented by major activities contained in other programme areas.

Sea-based activities

17.38 An estimated $84 million per year is needed to build waste reception facilities in ports in developing countries. This will require special funding mechanisms such as loans or grants from international agencies, including the Global Environmental Facility or a system of "Reception Facility Funds", with the assistance of IMO. Income should be raised from shipping to cover at least the operation and maintenance of these facilities, if not to reimburse the capital investment.

17.39 Provision of oil spill response materials and equipment, apart from the larger countries that have already invested hundreds of millions of dollars in stockpiles, is estimated at $50 million per year from 1993 to 2000. To this should be added $40 million per year for technical cooperation and capacity-building in developing countries, all with reference to global issues, including $6 million to strengthen international organizations.

(b) Scientific and technological means

17.37. National, subregional and regional action programmes will, where appropriate, require technology transfer in conformity with chapter 34, and financial resources, particularly where developing countries are concerned, including:[6]

(a) Assistance to industries in identifying and adopting clean production or cost-effective pollution control technologies;

(b) Planning development and application of low-cost and low-maintenance sewage installation and treatment technologies for developing countries;

(c) Equipment of laboratories to observe systematically human and other impacts on the marine environment;

(d) Identification of appropriate oil and chemical spill control materials, including low-cost locally available materials and techniques, suitable for pollution emergencies in developing countries;

(e) Study of the use of persistent organohalogens that are liable to accumulate in the marine environment to identify those that cannot be adequately controlled and to provide a basis for a decision on a time schedule for phasing them out as soon as practicable;

(f) Establishment of a clearing house on marine pollution control, including processes and technologies to address marine pollution control, and support their transfer to developing and other countries with demonstrated needs.

(c) Human resources development

17.38. States individually or in cooperation with each other and with the support of international organizations, whether subregional, regional or global, as appropriate, should:

(a) Provide training for critical personnel required for the adequate protection of the marine environment as identified by training needs' surveys at the national, regional or subregional levels;

(b) Promote the introduction of marine environmental protection topics into the curriculum of marine studies programmes;

(c) Establish training courses for oil and chemical spill response personnel, in cooperation, where appropriate, with the oil and chemical industries;

---

6   The introductory sentence to draft paragraph 17.40 of A/CONF.151/4 (22 April 1992) was replaced by decision of the Main Committee of UNCED on 10 June 1992. See A/CONF.151/L.3/Add.17 (12 June 1992). The former draft read as follows: "National, subregional and regional action programmes will, where appropriate, require [technological cooperation,] technology transfer and financial resources, particularly where developing countries are concerned, including:".

(d) Conduct workshops on environmental aspects of port operations and development;

(e) Strengthen and provide secure financing for new and existing specialized international centres of professional maritime education;

(f) States should, through bilateral and multilateral cooperation, support and supplement the national efforts of developing countries as regards human resource development in relation to prevention and reduction of degradation of the marine environment.

(d) Capacity-building

17.39. National planning and coordinating bodies should be given the capacity and authority to review all land-based activities and sources of pollution for their impacts on the marine environment and to propose appropriate control measures.

17.40. Research facilities should be strengthened or, where appropriate, developed in developing countries, for systematic observation of marine pollution, environmental impact assessment and development of control recommendations and should be managed and staffed by local experts.

17.41. Special arrangements will be needed to provide adequate financial and technical resources to assist developing countries in preventing and solving problems associated with activities that threaten the marine environment.

17.42. An international funding mechanism should be created for the application of appropriate sewage treatment technologies and building sewage treatment facilities, including grants or concessional loans from international agencies and appropriate regional funds, replenished at least in part on a revolving basis by user fees.

17.43. In carrying out these programme activities, particular attention needs to be given to the problems of developing countries which would bear an unequal burden because of their lack of facilities, expertise or technical capacities.

C. Sustainable use and conservation of marine living resources of the high seas.

Basis for action

17.44. Over the last decade, fisheries on the high seas have considerably expanded and currently represent approximately 5 per cent of total world landings. The provisions of the United Nations Convention on the Law of the Sea on the marine living resources of the high seas sets forth rights and obligations of States with respect to conservation and utilization of those resources.

17.45. However, management of high seas fisheries, including the adoption, monitoring and enforcement of effective conservation measures, is inadequate in many areas and some resources are overutilized. There are problems of un-regulated fishing, overcapitalization, excessive fleet size, vessel reflagging to escape controls, insufficiently selective gear, unreliable databases and lack of sufficient cooperation between States. Action by States whose nationals and vessels fish on the high seas as well as cooperation at the bilateral, subregion-al, regional and global levels, is essential particularly for highly migratory species and straddling stocks. Such action and cooperation should address in-adequacies in fishing practices, as well as in biological knowledge, fisheries statistics and improvement of systems for handling data. Emphasis should also be on multi-species management and other approaches which take into ac-count the relationships among species, especially in addressing depleted spe-cies, but also in identifying the potential of underutilized or unutilized populations.

Objectives

17.46. States commit themselves to the conservation and sustainable use of ma-rine living resources on the high seas. To this end, it is necessary to:

(a) Develop and increase the potential of marine living resources to meet hu-man nutritional needs, as well as social, economic and development goals;

(b) Maintain or restore populations of marine species at levels that can produce the maximum sustainable yield as qualified by relevant environmen-tal and economic factors, taking into consideration relationships among species;

(c) Promote the development and use of selective fishing gear and practices that minimize waste in the catch of target species and minimize by-catch of non-target species;

(d) Ensure effective monitoring and enforcement with respect to fishing activities;

(e) Protect and restore endangered marine species;

(f) Preserve habitats and other ecologically sensitive areas;

(g) Promote scientific research with respect to the marine living resources in the high seas.[7]

---

7   A subparagraph (h) was deleted by the Main Committee of UNCED; see A/CONF. 151/L.3/Add.17
     (12 June 1992). It read as follows:

     (h) Cooperate to ensure that high seas fishing does not have an adverse impact on the marine living
     resources under the national jurisdiction of coastal States.

17.47. Nothing in subparagraph 17.46 above restricts the right of a State or the competence of an international organization, as appropriate, to prohibit, limit or regulate the exploitation of marine mammals on the high seas more strictly than provided for in that paragraph. States shall cooperate with a view to the conservation of marine mammals and, in the case of cetaceans shall in particular work through the appropriate international organizations for their conservation, management and study.

17.48. The ability of developing countries to fulfil the above objectives is dependent upon their capabilities, including the financial, scientific and technological means at their disposal. Adequate financial, scientific and technological cooperation should be provided to support action by them to implement these objectives.

Activities

(a) Management-related activities

17.49. States should take effective action, including bilateral and multilateral cooperation, where appropriate at the subregional, regional and global level, to ensure that high seas fisheries are managed in accordance with the provisions of the United Nations Convention on the Law of the Sea. In particular, they should:

(a) Give full effect to these provisions with regard to fisheries populations whose ranges lie both within and beyond exclusive economic zones (straddling stocks);

(b) Give full effect to these provisions with regard to highly migratory species;

(c) Negotiate, where appropriate, international agreements for the effective management and conservation of fishery stocks;

(d) Define and identify appropriate management units;

(e) States should convene, as soon as possible, an intergovernmental conference under United Nations auspices, taking into account relevant activities at the subregional, regional and global levels, with a view to promoting effective implementation of the provisions of the United Nations Convention on the Law of the Sea on straddling fish stocks and highly migratory fish stocks. The conference, drawing, *inter alia*, on scientific and technical studies by FAO, should identify and assess existing problems related to the conservation and management of such fish stocks, and consider means of improving cooperation on fisheries among States, and formulate appropriate recommendations. The work and the results of the conference should be fully consistent with the provisions of the United Nations Convention on the Law of the Sea, in particular the rights and obligations of coastal States and States fishing on the high seas.[8]

17.50. States should ensure that fishing activities by vessels flying their flags in the high seas take place in a manner so as to minimize incidental catch.

17.51. States should take effective action consistent with international law to monitor and control fishing activities by vessels flying their flags on the high seas to ensure compliance with applicable conservation and management rules, including full, detailed, accurate and timely reporting of catches and effort.

17.52. States should take effective action, consistent with international law, to deter reflagging of vessels by their nationals as a means of avoiding compliance with applicable conservation and management rules for fishing activities on the high seas.

17.53. States should prohibit dynamiting, poisoning and other comparable destructive fishing practices.

17.54. States should fully implement General Assembly resolution 46/215 on large-scale pelagic drift-net fishing.

17.55. States should take measures to increase the availability of marine living resources as human food by reducing wastage, post-harvest losses and discards, and improving techniques of processing, distribution and transportation.

(b) Data and information

17.56. States, with the support of international organizations, whether subregional, regional or global, as appropriate, should cooperate to:

(a) Promote enhanced collection of data necessary for the conservation and sustainable use of the marine living resources of the high seas;

---

8   Draft paragraph 17.52(e) of A/CONF.151/4 (22 April 1992) was replaced by decision of the Main Committee of UNCED on 10 June 1992. See A/CONF.151/L.3/Add.17 (12 June 1992). The former draft read as follows: "Develop guidelines for better implementation of the provisions of the United Nations Convention on the Law of the Sea on high seas fisheries." Paragraphs 17.53 and 17.54 were also deleted in the same document. They read as follows:

17.53 States whose [nationals] [vessels] fish for straddling stocks on the high seas and the coastal States in whose exclusive economic zones such stocks occur, should cooperate with a view to agreeing on measures [applicable on the high seas] necessary to ensure the conservation and sustainable use of such stocks. Such measures should:

(a) Be consistent with measures applied by the coastal States within the exclusive economic zones;

(b) Give effect to the special interest and responsibility of the coastal State with respect to the portion of the straddling stocks beyond the exclusive economic zones;

[17.54 States whose [nationals] [vessels] fish for stocks of highly migratory species on the high seas and coastal States in whose exclusive economic zones such stocks occur should cooperate with a view to agreeing on measures [applicable on the high seas] necessary to ensure the conservation and management of such stocks. Such measures should:

(a) Fully recognize the sovereign rights of the coastal States in their exclusive economic zones;

(b) Take into account the special interest of the coastal States in these stocks outside their exclusive economic zones, thereby avoiding adverse impacts on such stocks within their exclusive economic zones.

(b) Exchange on a regular basis up-to-date data and information adequate for fisheries assessment;

(c) Develop and share analytical and predictive tools such as stock assessment and bioeconomic models;

(d) Establish or expand appropriate monitoring and assessment programmes.

(c) International and regional cooperation and coordination

17.57. States, through bilateral and multilateral cooperation and within the framework of subregional and regional fisheries bodies, as appropriate, and with the support of other international intergovernmental agencies, should assess high seas resource potentials and develop profiles of all stocks (target and non-target).

17.58. States should, where and as appropriate, ensure adequate coordination and cooperation in enclosed and semi-enclosed seas and between subregional, regional and global intergovernmental fisheries bodies.

17.59. Effective cooperation within existing subregional, regional or global fisheries bodies should be encouraged. Where such organizations do not exist, States should, as appropriate, cooperate to establish such organizations.

17.60. States with an interest in a high seas fishery regulated by an existing subregional and/or regional high seas fisheries organization of which they are not members should be encouraged to join that organization, where appropriate.

17.61. States recognize:

(a) The responsibility of the International Whaling Commission for the conservation and management of whale stocks and the regulation of whaling pursuant to the 1946 International Convention for the Regulation of Whaling;

(b) The work of the International Whaling Commission Scientific Committee in carrying out studies of large whales in particular, as well as of other cetaceans;

(c) The work of other organizations, such as the Inter-American Tropical Tuna Commission and the Agreement on Small Cetaceans in the Baltic and North Sea under the Bonn Convention, in the conservation, management and study of cetaceans and other marine mammals.

17.62. States should cooperate for the conservation, management and study of cetaceans.

Means of implementation

(a) Financing and cost evaluation

17.63. The Conference secretariat has estimated the average total annual cost (1993-2000) of implementing the activities of this programme to be about $12 million from the international community on grant or concessional terms. These are indicative and order-of-magnitude estimates only and have not been reviewed by Governments. Actual costs and financial terms, including any that are non-concessional, will depend upon, *inter alia*, the specific strategies and programmes Governments decide upon for implementation.[9]

(b) Scientific and technological means

17.64. States, with the support of relevant international organizations, where necessary, should develop collaborative technical and research programmes to improve understanding of the life cycles and migrations of species found on the high seas, including identifying critical areas and life stages.

17.65. States, with the support of relevant international organizations, whether subregional, regional or global, as appropriate, should:

(a) Develop databases on the high seas marine living resources and fisheries;

(b) Collect and correlate marine environmental data with high seas marine living resources data, including the impacts of regional and global changes brought about by natural causes and by human activities;

(c) Cooperate in coordinating research programmes to provide the knowledge necessary to manage high seas resources.

(c) Human resource development

17.66. Human resource development at the national level should be targeted at both development and management of high seas resources, including training in high seas fishing techniques and in high seas resource assessment, strengthening cadres of personnel to deal with the high seas resource management and conservation and related environmental issues, and training observers and inspectors to be placed on fishing vessels.

---

9   Draft paragraph 17.68 of A/CONF.151/4 (22 April 1992) was replaced by decision of the Main Committee of UNCED on 10 June 1992. See A/CONF.151/L.3/Add.17 (12 June 1992). The former draft read as follows:

The costs of developing sustainable uses of high seas resources should be borne by utilizing countries. The principal costs of research and management systems in the high seas should also be supported by the States [and the various users]. However, the catalytic funding required to improve the database and scientific knowledge, the effectiveness of fisheries management bodies, and the participation of all coastal countries, especially developing ones, in this effort is estimated at $12 million per year for this global issue, including $5 million to strengthen international and regional organizations.

(d) Capacity-building

17.67. States, with the support, where appropriate, of relevant international organizations, whether subregional, regional or global, should cooperate to develop or upgrade systems and institutional structures for monitoring, control and surveillance, as well as the research capacity for assessment of marine living resource populations.

17.68. Special support, including cooperation among States, will be needed to enhance the capacities of developing countries in the areas of data and information, scientific and technological means and human resource development in order to participate effectively in the conservation and sustainable utilization of high seas marine living resources.

D. Sustainable use and conservation of marine living resources under national jurisdiction

Basis for action

17.69. Marine fisheries yield 80 to 90 million tons of fish and shellfish per year, 95 percent of which is taken from waters under national jurisdiction. Yields have increased nearly fivefold over the past four decades. The provisions of the United Nations Convention on the Law of the Sea on marine living resources of the exclusive economic zone and other areas under national jurisdiction set forth rights and obligations of States with respect to conservation and utilization of those resources.

17.70. Marine living resources provide an important source of protein in many countries and their use is often of major importance to local communities and indigenous people. Such resources provide food and livelihoods to millions of people and, if sustainably utilized, offer increased potential to meet nutritional and social needs, particularly in developing countries. To realize this potential requires improved knowledge and identification of marine living resource stocks, particularly of underutilized and unutilized stocks and species, use of new technologies, better handling and processing facilities to avoid wastage and improved quality and training of skilled personnel to effectively manage and conserve the marine living resources of the exclusive economic zone and other areas under national jurisdiction. Emphasis should also be on multi-species management and other approaches that take into account the relationships among species.

17.71. Fisheries in many areas under national jurisdiction face mounting problems, including local overfishing, unauthorized incursions by foreign fleets, ecosystem degradation, overcapitalization and excessive fleet sizes, undervaluation of catch, insufficiently selective gear, unreliable databases, and increasing competition between artisanal and large-scale fishing, and between fishing and other types of activities.

17.72. Problems extend beyond fisheries. Coral reefs and other marine and coastal habitats such as mangroves and estuaries, are among the most highly diverse, integrated and productive of the Earth's ecosystems. They often serve important ecological functions, provide coastal protection, and are critical resources for food, energy, tourism and economic development. In many parts of the world, such marine and coastal systems are under stress or threatened from a variety of sources, both human and natural.

Objectives

17.73. Coastal States, particularly developing countries and States whose economies are overwhelmingly dependent on the exploitation of the marine living resources of their exclusive economic zones, should obtain the full social and economic benefits from sustainable utilization of marine living resources within their exclusive economic zones and other areas under national jurisdiction.

17.74. States commit themselves to the conservation and sustainable use of marine living resources under national jurisdiction. To this end, it is necessary to:

(a) Develop and increase the potential of marine living resources to meet human nutritional needs, as well as social, economic and development goals;

(b) Take into account traditional knowledge and interests of local communities, small-scale artisanal fisheries and indigenous people in development and management programmes;

(c) Maintain or restore populations of marine species at levels that can produce the maximum sustainable yield as qualified by relevant environmental and economic factors, taking into consideration relationships among species;

(d) Promote the development and use of selective fishing gear and practices that minimize waste in the catch of target species and minimize by-catch of non-target species;

(e) Protect and restore endangered marine species;

(f) Preserve rare or fragile ecosystems as well as habitats and other ecologically sensitive areas.

17.75. Nothing in paragraph 17.74 above restricts the right of a coastal State or the competence of an international organization, as appropriate, to prohibit, limit or regulate the exploitation of marine mammals more strictly than provided for in that paragraph. States shall cooperate with a view to the conservation of marine mammals and in the case of cetaceans shall in particular work through the appropriate international organizations for their conservation, management and study.

17.76. The ability of developing countries to fulfil the above objectives is dependent upon their capabilities, including the financial, scientific and technological means at their disposal. Adequate financial, scientific and technological cooperation should be provided to support action by them to implement these objectives.

Activities

(a) Management-related activities

17.77. States should ensure that marine living resources of the exclusive economic zone and other areas under national jurisdiction are conserved and managed in accordance with the provisions of the United Nations Convention on the Law of the Sea.

17.78. States, in implementing the provisions of the United Nations Convention on the Law of the Sea, should address the issues of straddling stocks and highly migratory species, and, taking fully into account the objective set out in paragraph 17.73, access to the surplus of allowable catches.[10]

17.79. Coastal States, individually or through bilateral and/or multilateral cooperation and with the support, as appropriate of international organizations, whether subregional, regional or global, should *inter alia*:

(a) Assess the potential of marine living resources, including underutilized or unutilized stocks and species, by developing inventories, where necessary, for their conservation and sustainable use;

(b) Implement strategies for the sustainable use of marine living resources, taking into account the special needs and interests of small-scale artisanal fisheries, local communities and indigenous people to meet human nutritional and other development needs;

(c) Implement, in particular in developing countries, mechanisms to develop mariculture, aquaculture and small-scale, deep-sea and oceanic fisheries within areas under national jurisdiction where assessments show that marine living resources are potentially available;

(d) Strengthen their legal and regulatory frameworks, where appropriate, including management, enforcement and surveillance capabilities, to regulate activities related to the above strategies;

(e) Take measures to increase the availability of marine living resources as human food by reducing wastage, post-harvest losses and discards, and improving techniques of processing, distribution and transportation;

---

10   Draft paragraph 17.83 or 17.84 bis options of A/CONF.151/4 (22 April 1992) was replaced by decision of the Main Committee of UNCED on 10 June 1992. See A/CONF.151/L.3/Add.17 (12 June 1992). The former draft read as follows:

    [[17.83 or 17.84bis] States should give attention to issues related to the conservation and management of straddling stocks, migratory species and access to surplus.]

    [[17.83 or 17.84bis] States should implement the provisions of the United Nations Convention on the Law of the Sea with regard to straddling stocks, migratory species and access to surplus.]

(f) Develop and promote the use of environmentally sound technology under criteria compatible with the sustainable use of marine living resources, including assessment of environmental impact of major new fishery practices;

(g) Enhance the productivity and utilization of their marine living resources for food and income;

17.80. Coastal States should explore the scope for expanding recreational and tourist activities based on marine living resources, including those for providing alternative sources of income. Such activities should be compatible with conservation and sustainable development policies and plans.

17.81. Coastal States should support the sustainability of small-scale artisanal fisheries. To this end, they should, as appropriate:

(a) Integrate small-scale artisanal fisheries development in marine and coastal planning, taking into account the interests and, where appropriate, encouraging representation of fishermen, small-scale fisherworkers, women, local communities and indigenous people;

(b) Recognize the rights of small-scale fishworkers and the special situation of indigenous people and local communities, including their rights to utilization and protection of their habitats on a sustainable basis;

(c) Develop systems for the acquisition and recording of traditional knowledge concerning marine living resources and environment and promote the incorporation of such knowledge into management systems.

17.82. Coastal States should ensure that, in the negotiation and implementation of international agreements on the development or conservation of marine living resources, the interests of local communities and indigenous people are taken into account, in particular their right to subsistence.

17.83. Coastal States, with the support, as appropriate, of international organizations should conduct analyses of the potential for aquaculture in marine and coastal areas under national jurisdiction and apply appropriate safeguards as to the introduction of new species.

17.84. States should prohibit dynamiting, poisoning and other comparable destructive fishing practices.

17.85. States should identify marine ecosystems exhibiting high levels of biodiversity and productivity and other critical habitat areas and provide necessary limitations on use in these areas, through, *inter alia*, designation of protected areas. Priority should be accorded, as appropriate, to:

(a) Coral reef ecosystems;

(b) Estuaries;

(c) Temperate and tropical wetlands, including mangroves;

(d) Seagrass beds;

(e) Other spawning and nursery areas.

(b) Data and information

17.86. States, individually or through bilateral and multilateral cooperation and with the support, as appropriate, of international organizations, whether subregional, regional or global, should:

(a) Promote enhanced collection and exchange of data necessary for the conservation and sustainable use of the marine living resources under national jurisdiction;

(b) Exchange on a regular basis up-to-date data and information necessary for fisheries assessment;

(c) Develop and share analytical and predictive tools such as stock assessment and bioeconomic models;

(d) Establish or expand appropriate monitoring and assessment programmes;

(e) Complete or update marine biodiversity, marine living resource and critical habitat profiles of exclusive economic zones and other areas under national jurisdiction, taking account of changes in the environment brought about by natural causes and human activities.

(c) International and regional cooperation and coordination

17.87. States, through bilateral and multilateral cooperation, and with the support of relevant United Nations and other international organizations, should cooperate to:

(a) Develop financial and technical cooperation to enhance the capacities of developing countries in small-scale and oceanic fisheries as well as coastal aquaculture and mariculture;

(b) Promote the contribution of marine living resources to eliminate malnutrition and to achieve food self-sufficiency in developing countries, *inter alia*, by minimizing post harvest losses and managing stocks for guaranteed sustainable yields;

(c) Develop agreed criteria for the use of selective fishing gear and practices to minimize waste of catch of target species and minimize by-catch of non-target species;

(d) Promote seafood quality, including through national quality assurance systems for seafood, in order to promote access to markets, improve consumer confidence and maximize economic returns.

17.88. States should, where and as appropriate, ensure adequate coordination and cooperation in enclosed and semi-enclosed seas and between subregional, regional and global intergovernmental fisheries bodies.

17.89. States recognize:

(a) The responsibility of the International Whaling Commission for the conservation and management of whale stocks and the regulation of whaling pursuant to the 1946 International Convention for the Regulation of Whaling;

(b) The work of the International Whaling Commission Scientific Committee in carrying out studies of large whales in particular, as well as of other cetaceans;

(c) The work of other organizations, such as the Inter-American Tropical Tuna Commission and the Agreement on Small Cetaceans in the Baltic and North Sea under the Bonn Convention, in the conservation, management and study of cetaceans and other marine mammals.

17.90. States should cooperate for the conservation, management and study of cetaceans.

Means of implementation

(a) Financing and cost evaluation

17.91. The Conference secretariat has estimated the average total annual cost (1993-2000) of implementing the activities of this programme to be about $6 billion, including about $60 million from the international community on grant or concessional terms. These are indicative and order-of-magnitude estimates only and have not been reviewed by Governments. Actual costs and financial terms, including any that are non-concessional, will depend upon, *inter alia*, the specific strategies and programmes Governments decide upon for implementation.[11]

(b) Scientific and technological means

17.92. States, with the support of relevant intergovernmental organizations, as appropriate, should:

(a) Provide for the transfer of environmentally sound technologies to develop fisheries, aquaculture and mariculture, particularly to developing countries;

(b) Accord special attention to mechanisms for transferring resource information and improved fishing and aquaculture technologies to fishing communities at the local level;

---

11   Draft paragraph 17.96 of A/CONF.151/4 (22 April 1992) was replaced by decision of the Main Committee of UNCED on 10 June 1992. See A/CONF.151/L.3/Add.17 (12 June 1992). The former draft read as follows:

       The total cost to restructure the fisheries sector is estimated at up to $6 billion per year, excluding investments needed to organize sector reconversion to reduce overcapitalization. The catalytic funding proposed to implement the above activities at the national and regional levels is on the order of $60 million annually to accelerate development and improve management, including $4 million to strengthen regional and international organizations.

(c) Promote the study, scientific assessment and use of appropriate traditional management systems;

(d) Consider observing, as appropriate, the FAO/ICES Code of Practice for Consideration of Transfer and Introduction of Marine and Freshwater Organisms;

(e) Promote scientific research on marine areas of particular importance for marine living resources, such as areas of high diversity, endemism and productivity and migratory stopover points.

(c) Human resource development

17.93. States individually, or through bilateral and multilateral cooperation and with the support of relevant international organizations, whether subregional, regional or global, as appropriate, should encourage and provide support for developing countries, *inter alia*, to:

(a) Expand multidisciplinary education, training and research on marine living resources, particularly in social and economic sciences;

(b) Create training opportunities at national and regional levels to support artisanal (including subsistence) fisheries, to develop small-scale use of marine living resources and to encourage equitable participation of local communities, small-scale fish workers, women and indigenous people;

(c) Introduce topics relating to the importance of marine living resources in educational curricula at all levels.

(d) Capacity-building

17.94. Coastal States, with the support of relevant subregional, regional and global agencies, where appropriate, should:

(a) Develop research capacities for assessment of marine living resource populations and monitoring;

(b) Provide support to local fishing communities, in particular those which rely on fishing for subsistence, indigenous people and women, including, as appropriate, the technical and financial assistance to organize, maintain, exchange and improve traditional knowledge of marine living resources and fishing techniques, and upgrade knowledge on marine ecosystems;

(c) Establish sustainable aquaculture development strategies, including environmental management in support of rural fish-farming communities;

(d) Develop and strengthen, where the need may arise, institutions capable of implementing the objectives and activities related to the conservation and management of marine living resources.

17.95. Special support, including cooperation among States, will be needed to enhance the capacities of developing countries in the areas of data and information, scientific and technological means and human resource development in order to enable them to participate effectively in the conservation and sustainable use of marine living resources under national jurisdiction.

E. Addressing critical uncertainties for the management of the marine environment and climate change

Basis for action

17.96. The marine environment is vulnerable and sensitive to climate and atmospheric changes. Rational use and development of coastal areas, all seas and marine resources, as well as conservation of the marine environment, requires the ability to determine the present state of these systems and to predict future conditions. The high degree of uncertainty in present information inhibits effective management and limits the ability to make predictions and assess environmental change. Systematic collection of data on marine environmental parameters will be needed to apply integrated management approaches and to predict effects of global climate change and of atmospheric phenomena, such as ozone depletion, on living marine resources and the marine environment. In order to determine the role of the oceans and all seas in driving global systems and to predict natural and human-induced changes in marine and coastal environments, the mechanisms to collect, synthesize and disseminate information from research and systematic observation activities need to be restructured and reinforced considerably.

17.97. There are many uncertainties about climate change and particularly sealevel rise. Small increases in sealevel have the potential of causing significant damage to small islands and low-lying coasts. Response strategies should be based on sound data. A long-term cooperative research commitment is needed to provide the data required for global climate models and to reduce uncertainty. Meanwhile, precautionary measures should be undertaken to diminish the risks and effects, particularly on small islands and on low-lying and coastal areas of the world.

17.98. Increased ultraviolet radiation derived from ozone depletion has been reported in some areas of the world. An assessment of its effects in the marine environment is needed to reduce uncertainty and to provide a basis for action.

Objectives

17.99. States, in accordance with provisions of the United Nations Convention on the Law of the Sea on marine scientific research, commit themselves to improve the understanding of the marine environment and its role on global processes. To this end, it is necessary to:

(a) Promote scientific research on and systematic observation of the marine environment within the limits of national jurisdiction and high seas, including interactions with atmospheric phenomena, such as ozone depletion;

(b) Promote exchange of data and information resulting from scientific research and systematic observation and from traditional ecological knowledge and ensure its availability to policy makers and the public at the national level;

(c) Cooperate with a view to the development of standard inter-calibrated procedures, measuring techniques, data storage and management capabilities for scientific research on and systematic observation of the marine environment.

Activities

(a) Management-related activities

17.100. States should consider, *inter alia*:

(a) Coordinating national and regional observation programmes for coastal and near-shore phenomena related to climate change and for research parameters essential for marine and coastal management in all regions;

(b) Providing improved forecasts of marine conditions for the safety of inhabitants of coastal areas and for the efficiency of maritime operations;

(c) Cooperating with a view to adopt special measures to cope with and adapt to potential climate change and sealevel rise, including the development of globally accepted methodologies for coastal vulnerability assessment, modelling and response strategies particularly for priority areas, such as small islands and low-lying and critical coastal areas;

(d) Identifying ongoing and planned programmes of systematic observation of the marine environment, with a view to integrating activities and establishing priorities to address critical uncertainties for oceans and all seas;

(e) Initiating a programme of research to determine the marine biological effects of increased levels of ultraviolet rays due to the depletion of the stratospheric ozone layer and to evaluate the possible effects.

17.101. Recognizing the important role that oceans and all seas play in attenuating potential climate change, IOC and other relevant competent United Nations bodies, with the support of countries having the resources and expertise, should carry out analysis, assessments and systematic observation of the role of oceans as a carbon sink.

(b) Data and information

17.102. States should consider, *inter alia*:

(a) Increasing international cooperation particularly with a view to strengthening national scientific and technological capabilities for analysing, assessing and predicting global climate and environmental change;

(b) Supporting the role of the IOC in cooperation with WMO, UNEP and other international organizations in the collection, analysis and distribution of data and information from the oceans and all seas, including as appropriate, through the proposed Global Ocean Observing System, giving special attention to the need for IOC to develop fully the strategy for providing training and technical assistance for developing countries through its Training, Education and Mutual Assistance (TEMA) programme;

(c) Creating national multisectoral information bases, covering the results of research and systematic observation programmes;

(d) Linking these databases to existing data and information services and mechanisms, such as World Weather Watch and Earthwatch;

(e) Cooperating with the view to the exchange of data and information and its storage and archiving through the world and regional data centres;

(f) Cooperating to ensure full participation of developing countries, in particular, in any international scheme under the organs and organizations of the United Nations system for the collection, analysis and use of data and information.

(c) International and Regional Cooperation and Coordination

17.103. States should consider bilaterally and multilaterally and in cooperation with international organizations, whether subregional, regional, interregional or global, where appropriate:

(a) Providing technical cooperation in developing the capacity of coastal and island States for marine research and systematic observation and for using its results;

(b) Strengthening existing national institutions and creating, where necessary, international analysis and prediction mechanisms in order to prepare and exchange regional and global oceanographic analyses and forecasts and to provide facilities for international research and training at national, subregional and regional levels, where applicable.

17.104. In recognition of the value of Antarctica as an area for the conduct of scientific research, in particular research essential to understanding the global environment, States carrying out such research activities in Antarctica should, as provided for in Article III of the Antarctic Treaty, continue to:

(a) Ensure that data and information resulting from such research is freely available to the international community;

(b) Enhance access of the international scientific community and specialized agencies of the United Nations to such data and information including the encouragement of periodic seminars and symposia.

17.105. States should strengthen high-level inter-agency, subregional, regional and global coordination, as appropriate, and review mechanisms to develop and integrate systematic observation networks. This would include:

(a) Review of existing regional and global databases;

(b) Mechanisms to develop comparable and compatible techniques, validate methodologies and measurements, organize regular scientific reviews, develop options for corrective measures, agree on formats for presentation and storage, and communicate the information gathered to potential users;

(c) Systematic observation of coastal habitats and sealevel changes, inventories of marine pollution sources and reviews of fisheries statistics;

(d) Organization of periodic assessments of ocean and all seas and coastal area status and trends.

17.106. International cooperation, through relevant organizations within the United Nations system, should support countries to develop and integrate regional systematic long-term observation programmes, when applicable, into the Regional Seas Programmes in a coordinated fashion to implement, where appropriate, subregional, regional and global observing systems based on the principle of exchange of data. One aim should be the predicting of the effects of climate-related emergencies on existing coastal physical and socio-economic infrastructure.

17.107. Based on the results of research on the effects of the additional ultraviolet radiation reaching the Earth's surface, in the fields of human health, agriculture and marine environment, States and international organizations should consider taking appropriate remedial measures.

Means of Implementation

(a) Financing and cost evaluation

17.108. The Conference secretariat has estimated the average total annual cost (1993-2000) of implementing the activities of this programme to be about $750 million, including about $480 million from the international community on grant or concessional terms. These are indicative and order-of-magnitude estimates only and have not been reviewed by Governments. Actual costs and financial terms, including any that are non-concessional, will depend upon, *inter alia*, the specific strategies and programmes Governments decide upon for implementation.[12]

---

12   Draft paragraph 17.113 of A/CONF.151/4 (22 April 1992) was replaced by decision of the Main Committee of UNCED on 10 June 1992. See A/CONF.151/L.3/Add.17 (12 June 1992). The former draft read as follows:

   The estimate of costs to ensure participation in the implementation of the recommendations in this section needs to be reconsidered in the light of conclusions on financial matters.

17.109. Developed countries should provide the financing for the further development and implementation of the Global Ocean Observing System.

(b) Scientific and technological means

17.110. To address critical uncertainties through systematic coastal and marine observations and research, coastal States should cooperate in the development of procedures that allow for comparable analysis and soundness of data. They should also cooperate on a subregional and regional basis, through existing programmes where applicable, share infrastructure and expensive and sophisticated equipment, develop quality assurance procedures and develop human resources jointly. Special attention should be given to transfer of scientific and technological knowledge and means to support States, particularly developing countries, in the development of endogenous capabilities.

17.111. International organizations should support, when requested, coastal countries in implementing research projects on the effects of additional ultraviolet radiation.

(c) Human resource development

17.112. States, individually or through bilateral and multilateral cooperation and with the support, as appropriate, of international organizations whether subregional, regional or global, should develop and implement comprehensive programmes, particularly in developing countries for a broad and coherent approach to meeting their core human resource needs in the marine sciences.

(d) Capacity-building

17.113. States should strengthen or establish as necessary, national scientific and technological oceanographic commissions or equivalent bodies to develop, support and coordinate marine science activities and work closely with international organizations.

17.114. States should use existing subregional and regional mechanisms, where applicable, to develop knowledge of the marine environment, exchange information, organize systematic observations and assessments, and make most effective use of scientists, facilities and equipment. They should also cooperate in the promotion of endogenous research capabilities in developing countries.

F. Strengthening international, including regional, cooperation and coordination

Basis for action

17.115. It is recognized that the role of international cooperation is to support and supplement national efforts. Implementation of strategies and activities under the programme areas relative to marine and coastal areas and seas require effective institutional arrangements at national, subregional, regional and global levels, as appropriate. There are numerous national and international, including regional, institutions, both within and outside the United Nations system, with competence in marine issues, and there is a need to improve coordination and strengthen links among them. It is also important to ensure that an integrated and multisectoral approach to marine issues is pursued at all levels.

Objectives

17.116. States commit themselves, in accordance with their policies, priorities and resources, to promote institutional arrangements necessary to support the implementation of the programme areas in this chapter. To this end, it is necessary, as appropriate, to:

(a) Integrate relevant sectoral activities addressing environment and development in marine and coastal areas at national, subregional, regional and global levels, as appropriate;

(b) Promote effective information exchange and, where appropriate, institutional linkages between bilateral and multilateral national, regional, subregional and interregional institutions dealing with environment and development in marine and coastal areas;

(c) Promote within the United Nations system, regular intergovernmental review and consideration of environment and development issues with respect to marine and coastal areas;

(d) Promote the effective operation of coordinating mechanisms for the components of the United Nations system dealing with issues of environment and development in marine and coastal areas, as well as links with relevant international development bodies.

Activities

(a) Management-related activities

Global

17.117. The General Assembly should provide for regular consideration, within the United Nations system, at the intergovernmental level of general marine and coastal issues, including environment and development matters, and should request the Secretary-General and executive heads of United Nations agencies and organizations to:

(a) Strengthen coordination and develop improved arrangements among the relevant United Nations organizations with major marine and coastal responsibilities, including their subregional and regional components;

(b) Strengthen coordination between those organizations and other United Nations organizations, institutions and specialized agencies dealing with development, trade and other related economic issues, as appropriate;

(c) Improve representation of United Nations agencies dealing with the marine environment in United Nations system-wide coordination efforts;

(d) Promote, where necessary, greater collaboration between the United Nations agencies and subregional and regional coastal and marine programmes;

(e) Develop a centralized system to provide for information on legislation and advice on implementation of legal agreements on marine environmental and development issues.

17.118. States recognize that environmental policies should deal with the root causes of environmental degradation, thus preventing environmental measures from resulting in unnecessary restrictions to trade. Trade policy measures for environmental purposes should not constitute a means of arbitrary or unjustifiable discrimination or a disguised restriction on international trade. Unilateral actions to deal with environmental challenges outside the jurisdiction of the importing country should be avoided. Environmental measures addressing international environmental problems should, as far as possible, be based on an international consensus. Domestic measures targeted to achieve certain environmental objectives may need trade measures to render them effective. Should trade policy measures be found necessary for the enforcement of environmental policies, certain principles and rules should apply. These could include, *inter alia*: the principle of non-discrimination; the principle that the trade measure chosen should be the least trade-restrictive necessary to achieve the objectives; an obligation to ensure transparency in the use of trade measures related to the environment and to provide adequate notification of national regulations; and the need to give consideration to the special conditions and developmental requirements of developing countries as they move towards internationally agreed environmental objectives.

Subregional and regional

17.119. States should consider, as appropriate:

(a) Strengthening, and extending where necessary, intergovernmental regional cooperation, the Regional Seas Programmes of UNEP, regional and subregional fisheries organizations and regional commissions;

(b) Introduce, where necessary, coordination among relevant United Nations and other multilateral organizations at the subregional and regional levels, including consideration of co-location of their staff;

(c) Arrange for periodic intraregional consultations;

(d) Facilitate access to and use of expertise and technology through relevant national bodies to subregional and regional centres and networks, such as the Regional Centres for Marine Technology.

(b) Data and information

17.120. States should, where appropriate:

(a) Promote exchange of information on marine and coastal issues;

(b) Strengthen the capacity of international organizations to handle information and support the development of national, subregional and regional data and information systems, where appropriate. This could also include networks linking countries with comparable environmental problems;

(c) Further develop existing international mechanisms such as Earthwatch and GESAMP.

Means of implementation

(a) Financing and cost evaluation

17.121. The Conference secretariat has estimated the average total annual cost (1993-2000) of implementing the activities of this programme to be about $50 million from the international community on grant or concessional terms. These are indicative and order-of-magnitude estimates only and have not been reviewed by Governments. Actual costs and financial terms, including any that are non-concessional, will depend upon, *inter alia*, the specific strategies and programmes Governments decide upon for implementation.[13]

(b) Scientific and technological means, human resource development and capacity-building

17.122. The means of implementation outlined in the other programme areas on marine and coastal issues, under the sections on Scientific and technological means, human resource development and capacity-building are entirely relevant for this programme area as well. Additionally, States should, through international cooperation, develop a comprehensive programme for meeting the core human resource needs in marine sciences at all levels.

G. Sustainable development of small islands

Basis for action

17.123. Small island developing States, and islands supporting small communities are a special case both for environment and development. They are ecologi-

---

13 Draft paragraph 17.126 of A/CONF.151/4 (22 April 1992) was replaced by decision of the Main Committee of UNCED on 10 June 1992. See A/CONF.151/L.3/Add.6 (12 June 1992). The former draft read as follows:

The proposed cost for strengthening regional cooperation is $12/million per year in additional support for international organizations and regional coordinating units, and at least $25/million annually in further direct support to activities at the regional level. Improving international coordination and strengthening the global role of the United Nations system to implement Agenda 21 in oceans and coastal areas would cost a proposed $12/million per year, which would approximately double present expenditures and would catalyse and coordinate much larger national expenditures.

cally fragile and vulnerable. Their small size, limited resources, geographic dispersion and isolation from markets, place them at a disadvantage economically and prevent economies of scale. For small island developing States the ocean and coastal environment is of strategic importance and constitutes a valuable development resource.

17.124. Their geographic isolation has resulted in their habitation of a comparatively large number of unique species of flora and fauna, giving them a very high share of global biodiversity. They also have rich and diverse cultures with special adaptations to island environments and knowledge of the sound management of island resources.

17.125. Small island developing States have all the environmental problems and challenges of the coastal zone concentrated in a limited land area. They are considered extremely vulnerable to global warming and sealevel rise with certain small low-lying islands facing the increasing threat of the loss of their entire national territories. Most tropical islands are also now experiencing the more immediate impacts of increasing frequency of cyclones, storms and hurricanes associated with climate change. These are causing major set-backs to their socio-economic development.

17.126. Because small island development options are limited, there are special challenges to planning for and implementing sustainable development. Small island developing States will be constrained in meeting these challenges without the cooperation and assistance of the international community.

Objectives

17.127. States commit themselves to addressing the problems of sustainable development of small island developing States. To this end, it is necessary:

(a) To adopt and implement plans and programmes to support the sustainable development and utilization of their marine and coastal resources, including meeting essential human needs, maintaining biodiversity and improving the quality of life for island people;

(b) To adopt measures which will enable small island developing States to cope effectively, creatively and sustainably with environmental change and to mitigate impacts and reduce the threats posed to marine and coastal resources.

Activities

(a) Management-related activities

17.128. Small island developing States, with the assistance as appropriate of the international community and on the basis of existing work of national and international organizations, should:

(a) Study the special environmental and developmental characteristics of small islands, producing an environmental profile and inventory of their natural resources, critical marine habitats and biodiversity;

(b) Develop techniques for determining and monitoring the carrying capacity of small islands under different development assumptions and resource constraints;

(c) Prepare medium- and long-term plans for sustainable development that emphasize multiple use of resources, integrate environmental considerations with economic and sectoral planning and policies, define measures for maintaining cultural and biological diversity and conserve endangered species and critical marine habitats;

(d) Adapt coastal area management techniques, such as planning, siting and environmental impact assessments, using Geographic Information Systems (GIS), suitable to the special characteristics of small islands, taking into account the traditional and cultural values of indigenous people of island countries;

(e) Review the existing institutional arrangements and identify and undertake appropriate institutional reforms essential to the effective implementation of sustainable development plans, including intersectoral coordination and community participation in the planning process;

(f) Implement sustainable development plans, including the review and modification of existing unsustainable policies and practices;

(g) Based on precautionary and anticipatory approaches, design and implement rational response strategies to address the environmental, social and economic impacts of climate change and sealevel rise, and prepare appropriate contingency plans;

(h) Promote environmentally sound technology for sustainable development within small island developing States and identify technologies that should be excluded because of their threats to essential island ecosystems.

(b) Data and information

17.129. Additional information on the geographic, environmental, cultural and socio-economic characteristics of islands should be compiled and assessed to assist in the planning process. Existing island databases should be expanded and geographic information systems developed and adapted to suit the special characteristics of islands.

(c) International and regional cooperation and coordination

17.130. Small island developing States, with the support, as appropriate, of international organizations, whether subregional, regional or global, should develop and strengthen inter-island, regional and interregional cooperation and information exchange, including periodic regional and global meetings on sustainable development of small island developing States with the first global conference on the sustainable development of small island developing States, to be held in 1993.

17.131. International organizations, whether subregional, regional or global, must recognize the special development requirements of small island developing States and give adequate priority in the provision of assistance, particularly with respect to the development and implementation of sustainable development plans.

Means of Implementation

(a) Financing and Cost Evaluation

17.132. The Conference secretariat has estimated the average total annual cost (1993-2000) of implementing the activities of this programme to be about $130 million, including about $50 million from the international community on grant or concessional terms. These are indicative and order-of-magnitude estimates only and have not been reviewed by Governments. Actual cost and financial terms, including any that are non-concessional, will depend upon, *inter alia*, the specific strategies and programmes Governments decide upon for implementation.[14]

(b) Scientific and technical means

17.133. Centres for the development and diffusion of scientific information and advice on technical means and technologies appropriate to small island developing States, especially with reference to the management of the coastal zone, the exclusive economic zone and marine resources, should be established or strengthened, as appropriate, on a regional basis.

(c) Human resource development

17.134. Since populations of small island developing States cannot maintain all necessary specializations, training for integrated coastal management and development should aim to produce cadres of managers or scientists, engineers and coastal planners able to integrate the many factors that need to be considered in integrated coastal management. Resource users should be prepared to execute both management and protection functions and to apply the polluter pays principle and support the training of their personnel. Educational systems

---

14   Paragraph 17.132, formerly para. 17.137 of A/CONF. 151/4 (Part II), p. 171, was revised by the main committee of UNED. It formerly read as follows:

Technical cooperation costs to implement these activities amount to $7 million per year. A programme on integrated planning for sustainable development of islands will cost about $130 million per year, to be financed by private and public sources. About $40 million could come from the international community. Since many small islands will never develop an adequate economic or population base to provide all of the services necessary for a reasonable quality of life, some external support will frequently be required on a continuing basis. In addition, the need to maintain the island share of global biodiversity will further limit development options and should be supported by the international community with at least $3 million per year.

should be modified to meet these needs and special training programmes developed in integrated island management and development. Local planning should be integrated in educational curricula of all levels and public awareness campaigns developed with the assistance of non-governmental organizations and indigenous coastal populations.

(d) Capacity-building

17.135. The total capacity of small island developing States will always be limited. Existing capacity must therefore be restructured to efficiently meet the immediate needs for sustainable development and integrated management. At the same time, adequate and appropriate assistance from the international community must be directed at strengthening the full range of human resources needed on a continuous basis to implement sustainable development plans.

17.136. New technologies which can increase the output and range of capability of the limited human resources should be employed to increase the capacity of very small populations to meet their needs. The development and application of traditional knowledge to improve the capacity of countries to implement sustainable development should be fostered.

Chapter 18

Protection of the Quality and Supply of Freshwater Resources: Application of Integrated Approaches to the Development, Management and Use of Water Resources

INTRODUCTION

18.1. Freshwater resources are an essential component of the earth's hydrosphere and an indispensable part of all terrestrial ecosystems. The freshwater environment is characterized by the hydrological cycel, including floods and droughts, which in some regions have become more extreme and dramatic in their consequences. Global climate change and atmospheric pollution could also have an impact on freshwater resources and their availability and, through sea-level rise, threaten low-lying coastal areas and small island ecosystems.

18.2. Water is needed in all aspects of life. The general objective is to make certain that adequate supplies of water of good quality are maintained for the entire population of this planet, while preserving the hydrological, biological and chemical functions of ecosystems, adapting human activities within the capacity limits of nature and combating vectors of water-related diseases. Innovative technologies, including the improvement of indigenous technologies, are needed to fully utilize limited water resources and to safeguard those resources against pollution.

18.3. The widespread scarcity, gradual destruction and aggravated pollution of freshwater resources in many world regions, along with the progressive encroachment of incompatible activities, demand integrated water resources planning and management. Such integration must cover all types of interrelated freshwater bodies, including both surface water and groundwater, and duly consider water quantity and quality aspects. The multisectoral nature of water resources development in the context of socio-economic development must be recognized, as well as the multi-interest utilization of water resources for water supply ans sanitation, agriculture, industry, urban development, hydropower generation, inland fisheries, transportation, recreation, low and flat lands management and other activities. Rational water utilization schemes for the development of surface and underground water-supply sources and other potenttial sources have to be supported by concurrent water conservation and wastage minimization measures. Priority, however, must be accorded to flood prevention and control measures, as well as sedimentation control, where required.

18.4. Transboundary water resources and their use are of great importance to riparian States. In this connection, cooperation among those States may be desirable in conformity with existing agreements and/or other relevant arrangements, taking into account the interests of all riparian States concerned.

18.5. The following programme areas are proposed for the freshwater sector:

(a) Integrated water resources development and management;

(b) Water resources assessment;

(c) Protection of water resources, water quality and aquatic ecosystems;

(d) Drinking-water supply and sanitation;

(e) Water and sustainable development;

(f) Water for sustainable food production and rural development;

(g) Impacts of climate change on water resources.

Editor's Note: Draft paragraphs 18.1 to 18.15 of A/CONF.151/4 (22 April 1992) were replaced by decision of the Main Committee of UNCED on 10 June 1992. See A/CONF.151/L.3/Add.18 (11 June 1992). The former draft read as follows:

18.1. Effectively integrated management of water resources is important to all socio-economic sectors relying on water. Rational allocation prevents conflict and enhances the social development of local communities as well as economic planning and productivity. Efficient demand management allows water-using sectors to make long-term savings on water costs and stimulates resource-conscious production technologies. Health conditions and environmental quality should also improve, either as a result of integrated development planning or as a beneficial consequence of improved environmental or social conditions.

Linkages to other environmental and developmental issues

18.2. Water is a finite resource, essential for the sustenance of life on earth. Virtually all the environmental issues listed in General Assembly resolution 44/228 are directly or indirectly linked to freshwater issues. With increases in economic activities and the consequent potential for stress on ecosystems and natural resource stocks, the study and recognition of linkages between freshwater issues and other sectoral and cross-sectoral issues is becoming increasingly important. Socio-economic pursuit/including urbanization, industrial production and agricultural activities/has reached a stage where freshwater issues have often become the limiting factor for sustainable development. Freshwaters/rivers, reservoirs, lakes and groundwaters [polar ice mass and glaciers] are in contact with other ecosystems and are used in a variety of human activities, many of which would not be possible without a freshwater supply of adequate quality and quantity.

18.3. Poor land-use management, including deforestation, non-sustainable agriculture, mining and urbanization, could lead to a considerable increase in erosion problems and related soil loss in the river basins. The sedimentation in large reservoirs may have serious adverse effects downstream by reducing the quantity of natural nutrients available to agricultural land or to coastal waters. The loss of nutrients can lead to increased fertilizer use and decreases in coastal fishery yields. Acidification of surface and some groundwaters owing to atmospheric deposition of air pollutants can lead to depletion of freshwater living resources, contributing to the loss of biodiversity. Construction of dams for hydropower and irrigation, water channelization, over-abstraction from aquifers, use of water bodies as open sewers for the discharge of both domestic and industrial wastes can lead to the salinization of rivers, lakes, and soils, salt intrusions in coastal aquifers, and serious water pollution problems. Should climate change occur as a result of global warming, it would affect low-lying island freshwater resources and may affect the world's freshwater resources through [the melting of ice mass in the Arctic and Antarctic regions and] changes in the hydrologic cycle, resulting in changes in precipitation, with possible decreases in many areas of the Northern Hemisphere, accompanying decreases in soil moisture and annual river runoff. Even in the absence of global warming, a natural variation in precipitation may be expected, as in the past, resulting in periodic drought which can impact water availability, with consequent negative implications for economy and development. Because of these concerns, an integrated approach to freshwater management seems vital, along with, for example, an integrated approach to pollution control, the optimal use of water and a holistic approach to the conservation of ecosystems.

18.4. Transboundary water resources and their use are of great importance to riparian States. In this connection, cooperation among these States may be desirable in conformity with existing agreements and/or other relevant arrangements, taking into account the interests of all riparian States concerned.

18.5. Water-related diseases are still a major health problem, especially in the developing countries. Diseases caused by the microbiological pollution of water supplies or transmitted by water-associated vectors, and those related to inadequate sanitation and the absence of clean water, are widespread. With water use per capita expected to increase significantly in developing countries with high economic or population growth rates, the volume of waste requiring treatment is expected to present a growing problem. Likewise, the application of water-intensive production techniques and other high water-use consumption patterns are of concern in certain countries, particularly industrial ones. To ignore the interactions and linkages between freshwater issues and other sectoral issues could result in severe social, economic or human health consequences. Therefore, the provision of water supply and sanitation in developing countries is not only a vital ingredient of economic and social development but also an important element of environmental protection.

GENERAL OBJECTIVES

18.6. Water is needed in aspects of life. The general objective is to ascertain and maintain adequate supplies of water of good quality for all the population of this planet, preserving the hydrological, biological and chemical functions of the ecosystems, adapting human activities to the capacity limits of nature and combating vectors of disease related to water.

18.7. Freshwater resources are an essential component of the earth's hydrosphere and an indispensable part of all terrestrial ecosystems. The freshwater environment is characterized by its hydrological regime, including floods and droughts which, in some regions, have become more extreme and dramatic in their consequences in recent years. Global climate changes could also have their impact on freshwater resources and their availability and, through sealevel rise and atmospheric pollution, threaten coastal aquifers and small island ecosystems.

18.8. Freshwaters are a finite resource, not only indispensable for the sustenance of life on earth but also of vital importance to all socio-economic sectors. Development is not possible without considerable exploitation of water sources in relation to other land use activities and the control of deforestation and desertification. Priority must be given to the sustenance of land/water ecosystems, with particular attention to wetlands and biodiversity, and the satisfaction of basic human needs for drinking water, health protection and food security. For any water utilization beyond this, freshwater resources have to be considered as an economic good with an opportunity cost in alternative uses.

18.9. The Mar del Plata Action Plan, which emerged from the United Nations Water Conference in 1977, remains generally valid as the common basis for national and international action programmes in the freshwater sector. The review of progress achieved in its implementation and resulting strategies for the 1990s are reflected in Economic and Social Council resolution 1991/85. Agenda 21 in this sector, as presented hereunder, is based on these strategies, on the results of the Global Consultation on Safe Water and Sanitation for the 1990s, held at New Delhi in September 1990 (see General Assembly resolution 45/181) and on the recommendations that emerged from the International Conference on Water and the Environment, held in Dublin in January 1992, and on the results of the Preparatory Committee.

18.10. The widespread scarcity of freshwater resources, the progressive encroachment of incompatible activities and the gradual destruction of freshwater resources and their aggravating pollution in many world regions demands truly integrated water resources planning and management. The multisectoral nature of water resources development in the context of socio-economic development must be recognized as well as the multi-interest utilization of water resources for agriculture, industry, urban development, hydropower, inland fisheries, transportation, recreation and other activities. Rational water utilization schemes for the development of surface and underground water supply sources and other potential sources have to be supported by concurrent water conservation and wastage minimization measures.

18.11. Integrated water resources management necessitates appropriate mechanisms at the global, regional, national and local levels for implementing, coordinating and funding the related strategies and action programmes. Management of water resources should, as far as possible, take place in a river basin context (catchment level). [The options proposed by the International Conference on Water and the Environment/Development Issues for the 21st Century, held in Dublin, January 1992, has provided an input to identifying suitable implementation mechanisms.]

18.12. Capacity-building is a prerequisite to integrated water resources management. Technical solutions will not achieve programme objectives on their own without suitable attention given to the human factor. The Symposium on a Strategy for Water Resources Capacity-Building, held at Delft in June 1991, recognized the importance of capacity-building for integrated and sustainable development of water resources at all levels. Capacity-building consists of four basic elements:

(a) Creating an enabling environment with appropriate policy and legal frameworks;

(b) Institutional strengthening and development, including local community participation;

(c) Human resources development, including the strengthening of managerial systems and water users interests;

(d) Awareness building and education at all levels of society, [including, *inter alia*, the consideration of a United Nations World Water Day].

18.13. [Adequate new and additional financial resources are indispensable for the effective utilization and protection of freshwater resources. Pursuant to the recognition of water as an economic good, but with priority to the satisfaction of basic needs, internal revenues have to be generated through cost-recovery schemes, water tariffs, taxes etc. for uses implying productive activities, reflecting marginal and opportunity costs. In addition, external support will be required for water resources development from multilateral or bilateral sources (external support agencies) and from the private sector.]

18.14. Innovative technologies, including the improvement of indigenous techniques, are much needed to fully utilize limited water resources and to safeguard them against pollution. Implementation of Agenda 21 in the water sectors must therefore be supported by broad-based research and development programmes allowing for new technological solutions to be developed and field-tested. Technology [transfer on preferential and concessional terms] and [cooperation and diffusion] on all aspects of integrated water resources management is to be built into each programme area.]

18.15. In accordance with the general objectives, the following programme areas are proposed for the freshwater sector:

(a) Integrated water resources development and management;

(b) Water resources assessment;

(c) Protection of water resources, water quality and aquatic ecosystems;

(d) Drinking water supply and sanitation;

(e) Water and sustainable urban development;

(f) Water for sustainable food production and rural development;

(g) Impacts of climate change on water resources.

PROGRAMME AREAS

A. Integrated water resources development and management

Basis for action

18.6. The extent to which water resources development contributes to economic productivity and social well-being is not usually appreciated, although all social and economic activities rely heavily on the supply and quality of freshwater. As populations and economic activities grow, many countries are rapidly reaching conditions of water scarcity or facing limits to economic development. Water demands are increasing rapidly, with 70-80 per cent for irrigation, less than 20 per cent for industry and a mere 6 per cent for domestic consumption. The holistic management of fresh water as a finite and vulnerable resource, and the integration of sectoral water plans and programmes within the framework of national economic and social policy, is of paramount importance for action in the 1990s and beyond. The fragmentation of responsibilities for water resources development among sectoral agencies is proving, however, to be an even greater impediment to promoting integrated water management than had been anticipated. Effective implementation and coordination mechanisms are required.

Objectives

18.7. The overall objective is to satisfy the freshwater needs of all countries for their sustainable development.

18.8. Integrated water resources management is based on the perception of water as an integral part of the ecosystem, a natural resource and a social and economic good, whose quantity and quality determine the nature of its utilization. To this end, water resources have to be protected, taking into account the functioning of aquatic ecosystems and the perenniality of the resource, in order to satisfy or reconcile water needs in human activities. In developing and using water resources, priority has to be given to the satisfaction of basic needs and the safeguarding of ecosystems. Beyond these requirements, however, water users should be charged appropriately.

18.9. Integrated water resources management, including the integration of land- and water-related aspects, should be carried out at the catchment basin or sub-basin. Four principal objectives should be pursued, as follows:

(a) To promote a dynamic, interactive, iterative and multisectoral approach to water resources management, including the identification and protection of potential sources of freshwater supply, that integrates technological, socio-economic, environmental and human health considerations;

(b) To plan for the sustainable and rational utilization, protection, conservation and management of water resources based on community needs and priorities and within the framework of national economic development policy;

(c) To design, implement and evaluate projects and programmes that are both economically efficient and socially appropriate within clearly defined strategies, based on an approach of full public participation, including that of women, youth, indigenous people and local communities in water management policy-making and decision-making;

(d) To identify and strengthen or develop, as required, in particular in developing countries, the appropriate institutional, legal and financial mechanisms to ensure that water policy and its implementation are a catalyst for sustainable social progress and economic growth.

18.10. In the case of transboundary water resources, there is a need for riparian States to formulate water resource strategies, prepare water resource action programmes and consider, where appropriate, the harmonization of those strategies and action programmes.

18.11. All States, according to their capacity and available resources, and through bilateral or multilateral cooperation, including through the United Nations and other relevant organizations as appropriate, could set the following targets:

(a) By the year 2000:

(i) To have designed and initiated costed and targeted national action programmes, and to have put in place appropriate institutional structures and legal instruments;

(ii) To have established efficient water-use programmes to attain sustainable resource utilization patterns;

(b) By the year 2025:

(i) To have achieved subsectoral targets of all freshwater programme areas.

It is understood that the fulfilment of the targets quantified in (i) and (ii) above will depend upon new and additional financial resources that will be made available to developing countries in accordance with the relevant provisions of General Assembly resolution 44/228.

Activities

18.12. All States, according to their capacity and available resources, and through bilateral or multilateral cooperation, including through the United Nations and other relevant organizations as appropriate, could implement the following activities to improve integrated water resources management:

(a) Formulation of costed and targeted national action plans and investment programmes;

(b) Integration of measures for the protection and conservation of potential sources of freshwater supply, including the inventorying of water resources, with land-use planning, forest resource utilization, protection of mountain slopes and riverbanks and other relevant development and conservation activities;

(c) Development of interactive databases, forecasting models, economic planning models and methods for water management and planning, including environmental impact assessment methods;

(d) Optimization of water resources allocation under physical and socio-economic constraints;

(e) Implementation of allocation decisions through demand management, pricing mechanisms and regulatory measures;

(f) Flood and drought management, including risk analysis and environmental and social impact assessment;

(g) Promotion of schemes for rational water use through public awareness-raising, educational programmes and levying of water tariffs and other economic instruments;

(h) Mobilization of water resources, particularly in arid and semi-arid areas;

(i) Promotion of international scientific research cooperation on freshwater resources;

(j) Development of new and alternative sources of water supply such as sea-water desalination, artificial groundwater recharge, use of marginal-quality water, waste-water reuse and water recycling;

(k) Integration of water (including surface and underground water resources) quantity and quality management;

(l) Promotion of water conservation through improved water-use efficiency and wastage minimization schemes for all users, including the development of water-saving devices;

(m) Support to water users groups to optimize local water resources management;

(n) Development of public participatory techniques and their implementation in decision-making, particularly the enhancement of the role of women in water resources planning and management;

(o) Development and strengthening, as appropriate, of cooperation, including mechanisms where appropriate, at all levels concerned, namely:

(i) At the lowest appropriate level, delegation of water resources management, generally, to such a level, in accordance with national legislation, including decentralization of government services to local authorities, private enterprises and communities;

(ii) At the national level, integrated water resources planning and management in the framework of the national planning process and, where appropriate, establishment of independent regulation and monitoring of freshwater, based on national legislation and economic measures;

(iii) At the regional level, consideration, where appropriate, of the harmonization of national strategies and action programmes;

(iv) At the global level, improved delineation of responsibilities, division of labour and coordination of international organizations and programmes, including facilitating discussions and sharing experiences in areas related to water resources management;

(p) Dissemination of information, including operational guidelines, and promotion of education for water users, including the consideration by the United Nations of a World Water Day.[1]

---

1   Draft paragraph 18.22(p) of A/CONF.151/4 (22 April 1992) was replaced by decision of the Main Committee of UNCED on 10 June 1992. See A/CONF.151/L.3/Add.18 (11 June 1992). The former draft read as follows:

The dissemintation of information, including operational guidelines, and the promotion of education for water users.

Means of implementation

(a) Financing and cost evaluation

18.13. The Conference secretariat has estimated the average total annual cost (1993-2000) of implementing the activities of this programme to be about $115 million from the international community on grant or concessional terms. These are indicative and order-of-magnitude estimates only and have not been reviewed by Governments. Actual costs and financial terms, including any that are non-concessional, will depend upon, *inter alia*, the specific strategies and programmes Governments decide upon for implementation.[2]

(b) Scientific and technological means

18.14. The development of interactive databases, forecasting methods and economic planning models appropriate to the task of managing water resources in an efficient and sustainable manner will require the application of new techniques such as geographical information systems and expert systems to gather, assimilate, analyse and display multisectoral information and to optimize decision-making. In addition, the development of new and alternative sources of water-supply and low-cost water technologies will require innovative applied research. This will involve the transfer, adaption and diffusion of new techniques and technology among developing countries, as well as the development of endogenous capacity, for the purpose of being able to deal with the added dimension of integrating engineering, economic, environmental and social aspects of water resources management and predicting the effects of human impact.

18.15. Pursuant to the recognition of water as a social and an economic good, the various available options for charging water users (including domestic, urban, industrial and agricultural water-user groups) have to be further evaluated and field-tested. Further development is required on economic instruments that take into account opportunity costs and environmental externalities. Field studies on the willingness to pay should be conducted in rural and urban situations.

18.16. Water resources development and management should be planned in an integrated manner, taking into account long-term planning needs as well as those with narrower horizons, that is to say, they should incorporate environmental, economic and social considerations based on the principle of sustainability; include the requirements of all users as well as those relating to the

---

2   Draft paragraph 18.23 of A/CONF.151/4 (22 April 1992) was replaced by decision of the Main Committee of UNCED on 10 June 1992. See A/CONF.151/L.3/Add.18 (11 June 1992). The former draft read as follows:

   During the period 1993 to 2000, an annual amount of about $ 100 million of international financing is required to support national development in this programme area. The strengthening of international institutions in support of the planning and initiation phases at the country level requires the allocation of about $ 10 million per year. The transboundary and global freshwater issues require financial support in the order of $ 5 million annually for the executing of national, regional and global authorities and organizations. The total annual financing requirements in this programme area amount to $ 115 million.

prevention and mitigation of water-related hazards; and constitute an integral part of the socio-economic development planning process. A prerequisite for the sustainable management of water as a scarce vulnerable resource is that its full costs should be acknowledged in all planning and development. Planning considerations should reflect benefits investment, environmental protection and operation costs, as well as the opportunity costs reflecting the most valuable alternative use of water. Actual charging need not necessarily burden all beneficiaries with these considerations. Charging mechanisms should, however, reflect as far as possible both the true cost of water when used as an economic good and the ability of the communities to pay.

18.17. The role of water as a social, economic and life-sustaining good should be reflected in demand management mechanisms and implemented through water conservation and re-use, resource assessment, and financial instruments.

18.18. The setting of afresh priorities for private and public investment strategies should take place taking into account (a) maximum utilization of existing projects, through maintenance, rehabilitation and optimal operation; (b) new or alternative clean technologies; and (c) environmentally and socially benign hydro-power.

(c) Human resources development

18.19. The delegation of water resources management to the lowest appropriate level necessitates the education and training of water management staff at all levels, and ensuring that women participate equally in these education and training programmes. Particular emphasis has to be placed on the introduction of public participatory techniques, including enhancement of the role of women, youth, indigenous people, local communities. Skills related to various water management functions have to be developed by municipal government and water authorities and also in the private sector, local/national non-governmental organizations, cooperatives, corporations and other water user groups. Education of the public in the importance of water and its proper management is also needed.[3]

18.20. To implement these principles, communities need to have adequate capacities. Those who establish the framework for water development and management at any level, whether international, national or local, need to ensure

---

3   The second sentence of draft paragraph 18.29 of A/CONF.151/4 (22 April 1992) was replaced by decision of the Main Committee of UNCED on 10 June 1992. See A/CONF.151/L.3/Add.186 (11 June 1992). The former draft read as follows:

   Particular emphasis has to be placed on the introduction of public participatory techniques, including enhancement of the role of women, youth, indigenous people, local communities and people under occupation.

that the means exist to build those capacities. The means will vary from case to case. They usually include:

(a) Awareness-creation programmes, including mobilizing commitment and support at all levels and initiating global and local action to promote such programmes;

(b) The training of water managers at all levels so that they have an appropriate understanding of all the elements necessary for their decisions;

(c) The strengthening of training capacities in developing countries;

(d) Appropriate training of the necessary professionals, including extension workers;

(e) Improvement of career structures;

(f) Sharing of appropriate knowledge and technology, both for the collection of data and for the implementation of planned development; this should include non-polluting technologies and the knowledge needed to extract the best performance from the existing investment system.

(d) Capacity-building

18.21. Institutional capacity for implementing integrated water management should be reviewed and developed when there is a clear demand. Existing administrative structures will often be quite capable of achieving local water resources management, but the need may arise for new institutions based upon, e.g., river catchment areas, district development councils or local community committees. Although water is managed at various levels in the socio-political system, demand-driven management requires the development of water-related institutions at appropriate levels, taking into account the need for integration with land use management.

18.22. In creating the enabling environment for lowest appropriate-level management, the role of Government includes mobilization of financial and human resources, legislation, standard-setting and other regulatory functions, monitoring and assessment of the use of water and land resources, and creating opportunities for public participation. International agencies and donors have an important role to play to support developing countries in creating the required enabling environment for integrated water resources management. This should include, as appropriate, donor support to local levels in developing countries, including community-based institutions, non-governmental organizations and women's groups.

B. Water resources assessment

Basis for action

18.23. Water resources assessment, including the identification of potential sources of freshwater supply, is the continuing determination of sources, extent, dependability and quality of water resources and of the human activities which affect these resources. It is the practical basis for their sustainable management and a prerequisite for evaluation of the possibilities for this development. There is, however, growing concern that at a time when more precise and reliable information is needed about water resources, hydrological services and related bodies are less able to provide this information, especially information on groundwater and water quality. Major impediments are the lack of financial resources for water resources assessment, the fragmented nature of hydrological services and the insufficient numbers of qualified staff. At the same time, the advancing technology for data capture and management is increasingly difficult to access for developing countries. Establishment of national databases is, however, vital to water resources assessment and for mitigating the effects of floods, droughts, desertification and pollution.

Objectives

18.24. Based upon the Mar del Plata Action Plan, this programme area is extended into the 1990s and beyond with the overall objective of ensuring the assessment and forecasting of the quantity and quality of water resources, in order to estimate the total quantity of water resources available and their future supply potential, to reflect their current quality status, to predict possible conflicts between supply and demand and to provide a scientific database for rational water resource utilization.

18.25. Five specific objectives are set, accordingly, as follows:

(a) To make available to all countries water resource assessment technology that is appropriate to their needs, irrespective of their level of development, including methods for the impact assessment of climate change on freshwaters;

(b) To have all countries, according to their financial means, allocate to water resource assessment financial resources in line with the economic and social needs for water resources data;

(c) To ensure that the assessment information is fully utilized in the development of water management policies;

(d) To have all countries establish the institutional arrangements needed to ensure the efficient collection, processing, storage, retrieval and dissemination to users of information about the quality and quantity of available water resources at the level of catchments and groundwater aquifers in an integrated manner;

(e) To have sufficient numbers of appropriately qualified and capable staff recruited and retained by water resource assessment agencies, and provided with the training and retraining they need to carry out their responsibilities successfully.

18.26. All States, according to their capacity and available resources, and through bilateral or multilateral cooperation, including through the United Nations and other relevant organizations, as appropriate, could set the following targets:

(a) By the year 2000, to have studied in detail the feasibility of installing water resources assessment services;

(b) As a long-term target, to have fully operational services available based upon high-density hydrometric networks.

Activities

18.27. All States, according to their capacity and available resources, and through bilateral or multilateral cooperation, including through the United Nations and other relevant organizations, as appropriate, could undertake the following activities:

(a) Institutional framework:

(i) Establish appropriate policy frameworks and national priorities;

(ii) Establish and strengthen the institutional capabilities of countries, including legislative and regulatory arrangements, that are required to ensure the adequate assessment of their water resources and the provision of flood and drought forecasting services;

(iii) Establish and maintain effective cooperation at the national level between the various agencies responsible for the collection, storage and analysis of hydrological data;

(iv) Cooperate in the assessment of transboundary water resources, subject to the prior agreement of each riparian State concerned;

(b) Data systems:

(i) Review existing data collection networks and assess their adequacy, including those that provide real time data for flood and drought forecasting;

(ii) Improve networks to meet accepted guidelines for the provision of data on water quantity and quality for surface and groundwater, as well as relevant land use data;

(iii) Apply standards and other means to ensure data compatibility;

(iv) Upgrade facilities and procedures used to store, process and analyse hydrological data and make such data and the forecasts derived from them available to potential users;

(v) Establish databases on the availability of all types of hydrological data at the national level;

(vi) Implement "data rescue" operations, e.g., establishment of national archives of water resources;

(vii) Implement appropriate well-tried techniques for the processing of hydrological data;

(viii) Derive area-related estimates from point hydrological data;

(ix) Assimilate remotely sensed data and the use, where appropriate, of geographical information systems;

(c) Data dissemination:

(i) Identify the need for water resources data for various planning purposes;

(ii) Analyse and present data and information on water resources in the forms required for planning and management of countries' socio-economic development, for use in environmental protection strategies and in the design and operation of specific water-related projects;

(iii) Provide forecasts and warnings of flood and drought to the general public and civil defense;

(d) Research and development:

(i) Establish or strengthen research and development programmes at the national, subregional, regional and international levels in support of water resources assessment activities;

(ii) Monitor research and development activities to ensure that they make full use of local expertise and other local resources and that they are appropriate for the needs of the country or countries concerned.

Means of implementation

(a) Financing and cost evaluation

18.28. The Conference secretariat has estimated the average total annual cost (1993-2000) of implementing the activities of this programme to be about $355 million, including about $145 million from the international community on grant or concessional terms. These are indicative and order of magnitude estimates only and have not been reviewed by Governments. Actual costs and financial terms, including any that are non-concessional, will depend upon, *inter alia*, the specific strategies and programmes Governments decide upon for implementation.[4]

---

4   Draft paragraph 18.38 of A/CONF.151/4 (22 April 1992) was replaced by decision of the Main
     Committee of UNCED on 10 June 1992. See A/CONF.151/L.3/Add.18 (11 June 1992). The for-
     mer draft read as follows:

     In order to attain the programme area targets as stated above by the year 2000, total average annual
     funding in the order of $ 350 million is required, including contributions from external sources of
     $ 140 million annually. The strengthening of international institutions for the development and ex-
     change of information and technology requires about $ 5 million per year. The total international fi-
     nancing needs for the years 1993 to 2000 for this programme area amount to $ 145 million annually.

(b) Scientific and technological means

18.29. Important research needs include (a) development of global hydrologic models in support of analysis of climate change impact and of macroscale water resources assessment; (b) closing the gap between terrestrial hydrology and ecology at different scales, including the critical water-related processes behind loss of vegetation, land degradation and its restoration; and (c) study of the key processes in water quality genesis, closing the gap between hydrological flows and biogeochemical processes. The research models should build upon hydrological balance studies and also include the consumptive use of water. This approach should also, when appropriate, be applied at the catchment level.

18.30. Water resources assessment necessitates the strengthening of existing systems for technology transfer, adaptation and diffusion, and the development of new technology for use under field conditions, as well as the development of endogenous capacity. Prior to the above activities, it is necessary to prepare catalogues of the water resources information held by government services, private sector, educational institutes, consultants, local water-use organizations and others.

(c) Human resource development

18.31. Water resources assessment requires the establishment and maintenance of a body of well-trained and motivated staff sufficient to undertake the above activities. Education and training programmes should be established or strengthened at the local, national, subregional or regional levels designed to ensure an adequate supply of these trained personnel. In addition, the provision of attractive terms of employment and career paths for professional and technical staff should be encouraged. Human resource needs should be monitored periodically, including all levels of employment. Plans have to be established to meet those needs through education and training opportunities, and international programmes of courses and conferences.

18.32. Because well-trained people are particularly important to water resources assessment and hydrological forecasting, personnel matters should receive special attention in this area. The aim should be to attract and retain personnel to work on water resources assessment who are sufficient in number and adequate in their level of education to ensure the effective implementation of the activities that are planned. Education may be called for at both the national and the international level, while adequate terms of employment are a national responsibility.

18.33. Recommended actions include:

(a) Identifying education and training needs geared to the specific requirements of countries;

(b) Establishing and strengthening education and training programmes on water-related topics, within an environmental and developmental context, for all categories of staff involved in water resources assessment activities, using advanced educational technology, where appropriate, and involving both men and women;

(c) Developing sound recruitment, personnel and pay policies for staff of national and local water agencies.

(d) Capacity-building

18.34. The conduct of water resources assessment on the basis of operational national hydrometric networks requires an enabling environment at all levels. The following national support action is necessary for enhanced national capacities:

(a) Review of the legislative and regulatory basis of water resources assessment;

(b) Facilitation of close collaboration between water sector agencies, particularly between information producers and users;

(c) Implementation of water management policies based upon realistic appraisals of water resource conditions and trends;

(d) Strengthening of the managerial capabilities of water users groups, including women, youth, indigenous people and local communities, to improve water use efficiency at the local level.

C. Protection of water resources, water quality and aquatic ecosystems

Basis for action

18.35. Freshwater is a unitary resource. Long-term development of global freshwater requires holistic management of the resources and a recognition of the interconnectedness of the elements that comprise freshwater and its quality. There are few regions of the world that are still exempt from problems of loss of potential sources of freshwater supply and of degraded water quality and the pollution of surface and groundwater sources. Major problems affecting the water quality of rivers and lakes arise, in variable order of importance according to different situations, from inadequately treated domestic sewage, inadequate controls on the discharges of industrial waste waters, the loss and destruction of catchment areas, siting of industrial plants, deforestation, uncontrolled shifting cultivation and poor agricultural practices, giving rise to the leaching of nutrients and pesticides. Aquatic ecosystems are disturbed and the living freshwater resources are threatened. Under certain circumstances, aquatic ecosystems are also affected by agricultural water resource development projects such as dams, river diversions, water installations and irrigation schemes. Erosion, sedimentation, deforestation and desertification have led to increased land degradation, and the creation of reservoirs has, in some cases, resulted in adverse effects on ecosystems. Many of these problems have arisen from a development model that is environmentally destructive and from a lack of public awareness and education about surface and groundwater resource protection. Ecological and human health effects are the measurable consequences, although the means to monitor them are inadequate or non-existent in many countries. There is a widespread lack of perception of the linkages between the development, management, use and treatment of water resources and aquatic ecosystems. A preventive approach, where appropriate, is crucial to avoid costly subsequent measures to rehabilitate, treat and develop new water supplies.

Objectives

18.36. The complex interconnected nature of freshwater systems demands that freshwater management be holistic, taking a catchment management approach, and be based on a balanced consideration of the needs of people and the environment. The Mar del Plata Action Plan has already recognized the intrinsic linkage between water resource development projects and their important repercussions of a physical, chemical, biological, health and socio-economic nature. The overall environmental health objective was set:

> "to evaluate the consequences which the various users of water have on the environment, to support measures aimed at controlling water-related diseases, and to protect ecosystems".

18.37. The extent and severity of contamination of unsaturated zones and aquifers have long been underestimated owing to the relative inaccessibility of aquifers and the lack of reliable information on aquifer systems. The protection of groundwater is therefore an essential element of water resource management.

18.38. Three objectives will have to be pursued concurrently to integrate water quality aspects into water resource management:

(a) Maintenance of ecosystem integrity, a management principle to preserve aquatic ecosystems, including the living resources, and to protect them effectively from any form of degradation on a drainage basin basis;

(b) Public health protection, a task requiring not only the provision of safe drinking water but also the control of disease vectors in the aquatic environment;

(c) Human resources development, a key to capacity-building and a prerequisite for implementing water quality management.

18.39. All States, according to their capacity and available resources, through bilateral or multilateral cooperation, including through the United Nations and other relevant organizations, as appropriate, could set the following targets:

(a) To identify those surface and groundwater resources that could be developed for use on a sustainable basis and other major water dependent resources that can be developed and, simultaneously, have initiated programmes for the protection, conservation and rational use of these resources on a sustainable basis;

(b) To identify all potential sources of water supply and prepared outlines for their protection, conservation and rational use;

(c) To initiate effective water pollution prevention and control programmes, based on an appropriate mixture of pollution reduction-at-source strategies, environmental impact assessments, enforceable standards for major point-source discharges and high-risk non-point sources, commensurate with their socio-economic development;

(d) To participate, as far as appropriate, in international water quality monitoring and management programmes such as the Global Water Quality Monitoring Programme GEMS/WATER, the UNEP Environmentally Sound Management of Inland Waters, the FAO regional inland fishery bodies, and the RAMSAR Convention on Wetlands of International Importance Especially As Waterfowl Habitat;

(e) To reduce the prevalence of water-associated diseases, starting with the eradication of dracunculiasis (Guinea worm) and onchocerciasis (river blindness) by the year 2000;

(f) To establish, according to capacities and needs, biological, health, physical and chemical quality criteria for all water bodies (surface and groundwater), with a view to an ongoing improvement of water quality;

(g) To adopt an integrated approach to environmentally sustainable management of water resources, including the protection of aquatic ecosystems and freshwater living resources;

(h) To put in place strategies for the environmentally sound management of freshwaters and related coastal ecosystems, including the consideration of fisheries, aquaculture, animal grazing, agricultural activities and biodiversity.

Activities

18.40. All States, according to their capacity and available resources, and through bilateral or multilateral cooperation, including through United Nations and other relevant organizations, as appropriate, could implement the following activities:

(a) Water resources protection and conservation:

(i) Establishment and strengthening of technical and institutional capacities to identify and protect potential sources of water supply within all sectors of society;

(ii) Identification of potential sources of water supply and preparation of national profiles;

(iii) Preparation of national plans for water resources protection and conservation;

(iv) Rehabilitation of important but degraded catchment areas, particularly on small islands;

(v) Strengthening of administrative and legislative measures to prevent encroachment into existing and potentially usable catchment areas;

(b) Water pollution prevention and control:

(i) Application of the polluter pays principle, where appropriate, to all kinds of sources, including on-site and off-site sanitation;

(ii) Promotion of the construction of treatment facilities for domestic sewage, industrial effluents, and the development of appropriate technologies, taking into account sound traditional and indigenous practices;

(iii) Establishment of standards for the discharge of effluents and for the receiving waters;

(iv) Introduction of the precautionary approach in water quality management, where appropriate, with a focus on pollution minimization and prevention through use of new technologies, product and process change, pollution reduction at source, effluent reuse, recycling and recovery, treatment and environmentally safe disposal;

(v) Mandatory environmental impact assessment on all major water resource development projects potentially impairing water quality and aquatic ecosystems, combined with the delineation of appropriate remedial measures and a strengthened control of new industrial installations, solid waste landfills and infrastructure development projects;

(vi) Use of risk assessment and risk management in reaching decisions in this area and ensuring compliance with those decisions;

(vii) Identification and application of best environmental practices at reasonable cost to avoid diffuse pollution, i.e., through a limited, rational and planned use of nitrogenous fertilizers and other agrochemicals (pesticides, herbicides) in agricultural practices;

(viii) Encouragement and promotion of the use of adequately treated and purified waste waters in agriculture, aquaculture, industry and other sectors;

(c) Development and application of clean technology:

(i) Control of industrial waste discharges, including low-waste production technologies and water recirculation, in an integrated way and by applying precautionary measures derived from a broad-based life-cycle analysis;

(ii) Treatment of municipal waste water for safe reuse in agriculture and aquaculture;

(iii) Development of biotechnology, including for waste treatment, production of biofertilizers and other activities;

(iv) Development of appropriate methods for water pollution control, taking into account sound traditional and indigenous practices;

(d) Groundwater protection:

(i) Developing agricultural practices that do not degrade groundwaters;

(ii) Application of the necessary measures to mitigate saline intrusion into aquifers of small islands and coastal plains as a consequence of sealevel rise or of overexploitation of coastal aquifers;

(iii) Prevention of aquifer pollution through the regulation of toxic substances that permeate the ground and the establishment of protection zones in groundwater recharge and abstraction areas;

(iv) Design and management of landfills based upon sound hydrogeological information and impact assessment, using best practicable and best available technology;

(v) Promotion of measures to improve the safety and integrity of wells and wellhead areas to reduce intrusion of biological pathogens and hazardous chemicals into aquifers at well sites;

(vi) Water quality monitoring, as needed, of surface and groundwaters potentially affected by sites storing toxic and hazardous materials;

(e) Protection of aquatic ecosystems:

(i) Rehabilitation of polluted and degraded water bodies to restore aquatic habitats and ecosystems;

(ii) Rehabilitation programmes for agricultural lands and for other users, taking into account equivalent action for the protection and use of groundwater resources, important for agricultural productivity and for the biodiversity of the tropics;

(iii) Conservation and protection of wetlands owing to their ecological and habitat importance for many species, and taking into account social and economic factors;

(iv) Control of noxious aquatic species that may destroy some other water species;

(f) Protection of freshwater living resources:

(i) Control and monitoring of water quality to allow for the sustainable development of inland fisheries;

(ii) Protection of ecosystems from pollution and degradation for the development of freshwater aquaculture projects;

(g) Monitoring and surveillance of water resources and waters receiving wastes:

(i) Establishment of networks for the monitoring and continuous surveillance of waters receiving wastes and of point and diffuse sources of pollution;

(ii) Promotion and extension of the application of geographical information systems environmental impact assessments;

(iii) Surveillance of pollution sources to improve the compliance with standards and regulations and to regulate the issue of discharge permits;

(iv) Monitoring of the utilization of chemicals in agriculture that may have an adverse environmental effect;

(v) Rational land use to prevent land degradation, erosion and siltation of lakes and other water bodies;

(h) Development of national and international legal instruments for water quality protection that may be required to protect the quality of water resources, as appropriate, particularly for:

(i) Monitoring and control of pollution and its effects in national and transboundary waters;

(ii) Control of long-range atmospheric transport of pollutants;

(iii) Control of accidental and/or deliberate spills in national and/or transboundary water bodies;

(iv) Environmental impact assessment.

Means of implementation

(a) Financing and cost evaluation

18.41. The Conference secretariat has estimated the average total annual cost (1993-2000) of implementing the activities of this programme to be about $1 billion, including about $340 million from the international community on grant or concessional terms. These are indicative and order of magnitude estimates only and have not been reviewed by Governments. Actual costs and financial terms, including any that are non-concessional, will depend upon, *inter alia,* the specific strategies and programmes Governments decide upon for implementation.[5]

---

5   Draft paragraph 6.6 of A/CONF.151/4 (22 April 1992) was replaced by decision of the Main Committee of UNCED on 10 June 1992. See A/CONF.151/L.3/Add.6 (12 June 1992). The former draft read as follows:

Funds for pollution control have to be generated ultimately within each river basin and/or country through cost recovery and economic or fiscal instruments. The "polluter pays principle" has to be adopted in conformity with the notion of water as a social and an economic good. Total costs, including those financed nationally, are estimated at about $ 1.0 billion annually for the period 1993 to 2000. Of this amount, about $ 330 million would be needed annually from international sources.

Former paragraph 18.52, that appealed as an additional paragraph at this point, read as follows:

18.42. The assessment of global environmental issues also includes water quality and aquatic ecosystems monitoring and assessment. River monitoring for global flux estimates is covered under programme area B already, and the necessary funds indicated there. About $ 10 million annually would be needed in addition to this to strengthen international institutions. The total financing requirement for this programme area amounts to $ 340 million annually.

(b) Scientific and technological means

18.42. States should undertake cooperative research projects to develop solutions to technical problems that are appropriate for the conditions in each watershed or country. States should consider strengthening and developing national research centres linked through networks, supported by regional water research institutes. The North-South twinning of research centres and field studies by international water research institutions should be actively promoted. It is important that a minimum percentage of funds for water resource development projects is allocated to research and development, particularly in externally funded projects.

18.43. Monitoring and assessment of complex aquatic systems often require multidisciplinary studies involving several institutions and scientists in a joint programme. International water quality programmes, such as GEMS/WATER, should be oriented towards the water quality of developing countries. User-friendly software, GIS and GRID methods should be developed for the handling, analysis and interpretation of monitoring data and for the preparation of management strategies.

(c) Human resource development

18.44. Innovative approaches should be adopted for professional and managerial staff training in order to cope with changing needs and challenges. Flexibility and adaptability to emerging water pollution issues should be developed. Training activities should be undertaken periodically at all levels within the organizations responsible for water quality management, and innovative teaching techniques adopted for specific aspects of water quality monitoring and control, including development of training skills, in-service training, problem-solving workshops and refresher training courses.

18.45. Suitable approaches include strengthening and improving the human resource capabilities of local governments in managing water protection, treatment and use, particularly in urban areas, and the establishment of national and regional technical and engineering courses on water quality protection and control subjects at existing schools, and education/training courses for laboratory and field technicians, women and other water user groups for water resources protection and conservation.

(d) Capacity-building

18.46. The effective protection of water resources and ecosystems from pollution requires considerable upgrading of most countries' present capacities. Water quality management programmes require a certain minimum infrastructure and staff to identify and implement technical solutions and to enforce regulatory action. One of the key problems today and for the future is the sustained operation and maintenance of these facilities. In order not to allow resources gained from previous investments to deteriorate further, immediate action is required in a number of areas.

D. Drinking water supply and sanitation

Basis for action

18.47. Safe water supplies and environmental sanitation are vital for protecting the environment, improving health and alleviating poverty. Safe water is also crucial to many traditional and cultural activities. An estimated 80 per cent of all diseases and over one third of deaths in developing countries are caused by the consumption of contaminated water, and on average as much as one tenth of each person's productive time is sacrificed to water-related diseases. Concerted efforts during the 1980s brought water and sanitation services to hundreds of millions of the world's poorest people. The most outstanding of these efforts is the launching in 1981 of the United Nations International Drinking Water Supply and Sanitation Decade, which resulted from the Mar del Plata Action Plan adopted by the United Nations Water Conference in 1977. The commonly agreed premise was that "all peoples, whatever their stage of development and their social and economic conditions, have the right to have access to drinking water in quantities and of a quality equal to their basic needs". The target of the Decade was to provide safe drinking water and sanitation to underserved urban and rural areas by 1990. But even the unprecedented progress achieved during the Decade was not enough. One in three people in the developing world still lacks these two most basic requirements for health and dignity. It is also recognized that human excreta and sewage are important causes of the deterioration of water quality in developing countries, and the introduction of available technologies, including appropriate technologies, and the construction of sewage treatment facilities could bring significant improvement.

Objectives

18.48. The New Delhi Statement formalized the need to provide, on a sustainable basis, access to safe water in sufficient quantities and proper sanitation for all, emphasizing the "some for all rather than more for some" approach. Four guiding principles provide for the programme objectives:

(a) Protection of the environment and safeguarding of health through the integrated management of water resources and liquid and solid wastes;

(b) Institutional reforms promoting an integrated approach and including changes in procedures, attitudes and behaviour, and the full participation of women at all levels in sector institutions;

(c) Community management of services, backed by measures to strengthen local institutions in implementing and sustaining water and sanitation programmes;

(d) Sound financial practices, achieved through better management of existing assets, and widespread use of appropriate technologies.

18.49. Past experience has shown that specific targets should be set by each individual country. At the World Summit for Children, in September 1990, heads of State or Government called for both universal access to water supply and sanitation and the eradication of guinea worm disease by 1995. Even for the more realistic target of achieving full coverage in water supply by 2025, it is estimated that annual investments must reach double the current levels. One realistic strategy to meet present and future needs, therefore, is to develop lower cost but adequate services that can be implemented and sustained at the community level.

Activities

18.50. All States, according to their capacity and available resources, and through bilateral or multilateral cooperation, including through the United Nations and other relevant organizations, as appropriate, could implement the following activities:

(a) Environment and health:

(i) Establishment of protected areas for sources of drinking water supply;

(ii) Sanitary disposal of excreta and sewage, using appropriate systems to treat waste waters in urban and rural areas;

(iii) Expansion of urban and rural water supply and, in addition to the reticulated water supply system, develop and expand rainwater catchment systems, particularly on small islands;

(iv) Building and expansion, where appropriate, of sewage treatment facilities and drainage systems;

(v) Treatment and safe reuse of domestic and industrial waste waters in urban and rural areas;

(vi) Control of water-associated diseases;

(b) People and institutions:

(i) Strengthening the functioning of Governments in water resources management and, at the same time, giving full recognition to the role of local authorities;

(ii) Encouraging water development and management based on a participatory approach, involving users, planners and policy makers at all levels;

(iii) Applying the principle that decisions are taken at the lowest appropriate level, with public consultation and involvement of users in the planning and implementation of water projects;

(iv) Human resource development at all levels, including special programmes for women;

(v) Broad-based education programmes, with particular emphasis on hygiene, local management and risk reduction;

(vi) International support mechanisms for programme funding, implementation, and follow-up;[6]

(c) National and community management:

(i) Support and assist communities in managing their own systems on a sustainable basis;

(ii) Encouragement of the local population, especially women, youth, indigenous people and local communities in water management;

(iii) Linkages between national water plans and community management of local waters;

(iv) Integration of community management of water in the context of overall planning;

(v) Promotion of primary health and environmental care at the local level, including training for local communities in appropriate water management techniques and primary health care;

(vi) Assisting service agencies to be more cost-effective and responsive to consumer needs;

(vii) More attention to be given to underserved rural and low-income peri-urban areas;

(viii) Rehabilitation of defective systems, reduction of wastage and safe reuse of water and waste water;[7]

(ix) Programmes for rational water use and ensured operation and maintenance;

(x) Research and development of appropriate technical solutions;

(xi) Substantially increase urban treatment capacity commensurate with increasing loads;[8]

---

6   Draft paragraph 18.61(b)(vi) of A/CONF.151/4 (22 April 1992) included brackets around the entire text of paragraph 18.61(b)(vi). The brackets were deleted by decision of the Main Committee of UNCED on 10 June 1992. See A/CONF./151/L.3/Add.18 (11 June 1992).

7   Draft paragraph 18.61(c)(viii) of A/CONF.151/4 (22 April 1992) was revised by decision of the Main Committee of UNCED on 10 June 1992. See A/CONF.151/L.3/Add.18 (11 June 1992). The former draft read as follows:

Rehabilitation of defective systems, reduction of wastage and safe reuse of water and waste water [through additional international financing];

8   Draft paragraph 18.61(c)xi) of A/CONF.151/4 (22 April 1992) was replaced by decision of the Main Committee of UNCED on 10 June 1992. See A/CONF.151/L.3/Add.18 (11 June 1992). The former draft read as follows:

[International efforts of solidarity by the developed countries with the developing countries in granting new and additional financial resources in accordance with General Assembly resolution 44/228 in order to install treatment plants for urban waste waters];

(d) Awareness creation and public information/participation:

(i) Strengthening of sector monitoring and information management at subnational and national levels;

(ii) Annual processing, analysis and publishing of monitoring results at national and local levels as a sector management and advocacy/awareness creation tool;

(iii) Use of limited sector indicators at regional and global levels to promote the sector and raise funds;

(iv) Improve sector coordination, planning and implementation, with assistance of improved monitoring and information management, to increase the sector's absorptive capacity, particularly in community-based self-help projects.

Means of implementation

(a) Financing and cost evaluation

18.51. The Conference secretariat has estimated the average total annual cost (1993-2000) of implementing the activities of this programme to be about $20 billion, including about $7.4 billion from the international community on grant or concessional terms. These are indicative and order of magnitude estimates only and have not been reviewed by Governments. Actual costs and financial terms, including any that are non-concessional, will depend upon, *inter alia*, the specific strategies and programmes Governments decide upon for implementation.[9]

(b) Scientific and technological means

18.52. To ensure the feasibility, acceptability and sustainability of planned water supply services, adopted technologies should be responsive to the needs and constraints imposed by the conditions of the community concerned. Thus, design criteria involve technical, health, social, economic, provincial, institutional and environmental aspects that determine the characteristics, magnitude and cost of the planned system. Relevant international support programmes should address the developing countries concerning, *inter alia*:

(a) Pursuit of low-cost scientific and technological means, as far as practicable;

---

9   Draft paragraph 18.62 of A/CONF.151/4 (22 April 1992) was replaced by decision of the Main Committee of UNCED on 10 June 1992. See A/CONF.151/L.3/Add.18 (11 June 1992). The former draft read as follows:

Accelerated development is necessary to reach the desired coverage of water supply and basic sanitation services by the year 2000. The rate of investment for the years until 2000 has, at least, to be doubled to a total of $ 20 billion annually to achieve complete service coverage. The external component should be maintained at no less than one third of this, i.e. at about $ 6.7 billion annually. The improved operation, maintenance and management of systems and the full utilization of the investments made requires the allocation of external support in the order of $ 0.7 billion. The total external funding needs until the year 2000 are, therefore, $ 7.4 billion annually.

(b) Utilization of traditional and indigenous practices, as far as practicable, to maximize and sustain local involvement;

(c) Assistance to country-level technical/scientific institutes to facilitate curricula development to support fields critical to the water and sanitation sector.

(c) Human resource development

18.53. To effectively plan and manage water supply and sanitation at the national, provincial, district and community level, and to utilize funds most effectively, trained professional and technical staff must be developed within each country in sufficient numbers. To do this, countries must establish manpower development plans, taking into consideration present requirements and planned developments. Subsequently, the development and performance of country-level training institutions should be enhanced so that they can play a pivotal role in capacity-building. It is also important that countries provide adequate training for women in the sustainable maintenance of equipment, water resource management and environmental sanitation.

(d) Capacity-building

18.54. The implementation of water supply and sanitation programmes is a national responsibility. To varying degrees, responsibility for the implementation of projects and the operating of systems should be delegated to all administrative levels right down to the community and individual served. This also means that national authorities, together with the agencies and bodies of the United Nations system and other external support agencies in providing support to national programmes, should develop mechanisms and procedures to collaborate at all levels. This is particularly important if full advantage is to be taken of community-based approaches and self-reliance as tools to sustainability. This entails a high degree of community participation, involving women, in the conception, planning, decision-making, implementation and evaluation of projects for domestic water supply and sanitation.

18.55. Overall national capacity-building at all administrative levels, including institutional development, coordination, human resources, community participation, health and hygiene education, literacy etc., have to be developed as fundamental to any efforts to improve health and socio-economic development through water supply and sanitation and their impact on the human environment. Capacity-building should therefore be one of the underlying keys in implementation strategies. Institutional capacity-building should be considered as equally important as sector supplies and equipment, so that funds can be directed to both aspects. This can be undertaken at the planning or programme/project formulation stage with clear definition of objectives and targets in this regard. In this respect, technical cooperation among developing countries is crucial, owing to available wealth of information and experience, and to avoid reinventing the wheel. This has proved cost-effective in many country projects already.

E. Water and sustainable urban development

Basis for action

18.56. Early in the next century, more than half of the world's population will be living in urban areas. By 2025, that proportion will have risen to 60 per cent, some 5 billion people. Rapid urban population growth and industrialization are putting severe strains on the water resources and environmental protection capabilities of many cities. Special attention needs to be given to the growing effects of urbanization on water demands and usage, and on the critical role played by local and municipal authorities in managing the supply, use and overall treatment of water, particularly in developing countries for which special support is needed. Scarcity of freshwater resources and the escalating costs of developing new resources have a considerable impact on national industrial, agricultural and human settlement development and economic growth. Better management of urban water resources, including the elimination of unsustainable consumption patterns, can make a substantial contribution to the alleviation of poverty and improvement of the health and quality of life of the urban and rural poor. A high proportion of large urban agglomerations are located around estuaries and in coastal zones, leading to pollution from municipal and industrial discharges combined with overexploitation of available water resources and threatening the marine environment and the supply of freshwater resources.

Objectives

18.57. The development objective of this programme is to support local and central governments' efforts and capacities to sustain national development and productivity through environmentally sound management of water resources for urban use. Supporting this objective is the identification and implementation of strategies and actions to ensure the continued supply of affordable water for present and future needs, and to reverse current trends of resource degradation and depletion.

18.58. All States, according to their capacity and available resources, and through bilateral or multilateral cooperation, including through the United Nations and other relevant organizations, as appropriate, could set the following targets:

(a) By the year 2000, ensure that all urban residents have access to at least 40 litres per capita per day of safe water and that 75 per cent of the urban population are provided with on-site or community facilities for sanitation;

(b) By the year 2000, have established and applied quantitative and qualitative discharge standards for municipal and industrial effluents;

(c) By the year 2000, have 75 per cent of solid waste generated in urban areas collected and recycled or disposed of in an environmentally safe way.

Activities

18.59. All States, according to their capacity and available resources, and through bilateral or multilateral cooperation, including through the United Nations and other relevant organizations, as appropriate, could implement the following activities:

(a) Protection of water resources from depletion, pollution and degradation:

(i) Introduction of sanitary waste disposal facilities based on environmentally sound low-cost and upgradable technologies;

(ii) Implementation of urban storm water runoff and drainage programmes;

(iii) Promotion of recycling and reuse of waste water and solid wastes;

(iv) Control of industrial pollution sources to protect water resources;

(v) Protection of watersheds from depletion and degradation of their forest cover and from harmful upstream activities;

(vi) Promotion of research into the contribution of forests to sustainable water resources development;

(vii) Encouragement of best management practices for the use of agrochemicals with a view to minimizing their impact on water resources;

(b) Efficient and equitable allocation of water resources:

(i) Reconciliation of city development planning with the availability and sustainability of water resources;

(ii) Satisfaction of the basic water needs of the urban population;

(iii) Introduction of water tariffs, by taking into account the circumstances in each country and where affordable, which reflect the marginal and opportunity cost of water, especially for productive activities;

(c) Institutional/legal/management reforms:

(i) Adoption of a city-wide approach to the management of water resources;

(ii) Promotion at the national and local level of the elaboration of land use plans that give due consideration to water resources development;

(iii) Utilization of the skills and potential of non-governmental organizations and the private sector and local people, taking into account the public and strategic interests in water resources;

(d) Promotion of public participation:

(i) Initiation of public awareness campaigns to encourage the public towards rational water utilization;

(ii) Sensitization of the public for the protection of water quality within the urban environment;

(iii) Promotion of public participation for the collection, recycling and elimination of wastes;

(e) Support to local capacity-building:

(i) Development of legislation and policies to promote investments in urban water and waste management, reflecting the major contribution of cities to national economic development;

(ii) Provision of seed money and technical support to the local handling of materials supply and services;

(iii) Encouragement, to the extent possible, of autonomy and financial viability of city water, solid waste and sewerage utilities;

(iv) Creation and maintenance of a cadre of professionals and semi-professionals, for water, waste water and solid waste management;

(f) Provision of enhanced access to sanitary services:

(i) Implement water, sanitation and waste management programmes focused on the urban poor;

(ii) Make low-cost water supply and sanitation technology choices available;

(iii) Base choice of technology and service levels on user preferences and willingness to pay;

(iv) Mobilize and facilitate the active involvement of women in water management teams;

(v) Encourage and equip local water association and water committees to manage community water supply systems and communal latrines, with technical back-up available when required;

(vi) Consider the merits and practicality of rehabilitating existing malfunctioning systems and correcting operation and maintenance inadequacies.

Means of implementation

(a) Financing and cost evaluation

18.60. The Conference secretariat has estimated the average total annual cost (1993-2000) of implementing the activities of this programme to be about $20 billion, including about $4.5 from the international community on grant or concessional terms. These are indicative and order of magnitude estimates only and have not been reviewed by Governments. Actual costs and financial terms, including any that are non-concessional, will depend upon, *inter alia*, the specific strategies and programmes Governments decide upon for implementation.[10]

(b) Scientific and technological means

18.61. The 1980s saw considerable progress in the development and application of low-cost water supply and sanitation technologies. The programme envisages continuation of this work, with particular emphasis on development of appropriate sanitation and waste disposal technologies for low-income high-density urban settlements. There should also be international information exchange, to ensure a widespread recognition among sector professionals of the availability and benefits of appropriate low-cost technologies. The public awareness campaigns will also include components to overcome user resistance to "second class" services, emphasizing the benefits of reliability and sustainability.

(c) Human resource development

18.62. Implicit in virtually all the elements of this programme is the need for progressive enhancement of the training and career development of personnel at all levels in sector institutions. Specific programme activities will involve the training and retention of staff with skills in community involvement, low-cost technology, financial management, and integrated planning of urban water resources management. Special provision should be made for mobilizing and facilitating the active participation of women, youth, indigenous people and local communities in water management teams, and for supporting the development of water associations and water committees, with appropriate training of treasurers, secretaries, caretakers etc. Special education and training programmes for women should be launched with regard to the protection of water resources and water quality within urban areas.

(d) Capacity-building

18.63. In combination with human resource development, strengthening of institutional, legislative and management structures are key elements of the programme. A prerequisite for progress in enhancing access to water and sanitation services is the establishment of an institutional framework that ensures that the real needs and potential contributions of currently unserved populations are reflected in urban development planning. The multisectoral approach, which is a vital part of urban water resources management, requires institutional linkages at national and city levels, and the programme includes proposals for

---

10   Draft paragraph 18.71 of A/CONF.151/4 (22 April 1992) was replaced by decision of the Main Committee of UNCED on 10 June 1992. See A/CONF.151/L.3/Add.18 (11 June 1992). The former draft read as follows:

Total costs incurring for the installation of sewage collection and treatment facilities amount to about $ 9 billion annually, including about $ 1.8 billion in external financing. The needs for urban drainage programmes are also about $ 9 billion annually, including about $ 2.3 billion in international funding. Operation and maintenance and related capacity-building measures require about $ 1.8 billion annually, including about $ 0.4 billion in international financial support. The total external financing requirements amount to about $ 4.5 billion annually.

establishing intersectoral planning groups. Proposals for greater pollution control and prevention depend for their success on the right combination of economic and regulatory mechanisms, backed by adequate monitoring and surveillance and supported by enhanced capacity to address environmental issues on the part of local governments.

18.64. Establishment of appropriate design standards, water quality objectives and discharge consents is therefore among the proposed activities. The programme also includes support for strengthening the capability of water and sewerage agencies, and for developing their autonomy and financial viability. Operation and maintenance of existing water and sanitation facilities has been recognized as a serious shortcoming in many countries. Technical and financial support is needed to help countries to correct present inadequacies and build up the capacity to operate and maintain rehabilitated and new systems.

F. Water for sustainable food production and rural development

Basis for action

18.65. Sustainability of food production increasingly depends on sound and efficient water use and conservation practices consisting primarily of irrigation development and management, including water management in rainfed areas, livestock water supply, inland fisheries and agro-forestry. Achieving food security is a high priority in many countries, and agriculture must not only provide food for rising populations, but also save water for other uses. The challenge is to develop and apply water-saving technology and management methods, and, through capacity-building, enable communities to introduce institutions and incentives for the rural population to adopt new approaches, for both rainfed and irrigated agriculture. The rural population must also have better access to a potable water supply and to sanitation services. It is an immense task, but not an impossible one, provided appropriate policies and programmes are adopted at all levels—local, national and international. While significant expansion of the area under rainfed agriculture has been achieved during the past decade, the productivity response and sustainability of irrigation systems have been constrained by problems of water-logging and salinization. Financial and market constraints are also a common problem. Soil erosion, mismanagement and overexploitation of natural resources and acute competition for water, have all influenced the extent of poverty, hunger and famine in the developing countries. Soil erosion caused by overgrazing of livestock is also often responsible for the siltation of lakes. The development of irrigation schemes is most often not supported by environmental impact assessments identifying hydrological consequences within watersheds and owing to interbasin transfers, nor by the assessment of social impacts on peoples in river valleys.

18.66. The non-availability of water supplies of suitable quality is a significant limiting factor to livestock production in many countries and improper disposal of animal wastes can in certain circumstances result in pollution of water supplies for both humans and animals. The drinking water requirements of live-stock vary according to species and environment in which they are kept. It is estimated that the current global livestock drinking water requirement is about 60 billion litres a day and, based on livestock population growth estimates, this daily requirement is predicted to increase by 0.4 billion litres per annum in the foreseeable future.

18.67. Freshwater fisheries in lakes and streams are an important source of food and protein. Fisheries of inland waters should be managed to maximize the yield of aquatic food organisms in an environmentally sound manner. This re-quires the conservation of water quality and quantity, as well as the functional morphology of the aquatic environment. On the other hand, fishing and aqua-culture themselves may damage the aquatic ecosystem and hence their develop-ment should conform to guidelines for impact limitation. Present levels of production from inland fisheries, both from fresh and brackish water, are about 7 million tons per year and could increase to 16 million tons per year by the year 2000; however, any increase in environmental stress could jeopardize this rise.

Objectives

18.68. The key strategic principles for holistic and integrated environmentally sound management of water resources in the rural context are set forth as follows:

(a) Water should be regarded as a finite resource that has an economic value with significant social and economic implications, taking into consideration the importance of meeting basic needs;

(b) Local communities must participate in all phases of water management, ensuring the full involvement of women in view of their crucial role in the practical day-to-day supply, management and use of water;

(c) Water resource management must be developed within a comprehensive set of policies for (i) human health; (ii) food production, preservation and dis-tribution; (iii) disaster mitigation plans; (iv) environmental protection and conservation of the natural resource base;

(d) The need to recognize and actively support the role of rural populations, with particular emphasis on women.

18.69. An International Action Programme on Water and Sustainable Agricul-tural Development (IAP-WASAD) has been initiated by FAO in cooperation with other international organizations. The main objective of the Action Programme is to assist developing countries in planning, developing and managing water re-sources on an integrated basis to meet the present and future needs for agricul-tural production, taking into account environmental considerations.

18.70. The Action Programme has developed a framework for sustainable water use in the agricultural sector and identified priority areas for action at national, regional and global levels. Quantitative targets for new irrigation development, improvement of existing irrigation schemes and reclamation of waterlogged and salinized lands through drainage for 130 developing countries are estimated on the basis of food requirements, agro-climatic zones and availability of water and land.

18.71. The FAO global projections for irrigation, drainage and small-scale water programmes by the year 2000 for 130 developing countries are: (a) 15.2 million hectares of new irrigation development; (b) 12 million hectares of improvement/modernization of existing schemes; (c) 7 million hectares installed with drainage and water control facilities; and (d) 10 million hectares of small-scale water programmes and conservation.

18.72. The development of new irrigation areas at the above level may give rise to environmental concerns as this may imply the destruction of wetlands, water pollution, increased sedimentation and a reduction in biodiversity. Therefore, new irrigation schemes should be accompanied by an environmental impact assessment in case significant negative environmental impacts are expected and also depending upon the scale of the scheme. When considering proposals for new irrigation schemes, consideration should also be given to a more rational exploitation, and increasing the efficiency or productivity, of any existing schemes capable of serving the same localities. Technologies for new irrigation schemes should be thoroughly evaluated, including their potential conflicts with other land uses. The active involvement of water users groups is a supporting objective.

18.73. It should be ensured that rural communities of all countries, according to their capacities and available resources and taking advantage of international cooperation as appropriate, will have access to safe water in sufficient quantities and adequate sanitation to meet their health needs and maintain the essential qualities of their local environments.

18.74. The objectives with regard to water management for inland fisheries and aquaculture include conservation of water quality and quantity requirements for optimum production and prevention of water pollution by aquacultural activities. The Action Programme seeks to assist member countries in managing the fisheries of inland waters through the promotion of sustainable management of capture fisheries as well as the development of environmentally sound approaches to intensification of aquaculture.

18.75. The objectives with regard to water management for livestock supply are twofold: provision of adequate amounts and safeguarding of drinking-water quality in accordance with the specific needs of different animal species. This entails maximum salinity tolerance levels and the absence of pathogenic organisms. No global targets can be set owing to large regional and intra-country variations.

Activities

18.76. All States, according to their capacity and available resources, and through bilateral or multilateral cooperation, including through the United Nations and other relevant organizations, as appropriate, could implement the following activities:

(a) Water supply and sanitation for the unserved rural poor:

(i) Establish national policies and budget priorities with regard to increasing service coverage;

(ii) Promote appropriate technologies;

(iii) Introduce suitable cost-recovery mechanisms, taking into account efficiency and equity through demand management mechanisms;

(iv) Promote community ownership and rights to water supply and sanitation facilities;

(v) Establish monitoring and evaluation systems;

(vi) Strengthen the rural water supply and sanitation sector with emphasis on institutional development, efficient management and an appropriate framework for financing of the services;

(vii) Increase hygiene education and eliminate disease transmission foci;

(viii) Adopt appropriate technologies for water treatment;

(ix) Adopt wide-scale environmental management measures to control disease vectors;

(b) Water-use efficiency:

(i) Increase of efficiency and productivity in agricultural water use for better utilization of limited water resources;

(ii) Strengthening of water and soil management research under irrigation and rainfed conditions;

(iii) Monitoring and evaluation of irrigation project performance to ensure, *inter alia,* the optimal utilization and proper maintenance of the project;

(iv) Support to water users groups with a view to improving management performance at the local level;

(v) Supporting the appropriate use of relatively brackish water for irrigation;

(c) Waterlogging, salinity control and drainage:

(i) Introduction of surface drainage in rainfed agriculture to prevent temporary waterlogging and flooding of lowlands;

(ii) Introduction of artificial drainage in irrigated and rainfed agriculture;

(iii) Encouragement of conjunctive use of surface and groundwaters, including monitoring and water balance studies;

(iv) Practising of drainage in irrigated areas of arid and semi-arid regions;

(d) Water quality management:

(i) Establishment and operation of cost-effective water quality monitoring systems for agricultural water uses;

(ii) Prevention of adverse effects of agricultural activities on water quality for other social and economic activities and on wetlands, *inter alia*, through optimal use of on-farm inputs and the minimization of the use of external inputs in agricultural activities;

(iii) Establishment of biological, physical and chemical water quality criteria for agricultural water users and for marine and riverine ecosystems;

(iv) Minimization of soil run-off and sedimentation;

(v) Proper disposal of sewage from human settlements and of manure produced by intensive livestock breeding;

(vi) Minimize adverse effects from agricultural chemicals by use of integrated pest management;

(vii) Education of communities about the pollution impacts of the use of fertilizers and chemicals on water quality, food safety and human health risks;

(e) Water resources development programmes:

(i) Development of small-scale irrigation, water supply for humans and livestock and for water and soil conservation;

(ii) Formulation of large-scale and long-term irrigation development programmes, taking into account their effects on the local level, the economy and the environment;

(iii) Promotion of local initiatives for the integrated development and management of water resources;

(iv) Provision of adequate technical advice and support and enhancement of institutional collaboration at the local community level;

(v) Promotion of a farming approach for land and water management that takes account of the level of education, the capacity to mobilize local communities, and the ecosystem requirements of arid and semi-arid regions;

(vi) Planning and development of multi-purpose hydro-electric power schemes, making sure that environmental concerns are duly taken into account;

(f) Scarce water resources management:

(i) Development of long-term strategies and practical implementation programmes for agricultural water use under scarcity conditions with competing demands for water;

(ii) Recognition of water as a social, economic and strategic good in irrigation planning and management;

(iii) Formulation of specialized programmes focused on drought preparedness, with emphasis on food scarcity and environmental safeguards;

(iv) Promotion and enhancement of waste water reuse in agriculture;

(g) Water supply for livestock:

(i) Improve quality of water available to livestock, taking into account their tolerance limits;

(ii) Increase the quantity of water sources available to livestock, and in particular those in extensive grazing systems, in order to both reduce the distance needed to travel for water and to prevent overgrazing around water sources;

(iii) Prevent contamination of water sources with animal excrement in order to prevent the spread of diseases and in particular zoonosis;

(iv) Encourage multiple use of water supplies through promotion of integrated agro-livestock-fishery systems;

(v) Encourage water spreading schemes to increase water retention of extensive grasslands to stimulate forage production and prevent run-off;

(h) Inland fisheries:

(i) Develop the sustainable management of fisheries as part of national water resources planning;

(ii) Study specific aspects of the hydro-biology and environmental requirements of key inland fish species in relation to varying water regimes;

(iii) Prevent, mitigate or rehabilitate aquatic environments subjected to modification by other users for the sustainable use and conservation of biological diversity of living aquatic resources;

(iv) Develop and disseminate environmentally sound water resources development and management methodologies for the intensification of fish yield from inland waters;

(v) Establish and maintain adequate systems for the collection and interpretation of data on water quality, quantity and channel morphology related to management and the state of living aquatic resources, including fisheries;

(i) Aquaculture development:

(i) Develop environmentally sound aquaculture technologies that are compatible with local, regional and national water resources management plans and taking into consideration social factors;

(ii) Introduce appropriate aquaculture techniques and related water development and management practices in countries not yet experienced in aquaculture;

(iii) Assess environmental impacts of aquaculture with specific reference to commercialized culture units and potential water pollution from processing centres;

(iv) Evaluate economic feasibility of aquaculture in relation to alternative use of water, taking into consideration the use of marginal quality water and investment and operational requirements.

Means of implementation

(a) Financing and cost evaluation

18.77. The Conference secretariat has estimated the average total annual cost (1993-2000) of implementing the activities of this programme to be about $13.2 billion, including about $4.5 billion from the international community on grant or concessional terms. These are indicative and order of magnitude estimates only and have not been reviewed by Governments. Actual costs and financial terms, including any that are non-concessional, will depend upon, *inter alia*, the specific strategies and programmes Governments decide upon for implementation.[11]

(b) Scientific and technological means

18.78. There is an urgent need for countries to monitor water resources and water quality, water and land use and crop production; compile inventories of type and extent of agricultural water development and their present and future contributions to sustainable agricultural development; evaluate the potential for fisheries and aquaculture development; and improve the availability and dissemination of data to planners, technicians, farmers and fishermen. Priority requirements for research are as follows:

(a) Identify critical areas for water-related adaptive research;

(b) Strengthen the adaptive research capacities of institutions in developing countries;

---

11   Draft paragraph 18.88 of A/CONF.151/4 (22 April 1992) was replaced by decision of the Main Committee of UNCED on 10 June 1992. See A/CONF.151/L.3/Add.18 (11 June 1992). The former draft read as follows:

During the period 1993 to 2000, total annual costs for investments and technical support in this programme area are estimated at about $ 13.2 billion, of which about $ 4.5 billion would have to come from international sources. This includes also about $ 10 million annually to strengthen international, global and regional organizations.

(c) Enhance translation of water-related farming and fishing systems research results into practical and accessible technologies and provide the support needed for their quick adoption at the field level.

18.79. Transfer of technology, both horizontal and vertical, needs to be strengthened. Mechanisms to provide credit, input supplies, markets, appropriate pricing and transportation must be developed jointly by countries and external support agencies. Integrated rural water supply infrastructure including facilities for water-related education and training and support services for agriculture, should be expanded for multiple uses and assist in developing the rural economy.

(c) Human resource development

18.80. Education and training of human resources should be actively pursued at the national level through: (a) assessment of current and long-term human resources management and training needs; (b) establishment of a national policy for human resources development; and (c) initiation and implementation of training programmes for staff at all levels as well as for farmers. The necessary actions are as follows:

(a) Assess training needs for agricultural water management;

(b) Increase formal and informal training activities;

(c) Develop practical training courses for improving the ability of extension services to disseminate technologies and strengthen farmers' capabilities, with special reference to small-scale producers;

(d) Train staff at all levels, including farmers, fishermen and members of local communities, with particular reference to women;

(e) Increase the opportunities for career development to enhance the capabilities of administrators and officers at all levels involved in land and water-management programmes.

(d) Capacity-building

18.81. The importance of a functional and coherent institutional framework at the national level to promote water and sustainable agricultural development has been generally fully recognized at present. In addition, an adequate legal framework of rules and regulations should be in place to facilitate actions on agricultural water use, drainage, water quality management, small-scale water programmes and the functioning of water users' and fishermen's associations. Legislation specific to the needs of the agricultural water sector should be consistent with, and stem from, general legislation for the management of water resources. Actions should be pursued in the following areas:

(a) Improvement of water-use policies related to agriculture, fisheries and rural development and of legal frameworks for implementing such policies;

(b) Review, strengthening and restructuring, if required, of existing institutions in order to enhance their capacities in water-related activities, while recognizing the need to manage water resources at the lowest appropriate level;

(c) Review and strengthening, where necessary, of organizational structure, functional relationships and linkages among ministries and departments within a ministry;

(d) Provision of specific measures that require support for institutional strengthening, *inter alia,* through long-term programme budgeting, staff training, incentives, mobility, equipment and coordination mechanisms;

(e) Enhancement of involvement of the private sector, where appropriate, in human resource development and provision of infrastructure;

(f) Transfer of existing and new water use technologies by creating mechanisms for cooperation and information exchange among national and regional institutions.

G. Impacts of climate change on water resources

Basis for action

18.82. There is uncertainty in the prediction of climate change at the global level; the uncertainties increase greatly at the regional, national and local levels and yet it is at the national level that the most important decisions would need to be made. Higher temperatures or decreased precipitation would lead to decreased water supplies and increased water demands, and it may cause deterioration of the quality of freshwater bodies, putting strains on the already fragile balance between supply and demand in many countries. Even where precipitation might increase, there is no guarantee that it would occur at the time of year when it can be used and in addition there may be a likelihood of increased flooding. Any rise in sealevel will often cause the intrusion of salt water in estuaries, small islands and coastal aquifers and the flooding of low-lying coastal areas; this puts low-lying countries at great risk.

18.83. The Ministerial Declaration of the Second World Climate Conference states that "the potential impact of such climate change could pose an environmental threat of an up to now unknown magnitude; and could even threaten survival in some small island States and in low-lying coastal, arid and semi-arid areas". The Conference recognized that among the most important impacts of climate change were its effects on the hydrological cycle and water management systems and, through these, on socio-economic systems. Increase in incidence of extremes, such as floods and droughts, would cause increased frequency and severity of disasters. The Conference therefore called for a strengthening of the necessary research and monitoring programmes and the exchange of relevant data and information, these actions to be undertaken at the national, regional and international levels.

Objectives

18.84. The very nature of this topic calls first and foremost for more information about and greater understanding of the threat being faced. This topic may be translated into the following objectives, consistent with the United Nations Framework Convention on Climate Change:[12]

(a) To understand and quantify the threat of the impact of climate change on freshwater resources;

(b) To facilitate the implementation of effective national counter-measures, as and when the threatening impact is seen as sufficiently confirmed to justify such action;

(c) To study the potential impacts of climate change on areas prone to droughts and floods.

Activities

18.85. All States, according to their capacity and available resources, and through bilateral or multilateral cooperation, including through the United Nations and other relevant organizations, as appropriate, could implement the following activities:

(a) Monitor the hydrological regime, including soil moisture, groundwater balance, penetration and transpiration of water quality, and related climate factors, especially in those regions and countries most likely to suffer from the adverse effects of climate change, where the localities vulnerable to these effects should be defined;

(b) Develop and apply techniques and methodologies for assessing the potential adverse effects of climate change, through changes in temperature, precipitation and sea level rise on freshwater resources and the flood risk;

(c) Initiate case-studies to establish whether there are linkages between climate changes and the current occurrences of droughts and floods in certain regions;

(d) Assess the resulting social, economic and environmental impacts;

(e) Develop and initiate response strategies to counter the adverse effects that are identified, including changing groundwater levels, and the mitigation of saline intrusion into aquifers;

---

12   The introductory phrase to draft paragraph 18.95 of A/CONF.151/4 (22 April 1992) was replaced by decision of the Main Committee of UNCED on 10 June 1992. See A/CONF.151/L.3/Add.18 (11 June 1992). The former draft read as follows:

The very nature of this topic calls first and foremost for more information about and greater understanding of the threat that is being faced. [Subject to the outcome of the Intergovernmental Negotiating Committee on a Framework Convention for Climate Change] this may be translated into the following objectives:

(f) Develop agricultural activities based on brackish water use;

(g) Contribute to the research activities under way within the framework of current international programmes.

Means of implementation

(a) Financing and cost evaluation

18.86. The Conference secretariat has estimated the average total annual cost (1993-2000) of implementing the activities of this programme to be about $100 million, including about $40 million from the international community on grant or concessional terms. These are indicative and order of magnitude estimates only and have not been reviewed by Governments. Actual costs and financial terms, including any that are non-concessional, will depend upon, *inter alia,* the specific strategies and programmes Governments decide upon for implementation.[13]

(b) Scientific and technological means

18.87. Monitoring of climate change and its impact on freshwater bodies must be closely integrated with national and international programmes for monitoring the environment, in particular those concerned with the atmosphere, as discussed under other sections of Agenda 21, and with the hydrosphere, as discussed under programme area B above. The analysis of data for indication of climate change as a basis for developing remedial measures is a complex task. Extensive research is necessary in this area and due account has to be taken of the work of the International Panel on Climate Change (IPCC), the World Climate Programme, the International Geosphere-Biosphere Programme (IGBP) and other relevant international programmes.

18.88. The development and implementation of response strategies requires innovative use of technological means and engineering solutions, including the installation of flood and drought warning systems and the construction of new water-resource development projects such as dams, aqueducts, well fields, waste water treatment plants, desalination works, levees, banks and drainage channels. There is also a need for coordinated research networks such as the IGBP/START network.

---

13   Draft paragraph 18.97 of A/CONF.151/4 (22 April 1992) was replaced by decision of the Main Committee of UNCED on 10 June 1992. See A/CONF.151/L.3/Add.18 (11 June 1992). The former draft read as follows:

During the years 1993 to 2000, national programmes to assess and mitigate the effects of climate change will incur costs of about $ 100 million annually, of which about $ 40 million would have to come from international sources. Joint international research and case-studies require an additional $ 4 million annually.

(c) Human resource development

18.89. The developmental work and innovation depend for their success on good academic training and staff motivation. International projects can help by enumerating alternatives, but each country needs to establish and implement the necessary policies and to develop its own expertise in the scientific and engineering challenges to be faced, plus a body of dedicated individuals who are able to interpret the complex issues concerned for those required to make policy decisions. These specialized personnel need to be trained, hired and retained in service where they can serve their countries in these tasks.

(d) Capacity-building

18.90. There is a need, however, to build a capacity at the national level to develop, review and implement response strategies. Construction of major engineering works and installation of forecasting systems will require significant strengthening of the agencies responsible, whether in the public or the private sector. Most critical is the requirement for a socio-economic mechanism which can review predictions of the impact of climate change and possible response strategies and make the necessary judgements and decisions.

Chapter 19

Environmentally Sound Management of Toxic Chemicals, Including Prevention of Illegal International Traffic in Toxic and Dangerous Products

INTRODUCTION

19.1. A substantial use of chemicals is essential to meet the social and economic goals of the world community and today's best practice demonstrates that they can be used widely in a cost-effective manner, and with a high degree of safety. However, a great deal remains to be done to assure the environmentally sound management of toxic chemicals, within the principles of sustainable development and improved quality of life for humankind. Two of the major problems, particularly in developing countries, are (a) lack of sufficient scientific information for the assessment of risks entailed by the use of a great number of chemicals, and (b) lack of resources for assessment of chemicals for which data are at hand.

19.2. Gross chemical contamination, with grave damage to human health, genetic structures and reproductive outcomes, and the environment, has in recent times been continuing within some of the world's most important industrial areas. Restoration will require major investment and development of new techniques. The long-range effects of pollution, extending even to the fundamental chemical and physical processes of the Earth's atmosphere and climate, are becoming understood only recently and the importance of those effects is becoming recognized only recently as well.

19.3. A considerable number of international bodies are involved in work on chemical safety. In many countries work programmes for the promotion of chemical safety are in place. Such work has international implications, as chemical risks do not respect national boundaries. However, a significant strengthening of both national and international efforts is needed to achieve an environmentally sound management of chemicals.

19.4. Six programme areas are proposed:

(a) Expanding and accelerating international assessment of chemical risks;

(b) Harmonization of classification and labelling of chemicals;

(c) Information exchange on toxic chemicals and chemical risks;

(d) Establishment of risk reduction programmes;

(e) Strengthening of national capabilities and capacities for management of chemicals;

(f) Prevention of illegal international traffic in toxic and dangerous products.

In addition, a short final section G deals with the enhancement of cooperation related to several programmes areas.

19.5. The six programme areas are together dependent for their successful implementation on intensive international work and improved coordination of current international activities, as well as on the identification and application of technical, scientific, educational and financial means, in particular for developing countries. To varying degrees, the programme areas involve hazard assessment (based on the intrinsic properties of chemicals), risk assessment (including assessment of exposure), risk acceptability and risk management.

19.6. Collaboration on chemical safety between the United Nations Environment Programme (UNEP), the International Labour Organisation (ILO) and the World Health Organization (WHO) in the International Programme on Chemical Safety (IPCS) should be the nucleus for international cooperation on environmentally sound management of toxic chemicals. All efforts should be made to strengthen this programme. Cooperation with other programmes, such as those of the Organisation for Economic Cooperation and Development (OECD) and the European Communities (EC) and other regional and governmental chemical programmes, should be promoted.

19.7. Increased coordination of United Nations bodies and other international organizations involved in chemicals assessment and management should be further promoted. Within the framework of IPCS, an intergovernmental meeting, convened by the Executive Director of UNEP, was held in London in December 1991 to further explore this matter (see paras. 19.75 and 19.76).

19.8. The broadest possible awareness of chemical risks is a prerequisite for achieving chemical safety. The principle of the right of the community and of workers to know those risks should be recognized. However, the right to know the identity of hazardous ingredients should be balanced with industry's right to protect confidential business information. (Industry, as referred to in this chapter, shall be taken to include large industrial enterprises and transnational corporations as well as domestic industries.) The industry initiative on responsible care and product stewardship should be developed and promoted. Industry should apply adequate standards of operation in all countries in order not to damage human health and the environment.

19.9. There is international concern that part of the international movement of toxic and dangerous products is being carried out in contravention of existing national legislation and international instruments, to the detriment of the environment and public health of all countries, particularly developing countries.

19.10. In resolution 44/226 of 22 December 1989, the General Assembly requested each regional commission, within existing resources, to contribute to the prevention of the illegal traffic in toxic and dangerous products by monitoring and making regional assessments of that illegal traffic and its environmental and health implications. The Assembly also requested the regional commissions to interact among themselves and to cooperate with the United Nations Environment Programme, with a view to maintaining efficient and coordinated monitoring and assessment of the illegal traffic in toxic and dangerous products.

PROGRAMME AREAS

A. Expanding and accelerating the international assessment of chemical risks

19.11. Assessing the risks to human health and the environment hazards that a chemical may cause is a prerequisite to planning for its safe and beneficial use. Among the approximately 100,000 chemical substances in commerce and the thousands of substances of natural origin with which human beings come into contact, many appear as pollutants and contaminants in food, commercial products and the various environmental media. Fortunately, exposure to most chemicals (some 1,500 cover over 95 per cent of total world production) is rather limited, as most are used in very small amounts. However, a serious problem is that even for a great number of chemicals characterized by high-volume production, crucial data for risk assessment are often lacking. Within the framework of the OECD chemicals programme such data are now being generated for a number of chemicals.

19.12. Risk assessment is resource-intensive. It could be made cost-effective by strengthening international cooperation and better coordination, thereby making the best use of available resources and avoiding unnecessary duplication of effort. However, each nation should have a critical mass of technical staff with experience in toxicity testing and exposure analysis, which are two important components of risk assessment.

Objectives

19.13. The objectives of this programme area are:

(a) To strengthen international risk assessment. Several hundred priority chemicals or groups of chemicals, including major pollutants and contaminants of global significance, should be assessed by the year 2000, using current selection and assessment criteria;

(b) To produce guidelines for acceptable exposure for a greater number of toxic chemicals, based on peer review and scientific consensus distinguishing between health- or environment-based exposure limits and those relating to socio-economic factors.

Activities

(a) Management-related activities

19.14. Governments, through the cooperation of relevant international organizations and industry, where appropriate, should:

(a) Strengthen and expand programmes on chemical risk assessment within the United Nations system IPCS [International Programme on Chemical Safety] (UNEP, ILO, WHO) and the Food and Agriculture Organization of the United Nations (FAO), together with other organizations, including the Organisation for Economic Cooperation and Development (OECD), based on an agreed approach to data quality assurance, application of assessment criteria, peer review and linkages to risk management activities, taking into account the precautionary approach;

(b) Promote mechanisms to increase collaboration among Government, industry, academia and relevant non-governmental organizations, involved in the various aspects of risk assessment of chemicals and related processes, in particular the promoting and coordinating research activities to improve understanding of the mechanisms of action of toxic chemicals;

(c) Encourage the development of procedures for the exchange by countries of their assessment reports on chemicals with other countries for use in national chemical assessment programmes.

(b) Data and information

19.15. Governments, through the cooperation of relevant international organizations and industry, where appropriate, should:

(a) Give high priority to hazard assessment of chemicals, that is, of their intrinsic properties as the appropriate basis for risk assessment;

(b) Generate data necessary for assessment, building *inter alia*, on programmes of IPCS (UNEP, WHO, ILO), FAO, OECD and EC and on established programmes of [sic] other regions and Governments. Industry should participate actively.

19.16. Industry should provide data for substances produced that are needed specifically for the assessment of potential risks to human health and the environment. Such data should be made available to relevant national competent authorities and international bodies and other interested parties involved in hazard and risk assessment, and to the greatest possible extent to the public also, taking into account legitimate claims of confidentiality.

(c) International and regional cooperation and coordination

19.17. Governments, through the cooperation of relevant international organizations and industry, where appropriate, should:

(a) Develop criteria for priority-setting for chemicals of global concern with respect to assessment;

(b) Review strategies for exposure assessment and environmental monitoring to allow for the best use of available resources, to ensure compatibility of data and to encourage coherent national and international strategies for that assessment.

Means of implementation

(a) Financial and cost evaluation

19.18. Most of the data and methods for chemical risk assessment are generated in the developed countries and an expansion and acceleration of the assessment work will call for a considerable increase in research and safety testing by industry and research institutions. The cost projections address the needs to strengthen the capacities of relevant United Nations bodies and are based on current experience in IPCS. It should be noted that there are considerable costs, often not possible to quantify, that are not included. These comprise costs to industry and Governments of generating the safety data underlying the assessments and costs to Governments of providing background documents and draft assessment statements to IPCS, the International Register of Potentially Toxic Chemicals (IRPTC) and OECD. They also include the cost of accelerated work in non-United Nations bodies such as OECD and EC.[1]

19.19. The Conference secretariat has estimated the average total annual cost (1993-2000) of implementing the activities of this programme to be about $30 million from the international community on grant or concessional terms. These are indicative and order-of-magnitude estimates only and have not been reviewed by Governments. Actual costs and financial terms, including any that are non-concessional, will depend upon, *inter alia*, the specific strategies and programmes Governments decide upon for implementation.[2]

---

1   Draft paragraph 19.18 of A/CONF./151/4 (22 April 1992) included brackets around the entire text of paragraph 19.18. The brackets were deleted by decision of the Main Committee of UNCED on 10 June 1992. See A/CONF.151/L.3/Add.19 (12 June 1992).

2   Draft paragraph 19.19 of A/CONF.151/4 (22 April 1992) was replaced by decision of the Main Committee of UNCED on 10 June 1992. See A/CONF.151/L.3/Add.19 (12 June 1992). The former draft read as follows:

The estimated international costs, about $ 30 million annually, are based on the assumption that a complete evaluation of 500 chemicals will be made in the period 1993-2000.

(b) Scientific and technological means

19.20. Major research efforts should be launched in order to improve methods for assessment of chemicals as work towards a common framework for risk assessment and to improve procedures for using toxicological and epidemiological data to predict the effects of chemicals on human health and the environment, so as to enable decision makers to adopt adequate policies and measures to reduce risks posed by chemicals.

19.21. Activities include:

(a) Strengthening research on safe/safer alternatives to toxic chemicals that pose an unreasonable and otherwise unmanageable risk to the environment or human health and those that are toxic, persistent and bio-accumulative and that cannot be adequately controlled;

(b) Promotion of research on, and validation of, methods constituting a replacement for those using test animals (thus reducing the use of animals for testing purposes);

(c) Promotion of relevant epidemiological studies with a view to establishing a cause-and-effect relationship between exposure to chemicals and the occurrence of certain diseases;

(d) Promotion of ecotoxicological studies with the aim of assessing the risks of chemicals to the environment.

(c) Human resource development

19.22. International organizations, with the participation of Governments and non-governmental organizations, should launch training and education projects involving women and children, who are at greatest risk, in order to enable countries, and particularly developing countries, to make maximum national use of international assessments of chemical risks.

(d) Capacity-building

19.23. International organizations, building on past, present and future assessment work, should support countries, particularly developing countries, in developing and strengthening risk assessment capabilities at national and regional levels to minimize, and as far as possible control and prevent, risk in the manufacturing and use of toxic and hazardous chemicals. Technical cooperation and financial support or other contributions should be given to activities aimed at expanding and accelerating the national and international assessment and control of chemical risks to enable the best choice of chemicals.[3]

---

3   Draft paragraph 19.23 of A/CONF.151/4 (22 April 1992) included brackets around the word "financial." The brackets were deleted by decision of the Main Committee of UNCED on 10 June 1992. See A/CONF.151/L.3/Add.19 (12 June 1992).

B. Harmonization of classification and labelling of chemicals

Basis for action

19.24. Adequate labelling of chemicals and the dissemination of safety data sheets such as ICSCs (International Chemical Safety Cards) and similarly written materials, based on assessed hazards to health and environment, are the simplest and most efficient way of indicating how to handle and use chemicals safely.

19.25. For the safe transport of dangerous goods, including chemicals, a comprehensive scheme elaborated within the United Nations system is in current use. This scheme mainly takes into account the acute hazards of chemicals.

19.26. Globally harmonized hazard classification and labelling systems are not yet available to promote the safe use of chemicals, *inter alia*, at the workplace or in the home. Classification of chemicals can be made for different purposes and is a particularly important tool in establishing labelling systems. There is a need to develop harmonized hazard classification and labelling systems, building on ongoing work.

Objectives

19.27. A globally harmonized hazard classification and compatible labelling system, including material safety data sheets and easily understandable symbols, should be available, if feasible, by the year 2000.

Activities

(a) Management-related activities

19.28. Governments, through the cooperation of relevant international organizations and industry, where appropriate, should launch a project with a view to establishing and elaborating a harmonized classification and compatible labelling system for chemicals for use in all United Nations official languages including adequate pictograms. Such a labelling system should not lead to the imposition of unjustified trade barriers. The new system should draw on current systems to the greatest extent possible; it should be developed in steps and should address the subject of compatibility with labels of various applications.

(b) Data and information

19.29. International bodies including, *inter alia*, IPCS (UNEP, ILO and WHO), FAO, the International Maritime Organization (IMO), the United Nations Committee of Experts on the Transport of Dangerous Goods and OECD, in cooperation with regional and national authorities having existing classification and labelling and other information-dissemination systems, should establish a coordinating group to:

(a) Evaluate and, if appropriate, undertake studies of existing hazard classification and information systems to establish general principles for a globally harmonized system;

(b) Develop and implement a work plan for the establishment of a globally harmonized hazard classification system. The plan should include a description of the tasks to be completed, deadline for completion and assignment of tasks to the participants in the coordinating group;

(c) Elaborate a harmonized hazard classification system;

(d) Draft proposals for standardization of hazard communication terminology and symbols in order to enhance risk management of chemicals and facilitate both international trade and translation of the information into the end-user's language;

(e) Elaborate a harmonized labelling system.

Means of implementation

(a) Financial and cost evaluation

19.30. The Conference secretariat has included the technical assistance costs related to this programme in estimates provided in programme area E. They estimate the average total annual cost (1993-2000) for strengthening international organizations to be about $3 million from the international community on grant or concessional terms. These are indicative and order-of-magnitude estimates only and have not been reviewed by Governments. Actual costs and financial terms, including any that are non-concessional, will depend upon, *inter alia*, the specific strategies and programmes Governments decide upon for implementation.[4]

(b) Human resource development

19.31. Governments and institutions and non-governmental organizations, with the collaboration of appropriate organizations and programmes of the United

---

4   Draft paragraphs 19.30 and 19.31 of A/CONF.151/4 (22 April 1992) were replaced by decision of the Main Committee of UNCED on 10 June 1992. See A/CONF.151/L.3/Add.19 (12 June 1992). The former draft read as follows:

    19.30 A step-by-step international cooperative approach to harmonize the main existing systems, with subsequent or concurrent adoption of the resulting system, wholly or in part, by all member States before the year 2000, would limit additional costs for the work required to reconcile these systems and for assisting developing countries in implementing compatible classification and labelling schemes. Around $3 million would be needed annually to strengthen the capacities of international organizations to coordinate the work of harmonization. Additional costs for technical assistance to strengthen national capacities related to work to be undertaken under this programme area are included in the costing of programme area E.

    19.31 The benefits from these expenditures would far exceed the costs.

Nations, should launch training courses and information campaigns to facilitate the understanding and use of a new harmonized classification and compatible labelling system for chemicals.

(c) Capacity-building

19.32. In strengthening national capacities for management of chemicals, including development and implementation of, and adaptation to, new classification and labelling systems, the creation of trade barriers should be avoided and the limited capacities and resources of a large number of countries, particularly developing countries, for implementing such a system, should be taken into full account.

C. Information exchange on toxic chemicals and chemical risks

Basis for action

19.33. The following activities, related to information exchange on the benefits as well as the risks associated with the use of chemicals, are aimed at enhancing the sound management of toxic chemicals through the exchange of scientific, technical, economic and legal information.

19.34. The *London Guidelines for the Exchange of Information on Chemicals in International Trade* are a set of guidelines adopted by Governments with a view to increasing chemical safety through the exchange of information on chemicals. Special provisions have been included in the guidelines with regard to the exchange of information on banned and severely restricted chemicals.

19.35. The export to developing countries of chemicals that have been banned in producing countries or whose use has been severely restricted in some industrialized countries has been the subject of concern, as some importing countries lack the ability to ensure safe use, owing to inadequate infrastructure for controlling the importation, distribution, storage, formulation and disposal of chemicals.

19.36. In order to address this issue, provisions for Prior Informed Consent (PIC) procedures were introduced in 1989 in the London Guidelines (UNEP) and in the International Code of Conduct on the Distribution and Use of Pesticides (FAO). In addition a joint FAO/UNEP programme has been launched for the operation of the PIC procedures for chemicals, including the selection of chemicals to be included in the PIC procedure and preparation of PIC decision guidance documents. The ILO chemicals convention calls for communication between exporting and importing countries when hazardous chemicals have been prohibited for reasons of safety and health at work. Within the General Agreement on Tariffs and Trade (GATT) framework, negotiations have been pursued with a view to creating a binding instrument on products banned or severely restricted in the domestic market. Further, the GATT Council has agreed, as stated in its decision contained in C/M/251, to extend the mandate of the working group for a period of three months, to begin from the date of the group's next meeting, and has authorized the Chairman to hold consultations on timing with respect to convening this meeting.

19.37. Notwithstanding the importance of the PIC procedure, information exchange on all chemicals is necessary.

Objectives

19.38. The objectives of the programme area are:

(a) To promote intensified exchange of information on chemical safety, use and emissions between all involved parties;

(b) To achieve by the year 2000, as feasible, full participation in and implementation of the PIC procedure, including possible mandatory applications through legally binding instruments contained in the amended London Guidelines and in the FAO International Code of Conduct, taking into account the experience gained within PIC procedure.

Activities

(a) Management-related activities

19.39. Governments and relevant international organizations with the cooperation of industry should:

(a) Strengthen national institutions responsible for information exchange on toxic chemicals and promote the creation of national centres where these centres do not exist;

(b) Strengthen international institutions and networks such as the IRPTC, responsible for information exchange on toxic chemicals;

(c) Establish technical cooperation with, and provide information to, other countries, especially those with shortages of technical expertise, including training in the interpretation of relevant technical data, such as Environmental Health Criteria Documents, Health and Safety Guides and International Chemical Safety Cards (published by IPCS); monographs on the Evaluation of Carcinogenic Risks of Chemicals to Humans (published by the International Agency for Research on Cancer (IARC)); and decision guidance documents (provided through the FAO/UNEP joint programme on PIC), as well as those submitted by industry and other sources;

(d) Implement the PIC procedures as soon as possible and, in the light of experience gained, invite relevant international organizations, such as UNEP, GATT, FAO, WHO and others, in their respective area of competence to consider working expeditiously towards the conclusion of legally binding instruments.

(b) Data and information

19.40. Governments and relevant international organizations with the cooperation of industry should:

(a) Assist in the creation of national chemical information systems in developing countries and improve access to existing international systems;

(b) Improve databases and information systems on toxic chemicals, such as emission inventory programmes, through provision of training in the use of those systems as well as software, hardware and other facilities;

(c) Provide knowledge and information on severely restricted or banned chemicals to importing countries to enable them to judge and take decisions on whether to import, and how to handle, those chemicals and establish joint responsibilities in trade of chemicals between importing and exporting countries;

(d) Provide data necessary to assess risks to human health and the environment of possible alternatives to banned or severely restricted chemicals.

19.41. United Nations organizations should provide, as far as possible, all international information material on toxic chemicals in all United Nations official languages.

(c) International and regional cooperation and coordination

19.42. Governments and relevant international organizations with the cooperation of industry should cooperate in establishing, strengthening and expanding, as appropriate, the network of designated national authorities for exchange of information on chemicals and establish a technical exchange programme to produce a core of trained personnel within each participating country.

Means of implementation

(a) Financing and cost evaluation

19.43. The Conference secretariat has estimated the average total annual cost (1993-2000) of implementing the activities of this programme to be about $10 million from the international community on grant or concessional terms. These are indicative and order-of-magnitude estimates only and have not been reviewed by Governments. Actual costs and financial terms, including any that are non-concessional, will depend upon, *inter alia*, the specific strategies and programmes Governments decide upon for implementation.[5]

---

5   Draft paragraph 19.44 of A/CONF.151/4 (22 April 1992) was replaced by decision of the Main Committee of UNCED on 10 June 1992. See A/CONF.151/L.3/Add.19 (12 June 1992). The former draft read as follows:

Annual international financing of about $ 10 million will be needed: $ 7 million for technical assistance and $ 3 million for strengthening international institutions.

D. Establishment of risk reduction programmes

Basis for action

19.44. There are often alternatives to toxic chemicals currently in use. Thus, risk reduction can sometimes be achieved by using other chemicals or even non-chemical technologies. The classic example of risk reduction is the substitution of harmless or less harmful substances for harmful ones. Establishment of pollution prevention procedures and setting standards for chemicals in each environmental medium, including food and water, and in consumer goods, constitute another example of risk reduction. In a wider context, risk reduction involves broad-based approaches to reducing the risks of toxic chemicals, taking into account the entire life cycle of the chemicals. Such approaches could encompass both regulatory and non-regulatory measures, such as promotion of the use of cleaner products and technologies, pollution prevention procedures and programmes, emission inventories, product labelling, use limitations, economic incentives, procedures for safe handling and exposure regulations, and the phasing out or banning of chemicals that pose unreasonable and otherwise unmanageable risks to human health and the environment and of those that are toxic, persistent and bio-accumulative and whose use cannot be adequately controlled.

19.45. In the agricultural area, integrated pest management, including the use of biological control agents as alternatives to toxic pesticides, is one approach to risk reduction.

19.46. Other areas of risk reduction encompass the prevention of chemical accidents, prevention of poisoning by chemicals and the undertaking of toxico-vigilance and coordination of clean-up and rehabilitation of areas damaged by toxic chemicals.

19.47. The OECD Council has decided that OECD member countries should establish or strengthen national risk reduction programmes. The International Council of Chemical Associations (ICCA) has introduced initiatives regarding responsible care and product stewardship aimed at reduction of chemical risks. The Awareness and Preparedness for Emergencies at Local Level (APELL) programme of UNEP is designed to assist decision makers and technical personnel in improving community awareness of hazardous installations and preparing response plans. ILO has published a Code of Practice on the prevention of major industrial accidents and is preparing an international instrument on the prevention of industrial disasters for eventual adoption in 1993.

Objectives

19.48. The objective of the programme area is to eliminate unacceptable or unreasonable risks and, to the extent economically feasible, to reduce risks posed by toxic chemicals, by employing a broad-based approach involving a wide range of risk reduction options and by taking precautionary measures derived from a broad-based life-cycle analysis.

Activities

(a) Management-related activities

19.49. Governments, through the cooperation of relevant international organizations and industry, where appropriate, should:

(a) Consider adopting policies based on accepted producers liability principles, where appropriate, as well as precautionary, anticipatory and life-cycle approaches to chemical management, covering manufacturing, trade, transport, use and disposal;

(b) Undertake concerted activities to reduce risks for toxic chemicals, taking into account the entire life cycle of the chemicals. These activities could encompass both regulatory and non-regulatory measures, such as promotion of the use of cleaner products and technologies; emission inventories; product labelling; use limitations; economic incentives; and the phasing out or banning of toxic chemicals that pose an unreasonable and otherwise unmanageable risk to the environment or human health and those that are toxic, persistent and bio-accumulative and whose use cannot be adequately controlled;

(c) Adopt policies and regulatory and non-regulatory measures to identify, and minimize exposure to, toxic chemicals by replacing them with less toxic substitutes and ultimately phasing out the chemicals that pose unreasonable and otherwise unmanageable risk to human health and the environment and those that are toxic, persistent and bio-accumulative and whose use cannot be adequately controlled;

(d) Increase efforts to identify national needs for standard setting and implementation in the context of the FAO/WHO Codex Alimentarius in order to minimize adverse effects of chemicals in food;

(e) Develop national policies and adopt the necessary regulatory framework for prevention of accidents, preparedness and response, *inter alia,* through land-use planning, permit systems and reporting requirements on accidents, and work with OECD/UNEP international directory of regional response centres and the APELL programme;

(f) Promote establishment and strengthening, as appropriate, of national poison control centres to ensure prompt and adequate diagnosis and treatment of poisonings;

(g) Reduce the over-dependence on the use of agricultural chemicals through alternative farming practices, integrated pest management or other appropriate means;

(h) Require manufacturers, importers and others handling toxic chemicals to develop, with the cooperation of producers of such chemicals, where applicable, emergency response procedures and preparation of on-site and off-site emergency response plans;

(i) Identify, assess, reduce and minimize, or eliminate as far as feasible by environmentally sound disposal practices, risks from storage of outdated chemicals.

19.50. Industry should be encouraged to:

(a) Develop an internationally agreed upon code of principles for the management of trade in chemicals, recognizing in particular the responsibility for making available information on potential risks and environmentally sound disposal practices if those chemicals become wastes, in cooperation with Governments and relevant international organizations and appropriate agencies of the United Nations system;

(b) Develop application of a "responsible care" approach by producers and manufacturers towards chemical products, taking into account the total life cycle of such products;

(c) Adopt, on a voluntary basis, community right-to-know programmes based on international guidelines, including sharing of information on causes of accidental and potential releases and means of preventing them, and reporting on annual routine emissions of toxic chemicals to the environment in the absence of host country requirements.

(b) Data and information

19.51. Governments, through the cooperation of relevant international organizations and industry, where appropriate, should:

(a) Promote exchange of information on national and regional activities to reduce the risks of toxic chemicals;

(b) Cooperate in the development of communication guidelines on chemical risks at the national level to promote information exchange with the public and the understanding of risks.

(c) International and regional cooperation and coordination

19.52. Governments, through the cooperation of relevant international organizations and industry, where appropriate, should:

(a) Collaborate to develop common criteria to determine which chemicals are suitable candidates for concerted risk reduction activities;

(b) Coordinate concerted risk reduction activities;

(c) Develop guidelines and policies for the disclosure by manufacturers, importers and others using toxic chemicals of toxicity information declaring risks and emergency response arrangements;

(d) Encourage large industrial enterprises including transnational corporations and other enterprises wherever they operate to introduce policies demonstrating the commitment, with reference to the environmentally sound management of toxic chemicals, to adopt standards of operation equivalent or not less stringent than in the country of origin.

(e) Encourage and support the development and adoption by small- and medium-size industries of relevant procedures for risk reduction in their activities;

(f) Develop regulatory and non-regulatory measures and procedures aimed at preventing the export of chemicals that are banned, severely restricted, withdrawn or not approved for health or environmental reasons, except when such export has received prior written consent from the importing country or is otherwise in accordance with the PIC procedure;

(g) Encourage national and regional work to harmonize evaluation of pesticides;

(h) Promote and develop mechanisms for the safe production, management and use of dangerous materials, formulating programmes to substitute for them with safer alternatives, where appropriate;

(i) Formalize networks of emergency response centres;

(j) Encourage industry, with the help of multilateral cooperation, to phase out as appropriate, and dispose of any banned chemicals that are still in stock or in use in an environmentally sound manner, including safe reuse, where approved and appropriate.

Means of implementation

(a) Financial and cost evaluation

19.53. The Conference secretariat has included most costs related to this programme in estimates provided for programme areas A and E. They estimate other requirements for training and strengthening the emergency and poison control centres to be about $4 million annually from the international community on grant or concessional terms. These are indicative and order-of-magnitude estimates only and have not been reviewed by Governments. Actual costs and financial terms, including any that are non-concessional, will depend upon, *inter alia*, the specific strategies and programmes Governments decide upon for implementation.[6]

---

6   Draft paragraph 19.54 of A/CONF.151/4 (22 April 1992) was replaced by decision of the Main Committee of UNCED on 10 June 1992. See A/CONF.151/L.3/Add.19 (12 June 1992). The former draft read as follows:

Risk assessment is a prerequisite for many actions needed to meet the objectives of this programme area. These costs are included in estimates for programme areas A and E and part of the costs of national-level programmes are included under programme area E. About $ 4 million will be needed annually from the international community for training and strengthening the emergency and poison control centres.

(b) Scientific and technological means

19.54. Governments, in cooperation with relevant international organizations and programmes, should:

(a) Promote technology that would minimize release of, and exposure to, toxic chemicals in all countries;

(b) Carry out national reviews, as appropriate, of previously accepted pesticides whose acceptance was based on criteria now recognized as insufficient or outdated and of their possible replacement with other pest control methods, particularly in the case of pesticides that are toxic, persistent and/or bio-accumulative.

E. Strengthening of national capabilities and capacities for management of chemicals

Basis for action

19.55. Many countries lack national systems to cope with chemical risks. Most countries lack scientific means of collecting evidence of misuse and of judging the impact of toxic chemicals on the environment, because of the difficulties involved in the detection of many problematic chemicals and systematically tracking their flow. Significant new uses are among the potential hazards to human health and the environment in developing countries. In several countries with systems in place there is an urgent need to make the systems more efficient.

19.56. Basic elements for sound management of chemicals are: (a) adequate legislation, (b) information gathering and dissemination, (c) capacity for risk assessment and interpretation, (d) establishment of risk management policy, (e) capacity for implementation and enforcement, (f) capacity for rehabilitation of contaminated sites and poisoned persons, (g) effective education programmes and (h) capacity to respond to emergencies.

19.57. As management of chemicals takes place within a number of sectors related to various national ministries, experience suggests that a coordinating mechanism is essential.

Objective

19.58. By the year 2000, national systems for environmentally sound management of chemicals, including legislation and provisions for implementation and enforcement, should be in place in all countries to the extent possible.

Activities

(a) Management-related activities

19.59. Governments, where appropriate and with the collaboration of relevant intergovernmental organizations, agencies and programmes of the United Nations, should:

(a) Promote and support multidisciplinary approaches to chemical safety problems;

(b) Consider the need to establish and strengthen, where appropriate, a national coordinating mechanism to provide a liaison for all parties involved in chemical safety activities (for example, agriculture, environment, education, industry, labour, health, transportation, police, civil defence, economic affairs, research institutions, and poison control centres);

(c) Develop institutional mechanisms for the management of chemicals, including effective means of enforcement;

(d) Establish and develop or strengthen, where appropriate, networks of emergency response centres, including poison control centres;

(e) Develop national and local capabilities to prepare for and respond to accidents by taking into account the UNEP APELL programme and similar programmes on accident prevention, preparedness and response, where appropriate, including regularly tested and updated emergency plans;

(f) Develop, in cooperation with industry, emergency response procedures, identifying necessary means and equipment in industries and plants necessary to reduce impacts of accidents.

(b) Data and information

19.60. Governments should:

(a) Direct information campaigns such as programmes providing information about chemical stockpiles, environmentally safer alternatives and emission inventories that could also be a tool for risk reduction, to the general public to increase the awareness of problems on chemical safety;

(b) Establish, in conjunction with IRPTC, national registers and databases, including safety information, for chemicals;

(c) Generate field monitoring data for toxic chemicals of high environmental importance;

(d) Cooperate with international organizations, where appropriate, to effectively monitor and control the generation, manufacturing, distribution, transportation and disposal activities relating to toxic chemicals, to foster preventive and precautionary approaches and ensure compliance with safety management rules, and provide accurate reporting of relevant data.

(c) International and regional cooperation and coordination

19.61. Governments, with the cooperation of international organizations, where appropriate, should:

(a) Prepare guidelines, where not already available, with advice and checklists for enacting legislation in the chemical safety field;

(b) Support countries, particularly developing countries, in developing and further strengthening national legislation and its implementation;

(c) Consider adoption of community right-to-know or other public information-dissemination programmes, when appropriate, as possible risk reduction tools. Appropriate international organizations, in particular UNEP, OECD, ECE, and other interested parties, should consider the possibility of developing a guidance document on the establishment of such programmes for use by interested Governments. The document should build on existing work on accidents and include new guidance on toxic emission inventories and risk communication. Such guidance should include harmonization of requirements, definitions and data elements to promote uniformity and allow sharing of data internationally;

(d) Build on past, present and future risk assessment work at an international level, to support countries, particularly developing countries in developing and strengthening risk assessment capabilities at national and regional levels to minimize risk in the manufacturing and use of toxic chemicals;

(e) Promote implementation of UNEP's APELL programme and, in particular, use of an OECD/UNEP international directory of emergency response centres;

(f) Cooperate with all countries, particularly developing countries, in the setting up of an institutional mechanism at the national level and the development of appropriate tools for management of chemicals;

(g) Arrange information courses at all levels of production and use, aimed at staff working on chemical safety issues;

(h) Develop mechanisms to make maximum use in countries of internationally available information;

(i) Invite UNEP to promote principles for accident prevention, preparedness and response for Governments, industry and the public, building on the ILO, OECD and ECE work in this area.

Means of implementation

(a) Financing and cost evaluation

19.62. The Conference secretariat has estimated the average total annual cost (1993-2000) of implementing the activities of this programme to be about $600 million, including $150 million from the international community on grant or concessional terms. These are indicative and order-of-magnitude estimates only and have not been reviewed by Governments. Actual costs and financial terms, including any that are non-concessional, will depend upon, *inter alia*, the specific strategies and programmes Governments decide upon for implementation.[7]

(b) Scientific and technological means

19.63. International organizations should:

(a) Promote the establishment and strengthening of national laboratories to ensure the availability of adequate national control in all countries regarding the importation, manufacture and use of chemicals;

(b) Promote translation, where feasible, of internationally prepared documents on chemical safety into local languages and support various levels of regional activities related to technology transfer and information exchange.

(c) Human resource development

19.64. International organizations should:

(a) Enhance technical training for developing countries in relation to risk management of chemicals;

(b) Promote translation where feasible of internationally prepared documents on chemical safety into local languages and support various levels of regional activities related to technology transfer and information exchange.[8]

19.65. Governments should organize, in collaboration with industry and trade unions, training programmes in the management of chemicals, including emergency response, targeted at all levels. In all countries basic elements of chemical safety principles should be included in the primary education curricula.

F. Prevention of illegal international traffic in toxic and dangerous products

19.66. There is currently no global international agreement on traffic in toxic and dangerous products (toxic and dangerous products are those that are banned, severely restricted, withdrawn or not approved for use or sale by Gov-

---

7   Draft paragraph 19.63 of A/CONF.151/4 (22 April 1992) was replaced by decision of the Main Committee of UNCED. See A/CONF.151/L.3/Add.19 (12 June 1992). The prior text read as follows:

    National annual costs for regulatory efforts, including enforcement, have been estimated as a proportion of the value of chemicals manufactured or imported. On this basis the annual requirements in developing countries would amount to $ 500-600 million. It is suggested that $100-150 million be provided as concessional finance for this purpose to developing countries by the international community.

8   Paragraph 19.64(b) was revised by the Main Committee at UNCED; see A/CONF. 151/L.31 add 19 (12 June 1992). The former text read as follows:

    Promote and increase support for research activities at the local level by providing grants and fellowships for studies at recognized research institutions active in disciplines of importance for chemical safety programmes.

ernments in order to protect public health and the environment). However, there is international concern that illegal international traffic in these products is detrimental to public health and the environment, particularly in developing countries, as acknowledged by the General Assembly in Resolutions 42/183 and 44/226. Illegal traffic refers to traffic that is carried out in contravention of a country's laws or relevant international legal instruments. The concern also relates to the transboundary movements of those products that are not carried out in accordance with applicable internationally adopted guidelines and principles. Activities under this programme area are intended to improve detection and prevention of the traffic concerned.

19.67. Further strengthening of international and regional cooperation is needed to prevent illegal transboundary movement of toxic and dangerous products. Furthermore, capacity-building at the national level is needed to improve monitoring and enforcement capabilities involving recognition of the fact that appropriate penalties may need to be imposed under an effective enforcement programme. Other activities envisaged in the present chapter (for example, under paragraph 19.39 (d)) will also contribute to achieving these objectives.

Objectives

19.68. The objectives of the programme are:

(a) To reinforce national capacities to detect and halt any illegal attempt to introduce toxic and dangerous products into the territory of any State, in contravention of national legislation and relevant international legal instruments;

(b) To assist all countries, particularly developing countries, in obtaining all appropriate information concerning illegal traffic in toxic and dangerous products.

Activities

(a) Management-related activities

19.69. Governments, according to their capacities and available resources and with the cooperation of the United Nations and other relevant organizations, as appropriate, should:

(a) Adopt, where necessary, and implement legislation to prevent the illegal import and export of toxic and dangerous products;

(b) Develop appropriate national enforcement programmes to monitor compliance with such legislation, and detect and deter violations through appropriate penalties.

(b) Data and information

19.70. Governments should develop, as appropriate, national alert systems to assist in detecting illegal traffic in toxic and dangerous products; local communities, and others could be involved in the operation of such a system.

19.71. Governments should cooperate in the exchange of information on illegal transboundary movements of toxic and dangerous products and should make such information available to appropriate United Nations bodies, such as UNEP and the regional commissions.

(c) International and regional cooperation and coordination

19.72. Further strengthening of international and regional cooperation is needed to prevent illegal transboundary movement of toxic and dangerous products.

19.73. The regional commissions, in cooperation with and relying upon expert support and advice from UNEP and other relevant bodies of the United Nations, should monitor, on the basis of data and information provided by Governments, and on a continuous basis make regional assessments of, the illegal traffic in toxic and dangerous products and its environmental, economic and health implications, in each region, drawing upon the results and experience gained in the joint UNEP/ESCAP [Economic and Social Commission for Asia and the Pacific] preliminary assessment of illegal traffic, expected to be completed in August 1992.

19.74. Governments and international organizations, as appropriate, should cooperate with developing countries in strengthening their institutional and regulatory capacities in order to prevent illegal import and export of toxic and dangerous products.

G. Enhancement of international cooperation relating to several of the programme areas

19.75. A meeting of government-designated experts, held in London in December 1991, made recommendations for increased coordination among United Nations bodies and other international organizations involved in chemical risk assessment and management. That meeting called for the taking of appropriate measures to enhance the role of IPCS and establish an intergovernmental forum on chemical risk assessment and management.

19.76. To further consider the recommendations of the London meeting and initiate action on them, as appropriate, the Executive Heads of WHO, ILO and UNEP are invited to convene an intergovernmental meeting within one year, which could constitute the first meeting of the intergovernmental forum.

Chapter 20

Environmentally Sound Management of Hazardous Wastes Including Prevention of Illegal International Traffic in Hazardous Wastes

INTRODUCTION

20.1. Effective control of the generation, storage, treatment, recycling and re-use, transport, recovery and disposal of hazardous wastes is of paramount importance for proper health, environmental protection and natural resource management, and sustainable development. This will require the active cooperation and participation of the international community, Governments and industry. Industry, as referred to in this paper, shall include large industrial enterprises, including transnational corporations and domestic industry.[1]

20.2. Prevention of the generation of hazardous wastes and the rehabilitation of contaminated sites are the key elements, and both require knowledge, experienced people, facilities, financial resources, and technical and scientific capacities.

20.3. The activities outlined in the present chapter are very closely related to, and have implications for, many of the programme areas described in other chapters, so that an overall integrated approach to hazardous waste management is necessary.

20.4. There is international concern that part of the international movement of hazardous wastes is being carried out in contravention of existing national legislation and international instruments to the detriment of the environment and public health of all countries, particularly developing countries.

20.5. In section I of resolution 44/226 of 22 December 1989, the General Assembly requested each regional commission, within existing resources, to contribute to the prevention of the illegal traffic in toxic and dangerous products and wastes by monitoring and making regional assessments of that illegal traffic and

---

1   The preceding two sentences of draft paragraph 20.1 of A/CONF.151/4 (22 April 1992) were added by decision of the Main Committee of UNCED on 10 June 1992. See A/CONF.151/L.3/Add.20 (12 June 1992).

its environmental and health implications. The Assembly also requested the regional commissions to interact among themselves and cooperate with the United Nations Environment Programme (UNEP), with a view to maintaining efficient and coordinated monitoring and assessment of the illegal traffic in toxic and dangerous products and wastes.

Overall objective

20.6. Within the framework of integrated life-cycle management, the overall objective is to prevent to the extent possible, and minimize, the generation of hazardous wastes, as well as to manage those wastes in such a way that they do not cause harm to health and the environment.

Overall targets

20.7. The overall targets are:

(a) Preventing or minimizing the generation of hazardous wastes as part of an overall integrated cleaner production approach; eliminating or reducing to a minimum transboundary movements of hazardous wastes, consistent with the environmentally sound and efficient management of those wastes: and ensuring that environmentally sound hazardous waste management options are pursued to the maximum extent possible within the country of origin (the self-sufficiency principle). The transboundary movements that take place should be based on environmental and economic grounds and upon agreements between the States concerned;

(b) Ratification of the Basel Convention on the Control of Transboundary Movements of Hazardous Wastes and their Disposal and the expeditious elaboration of related protocols, such as the protocol on liability and compensation, mechanisms and guidelines to facilitate the implementation of the Basel Convention;

(c) Ratification and full implementation by the countries concerned of the Bamako Convention on the Ban on the Import into Africa and the Control of Transboundary Movement of Hazardous Wastes within Africa and the expeditious elaboration of a protocol on liability and compensation;

(d) Elimination of the export of hazardous wastes to countries that, individually or through international agreements, prohibit the import of such wastes, such as, the contracting parties to the Bamako Convention, to the fourth Lomé Convention or other relevant conventions, where such prohibition is provided for.

20.8. The following programme areas are included in this chapter:

(a) Promoting the prevention and minimization of hazardous waste;

(b) Promoting and strengthening institutional capacities in hazardous waste management;

(c) Promoting and strengthening international cooperation in the management of transboundary movements of hazardous wastes;

(d) Preventing illegal international traffic in hazardous wastes.

PROGRAMME AREAS

A. Promoting the prevention and minimization of hazardous waste

Basis for action

20.9. Human health and environmental quality are undergoing continuous degradation by the increasing amount of hazardous wastes being produced. There are increasing direct and indirect costs to society and to individual citizens in connection with the generation, handling and disposal of such wastes. It is therefore crucial to enhance knowledge and information on the economics of prevention and management of hazardous wastes, including the impact in relation to the employment and environmental benefits, in order to ensure that the necessary capital investment is made available in development programmes through economic incentives. One of the first priorities in hazardous waste management is minimization, as part of a broader approach to change industrial processes and consumer patterns through pollution prevention and cleaner production strategies.

20.10. Among the most important factors in these strategies is the recovery of hazardous wastes and their transformation into useful material. Technology application, modification and development of new low waste technologies are therefore currently a central focus of hazardous waste minimization.

Objectives

20.11. The objectives of this programme are:

(a) To reduce the generation of hazardous wastes, to the extent feasible, as part of an integrated cleaner production approach;

(b) To optimize the use of materials by utilizing, where practicable and environmentally sound, the residues from production processes;

(c) To enhance knowledge and information on the economics of prevention and management of hazardous wastes.

20.12. To achieve those objectives, and thereby reduce the impact and cost of industrial development, countries that can afford to adopt the requisite technologies without detriment to their development should establish policies that include:

(a) Integration of cleaner production approaches and hazardous waste minimization in all planning, and the adoption of specific goals;

(b) Promotion of the use of regulatory and market mechanisms;

(c) Establishment of an intermediate goal for the stabilization of the quantity of hazardous waste generated;

(d) Establishment of long-term programmes and policies including targets where appropriate for reducing the amount of hazardous waste produced per unit of manufacture;

(e) Achievement of a qualitative improvement of waste streams, mainly through activities aimed at reducing their hazardous characteristics;

(f) Facilitation of the establishment of cost-effective policies and approaches to hazardous waste prevention and management, taking into consideration the state of development of each country.

Activities

(a) Management-related activities

20.13. The following activities should be undertaken:

(a) Governments should establish or modify standards or purchasing specifications to avoid discrimination against recycled materials, provided that those materials are environmentally sound;

(b) Governments, according to their possibilities and with the help of multilateral cooperation, should provide economic or regulatory incentives, where appropriate, to stimulate industrial innovation towards cleaner production methods, to encourage industry to invest in preventive and/or recycling technologies so as to ensure environmentally sound management of all hazardous wastes, including recyclable wastes, and to encourage waste minimization investments;

(c) Governments should intensify research and development activities on cost-effective alternatives for processes and substances that currently result in the generation of hazardous wastes that pose particular problems for environmentally sound disposal or treatment, the possibility of ultimate phase-out of those substances that present an unreasonable or otherwise unmanageable risk and are toxic, persistent and bioaccumulative to be considered as soon as practicable. Emphasis should be given to alternatives that could be economically accessible to developing countries;

(d) Governments according to their capacities and available resources and with the cooperation of the United Nations and other relevant organizations and industries, as appropriate, should support the establishment of domestic facilities to handle hazardous wastes of domestic origin;

(e) Governments of developed countries should promote the transfer of environmentally sound technologies and know-how on clean technologies and low-waste production to developing countries in conformity with chapter 34, which will bring about changes to sustain innovation. Governments should cooperate with industry to develop guidelines and codes of conduct, where appropriate, leading to cleaner production through sectoral trade industry associations;

(f) Governments should encourage industry to treat, recycle, reuse and dispose of wastes at the source of generation, or as close as possible thereto, whenever hazardous waste generation is unavoidable and when it is both economically and environmentally efficient to do so;

(g) Governments should encourage technology assessments, for example through the use of technology assessment centres;

(h) Governments should promote cleaner production through the establishment of centres providing training and information on environmentally sound technologies;

(i) Industry should establish environmental management systems, including environmental auditing of its production or distribution sites, in order to identify where the installation of cleaner production methods is needed;

(j) A relevant and competent United Nations organization should take the lead, in cooperation with other organizations, to develop guidelines for estimating the costs and benefits of various approaches to the adoption of cleaner production and waste minimization and environmentally sound management of hazardous wastes, including rehabilitation of contaminated sites, taking into account, where appropriate, the report of the 1991 Nairobi meeting of government-designated experts on an international strategy and an action programme, including technical guidelines for the environmentally sound management of hazardous wastes; in particular in the context of the work of the Basel Convention, being developed under the UNEP secretariat;

(k) Governments should establish regulations that lay down the ultimate responsibility of industries for environmentally sound disposing of the hazardous wastes their activities generate.

(b) Data and information

20.14. The following activities should be undertaken:

(a) Governments, assisted by international organizations, should establish mechanisms for assessing the value of existing information systems;

(b) Governments should establish nationwide and regional information collection and dissemination clearing-houses and networks that are easy for Government institutions and industry and other non-governmental organizations to access and use;

(c) International organizations, through the UNEP Cleaner Production Programme and ICPIC, should extend and strengthen existing systems for collection of cleaner production information;

(d) All United Nations organs and organizations should promote the use and dissemination of information collected through the Cleaner Production network;

(e) OECD should, in cooperation with other organizations, undertake a comprehensive survey of, and disseminate information on, experiences of member countries in adopting economic regulatory schemes and incentive mechanisms for hazardous waste management and for the use of clean technologies that prevent such wastes from being generated;

(f) Governments should encourage industries to be transparent in their operations and provide relevant information to the communities that might be affected by the generation, management and disposal of hazardous wastes.

(c) International and regional cooperation and coordination

20.15. International/regional cooperation should encourage the ratification by States of the Basel and Bamako Conventions and promote the implementation of those Conventions. Regional cooperation will be necessary for the development of similar conventions in regions other than Africa, if so required. In addition there is a need for effective coordination of international regional and national policies and instruments. Another activity proposed is cooperating in monitoring the effects of the management of hazardous wastes.

Means of implementation

(a) Financing and cost evaluation

20.16. The Conference secretariat has estimated the average total annual cost (1993-2000) of implementing the activities of this programme to be about $750 million from the international community on grant or concessional terms. These are indicative and order-of-magnitude estimates only and have not been reviewed by Governments. Actual costs and financial terms, including any that are non-concessional, will depend upon, *inter alia*, the specific strategies and programmes Governments decide upon for implementation.[2]

---

2   Draft paragraphs 20.16 and 20.17 of A/CONF.151/4 (22 April 1992) were replaced by decision of the Main Committee of UNCED on 10 June 1992. See A/CONF.151/L.3/Add.20 (12 June 1992). The former draft read as follows:

20.16. It is estimated that the annual cost of improving the national capacity of developing countries through contributions from the international community and industry to implement this programme area will be approximately $740 million. This includes the establishment of national centres to promote cleaner production activities, research and training activities and activities related to the use of economic instruments in waste management, amounting to about $380 million per year, and the launching of demonstration projects for about $360 million per year. This amount may depend on the rate of implementation of such projects at the country level; the participation of the industry should be an integral part of implementation.

20.17. The annual cost of strengthening international institutions, including their activities on the strengthening of information exchange systems and the enhancement of knowledge and information on the economics of prevention and management of hazardous wastes, will be about $10 million.

(b) Scientific and technological means

20.17. The following activities related to technology development and research should be undertaken:

(a) Governments, according to their capacities and available resources and with the cooperation of the United Nations and other relevant organizations, and industries, as appropriate, should significantly increase financial support for cleaner technology research and development programmes, including the use of biotechnologies;

(b) States, with the cooperation of international organizations where appropriate, should encourage industry to promote and undertake research into the phase-out of the processes that pose the greatest environmental risk based on hazardous wastes generated;

(c) States should encourage industry to develop schemes to integrate the cleaner production approach into the design of products and their management practices;

(d) States should encourage industry to exercise environmentally responsible care through hazardous waste reduction and by ensuring the environmentally sound reuse, recycling and recovery of hazardous wastes, as well as their final disposal.

(c) Human resource development

20.18. The following activities should be undertaken:

(a) Governments, international organizations and industry should encourage industrial training programmes, incorporating hazardous waste prevention and minimization techniques and launching demonstration projects at the local level to develop "success stories" in cleaner production;

(b) Industry should integrate cleaner production principles and case examples into training programmes and establish demonstration projects/networks by sector/country;

(c) All sectors of society should develop cleaner production awareness campaigns and promote dialogue and partnership with industry and other actors.

(d) Capacity-building

20.19. The following activities should be undertaken:

(a) Governments of developing countries, in cooperation with industry and with the cooperation of appropriate international organizations, should develop inventories of hazardous waste production, in order to identify their needs with respect to technology transfer and implementation of measures for the sound management of hazardous wastes and their disposal;

(b) Governments should include in national planning and legislation an integrated approach to environmental protection, driven by prevention and source reduction criteria, taking into account the "polluter-pays" principle, and adopt programmes for hazardous waste reduction, including targets and adequate environmental control;

(c) Governments should work with industry on sector-by-sector cleaner production and hazardous waste minimization campaigns, as well as on the reduction of such wastes and other emissions;

(d) Governments should take the lead in establishing and strengthening, as appropriate, national procedures for environmental impact assessment taking into account the cradle to grave approach to the management of hazardous wastes, in order to identify options for minimizing the generation of hazardous wastes, through safer handling, storage, disposal and destruction;

(e) Governments, in collaboration with industry and appropriate international organizations, should develop procedures for monitoring the application of the cradle to grave approach, including environmental audits;

(f) Bilateral and multinational development assistance agencies should substantially increase funding for cleaner technology transfer to developing countries, including small and medium-sized enterprises.[3]

B. Promoting and strengthening institutional capacities in hazardous waste management

Basis for action

20.20. Many countries lack the national capacity to handle and manage hazardous wastes. This is primarily due to inadequate infrastructure, deficiencies in regulatory frameworks, insufficient education and training programmes and lack of coordination between the different ministries and institutions involved in various aspects of waste management. In addition, there is a lack of knowledge about environmental contamination and pollution and the associated health risk from the exposure of populations, especially women and children, and ecosystems to hazardous wastes; assessment of risks; and the characteristics of wastes. Steps need to be taken immediately to identify populations at high risk and to take remedial measures, where necessary. One of the main priorities in ensuring environmentally sound management of hazardous wastes is to provide awareness, education and training programmes covering all levels of society. There is also a need to undertake research programmes to understand the nature of hazardous wastes, to identify their potential environmental effects and

---

3   Paragraph 20.19(f) was revised by the Main Committee at UNCED. See A/CONF. 151/L.3/Add. 20 (12 June 1992) p. 2. The prior text read as follows in A/CONF. 151/4 (Part II), p. 244:

   (vi) Bilateral and multilateral development assistance agencies should substantially increase funding for cleaner technology transfer to developing countries and [economies in transition,] including small- and medium-sized enterprises.

to develop technologies to safely handle these wastes. Finally, there is a need to strengthen the capacities of institutions that are responsible for the management of hazardous wastes.

Objectives

20.21. The objectives in this programme area are:

(a) To adopt appropriate coordinating, legislative and regulatory measures at the national level for the environmentally sound management of hazardous wastes, including the implementation of international and regional conventions;

(b) To establish public awareness and information programmes on hazardous waste issues and to ensure that basic education and training programmes are provided for industry and government workers in all countries;

(c) To establish comprehensive research programmes on hazardous wastes in countries;

(d) To strengthen service industries to enable them to handle hazardous wastes and to build up international networking;

(e) To develop endogenous capacities in all developing countries to educate and train staff at all levels in environmentally sound hazardous waste handling, and monitoring and in environmentally sound management;

(f) To promote human exposure assessment with respect to hazardous waste sites and identify remedial measures required;

(g) To facilitate the assessment of impacts and risks of hazardous wastes on human health and the environment by establishing appropriate procedures, methodologies, criteria and/or effluent-related guidelines and standards;

(h) To improve knowledge regarding the effects of hazardous wastes on human health and the environment;

(i) To make information available to Governments and to the general public on the effects of hazardous wastes, including infectious wastes, on human health and the environment.

Activities

(a) Management-related activities

20.22. The following activities should be undertaken:

(a) Governments should establish and maintain inventories, including computerized inventories, of hazardous wastes and their treatment/disposal sites, as well as of contaminated sites that require rehabilitation, and assess the exposure and risk to human health and the environment; they should also identify the measures required to clean up the disposal sites. Industry should make the necessary information available;

(b) Governments, industry and international organizations should collaborate in developing guidelines and easy-to-implement methods for the characterization and classification of hazardous wastes;

(c) Governments should carry out exposure and health assessments of populations residing near uncontrolled hazardous waste sites and initiate remedial measures;

(d) International organizations should develop improved health-based criteria, taking into account national decision-making processes, and assist in the preparation of practical technical guidelines for the prevention, minimization and safe handling and disposal of hazardous wastes;

(e) Governments of developing countries should encourage interdisciplinary and intersectoral groups, in cooperation with international organizations and agencies, to implement training and research activities related to evaluation, prevention and control of hazardous waste health risks. Such groups should serve as models to develop similar regional programmes;

(f) Governments, according to their capacities and available resources and with the cooperation of the United Nations and other relevant organizations as appropriate, should encourage as far as possible the establishment of combined treatment/disposal facilities for hazardous wastes in small- and medium-sized industries;

(g) Governments should promote identification and clean-up of sites of hazardous wastes in collaboration with industry and international organizations. Technologies, expertise and financing should be available for this purpose, as far as possible and when appropriate with the application of the "polluter-pays" principle;

(h) Governments should ascertain that their military establishments conform to their nationally applicable environmental norms in the treatment and disposal of hazardous wastes.[4]

(b) Data and information

20.23. The following activities should be undertaken:

(a) Governments, international and regional organizations and industry should facilitate and expand the dissemination of technical and scientific information dealing with the various health aspects of hazardous wastes, and promote its application;

(b) Governments should establish notification systems and registries of exposed populations and of adverse health effects and databases on risk assessments of hazardous wastes;

---

4   Paragraph 20.22(h) was revised by decision of the Main Committee of UNCED to this effect, after The Representative of Sweden informed the Committee of his consultations. See A/CONF. 151/L.3/Add. 20, para. 3. The Representatives of Egypt and Mexico expressed reservations on the paragraph. *Id.*, para 4.

(c) Governments should endeavour to collect information on those who generate or dispose/recycle hazardous wastes and provide such information to the individuals and institutions concerned.

(c) International and regional cooperation and coordination

20.24. Governments, according to their capacities and available resources and with the cooperation of the United Nations and other relevant organizations, as appropriate, should:

(a) Promote and support the integration and operation, at the regional and local levels as appropriate, of institutional and interdisciplinary groups that collaborate, according to their capabilities, in activities oriented towards strengthening risk assessment, risk management and risk reduction with respect to hazardous wastes;

(b) Support capacity-building and technological development and research in developing countries in connection with human resource development, with particular support to be given to consolidating the networks;

(c) Encourage self-sufficiency in hazardous waste disposal in the country of origin to the extent environmentally sound and feasible. The transboundary movements that take place should be on environmental and economic grounds and based upon agreements between all States concerned.

Means of implementation

(a) Financing and cost evaluation

20.25. The Conference secretariat has estimated the average total annual cost (1993-2000) of implementing the activities of this programme to be about $18.5 billion on a global basis with about $3.5 billion related to developing countries, including about $500 million from the international community on grant or concessional terms. These are indicative and order-of-magnitude estimates only and have not been reviewed by Governments. Actual costs and financial terms, including any that are non-concessional, will depend upon, *inter alia*, the specific strategies and programmes Governments decide upon for implementation.[5]

---

5   Draft paragraph 20.26 of A/CONF.151/4 (22 April 1992) was replaced by decision of the Main Committee of UNCED on 12 June 1992. See A/CONF.151/L.3/Add.20. The former draft read as follows in A/CONF. 151/4 (Part II), p. 247:

      Total costs for management and safe disposal of hazardous wastes are roughly estimated to be about $12 billion per year for OECD countries, $3 billion per year for Eastern Europe and $3.5 billion per year for developing countries. An amount of $500 million per year should be made available through the international community to developing countries for the strengthening of their institutional capacities to safely manage and dispose of their hazardous wastes.

(b) Scientific and technological means

20.26. The following activities should be undertaken:

(a) Governments, according to their capacities and available resources and with the cooperation of the United Nations and other relevant organizations and industry as appropriate, should increase support for hazardous waste research management in developing countries;

(b) Governments, in collaboration with international organizations, should conduct research on the health effects of hazardous wastes in developing countries, including the long-term effects on children and women;

(c) Governments should conduct research aimed at the needs of small and medium-sized industries;

(d) Governments and international organizations in cooperation with industry should expand technological research on environmentally sound hazardous waste handling, storage, transport, treatment and disposal and on hazardous waste assessment, management and remediation;

(e) International organizations should identify relevant and improved technologies for handling, storage, treatment and disposal of hazardous wastes.

(c) Human resource development

20.27. Governments, according to their capacities and available resources and with the cooperation of the United Nations and other relevant organizations and industry as appropriate, should:

(a) Increase public awareness and information on hazardous waste issues and promote the development and dissemination of public information that the general public can understand;

(b) Increase the participation in hazardous waste management programmes by the general public, particularly women, including participation at grass-root levels;

(c) Develop training and education programmes for men and women in industry and Government aimed at specific real-life problems, for example, planning and implementing hazardous waste minimization programmes, conducting hazardous materials audits and establishing appropriate regulatory programmes;

(d) Promote the training of labour, industrial management and government regulatory staff in developing countries on technologies to minimize and manage hazardous wastes in an environmentally sound manner.

20.28. The following activities should also be undertaken:

(a) Governments, according to their capacities and available resources and with the cooperation of the United Nations, other organizations and non-governmental organizations, should collaborate in developing and disseminating educational materials concerning hazardous wastes and their effects on environment and human health, for use in schools, by women's groups and by the general public;

(b) Governments, according to their capacities and available resources and with the cooperation of the United Nations and other organizations, should establish or strengthen programmes for the environmentally sound management of hazardous wastes in accordance with, as appropriate, health and environmental standards, and extend surveillance systems for the purpose of identifying adverse effects on populations and the environment of exposure to hazardous wastes;

(c) International organizations should provide assistance to member States in assessing the health and environmental risks resulting from exposure to hazardous wastes, and in identifying their priorities for controlling the various categories or classes of wastes;

(d) Governments, according to their capacities and available resources and with the cooperation of the United Nations and other relevant organizations, should promote centres of excellence for training in hazardous waste management, building on appropriate national institutions and encouraging international cooperation, *inter alia*, including through institutional links between developed and developing countries.

(d) Capacity-building

20.29. Wherever they operate, transnational corporations and other large-scale enterprises should be encouraged to introduce policies and make commitments to adopt standards of operation with reference to hazardous waste generation and disposal that are equivalent to or no less stringent than standards in the country of origin, and Governments are invited to make efforts to establish regulations to require environmentally sound management of hazardous wastes.

20.30. International organizations should provide assistance to member States in assessing the health and environmental risks resulting from exposure to hazardous wastes and in identifying their priorities for controlling the various categories or classes of wastes.

20.31. Governments, according to their capacities and available resources and with the cooperation of the United Nations and other relevant organizations and industries, should:

(a) Support national institutions in dealing with hazardous wastes from the regulatory monitoring and enforcement perspectives, with such support including enabling them to implement international conventions;

(b) Develop industry-based institutions for dealing with hazardous wastes and service industries for handling hazardous wastes;

(c) Adopt technical guidelines for the environmentally sound management of hazardous wastes and support the implementation of regional and international conventions;

(d) Develop and expand international networking among professionals working in the area of hazardous wastes and maintain an information flow among countries;

(e) Assess the feasibility of establishing and operating national, subregional and regional hazardous wastes treatment centres. Such centres could be used for education and training, as well as for facilitation and promotion of the transfer of technologies for the environmentally sound management of hazardous wastes;

(f) Identify and strengthen relevant academic/research institutions or centres for excellence to enable them to carry out education and training activities in the environmentally sound management of hazardous wastes;

(g) Develop a programme for the establishment of national capacities and capabilities to educate and train staff at various levels in hazardous wastes management;

(h) Conduct environmental audits of existing industries to improve in-plant regimes for the management of hazardous wastes.

C. Promoting and strengthening international cooperation in the management of transboundary movements of hazardous wastes

Basis for action

20.32. In order to promote and strengthen international cooperation in the management, including control and monitoring, of transboundary movements of hazardous wastes, a precautionary approach should be applied. There is a need to harmonize the procedures and criteria used in various international and legal instruments. There is also a need to develop or harmonize existing criteria for identifying wastes dangerous to the environment and to build monitoring capacities.

Objectives

20.33. The objectives of this programme area are:

(a) To facilitate and strengthen international cooperation in the environmentally sound management of hazardous wastes, including control and monitoring of transboundary movements of such wastes, including wastes for recovery, by using internationally adopted criteria to identify and classify hazardous wastes and to harmonize relevant international legal instruments;

(b) To adopt a ban on or prohibit, as appropriate, the export of hazardous wastes to countries that do not have the capacity to deal with those wastes in an environmentally sound way, or that have banned the import of such wastes;

(c) To promote the development of control procedures for the transboundary movement of hazardous wastes destined for recovery operations under the Basel Convention that encourage environmentally and economically sound recycling options.

Activities

(a) Management-related activities

Strengthening and harmonizing criteria and regulations

20.34. Governments, according to their capacities and available resources and with the cooperation of United Nations and other relevant organizations, as appropriate, should:

(a) Incorporate the notification procedure called for in the Basel Convention and relevant regional conventions, as well as in their annexes, into national legislation;

(b) Formulate, where appropriate, regional agreements such as the Bamako Convention regulating the transboundary movement of hazardous wastes;

(c) Help promote the compatibility and complementarity of such regional agreements with international conventions and protocols;

(d) Strengthen national and regional capacities and capabilities to monitor and control the transboundary movement of hazardous wastes;

(e) Promote the development of clear criteria and guidelines, within the framework of the Basel Convention and regional conventions, as appropriate, for environmentally and economically sound operation in resource recovery, recycling, reclamation, direct use or alternative uses and for determination of acceptable recovery practices, including recovery levels where feasible and appropriate, with a view to preventing abuses and false presentation in the above operations;

(f) Consider setting up, at national and regional levels, as appropriate, systems for monitoring and surveillance of the transboundary movements of hazardous wastes;

(g) Develop guidelines for the assessment of environmentally sound treatment of hazardous wastes;

(h) Develop guidelines for the identification of hazardous wastes at the national level, taking into account existing internationally—and, where appropriate, regionally—agreed criteria and prepare a list of hazard profiles for the hazardous wastes listed in national legislation;

(i) Develop and use appropriate methods for testing, characterizing and classifying hazardous wastes and adopt or adapt safety standards and principles for managing hazardous wastes in an environmentally sound way.

Implementing of existing agreements

20.35. Governments are urged to ratify the Basel Convention and the Bamako Convention, as applicable, and to pursue the expeditious elaboration of related protocols, such as protocols on liability and compensation, and of mechanisms and guidelines to facilitate the implementation of the conventions.

Means of implementation

(a) Financing and cost evaluation

20.36. Because this programme area covers a relatively new field of operation and because of the lack so far of adequate studies on costing of activities under this programme, no cost estimate is available at present. However, the costs for some of the activities related to capacity-building that are presented under this programme could be considered to have been covered under the costing of programme area B above.

20.37. The interim secretariat for the Basel Convention should undertake studies in order to arrive at a reasonable cost estimate for activities to be undertaken initially until the year 2000.

(b) Capacity-building

20.38. Governments, according to their capacities and available resources and with the cooperation of United Nations and other relevant organizations, as appropriate, should:

(a) Elaborate or adopt policies for the environmentally sound management of hazardous wastes, taking into account existing international instruments;

(b) Make recommendations to the appropriate forums or establish or adapt norms, including the equitable implementation of the polluter pays principle, and regulatory measures to comply with obligations and principles of the Basel Convention, the Bamako Convention and other relevant existing or future agreements, including protocols, as appropriate, for setting appropriate rules and procedures in the field of liability and compensation for damage resulting from the transboundary movement and disposal of hazardous wastes;

(c) Implement policies for the implementation of a ban or prohibition, as appropriate, of exports of hazardous wastes to countries that do not have the capacity to deal with those wastes in an environmentally sound way or that have banned the import of such wastes;

(d) Study, in the context of the Basel Convention and relevant regional conventions, the feasibility of providing temporary financial assistance in the case of an emergency situation, in order to minimize damage from accidents arising from transboundary movements of hazardous wastes or during the disposal of those wastes.

D. Preventing illegal international traffic in hazardous wastes

Basis for action

20.39. The prevention of illegal traffic in hazardous wastes will benefit the environment and public health in all countries, particularly developing countries. It will also help to make the Basel Convention and regional international instruments, such as the Bamako Convention and the fourth Lomé Convention, more effective by promoting compliance with the controls established in those agreements. Article IX of the Basel Convention specifically addresses the issue of illegal shipments of hazardous wastes. Illegal traffic of hazardous wastes may cause serious threats to human health and the environment and impose a special and abnormal burden on the countries that receive such shipments.

20.40. Effective prevention requires action through effective monitoring, and the enforcement and imposition of appropriate penalties.

Objectives

20.41. The objectives of this programme area are:

(a) To reinforce national capacities to detect and halt any illegal attempt to introduce hazardous wastes into the territory of any State in contravention of national legislation and relevant international legal instruments;

(b) To assist all countries, particularly developing countries, in obtaining all appropriate information concerning illegal traffic in hazardous wastes;

(c) To cooperate, within the framework of the Basel Convention, in assisting countries that suffer the consequences of illegal traffic.

Activities

(a) Management-related activities

20.42. Governments, according to their capacities and available resources and with the cooperation of the United Nations and other relevant organizations, as appropriate, should:

(a) Adopt, where necessary, and implement legislation to prevent the illegal import and export of hazardous wastes;

(b) Develop appropriate national enforcement programmes to monitor compliance with such legislation, detect and deter violations through appropriate penalties and give special attention to those who are known to have conducted illegal traffic in hazardous wastes and to hazardous wastes that are particularly susceptible to illegal traffic.

(b) Data and information

20.43. Governments should develop as appropriate, an information network and alert system to assist in detecting illegal traffic in hazardous wastes. Local communities and others could be involved in the operation of such a network and system.

20.44. Governments should cooperate in the exchange of information on illegal transboundary movements of hazardous wastes and should make such information available to appropriate United Nations bodies such as UNEP and the regional commissions.

(c) International and regional cooperation

20.45. The regional commissions, in cooperation with and relying upon expert support and advice from UNEP and other relevant bodies of the United Nations system, taking full account of the Basel Convention, shall continue to monitor and assess the illegal traffic in hazardous wastes, including its environmental, economic and health implications, on a continuing basis, drawing upon the results and experience gained in the joint UNEP/ESCAP preliminary assessment of illegal traffic.

20.46. Countries and international organizations, as appropriate, should cooperate to strengthen institutional and regulatory capacities, in particular of developing countries in order to prevent the illegal import and export of hazardous wastes.

Chapter 21

Environmentally Sound Management of Solid Wastes and Sewage-Related Issues

INTRODUCTION

21.1. This chapter has been incorporated in Agenda 21 in response to General Assembly resolution 44/228, section I, paragraph 3, in which the Assembly affirmed that the Conference should elaborate strategies and measures to halt and reverse the effects of environmental degradation in the context of increased national and international efforts to promote sustainable and environmentally sound development in all countries, and to section I, paragraph 12 (g), of the same resolution, in which the Assembly affirmed that environmentally sound management of wastes was among the environmental issues of major concern in maintaining the quality of the Earth's environment and especially in achieving environmentally sound and sustainable development in all countries.

21.2. Programme areas included in the present chapter of Agenda 21 are closely related to the following programme areas of other chapters of Agenda 21:

(a) Protection of the quality and supply of freshwater resources: application of integrated approaches to the development, management and use of water resources (chapter 18);

(b) Promoting a sustainable pattern of human settlement development (chapter 7);

(c) Protecting and promoting human health conditions (chapter 6);

(d) Changing consumption patterns (chapter 4).

21.3. Solid wastes, as defined in this chapter, include all domestic refuse and non-hazardous wastes such as commercial and institutional wastes, street sweepings and construction debris. In some countries, the solid wastes management system also handles human wastes such as night-soil, ashes from incinerators, septic tank sludge and sludge from sewage treatment plants. If these wastes manifest hazardous characteristics they should be treated as hazardous wastes.

21.4. Environmentally sound waste management must go beyond the mere safe disposal or recovery of wastes that are generated and seek to address the root cause of the problem by attempting to change unsustainable patterns of production and consumption. This implies the application of the integrated life cycle management concept, which presents a unique opportunity to reconcile development with environmental protection.

21.5. Accordingly, the framework for requisite action should be founded on a hierarchy of objectives and focused on the four major waste-related programme areas, as follows:

(a) Minimizing wastes;

(b) Maximizing environmentally sound waste reuse and recycling;

(c) Promoting environmentally sound waste disposal and treatment;

(d) Extending waste service coverage.

21.6. The four programmes are interrelated and mutually supportive and must therefore be integrated in order to provide a comprehensive and environmentally responsive framework for managing municipal solid wastes. The mix and emphasis given to each of the four programme areas will vary according to the local socio-economic and physical conditions, rates of waste generation and waste composition. All sectors of society should participate in all the programme areas.

PROGRAMME AREAS

A. Minimizing wastes

Basis for action

21.7. Unsustainable patterns of production and consumption are increasing the quantities and variety of environmentally persistent wastes at unprecedented rates. The trend could significantly increase the quantities of wastes produced by the end of the century and increase quantities four to fivefold by the year 2025. A preventive waste management approach focused on changes in lifestyles and in production and consumption patterns offers the best chance for reversing current trends.

Objectives

21.8. The objectives in this area are:

(a) To stabilize or reduce the production of wastes destined for final disposal, over an agreed time-frame, by formulating goals based on waste weight, volume and composition and to induce separation to facilitate waste recycling and reuse;

(b) To strengthen procedures for assessing waste quantity and composition changes for the purpose of formulating operational waste minimization policies utilizing economic or other instruments to induce beneficial modifications of production and consumption patterns.

21.9. Governments, according to their capacities and available resources and with the cooperation of the United Nations and other relevant organizations, as appropriate, should:

(a) By the year 2000, ensure sufficient national, regional and international capacity to access, process and monitor waste trend information and implement waste minimization policies;[1]

(b) By the year 2000 have in place in all industrialized countries programmes to stabilize or reduce, if practicable, production of wastes destined for final disposal, including per capita wastes (where this concept applies), at the level prevailing at that date; developing countries as well should work towards that goal without jeopardizing their development prospects;[2]

(c) Apply by the year 2000, in all countries, in particular in industrialized countries, programmes to reduce the production of agrochemical wastes, containers and packaging materials, which do not meet hazardous characteristics.[3]

Activities

(a) Management-related activities

21.10. Governments should initiate programmes to achieve sustained minimization of waste generation. Non-governmental organizations and consumer groups should be encouraged to participate in such programmes, which could be drawn up with the cooperation of international organizations, where neces-

---

1   The footnote to draft paragraph 21.9(a) and the brackets around the text of paragraph 21.9(a) of A/CONF.151/4 (22 April 1992) were deleted by decision of the Main Committee of UNCED on 10 June 1992. See A/CONF.151/L.3/Add.43 (12 June 1992). The former draft footnote read as follows:

    Target dates mentioned in this document will be reexamined in light of the discussion on finance issues, technology transfer and comparable target setting in other Agenda 21 areas.

2   The footnote to draft paragraph 21.9(b) and the brackets around the text of paragraph 21.9(b) of A/CONF.151/4 (22 April 1992) were deleted by decision of the Main Committee of UNCED on 10 June 1992. See A/CONF.151/L.3/Add.43 (12 June 1992). The former draft footnote read as follows:

    Target dates mentioned in this document will be reexamined in light of the discussion on finance issues, technology transfer and comparable target setting in other Agenda 21 areas.

3   The footnote to draft paragraph 21.9(c) and the brackets around the text of paragraph 21.9(c) of A/CONF.151/4 (22 April 1992) were deleted by decision of the Main Committee of UNCED on 10 June 1992. See A/CONF.151/L.3/Add.43 (12 June 1992). The former draft footnote read as follows:

    Target dates mentioned in this document will be reexamined in light of the discussion on finance issues, technology transfer and comparable target setting in other Agenda 21 areas.

sary. These programmes should, wherever possible, build upon existing or planned activities and should:

(a) Develop and strengthen national capacities in research and design of environmentally sound technologies, as well as adopt measures to reduce wastes to a minimum;

(b) Provide for incentives to reduce unsustainable patterns of production and consumption;

(c) Develop, where necessary, national plans to minimize waste generation as part of overall national development plans;

(d) Emphasize waste minimization considerations in procurement within the United Nations system.

(b) Data and information

21.11. Monitoring is a key prerequisite for keeping track of changes in waste quantity and quality and their resultant impact on health and the environment. Governments, with the support of international agencies, should:

(a) Develop and apply methodologies for country-level waste monitoring;

(b) Undertake data gathering and analysis, establish national goals and monitor progress;

(c) Utilize data to assess environmental soundness of national waste policies as a basis for corrective action;

(d) Input information into global information systems.

(c) International and regional cooperation and coordination

21.12. The United Nations and intergovernmental organizations, with the collaboration of Governments, should help promote waste minimization by facilitating greater exchange of information, know-how and experience. The following is a non-exhaustive list of specific activities that could be undertaken:

(a) Identifying, developing and harmonizing methodologies for waste monitoring and transferring such methodologies to countries;

(b) Identifying and further developing the activities of existing information networks on clean technologies and waste minimization;

(c) Undertaking periodic assessment, collating and analysing country data and reporting systematically, in an appropriate United Nations forum, to the countries concerned;

(d) Reviewing the effectiveness of all waste minimization instruments and identifying potential new instruments that could be used and techniques by which they could be made operational at the country level. Guidelines and codes of practice should be developed;

(e) Undertaking research on the social and economic impacts of waste minimization at the consumer level.

Means of implementation

(a) Financing and cost evaluation

21.13. The Conference secretariat suggests that industrialized countries should consider investing in waste minimization the equivalent of about 1 per cent of the expenditures on solid wastes and sewage disposal. At current levels, this would amount to about $6.5 billion annually, including about $1.8 billion related to minimizing municipal solid wastes. Actual amounts would be determined by relevant municipal, provincial and national budget authorities based on local circumstances.[4]

(b) Scientific and technological means

21.14. Waste minimization technologies and procedures will need to be identified and widely disseminated. This work should be coordinated by national Governments, with the cooperation and collaboration of non-governmental organizations, research institutions and appropriate organizations of the United Nations, and could include the following:

(a) Undertaking a continuous review of the effectiveness of all waste minimization instruments and identifying potential new instruments that could be used and techniques by which instruments could be made operational at the country level. Guidelines and codes of practice should be developed;

(b) Promoting waste prevention and minimization as the principal objective of national waste management programmes;

(c) Promoting public education and a range of regulatory and non-regulatory incentives to encourage industry to change product design and reduce industrial process wastes through cleaner production technologies and good housekeeping practices and to encourage industries and consumers to use types of packaging that can be safely reused;

(d) Executing, in accordance with national capacities, demonstration and pilot programmes to optimize waste minimization instruments;

(e) Establishing procedures for adequate transport, storage, conservation and management of agricultural products, foodstuffs and other perishable

---

4   Draft paragraph 21.13 of A/CONF.151/4 (22 April 1992) was replaced by decision of the Main Committee of UNCED on 10 June 1992. See A/CONF.151/L.3/Add.21 (12 June 1992). The former draft read as follows:

It is suggested that industrialized countries invest 1 per cent of the revenues derived from total annual solid wastes and sewage towards waste minimization. At current levels this would amount to about $6.5 billion annually, of which $1.8 billion is required for minimizing municipal solid wastes, goods in order to reduce loss of those products, which results in the production of solid waste;

(f) Facilitating the transfer of waste-reduction technologies to industry, particularly in developing countries, and establishing concrete national standards for effluents and solid waste, taking into account, *inter alia*, raw material use and energy consumption.

(c) Human resource development

21.15. Human resource development for waste minimization not only should be targeted at professionals in the waste management sector but also should seek to obtain the support of citizens and industry. Human resources development programmes must therefore aim to raise consciousness and educate and inform concerned groups and the public in general. Countries should incorporate within school curricula, where appropriate, the principles and practices of preventing and minimizing wastes and material on the environmental impacts of waste.

B. Maximizing environmentally sound waste reuse and recycling

Basis for action

21.16. The exhaustion of traditional disposal sites, stricter environmental controls governing waste disposal and increasing quantities of more persistent wastes, particularly in industrialized countries, have all contributed to a rapid increase in the cost of waste disposal services. Costs could double or triple by the end of the decade. Some current disposal practices pose a threat to the environment. As the economics of waste disposal services change, waste recycling and resource recovery are becoming increasingly cost-effective. Future waste management programmes should take maximum advantage of resource-efficient approaches to the control of wastes. These activities should be carried out in conjunction with public education programmes. It is important that markets for products from reclaimed materials be identified in the development of reuse and recycling programmes.

Objectives

21.17. The objectives in this area are:

(a) To strengthen and increase national waste reuse and recycling systems;

(b) To create a model internal waste reuse and recycling programme for waste streams, including paper, within the United Nations system;

(c) To make available information, techniques and appropriate policy instruments to encourage and make operational waste reuse and recycling schemes.

21.18. Governments, according to their capacities and available resources and with the cooperation of the United Nations and other relevant organizations, as appropriate, should:

(a) By the year 2000, promote sufficient financial and technological capacities at the regional, national and local levels, as appropriate, to implement waste reuse and recycling policies and actions;[5]

(b) By the year 2000, in all industrialized countries and by the year 2010, in all developing countries, have a national programme, including, to the extent possible, targets for efficient waste reuse and recycling.[6]

Activities

(a) Management-related activities:

21.19. Governments and institutions and non-governmental organizations, including consumer, women's and youth groups, in collaboration with appropriate organizations of the United Nations, should launch programmes to demonstrate and make operational enhanced waste reuse and recycling. These programmes should, wherever possible, build upon existing or planned activities and should:

(a) Develop and strengthen national capacity to reuse and recycle an increasing proportion of wastes;

(b) Review and reform national waste policies to provide incentives for waste reuse and recycling;

(c) Develop and implement national plans for waste management that take advantage of, and give priority to, waste reuse and recycling;

(d) Modify existing standards or purchase specifications to avoid discrimination against recycled materials, taking into account the saving in energy and raw materials;

(e) Develop public education and awareness programmes to promote the use of recycled products.

---

5   The footnote to draft paragraph 21.18(a) and the brackets around the text of paragraph 21.18(a) of A/CONF.151/4 (22 April 1992) were deleted by decision of the Main Committee of UNCED on 10 June 1992. See A/CONF.151/L.3/Add.43 (12 June 1992). The former draft footnote read as follows:

   Target dates mentioned in this document will be reexamined in light of the discussion on finance issues, technology transfer and comparable target setting in other Agenda 21 areas.

6   The footnote to draft paragraph 21.18(b) and the brackets around the text of paragraph 21.18(b) of A/CONF.151/4 (22 April 1992) were deleted by decision of the Main Committee of UNCED on 10 June 1992. See A/CONF.151/L.3/Add.43 (12 June 1992). The former draft footnote read as follows:

   Target dates mentioned in this document will be reexamined in light of the discussion on finance issues, technology transfer and comparable target setting in other Agenda 21 areas.

(b) Data and information

21.20. Information and research is required to identify promising socially acceptable and cost-effective forms of waste reuse and recycling relevant to each country. For example, supporting activities undertaken by national and local government in collaboration with the United Nations and other international organizations could include:

(a) Undertaking an extensive review of options and techniques for reuse and recycling all forms of municipal solid wastes. Policies for reuse and recycling should be made an integral component of national and local waste management programmes;

(b) Assessing the extent and practice of waste reuse and recycling operations currently undertaken and identifying ways by which these could be increased and supported;

(c) Increasing funding for research pilot programmes to test various options for reuse and recycling, including the use of small-scale, cottage-based recycling industries; compost production; treated waste-water irrigation; and energy recovery from wastes;

(d) Producing guidelines and best practices for waste reuse and recycling;

(e) Intensifying efforts, at collecting, analysing and disseminating, to key target groups, relevant information on waste issues. Special research grants could be made available on a competitive basis for innovative research projects on recycling techniques;

(f) Identifying potential markets for recycled products.

(c) International and regional cooperation and coordination

21.21. States, through bilateral and multilateral cooperation, including through the United Nations and other relevant international organizations, as appropriate, should:

(a) Undertake a periodic review of the extent to which countries reuse and recycle their wastes;

(b) Review the effectiveness of techniques for and approaches to waste reuse and recycling and ways of enhancing their application in countries;

(c) Review and update international guidelines for the safe reuse of wastes;

(d) Establish appropriate programmes to support the small communities' waste reuse and recycling industries in developing countries.

Means of implementation

(a) Financing and cost evaluation

21.22. The Conference secretariat has estimated that if the equivalent of 1 per cent of waste-related municipal expenditures was devoted to safe waste reuse schemes, worldwide expenditures for this purpose would amount to $8 billion. The secretariat estimates the total annual cost (1993-2000) of implementing the activities of this programme area in developing countries to be about $850 million on grant or concessional terms. These are indicative and or-der-of-magnitude estimates only and have not been reviewed by Governments. Actual costs and financial terms, including any that are non-concessional, will depend upon, *inter alia*, the specific programmes proposed by international in-stitutions and approved by their governing bodies.[7]

(b) Scientific and technological means

21.23. The transfer of technology should support waste recycling and reuse by the following means:

(a) Including the transfer of recycling technologies, such as machinery for re-using plastics, rubber and paper, within bilateral and multilateral technical cooperation and aid programmes;

(b) Developing and improving existing technologies, especially indigenous technologies, and facilitating their transfer under ongoing regional and inter-regional technical assistance programmes;

(c) Facilitating the transfer of waste reuse and recycling technology.

21.24. Incentives for waste reuse and recycling are numerous. Countries could consider the following options to encourage industry, institutions, commercial establishments and individuals to recycle wastes instead of disposing of them:

(a) Offering incentives to local and municipal authorities that recycle the maximum proportion of their wastes;

(b) Providing technical assistance to informal waste reuse and recycling operations;

(c) Applying economic and regulatory instruments, including tax incentives, to support the principle that generators of wastes pay for their disposal;

---

7   Draft paragraphs 21.22 and 21.23 of A/CONF.151/4 (22 April 1992) were replaced by decision of the Main Committee of UNCED on 10 June 1992. See A/CONF.151/L.3/Add.21 (12 June 1992). The former draft read as follows:

21.22 If all countries devoted 1 per cent of waste-related municipal revenues to safe waste reuse schemes at current rates those revenues would constitute annual worldwide expenditures of about $8 billion, of which $2.3 billion would be required exclusively for reutilizing solid wastes. It is pro-posed that the international community direct $0.85 billion to accelerate safe waste reuse in devel-oping countries, of which $0.25 billion relates to solid wastes.

21.23 It is proposed that funding be increased to international organizations to enable them to sup-port these efforts by about $5 million annually. Half of this amount relates to solid wastes.

(d) Providing legal and economic conditions conducive to investments in waste reuse and recycling;

(e) Implementing specific mechanisms such as deposit/refund systems as incentives for reuse and recycling;

(f) Promoting the separate collection of recyclable parts of household wastes;

(g) Providing incentives to improve the marketability of technically recyclable waste;

(h) Encouraging the use of recyclable materials, particularly in packaging, where feasible;

(i) Encouraging the development of markets for recycled goods by establishing programmes.

(c) Human resource development

21.25. Training will be required to reorient current waste management practices to include waste reuse and recycling. Governments, in collaboration with United Nations international and regional organizations, should undertake the following indicative list of actions:

(a) Including waste reuse and recycling in in-service training programmes as integral components of technical cooperation programmes on urban management and infrastructure development;

(b) Expanding training programmes on water supply and sanitation to incorporate techniques and policies for waste reuse and recycling;

(c) Including the advantages and civic obligations associated with waste reuse and recycling in school curricula and relevant general educational courses;

(d) Encouraging non-governmental organizations, community-based organizations and women's, youth and public interest group programmes, in collaboration with local municipal authorities, to mobilize community support for waste reuse and recycling through focused community-level campaigns.

(d) Capacity-building

21.26. Capacity-building to support increased waste reuse and recycling should focus on the following areas:

(a) Making operational national policies and incentives for waste management;

(b) Enabling local and municipal authorities to mobilize community support for waste reuse and recycling by involving and assisting informal sector waste reuse and recycling operations and undertaking waste management planning that incorporates resource recovery practices.

C. Promoting environmentally sound waste disposal and treatment

Basis for action

21.27. Even when wastes are minimized, some wastes will still remain. Even after treatment, all discharges of wastes have some residual impact on the receiving environment. Consequently, there is scope for improving waste treatment and disposal practices such as, for example, avoiding the discharge of sludges at sea. In developing countries, the problem is of a more fundamental nature: less than 10 per cent of urban wastes receive some form of treatment and only a small proportion of treatment is in compliance with any acceptable quality standard. Faecal matter treatment and disposal should be accorded due priority given the potential threat of faeces to human health.

Objectives

21.28. The objective in this area is to treat and safely dispose of a progressively increasing proportion of the generated wastes.

21.29. Governments according to their capacities and available resources and with the cooperation of the United Nations and other relevant organizations, as appropriate, should:

(a) By the year 2000, establish waste treatment and disposal quality criteria, objectives and standards based on the nature and assimilative capacity of the receiving environment;[8]

(b) By the year 2000, establish sufficient capacity to undertake waste-related pollution impact monitoring and conduct regular surveillance, including epidemiological surveillance, where appropriate;[9]

(c) By the year 1995, industrialized countries, and by the year 2005, in developing countries, ensure that at least 50 per cent of all sewage, waste waters

---

8   The footnote to draft paragraph 21.30(a) and the brackets around the text of paragraph 21.30(a) of A/CONF.151/4 (22 April 1992) were deleted by decision of the Main Committee of UNCED on 10 June 1992. See A/CONF.151/L.3/Add.43 (12 June 1992). The former draft footnote read as follows:

Target dates mentioned in this document will be reexamined in light of the discussion on finance issues, technology transfer and comparable target setting in other Agenda 21 areas.

9   The footnote to draft paragraph 21.30(b) and the brackets around the text of paragraph 21.30(b) of A/CONF.151/4 (22 April 1992) were deleted by decision of the Main Committee of UNCED on 10 June 1992. See A/CONF.151/L.3/Add.43 (12 June 1992). The former draft footnote read as follows:

Target dates mentioned in this document will be reexamined in light of the discussion on finance issues, technology transfer and comparable target setting in other Agenda 21 areas.

and solid wastes are treated or disposed of in conformity with national or international environmental and health quality guidelines;[10]

(d) By the year 2025, dispose of all sewage, waste waters and solid wastes in conformity with national or international environmental quality guidelines.[11]

Activities

(a) Management-related activities

21.30. Governments, institutions and non-governmental organizations together with industries, in collaboration with appropriate organizations of the United Nations, should launch programmes to improve the control and management of waste-related pollution. These programmes should, wherever possible, build upon existing or planned activities and should:

(a) Develop and strengthen national capacity to treat and safely dispose of wastes;

(b) Review and reform national waste management policies to gain control over waste-related pollution;

(c) Encourage countries to seek waste disposal solutions within their sovereign territory and as close as possible to the sources of origin that are compatible with environmentally sound and efficient management. In a number of countries, transboundary movements take place to ensure that wastes are managed in an environmentally sound and efficient way. Such movements observe the relevant conventions, including those that apply to areas that are not under national jurisdiction;

(d) Develop human wastes management plans, giving due attention to the development and application of appropriate technologies and the availability of resources for implementation.

(b) Data and information

21.31. Standard setting and monitoring are two key elements essential for gaining control over waste-related pollution. The following specific activities are indicative of the kind of supportive actions that could be taken by international

---

10   The footnote to draft paragraph 21.30(c) and the brackets around the text of paragraph 21.30(c) of A/CONF.151/4 (22 April 1992) were deleted by decision of the Main Committee of UNCED on 10 June 1992. See A/CONF.151/L.3/Add.43 (12 June 1992). The former draft footnote read as follows:

Target dates mentioned in this document will be reexamined in light of the discussion on finance issues, technology transfer and comparable target setting in other Agenda 21 areas.

11   The footnote to draft paragraph 21.30(d) and the brackets around the text of paragraph 21.30(d) of A/CONF.151/4 (22 April 1992) were deleted by decision of the Main Committee of UNCED on 10 June 1992. See A/CONF.151/L.3/Add.43 (12 June 1992). The former draft footnote read as follows:

Target dates mentioned in this document will be reexamined in light of the discussion on finance issues, technology transfer and comparable target setting in other Agenda 21 areas.

bodies such as the United Nations Centre for Human Settlements (Habitat), the United Nations Environment Programme and the World Health Organization:

(a) Assembling and analysing the scientific evidence and pollution impacts of wastes in the environment in order to formulate and disseminate recommended scientific criteria and guidelines for environmentally sound management of solid wastes;

(b) Recommending national and, where relevant, local environmental quality standards based on scientific criteria and guidelines;

(c) Including within technical cooperation programmes and agreements the provision for monitoring equipment and for the requisite training in its use;

(d) Establishing an information clearing-house with extensive networks at the regional, national and local levels to collect and disseminate information on all aspects of waste management, including safe disposal.

(c) International and regional cooperation and coordination

21.32. States, through bilateral and multilateral cooperation, including through the United Nations and other relevant international organizations, as appropriate, should:

(a) Identify, develop and harmonize methodologies and environmental quality and health guidelines for safe waste discharge and disposal;

(b) Review and keep abreast of developments and disseminate information on the effectiveness of techniques and approaches to safe waste disposal and ways of supporting their application in countries.

Means of implementation

(a) Financing and cost evaluation

21.33. Safe waste disposal programmes are relevant to both developed and developing countries. In developed countries the focus is on improving facilities to meet higher environmental quality criteria, while in developing countries considerable investment is required to build new treatment facilities.[12]

21.34. The Conference secretariat has estimated the average total annual cost (1993-2000) of implementing the activities of this programme in developing countries to be about $15 billion, including about $3.4 billion from the international community on grant or concessional terms. These are indicative and order of magnitude estimates only and have not been reviewed by Governments. Actual costs and financial terms, including any that are non-concessional, will de-

---

12 Draft paragraph 21.34 of A/CONF.151/4 (22 April 1992) included brackets around the entire text of paragraph 21.34. The brackets were deleted by decision of the Main Committee of UNCED on 10 June 1992. See A/CONF.151/L.3/Add.21 (12 June 1992).

pend upon, *inter alia,* the specific strategies and programmes Governments decide upon for implementation.[13]

(b) Scientific and technological means

21.35. Scientific guidelines and research on various aspects of waste-related pollution control will be crucial for achieving the objectives of this programme. Governments, municipalities and local authorities, with appropriate international cooperation should:

(a) Prepare guidelines and technical reports on subjects such as the integration of land use planning in human settlements with waste disposal, environmental quality criteria and standards, waste treatment and safe disposal options, industrial waste treatment and landfill operations;

(b) Undertake research on critical subjects such as low-cost, low-maintenance waste-water treatment systems; safe sludge disposal options; industrial waste treatment; and low-technology, ecologically safe waste disposal options;

(c) Transfer of technologies, in conformity with the terms as well as the provisions of chapter 34, on industrial waste treatment processes through bilateral and multilateral technical cooperation programmes, and in cooperation with business and industry including large and transnational corporations, as appropriate.[14]

(d) Focus on the rehabilitation, operation and maintenance of existing facilities and technical assistance on improved maintenance practices and techniques followed by the planning and construction of waste treatment facilities;

(e) Establish programmes to maximize the source segregation and safe disposal of the hazardous components of municipal solid waste;

(f) Ensure the investment and provision of waste collection facilities with the concomitant provision of water services and with an equal and parallel investment and provision of waste treatment facilities.

---

13 Draft paragraphs 21.35 and 21.36 of A/CONF.151/4 (22 April 1992) were replaced by decision of the Main Committee of UNCED on 10 June 1992. See A/CONF.151/L.3/Add.21 (12 June 1992). The former draft read as follows:

21.35 Safe waste disposal programmes require a total annual investment in developing countries of $15.1 billion, of which $2.7 billion is required exclusively for the safe disposal of solid wastes. If the international community provided one third of this amount, about $3.4 billion annually would be required, of which about $1 billion relates to solid wastes.

21.36 About $5 million annually would be required to strengthen the capacity of international organizations to support these efforts. Half of this amount relates to solid wastes.

14 Draft paragraph 21.37(c) of A/CONF.151/4 (22 April 1992) was replaced by decision of the Main Committee of UNCED on 10 June 1992. See A/CONF.151/L.3/Add.21 (12 June 1992). The former draft read as follows: "(iii) Transfer technologies on industrial waste treatment processes through transnational corporations and bilateral and multilateral technical cooperation programmes."

(c) Human resources development

21.36. Training would be required to improve current waste management practices to include safe collection and waste disposal. The following is an indicative list of actions that should be undertaken by Governments, in collaboration with international agencies:

(a) Providing both formal and in-service training focused on pollution control, waste treatment and disposal technologies, and operating and maintaining of waste-related infrastructure. Intercountry staff exchange programmes should also be established;

(b) Undertaking the requisite training for waste-related pollution monitoring and control enforcement.

(d) Capacity-building

21.37. Institutional reforms and capacity-building will be indispensable if countries are to be able to quantify and mitigate waste-related pollution. Activities to achieve this objective should include:

(a) Creation and strengthening independent environmental control bodies at the national and local levels. International organizations and donors should support needed upgrading of manpower skills and provision of equipment;

(b) Empowering of pollution control agencies with the requisite legal mandate and financial capacities to carry out their duties effectively.

D. Extending waste service coverage

Basis for action

21.38. By the end of the century, over 2.0 billion people will be without access to basic sanitation, and an estimated half of the urban population in developing countries will be without adequate solid waste disposal services. As many as 5.2 million people, including 4 million children under five years of age, die each year from waste-related diseases. The health impacts are particularly severe for the urban poor. The health and environmental impacts of inadequate waste management, however, go beyond the unserved settlements themselves and result in water, land and air contamination and pollution over a wider area. Extending and improving waste collection and safe disposal services are crucial to gaining control over this form of pollution.

Objectives

21.39. The overall objective of this programme is to provide health-protecting, environmentally safe waste collection and disposal services to all people. Governments, according to their capacities and available resources and with the cooperation of the United Nations and other relevant organizations, as appropriate, should:

(a) By the year 2000, have the necessary technical, financial and human resource capacity to provide waste collection services commensurate with needs;[15]

(b) By the year 2025, provide all urban populations with adequate waste services;[16]

(c) By the year 2025, ensure that full urban waste service coverage is maintained and sanitation coverage achieved in all rural areas.[17]

Activities

(a) Management-related activities

21.40. Governments, according to their capacities and available resources and with the cooperation of the United Nations and other relevant organizations, as appropriate, should:

(a) Establish financing mechanisms for waste management service development in deprived areas, including appropriate modes of revenue generation;

(b) Apply the "polluter pays" principle, where appropriate, by setting waste management charges at rates that reflect the costs of providing the service and ensure that those who generate the wastes pay the full cost of disposal in an environmentally safe way;

(c) Encourage institutionalization of communities' participation in planning and implementation procedures for solid waste management.

---

15 The footnote to draft paragraph 21.41(a) and the brackets around the text of paragraph 21.41(a) of A/CONF.151/4 (22 April 1992) were deleted by decision of the Main Committee of UNCED on 10 June 1992. See A/CONF.151/L.3/Add.43 (12 June 1992). The former draft footnote read as follows:

   Target dates mentioned in this document will be reexamined in light of the discussion on finance issues, technology transfer and comparable target setting in other Agenda 21 areas.

16 The footnote to draft paragraph 21.41(b) and the brackets around the text of paragraph 21.41(b) of A/CONF.151/4 (22 April 1992) were deleted by decision of the Main Committee of UNCED on 10 June 1992. See A/CONF.151/L.3/Add.43 (12 June 1992). The former draft footnote read as follows:

   Target dates mentioned in this document will be reexamined in light of the discussion on finance issues, technology transfer and comparable target setting in other Agenda 21 areas.

17 The footnote to draft paragraph 21.41(c) and the brackets around the text of paragraph 21.41(c) of A/CONF.151/4 (22 April 1992) were deleted by decision of the Main Committee of UNCED on 10 June 1992. See A/CONF.151/L.3/Add.43 (12 June 1992). The former draft footnote read as follows:

   Target dates mentioned in this document will be reexamined in light of the discussion on finance issues, technology transfer and comparable target setting in other Agenda 21 areas.

(b) Data and information

21.41. Governments in collaboration with the United Nations and international organizations should undertake the following:

(a) Developing and applying methodologies for waste monitoring;

(b) Data gathering and analysis to establish goals and monitor progress;

(c) Inputting information into a global information system building upon existing systems;

(d) Strengthening the activities of existing information networks in order to disseminate focused information on the application of innovative and low-cost alternatives for waste disposal to targeted audiences.

(c) International and regional cooperation and coordination

21.42. Many United Nations and bilateral programmes exist that seek to provide water supply and sanitation services to the unserved. The Water and Sanitation Collaborative Council, a global forum, currently acts to coordinate development and encourage cooperation. Even so, given the ever-increasing numbers of unserved urban poor populations and the need to address, in addition, the problem of solid waste disposal, additional mechanisms are essential to ensure accelerated coverage of urban waste disposal services. The international community in general and selected United Nations organizations in particular should:

(a) Launch a settlement infrastructure and environment programme following the United Nations Conference on Environment and Development to coordinate the activities of all agencies of the United Nations system involved in this area and include a clearing-house for information dissemination on all waste management issues;

(b) Undertake and systematically report on progress in providing waste services to those without such services;

(c) Review the effectiveness of techniques for and approaches to increasing coverage and identify innovative ways of accelerating the process.

Means of implementation

(a) Financing and cost evaluation

21.43. The Conference secretariat has estimated the average total annual cost (1993-2000) of implementing the activities of this programme to be about $7.5 billion, including about $2.6 billion from the international community on grant or concessional terms. These are indicative and order-of-magnitude estimates only and have not been reviewed by Governments. Actual costs and financial terms, including any that are non-concessional, will depend upon, *inter alia*, the specific strategies and programmes Governments decide upon for implementation.[18]

(b) Scientific and technological means

21.44. Governments and institutions, together with non-governmental organizations, should, in collaboration with appropriate organizations of the United Nations system, launch programmes in different parts of the developing world to extend waste services to the unserved populations. These programmes should, wherever possible, build upon and reorient existing or planned activities.

21.45. Policy changes at the national and local levels could enhance the rate of waste service coverage extension. These changes should include the following:

(a) Giving full recognition to and using the full range of low-cost options for waste management, including, where appropriate, their institutionalization and incorporation within codes of practice and regulation;

(b) Assigning high priority to the extension of waste management services, as necessary and appropriate, to all settlements irrespective of their legal status, giving due emphasis to meeting the waste disposal needs of the unserved, especially the unserved urban poor;

(c) Integrating the provision and maintenance of waste management services with other basic services such as water-supply and storm-water drainage.

21.46. Research activities could be enhanced. Countries, in cooperation with appropriate international organizations and non-governmental organizations, should, for instance:

(a) Find solutions and equipment for managing wastes in areas of concentrated populations and on small islands. In particular, there is a need for appropriate refuse storage and collection systems and cost-effective and hygienic human waste disposal options;

(b) Prepare and disseminate guidelines, case-studies, policy reviews and technical reports on appropriate solutions and modes of service delivery to unserved low-income areas;

---

18   Draft paragraphs 21.45 and 21.46 of A/CONF.151/4 (22 April 1992) was replaced by decision of the Main Committee of UNCED on 10 June 1992. See A/CONF.151/L.3/Add.21 (12 June 1992). The former draft read as follows:

21.45 Extending waste service coverage to unserved populations is relevant mainly to developing countries. A total annual investment for extending waste service coverage in accordance with the schedule indicated in programme objectives is estimated at $7.5 billion of which $1.6 billion pertains to solid waste service expansion. Assuming one third of these costs was financed by the international community, the concessional assistance requirements would be about $2.6 billion, of which $0.6 billion relates to solid wastes services.

21.46 About $8 million annually will be needed to strengthen the capacity of international organizations to support these efforts. Half of this amount relates to solid wastes.

(c) Launch campaigns to encourage active community participation involving women's and youth groups in management of waste, particularly household waste;

(d) Promote intercountry transfer of relevant technologies, especially technologies for high-density settlements.

(c) Human resource development

21.47. International organizations and national and local Governments, in collaboration with non-governmental organizations, should provide focused training on low-cost waste collection and disposal options, particularly techniques for their planning and delivery. Intercountry staff exchange programmes among developing countries could form part of such training. Particular attention should be given to upgrading the status and skills of management-level personnel in waste management agencies.

21.48. Improvements in management techniques are likely to yield the greatest returns in terms of improving waste management service efficiency. The United Nations, international organizations and financial institutions should, in collaboration with national and local Governments, develop and render operational management information systems for municipal record keeping and accounting and for efficiency and effectiveness assessment.

(d) Capacity-building

21.49. Governments, institutions and non-governmental organizations, with the collaboration of appropriate organizations of the United Nations system, should develop capacities to implement programmes to provide waste collection and disposal services to the unserved populations. Some activities under the programmes should include the following:

(a) Establishing a special unit within current institutional arrangements to plan and deliver services to the unserved poor communities, with their involvement and participation;

(b) Making revisions to existing codes and regulations to permit the use of the full range of low-cost alternative technologies for waste disposal;

(c) Building institutional capacity and developing procedures for undertaking service planning and delivery.

Chapter 22

Safe and Environmentally Sound Management of Radioactive Wastes

PROGRAMME AREA

Promoting the safe and environmentally sound management of radioactive wastes

Basis for action

22.1. Radioactive wastes are generated in the nuclear fuel cycle as well as in nuclear applications (the use of radionuclides in medicine, research and industry). The radiological and safety risk from radioactive wastes vary from very low in short-lived, low-level wastes up to very large for high-level wastes. Annually about 200,000 m3 of low-level and intermediate-level waste and 10,000 m3 of high-level waste (as well as spent nuclear fuel destined for final disposal) is generated world wide from the nuclear power production. These volumes are increasing as more nuclear power units are taken into operation, nuclear facilities are decommissioned and the use of radionuclides increases. The high-level waste contains about 99 per cent of the radionuclides and thus represents the largest radiological risks. The waste volumes from nuclear applications are generally much smaller, typically some tens of cubic metres or less per year and country. However, the activity concentration, especially in sealed radiation sources, might be high, thus justifying very stringent radiological protection measures. The growth of waste volumes should continue to be kept under close review.

22.2. The safe and environmentally sound management of the radioactive wastes, including their minimization, transportation and disposal, is important, given their characteristics. In most countries with a substantive nuclear power programme technical and administrative measures have been taken to implement a waste management system. In many other countries, still only in preparation for a national nuclear programme or with only nuclear applications, such systems are still needed.

Objective

22.3. To ensure that radioactive wastes are safely managed, transported, stored and disposed of, with a view to protecting human health and the environment, within a wider framework of an interactive and integrated approach to radioactive waste management and safety.

Activities

(a) Management-related activities

22.4. States, in cooperation with relevant international organizations where appropriate, should:[1]

(a) Promote policies and practical measures to minimize and limit, where appropriate, the generation of radioactive wastes, and to provide for their safe processing, conditioning, transportation and disposal;

(b) Support efforts within IAEA to develop and promulgate radioactive waste safety standards or guidelines and codes of practice as an internationally accepted basis for the safe and environmentally sound management and disposal of radioactive wastes;

(c) Promote safe storage, transportation and disposal of radioactive wastes, as well as spent radiation sources and spent fuel from nuclear reactors, destined for final disposal, in all countries and in particular in developing countries, by facilitating the transfer of relevant technologies to those countries, and/or the return to the supplier of radiation sources after their use, in accordance with relevant international regulations or guidelines;

(d) Promote proper planning, including where appropriate environmental impact assessment, of safe and environmentally sound management of radioactive waste, including emergency procedures, storage, transportation and disposal, prior to and after activities which generate such waste.

(b) International and regional cooperation and coordination

22.5. States, in cooperation with relevant international organizations, where appropriate, should:

(a) Strengthen their efforts to implement the Code of Practice for International Transboundary Movement of Radioactive Waste and, under the auspices of IAEA, in cooperation with relevant international organizations dealing with different modes of transport, keep the question of such movements under active review, including the desirability of concluding a legally binding instrument;

(b) Encourage the London Dumping Convention to expedite work to complete studies on replacing the current voluntary moratorium on disposal of

---

1   This line read "should undertake the following activities" in the draft of para 22.4.

low-level radioactive wastes at sea by a ban, taking into account the precautionary approach, with a view to taking a well informed and timely decision on the issue;

(c) Not promote or allow the storage or disposal of high-level, intermediate-level and low-level radioactive wastes near the marine environment unless they determine that scientific evidence, consistent with the applicable internationally agreed principles and guidelines, shows that such storage or disposal poses no unacceptable risk to people and the marine environment or does not interfere with other legitimate uses of the sea, making, in the process of consideration, appropriate use of the concept of the precautionary approach.[2]

(d) Not export radioactive wastes to countries which individually or through international agreements prohibit the import of such wastes, such as the contracting parties to the Bamako Convention, to the fourth Lomé Convention, or to other relevant conventions, where such prohibition is provided for;

(e) Respect, in accordance with international law, the decisions as far as applicable to them taken by parties to other relevant regional environmental conventions dealing with other aspects of safe and environmentally sound management of radioactive wastes.

Means of implementation

(a) Financial and cost evaluation

22.6. The costs at national level to manage and dispose of radioactive wastes are considerable and will vary, depending on the technology used for disposal.

22.7 The Conference secretariat has estimated the average total annual cost (1993-2000) to international organizations to implement the activities of this programme to be about $8 million. Actual costs and financial terms, including any that are non-concessional, will depend upon, *inter alia*, the specific strategies and programmes Governments decide upon for implementation.[3]

---

2   Draft paragraph 22.5(c) of A/CONF.151/4 (22 April 1992) was replaced by decision of the Main Committee of UNCED on 10 June 1992. See A/CONF.151/L.3/Add.22 (12 June 1992). The former draft read as follows:

> (iii) Not promote or allow the storage or disposal of high-level, intermediate-level and low-level radioactive wastes near [and in] the marine environment unless scientific evidence, consistent with the applicable internationally agreed principles and guidelines, shows that such storage or disposal poses no unacceptable risk to people and the marine environment or does not interfere with other legitimate uses of the sea, making in this process of consideration appropriate use of the concept of precautionary approach;

> This revision was added after the Representative of the Netherlands informed the Committee of her consultations on this subparagraph.

3   Draft paragraph 22.7 was replaced by decision of The Main Committee of UNCED on 13 June 1993. See A/CONF. 151/L.3/Add. 22 (13 June 1993). The prior text read as follows:

> An annual cost of about $ 8 million will be needed to implement this programme through international organizations (mainly IAEA) to further develop international regulations, to promote research

(b) Scientific and technological means:

22.8. States should undertake the following activities in cooperation with international organizations where appropriate:

(a) Promote research and development of methods for the safe and environmentally sound treatment, processing and disposal, including deep geological disposal, of high-level radioactive waste;

(b) Conduct research and assessment programmes concerned with evaluating the health and environmental impact of radioactive waste disposal.

(c) Capacity-building, including human resources development

22.9. States, in cooperation with relevant international organizations should provide, as appropriate, assistance to developing countries to establish and/or strengthen radioactive waste management infrastructures, including legislation, organizations, trained manpower and facilities for the handling, processing, storage and disposal of wastes, generated from nuclear applications.

---

policies and international cooperation and to support developing countries to take preventive and corrective action.

Section 3: Strengthening the Role of Major Groups

Chapter 23

Preamble

23.1. Critical to the effective implementation of the objectives, policies and mechanisms agreed to by Governments in all programme areas of Agenda 21 will be the commitment and genuine involvement of all social groups.

23.2. One of the fundamental prerequisites for the achievement of sustainable development is broad public participation in decision-making. Furthermore, in the more specific context of environment and development, the need for new forms of participation has emerged. This includes the need of individuals, groups and organizations to participate in environmental impact assessment procedures and to know about and participate in decisions, particularly those that potentially affect the communities in which they live and work. Individuals, groups and organizations should have access to information relevant to environment and development held by national authorities, including information on products and activities that have or are likely to have a significant impact on the environment, and information on environmental protection measures.

23.3. Any policies, definitions or rules affecting access to and participation by non-governmental organizations in the work of United Nations institutions or agencies associated with the implementation of Agenda 21 must apply equally to all major groups.

23.4. The programme areas set out below address the means for moving towards real social partnership in support of common efforts to build environmental and economic security.

Chapter 24

Global Action for Women Towards Sustainable and Equitable Development

PROGRAMME AREA

Basis for action

24.1. The international community has endorsed several plans of action and conventions for the full, equal and beneficial integration of women in all development activities, in particular the Nairobi Forward-looking Strategies for the Advancement of Women, which emphasize women's participation in national and international ecosystem management and control of environment degradation. Several conventions, including the Convention on the Elimination of All Forms of Discrimination against Women (General Assembly resolution 34/180, annex) and conventions of the International Labour Organisation (ILO) and the United Nations Educational, Scientific and Cultural Organization (UNESCO) have also been adopted to end gender-based discrimination and ensure women access to land and other resources, education and safe and equal employment. Also relevant are the 1990 World Declaration on the Survival, Protection and Development of Children and its Plan of Action (A/45/625, annex). Effective implementation of these programmes will depend on the active involvement of women in economic and political decision-making and will be critical to the successful implementation of Agenda 21.

Objectives

24.2. The following objectives are proposed for national Governments:

(a) To implement the Nairobi Forward-looking Strategies for the Advancement of Women, particularly with regard to women's participation in national ecosystem management and control of environment degradation;

(b) To increase the proportion of women decision makers, planners, technical advisers, managers and extension workers in environment and development fields;

(c) To consider developing and issuing by the year 2000 a strategy of changes necessary to eliminate constitutional, legal, administrative, cultural, behavioural, social and economic obstacles to women's full participation in sustainable development and in public life;

(d) To establish by the year 1995, mechanisms at the national, regional and international levels to assess the implementation and impact of development and environment policies and programmes on women and ensure their contributions and benefits;

(e) To assess, review, revise and implement, where appropriate, curriculum and other educational material, with a view to promoting the dissemination to both men and women of gender-relevant knowledge and valuation of women's roles through formal and non-formal education, as well as through training institutions, in collaboration with non-governmental organizations;

(f) To formulate and implement clear government policies and national guidelines, strategies and plans for the achievement of equality in all aspects of society, including the promotion of women's literacy, education, training, nutrition, health and their participation in key decision-making positions and in management of the environment, particularly as it pertains to their access to resources, by facilitating better access to all forms of credit, particularly in the informal sector, taking measures towards ensuring women's access to property rights as well as agricultural inputs and implements;

(g) To implement, as a matter of urgency, in accordance with country-specific conditions, measures to ensure that women and men have the same right to decide freely and responsibly the number and spacing of their children and have access to information, education and means, as appropriate, to enable them to exercise this right in keeping with their freedom, dignity and personally held values;

(h) To consider adopting, strengthening and enforcing legislation prohibiting violence against women and take all necessary administrative, social and educational means to eliminate violence against women in all its forms.

Activities

24.3. Governments should take active steps to implement the following:

(a) Measures to review policies and establish plans to increase the proportion of women involved as decision makers, planners, managers, scientists and technical advisers in the design, development and implementation of policies and programmes for sustainable development;

(b) Measures to strengthen and empower women's bureaux, women's non-governmental organizations and women's groups in enhancing capacity-building for sustainable development;

(c) Measures to eliminate female illiteracy and to expand the enrolment of women and girls in educational institutions promoting the goal of universal access to primary and secondary education for girl children and for women, and increased educational and training opportunities for women and girls in sciences and technology, particularly at the post-secondary level;

(d) Programmes to promote the reduction of the heavy workload of women and girl children at home and outside through the establishment of more and affordable nurseries and kindergartens by Governments, local authorities, employers and other relevant organizations and the sharing of household tasks by men and women on an equal basis; environmentally sound technologies which have been designed, developed and improved in consultation with women; accessible and clean water; efficient fuel supply and adequate sanitation facilities;

(e) Programmes to establish and strengthen preventive and curative health facilities, which include women-centred, women-managed, safe and effective reproductive health care and affordable, accessible, responsible planning of family size and services, as appropriate, in keeping with freedom, dignity and personally held values. Programmes should focus on providing comprehensive health care, including pre-natal care, education and information on health and responsible parenthood, and should provide the opportunity for all women to fully breastfeed at least during the first four months post-partum. Programmes should fully support women's productive and reproductive roles and well-being and pay special attention to the need to provide equal and improved health care for all children and to reduce the risk of maternal and child mortality and sickness;

(f) Programmes to support and strengthen equal employment opportunities and equitable remuneration for women in the formal and informal sectors with adequate economic, political and social support systems and services, including child care, particularly day-care facilities and parental leave, and equal access to credit, land and other natural resources;

(g) Programmes to establish rural banking systems with a view to facilitating and increasing rural women's access to credit as well as agricultural inputs and implements;

(h) Programmes to develop consumer awareness and the active participation of women, emphasizing their crucial role in achieving changes necessary to reduce or eliminate unsustainable patterns of consumption and production, particularly in industrialized countries,[1] in order to encourage investment in environmentally sound productive activities and induce environmentally and socially friendly industrial development;

(i) Programmes to eliminate persistent negative images, stereotypes, attitudes and prejudices against women through changes in socialization patterns, the media, advertising, and formal and non-formal education;

(j) Measures to review progress made in these areas and prepare a review and appraisal report which includes recommendations to be submitted to the 1995 world conference on women.

---

1   Draft paragraph 24.3(h) of A/CONF.151/4 (22 April 1992) included brackets around the words "particularly in industrialized countries." The brackets were deleted by decision of the Main Committee of UNCED on 10 June 1992. See A/CONF.151/L.3/Add.24 (12 June 1992).

24.4. Governments are urged to ratify all relevant conventions pertaining to women if they have not already done so. Those that have ratified conventions should enforce and establish legal, constitutional and administrative procedures to transform agreed rights into domestic legislation and adopt measures to implement them in order to strengthen women's legal capacity for full and equal participation in issues and decisions on sustainable development.

24.5. States parties to the Convention on the Elimination of All Forms of Discrimination against Women should review and suggest amendments to it by the year 2000, with a view to strengthening its elements related to environment and development giving special attention to the issue of access and entitlements to natural resources, technology, creative banking facilities and low-cost housing, and the control of pollution and toxicity in the home and workplace. States Parties should also clarify the extent of the Convention's scope with respect to the issues of environment and development and request the Committee on the Elimination of Discrimination against Women to develop guidelines regarding the nature of reporting such issues, required under particular articles of the Convention.

(a) Areas requiring urgent action

24.6. Countries should take urgent measures to avert the ongoing rapid environmental and economic degradation in developing countries that generally affects the lives of women and children in rural areas suffering drought, desertification and deforestation, armed hostilities, (USA) natural disasters, toxic waste and the aftermath of the use of unsuitable agro-chemical products.[2]

24.7. In order to reach these goals, women should be fully involved in decision-making and in the implementation of sustainable development activities.

(b) Research, data collection and information dissemination

24.8. Countries should develop gender-sensitive databases, information systems and participatory action-oriented research and policy analyses with the collaboration of academic institutions and local women researchers on the following:

(a) Women's knowledge and experience of the management and conservation of natural resources for incorporation in the databases and information systems for sustainable development;

(b) The impact of structural adjustment programmes on women. In research done on structural adjustment programmes, special attention should be given to the differential impact on women especially in terms of cut-backs in

---

2   Draft paragraph 24.6 of A/CONF.151/4 (22 April 1992) was revised by decision of the Main Committee of UNCED on 10 June 1992. See A/CONF.151/L.3/Add.24 (12 June 1992). The former draft read as follows:

Countries should take urgent measures to avert the ongoing rapid environmental and economic degradation in developing countries that generally affects the lives of women and children in rural areas suffering drought, desertification and deforestation, [wars,] (USA) natural disasters, toxic waste and the aftermath of the use of unsuitable agro-chemical products.

social services, education and health and in the removal of subsidies on food and fuel;

(c) The impact on women of environmental degradation, particularly drought, desertification, toxic chemicals and armed hostilities;[3]

(d) Analysis of the structural linkages between gender relations, environment and development;

(e) The integration of the value of unpaid work, including work that is currently designated "domestic", in resource accounting mechanisms in order to better represent the true value of women's contribution to the economy, using revised guidelines for the United Nations System of National Accounts, to be issued in 1993;

(f) Measures to develop and include environmental, social and gender impact analyses as an essential step in the development and monitoring of programmes and policies;

(g) Programmes to create rural and urban training, research and resource centres in developing and developed countries that will serve to disseminate environmentally sound technologies to women.

(c) International and regional cooperation and coordination

24.9. The Secretary-General of the United Nations should review the adequacy of all United Nations institutions, including those with a special focus on the role of women in meeting development and environment objectives, and make recommendations for strengthening their capacities. Institutions which require special attention in this area include the Division for the Advancement of Women, the United Nations Development Fund for Women (UNIFEM), the International Research and Training Institute for the Advancement of Women (INSTRAW) and the women's programmes of regional commissions. The review should consider how the environment and development programmes of each United Nations organization could be strengthened to implement Agenda 21 and how to incorporate the role of women in programmes and decisions related to sustainable development.

24.10. Each United Nations organization should review the number of women in senior policy-level and decision-making posts and, where appropriate, adopt programmes to increase that number, in accordance with Economic and Social Council resolution 1991/17 on the improvement of the status of women in the Secretariat and the specialized agencies.

24.11. UNIFEM should establish regular consultations with donors in collaboration with the United Nations Children's Fund (UNICEF), with a view to promoting

---

3   Draft paragraph 24.8(c) of A/CONF.151/4 (22 April 1992) was replaced by decision of the Main Committee of UNCED on 10 June 1992. See A/CONF.151/L.3/Add.24 (12 June 1992). The former draft read as follows:

The impact on women of environmental degradation, particularly drought, desertification, toxic chemicals and [wars,];[.]

operational programmes and projects on sustainable development that will strengthen the participation of women, especially low-income women, in sustainable development and in decision-making. UNDP should establish a women's focal point on development and environment in each of its resident representative offices, to provide information and promote exchange of experience and information in these fields. United Nations organizations, Governments and non-governmental organizations involved in the follow-up to the United Nations Conference on Environment and Development and the implementation of Agenda 21 should ensure that gender considerations are fully integrated into all the policies, programmes and activities.

Means of implementation

Financing and cost evaluation

24.12. The Conference secretariat has estimated the average total annual cost (1993-2000) of implementing the activities of this programme to be about $40 million from the international community on grant or concessional terms. These are indicative and order of magnitude estimates only and have not been reviewed by Governments. Actual costs and financial terms, including any that are non-concessional, will depend upon, *inter alia*, the specific strategies and programmes Governments decide upon for implementation.[4]

---

4   Draft paragraphs 24.12 and 24.13 of A/CONF.151/4 (22 April 1992) were replaced by decision of the Main Committee of UNCED on 10 June 1992. See A/CONF.151/L.3/Add.24 (12 June 1992). The former draft read as follows:

24.12 Finance and cost evaluation

Studies suggest that the actual budgeting process in some countries results in underfunding of activities related to the participation of women in sustainable development. The following action would be necessary:

(a) At the national and international levels, financial policies and programme budgets of Governments, international organizations and aid agencies should be re-oriented and executed to ensure adequate funding for greater gender equity on an annual basis during the period 1993-2000;

(b) There will be a need for allocation of adequate funds by each country to conduct national reviews and prepare reports for the 1995 world conference on women. An average cost of $30,000 is estimated at the national level;

(c) Establishing gender-sensitive national databases and information and research activities would require $250,000 a year for two years on the average for each country, and $10,000 a year thereafter as expenditure for maintenance;

(d) Funding for the United Nations Development Fund for Women (UNIFEM) could be increased by about $10 million to give it enhanced capacity to manage technical cooperation activities. As part of an overall increase in funding for projects targeting issues related to women in sustainable development a strengthened UNIFEM would be able to manage projects in excess of $100 million annually by the year 2000.

24.13 The Secretary-General's review and production of a report will require additional staffing in the United Nations system for a period of at least two years at a cost not to exceed $2 million.

Chapter 25

Children and Youth in Sustainable Development

INTRODUCTION

25.1. Youth comprise nearly 30 per cent of the world's population. The involvement of today's youth in environment and development decision-making and in the implementation of programmes is critical to the long-term success of Agenda 21.

PROGRAMME AREAS

A. Advancing the Role of Youth and Actively Involving Them in the Protection of the Environment and the Promotion of Economic and Social Development

Basis for action

25.2. It is imperative that youth from all parts of the world participate actively in all relevant levels of decision-making processes because it affects their lives today and has implications for their futures. In addition to their intellectual contribution and their ability to mobilize support, they bring unique perspectives that need to be taken into account.

25.3. Numerous actions and recommendations within the international community have been proposed to ensure that youth are provided a secure and healthy future, including an environment of quality, improved standards of living and access to education and employment. These issues need to be addressed in development planning.

Objectives

25.4. Each country should, in consultation with its youth communities, establish a process to promote dialogue between the youth community and Government at all levels and to establish mechanisms that permit youth access to information and provide them with the opportunity to present their perspectives on government decisions, including the implementation of Agenda 21.

25.5. Each country, by the year 2000, should ensure that more than 50/per/cent of its youth, gender balanced, are enrolled in or have access to appropriate secondary education or equivalent educational or vocational training programmes by increasing participation and access rates on an annual basis.

25.6. Each country should undertake initiatives aimed at reducing current levels of youth unemployment, particularly where they are disproportionately high in comparison to the overall unemployment rate.

25.7. Each country and the United Nations should support the promotion and creation of mechanisms to involve youth representation in all United Nations processes in order to influence those processes.

25.8. Each country should combat human rights abuses against young people, particularly young women and girls, and should consider providing all youth with legal protection, skills, opportunities and the support necessary for them to fulfil their personal, economic and social aspirations and potentials.

Activities

25.9. National Governments, according to their strategies, should take measures to:

(a) Establish procedures allowing for consultation and possible participation of youth of both genders, by 1993, in decision-making processes, with regard to the environment, involving youth at the local, national and regional levels;

(b) Promote dialogue with youth organizations regarding the drafting and evaluation of environment plans and programmes or questions on development;

(c) Consider for incorporation into relevant policies the recommendations of international, regional and local youth conferences and other forums that offer youth perspectives on social and economic development and resource management;

(d) Ensure access for all youth to all types of education and, wherever appropriate, providing alternative learning structures; ensure that education reflects the economic and social needs of youth and incorporates the concepts of environmental awareness and sustainable development throughout the curricula; expand vocational training, implementing innovative methods aimed at increasing practical skills, such as environmental scouting;

(e) In cooperation with relevant ministries and organizations, including representatives of youth, develop and implement strategies for creating alternative employment opportunities and provide required training to young men and women;

(f) Establish task forces that include youth and youth non-governmental organizations to develop education and awareness programmes specifically targeted to the youth population on critical issues pertaining to youth. These task forces should use formal and non-formal educational methods to reach a maximum audience. National and local media, non-governmental organizations, businesses and other organizations should assist in these task forces;

(g) Give support to programmes, projects, networks, national organizations and youth non-governmental organizations to examine the integration of programmes in relation to their project requirements, encouraging the involvement of youth in project identification, design, implementation and follow-up;

(h) Include youth representatives in their delegations to international meetings, in accordance with the relevant General Assembly resolutions adopted in 1968, 1977, 1985 and 1989.

25.10. The United Nations and international organizations with youth programmes, should take measures to:

(a) Review their youth programmes and consider how coordination between them can be enhanced;

(b) Improve the dissemination of relevant information to Governments, youth organizations and other non-governmental organizations on current youth positions and activities; monitor and evaluate the application of Agenda 21;

(c) Promote the United Nations Trust Fund for the International Youth Year and collaborate with youth representatives in the administration of it, focusing particularly on the needs of youth from developing countries.

Means of implementation

Financing and cost evaluation

25.11. The Conference secretariat has estimated the average total annual cost (1993-2000) of implementing the activities of this programme to be about $1.5 million from the international community on grant or concessional terms. These are indicative and order of magnitude estimates only and have not been reviewed by Governments. Actual costs and financial terms, including any that are non-concessional, will depend upon, *inter alia*, the specific strategies and programmes Governments decide upon for implementation.[1]

---

1   Draft paragraph 25.11 of A/CONF.151/4 (22 April 1992) was replaced by decision of the Main Committee of UNCED on 10 June 1992. See A/CONF.151/L.3/Add.25 (12 June 1992). The former draft read as follows:

       Financing requirements for most of the activities are included in estimates for other programmes. Annual funding of about $1.5 million will be needed for youth-related activities in the United Nations.

B. Children in Sustainable Development

Basis for action

25.12. Children not only will inherit the responsibility of looking after the Earth, but in many developing countries they comprise nearly half the population. Furthermore, children in both developing and industrialized countries are highly vulnerable to the effects of environmental degradation. They are also highly aware supporters of environmental thinking. The specific interests of children need to be taken fully into account in the participatory process on environment and development in order to safeguard the future sustainability of any actions taken to improve the environment.

Objectives

25.13. National Governments, according to their policies, should take measures to:

(a) Ensure the survival, protection and development of children, in accordance with the goals endorsed by the 1990 World Summit for Children (A145/625, annex);

(b) Ensure that the interests of children are taken fully into account in the participatory process for sustainable development and environmental improvement.

Activities

25.14. Governments should take active steps to:

(a) Implement programmes for children designed to reach the child-related goals of the 1990s in the areas of environment and development, especially health, nutrition, education, literacy, and poverty alleviation;

(b) Ratify the Convention on the Rights of the Child (General Assembly Resolution 45/25 of 20 November 1989, annex), at the earliest moment and implement it by addressing the basic needs of youth and children;

(c) Promote primary environmental care activities that address the basic needs of communities, improve the environment for children at the household and community level and encourage the participation and empowerment of local populations, including women, youth, children and indigenous people, towards the objective of integrated community management of resources, especially in developing countries;

(d) Expand educational opportunities for children and youth, including education for environmental and developmental responsibility, with overriding attention to the education of the girl child;

(e) Mobilize communities through schools and local health centres so that children and their parents become effective focal points for sensitization of communities to environmental issues;

(f) Establish procedures to incorporate children's concerns into all relevant policies and strategies for environment and development at the local, regional and national levels, including those concerning allocation of and entitlement to natural resources, housing and recreation needs, and control of pollution and toxicity in both rural and urban areas.

25.15. International and regional organizations should cooperate and coordinate in the proposed areas. UNICEF [The United Nations Children's Fund] should maintain cooperation and collaboration with other organizations of the United Nations, Governments and non-governmental organizations to develop programmes for children and programmes to mobilize children in the activities outlined above.

Means of implementation

(a) Financing and cost evaluation

25.16. Financing requirements for most of the activities are included in estimates for other programmes.[2]

(b) Human resources development and capacity-building

25.17. The activities should facilitate capacity-building and training activities already contained in other chapters of Agenda 21.[3]

---

2   Draft paragraph 25.16 of A/CONF.151/4 (22 April 1992) included brackets around the entire text of 25.16. The brackets were deleted by decision of the Main Committee of UNCED on 10 June 1992. See A/CONF.151/L.3/Add.25 (12 June 1992).

3   Draft paragraph 25.17 of A/CONF.151/4 (22 April 1992) included brackets around the entire text of 25.17. The brackets were deleted by decision of the Main Committee of UNCED on 10 June 1992. See A/CONF.151/L.3/Add.25 (12 June 1992).

Chapter 26

Recognizing and Strengthening the Role of Indigenous People and Their Communities

PROGRAMME AREA

Basis for action

26.1. Indigenous people and their communities have an historical relationship with their lands and are generally descendants of the original inhabitants of such lands. In the context of this chapter the term "lands" is understood to include the environment of the areas which the people concerned traditionally occupy. Indigenous people and their communities represent a significant percentage of the global population. They have developed over many generations a holistic traditional scientific knowledge of their lands, natural resources and environment. Indigenous people and their communities shall enjoy the full measure of human rights and fundamental freedoms without hindrance or discrimination. Their ability to participate fully in sustainable development practices on their lands has tended to be limited as a result of factors of an economic, social and historical nature. In view of the interrelationship between the natural environment and its sustainable development and the cultural, social, economic and physical well-being of indigenous people, national and international efforts to implement environmentally sound and sustainable development should recognize, accommodate, promote and strengthen the role of indigenous people and their communities.

26.2. Some of the goals inherent in the objectives and activities of this programme area are already contained in such international legal instruments as the Indigenous and Tribal Peoples Convention (No. 169) of the International Labour Organisation (ILO) and are being incorporated into the draft universal declaration on indigenous rights, being prepared by the United Nations working group on indigenous populations. The International Year for the World's Indigenous People (1993) presents a timely opportunity to mobilize further international technical and financial cooperation.

Objectives

26.3. In full partnership with indigenous people and their communities, Governments and, where appropriate, intergovernmental organizations should aim at fulfilling the following objectives:

(a) Establishment of a process to empower indigenous people and their communities through measures that include:

(i) Adoption or strengthening of appropriate policies and/or legal instruments at the national level;

(ii) Recognition that the lands of indigenous people and their communities should be protected from activities that are environmentally unsound or that the indigenous people concerned consider to be socially and culturally inappropriate;

(iii) Recognition of their values, traditional knowledge and resource management practices with a view to promoting environmentally sound and sustainable development;

(iv) Recognition that traditional and direct dependence on renewable resources and ecosystems, including sustainable harvesting, continues to be essential to the cultural, economic and physical well-being of indigenous people and their communities;

(v) Development and strengthening of national dispute-resolution arrangements in relation to settlement of land and resource-management concerns;

(vi) Support for alternative environmentally sound means of production to ensure a range of choices on how to improve their quality of life so that they effectively participate in sustainable development;

(vii) Enhancement of capacity-building for indigenous communities, based on the adaptation and exchange of traditional experience, knowledge and resource-management practices, to ensure their sustainable development;

(b) Establishment, where appropriate, of arrangements to strengthen the active participation of indigenous people and their communities in the national formulation of policies, laws and programmes relating to resource management and other development processes that may affect them, and their initiation of proposals for such policies and programmes;

(c) Involvement of indigenous people and their communities at the national and local levels in resource management and conservation strategies and other relevant programmes established to support and review sustainable development strategies, such as those suggested in other programme areas of Agenda 21.

Activities

26.4. Some indigenous people and their communities may require, in accordance with national legislation, greater control over their lands, self-management of their resources, participation in development decisions affecting them, including, where appropriate, participation in the establishment or management of protected areas. The following are some of the specific measures which Governments could take:

(a) Consider the ratification and application of existing international conventions relevant to indigenous people and their communities (where not yet done), and provide support for the adoption by the General Assembly of a declaration on indigenous rights;

(b) Adopt or strengthen appropriate policies and/or legal instruments that will protect indigenous intellectual and cultural property and the right to preserve customary and administrative systems and practices.

26.5. United Nations organizations and other international development and finance organizations and Governments should, drawing on the active participation of indigenous people and their communities, as appropriate, take the following measures, *inter alia*, to incorporate their values, views and knowledge, including the unique contribution of indigenous women, in resource management and other policies and programmes that may affect them:

(a) Appoint a special "focal point" within each international agency, and organise annual interagency coordination meetings in consultation with Governments and indigenous organisations, as appropriate, and develop a procedure within and between operational agencies for assisting Governments in ensuring the coherent and coordinated incorporation of the views of indigenous people in the design and implementation of policies and programmes. Under this procedure, indigenous people and their communities should be informed, consulted and allowed to participate in national decision-making, in particular regarding regional and international cooperative efforts. In addition, these policies and programmes should take fully into account strategies based on local indigenous initiatives;

(b) Provide technical and financial assistance for capacity-building programmes to support the sustainable self-development of indigenous people and their communities;

(c) Strengthen research and education programmes aimed at:

(i) Achieving a better understanding of indigenous people's knowledge and management experience related to the environment, and applying this to contemporary development challenges;

(ii) Increasing the efficiency of indigenous people's resource management systems, for example, by promoting the adaptation and dissemination of suitable technological innovations;

(d) Contribute to the endeavours of indigenous people and their communities in resource management and conservation strategies (such as those that may be developed under appropriate projects funded through the Global Environmental Facility and Tropical Forestry Action Plan) and other programme areas of Agenda 21, including programmes to collect, analyse and use data and other information in support of sustainable development projects.

26.6. Governments, in full partnership with indigenous people and their communities should, where appropriate:

(a) Develop or strengthen national arrangements to consult with indigenous people and their communities with a view to reflecting their needs and incorporating their values and traditional and other knowledge and practices in national policies and programmes in the field of natural resource management and conservation and other development programmes affecting them;

(b) Cooperate at the regional level, where appropriate, to address common indigenous issues with a view to recognizing and strengthening their participation in sustainable development.

Means of Implementation

(a) Financing and cost evaluation

26.7. The Conference secretariat has estimated the average total annual cost (1993-2000) of implementing the activities of this programme to be about $3 million from the international community on grant or concessional terms. These are indicative and order of magnitude estimates only and have not been reviewed by Governments. Actual costs and financial terms, including any that are non-concessional, will depend upon, *inter alia*, the specific strategies and programmes Governments decide upon for implementation.[1]

(b) Legal and administrative frameworks

26.8. Governments should incorporate, in collaboration with the indigenous people affected, the rights and responsibilities of indigenous people and their

---

1   Draft paragraph 26.7 of A/CONF.151/4 (22 April 1992) was replaced by decision of the Main Committee of UNCED on 10 June 1992. See A/CONF.151/L.3/Add.26 (12 June 1992). The former draft read as follows:

   To implement the above activities, the United Nations system will require about $3 million annually for institutional strengthening.

communities in the legislation of each country, suitable to the country's specific situation. Developing countries may require technical assistance to implement these activities.[2]

(c) Human resource development

26.9. International development agencies and Governments should commit financial and other resources to education and training for indigenous people and their communities to develop their capacities to achieve their sustainable self-development, and to contribute to and participate in sustainable and equitable development at the national level. Particular attention should be given to strengthening the role of indigenous women.[3]

---

2   At The Main Committee of UNCED the Representative of the Netherlands informed The Committee that as a result of consultations paragraphs 26.8 and 26.9 would be amended to read as stated above. See A/CONF. 151/L.3/Add. 26 (12 June 1992). The prior text to 26.8 read as follows:

> 26.8.National Governments should incorporate, in collaboration with the indigenous people affected, the rights and responsibilities of indigenous people and their communities in national legal frameworks, including recognition of the need to protect their lands from unsustainable and inequitable development, and secure their access to and control over both their lands and natural resources. Developing countries may require technical assistance to implement these activities, such as in the demarcation of lands.

3   Draft paragraph 26.9 of A/CONF.151/4 (22 April 1992) was replaced by decision of the Main Committee of UNCED on 10 June 1992. See A/CONF.151/L.3/Add.26 (12 June 1992). The former draft read as follows:

> International development agencies and national Governments should commit additional resources to education and training for indigenous people and their communities to develop their capacities to achieve their sustainable self-development, contribute to and participate in sustainable and equitable development at the national level. Particular attention should be given to strengthening the role of indigenous women.

Chapter 27

Strengthening the Role of Non-Governmental Organizations: Partners for Sustainable Development

PROGRAMME AREA

Basis for action

27.1. Non-governmental organizations play a vital role in the shaping and implementation of participatory democracy. Their credibility lies in the responsible and constructive role they play in society. Formal and informal organizations, as well as grass-roots movements, should be recognized as partners in the implementation of Agenda 21. The nature of the independent role played by non-governmental organizations within a society calls for real participation; therefore, independence is a major attribute of non-governmental organizations and is the precondition of real participation.

27.2. One of the major challenges facing the world community as it seeks to replace unsustainable development patterns with environmentally sound and sustainable development is the need to activate a sense of common purpose on behalf of all sectors of society. The chances of forging such a sense of purpose will depend on the willingness of all sectors to participate in genuine social partnership and dialogue, while recognizing the independent roles, responsibilities and special capacities of each.

27.3. Non-governmental organizations, including those non-profit organizations representing groups addressed in the present section of Agenda 21, possess well-established and diverse experience, expertise and capacity in fields which will be of particular importance to the implementation and review of environmentally sound and socially responsible sustainable development, as envisaged throughout Agenda 21. The community of non-governmental organizations, therefore offers a global network which should be tapped, enabled and strengthened in support of efforts to achieve these common goals.

27.4. To ensure that the full potential contribution of non-governmental organizations is realized, the fullest possible communication and cooperation between international organizations, national and local governments and non-governmental organizations should be promoted in institutions mandated, and programmes designed to carry out Agenda 21. Non-governmental organizations will also need to foster cooperation and communication among themselves to reinforce their effectiveness as actors in the implementation of sustainable development.

Objectives

27.5. Society, Governments and international bodies should develop mechanisms to allow non-governmental organizations to play their partnership role responsibly and effectively in the process of environmentally sound and sustainable development.

27.6. With a view to strengthening the role of non-governmental organizations as social partners, the United Nations system and Governments should initiate a process, in consultation with non-governmental organizations, to review formal procedures and mechanisms for the involvement of these organizations at all levels from policy-making and decision-making to implementation.

27.7. By 1995, a mutually productive dialogue should be established at the national level between all Governments and non-governmental organizations and their self-organized networks to recognize and strengthen their respective roles in implementing environmentally sound and sustainable development.

27.8. Governments and international bodies should promote and allow the participation of non-governmental organizations in the conception, establishment and evaluation of official mechanisms and formal procedures designed to review the implementation of Agenda 21 at all levels.

Activities

27.9. The United Nations system, including international finance and development agencies, and all intergovernmental organizations and forums should, in consultation with non-governmental organizations, take measures to:

(a) Review and report on ways of enhancing existing procedures and mechanisms by which non-governmental organizations contribute to policy design, decision-making, implementation and evaluation at the individual agency level, in inter-agency discussions and in United Nations conferences;

(b) On the basis of subparagraph (a) above, enhance existing or, where they do not exist, establish, mechanisms and procedures within each agency to draw on the expertise and views of non-governmental organizations in policy and programme design, implementation and evaluation;

(c) Review levels of financial and administrative support for non-governmental organizations and the extent and effectiveness of their involvement in project and programme implementation, with a view to augmenting their role as social partners;

(d) Design open and effective means of achieving the participation of non-governmental organizations in the processes established to review and evaluate the implementation of Agenda 21 at all levels;

(e) Promote and allow non-governmental organizations and their self-organized networks to contribute to the review and evaluation of policies and programmes designed to implement Agenda 21, including support for developing country non-governmental organizations and their self-organized networks;

(f) Take into account the findings of non-governmental review systems and evaluation processes in relevant reports of the United Nations Secretary-General to the General Assembly, and of all pertinent United Nations organizations and other intergovernmental organizations and forums concerning implementation of Agenda 21, in accordance with the review process for Agenda 21;

(g) Provide access for non-governmental organizations to accurate and timely data and information to promote the effectiveness of their programmes and activities and their roles in support of sustainable development.

27.10. Governments should take measures to:

(a) Establish or enhance an existing dialogue with non-governmental organizations and their self-organized networks representing various sectors, which could serve to: (i) consider the rights and responsibilities of these organizations; (ii) efficiently channel integrated non-governmental inputs to the governmental policy development process; and (iii) facilitate non-governmental coordination in implementing national policies at the programme level;

(b) Encourage and enable partnership and dialogue between local non-governmental organizations and local authorities in activities aimed at sustainable development;

(c) Involve non-governmental organizations in national mechanisms or procedures established to carry out Agenda 21, making the best use of their particular capacities, especially in the fields of education, poverty alleviation and environmental protection and rehabilitation;

(d) Take into account the findings of non-governmental monitoring and review mechanisms in the design and evaluation of policies concerning the implementation of Agenda 21 at all levels;

(e) Review government education systems to identify ways to include and expand the involvement of non-governmental organizations in the field of formal and informal education and of public awareness;

(f) Make available and accessible to non-governmental organizations the data and information necessary for their effective contribution to research and to the design, implementation and evaluation of programmes.

Means of implementation

(a) Financing and cost evaluation

27.11. Depending on the outcome of review processes and the evolution of views as to how best to build partnership and dialogue between official organizations and groups of non-governmental organizations, relatively limited, but unpredictable, costs will be involved at the international and national levels in enhancing consultative procedure and mechanisms. Non-governmental organizations will also require additional funding in support of their establishment of, improvement of or contributions to Agenda 21 monitoring systems. These costs will be significant but cannot be reliably estimated on the basis of existing information.

(b) Capacity-building

27.12. The organizations of the United Nations system and other intergovernmental organizations and forums, bilateral programmes and the private sector, as appropriate, will need to provide increased financial and administrative support for non-governmental organizations and their self-organized networks, in particular those based in developing countries, contributing to the monitoring and evaluation of Agenda 21 programmes, and provide training for non-governmental organizations (and assist them to develop their own training programmes) at the international and regional levels to enhance their partnership role in programme design and implementation.[1]

27.13 Governments will need to promulgate or strengthen, subject to country specific conditions, any legislative measures necessary to enable the establishment by non-governmental organizations of consultative groups, and to ensure the right of non-governmental organizations to protect the public interest through legal action.[2]

---

1   Draft paragraph 27.12 of A/CONF.151/4 (22 April 1992) was replaced by decision of the Main Committee of UNCED on 10 June 1992. See A/CONF.151/L.3/Add.27 (12 June 1992). The former draft read as follows:

   The organizations of the United Nations system and other intergovernmental organizations and forums will need to provide increased financial and administrative support for non-governmental organizations and their self-organized networks contributing to the monitoring and evaluation of Agenda 21 programmes, and provide training for non-governmental organizations (and assist them to develop their own training programmes) at the international and regional levels to enhance their partnership role in programme design and implementation.

2   Draft paragraph 27.13 of A/CONF.151/4 (22 April 1992) was replaced by decision of the Main Committee of UNCED on 10 June 1992. See A/CONF.151/L.3/Add.27 (12 June 1992). The former draft read as follows:

   Governments will need to promulgate any legislative measures necessary to enable the establishment by non-governmental organizations of consultative groups, and to ensure [the right of non-governmental organizations to protect the public interest through legal action] or [access by non-governmental organizations with a recognized legal interest to judicial and administrative procedures].

Chapter 28

Local Authorities Initiatives in Support of Agenda 21

PROGRAMME AREA

Basis for action

28.1. Because so many of the problems and solutions being addressed by Agenda 21 have their roots in local activities, the participation and cooperation of local authorities will be a determining factor in fulfilling its objectives. Local authorities construct, operate and maintain economic, social and environmental infrastructure, oversee planning processes, establish local environmental policies and regulations, and assist in implementing national and subnational environmental policies. As the level of governance closest to the people, they play a vital role in educating, mobilizing and responding to the public to promote sustainable development.

Objectives

28.2. The following objectives are proposed for this programme area:

(a) By 1996, most local authorities in each country should have undertaken a consultative process with their populations and achieved a consensus on "a local Agenda 21" for the community;

(b) By 1993, the international community should have initiated a consultative process aimed at increasing cooperation between local authorities;

(c) By 1994, representatives of associations of cities and other local authorities should have increased levels of cooperation and coordination with the goal of enhancing the exchange of information and experience among local authorities;

(d) All local authorities in each country should be encouraged to implement and monitor programmes which aim at ensuring that women and youth are represented in decision-making, planning and implementation processes.

Activities

28.3. Each local authority should enter into a dialogue with its citizens, local organizations and private enterprises and adopt "a local Agenda 21". Through consultation and consensus-building, local authorities would learn from citizens and from local, civic, community, business and industrial organizations and acquire the information needed for formulating the best strategies. The process of consultation would increase household awareness of sustainable development issues. Local authority programmes, policies, laws and regulations to achieve Agenda 21 objectives would be assessed and modified, based on local programmes adopted. Strategies could also be used in supporting proposals for local, national, regional and international funding.

28.4. Partnerships should be fostered among relevant organs and organizations such as UNDP [U.N. Development Programme], the United Nations Centre for Human Settlements (Habitat) and the United Nations Environment Programme (UNEP), the World Bank, regional banks, the International Union of Local Authorities, the World Association of the Major Metropolises, Summit of Great Cities of the World, the United Towns Organization and other relevant partners, with a view to mobilizing increased international support for local authority programmes. An important goal would be to support, extend and improve existing institutions working in the field of local authority capacity-building and local environment management. For this purpose:

(a) Habitat and other relevant organs and organizations of the United Nations system are called upon to strengthen services in collecting information on strategies of local authorities, in particular for those that need international support;

(b) Periodic consultations involving both international partners and developing countries could review strategies and consider how such international support could best be mobilized. Such a sectoral consultation would complement concurrent country-focused consultations, such as those taking place in consultative groups and round tables.

28.5. Representatives of associations of local authorities are encouraged to establish processes to increase the exchange of information, experience and mutual technical assistance among local authorities.

Means of implementation

(a) Financing and cost evaluation

28.6. It is recommended that all parties reassess funding needs in this area. The Conference secretariat has estimated the average total annual cost (1993-2000) for strengthening international secretariat services for implementing the activities in this chapter to be about $1 million on grant or concessional terms. These are indicative and order of magnitude estimates only and have not been reviewed by Governments.[1]

(b) Human resource development and capacity-building

28.7. This programme should facilitate the capacity-building and training activities already contained in other chapters of Agenda 21.[2]

---

1   Draft paragraph 28.6 of A/CONF.151/4 (22 April 1992) was replaced by decision of the Main Committee of UNCED on 10 June 1992. See A/CONF.151/L.3/Add.28 (12 June 1992). The former draft read as follows:

    Financing for the first activity would be at the local level. In general, donors have not given high priority to funding for urban local authorities and the institutions that these local authorities have themselves established to provide them with training and support. International funding will play a catalytic role and be especially helpful in training, institution-building and in introducing new approaches to solving problems related to urban development and environment. In view of the projected increase in urban population and the increased proportion of income expected to be generated in urban communities, priority for funding urban programmes should be reassessed. Rather than estimate costs under this programme area the costs have been estimated in other parts of Agenda 21. UNDP and Habitat will need to be strengthened to provide secretariat services for the funding and information exchange functions. These costs are estimated at $1 million annually.

2   Draft paragraph 28.7 of A/CONF.151/4 (22 April 1992) included brackets around the entire text of paragraph 28.7. The brackets were deleted by decision of the Main Committee of UNCED on 10 June 1992. See A/CONF.151/L.3/Add.28 (12 June 1992).

Chapter 29

Strengthening the Role of Workers and Their Trade Unions

PROGRAMME AREA

Basis for action

29.1. Efforts to implement sustainable development will involve adjustments and opportunities at the national and enterprise levels, with workers foremost among those concerned. As their representatives, trade unions are vital actors in facilitating the achievement of sustainable development in view of their experience in addressing industrial change, the extremely high priority they give to protection of the working environment and the related natural environment, and their promotion of socially responsible and economic development. The existing network of collaboration among trade unions and their extensive membership provide important channels through which the concepts and practices of sustainable development can be supported. The established principles of tripartism provide a basis for strengthened collaboration between workers and their representatives, Governments and employers in the implementation of sustainable development.

Objectives

29.2. The overall objective is poverty alleviation and full and sustainable employment, which contribute to safe, clean and healthy environments—the working environment, the community and the physical environment. Workers should be full participants in the implementation and evaluation of activities related to Agenda 21.

29.3. To that end the following objectives are proposed for accomplishment by the year 2000:

(a) To promote ratification of relevant conventions of ILO [International Labour Organisation] and the enactment of legislation in support of those conventions;

(b) To establish bipartite and tripartite mechanisms on safety, health and sustainable development;

(c) To increase the number of environmental collective agreements aimed at achieving sustainable development;

(d) To reduce occupational accidents, injuries and diseases according to recognized statistical reporting procedures;

(e) To increase the provision of workers' education, training and retraining, particularly in the area of occupational health and safety and environment.

Activities

(a) Promoting freedom of association

29.4. For workers and their trade unions to play a full and informed role in support of sustainable development, Governments and employers should promote the rights of individual workers to freedom of association and the protection of the right to organize as laid down in ILO conventions. Governments should consider ratifying and implementing those conventions, if they have not already done so.

(b) Strengthening participation and consultation

29.5. Governments, business and industry should promote the active participation of workers and their trade unions in decisions on the design, implementation and evaluation of national and international policies and programmes on environment and development, including employment policies, industrial strategies, labour adjustment programmes and technology transfers.

29.6. Trade unions, employers and Governments should cooperate to ensure that the concept of sustainable development is equitably implemented.

29.7. Joint (employer/worker) or tripartite (employer/worker/Government) collaborative mechanisms at the workplace, community and national levels should be established to deal with safety, health and environment, including special reference to the rights and status of women in the workplace.

29.8. Governments and employers should ensure that workers and their representatives are provided with all relevant information to enable effective participation in these decision-making processes.

29.9. Trade unions should continue to define, develop and promote policies on all aspects of sustainable development.

29.10. Trade unions and employers should establish the framework for a joint environmental policy, and set priorities to improve the working environment and the overall environmental performance of enterprise.

29.11. Trade unions should:

(a) Seek to ensure that workers are able to participate in environmental audits at the workplace and in environmental impact assessments;

(b) Participate in environment and development activities within the local community and promote joint action on potential problems of common concern;

(c) Play an active role in the sustainable development activities of international and regional organizations, particularly within the United Nations system.

(c) Provide adequate training

29.12. Workers and their representatives should have access to adequate training to augment environmental awareness, ensure their safety and health, and improve their economic and social welfare. Such training should ensure that the necessary skills are available to promote sustainable livelihoods and improve the working environment. Trade unions, employers, Governments and international agencies should cooperate in assessing training needs within their respective spheres of activity. Workers and their representatives should be involved in the design and implementation of worker training programmes conducted by employers and Governments.

Means of implementation

(a) Financing and cost evaluation

29.13. The Conference secretariat has estimated the average total annual cost (1993-2000) of implementing the activities of this programme to be about $300 million from the international community on grant or concessional terms. These are indicative and order-of-magnitude estimates only and have not been reviewed by Governments. Actual costs and financial terms, including any that are non-concessional, will depend upon, *inter alia*, the specific strategies and programmes Governments decide upon for implementation.[1]

---

1   Draft paragraphs 29.13 and 29.14 of A/CONF.151/4 (22 April 1992) were replaced by decision of the Main Committee of UNCED on 10 June 1992. See A/CONF.151/L.3/Add.29 (12 June 1992). The former draft read as follows:

    29.13. Given the need to catalyse and support expanded activities in developing countries in support of freedom of association, expanded trade union participation, improvements in the working environment, and increased environment and development training for workers, approximately $300 million per year in international financing (at $3 million per country) will be required as an initial step. For the ILO to play an extended role in supporting these activities, additional resources of approximately $4.0 million per year will be required.

    29.14. It should be emphasized that these "costs" would in all likelihood lead to even more significant financial benefits.

(b) Capacity-building

29.14. Particular attention should be given to strengthening the capacity of each of the tripartite social partners (Governments and employers' and workers' organizations) to facilitate greater collaboration towards sustainable development.[2]

---

2   Draft paragraph 29.15 of A/CONF.151/4 (22 April 1992) included brackets around the entire text of paragraph 29.15. The brackets were deleted by decision of the Main Committee of UNCED on 10 June 1992. See A/CONF.151/L.3/Add.29 (12 June 1992).

Chapter 30

Strengthening the Role of Business and Industry

INTRODUCTION

30.1. Business and industry, including transnational corporations, play a crucial role in the social and economic development of a country. A stable policy regime enables and encourages business and industry to operate responsibly and efficiently and to implement longer-term policies. Increasing prosperity, a major goal of the development process, is contributed primarily by the activities of business and industry. Business enterprises, large and small, formal and informal, provide major trading, employment and livelihood opportunities. Business opportunities available to women are contributing towards their professional development, strengthening their economic role and transforming social systems. Business and industry, including transnational corporations, and their representative organizations, should be full participants in the implementation and evaluation of activities related to Agenda 21.

30.2. Through more efficient production processes, preventive strategies, cleaner production technologies and procedures throughout the product life cycle, hence minimizing or avoiding wastes, the policies and operations of business and industry, including transnational corporations, can play a major role in reducing impacts on resource use and the environment. Technological innovations, development, applications, transfer and the more comprehensive aspects of partnership and cooperation are to a very large extent within the province of business and industry.

30.3. Business and industry, including transnational corporations, should recognize environmental management as among the highest corporate priorities and as a key determinant to sustainable development. Some enlightened leaders of enterprises are already implementing "responsible care" and product stewardship policies and programmes, fostering openness and dialogue with employees and the public and carrying out environmental audits and assessments of compliance. These leaders in business and industry, including transnational corporations, are increasingly taking voluntary initiatives, promoting and implementing self-regulations and greater responsibilities in ensuring their activities have minimal impacts on human health and the environment. The regulatory regimes introduced in many countries, the growing consciousness of consumers and the general public and enlightened leaders of business and industry, including trans-national corporations, have all contributed to this. A positive contribution of business and industry, including transnational corporations, to sustainable de-velopment can increasingly be achieved by using economic instruments such as free market mechanisms in which the prices of goods and services should in-creasingly reflect the environmental costs of their input, production, use, recy-cling and disposal subject to country-specific conditions.

30.4. The improvement of production systems through technologies and pro-cesses that utilize resources more efficiently and at the same time produce less wastes—achieving more with less—is an important pathway towards sus-tainability for business and industry. Similarly, facilitating and encouraging inventiveness, competitiveness and voluntary initiatives are necessary for stimu-lating more varied, efficient and effective options. To address these major re-quirements and strengthen further the role of business and industry, including transnational corporations, the following two programmes are proposed.

PROGRAMME AREAS

A. Promoting Cleaner Production

Basis for action

30.5. There is increasing recognition that production, technology and manage-ment that use resources inefficiently, form residues that are not reused, dis-charge wastes that have adverse impacts on human health and the environment and manufacture products that when used have further impacts and are difficult to recycle, need to be replaced with technologies, good engineering and man-agement practices and know-how that would minimize waste throughout the product life cycle. The concept of cleaner production implies striving for opti-mal efficiencies at every stage of the product life cycle. A result would be the improvement of the overall competitiveness of the enterprise. The need for a transition towards cleaner production policies was recognized at the UNIDO-or-ganized ministerial-level Conference on Ecologically Sustainable Development, held at Copenhagen in October 1991.[1]

Objectives

30.6. Governments, business and industry, including transnational corporations, should aim to increase the efficiency of resource utilization, including increasing the reuse and recycling of residues, and to reduce the quantity of waste dis-charge per unit of economic output.

---

1   See A/CONF.151/PC/125. UNIDO is the U.N. Industrial Development Organization.

Activities

30.7. Governments, business and industry, including transnational corporations, should strengthen partnerships to implement the principles and criteria for sustainable development.

30.8. Governments should identify and implement an appropriate mix of economic instruments and normative measures such as laws, legislations and standards, in consultation with business and industry, including transnational corporations, that will promote the use of cleaner production, with special consideration for small and medium-sized enterprises. Voluntary private initiatives should also be encouraged.

30.9. Governments, business and industry, including transnational corporations, academia and international organizations, should work towards the development and implementation of concepts and methodologies for the internalization of environmental costs into accounting and pricing mechanisms.

30.10. Business and industry, including transnational corporations, should be encouraged:

(a) To report annually on their environmental records, as well as on their use of energy and natural resources;

(b) To adopt and report on the implementation of codes of conduct promoting the best environmental practice, such as the Business Charter on Sustainable Development of the International Chamber of Commerce and the chemical industry's responsible care initiative.

30.11. Governments should promote technological and know-how cooperation between enterprises, encompassing identification, assessment, research and development, management marketing and application of cleaner production.

30.12. Industry should incorporate cleaner production policies in its operations and investments, taking also into account its influence on suppliers and consumers.

30.13. Industry and business associations should cooperate with workers and trade unions to continuously improve the knowledge and skills for implementing sustainable development operations.

30.14. Industry and business associations should encourage individual companies to undertake programmes for improved environmental awareness and responsibility at all levels to make these enterprises dedicated to the task of improving environmental performance based on internationally accepted management practices.

30.15. International organizations should increase education, training and awareness activities relating to cleaner production, in collaboration with industry, academia and relevant national and local authorities.

30.16. International and non-governmental organizations, including trade and scientific associations, should strengthen cleaner production information dissemination by expanding existing databases such as UNEP International Cleaner Production Clearing House (ICPIC), UNIDO Industrial and Technological Information Bank (INTIB), and the ICC [International Chamber of Commerce] International Environment Bureau (IEB) and should forge networking of national and international information systems.[2]

B. Promoting responsible entrepreneurship

Basis for action

30.17. Entrepreneurship is one of the most important driving forces for innovations, increasing market efficiencies and responding to challenges and opportunities. Small and medium-sized entrepreneurs, in particular, play a very important role in the social and economic development of a country. Often, they are the major means for rural development, increasing off-farm employment and providing the transitional means for improving the livelihoods of women. Responsible entrepreneurship can play a major role in improving the efficiency of resource use, reducing risks and hazards, minimizing wastes and safeguarding environmental qualities.

Objectives

30.18. The following objectives are proposed:

(a) To encourage the concept of stewardship in the management and utilization of natural resources by entrepreneurs;

(b) To increase the number of entrepreneurs engaged in enterprises that subscribe to and implement sustainable development policies.

Activities

30.19. Governments should encourage the establishment and operations of sustainably managed enterprises. The mix would include regulatory measures,

---

2   The subheadings "Means of implementation" and "Financial and cost evaluation" and draft paragraphs 30.17 and 30.18 of A/CONF.151/4 (22 April 1992) were deleted by decision of the Main Committee of UNCED on 10 June 1992. See A/CONF.151/L.3/Add.30 (12 June 1992). The former draft reads as follows:

30.17. Although the investments for cleaner production will yield benefits for the enterprise, the costs involved could not be estimated [because of the evolving goal towards cleaner and cleaner production with improvements in technology and experience; the wide differences in operations among business and industry; and the range of options that could be considered for promoting cleaner production].

30.18. The implementation of cleaner production policies helps an enterprise to use resources more efficiently and discharge less wastes needing to be treated, hence accruing benefits for the enterprise [, thus it is expected that the major portion of the costs would be borne by the enterprise. The use of appropriate regulatory measures and economic instruments by Governments will help facilitate the speedier transition towards cleaner production.]

economic incentives and streamlining of administrative procedures to assure maximum efficiency in dealing with applications for approval in order to facilitate investment decisions, advice and assistance with information, infrastructural support and stewardship responsibilities.

30.20. Governments should encourage, in cooperation with the private sector, the establishment of venture capital funds for sustainable development projects and programmes.

30.21. In collaboration with business, industry, academia and international organizations, Governments should support training in the environmental aspects of enterprise management. Attention should also be directed towards apprenticeship schemes for youth.

30.22. Business and industry, including transnational corporations, should be encouraged to establish world-wide corporate policies on sustainable development, arrange for environmentally sound technologies to be available to affiliates owned substantially by their parent company in developing countries without extra external charges, encourage overseas affiliates to modify procedures in order to reflect local ecological conditions and share experiences with local authorities, national Governments and international organizations.

30.23. Large business and industry, including transnational corporations, should consider establishing partnership schemes with small and medium-sized enterprises to help facilitate the exchange of experience in managerial skills, market development and technological know-how, where appropriate, with the assistance of international organizations.

30.24. Business and industry should establish national councils for sustainable development and help promote entrepreneurship in the formal and informal sectors. The inclusion of women entrepreneurs should be facilitated.

30.25. Business and industry, including transnational corporations, should increase research and development of environmentally sound technologies and environmental management systems, in collaboration with academia and the scientific/engineering establishments, drawing upon indigenous knowledge, where appropriate.

30.26. Business and industry, including transnational corporations, should ensure responsible and ethical management of products and processes from the point of view of health, safety and environmental aspects. Towards this end, business and industry should increase self-regulation, guided by appropriate codes, charters and initiatives integrated into all elements of business planning and decision-making, and fostering openness and dialogue with employees and the public.

30.27. Multilateral and bilateral financial aid institutions should continue to encourage and support small- and medium-scale entrepreneurs engaged in sustainable development activities.

30.28. United Nations organizations and agencies should improve mechanisms for business and industry inputs, policy and strategy formulation processes, to ensure that environmental aspects are strengthened in foreign investment.

30.29. International organizations should increase support for research and development on improving the technological and managerial requirements for sustainable development, in particular for small and medium-sized enterprises in developing countries.

Means of implementation

Financing and cost evaluation

30.30. The activities included under this programme area are mostly changes in the orientation of existing activities and additional costs are not expected to be significant. The cost of activities by Governments and international organizations are already included in other programme areas.[3]

---

3   Paragraph 30.30 was proposed with two draft alternatives, A and B. In the draft of Agenda 21, Draft paragraph 30.32, alternative A, of A/CONF.151/4 (22 April 1992) was replaced by decision of the Main Committee of UNCED on 10 June 1992. See A/CONF.151/L.3/Add.30 (12 June 1992). The former draft read as follows:

Alternative A:

30.32. It is not possible to estimate the costs that might be incurred at the micro-economic level in global economies from implementing the various measures outlined in this programme. However, some changes may simply amount to changes in the orientation of existing activities and additional costs for Governments and international organizations may not be significant. These costs are also included in other areas.

Alternative B:

The activities included under this programme area are mostly changes in the orientation of existing activities and additional costs are not expected to be significant. The cost of activities by Governments and international organizations are already included in other programme areas. Draft paragraph 30.32, alternative B of A/CONF.151/4 (22 April 1992) included brackets around the entire text of paragraph 30.32, alternative B. The brackets were deleted by decision of the Main Committee of UNCED on 10 June 1992. See A/CONF.151/L.3/Add.30 (12 June 1992).

Chapter 31

Scientific and Technological Community

INTRODUCTION

31.1. The present chapter focuses on how to enable the scientific and techno-logical community, which includes, among others, engineers, architects, indus-trial designers, urban planners and other professionals and policy makers, to make a more open and effective contribution to the decision-making processes concerning environment and development. It is important that the role of science and technology in human affairs be more widely known and better un-derstood, both by decision makers who help determine public policy and by the general public. The cooperative relationship existing between the scientific and technological community and the general public should be extended and deepened into a full partnership. Improved communication and cooperation between the scientific and technological community and decision makers will facilitate greater use of scientific and technical information and knowledge in policies and programme implementation. Decision makers should create more favourable conditions for improving training and independent research in sus-tainable development. Existing multidisciplinary approaches will have to be strengthened and more interdisciplinary studies developed between the scien-tific and technological community and policy makers and with the general public to provide leadership and practical know-how to the concept of sustain-able development. The public should be assisted in communicating their senti-ments to the scientific and technological community concerning how science and technology might be better managed to affect their lives in a beneficial way. By the same token, the independence of the scientific and technological com-munity to investigate and publish without restriction and to exchange their findings freely must be assured. The adoption and implementation of ethical principles and codes of practice for the scientific and technological community that are internationally accepted could enhance professionalism and may im-prove and hasten recognition of the value of its contributions to environment and development, recognizing the continuing evolution and uncertainty of sci-entific knowledge.

PROGRAMME AREAS

A. Improving communication and cooperation among the scientific and technological community, decision-makers and the public

Basis for action

31.2. The scientific and technological community and policy makers should in-crease their interaction in order to implement strategies for sustainable devel-opment on the basis of the best available knowledge. This implies that decision makers should provide the necessary framework for rigorous research and for full and open communication of the findings of the scientific and technological community, and develop with it ways in which research results and the concerns stemming from the findings can be communicated to decision-making bodies so as to better link scientific and technical knowledge with strategic policy and programme formulation. At the same time, this dialogue would assist the scien-tific and technological community in developing priorities for research and pro-posing actions for constructive solutions.

Objectives

31.3. The following objectives are proposed:

(a) To extend and open up the decision-making process and broaden the range of developmental and environmental issues where cooperation at all levels between the scientific and technological community and decision mak-ers can take place;

(b) To improve the exchange of knowledge and concerns between the scientific and technological community and the general public in order to enable policies and programmes to be better formulated, understood and supported.

Activities

31.4. Governments should undertake the following activities:

(a) Review how national scientific and technological activities could be more responsive to sustainable development needs as part of an overall effort to strengthen national research and development systems, including through strengthening and widening the membership of national scientific and tech-nological advisory councils, organizations and committees to assure that:

(i) The full range of national needs for scientific and technological programmes are communicated to Governments and the public;

(ii) The various strands of public opinion are represented;

(b) Promote regional cooperative mechanisms to address regional needs for sustainable development. Such regional cooperative mechanisms could be facilitated through public/private partnerships and provide support to Governments, industry, non-governmental educational institutions and other domestic and international organizations, and by strengthening global professional networks;

(c) Improve and expand scientific and technical inputs through appropriate mechanisms to intergovernmental consultative, cooperative and negotiating processes towards international and regional agreements;

(d) Strengthen science and technology advice to the highest levels of the United Nations, and other international institutions, in order to ensure the inclusion of science and technology know-how in sustainable development policies and strategies;

(e) Improve and strengthen programmes for disseminating research results of universities and research institutions. This requires recognition of and greater support to the scientists, technologists and teachers who are engaged in communicating and interpreting scientific and technological information to policy makers, professionals in other fields and the general public. Such support should focus on the transfer of skills and the transfer and adaptation of planning techniques. This requires full and open sharing of data and information among scientists and decision makers. The publication of national scientific research reports and technical reports that are understandable and relevant to local sustainable development needs would also improve the interface between science and decision-making, as well as the implementation of scientific results;

(f) Improve links between the official and independent research sector and industry so that research may become an important element of industrial strategy;[1]

(g) Promote and strengthen the role of women as full partners in the science and technology disciplines;

(h) Develop and implement information technologies to enhance the dissemination of information for sustainable development.

Means of implementation

(a) Financing and cost evaluation

31.5. The Conference secretariat has estimated the average total annual cost (1993-2000) of implementing the activities of this programme to be about $15 million from the international community on grant or concessional

---

1   In subparagraph 31.4(f) the word "and" was inserted between the word "official" and the word "independent." See A/CONF. 151/L3/Add. (13 June 1992).

terms. These are indicative and order-of-magnitude estimates only and have not been reviewed by Governments. Actual costs and financial terms, including any that are non-concessional, will depend upon, *inter alia*, the specific strategies and programmes Governments decide upon for implementation.[2]

(b) Capacity-building

31.6. Intergovernmental panels on development and environmental issues should be organized, with emphasis on their scientific and technical aspects, and studies of responsiveness and adaptability in subsequent programmes of action.[3]

B. Promoting codes of practice and guidelines related to science and technology

Basis for action

31.7. Scientists and technologists have a special set of responsibilities which belong to them both as inheritors of a tradition and as professionals and members of disciplines devoted to the search for knowledge and to the need to protect the biosphere in the context of sustainable development.

31.8. Increased ethical awareness in environmental and developmental decision-making should help to place appropriate priorities for the maintenance and enhancement of life-support systems for their own sake, and in so doing ensure that the functioning of viable natural processes is properly valued by present and future societies. Therefore, a strengthening of the codes of practice and guidelines for the scientific and technological community would increase environmental awareness and contribute to sustainable development. It would build up the level of esteem and regard for the scientific and technological community and facilitate the "accountability" of science and technology.

---

2   Draft paragraph 31.5 of A/CONF.151/4 (22 April 1992) was replaced by decision of the Main Committee of UNCED on 10 June 1992. See A/CONF.151/L.3/Add.31 (13 June 1992). The former draft read as follows:

    Between $10 million and $15 million of international financing per year will be needed.

3   Draft paragraph 31.6 of A/CONF.151/4 (22 April 1992) was replaced by decision of the Main Committee of UNCED on 10 June 1992. See A/CONF.151/L.3/Add.31 (13 June 1992). The former draft read as follows:

    Intergovernmental panels on development and environmental issues should be organized, with emphasis on their scientific and technical aspects, and studies of responsiveness and adaptability in subsequent programmes of action[, drawing upon the experience of the Intergovernmental Panel on Climate Change.

Objectives

31.9. The objective should be to develop, improve and promote international acceptance of codes of practice and guidelines relating to science and technology in which the integrity of life-support systems is comprehensively accounted for and where the important role of science and technology in reconciling the needs of environment and development is accepted. To be effective in the decision-making process, such principles, codes of practice and guidelines must not only be agreed upon by the scientific and technological community, but also recognized by the society as a whole.

Activities

31.10. The following activities could be undertaken:

(a) Strengthening national and international cooperation, including the non-governmental sector, to develop codes of practice and guidelines regarding environmentally sound and sustainable development, taking into account the Rio Declaration and existing codes of practice and guidelines;

(b) Strengthening and establishing national advisory groups on environmental and developmental ethics, in order to develop a common value framework between the scientific and technological community and society as a whole, and promote continuous dialogue;

(c) Extending education and training in developmental and environmental ethical issues to integrate such objectives into education curricula and research priorities;

(d) Reviewing and amending relevant national and international environment and development legal instruments to ensure appropriate codes of practice and guidelines are incorporated into such regulatory machinery.

Means of implementation

(a) Financing and cost evaluation

31.11. The Conference secretariat has estimated the average total annual cost (1993-2000) of implementing the activities of this programme to be about $5 million from the international community on grant or concessional terms. These are indicative and order-of-magnitude estimates only and have not been reviewed by Governments. Actual costs and financial terms, including any that are non-concessional, will depend upon, *inter alia*, the specific strategies and programmes Governments decide upon for implementation.[4]

---

4   Draft paragraph 31.11 of A/CONF.151/4 (22 April 1992) was replaced by decision of the Main Committee of UNCED on 10 June 1992. See A/CONF.151/L.3/Add.31 (13 June 1992). The former draft read as follows:

About $5 million of international financing per year over the period 1993-2000 will be needed.

(b) Capacity-building

31.12. Codes of practice and guidelines, including on appropriate principles, should be developed for and by the scientific and technological community in the pursuit of its research activities and implementation of programmes aimed at sustainable development.[5]

---

5   The first sentence of draft paragraph 31.12 of A/CONF.151/4 (22 April 1992) was replaced by decision of the Main Committee of UNCED on 10 June 1992. See A/CONF.151/L.3/Add.31 (12 June 1992). The former draft read as follows:

    UNESCO might take the lead in implementing the above-mentioned activities, with the collaboration of other United Nations agencies and intergovernmental and non-governmental organizations.

Chapter 32

Strengthening the Role of Farmers[1]

INTRODUCTION

PROGRAMME AREA

Basis for action

32.1. Agriculture occupies one third of the land surface of the Earth, and is the central activity for much of the world's population. Rural activities take place in close contact with nature, adding value to it by producing renewable resources, while at the same time becoming vulnerable to overexploitation and improper management.

32.2. The rural household, indigenous people and their communities, and the family farmer, a substantial number of whom are women, have been the stewards of much of the Earth's resources. Farmers must conserve their physical environment as they depend on it for their sustenance. Over the past 20 years there has been impressive increase in aggregate agricultural production. Yet, in some regions, this increase has been outstripped by population growth or international debt or falling commodity prices. Further, the natural resources that sustain farming activity need proper care, and there is a growing concern about the sustainability of agricultural production systems.

32.3. A farmer-centred approach is the key to the attainment of sustainability in both developed and developing countries and many of the programme areas in Agenda 21 address this objective. A significant number of the rural population in developing countries depend primarily upon small-scale, subsistence-oriented agriculture based on family labour. However, they have limited access to resources, technology, alternative livelihood and means of production. As a result, they are engaged in the overexploitation of natural resources, including marginal lands.

---

1   In this chapter, all references to "farmers" include all rural people who derive their livelihood from activities such as farming, fishing and forest harvesting. The term "farming" also includes fishing and forest harvesting. [This note appears as an asterisk in chapter 32 of agenda 21.]

32.4. The sustainable development of people in marginal and fragile ecosystems is also addressed in Agenda 21. The key to the successful implementation of these programmes lies in the motivation and attitudes of individual farmers and government policies that would provide incentives to farmers to manage their natural resources efficiently and in a sustainable way. Farmers, particularly women, face a high degree of economic, legal and institutional uncertainties when investing in their land and other resources. The decentralization of decision-making towards local and community organizations is the key in changing people's behaviour and implementing sustainable farming strategies. This programme area deals with activities which can contribute to this end.

Objectives

32.5. The following objectives are proposed:

(a) To encourage a decentralized decision-making process through the creation and strengthening of local and village organizations that would delegate power and responsibility to primary users of natural resources;

(b) To support and enhance the legal capacity of women and vulnerable groups with regard to access, use and tenure of land;

(c) To promote and encourage sustainable farming practices and technologies;

(d) To introduce or strengthen policies that would encourage self-sufficiency in low-input and low-energy technologies, including indigenous practices, and pricing mechanisms that internalize environmental costs;

(e) To develop a policy framework that provides incentives and motivation among farmers for sustainable and efficient farming practices;

(f) To enhance the participation of farmers, men and women, in the design and implementation of policies directed towards these ends, through their representative organizations.

Activities

(a) Management-related activities

32.6. National Governments should:

(a) Ensure the implementation of the programmes on sustainable livelihoods, agriculture and rural development, managing fragile ecosystems, water use in agriculture, and integrated management of natural resources;

(b) Promote pricing mechanisms, trade policies, fiscal incentives and other policy instruments that positively affect individual farmer's decisions about an efficient and sustainable use of natural resources, and take full account of the impact of these decisions on household food security, farm incomes, employment and the environment;

(c) Involve farmers, and their representative organizations in the formulation of policy;

(d) Protect, recognize and formalize women's access to tenure and use of land, as well as rights to land, access to credit, technology, inputs and training;

(e) Support the formation of farmers' organizations by providing adequate legal and social conditions.

32.7. Support for farmers' organizations could be arranged as follows:

(a) National and international research centres should cooperate with farmers' organizations in developing location-specific environment-friendly farming techniques;

(b) National Governments, multilateral and bilateral development agencies and non-governmental organizations should collaborate with farmers' organizations in formulating agricultural development projects to specific agro-ecological zones.

(b) Data and information

32.8. Governments and farmers' organizations should:

(a) Initiate mechanisms to document, synthesize and disseminate local knowledge, practices and project experiences so that they will make use of the lessons of the past when formulating and implementing policies affecting farming, forest and fishing populations;

(b) Establish networks for the exchange of experiences with regard to farming that help to conserve land, water and forest resources, minimize the use of chemicals and reduce or reutilize farm wastes;

(c) Develop pilot projects and extension services that would seek to build on the needs and knowledge base of women farmers.

(c) International and regional cooperation

32.9. FAO [Food and Agricultural Organization], IFAD [International Fund for Agricultural Development], WFP [World Food Programme], the World Bank, the regional development banks and other international organizations involved in rural development should involve farmers and their representatives in their deliberations, as appropriate.

32.10. Representative organizations of farmers should establish programmes for the development and support of farmers' organizations, particularly in developing countries.

Means of implementation

(a) Financing and cost evaluation

32.11. The financing needed for this programme area is estimated in chapter 14 (Promoting sustainable agriculture and rural development), particularly in the programme area entitled "Ensuring people's participation and promoting human resource development for sustainable agriculture". The costs shown under chapters 3 (Combating poverty), 12 (Managing fragile ecosystems: combating desertification and drought), and 13 (Managing fragile ecosystems: sustainable mountain development) are also relevant to this programme area.[2]

(b) Scientific and technological means

32.12. Governments and appropriate international organizations, in collaboration with national research organizations and non-governmental organizations should, as appropriate:

(a) Develop environmentally sound farming technologies that enhance crop yields, maintain land quality, recycle nutrients, conserve water and energy and control pests and weeds;

(b) Conduct studies of high-resource and low-resource agriculture to compare their productivity and sustainability. The research should preferably be conducted under various environmental and sociological settings;

(c) Support research on mechanization that would optimize human labour and animal power and hand-held and animal-drawn equipment that can be easily operated and maintained. The development of farm technologies should take into account farmers' available resources and the role of animals in farming households and the ecology.[3]

---

2   Paragraph 32.11 was revised by decision of The Main Committee of UNCED. The former text read as follows:

> The financing needed for this programme area is estimated in sustainable agricultural and rural development, particularly in the programme area entitled "Ensuring people's participation and promoting human resource development". The cost shown under the chapters on sustainable mountain development, combating desertification and drought, and combating poverty and meeting basic needs are also relevant for this programme area.

3   Draft paragraph 32.12 of A/CONF.151/4 (22 April 1992) included brackets around the entire text of paragraph 32.12. The brackets were deleted by decision of the Main Committee of UNCED on 10 June 1992. See A/CONF.151/L.3/Add.32 (13 June 1992).

(c) Human resource development

32.13.[4] Governments, with the support of multilateral and bilateral development agencies and scientific organizations, should develop curricula for agricultural colleges and training institutions that would integrate ecology into agricultural science. Interdisciplinary programmes in agricultural ecology are essential to the training of a new generation of agricultural scientists and field-level extension agents.[5]

(d) Capacity-building

32.14. Governments should, in the light of each country's specific situation:[6]

(a) Create the institutional and legal mechanisms to ensure effective land tenure to farmers.[7] The absence of legislation indicating land rights has been an obstacle in taking action against land degradation in many farming communities in developing countries;

(b) Strengthen rural institutions that would enhance sustainability through locally managed credit systems and technical assistance, local production

---

4   Draft paragraph 32.13 of A/CONF.151/4 (22 April 1992) was replaced by decision of the Main Committee of UNCED on 10 June 1992. See A/CONF.151/L.3/Add.32 (13 June 1992). The former draft read as follows:

32.13 National Governments and appropriate international organizations[, in collaboration with national research organizations] and non-governmental organizations, should:

(a) Develop farming technologies that enhance [sustainable] crop yields and [profitability] intensity or [crop intensity], maintain land quality, recycle nutrients, conserve water and energy and control pests [and weeds];

(b) Conduct studies of high-input and low-input agriculture to compare their productivity and sustainability. The research should be conducted under various environmental and sociological settings;

(c) Support research on mechanization that would optimize human labour and animal power and hand-held and animal-drawn equipment that can be easily operated and maintained. The development of farm technologies should take into account farmers' available resources and the role of animals to farming households and the ecology.

5   Draft paragraph 32.13, formerly 31.14 of A/CONF.151/4 (22 April 1992), included brackets around the entire text of paragraph 32.14 and included the word "National" before "Governments". The brackets and the word were deleted by decision of the Main Committee of UNCED on 10 June 1992. See A/CONF.151/L.3/Add.32 (13 June 1992).

6   The introductory phrase of draft paragraph 32.15 of A/CONF.151/4 (22 April 1992) was replaced by decision of the Main Committee of UNCED on 10 June 1992. See A/CONF.151/L.3/Add.32 (13 June 1992). The former draft read as follows: "National Governments should:".

7   The first sentence of draft paragraph 32.15(a) of A/CONF.151/4 (22 April 1992) was replaced by decision of the Main Committee of UNCED on 10 June 1992. See A/CONF.151/L.3/Add.32 (13 June 1992). The former draft read as follows:

Create the institutional and legal mechanisms to give effective land tenure to farmers [who demonstrate they are conserving and utilizing resources properly] or farmers [with a view to] conserving and utilizing resources properly or [to forest harvesting and fishing rights to those who are working towards sustainable management of resources].

and distribution facilities for inputs, appropriate equipment and small-scale processing units, and marketing and distribution systems;

(c) Establish mechanisms to increase access of farmers, in particular women and farmers from indigenous groups, to agricultural training, credit and use of improved technology for ensuring food security.[8]

---

8 Draft paragraphs 32.15(b) and 32.15(c) of A/CONF.151/4 (22 April 1992) were replaced by decision of the Main Committee of UNCED on 10 June 1992. See A/CONF.151/L.3/Add.32 (13 June 1992). The former draft with alternative revisions read as follows:

Alternate [(b) Strengthen rural institutions that would enhance sustainability through locally managed credit systems and technical assistance, small facilties for producing inputs, appropriate equipment and small-scale processing units, and marketing and distribution systems;]

or

(b) Strengthen farmer institutions that would enhance locally-managed credit systems, small facilities for producing agricultural inputs, [small-scale processing units] and agricultural equipment, and marketing [and distribution] systems;

(c) Establish mechanisms to increase [women and indigenous groups'] or [farmers'] access to agricultural training, [credit] and use of improved [appropriate] or [farming] technology for ensuring food security.

Section 4. Means of Implementation

Chapter 33

Financial Resources and Mechanisms[1]

INTRODUCTION

33.1. The General Assembly, in resolution 44/228 of 22 December 1989, *inter alia*, decided that the United Nations Conference on Environment and Development should:

Identify ways and means of providing new and additional financial resources, particularly to developing countries, for environmentally sound development programmes and projects in accordance with national development objectives, priorities and plans and to consider ways of effectively monitoring the provision of such new and additional financial resources, particularly to developing countries, so as to enable the international community to take further appropriate action on the basis of accurate and reliable data;

Identify ways and means of providing additional financial resources for measures directed towards solving major environmental problems of global concern and especially of supporting those countries, in particular developing countries, for which the implementation of such measures would entail a special or abnormal burden, owing, in particular, to their lack of financial resources, expertise or technical capacity;

Consider various funding mechanisms, including voluntary ones, and examine the possibility of a special international fund and other innovative ap-

---

1 The Main Committee considered chapter 33 of Agenda 21 at its 8th meeting, on 10 June 1992.

At that meeting the issue coordinator, Mr. Rubens Ricupero (Brazil), introduced the text of the chapter, which had been prepared in the contact group on financial resources and mechanisms and which read as set forth here. No text for a draft Chapter 33 was included in the draft of Agenda 21, A/CONF. 151/4 (Part IV) 27 April 1992. That draft noted that the Chapter "will be finalized following consultations at the conference."

proaches, with a view to ensuring, on a favourable basis, the most effective and expeditious transfer of environmentally sound technologies to developing countries;

Quantify the financial requirements for the successful implementation of Conference decisions and recommendations and identify possible sources, including innovative ones, of additional resources.

33.2. This chapter deals with the financing of the implementation of Agenda 21, which reflects a global consensus integrating environmental considerations into an accelerated development process. For each of the other chapters, the secretariat of the Conference has provided indicative estimates of the total costs of implementation for developing countries and the requirements for grant or other concessional financing needed from the international community. These describe the need for a substantially increased effort both by countries themselves and by the international community.

Basis for Action

33.3. Economic growth, social development and poverty eradication are the first and overriding priorities in developing countries and are themselves essential to meeting national and global sustainability objectives. In the light of the global benefits to be realized by the implementation of Agenda 21 as a whole, the provision to developing countries of effective means, *inter alia*, financial resources and technology, without which it will be difficult for them to fully implement their commitments, will serve the common interests of developed and developing countries and of humankind in general, including future generations.

33.4. The cost of inaction could outweigh the financial costs of implementing Agenda 21. Inaction will narrow the choices of future generations.

33.5. For dealing with environmental issues, special efforts will be required. Global and local environmental issues are interrelated. The United Nations Framework Convention on Climate Change and the Convention on Biological Diversity address two of the most important global issues.

33.6. Economic conditions, both domestic and international, that encourage free trade and access to markets will help make economic growth and environmental protection mutually supportive for all countries, particularly for developing countries and countries undergoing the process of transition to a market economy (see chapter 2 for a fuller discussion of these issues).

33.7. International cooperation for sustainable development should also be strengthened in order to support and complement the efforts of developing countries, particularly the least developed countries.

33.8. All countries should assess how to translate Agenda 21 into national policies and programmes through a process that will integrate environment and development considerations. National and local priorities should be established by means that include public participation and community involvement, promoting equal opportunity for men and women.

33.9. For an evolving partnership among all countries of the world, including, in particular, between developed and developing countries, sustainable development strategies and enhanced and predictable levels of funding in support of longer term objectives are required. For that purpose, developing countries should articulate their own priority actions and needs for support and developed countries should commit themselves to addressing these priorities. In this respect, consultative groups and roundtables and other nationally based mechanisms can play a facilitative role.

33.10. The implementation of the huge sustainable development programmes of Agenda 21 will require the provision to developing countries of substantial new and additional financial resources. Grant or concessional financing should be provided according to sound and equitable criteria and indicators. The progressive implementation of Agenda 21 should be matched by the provision of such necessary financial resources. The initial phase will be accelerated by substantial early commitments of concessional funding.

Objectives

33.11. The objectives are as follows:

(a) To establish measures concerning financial resources and mechanisms for implementation of Agenda 21.

(b) To provide new and additional financial resources that are both adequate and predictable.

(c) To seek full use and continuing qualitative improvement of funding mechanisms to be utilized for the implementation of Agenda 21.

Activities

33.12. Fundamentally, the activities of this chapter are related to the implementation of all the other chapters of Agenda 21.

Means of Implementation

33.13. In general, the financing for the implementation of Agenda 21 will come from a country's own public and private sectors. For developing countries, particularly the least developed countries, ODA is a main source of external funding, and substantial new and additional funding for sustainable development and implementation of Agenda 21 will be required. Developed countries reaffirm their commitments to reach the accepted United Nations target of 0.7 per cent of GNP for ODA and, to the extent that they have not yet achieved that target, agree to augment their aid programmes in order to reach that target as soon as possible and to ensure prompt and effective implementation of Agenda 21. Some countries have agreed to reach the target by the year 2000. It was decided that the

Commission on Sustainable Development would regularly review and monitor progress towards this target. This review process should systematicaly combine the monitoring of the implementation of Agenda 21 with a review of the financial resources available. Those countries that have already reached the target are to be commended and encouraged to continue to contribute to the common effort to make available the substantial additional resources that have to be mobilized. Other developed countries, in line with their support for reform efforts in developing countries, agree to make their best efforts to increase their level of ODA. In this context, the importance of equitable burden-sharing among developed countries is recognized. Other countries, including those undergoing the process of transition to a market economy, may voluntarily augment the contributions of the developed countries.

33.14. Funding for Agenda 21 and other outcomes of the Conference should be provided in a way that maximizes the availability of new and additional resources and that uses all available funding sources and mechanisms. These include, among others:

(a) The multilateral development banks and funds:

(i) *The International Development Association (IDA)*. Among the various issues and options that IDA deputies will examine in connection with the forthcoming tenth replenishment of IDA, the statement made by the President of the World Bank at the United Nations Conference on Environment and Development should be given special consideration in order to help the poorest countries meet their sustainable development objectives as contained in Agenda 21;[2]

(ii) *Regional and subregional development banks*. The regional and subregional development banks and funds should play an increased and more effective role in providing resources on concessional or other favourable terms needed to implement Agenda 21;

(iii) *The Global Environment Facility*, managed jointly by the World Bank, UNDP and UNEP, whose additional grant and concessional funding is designed to achieve global environmental benefits, should cover the agreed incremental costs of relevant activities under Agenda 21, in particular for developing countries. Therefore, it should be restructured so as to, *inter alia*:

Encourage universal participation;

Have sufficient flexibility to expand its scope and coverage to relevant programme areas of Agenda 21, with global environmental benefits, as agreed;

---

2   The former draft read as follows:

International Development Association (IDA). In order to help poorer countries meet their sustainable development objectives as contained in Agenda 21, IDA [should be replenished, with a substantial Earth Increment in addition to the volume of resources needed to maintain the IDA-9 funding level in real terms] [should consider a special "Earth Increment" to the tenth replenishment]. This could be used to increase funding for policies and projects which are country driven and consistent with national plans designed to support sustainable development. This increment could be financed in part by a use of funds from the IBRD net income;

Ensure a governance that is transparent and democratic in nature, including in terms of decision-making and operations, by guaranteeing a balanced and equitable representation of the interests of developing countries and giving due weight to the funding efforts of donor countries;

Ensure new and additional financial resources on grant and concessional terms, in particular to developing countries;

Ensure predictability in the flow of funds by contributions from developed countries, taking into account the importance of equitable burden-sharing;

Ensure access to and disbursement of the funds under mutually agreed criteria without introducing new forms of conditionality;

(b) *The relevant specialized agencies, other United Nations bodies and other international organizations*, which have designated roles to play in supporting national Governments in implementing Agenda 21;

(c) *Multilateral institutions for capacity-building and technical cooperation*. Necessary financial resources should be provided to UNDP to use its network of field offices and its broad mandate and experience in the field of technical cooperation for facilitating capacity-building at the country level, making full use of the expertise of the specialized agencies and other United Nations bodies within their respective areas of competence, in particular UNEP and including the multilateral and regional development banks;

(d) *Bilateral assistance programmes*. These programmes will need to be strengthened in order to promote sustainable development;

(e) *Debt relief*. It is important to achieve durable solutions to the debt problems of low- and middle-income developing countries in order to provide them with the needed means for sustainable development. Measures to address the continuing debt problems of low- and middle-income countries should be kept under review. All creditors in the Paris Club should promptly implement the agreement of December 1991 to provide debt relief for the poorest heavily indebted countries pursuing structural adjustment; debt relief measures should be kept under review so as to address the continuing difficulties of those countries;

(f) *Private funding*. Voluntary contributions through non-governmental channels, which have been running at about 10 per cent of ODA, might be increased.

33.15. *Investment*. Mobilization of higher levels of foreign direct investment and technology transfers should be encouraged through national policies that promote investment and through joint ventures and other modalities.

33.16. *Innovative financing*. New ways of generating new public and private financial resources should be explored, in particular:

(a) Various forms of debt relief, apart from official or Paris Club debt, including greater use of debt swaps;

(b) The use of economic and fiscal incentives and mechanisms;

(c) The feasibility of tradeable permits;

(d) New schemes for fund-raising and voluntary contributions through private channels, including non-governmental organizations;

(e) The reallocation of resources presently committed to military purposes.

33.17. A supportive international and domestic economic climate conducive to sustained economic growth and development is important, particularly for developing countries, in order to achieve sustainability.

33.18. The secretariat of the Conference has estimated the average annual costs (1993-2000) of implementing in developing countries the activities in Agenda 21 to be over $600 billion, including about $125 billion on grant or concessional terms from the international community. These are indicative and order-of-magnitude estimates only, and have not been reviewed by Governments. Actual costs will depend upon, *inter alia*, the specific strategies and programmes Governments decide upon for implementation.

33.19. Developed countries and others in a position to do so should make initial financial commitments to give effect to the decisions of the Conference. They should report on such plans and commitments to the United Nations General Assembly at its forty-seventh session, in 1992.

33.20. Developing countries should also begin to draw up national plans for sustainable development to give effect to the decisions of the Conference.

33.21. Review and monitoring of the financing of Agenda 21 is essential. Questions related to the effective follow-up of the Conference are discussed in chapter 38 (International institutional arrangements). It will be important to review on a regular basis the adequacy of funding and mechanisms, including efforts to reach agreed objectives of the present chapter, including targets where applicable.[3]

---

3   The entire text of chapter 33 was adopted by decision of the Main Committee of UNCED on 10 June 1992. See A/CONF.151/L.3/Add.33 (11 June 1992).

Chapter 34

Transfer of Environmentally Sound Technology, Cooperation and Capacity-Building[1]

INTRODUCTION

34.1. Environmentally sound technologies protect the environment, are less polluting, use all resources in a more sustainable manner, recycle more of their wastes and products, and handle residual wastes in a more acceptable manner than the technologies for which they were substitutes.[2]

34.2. Environmentally sound technologies in the context of pollution are "process and product technologies" that generate low or no waste, for the prevention of pollution. They also cover "end of the pipe" technologies for treatment of pollution after it has been generated.

34.3. Environmentally sound technologies are not just individual technologies, but total systems which include know-how, procedures, goods and services, and equipment as well as organizational and managerial procedures. This implies that when discussing transfer of technologies, the human resource development and local capacity building aspects of technology choices, including gender-rele-

---

1   The title of chapter 34 of A/CONF.151/4 (22 April 1992) was replaced by decision of the Main Committee of UNCED on 10 June 1992. See A/CONF.151/L.3/Add.34 and A/CONF.151/L.3/Add. 44 (13 June 1992). The former draft alternative titles read as follows:
     "[ENVIRONMENTALLY [SAFE AND] SOUND TECHNOLOGY: TRANSFER, COOPERATION AND CAPACITY BUILDING]
     OR
     [TRANSFER OF ENVIRONMENTALLY [SAFE AND] SOUND TECHNOLOGY; REQUISITE COOPERATION AND CAPACITY BUILDING THEREUNDER]
     OR
     [COOPERATION IN AND RELATED TO THE ACCESS TO AND THE TRANSFER OF ENVIRONMENTALLY [SAFE AND] SOUND TECHNOLOGY]
     OR
     [COOPERATION IN AND RELATED TO THE TRANSFER OF ENVIRONMENTALLY [SAFE AND] SOUND TECHNOLOGY]".

2   Draft paragraph 34.1 of A/CONF.151/4 (22 April 1992) was replaced by decision of the Main Committee of UNCED on 10 June 1992. See A/CONF.151/L.3/Add.34 and A/CONF.151/L.3/Add.44 (13 June 1992). The former draft read as follows:
     Environmentally [safe and] sound technologies protect the environment, are less polluting, less [energy and] resource intensive, use [renewable] [all] resources in a more sustainable manner, recycle more of their wastes and products, and handle residual wastes in a more acceptable manner than the technologies for which they were substitutes.

vant aspects, should also be addressed. Environmentally sound technologies should be compatible with nationally determined socio-economic, cultural, and environmental priorities.

34.4. There is a need for favourable access to and transfer of environmentally sound technologies, in particular to developing countries, through supportive measures that promote technology cooperation and that should enable transfer of necessary technological know-how as well as building up of economic, technical, and managerial capabilities for the efficient use and further development of transferred technology. Technology cooperation involves joint efforts by enterprises and Governments, both suppliers of technology and its recipients. Therefore, such cooperation entails an iterative process involving Government, the private sector, and research and development facilities to ensure the best possible results from transfer of technology. Successful long-term partnerships in technology cooperation necessarily require continuing systematic training and capacity building at all levels over an extended period of time.

34.5. The activities proposed in this chapter aim at improving conditions and processes on information, access to and transfer of technology (including the state-of-the-art technology and related know-how), in particular to developing countries, as well as on capacity building and cooperative arrangements and partnerships in the field of technology, in order to promote sustainable development. New and efficient technologies will be essential to increase the capabilities, in particular of developing countries, to achieve sustainable development, sustain the world's economy, protect the environment, and alleviate poverty and human suffering. Inherent in these activities is the need to address the improvement of technology currently used and its replacement, when appropriate, with more accessible and more environmentally sound technology.

Basis for action

34.6. This chapter of Agenda 21 is without prejudice to specific commitments and arrangements on transfer of technology to be adopted in specific international instruments.

34.7. The availability of scientific and technological information and access and transfer of environmentally sound technology are essential requirements for sustainable development. Providing adequate information on the environmental aspects of present technologies consists of two interrelated components: upgrading information on present and state-of-the-art technologies, including their environmental risks, and improving access to environmentally sound technologies.

34.8. The primary goal of improved access to technology information is to enable informed choices, leading to access to and transfer of such technologies and the strengthening of countries' own technological capabilities.

34.9. A large body of useful technological knowledge lies in the public domain. There is a need for the access of developing countries to such technologies as are not covered by patents or lie in the public domain. Developing countries would also need to have access to the know-how and expertise required for the effective utilization of the aforesaid technologies.

34.10. Consideration must be given to the role of patent protection and intellectual property rights along with examination of their impact on the access to and transfer of environmentally sound technology in particular to developing countries as well as to further exploring efficiently the concept of assured access for developing countries to environmentally sound technology in its relation to proprietary rights with a view to developing effective responses to the needs of developing countries in this area.

34.11. Proprietary technology is available through commercial channels, and international business is an important vehicle for technology transfer. Tapping this pool of knowledge and recombining it with local innovations to generate alternative technologies should be pursued. At the same time that concepts and modalities for assured access to environmentally sound technologies, including state-of-the-art technologies, in particular by developing countries, continued to be explored, enhanced access to environmentally solid technologies should be promoted, facilitated and financed as appropriate, while providing fair incentives to innovators that promote research and development of new environmentally sound technologies.[3]

34.12. Recipient countries require technology and strengthened support to help further develop their scientific, technological, professional and related capacities, taking into account existing technologies and capacities. This support would enable countries, in particular developing countries, to make more rational technology choices. These countries could then better assess environmentally sound technologies prior to their transfer and properly apply and manage them, as well as improve upon already present technologies and adapt them to suit their specific development needs and priorities.

34.13. A critical mass of research and development capacity is crucial to the effective dissemination and use of environmentally sound technologies and their generation locally. Education and training programmes should reflect the needs of specific goal-oriented research activities and should work to produce specialists literate in environmentally sound technology and with an interdisciplinary outlook. Achieving this critical mass involves building the capabilities of craftspersons, technicians and middle-level managers, scientists, engineers and edu-

---

3   Draft paragraph 34.10 of A/CONF.151/4 (22 April 1992) was replaced by decision of the Main Committee of UNCED on 10 June 1992. See A/CONF.151/L.3/Add.34 (11 June 1992). The former draft read as follows:

Proprietary technology is available through commercial channels, and international business is an important vehicle for technology transfer. Tapping this pool of knowledge and recombining it with local innovations to generate alternative technologies should be pursued. At the same time, [assured] access to the environmentally [safe and] sound technologies, including state-of-the-art technologies, in particular by developing countries, should be [ensured,] promoted, facilitated and financed as appropriate, while providing fair incentives to innovators that promote research and development of new environmentally [safe and] sound technologies.

cators, as well as developing their corresponding social or managerial support systems. Transferring environmentally sound technologies also involves innovatively adapting and incorporating them into the local or national culture.

Objectives

34.14. The following objectives are proposed:

(a) To help to ensure the access, in particular of developing countries, to scientific and technological information, including information on state-of-the-art technologies;

(b) To promote, facilitate, and finance, as appropriate, the access to and the transfer of environmentally sound technologies and corresponding know-how, in particular to developing countries, on favourable terms, including on concessional and preferential terms as mutually agreed, taking into account the need to protect intellectual property rights as well as the special needs of developing countries for the implementation of Agenda 21;

(c) To facilitate the maintenance and promotion of environmentally sound indigenous technologies that may have been neglected or displaced, in particular in developing countries, paying particular attention to their priority needs and taking into account the complementary roles of men and women;

(d) To support endogenous capacity-building in particular in developing countries, so they can assess, adopt, manage and apply environmentally sound technologies. This could be achieved through *inter alia*:

(i) Human resource development;

(ii) Strengthening of institutional capacities for research and development and programme implementation;

(iii) Integrated sector assessments of technology needs, in accordance with countries' plans, objectives and priorities as foreseen in the implementation of Agenda 21 at the national level;

(e) To promote long-term technological partnerships between holders of environmentally sound technologies and potential users.

Activities

(a) Development of international information networks which link national, subregional, regional and international systems

34.15. Existing national, subregional, regional and international information systems should be developed and linked through regional clearing-houses covering broad-based sectors of the economy such as agriculture, industry and energy. Such a network might, *inter alia*, include national, subregional and regional patent offices that are equipped to produce reports on state-of-the-art technology. The clearing-house networks would disseminate information on available technologies, their sources, their environmental risks, and the broad terms under which they may be acquired. They would operate on an information-demand basis and focus on the information needs of the end-users. They would take into account the positive roles and contributions of international, regional and subregional organizations, business communities, trade associations, non-governmental organizations, national Governments, and newly established or strengthened national networks.

34.16. The international and regional clearing-houses would take the initiative, where necessary, in helping users to identify their needs and in disseminating information that meets those needs, including the use of existing news, public information, and communication systems. The disseminated information would highlight and detail concrete cases where environmentally sound technologies were successfully developed and implemented. In order to be effective, the clearing-houses need to provide not only information, but also referrals to other services, including sources of advice, training, technologies and technology assessment. The clearing-houses would thus facilitate the establishment of joint ventures and partnerships of various kinds.

34.17. An inventory of existing and international or regional clearing-houses or information exchange systems should be undertaken by the relevant United Nations bodies. The existing structure should be strengthened and improved when necessary. Additional information systems should be developed, if necessary, in order to fill identified gaps in this international network.

(b) Support of and promotion access to transfer of technology

34.18. Governments and international organizations should promote, and encourage the private sector to promote, effective modalities for the access and transfer, in particular to developing countries, of environmentally sound technologies by activities including the following:

(a) Formulation of policies and programmes for the effective transfer of environmentally sound technologies that are publicly owned or in the public domain;

(b) Creation of favourable conditions to encourage the private as well as public sector to innovate, market and use environmentally sound technologies;

(c) Examination by Governments and, where appropriate, by relevant organizations of existing policies, including subsidies and tax policies, and regulations to determine whether they encourage or impede the access to, transfer of and introduction of environmentally sound technologies;

(d) Addressing, in a framework which fully integrates environment and development, barriers to the transfer of privately owned environmentally sound technologies and adoption of appropriate general measures to reduce such barriers while creating specific incentives, fiscal or otherwise, for the transfer of such technologies;

(e) In the case of privately owned technologies, the adoption of the following measures, in particular for developing countries:

(i) Creation and enhancement by developed countries, as well as other countries which might be in a position to do so, of appropriate incentives, fiscal or otherwise, to stimulate the transfer of environmentally sound technology by companies, in particular to developing countries, as integral to sustainable development;

(ii) Enhancement of the access to and transfer of patent protected environmentally sound technologies, in particular to developing countries;

(iii) Purchase of patents and licenses on commercial terms for their transfer to developing countries on non-commercial terms as part of development cooperation for sustainable development, taking into account the need to protect intellectual property rights;

(iv) In compliance with and under the specific circumstances recognized by the relevant international conventions adhered to by States, undertaking measures to prevent the abuse of intellectual property rights, including rules with respect to their acquisition through compulsory licensing, with the provision of equitable and adequate compensation.[4]

(v) Provision of financial resources to acquire environmentally sound technologies in order to enable in particular developing countries to implement measures to promote sustainable development that would entail a special or abnormal burden to them;[5]

(f) Development of mechanisms for the access to and transfer of environmentally sound technologies, in particular to developing countries, while taking into account development in the process of negotiating an international code of conduct on transfer of technology, as decided by UNCTAD at its eighth session, held at Cartagena de Indias, Colombia, in February 1992.[6]

---

4   Draft paragraph 34.21(e)(iv) of A/CONF.151/4 (22 April 1992) was replaced by decision of the Main Committee of UNCED on 10 June 1992. See A/CONF.151/L.3/Add.34 (11 June 1992). The former draft read as follows: "Compulsory acquisition with the provision of equitable and adequate compensation, in accordance with international conventions adhered to by States;".

5   Draft paragraph 34.21(e)(v) of A/CONF.151/4 (22 April 1992) included brackets around the entire text of paragraph 34.21(e)(v). The brackets were deleted by decision of the Main Committee of UNCED on 10 June 1992. See A/CONF.151/L.3/Add.34 (11 June 1992).

6   Draft paragraph 34.21(f) of A/CONF.151/4 (22 April 1992) was replaced by decision of the Main Committee of UNCED on 10 June 1992. See A/CONF.151/L.3/Add.34 (11 June 1992). The former draft read as follows:

     Develop mechanisms for the access to and transfer of environmentally [safe and] sound technologies, in particular to developing countries [including in negotiating an International Code of Conduct on Transfer of Technology].

(c) Improvement of the capacity to develop and manage environmentally sound technologies

34.19. Frameworks at subregional, regional and international levels should be established and/or strengthened for the development, transfer and application of environmentally sound technologies and corresponding technical know-how with a special focus on developing countries' needs, by adding such functions to already existing bodies. Such frameworks would facilitate initiatives from both developing and developed countries to stimulate the research, development and transfer of environmentally sound technologies, often through partnerships within and among countries and between the scientific and technological community, industry and Governments.

34.20. National capacities to assess, develop, manage and apply new technologies should be developed. This will require strengthening existing institutions, training of personnel at all levels, and education of the end-user of the technology.

(d) Establishment of a collaborative network of research centres

34.21. A collaborative network of national, subregional, regional and international research centres on environmentally sound technology should be established to enhance the access to and development, management and transfer of environmentally sound technologies, including transfer and cooperation among developing countries and between developed and developing countries, primarily based on existing subregional or regional research, development and demonstration centres which are linked with the national institutions, in close cooperation with the private sector.

(e) Support for programmes of cooperation and assistance

34.22. Support should be provided for programmes of cooperation and assistance, including those provided by United Nations agencies, international organizations, and other appropriate public and private organizations, in particular to developing countries, in the areas of research and development, technological and human resources capacity-building in the fields of training, maintenance, national technology needs assessments, environmental impact assessments, and sustainable development planning.

34.23. Support should also be provided for national, subregional, regional, multilateral and bilateral programmes of scientific research, dissemination of information and technology development among developing countries, including through the involvement of both public and private enterprises and research facilities, as well as funding for technical cooperation among developing countries' programmes in this area. This should include developing links among these facilities to maximize their efficiency in understanding, disseminating and implementing technologies for sustainable development.

34.24. The development of global, regional and subregional programmes should include identification and evaluation of regional, subregional and national need-based priorities. Plans and studies supporting these programmes should provide the basis for potential financing by multilateral development banks, bilateral organizations, private sector interests and non-governmental organizations.

34.25. Visits should be sponsored and, on a voluntary basis, the return of qualified experts from developing countries in the field of environmentally sound technologies who are currently working in developed country institutions should be facilitated.

(f) Technology assessment in support of the management of environmentally sound technology

34.26. The international community, in particular United Nations agencies, international organizations, and other appropriate and private organizations should help exchange experiences and develop capacity for technology needs assessment, in particular in developing countries, to enable them to make choices based on environmentally sound technologies. They should:

(a) Build up technology assessment capacity for the management of environmentally sound technology, including environmental impact and risk assessment, with due regard to appropriate safeguards on the transfer of technologies subject to prohibition on environmental or health grounds;

(b) Strengthen the international network of regional, subregional or national environmentally sound technology assessment centres, coupled with clearing-houses, to tap the technology assessment sources mentioned above for the benefit of all nations. These centres could, in principle, provide advice and training for specific national situations and promote the building up of national capacity in environmentally sound technology assessment. The possibility of assigning this activity to already existing regional organizations should be fully explored before creating entirely new institutions, and funding of this activity through public-private partnerships should also be explored, as appropriate.

(g) Collaborative arrangements and partnerships

34.27. Long-term collaborative arrangements should be promoted between enterprises of developed and developing countries for the development of environmentally sound technologies. Multinational companies, as repositories of scarce technical skills needed for the protection and enhancement of the environment, have a special role and interest in promoting cooperation in and related to technology transfer, as they are important channels for such transfer, and for building a trained human resource pool and infrastructure.

34.28. Promote joint ventures between suppliers and recipients of technologies, taking into account developing countries' policy priorities and objectives. Together with direct foreign investment, these ventures could constitute important channels of transferring environmentally sound technologies. Through such joint ventures and direct investment, sound environmental management practices could be transferred and maintained.

Means of implementation

Financing and cost evaluation

34.29. The Conference secretariat has estimated the average total annual cost (1993-2000) of implementing the activities of this programme to be between $450 million and $600 million from the international community on grant or concessional terms. These are indicative and order-of-magnitude estimates only and have not been reviewed by Governments. Actual costs and financial terms, including any that are non-concessional, will depend upon, *inter alia*, the specific strategies and programmes Governments decide upon for implementation.[7]

---

7   Draft paragraphs 34.29-34.33, formerly 34.34-34.38 of A/CONF.151/4 (22 April 1992), were replaced by decision of the Main Committee of UNCED on 10 June 1992. See A/CONF.151/L.3/Add.34 (11 June 1992). The former draft read as follows:

> 34.34. The financial resources necessary to implement the international networks would be derived from a selection of existing funds and those to be additionally established. The running costs for international information networks would amount to approximately $ 150-200 million to be borne by the international community per year.

> 34.35. Given the nature of purchasing of patents and licenses as described in paragraph 21(e)(iii) and provision of financial resources to acquire environmentally [safe and] sound technologies as described in paragraph 21(e)(v), and the lack of actual experience, there are no solid grounds for estimating the costs of such activities.

> 34.36. A very rough estimate of costs to be borne by the international community for the activities in paragraphs 22 to 28 would be $ 250-300 million per year.

> 34.37. A very rough estimate of costs for the activities in paragraphs 29 to 31 would be $ 50-100 million per year.

> 34.3.8 The activities in promoting collaborative arrangements and partnerships in paragraphs 32 to 33 do not involve international financing on a concessional basis.

    Draft Chapter 34 of A/CONF.151/4 (22 April 1992) included the bracketed words [safe and] prior to the words "sound technology" and "sound technologies" each time those words appeared. The bracketed words [safe and] were deleted by decision of the Main Committee of UNCED on 10 June 1992. See A/CONF.151/L.3/Add.44 (13 June 1992).

Chapter 35

Science for Sustainable Development

INTRODUCTION

35.1. This chapter focuses on the role and the use of the sciences in supporting the prudent management of the environment and development for the daily survival and future development of humanity. The programme areas proposed herein are intended to be over-arching, in order to support the specific scientific requirements identified in the other Agenda 21 chapters. One role of the sciences should be to provide information to better enable formulation and selection of environment and development policies in the decision-making process. In order to fulfil this requirement, it will be essential to enhance scientific understanding, improve long-term scientific assessments, strengthen scientific capacities in all countries and ensure that the sciences are responsive to emerging needs.

35.2. Scientists are improving their understanding in areas such as climatic change, growth in rates of resource consumption, demographic trends, and environmental degradation. Changes in those and other areas need to be taken into account in working out long-term strategies for development. A first step towards improving the scientific basis for these strategies is a better understanding of land, oceans, atmosphere and their interlocking water, nutrient and biogeochemical cycles and energy flows which all form part of the Earth system. This is essential if a more accurate estimate of the carrying capacity of the planet Earth and of its resilience under the many stresses placed upon it by human activities is to be provided. The sciences can provide this understanding through increased research into the underlying ecological processes and through the application of modern, effective and efficient tools that are now available, such as remote-sensing devices, robotic monitoring instruments and computing and modelling capabilities. The sciences are playing an important role in linking the fundamental significance of the Earth system as life support to appropriate strategies for development which build on its continued functioning. The sciences should continue to play an increasing role in providing for improvement in the efficiency of resource utilization and in finding new development practices, resources, and alternatives. There is need for the sciences constantly to reassess and promote less intensive trends in resource utilization, including less intensive utilization of energy in industry, agriculture, and transportation. Thus, the sciences are increasingly being understood as an essential component in the search for feasible pathways towards sustainable development.

35.3. Scientific knowledge should be applied to articulate and support the goals of sustainable development, through scientific assessments of current conditions and future prospects for the Earth system. Such assessments, based on existing and emerging innovations within the sciences, should be used in the decision-making process and in the interactive processes between the sciences and policy-making. There needs to be an increased output from the sciences in order to enhance understanding and facilitate interaction between science and society. An increase in the scientific capacity and capability to achieve these goals will also be required, particularly in developing countries. Of crucial importance is the need for scientists in developing countries to participate fully in international scientific research programmes dealing with the global problems of environment and development so as to allow all countries to participate on equal footing in negotiations on global environmental and developmental issues. In the face of threats of irreversible environmental damage, lack of full scientific understanding should not be an excuse for postponing actions which are justified in their own right. The precautionary approach could provide a basis for policies relating to complex systems that are not yet fully understood and whose consequences of disturbances cannot yet be predicted.

35.4. The programme areas, which are in harmony with the conclusions and recommendations of the International Conference on an Agenda of Science for Environment and Development into the 21st Century (ASCEND 21) are:

(a) Strengthening the scientific basis for sustainable management;

(b) Enhancing scientific understanding;

(c) Improving long-term scientific assessment;

(d) Building up scientific capacity and capability.

PROGRAMME AREAS

A. Strengthening the scientific basis for sustainable management

Basis for action

35.5. Sustainable development requires taking longer-term perspectives, integrating local and regional effects of global change into the development process, and using the best scientific and traditional knowledge available. The development process should be constantly re-evaluated, in light of the findings of scientific research, to ensure that resource utilization has reduced impacts on the Earth system. Even so, the future is uncertain, and there will be surprises. Good environmental and developmental management policies must therefore be scientifically robust, seeking to keep open a range of options to ensure flexibility of response. The precautionary approach is important. Often, there is a communication gap among scientists, policy makers, and the public at large, whose interests are articulated by both governmental and non-governmental organizations. Better communication is required among scientists, decision makers, and the general public.

Objectives

35.6. The primary objective is for each country with the support of international organizations, as requested, to identify the state of its scientific knowledge and its research needs and priorities in order to achieve, as soon as possible, substantial improvements in:

(a) Large-scale widening of the scientific base and strengthening of scientific and research capacities and capabilities—in particular, those of developing countries—in areas relevant to environment and development;

(b) Environmental and developmental policy formulation, building upon the best scientific knowledge and assessments, and taking into account the need to enhance international cooperation and the relative uncertainties of the various processes and options involved;

(c) The interaction between the sciences and decision-making, using the precautionary approach, where appropriate, to change the existing patterns of production and consumption and to gain time for reducing uncertainty with respect to the selection of policy options;

(d) The generation and application of knowledge, especially indigenous and local knowledge, to the capacities of different environments and cultures, to achieve sustained levels of development, taking into account interrelations at the national, regional and international levels;

(e) Improving cooperation between scientists by promoting interdisciplinary research programmes and activities;

(f) Participation of people in setting priorities and in decision-making relating to sustainable development.

Activities

35.7. Countries, with the assistance of international organizations, where required, should:

(a) Prepare an inventory of their natural and social science data holdings relevant to the promotion of sustainable development;

(b) Identify their research needs and priorities in the context of international research efforts;

(c) Strengthen and design appropriate institutional mechanisms at the highest appropriate local, national, subregional and regional levels and within the United Nations system for developing a stronger scientific basis for the improvement of environmental and developmental policy formulation consistent with long-term goals of sustainable development. Current research in this area should be broadened to include more involvement of the public in establishing long-term societal goals for formulating the sustainable development scenarios;

(d) Develop, apply and institute the necessary tools for sustainable development, with regard to:

(i) Quality-of-life indicators covering, for example, health, education, social welfare, state of the environment, and the economy;

(ii) Economic approaches to environmentally sound development and new and improved incentive structures for better resource management;

(iii) Long-term environmental policy formulation, risk management and environmentally sound technology assessment;

(e) Collect, analyse and integrate data on the linkages between the state of ecosystems and the health of human communities in order to improve knowledge of the cost and benefit of different development policies and strategies in relation to health and the environment, particularly in developing countries;

(f) Conduct scientific studies of national and regional pathways to sustainable development, using comparable and complementary methodologies. Such studies, coordinated by an international science effort, should to a large extent involve local expertise and be conducted by multidisciplinary teams from regional networks and/or research centres, as appropriate and according to national capacities and the available resources;

(g) Improve capabilities for determining scientific research priorities at the national, regional and global levels to meet the needs of sustainable development. This is a process that involves scientific judgements regarding short-term and long-term benefits and possible long-term costs and risks. It should be adaptive and responsive to perceived needs and be carried out via transparent, "user-friendly", risk-evaluation methodologies;

(h) Develop methods to link the findings of the established sciences with the indigenous knowledge of different cultures. The methods should be tested using pilot studies. They should be developed at the local level and should concentrate on the links between the traditional knowledge of indigenous groups and corresponding, current "advanced science", with particular focus on disseminating and applying the results to environmental protection and sustainable development.

Means of implementation

(a) Financing and cost evaluation

35.8. The Conference secretariat has estimated the average total annual cost (1993-2000) of implementing the activities of this programme to be about $150 million, including about $30 million from the international community on grant or concessional terms. These are indicative and order-of-magnitude estimates only and have not been reviewed by Governments. Actual costs and financial terms, including any that are non-concessional, will depend upon, *inter alia*, the specific strategies and programmes Governments decide upon for implementation.[1]

(b) Scientific and technological means

35.9. The scientific and technological means include the following:

(a) Supporting new scientific research programmes, including their socio-economic and human aspects, at the community, national, subregional, regional and global levels, to complement and encourage synergies between traditional and conventional scientific knowledge and practices and strengthening interdisciplinary research related to environmental degradation and rehabilitation;

(b) Setting up demonstration models of different types (e.g., socio-economic, environmental conditions) to study methodologies and formulate guidelines;

(c) Supporting research by developing relative-risk evaluation methods to assist policy makers in ranking scientific research priorities.

B. Enhancing scientific understanding

Basis for action

35.10. In order to promote sustainable development, more extensive knowledge is required of the Earth's carrying capacity, including the processes that could either impair or enhance its ability to support life. The global environment is changing more rapidly than at any time in recent centuries; as a result, surprises may be expected, and the next century could see significant environmental changes. At the same time, the human consumption of energy, water and non-renewable resources is increasing, on both a total and a per capita basis, and shortages may ensue in many parts of the world even if environmental conditions were to remain unchanged. Social processes are subject to multiple variations across time and space, regions and culture. They both affect and are

---

1   Draft paragraph 35.8 of A/CONF.151/4 (22 April 1992) was replaced by decision of the Main Committee of UNCED on 10 June 1992. See A/CONF.151/L.3/Add.35 (12 June 1992). The former draft read as follows:

Financing and cost evaluation: The cost of this programme area is estimated to be about $40 million per year over the 1993-2000 period, which includes $15 million in international assistance.

influenced by changing environmental conditions. Human factors are key driving forces in these intricate sets of relationships and exert their influence directly on global change. Therefore, study of the human dimensions of the causes and consequences of environmental change and of more sustainable development paths is essential.

Objectives

35.11. One key objective is to improve and increase the fundamental understanding of the linkages between human and natural environmental systems and improve the analytical and predictive tools required to better understand the environmental impacts of development options by:

(a) Carrying out research programmes in order better to understand the carrying capacity of the Earth as conditioned by its natural systems, such as the biogeochemical cycles, the atmosphere/hydrosphere/lithosphere/cryosphere system, the biosphere and biodiversity, the agro-ecosystem and other terrestrial and aquatic ecosystems;

(b) Developing and applying new analytical and predictive tools in order to assess more accurately the ways in which the Earth's natural systems are being increasingly influenced by human actions, both deliberate and inadvertent, and demographic trends, and the impact and consequences of those actions and trends;

(c) Integrating physical, economic and social sciences in order better to understand the impacts of economic and social behaviour on the environment and of environmental degradation on local and global economies.

Activities

35.12. The following activities should be undertaken:

(a) Support development of an expanded monitoring network to describe cycles (for example, global, biogeochemical and hydrological cycles) and test hypotheses regarding their behaviour, and improve research into the interactions among the various global cycles and their consequences at national, subregional, regional and global levels as guides to tolerance and vulnerability;

(b) Support national, subregional, regional and international observation and research programmes in global atmospheric chemistry and the sources and sinks of greenhouse gases, and ensure that the results are presented in a publicly accessible and understandable form;

(c) Support national, subregional, regional and international research programmes on marine and terrestrial systems, strengthen global terrestrial databases of their components, expand corresponding systems for monitoring their changing states and enhance predictive modelling of the earth system and its subsystems, including modelling of the functioning of these systems assuming different intensities of human impact. The research programmes should include the programmes mentioned in other Agenda 21 chapters which support mechanisms for cooperation and coherence of research programmes on global change;

(d) Encourage coordination of satellite missions, the networks, systems and procedures for processing and disseminating their data; develop the interface with the research users of Earth observation data and with the United Nations EARTHWATCH system;

(e) Develop the capacity for predicting the responses of terrestrial, freshwater, coastal and marine ecosystems and biodiversity to short- and long-term perturbations of the environment, and develop further restoration ecology;

(f) Study the role of biodiversity and the loss of species in the functioning of ecosystems and the global life-support system;

(g) Initiate a global observing system of parameters needed for the rational management of coastal and mountain zones and significantly expand freshwater quantity/quality monitoring systems, particularly in developing countries;

(h) In order to understand the Earth as a system, develop Earth observation systems from space which will provide integrated, continuous and long-term measurements of the interactions of the atmosphere, hydrosphere and lithosphere, and develop a distribution system for data which will facilitate the utilization of data obtained through observation;

(i) Develop and apply systems and technology that automatically collect, record and transmit data and information to data and analysis centres, in order to monitor marine, terrestrial and atmospheric processes and provide advance warning of natural disasters;

(j) Enhance the contribution of the engineering sciences to multidisciplinary research programmes on the Earth system, in particular with regard to increasing emergency preparedness and reducing the negative effects of major natural disasters;

(k) Intensify research to integrate physical, economic and social sciences to better understand the impacts of economic and social behaviour on the environment and of environmental degradation on local and global economies, in particular:

(i) Develop research on human attitudes and behaviour as driving forces central to an understanding of the causes and consequences of environmental change and resource use;

(ii) Promote research on human, economic and social responses to global change;

(l) Support development of new user-friendly technologies and systems that facilitate the integration of multidisciplinary, physical, chemical, biological and social/human processes which, in turn, provide information and knowledge for decision makers and the general public.

Means of implementation

(a) Financing and cost evaluation

35.13. The Conference secretariat has estimated the average total annual cost (1993-2000) of implementing the activities of this programme to be about $2 billion, including about $1.5 billion from the international community on grant or concessional terms. These are indicative and order-of-magnitude estimates only and have not been reviewed by Governments. Actual costs and financial terms, including any that are non-concessional, will depend upon, *inter alia*, the specific strategies and programmes Governments decide upon for implementation.[2]

(b) Scientific and technological means

35.14. The scientific and technological means include the following:

(a) Supporting and using the relevant national research activities of academia, research institutes and governmental and non-governmental organizations, and promoting their active participation in regional and global programmes, particularly in developing countries;

(b) Increasing the use of appropriate enabling systems and technologies, such as supercomputers, space-based observational technology, Earth- and ocean-based observational technologies, data management and database technologies and, in particular, developing and expanding the Global Climate Observing System.

C. Improving long-term scientific assessment

Basis for action

35.15. Meeting scientific research needs in the environment/development field is only the first step in the support that the sciences can provide for the sustainable development process. The knowledge acquired may then be used to provide scientific assessments (audits) of the current status and for a range of possible future conditions. This implies that the biosphere must be maintained in a healthy state and that losses in biodiversity must be slowed down. Although many of the long-term environmental changes that are likely to affect people

---

2　Draft paragraph 35.13 of A/CONF.151/4 (22 April 1992) was replaced by decision of the Main Committee of UNCED on 10 June 1992. See A/CONF.151/L.3/Add.35 (12 June 1992). The former draft read as follows:

Financing and cost evaluation: It is estimated that this programme area, which is primarily related to global environmental issues, will cost about $1 billion per year over the period 1993-2000, of which about $750 million should be in international financing, building on ongoing and newly started programmes and activities.

and the biosphere are global in scale, key changes can often be made at the national and local levels. At the same time, human activities at the local and regional levels often contribute to global threats—e.g., stratospheric ozone depletion. Thus scientific assessments and projections are required at the global, regional and local levels. Many countries and organizations already prepare reports on the environment and development which review current conditions and indicate future trends. Regional and global assessments could make full use of such reports but should be broader in scope and include the results of detailed studies of future conditions for a range of assumptions about possible future human responses, using the best available models. Such assessments should be designed to map out manageable development pathways within the environmental and socio-economic carrying capacity of each region. Full use should be made of traditional knowledge of the local environment.

Objectives

35.16. The primary objective is to provide assessments of the current status and trends in major developmental and environmental issues at the national, subregional, regional and global levels on the basis of the best available scientific knowledge in order to develop alternative strategies, including indigenous approaches, for the different scales of time and space required for long-term policy formulation.

Activities

35.17. The following activities should be undertaken:

(a) Coordinate existing data- and statistics-gathering systems relevant to developmental and environmental issues so as to support preparation of long-term scientific assessments—for example, data on resource depletion, import/export flows, energy use, health impacts and demographic trends; apply the data obtained through the activities identified in programme area B to environment/development assessments at the global, regional and local levels; promote the wide distribution of the assessments in a form that is responsive to public needs and can be widely understood;

(b) Develop a methodology to carry out national and regional audits and a five-year global audit on an integrated basis. The standardized audits should help to refine the pattern and character of development, examining in particular the capacities of global and regional life-supporting systems to meet the needs of human and non-human life forms and identifying areas and resources vulnerable to further degradation. This task would involve the integration of all relevant sciences at the national, regional, and global levels, and would be organized by governmental agencies, non-governmental organizations, universities and research institutions, assisted by international governmental and non-governmental organizations and United Nations bodies, when necessary and as appropriate. These audits should then be made available to the general public.

Means of implementation

(a) Financing and cost evaluation

35.18. The Conference secretariat has estimated the average total annual cost (1993-2000) of implementing the activities of this programme to be about $35 million, including about $18 million from the international community on grant or concessional terms. These are indicative and order-of-magnitude estimates only and have not been reviewed by Governments. Actual costs and financial terms, including any that are non-concessional, will depend upon, *inter alia*, the specific strategies and programmes Governments decide upon for implementation.[3]

35.19. With regard to the existing data requirements under programme area A, support should be provided for national data collection and warning systems. This would involve setting up database, information and reporting systems, including data assessment and information dissemination in each region.

D. Building up scientific capacity and capability

Basis for action

35.20. In view of the increasing role the sciences have to play in dealing with the issues of environment and development, it is necessary to build up scientific capacity and strengthen such capacity in all countries—particularly in developing countries—to enable them to participate fully in the generation and application of the results of scientific research and development concerning sustainable development. There are many ways to build up scientific and technological capacity. Some of the most important of them are the following: education and training in science and technology; assistance to developing countries to improve infrastructures for research and development which could enable scientists to work more productively; development of incentives to encourage research and development; and greater utilization of their results in the productive sectors of the economy. Such capacity-building would also form the basis for improving public awareness and understanding of the sciences. Special emphasis must be put on the need to assist developing countries to strengthen their capacities to study their own resource bases and ecological systems and manage them better in order to meet national, regional and global challenges. Furthermore, in view of the size and complexity of global environmental problems, a need for more specialists in several disciplines has become evident world wide.

---

3   Draft paragraph 35.18 of A/CONF.151/4 (22 April 1992) was replaced by decision of the Main Committee of UNCED on 10 June 1992. See A/CONF.151/L.3/Add.35 (12 June 1992). The former draft read as follows:

Financing and cost evaluation: The cost of this programme area is estimated to be about $35 million per year over the period 1993-2000, of which $18 million will be needed from international sources.

Objectives

35.21. The primary objective is to improve the scientific capacities of all countries—in particular, those of developing countries—with specific regard to:

(a) Education, training and facilities for local research and development and human resource development in basic scientific disciplines and in environment-related sciences, utilizing where appropriate traditional and local knowledge of sustainability;

(b) A substantial increase by the year 2000 in the number of scientists—particularly women scientists—in those developing countries where their number is at present insufficient;

(c) Reducing significantly the exodus of scientists from developing countries and encouraging those who have left to return;

(d) Improving access to relevant information for scientists and decision makers, with the aim of improving public awareness and participation in decision-making;

(e) Involvement of scientists in national, regional and global environmental and developmental research programmes, including multidisciplinary research;

(f) Periodic academic update of scientists from developing countries in their respective fields of knowledge.

Activities

35.22. The following activities should be undertaken:

(a) Promote the education and training of scientists, not only in their disciplines but also in their ability to identify, manage and incorporate environmental considerations into research and development projects; ensure that a sound base in natural systems, ecology and resource management is provided; and develop specialists capable of working in interdisciplinary programmes related to environment and development, including the field of applied social sciences;

(b) Strengthen the scientific infrastructure in schools, universities and research institutions—particularly those in developing countries—by the provision of adequate scientific equipment and access to current scientific literature, for the purpose of achieving and sustaining a critical mass of highly qualified scientists in these countries;

(c) Develop and expand national scientific and technological databases, processing data in unified formats and systems, and allowing full and open access to the depository libraries of regional scientific and technological information networks. Promote submission of scientific and technological information and databases to global or regional data centres and network systems;

(d) Develop and expand regional and global scientific and technological information networks which are based on and linked to national scientific and technological databases; collect, process and disseminate information from regional and global scientific programmes; expand activities to reduce information barriers due to language differences. Increase the applications—particularly in developing countries—of computer-based retrieval systems in order to cope with the growth of scientific literature;

(e) Develop, strengthen and forge new partnerships among national, regional and global capacities to promote the full and open exchange of scientific and technological data and information and to facilitate technical assistance related to environmentally sound and sustainable development. This should be done through the development of mechanisms for the sharing of basic research, data and information, and the improvement and development of international networks and centres, including regional linking with national scientific databases, for research, training and monitoring. Such mechanisms should be designed so as to enhance professional cooperation among scientists in all countries and to establish strong national and regional alliances between industry and research institutions;

(f) Improve and develop new links between existing networks of natural and social scientists and universities at the international level in order to strengthen national capacities in the formulation of policy options in the field of environment and development;

(g) Compile, analyse and publish information on indigenous environmental and developmental knowledge, and assist the communities that possess such knowledge to benefit from them.

Means of implementation

(a) Financing and cost evaluation

35.23. The Conference secretariat has estimated the average total annual cost (1993-2000) of implementing the activities of this programme to be about $750 million, including about $470 million from the international community on grant or concessional terms. These are indicative and order-of-magnitude estimates only and have not been reviewed by Governments. Actual costs and financial terms, including any that are non-concessional, will depend upon, *inter alia*, the specific strategies and programmes Governments decide upon for implementation.[4]

---

4   Draft paragraph 35.23 of A/CONF.151/4 (22 April 1992) was replaced by decision of the Main Committee of UNCED on 10 June 1992. See A/CONF.151/L.3/Add.35 (12 June 1992). The former draft read as follows:

Financing and cost evaluation: The cost of this programme area is estimated to be about $750 million per year for the period 1993-2000, of which $470 million will be needed from international sources, keeping absorptive capacity in view.

(b) Scientific and technological means

35.24. Such means include increasing and strengthening regional multidisciplinary research and training networks and centres making optimal use of existing facilities and associated sustainable development and technology support systems in developing regions. Promote and use the potential of independent initiatives and indigenous innovations and entrepreneurship. The function of such networks and centres could include, for example:

(a) Support and coordination of scientific cooperation among all nations in the region;

(b) Linking with monitoring centres and carrying out assessment of environmental and developmental conditions;

(c) Support and coordination of national studies of pathways towards sustainable development;

(d) Organization of science education and training;

(e) Establishment and maintenance of information, monitoring and assessment systems and databases.

(c) Capacity-building

35.25. Capacity-building includes the following:

(a) Creating conditions (e.g., salaries, equipment, libraries) to ensure that the scientists will work effectively in their home countries;

(b) Enhancing national, regional and global capacities for carrying out scientific research and applying scientific and technological information to environmentally sound and sustainable development. This includes a need to increase financial resources to global and regional scientific and technological information networks, as may be appropriate, so that they will be able to function effectively and efficiently in satisfying the scientific needs of developing countries. Ensure the capacity-building of women by recruiting more women in research and research training.

Chapter 36

Promoting Education, Public Awareness and Training

INTRODUCTION

36.1. Education, raising of public awareness and training are linked to virtually all areas in Agenda 21, and even more closely to the ones on meeting basic needs, capacity-building, data and information, science, and the role of major groups. This chapter sets out broad proposals, while specific suggestions related to sectoral issues are contained in other chapters. The Declaration and Recommendations of the Tbilisi Intergovernmental Conference on Environmental Education[1] organized by UNESCO [UN Educational, Scientific and Cultural Organization] and UNEP [UN Environment Programme] and held in 1977, have provided the fundamental principles for the proposals in this document.

36.2. Programme areas described in the present chapter are:

(a) Reorienting education towards sustainable development;

(b) Increasing public awareness;

(c) Promoting training.

PROGRAMME AREAS

A. Reorienting education towards sustainable development

Basis for action

36.3. Education, including formal education, public awareness and training should be recognized as a process by which human beings and societies can reach their fullest potential. Education is critical for promoting sustainable development and improving the capacity of the people to address environment and development issues. While basic education provides the underpinning for any environmental and development education, the latter needs to be incorporated as an essential part of learning. Both formal and non-formal education are

---

1 *Intergovernmental Conference on Environmental Education: Final Report* (Paris, UNESCO, 1978), chap. III.

indispensable to change people's attitudes so that they have the capacity to assess and address their sustainable development concerns. It is also critical for achieving environmental and ethical awareness, values and attitudes, skills and behaviour consistent with sustainable development and for effective public participation in decision-making. To be effective, environment and development education should deal with the dynamics of both the physical/biological and socio/economic environment and human (which may include spiritual) development, be integrated in all disciplines, and should employ formal and non-formal methods and effective means of communication.

Objectives

36.4. Recognizing that countries, regional and international organizations will develop their own priorities and schedules for implementation in accordance with their needs, policies and programmes, the following objectives are proposed:

(a) To endorse the recommendations arising from the World Conference on Education for All: Meeting Basic Learning Needs[2] and to strive to ensure universal access to basic education, and to achieve primary education for at least 80 per cent of girls and 80 per cent of boys of primary school-age through formal schooling or non-formal education and to reduce the adult illiteracy rate to at least half of its 1990 level. Efforts should focus on reducing the high illiteracy levels and redressing the lack of basic education among women and should bring their literacy levels into line with those of men;

(b) To achieve environmental and development awareness in all sectors of society on a world-wide scale as soon as possible;

(c) To strive to achieve the accessibility of environmental and development education, linked to social education, from primary school age through adulthood to all groups of people;

(d) To promote integration of environment and development concepts, including demography, in all educational programmes, in particular the analysis of the causes of major environment and development issues in a local context, drawing on the best available scientific evidence and other appropriate sources of knowledge, and giving special emphasis to the further training of decision makers at all levels.

Activities

36.5. Recognizing that countries and regional and international organizations will develop their own priorities and schedules for implementation in accor-

---

2   *Final Report of the World Conference on Education for All: Meeting Basic Learning Needs, Jomtien, Thailand, 5-9 March 1990* (New York, Inter-Agency Commission (UNDP, UNESCO, UNICEF, World Bank) for the World Conference on Education for All, 1990).

dance with their needs, policies and programmes, the following activities are proposed.

(a) All countries are encouraged to endorse the recommendations of the Jomtien Conference and strive to ensure its Framework for Action. This would encompass the preparation of national strategies and actions for meeting basic learning needs, universalizing access and promoting equity, broadening the means and scope of education, developing a supporting policy context, mobilizing resources and strengthening international cooperation to redress existing economic, social and gender disparities which interfere with these aims. Non-governmental organizations can make an important contribution in designing and implementing educational programmes and should be recognized;

(b) Governments should strive to update or prepare strategies aimed at integrating environment and development as a cross-cutting issue into education at all levels within the next three years. This should be done in cooperation with all sectors of society. The strategies should set out policies and activities, and identify needs, cost, means and schedules for their implementation, evaluation and review. A thorough review of curricula should be undertaken to ensure a multidisciplinary approach, with environment and development issues and their socio-cultural and demographic aspects and linkages. Due respect should be given to community-defined needs and diverse knowledge systems, including science, cultural and social sensitivities;

(c) Countries are encouraged to set up national advisory environmental education coordinating bodies or round tables representative of various environmental, developmental, educational, gender and other interests, including non-governmental organizations, to encourage partnerships, help mobilize resources, and provide a source of information and focal point for international ties. These bodies would help mobilize and facilitate different population groups and communities to assess their own needs and to develop the necessary skills to create and implement their own environment and development initiatives;

(d) Educational authorities, with the appropriate assistance from community groups or non-governmental organizations, are recommended to assist or set up pre-service and in-service training programmes for all teachers, administrators, and educational planners, as well as non-formal educators in all sectors, addressing the nature and methods of environmental and development education and making use of relevant experience of non-governmental organizations;

(e) Relevant authorities should ensure that every school is assisted in designing environmental activity work plans, with the participation of students and staff. Schools should involve schoolchildren in local and regional studies on environmental health, including safe drinking water, sanitation and food and ecosystems and in relevant activities, linking these studies with services and research in national parks, wildlife reserves, ecological heritage sites etc.;

(f) Educational authorities should promote proven educational methods and the development of innovative teaching methods for educational settings. They should also recognize appropriate traditional education systems in local communities;

(g) Within two years the United Nations system should undertake a comprehensive review of its educational programmes, encompassing training and public awareness, to reassess priorities and reallocate resources. The UNESCO/UNEP International Environmental Education Programme should, in cooperation with the appropriate bodies of the United Nations system, Governments, non-governmental organizations and others, establish a programme within two years to integrate the decisions of the Conference into the existing United Nations framework adapted to the needs of educators at different levels and circumstances. Regional organizations and national authorities should be encouraged to elaborate similar parallel programmes and opportunities by conducting an analysis of how to mobilize different sectors of the population in order to assess and address their environmental and development education needs;

(h) There is a need to strengthen, within five years, information exchange by enhancing technologies and capacities necessary to promote environment and development education and public awareness. Countries should cooperate with each other and with the various social sectors and population groups to prepare educational tools that include regional environment and development issues and initiatives, using learning materials and resources suited to their own requirements;

(i) Countries could support university and other tertiary activities and networks for environmental and development education. Cross-disciplinary courses could be made available to all students. Existing regional networks and activities and national university actions which promote research and common teaching approaches on sustainable development should be built upon, and new partnerships and bridges created with the business and other independent sectors, as well as with all countries for technology, know-how, and knowledge exchange;

(j) Countries, assisted by international organizations, non-governmental organizations and other sectors, could strengthen or establish national or regional centres of excellence in interdisciplinary research and education in environmental and developmental sciences, law and the management of specific environmental problems. Such centres could be universities or existing networks in each country or region, promoting cooperative research and information sharing and dissemination. At the global level these functions should be performed by appropriate institutions;

(k) Countries should facilitate and promote non-formal education activities at the local, regional and national level by cooperating with and supporting the efforts of non-formal educators and other community-based organizations. The appropriate bodies of the United Nations system in cooperation with non-governmental organizations should encourage the development of an international network for the achievement of global educational aims. At the national and local level, public and scholastic forums should discuss environmental and development issues, and suggest sustainable alternatives to policy makers;

(l) Educational authorities, with appropriate assistance of non-governmental organizations, including women's and indigenous peoples' organizations, should promote all kinds of adult education programmes for continuing education in environment and development, basing activities around elementary/secondary schools and local problems. These authorities and industry should encourage business, industrial and agricultural schools to include such topics in their curricula. The corporate sector could include sustainable development in their education and training programmes. Programmes at a post-graduate level should include specific courses aiming at the further training of decision makers;

(m) Governments and educational authorities should foster opportunities for women in non-traditional fields and eliminate gender stereotyping in curricula. This could be done by improving enrolment opportunities, by including females in advanced programmes as students and instructors, reforming entrance and teacher staffing policies and providing incentives for establishing child-care facilities, as appropriate. Priority should be given to education of young females and to programmes promoting literacy among women;

(n) Governments should affirm the rights of indigenous people, by legislation if necessary, to use their experience and understanding of sustainable development to play a part in education and training;

(o) The United Nations could maintain a monitoring and evaluative role regarding decisions of the United Nations Conference on Environment and Development on education and awareness, through the relevant United Nations agencies. With Governments and non-governmental organizations, as appropriate, it should present and disseminate decisions in a variety of forms, and should ensure the continuous implementation and review of the educational implications of Conference decisions, in particular through relevant events and conferences.

Means of implementation

(a) Financing and cost evaluation

36.6. The Conference secretariat has estimated the average total annual cost (1993-2000) of implementing the activities of this programme to be about $8 billion to $9 billion, including about $3.5 billion to $4.5 billion from the international community on grant or concessional terms. These are indicative and order-of-magnitude estimates only and have not been reviewed by Governments. Actual costs and financial terms, including any that are non-concessional, will depend upon, *inter alia*, the specific strategies and programmes Governments decide upon for implementation.[3]

36.7. In the light of country-specific situations, more support for education, training and public awareness activities related to environment and development could be provided, in appropriate cases, through measures such as the following:[4]

(a) Giving higher priority to those sectors in budget allocations, protecting them from structural cutting requirements;

(b) Shifting allocations within existing education budgets in favour of primary education, with focus on environment and development;

(c) Promoting conditions where a larger share of the cost is borne by local communities, with rich communities assisting poorer ones;

(d) Obtaining additional funds from private donors concentrating on the poorest countries, and those with rates of literacy below 40 per cent;

(e) Encouraging debt for education swaps;

(f) Lifting restrictions on private schooling and increase the flow of funds from and to non-governmental organizations, including small-scale grass-roots organizations;

(g) Promoting the effective use of existing facilities, for example, multiple school shifts, fuller development of open universities and other long-distance teaching;

(h) Facilitating low-cost or no-cost use of mass media for education purposes;

(i) Encouraging twinning of universities in developed and developing countries.

---

3   Paragraph 36.6 was revised by decision of the Main Committee of UNCED. See A/CONF. 151/L.3/Add. 36. The prior text read as follows in A/CONF. 151/4 (Part IV), p. 28:

    36.6. Total financing required for basic education is $7 to $8 billion per annum, of which $3 to $4 billion is needed from the international community. For environmental and development education total costs are around $1 billion, including about $500 million to be obtained from the international community; $10 million would be required for strengthening international institutions. Resources allocation should be based on the needs of all learners and be a transparent process which includes all sectors of society decision-making. Decision-making and accountability on adequate resource allocation and spending for education should be transparent.

4   Draft paragraph 36.22 of A/CONF.151/4/ (22 April 1992) was replaced by decision of the Main Committee of UNCED on 10 June 1992. See A/CONF.151/L.3/Add 36 (12 June 1992). The former draft read as follows: "More support for education, training and public awareness activities related to environment and development could be provided, in particular, through the following measures:".

B. Increasing Public Awareness

Basis for action

36.8. There is still a considerable lack of awareness of the interrelated nature of all human activities and the environment, due to inaccurate or insufficient information. Developing countries in particular lack relevant technologies and expertise. There is a need to increase public sensitivity to environment and development problems and involvement in their solutions and foster a sense of personal environmental responsibility and greater motivation and commitment towards sustainable development.

Objective

36.9. The objective is to promote broad public awareness as an essential part of a global education effort to strengthen attitudes, values and actions which are compatible with sustainable development. It is important to stress the principle of devolving authority, accountability and resources to the most appropriate level with preference given to local responsibility and control over awareness-building activities.

Activities

36.10. Recognizing that countries, regional and international organizations will develop their own priorities and schedules for implementation in accordance with their needs, policies and programmes, the following activities are proposed:

(a) Countries should strengthen existing advisory bodies or establish new ones for public environment and development information, and should coordinate activities with, among others, the United Nations, non-governmental organizations and important media. They should encourage public participation in discussions of environmental policies and assessments. Governments should also facilitate and support national to local networking of information through existing networks;

(b) The United Nations system should improve its outreach in the course of a review of its education and public awareness activities to promote greater involvement and coordination of all parts of the system, especially its information bodies and regional and country operations. Systematic surveys of the impact of awareness programmes should be conducted, recognizing the needs and contributions of specific community groups;

(c) Countries and regional organizations should be encouraged, as appropriate, to provide public environmental and development information services for raising the awareness of all groups, the private sector and particularly decision makers;

(d) Countries should stimulate educational establishments in all sectors, especially the tertiary sector, to contribute more to awareness building. Educational materials of all kinds and for all audiences should be based on the best available scientific information, including the natural, behavioural and social sciences, and taking into account aesthetic and ethical dimensions;

(e) Countries and the United Nations system should promote a cooperative relationship with the media, popular theatre groups, and entertainment and advertising industries by initiating discussions to mobilize their experience in shaping public behaviour and consumption patterns and making wide use of their methods. Such cooperation would also increase the active public participation in the debate on the environment. UNICEF should make child-oriented material available to media as an educational tool, ensuring close cooperation between the out-of-school public information sector and the school curriculum, for the primary level. UNESCO, UNEP and universities should enrich pre-service curricula for journalists on environment and development topics;

(f) Countries, in cooperation with the scientific community, should establish ways of employing modern communication technologies for effective public outreach. National and local educational authorities, and relevant United Nations agencies should expand, as appropriate, the use of audio-visual methods, especially in rural areas in mobile units, by producing television and radio programmes for developing countries, involving local participation, employing interactive multimedia methods and integrating advanced methods with folk media;

(g) Countries should promote, as appropriate, environmentally sound leisure and tourism activities, building on The Hague Declaration of Tourism (1989) and the current programmes of the World Tourism Organization and UNEP, making suitable use of museums, heritage sites, zoos, botanical gardens, national parks, and other protected areas;

(h) Countries should encourage non-governmental organizations to increase their involvement in environmental and development problems, through joint awareness initiatives and improved interchange with other constituencies in society;

(i) Countries and the United Nations system should increase their interaction with and include, as appropriate, indigenous people in the management, planning and development of their local environment, and should promote dissemination of traditional and socially learned knowledge through means based on local customs, especially in rural areas, integrating these efforts with the electronic media, whenever appropriate;

(j) UNICEF, UNESCO, UNDP and non-governmental organizations should develop support programmes to involve young people and children in environment and development issues, such as children's and youth hearings, building on decisions of the World Summit for Children (A/45/625, annex);

(k) Countries, the United Nations and non-governmental organizations should encourage mobilization of both men and women in awareness campaigns, stressing the role of the family in environmental activities, women's contribution to transmission of knowledge and social values and the development of human resources;

(l) Public awareness should be heightened regarding the impacts of violence in society.

Means of implementation

Financing and cost evaluation

36.11. The Conference secretariat has estimated the average total annual cost (1993-2000) of implementing the activities of this programme to be about $1.2 billion, including about $110 million from the international community on grant or concessional terms. These are indicative and order-of-magnitude estimates only and have not been reviewed by Governments. Actual costs and financial terms, including any that are non-concessional, will depend upon, *inter alia*, the specific strategies and programmes Governments decide upon for implementation.[5]

C. Promoting Training

Basis for action

36.12. Training is one of the most important tools to develop human resources and facilitate the transition to a more sustainable world. It should have a job-specific focus, aimed at filling gaps in knowledge and skill that would help individuals find employment and be involved in environmental and development work. At the same time, training programmes should promote a greater awareness of environment and development issues as a two-way learning process.

Objectives

36.13. The following objectives are proposed:

(a) To establish or strengthen vocational training programmes that meet the needs of environment and development with ensured access to training opportunities, regardless of social status, age, gender, race or religion;

---

5   Draft paragraph 36.38 of A/CONF.151/4 (22 April 1992) was replaced by decision of the Main Committee of UNCED on 10 June 1992. See A/CONF.151/L.3/Add.36 (12 June 1992). The former draft read as follows:

   36.38 Total financing required to implement these activities would be around $1.2 billion per annum, including $100 million to be obtained from the international community; $10 million are needed for strengthening international institutions.

(b) To promote a flexible and adaptable workforce of various ages equipped to meet growing environment and development problems and changes arising from the transition to a sustainable society;

(c) To strengthen national capacities, particularly in scientific education and training, to enable Governments, employers and workers to meet their environmental and development objectives and to facilitate the transfer and assimilation of new environmentally sound, socially acceptable and appropriate technology and know-how;

(d) To ensure that environmental and human ecological considerations are integrated at all managerial levels and in all functional management areas, such as marketing, production and finance.

Activities

36.14. Countries with the support of the United Nations system should identify workforce training needs and assess measures to be taken to meet those needs. A review of progress in this area could be undertaken by the United Nations system in 1995.

36.15. National professional associations are encouraged to develop and review their codes of ethics and conduct to strengthen environmental connections and commitment. The training and personal development components of programmes sponsored by professional bodies should ensure incorporation of skills and information on the implementation of sustainable development at all points of policy- and decision-making.

36.16. Countries and educational institutions should integrate environmental and developmental issues into existing training curricula and promote the exchange of their methodologies and evaluations.

36.17. Countries should encourage all sectors of society, such as industry, universities, government officials and employees, non-governmental organizations and community organizations, to include an environmental management component in all relevant training activities, with emphasis on meeting immediate skill requirements through short-term formal and in-plant vocational and management training. Environmental management training capacities should be strengthened, and specialized "training of trainers" programmes should be established to support training at the national and enterprise levels. New training approaches for existing environmentally sound practices should be developed that create employment opportunities and make maximum use of local resource-based methods.

36.18. Countries should strengthen or establish practical training programmes for graduates from vocational schools, high schools and universities, in all countries, to enable them to meet labour market requirements and to achieve sustainable livelihoods. Training and retraining programmes should be established to meet structural adjustments which have an impact on employment and skill qualifications.

36.19. Governments are encouraged to consult with people in isolated situations, whether geographically, culturally or socially, to ascertain their needs for training to enable them to contribute more fully to developing sustainable work practices and lifestyles.

36.20. Governments, industry, trade unions, and consumers should promote an understanding of the interrelationship between good environment and good business practices.

36.21. Countries should develop a service of locally trained and recruited environmental technicians able to provide local people and communities, particularly in deprived urban and rural areas, with the services they require, starting from primary environmental care.

36.22. Countries should enhance the ability to gain access to analyse and effectively use information and knowledge available on environment and development. Existing or established special training programmes should be strengthened to support information needs of special groups. The impact of these programmes on productivity, health, safety and employment should be evaluated. National and regional environmental labour-market information systems should be developed that would supply, on a continuing basis, data on environmental job and training opportunities. Environment and development training resource-guides should be prepared and updated, with information on training programmes, curricula, methodologies and evaluation results at the local, national, regional and international levels.

36.23. Aid agencies should strengthen the training component in all development projects, emphasizing a multidisciplinary approach, promoting awareness and providing the necessary skills for transition to a sustainable society. The environmental management guidelines of UNDP for operational activities of the United Nations system may contribute to this end.

36.24. Existing networks of employers' and workers' organizations, industry associations and non-governmental organizations should facilitate the exchange of experience concerning training and awareness programmes.

36.25. Governments, in cooperation with relevant international organizations, should develop and implement strategies to deal with national, regional and local environmental threats and emergencies, emphasizing urgent practical training and awareness programmes for increasing public preparedness.

36.26. The United Nations system, as appropriate, should extend its training programmes, particularly its environmental training and support activities for employers' and workers' organizations.

Means of implementation

(a) Financing and cost evaluation

36.27. The Conference secretariat has estimated the average total annual cost (1993-2000) of implementing the activities of this programme to be about $5 billion, including about $2 billion from the international community on grant or concessional terms. These are indicative and order-of-magnitude estimates only and have not been reviewed by Governments. Actual costs and financial terms, including any that are non-concessional, will depend upon, *inter alia*, the specific strategies and programmes Governments decide upon for implementation.[6]

---

6   Draft paragraph 36.54 of A/CONF.151/4 (22 April 1992) was replaced by decision of the Main Committee of UNCED on 10 June 1992. See A/CONF.151/L.3/Add.36 (12 June 1992). The former draft read as follows:

   36.54. Total financing required to implement these activities would be $5 billion per annum, including $2 billion to be obtained from international sources. Strengthening international institutions would require about $30 million.

Chapter 37

National Mechanisms and International Cooperation for Capacity-Building in Developing Countries

PROGRAMME AREA

Basis for action

37.1. The ability of a country to follow sustainable development paths is determined to a large extent by the capacity of its people and its institutions as well as by its ecological and geographical conditions. Specifically, capacity-building encompasses the country's human, scientific, technological, organizational, institutional and resource capabilities. A fundamental goal of capacity-building is to enhance the ability to evaluate and address the crucial questions related to policy choices and modes of implementation among development options, based on an understanding of environmental potentials and limits and of needs as perceived by the people of the country concerned. As a result, the need to strengthen national capacities is shared by all countries.

37.2. Building endogenous capacity to implement Agenda 21 will require the efforts of the countries themselves in partnership with relevant United Nations organizations, as well as with developed countries. The international community at the national, subregional and regional levels, municipalities, non-governmental organizations, universities and research centres, and business and other private institutions and organizations could also assist in these efforts. It is essential for individual countries to identify priorities and determine the means for building capacity and capability to implement Agenda 21, taking into account their environmental and economic needs. Skills, knowledge and technical know-how at the individual and institutional levels are necessary for institution-building, policy analysis and development management, including the assessment of alternative courses of action with a view to enhancing access to and transfer of technology and promoting economic development. Technical cooperation, including that related to technology transfer and know-how, encompasses the whole range of activities to develop or strengthen individual and group capacities and capabilities. It should serve the purpose of long-term capacity-building and needs to be managed and coordinated by the countries themselves. Technical cooperation, including that related to technology transfer and know-how, is effective only when it is derived from and related to a country's own strategies and priorities on environment and development and when development agencies and Governments define improved and consistent policies and procedures to support this process.

Objectives

37.3. The overall objectives of endogenous capacity-building in this programme area are to develop and improve national and related subregional and regional capacities and capabilities for sustainable development, with the involvement of the non-governmental sectors. The programme should assist by:

(a) Promoting an ongoing participatory process to define country needs and priorities in promoting Agenda 21 and to give importance to technical and professional human resource development and development of institutional capacities and capabilities on the agenda of countries, with due recognition of the potential for optimal use of existing human resources as well as enhancement of the efficiency of existing institutions and non-governmental organizations, including scientific and technological institutions;

(b) Reorienting and reprioritizing technical cooperation and, in that process, setting new priorities in the field, including that related to transfer of technology and know-how processes while giving due attention to the specific conditions and individual needs of recipients, and improving coordination among providers of assistance to support countries' own programmes of action. This coordination should also include non-governmental organizations and scientific and technological institutions, as well as business and industry whenever appropriate;

(c) Shifting time horizons in programme planning and implementation addressing the developing and strengthening of institutional structures to permit an enhancement of their ability to respond to new longer-term challenges rather than concentrating only on immediate problems;

(d) Improving and reorienting existing international multilateral institutions with responsibilities for environment and/or development matters to ensure that those institutions have the capability and capacity to integrate environment and development;

(e) Improving institutional capacity and capability, both public and private, in order to evaluate the environmental impact of all development projects.

37.4. Specific objectives include the following:

(a) Each country should aim to complete, as soon as practicable, if possible by 1994, a review of capacity- and capability-building requirements for devising national sustainable development strategies, including those for generating and implementing its own Agenda 21 action programme;

(b) By 1997, the Secretary-General should submit to the General Assembly a report on achievement of improved policies, coordination systems and procedures for strengthening the implementation of technical cooperation programmes for sustainable development, as well as on additional measures required to strengthen such cooperation. That report should be prepared on the basis of information provided by countries, international organizations, environment and development institutions, donor agencies and non-governmental partners.

Activities

(a) Building a national consensus and formulate capacity-building strategies for implementing Agenda 21

37.5. As an important aspect of overall planning, each country should seek internal consensus at all levels of society on policies and programmes needed for short- and long-term capacity-building to implement its Agenda 21 programme. This consensus should result from a participatory dialogue of relevant interest groups and lead to an identification of skill gaps, institutional capacities and capabilities, technological and scientific requirements and resource needs to enhance environmental knowledge and administration to integrate environment and development. UNDP [UN Development Programme] in partnership with relevant specialized agencies and other international intergovernmental and non-governmental organizations could assist, upon request of Governments, in the identification of the requirements for technical cooperation, including those related to technology transfer and know-how and development assistance for the implementation of Agenda 21. The national planning process together, where appropriate, with national sustainable development action plans or strategies should provide the framework for such cooperation and assistance. UNDP should use and further improve its network of field offices and its broad mandate to provide assistance, using its experience in the field of technical cooperation for facilitating capacity-building at the country and regional levels and making full use of the expertise of other bodies, in particular UNEP, the World Bank and regional commissions and development banks, as well as relevant international intergovernmental and non-governmental organizations.

(b) Identification of national sources and presentation of requests for technical cooperation, including that related to transfer of technology and know-how in the framework of sector strategies

37.6 Countries desiring arrangements for technical cooperation, including that related to technology transfer and know-how, with international organizations and donor institutions should formulate requests in the framework of long-term sector or subsector capacity-building strategies. Strategies should, as appropriate, address policy adjustments to be implemented, budgetary issues, cooperation and coordination among institutions, human resource requirements, and technology and scientific equipment requirements. They should cover public and private sector needs and consider strengthening scientific training and educational and research programmes, including such training in the developed countries and the strengthening of centres of excellence in developing countries. Countries could designate and strengthen a central unit to organize and coordinate technical cooperation, linking it with the priority-setting and the resource allocation process.

(c) Establishment of a review mechanism of technical cooperation in and related to technology transfer and know-how

37.7. Donors and recipients, the organizations and institutions of the United Nations system, and international public and private organizations should review the development of the cooperation process as it relates to technical cooperation, including that related to activities for the transfer of technology and know-how linked to sustainable development. To facilitate this process the Secretary-General could undertake, taking into account work carried out by UNDP and other organizations in preparation for the United Nations Conference on Environment and Development, consultations with developing countries, regional organizations, organizations and institutions of the United Nations system, including regional commissions, and multilateral and bilateral aid and environment agencies, with a view to further strengthening the endogenous capacities of countries and improving technical cooperation, including that related to the technology transfer and know-how process. The following aspects should be reviewed:

(a) Evaluation of existing capacity and capability for the integrated management of environment and development, including technical, technological and institutional capacities and capabilities, and facilities to assess the environmental impact of development projects; and evaluation of abilities to respond to and link up with needs for technical cooperation, including that related to technology transfer and know-how, of Agenda 21 and the global conventions on climate change and biological diversity;

(b) Assessment of the contribution of existing activities in technical cooperation, including that related to transfer of technology and know-how, towards strengthening and building national capacity and capability for integrated environment and development management and an assessment of the means of improving the quality of international technical cooperation, including that related to technology transfer and know-how;

(c) A strategy for shifting to a capacity- and capability-building thrust that recognizes the need for the operational integration of environment and development with longer-term commitments, having as a basis the set of national programmes established by each country, through a participatory process;

(d) Consideration of greater use of long-term cooperative arrangements between municipalities, non-governmental organizations, universities, training and research centres and business, public and private institutions with counterparts in other countries or within countries or regions. Programmes such as the Sustainable Development Networks of UNDP should be assessed in this regard;

(e) Strengthening of the sustainability of projects by including in the original project design consideration of environmental impacts, the costs of institution-building, human resource development and technology needs, as well as financial and organizational requirements for operation and maintenance;

(f) Improvement of technical cooperation, including that related to transfer of technology and know-how and management processes, by giving greater attention to capacity- and capability-building as an integral part of sustainable development strategies for environment and development programmes both in country-related coordination processes, such as consultative groups and round tables, and in sectoral coordination mechanisms to enable developing countries to participate actively in obtaining assistance from different sources.

(d) Enhancement of the expertise and collective contribution of the United Nations system for capacity- and capability-building initiatives

37.8. Organizations, organs, bodies and institutions of the United Nations system, together with other international and regional organizations and the public and private sectors, could, as appropriate, strengthen their joint activities in technical cooperation, including that related to technology transfer and know-how, in order to address linked environment and development issues and to promote coherence and consistency of action. Organizations could assist and reinforce countries, particularly least developed countries, upon request, on matters relating to national environmental and developmental policies, human resource development and fielding of experts, legislation, natural resources and environmental data.

37.9. UNDP, the World Bank and regional multilateral development banks, as part of their participation in national and regional coordination mechanisms, should assist in facilitating capacity- and capability-building at the country level, drawing upon the special expertise and operational capacity of UNEP [UN Environment Programme] in the environmental field as well as of the specialized agencies, organizations of the United Nations system and regional and subregional organizations in their respective areas of competence. For this purpose UNDP should mobilize funding for capacity and capability-building, utilizing its network of field offices and its broad mandate and experience in the field of technical cooperation, including that related to technology transfer and know-how. UNDP, together with these international organizations, should at the same time continue to develop consultative processes to enhance mobilization and coordination of funds from the international community for capacity and capability-building, including the establishment of an appropriate database. These responsibilities may need to be accompanied by strengthening of the capacities of UNDP.

37.10. The national entity in charge of technical cooperation, with the assistance of UNDP resident representatives and UNEP representatives, should establish a small group of key actors to steer the process, giving priority to the country's own strategies and priorities. The experience gained through existing planning exercises such as the national reports for the United Nations Conference on Environment and Development, national conservation strategies and environment action plans should be fully used and incorporated into a country-driven, participatory and sustainable development strategy. This should be complemented with information networks and consultations with donor organizations in order to improve coordination, as well as access to the existing body of scientific and technical knowledge and information available in institutions elsewhere.

(e) Harmonization of the delivery of assistance at the regional level

37.11. At the regional level, existing organizations should consider the desirability of improved regional and subregional consultative processes and round-table meetings to facilitate the exchange of data, information and experience in the implementation of Agenda 21. UNDP, building on the results of the regional surveys on capacity-building that those regional organizations carried out on the United Nations Conference on Environment and Development initiative, and in collaboration with existing regional, subregional or national organizations with potential for regional coordination, should provide a significant input for this purpose. The relevant national unit should establish a steering mechanism. A periodic review mechanism should be established among the countries of the region with the assistance of the appropriate relevant regional organizations and the participation of development banks, bilateral aid agencies and non-governmental organizations. Other possibilities are to develop national and regional research and training facilities building on existing regional and subregional institutions.

Means of implementation

Financing and cost evaluation

37.12. The cost of bilateral expenditures to developing countries for technical cooperation, including that related to transfer of technology and know-how, is about $15 billion or about 25 per cent of total official development assistance.

The implementation of Agenda 21 will require a more effective use of these funds and additional funding in key areas.[1]

37.13. The Conference secretariat has estimated the average total annual cost (1993-2000) of implementing the activities of this programme to be between $300 million and $1 billion from the international community on grant or concessional terms. These are indicative and order-of-magnitude estimates only and have not been reviewed by Governments. Actual costs and financial terms, including any that are non-concessional, will depend upon, *inter alia*, the specific strategies and programmes Governments decide upon for implementation.[2]

---

1   Draft paragraph 37.12 of A/CONF.151/4 (22 April 1992) was replaced by decision of the Main Committee of UNCED on 10 June 1992. See A/CONF.151/L.3/Add.37 (12 June 1992). The former draft read as follows:

> The cost of bilateral expenditures to developing countries for technical cooperation, including that related to technology transfer and know-how, is about $15 billion, or about 25 per cent of total official development assistance. The implementation of Agenda 21 will require a more effective use of these funds and additional funding in key areas. [Specific funding requirements are included in each programme area. Support for the Secretary-General's consultative process will require approximately $1 million.]

2   Draft paragraph 37.13 of A/CONF.151/4 (22 April 1992) was replaced by decision of the Main Committee of UNCED on 10 June 1992. See A/CONF.151/L.3/Add.37 (12 June 1992). The former draft read as follows:

> 37.13. As reflected in paragraph 9, there is a need for a new funding mechanism [coordinated by the United Nations Development Programme] to provide lead and catalytic funding to give effect to a major capacity-building initiative. Amounts suggested could be in the range of $300-$500 million per year, rising over five years to some $1 billion per year. This would include the establishment of a consultative group process that could be managed by the United Nations Development Programme and assisted by a technical advisory committee to mobilize funding from all sources for capacity- and capability-building.

Chapter 38

International Institutional Arrangements

Basis for action

38.1. The mandate of the United Nations Conference on Environment and Development emanates from General Assembly resolution 44/228 in which the Assembly, *inter alia*, affirmed that the Conference should elaborate strategies and measures to halt and reverse the effects of environmental degradation in the context of increased national and international efforts to promote sustainable and environmentally sound development in all countries and that the promotion of economic growth in developing countries is essential to address problems of environmental degradation. The intergovernmental follow-up to the Conference process shall be within the framework of the United Nations system, with the General Assembly being the supreme policy-making forum that would provide overall guidance to Governments, United Nations system and relevant treaty bodies. At the same time, Governments, as well as regional economic and technical cooperation organizations, have a responsibility to play an important role in the follow-up to the Conference. Their commitments and actions should be adequately supported by the United Nations system and multilateral financial institutions. Thus, national and international efforts would mutually benefit from one another.

38.2. In fulfilling the mandate of the Conference, there is a need for institutional arrangements within the United Nations system in conformity with, and providing input into, the restructuring and revitalization of the United Nations in the economic, social and related fields, and the overall reform of the United Nations, including ongoing changes in the Secretariat. In the spirit of reform and revitalization of the United Nations system, implementation of Agenda 21 and other conclusions of the Conference shall be based on an action- and result-oriented approach and consistent with the principles of universality, democracy, transparency, cost-effectiveness and accountability.

38.3. The United Nations system, with its multisectoral capacity and the extensive experience of a number of specialized agencies in various spheres of international cooperation in the field of environment and development, is uniquely positioned to assist Governments to establish more effective patterns of economic and social development with a view to achieving the objectives of Agenda 21 and sustainable development.

38.4. All agencies of the United Nations system have a key role to play in the implementation of Agenda 21 within their respective competence. To ensure proper coordination and avoid duplication in the implementation of Agenda 21, there should be an effective division of labour between various parts of the United Nations system based on their terms of reference and comparative advantages. Member States, through relevant governing bodies, are in a position to ensure that these tasks are carried out properly. In order to facilitate evaluation of agencies' performance and promote knowledge of their activities, all bodies of the United Nations system should be required to elaborate and publish reports of their activities on the implementation of Agenda 21 on a regular basis. Serious and continuous reviews of their policies, programmes, budgets and activities will also be required.

38.5. The continued active and effective participation of non-governmental organizations, the scientific community and the private sector, as well as local groups and communities, are important in the implementation of Agenda 21.

38.6. The institutional structure envisaged below will be based on agreement on financial resources and mechanisms, technology transfer, the Earth Charter/Rio Declaration and Agenda 21. In addition, there has to be an effective link between substantive action and financial support, and this requires close and effective cooperation and exchange of information between the United Nations system and the multilateral financial institutions for the follow-up of Agenda 21 within the institutional arrangement.

Objectives

38.7. The overall objective is the integration of environment and development issues at national, sub-regional, regional and international levels, including in the United Nations system institutional arrangements.

38.8. Specific objectives shall be:

(a) To ensure and review the implementation of Agenda 21 so as to achieve sustainable development in all countries;

(b) To enhance the role and functioning of the United Nations system in the field of environment and development. All relevant agencies, organizations and programmes of the United Nations system should adopt concrete programmes for the implementation of Agenda 21 and also provide policy-guidance for United Nations activities or advice to Governments upon request, within their respective areas of competence;

(c) To strengthen cooperation and coordination on environment and development in the United Nations system;

(d) To encourage interaction and cooperation between the United Nations system and other intergovernmental and non-governmental subregional, regional and global institutions and non-governmental organizations in the field of environment and development;

(e) To strengthen institutional capabilities and arrangements required for the effective implementation, follow-up and review of Agenda 21;

(f) To assist in the strengthening and coordination of national, subregional and regional capacities and actions in the areas of environment and development;

(g) To establish effective cooperation and exchange of information between the United Nations organs, organizations, programmes and the multilateral financial bodies, within the institutional arrangements for the follow-up of Agenda 21;

(h) To respond to continuing and emerging issues relating to environment and development;

(i) To ensure that any new institutional arrangements would support revitalization, clear division of responsibilities and the avoidance of duplication in the United Nations system and depend to the maximum extent possible upon existing resources.

Institutional Structure

A. General Assembly

38.9. The General Assembly, as the highest level intergovernmental mechanism, is the principal policy-making and appraisal organ on matters relating to the follow-up of the Conference. The Assembly would organize a regular review of the implementation of Agenda 21. In fulfilling this task, the Assembly could consider the timing, format and organizational aspects of such a review. In particular, the Assembly could consider holding a special session not later than 1997 for the overall review and appraisal of Agenda 21, with adequate preparations at a high level.

B. Economic and Social Council

38.10. The Economic and Social Council, in the context of its Charter role *vis-á-vis* the General Assembly and the ongoing restructuring and revitalization of the United Nations in the economic, social and related fields, would assist the General Assembly through overseeing system-wide coordination, overview on the implementation of Agenda 21 and making recommendations in this regard. In addition, the Council would undertake the task of directing system-wide coordination and integration of environmental and developmental aspects in the United Nations' policies and programmes and make appropriate recommendations to the General Assembly, specialized agencies concerned and Member States. Appropriate steps should be taken to obtain regular reports from specialized agencies on their plans and programmes related to the implementation of Agenda 21, pursuant to Article 64 of the Charter of the United Nations. The Economic and Social Council should organize a periodic review of the work of the Commission on Sustainable Development envisaged in paragraph 38.11, as well as of system-wide activities to integrate environment and development, making full use of its high-level and coordination segments.[1]

C. Commission on Sustainable Development

38.11. In order to ensure the effective follow-up of the Conference, as well as to enhance international cooperation and rationalize the intergovernmental decision-making capacity for the integration of environment and development issues and to examine the progress in the implementation of Agenda 21 at the national, regional and international levels, a high-level Commission on Sustainable Development should be established in accordance with Article 68 of the Charter of the United Nations. This Commission would report to the Economic and Social Council in the context of the Council's role under the Charter *vis-á-vis* the General Assembly. It would consist of representatives of States elected as members with due regard to equitable geographical distribution. Representatives of non-member States of the Commission would have observer status. The Commission should provide for the active involvement of organs, programmes and organizations of the United Nations system, international financial institutions and other relevant intergovernmental organizations, and encourage the participation of non-governmental organizations, including industry and the business and scientific communities. The first meeting of the Commission should be convened no later than 1993. The Commission should be supported by the secretariat envisaged in paragraph 38.19. Meanwhile the Secretary-General of the United Nations is requested to ensure adequate interim administrative secretariat arrangements.

38.12. The General Assembly, at its forty-seventh session, should determine specific organizational modalities for the work of this Commission, such as its membership, its relationship with other intergovernmental United Nations bodies dealing with matters related to environment and development, and the frequency, duration and venue of its meetings. These modalities should take into account the ongoing process of revitalization and restructuring of the work of the United Nations in the economic, social and related fields, in particular measures recommended by the General Assembly in resolutions 45/264 of 13 May 1991 and 46/235 of 13 April 1992 and other relevant Assembly resolutions. In this respect, the Secretary-General of the United Nations, with the assistance of the Secretary-General of the United Nations Conference on Environment and Development, is requested to prepare for the Assembly a report with appropriate recommendations and proposals.[2]

---

1   The final sentence of draft paragraph 38.10 of A/CONF.151/4 (22 April 1992) was added by decision of the Main Committee of UNCED on 10 June 1992. See A/CONF.151/L.3/Add.38 (11 June 1992).

2   The former draft of paragraphs 38.11 and 38.12 read as follows:

        38.11. In order to enhance and rationalize the intergovernmental decision-making capacity for integration of environment and development issues and to ensure effective follow up to UNCED and the

38.13. The Commission on Sustainable Development should have the following functions:

(a) To monitor progress in the implementation of Agenda 21 and activities related to the integration of environmental and developmental goals throughout the United Nations system through analysis and evaluation of reports from all relevant organs, organizations, programmes and institutions of the United Nations system dealing with various issues of environment and development, including those related to finance;

(b) To consider information provided by Governments, including, for example, information in the form of periodic communications or national reports regarding the activities they undertake to implement Agenda 21, the problems they face, such as problems related to financial resources and technology transfer, and other environment and development issues they find relevant;[3]

(c) To review the progress in the implementation of the commitments contained in Agenda 21, including those related to provision of financial resources and transfer of technology;

(d) To receive and analyse relevant input from competent non-governmental organizations, including the scientific and the private sector, in the context of the overall implementation of Agenda 21;

(e) To enhance the dialogue within the framework of the United Nations, with non-governmental organizations and the independent sector, as well as other entities outside the United Nations system;

---

implementation of Agenda 21, provision shall be made within the framework of the General Assembly and the Economic and Social Council. This should provide for active involvement from organs, programmes and organizations of the United Nations system, Governments and non-governmental organizations including industry, business and scientific communities. It could take the form of either:

(i) a high-level Commission on Sustainable Development as the main subsidiary organ of the General Assembly and the ECOSOC for the integration of environment and development issues that will report directly to the General Assembly on matters of substance and through ECOSOC to the General Assembly on matters related to coordination. It would consist of States elected as members of this Commission;

or

(ii) The full use of a revitalized ECOSOC, in accordance with General Assembly resolution 45/264, with a recommendation for either the establishment of a subsidiary mechanism such as, in particular, a third sessional committee, or the full utilization of its new high level and coordination segments.

38.12. On the basis of the conclusions of UNCED, the 47th session of the General Assembly should determine specific modalities for the work and other organizational aspects of institutional arrangements agreed at the Conference, in conjunction with a review of the complementarity between the role of ECOSOC and the General Assembly in accordance with General Assembly resolution 45/264. In this respect, the Secretary-General is requested to prepare a report with appropriate recommendations taking into account institutional objectives and functions decided by UNCED.

3   Paragraph 38.13(b) was replaced by decision of the Main Committee of UNCED. See A/CONF. 151/L.3/Add. 38, p. 2-3 (11 June 1992).

(f) To consider, where appropriate, information regarding the progress made in the implementation of environmental conventions, which could be made available by the relevant Conferences of Parties;[4]

(g) To provide appropriate recommendations to the General Assembly through the Economic and Social Council on the basis of an integrated consideration of the reports and issues related to the implementation of Agenda 21;[5]

(h) To consider, at an appropriate time, the results of the review to be conducted expeditiously by the Secretary-General of all recommendations of the Conference for capacity-building programmes, information networks, task forces and other mechanisms to support the integration of environment and development at regional and sub-regional levels.

38.14. Within the intergovernmental framework, consideration should be given to allowing non-governmental organizations, including those related to major groups, particularly women's groups, committed to the implementation of Agenda 21 to have relevant information available to them, including information, reports and other data produced within the United Nations system.

D. The Secretary-General

38.15. Strong and effective leadership on the part of the Secretary-General is crucial, since he/she would be the focal point of the institutional arrangements within the United Nations system for the successful follow-up to the Conference and for the implementation of Agenda 21.

E. High-level inter-agency coordination mechanism

38.16. Agenda 21, as the basis for action by the international community to integrate environment and development, should provide the principal framework for coordination of relevant activities within the United Nations system. To ensure effective monitoring, coordination and supervision of the involvement of the United Nations system in the follow-up to the Conference, there is a need for a coordination mechanism under the direct leadership of the Secretary-General.

38.17. This task should be given to the Administrative Committee on Coordination (ACC), headed by the Secretary-General. ACC would thus provide a vital link and interface between the multilateral financial institutions and other United

---

4   Paragraph 38.13(f) was replaced with the above text at UNCED. A/CONF. 151/L.3/ Add. 38, p. 2. It proposed alternativies as follows: [To consider reports presented by relevant treaty bodies on the implementation of environmental conventions;] [To consider reports on implementation of environmental conventions which the relevant conferences of parties may wish to provide;]

5   The words "Through the Economic and Social Council" were added to paragraph 38.13(g) by the Main Committee of UNCED on June 11, 1992. See A/CONF. 151/L.3/Add. 38, p. 3 (11 June 1992).

Nations bodies at the highest administrative level. The Secretary-General should continue to revitalize the functioning of the Committee. All heads of agencies and institutions of the United Nations system shall be expected to cooperate with the Secretary-General fully in order to make ACC work effectively in fulfilling its crucial role and ensure successful implementation of Agenda 21. ACC should consider establishing a special task force, subcommittee or sustainable development board, taking into account the experience of the Designated Officials for Environmental Matters (DOEM) and the Committee of International Development Institutions on Environment (CIDIE), as well as the respective roles of UNEP [UN Environment Programme] and UNDP [UN Development Programme]. Its report should be submitted to the relevant intergovernmental bodies.

F. High-level advisory body

38.18. Intergovernmental bodies, the Secretary-General and the United Nations system as a whole may also benefit from the expertise of a high-level advisory board consisting of eminent persons knowledgeable about environment and development, including relevant sciences, appointed by the Secretary-General in their personal capacity. In this regard, the Secretary-General should make appropriate recommendations to the General Assembly at its forty-seventh session.

G. Secretariat support structure

38.19. A highly qualified and competent secretariat support structure within the United Nations Secretariat, drawing, *inter alia*, on the expertise gained in the Conference preparatory process is essential for the follow-up to the Conference and the implementation of Agenda 21. This secretariat support structure should provide support to the work of both intergovernmental and inter-agency coordination mechanisms. Concrete organizational decisions fall within the competence of the Secretary-General as the chief administrative officer of the Organization, who is requested to report on the provisions to be made, covering staffing implications, as soon as practicable, taking into account gender balance as defined in Article 8 of the Charter of the United Nations, and the need for the best use of existing resources in the context of current and ongoing restructuring of the United Nations Secretariat.

H. Organs, programmes and organizations of the United Nations system

38.20. In the follow-up to the Conference, in particular implementation of Agenda 21, all relevant organs, programmes and organizations of the United Nations system will have an important role within their respective areas of expertise and mandates in supporting and supplementing national efforts. Coordination and mutual complementarity of their efforts to promote integration of environment and development can be enhanced through countries encouraging to maintain consistent positions in the various governing bodies.

1. United Nations Environment Programme

38.21. In the follow-up to the Conference, there will be a need for an enhanced and strengthened role for UNEP and its Governing Council. The Governing Council should, within its mandate, continue to play its role with regard to policy guidance and coordination in the field of the environment, taking into account the development perspective.

38.22. Priority areas on which UNEP should concentrate include the following:

(a) Strengthening its catalytic role in stimulating and promoting environmental activities and considerations throughout the United Nations system;

(b) Promoting international cooperation in the field of environment and recommending, as appropriate, policies to this end;

(c) Developing and promoting the use of such techniques as natural resource accounting and environmental economics;

(d) Environmental monitoring and assessment, both through improved participation by the United Nations system agencies in the Earthwatch programme and expanded relations with private scientific and non-governmental research institutes; strengthening and making operational its early warning function;

(e) Coordination and promotion of relevant scientific research with a view to providing a consolidated basis for decision-making;

(f) Dissemination of environmental information and data to Governments and to organs, programmes and organizations of the United Nations system;

(g) Raising general awareness and action in the area of environmental protection through collaboration with the general public, non-governmental entities and intergovernmental institutions;

(h) Further development of international environmental law, in particular conventions and guidelines, promotion of its implementation, and coordinating functions arising from an increasing number of international legal agreements, *inter alia*, the functioning of the secretariats of the Conventions, taking into account the need for the most efficient use of resources, including possible co-location of secretariats established in the future;

(i) Further development and promotion of the widest possible use of environmental impact assessments, including activities carried out under the auspices of specialized agencies of the United Nations system, and in connection with every significant economic development project or activity;

(j) Facilitation of information exchange on environmentally sound technologies, including legal aspects, and provision of training;

(k) Promotion of sub-regional and regional cooperation and support to relevant initiatives and programmes for environmental protection, including playing a major contributing and coordinating role in the regional mechanisms in the field of environment identified for the follow-up to the Conference;

(l) Provision of technical, legal and institutional advice to Governments, upon request in establishing and enhancing their national legal and institutional frameworks, in particular, in cooperation with UNDP capacity-building efforts;

(m) Support to Governments, upon request, and development agencies and organs in the integration of environmental aspects into their development policies and programmes, in particular through provision of environmental, technical and policy advice during programme formulation and implementation;

(n) Further developing assessment and assistance in cases of environmental emergencies.

38.23. In order to perform all of these functions, while retaining its role as the principal body within the United Nations system in the field of environment and taking into account the development aspects of environmental questions, UNEP would require access to greater expertise and provision of adequate financial resources and it would require closer cooperation and collaboration with development and other relevant organs of the United Nations system. Furthermore, the regional offices of UNEP should be strengthened without weakening its headquarters in Nairobi, and UNEP should take steps to reinforce and intensify its liaison and interaction with UNDP and the World Bank.

2. United Nations Development Programme

38.24. UNDP, like UNEP, also has a crucial role in the follow-up to the United Nations Conference on Environment and Development. Through its network of field offices it would foster the United Nations system's collective thrust in support of the implementation of Agenda 21, at the country, regional, interregional and global levels, drawing on the expertise of the specialized agencies and other United Nations organizations and bodies involved in operational activities. The role of the resident representative/resident coordinator of UNDP needs to be strengthened in order to coordinate the field-level activities of the United Nations operational activities.

38.25. Its role should include the following:

(a) Acting as the lead agency in organizing United Nations system efforts towards capacity-building at the local, national and regional levels;

(b) Mobilizing donor resources on behalf of Governments for capacity-building in recipient countries and, where appropriate, through the use of the UNDP round-table mechanisms;

(c) Strengthening its own programmes in support of follow-up to the Conference without prejudice to the fifth programme cycle;

(d) Assisting recipient countries, upon request, in the establishment and strengthening of national coordination mechanisms and networks related to activities for the follow-up of the Conference;

(e) Assisting recipient countries, upon request, in coordinating the mobilization of domestic financial resources;

(f) Promoting and strengthening the role and involvement of women, youth and other major groups, in recipient countries in the implementation of Agenda 21.

3. United Nations Conference on Trade and Development

38.26. UNCTAD should play an important role in the implementation of Agenda 21 as extended at its eighth session, taking into account the importance of the interrelationships between development, international trade and the environment and in accordance with its mandate in the area of sustainable development.

4. United Nations Sudano-Sahelian Office

38.27. The role of the United Nations Sudano-Sahelian Office (UNSO), with added resources that may become available, operating under the umbrella of UNDP and with the support of UNEP, should be strengthened so that it can assume an appropriate major advisory role and participate effectively in the implementation of Agenda 21 provisions related to combating drought and desertification and to land resource management. In this context, the experience gained could be used by all other countries affected by drought and desertification, in particular those in Africa, with special attention to countries most affected or classified as least developed countries.

5. Specialized agencies of the United Nations system and related organizations and other relevant intergovernmental organizations

38.28. All specialized agencies of the United Nations system, related organizations and other relevant intergovernmental organizations within their respective fields of competence have an important role to play in the implementation of relevant parts of Agenda 21 and other decisions of the Conference. Their governing bodies may consider ways of strengthening and adjusting activities and programmes in line with Agenda 21, in particular, regarding projects for promoting sustainable development. Furthermore, they may consider establishing special arrangements with donors and financial institutions for project implementation that may require additional resources.

I. Regional and subregional cooperation and implementation

38.29. Regional and subregional cooperation will be an important part of the outcome of the Conference. The regional commissions, regional development banks and regional economic and technical cooperation organizations, within their respective agreed mandates, can contribute to this process by:

(a) Promoting regional and subregional capacity-building;

(b) Promoting the integration of environmental concerns in regional and sub-regional development policies;

(c) Promoting regional and subregional cooperation, where appropriate, re-garding transboundary issues related to sustainable development.

38.30. The regional commissions, as appropriate, should play a leading role in coordinating regional and subregional activities by sectoral and other United Nations bodies and shall assist countries in achieving sustainable development. The commissions and regional programmes within the United Nations system, as well as other regional organizations, should review the need for modification of ongoing activities, as appropriate, in light of Agenda 21.

38.31. There must be active cooperation and collaboration among the regional commissions and other relevant organizations, regional development banks, non-governmental organizations and other institutions at the regional level. UNEP and UNDP, together with the regional commissions, would have a crucial role to play, especially in providing the necessary assistance, with particular emphasis on building and strengthening the national capacity of Member States.

38.32. There is a need for closer cooperation between UNEP and UNDP, together with other relevant institutions, in the implementation of projects to halt environmental degradation or its impact and to support training programmes in environmental planning and management for sustainable development at the regional level.

38.33. Regional intergovernmental technical and economic organizations have an important role to play in helping Governments to take coordinated action in solving environment issues of regional significance.

38.34. Regional and subregional organizations should play a major role in the implementation of the provisions of Agenda 21 provisions related to combating drought and desertification. UNEP, UNDP and UNSO should assist and cooperate with those relevant organizations.

38.35. Cooperation between regional and subregional organizations and relevant organizations of the United Nations system should be encouraged, where appropriate, in other sectoral areas.

J. National implementation

38.36. States have an important role to play in the follow-up of the Conference and the implementation of Agenda 21. National level efforts should be undertaken by all countries in an integrated manner so that both environment and development concerns can be dealt with in a coherent manner.

38.37. Policy decisions and activities at the national level, tailored to support and implement Agenda 21, should be supported by the United Nations system upon request.

38.38. Furthermore, States could consider the preparation of national reports. In this context, the organs of the United Nations system should, upon request, assist countries, in particular developing countries. Countries could also consider the preparation of national action plans for the implementation of Agenda 21.

38.39. Existing assistance consortia, consultative groups and round tables should make greater efforts to integrate environmental considerations and related development objectives into their development assistance strategies and should consider reorienting and appropriately adjusting their memberships and operations to facilitate this process and better support national efforts to integrate environment and development.

38.40. States may wish to consider setting up a national coordination structure responsible for the follow-up of Agenda 21. Within this structure, which would benefit from the expertise of non-governmental organizations, submissions and other relevant information could be made to the United Nations.

K. Cooperation between United Nations bodies and international financial organizations

38.41. The success of the follow-up to the Conference is dependent upon an effective link between substantive action and financial support, and this requires close and effective cooperation between United Nations bodies and the multilateral financial organizations. The Secretary-General and heads of United Nations programmes, organizations and the multi-lateral financial organizations have a special responsibility in forging such a cooperation, not only through the United Nations high-level coordination mechanism (Administrative Committee on Coordination) but also at regional and national levels. In particular, representatives of multilateral financial institutions and mechanisms, as well as IFAD, should actively be associated with deliberations of the intergovernmental structure responsible for the follow-up to Agenda 21.

L. Non-governmental organizations

38.42. Non-governmental organizations and major groups are important partners in the implementation of Agenda 21. Relevant non-governmental organizations, including scientific community, the private sector and women's groups, should be given opportunities to make their contributions and establish appropriate relationships with the United Nations system. Support should be provided for developing countries' non-governmental organizations and their self-organized networks.

38.43. The United Nations system, including international finance and development agencies, and all intergovernmental organizations and forums should, in consultation with non-governmental organizations take measures to:

(a) Design open and effective means to achieve the participation of non-governmental organizations, including those related to major groups, in the process established to review and evaluate the implementation of Agenda 21 at all levels and promote their contribution to it;

(b) Take into account the findings of review systems and evaluation processes of non-governmental organizations in relevant reports of the Secretary-General to the General Assembly and all pertinent United Nations agencies and intergovernmental organizations and forums concerning implementation of Agenda 21 in accordance with its review process.

38.44. Procedures should be established for an expanded role for non-governmental organizations, including those related to major groups, with accreditation based on the procedures used in the Conference. Such organizations should have access to reports and other information produced by the United Nations system. The General Assembly, at an early stage, should examine ways of enhancing the involvement of non-governmental organizations within the United Nations system in relation to the follow-up process of the Conference.

38.45. The Conference takes note of other institutional initiatives for the implementation of Agenda 21, such as the proposal to establish a non-governmental Earth Council and the proposal to appoint a guardian for future generations, as well as other initiatives taken by local governments and business sectors.

Chapter 39

International Legal Instruments and Mechanisms

Basis for action

39.1. The recognition that the following vital aspects of the universal, multilateral and bilateral treaty-making process should be taken into account:

(a) The further development of international law on sustainable development, giving special attention to the delicate balance between environmental and developmental concerns;

(b) The need to clarify and strengthen the relationship between existing international instruments or agreements in the field of environment and relevant social and economic agreements or instruments, taking into account the special needs of developing countries;

(c) At the global level, the essential importance of the participation in and the contribution of all countries, including the developing countries, to treaty-making in the field of international law on sustainable development. Many of the existing international legal instruments and agreements in the field of environment have been developed without adequate participation and contribution of developing countries, and thus may require review in order to reflect the concerns and interests of developing countries and to ensure a balanced governance of such instruments and agreements;

(d) Developing countries should also be provided with technical assistance in their attempts to enhance their national legislative capabilities in the field of environmental law;

(e) Future projects for the progressive development and codification of international law on sustainable development should take into account the ongoing work of the International Law Commission;

(f) Any negotiations for the progressive development and codification of international law concerning sustainable development should, in general, be conducted on a universal basis, taking into account special circumstances in the various regions.

Objectives

39.2. The overall objective of the review and development of international environmental law should be to evaluate and to promote the efficacy of that law and to promote the integration of environment and development policies through effective international agreements or instruments taking into account both universal principles and the particular and differentiated needs and concerns of all countries.

39.3. Specific objectives are:

(a) To identify and address difficulties which prevent some States, in particular developing countries, from participating in or duly implementing international agreements or instruments and, where appropriate, to review or revise them with the purposes of integrating environmental and developmental concerns and laying down a sound basis for the implementation of these agreements or instruments;

(b) To set priorities for future law-making on sustainable development at the global, regional or subregional level, with a view to enhancing the efficacy of international law in this field through, in particular, the integration of environmental and developmental concerns;

(c) To promote and support the effective participation of all countries concerned, in particular developing countries, in the negotiation, implementation, review and governance of international agreements or instruments, including appropriate provision of technical and financial assistance and other available mechanisms for this purpose, as well as the use of differential obligations where appropriate;

(d) To promote, through the gradual development of universally and multilaterally negotiated agreements or instruments, international standards for the protection of the environment that take into account the different situations and capabilities of countries. States recognize that environmental policies should deal with the root causes of environmental degradation, thus preventing environmental measures from resulting in unnecessary restrictions to trade. Trade policy measures for environmental purposes should not constitute a means of arbitrary or unjustifiable discrimination or a disguised restriction on international trade. Unilateral actions to deal with environmental challenges outside the jurisdiction of the importing country should be avoided. Environmental measures addressing international environmental problems should, as far as possible, be based on an international consensus. Domestic measures targeted to achieve certain environmental objectives may need trade measures to render them effective. Should trade policy measures be found necessary for the enforcement of environmental policies, certain principles and rules should apply. These could include, *inter alia*, the principle of non-discrimination; the principle that the trade measure chosen should be the least trade-restrictive necessary to achieve the objectives; an obligation to ensure transparency in the use of trade measures related to the environment and to provide adequate notification of national regulations; and the need to give consideration to the special conditions and development requirements of developing countries as they move towards internationally agreed environmental objectives;[1]

(e) To ensure the effective, full and prompt implementation of legally binding instruments and to facilitate timely review and adjustment of agreements or instruments by the parties concerned, taking into account the special needs and concerns of all countries, in particular developing countries;[2]

(f) To improve the effectiveness of institutions, mechanisms and procedures for the administration of agreements and instruments;

(g) To identify and prevent actual or potential conflicts, particularly between environmental and social/economic agreements or instruments, with a view to ensuring that such agreements or instruments are consistent. Where conflicts arise, they should be appropriately resolved;

(h) To study and consider the broadening and strengthening of the capacity of mechanisms, *inter alia*, in the United Nations system, to facilitate, where appropriate and agreed to by the parties concerned, the identification, avoidance and settlement of international disputes in the field of sustainable development, duly taking into account existing bilateral and multilateral agreements for the settlement of such disputes.[3]

Activities

39.4. Activities and means of implementation should be considered in the light of the above basis for action and objectives without prejudice to the right of every State to put forward suggestions in this regard in the General Assembly.

---

1   Draft paragraph 39.3(d) of A/CONF.151/4 (22 April 1992) was replaced by decision of the Main Committee of UNCED on 10 June 1992. See A/CONF.151/L.3/Add.39 (11 June 1992). The former draft read as follows:

> To promote, through the gradual development of universally and multilaterally negotiated agreements or instruments, international standards for the protection of the environment that take into account the different situations and capabilities of countries [, thus avoiding the possible use of unilaterally set environmental standards as barriers to trade] in order to establish a framework for coexistence between environmental measures and international trade rules, and thus aiming at preventing the use of environmental measures for protectionist purposes.

2   Draft paragraph 39.3(e) of A/CONF.151/4 (22 April 1992) was revised by decision of the Main Committee of UNCED on 10 June 1992. See A/CONF.151/L.3/Add.39 (11 June 1992). The former draft read as follows:

> To ensure the effective and appropriate implementation [and compliance,] and to facilitate timely review and adjustment of agreements or instruments by the parties concerned, taking into account the special needs and concerns of all countries, in particular developing countries.

3   Draft paragraph 39.3(h) of A/CONF.151/4 (22 April 1992) was replaced by decision of the Main Committee of UNCED on 10 June 1992. See A/CONF.151/L.3/Add.39 (11 June 1992). The former draft read as follows:

> To study and consider the broadening and strengthening of mechanisms to identify [, prevent] and settle international disputes in the field of sustainable development, duly taking into account existing bilateral and multilateral agreements for the settlement of such disputes.

These suggestions could be reproduced in a separate compilation on sustainable development.

A. Review, assessment and fields of action in international law for sustainable development

39.5. While ensuring the effective participation of all countries concerned, Parties should at periodic intervals review and assess both the past performance and effectiveness of existing international agreements or instruments as well as the priorities for future lawmaking on sustainable development. This may include an examination of the feasibility of elaborating general rights and obligations of States, as appropriate, in the field of sustainable development, as provided by General Assembly resolution 44/228. In certain cases, attention should be given to the possibility of taking into account varying circumstances through differential obligations or gradual application. As an option for carrying out this task, earlier UNEP practice may be followed whereby legal experts designated by Governments could meet at suitable intervals, to be decided later, with a broader environmental and developmental perspective.

39.6. Measures in accordance with international law should be considered to address, in times of armed conflict, large-scale destruction of the environment that cannot be justified under international law. The General Assembly and its Sixth Committee are the appropriate forums to deal with this subject. The specific competence and role of the International Committee of the Red Cross should be taken into account.[4]

39.7. In view of the vital necessity of ensuring safe and environmentally sound nuclear power, and in order to strengthen international cooperation in this field, efforts should be made to conclude the ongoing negotiations for a nuclear safety convention in the framework of the International Atomic Energy Agency.[5]

---

4   Draft paragraph 39.6(a) of A/CONF.151/4 (22 April 1992) was replaced by decision of the Main Committee of UNCED on 10 June 1992. See A/CONF.151/L.3/Add.39 (11 June 1992). The former draft read as follows:

> 39.6 (a) In view of the importance of full compliance with the relevant rules of international law, all appropriate means should be considered to prevent any wilfully caused large-scale destruction of the environment [in times of war], which cannot be justified under international law. The General Assembly and its Sixth Committee as well as, in particular, the expert meetings of the International Committee of the Red Cross, are the appropriate fora to deal with this subject.

5   Draft paragraph 39.6(b) of A/CONF.151/4 (22 April 1992) was replaced by decision of the Main Committee of UNCED on 10 June 1992. See A/CONF.151/L.3/Add.39 (11 June 1992). The former draft read as follows:

> In view of the vital necessity of continuing to promote the highest level of safe and environmentally sound management of nuclear power worldwide, international cooperation should be strengthened by a step-by-step approach to a nuclear safety convention and its implementation. The relevant work already under way at the International Atomic Energy Agency should be welcomed and it is emphasized that there is a necessity to pass a nuclear safety convention in the framework of IAEA.

B. Implementation mechanisms[6]

39.8. The Parties to international agreements should consider procedures and mechanisms to promote and review their effective, full and prompt implementation.[7] To that effect, States could, *inter alia*:

(a) Establish efficient and practical reporting systems on the effective, full and prompt implementation of international legal instruments;[8]

(b) Consider appropriate ways in which relevant international bodies, such as UNEP, might contribute towards the further development of such mechanisms.

C. Effective participation in international lawmaking

39.9. In all these activities and others that may be pursued in the future, based on the above basis for action and objectives, the effective participation of all countries, in particular developing countries, should be ensured through appropriate provision of technical assistance and/or financial assistance. Developing countries should be given "headstart" support not only in their national efforts to implement international agreements or instruments, but also to participate effectively in the negotiation of new or revised agreements or instruments and in the actual international operation of such agreements or instruments. Support should include assistance in building up expertise in international law particularly in relation to sustainable development, and in assuring access to the necessary reference information and scientific/technical expertise.[9]

---

6   The former title of Section B of Chapter 39 of A/CONF.151/4 (22 April 1992) included the words "and compliance". The brackets were deleted by decision of the Main Committee of UNCED on 10 June 1992. See A/CONF.151/L.3/Add.39 (11 June 1992).

7   The first sentence of draft paragraph 39.7 of A/CONF.151/4 (22 April 1992) was revised by decision of the Main Committee of UNCED on 10 June 1992. See A/CONF.151/L.3/Add.39 (11 June 1992). The former draft read as follows:

The Parties to international agreements should consider procedures and mechanisms to promote and review implementation [and compliance].

8   Draft paragraph 39.7(a) of A/CONF.151/4 (22 April 1992) was revised by decision of the Main Committee of UNCED on 10 June 1992. See A/CONF.151/L.3/Add.39 (11 June 1992). The former draft read as follows:

Establish efficient and practical reporting systems on the implementation of [and compliance with] international legal instruments; and

9   The final sentence of draft paragraph 39.8 of A/CONF.151/4 (22 April 1992) was revised by decision of the Main Committee of UNCED on 10 June 1992. See A/CONF.151/L.3/Add.39 (11 June 1992). The former draft read as follows:

Support should include assistance in building up expertise in international law particularly in relation to sustainable development, and in assuring access to the necessary reference information and scientific/technical expertise [on fair and equitable terms.]

D. Disputes in the field of sustainable development[10]

39.10. In the area of avoidance and settlement of disputes, States should further study and consider methods to broaden and make more effective the range of techniques available at present, taking into account, among others, relevant experience under existing international agreements, instruments or institutions and, where appropriate, their implementing mechanisms such as modalities for dispute avoidance and settlement. This may include mechanisms and procedures for the exchange of data and information, notification and consultation regarding situations that might lead to disputes with other States in the field of sustainable development and for effective peaceful means of dispute settlement in accordance with the Charter of the United Nations, including, where appropriate, recourse to the International Court of Justice, and their inclusion in treaties relating to sustainable development.[11]

---

10 The title of section D of chapter 39 of A/CONF.151/4 (22 April 1992) was replaced by decision of the Main Committee of UNCED on 10 June 1992. See A/CONF.151/L.3/Add.39 (11 June 1992). The former draft read as follows:

Dispute [prevention and] settlement

11 Draft paragraph 39.9 of A/CONF.151/4 (22 April 1992) was replaced by decision of the Main Committee of UNCED on 10 June 1992. See A/CONF.151/L.3/Add.39 (11 June 1992). The former draft read as follows:

In the area of [prevention and] settlement of disputes, States should further study and consider methods to broaden and make more effective the range of techniques available at present, taking into account, among others, relevant experience under existing international agreements or instruments and, where appropriate, their implementing mechanisms such as modalities for dispute [prevention and] settlement. This may include [, inter alia,] mechanisms and procedures for the exchange of data and information [, notification, consultation and fact-finding] regarding situations that might lead to disputes with other States in the field of sustainable development; and consideration of the inclusion in treaties relating to sustainable development, of clauses providing for the effective peaceful settlement of disputes. [Existing institutions, in particular the International Court of Justice, should also play a role in this field].

Chapter 40

Information for Decision-Making

INTRODUCTION

40.1. In sustainable development, everyone is a user and provider of information considered in the broad sense that includes data, information, appropriately packaged experience and knowledge. The need for information arises at all levels, from that of senior decision makers at the national and international levels to the grass-roots and individual levels. The following two programme areas need to be implemented to ensure that decisions are based increasingly on sound information:

(a) Bridging the data gap;

(b) Improving information availability.

PROGRAMME AREAS

A. Bridging the data gap

Basis for action

40.2. While considerable data already exist, as the various sectoral chapters of Agenda 21 indicate, more and different types of data need to be collected, at local, provincial, national and international levels, indicating the status and trends of the planet's ecosystem, natural resource, pollution and socio-economic variables. The gap in the availability, quality, coherence, standardization and accessibility of data between the developed and the developing world has been increasing, seriously impairing the capacities of countries to make informed decisions concerning environment and development.

40.3. There is a general lack of capacity, particularly in developing countries, and in many areas at the international level, for the collection and assessment of data, for their transformation into useful information and for their dissemination. There is also need for improved coordination among environmental, demographic, social and developmental data and information activities.

40.4. Commonly used indicators such as the gross national product (GNP) and measurements of individual resource or pollution flows do not provide adequate indications of sustainability. Methods for assessing interactions between different sectoral environmental, demographic, social and developmental parameters are not sufficiently developed or applied. Indicators of sustainable development need to be developed to provide solid bases for decision-making at all levels and to contribute to a self-regulating sustainability of integrated environment and development systems.

Objectives

40.5. The following objectives are important:

(a) To achieve more cost-effective and relevant data collection and assessment by better identification of users, in both the public and private sectors, and of their information needs at local, provincial, national and international levels;

(b) To strengthen local, provincial, national and international capacity to collect and use multisectoral information in decision-making processes and to enhance capacities to collect and analyse data and information for decision-making, particularly in developing countries;

(c) To develop or strengthen local, provincial, national and international means of ensuring that planning for sustainable development in all sectors is based on timely, reliable and usable information;

(d) To make relevant information accessible in the form and at the time required to facilitate its use.

Activities

(a) Development of indicators of sustainable development

40.6. Countries at the national level and international governmental and non-governmental organizations at the international level should develop the concept of indicators of sustainable development in order to identify such indicators. In order to promote the increasing use of some of those indicators in satellite accounts, and eventually in national accounts, the development of indicators needs to be pursued by the Statistical Office of the United Nations Secretariat, as it draws upon evolving experience in this regard.

(b) Promotion of global use of indicators of sustainable development

40.7. Relevant organs and organizations of the United Nations system, in cooperation with other international governmental, intergovernmental and non-governmental organizations, should use a suitable set of sustainable development indicators and indicators related to areas outside of national jurisdiction, such as the high seas, the upper atmosphere and outer space. The organs and organizations of the United Nations system, in coordination with other relevant international organizations, could provide recommendations for harmonized development of indicators at the national, regional and global levels, and for incorporation of a suitable set of these indicators in common, regularly updated, and widely accessible reports and databases, for use at the international level, subject to national sovereignty considerations.

(c) Improvement of data collection and use

40.8. Countries and, upon request, international organizations should carry out inventories of environmental, resource and developmental data, based on national/global priorities for sustainable development management. They should determine the gaps and organize activities to fill those gaps. Within the organs and organizations of the United Nations system and relevant international organizations, data-collection activities, including those of Earthwatch and World Weather Watch, need to be strengthened, especially in the areas of urban air, freshwater, land resources (including forests and rangelands), desertification, other habitats, soil degradation, biodiversity, the high seas and the upper atmosphere. Countries and international organizations should make use of new techniques of data collection, including satellite-based remote sensing. In addition to the strengthening of existing development-related data collection, special attention needs to be paid to such areas as demographic factors, urbanization, poverty, health and rights of access to resources, as well as special groups, including women, indigenous peoples, youth, children and the disabled, and their relationships with environment issues.

(d) Improvement of methods of data assessment and analysis

40.9. Relevant international organizations should develop practical recommendations for coordinated, harmonized collection and assessment of data at the national and international levels. National and international data and information centres should set up continuous and accurate data-collection systems and make use of geographic information systems, expert systems, models and a variety of other techniques for the assessment and analysis of data. These steps will be particularly relevant, as large quantities of data from satellite sources will need to be processed in the future. Developed countries and international organizations, as well as the private sector, should cooperate, in particular with developing countries, upon request, to facilitate their acquiring these technologies and this know-how.

(e) Establishment of a comprehensive information framework

40.10. Governments should consider undertaking the necessary institutional changes at the national level to achieve the integration of environmental and developmental information. At the international level, environmental assessment activities need to be strengthened and coordinated with efforts to assess development trends.

(f) Strengthening of the capacity for traditional information

40.11. Countries, with the cooperation of international organizations, should establish supporting mechanisms to provide local communities and resource users with the information and know-how they need to manage their environment and resources sustainably, applying traditional and indigenous knowledge and approaches when appropriate. This is particularly relevant for rural and urban populations and indigenous, women's and youth groups.

Means of implementation

(a) Financing and cost evaluation[1]

40.12. The secretariat of the Conference has estimated the average total annual cost (1993-2000) of implementing the activities of this programme to be about $1.9 billion from the international community on grant or concessional terms. These are indicative and order-of-magnitude estimates only and have not been reviewed by Governments. Actual costs and financial terms, including any that are non-concessional, will depend upon, *inter alia*, the specific strategies and programmes Governments decide upon for implementation.[2]

(b) Institutional means

40.13. Institutional capacity to integrate environment and development and to develop relevant indicators is lacking at both the national and international levels. Existing institutions and programmes such as the Global Environmental Monitoring System (GEMS) and the Global Resource Information Database (GRID) within UNEP and different entities within the systemwide Earthwatch will need to be considerably strengthened. Earthwatch has been an essential element for environment-related data. While programmes related to development data exist in a number of agencies, there is insufficient coordination between them. The activities related to development data of agencies and institutions of the United Nations system should be more effectively coordinated perhaps

---

1 Draft paragraph 40.12 of A/CONF.151/4 (22 April 1992) was deleted by decision of the Main Committee of UNCED on 10 June 1992. See A/CONF.151/L.3/Add.40 (12 June 1992). The former draft read as follows:

   40.12. Financing will have to be increased, particularly for environmental data gathering/assessment at both the national and international levels [, although some redeployment and greater efficiency in the use of existing funds may be possible by better targeting information needs and associated data-collection and assessment activities.

2 Draft paragraph 40.12, formerly paragraph 40.13 of A/CONF.151/4 (22 April 1992), was replaced by decision of the Main Committee of UNCED on 10 June 1992. See A/CONF.151/L.3/Add.40 (12 June 1992). The former draft read as follows:

   The activities for data collection and assessments are expected to require international funding on the order of $1.5 billion per year for global activities, $300 million per year for accelerated development efforts and $70 million per year for international activities. In other chapters, the funding requirements of monitoring and assessment activities have been costed in other programme areas, except for that of the setting up of national monitoring centres in developing countries, for which external costs are estimated to be up to $20 million per year, depending on the number of such centres established.

STRATEGIES TOWARD SUSTAINABLE DEVELOPMENT

through an equivalent and complementary "Development Watch", which with the existing Earthwatch should be coordinated through an appropriate office within the United Nations to ensure the full integration of environment and development concerns.

(c) Scientific and technological means

40.14. Regarding transfer of technology, with the rapid evolution of data-collection and information technologies it is necessary to develop guidelines and mechanisms for the rapid and continuous transfer of those technologies, particularly to developing countries in conformity with chapter 34 (Transfer of environmentally sound technology, cooperation and capacity-building), and for the training of personnel in their utilization.[3]

(d) Human resources development

40.15. International cooperation for training in all areas and at all levels will be required, particularly in developing countries. That training will have to include technical training of those involved in data collection, assessment and transformation, as well as assistance to decision makers concerning how to use such information.

(e) Capacity-building

40.16. All countries, particularly developing countries, with the support of international cooperation, should strengthen their capacity to collect, store, organize, assess and use data in decision-making more effectively.

B. Improving availability of information

Basis for action

40.17. There already exists a wealth of data and information that could be used for the management of sustainable development. Finding the appropriate information at the required time and at the relevant scale of aggregation is a difficult task.

40.18. Information within many countries is not adequately managed, because of shortages of financial resources and trained manpower, lack of awareness of the value and availability of such information and other immediate or pressing problems, especially in developing countries. Even where information is avail-

---

3   Draft paragraph 40.15 of A/CONF.151/4 (22 April 1992) was replaced by decision of the Main Committee of UNCED on 10 June 1992. See A/CONF.151/L.3/Add.40 (12 June 1992). The former draft read as follows:

    Regarding [transfer of [safe and sound] technology]/[technology cooperation], with the rapid evolution of data-collection and information technologies it is necessary to develop guidelines and mechanisms for the rapid and continuous transfer of those technologies, particularly to developing countries [on concessional and preferential terms] and for the training of personnel in their utilization.

able, it may not be easily accessible, either because of the lack of technology for effective access or because of associated costs, especially for information held outside the country and available commercially.

Objectives

40.19. Existing national and international mechanisms of information process-ing and exchange, and of related technical assistance, should be strengthened to ensure effective and equitable availability of information generated at the local, provincial, national and international levels, subject to national sovereignty and relevant intellectual property rights.

40.20. National capacities should be strengthened, as well as capacities within Governments, non-governmental organizations and the private sector, in infor-mation handling and communication, particularly within developing countries.

40.21. Full participation of, in particular, developing countries should be en-sured in any international scheme under the organs and organizations of the United Nations system for the collection, analysis and use of data and information.

Activities

(a) Production of information usable for decision-making

40.22. Countries and international organizations should review and strengthen information systems and services in sectors related to sustainable development, at the local, provincial, national and international levels. Special emphasis should be placed on the transformation of existing information into forms more useful for decision-making and on targeting information at different user groups. Mechanisms should be strengthened or established for transforming sci-entific and socio-economic assessments into information suitable for both planning and public information. Electronic and non-electronic formats should be used.

(b) Establishment of standards and methods for handling information

40.23. Governments should consider supporting the efforts of governmental as well as non-governmental organizations to develop mechanisms for efficient and harmonized exchange of information at the local, national, provincial and international levels, including revision and establishment of data, access and dis-semination formats, and communication interfaces.

(c) Development of documentation about information

40.24. The organs and organizations of the United Nations system, as well as other governmental and non-governmental organizations, should document and share information about the sources of available information in their respective organizations. Existing programmes, such as those of the Advisory Committee for the Coordination of Information Systems (ACCIS) and the International Environmental Information System (INFOTERRA), should be reviewed and strengthened as required. Networking and coordinating mechanisms should be encouraged between the wide variety of other actors, including arrangements with non-governmental organizations for information sharing and donor activities for sharing information on sustainable development projects. The private sector should be encouraged to strengthen the mechanisms of sharing its experience and information on sustainable development.

(d) Establishment and strengthening of electronic networking capabilities

40.25. Countries, international organizations, including organs and organizations of the United Nations system, and non-governmental organizations should exploit various initiatives for electronic links to support information sharing, to provide access to databases and other information sources, to facilitate communication for meeting broader objectives, such as the implementation of Agenda 21, to facilitate intergovernmental negotiations, to monitor conventions and efforts for sustainable development, to transmit environmental alerts, and to transfer technical data. These organizations should also facilitate the linkage of different electronic networks and the use of appropriate standards and communication protocols for the transparent interchange of electronic communications. Where necessary, new technology should be developed and its use encouraged to permit participation of those not served at present by existing infrastructure and methods. Mechanisms should also be established to carry out the necessary transfer of information to and from non-electronic systems to ensure the involvement of those not able to participate in this way.

(e) Making use of commercial information sources

40.26. Countries and international organizations should consider undertaking surveys of information available in the private sector on sustainable development and of present dissemination arrangements to determine gaps and how those gaps could be filled by commercial or quasi-commercial activity, particularly activities in and/or involving developing countries where feasible. Whenever economic or other constraints on supplying and accessing information arise, particularly in developing countries, innovative schemes for subsidizing such information-related access or removing the non-economic constraints should be considered.

Means of implementation

(a) Financing and cost evaluation

40.27. The secretariat of the Conference has estimated the average total annual cost (1993-2000) of implementing the activities of this programme to be about $165 million from the international community on grant or concessional terms. These are indicative and order-of-magnitude estimates only and have not been reviewed by Governments. Actual costs and financial terms, including any that

are non-concessional, will depend upon, *inter alia*, the specific strategies and programmes Governments decide upon for implementation.[4]

(b) Institutional means

40.28. The institutional implications of this programme concern mostly the strengthening of already existing institutions, as well as the strengthening of co-operation with non-governmental organizations, and need to be consistent with the overall decisions on institutions made by the United Nations Conference on Environment and Development.

(c) Capacity-building

40.29. Developed countries and relevant international organizations should co-operate, in particular with developing countries, to expand their capacity to receive, store and retrieve, contribute, disseminate, use and provide appropriate public access to relevant environmental and developmental information, by providing technology and training to establish local information services and by supporting partnership and cooperative arrangements between countries and on the regional or subregional level.

(d) Scientific and technological means

40.30. Developed countries and relevant international organizations should support research and development in hardware, software and other aspects of information technology, in particular in developing countries, appropriate to their operations, national needs and environmental contexts.

---

4   Draft paragraph 40.28 of A/CONF.151/4 (22 April 1992) was replaced by decision of the Main Committee of UNCED on 10 June 1992. See A/CONF.151/L.3/Add.40 (12 June 1992). The former draft read as follows:

> This programme area involves strengthening existing country and international programmes. About $130 million per year will be needed for technical cooperation activities with and relating to developing countries and up to $35 million per year for strengthening activities in international organizations.

MILLENNIUM DECLARATION
AND
REPORT

Millennium Declaration

UN Res. 55/2

Resolution adopted by the General Assembly

[without reference to a Main Committee (A/55/L.2)]

8th plenary meeting
8 September 2000

The General Assembly

Adopts the following Declaration:

I. Values and Principles

1. We, heads of State and Government, have gathered at United Nations Headquarters in New York from 6 to 8 September 2000, at the dawn of a new millennium, to reaffirm our faith in the Organization and its Charter as indispensable foundations of a more peaceful, prosperous and just world.

2. We recognize that, in addition to our separate responsibilities to our individual societies, we have a collective responsibility to uphold the principles of human dignity, equality and equity at the global level. As leaders we have a duty therefore to all the world's people, especially the most vulnerable and, in particular, the children of the world, to whom the future belongs.

3. We reaffirm our commitment to the purposes and principles of the Charter of the United Nations, which have proved timeless and universal. Indeed, their relevance and capacity to inspire have increased, as nations and peoples have become increasingly interconnected and interdependent.

4. We are determined to establish a just and lasting peace all over the world in accordance with the purposes and principles of the Charter. We rededicate ourselves to support all efforts to uphold the sovereign equality of all States, respect for their territorial integrity and political independence, resolution of disputes by peaceful means and in conformity with the principles of justice and international law, the right to self-determination of peoples which remain under colonial domination and foreign occupation, non-interference in the internal affairs of States, respect for human rights and fundamental freedoms, respect for

the equal rights of all without distinction as to race, sex, language or religion and international cooperation in solving international problems of an economic, social, cultural or humanitarian character.

5. We believe that the central challenge we face today is to ensure that globalization becomes a positive force for all the world's people. For while globalization offers great opportunities, at present its benefits are very unevenly shared, while its costs are unevenly distributed. We recognize that developing countries and countries with economies in transition face special difficulties in responding to this central challenge. Thus, only through broad and sustained efforts to create a shared future, based upon our common humanity in all its diversity, can globalization be made fully inclusive and equitable. These efforts must include policies and measures, at the global level, which correspond to the needs of developing countries and economies in transition and are formulated and implemented with their effective participation.

6. We consider certain fundamental values to be essential to international relations in the twenty-first century. These include:

- **Freedom**. Men and women have the right to live their lives and raise their children in dignity, free from hunger and from the fear of violence, oppression or injustice. Democratic and participatory governance based on the will of the people best assures these rights.

- **Equality**. No individual and no nation must be denied the opportunity to benefit from development. The equal rights and opportunities of women and men must be assured.

- **Solidarity**. Global challenges must be managed in a way that distributes the costs and burdens fairly in accordance with basic principles of equity and social justice. Those who suffer or who benefit least deserve help from those who benefit most.

- **Tolerance**. Human beings must respect one other, in all their diversity of belief, culture and language. Differences within and between societies should be neither feared nor repressed, but cherished as a precious asset of humanity. A culture of peace and dialogue among all civilizations should be actively promoted.

- **Respect for nature**. Prudence must be shown in the management of all living species and natural resources, in accordance with the precepts of sustainable development. Only in this way can the immeasurable riches provided to us by nature be preserved and passed on to our descendants. The current unsustainable patterns of production and consumption must be changed in the interest of our future welfare and that of our descendants.

- **Shared responsibility**. Responsibility for managing worldwide economic and social development, as well as threats to international peace and security, must be shared among the nations of the world and should be exercised multilaterally. As the most universal and most representative organization in the world, the United Nations must play the central role.

7. In order to translate these shared values into actions, we have identified key objectives to which we assign special significance.

II. Peace, Security and Disarmament

8. We will spare no effort to free our peoples from the scourge of war, whether within or between States, which has claimed more than 5 million lives in the past decade. We will also seek to eliminate the dangers posed by weapons of mass destruction.

9. We resolve therefore:

- To strengthen respect for the rule of law in international as in national affairs and, in particular, to ensure compliance by Member States with the decisions of the International Court of Justice, in compliance with the Charter of the United Nations, in cases to which they are parties.

- To make the United Nations more effective in maintaining peace and security by giving it the resources and tools it needs for conflict prevention, peaceful resolution of disputes, peacekeeping, post-conflict peace-building and reconstruction. In this context, we take note of the report of the Panel on United Nations Peace Operations[1] and request the General Assembly to consider its recommendations expeditiously.

- To strengthen cooperation between the United Nations and regional organizations, in accordance with the provisions of Chapter VIII of the Charter.

- To ensure the implementation, by States Parties, of treaties in areas such as arms control and disarmament and of international humanitarian law and human rights law, and call upon all States to consider signing and ratifying the Rome Statute of the International Criminal Court.[2]

- To take concerted action against international terrorism, and to accede as soon as possible to all the relevant international conventions.

- To redouble our efforts to implement our commitment to counter the world drug problem.

- To intensify our efforts to fight transnational crime in all its dimensions, including trafficking as well as smuggling in human beings and money laundering.

---

1   A/55/305-S/2000/809; see *Official Records of the Security Council, Fifty-fifth Year, Supplement for July, August and September 2000*, document S/2000/809.
2   A/CONF.183/9.

- To minimize the adverse effects of United Nations economic sanctions on innocent populations, to subject such sanctions regimes to regular reviews and to eliminate the adverse effects of sanctions on third parties.

- To strive for the elimination of weapons of mass destruction, particularly nuclear weapons, and to keep all options open for achieving this aim, including the possibility of convening an international conference to identify ways of eliminating nuclear dangers.

- To take concerted action to end illicit traffic in small arms and light weapons, especially by making arms transfers more transparent and supporting regional disarmament measures, taking account of all the recommendations of the forthcoming United Nations Conference on Illicit Trade in Small Arms and Light Weapons.

- To call on all States to consider acceding to the Convention on the Prohibition of the Use, Stockpiling, Production and Transfer of Anti-personnel Mines and on Their Destruction,[3] as well as the amended mines protocol to the Convention on conventional weapons.[4]

10. We urge Member States to observe the Olympic Truce, individually and collectively, now and in the future, and to support the International Olympic Committee in its efforts to promote peace and human understanding through sport and the Olympic Ideal.

III. Development and Poverty Eradication

11. We will spare no effort to free our fellow men, women and children from the abject and dehumanizing conditions of extreme poverty, to which more than a billion of them are currently subjected. We are committed to making the right to development a reality for everyone and to freeing the entire human race from want.

12. We resolve therefore to create an environment—at the national and global levels alike—which is conducive to development and to the elimination of poverty.

13. Success in meeting these objectives depends, *inter alia*, on good governance within each country. It also depends on good governance at the international level and on transparency in the financial, monetary and trading systems. We are committed to an open, equitable, rule-based, predictable and non-discriminatory multilateral trading and financial system.

14. We are concerned about the obstacles developing countries face in mobilizing the resources needed to finance their sustained development. We will there-

---

3   See CD/1478.

4   Amended protocol on prohibitions or restrictions on the use of mines, booby-traps and other devices (CCW/CONF.I/16 (Part I), annex B).

fore make every effort to ensure the success of the High-level International and Intergovernmental Event on Financing for Development, to be held in 2001.

15. We also undertake to address the special needs of the least developed countries. In this context, we welcome the Third United Nations Conference on the Least Developed Countries to be held in May 2001 and will endeavour to ensure its success. We call on the industrialized countries:

- To adopt, preferably by the time of that Conference, a policy of duty- and quota-free access for essentially all exports from the least developed countries;

- To implement the enhanced programme of debt relief for the heavily indebted poor countries without further delay and to agree to cancel all official bilateral debts of those countries in return for their making demonstrable commitments to poverty reduction; and

- To grant more generous development assistance, especially to countries that are genuinely making an effort to apply their resources to poverty reduction.

16. We are also determined to deal comprehensively and effectively with the debt problems of low- and middle-income developing countries, through various national and international measures designed to make their debt sustainable in the long term.

17. We also resolve to address the special needs of small island developing States, by implementing the Barbados Programme of Action[5] and the outcome of the twenty-second special session of the General Assembly rapidly and in full. We urge the international community to ensure that, in the development of a vulnerability index, the special needs of small island developing States are taken into account.

18. We recognize the special needs and problems of the landlocked developing countries, and urge both bilateral and multilateral donors to increase financial and technical assistance to this group of countries to meet their special development needs and to help them overcome the impediments of geography by improving their transit transport systems.

19. We resolve further:

- To halve, by the year 2015, the proportion of the world's people whose income is less than one dollar a day and the proportion of people who suffer from hunger and, by the same date, to halve the proportion of people who are unable to reach or to afford safe drinking water.

---

5   Programme of Action for the Sustainable Development of Small Island Developing States (*Report of the Global Conference on the Sustainable Development of Small Island Developing States, Bridgetown, Barbados, 25 April-6 May 1994* (United Nations publication, Sales No. E.94.I.18 and corrigenda), chap. I, resolution 1, annex II).

- To ensure that, by the same date, children everywhere, boys and girls alike, will be able to complete a full course of primary schooling and that girls and boys will have equal access to all levels of education.

- By the same date, to have reduced maternal mortality by three quarters, and under-five child mortality by two thirds, of their current rates.

- To have, by then, halted, and begun to reverse, the spread of HIV/AIDS, the scourge of malaria and other major diseases that afflict humanity.

- To provide special assistance to children orphaned by HIV/AIDS.

- By 2020, to have achieved a significant improvement in the lives of at least 100 million slum dwellers as proposed in the "Cities Without Slums" initiative.

20. We also resolve:

- To promote gender equality and the empowerment of women as effective ways to combat poverty, hunger and disease and to stimulate development that is truly sustainable.

- To develop and implement strategies that give young people everywhere a real chance to find decent and productive work.

- To encourage the pharmaceutical industry to make essential drugs more widely available and affordable by all who need them in developing countries.

- To develop strong partnerships with the private sector and with civil society organizations in pursuit of development and poverty eradication.

- To ensure that the benefits of new technologies, especially information and communication technologies, in conformity with recommendations con- tained in the ECOSOC 2000 Ministerial Declaration,[6] are available to all.

IV. Protecting our Common Environment

21. We must spare no effort to free all of humanity, and above all our children and grandchildren, from the threat of living on a planet irredeemably spoilt by human activities, and whose resources would no longer be sufficient for their needs.

22. We reaffirm our support for the principles of sustainable development, in- cluding those set out in Agenda 21,[7] agreed upon at the United Nations Confer- ence on Environment and Development.

---

6   E/2000/L.9.

7   *Report of the United Nations Conference on Environment and Development, Rio de Janeiro, 3-14 June 1992* (United Nations publication, Sales No. E.93.I.8 and corrigenda), vol. I: *Resolutions adopted by the Conference*, resolution 1, annex II.

23. We resolve therefore to adopt in all our environmental actions a new ethic of conservation and stewardship and, as first steps, we resolve:

- To make every effort to ensure the entry into force of the Kyoto Protocol, preferably by the tenth anniversary of the United Nations Conference on Environment and Development in 2002, and to embark on the required reduction in emissions of greenhouse gases.

- To intensify our collective efforts for the management, conservation and sustainable development of all types of forests.

- To press for the full implementation of the Convention on Biological Diversity[8] and the Convention to Combat Desertification in those Countries Experiencing Serious Drought and/or Desertification, particularly in Africa.[9]

- To stop the unsustainable exploitation of water resources by developing water management strategies at the regional, national and local levels, which promote both equitable access and adequate supplies.

- To intensify cooperation to reduce the number and effects of natural and man-made disasters.

- To ensure free access to information on the human genome sequence.

V. Human Rights, Democracy and Good Governance

24. We will spare no effort to promote democracy and strengthen the rule of law, as well as respect for all internationally recognized human rights and fundamental freedoms, including the right to development.

25. We resolve therefore:

- To respect fully and uphold the Universal Declaration of Human Rights.[10]

- To strive for the full protection and promotion in all our countries of civil, political, economic, social and cultural rights for all.

- To strengthen the capacity of all our countries to implement the principles and practices of democracy and respect for human rights, including minority rights.

- To combat all forms of violence against women and to implement the Convention on the Elimination of All Forms of Discrimination against Women.[11]

- To take measures to ensure respect for and protection of the human rights of migrants, migrant workers and their families, to eliminate the increasing acts

---

8   See United Nations Environment Programme, *Convention on Biological Diversity* (Environmental Law and Institution Programme Activity Centre), June 1992.

9   A/49/84/Add.2, annex, appendix II.

10   Resolution 217 A (III).

11   Resolution 34/180, annex.

of racism and xenophobia in many societies and to promote greater harmony and tolerance in all societies.

- To work collectively for more inclusive political processes, allowing genuine participation by all citizens in all our countries.

- To ensure the freedom of the media to perform their essential role and the right of the public to have access to information.

VI. Protecting the Vulnerable

26. We will spare no effort to ensure that children and all civilian populations that suffer disproportionately the consequences of natural disasters, genocide, armed conflicts and other humanitarian emergencies are given every assistance and protection so that they can resume normal life as soon as possible.

We resolve therefore:

- To expand and strengthen the protection of civilians in complex emergencies, in conformity with international humanitarian law.

- To strengthen international cooperation, including burden sharing in, and the coordination of humanitarian assistance to, countries hosting refugees and to help all refugees and displaced persons to return voluntarily to their homes, in safety and dignity and to be smoothly reintegrated into their societies.

- To encourage the ratification and full implementation of the Convention on the Rights of the Child[12] and its optional protocols on the involvement of children in armed conflict and on the sale of children, child prostitution and child pornography.[13]

VII. Meeting the Special Needs of Africa

27. We will support the consolidation of democracy in Africa and assist Africans in their struggle for lasting peace, poverty eradication and sustainable development, thereby bringing Africa into the mainstream of the world economy.

28. We resolve therefore:

- To give full support to the political and institutional structures of emerging democracies in Africa.

- To encourage and sustain regional and subregional mechanisms for preventing conflict and promoting political stability, and to ensure a reliable flow of resources for peacekeeping operations on the continent.

- To take special measures to address the challenges of poverty eradication and sustainable development in Africa, including debt cancellation, improved

---

12   Resolution 44/25, annex.

13   Resolution 54/263, annexes I and II.

market access, enhanced Official Development Assistance and increased flows of Foreign Direct Investment, as well as transfers of technology.

- To help Africa build up its capacity to tackle the spread of the HIV/AIDS pandemic and other infectious diseases.

VIII. Strengthening the United Nations

29. We will spare no effort to make the United Nations a more effective instrument for pursuing all of these priorities: the fight for development for all the peoples of the world, the fight against poverty, ignorance and disease; the fight against injustice; the fight against violence, terror and crime; and the fight against the degradation and destruction of our common home.

30. We resolve therefore:

- To reaffirm the central position of the General Assembly as the chief deliberative, policy-making and representative organ of the United Nations, and to enable it to play that role effectively.

- To intensify our efforts to achieve a comprehensive reform of the Security Council in all its aspects.

- To strengthen further the Economic and Social Council, building on its recent achievements, to help it fulfil the role ascribed to it in the Charter.

- To strengthen the International Court of Justice, in order to ensure justice and the rule of law in international affairs.

- To encourage regular consultations and coordination among the principal organs of the United Nations in pursuit of their functions.

- To ensure that the Organization is provided on a timely and predictable basis with the resources it needs to carry out its mandates.

- To urge the Secretariat to make the best use of those resources, in accordance with clear rules and procedures agreed by the General Assembly, in the interests of all Member States, by adopting the best management practices and technologies available and by concentrating on those tasks that reflect the agreed priorities of Member States.

- To promote adherence to the Convention on the Safety of United Nations and Associated Personnel.[14]

- To ensure greater policy coherence and better cooperation between the United Nations, its agencies, the Bretton Woods Institutions and the World Trade Organization, as well as other multilateral bodies, with a view to achieving a fully coordinated approach to the problems of peace and development.

---

14   Resolution 49/59, annex.

- To strengthen further cooperation between the United Nations and national parliaments through their world organization, the Inter-Parliamentary Union, in various fields, including peace and security, economic and social development, international law and human rights and democracy and gender issues.

- To give greater opportunities to the private sector, non-governmental organizations and civil society, in general, to contribute to the realization of the Organization's goals and programmes.

31. We request the General Assembly to review on a regular basis the progress made in implementing the provisions of this Declaration, and ask the Secretary-General to issue periodic reports for consideration by the General Assembly and as a basis for further action.

32. We solemnly reaffirm, on this historic occasion, that the United Nations is the indispensable common house of the entire human family, through which we will seek to realize our universal aspirations for peace, cooperation and development. We therefore pledge our unstinting support for these common objectives and our determination to achieve them.

Millennium Report

We the Peoples: The Role of the United Nations in the Twenty-First Century

UN General Assembly Report 54/2000

Report of the Secretary-General

The Millennium Assembly of the United Nations

I. New Century, New Challenges

The arrival of the new millennium is an occasion for celebration and reflection.

The world did celebrate as the clock struck midnight on New Year's Eve, in one time zone after another, from Kiribati and Fiji westward around the globe to Samoa. People of all cultures joined in—not only those for whom the millennium might be thought to have a special significance. The Great Wall of China and the Pyramids of Giza were lit as brightly as Manger Square in Bethlehem and St. Peter's Square in Rome. Tokyo, Jakarta and New Delhi joined Sydney, Moscow, Paris, New York, Rio de Janeiro and hundreds of other cities in hosting millennial festivities. Children's faces reflected the candlelight from Spitsbergen in Norway to Robben Island in South Africa. For 24 hours the human family celebrated its unity through an unprecedented display of its rich diversity.

The Millennium Summit affords an opportunity for reflection. The General Assembly convened this gathering of Heads of State and Government to address the role of the United Nations in the twenty-first century. Both the occasion and the subject require us to step back from today's headlines and take a broader, longer-term view—of the state of the world and the challenges it poses for this Organization.

There is much to be grateful for. Most people today can expect to live longer than their parents, let alone their more remote ancestors. They are better nourished, enjoy better health, are better educated, and on the whole face more favourable economic prospects.

There are also many things to deplore, and to correct. The century just ended was disfigured, time and again, by ruthless conflict. Grinding poverty and striking inequality persist within and among countries even amidst unprecedented wealth. Diseases, old and new, threaten to undo painstaking progress. Nature's life-sustaining services, on which our species depends for its survival, are being seriously disrupted and degraded by our own everyday activities.

The world's people look to their leaders, when they gather at the Millennium Summit, to identify and act on the major challenges ahead.

The United Nations can succeed in helping to meet those challenges only if all of us feel a renewed sense of mission about our common endeavour. We need to remind ourselves why the United Nations exists—for what, and for whom. We also need to ask ourselves what kind of United Nations the world's leaders are prepared to support, in deeds as well as words. Clear answers are necessary to energize and focus the Organization's work in the decades ahead. It is those answers that the Millennium Summit must provide.

Of course, the United Nations exists to serve its Member States. It is the only body of its kind with universal membership and comprehensive scope, and encompassing so many areas of human endeavour. These features make it a uniquely useful forum—for sharing information, conducting negotiations, elaborating norms and voicing expectations, coordinating the behaviour of states and other actors, and pursuing common plans of action. We must ensure that the United Nations performs these functions as efficiently and effectively as possible.

The United Nations is more than a mere tool, however. As its Charter makes clear, the United Nations was intended to introduce new principles into international relations, making a qualitative difference to their day-to-day conduct. The Charter's very first Article defines our purposes: resolving disputes by peaceful means; devising cooperative solutions to economic, social, cultural and humanitarian problems; and broadly encouraging behaviour in conformity with the principles of justice and international law. In other words, quite apart from whatever practical tasks the United Nations is asked to perform, it has the avowed purpose of transforming relations among states, and the methods by which the world's affairs are managed.

Nor is that all. For even though the United Nations is an organization of states, the Charter is written in the name of "we the peoples". It reaffirms the dignity and worth of the human person, respect for human rights and the equal rights of men and women, and a commitment to social progress as measured by better standards of life, in freedom from want and fear alike. Ultimately, then, the United Nations exists for, and must serve, the needs and hopes of people everywhere.

For its first 45 years, the United Nations lived in the grip of the cold war, prevented from fulfilling some of its core missions but discovering other critical tasks in that conflict's shadow. For 10 years now, the United Nations has been buffeted by the tumultuous changes of the new era, doing good work in many instances but falling short in others. Now, the Millennium Summit offers the world's leaders an unparalleled opportunity to reshape the United Nations well into the twenty-first century, enabling it to make a real and measurable difference to people's lives.

I respectfully submit the present report to Member States to facilitate their preparations for the Summit and to stimulate their subsequent deliberations at the Summit. The report identifies some of the pressing challenges faced by the world's people that fall within the United Nations ambit. It proposes a number of priorities for Member States to consider, and it recommends several immediate steps that we can take at the Summit itself, to lift people's spirits and improve their lives.

All these proposals are set in the context of globalization, which is transforming the world as we enter the twenty-first century. In this new era, people's actions constantly—if often unwittingly—affect the lives of others living far away. Globalization offers great opportunities, but at present its benefits are very unevenly distributed while its costs are borne by all.

Thus the central challenge we face today is to ensure that globalization becomes a positive force for all the world's people, instead of leaving billions of them behind in squalor. Inclusive globalization must be built on the great enabling force of the market, but market forces alone will not achieve it. It requires a broader effort to create a shared future, based upon our common humanity in all its diversity.

That in turn requires that we think afresh about how we manage our joint activities and our shared interests, for many challenges that we confront today are beyond the reach of any state to meet on its own. At the national level we must govern better, and at the international level we must learn to govern better together. Effective states are essential for both tasks, and their capacity for both needs strengthening. We must also adapt international institutions, through which states govern together, to the realities of the new era. We must form coalitions for change, often with partners well beyond the precincts of officialdom.

No shift in the way we think or act can be more critical than this: we must put people at the centre of everything we do. No calling is more noble, and no responsibility greater, than that of enabling men, women and children, in cities and villages around the world, to make their lives better. Only when that begins to happen will we know that globalization is indeed becoming inclusive, allowing everyone to share its opportunities.

We must do more than talk about our future, however. We must start to create it, now. Let the Millennium Summit signal the renewed commitment of Member States to their United Nations, by agreeing on our common vision. Let the world's leaders prove their commitment by acting on it as soon as they return home.

II. Globalization and Governance

In the early years of the United Nations, the General Assembly's timely adjournment could be predicted with precision: its absolute limit was fixed by the year's last voyage of the *Queen Mary*. That world, clearly, was a very different place from today's.

Indeed, when the United Nations was founded two thirds of the current Members did not exist as sovereign states, their people still living under colonial rule. The planet hosted a total population of fewer than 2. 5 billion, compared to 6 billion today. Trade barriers were high, trade flows minuscule and capital controls firmly in place. Most big companies operated within a single country and produced for their home market. The cost of transoceanic telephone calls was prohibitive for the average person and limited even business use to exceptional circumstances. The annual output of steel was a prized symbol of national economic prowess. The world's first computer had just been constructed; it filled a large room, bristled with 18, 000 electron tubes and half a million solder joints, and had to be physically rewired for each new task. Ecology was a subject confined to the study of biology, and references to cyberspace would not have been found even in science fiction.

We know how profoundly things have changed. World exports have increased tenfold since 1950, even after adjusting for inflation, consistently growing faster than world GDP. Foreign investment has risen more rapidly; sales by multinational firms exceed world exports by a growing margin, and transactions among corporate affiliates are a rapidly expanding segment of world trade. Foreign exchange flows have soared to more than $1. 5 trillion daily, up from $15 billion in 1973 when the regime of fixed exchange rates collapsed. A recent transnational telecommunications takeover created a firm whose market value exceeds the GDP of nearly half of all United Nations Members, though it ranks only as the world's fourth most valuable company. Today rushed General Assembly delegates can cross the Atlantic in less than four hours—and, if they so wish, conduct affairs of state on the Internet or telephone all the way.

This is the world of globalization—a new context for and a new connectivity among economic actors and activities throughout the world. Globalization has been made possible by the progressive dismantling of barriers to trade and capital mobility, together with fundamental technological advances and steadily declining costs of transportation, communication and computing. Its integrative logic seems inexorable, its momentum irresistible. The benefits of globalization are plain to see: faster economic growth, higher living standards, accelerated innovation and diffusion of technology and management skills, new economic opportunities for individuals and countries alike.

Why, then, has globalization begun to generate a backlash, of which the events surrounding last November's World Trade Organization meeting in Seattle were but the most recent and highly visible manifestation?

Few people, groups or governments oppose globalization as such. They protest against its disparities. First, the benefits and opportunities of globalization remain highly concentrated among a relatively small number of countries and are spread unevenly within them. Second, in recent decades an imbalance has emerged between successful efforts to craft strong and well-enforced rules facilitating the expansion of global markets, while support for equally valid social objectives, be they labour standards, the environment, human rights or poverty reduction, has lagged behind.

More broadly, for many people globalization has come to mean greater vulnerability to unfamiliar and unpredictable forces that can bring on economic instability and social dislocation, sometimes at lightning speed. The Asian financial crisis of 1997-1998 was such a force—the fifth serious international monetary and financial crisis in just two decades. There is mounting anxiety that the integrity of cultures and the sovereignty of states may be at stake. Even in the most powerful countries, people wonder who is in charge, worry for their jobs and fear that their voices are drowned out in globalization's sweep.

Underlying these diverse expressions of concern is a single, powerful message: globalization must mean more than creating bigger markets. The economic sphere cannot be separated from the more complex fabric of social and political life, and sent shooting off on its own trajectory. To survive and thrive, a global economy must have a more solid foundation in shared values and institutional practices—it must advance broader, and more inclusive, social purposes.

A. The Challenge in 1945

This view was firmly embraced by the world's leaders who gathered in the waning days of the Second World War to rebuild a viable international order. They knew fully how an earlier era of economic globalization, in some respects as economically interdependent as ours, eroded steadily before collapsing completely under the shock of 1914. That global era rested on a political structure of imperialism, denying subject peoples and territories the right of self-rule.

Moreover, the major powers lacked adequate means for international political adjustment and peaceful change. To stabilize the European balance of power, for example, those powers resorted to carving up the African continent. In the economic sphere, the best they could do to achieve international financial stability was to hold levels of domestic economic activity hostage to shifts in their external balance of payments—contracting when in deficit, expanding when in surplus. This practice became untenable once the franchise was extended to ordinary people and governments began to respond gradually—and at first grudgingly—to people's needs for steady jobs and stable prices.

From the 20 years' crisis between the wars, however, the architects of the post1945 world learned how utterly destructive it was for countries to turn their backs altogether on economic interdependence. Unrestrained economic nationalism and "beggar-my-neighbour" policies took root almost everywhere in the 1930s, spilling over into political revanchism, totalitarianism and militarism in some countries, isolationism in others. The League of Nations was critically wounded from the start, and in the face of those forces it stood no chance.

Our predecessors, therefore, wisely chose a course of openness and cooperation. They established the United Nations, the Bretton Woods institutions, the General Agreement on Tariffs and Trade (later subsumed into the World Trade Organization) and a host of other organizations whose job it was to make the overall system work. Some supported decolonization, though the struggle for independence, which the United Nations was proud to promote, took too many years and cost too many lives. In the industrialized countries, domestic support for open markets was secured by constructing social safety nets and providing adjustment assistance to adversely affected groups and industries. We benefit from that legacy still.

Here, however, is the crux of our problem today: while the post-war multilateral system made it possible for the new globalization to emerge and flourish, globalization, in turn, has progressively rendered its designs antiquated. Simply put, our postwar institutions were built for an inter-*national* world, but we now live in a *global* world. Responding effectively to this shift is the core institutional challenge for world leaders today. The Millennium Summit can help show the way.

B. The Challenge Today

How far we have moved from a strictly international world is evidenced by the changed nature of threats to peace and security faced by the world's people today. The provisions of the Charter presupposed that external aggression, an attack by one state against another, would constitute the most serious threat; but in recent decades far more people have been killed in civil wars, ethnic cleansing and acts of genocide, fuelled by weapons widely available in the global arms bazaar. Technologies of mass destruction circulate in a netherworld of illicit markets, and terrorism casts shadows on stable rule. We have not yet adapted our institutions to this new reality.

Much the same is true in the economic realm. Here, the post-war institutional arrangements were premised on a world made up of separate national economies, engaged in external transactions, conducted at arms length. Globalization contradicts each of these expectations. It is hardly surprising, therefore, that the trade regime is under such stress—it increasingly deals with traditionally "domestic" matters rather than border barriers. Nor are we surprised that calls for a new financial architecture are so insistent.

Globalization constrains the ability of industrialized countries to cushion the adverse domestic effects of further market opening. The developing countries had never enjoyed that privilege to begin with. As a result, the public in both now feels exposed and insecure.

Globalization has also created new vulnerabilities to old threats. Criminal networks take advantage of the most advanced technologies to traffic around the world in drugs, arms, precious metals and stones—even people. Indeed, these elements of "uncivil society" are constructing global conglomerates of illicit activities.

Diseases have shaped history for millennia, spread by traders, invaders and natural carriers. But the most recent upsurge in the global transmission of pathogens, above all HIV/AIDS, has hit with a velocity and scope made possible only by open borders and unprecedented mobility.

Entirely new dimensions of globalization have emerged as well. While transborder pollution has been on the international agenda for decades, once the cumulative effects of industrialization were understood to affect global climate change, the world entered—literally, became enveloped by—a wholly new context in which conventional institutional remedies fare poorly.

The revolution in global communications has created new expectations that humanitarian suffering will be alleviated and fundamental rights vindicated. Neither governments nor international institutions have yet sorted out either the full implications of these expectations or how to meet them.

The communications revolution is being felt in other ways, too. The Internet is the fastest growing instrument of communication in the history of civilization, and it may be the most rapidly disseminating tool of any kind ever. The convergence of information technology, the Internet and e-commerce may well become as transformative as the industrial revolution. They will continue to alter the world's economic landscape and reconfigure organizational structures. They will change the way many people work and live. They already make it possible to leapfrog existing barriers to development, as entrepreneurs from Bangalore to Guadalajara and São Paulo will testify, and the range of such opportunities can be vastly expanded.

Perhaps most important, these technologies enable people to be connected directly who otherwise might remain divided by distance, culture and economic stratification, potentially creating, thereby, a better understanding of who we, the peoples, are. But none of these possibilities exists for those without access to the technology, either because the necessary infrastructure or capital is lacking, or because regulatory environments stand in the way.

And so the challenge is clear: if we are to capture the promises of globalization while managing its adverse effects, we must learn to govern better, and we must learn how better to govern together. The Millennium Summit, therefore, takes place at a compelling moment, not merely in symbolic but also in practical terms.

C. Governing Better Together

What do we mean by "governance" when applied to the international realm? What are some of its desirable attributes if our aim is to successfully manage the transition from an international to a global world?

In the minds of some, the term still conjures up images of world government, of centralized bureaucratic behemoths trampling on the rights of people and states. Nothing is less desirable. Weak states are one of the main impediments to effective governance today, at national and international levels alike. For the good of their own people and for the sake of our common aims, we must help to strengthen the capacity of those states to govern, not undermine them further. Moreover, the very notion of centralizing hierarchies is itself an anachronism in our fluid, highly dynamic and extensively networked world—an outmoded remnant of nineteenth century mindsets.

By the same token, states need to develop a deeper awareness of their dual role in our global world. In addition to the separate responsibilities each state bears towards its own society, states are, collectively, the custodians of our common life on this planet—a life the citizens of *all* countries share. Notwithstanding the institutional turmoil that is often associated with globalization, there exists no other entity that competes with or can substitute for the state. Successfully managing globalization, therefore, requires—first and foremost—that states act in a manner consistent with their dual role.

This implies, in turn, that decision-making structures through which governance is exercised internationally must reflect the broad realities of our times. The United Nations Security Council is an obvious case in point. Based on the distribution of power and alignments in 1945, the composition of the Council today does not fully represent either the character or the needs of our globalized world. The same holds in some major economic forums: all countries are consumers of globalization's effects; all must have a greater say in the process itself.

The unique role of the United Nations in the new global era derives from our universal membership and scope, and from the shared values embodied in our Charter. It is our job to ensure that globalization provides benefits, not just for some, but for all; that peace and security hold, not only for a few, but for the many; that opportunities exist, not merely for the privileged, but for every human being everywhere. More than ever, the United Nations is needed to broker differences among states in power, culture, size and interest, serving as the place where the cause of common humanity is articulated and advanced. More than ever, a robust international legal order, together with the principles and practices of multilateralism, is needed to define the ground rules of an emerging global civilization within which there will be room for the world's rich diversity to express itself fully.

Better governance means greater participation, coupled with accountability. Therefore, the international public domain—including the United Nations—must be opened up further to the participation of the many actors whose contributions are essential to managing the path of globalization. Depending on the issues at hand, this may include civil society organizations, the private sector, parliamentarians, local authorities, scientific associations, educational institutions and many others.

Global companies occupy a critical place in this new constellation. They, more than anyone, have created the single economic space in which we live; their decisions have implications for the economic prospects of people and even nations around the world. Their rights to operate globally have been greatly expanded by international agreements and national policies, but those rights must be accompanied by greater responsibilities—by the concept and practice of global corporate citizenship. The marks of good citizenship may vary depending upon circumstances, but they will exhibit one common feature: the willingness by firms, wherever possible and appropriate, to pursue "good practices" as defined by the broader community, rather than taking advantage of the weaker regulatory systems or unequal bargaining positions of host countries.

The more integrated global context also demands a new degree of policy coherence, while important gaps must be filled. The international financial architecture needs strengthening, as does the multilateral trade regime. Greater consistency must be achieved among macroeconomic, trade, aid, financial and environmental policies, so that all support our common aim of expanding the benefits of globalization. Conflict prevention, post-conflict peace-building, humanitarian assistance and development policies need to become more effectively integrated. In short, it is exceedingly difficult to successfully navigate the transition to a more global world with incomplete and incompatible policy fragments.

Formal institutional arrangements may often lack the scope, speed and informational capacity to keep up with the rapidly changing global agenda. Mobilizing the skills and other resources of diverse global actors, therefore, may increasingly involve forming loose and temporary global policy networks that cut across national, institutional and disciplinary lines. The United Nations is well situated to nurture such informal "coalitions for change" across our various areas of responsibility. Many of the networks can be virtual, overcoming, thereby, the usual constraints imposed by distance and time. The essential role that formal governance structures must continue to play is normative: defining objectives, setting standards and monitoring compliance.

For the United Nations, success in meeting the challenges of globalization ultimately comes down to meeting the needs of peoples. It is in their name that the Charter was written; realizing their aspirations remains our vision for the twenty-first century.

D. The Peoples' Concerns

But who are *we*, the peoples? And what are our common concerns?

Let us imagine, for a moment, that the world really is a "global village"—taking seriously the metaphor that is often invoked to depict global interdependence. Say this village has 1, 000 individuals, with all the characteristics of today's human race distributed in exactly the same proportions. What would it look like? What would we see as its main challenges?

Some 150 of the inhabitants live in an affluent area of the village, about 780 in poorer districts. Another 70 or so live in a neighbourhood that is in transition. The average income per person is $6, 000 a year, and there are more middle income families than in the past. But just 200 people dispose of 86 per cent of all the wealth, while nearly half of the villagers are eking out an existence on less than $2 per day.

Men outnumber women by a small margin, but women make up a majority of those who live in poverty. Adult literacy has been increasing. Still, some 220 villagers—two thirds of them women—are illiterate. Of the 390 inhabitants under 20 years of age, three fourths live in the poorer districts, and many are looking desperately for jobs that do not exist. Fewer than 60 people own a computer and only 24 have access to the Internet. More than half have never made or received a telephone call.

Life expectancy in the affluent district is nearly 78 years, in the poorer areas 64 years—and in the very poorest neighbourhoods a mere 52 years. Each marks an improvement over previous generations, but why do the poorest lag so far behind? Because in their neighbourhoods there is a far higher incidence of infectious diseases and malnutrition, combined with an acute lack of access to safe water, sanitation, health care, adequate housing, education and work.

There is no predictable way to keep the peace in this village. Some districts are relatively safe while others are wracked by organized violence. The village has suffered a growing number of weather-related natural disasters in recent years, including unexpected and severe storms, as well as sudden swings from floods to droughts, while the average temperature is perceptibly warmer. More and more evidence suggests that there is a connection between these two trends, and that warming is related to the kind of fuel, and the quantities of it, that the people and businesses are using. Carbon emissions, the major cause of warming, have quadrupled in the last 50 years. The village's water table is falling precipitously, and the livelihood of one sixth of the inhabitants is threatened by soil degradation in the surrounding countryside.

Who among us would not wonder how long a village in this state can survive without taking steps to ensure that all its inhabitants can live free from hunger and safe from violence, drinking clean water, breathing clean air, and knowing that their children will have real chances in life?

That is the question we have to face in our real world of 6 billion inhabitants. Indeed, questions like it were raised by the civil society participants at hearings held by the United Nations regional commissions in preparation for the Millennium Assembly—in Addis Ababa, Beirut, Geneva, Tokyo and Santiago.

Similar sentiments were expressed last autumn in the largest survey of public opinion ever conducted—of 57, 000 adults in 60 countries, spread across all six continents (see box 1).

Strikingly, the centrality of human rights to peoples' expectations about the future role of the United Nations was stressed both at the hearings and in the survey. The current level of performance, especially of governments, was judged to be unsatisfactory.

The respondents in the Millennium Survey expressed equally strong views about the environment. Fully two thirds of them, worldwide, said their governments had not done enough to protect the environment. In only 5 countries out of 60 was the majority satisfied with the government's efforts in this respect; people in developing countries were among the most critical.

The hearings and the survey alike gave the United Nations a mixed overall assessment. In the sampling of public opinion, governments received even lower ratings than the United Nations. In most countries a majority said their elections were free and fair, but as many as two thirds of all respondents felt that their country, nevertheless, was not governed by the will of the people. Even in the world's oldest democracies many citizens expressed deep dissatisfaction.

Let there be no mistake. We have many success stories to tell and positive trends to report—and I shall do both throughout this report. The United Nations global conferences in the 1990s, for example, laid a solid foundation of goals and action plans—in the areas of environment and development, human rights, women, children, social development, population, human settlements and food security. At the national level, economic restructuring and political reforms are more widespread today than ever.

The world's people are nevertheless telling us that our past achievements are not enough, given the scale of the challenges we face. We must do more, and we must do it better.

The challenges I highlight below are not exhaustive. I have focused on strategic priority areas where, in my view, we can and must make a real difference to help people lead better lives. The challenges are clustered into three broad categories.

Two are founding aims of the United Nations whose achievement eludes us still: freedom from want, and freedom from fear. No one dreamed, when the Charter was written, that the third—leaving to successor generations an environmentally sustainable future—would emerge as one of the most daunting challenges of all.

Box 1
Voices of the People: The World's Largest Ever Public Opinion Survey

In 1999, Gallup International sponsored and conducted a Millennium Survey of 57, 000 adults in 60 countries.

What matters most in life

- People everywhere valued good health and a happy family life more highly than anything else. Where economic performance was poor, they also stressed jobs.
- Where there was conflict, people expressed a strong desire to live without it. Where corruption was endemic, people condemned it.

Human rights

- Respondents showed widespread dissatisfaction with the level of respect for human rights.
- In one region fewer than one in 10 citizens believed that human rights were being fully respected, while one third believed they were not observed at all.
- Discrimination by race and gender were commonly expressed concerns.

Environment

- Two thirds of all the respondents said their government had done too little to redress environmental problems in their country.
- Respondents in the developing countries were among the most critical of their government's actions in this respect.

The United Nations

- The survey showed that most people around the globe consider the protection of human rights to be the most important task for the United Nations. The younger the respondents, the greater the importance assigned to this goal.
- United Nations peacekeeping and the provision of humanitarian assistance were also stressed.
- Globally, less than half of those interviewed judged the performance of the United Nations to be satisfactory, although a majority of the young were favourably inclined.

Democracy

- In most countries the majority said their elections were free and fair.
- Despite this, two thirds of all respondents considered that their country was not governed by the will of the people. This opinion held even in some of the oldest democracies in the world.

III. Freedom from Want

In the past half-century the world has made unprecedented economic gains. Countries that a mere generation ago were struggling with underdevelopment are now vibrant centres of global economic activity and domestic well-being. In just two decades, 15 countries, whose combined populations exceed 1. 6 billion, have halved the proportion of their citizens living in extreme poverty. Asia has made an astounding recovery from the financial crisis of 1997-1998, demonstrating the staying power of its economies—though Asia's poor have not yet regained lost ground.

Chief among the human development success stories since the 1960s are the increase in life expectancy in developing countries, from 46 to 64 years; the halving of infant mortality rates; an increase of more than 80 per cent in the proportion of children enrolled in primary school; and the doubling of access to safe drinking water and basic sanitation.

While more of us enjoy better standards of living than ever before, many others remain desperately poor. Nearly half the world's population still has to make do on less than $2 per day. Approximately 1. 2 billion people—500 million in South Asia and 300 million in Africa—struggle on less than $1 (see figure 1; for other measures of poverty, see figure 2). People living in Africa south of the Sahara are almost as poor today as they were 20 years ago. With that kind of deprivation comes pain, powerlessness, despair and lack of fundamental freedom—all of which, in turn, perpetuate poverty. Of a total world labour force of some 3 billion, 140 million workers are out of work altogether, and a quarter to a third are underemployed.

The persistence of income inequality over the past decade is also troubling. Globally, the 1 billion people living in developed countries earn 60 per cent of the world's income, while the 3. 5 billion people in low-income countries earn less than 20 per cent. Many countries have experienced growing internal inequality, including some of those in transition from communism. In the developing world, income gaps are most pronounced in Latin America, followed closely by sub-Saharan Africa.

Extreme poverty is an affront to our common humanity. It also makes many other problems worse. For example, poor countries—especially those with significant inequality between ethnic and religious communities—are far more likely to be embroiled in conflicts than rich ones. Most of these conflicts are internal, but they almost invariably create problems for neighbours or generate a need for humanitarian assistance.

Moreover, poor countries often lack the capacity and resources to implement environmentally sound policies. This undermines the sustainability of their people's meagre existence, and compounds the effects of their poverty.

Figure 1 Population living on less than $1 per day, 1990–1998 (Millions)

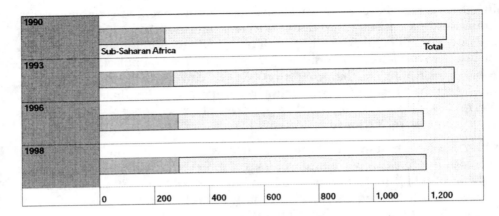

Note: Data for 1998 are estimated.

Source: World Bank, *World Development Indicators 1999.*

Figure 2 Measures of poverty (Millions)

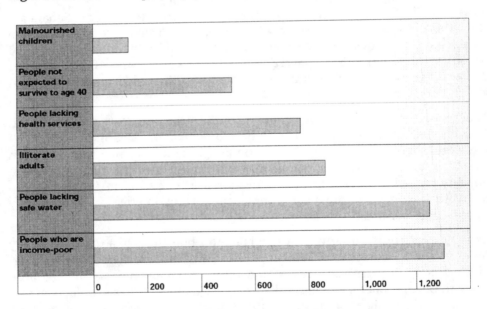

Source: United Nations Development Programme, *Human Development Report 1997.*

Unless we redouble and concert our efforts, poverty and inequality may get worse still. World population recently reached 6 billion. It took only 12 years to add the last billion, the shortest such span in history. By 2025, we can expect a further 2 billion—almost all in developing countries, and most of them in the poorest (see figure 3). We must act now.

Figure 3 World population projections, 1950–2050 (Billions)

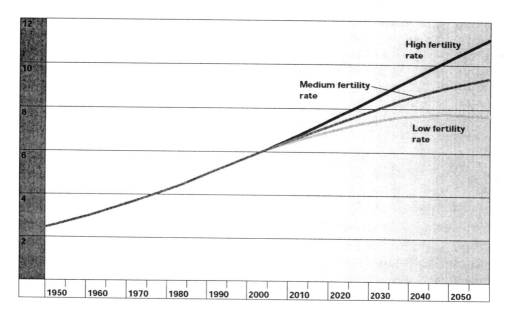

Source: United Nations Department of Economic and Social Affairs, *Critical Trends: Global Change and Sustainable Development,* 1997.

I call on the international community at the highest level—the Heads of State and Government convened at the Millennium Summit—to adopt the target of halving the proportion of people living in extreme poverty, and so lifting more than 1 billion people out of it, by 2015. I further urge that no effort be spared to reach this target by that date in every region, and in every country.

History will judge political leaders in the developing countries by what they did to eradicate the extreme poverty of their people—by whether they enabled their people to board the train of a transforming global economy, and made sure that everyone had at least standing room, if not a comfortable seat. By the same token, history will judge the rest of us by what we did to help the world's poor board that train in good order.

There is a growing consensus on what must be done for us to reach this paramount goal—and it can be reached. I wish to highlight a number of specific areas for particular attention by the Summit.

A. Achieving Sustained Growth

Our only hope of significantly reducing poverty is to achieve sustained and broadbased income growth. South Asia, and even more so sub-Saharan Africa, will have to make significant gains.

The latest poverty figures illustrate the challenge. They show a decrease in the overall number of people living on $1 a day. A closer look reveals that this is due almost entirely to progress in East Asia, notably China, where poverty reduction is closely associated with strong rates of growth. Indeed, recent studies show an almost perfect correlation between growth and poverty reduction in poor countries—a 1 per cent increase in GDP brings a corresponding increase in the incomes of the poorest 20 per cent of the population. Only in the societies with the greatest inequalities does growth fail to benefit the poor.

So what are some of the critical ingredients of success?

Expanding access to the opportunities of globalization is one. Those countries that have achieved higher growth are those that have successfully integrated into the global economy and attracted foreign investment. Over the past 25 years, Asia has grown at an annual rate of 7 per cent and Latin America at 5 per cent. The countries that have been largely left out of globalization have fared the worst. That includes substantial parts of sub-Saharan Africa.

Some people fear that globalization makes inequality worse. The relationship between the two is complex. With the exception of the economies in transition, recent increases in income gaps are largely the result of technological changes that favour higher skilled workers over less skilled ones. As the economic benefits of education and skills increase, so does income inequality between the people who have them and those who do not. This is true both within and among countries. Globalization may exacerbate these differences, but it does not cause them. Increased global competition may also restrain income gains in relatively higher wage countries, though to date this effect has been felt mainly in the industrialized countries.

Another major source of income inequality within countries is gender discrimination in wages, property rights and access to education. Here globalization, on the whole, may be having some positive effects.

In the developing countries, the labour force engaged in global production typically includes a large proportion of women—whether in textiles, electronics, data processing or chip manufacturing. In many cases, these women work in conditions and for wages that are appalling, and which we must strive to improve. But the fact of their employment also has important benefits.

These new employment opportunities enable women to expand the range of critical choices open to them. They can delay marriage, for example, as a result of which fertility rates often decline. They and their children often gain access to more and better nutrition, health care and education. As the survival rates of their children increase, fertility rates will decline further. The increase in female employment and earnings may also lead to changes in the perceived "social value" of a female child, which means that parents and society at large may become more willing to give girls greater access to education, health care and nutrition.

It is now widely accepted that economic success depends in considerable measure on the quality of governance a country enjoys. Good governance comprises the rule of law, effective state institutions, transparency and accountability in the management of public affairs, respect for human rights, and the participation of all citizens in the decisions that affect their lives. While there may be debates about the most appropriate forms they should take, there can be no disputing the importance of these principles.

A fair and transparent public expenditure and taxation system is another key ingredient. Revenues must be used wisely to help the poor, and to make sound investments in physical and social infrastructure for all. Excessive regulation, by contrast, impedes economic performance and slows growth.

Certain practices clearly do not constitute good governance by any definition. If a succession of military dictators in a resource-rich country in a poor part of the world siphon off as much as $27 billion of the public's money, economic performance and the poor are likely to suffer. Those responsible for such abuses, and the international banks that eagerly transfer their funds to safe havens, must be held accountable.

Other forms of institutionalized corruption are far less extreme but may, nevertheless, seriously distort economic incentives, limit economic growth and result in low levels of support for the poor.

Nothing is more inimical to pro-growth, anti-poverty objectives than armed conflict. It must pain us all beyond description to see a war between two of Africa's poorest countries drag on into yet a third year, having already taken an estimated 55, 000 lives, and with 8 million people in one of the countries threatened by famine. Internal conflicts in other parts of Africa have lasted even longer, and have destroyed the lives and livelihoods of many more millions of Africans.

Sustained and broad-based growth also requires investments in health and education, as well as other social policies. The United Nations conferences in the 1990s spelled these out in considerable detail; I shall recommend both a health and an education initiative.

Better-educated and healthier people are empowered to make better choices and lead fuller lives, which also makes them more productive and their economies more competitive. Similarly, all the evidence indicates that extending equal opportunities to women and girls has multiplier effects for entire families and even communities. As a supplement to universal social programmes, school lunches and other targeted initiatives for the poor have an economic as well as a social purpose.

Finally, appropriate levels and types of support from the global community—public and private—are needed for development targets to be reached. I shall address this dimension of the challenge separately.

In short, experience confirms some fundamental truths: growth is a necessary, though not sufficient, condition for reducing poverty and income inequality. The surest route to growth is through successfully engaging in the global economy. But that must be combined with effective social policies: advances in education for all, health for all and gender equality. Success rests on a strong foundation in governance. And it requires external support.

B. Generating Opportunities for the Young

More than 1 billion people today are between the ages of 15 and 24; in fact, nearly 40 per cent of the world's population is below the age of 20. Many of these young people already are, or are about to start, having children of their own. Most of the resulting youth bulge—nearly 98 per cent—will occur in the developing world.

Demography is not destiny, but this is a formidable challenge—not so much because of the sheer number of people as because of the context of poverty and deprivation in which they will have to live unless we take decisive action now. If I had one wish for the new millennium, it would be that we treat this challenge as an opportunity for all, not a lottery in which most of us will lose.

Young people are a source of creativity, energy and initiative, of dynamism and social renewal. They learn quickly and adapt readily. Given the chance to go to school and find work, they will contribute hugely to economic development and social progress.

Were we to fail to give them these opportunities, at best we would be complicit in an unforgivable waste of human potential. At worst, we would be contributing to all the evils of youth without hope: loss of morale, and lives that are socially unproductive and potentially destructive—of the individuals themselves, their communities and even fragile democracies.

Education

Education is the key to the new global economy, from primary school on up to life-long learning. It is central to development, social progress and human freedom.

Educational levels in developing countries have climbed dramatically in the past half-century. Indeed, East Asia's rapid reduction of poverty has had a great deal to do with its investments in education. But we still have a long way to go. While a majority of the world's children are attending school, more than 130 million primary-school-age children in developing countries are not—of whom more than half live in India, Bangladesh, Pakistan, Nigeria and Ethiopia.

Moreover, to enable families living in poverty to survive, a quarter of a billion children aged 14 and under, both in and out of school, now work, often in hazardous or unhealthy conditions. They toil in urban sweatshops; on farms or as domestic servants; selling gum or cleaning shoes in urban streets; clambering down dangerous mine shafts; and—in distressing numbers—bonded or sold into sexual services. Having approved the International Labour Organization convention on the worst forms of child labour, Member States must now implement it fully.

Providing primary education for the 130 million children in developing countries who do not now enjoy it would add an estimated $7 billion a year to educational costs, over a 10-year period. More than buildings are required, however. Schools must be accessible, have qualified teachers and offer such amenities as textbooks and supplies for the poor.

About 60 per cent of children not in school are girls. Female enrolment in rural areas remains shockingly low. Short-changing girls is not only a matter of gender discrimination; it is bad economics and bad social policy. Experience has shown, over and over again, that investments in girls' education translate directly and quickly into better nutrition for the whole family, better health care, declining fertility, poverty reduction and better overall economic performance. Indeed, world leaders, at United Nations conferences throughout the 1990s, have acknowledged that poverty cannot be overcome without specific, immediate and sustained attention to girls' education.

Yet the gap between numbers of boys and girls in school remains significant in 47 countries even at the primary level. In some instances, efforts to increase overall enrolments have widened it.

Individual families in poverty face stark choices. Schooling is often expensive, girls are a traditional source of free household labour and parents are not confident that an educated daughter will benefit the family as much as an educated son. To overcome this difference between household priorities and those of society at large, families need support from their local communities and governments, backed by the wider world. Generating employment opportunities for women would have a similar effect.

Universal access to primary and secondary school education is vital, and can only be achieved by closing the education gender gap. UNICEF, with other United Nations partners, has developed an initiative that encompasses both primary and secondary levels. Its success depends both on national strategies and plans and on international financial support. I ask all governments to work with us to make it succeed. And I propose that we go a step further:

I urge the Millennium Summit to endorse the objectives of demonstrably narrowing the gender gap in primary and secondary education by 2005 and of ensuring that, by 2015 all children complete a full course of primary education.

Employment

Education is the first step. Creating employment opportunities is the next.

The world faces a major challenge of youth unemployment—and it is liable to get even worse with the coming youth bulge. According to International Labour Organization estimates, 60 million young people are searching for work but cannot find any; about 80 per cent of them are in developing countries and economies in transition. Those in the 15 to 24 age cohort are nearly twice as likely to be unemployed as adults; in some developing countries the ratio is higher. Young workers are also more likely than older ones to be last hired, first fired; and they are less likely to be protected by legislation.

Joblessness among the young can be devastating, and governments have tried, in a number of ways, to deal with it. But policies targeted at young people, including preferential hiring, have proved largely unsuccessful for the simple reason that they are economically unsustainable.

The problem is one of inadequate aggregate demand. Low-growth economies cannot generate sufficient employment opportunities to hire their own young people. This failure, in turn, further depresses growth and perpetuates poverty. No one has yet discovered any easy or obvious solutions to this self-perpetuating cycle.

Together with the heads of the World Bank and the International Labour Organization, I am convening a high-level policy network on youth employment—drawing on the most creative leaders in private industry, civil society and economic policy to explore imaginative approaches to this difficult challenge.

I will ask this policy network to propose a set of recommendations that I can convey to world leaders within a year. The possible sources of solutions will include the Internet and the informal sector, especially the contribution that small enterprises can make to employment generation.

C. Promoting Health and Combating HIV/AIDS

In recent decades, innovations in medicine, progress in basic health care and enabling social policies have brought dramatic increases in life expectancy and sharp declines in infant mortality. Better health, in turn, stimulates economic growth while reducing poverty and income inequality. In fact, investments in health care are particularly beneficial to the poor, who are largely dependent for their livelihoods on their own labour.

Not all regions have achieved the same level of progress. East Asia has done best, sub-Saharan Africa the least well. Lack of access to basic health care is one of the main reasons poor people stay poor. In most low-income countries, health spending is often less than $10 per person per year. In Africa, the high burden of disease not only requires families to stretch their meagre resources but also locks them into a high-fertility, high-mortality poverty trap.

In some of the transition economies, a precipitous fall in life expectancy has occurred in recent years, reflecting reduced public spending on health care and a more general erosion of social services.

Although more than $56 billion a year is spent globally on health research, less than 10 per cent is aimed at the health problems affecting 90 per cent of the world's population. Pneumonia, diarrhoea, tuberculosis and malaria—all of great concern to developing countries—receive less than 1 per cent of global health research budgets.

The results are shattering. Malaria alone takes two lives every minute of every day—mainly children under 5 and pregnant women. The Roll Back Malaria campaign, led by the World Health Organization, deserves full support as it seeks to control and prevent this deadly disease.

More generally, wider access to essential drugs, vaccines and such simple and cost-effective interventions as insecticide-treated bed nets could sharply reduce high mortality and disability rates among poor people around the world.

It is beyond the scope of this report to explore all of these challenges. I wish here to focus on a specific health crisis that threatens to reverse a generation of accomplishments in human development, and which is rapidly becoming a social crisis on a global scale: the spread of HIV/AIDS.

Some 50 million people have been infected with HIV since the early 1970s; 16 million have died. In 1999 alone, 5. 6 million people became infected with HIV, half of them under 25 years old. It is a disease that attacks the young disproportionately, its worst effects are concentrated in poor countries and it has a hideous potential to expand.

Of nearly 36 million people now living with HIV/AIDS worldwide, more than 23 million are in sub-Saharan Africa. In Côte d'Ivoire, a teacher dies of AIDS every school day. The average child born in Botswana today has a life expectancy of 41 years, when without AIDS it would have been 70 years. In the worst hit cities of southern Africa, 40 per cent of pregnant women are HIV-positive.

In that same region, more than one child in every 10 has already lost its mother to AIDS. By 2010, it is estimated that there will be 40 million orphans in sub-Saharan Africa, largely because of HIV/AIDS. Those children are far less likely to continue schooling or be immunized than their peers, and much more likely to suffer serious malnutrition. Tragically, it is no longer unusual to see orphans under the age of 15 heading households.

Government projections in Zimbabwe indicate that HIV/AIDS will consume 60 per cent of the nation's health budget by 2005, and even that will be wholly inadequate. AIDS is decimating the ranks of the skilled and educated during their prime years, with what are bound to be tragic implications for every affected country and for the entire region.

And the epidemic is spreading far beyond Africa. In Asia, new HIV infections increased by 70 per cent between 1996 and 1998. India is now estimated to have more people living with HIV than any other country in the world. In short, the crisis has become global.

Building on the agreement reached by the General Assembly at its special session on population and development, held in 1999, I propose a strategy to contain and reduce the spread of HIV/AIDS, focused on young men and women between the ages of 15 and 24, and to provide better care for those living with the illness.

The active support of governments is critical. Large-scale prevention programmes have had some success in several developing countries, including Senegal, Thailand and Uganda. Such efforts, however, are rare, and typically underfunded. In too many countries an official conspiracy of silence about AIDS has denied people information that could have saved their lives. We must empower young people to protect themselves through information and a supportive social environment that reduces their vulnerability to infection.

As a next step, ready access to essential services and preventive technologies must be provided, including male and female condoms. Preventing mother-to-child transmission is especially important. It could avert half a million new infections in babies every year. There is evidence that a drug called nevaripine is both effective and relatively inexpensive. A $4 single dose—along with the cost of testing and voluntary counselling—may be nearly as effective as more complicated and far more expensive regimens. If so, it should be made universally available.

The world's leaders must act to protect their young people and children from avoidable premature illness and mortality due to HIV. UNAIDS will work with governments and other partners to develop and implement national plans of action. Indeed, I would urge that every seriously affected country have a national plan of action in place within one year of the Summit. In addition:

I recommend that the Millennium Summit adopt as an explicit goal the reduction of HIV infection rates in persons 15 to 24 years of age—by 25 per cent within the most affected countries before the year 2005 and by 25 per cent globally before 2010.

To that end, I recommend further that governments set explicit prevention targets: by 2005 at least 90 per cent, and by 2010 at least 95 per cent, of young men and women must have access to the information, education and services they need to protect themselves against HIV infection.

Finally, the world desperately needs a vaccine against HIV. Of the $2 billion spent on research for the treatment of AIDS to date, only $250 million has been spent on creating vaccines, few of which are potentially useful for poor countries, where about 95 per cent of HIV infections occur.

Therefore, I challenge the developed countries to work with their pharmaceutical industries and other partners to develop an effective and affordable vaccine against HIV.

The scientific challenges and financial needs are daunting, but I believe that innovative public-private partnerships, supported by public incentive systems, can stimulate the increased investments so desperately needed. The Global Alliance for Vaccines and Immunization serves as a model of what such partnerships can achieve (see box 2).

Finally, we must also ensure that systems of care and support for the 36 million people who live with HIV/AIDS are improved. Even relatively inexpensive treatments and better care can help in the fight against the symptoms of AIDS, and can make it possible for people with AIDS to live longer, more productive and more dignified lives. Moreover, governments, the pharmaceutical industry and international institutions working together must make HIV-related drugs more widely accessible to developing countries.

Box 2 The Global Alliance for Vaccines and Immunization

At the start of the new millennium a quarter of the world's children, most of them in poor countries, remain unprotected against the six core diseases: polio, diphtheria, whooping cough, measles, tetanus and tuberculosis. Those children are 10 times more likely to die from these diseases than children protected by vaccines.

The Global Alliance for Vaccines and Immunization (GAVI) was formed in 1999 with the mission of ensuring that all the world's children are protected against vaccine-preventable diseases.

The Alliance is a creative coalition of national governments, development banks, business leaders, philanthropic foundations, the World Health Organization, the World Bank group and UNICEF. Its strategic objectives include:

- Improving access to sustainable immunization services;
- Accelerating the research and development of new vaccines for diseases that are especially prevalent in developing countries, such as HIV/AIDS, malaria, tuberculosis and diarrhoea;
- Expanding the use of all existing cost-effective vaccines;
- Making immunization a centrepiece in the design and assessment of international development efforts.

In January 2000, GAVI launched the Global Fund for Children's Vaccines at the World Economic Forum in Davos. The Fund, assisted by a $750 million grant from the Bill and Melinda Gates Foundation, will provide resources to expand the reach of existing vaccines and to strengthen the infrastructures necessary to deliver vaccines in the poorest countries. The Fund will also support research for developing new vaccines.

The Global Alliance for Vaccines and Immunization exemplifies the value of public-private sector cooperation in finding global solutions to global problems.

D. Upgrading the Slums

During the next generation, the global urban population will double, from 2. 5 billion to 5 billion people. Almost all of the increase will be in developing countries. Cities are often described as cradles of civilization, and sources of cultural and economic renaissance but, for the roughly one third of the developing world's urban population that lives in extreme poverty, they are anything but that. Most of these urban poor have no option but to find housing in squalid and unsafe squatter settlements or slums. And even though the population of cities, like countries, has on average become older, slum dwellers are getting younger.

Slums go by various names—*favelas, kampungs, bidonvilles, tugurios, gecikondus*—but the meaning is everywhere the same: miserable living conditions. Slums lack basic municipal services, such as water, sanitation, waste collection and storm drainage. Typically, there are no schools or clinics within easy reach, no places for the community to meet and socialize, no safe areas for children to play. Slum dwellers live and work in conditions of pervasive insecurity—exposed to disease, crime and environmental hazards.

Such slums and squatter settlements are only partially caused by inherent resource scarcities. Also to blame are poorly functioning markets for property and land, unresponsive financial systems, failed policies, corruption and a fundamental lack of political will. And yet these cities-within-cities are wellsprings of entrepreneurial energy that can be mobilized to provide welfare improvements for their inhabitants and for society at large.

The World Bank and the United Nations have joined forces to respond to this challenge, by building a global alliance of cities and their development partners. An ambitious "Cities without Slums" action plan was launched in December 1999, with President Nelson Mandela as its patron. It aims to improve the lives of 100 million slum dwellers by 2020. (The key features of this plan are presented in table 1.) It requires world leaders to commit themselves to, and the international development community to focus on, improving the living conditions of the urban poor.

I strongly support the Cities without Slums initiative and ask all Member States to endorse it and to act on it.

Table 1 Cities Without Slums action plan

Actions	2000	2001	2006–20
	• Mobilize global political and financial commitments to slum-upgrading and gear up the capacity to support large-scale actions	• 20 citywide and nationwide programmes underway in five regions changing the lives of 5 million urban poor	• 50 nationwide programmes launched with slum improvements—a central element of urban development strategies in most countries • 100 million slum residents provided with basic services • Slum formation stopped
Support in grants	$ 4 million	$ 111 million	$180 million
Urban budget Increment	$ 3.5 million	$ 35 million	$100 million
Upgrading investment	$ 200 million	$ 2, 300 million	$ 47, 500 million

Source: Cities Alliance for Cities Without Slums, The World Bank, United Nations Centre for Human Settlements (HABITAT), 1999.

E. Including Africa

Nowhere is a global commitment to poverty reduction needed more than in Africa south of the Sahara, because no region of the world endures greater human suffering. The latest estimates indicate that sub-Saharan Africa has the largest proportion of people who live on less than $1 a day. Growth in per capita income averaged 1. 5 per cent in the 1960s, 0. 8 per cent in the 1970s, and minus 1. 2 per cent in the 1980s. In the 1990s, the region grew more slowly than any other group of middle-or low-income countries.

Today, per capita income is just $500 a year. Private capital flows to Africa are a tiny fraction of global flows, and for some countries capital flight is several times their GDP. Total outstanding external debts often exceed the entire gross national product, and it is not unusual for debt servicing requirements to exceed 25 per cent of export earnings. Reversing these trends poses an enormous challenge to both domestic and international policy makers, and the difficulty of the task is multiplied manifold by the severity of Africa's AIDS crisis.

Extractive industries dominate the region's economy and resources are being depleted at an alarming rate. Infrastructure requirements are enormous, particularly in the areas of power generation and telecommunications. Electrical power consumption, per person, is the lowest in the world. Africa has 14 telephone lines per 1, 000 people, and less than half of 1 per cent of all Africans have used the Internet. A mere 17 per cent of road surfaces is paved. And the list goes on.

Yet Mozambique topped the world's GDP growth last year—before its recent devastating floods. Higher commodity prices, of course, were a significant factor, but Mozambique, utterly impoverished and in the grip of an apparently intractable civil war only a few years ago, has taken great strides thanks to its own efforts. Botswana, ranked second on the list, and several other countries in the region have enjoyed good economic performance and good governance for some time. What, precisely, are the impediments elsewhere?

In economic terms, African productivity has suffered because economic regimes tend to be tightly controlled and inefficiently managed by the state. This results in high trade barriers, and poor delivery of public services. It also means that corruption is widespread. Firms in the private sector are unable to compete internationally because they lack access to appropriate technology and information.

The agricultural sector in Africa has yet to experience a Green Revolution. Unlike the rest of the world, yields of basic food commodities have not increased significantly. Variable rainfall, highly weathered soils, disease and pests have taken their toll. Agricultural technologies developed in other climatic and ecological zones have not transferred well into the region. Inputs like fertilizer are often controlled by state monopolies and are not available to farmers at competitive prices. Fertilizer prices in the early 1990s, for example, were estimated to be two to four times higher in Africa than in Asia. The poor infrastructure restricts the ability to move goods, so that transportation and shipping costs remain prohibitive.

Africa's agricultural sector thus remains unable to generate a steady and inexpensive source of food for urban populations. Indeed, much of sub-Sahara's food supply is imported. Its urban centres remain small by international standards, and they have not provided the human capital necessary to fuel industrial expansion.

I challenge the foremost experts in the world to think through the barrier of low agricultural productivity in Africa. I implore the great philanthropic foundations—which have stimulated so much good and practical research on agriculture—to rise to this vital challenge.

In many African countries there are political obstacles to economic progress as well. I addressed these issues in a report to the Security Council in April 1998. They boil down to a "winner-takes-all" attitude to political competition, the control of society's wealth and resources, and to the power of patronage and the prerogatives of office. It is coupled in too many instances with appalling violations of fundamental rights and a readiness to resort to force to resolve disputes or hold on to power.

Only Africans, I concluded in that report, can break out of these vicious cycles. I am gratified that so many have chosen to do so, and that rulers who had perpetrated crimes against their own people are increasingly being held accountable for them. Yet inexplicably, even today, relatively few African governments show the necessary commitment to poverty reduction in their national economic and social policies.

We do have the chance to turn things around. There are many positive developments in Africa, and the international community has demonstrated a growing interest in assisting those African countries still afflicted by turmoil and tragedy. We must not let up now.

F. Building Digital Bridges

The world has entered the early phases of another technological revolution. We see it in the area of medicines and pharmaceuticals, and in biotechnology. These new frontiers raise both hopes and fears. Better health and greater food security are within our reach, but in seizing the opportunities biotechnology presents we must not neglect the inherent risks. In particular, we must ensure that free access is provided to the information compiled by researchers deciphering the genetic code. The genetic key to human life belongs to all humanity.

I wish to focus here on a technological shift that is already transforming social and economic life: the digital revolution. Fundamental changes are occurring in the communications and information industries, and at near-lightning speed (see figure 4).

Figure 4 Growth of information technologies (Millions)

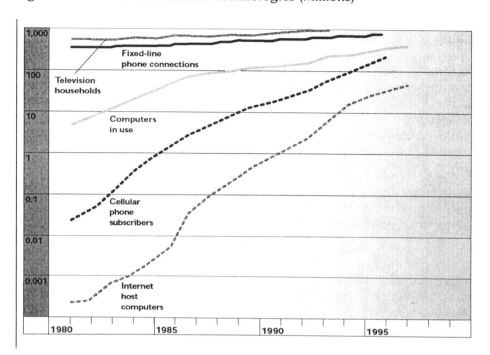

Source: Worldwatch Institute, International Telecommunication Union 2000.

It took 38 years for radio to reach 50 million people, and 13 years for television. The same number of people adopted the Internet in just four years. There were 50 pages on the World Wide Web in 1993; today there are more than 50 million. A mere 143 million people logged on to the Internet in 1998; by 2001 the number of users will climb to 700 million. The market for e-commerce was $2. 6 billion in 1996; it is expected to grow to $300 billion by 2002. And the Internet already has a far wider range of applications than any previous tool of communication ever invented.

At present, a yawning digital divide still exists in the world. There are more computers in the United States of America than in the rest of the world combined. There are as many telephones in Tokyo as in all of Africa.

The digital divide can—and will—be bridged. Already, the city of Bangalore in India has become a dynamic hub of innovation, boasting more than 300 high-tech companies. India's software exports alone will exceed $4 billion this year—about 9 per cent of India's total exports—and industry sources project that they will reach $50 billion by 2008 (see box 3.)

Costa Rica's economic growth surged to 8. 3 per cent in 1999, the highest in Latin America, fuelled by exports from the microchip industry, which now accounts for 38 per cent of all exports. I could give many other examples of developing countries seizing the opportunity of this revolution. It holds great promise for economic growth and development, potentially for all countries.

Box 3 India and the Information Revolution

No developing country has benefited more from the digital revolution than India, whose software industry is expected to increase about eightfold, to $85 billion, by 2008. The industry has generated a significant amount of employment and wealth, creating a new cadre of high-technology entrepreneurs. One Indian company, Infosys Technologies, has seen a tenfold increase in its value since it was listed on the United States Nasdaq stock exchange in March 1999.

The software revolution in India has been accelerated by foreign investment and assisted by economic liberalization and the creation of government-supported software technology parks. India also has a great number of globally mobile software professionals.

Indian companies have become world leaders in designing portals and web-based applications, and they have successfully sidestepped bureaucratic delays and outdated infrastructure by building their own telecommunications systems and beaming their software products by satellite around the world. Access to the Internet in India is also increasing rapidly and it is estimated that about 6 million people in India will be using the Internet by 2001, aided by the deregulation of the telecommunications and information technology sectors.

Yet India, like so many other countries, continues to face the challenge of the "digital divide". There remains a huge gap within the country between those who are part of the Internet revolution and those who are not. On the eve of India's fiftieth anniversary as a constitutional republic, the President of India warned that his country has "one of the world's largest reservoirs of technical personnel but also the world's largest number of illiterates, the largest number of people below the poverty line, and the largest number of children suffering from malnutrition. "

India's success in embracing the Information Revolution is directly related to its success in producing large numbers of highly qualified technical and science graduates. The information networks these graduates are now building have a huge potential for spreading the benefits of education to the less fortunate.

To fully appreciate how the digital revolution can stimulate economic growth and development, we need to grasp several of its core features. First, it has created a brand new economic sector that simply did not exist before. As the countries at its forefront devote ever larger shares of their economies to this sector, a high-value space is opened up for others to occupy, and so on successively throughout the world economy. This, indeed, is how the so-called emerging economies first "emerged" when other sectors were vacated. Globalization facilitates such shifts.

Second, the capital that matters most in the digital revolution increasingly is intellectual capital. Hardware costs are declining. The shift from hardware to software as the cutting edge of the industry helps to overcome what has been a major impediment to development—the shortage of finance. It also improves the chances for poor countries to leapfrog some long and painful stages in the development process. Clearly, the requisite intellectual capital is not universally available, but it is far more widespread in the developing world and in the transition economies than is finance capital.

Third, the digital revolution, besides creating a new economic sector, is also a means to transform and enhance many other activities. Mauritius, for example, uses the Internet to position its textile industry globally. The UNCTAD Trade Point Programme allows participants to trade products on-line. The Government of Mali has established an intranet to provide more effective administrative services. And there are many other opportunities: for telemedicine and distance learning; for "virtual" banking coupled with microcredit; for checking weather forecasts before planting and crop prices before harvesting; for having the world's largest library at your fingertips; and so on. The information technology sector, in short, can transform many if not most other sectors of economic and social activity.

Finally, the core product in this sector—information—has unique attributes, not shared by others. The steel used to construct a building, or the boots worn by the workers constructing it, cannot be consumed by anyone else. Information is different. Not only is it available for multiple uses and users, it becomes more valuable the more it is used. The same is true of the networks that link up different sources of information. We in the policy-making world need to understand better how the economics of information differs from the economics of inherently scarce physical goods—and use it to advance our policy goals.

This is not to say that the transition will be easy for developing countries, especially the very poor. Lack of resources and skills is part of the problem, inadequate basic infrastructure another, illiteracy and language a third, and, of course, there are concerns about privacy and content. Technical solutions will become available for many of these problems, including wireless access, and even simple automatic translation programmes, enabling us to communicate and engage in e-commerce across language barriers.

For the immediate future, the individual consumer model of using information technology that prevails in the industrialized countries will prove too expensive for many developing ones. But that constraint, too, can be overcome. Public telecentres have been established in places from Peru to Kazakhstan. In Egypt, for example, the United Nations Development Programme has helped to create Technology Access Community Centres to bring the Internet and fax service to poor and rural areas. With help from civil society organizations and the private sector, we can expand these pilot programmes to reach even the remotest corners of the globe.

There is however no easy fix for the institutional impediments in many developing countries, above all unsupportive regulatory environments and exorbitant charges imposed by national authorities.

I encourage Member States to review their policies and arrangements in this area, to make sure that they are not denying their people the opportunities offered by the digital revolution.

As a concrete demonstration of how we can build bridges over digital divides, I am pleased to announce a new Health Inter-Network for developing countries.

This network will establish and operate 10, 000 on-line sites in hospitals, clinics and public health facilities throughout the developing world. It aims to provide access to relevant up-to-date health and medical information, tailored for specific countries or groups of countries. The equipment and Internet access, wireless where necessary, will be provided by a consortium in cooperation with other foundation and corporate partners. Training and capacity-building in developing countries is an integral part of the project. The World Health Organization is leading the United Nations side in developing this initiative with external partners, including the United Nations Foundation.

I am also announcing a second digital bridges initiative: a United Nations Information Technology Service, which I propose to call UNITeS.

This will be a consortium of high-tech volunteer corps, including Net Corps Canada and Net Corps America, which United Nations Volunteers will help to coordinate. UNITeS will train groups in developing countries in the uses and opportunities of information technology, and stimulate the creation of additional digital corps in the North and South. We are currently exploring external sources of funding to support UNITeS.

G. Demonstrating Global Solidarity

Creating an inclusive global market is one of humanity's central challenges in the twenty-first century. We are all impoverished if the poor are denied opportunities to make a living. And it is within our power to extend these opportunities to all.

The rich countries have an indispensable role to play by further opening their markets, by providing deeper and faster debt relief, and by giving more and better-focused development assistance.

Trade access

Despite decades of liberalization, the world trading system remains burdened with tariffs and quotas. Most industrialized countries still protect their markets for agricultural products heavily, and all protect textiles—the two sectors in which the developing countries have a recognized comparative advantage. Moreover, agricultural subsidies in the industrialized countries drive down world prices, hurting farmers in poor countries even more.

Everybody pays a high price for these practices. The estimated cost per job "saved" in industrialized countries ranges from $30, 000 to $200, 000, depending on the industry. Global economic losses from agricultural protectionism may be as high as $150 billion per year—about $20 billion of it in lost exports for developing countries. Developing countries also cause a great deal of damage to themselves, however, by their own protectionist policies, in agriculture and elsewhere.

Rather than trying to freeze declining industries in place, which always fails in the long run, political leaders should make the case for upgrading skills through education and training, and for providing adjustment assistance.

The tenth session of the United Nations Conference on Trade and Development, held recently in Bangkok, highlighted the need for better market access for the agricultural and industrial products exported by the least developed countries. That would be particularly helpful to sub-Saharan Africa.

I urge the industrialized countries to consider granting duty-free and quota-free access for essentially all exports from the least developed countries—and to be prepared to endorse that commitment at the Third United Nations Conference on the Least Developed Countries in March 2001.

A related issue of trade linkages has emerged in recent years. I refer to the desire of some to make trade liberalization conditional on the developing countries' meeting certain standards in the areas of labour, the environment and human rights. This issue must be handled with great care so that it does not become yet another pretext for protectionism.

I propose a different course. First, in most of these areas agreements already exist on universal values and common standards—the fruit of many conferences and long negotiations. What is needed now is for states to live up to their obligations, and for the relevant United Nations agencies to be given the resources and support to help them. If that means that the world should have a more robust global environmental organization, for example, or that the International Labour Organization needs to be strengthened, then let us consider those possibilities.

Second, global companies must play a leadership role. At relatively little if any cost to themselves, they can, in their own corporate domains, apply good practices everywhere they operate. This would have a beneficial demonstration effect throughout the world. That is why I have invited the business community to join me in a "Global Compact" to enact in their own corporate practices a set of core values in three areas: labour standards, human rights and the environment (see box 4). This initiative has been endorsed by a wide variety of business associations, labour groups and non-governmental organizations—and I hope to announce soon the first business leaders who are joining us to make the Global Compact an everyday reality.

Box 4—The Global Compact: A Framework for United Nations– Private Sector Partnerships

Launched by the Secretary-General early in 1999, the Global Compact is a joint undertaking of the International Labour Organization, the United Nations Environment Programme and the Office of the United Nations High Commissioner for Human Rights.

The Compact seeks to engage corporations in the promotion of equitable labour standards, respect for human rights and the protection of the environment. Corporations are asked to translate commitments to general principles in these three areas into concrete management practices. The Global Compact is based on the conviction that weaving universal values into the fabric of global markets and corporate practices will help advance broad societal goals while securing open markets.

To help pursue this ambitious agenda the Compact team at the United Nations has created a web site that provides information on the Compact and access to extensive United Nations country-based data banks. It describes corporate "best practice" in the areas of human rights, labour standards and protection of the environment, and promotes dialogue on supportive partnership programmes. The web site can be accessed at http//:unglobalcompact. org.

The Global Compact is actively supported by:

- Global business associations: the International Chamber of Commerce, the International Organization of Employers, the World Business Council on Sustainable Development, the Prince of Wales Business Leaders Forum and Business for Social Responsibility.

- Other global associations that have joined, or are considering doing so, include: the International Fertilizer Industry Association, the International Federation of Consulting Engineers, the World Federation of Sporting Goods Industry, the International Iron and Steel Institute, the International Petroleum Industry Environmental Conservation Association and the International Council of Chemical Associations.

- The International Confederation of Free Trade Unions.

- Issue-oriented non-governmental organizations dealing with the environment, human rights and development.

Debt relief

High levels of external debt are a crushing burden on economic growth in many of the poorest countries. Debt servicing requirements in hard currency prevent them from making adequate investments in education and health care, and from responding effectively to natural disasters and other emergencies. Debt relief for those heavily indebted poor countries must, therefore, be an integral part of the international community's contribution to development.

Repeated rescheduling of these countries' bilateral debts has not significantly reduced their overall indebtedness. In 1996, therefore, the international donor community launched an initiative to reduce these countries' debt to sustainable levels—the so-called HIPC initiative. In the three years since its adoption, however, only four countries have fully qualified. Another nine are reaching that point, while five others are engaged in preliminary discussions. But progress has been slow.

A proposed expansion of the HIPC programme—agreed by the Cologne Summit of the G-8 in June 1999 and endorsed by the international financial institutions in September—provides for deeper, faster and broader debt relief. But it has yet to be implemented. Other obstacles remain. For instance, there is no mechanism for handling the large-scale restructuring of debt owed to foreign lenders by many private borrowers in the banking and corporate sector in developing countries.

I call upon the donor countries and the international financial institutions to consider wiping off their books all official debts of the heavily indebted poor countries in return for those countries making demonstrable commitments to poverty reduction.

In designing such national poverty reduction programmes, governments are encouraged to consult closely with civil society.

I would go a step further and propose that, in the future, we consider an entirely new approach to handling the debt problem. The main components of such an approach could include immediate cancellation of the debts owed by countries that have suffered major conflicts or natural disasters; expanding the number of countries in the HIPC scheme by allowing them to qualify on grounds of poverty alone; pegging debt repayments at a maximum percentage of foreign exchange earnings; and establishing a debt arbitration process to balance the interests of creditors and sovereign debtors and introduce greater discipline into their relations.

Let us, above all, be clear that, without a convincing programme of debt relief to start the new millennium, our objective of halving world poverty by 2015 will be only a pipe dream.

Official development assistance

Development assistance—the third pillar of support by the international community—has been in steady decline for several decades. There are some signs that this decline has now begun to flatten out but, despite recent increases by five countries, no general upward momentum is yet visible (see figure 5). While it is true that private investment flows have increased significantly, many poor countries are not yet fully equipped to attract such investment.

Figure 5 Financial flows to developing countries (Billions of United States dollars—constant 1995 dollars)

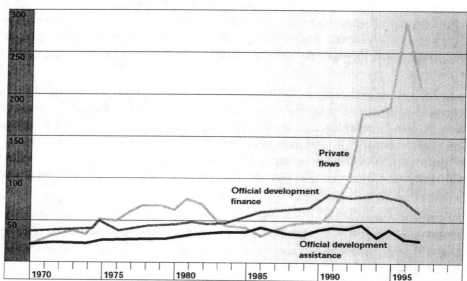

Source: World Bank, *Global Development Finance 1998.*

Additional aid flows should be deployed to support the kinds of priorities I have described: programmes that encourage growth and help the poor. Aid should also promote domestic and foreign investment opportunities. For example, it could perhaps be used to offset some of the risk premium of private investment in poor countries. The private sector can also be helpful in providing pre-investment assistance—as in the case of the partnership between UNCTAD and the International Chamber of Commerce to produce investment guides for the least developed countries (see box 5).

If external assistance programmes are to yield the best results, their administrative burdens on the countries they are supposed to help must be significantly reduced, and those countries must play a full part in designing them. The United Nations Development Assistance Framework is a useful—and by all accounts, a successful—step in that direction (see box 6)—as are changes recently introduced by other agencies, including the World Bank. But bilateral programmes still need to be far better coordinated.

As a result of globalization, the world's commitment to the poor is slowly coming to be seen, not only as a moral imperative but also as a common interest. Each country must still take primary responsibility for its own programmes of economic growth and poverty reduction. But ridding the world of the scourge of extreme poverty is a challenge to every one of us. It is one that we must not fail to meet.

Box 5 Attracting Investment to the Poorest Countries: a United Nations/ Private Sector Initiative

Foreign direct investment (FDI) contributes greatly to economic growth in developing countries. Most of this investment goes to the industrialized world, but an increasing share, about one quarter of the total, is now going to developing countries. In the last 10 years these private capital flows have become a far more important source of development finance for many developing countries than official development assistance.

But FDI does not flow equally to all parts of the developing world. Asia receives almost 20 times more foreign investment than sub-Saharan Africa, where the need is greatest.

Why do the poorest and most needy countries get the lowest levels of private capital investment? The reasons are complex. Poorly functioning capital and labour markets, weak governance, and high costs of transportation are part of the problem. But even when developing countries undertake the reforms necessary to address these problems they often still do not receive the FDI they so desperately need.

Often, the key challenge is to inform prospective investors that the needed reforms have been made, and that real investment opportunities exist. Doing precisely that is a major goal of the joint initiative undertaken by the United Nations Conference on Trade and Development (UNCTAD) and the International Chamber of Commerce (ICC).

This initiative includes publication of a series of investment guides, describing investment opportunities and conditions in the least developed countries, and promoting dialogue between governments and potential investors. A central objective is to help strengthen the capacity of the poorest countries to attract investment.

Twenty-eight companies—household names in many parts of the world—are supporting the partnership and contributing to the UNCTAD-ICC project, as are China, Finland, France, India and Norway.

The UNCTAD-ICC project is one of many public-private cooperative projects now being pursued at the United Nations. With aid flows having declined in the 1990s such collaboration is becoming an increasingly important means of assisting the development process in the poorest countries.

Box 6 Cooperating for development: the United Nations Development Assistance Framework

Development cooperation has changed dramatically in the last decade, with much greater emphasis being placed on human rights, human development and environmental concerns. Demands for assistance have increased; resources to meet those demands have declined.

The United Nations has increasingly been required to do more with less. This, in turn, has required greater collaboration between our agencies and more partnerships with actors in civil society and the private sector. As the number of development agencies and non-governmental organizations in the field has increased, the need for better coordination has grown commensurately.

To bring greater collaboration, coherence and impact to the Organization's work at the country level, the United Nations Development Assistance Framework (UNDAF) was introduced in 1997 as part of the Secretary-General's reform package. UNDAF is a common framework with a common vision and is based on a common country assessment.

UNDAF seeks to improve coordination and avoid duplication of effort between United Nations agencies, national governments and other partners in support of country priorities. It is currently being implemented in 74 countries around the world, each under the leadership of the United Nations Resident Coordinator. It is part of a broader trend in the United Nations system to treat issues like development in a more comprehensive way.

UNDAF also represents a shift in development planning and implementation from Headquarters to the country level. In India, for example, UNDAF facilitated collaboration between the United Nations and the Government in dealing with the twin challenges of gender and decentralization. In Romania, UNDAF helped elaborate the first National Strategy on Poverty, which in turn enabled the Government to mobilize additional resources from other donors.

In its short existence, the achievements of UNDAF clearly demonstrate that agencies operating cooperatively can achieve far more than when they act on their own.

IV. Freedom from Fear

The world is now in the fifty-fifth year without war among the major powers—the longest such period in the entire history of the modern system of states. In the area of Europe that now comprises the European Union—where most modern wars started—a security community has emerged: an association of states characterized by dependable expectations that disputes will be resolved by peaceful means.

Moreover, nearly five decades of cold war—sustained by a nuclear balance of terror that could have annihilated us all instantly—have passed. Some observers have lamented that fact, claiming that bipolarity was stable, predictable and helped keep the peace. But that was hardly true in the developing world: there the cold war was a period of frequent armed conflict fuelled by both sides in the bipolar world. Once the cold war ended, that source of external political and material support ceased to exist.

Freeing the United Nations from the shackles of the cold war also enabled it to play a more significant role. The 1990s saw an upsurge both in our peacekeeping and in our peacemaking activities: three times more peace agreements were negotiated and signed during that decade than in the previous three combined.

The frequency of inter-state warfare has been declining for some time. (For the corresponding decline in refugee numbers, see figure 6.) Economic globalization has largely eliminated the benefits of territorial acquisition, while the destructiveness of modern warfare has increased its costs. The near-doubling in the number of democracies since 1990 has been equally important, because established democratic states, for a variety of reasons, rarely fight each other militarily (see figure 7).

Figure 6 Global refugee population, 1965–1998 (Millions)

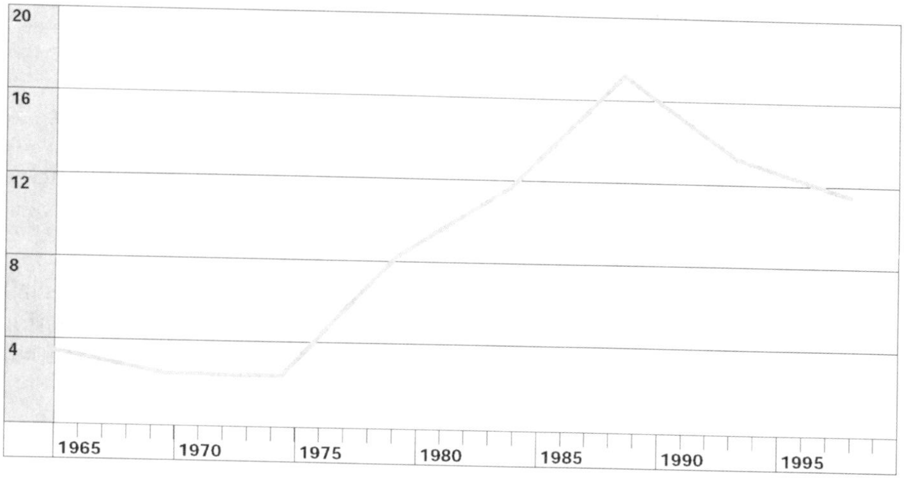

Source: UNHCR, 2000.

Wars since the 1990s have been mainly internal. They have been brutal, claiming more than 5 million lives. They have violated, not so much borders, as people. Humanitarian conventions have been routinely flouted, civilians and aid workers have become strategic targets, and children have been forced to become killers. Often driven by political ambition or greed, these wars have preyed on ethnic and religious differences, they are often sustained by external economic interests, and they are fed by a hyperactive and in large part illicit global arms market.

In the wake of these conflicts, a new understanding of the concept of security is evolving. Once synonymous with the defence of territory from external attack, the requirements of security today have come to embrace the protection of communities and individuals from internal violence.

Figure 7 Democratic, autocratic and transitional polities, 1946–1998

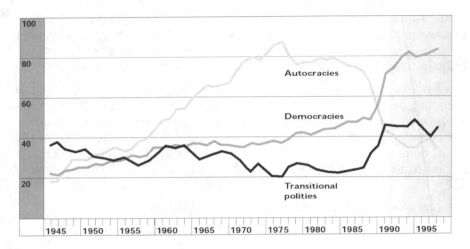

Source: Marshall, derived from data from the Polity III dataset, Center for International Development and Conflict Management, University of Maryland, 1999.

The need for a more human-centred approach to security is reinforced by the continuing dangers that weapons of mass destruction, most notably nuclear weapons, pose to humanity: their very name reveals their scope and their intended objective, if they were ever used.

As we look ahead, we can see real risks that resource depletion, especially freshwater scarcities, as well as severe forms of environmental degradation, may increase social and political tensions in unpredictable but potentially dangerous ways.

In short, these new security challenges require us to think creatively, and to adapt our traditional approaches to better meet the needs of our new era. But one time-honoured precept holds more firmly today than ever: it all begins with prevention.

A. Preventing Deadly Conflicts

There is near-universal agreement that prevention is preferable to cure, and that strategies of prevention must address the root causes of conflicts, not simply their violent symptoms. Consensus is not always matched by practical actions, however. Political leaders find it hard to sell prevention policies abroad to their public at home, because the costs are palpable and immediate, while the benefits—an undesirable or tragic future event that does not occur—are more difficult for the leaders to convey and the public to grasp. Thus prevention is, first and foremost, a challenge of political leadership.

If we are to be successful at preventing deadly conflicts, we must have a clear understanding of their causes. Not all wars are alike; therefore no single strategy will be universally effective. What is different about the wars that people have suffered since the beginning of the 1990s?

Several major conflicts in the past decade were wars of post-communist succession, in which callous leaders exploited the most primitive forms of ethnic nationalism and religious differences to retain or acquire power. Some of those conflicts have already receded into the history books—along with those leaders—and it is to be hoped that the remainder soon will. The majority of wars today are wars among the poor. Why is this the case?

Poor countries have fewer economic and political resources with which to manage conflicts. They lack the capacity to make extensive financial transfers to minority groups or regions, for example, and they may fear that their state apparatus is too fragile to countenance devolution. Both are routine instruments in richer countries.

What this means is that every single measure I described in the previous section—every step taken towards reducing poverty and achieving broad-based economic growth—is a step towards conflict prevention. All who are engaged in conflict prevention and development, therefore—the United Nations, the Bretton Woods institutions, governments and civil society organizations—must address these challenges in a more integrated fashion.

We can do more. In many poor countries at war, the condition of poverty is coupled with sharp ethnic or religious cleavages. Almost invariably, the rights of subordinate groups are insufficiently respected, the institutions of government are insufficiently inclusive and the allocation of society's resources favours the dominant faction over others.

The solution is clear, even if difficult to achieve in practice: to promote human rights, to protect minority rights and to institute political arrangements in which all groups are represented. Wounds that have festered for a long time will not heal overnight. Nor can confidence be built or dialogues develop while fresh wounds are being inflicted. There are no quick fixes, no short cuts. Every group needs to become convinced that the state belongs to all people.

Some armed conflicts today are driven by greed, not grievance. Whereas war is costly for society as a whole, it nevertheless may be profitable for some. In such cases, often the control over natural resources is at stake, drugs are often involved, the conflicts are abetted by opportunistic neighbours, and private sector actors are complicit—buying ill-gotten gains, helping to launder funds and feeding a steady flow of weapons into the conflict zone.

The best preventive strategy in this context is transparency: "naming and shaming". Civil society actors have an enormous role to play in this regard, but governments and the Security Council must exercise their responsibility. Greater social responsibility on the part of global companies, including banks, is also essential.

Finally, successful strategies for prevention require us to ensure that old conflicts do not start up again, and that the necessary support is provided for post-conflict peace-building. I regret to say that we do not fully enjoy that level of support in most of our missions.

While prevention is the core feature of our efforts to promote human security, we must recognize that even the best preventive and deterrence strategies can fail. Other measures, therefore, may be called for. One is to strengthen our commitment to protecting vulnerable people.

B. Protecting the Vulnerable

Despite the existence of numerous international conventions intended to protect the vulnerable, the brutalization of civilians, particularly women and children, continues in armed conflicts. Women have become especially vulnerable to violence and sexual exploitation, while children are easy prey for forced labour and are often coerced into becoming fighters. Civilian populations and infrastructure have become covers for the operations of rebel movements, targets for reprisal and victims of the chaotic brutalities that too often follow breakdowns in state authority. In the most extreme cases, the innocent become the principal targets of ethnic cleansers and *genocidaires*.

International conventions have traditionally looked to states to protect civilians, but today this expectation is threatened in several ways. First, states are sometimes the principal perpetrators of violence against the very citizens that humanitarian law requires them to protect. Second, non-state combatants, particularly in collapsed states, are often either ignorant or contemptuous of humanitarian law. Third, international conventions do not adequately address the specific needs of vulnerable groups, such as internally displaced persons, or women and children in complex emergencies.

To strengthen protection, we must reassert the centrality of international humanitarian and human rights law. We must strive to end the culture of impunity—which is why the creation of the International Criminal Court is so important. We must also devise new strategies to meet changing needs.

New approaches in this area could include establishing a mechanism to monitor compliance by all parties with existing provisions of international humanitarian law. Stronger legal standards are needed to provide for the protection of humanitarian workers. Consideration should also be given to an international convention regulating the actions of private and corporate security firms, which we see involved in internal wars in growing numbers.

Greater use of information technology can also help to reduce the pain and burdens of complex emergencies for the people involved; one example is a programme called "Child Connect", which helps reunite children and parents who have been separated in wars and natural disaster (see box 7).

Of one thing we may be certain: without protecting the vulnerable, our peace initiatives will be both fragile and illusory.

Box 7 Child Connect: Using the Information Revolution to Find Lost Children

In wars and natural disasters children often get separated from their parents and reuniting them can pose an immense challenge for aid agencies. The International Rescue Committee's "Child Connect" project was designed to solve this problem. The project uses a shared database open to all the agencies in the field seeking to reunite lost children with their parents. These agencies can submit data and photographs of unaccompanied children as well as search requests from parents. Search procedures that once took months can now be completed in minutes, saving both children and parents much heartache.

For Child Connect to realize its potential, all the tracing agencies in a region need to be able to submit and review the lost-and-found data on a regular basis. The easiest way to do this, of course, is via the Internet, but armed conflicts rarely occur in places with robust Internet or communications infrastructures.

In Kosovo, the International Rescue Committee created a shared satellite/wireless Internet network in Pristina (www. ipko. org). Every United Nations agency, the Organization for Security and Cooperation in Europe, several national missions, and the majority of non-governmental organizations are connected to the Internet 24 hours per day via the network.

Because the marginal cost of this technology is so low, the project is also able to provide free Internet access to the university, hospital, libraries, schools, local media and local non-governmental organizations. So not only are international organizations getting robust communications links and saving money, they are helping to support Kosovar civil society and build a long-term Internet infrastructure for Kosovo. The project has now been turned over to an independent local non-governmental organization that is already completely self-sustaining.

This project can serve as a model for future humanitarian emergencies. By building a shared Internet infrastructure, international organizations will benefit from more reliable communications at a much lower cost and they will be able to take advantage of shared access to databases and other Internet-based applications to improve their effectiveness.

When the crisis ends, the infrastructure can be left in place and local people trained to maintain it.

C. Addressing the Dilemma of Intervention

In my address to the General Assembly last September, I called on Member States to unite in the pursuit of more effective policies to stop organized mass murder and egregious violations of human rights. Although I emphasized that intervention embraced a wide continuum of responses, from diplomacy to armed action, it was the latter option that generated most controversy in the debate that followed.

Some critics were concerned that the concept of "humanitarian intervention" could become a cover for gratuitous interference in the internal affairs of sovereign states. Others felt that it might encourage secessionist movements deliberately to provoke governments into committing gross violations of human rights in order to trigger external interventions that would aid their cause. Still others noted that there is little consistency in the practice of intervention, owing to its inherent difficulties and costs as well as perceived national interests—except that weak states are far more likely to be subjected to it than strong ones.

I recognize both the force and the importance of these arguments. I also accept that the principles of sovereignty and non-interference offer vital protection to small and weak states. But to the critics I would pose this question: if humanitarian intervention is, indeed, an unacceptable assault on sovereignty, how should we respond to a Rwanda, to a Srebrenica—to gross and systematic violations of human rights that offend every precept of our common humanity?

We confront a real dilemma. Few would disagree that both the defence of humanity and the defence of sovereignty are principles that must be supported. Alas, that does not tell us which principle should prevail when they are in conflict.

Humanitarian intervention is a sensitive issue, fraught with political difficulty and not susceptible to easy answers. But surely no legal principle—not even sovereignty—can ever shield crimes against humanity. Where such crimes occur and peaceful attempts to halt them have been exhausted, the Security Council has a moral duty to act on behalf of the international community. The fact that we cannot protect people everywhere is no reason for doing nothing when we can. Armed intervention must always remain the option of last resort, but in the face of mass murder it is an option that cannot be relinquished.

D. Strengthening Peace Operations

With the end of the cold war confrontation and the paralysis it had induced in the Security Council, the decade of the 1990s became one of great activism for the United Nations. More peace operations were mounted in that decade than in the previous four combined, and we developed new approaches to post-conflict peace-building and placed new emphasis on conflict prevention.

While traditional peacekeeping had focused mainly on monitoring ceasefires, today's complex peace operations are very different. Their objective, in essence, is to assist the parties engaged in conflict to pursue their interests through political channels instead. To that end, the United Nations helps to create and strengthen political institutions and to broaden their base. We work alongside governments, non-governmental organizations and local citizens' groups to provide emergency relief, demobilize former fighters and reintegrate them into society, clear mines, organize and conduct elections, and promote sustainable development practices.

International assistance to rebuild the economy is an essential complement to this work. People will quickly become disillusioned with fledgling institutions, and even the peace process itself, if they see no prospect for any material improvement in their condition. Post-conflict peace-building has helped to prevent the breakdown of numerous peace agreements, and to build the foundations for sustainable peace.

We can claim significant successes among our peace operations in the last decade or so, beginning with Namibia in the late 1980s, and including Mozambique, El Salvador, the Central African Republic, Eastern Slavonia, the former Yugoslav Republic of Macedonia and, at least partially, Cambodia. We also encountered tragic failures, none more so than Rwanda and the fall of Srebrenica and the other safe areas in Bosnia. The many reasons for those failures, including those attributable to the United Nations Secretariat, are discussed frankly and in considerable detail in two reports I issued late last year.

The structural weaknesses of United Nations peace operations, however, only Member States can fix. Our system for launching operations has sometimes been compared to a volunteer fire department, but that description is too generous. Every time there is a fire, we must first find fire engines and the funds to run them before we can start dousing any flames. The present system relies almost entirely on last minute, ad hoc arrangements that guarantee delay, with respect to the provision of civilian personnel even more so than military.

Although we have understandings for military standby arrangements with Member States, the availability of the designated forces is unpredictable and very few are in a state of high readiness. Resource constraints preclude us even from being able to deploy a mission headquarters rapidly.

On the civilian side, we have been starkly reminded in Kosovo and East Timor how difficult it is to recruit qualified personnel for missions. Where do we find police officers quickly, or judges, or people to run correctional institutions—to focus only on law enforcement needs? A more systematic approach is necessary here as well.

To bring greater clarity to where we stand and how we can hope to progress with regard to United Nations peace operations, I have established a high-level panel, which will review all aspects of peace operations, from the doctrinal to the logistical. It will suggest ways forward that are acceptable politically and make sense operationally.

I expect that the panel's report will be completed in time to enable the Millennium Assembly to consider its recommendations.

E. Targeting Sanctions

During the 1990s, the United Nations established more sanctions regimes than ever before. Sanctions, an integral element of the collective security provisions of the Charter, offer the Security Council an important instrument to enforce its decisions, situated on a continuum between mere verbal condemnation and recourse to armed force. They include arms embargoes, the imposition of trade and financial restrictions, interruptions of relations by air and sea, and diplomatic isolation.

Sanctions have had an uneven track record in inducing compliance with Security Council resolutions. In some cases, little if any effort has gone into monitoring and enforcing them. In many cases, neighbouring countries that bear much of the loss from ensuring compliance have not been helped by the rest of the international community and, as a result, have allowed sanctions to become porous.

When robust and comprehensive economic sanctions are directed against authoritarian regimes, a different problem is encountered. Then it is usually the people who suffer, not the political elites whose behaviour triggered the sanctions in the first place. Indeed, those in power, perversely, often benefit from such sanctions by their ability to control and profit from black market activity, and by exploiting them as a pretext for eliminating domestic sources of political opposition.

Because economic sanctions have proved to be such a blunt and even counter-productive instrument, a number of governments, and numerous civil society organizations and think tanks around the world, have explored ways to make them smarter by better targeting them. Switzerland has led an effort to design instruments of targeted financial sanctions, including drafting model national legislation required to implement them, and Germany is supporting work on how to make arms embargoes and other forms of targeted boycotts more effective. The United Kingdom of Great Britain and Northern Ireland and Canada have also contributed to the debate on how to target sanctions more effectively.

These efforts are now sufficiently well advanced to merit serious consideration by Member States. I invite the Security Council, in particular, to bear them in mind when designing and applying sanctions regimes.

F. Pursuing Arms Reductions

The post-cold-war era has seen both gains and setbacks in the realm of disarmament. On the positive side, the Ottawa Convention banning landmines and the Chemical Weapons Convention have both entered into force. The Comprehensive Nuclear-TestBan Treaty has been concluded, nuclear safeguards have been strengthened and nuclear-weapon-free zones now embrace all of the southern hemisphere. Nuclear weapons numbers have almost halved since 1982, and world military expenditures declined by some 30 per cent between 1990 and 1998 (see figures 8 and 9).

The rest of the picture is much less encouraging. Little meaningful progress has been achieved in limiting the proliferation of small arms. The nuclear non-proliferation regime has suffered major blows as a result of clandestine nuclear weapon programmes, the nuclear tests in South Asia and the unwillingness of key states to ratify the Comprehensive Nuclear-Test-Ban Treaty.

Figure 8 Nuclear stockpiles, estimated, 1950–2000 (Thousands of weapons)

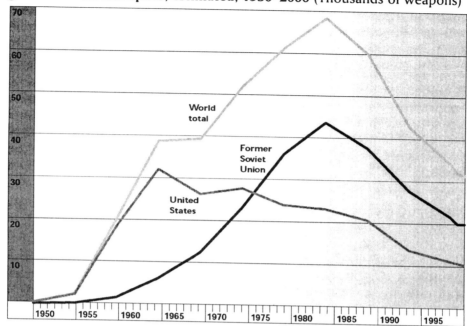

Source: Natural Resources Defense Council, 2000.

Figure 9 World military expenditures, 1989–1998 (Billions of United States dollars—constant 1995 dollars)

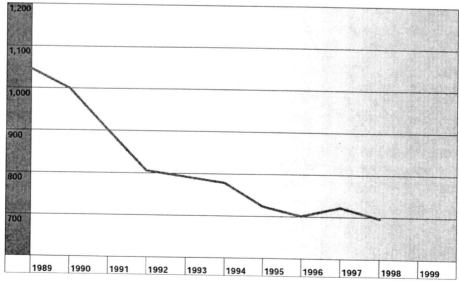

Note: 1991 estimated.

Source: Stockholm Peace Research Institute, *SIPRI Yearbook 1999.*

Advances in biotechnology are increasing the potential threat posed by biological weapons, while negotiations on a verification regime for the Biological Weapons Convention are being unnecessarily prolonged. For three years in a row now, the Conference on Disarmament in Geneva has not engaged in any negotiations because its members have been unable to agree on disarmament priorities.

I cannot here review the entire arms control spectrum. Instead, I focus on two categories of weapon that are of special concern: small arms and light weapons, because they currently kill most people in most wars; and nuclear weapons, because of their continuing terrifying potential for mass destruction.

Small arms

The death toll from small arms dwarfs that of all other weapons systems—and in most years greatly exceeds the toll of the atomic bombs that devastated Hiroshima and Nagasaki. In terms of the carnage they cause, small arms, indeed, could well be described as "weapons of mass destruction". Yet there is still no global non-proliferation regime to limit their spread, as there is for chemical, biological and nuclear weapons.

Small arms proliferation is not merely a security issue; it is also an issue of human rights and of development. The proliferation of small arms sustains and exacerbates armed conflicts. It endangers peacekeepers and humanitarian workers. It undermines respect for international humanitarian law. It threatens legitimate but weak governments and it benefits terrorists as well as the perpetrators of organized crime.

Much of the cold war's small arms surplus finished up in the world's most dangerous conflict zones and, as the number of weapons in circulation increased, their price declined, making access to them ever easier even in the poorest countries. In parts of Africa in the mid-1990s, for example, deadly assault rifles could be bought for the price of a chicken or a bag of maize. Reducing the toll caused by these weapons will be difficult, not least because of the extraordinary number in circulation, which some estimates put as high as 500 million.

An estimated 50 to 60 per cent of the world's trade in small arms is legal—but legally exported weapons often find their way into the illicit market. The task of effective proliferation control is made far harder than it needs to be because of irresponsible behaviour on the part of some states and lack of capacity by others, together with the shroud of secrecy that veils much of the arms trade. Member States must act to increase transparency in arms transfers if we are to make any progress. I would also urge that they support regional disarmament measures, like the moratorium on the importing, exporting or manufacturing of light weapons in West Africa.

Even if all arms transfers could be eliminated, however, the problem posed by the many millions of illicitly held small arms already in circulation in the world's war zones would remain.

Because most conflict-prone poor countries lack the capacity to detect and seize illicit weapons, a more promising path may be the use of market incentives. Outright buy-back programmes may simply stimulate arms imports from neighbouring countries, but non-monetary reimbursement schemes have worked in Albania, El Salvador, Mozambique and Panama. In return for weapons, individuals may receive tools, such as sewing machines, bicycles, hoes and construction materials, and entire communities have been provided with new schools, health-care services and road repairs.

Not only governments but also the private sector can and should help fund such programmes. This would be both a helpful and an appropriate contribution by major international corporations that have a presence in conflict-prone regions.

Controlling the proliferation of illicit weapons is a necessary first step towards the non-proliferation of small arms. These weapons must be brought under the control of states, and states must be held accountable for their transfer. The United Nations is convening a conference on the illicit trade in small arms and light weapons in 2001, in which I hope civil society organizations will be invited to participate fully.

I urge Member States to take advantage of this conference to start taking serious actions that will curtail the illicit traffic in small arms.

The many recent expressions of concern about small arms proliferation are a welcome sign that the importance of the issue is being recognized, but words alone do nothing to prevent the ongoing slaughter of innocent people. Dialogue is critical, but we must match the rhetoric of concern with the substance of practical action.

Nuclear weapons

Let me now turn to nuclear weapons. When the bipolar balance of nuclear terror passed into history, the concern with nuclear weapons also seemed to drift from public consciousness. But some 35, 000 nuclear weapons remain in the arsenals of the nuclear powers, with thousands still deployed on hair-trigger alert. Whatever rationale these weapons may once have had has long since dwindled. Political, moral and legal constraints on actually using them further undermine their strategic utility without, however, reducing the risks of inadvertent war or proliferation.

The objective of nuclear non-proliferation is not helped by the fact that the nuclear weapon states continue to insist that those weapons in their hands enhance security, while in the hands of others they are a threat to world peace.

If we were making steady progress towards disarmament, this situation would be less alarming. Unfortunately the reverse is true. Not only are the Strategic Arms Reduction Talks stalled, but there are no negotiations at all covering the many thousands of so-called tactical nuclear weapons in existence, or the weapons of any nuclear power other than those of the Russian Federation and the United States of America.

Moreover, unless plans to deploy missile defences are devised with the agreement of all concerned parties, the progress achieved thus far in reducing the number of nuclear weapons may be jeopardized. Confidence-building is required to reassure states that their nuclear deterrent capabilities will not be negated.

Above all else, we need a reaffirmation of political commitment at the highest levels to reduce the dangers that arise both from existing nuclear weapons and from further proliferation.

To help focus attention on the risks we confront and on the opportunities we have to reduce them, I propose that consideration be given to convening a major international conference that would help to identify ways of eliminating nuclear dangers.

V. Sustaining Our Future

The founders of the United Nations set out, in the words of the Charter, to promote social progress and better standards of life in larger freedom—above all, freedom from want and freedom from fear. In 1945, they could not have anticipated, however, the urgent need we face today to realize yet a third: the freedom of future generations to sustain their lives on this planet. We are failing to provide that freedom. On the contrary, we have been plundering our children's future heritage to pay for environmentally unsustainable practices in the present.

The natural environment performs for us, free of charge, basic services without which our species could not survive. The ozone layer screens out ultraviolet rays from the sun that harm people, animals and plants. Ecosystems help purify the air we breathe and the water we drink. They convert wastes into resources and reduce atmospheric carbon levels that would otherwise contribute to global warming. Biodiversity provides a bountiful store of medicines and food products, and it maintains genetic variety that reduces vulnerability to pests and diseases. But we are degrading, and in some cases destroying, the ability of the environment to continue providing these life-sustaining services for us.

During the past hundred years, the natural environment has borne the stresses imposed by a fourfold increase in human numbers and an eighteen-fold growth in world economic output. With world population projected to increase to nearly 9 billion by 2050, from the current 6 billion, the potential for doing irreparable environmental harm is obvious. One of two jobs worldwide—in agriculture, forestry and fisheries—depends directly on the sustainability of ecosystems. Even more important, so does the planet's health—and our own.

Environmental sustainability is everybody's challenge. In the rich countries, the byproducts of industrial and agribusiness production poison soils and waterways. In the developing countries, massive deforestation, harmful farming practices and uncontrolled urbanization are major causes of environmental degradation. Carbon dioxide emissions are widely believed to be a major source of global climate change, and the burning of fossil fuels is their main source. The one fifth of the world's population living in the industrialized countries accounts for nearly 60 per cent of the world's total consumption of energy, but the developing world's share is rising rapidly.

Our goal must be to meet the economic needs of the present without compromising the ability of the planet to provide for the needs of future generations.

We have made progress since 1972, when the United Nations convened the first global conference ever to address environmental issues. That conference stimulated the creation of environmental ministries throughout the world, established the United Nations Environment Programme and led to a vast increase in the number of civil society organizations promoting environmental concerns.

Twenty years later, the United Nations Conference on Environment and Development provided the foundations for agreements on climate change, forests and biodiversity. It adopted an indicative policy framework intended to help achieve the goal of sustainable development—in rich and poor countries alike.

Perhaps the single most successful international environmental agreement to date has been the Montreal Protocol, in which states accepted the need to phase out the use of ozone-depleting substances (see box 8).

Nevertheless, we must face up to an inescapable reality: the challenges of sustainability simply overwhelm the adequacy of our responses. With some honourable exceptions, our responses are too few, too little and too late.

This section is intended to convey that reality to the Millennium Summit with a particular sense of urgency. The fact that environmental issues were never seriously considered in the nearly 18 months during which the General Assembly debated which subjects to include in the Summit's agenda makes it plain how little priority is accorded to these extraordinarily serious challenges for all humankind. Leadership at the very highest level is imperative if we are to bequeath a liveable Earth to our children—and theirs.

The 10-year follow-up to the Conference on Environment and Development will be held in 2002. It is my hope that the world's leaders will take advantage of the time remaining to revitalize the sustainability debate and to prepare the ground for the adoption of concrete and meaningful actions by that time.

Box 8 Protecting the Ozone Layer: An Environmental Success Story

In the early 1970s evidence had accumulated showing that chlorofluorocarbons (CFCs) were damaging the ozone layer in the stratosphere and increasing the amount of ultraviolet B (UV-B) radiation reaching Earth's surface. Since the ozone layer protects humans, animals and plants from the damaging effects of UV-B radiation, the steady increase in CFCs and other ozone-depleting substances constituted a major potential health hazard. But it took a decade and a half of increasingly intensive effort to achieve an agreement that would resolve the problem.

The 1987 Montreal Protocol on Substances that Deplete the Ozone Layer was a landmark international environmental agreement. It has been remarkably successful. Production of the most damaging ozone-depleting substances was eliminated, except for a few critical uses, by 1996 in developed countries and should be phased out by 2010 in developing countries. Without the Protocol the levels of ozone-depleting substances would have been five times higher than they are today, and surface UV-B radiation levels would have doubled at mid-latitudes in the northern hemisphere. On current estimates the CFC concentration in the ozone layer is expected to recover to pre-1980 levels by the year 2050.

Prior to the Protocol intergovernmental negotiations on their own failed to mobilize sufficient support for the far-reaching measures that were needed. But intensive lobbying by civil society organizations, the presentation of overwhelming scientific evidence—and the discovery of the huge ozone hole over Antarctica—eventually created the consensus necessary for the agreement to be signed.

A. Coping with Climate Change

Spurred by a quadrupling of carbon emissions during the past half-century alone, Earth's atmosphere is warming at an increasing rate (see figure 10). The hottest 14 years since systematic measurements began in the 1860s have all occurred in the past two decades; the summer of 1998 was the hottest on record, and the winter of 19992000 may turn out to be the warmest. Average temperatures are projected to increase further, by 1. 2° to 3. 5° C (2° to 6° F) over the course of the present century—which would melt glaciers and the polar ice caps, raise sea levels and pose threats to hundreds of millions of coastal dwellers while drowning low-lying islands altogether.

Portents of this future are already visible. As the warming trend has accelerated, weather patterns have become more volatile and more extreme, while the severity of weather-related disasters has escalated. The cost of natural disasters in 1998 alone exceeded the cost of all such disasters in the entire decade of the 1980s (see figure 11). Tens of thousands of mostly poor people were killed that year, and an estimated 25 million "environmental refugees" were forced from their homes. The damage wrought by these disasters has been exacerbated by unsustainable environmental practices and the fact that more and more poor people have little choice but to live in harm's way—on flood plains and unstable hillsides and in unsafe buildings.

Figure 10 Average temperature at the Earth's surface, 1860–1998 (Degrees celsius)

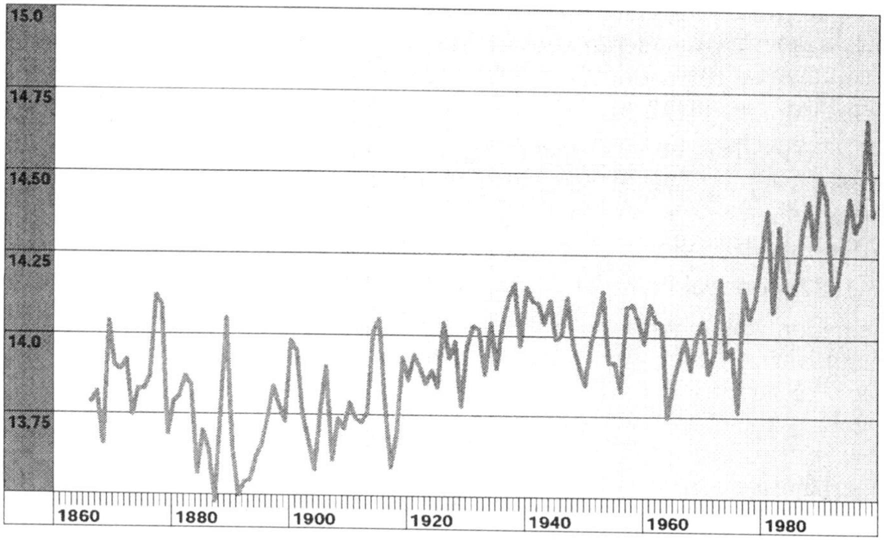

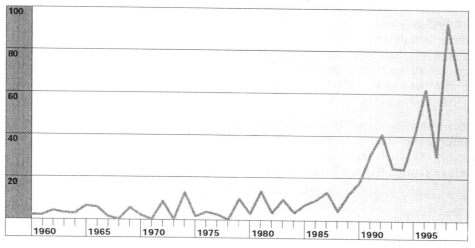

Source: Goddard Institute, Worldwatch Institute, 1999.

Figure 11 Economic losses from weather-related natural disasters worldwide, 1960–1998 (Billions of United States dollars, 1997)

Source: Munich Re Group.

Reducing the threat of global warming requires, above all, that carbon emissions be reduced. The burning of fossil fuels, which still provide more than 75 per cent of energy worldwide, produces most of these emissions. The rapidly expanding number of automobiles around the globe threatens an even greater escalation in emissions. The need to promote energy-efficiency and greater reliance on renewable resources is obvious.

Further development of fuel cell, wind turbine, photovoltaic and cogeneration technologies will help. In the developing world, particularly in rural areas that are not connected to energy grids, the rapidly falling costs of solar cells and wind power have the potential to bring energy to the poor at reasonable costs, thereby also enhancing agricultural productivity and generating income.

Stabilizing levels of carbon dioxide in the atmosphere to a range that is considered safe will require overall reductions on the order of 60 per cent or more in the emission of the "greenhouse gases" that are responsible for global warming. Thus far, the international community has not found the political will needed to make the necessary changes.

Implementing the 1997 Kyoto Protocol would mark a significant advance by binding the industrialized countries to verifiable emission limitation and reduction targets averaging 5 per cent below 1990 levels, to be achieved over the period 2008-2012. Recognizing the economic roots of the climate change problem, the Protocol seeks to engage the private sector in the search for solutions. It does so by the use of market mechanisms that provide incentives for cutting emissions, and which stimulate investment and technology flows to developing countries that will help them achieve more sustainable patterns of industrialization (see box 9).

Box 9 Using Economic Incentives to Reduce Global Warming and Promote Investment in Developing Countries

Addressing the challenge of climate change is one of the most important tasks of the twenty-first century. It will require major reductions in emissions of the so-called greenhouse gases that cause global warming. This in turn will require cleaner and more efficient technologies in the energy, transport and industrial industries if the greenhouse reduction targets specified by the 1997 Kyoto Protocol are to be met. Reductions can be achieved in a number of ways. One of the most ingenious of these, the Clean Development Mechanism (CDM), provides benefits for both industrial and developing countries.

The CDM allows industrial countries to gain emissions credits for climate-friendly investments in developing countries where these would reduce pre-existing levels of greenhouse emissions. Emission credits count towards the reduction targets that the industrial states have to meet.

The prospect of gaining emission credit provides incentives for rich countries to make energy-saving investments in poor countries. The fact that the emissions savings have to be verified and certified provides incentives to create a new service industry dedicated to this task. The climate-friendly investment helps build sustainability in the developing country.

The CDM and other Kyoto mechanisms seek to use incentives to engage the private sector in the vital task of reducing global warming. They are very much in tune with the spirit of the times.

Although the first generation of Kyoto targets represent just one step towards what is needed to reduce global warming, their achievement would result in a sharp reduction in current rates of increase of greenhouse gas emissions by the industrialized countries (see figure 12). Early action is essential. Without success, there will be little incentive for the further rounds of emission limitations that must follow, in which the developing countries will need to become progressively engaged.

I call upon the Millennium Summit to promote the adoption and implementation of the Kyoto Protocol. Specifically, I urge those states whose ratifications are needed to bring it into effect to take the necessary action in time for entry into force by 2002, as a fitting celebration of our progress since Stockholm in 1972 and Rio in 1992.

In several other areas, there are severe challenges for which we still lack remotely adequate responses.

Figure 12 Projected impact of the Kyoto Protocol on emissions of greenhouse gases (Gigatons of carbon)

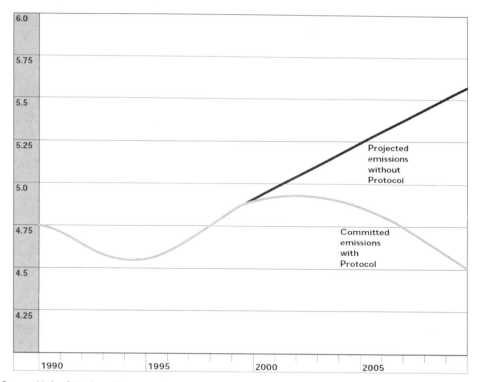

Source: United Nations Framework Convention on Climate Change secretariat, 2000.

B. Confronting the Water Crisis

Global freshwater consumption rose sixfold between 1900 and 1995—more than twice the rate of population growth. About one third of the world's population already lives in countries considered to be "water stressed"—that is, where consumption exceeds 10 per cent of total supply. If present trends continue, two out of every three people on Earth will live in that condition by 2025.

Groundwater supplies about one third of the world's population. The unsustainable, but largely unnoticed, exploitation of these water resources is a particular source of concern. The withdrawal of groundwater in quantities greater than nature's ability to renew it is widespread in parts of the Arabian Peninsula, China, India, Mexico, the former Soviet Union and the United States. In some cases, water tables are falling by 1 to 3 metres a year. In a world where 30 to 40 per cent of food production comes from irrigated lands, this is a critical issue for food security.

There is already fierce national competition over water for irrigation and power generation in some of the world's regions, which is likely to worsen as populations continue to grow. Today, the Middle East and North Africa are most seriously affected by water scarcity, but sub-Saharan Africa will join them over the next half-century as its population doubles and even triples.

Sheer shortages of freshwater are not the only problem. Fertilizer run-off and chemical pollution threaten both water quality and public health. More than one fifth of freshwater fish stocks are already vulnerable or endangered because of pollution or habitat modification.

The most serious immediate challenge is the fact that more than 1 billion people lack access to safe drinking water, while half of humanity lacks adequate sanitation. In many developing countries, rivers downstream from large cities are little cleaner than open sewers. The health impact is devastating.

Unsafe water and poor sanitation cause an estimated 80 per cent of all diseases in the developing world. The annual death toll exceeds 5 million, 10 times the number killed in wars, on average, each year. More than half of the victims are children. No single measure would do more to reduce disease and save lives in the developing world than bringing safe water and adequate sanitation to all.

The World Water Forum's Ministerial Conference, which met in March 2000, recommended a set of realistically achievable targets on water and sanitation. I ask the Millennium Summit to endorse these targets and to build on them in the years ahead.

Specifically, I urge the Summit to adopt the target of reducing by half, between now and 2015, the proportion of people who lack sustainable access to adequate sources of affordable and safe water.

To arrest the unsustainable exploitation of water resources, we require water management strategies at national level and local levels. They should include pricing structures that promote both equity and efficiency. We need a "Blue Revolution" in agriculture that focuses on increasing productivity per unit of water—"more crop per drop"—together with far better watershed and flood plain management. But none of this will happen without public awareness and mobilization campaigns, to bring home to people the extent and causes of current and impending water crises.

C. Defending the Soil

In principle, there is no reason why Earth could not support far more than its present population. In reality, however, the distribution of good soils and favourable growing conditions does not match that of populations. Increasing land degradation exacerbates that problem. Nearly 2 billion hectares of land—an area about the combined size of Canada and the United States—is affected by human-induced degradation of soils, putting the livelihoods of nearly 1 billion people at risk. The major culprits are irrigation-induced salinization, soil erosion caused by overgrazing and deforestation, and biodiversity depletion. The direct cost alone, in terms of annual income forgone, has been estimated at more than $40 billion a year.

Each year an additional 20 million hectares of agricultural land becomes too degraded for crop production, or is lost to urban sprawl. Yet over the next 30 years the demand for food in the developing countries is expected to double. New land can and will be farmed, but much of it is marginal and, therefore, even more highly susceptible to degradation.

Increases in farm productivity, boosted by new high-yield plant varieties and a ninefold increase in fertilizer use, have prevented the Doomsday scenarios of global famine that were predicted in the 1970s—but often at considerable environmental cost. The rate of increase in global agricultural productivity slowed dramatically in the 1990s, and sub-Saharan Africa never enjoyed its benefits. The absence of secure land tenure is also a serious impediment to improved agricultural productivity and soil management.

Meanwhile, world population is expected to increase by more than 3 billion by mid-century, with the biggest growth coming in the countries that already contain the largest number of hungry people and the most stressed farmlands.

Thus the world faces a real threat to future global food security. Plant scientists currently are unable to repeat the huge gains in plant yields they achieved in recent decades, land degradation is increasing, returns from fertilizer application are diminishing in many areas and there are serious constraints on expanding irrigation.

Advances in agricultural biotechnology may help developing countries by creating drought-, salt- and pest-resistant crop varieties. But the environmental impact of biotechnology has yet to be fully evaluated and many questions, in particular those related to biosafety, remain to be answered.

I intend to convene a high-level global public policy network to address these and related controversies concerning the risks and opportunities associated with the increased use of biotechnology and bioengineering.

Of course, not every country has to produce all its own food. Shortfalls in supply can be met by imports from food-surplus countries, an increasingly common practice. But, apart from emergency aid, this is a solution to food production deficits only if the countries and people in need of food have the purchasing power to acquire it. According to the Food and Agriculture Organization of the United Nations, no fewer than 82 countries lack those resources.

D. Preserving Forests, Fisheries and Biodiversity

Increasing populations and economic growth continue to drive a seemingly insatiable global demand for forest products. Some 65 million hectares of forest were lost in the developing world between 1990 and 1995 because of over-harvesting, conversion into agricultural land, disease and fire. The high demand for timber in the industrialized countries was a major factor behind this depletion.

Nevertheless, growing demand need not necessarily generate ever-greater destruction of forests. Major efficiency gains can be achieved in the production of paper and wood products; greater use of recycling can conserve materials and electronic publishing can save paper. Reforestation provides for future timber needs and helps to absorb carbon from the atmosphere, thus reducing global warming. It enhances flood control and helps to prevent soil erosion.

The need to preserve biodiversity is a less self-evident conservation issue than polluted beaches, burning forests or expanding deserts. But it is as critical, if not more so. Conserving agricultural biodiversity is essential for long-term food security, because wild plants are genetic sources of resistance to disease, drought and salinization.

Biodiversity is not only important for agriculture. Plant-based medicines provide more than 3 billion people with their primary health care and comprise a multi-billion dollar a year global industry. But as scientific and commercial awareness of the value of plant-based medicines grows, the plants are coming under increasing threat. According to a recent survey of nearly a quarter of a million plant species, one in every eight is at risk of extinction. The survival of some 25 per cent of the world's mammal species and 11 per cent of bird species is also threatened. As long as deforestation, land and water degradation, and monoculture cropping continue to increase, the threats to biodiversity will continue to grow.

Ocean fisheries continue to be stressed despite the large number of regulatory agreements in place. Fish catches have increased nearly fivefold during the last half-century, but almost 70 per cent of ocean fisheries are either fully exploited or over-fished. Unregulated, winner-take-all fishing practices using so-called factory ships, often heavily state subsidized, cause overexploitation of ocean fisheries and can also destroy the livelihoods of small fishing communities, particularly in the developing world. Coastal waters can be protected from unregulated foreign fishing fleets, but they confront different threats. Fish breeding stocks and nursery grounds are threatened in many regions by the growing degradation of coral reefs. More than half the world's coral reefs are currently at risk as the result of human activities.

The complete collapse of many once-valuable fisheries provides compelling evidence that a more sustainable and equitable ocean governance regime is needed. The importance of conservation is increasingly recognized, but it can flourish only if governments and the fishing industry work cooperatively to support it.

E. Building a New Ethic of Global Stewardship

The ecological crises we confront have many causes. They include poverty, negligence and greed—and above all, failures of governance. These crises do not admit of easy or uniform solutions.

Moreover, there is every reason to expect that unpleasant ecological surprises lie ahead. It is worth recalling that neither global warming nor ozone depletion were on the agenda of the 1972 United Nations Conference on the Human Environment in Stockholm. Nor would anyone in 1970 have predicted that the cost of natural disasters would increase 900 per cent between the 1960s and 1990s.

It is true that technological breakthroughs that are unimaginable today may solve some of the environmental challenges we confront. Perhaps they will, and we should surely provide incentives to increase the likelihood of their occurring. But it would be foolish to count on them and to continue with business as usual.

So the question remains, what should our priorities be? I recommend four. First, major efforts in public education are needed. Real understanding of the challenges we face is alarmingly low. As more and more of us live in cities, insulated from nature, the need for greater awareness grows. Consumers everywhere have to understand that their choices often have significant environmental consequences.

Much of the burden of consciousness-raising to date has fallen on civil society organizations. With energy, commitment, but few resources, non-governmental organizations have advocated environmental issues in public debates almost everywhere. Schools and universities also have a critical role to play in raising public consciousness, and governments themselves must step up their contributions.

Second, environmental issues must be fundamentally repositioned in the policy-making process. Governments typically treat the environment as an isolated category, assigned to a relatively junior ministry. This is a major obstacle to achieving sustainable development. Instead, the environment must become better integrated into mainstream economic policy. The surest way to achieve that goal is to modify systems of national accounts so that they begin to reflect true environmental costs and benefits—to move towards "green" accounting.

Today, when factories produce goods but in the process pump pollutants into rivers or the atmosphere, national accounts measure the value of the goods but not the costs inflicted by the pollutants. In the long run, these unmeasured costs may greatly exceed the measured short-term benefits. Only when they reflect a fuller accounting can economic policies ensure that development is sustainable.

The System of Integrated Environmental and Economic Accounting, pioneered by the United Nations in 1993, is a response to this challenge. It augments traditional national accounts with natural resource and pollution flow accounts. This additional information enables governments to formulate and monitor economic policies more effectively, enact more effective environmental regulations and resource management strategies, and use taxes and subsidies more efficiently.

Although this system of green accounting is still a work in progress, it is already employed by national governments. The Government of the Philippines started using it in 1995. Another 20 or so countries, North and South, are using elements of it. I encourage governments to consider this system of green accounting carefully and identify ways to incorporate it into their own national accounts.

Third, only governments can create and enforce environmental regulations, and devise more environment-friendly incentives for markets to respond to. To cite but one example, governments can make markets work for the environment by cutting the hundreds of billions of dollars that subsidize environmentally harmful activities each and every year. Another is by making greater use of "green taxes", based on the "polluter pays" principle.

Creating new incentives also encourages the emergence of entirely new industries, devoted to achieving greater energy efficiency and other environment-friendly practices. The success of the Montreal Protocol, for instance, has created a large market for ozone-safe refrigerators and air conditioners. Nothing would be more foolish than neglecting the enormously positive role the private sector can play in promoting environmental change.

Finally, it is impossible to devise effective environmental policy unless it is based on sound scientific information. While major advances in data collection have been made in many areas, large gaps in our knowledge remain. In particular, there has never been a comprehensive global assessment of the world's major ecosystems. The planned Millennium Ecosystem Assessment, a major international collaborative effort to map the health of our planet, is a response to this need. It is supported by many governments, as well as UNEP, UNDP, FAO and UNESCO (see box 10).

I call on Member States to help provide the necessary financial support for the Millennium Ecosystem Assessment and to become actively engaged in it.

Different regions of the world face very different environmental problems, which require different solutions. But the peoples of our small planet share at least one common view about their predicament: they want their governments to do more to protect their environment. They ask that for themselves, and even more so for their children—and for the future of the planet itself. Given the extraordinary risks humanity confronts, the start of the new century could not be a more opportune time to commit ourselves—peoples as well as governments—to a new ethic of conservation and stewardship.

Box 10 Why We Need a Millennium Assessment of Global Ecosystems

During the past three decades we have become increasingly aware that the natural ecosystems on which human life depends are under threat. But we still lack detailed knowledge of the extent of the damage—or its causes. Indeed in some cases, data on freshwater quality, for example, we now have less information than we did 20 years ago because of short-sighted cuts in environmental monitoring programmes.

Good environmental policy must be based on reliable scientific data. To ensure that this data is available to policy makers we need a truly comprehensive global evaluation of the condition of the five major ecosystems: forests, freshwater systems, grasslands, coastal areas and agro-ecosystems.

The proposed Millennium Ecosystem Assessment seeks to produce just such an evaluation. An initiative of the World Resources Institute, the World Bank, the United Nations Development Programme and the United Nations Environment Programme among others, it will draw on and collate existing sources of data and promote new research to fill the missing knowledge gaps.

The Millennium Ecosystem Assessment promises important benefits to many stakeholders. It will provide the parties to various international ecosystem conventions with access to the data they need to evaluate progress towards meeting convention goals. National governments will gain access to information needed to meet reporting requirements under international conventions. The Assessment will strengthen capacity for integrated ecosystem management policies and provide developing nations with better access to global data sets. The private sector will benefit by being able to make more informed forecasts. And it will provide civil society organizations with the information they need to hold corporations and governments accountable for meeting their environmental obligations.

The Millennium Ecosystem Assessment is an outstanding example of the sort of international scientific and political cooperation that is needed to further the cause of sustainable development.

VI. Renewing the United Nations

The United Nations alone can meet none of the challenges I have described. They affect the entire international community, and they require all of us to do our part. But without a strong and effective Organization, the peoples of the world will find meeting these challenges immeasurably more difficult.

Whether the world's peoples have such an organization at their disposal depends ultimately, now as in the past, on the commitment of their governments to it. Now, as then, the Member States are the very foundation of the United Nations.

As we prepare for the Millennium Summit, we must reaffirm our founding purposes. But we must also think imaginatively how to strengthen the United Nations so that it can better serve states and people alike in the new era.

Today, global affairs are no longer the exclusive province of foreign ministries, nor are states the sole source of solutions for our small planet's many problems. Many diverse and increasingly influential non-state actors have joined with national decision makers to improvise new forms of global governance. The more complex the problem at hand—whether negotiating a ban on landmines, setting limits to emissions that contribute to global warming, or creating an International Criminal Court—the more likely we are to find non-governmental organizations, private sector institutions and multilateral agencies working with sovereign states to find consensus solutions.

I believe two strategies will be essential to realize the potential of our Organization in the years ahead.

First, while our own resources as an organization are tightly constrained, those of the communities we serve are much greater. We must strive, not to usurp the role of other actors on the world stage, but to become a more effective catalyst for change and coordination among them. Our most vital role will be to stimulate collective action at the global level.

Second, the United Nations—like all other institutions in the world today—must fully exploit the great promise of the Information Age. The digital revolution has unleashed an unprecedented wave of technological change. Used responsibly, it can greatly improve our chances of defeating poverty and better meeting our other priority objectives. If this is to happen, we in the United Nations need to embrace the new technologies more wholeheartedly than we have in the past.

A. Identifying our Core Strengths

When it was created more than half a century ago, in the convulsive aftermath of world war, the United Nations reflected humanity's greatest hopes for a just and peaceful global community. It still embodies that dream. We remain the only global institution with the legitimacy and scope that derive from universal membership, and a mandate that encompasses development, security and human rights as well as the environment. In this sense, the United Nations is unique in world affairs.

We are an organization without independent military capability, and we dispose of relatively modest resources in the economic realm. Yet our influence and impact on the world is far greater than many believe to be the case—and often more than we ourselves realize. This influence derives not from any exercise of power, but from the force of the values we represent; our role in helping to establish and sustain global norms; our ability to stimulate global concern and action; and the trust we enjoy for the practical work we do on the ground to improve people's lives.

The importance of principles and norms is easily underestimated; but in the decades since the United Nations was created, the spreading acceptance of new norms has profoundly affected the lives of many millions of people. War was once a normal instrument of statecraft; it is now universally proscribed, except in very specific circumstances. Democracy, once challenged by authoritarianism in various guises, has not only prevailed in much of the world, but is now generally seen as the most legitimate and desirable form of government. The protection of fundamental human rights, once considered the province of sovereign states alone, is now a universal concern transcending both governments and borders.

The United Nations conferences of the 1990s were sometimes marked by discord, but they have played a central role in forging normative consensus and spelling out practical solutions on the great issues of the day. Nowhere else has it been possible for the international community as a whole to sketch out responses to the dawning challenge of globalization on which all, or almost all, could agree. Indeed, it is on those responses that this report seeks to build.

More recently we have seen an upsurge of transnational single-issue campaigns to strengthen norms and build legal regimes, leading for instance to the convention banning landmines or to last year's agreement on enhanced debt relief for the most heavily indebted poor countries. These campaigns, often conducted in concert with the United Nations, have helped to raise—and alter—the consciousness of the international community and to change the behaviour of states on many critical global issues.

The United Nations plays an equally important, but largely unsung, role in creating and sustaining the global rules without which modern societies simply could not function. The World Health Organization, for example, sets quality criteria for the pharmaceutical industry worldwide. The World Meteorological Office collates weather data from individual states and redistributes it, which in turn improves global weather forecasting. The World Intellectual Property Organization protects trademarks and patents outside their country of origin. The rights for commercial airlines to fly over borders derive from agreements negotiated by the International Civil Aviation Organization. The United Nations Statistical Commission helps secure uniformity in accounting standards.

Indeed, it is impossible to imagine our globalized world without the principles and practice of multilateralism to underpin it. An open world economy, in the place of mercantilism; a gradual decrease in the importance of competitive military alliances coupled with a Security Council more often able to reach decisions; the General Assembly or great gatherings of states and civil society organizations addressing humanity's common concerns—these are some of the signs, partial and halting though they may be, of an indispensable multilateral system in action.

Taking a long-term view, the expansion of the rule of law has been the foundation of much of the social progress achieved in the last millennium. Of course, this remains an unfinished project, especially at the international level, and our efforts to deepen it continue. Support for the rule of law would be enhanced if countries signed and ratified international treaties and conventions. Some decline to do so for reasons of substance, but a far greater number simply lack the necessary expertise and resources, especially when national legislation is needed to give force to international instruments.

Therefore, I am asking all relevant United Nations entities to provide the necessary technical assistance that will make it possible for every willing state to participate fully in the emerging global legal order.

We will provide special facilities at the Millennium Summit for Heads of State or Government to add their signatures to any treaty or convention of which the Secretary-General is the depositary.

As global norms evolve, institutions have evolved with them. In recent years, for example, we have witnessed the creation of ad hoc tribunals for Rwanda and the former Yugoslavia, in response to the international community's growing concern about gross violations of human rights and its determination to end the "culture of impunity".

I strongly urge all countries to sign and ratify the Rome Statute of the International Criminal Court, so as to consolidate and extend the gains we have achieved in bringing to justice those responsible for crimes against humanity.

The United Nations must also adapt itself to the changing times. One critical area, to which I have already referred, is reform of the Security Council. The Council must work effectively, but it must also enjoy unquestioned legitimacy. Those two criteria define the space within which a solution must be found. I **urge Member States to tackle this challenge without delay.**

We also need to adapt our deliberative work so that it can benefit fully from the contributions of civil society. Already, civil society organizations have made an important contribution to articulating and defending global norms. (For the number of nongovernmental organizations, see figure 13.) It is clear that the United Nations and the world's people have much to gain from opening the Organization further to this vital source of energy and expertise—just as we have gained from closer institutional links and practical cooperation with national parliaments.

I would ask the General Assembly, therefore, to explore ways of improving these relationships. As a first step, an expert group, including representatives of civil society organizations, might be asked to prepare a study of innovative "best practices" in how those organizations contribute to the work of the United Nations in all its aspects. Such a study could form the basis for adopting new ways of involving civil society more fully in our common endeavours.

Partnerships with the private sector and foundations have also become extremely important to our recent successes, as I have noted in several instances in this report.

Figure 13 Number of international non-governmental organizations (Thousands)

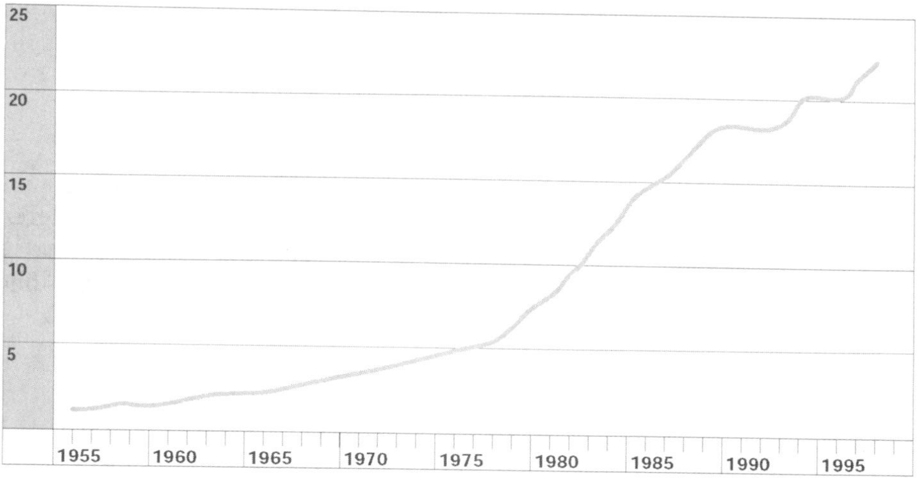

Source: Union of International Organizations and Worldwatch Institute, 1996–1999.

B. Networking for Change

The rapid pace of change today frequently exceeds the capacity of national and international institutions to adapt. So many things are changing at once that no organization on its own can keep track of them all—especially as the changes generally cut across traditional boundaries between academic disciplines and professional fields of expertise.

Part of the solution may be found in the emergence of "global policy networks". These networks—or coalitions for change—bring together international institutions, civil society and private sector organizations, and national governments, in pursuit of common goals.

Sometimes international organizations are in the lead—the World Health Organization, for example, in the Roll Back Malaria campaign, or my own office in the case of the Global Compact with the private sector.

In other instances a few national governments and non-governmental organizations are the driving force, as was the case with the campaign to ban landmines. In the Global Alliance for Vaccines and Immunization the private sector and philanthropic foundations are the major players. In every case, these loose creative coalitions give new meaning to the phrase "we the peoples", by showing that global governance is not a zero-sum game. All the partners in such a network see their influence increase.

States, in particular, gain from joining global policy networks because they can achieve cooperatively what is impossible unilaterally.

Though they can take many different forms, global policy networks share a number of characteristics. They are non-hierarchical and give voice to civil society. They help set global policy agendas, frame debates and raise public consciousness. They develop and disseminate knowledge, making extensive use of the Internet. They make it easier to reach consensus and negotiate agreements on new global standards, as well as to create new kinds of mechanisms for implementing and monitoring those agreements.

Our involvement with global policy networks has been extensive but largely unplanned. We need a more focused and systematic approach. We need to determine how best to help governments, civil society and the private sector to work together to ensure that policy networks succeed in achieving their—and our—goals.

C. Making Digital Connections

Earlier in this report, I discussed the vital importance of bridging the global digital divide. Here, I want to suggest how the Information Revolution can and must benefit the United Nations itself.

Ten years ago getting information from—or to—the developing world was costly and time-consuming. But today the World Wide Web is changing that. We can now read newspapers on-line from every corner of the world within seconds of their publication. We can find and download information from national government departments, leading overseas research institutions and key non-governmental organizations just as quickly.

This is not all. Increased global connectivity also means that every year the vast electronic treasure house of information available on the United Nations web site becomes accessible at no cost to millions more people. The popularity of our web site is extraordinary—it received more than 100 million "hits" last year.

The Internet also makes it possible for us to hold interactive global electronic conferences, which not only save airfares, hotel bills and conference costs, but can as easily and cheaply host 10, 000 participants as 10. Within the Secretariat, we can substitute electronic "meetings" for many face-to-face ones, thereby making far more efficient use of staff time. This is increasingly the practice in modern organizations that have embraced the Information Revolution.

Finally, the Information Revolution has the potential to radically improve the efficiency of our field operations. Wireless communications work even under the worst conditions, including natural disasters and emergencies.

I am pleased to announce the launch of a new disaster response programme, which will provide and maintain mobile and satellite telephones as well as microwave links for humanitarian relief workers.

This initiative will be led by Ericsson, in partnership with United Nations entities and the International Federation of Red Cross and Red Crescent Societies (see box 11).

Box 11 First on the Ground: Communications in Disaster Relief Operations

---

The dramatic growth in the scope and severity of natural disasters over the past three decades has placed ever-increasing demands on disaster relief organizations. To meet these demands, disaster relief operations have become larger and more complex, involving increasing numbers of players. This in turn has increased demand for more effective communications in the field.

Local communication systems are often extensively damaged in disasters. Unfortunately the communication systems used by different agencies and non-governmental organizations vary widely in quality and often suffer compatibility problems. The need for improvement is widely recognized, but for many agencies and non-governmental organizations acquisition of more effective systems has simply been too costly.

Responding to this challenge the Ericsson corporation has launched a major Disaster Response Programme that, among other initiatives, will provide and maintain mobile and satellite phones to agency and local humanitarian relief workers. The company will help install microwave links and other measures to improve existing communication networks—or it will build new ones where none exists. The Disaster Response Programme will rely heavily on support from Ericsson's offices in more than 140 countries worldwide and will focus on disaster preparation as well as response.

This generous exercise in global corporate citizenship and private-public cooperation will greatly benefit United Nations agencies and their partners and help improve the provision of services to disaster victims everywhere.

Logistical planning and operations in complex emergencies can also benefit from better use of available technology. In Kosovo, for example, the International Rescue Committee created a shared satellite/wireless Internet network in

Pristina. Every United Nations agency, the Organization for Security and Cooperation in Europe, several national missions and the majority of non-governmental organizations are connected via the network around the clock.

Up to now, however, the United Nations has scarcely tapped the potential of the Information Revolution. We remain handicapped by a change-resistant culture, inadequate information technology infrastructure, lack of training and, above all, failure to understand the great benefits that information technology can provide when used creatively. We need to update and upgrade our internal information technology capacity. There is enormous scope for the entire United Nations system to become better integrated, on-line, providing the world's people with information and data of concern to them.

In cooperation with other members of the United Nations family, I shall pursue these objectives with great vigour. I will also be appealing to the information technology industry for assistance in rebuilding the United Nations information technology infrastructure and capacity.

D. Advancing the Quiet Revolution

If the international community were to create a new United Nations tomorrow, its make-up would surely be different from the one we have. In 2000, our structure reflects decades of mandates conferred by Member States and, in some cases, the legacy of deep political disagreements. While there is widespread consensus on the need to make the United Nations a more modern and flexible organization, unless Member States are willing to contemplate **real structural reform**, there will continue to be severe limits to what we can achieve.

When the scope of our responsibilities and the hopes invested in us are measured against our resources, we confront a sobering truth. The budget for our core functions—the Secretariat operations in New York, Geneva, Nairobi, Vienna and five regional commissions—is just $1. 25 billion a year. That is about 4 per cent of New York City's annual budget—and nearly a billion dollars less than the annual cost of running Tokyo's Fire Department. Our resources simply are not commensurate with our global tasks.

Our difficulties in coping with stagnant budgets and non-payment of dues are well known. Less well understood are the strains that Member States impose on us by adding new mandates without adding new resources. We can do more with less, but only up to a point. Sooner or later the quality of our work must suffer.

The constraints are not only financial. In many areas we cannot do our job because disagreements among Member States preclude the consensus needed for effective action. This is perhaps most obvious with respect to peace operations, but it affects other areas as well. Moreover, the highly intrusive and excessively detailed mode of oversight that Member States exercise over our programme activities makes it very difficult for us to maximize efficiency or effectiveness.

The "quiet revolution" I launched in 1997 was designed to make the United Nations a leaner and more effective organization. Since then we have streamlined management procedures, shifted resources from administration to development work, introduced cabinet-style management and greatly improved coordination among the far-flung members of the United Nations family.

To reduce the built-in bias towards institutional inertia that has afflicted our work, and to facilitate the strategic redeployment of resources, I have proposed **time limits or "sunset provisions"** for initiatives involving new organizational structures or major commitments of funds. The General Assembly has not yet accepted this proposal; **I urge it to do so**.

Furthermore, a more people-oriented United Nations must be a more **results-based organization,** both in its staffing and its allocation of resources. We are making slow progress in the direction of a results-based budgeting system, one focused on outcomes rather than inputs and processes. When fully implemented this will encourage greater efficiency and flexibility, while at the same time enhancing transparency and the Secretariat's accountability to Member States. **Here, too, the General Assembly's support is necessary.**

To sum up, the United Nations of the twenty-first century must continue to be guided by its founding principles. It must remain an Organization dedicated to the interests of its Member States and of their peoples. Our objectives will not change: peace, prosperity, social justice and a sustainable future. But the means we use to achieve those ends must be adapted to the challenges of the new era.

In future, the United Nations must increasingly serve as a catalyst for collective action, both among its Member States and between them and the vibrant constellation of new non-state actors. We must continue to be the place where new standards of international conduct are hammered out, and broad consensus on them is established. We must harness the power of technology to improve the fortunes of developing countries. Finally, we ourselves, as an organization, must become more effective, efficient, and accessible to the world's peoples. When we fail, we must be our own most demanding critics.

Only by these means can we become a global public trust for all the world's peoples.

For Consideration by the Summit

The purposes and principles of the United Nations are set out clearly in the Charter, and in the Universal Declaration of Human Rights. Their relevance and capacity to inspire have in no way diminished. If anything they have increased, as peoples have become interconnected in new ways, and the need for collective responsibility at the global level has come to be more widely felt. The following values, which reflect the spirit of the Charter, are—I believe—shared by all nations, and are of particular importance for the age we are now entering:

Freedom. Men and women have the right to live their lives and raise their children in dignity, free from hunger and squalor and from the fear of violence or oppression. These rights are best assured by representative government, based on the will of the people.

Equity and solidarity. No individual and no nation must be denied the opportunity to benefit from globalization. Global risks must be managed in a way that shares the costs and burdens fairly. Those who suffer, or who benefit least, are entitled to help from those who benefit most.

Tolerance. Human beings must respect each other, in all their diversity of faith, culture and language. Differences within and between societies should be neither feared nor repressed, but cherished.

Non-violence. Disputes between and within nations should be resolved by peaceful means, except where use of force is authorized by the Charter.

Respect for nature. Prudence should be shown in handling all living species and natural resources. Only so can the immeasurable riches we inherit from nature be preserved and passed on to our descendants.

Shared responsibility. States must act together to maintain international peace and security, in accordance with the Charter. The management of risks and threats that affect all the world's peoples should be considered multilaterally.

* * *

In applying these values to the new century, our priorities must be clear.

First, we must spare no effort to free our fellow men and women from the abject and dehumanizing poverty in which more than 1 billion of them are currently confined. Let us resolve therefore:

- To halve, by the time this century is 15 years old, the proportion of the world's people (currently 22 per cent) whose income is less than one dollar a day.

- To halve, by the same date, the proportion of people (currently 20 per cent) who are unable to reach, or to afford, safe drinking water.

- That by the same date all children everywhere, boys and girls alike, will be able to complete a full course of primary schooling; and that girls and boys will have equal access to all levels of education.

- That by then we will have halted, and begun to reverse, the spread of HIV/AIDS.

- That, by 2020, we will have achieved significant improvement in the lives of at least 100 million slum dwellers around the world.

- To develop strategies that will give young people everywhere the chance of finding decent work.

- To ensure that the benefits of new technology, especially information technology, are available to all.

- That every national government will from now on commit itself to national policies and programmes directed specifically at reducing poverty, to be developed and applied in consultation with civil society.

At the international level, the more fortunate countries owe a duty of solidarity to the less fortunate. Let them resolve therefore:

- To grant free access to their markets for goods produced in poor countries—and, as a first step, to be prepared, at the Third United Nations Conference on the Least Developed Countries in March 2001, to adopt a policy of duty-free and quota-free access for essentially all exports from the least developed countries.

- To remove the shackles of debt which currently keep many of the poorest countries imprisoned in their poverty—and, as first steps, to implement the expansion of the debt relief programme for heavily indebted poor countries agreed last year without further delay, and to be prepared to cancel all official debts of the heavily indebted poor countries, in return for those countries making demonstrable commitments to poverty reduction.

- To grant more generous development assistance, particularly to those countries which are genuinely applying their resources to poverty reduction.

- To work with the pharmaceutical industry and other partners to develop an effective and affordable vaccine against HIV; and to make HIV-related drugs more widely accessible in developing countries.

At both the national and international levels, private investment has an indispensable role to play. Let us resolve therefore:

- To develop strong partnerships with the private sector to combat poverty in all its aspects.

Extreme poverty in sub-Saharan Africa affects a higher proportion of the population than in any other region. It is compounded by a higher incidence of conflict, HIV/AIDS and many other ills. Let us resolve therefore:

- That in all our efforts we will make special provision for the needs of Africa, and give our full support to Africans in their struggle to overcome the continent's problems.

For my part, I have announced four new initiatives in the course of this report:

- A Health InterNetwork, to provide hospitals and clinics in developing countries with access to up-to-date medical information.

- A United Nations Information Technology Service (UNITeS), to train groups in developing countries in the uses and opportunities of information technology.

- A disaster response initiative, "First on the Ground", which will provide uninterrupted communications access to areas affected by natural disasters and emergencies.

- A global policy network to explore viable new approaches to the problem of youth employment.

Second, we must spare no effort to free our fellow men and women from the scourge of war—as the Charter requires us to do—and especially from the violence of civil conflict and the fear of weapons of mass destruction, which are the two great sources of terror in the present age. Let us resolve therefore:

- To strengthen respect for law, in international as in national affairs, in particular the agreed provisions of treaties on the control of armaments, and international humanitarian and human rights law. I invite all governments that have not done so to sign and ratify the various conventions, covenants and treaties which form the central corpus of international law.

- To make the United Nations more effective in its work of maintaining peace and security, notably by

  - Strengthening the capacity of the United Nations to conduct peace operations.

  - Adopting measures to make economic sanctions adopted by the Security Council less harsh on innocent populations, and more effective in penalizing delinquent rulers.

- To take energetic action to curb the illegal traffic in small arms, notably by

  - Creating greater transparency in arms transfers. Supporting regional disarmament measures, such as the moratorium on the importing, exporting or manufacturing of light weapons in West Africa.

- Extending to other areas—especially post-conflict situations—the "weapons for goods" programmes that have worked well in Albania, El Salvador, Mozambique and Panama.

- To examine the possibility of convening a major international conference to identify ways of eliminating nuclear dangers.

Third, we must spare no effort to free our fellow men and women, and above all our children and grandchildren, from the danger of living on a planet irredeemably spoilt by human activities, and whose resources can no longer provide for their needs. Given the extraordinary risks humanity confronts, let us resolve:

- To adopt a new ethic of conservation and stewardship; and, as first steps:

  - To adopt and ratify the Kyoto Protocol, so that it can enter into force by 2002, and to ensure that its goals are met, as a step towards reducing emissions of greenhouse gases.

  - To consider seriously incorporating the United Nations system of "green accounting" into national accounts.

  - To provide financial support for, and become actively engaged in, the Millennium Ecosystem Assessment.

Finally, we must spare no effort to make the United Nations a more effective instrument in the hands of the world's peoples for pursuing all three of these priorities—the fight against poverty, ignorance and disease; the fight against violence and terror; and the fight against the degradation and destruction of our common home. Let us resolve therefore:

- To reform the Security Council, in a way that both enables it to carry out its responsibilities more effectively and gives it greater legitimacy in the eyes of all the world's peoples.

- To ensure that the Organization is given the necessary resources to carry out its mandates.

- To ensure that the Secretariat makes best use of those resources in the interests of all Member States, by allowing it to adopt the best management practices and technologies available, and to concentrate on those tasks that reflect the current priorities of Member States.

- To give full opportunities to non-governmental organizations and other non-state actors to make their indispensable contribution to the Organization's work.

* * *

I believe that these priorities are clear, and that all these things are achievable if we have the will to achieve them. For many of the priorities, strategies have already been worked out, and are summarized in this report. For others, what is needed first is to apply our minds, our energies and our research budgets to an intensive quest for workable solutions.

No state and no organization can solve all these problems by acting alone. Nor however, should any state imagine that others will solve them for it, if its own government and citizens do not apply themselves wholeheartedly to the task. Building a twenty-first century safer and more equitable than the twentieth is a task that requires the determined efforts of every state and every individual. In inspiring and coordinating those efforts, a renewed United Nations will have a vital and exalting role to play.

MONTERREY CONSENSUS OF THE INTERNATIONAL CONFERENCE ON FINANCING FOR DEVELOPMENT AND FOLLOW-UP REPORT

United Nations Report of the International Conference on Financing for Development

Monterrey, Mexico, 18-22 March 2002

UN Doc. A/CONF. 198/11

Chapter I
Resolutions Adopted by the Conference

Resolution 1*
Monterrey Consensus of the International Conference on Financing for Development

The International Conference on Financing for Development,

Having met in Monterrey, Mexico, from 18 to 22 March 2002,

1. *Adopts* the Monterrey Consensus of the International Conference on Financing for Development, which is annexed to the present resolution;

2. *Recommends* to the General Assembly that it endorse the Monterrey Consensus as adopted by the Conference.

* Adopted at the 5th plenary meeting, on 22 March 2002; for the discussion, see chap. VI.

Annex
Monterrey Consensus of the International Conference on Financing for Development

Contents

Chapter	Paragraphs
I. Confronting the Challenges of Financing for Development: A Global Response	1-9
II. Leading Actions	10-67
A. Mobilizing Domestic Financial Resources for Development	10-19
B. Mobilizing International Resources for Development: Foreign Direct Investment and Other Private Flows	20-25
C. International Trade as an Engine for Development	26-38
D. Increasing International Financial and Technical Cooperation for Development	39-46
E. External Debt	47-51
F. Addressing Systemic Issues: Enhancing the Coherence and Consistency of the International Monetary, Financial and Trading Systems in Support of Development	52-67
III. Staying Engaged	68-73

I. Confronting the Challenges of Financing for Development: A Global Response

1. We the heads of State and Government, gathered in Monterrey, Mexico, on 21 and 22 March 2002, have resolved to address the challenges of financing for development around the world, particularly in developing countries. Our goal is to eradicate poverty, achieve sustained economic growth and promote sustainable development as we advance to a fully inclusive and equitable global economic system.

2. We note with concern current estimates of dramatic shortfalls in resources required to achieve the internationally agreed development goals, including those contained in the United Nations Millennium Declaration.[1]

3. Mobilizing and increasing the effective use of financial resources and achieving the national and international economic conditions needed to fulfil internationally agreed development goals, including those contained in the Millennium Declaration, to eliminate poverty, improve social conditions and raise living standards, and protect our environment, will be our first step to ensuring that the twenty-first century becomes the century of development for all.

---

1   General Assembly resolution 55/2.

4. Achieving the internationally agreed development goals, including those contained in the Millennium Declaration, demands a new partnership between developed and developing countries. We commit ourselves to sound policies, good governance at all levels and the rule of law. We also commit ourselves to mobilizing domestic resources, attracting international flows, promoting international trade as an engine for development, increasing international financial and technical cooperation for development, sustainable debt financing and external debt relief, and enhancing the coherence and consistency of the international monetary, financial and trading systems.

5. The terrorist attacks on 11 September 2001 exacerbated the global economic slowdown, further reducing growth rates. It has now become all the more urgent to enhance collaboration among all stakeholders to promote sustained economic growth and to address the long-term challenges of financing for development. Our resolve to act together is stronger than ever.

6. Each country has primary responsibility for its own economic and social development, and the role of national policies and development strategies cannot be overemphasized. At the same time, domestic economies are now interwoven with the global economic system and, inter alia, the effective use of trade and investment opportunities can help countries to fight poverty. National development efforts need to be supported by an enabling international economic environment. We encourage and support development frameworks initiated at the regional level, such as the New Partnership for Africa's Development and similar efforts in other regions.

7. Globalization offers opportunities and challenges. The developing countries and countries with economies in transition face special difficulties in responding to those challenges and opportunities. Globalization should be fully inclusive and equitable, and there is a strong need for policies and measures at the national and international levels, formulated and implemented with the full and effective participation of developing countries and countries with economies in transition to help them respond effectively to those challenges and opportunities.

8. In the increasingly globalizing interdependent world economy, a holistic approach to the interconnected national, international and systemic challenges of financing for development—sustainable, gender-sensitive, people-centred development—in all parts of the globe is essential. Such an approach must open up opportunities for all and help to ensure that resources are created and used effectively and that strong, accountable institutions are established at all levels. To that end, collective and coherent action is needed in each interrelated area of our agenda, involving all stakeholders in active partnership.

9. Recognizing that peace and development are mutually reinforcing, we are determined to pursue our shared vision for a better future, through our individual efforts combined with vigorous multilateral action. Upholding the Charter of the United Nations and building upon the values of the Millennium Declaration, we

commit ourselves to promoting national and global economic systems based on the principles of justice, equity, democracy, participation, transparency, accountability and inclusion.

II. Leading Actions

A. Mobilizing Domestic Financial Resources for Development

10. In our common pursuit of growth, poverty eradication and sustainable development, a critical challenge is to ensure the necessary internal conditions for mobilizing domestic savings, both public and private, sustaining adequate levels of productive investment and increasing human capacity. A crucial task is to enhance the efficacy, coherence and consistency of macroeconomic policies. An enabling domestic environment is vital for mobilizing domestic resources, increasing productivity, reducing capital flight, encouraging the private sector, and attracting and making effective use of international investment and assistance. Efforts to create such an environment should be supported by the international community.

11. Good governance is essential for sustainable development. Sound economic policies, solid democratic institutions responsive to the needs of the people and improved infrastructure are the basis for sustained economic growth, poverty eradication and employment creation. Freedom, peace and security, domestic stability, respect for human rights, including the right to development, and the rule of law, gender equality, market-oriented policies, and an overall commitment to just and democratic societies are also essential and mutually reinforcing.

12. We will pursue appropriate policy and regulatory frameworks at our respective national levels and in a manner consistent with national laws to encourage public and private initiatives, including at the local level, and foster a dynamic and well functioning business sector, while improving income growth and distribution, raising productivity, empowering women and protecting labour rights and the environment. We recognize that the appropriate role of government in market-oriented economies will vary from country to country.

13. Fighting corruption at all levels is a priority. Corruption is a serious barrier to effective resource mobilization and allocation, and diverts resources away from activities that are vital for poverty eradication and economic and sustainable development.

14. We recognize the need to pursue sound macroeconomic policies aimed at sustaining high rates of economic growth, full employment, poverty eradication, price stability and sustainable fiscal and external balances to ensure that the benefits of growth reach all people, especially the poor. Governments should attach priority to avoiding inflationary distortions and abrupt economic fluctuations that negatively affect income distribution and resource allocation. Along

with prudent fiscal and monetary policies, an appropriate exchange rate regime is required.

15. An effective, efficient, transparent and accountable system for mobilizing public resources and managing their use by Governments is essential. We recognize the need to secure fiscal sustainability, along with equitable and efficient tax systems and administration, as well as improvements in public spending that do not crowd out productive private investment. We also recognize the contribution that medium-term fiscal frameworks can make in that respect.

16. Investments in basic economic and social infrastructure, social services and social protection, including education, health, nutrition, shelter and social security programmes, which take special care of children and older persons and are gender sensitive and fully inclusive of the rural sector and all disadvantaged communities, are vital for enabling people, especially people living in poverty, to better adapt to and benefit from changing economic conditions and opportunities. Active labour market policies, including worker training, can help to increase employment and improve working conditions. The coverage and scope of social protection needs to be further strengthened. Economic crises also underscore the importance of effective social safety nets.

17. We recognize the need to strengthen and develop the domestic financial sector, by encouraging the orderly development of capital markets through sound banking systems and other institutional arrangements aimed at addressing development financing needs, including the insurance sector and debt and equity markets, that encourage and channel savings and foster productive investments. That requires a sound system of financial intermediation, transparent regulatory frameworks and effective supervisory mechanisms, supported by a solid central bank. Guarantee schemes and business development services should be developed for easing the access of small and medium-sized enterprises to local financing.

18. Microfinance and credit for micro-, small and medium-sized enterprises, including in rural areas, particularly for women, as well as national savings schemes, are important for enhancing the social and economic impact of the financial sector. Development banks, commercial and other financial institutions, whether independently or in cooperation, can be effective instruments for facilitating access to finance, including equity financing, for such enterprises, as well as an adequate supply of medium- and long-term credit. In addition, the promotion of private-sector financial innovations and public-private partnerships can also deepen domestic financial markets and further develop the domestic financial sector. The prime objective of pension schemes is social protection, but when those schemes are funded they can also be a source of savings. Bearing in mind economic and social considerations, efforts should be made to incorporate the informal sector into the formal economy, wherever feasible. It is also important to reduce the transfer costs of migrant workers' remittances and create opportunities for development-oriented investments, including housing.

19. It is critical to reinforce national efforts in capacity-building in developing countries and countries with economies in transition in such areas as institutional infrastructure, human resource development, public finance, mortgage finance, financial regulation and supervision, basic education in particular, public administration, social and gender budget policies, early warning and crisis prevention, and debt management. In that regard, particular attention is required to address the special needs of Africa, the least developed countries, small island developing States and landlocked developing countries. We reaffirm our commitment to the Programme of Action for the Least Developed Countries for the Decade 2001–2010,[2] adopted by the Third United Nations Conference on the Least Developed Countries, held in Brussels from 14 to 20 May 2001, and the Global Programme of Action for the Sustainable Development of Small Island Developing States.[3] International support for those efforts, including technical assistance and through United Nations operational activities for development, is indispensable. We encourage South-South cooperation, including through triangular cooperation, to facilitate exchange of views on successful strategies, practices and experience and replication of projects.

B. Mobilizing International Resources for Development: Foreign Direct Investment and Other Private Flows

20. Private international capital flows, particularly foreign direct investment, along with international financial stability, are vital complements to national and international development efforts. Foreign direct investment contributes toward financing sustained economic growth over the long term. It is especially important for its potential to transfer knowledge and technology, create jobs, boost overall productivity, enhance competitiveness and entrepreneurship, and ultimately eradicate poverty through economic growth and development. A central challenge, therefore, is to create the necessary domestic and international conditions to facilitate direct investment flows, conducive to achieving national development priorities, to developing countries, particularly Africa, least developed countries, small island developing States, and landlocked developing countries, and also to countries with economies in transition.

21. To attract and enhance inflows of productive capital, countries need to continue their efforts to achieve a transparent, stable and predictable investment climate, with proper contract enforcement and respect for property rights, embedded in sound macroeconomic policies and institutions that allow businesses, both domestic and international, to operate efficiently and profitably and with maximum development impact. Special efforts are required in such priority areas as economic policy and regulatory frameworks for promoting and protecting investments, including the areas of human resource development, avoidance of

---

2   A/CONF.191/11.

3   *Report of the Global Conference on the Sustainable Development of Small Island Developing States, Bridgetown, Barbados, 25 April–6 May 1994* (United Nations publication, Sales No. E.94.I.18 and corrigenda), chap. I, resolution 1, annex II.

double taxation, corporate governance, accounting standards, and the promotion of a competitive environment. Other mechanisms, such as public/private partnerships and investment agreements, can be important. We emphasize the need for strengthened, adequately resourced technical assistance and productive capacity-building programmes, as requested by recipients.

22. To complement national efforts, there is the need for the relevant international and regional institutions as well as appropriate institutions in source countries to increase their support for private foreign investment in infrastructure development and other priority areas, including projects to bridge the digital divide, in developing countries and countries with economies in transition. To this end, it is important to provide export credits, co-financing, venture capital and other lending instruments, risk guarantees, leveraging aid resources, information on investment opportunities, business development services, forums to facilitate business contacts and cooperation between enterprises of developed and developing countries, as well as funding for feasibility studies. Inter-enterprise partnership is a powerful means for transfer and dissemination of technology. In this regard, strengthening of the multilateral and regional financial and development institutions is desirable. Additional source country measures should also be devised to encourage and facilitate investment flows to developing countries.

23. While Governments provide the framework for their operation, businesses, for their part, are expected to engage as reliable and consistent partners in the development process. We urge businesses to take into account not only the economic and financial but also the developmental, social, gender and environmental implications of their undertakings. In that spirit, we invite banks and other financial institutions, in developing countries as well as developed countries, to foster innovative developmental financing approaches. We welcome all efforts to encourage good corporate citizenship and note the initiative undertaken in the United Nations to promote global partnerships.

24. We will support new public/private sector financing mechanisms, both debt and equity, for developing countries and countries with economies in transition, to benefit in particular small entrepreneurs and small and medium-size enterprises and infrastructure. Those public/private initiatives could include the development of consultation mechanisms between international and regional financial organizations and national Governments with the private sector in both source and recipient countries as a means of creating business-enabling environments.

25. We underscore the need to sustain sufficient and stable private financial flows to developing countries and countries with economies in transition. It is important to promote measures in source and destination countries to improve transparency and the information about financial flows. Measures that mitigate the impact of excessive volatility of short-term capital flows are important and must be considered. Given each country's varying degree of national capacity, managing national external debt profiles, paying careful attention to currency

and liquidity risk, strengthening prudential regulations and supervision of all financial institutions, including highly leveraged institutions, liberalizing capital flows in an orderly and well sequenced process consistent with development objectives, and implementation, on a progressive and voluntary basis, of codes and standards agreed internationally, are also important. We encourage public/private initiatives that enhance the ease of access, accuracy, timeliness and coverage of information on countries and financial markets, which strengthen capacities for risk assessment. Multilateral financial institutions could provide further assistance for all those purposes.

C. International Trade as an Engine for Development

26. A universal, rule-based, open, non-discriminatory and equitable multilateral trading system, as well as meaningful trade liberalization, can substantially stimulate development worldwide, benefiting countries at all stages of development. In that regard, we reaffirm our commitment to trade liberalization and to ensure that trade plays its full part in promoting economic growth, employment and development for all. We thus welcome the decisions of the World Trade Organization to place the needs and interests of developing countries at the heart of its work programme, and commit ourselves to their implementation.

27. To benefit fully from trade, which in many cases is the single most important external source of development financing, the establishment or enhancement of appropriate institutions and policies in developing countries, as well as in countries with economies in transition, is needed. Meaningful trade liberalization is an important element in the sustainable development strategy of a country. Increased trade and foreign direct investment could boost economic growth and could be a significant source of employment.

28. We acknowledge the issues of particular concern to developing countries and countries with economies in transition in international trade to enhance their capacity to finance their development, including trade barriers, trade-distorting subsidies and other trade-distorting measures, particularly in sectors of special export interest to developing countries, including agriculture; the abuse of anti-dumping measures; technical barriers and sanitary and phytosanitary measures; trade liberalization in labour intensive manufactures; trade liberalization in agricultural products; trade in services; tariff peaks, high tariffs and tariff escalation, as well as non-tariff barriers; the movement of natural persons; the lack of recognition of intellectual property rights for the protection of traditional knowledge and folklore; the transfer of knowledge and technology; the implementation and interpretation of the Agreement on Trade-Related Aspects of Intellectual Property Rights[4] in a manner supportive of public health; and the need for special and differential treatment provisions for developing countries in trade agreements to be made more precise, effective and operational.

---

4   *The Results of the Uruguay Round of Multilateral Trade Negotiations: The Legal Texts* (Geneva, GATT secretariat, 1994), annex 1C.

29. To ensure that world trade supports development to the benefit of all countries, we encourage the members of the World Trade Organization to implement the outcome of its Fourth Ministerial Conference, held in Doha, Qatar from 9 to 14 November 2001.

30. We also undertake to facilitate the accession of all developing countries, particularly the least developed countries, as well as countries with economies in transition, that apply for membership of the World Trade Organization.

31. We will implement the commitments made in Doha to address the marginalization of the least developed countries in international trade as well as the work programme adopted to examine issues related to the trade of small economies.

32. We also commit ourselves to enhancing the role of regional and subregional agreements and free trade areas, consistent with the multilateral trading system, in the construction of a better world trading system. We urge international financial institutions, including the regional development banks, to continue to support projects that promote subregional and regional integration among developing countries and countries with economies in transition.

33. We recognize the importance of enhanced and predictable access to all markets for the exports of developing countries, including small island developing States, landlocked developing countries, transit developing countries and countries in Africa, as well as countries with economies in transition.

34. We call on developed countries that have not already done so to work towards the objective of duty-free and quota-free access for all least developed countries' exports, as envisaged in the Programme of Action for the Least Developed Countries adopted in Brussels. Consideration of proposals for developing countries to contribute to improved market access for least developed countries would also be helpful.

35. We further recognize the importance for developing countries as well as countries with economies in transition of considering reducing trade barriers among themselves.

36. In cooperation with the interested Governments and their financial institutions and to further support national efforts to benefit from trade opportunities and effectively integrate into the multilateral trading system, we invite multilateral and bilateral financial and development institutions to expand and coordinate their efforts, with increased resources, for gradually removing supply-side constraints; improve trade infrastructure; diversify export capacity and support an increase in the technological content of exports; strengthen institutional development and enhance overall productivity and competitiveness. To that end, we further invite bilateral donors and the international and regional financial institutions, together with the relevant United Nations agencies, funds and programmes, to reinforce the support for trade-related training, capacity and institution building and trade-supporting services. Special consideration should

be given to least developed countries, landlocked developing countries, small island developing States, African development, transit developing countries and countries with economies in transition, including through the Integrated Framework for Trade-Related Technical Assistance to Least Developed Countries and its follow-up, the Joint Integrated Technical Assistance Programme, the World Trade Organization Doha Development Agenda Global Trust Fund, as well as the activities of the International Trade Centre.

37. Multilateral assistance is also needed to mitigate the consequences of depressed export revenues of countries that still depend heavily on commodity exports. Thus, we recognize the recent review of the International Monetary Fund Compensatory Financing Facility and will continue to assess its effectiveness. It is also important to empower developing country commodity producers to insure themselves against risk, including against natural disasters. We further invite bilateral donors and multilateral aid agencies to strengthen their support to export diversification programmes in those countries.

38. In support of the process launched in Doha, immediate attention should go to strengthening and ensuring the meaningful and full participation of developing countries, especially the least developed countries, in multilateral trade negotiations. In particular, developing countries need assistance in order to participate effectively in the World Trade Organization work programme and negotiating process through the enhanced cooperation of all relevant stakeholders, including the United Nations Conference on Trade and Development, the World Trade Organization and the World Bank. To those ends, we underscore the importance of effective, secure and predictable financing of trade-related technical assistance and capacity-building.

D. Increasing International Financial and Technical Cooperation for Development

39. Official development assistance (ODA) plays an essential role as a complement to other sources of financing for development, especially in those countries with the least capacity to attract private direct investment. ODA can help a country to reach adequate levels of domestic resource mobilization over an appropriate time horizon, while human capital, productive and export capacities are enhanced. ODA can be critical for improving the environment for private sector activity and can thus pave the way for robust growth. ODA is also a crucial instrument for supporting education, health, public infrastructure development, agriculture and rural development, and to enhance food security. For many countries in Africa, least developed countries, small island developing States and landlocked developing countries, ODA is still the largest source of external financing and is critical to the achievement of the development goals and targets of the Millennium Declaration and other internationally agreed development targets.

40. Effective partnerships among donors and recipients are based on the recognition of national leadership and ownership of development plans and, within

that framework, sound policies and good governance at all levels are necessary to ensure ODA effectiveness. A major priority is to build those development partnerships, particularly in support of the neediest, and to maximize the poverty reduction impact of ODA. The goals, targets and commitments of the Millennium Declaration and other internationally agreed development targets can help countries to set short- and medium-term national priorities as the foundation for building partnerships for external support. In that context, we underline the importance of the United Nations funds, programmes and specialized agencies, and we will strongly support them.

41. We recognize that a substantial increase in ODA and other resources will be required if developing countries are to achieve the internationally agreed development goals and objectives, including those contained in the Millennium Declaration. To build support for ODA, we will cooperate to further improve policies and development strategies, both nationally and internationally, to enhance aid effectiveness.

42. In that context, we urge developed countries that have not done so to make concrete efforts towards the target of 0.7 per cent of gross national product (GNP) as ODA to developing countries and 0.15 to 0.20 per cent of GNP of developed countries to least developed countries, as reconfirmed at the Third United Nations Conference on Least Developed Countries, and we encourage developing countries to build on progress achieved in ensuring that ODA is used effectively to help achieve development goals and targets. We acknowledge the efforts of all donors, commend those donors whose ODA contributions exceed, reach or are increasing towards the targets, and underline the importance of undertaking to examine the means and time frames for achieving the targets and goals.

43. Recipient and donor countries, as well as international institutions, should strive to make ODA more effective. In particular, there is a need for the multilateral and bilateral financial and development institutions to intensify efforts to:

- Harmonize their operational procedures at the highest standard so as to reduce transaction costs and make ODA disbursement and delivery more flexible, taking into account national development needs and objectives under the ownership of the recipient country;

- Support and enhance recent efforts and initiatives, such as untying aid, including the implementation of the Organisation for Economic Cooperation and Development/Development Assistance Committee recommendation on untying aid to the least developed countries, as agreed by the Organisation for Economic Cooperation and Development in May 2001. Further efforts should be made to address burdensome restrictions;

- Enhance the absorptive capacity and financial management of the recipient countries to utilize aid in order to promote the use of the most suitable aid delivery instruments that are responsive to the needs of developing countries and to the need for resource predictability, including budget support mechanisms, where appropriate, and in a fully consultative manner;

- Use development frameworks that are owned and driven by developing countries and that embody poverty reduction strategies, including poverty reduction strategy papers, as vehicles for aid delivery, upon request;

- Enhance recipient countries' input into and ownership of the design, including procurement, of technical assistance programmes; and increase the effective use of local technical assistance resources;

- Promote the use of ODA to leverage additional financing for development, such as foreign investment, trade and domestic resources;

- Strengthen triangular cooperation, including countries with economies in transition, and South-South cooperation, as delivery tools for assistance;

- Improve ODA targeting to the poor, coordination of aid and measurement of results.

We invite donors to take steps to apply the above measures in support of all developing countries, including immediately in support of the comprehensive strategy that is embodied in the New Partnership for Africa's Development and similar efforts in other regions, as well as in support of least developed countries, small island developing States and landlocked developing countries. We acknowledge and appreciate the discussions taking place in other forums on proposals to increase the concessionality of development financing, including greater use of grants.

44. We recognize the value of exploring innovative sources of finance provided that those sources do not unduly burden developing countries. In that regard, we agree to study, in the appropriate forums, the results of the analysis requested from the Secretary-General on possible innovative sources of finance, noting the proposal to use special drawing rights allocations for development purposes. We consider that any assessment of special drawing rights allocations must respect the International Monetary Fund's Articles of Agreement and the established rules of procedure of the Fund, which requires taking into account the global need for liquidity at the international level.

45. Multilateral and regional development banks continue to play a vital role in serving the development needs of developing countries and countries with economies in transition. They should contribute to providing an adequate supply of finance to countries that are challenged by poverty, follow sound economic policies and may lack adequate access to capital markets. They should also mitigate the impact of excessive volatility of financial markets. Strengthened regional development banks and subregional financial institutions add flexible financial support to national and regional development efforts, enhancing ownership and overall efficiency. They also serve as a vital source of knowledge and expertise on economic growth and development for their developing member countries.

46. We will ensure that the long-term resources at the disposal of the international financial system, including regional and subregional institutions and funds, allow them to adequately support sustained economic and social development, technical assistance for capacity-building, and social and environmental protection schemes. We will also continue to enhance their overall lending effectiveness through increased country ownership, operations that raise productivity and yield measurable results in reducing poverty, and closer coordination with donors and the private sector.

E. External Debt

47. Sustainable debt financing is an important element for mobilizing resources for public and private investment. National comprehensive strategies to monitor and manage external liabilities, embedded in the domestic preconditions for debt sustainability, including sound macroeconomic policies and public resource management, are a key element in reducing national vulnerabilities. Debtors and creditors must share the responsibility for preventing and resolving unsustainable debt situations. Technical assistance for external debt management and debt tracking can play an important role and should be strengthened.

48. External debt relief can play a key role in liberating resources that can then be directed towards activities consistent with attaining sustainable growth and development, and therefore, debt relief measures should, where appropriate, be pursued vigorously and expeditiously, including within the Paris and London Clubs and other relevant forums. Noting the importance of re-establishing financial viability for those developing countries facing unsustainable debt burdens, we welcome initiatives that have been undertaken to reduce outstanding indebtedness and invite further national and international measures in that regard, including, as appropriate, debt cancellation and other arrangements.

49. The enhanced Heavily Indebted Poor Countries Initiative provides an opportunity to strengthen the economic prospects and poverty reduction efforts of its beneficiary countries. Speedy, effective and full implementation of the enhanced Initiative, which should be fully financed through additional resources, is critical. Heavily indebted poor countries should take the policy measures necessary to become eligible for the Initiative. Future reviews of debt sustainability should also bear in mind the impact of debt relief on progress towards the achievement of the development goals contained in the Millennium Declaration. We stress the importance of continued flexibility with regard to the eligibility criteria. Continued efforts are needed to reduce the debt burden of heavily indebted poor countries to sustainable levels. The computational procedures and assumptions underlying debt sustainability analysis need to be kept under review. Debt sustainability analysis at the completion point needs to take into account any worsening global growth prospects and declining terms of trade. Debt relief arrangements should seek to avoid imposing any unfair burdens on other developing countries.

50. We stress the need for the International Monetary Fund and the World Bank to consider any fundamental changes in countries' debt sustainability caused by natural catastrophes, severe terms of trade shocks or conflict, when making policy recommendations, including for debt relief, as appropriate.

51. While recognizing that a flexible mix of instruments is needed to respond appropriately to countries' different economic circumstances and capacities, we emphasize the importance of putting in place a set of clear principles for the management and resolution of financial crises that provide for fair burden-sharing between public and private sectors and between debtors, creditors and investors. We encourage donor countries to take steps to ensure that resources provided for debt relief do not detract from ODA resources intended to be available for developing countries. We also encourage exploring innovative mechanisms to comprehensively address debt problems of developing countries, including middle-income countries and countries with economies in transition.

F. Addressing Systemic Issues: Enhancing the Coherence and Consistency of the International Monetary, Financial and Trading Systems in Support of Development

52. In order to complement national development efforts, we recognize the urgent need to enhance coherence, governance, and consistency of the international monetary, financial and trading systems. To contribute to that end, we underline the importance of continuing to improve global economic governance and to strengthen the United Nations leadership role in promoting development. With the same purpose, efforts should be strengthened at the national level to enhance coordination among all relevant ministries and institutions. Similarly, we should encourage policy and programme coordination of international institutions and coherence at the operational and international levels to meet the Millennium Declaration development goals of sustained economic growth, poverty eradication and sustainable development.

53. Important international efforts are under way to reform the international financial architecture. Those efforts need to be sustained with greater transparency and the effective participation of developing countries and countries with economies in transition. One major objective of the reform is to enhance financing for development and poverty eradication. We also underscore our commitment to sound domestic financial sectors, which make a vital contribution to national development efforts, as an important component of an international financial architecture that is supportive of development.

54. Strong coordination of macroeconomic policies among the leading industrial countries is critical to greater global stability and reduced exchange rate volatility, which are essential to economic growth as well as for enhanced and predictable financial flows to developing countries and countries with economies in transition.

55. The multilateral financial institutions, in particular the International Monetary Fund, need to continue to give high priority to the identification and prevention of potential crises and to strengthening the underpinnings of international financial stability. In that regard, we stress the need for the Fund to further strengthen its surveillance activities of all economies, with particular attention to short-term capital flows and their impact. We encourage the International Monetary Fund to facilitate the timely detection of external vulnerability through well designed surveillance and early warning systems and to coordinate closely with relevant regional institutions or organizations, including the regional commissions.

56. We stress the need for multilateral financial institutions, in providing policy advice and financial support, to work on the basis of sound, nationally owned paths of reform that take into account the needs of the poor and efforts to reduce poverty, and to pay due regard to the special needs and implementing capacities of developing countries and countries with economies in transition, aiming at economic growth and sustainable development. The advice should take into account social costs of adjustment programmes, which should be designed to minimize negative impact on the vulnerable segments of society.

57. It is essential to ensure the effective and equitable participation of developing countries in the formulation of financial standards and codes. It is also essential to ensure implementation, on a voluntary and progressive basis, as a contribution to reducing vulnerability to financial crisis and contagion.

58. Sovereign risk assessments made by the private sector should maximize the use of strict, objective and transparent parameters, which can be facilitated by high-quality data and analysis.

59. Noting the impact of financial crisis or risk of contagion in developing countries and countries with economies in transition, regardless of their size, we underline the need to ensure that the international financial institutions, including the International Monetary Fund, have a suitable array of financial facilities and resources to respond in a timely and appropriate way in accordance with their policies. The International Monetary Fund has a range of instruments available and its current financial position is strong. The contingent credit line is an important signal of the strength of countries' policies and a safeguard against contagion in financial markets. The need for special drawing rights allocations should be kept under review. In that regard, we also underline the need to enhance the stabilizing role of regional and subregional reserve funds, swap arrangements and similar mechanisms that complement the efforts of international financial institutions.

60. To promote fair burden-sharing and minimize moral hazard, we would welcome consideration by all relevant stakeholders of an international debt workout mechanism, in the appropriate forums, that will engage debtors and creditors to come together to restructure unsustainable debts in a timely and ef-

ficient manner. Adoption of such a mechanism should not preclude emergency financing in times of crisis.

61. Good governance at all levels is also essential for sustained economic growth, poverty eradication and sustainable development worldwide. To better reflect the growth of interdependence and enhance legitimacy, economic governance needs to develop in two areas: broadening the base for decision-making on issues of development concern and filling organizational gaps. To complement and consolidate advances in those two areas, we must strengthen the United Nations system and other multilateral institutions. We encourage all international organizations to seek to continually improve their operations and interactions.

62. We stress the need to broaden and strengthen the participation of developing countries and countries with economies in transition in international economic decision-making and norm-setting. To those ends, we also welcome further actions to help developing countries and countries with economies in transition to build their capacity to participate effectively in multilateral forums.

63. A first priority is to find pragmatic and innovative ways to further enhance the effective participation of developing countries and countries with economies in transition in international dialogues and decision-making processes. Within the mandates and means of the respective institutions and forums, we encourage the following actions:

- International Monetary Fund and World Bank: to continue to enhance participation of all developing countries and countries with economies in transition in their decision-making, and thereby to strengthen the international dialogue and the work of those institutions as they address the development needs and concerns of these countries;

- World Trade Organization: to ensure that any consultation is representative of its full membership and that participation is based on clear, simple and objective criteria;

- Bank for International Settlements, Basel Committees and Financial Stability Forum: to continue enhancing their outreach and consultation efforts with developing countries and countries with economies in transition at the regional level, and to review their membership, as appropriate, to allow for adequate participation;

- Ad hoc groupings that make policy recommendations with global implications: to continue to improve their outreach to non-member countries, and to enhance collaboration with the multilateral institutions with clearly defined and broad-based intergovernmental mandates.

64. To strengthen the effectiveness of the global economic system's support for development, we encourage the following actions:

- Improve the relationship between the United Nations and the World Trade Organization for development, and strengthen their capacity to provide technical assistance to all countries in need of such assistance;

- Support the International Labour Organization and encourage its ongoing work on the social dimension of globalization;

- Strengthen the coordination of the United Nations system and all other multilateral financial, trade and development institutions to support economic growth, poverty eradication and sustainable development worldwide;

- Mainstream the gender perspective into development policies at all levels and in all sectors;

- Strengthen international tax cooperation, through enhanced dialogue among national tax authorities and greater coordination of the work of the concerned multilateral bodies and relevant regional organizations, giving special attention to the needs of developing countries and countries with economies in transition;

- Promote the role of the regional commissions and the regional development banks in supporting policy dialogue among countries at the regional level on macroeconomic, financial, trade and development issues.

65. We commit ourselves to negotiating and finalizing as soon as possible a United Nations convention against corruption in all its aspects, including the question of repatriation of funds illicitly acquired to countries of origin, and also to promoting stronger cooperation to eliminate money-laundering. We encourage States that have not yet done so to consider signature and ratification of the United Nations Convention against Transnational Organized Crime.[5]

66. We urge as a matter of priority all States that have not yet done so to consider becoming parties to the International Convention for the Suppression of the Financing of Terrorism,[6] and call for increased cooperation with the same objective.

67. We attach priority to reinvigorating the United Nations system as fundamental to the promotion of international cooperation for development and to a global economic system that works for all. We reaffirm our commitment to enabling the General Assembly to play effectively its central role as the chief deliberative, policy-making and representative organ of the United Nations, and to further strengthening the Economic and Social Council to enable it to fulfil the role ascribed to it in the Charter of the United Nations.

---

5   General Assembly resolution 55/25.
6   General Assembly resolution 54/109, annex.

III. Staying Engaged

68. To build a global alliance for development will require an unremitting effort. We thus commit ourselves to keeping fully engaged, nationally, regionally and internationally, to ensuring proper follow-up to the implementation of agreements and commitments reached at the present Conference, and to continuing to build bridges between development, finance, and trade organizations and initiatives, within the framework of the holistic agenda of the Conference. Greater cooperation among existing institutions is needed, based on a clear understanding and respect for their respective mandates and governance structures.

69. Building on the successful experience of the Conference and the process leading up to it, we shall strengthen and make fuller use of the General Assembly and the Economic and Social Council, as well as the relevant intergovernmental/governing bodies of other institutional stakeholders, for the purposes of conference follow-up and coordination, by substantively connecting, in ascending series, the following elements:

(a) Interactions between representatives of the Economic and Social Council and the directors of the executive boards of the World Bank and the International Monetary Fund can serve as preliminary exchanges on matters related to follow-up to the Conference and preparations for the annual spring meeting between those institutions. Similar interactions can also be initiated with representatives of the appropriate intergovernmental body of the World Trade Organization;

(b) We encourage the United Nations, the World Bank and the International Monetary Fund, with the World Trade Organization, to address issues of coherence, coordination and cooperation, as a follow-up to the Conference, at the spring meeting between the Economic and Social Council and the Bretton Woods institutions. The meeting should include an intergovernmental segment to address an agenda agreed to by the participating organizations, as well as a dialogue with civil society and the private sector;

(c) The current high-level dialogue on strengthening international cooperation for development through partnership, held every two years in the General Assembly, would consider the financing for development-related reports coming from the Economic and Social Council and other bodies, as well as other financing for development-related issues. It would be reconstituted to enable it to become the intergovernmental focal point for the general follow-up to the Conference and related issues. The high-level dialogue would include a policy dialogue, with the participation of the relevant stakeholders, on the implementation of the results of the Conference, including the theme of coherence and consistency of the international monetary, financial and trading systems in support of development;

(d) Appropriate modalities to enable participation in the reconstituted high-level dialogue by all relevant stakeholders, as necessary, will be considered.

70. To support the above elements at the national, regional and international levels, we resolve:

- To continue to improve our domestic policy coherence through the continued engagement of our ministries of development, finance, trade and foreign affairs, as well as our central banks;

- To harness the active support of the regional commissions and the regional development banks;

- To keep the financing for development process on the agenda of the intergovernmental bodies of all main stakeholders, including all United Nations funds, programmes and agencies, including the United Nations Conference on Trade and Development.

71. We recognize the link between financing of development and attaining internationally agreed development goals and objectives, including those contained in the Millennium Declaration, in measuring development progress and helping to guide development priorities. We welcome in that regard the intention of the United Nations to prepare a report annually. We encourage close cooperation between the United Nations, the World Bank, the International Monetary Fund and the World Trade Organization in the preparation of that report. We shall support the United Nations in the implementation of a global information campaign on the internationally agreed development goals and objectives, including those contained in the Millennium Declaration. In that respect, we would like to encourage the active involvement of all relevant stakeholders, including civil society organizations and the private sector.

72. To underpin those efforts, we request the Secretary-General of the United Nations to provide—with collaboration from the secretariats of the major institutional stakeholders concerned, fully utilizing the United Nations System Chief Executives Board for Coordination mechanism—sustained follow-up within the United Nations system to the agreements and commitments reached at the present Conference and to ensure effective secretariat support. That support will build on the innovative and participatory modalities and related coordination arrangements utilized in the preparations of the Conference. The Secretary-General of the United Nations is further requested to submit an annual report on those follow-up efforts.

73. We call for a follow-up international conference to review the implementation of the Monterrey Consensus. The modalities of that conference shall be decided upon not later than 2005.

Resolution 2*
Expression of thanks to the people and Government of Mexico

* Adopted at the 6th plenary meeting, on 22 March 2002; for the discussion, see chap. IX.

The International Conference on Financing for Development,

Having met in Monterrey, Mexico, from 18 to 22 March 2002, at the invitation of the Government of Mexico,

1. *Expresses its deep appreciation* to His Excellency Vicente Fox, President of Mexico, for his outstanding contribution, as President of the International Conference on Financing for Development, to the successful outcome of the Conference;

2. *Expresses its profound gratitude* to the Government of Mexico for having made it possible for the Conference to be held in Mexico and for the excellent facilities, staff and services so graciously placed at its disposal;

3. *Requests* the Government of Mexico to convey to the city of Monterrey and to the people of Mexico the gratitude of the Conference for the hospitality and warm welcome extended to the participants.

Resolution 3*
Credentials of representatives to the International Conference on Financing for Development

* Adopted at the 6th plenary meeting, on 22 March 2002; for the discussion, see chap. VII.

The International Conference on Financing for Development,

Having considered the report of the Credentials Committee and the recommendation contained therein,

Approves the report of the Credentials Committee.

Chapter II
Attendance and Organization of Work

A. Date and Place of the Conference

1. The International Conference on Financing for Development was held at Monterrey, Mexico, from 18 to 22 March 2002, in conformity with General Assembly resolutions 55/245 A and 55/245 B of 21 March 2001. The Conference held 6 plenary meetings.

B. Attendance

2. The following States were represented at the Conference:

Afghanistan	Costa Rica
Albania	Côte d'Ivoire
Algeria	Croatia
Andorra	Cuba
Angola	Cyprus
Antigua and Barbuda	Czech Republic
Argentina	Denmark
Armenia	Djibouti
Australia	Dominican Republic
Austria	Ecuador
Azerbaijan	Egypt
Bahamas	El Salvador
Bahrain	Equatorial Guinea
Bangladesh	Eritrea
Barbados	Estonia
Belarus	Ethiopia
Belgium	European Community
Belize	Fiji
Benin	Finland
Bhutan	France
Bolivia	Gabon
Bosnia and Herzegovina	Gambia
Botswana	Georgia
Brazil	Germany
Brunei Darussalam	Ghana
Bulgaria	Greece
Burkina Faso	Grenada
Burundi	Guatemala
Cambodia	Guinea
Cameroon	Guinea-Bissau
Canada	Guyana
Cape Verde	Haiti
Central African Republic	Holy See
Chad	Honduras
Chile	Hungary
China	Iceland
Colombia	India
Comoros	Indonesia
Congo	Iran (Islamic Republic of)
Cook Islands	Iraq

Ireland
Israel
Italy
Jamaica
Japan
Jordan
Kazakhstan
Kenya
Kuwait
Kyrgyzstan
Lao People's Democratic Republic
Latvia
Lebanon
Lesotho
Libyan Arab Jamahiriya
Liechtenstein
Lithuania
Luxembourg
Madagascar
Malawi
Malaysia
Maldives
Mali
Malta
Marshall Islands
Mauritania
Mauritius
Mexico
Micronesia (Federated States of)
Monaco
Mongolia
Morocco
Mozambique
Myanmar
Namibia
Nauru
Nepal
Netherlands
New Zealand
Nicaragua
Niger
Nigeria
Norway

Oman
Pakistan
Palau
Panama
Paraguay
Peru
Philippines
Poland
Portugal
Qatar
Republic of Korea
Republic of Moldova
Romania
Russian Federation
Rwanda
Saint Kitts and Nevis
Saint Lucia
Saint Vincent and the Grenadines
Samoa
Saudi Arabia
Senegal
Seychelles
Sierra Leone
Singapore
Slovakia
Slovenia
Solomon Islands
Somalia
South Africa
Spain
Sri Lanka
Sudan
Suriname
Swaziland
Sweden
Switzerland
Syrian Arab Republic
Thailand
The former Yugoslav Republic of
  Macedonia
Togo
Tonga
Trinidad and Tobago

Tunisia	United Republic of Tanzania
Turkey	United States of America
Turkmenistan	Uruguay
Tuvalu	Venezuela
Uganda	Viet Nam
Ukraine	Yemen
United Arab Emirates	Yugoslavia
United Kingdom of Great Britain	Zambia
and Northern Ireland	Zimbabwe

3. The following associate members of the regional commissions were represented by observers: Puerto Rico and United States Virgin Islands.

4. The secretariats of the following regional commissions were represented:

Economic Commission for Europe

Economic and Social Commission for Asia and the Pacific

Economic Commission for Latin America and the Caribbean

Economic Commission for Africa

Economic and Social Commission for Western Asia

5. The following United Nations bodies and programmes were represented:

United Nations

United Nations Conference on Trade and Development

United Nations Development Programme

United Nations Centre for Human Settlements

United Nations Environment Programme

United Nations Children's Fund

United Nations Population Fund

World Food Programme

United Nations Development Fund for Women

Joint United Nations Programme on HIV/AIDS

6. The following specialized agencies and related organizations were represented:

International Labour Organization

Food and Agriculture Organization of the United Nations

World Health Organization

World Bank

International Monetary Fund

World Intellectual Property Organization

International Fund for Agricultural Development

United Nations Industrial Development Organization

World Trade Organization

7. The following intergovernmental organizations were represented:

Andean Community

Arab Bank for Economic Development in Africa

African Development Bank

Asian Development Bank

Caribbean Community

Central American Bank for Economic Integration

Common Fund for Commodities

Commonwealth Secretariat

Council of Europe Development Bank

European Bank for Reconstruction and Development

Eastern Caribbean Central Bank

European Commission

Financial Stability Forum

Inter-American Development Bank

International Organization of the Francophonie

International Federation of Red Cross and Red Crescent Societies

International Union for the Conservation of Nature and Natural Resources

Interparliamentary Union

The OPEC Fund for International Development

Organization of African Unity

Organization for Economic Cooperation and Development

8. The Preparatory Committee for the Conference accredited a number of business entities/organizations to the substantive preparatory process and the Conference. The accredited business entities/organizations are listed in documents A/AC.257/30 and Add.1 and 2; additional accreditations are listed in decision 4/7 of the Preparatory Committee (see A/CONF.198/5, chap. VIII, sect. B).

9. A large number of non-governmental organizations attended the Conference. The accredited non-governmental organizations are listed in documents A/AC.257/10 and Add.1–5, and in Committee decision 4/6 (see A/CONF.198/5, chap. VIII, sect. B). The Conference also accredited two additional nongovernmental organizations (see para. 16 below).

10. Other entities having received a standing invitation and participating as observers are the International Federation of Red Cross and Red Crescent Societies and the Sovereign Military Order of Malta.

C. Opening of the Conference and Election of the President of the Conference and Co-Presidents of the High-Level and Ministerial Segments

11. The Conference was declared open by the Under-Secretary-General for Economic and Social Affairs on behalf of the Secretary-General of the United Nations.

12. At the 1st plenary meeting, on 18 March, the Under-Secretary-General, on behalf of the Secretary-General, presided over the election of the following officers by acclamation:

President of the Conference

Vicente Fox, President of Mexico

Co-Presidents of the ministerial segment

Jorge G. Castañeda Gutman, Minister of Foreign Affairs of Mexico, Francisco Gil Diaz, Minister of Finance of Mexico, and Luis Ernesto Derbez Bautista, Minister of Trade of Mexico

Co-Presidents of the high-level officials segment

Miguel Hakim Simón, Vice Minister of Foreign Affairs of Mexico, Agustin Carstens Carstens, Vice Minister of Finance of Mexico, and Luis Fernando de la Calle, Vice-Minister of Trade of Mexico

D. Adoption of the Rules of Procedure

13. At its 1st plenary meeting, on 18 March, on the recommendation of its Preparatory Committee and as approved by the General Assembly in its decision 56/446, the Conference adopted the provisional rules of procedure (A/CONF.198/2).

E. Adoption of the Agenda and Other Organizational Matters

14. At its 1st plenary meeting, on 18 March, the Conference adopted the provisional agenda (A/CONF.198/1/Rev.1) as recommended by its Preparatory Committee in its decision 4/2 (see A/CONF.198/5, chap. VIII, sect. A). The agenda as adopted was as follows:

1. Opening of the Conference.

2. Election of the President.

3. Adoption of the rules of procedure.

4. Adoption of the agenda and other organizational matters.

5. Election of officers other than the President.

6. Organization of work, including the establishment of [the Main Committee,] the high-level officials segment, the ministerial segment and the summit segment.

7. Credentials of representatives to the Conference:

    (a) Appointment of members of the Credentials Committee;

    (b) Report of the Credentials Committee.

8. High-level officials segment:

    (a) General exchange of views;

    (b) Consideration of the draft Monterrey consensus;

    (c) Reports on activities by relevant stakeholders.

9. Ministerial segment:

    (a) General exchange of views;

    (b) Consideration of the draft Monterrey consensus;

    (c) Reports of business and civil society forums;

    (d) Ministerial round tables.

10. Summit segment:

    (a) General exchange of views;

    (b) Consideration of the draft Monterrey consensus;

    (c) Summit round tables.

11. Adoption of the Monterrey Consensus.

12. Adoption of the report of the Conference.

F. Accreditation of Intergovernmental Organizations

15. At its 1st plenary meeting, on 18 March, the Conference approved the accreditation of the following six intergovernmental organizations as recommended by the Bureau of its Preparatory Committee: Commonwealth Foundation, Banque des états de l'Afrique centrale, Partners in Population and Development: a South-South Initiative, International Association of Economic and Social Councils and Similar Institutions, Eastern Caribbean Central Bank and Financial Stability Forum.

G. Accreditation of Non-Governmental Organizations

16. At its 1st plenary meeting, on 18 March, the Conference approved the accreditation of the following two non-governmental organizations as recom-

mended by the Bureau of its Preparatory Committee: Institute for International Economics, Center for Global Development.

H. Election of Officers Other Than the President

17. At the 1st plenary meeting, on 18 March, the Co-President informed the Conference of the recommendations concerning the composition of the General Committee and the distribution of posts therein.

18. At the same meeting, the Conference elected Vice-Presidents from the following regional groups:

African Group of States

(five Vice-Presidents) Cameroon, Egypt, Ghana, Sudan, Namibia

Asian Group of States

(five Vice-Presidents) Bangladesh, Islamic Republic of Iran, Japan, Pakistan, Thailand

Eastern European Group of States

(five Vice-Presidents) Bulgaria, Czech Republic, Poland, Romania, the former Yugoslav Republic of Macedonia

Latin American and Caribbean Group of States

(four Vice-Presidents) Chile, El Salvador, Saint Lucia, Trinidad and Tobago

Western European and other States

(five Vice-Presidents) Denmark, France, Sweden, Turkey, United States of America

19. At the same meeting, the Conference also elected an ex officio Vice-President from the host country, Jorge Castañeda Gutman, Minister of Foreign Affairs of Mexico.

20. Also at the same meeting, the Co-President informed the Conference that more consultations were needed to elect one of the Vice-Presidents of the Conference to also serve as Rapporteur-General of the Conference.

21. At its 4th plenary meeting, on 21 March 2002, the Conference elected Hazem Fahmy (Egypt) the Rapporteur-General of the Conference.

I. Organization of Work, Including the Establishment of [the Main Committee,] the High-Level Officials Segment, the Ministerial Segment and the Summit Segment

22. At the 1st plenary meeting, on 18 March, in accordance with the recommendations of the Preparatory Committee contained in its decision 4/3 (see A/CONF.198/5, chap. VIII, sect. A), the Conference approved its organization of work as contained in document A/CONF.198/4/Rev.1.

23. At the same meeting, the Conference endorsed the proposals contained in document A/CONF.198/4/Rev.1 regarding the exchange of views and the composition of the Bureau of the General Committee and the high-level officials, ministerial and summit segments.

24. Also at the same meeting, the Conference approved the proposed timetable of work for the Conference as contained in document A/CONF.198/4/Rev.1 and orally revised.

J. Credentials of Representatives to the Conference

25. At the 1st plenary meeting, on 18 March, in accordance with rule 4 of the rules of procedure of the Conference and on the proposal of the Co-Chairman, it was decided that the composition of the Credentials Committee would be based on that of the Credentials Committee of the General Assembly of the United Nations at its fifty-sixth session, as follows: China, Denmark, Jamaica, Lesotho, Russian Federation, Senegal, Singapore, United States of America and Uruguay. With regard to the report of the Credentials Committee, it was the understanding that if one of those States did not participate in the Conference, it would be replaced by another State from the same regional group.

Chapter III
Report of the High-Level Officials Segment

1. At its 1st plenary meeting, on 18 March, in accordance with the recommendations of the Preparatory Committee contained in its decision 4/3 (see A/CONF.198/5, chap. VIII, sect. A), the Conference approved the organization of work as set out in document A/CONF.198/4/Rev.1, and decided to establish a high-level officials segment. The Conference also decided to allocate agenda item 8, "High-level officials segment", to the high-level officials segment.

A. General Exchange of Views

2. At its 1st plenary meeting, on 18 March, the high-level officials segment considered agenda item 8 (a), "General exchange of views", and heard statements by the Executive Secretaries of the Economic Commission for Europe, the Economic and Social Commission for Asia and the Pacific, the Economic Commission for Latin America and the Caribbean, the Economic Commission for Africa and the Economic and Social Commission for Western Asia.

3. At the 2nd plenary meeting, on 18 March, statements were made by the Vice-President of the Islamic Development Bank and the Vice-Governor of the Development Bank of the Council of Europe.

B. Consideration of the Draft Monterrey Consensus

4. At the 1st plenary meeting, on 18 March, the high-level officials segment considered agenda item 8 (b), "Consideration of the draft Monterrey Consensus";

for its consideration of the sub-item, it had before it a note by the Secretariat transmitting the draft outcome of the Conference (A/CONF.198/3).

5. At the same meeting, the high-level segment approved the draft Monterrey Consensus as contained in document A/CONF.198/3 and transmitted it to the ministerial segment for its consideration.

C. Reports on Activities by Relevant Stakeholders

6. At the 1st plenary meeting, on 18 March, the high-level officials segment considered agenda item 8 (c), "Reports on activities by relevant stakeholders", and heard statements by the Co-Chairmen of the Preparatory Committee for the Conference.

7. At the 2nd plenary meeting, on 18 March, statements were made by the Chairman of the Commission on Sustainable Development acting as the preparatory committee for the World Summit for Sustainable Development and the Co-Chairpersons of the Ministerial Seminar of the Global Environment Facility.

Chapter IV
Report of the Ministerial Segment

1. At its 2nd meeting, on 18 March, the Conference, in accordance with the recommendations of the Preparatory Committee contained in its decision 4/3 (see A/CONF.198/5, chap. VIII, sect. A), approved the organization of work as set out in document A/CONF.198/4/Rev.1, and decided to establish a ministerial segment. The Conference also decided to allocate agenda item 9, "Ministerial segment", to the ministerial segment.

A. General Exchange of Views

2. At the 2nd meeting, on 18 March, the ministerial segment considered agenda item 9 (a), "General exchange of views", and heard statements by the following representatives of intergovernmental economic, financial, monetary and trade bodies and regional development banks: the Chairman of the Development Committee, the President of the Economic and Social Council, the Chairman of the G–10, the Chairman of the G–20, the Chairman of the G–24, the Chairman of the Financial Stability Forum and the representative of the Asian Development Bank.

3. At the same meeting, statements were made by the following representatives of United Nations bodies and intergovernmental organizations: the Administrator of the United Nations Development Programme (UNDP), the Secretary-General of the United Nations Conference on Trade and Development (UNCTAD), the President of the International Fund for Agricultural Development (IFAD), the Executive Director of the United Nations Children's Fund (UNICEF), the Executive Director of the United Nations Environment Programme (UNEP), the Director-General of the United Nations Industrial Development Organization

(UNIDO), the Executive Director of the United Nations Population Fund (UNFPA), the Deputy Secretary-General of the Organisation for Economic Cooperation and Development (OECD), the Assistant Secretary-General of the Organization of African Unity, the Assistant Secretary-General of the Caribbean Community (CARICOM), the Chief Economist of the Commonwealth Secretariat, the head of delegation of the Organisation Internationale de la Francophonie, the Managing Director of the Common Fund for Commodities, the President of the Latin American Parliament, the Executive Director of the United Nations Human Settlements Programme (Habitat), the Assistant Director-General of the Food and Agriculture Organization of the United Nations (FAO), the Deputy Executive Director of the World Food Programme (WFP), the Executive Director of the United Nations Development Fund for Women (UNIFEM), the head of delegation of the International Labour Organization (ILO), the Director of Strategy of the World Health Organization and the Director-General of the Global Programme HIV/AIDS.

B. Report of Business and Civil Society Forums

4. At the second meeting, on 18 March, the ministerial segment considered agenda item 9 (c), "Report of business and civil society forums", and heard statements by the Secretary-General of the International Chamber of Commerce (on behalf of the International Business Forum), the President of ALCADECO (on behalf of the Civil Society Forum), the representative of the Mexican Senate (on behalf of the Parliamentarians Forum) and the Mayor of Monterrey (on behalf of the Local Authorities Forum).

C. Consideration of the Draft Monterrey Consensus

5. At the second meeting, on 18 March, the ministerial segment considered sub-item 9 (b), "Consideration of the draft Monterrey Consensus"; for its consideration of the sub-items, it had before it a note by the Secretariat transmitting the draft outcome of the Conference (A/CONF.198/3), which it transmitted to the summit segment for adoption.

D. Ministerial Round Tables

6. In accordance with General Assembly decision 56/445 the ministerial segment held eight multi-stakeholder round tables: on Tuesday, 19 March, and Wednesday, 20 March, two simultaneous round tables were held each morning and afternoon. The theme of the ministerial round tables held on 19 March was "Partnerships in financing for development"; the theme for those held on 20 March was "Coherence for development". An account of the ministerial round tables is set out below.

Ministerial round table A.1
Partnership in financing for development

7. The Co-Chairmen of round table A.1, Paa Kwesi Nduom, Minister for Economic Planning and Regional Cooperation (Ghana), Charles Josselin, Minister for Cooperation and Francophonie (France), and Heidemarie Wieczorek-Zeul, Federal Minister of Economic Cooperation and Development (Germany), opened the ministerial round table and made introductory statements.

8. Statements were made by the representatives of Algeria, Antigua and Barbuda, the Republic of Korea, Argentina, Canada, Bolivia, the United States of America, Viet Nam, Nepal, Greece, Samoa, Bhutan, China, Norway, Ukraine, Sri Lanka, Portugal, Burkina Faso, Bangladesh, Brazil, Lithuania, Belize, Angola, Botswana, Chile, Cape Verde and the Sudan.

9. Statements were made by the following institutional stakeholder participants: Economic and Social Commission for West Asia, United Nations Industrial Development Organization, World Bank and International Monetary Fund.

10. Statements were made by the following business sector participants: Suez Infrastructure Leasing and Financial Services, Deutsche Bank Research, and Barra Mexicana Colegio de Abogados, Von Wobeser y Sierra.

11. Statements were made by the following civil society participants: United Nations Association—Dominican Republic, Friedrich Ebert Foundation, United Nations Association—Denmark, Asociación de Economistas de America Latina y el Caribe/Brasil, International Gender and Trade Network, Center of Concern, and Forum for African Alternatives (EcuTeam). The Co-Chairmen made concluding remarks.

12. The summary prepared by the Co-Chairmen (A/CONF.198/8/Add.4) read as follows:

"1. We began with a fundamental agreement: attaining the millennium development goals is a most urgent priority and partnership is at the root of the system of international cooperation that can turn those goals into reality. Ministers and senior officials of Governments, senior representatives of international organizations, business leaders and representatives of nongovernmental organizations were thus able to hold a rich and focused round-table discussion on how to maximize the effectiveness of the contributions to financing for development of a wide variety of traditional and innovative partnerships between official entities, and between official entities and private enterprises and civil society.

"**Public-public partnerships**

"2. The vast majority of speakers expressed their concern about the inadequacy of official development assistance to developing countries in the face of the urgent need to meet the targets agreed by the international community at the Millennium Summit of the United Nations General Assembly. It was recognized that despite their efforts, some developing countries will not be able to attract enough private capital flows or to amass sufficient domestic resources to finance their developmental needs. For those countries, ODA will continue to be an important source of resources. While welcoming recently announced ODA initiatives, speakers urged donor countries to increase both the level and the efficiency of ODA for the mutual benefit of both donor and recipient countries.

"3. It was recognized that ODA resources have not always been targeted at the poorer countries but have often been driven by geopolitical considerations. In that respect, it was suggested that donor ODA practices and policies need to be changed. The need was underlined for increased coordination among donor countries to support the priorities and programmes of recipient countries and efficient public partnerships. A long-term planning framework, such as the poverty reduction strategy paper, should originate in the recipient country and be the basis for increased dialogue and consultation between the recipient country and its donors. Transparency and accountability are essential for the success of that process.

"4. Participants stressed the need to improve the policy coherence and consistency of donor countries as a means to improve ODA efficiency. While welcoming recent initiatives in that area, such as the Cotonou Agreement of the European Union and the African, Caribbean and Pacific Group of developing countries and the African Growth and Opportunity Act of the United States, several speakers voiced their concern about on-going protectionist practices in donor countries, which mitigate the potential positive impact that ODA can have on developing countries and reduce opportunities for faster economic growth through increased trade. In addition, the view was expressed that such practices indicate a lack of commitment to trade liberalization, a condition often imposed on developing countries in their negotiations with international financial organizations, and could represent a serious impediment to the new development agenda for trade negotiations launched in Doha in November 2001.

"5. Lack of market access by developing countries to the markets of developed countries is considered a great obstacle to development. At the same time, additional efforts are necessary to overcome supply-side constraints in developing countries and enhance their productive capacities.

"6. The importance of regional integration was also highlighted, as well as the possibility that public-public partnerships could be explored to provide solutions to common problems not only in the economic domain but also in the areas of health and education, among others. Several speakers placed great hopes on the New Partnership for Africa's Development as an answer to the continent's developmental quest. While the Partnership is a home-grown initiative, there is recognition that African countries will need assistance in the implementation process. Accordingly, the Partnership could be considered as a model for a new framework of cooperation among major development partners.

"7. Several participants expressed support for the proposal that ODA be used to promote foreign direct investment and facilitate the integration of developing countries in international trade. Such measures would maximize potential synergies in the generation of additional resources for development. In that sense, capacity-building is considered essential.

"8. Speakers also expressed their concern that the conditionality for official flows to developing countries is not uniformly applied, and they urged greater consistency of such requirements. In addition, it was felt that conditionality should not go beyond what has been agreed in international forums.

"9. The debt overhang continues to represent a serious impediment to growth in developing countries because it discourages private flows and represents a significant drain on scarce local resources. In the past few years, the international community has witnessed a series of significant initiatives to relieve the external debt burden, particularly of the highly indebted poor countries. However, participants suggested that more needs to be done and greater flexibility must be exerted in establishing debt sustainability because countries are continuously subjected to external shocks, such as the recent global slowdown and sharp fall in commodity prices.

"**Public-private partnerships**

"10. It was stressed that the effectiveness of public-private partnerships depends crucially on a supportive institutional environment, including a modern judicial system. A modern legal system is seen as one of the most important structural changes because it enhances governance by providing increased transparency and accountability, which would help curtail corruption where it is a problem. Accordingly, the development of a strong justice system should be supported by technical assistance.

"11. It was emphasized that to increase private investment, including foreign direct investment, more government or public-private investment in infrastructure is needed. There were also suggestions to increase the role of regional development banks in trade financing and project financing, together with the private sector. Several examples of successful collaboration between public and private sectors were given, including infrastructure development (water supply, telecommunications), education, research and development, and foreign equity investment in small and medium-sized enterprises.

"**Overall considerations**

"12. Several speakers emphasized that broader institutional considerations need to be in place for the above partnerships to be effective. They should make it possible to realize the right to development in a just society, with gender equality. By emphasizing the social dimensions of sustainable development and mobilizing public support in developing and developed countries, civil society is making an important contribution to that process.

"13. Problems of global economic governance were also discussed, including the increased participation of developing countries. The participants pointed to the need for more cooperation, coherence and consistency among different international economic organizations. In addition, some speakers argued that there is a gap in global economic governance because a global economic forum is lacking. Accordingly, it was suggested that treaties, such as those on global environmental issues, could serve as a model for more formal partnerships. In addition, some speakers suggested that partnerships in economic governance could be solidified through the establishment of an Economic Security Council."

Ministerial round table A.2
Partnerships in financing for development

13. The Co-Chairmen, Didier Opertti-Badan, Minister of Foreign Affairs (Uruguay) and Myoung-Ho Shin, Vice-President of the Asian Development Bank, opened the ministerial round table and made introductory statements.

14. Statements were made by the representatives of the United Kingdom of Great Britain and Northern Ireland, Italy, Cuba, Denmark, Ecuador, Tunisia, El Salvador, the Dominican Republic, Monaco, Nepal, Colombia, Djibouti, the Lao People's Democratic Republic (on behalf of the landlocked developing countries), New Zealand (on behalf of the Pacific Islands), Egypt, Costa Rica, Malta and the Syrian Arab Republic.

15. The following representatives of the institutional stakeholders made statements: Food and Agricultural Organization of the United Nations, Organisation for Economic Cooperation and Development, Economic and Social Commission for Asia and the Pacific, World Bank, International Monetary Fund.

16. The following representatives of the business sector made statements: Grupo Emyco, Samuels Associates, Potomac Associates, Moody's Investor Service, Evian Group, Uganda Small Business Enterprise, Grameen Phone.

17. The following representatives of civil society made statements: International Confederation of Free Trade Unions, Quaker United Nations Office, World Association of Former United Nations Interns and Fellows, KULU Women in Development/WEDO. The Co-Chairmen made concluding remarks.

18. The summary prepared by the Co-Chairmen (A/CONF.198/8/Add.1) read as follows:

"1. The round table held a very rich debate on the main issues before the International Conference on Financing for Development and on the theme "Partnerships in financing for development". A summary of the discussion is set out below.

"**General considerations**

"2. The general considerations of the round table were as follows:

- Ministers expressed strong support of the draft Monterrey Consensus, in particular of the domestic and international reforms that it advocates. The draft Consensus has put financing at the top of the international agenda;

- Ministers focused on the implementation of the draft Monterrey Consensus. They were of the view that an effective and rapid implementation of the draft Monterrey Consensus is critical to spur economic growth worldwide and eradicate poverty;

- It was noted that implementation will require major national and international efforts, and that substantial technical efforts should be accompanied by a strong and persistent political will. The participation of heads of State and Government in the Conference augur well for such political will;

- Partnership was seen as critical. However, partnerships must go hand in hand with country ownership. No single partner—whether a country or an institution—can do enough. Several dimensions of partnership are considered to be key to development. Public-private partnership is at the core of rapid economic growth. Partnership between countries and development organizations, as well as among the latter, are also crucial for sustainable development. Partnership between aid agencies and NGOs also make a major contribution to development efforts;

- Participants stressed that the millennium development goals are the driving force of the new unprecedented international effort for mobilizing financing for development. Considerable progress has been made in the last 30 years in the areas of health, education and other basic social services. Yet the numbers of the poor and the illiterate remain far too high, and international goals in the areas of health and basic social services are far from being achieved. The situation in least developed countries and landlocked developing countries calls for particular attention. Commitments to help those countries, other developing countries and countries with economies in transition to develop and integrate with the world economy must be implemented;

• Some ministers were of the view that the draft Monterrey Consensus should have been more explicit in addressing the social agenda and the financing of pro- grammes in social sectors. They also pointed to the need to address unemploy- ment, pay greater attention to the informal sector of the economy and support small entrepreneurs. In that regard, particular attention must be paid to rural ar- eas, where the majority of the poor live;

• Many ministers stressed the importance of education for all, particularly girls and women. Positive change requires education at all levels, particularly universal pri- mary education for boys and girls, as called for in the United Nations Millennium Declaration. The implementation of the Conference outcome must be pursued in a human rights framework.

"Main issues discussed

"3. Alongside support of the draft Monterrey Consensus by all ministers, discussion focused on a number of key issues. There was agreement that good governance forms the basis for mobilizing both domestic and international resources for developing countries. It was pointed out that effective efforts to eradicate corruption are essen- tial for good governance in all countries, and that those efforts are the joint responsi- bilities of developing and developed countries. Allocation of government resources to military uses diverts funds from development expenditures. With regard to interna- tional private resources, foreign direct investment was seen as preferable to short- term capital and more volatile credit. Many participants pointed out that the improve- ment of market access for agricultural products represents an important contribution to financing for development. There was general agreement that effective progress in implementing the Doha Ministerial Declaration, particularly the liberalization of trade in agriculture, is crucial. In that regard, it was stressed that mechanisms should be de- veloped to support the effective functioning of small entrepreneurs in a globalized economy, and that care must be taken to ensure that entrepreneurs benefit from in- ternational assistance. Many urged the rapid implementation of the enhanced heavily indebted poor countries (HIPC) initiative and efforts by donor countries to increase of- ficial development assistance to reach 0.7 per cent of gross national product. At the same time, ministers emphasized that the quality of ODA needs to be enhanced through improved coordination of donor efforts and conditions, the untying of aid and improved capacity of recipient countries to use aid effectively. A major inter- national effort to assist developing countries in capacity-building in all areas was iden- tified as an integral part of development assistance. Ministers underscored the importance of achieving consistency and coherence of the international monetary, trading and financial systems, as well as in the policies of developed countries, which can affect the international economic conditions that impact the economies of developing countries. They also emphasized the importance of reform of the Bretton Woods institutions and increased participation of developing countries in economic decision-making.

"Proposals additional to those contained in the draft Monterrey Consensus

"4. The following represent proposals made by various participants:

• Extended use of regional swap network for central banks;

• Regional banks to create new credit lines for emergency loans and to increase loans to the social sector;

• Debt cancellation for IDA-non-HIPCs;

• More extensive use of debt swaps;

- International Monetary Fund/World Bank/Organisation for Economic Cooperation and Development international dialogue on taxation;
- Industrialized countries should open labour markets to workers from developing countries;
- Establish international standards of partnership;
- Strengthen various global information clearinghouses for use by domestic and international investors;
- Improvement of private credit rating methodology."

Ministerial round table A.3
Partnerships in financing for development

19. The Co-Chairmen, Shaukat Aziz, Minister of Finance (Pakistan) and Mark Malloch Brown, Administrator of the United Nations Development Programme, opened the ministerial round table.

20. Statements were made by the representatives of Japan, Morocco, Australia, Guyana, Guatemala, the United States of America, Mali, Czech Republic, Liechtenstein, Iceland, Finland, Ireland, Honduras, Netherlands, Panama, the Russian Federation, Switzerland, South Africa, Jamaica, Yugoslavia, Namibia, Mexico and Ethiopia.

21. The following representatives of institutional stakeholders made statements: UNAIDS, Common Fund for Commodities, Economic Commission for Europe, European Commission.

22. The following representatives of the business sector made statements: International Chamber of Commerce, AMBAC Financial Group, Daimler Chrysler, Securities Industries Association, Cisneros Group of Companies, Union Bank of the Philippines.

23. The following representatives of civil society made statements: Carter Center, World Confederation of Labour, United Methodist Church, Social Watch Asia, Swedish Labor Organization, Maryknoll Sisters of St. Dominic, Center for Global Development, Instituto Braziliero de Analysis Sociais e Economicas.

24. The summary prepared by the Co-Chairmen (A/CONF.198/8/Add.2) read as follows:

"1. Ministers regarded the draft Monterrey Consensus as the embodiment of a new partnership for development, although a number of participants felt that it is not sufficiently far-reaching. There was broad agreement that its adoption must be followed by a strong focus on implementation and translation from words into action if it is to become a meaningful global initiative. Political will and leadership—in both the developed and the developing countries—will be key factors determining its ultimate success.

"2. The need to ensure national ownership of development was underlined. The development process must be fully inclusive and the concerns of all must be taken into account in the formulation and implementation of strategies, programmes and projects. External assistance should be regarded as economic cooperation rather than "aid", not as a permanent crutch but as a means of helping developing countries to help themselves. It is of the utmost importance that recipient countries themselves design programmes of reform and poverty eradication and fully own them. Donor countries should support implementation of such programmes instead of requiring recipient countries to follow any donor-designed reforms. The experience of Ireland with the aid received from its European partners was hailed as a good example of ownership, in which the recipient was encouraged to set its own developmental priorities, which were then supported by its partners. The New Partnership for Africa's Development was recognized as an important recent initiative fully owned by the developing countries involved.

"3. Within the framework of ownership, partnerships entail a clear understanding of the reciprocal commitments and mutual obligations of all parties involved in development. Ministers endorsed the concept of partnership as a central principle of international development cooperation, but felt that further work will be required to refine the new commitment to partnership into concrete results.

"4. Different aspects of the concept of partnership were stressed, including partnerships between developing countries, among developing countries and between the public and the private business sectors, as well as those involving various branches of civil society, including NGOs and trade unions. One of the key aspects of the concept of partnership is the need to fully recognize the role and contribution of those civil society partners. Participants also emphasized the need to incorporate the gender perspective into all development programmes and projects.

"5. Several examples were provided of the need for and benefits of partnerships within countries. It was recognized that the State's responsibility for development must be shared with a range of other stakeholders within and outside the countries. The private sector has a comparative advantage in some areas, although there are a number of risks and activities that are best left in the realm of the State. In some cases, public-private partnerships provide a means of taking advantage of the strengths of both parties. Several participants provided examples of such public-private collaboration.

"6. Official development assistance was universally recognized as indispensable to meeting the millennium development goals, particularly in the poorest countries. Attention should be focused on supporting national efforts to improve education and health, including AIDS, but there is also a manifest need for capacity-building, including in the management of ODA; some participants felt that infrastructure development no longer receives adequate attention in aid programmes.

"7. The accountability of both donors and recipients of aid was widely stressed. Recipients of aid should be accountable to both their citizens and donors in terms of commitment to sound governance and policies, but donors are also accountable to recipients in many ways, including in such respects as the volume, quality and effectiveness of their aid. Developed countries should make their own accountability a priority rather than leaving it to NGOs.

"8. The need to enhance coherence and coordination in international development assistance was emphasized. Developing countries are often required to comply with varying conditions in order to receive aid because donors' priorities and procedures differ. Improved coordination among donors could reduce the burden on recipient countries, particularly small States.

"9. Many ministers emphasized that public awareness about the importance of closing the poverty gap needs to be raised in the developed countries. There is a need to increase recognition of the need for and effectiveness of ODA in order to increase public support for additional flows. The Conference has already had a positive impact in that respect; the media could be an important partner in continuing that effort. Appreciation was expressed for the proposed increases in flows that have been announced by some major donors in the days prior to the Conference, but there is concern that ODA will still fall far short of both the estimates of the flows required to ensure that the millennium development goals are met and the target of 0.7 per cent of gross national product.

"10. There was an emphasis on the need for coherence among the trade, finance and development policies of developed countries. Several participants highlighted the impediments to development in developing countries created by protectionism and domestic subsidies in the developed countries.

"Proposals going beyond the draft Monterrey Consensus

"11. The following represent proposals made by various participants:

- One delegation clarified an earlier announcement regarding an increase in its country's future aid flows;

- One delegation announced that its country would be proposing a global lottery;

- A number of recipient countries recommended that donors delegate full responsibility for the management of their external assistance programmes to their offices in recipient countries;

- It was also proposed that donors pool their resources into a single fund at the country level;

- There was a suggestion that the international financial institutions report on donor countries' performance in terms of volume and quality of aid given, as well as on other development-related policies towards developing countries, such as trade;

- Two private-sector enterprises made proposals concerning learning frameworks and learning networks to build capacity for entrepreneurship and organizational skills in developing countries;

- It was suggested that the United Nations is in an advantageous position to raise public awareness of the need for additional aid flows."

Ministerial round table A.4
Partnerships in financing for development

25. The Co-Chairmen, Mugur Isarescu, Governor of the National Bank of Romania, and K. Y. Amoako, Executive Secretary of the Economic Commission for Africa, opened the round table.

26. Statements were made by the representatives of Brazil, the Philippines, the former Yugoslav Republic of Macedonia, Mozambique, Peru, India, Suriname, Spain, Slovakia, Sweden, Cameroon, Austria, Tuvalu, Venezuela, Turkey, Brunei Darussalam, Saint Lucia, Georgia, Mauritius, Senegal, Sierra Leone, Singapore, Mongolia, Trinidad and Tobago, and Tonga.

27. The following representatives of institutional stakeholders made statements: United Nations Human Settlements Programme (Habitat), Economic Commission for Latin America and the Caribbean, United Nations Development Programme.

28. The following representatives of the business sector made statements: Frank Russell Company, African Business Round Table, Spring Investment Corporation, Financial Services Volunteer Corps.

29. The following representatives of civil society made statements: Japan Network on Debt and Poverty, Church of Norway (EcuTeam), KARAT Coalition, World Council of Churches (EcuTeam), National Association of Economists, Development Network of Indigenous Volunteer Associations. The Co-Chairmen made concluding remarks.

30. The summary prepared by the Co-Chairmen (A/CONF.198/8/Add.3) read as follows:

"1. The draft Monterrey Consensus was welcomed as a historical instrument and a turning point in the global partnership for development.

"2. Participants emphasized that partnership is a critical element for poverty eradication and the achievement of the millennium development goals. Several dimensions of partnerships are considered key to people-centred sustainable development. At the national level, partnerships should be based on shared responsibilities and complementarity of efforts and roles of the State, the private sector and civil society. At the global level, developed and developing countries should pursue development as a joined responsibility. Partnerships among countries, development organizations, civil society and business are considered to be essential for achieving greater coherence and accelerating development. Delegates also strongly encouraged public/private partnerships as effective ways to create a favourable climate for socially responsible investment. A number of speakers stressed the important role of the private sector in wealth creation, and called for stronger partnerships between transnational corporations and national entrepreneurs to promote investment and growth.

"3. There was strong support for the domestic and international reforms advocated in the draft Monterrey Consensus, including, at the domestic level, solid democratic institutions, respect for human rights, gender equality, good governance, sound macroeconomic policies and an enabling environment for private investment (both domestic and foreign). At the international level, effective progress on trade liberalization along the lines of the Doha Ministerial Declaration, especially enhanced market access for developing countries, substantially increased quantity and quality of official development assistance, external debt relief, efforts to stabilize international financial markets and enhanced capacity-building in developing countries, were seen as crucial.

"4. With regard to ODA, the recent initiatives announced by some developed countries to increase their development assistance were welcomed as promising steps in the right direction. At the same time, several participants emphasized the need to increase the effectiveness of ODA through such measures as the untying of aid, improved coordination of donor efforts, increased country ownership and enhanced absorptive capacity of the recipient countries.

"5. Rapid and effective implementation of the draft Monterrey Consensus was the focus of many interventions. Building partnerships should be part of the process of staying engaged as a long-term commitment.

"6. The special needs of Africa, the least developed countries and the small island developing States were emphasized. Investment in those countries needs to be encouraged, including through the catalysing effect of ODA flows. The importance of the

New Partnership for Africa's Development was stressed as a key partnership that should be supported by the international community.

"Proposals additional to those contained in the draft Monterrey Consensus

"7. Alongside the support for the draft Monterrey Consensus in general terms, the following concrete proposals were put forward:

- Creation of a forum for business entities from North and South under the auspices of the World Bank and the regional development banks;

- Doubling ODA as a first step towards meeting the 0.7 per cent target to achieve the millennium development goals;

- Capacity-building reforms, with a special focus on post-conflict countries;

- Creation of an international task force focusing on global public goods;

- Creation of a permanent consultative forum among developing and developed countries on financial and debt issues;

- Ensuring greater participation of developing countries in decision-making on international economic and financial issues;

- Reducing expenditure on defence and increasing public spending on social sectors, in particular for human resource development;

- Enhanced International Monetary Fund and World Bank support for regional and subregional reserve funds and development banks;

- Additional efforts to move towards sustainable debt levels of developing countries;

- Strengthening the resources of the international financial institutions and the United Nations system and increasing coordination and coherence of actions among them;

- Further consideration of private sector proposals made at the Conference;

- A reassessment of conditionalities;

- Addressing the issue of subsidies, particularly in agriculture;

- New and innovative sources of financing, including a currency transaction tax and tax incentives for private flows;

- Gender mainstreaming at all levels and in all policies;

- Establishment of an entity to issue guarantees for capital markets risk coverage in sub-Saharan Africa;

- Establishment of a global forum on taxation;

- Development of mechanisms for debt arbitration among creditor and debtor countries."

Ministerial round table B.1
Coherence for development

31. The Co-Chairmen, Jan Kavan, Deputy Prime Minister and Minister of Foreign Affairs (Czech Republic), and Rubens Ricupero, Secretary-General of the United Nations Conference on Trade and Development, opened the ministerial round table and made introductory statements.

32. Statements were made by the representatives of China, the United States of America, Saint Lucia, Trinidad and Tobago, India, Denmark, Jordan, Malaysia, Angola, Australia, Slovenia, Sri Lanka, Suriname, Venezuela, Iraq, Lesotho, Egypt, Bangladesh, Sweden, Rwanda, Saint Vincent and the Grenadines, Ireland, Uruguay, Viet Nam, Peru, Chad, Ethiopia and Botswana.

33. The following representatives of institutional stakeholders made statements: European Commission, Financial Stability Forum, World Bank, World Food Programme, United Nations Population Fund, World Trade Organization.

34. The following representatives of the business sector made statements: Business Council for the United Nations, Samuels Associates, Capital Markets Credit Society, Calvert Funds, AB Volvo, State Street Global Investor Services Group, Allied Zurich.

35. The following representatives of civil society made statements: African Network for Environmental and Economic Justice, Congregación de la Sagrada Familia, Catholic Committee against Hunger and for Development, Women's International Coalition for Economic Justice, Network for African Women Economists. The Co-Chairmen summarized the discussion.

36. The summary prepared by the Co-Chairmen (A/CONF.198/8/Add.6) read as follows:

"1. The round table began with the recognition that the International Conference on Financing for Development needs to successfully address the matter of coherence. Policy-making in both individual Governments and intergovernmental settings has become specialized into more or less related entities that cooperate imperfectly. In many cases, the difficulty is not lack of information but unresolved differences in policy preferences that lead Governments or international organizations into inconsistent actions. Our discussion focused on coherence difficulties both in national Governments and internationally. Certain participants in our round table also announced a significant initiative.

"**Domestic coherence**

"2. Participants noted that the search for coherence is not a new phenomenon and that additional efforts are required. However, in approaching the issue, all dimensions of development and all stakeholders and partners should be considered in a comprehensive and holistic approach, in which all players should reinforce each other. For instance, lack of cohesion in the international sphere can undermine efforts to enhance cohesion at the domestic level.

"3. Some participants considered that despite its importance, enhancing coherence should not be pursued at the expense of addressing specific problems. Sometimes painful policy reforms are necessary and they should not be dismissed under the false pretence that they undermine consistency. On the other hand, it was widely recognized that developing countries are overburdened by a vast array of donor and creditor requirements. Seeking to implement them drains scarce resources and they thus need to be simplified.

"4. Considerable attention was devoted to the need to promote and enhance cohesion at the national level, both in developed and developing countries. Some speakers noted that achieving that goal would be a major challenge. The process involves numerous actors who may have conflicting interests and objectives—the national, regional and local levels of government and public institutions, the private sector and civil society.

"5. Participants considered that a clear vision or development strategy, formulated at the country level, that brings all stakeholders together in a spirit of true partnership and cooperation, could have an important bearing on improving coherence. In addition, it was stressed that such a vision should be based on respect for and support of human rights, promotion of gender equality and protection of the environment. The global compact launched by the Secretary-General of the United Nations and the increased attention by large institutional investors, such as pension funds to good corporate citizenship by the firms in which they invest, were cited as examples of relevant actions by different stakeholders.

"6. Some speakers highlighted the importance of public sector reform as a means to improve coherence at the national level. As the role of government has evolved in a number of countries, the State has become less a direct producer and more an enabler of economic activity. This requires that government have a strong institutional, supervisory and regulatory capacity, for example for the development of an effective financial sector, which is central to successful domestic resource mobilization. Adequate financial and technical support from the international community is also considered necessary to enable such reforms.

"7. Some speakers noted that although foreign direct investment (FDI) is important for development, simply attracting FDI does not automatically imply faster growth. There is a need for complementary domestic policies to link the operations of foreign firms to the domestic economy and thereby increase its benefits for the country concerned.

"8. One means of reducing inconsistencies is to increase the transparency of business and government practices and share information fully. Accordingly, representatives of the business sector put forward a series of proposals, including the establishment of a global information clearing house, the promotion of investment guidelines in least developed countries, enhancing developing countries' access to equity and debt financing, new mechanisms for infrastructure financing, and strengthening small and medium-sized enterprises in developing countries.[7]

"International coherence

"9. Participants stressed the importance of better coherence between national development efforts and international cooperation. It was argued that the major industrial countries should pay more attention to the consequences of their macroeconomic policies for the rest of the world. It was also observed that combating corruption requires cooperation between developing and developed countries, especially if developing countries are to recover illicitly removed funds.

"10. A large majority of speakers expressed concern about incoherence between trade and development policies. It was emphasized that structural reforms in developing countries, including foreign trade liberalization, have not been accompanied by adequate measures in industrial countries to open up their economies. Moreover, developed countries still heavily subsidize the export of many products, and developing countries that are efficient producers of those products have had to compete in third countries against those subsidized exports. Hence, the efforts of many developing

---

7   See paper entitled "Strengthening financing for development: proposals from the private sector", compiled by the United Nations-sanctioned business interlocutors to the International Conference on Financing for Development, March 2002.

countries to modernize their economies are held back by the lost opportunity to earn sufficient financial resources from exports. In addition, many developing countries do not have the capacity to adequately participate in negotiations to further liberalize trade in a balanced way, as in the case of agriculture in the World Trade Organization (WTO). It is recognized that technical cooperation to assist those countries in trade negotiations should be a priority.

"11. Problems of cohesion in official development assistance were also highlighted. The participants argued that although in the 1990s the developed countries experienced strong growth, in that period the volume of ODA declined, which, according to one speaker, represented a fundamental incoherence. It was also stressed that unlike the time-bound commitments contained in the adjustment programmes that developing countries arrange with multilateral creditors, most donors have not set a timetable for increasing ODA. Moreover, it was stressed that donors should streamline and harmonize procedures and not lightly or frequently change priorities of assistance, which sends conflicting and confusing messages to the recipients.

"12. The participants tried to find ways to better link national and international development efforts. It was agreed that that could be achieved if respective goals were clear and shared. Developing countries should be assisted to build the capacity to determine their own viable development programmes, which should be supported by the international community. Poverty reduction strategy papers are considered to be a move in the right direction.

"13. The need to improve coherence among the international agencies was also emphasized as one of the most critical issues. It was stressed that member countries often speak in different voices in different organizations and that those organizations can speak in different voices to individual countries. In addition, the economic programmes for developing countries do not always take due account of domestic conditions. A standardized approach should be avoided.

"14. There should also be more coherence among donors at the operational level, for example to simplify procedures and cut costs of implementation. Furthermore, policies of international development institutions have not always produced expected outcomes. For instance, the retreat of public financing from infrastructure projects has led to substantial reductions in that important component of investment. It was argued that the regional development banks should increase their activities in that sphere and that consideration should be given to strengthening regional financial cooperation for development.

"15. At the same time, speakers stressed that there have been positive developments in the closer cooperation of international organizations, including Bretton Woods institutions, WTO and the United Nations and its agencies and programmes. It was suggested that the United Nations play a central role in monitoring, assessing and coordinating international development cooperation, and that the relationship between WTO and the United Nations be put on the same basis as that between the United Nations and the Bretton Woods institutions.

"A specific proposal

"16. China and the United States of America announced a notable initiative during the round table as a follow-up to the Conference. They intend to bring together Governments and enterprises in Shanghai, China, in November 2002 in order to help better realize the potential contribution of foreign direct investment to economic growth and development."

Ministerial round table B.2
Coherence for development

37. The Co-Chairmen, Trevor Manuel, Minister of Finance (South Africa), and Eveline Herfkens, Minister for Development Cooperation (Netherlands), opened the ministerial round table and made introductory statements.

38. Statements were made by the representatives of Mozambique, Pakistan, Guyana, Norway, the Philippines, the former Yugoslav Republic of Macedonia, Panama, Liechtenstein, Yemen, Portugal, Mali, Cambodia, Haiti, the Lao People's Democratic Republic, Tunisia, Switzerland, the Congo and the Russian Federation.

39. The following representatives of institutional stakeholders made statements: World Trade Organization, International Monetary Fund, World Bank, United Nations, United Nations Development Fund for Women, Latin American Economic System, IUCN-World Conservation Union and International Fund for Agricultural Development.

40. The following representatives of the business sector made statements: Soros Fund Management, BRED Banque Populaire, ESKOM, Eurorient, Money Matters Institute.

41. The following representatives of civil society made statements: Instituto Braziliero de Analysis Sociais e Econo-micas, Bretton Woods Project, Third World Network, Oxfam International, Espacio Autónomo, CIDSE and All Pakistan Federation of Labour.

42. The summary prepared by the Co-Chairmen (A/CONF.198/8/Add.8) read as follows:

"1. The round table had a highly interactive and lively discussion on enhancing coherence for development. Many dimensions of coherence were addressed, both national and international, in particular coherence among international institutions and among international institutions and developing countries.

"General considerations

"2. A key thrust of the debate was that the millennium development goals, the draft Monterrey Consensus and the sustainable development agenda have provided major impetus to achieving greater coherence in the development policies and actions of all partners. There is now broad consensus that more coherence is needed. But that has to be translated into concrete implementation and actions.

"3. Ministers and stakeholders noted that the current approach adopted by many countries of giving uncoordinated directives from individual ministries to the various international institutions creates problems for good global governance. Coherence must start at home. Otherwise, such lack of coherence is exported to the international systems and hinders the efforts to guide globalization so that it supports the millennium development goals. In the end however, coherence must be established worldwide.

"4. A major challenge today is how to introduce a pro-poor focus in trade policies and the international trading system and ensure that they better support development goals. The agricultural and energy policies of developed countries must be submitted to the same scrutiny on policy coherence. The most restrictive trade barriers are a burden on the products of the poor. In particular, agricultural subsidies could be better spent on investing in millennium development goals.

"5. Coherence in cooperation policies should accompany country ownership of national poverty reduction strategies. Some progress has been made, but we need increased efforts in that area. Often, lack of coherence in national policies reflects the insufficient administrative capacity of a country to make policies in today's complex conditions. Once national poverty-focused strategies are formulated, with adequate participation by all stakeholders, donors should be more flexible and finance strategies with a predictable, multi-year commitment, preferably in common pool mechanisms.

"6. Countries' poverty reduction strategies—notably the poverty reduction strategy papers—are excellent tools for countries to foster policy coherence and make education, health and defence budgets add up to one integrated budget with a poverty focus. Coherence between macroeconomic policies and microeconomic policies is crucial for sustainable development. Yet a proper analysis of what pro-poor policy contains is country specific. Countries other than the highly indebted poor countries should also consider formulating poverty reduction strategy papers in order to reduce poverty in a comprehensive manner.

"7. At the national level, transparency and communication, as well as consultation with all partners at local and other levels, are critical to improved coherence. Thus, transparent and sound governance at the national level goes a long way towards ensuring policy coherence.

"**Main issues**

"8. The lack of policy coherence at the national level in developing countries reflects both a lack of capacity and, in many cases, incoherence among donors. Increased coherence in developing countries requires a major cooperation effort for capacity-building. A coherent approach by developed countries to support development requires removing obstacles to the exports of developing countries and providing market access, particularly in the areas of agriculture, manufacturing and services. Often, inconsistency arises from conditionalities imposed by donor countries and institutions. One country reported that it had to comply with some 160 conditions for obtaining support to its poverty reduction strategy. It was considered important for donors to show flexibility and help countries to respond to new situations or needs of an urgent nature. Double standards should be avoided, and all countries should impose on their own actions the same scrutiny and goals that they impose on others.

"9. When international financial volatility originates in developed countries, the demand for liberalization of the capital account worsens rather than improves financial conditions and stability in developing countries. It was stressed that the International Monetary Fund (IMF) does not currently call for indiscriminate liberalization of the capital account in developing countries but rather for the appropriate sequencing of strengthening of the financial sector and capital account liberalization.

"10. Coherence between macroeconomic and microeconomic policies in developing countries is crucial for achieving development. That includes supporting poverty reduction priorities with budget levels that accommodate pro-poor spending and establishing coherence between social and economic development policies and between public investment and private investment policies. Linkage between trade and development policies must also be made in development strategies, and the link between trade and poverty needs to be assessed.

"11. Coherence must be ensured between business actions and national plans. New initiatives, such as the New Partnership for Africa's Development, could be a driving force for mobilizing the contribution of the private sector to development.

"12. Gender blindness is an obvious example of lack of coherence. Trade liberalization may have negative consequences for women. Improved participation of women in economic policy-making must be ensured. Girls' education is one of the most effective means to reduce poverty.

"13. Reference was also made to the issue of incoherence in the policy advice provided by IMF, i.e., its article one on full employment.

"14. There is a need to formulate a single set of issues for the Bretton Woods institutions, the World Trade Organization and the United Nations. WTO members should invite their representatives to subscribe to the millennium development goals as a charter since the Marrakech Agreement Establishing WTO describes trade as a means to development.

"15. The multilateral organizations and bilateral donors still have fragmented priorities and strategies that undermine coherence. Ad hoc contributions to subprogrammes of the specialized agencies create even more fragmentation rather than a coherent United Nations strategy.

"16. In the United Nations, ongoing reform efforts aim to reduce the fragmentation of its operations and improve coherence in its day-to-day work, but more remains to be done. The United Nations needs help from donor countries in that respect through an increase in their core contributions. One participant suggested that at the next General Assembly, a request be made that the Secretary-General explore the idea of establishing an economic and social security council, with comparable functions to those of the Security Council. At the same time, there is a need to ensure that the Economic and Social Council is focused on the key issues of development.

"17. Coherence at the multilateral level requires the full participation of developing countries. In WTO, there has been progressive transparency in its operations, and there is now a requirement that all members participate better in decision-making. The more members understand trade issues and how they impact their development, the better their participation and coherence of decisions. The draft Monterrey Consensus and the International Conference on Financing for Development are definite steps forward in the participation of all stakeholders and in improving coherence.

"**Looking ahead**

"18. The following issues were revised:

- What do we focus on now in terms of how we want international institutions to be? Who should be doing the thinking now since the existing institutions are not the places that should be doing it? Who will provide the political leadership for listening to new ideas and changing institutions?

- Is there a true sense of multilateralism? Can large countries choose to opt out or are there the same rules and standards for all countries?

- The issues discussed need a lot of creative thinking. The focus on the millennium development goals and the road map for their implementation can provide us with strong guidance for coherence. Upcoming events—the World Summit on Sustainable Development to be held in Johannesburg, the Development Committee meeting to be held at the World Bank-IMF meetings and the Economic and Social Council-Bretton Woods institutions high-level dialogue—will provide opportunities for bringing those issues forward after some further thinking and continuing the momentum that was generated at this round table. Accordingly, we will submit the main findings of the round table to the high-level dialogue.

"Recommendations

"19. The following recommendations were made:

- There is a need to establish at the developing country level one coordination (or central contact) point for economic cooperation to give a sense of direction and ensure coherence between donors and domestic policy. Periodic briefing of donors and discussion with domestic stakeholders should be part of such a mechanism;

- There is a need to develop a single matrix for development, including national authorities, official development assistance, technical assistance and foreign direct investment, partly to avoid donors operating in the jurisdictions of ministries, and to reconcile national and international agendas;

- When countries come up with credible PRSPs, based on broad consultation with stakeholders, donors should be ready to provide more flexible financing;

- In developed countries, to confront the conflicts between national issues (interests) and the requirements to assist development (global issue) it is necessary to give a new public dimension to the global fight against poverty;

- The Organisation for Economic Cooperation and Development ministerial meeting held in June 2000 subscribed to policy coherence, which should now be followed up by an implementation plan;

- The European Union, already committed to enhance coherence in Maastricht in 1992, should pursue that commitment more vigorously;

- It is crucial to review progress in national and international efforts in order to achieve the millennium development goals and reduce inequity;

- The Bretton Woods institutions and WTO must help to build partnerships for enhancing countries capacities in the area of sustainable development;

- WTO should ensure that its work more clearly supports the pursuit of the millennium development goals and poverty eradication;

- The Philadelphia coordinating mechanism, which brings together Bretton Woods institutions executive directors and delegates to the United Nations, should be expanded to Geneva-based institutions and could be broadened to include other developed countries;

- The Economic and Social Council must focus on key topical issues of the day. It has an important role to play in the follow-up to the Monterrey Conference and in helping to keep the focus on coherence and coordination in pursuit of the millennium development goals."

Ministerial round table B.3
Coherence for development

43. The Co-Chairmen, Ram Sharan Mahat, Minister of Finance (Nepal), and Enrique Iglesias, President of the Inter-American Development Bank, opened the ministerial round table and made introductory statements.

44. Statements were made by the representatives of Ecuador, Cuba, Spain (also on behalf of the European Union), Zambia, Iceland, Turkey, Japan, Ukraine, Cam-

eroon, El Salvador, Malaysia, the Dominican Republic, Luxembourg, Colombia, Ghana, Guatemala, Belgium, Costa Rica, Grenada and Azerbaijan.

45. The following representatives of institutional stakeholders made statements: Pacific Island Forum, World Bank, the Economic Commission for Latin American and the Caribbean (on behalf of the United Nations), International Monetary Fund.

46. The following representatives of the business sector made statements: Business Council for Sustainable Development (Mexico), Business Council for the United Nations.

47. The following representatives of civil society made statements: Third World Network, World Council of Churches (EcuTeam), African Center for Empowerment Gender and Advocacy, Intermon Oxfam, Campaign to Reform the World Bank, WFUNA/UNA-Argentina, ATTAC/Norwegian Forum for Environment and Development. The Co-Chairmen summarized the discussion.

48. The summary prepared by the Co-Chairmen (A/CONF.198/8/Add.7) read as follows:

"1. Various dimensions of coherence were addressed—national, regional and international—among international institutions, among international institutions and developing countries, and among objectives and instruments. Coherence among the economic, human, gender, social and environmental dimensions is seen as essential. Striking the balance among those different agendas will be a key challenge for the World Summit on Sustainable Development. In that sense, the success of the International Conference on Financing for Development and the Summit are closely related.

"2. The millennium development goals provide a broad framework for coherence not only among policies and programmes of countries but also among multilateral institutions. The commitment to the substance and the spirit of the draft Monterrey Consensus and its follow-up should give new impetus to the mobilization of resources for their effective implementation. Since broad consensus has emerged on the need for coherence, attention should now focus on practical and effective measures for its promotion. In the end, coherence will be measured by its ability to reduce the number of people living in poverty.

"3. Several speakers stressed that coherence must start at home, especially among different ministries and other stakeholders, if directives to international institutions are to be equally coherent. No single actor or policy can succeed on its own but only in an effective combination of efforts. In that regard, better governance and coordination are essential to improve coherence within and among countries and institutions in the delivery and effective use of development assistance. The role of nationally owned policies as a framework for coherence, including in relation to poverty reduction strategy papers, was also emphasized. The need for coherence between national policies and multilaterally agreed commitments was further stressed. Cooperation among countries on issues that need to be addressed at the regional level can also enhance coherence of policies and actions.

"4. At the global level, increased participation of developing countries in international decision-making was seen as critical for coherence. Moreover, an effective strategy for development should seek to reduce existing asymmetries in access to capital and technology as well as between mobility of capital and restrictions to labour movements. The vulnerability of developing countries to external shocks and the frequency and more pronounced nature of economic cycles in those countries should also be addressed through a more coherent response that encompasses macroeconomic, financial, trade and social measures. Similarly, increased official development assistance for low-income countries should not come at the expense of flows directed to middle-income countries, otherwise poverty levels in the latter would inevitably rise. External debt burdens should be sustainable and consistent with poverty reduction goals.

"5. Speakers pointed out the importance of strengthening coherence between the United Nations, the Bretton Woods institutions and the World Trade Organization, as well as regional financial institutions. Development should be placed at the centre of the global political agenda. The dialogue on development among all stakeholders, including decision makers, in the political, development, finance and trade areas spurred by the Monterrey process was welcomed, and the importance of continuing it as a major new trend was stressed.

"6. It was considered that coherence in the international trading system requires the removal of obstacles to developing countries' exports, especially in agriculture and textiles. The Doha Ministerial Declaration and upcoming trade negotiations were seen as an opportunity to make the international trading system more responsive to the development needs of developing countries and more sensitive to the social and environmental dimensions.

"7. The need for greater investment to prevent the conflict situation that has affected many developing countries was also stressed. The conflict situation has deepened and expanded poverty, enriching only those who benefit from the arms trade.

"8. A better understanding of the relationship and exploitation of the synergies between the millennium development goals and other relevant policies will require further analytical work.

"**Proposals and recommendations**

"9. The following proposals and recommendations were made:

- Establish a "global compact for coherence" of commitments by developed and developing countries;

- Address consistency in donor countries between national interests and constraints, on the one hand, and development assistance goals on the other;

- Harmonize policies, actions and procedures of various institutions to align them with the millennium development goals and their implementation, as well as for monitoring and assessing results;

- As the most inclusive and participatory forum, the United Nations should remain at the centre of discussion on the promotion of coherence among development cooperation, macroeconomic and social policies;

- Fully utilize the potential of the Economic and Social Council to promote meaningful dialogue for policy coherence;

- Further strengthen the United Nations Development Assistance Framework and United Nations Development Group mechanisms;

- Establish a clearing house at the national level to share information, enhance coordination among different ministries and other actors and build on the outcomes of various United Nations conferences;

- Ensure that development cooperation policies do not directly or indirectly support arms purchases that lead to conflicts. Exploitation of conflicts for financial gains should be prevented through the development of global ethics;

- Promote the democratization of global governance;

- Ensure balance between macroeconomic reform programmes and the social agenda;

- ODA should be supportive of recipient countries' national strategies and should be untied."

Ministerial round table B.4
Coherence in development

49. The Co-Chairmen, Owen A. Arthur, Prime Minister and Minister of Finance (Barbados), and Jean Lemierre, President of the European Bank for Reconstruction and Development, opened the ministerial round table and made introductory statements.

50. Statements were made by the representatives of the United States, Brazil, Canada, Côte d'Ivoire, Algeria, Morocco, Finland, the Holy See, Benin, Burkina Faso, Chile, Austria, Djibouti, the Bahamas, Kenya, Armenia, the United Kingdom of Great Britain and Northern Ireland, Argentina, Belize and Yugoslavia.

51. The following representatives of institutional stakeholders made statements: Organisation for Economic Cooperation and Development, Islamic Development Bank, International Labour Organization, World Bank.

52. The following representatives of the business sector made statements: Grupo IMSA, World Economic Forum, Business Council on Sustainable Development—Argentina, China Online, FireXchange.

53. The following representatives of civil society made statements: InterAction, World Economy, Ecology and Development, Grupo Género y Economía, Environmental Development Action in the Third World, Institute for Agriculture and Trade Policy, Action for Economic Reform.

54. The summary prepared by the Co-Chairmen (A/CONF.198/8/Add.5) read as follows:

"1. The round table produced a rich debate on many aspects and dimensions of coherence and its relevance to development. There was a widespread view that the draft Monterrey Consensus provides a sound framework for a coherent approach to development and the achievement of the millennium development goals.

"General aspects

"2. Participants welcomed the impetus provided by the draft Monterrey Consensus and emphasized that more coherent policies and efforts are needed at all levels. Coherence requires a long-term approach and must be built on a set of sound domestic policies, democracy, the rule of law, the enforceability of contracts and anti-corruption measures. A supportive international environment is seen as crucial. Multiple conditionalities, protectionism, domestic subsidies and inadequate coordination in the development policies of international institutions are hindering efforts to create a global economic system that supports the achievement of the internationally agreed development goals.

"3. Ministers and other stakeholders stressed that coherence implies partnership at all levels. The coordination of efforts to rapidly implement the goals set out in the draft Monterrey Consensus is the duty of each and every party. There is a need for clarity in the responsibilities of all stakeholders to coordinate efforts and to improve broad-based policy dialogue. Transparency and accountability must be the underlying principles in that endeavour.

"4. Coherence must be people-centred and aim at a higher quality of sustainable liveli-hoods. It was stressed that true coherence relies on the citizen, who must be inte-grated through an appropriate institutional framework. Everyone must be able to participate in order to support a well-functioning political process. Coherence is a coming together of all parties and in all sectors—in an early and broad manner.

"5. Coherence and diversity work together. Participants stressed that development strategies must recognize different policy environments. Pluralism and heterodox ap-proaches should be encouraged, but all forces must be brought together, which re-quires an environment that is conducive to better and more transparent coordination of efforts.

"6. Resources are an important aspect of coherence. The recent European Union and United States initiatives to increase spending on official development assistance are welcome as first promising steps in the right direction. The effectiveness of aid has in-creased in the past few years, but more remains to be done to enhance the absorptive capacity of developing countries, including through private/public partnerships. Every country is responsible for its own development, and it is crucial for development strategies to be owned by individual developing countries. However, development re-quires much more than aid. Coherence implies joint efforts to address domestic re-source mobilization, trade issues, debt problems and the reform of the international financial architecture.

"Main issues discussed

"7. Many participants stressed the need to address the inconsistencies in the overall approach to development. A coherent approach would imply the use of a variety of in-struments and policies that do not conflict with each other. A fundamental problem in that respect lies in the incoherence between the development assistance and trade policies of developed countries. Protectionism, especially in the agricultural and agro-industrial sectors, creates distortions in international trade, and by penalizing competitive producers in developing countries that have comparative advantages in those sectors represents an obstacle to growth. The agreements reached at Doha, if fully implemented, represented an opportunity to advance towards a more develop-ment-oriented series of trade negotiations. However, as one minister noted, capacity constraints could be an obstacle preventing many developing countries from reaping the benefits that more accessible markets make possible through optimizing the scale of production.

"8. The combination of liberalized and increasingly volatile capital flows, particularly short-term flows, with an international financial system that is designed for a world with capital controls and far less integrated financial markets, is another source of in-coherence that needs to be addressed. One reflection of that problem is the repeated occurrence of international financial crises, which are often preceded by large capital inflows and revel underlying vulnerabilities and shortcomings at both the national and international levels. Coherence in the financial sense requires measures in developing and developed countries, as well as at the international level. Such measures should include international financial regulations for institutional investors, highly leveraged financial institutions and off-shore financial centres.

"9. Several ministers referred to the crisis in Argentina as a dramatic example of the urgent need to address incoherence at the international level. Some ministers expressed their solidarity with the Argentine people and its Government, and emphasized the need to support the Government in its pursuance of economic reforms amid extremely difficult circumstances.

"10. Conditionality attached to development aid could be a source of incoherence and needs to be addressed, according to several participants. In many cases, multiple and conflicting conditionalities can impose a heavy burden on recipient countries, and their absorptive capacity needs to be taken into account in that respect. Improved coordination among donors is essential. It was also stressed that conditionality needs to be applied in such a way that the people of developing countries are not penalized for the failure of their leaders to meet basic performance criteria for aid. It was also felt that effective development assistance requires donors and recipients to share the same goals, as well as a full commitment by Governments of recipient countries to those goals, particularly to poverty eradication. Ministers also addressed the need to avoid confusion between the goals of ODA and those of private economic activity, for example by avoiding the use of ODA to subsidize private business and to mitigate its inherent risk.

"11. Ministers had a broad discussion on the coherence of policies at different levels and with different approaches. One key issue was the coherence and coordination of the macroeconomic policies of the main advanced countries, which was seen as an essential ingredient of global macroeconomic stability and sustained, effective development policies, which would benefit all, particularly the developing countries. It was also viewed as a key aspect of the establishment of an enabling international environment, without which the development efforts of developing countries cannot succeed.

"12. Another aspect of policy coherence concerns development policies in the developing countries, particularly between macroeconomic and sectoral policies. For example, the subsidization of certain sectors can exacerbate fiscal burdens and lead to distortions in economic activity. One key aspect of policy coherence raised by one minister was the importance of public awareness of and support for economic policy and reform options. Even if policies are technically sound, they cannot succeed without the support of the people.

"**Proposals**

"13. The following proposals were made:

- An international taxation organization should be created to tackle issues of international coordination of tax policies, with a possible extension to issues concerning foreign direct investment (FDI);

- A committee should be established to harmonize the evaluation of procedures by the international financial institutions;

- The United Nations should study the positive and negative aspects of FDI and how to maximize its benefits for developing countries while limiting its negative impacts;

- Enhancing the civil service's effectiveness should become one of the priorities of official development assistance, inter alia, because it is needed for the development of the private sector;

- An index of sustainability of enterprises of developing countries, along the lines of the one that is already in place for developed countries, should be developed. That initiative would help to improve the triple social-environmental-economic bottom line at the national level;

- The international high-level economic dialogue now carried out under the Group of Eight Major Industrialized Countries grouping should be opened to include other groupings and the widening of the agenda."

Chapter V
Report of the Summit Segment

1. At its 1st plenary meeting, on 18 March, in accordance with the recommendations of the Preparatory Committee contained in its decision 4/3 (see A/CONF.198/5, chap. VIII, sect. A), the International Conference on Financing for Development approved the organization of work as set out in document A/CONF.198/4/Rev.1, and decided to establish a summit segment. The Conference also decided to allocate agenda items 10, "Summit segment", 11, "Adoption of the Monterrey Consensus" and 12, "Adoption of the report of the Conference", to the summit segment.

A. General Exchange of Views

2. The summit segment held a general exchange of views at its 3rd to 6th meetings, on 21 and 22 March 2002.

3. At the 3rd meeting, Vicente Fox, President of Mexico and President of the Conference, declared open the summit segment of the Conference and addressed the Conference.

4. At the same meeting, Kofi Annan, Secretary-General of the United Nations, addressed the Conference.

5. Also at the same meeting, addresses were made by Han Seung-Soo (Republic of Korea), President of the General Assembly, James D. Wolfensohn, President of the World Bank, Horst Köhler, Managing Director of the International Monetary Fund and Mike Moore, Director-General of the World Trade Organization.

6. At the same meeting, statements were made by Hugo Chávez Frías, President of Venezuela (on behalf of the Group of 77 and China); José María Aznar, President of the Government of Spain (on behalf of the European Union); Olusegun Obasanjo, President of Nigeria; Alejandro Toledo Manrique, President of Peru; Leo Falcam, President of the Federated States of Micronesia; Agbéyomé Messan Kodjo, Prime Minister of Togo; Guy Verhofstadt, Prime Minister of Belgium; Jean Chrétien, Prime Minister of Canada; José Maria Pereira Neves, Prime Minister of Cape Verde; Thabo Mbeki, President of South Africa; Tommy Remengesau, Jr., President of Palau; Enrique Bolaños Geyer, President of Nicaragua; Fidel Castro Ruz, President of Cuba; Francisco Guillermo Flores Pérez, President of El Salvador; Boris Trajkovski, President of the former Yugoslav Republic of Macedonia; Jorge Battle Ibáñez, President of Uruguay; Festus Mogae, President of Botswana;

Ricardo Maduro Joest, President of Honduras; Hipólito Mejía Domínguez, President of the Dominican Republic; Pascoal Manuel Mocumbi, Prime Minister of Mozambique; King Abdullah Bin Al Hussein, King of Jordan; Abderrahman Youssoufi, Prime Minister of Morocco; Miguel Ángel Rodríguez Echeverría, President of Costa Rica; Ralph Gonsalves, Prime Minister of Saint Vincent and the Grenadines and Minister for Finance, Planning, Economic Development, Labour, Information, the Grenadines and Legal Affairs; Stjepan Mesi, President of Croatia; Tarja Halonen, President of Finland; and Ion Iliescu, President of Romania.

7. At the 4th meeting, statements were made by Andrés Pastrana Arango, President of the Republic of Colombia; Kjell Magne Bondevik, Prime Minister of Norway; Thaksin Shinawatra, Prime Minister of Thailand; Abdoulaye Wade, President of Senegal; Abdelaziz Bouteflika, President of Algeria; Mireya Elisa Moscoso Rodríguez, President of Panama; Mohamed Ghannouchi, Prime Minister of Tunisia; El Hadj Omar Bongo, President of Gabon; Nagoum Yamassoum, Prime Minister of Chad; Owen Arthur, M.P., Prime Minister and Minister for Finance and Economic Affairs of Barbados; Eduardo Duhalde, President of Argentina; Jorge Quiroga Ramírez, President of Bolivia; Charles Goerens, Minister for Cooperation and Humanitarian Action of Luxembourg; Teofisto Guingona, Jr., Vice-President and Minister for Foreign Affairs of the Philippines; Majozi Sithole, Minister of Finance of Swaziland; Donald Kaberuka, Minister of Finance and Economic Planning of Rwanda; Roni Milo, Minister for Regional Cooperation of Israel; Saufatu Sopoanga, Minister of Finance, Economic Planning and Industries of Tuvalu; Jakaya Kikwete, M.P., Minister for Foreign Affairs and International Cooperation of the United Republic of Tanzania; Ibrahim Al-Assaf, Minister of Finance and National Economy of Saudi Arabia; Lyonpo Yeshey Zimba, Minister of Finance of Bhutan; Xiang Huaicheng, Minister of Finance and Representative of the President of China, Jiang Zeming; Volodymyr Pershyn, State Secretary, Ministry of Economy and for European Integration of Ukraine; Shaukat Aziz, Minister of Finance of Pakistan; Kermechend Raghoebarsing, Minister of Planning and Development Cooperation of Suriname; Joseph Henry Mensah, Senior Minister for Government and Business of Ghana; Joseph Deiss, Minister for Foreign Affairs of Switzerland; Carlos Julio Emanuel, Minister of Economy and Finance of Ecuador; El Hadj Oumar Kouyaté, Minister of State for Planning of Guinea; M. Saifur Rahman, Minister of Finance and Planning of Bangladesh; Mohamed Ould Nany, Minister of Economic Affairs and Development of Mauritania; Per Srig Moller, Minister for Foreign Affairs of Denmark; John Dalli, Minister of Finance of Malta; Bosse Ringholm, Minister of Finance of Sweden; Raymond Lim, Minister of State for Foreign Affairs and Trade and Industry of Singapore; Liz O'Donnell, T.D., Minister for Development Cooperation of Ireland; Abdullah bin Khalid Al-Attiayh, Governor of the Central Bank of Qatar; Julian Hunte, Minister for External Affairs of Saint Lucia; Delia Grybauskaite, Minister of Finance of Lithuania; Mpho Malie, Minister of Finance and Planning of Lesotho; Heidemarie Wieczorek-Zeul, Federal Minister for Economic Cooperation and Development of Germany; Francois Xavier Ngoubeyou, Minister of State for External Relations of the Republic of

Cameroon; Maris Riekstiņš, Secretary of State of the Ministry for Foreign Affairs of Latvia; Andreas Loverdos, Vice-Minister for Foreign Affairs of Greece; Anne Konate, Vice-Minister in charge of Economic Development of Burkina Faso; Franz Morak, State Secretary of Austria; Maskarim Wibisono, Vice-Minister for Foreign Affairs for Foreign Economic Relations of Indonesia; Jelica Minic, Vice-Federal Minister for Foreign Affairs of Yugoslavia; Archbishop Renato Martino, Chairman of the Delegation of the Holy See; Madina Jarbussynova, Chairperson of the Delegation of Kazakhstan; Warnasena Rasaputram, Chairman of the Delegation of Sri Lanka; Mohammad Abdulhassan, Chairman of the Delegation of Kuwait; Nouhad Mahmoud, Chairman of the Delegation of Lebanon; Altai Efendiev, Chairman of the Delegation of Azerbaijan; Fredrick Pitcher, Chairman of the Delegation of Nauru; and Guyla Nemeth, Chairman of the Delegation of Hungary.

8. At the 5th meeting, statements were made by Andranik Margaryan, Prime Minister of Armenia; Ricardo Lagos, President of Chile; Jacques Chirac, President of France; George W. Bush, President of the United States of America; Alfonso Portillo Cabrera, President of Guatemala; Romano Prodi, President of the European Commission; Vasile Tarlev, Prime Minister of the Republic of Moldova; Hubert Ingraham, Prime Minister of the Bahamas; Jin Nyum, Deputy Prime Minister and Minister of Finance and Economy of the Republic of Korea; Marek Belka, Deputy Prime Minister and Minister of Finance of Poland; Jan Kavan, Deputy Prime Minister and Minister for Foreign Affairs of the Czech Republic; Ivan Míkloš, Deputy Prime Minister for Economic Affairs of Slovakia; José Antonio Moreno Ruffinelli, Minister for Foreign Affairs of Paraguay; Anil Kumarsingh Gayan, Minister for Foreign Affairs and Regional Cooperation of Mauritius; Samuel Insanally, Minister for Foreign Affairs of Guyana; Mohamed Mahdi Salih, Minister of Trade of Iraq; Eveline Herfkens, Minister for Development Cooperation of the Netherlands; Ch. Ulaan, Minister of Finance and Economics of Mongolia; Soukanh Mahalath, Minister of Finance of the Lao People's Democratic Republic; Kristiina Ojuland, Minister for Foreign Affairs of Estonia; Kadi Sesay, Minister of Development and Economic Planning of Sierra Leone; Aboudramane Sangaré, Minister of State and Minister for Foreign Affairs of Côte d'Ivoire; Tahmaseb Mazaheri, Minister for Economic Affairs and Finance of the Islamic Republic of Iran; K. D. Knight, M.P., Minister for Foreign Affairs and Foreign Trade of Jamaica; Matt Robson, Minister for Disarmament and Arms Control and Associate Minister for Foreign Affairs and Trade for Official Development Assistance of New Zealand; Ram Sharan Mahat, Minister of Finance of Nepal; Datuk Azmi Khalid, Minister of Rural Development of Malaysia; Chris Gallus, Minister for Development Cooperation of Australia; Mulu Ketsela, Minister of State, Ministry of Finance and Economic Development of Ethiopia; David Aptsiauri, Vice-Minister for Foreign Affairs of Georgia; Sergei Kolotukhin, Vice-Minister of Finance of the Russian Federation; Alfredo Mantica, Vice-Minister for Foreign Affairs of Italy; Amraiya Naidu, Chairman of the Delegation of Fiji; Sheelagh de Osuna, Chairperson of the Delegation of Trinidad and Tobago; Guy Razafinony, Chairman of the Delegation of Madagascar; Tuiloma Neroni Slade, Chairman of the Delegation of

Samoa; Barrie Ireton, Chairman of the Delegation of the United Kingdom of Great Britain and Northern Ireland; Luis Marques Amado, Minister of State for Foreign Affairs and Cooperation of Portugal; Kemal Dervis, Minister of State of Turkey.

9. At the same meeting, the representative of Mesa Directiva del Senado de Mexico (Parliamentarians Forum) made a statement.

10. At the 6th meeting, statements were made by Jean Bertrand Aristide, President of the Republic of Haiti; Kessai Note, President of the Republic of the Marshall Islands; Hama Amadou, Prime Minister of the Republic of the Niger; John Briceño, Deputy Prime Minister of Belize; Ahmed Mohamed Sofan, Minister of Planning and Development of Yemen; Friday Jumbe, Minister of Finance and Economic Planning of Malawi; Christopher Obure, M.P., Minister of Finance of Kenya; Abdurrahman Mohamed Shalghem, Secretary of the General People's Committee for Foreign Liaison and International Cooperation of the Libyan Arab Jamahiriya; Woldal Futur, Minister of Planning and Development of Eritrea; Fayza Aboulnaga, Minister of State for Foreign Affairs of Egypt; Cham Prasidh, Minister of Commerce of Cambodia; Tran Xuan Gia, Minister of Planning and Investment of Viet Nam; Arun Shourie, Minister for Privatization of India; Bruno Amoussou, Senior Minister in charge of the Coordination of Government Action, Planning and Development, Personal Representative of the Head of State of Benin (on behalf of the least developed countries); Khin Maung Thein, Minister for Finance and Revenue of Myanmar; Geir Haarde, Minister of Finance of Iceland; Mohamed Jaleel, Minister of Finance and Treasury of Maldives; Anton Rop, Minister of Finance of Slovenia; Famara Jatta, Secretary of State for Finance and Economic Affairs of the Gambia; Gaston Browne, Minister of Planning of Antigua and Barbuda; Celso Lafer, Minister for External Relations of Brazil; Timothy Harris, Minister for Foreign Affairs of Saint Kitts and Nevis; Shigeru Uetake, Senior Vice-Minister for Foreign Affairs of Japan; Anne Konate, Minister in charge of Economic Development of Burkina Faso; Pehin Dato Ahmad Wally Skinner, Deputy Minister of Finance of Brunei Darussalam; Shaikh Ebrahim Bin Khalifa Al-Khalifa, Under-Secretary of the Ministry of Finance and National Economy of Bahrain; Stefan Sotirov, Director Minister of Finance of Bulgaria; Patrick Kalifungwa, M.P., Deputy Minister of Finance and National Planning of Zambia; Abdulaziz Al-Shamsi, head of the delegation of the United Arab Emirates; Jacques Boisson, head of the delegation of Monaco; Martin Andjaba, head of the delegation of Namibia; Sotirios Zacheos, head of the delegation of Cyprus; Sergei Ling, head of the delegation of Belarus; Mikhail Wehbe, head of the delegation of the Syrian Arab Republic; Jaume Gaytán, head of the delegation of Andorra; Mubarak Hussein Rahmtalla, head of the delegation of the Sudan; Lamuel Stanislaus, head of the delegation of Grenada; Jadranko Prliæ, Vice-Minister for Foreign Trade and Economic Affairs of Bosnia and Herzegovina.

11. At the same meeting, statements were also made by the representatives of the International Chamber of Commerce (Business Forum) and the Civil Society Forum.

B. Consideration of the Draft Monterrey Consensus

12. At the 6th meeting, the summit segment considered sub-item 10 (b), "Consideration of the draft Monterrey Consensus"; for its consideration of the sub-item, it had before it a note by the Secretariat transmitting the draft outcome of the Conference (A/CONF.198/3), which it transmitted to the Conference for adoption.

C. Summit Round Tables

13. In accordance with General Assembly decision 56/445, the summit segment held four round tables on Thursday, 21 March, two in the morning and two in the afternoon. The theme of the summit round tables was "Looking ahead". An account of the summit round tables is set out below.

Summit round table C.1
Looking ahead

14. The Co-Chairmen, Guy Verhofstadt, Prime Minister of Belgium, José María Aznar López, President of Spain, and James Wolfensohn, President of the World Bank, opened the summit round table and made introductory statements.

15. Statements were made by the representatives of Nigeria, the United States of America, the Czech Republic, India, Guyana, Cuba, Australia, Sweden, Kenya, New Zealand, the United Kingdom of Great Britain and Northern Ireland, Nepal, Togo, Maldives and Algeria.

16. Statements were made by the following institutional stakeholder participants: United Nations, International Monetary Fund, World Health Organization, United Nations Development Programme (UNDP) and the OPEC Fund for International Development.

17. Statements were made by the following business sector participants: Institute of Liberty and Democracy, ONDEO Suez, Cisneros Group of Companies, Total Fina Elf, and Calvert Funds.

18. Statements were made by the following civil society participants: Jubilee Debt Program, Country Women Association of Nigeria (COWAN), Asociación Nacional de Economistas y Contadores de Cuba, International Confederation of Free Trade Unions/Africa, Canadian Labour Congress, Center for Development Studies/Arab NGO Network for Development and Mexican Action Network for Free Trade.

19. The Co-Chairmen made concluding remarks. The summary prepared by the Co-Chairmen (A/CONF.198/8/Add.11) read as follows:

"1. Our perception is that in building up to the International Conference on Financing for Development, the international community has created the political space for unprecedented dialogue among all relevant stakeholders on financing for development. Certainly, the dialogue has not yet solved the key concerns of policy makers or policy advocates. However, we have seen actions on some issues that go beyond what only recently were called 'the narrow limits of the possible'. The Monterrey Conference has been a process of convergence, albeit far from complete.

"2. Today, multiple stakeholders have managed to hold a rich discussion of their respective priorities, prescriptions and concerns. Heads of State and other senior policy makers, along with stakeholders from intergovernmental organizations, the private sector and civil society organizations, have been able to focus on priorities for advancing private and official financing for development and on conditions for effectively 'staying engaged'.

"Private resources and investment

"3. For private investment to play its role in development, an enabling environment is essential. Well established property rights are seen as indispensable for productive private investment and fully mobilizing domestic resources. However, the practical institution of effective property rights for all people, especially the poor, could be a long and complex process.

"4. Some speakers noted that investment incentives need to be carefully designed. They may reduce risk for certain undertakings but should not completely insulate private investors from risk. It was suggested that sovereign guarantees of foreign investment be the exception and not the rule. Otherwise, they could lead to irresponsible investor behaviour and budgetary losses. Increasing information flows to investors, such as through an Internet-based clearing house, is a promising avenue of support of private investment.

"5. Several speakers considered that neither private nor official investors will undertake some types of essential investments, such as large infrastructure projects, on their own. They suggested that official development assistance continue to finance infrastructure investments, including co-financing with private investment, such as for water supply projects for the benefit of the poor. Important benefits are seen in the participation of users in the operation and maintenance of infrastructure facilities after they are built. It was also stressed that collaboration between the public and private sectors should be performance-oriented and accompanied by mutual accountability and transparency.

"6. It was further stressed that other types of alliances between the public and private sectors could work successfully. Examples were given of successfully applying advanced information technology to assist developing countries in increasing education in Latin America. Public-private alliances are also helping poor communities to improve health care.

"7. Participants noted a growing tendency of multinational corporations to make their operations in emerging markets more transparent and socially responsible, reflecting the changing demands of institutional shareholders, such as pension funds, as well as awareness by many corporations themselves of the need to change the ways they do business. In addition, government policies in developed countries towards the foreign behaviour of their multinational enterprises have been changing, albeit with a lag, and some speakers sought further progress in that area.

"Public resources and investment

"8. Several speakers noted that the commitment to the millennium development goals have imposed fundamental responsibilities on Governments. Investing in people—including in education, health, basic social infrastructure and social security programmes—is vital for overcoming poverty. It is also a very productive investment for economic growth. However, sustained government stewardship over those investments is required for efforts in those areas to be effective.

"9. Several participants pointed out that the current substantial gap between external financing levels and needs puts at risk the success of the New Partnership for Africa's Development. A number of speakers stressed that adequate international attention is also required to combat poverty in the developing countries of Asia, Latin America and the Pacific.

"10. ODA is recognized as an essential complement to domestic resources in the effort to reach the millennium development goals. ODA, when properly and effectively used and guided primarily by the needs of developing countries, can have a major impact, as illustrated by some speakers, who gave examples of countries moving from recipient to donor status. Both the quantity and quality of ODA are critical. The Monterrey Conference has clearly focused on both, and has already produced some concrete results. Recent donor initiatives to significantly increase ODA levels, while steps in the right direction, are felt to be insufficient and calls were made for additional support. Several speakers also stressed the need to enhance ODA effectiveness through the efforts of donors and recipients and such measures as untying of aid, improved donor coordination and increased country ownership. Several speakers emphasized that capacity-building is essential for long-term sustainability. Some of the expenditure on armaments could be usefully utilized for development purposes.

"11. Debt relief is also seen as holding the potential to release essential resources for poverty eradication and sustainable human development. The enhanced initiative for the heavily indebted poor countries has provided some progress, but there were also calls for further efforts to relieve developing countries of their unsustainable debt burden, including streamlining debt-relief mechanisms and strengthening the relationship between debt relief and development programmes. The United Nations and the Bretton Woods institutions were called upon to explore new approaches, such as collective debt cancellation by groups of countries and revised criteria for debt sustainability. There is also interest in developing the proposals for a new sovereign debt restructuring mechanism.

"12. It was also suggested that innovative sources of financing, such as environmental taxes and taxes on currency transactions, be seriously considered, particularly in support of global public goods. In addition, it was suggested that the 1997 International Monetary Fund agreement for a special equity allocation of special drawing rights be implemented now. Moreover, significant efforts should be made to track down illicitly transferred public funds and repatriate them, within the context of a coordinated effort to combat corruption, including through an international convention on corruption.

"Staying engaged

"13. Many speakers wanted to capitalize on the positive spirit of the Monterrey Conference. Key concepts in the new dynamic between North and South are partnership, solidarity and good governance. Democracy, the rule of law, accountability, transparency and the fight against corruption are considered essential prerequisites for financing for development.

"14. Ways were suggested to nurture and maintain the spirit of the Monterrey Conference for an effective follow-up to the Conference. A common interest in that regard is to turn the concept of mutual accountability into concrete practice at the international as well as at the national level.

"15. According to several speakers, a first step at the international level is to institute frank and timely monitoring of the implementation of commitments and further requirements of the key partners in development, including developing countries, donor Governments and multilateral institutions, along with other stakeholders. Such monitoring, it was suggested, should be comprehensive and take a coherent approach to the financing of development. The monitoring of the millennium development goals could also make an important contribution in that regard.

"16. The efforts of the United Nations to draw all relevant stakeholders together during the preparatory process to the Monterrey Conference has shown the potential results of close collaboration that should be enhanced in the follow-up to the Conference. It was also suggested that the democratization of global governance could be strengthened by making greater use of regional groupings of countries as intermediate forums to develop proposals and build consensus among Governments on the great challenges of tomorrow.

"17. There is a distinct sense that the world must make the effort now, not later, to make the commitments made at Monterrey real in order to strengthen development and finally begin to conquer global poverty. The terrorist attacks of 11 September 2001 have had a profound impact on the world. There is no place to hide. There is no time to lose. We need to instil a sense of urgency in the public on the issue of poverty reduction. In conclusion, it was noted that although all of the stakeholders may not agree on everything there is a strong sense that the overriding objective of poverty reduction is shared by all."

Summit round table C.2
Looking ahead

20. The Co-Chairmen, Thabo Mbeki, President of South Africa, and Horst Köhler, Managing Director of the International Monetary Fund, opened the round table and made introductory statements.

21. Statements were made by the representatives of Zambia, Germany, France, Finland, Denmark, Rwanda, Fiji, Panama, Ireland, Haiti and Morocco.

22. The following representatives of institutional stakeholders made statements: United Nations Conference on Trade and Development, World Bank, World Trade Organization and United Nations.

23. The following representatives of the business sector made statements: International Chamber of Commerce, Ultraquimia Group and FUNDES.

24. The following representatives of civil society made statements: Women's Environment and Development Organization, Women's Eyes on the Multilaterals/ALCADECO, Oxfam International, North-South Institute/Social Watch, International Confederation of Free Trade Unions, African Forum and Network on Debt and Development, and Iniciativa Cartagena/Women's Popular Education Network.

25. The Co-Chairmen made concluding remarks. The summary prepared by the Co-Chairmen (A/CONF.198/8/Add.12) read as follows:

"1. There was broad agreement among speakers that the draft Monterrey Consensus marks an important and substantial step towards achieving the millennium development goals. Looking ahead, the challenge is to maintain the momentum and translate those goals and the draft Monterrey Consensus into concrete actions to provide the resources that will produce meaningful results for the world's poor. Even if the resources were to become available, the required results would not necessarily be forthcoming. All stakeholders must assume their share of the responsibility for translating principles and commitment into action, and should do so without delay. It is necessary to solidify progress in the months ahead so that further concrete implementation measures can be agreed upon at the World Summit for Sustainable Development, to be held in Johannesburg in August 2002.

"2. One of the underlying principles behind the vision of the draft Monterrey Consensus is that of shared responsibilities and mutual commitment. The developing countries are committing themselves to taking full responsibility for their own development by undertaking structural reforms, with sound policies, good governance, gender mainstreaming, respect for human rights and the protection of the environment as indispensable underpinnings. The international community is committing itself to supporting developing countries' efforts through enhanced resource flows and a more development-friendly international environment. Such a 'two pillar' approach also underpins the New Partnership for Africa's Development.

"3. Having developed international consensus on principles, Governments must build within their countries—both developed and developing—the public support necessary to translate their collective vision into action. That would require political leadership—in the developing countries to overcome the many difficulties in undertaking institutional and policy reform, and in the developed countries to develop engagement and solidarity with the developing countries in their efforts to reduce poverty. It would also require a coordinated effort on the part of all stakeholders and all segments of society to support the formulation, implementation and monitoring of development programmes and activities.

"4. In the developed countries, the citizenry at large will have to be convinced that development and the reduction of poverty must be matters of concern in national policy, and that addressing those concerns will require resources and structural change. Some participants pointed to the wide support for development in some developed countries in terms of both commitment of resources and willingness to undertake necessary reforms. However, in most cases, particularly in the area of trade liberalization, considerable additional efforts are required for the population to become as aware of the need for change as they are in developing countries.

"5. There was general appreciation for the increases in official development assistance announced in preceding days, but also concern that total ODA will still fall far below both what is required to ensure that the millennium development goals are met, as well as the longstanding target of devoting 0.7 per cent of the gross national product of developed countries to ODA. Most participants underlined the need to achieve that target; one Minister called for each country to establish a timetable for doing so. It was suggested that such expenditures be regarded as an investment in the future rather than a current cost. The challenges of fully financing the heavily indebted poor countries initiative and the United Nations initiative on AIDS, malaria and tuberculosis were highlighted by some participants. A few were disappointed that the draft Monterrey Consensus does not propose the use of other innovative sources of development finance, such as issues of special drawing rights and various forms of international taxation. A few other participants regretted that the draft Consensus did not address global public goods and indicated that they would be pursuing the matter in other forums.

"6. It was emphasized that ODA is only one component of the developed countries' contribution to development, and that other elements should be not only consistent but complementary and reinforcing. Particular attention was focused on the impediments to growth and poverty reduction created by the trade barriers and subsidies of developed countries. It was pointed out that, if such measures were abolished, developing countries could realize far greater revenue than they would receive in ODA. It was incumbent on developed countries to remove such impediments to growth, particularly for the poorest countries.

"7. External debt was viewed as another major constraint to achieving the millennium development goals in many countries, particularly the least developed countries. Some participants emphasized the need for additional measures to deal with the external debt problem. Reduced debt service obligations are considered to be crucial for being able to allocate additional domestic resources to anti-poverty purposes, such as health and education. Speakers called for a long-term effort to vigorously pursue debt relief for countries facing unsustainable debt burdens, with a few advocating full debt cancellation.

"8. Several participants elaborated on the potential contribution of the private sector to development and poverty eradication. Developing countries need to create conditions to support entrepreneurship, particularly in small and medium-sized enterprises, including farms, and to encourage private investment, including foreign direct investment. Concern was expressed about the low levels of FDI in countries where it is needed most, particularly in Africa. In some instances, countries have made considerable efforts to fulfil the conditions for attracting FDI but have made little impact on flows or the perceptions of risk of investors. A number of participants, however, questioned the value of FDI, saying that it does not always necessarily contribute to development and poverty reduction.

"9. The need to develop adequate institutional capacity was noted and the complexities of achieving that objective were highlighted. One speaker pointed out that the institutions that are currently considered to be prerequisites for development arose in industrialized countries as a result and not as a precondition of development. In addition, the level of economic development itself sets the limits to what can be achieved and replicated at the level of institutional development, and the same arrangements are not necessarily optimal for all countries.

"10. Some participants also addressed the need to re-examine the representation of developing countries in the international financial institutions and the need for better gender balance.

"11. The process leading to the Monterrey Conference was based on a new partnership, involving dialogue and consultations, and enhanced transparency and sharing of information among the various development partners and stakeholders, all of which contributed to trust and consensus building. Participants welcomed the improved cooperation among the various multilateral organizations that had resulted from the financing for development process. It is imperative to stay engaged and further improve global policy coherence. The preparations for the upcoming Summit in Johannesburg will be part of that process, but the dialogue will also have to be sustained and enriched over the longer term. Some participants felt that, in order to enhance policy coherence at the global level, the international community should continue its efforts to improve global governance. Regional consultative mechanisms could contribute to this process.

"12. It was recognized that the draft Monterrey Consensus will require an effective monitoring system to follow up on the commitments by countries, international institutions, the business sector and civil society to ensure that the millennium development goals are achieved by 2015. There was support for the establishment of a formal mechanism for that purpose, and it was suggested that that could be a responsibility of the United Nations, in full and active cooperation with the International Monetary Fund, the World Bank, the World Trade Organization and other stakeholders. It was stressed, however, that such an exercise should not be accusatory but rather a means for all stakeholders to monitor and evaluate their own contributions and exchange views."

Summit round table C.3
Looking ahead

26. The Co-Chairmen, Miguel Rodríguez Echeverría, President of Costa Rica, Alejandro Toledo Manrique, President of Peru, and Mike Moore, Director-General of the World Trade Organization, opened the summit round table and made introductory statements.

27. Statements were made by the representatives of Argentina, Austria, China, Canada, Japan, Saint Lucia, the Republic of Korea, Suriname, Lesotho, Venezuela, Yemen, Turkey, Iraq, Italy and Ghana.

28. Statements were made by the following institutional stakeholder participants: Organisation for Economic Cooperation and Development/Development Assistance Committee, Common Fund for Commodities, World Bank, European Commission and International Monetary Fund.

29. Statements were made by the following business sector participants: Samuels Associates, Zurich Group, Fundación Merced, Infrastructure Leasing and Financial Services, and Bank of the Philippines.

30. Statements were made by the following civil society participants: International Confederation of Free Trade Unions/ORIT, Development Alternatives with Women for a new Era, African Women's Economic Policy Network, International Council for Social Welfare, Rural Reconstruction Nepal, Liberal Society Institute and South African Council of Churches (Ecumenical Team).

31. The Co-Chairmen made concluding remarks. The summary prepared by the Co-Chairmen (A/CONF.198/8/Add.10) read as follows:

"1. After participating in the opening of the debate, Alejandro Toledo Manrique, President of Peru and Co-Chair of the round table, had to leave the session prematurely due to the events that had taken place in his country. Participants expressed their solidarity with the President and people of Peru.

"2. The round table generated a rich exchange on the salient issues in terms of 'looking ahead' beyond the International Conference on Financing for Development. The main thrust of the discussion is summarized below.

"**General considerations**

"3. Participants agreed that the commitments contained in the draft Monterrey Consensus are clear and that their implementation is the responsibility of all. To translate the draft Consensus into action will involve a process of arriving at politically acceptable decisions at the national and international levels. There is a need for strong political will. Some participants noted that there is room for optimism in that regard because there has been a growing common intellectual base for moving forward on the draft Consensus.

"4. Many participants affirmed their commitment to eradicating terrorism, within the bounds of the law, wherever it arises. Global security and the health of the world economy are closely linked since insecurity discourages private national and international investment.

"5. The discussion reiterated the importance of coherence, partnership, ownership and participation in effective implementation of the draft Monterrey Consensus and working towards achieving the millennium development goals. There is a need for co-ordinated efforts to strengthen governance and participation in decision-making at the national and international levels while pursuing coherent development, trade and economic cooperation policies.

"6. Several participants underscored the major potential contribution of trade to de-velopment and poverty reduction in developing countries and the huge cost that subsidies and trade barriers in developed countries have imposed on developing countries.

"7. Participants welcomed the new aid commitments resulting from the Monterrey Conference, while noting that they represent only a first step in efforts to increase aid to achieve the millennium development goals. There was general agreement that im-proving the effectiveness of aid is the responsibility of donor and recipient countries, and involves improved coordination and capacity as well as national ownership of programmes.

"8. It was noted by some participants that the time frame for implementation of the draft Monterrey Consensus is not sufficiently explicit. Some participants felt strongly that there is insufficient consideration of human rights, labour rights, working condi-tions, fair pay and social protection in the draft Monterrey Consensus. Some also emphasized the need for greater consideration of women's participation in deci-sion-making at all levels and the importance of assessing the gender impact of eco-nomic and social policies. It was emphasized that poverty reduction and the provision of health services, education, employment opportunities and justice for all are necessary for strengthening democracy.

"9. Participants underscored the importance of the follow-up to the Monterrey Con-ference as well as more specific modalities of implementation.

"Main issues discussed

"10. Delegates agreed that the Monterrey Conference represents a key turning point in building the momentum for change in development assistance. The recent initia-tives announced by developed countries could be signalling a reversal of the long trend of declining official development assistance. The groundwork has now been laid for that reversal to be sustained over the long term: developing countries are more ex-plicit about their responsibilities and the need for sound policies and good gover-nance, and developed countries needed to prove the sincerity of their commitments, not just in the field of ODA. In large part, that mutual understanding is the result of common learning in the course of finding a new relationship between developed and developing countries throughout the last half century.

"11. Specific challenges of great importance remain ahead for ODA: it should be effec-tive and should also be delivered efficiently. It should prioritize capacity-building, whether for people—such as in the access to technologies—or at the governmental level—e.g., developing countries' capacity to take part in increasingly complex trade negotiations. It should also take into account the need to enhance productivity and di-versification in the agricultural sector.

"12. Delegates noted that an essential aspect of coherence consists in a more effective division of labour and development of partnerships between international organizations, in which the respective comparative advantages would be taken into account in the implementation of development strategies. In that light, the World Trade Organization highlighted its commitment to tap into the expertise of other international organizations, such as the United Nations Industrial Development Organization, the United Nations Conference on Trade and Development and the United Nations Development Programme.

"13. To many delegates, the Monterrey Conference embodies a crucial first stepping stone in the road to a new international financial architecture. In order to be truly instrumental in the process of financing development, the new architecture will have to be more participatory and embody two key principles: prevention and stability. Stable and transparent financial flows and capital markets, at both the domestic and the international levels, are widely seen as a prerequisite for a sustained implementation of development strategies, since episodes of financial turbulence have too often interrupted social progress. Also, the institutionalization of good governance practices by developing countries at the domestic level requires a long-term approach that is incompatible with excessive volatility of financial flows, particularly short-term flows. In that light, the building of institutional capacities for prevention of financial crises at the international level is seen as essential. Accordingly, a mechanism to deal in a fair and transparent way with the problem of external over-indebtedness of developing countries was considered by delegates to be a key aspect of the latter.

"14. Participants considered that the excessive volume of external debt of the developing countries must be tackled in a coherent way. External debt should not constitute a permanent and increasing drain on financial resources that would otherwise be available for development purposes. Some participants called for the cancellation of the external debt of the poorest countries. The heavily indebted poor countries initiative was commended by participants as a first step in advancing towards a solution; however, in order to enhance its coherence with other aspects of the international development strategies, progress still needs to be made by broadening the criteria for eligibility of countries and enhancing the volume of debt relief that it provides. True ownership of debt reduction strategies and their connected poverty eradication programmes by the recipient countries was also considered a key element of success. Special consideration should be given to avoid placing undue burdens on creditor developing countries. The final aim is to ensure that a country's level of external debt can be sustainable in the long run without compromising economic and social objectives.

"15. Many participants drew attention to the enormous costs that are caused by protectionism for developed and developing countries alike, particularly in the area of agricultural products, textiles and other labour intensive goods. The agreements reached at Doha represent a historical opportunity to start building developmental concerns into the trade liberalization agenda, and developed countries now have a golden opportunity to live up to their commitments. But developing countries also have their part to play in the trade agenda, notably in the field of integration, in a manner that is compatible with WTO rules. That would make their markets large enough to achieve the scale economies necessary, and it is also linked with the need to attract foreign direct investment inflows: one of the reasons that FDI has shied away from Africa, for example, is the pervasive high degree of trade protectionism among Africans themselves, which in too many cases represents an obstacle to an efficient scale of production. Another factor that represents a key obstacle to FDI is the lack of certainty and predictability of the legal and institutional framework, underlining the key importance of good governance policies at the domestic level.

"**Proposals**

"16. The following proposals were put forward:

- Establish a strong and effective mechanism for monitoring the implementation of the draft Monterrey Consensus;

- The United Nations should play the lead role in the follow-up to the Monterrey Conference;

- Establish a permanent consultation and discussion forum between developed and developing countries on monetary and financial issues;

- Establish an annual forum for the follow-up to the Monterrey Conference;

- Pursue an arrangement between the United Nations and WTO to bring WTO into the United Nations system to improve coherence;

- Set up an international task force to advance thinking on global public goods and their financing;

- Establish an international humanitarian fund financed from traditional and non-traditional sources, including taxes on speculative capital flows and confiscation of the proceeds of drug trafficking;

- Establish an international economic/financial crisis prevention mechanism comparable to the Secretary-General's proposed early warning mechanism for conflicts in the Security Council."

Summit round table C.4
Looking ahead

32. The Co-Chairmen, Ion Iliescu, President of Romania, and Thaksin Shinavatra, Prime Minister of Thailand, opened the round table and made introductory statements.

33. Statements were made by the representatives of Monaco, Malaysia, Colombia, Singapore, Brazil, Slovakia, Bangladesh, Pakistan, Belize, Switzerland, the Sudan and the Islamic Republic of Iran.

34. The following representatives of institutional stakeholders made statements: Commonwealth Secretariat, Organisation for Economic Cooperation and Development, World Bank, United Nations, and International Federation of Red Cross and Red Crescent Societies.

35. The following representatives of the business sector made statements: GTFI Fund Management, Electrolux, Potomac Associates, Cisneros Group of Companies, Calvert Funds, and African Business Round Table.

36. The following representatives of civil society made statements: World Confederation of Labor, Southern and Eastern African Trade Negotiations, Red Thread/Women's Environment and Development Organization, Instituto del Tercer Mundo/Social Watch, Gender and Economic Reforms in Africa, Development Alternatives with Women for a New Era/Iniciativa Cartagena, and Red Latinoamericano de Mujeres Transformando la Economia.

37. The Co-Chairmen made concluding remarks. The summary prepared by the Co-Chairmen (A/CONF.198/8/Add.9) read as follows:

"1. The round table had a very rich and substantive debate, a further testimony of the commitments of leaders of government and civil society at large to financing for development.

"2. A key message of the debate was strong support for the draft Monterrey Consensus. The International Conference on Financing for Development has managed to involve the international community and a range of partners in the first ever debate on how to finance development. It will give impetus to the implementation of the millennium development goals.

"3. Globalization unites us in one world. Poverty in one place is poverty everywhere. Globalization should be made truly inclusive, and should benefit all nations and partners more equitably to reduce poverty.

"4. The Conference has started forging crucial alliances between developing and developed countries and all partners. Those alliances aim to achieve the goals of halving poverty, reducing the gap between poor and rich countries, building social justice and gearing the international financial, trade and economic systems towards the achievement of the goals set at the Millennium Summit of the United Nations General Assembly.

"5. The new global partnership for development now has to be translated into concrete actions. We must now not only look ahead but move ahead.

"6. That will entail carrying forward the set of reforms and policies agreed to in Monterrey. There is growing consensus that reforms are necessary at both the national and international levels to ensure a stable and conducive environment for development.

"7. At the domestic level, countries have an obligation to work to eradicate poverty. Policies have to reconcile the concern for longer-term development goals and structural reform with the need to respond to the urgent needs of the poor. The benefits of development should target those most in need, particularly people at the grass-roots level, who should be provided with greater access to capital and information technologies. Good governance, sound policies and strengthening of the financial sector are crucial for development and for attracting investments. Gender should be mainstreamed in all policies. It is important to ensure broad participation and transparency in devising policies and initiatives at both the national and international levels.

"8. A major international effort is called for to give countries the tools to move forward in development and poverty eradication. Official development assistance, trade and foreign direct investment are three essential tools for development financing.

"9. The promises of the Doha Ministerial Declaration for a meaningful trade liberalization, supportive of development, must be fulfilled. A major effort is required by developed countries for liberalizing trade in agriculture and reducing subsidies. Some speakers stressed the importance of labour standards and the role of the International Labour Organization in that regard. Others advised against linking trade discussions with those on environmental and labour standards.

"10. Greater coherence and coordination at all levels is essential. Efforts to build a more stable and participatory international system must be pursued. Reform of the international financial architecture is crucial and must be pursued to foster international financial stability and help to build an international financial environment supportive of development. Standards and codes are essential for the conduct of international financial relations, but they also need to take into account the readiness of the domestic institutions in each country.

"11. The commitment expressed by some countries to increase ODA are welcomed. It is essential that all donors renew their commitments to increase ODA and reach agreed targets. Further progress is needed to solve the problems of poor countries' external debt.

"12. International efforts to build the capacity of developing countries are essential. Development cooperation must be conducted in the context of country-owned frameworks.

"13. The international community should support the New Partnership for Africa's Development as the new strategy for reviving development in the continent.

"14. The key role and responsibilities of the business sector in development were underscored. Small and medium-sized enterprises are especially important for creating employment, helping to reduce poverty and supporting growth.

"15. We need to set up some concrete mechanisms for the follow-up to the Monterrey Conference.

"16. The United Nations, the Bretton Woods institutions, the World Trade Organization and other international institutions have an important role in the implementation and follow-up to the Conference. The structures and functions of those institutions, notably the Bretton Woods institutions and WTO, may need to evolve to respond to a rapidly changing environment so as to best carry forward the goals of the Conference.

"17. Developing countries need to be given a greater voice in international financial institutions. Reform in that regard must be pursued. It is hoped that the Monterrey Conference will lead to developing a new, more equitable system of international governance.

"18. The presence of so many heads of state and government as well as leaders of business and civil society in Monterrey augurs well for the future implementation of the Conference and for the upcoming World Summit on Sustainable Development.

"**Proposals**

"19. A number of proposals and ideas were put forward in the course of the discussions of the round table to reinforce or carry forward the commitments of the draft Monterrey Consensus, including the following:

- An action plan and a follow-up mechanism should be developed for implementing the Conference;
- Compacts should be established between recipients and donors to monitor policies;
- An external gender monitoring group could be set up to monitor the integration of gender perspectives in efforts to promote coherence and coordination in the achievement of the millennium development goals;
- An international debt workout system was called for;
- Proposals made by the business sector, such as the creation of a global information clearing house or venture capital funds to help support enterprise creation, should be considered in the follow-up to the Monterrey Conference;
- The United Nations should help to coordinate and disseminate private-sector development initiatives, such as in the education or distant-learning fields;

- A global development corporation could be set up by the United Nations, with private sector participation, to support the creation of small and medium-sized enterprises in developing countries;
- Mechanisms for mobilizing resources to achieve the millennium development goals, such as taxation on speculative capital and on carbon emissions and a new allocation of special drawing rights should be studied and followed up;
- Efforts to combat corruption and illicit drugs should be actively pursued;
- Human rights commitments should guide the implementation of the draft Monterrey Consensus;
- The United Nations, in particular the Economic and Social Council, should be at the centre of the follow-up process, which should be accountable and should empower the international community to oversee globalization."

Chapter VI
Adoption of the Monterrey Consensus

1. On the recommendation of its Preparatory Committee at its fourth session and as endorsed by its high-level officials, ministerial and summit segments, the Conference considered the draft Monterrey Consensus transmitted to it in a note by the Secretariat (A/CONF.198/3).

2. At its 5th plenary meeting, on 22 March 2002, on the recommendation of the President of the Conference, the Conference unanimously adopted the Monterrey Consensus of the International Conference on Financing for Development and recommended it for endorsement by the General Assembly (for the text, see chap. I, resolution 1).

Chapter VII
Report of the Credentials Committee

1. At its 1st plenary meeting, on 18 March 2002, the Conference, in accordance with rule 4 of its rules of procedure, appointed a Credentials Committee with the same composition as that of the Credentials Committee of the General Assembly of the United Nations at its fifty-sixth session, namely, China, Denmark, Jamaica, Lesotho, the Russian Federation, Senegal, Singapore, the United States of America and Uruguay.

2. The Credentials Committee held one meeting, on 20 March 2002.

3. The Committee had before it a memorandum by the Secretary of the Conference dated 20 March 2002 on the credentials of representatives of States and of the European Community to the Conference. A representative of the Office of Legal Affairs of the United Nations Secretariat made a statement relating to the memorandum, in which, inter alia, he updated the memorandum to indicate credentials and communications received subsequent to its preparation.

4. As noted in paragraph 1 of the memorandum and in the statement relating thereto, formal credentials of representatives to the Conference, in the form re-

quired by rule 3 of the rules of procedure of the Conference, had been received as of the time of the meeting of the Credentials Committee from the following 41 States and the European Community: Algeria, Bahamas, Barbados, Belarus, Burkina Faso, Cambodia, China, Colombia, Cook Islands, Cyprus, Czech Republic, Dominican Republic, Eritrea, Finland, Guinea-Bissau, Holy See, Iceland, Iraq, Lao People's Democratic Republic, Libyan Arab Jamahiriya, Malaysia, Monaco, Mongolia, Morocco, Myanmar, Nicaragua, Republic of Korea, Russian Federation, Singapore, South Africa, Spain, Sudan, Suriname, Swaziland, Sweden, Tunisia, Turkey, Ukraine, Uruguay, Yugoslavia and Zimbabwe.

5. As noted in paragraph 2 of the memorandum and in the statement relating thereto, information concerning the appointment of the representatives of States to the Conference had been communicated to the Secretary-General of the United Nations, as of the time of the meeting of the Credentials Committee, by means of a cable or a telefax from the head of State or Government or the Minister for Foreign Affairs, or by means of a letter or note verbale from the mission concerned, by the following 138 States: Afghanistan, Albania, Andorra, Angola, Antigua and Barbuda, Argentina, Armenia, Australia, Austria, Azerbaijan, Bahrain, Bangladesh, Belgium, Belize, Benin, Bhutan, Bolivia, Botswana, Brazil, Brunei Darussalam, Bulgaria, Burundi, Cameroon, Canada, Cape Verde, Central African Republic, Chad, Chile, Comoros, Congo, Costa Rica, Côte d'Ivoire, Croatia, Cuba, Denmark, Djibouti, Ecuador, Egypt, El Salvador, Equatorial Guinea, Estonia, Ethiopia, Fiji, France, Gabon, Gambia, Georgia, Germany, Ghana, Greece, Grenada, Guatemala, Guinea, Guyana, Haiti, Honduras, India, Indonesia, Iran (Islamic Republic of), Ireland, Israel, Italy, Jamaica, Japan, Jordan, Kazakhstan, Kenya, Kuwait, Kyrgyzstan, Latvia, Lebanon, Lesotho, Liechtenstein, Lithuania, Luxembourg, Madagascar, Malawi, Maldives, Mali, Malta, Marshall Islands, Mauritania, Mauritius, Mexico, Micronesia (Federated States of), Mozambique, Namibia, Nauru, Nepal, Netherlands, New Zealand, Niger, Nigeria, Norway, Oman, Pakistan, Palau, Panama, Paraguay, Peru, Philippines, Poland, Portugal, Qatar, Republic of Moldova, Romania, Rwanda, Saint Kitts and Nevis, Saint Lucia, Saint Vincent and the Grenadines, Samoa, Saudi Arabia, Senegal, Seychelles, Sierra Leone, Slovakia, Slovenia, Solomon Islands, Somalia, Sri Lanka, Switzerland, Syrian Arab Republic, Thailand, the former Yugoslav Republic of Macedonia, Togo, Tonga, Trinidad and Tobago, Turkmenistan, Tuvalu, Uganda, United Arab Emirates, United Kingdom of Great Britain and Northern Ireland, United Republic of Tanzania, United States of America, Venezuela, Viet Nam, Yemen and Zambia.

6. As noted in paragraph 3 of the memorandum and in the statement relating thereto, the following two States participating in the Conference had not, as of the time of the meeting of the Credentials Committee, communicated to the Secretary-General any information regarding their representatives to the Conference: Bosnia and Herzegovina, and Hungary.

7. The Committee decided to accept the credentials of the representatives of all States listed in the above-mentioned memorandum and the statement relating thereto and the European Community, on the understanding that formal credentials for the representatives of the States referred to in paragraphs 6 and 7 above

would be communicated to the Secretary-General as soon as possible. The Secretary-General subsequently received the credentials of Bosnia and Herzegovina and Hungary.

8. The Committee adopted the following draft resolution without a vote:

"*The Credentials Committee*,

"*Having examined* the credentials of the representatives to the International Conference on Financing for Development referred to in the memorandum of the Secretary of the Conference dated 20 March 2002,

"*Accepts* the credentials of the representatives of the States and of the European Community referred to in the above-mentioned memorandum."

9. The Committee decided, without a vote, to recommend to the Conference the adoption of a draft resolution approving the report of the Committee.

Action taken by the Conference

10. At its 6th plenary meeting, on 22 March 2002, the Conference considered the report of the Credentials Committee (A/CONF.198/7).

11. The Conference adopted the draft resolution recommended by the Committee in its report (for the text, see chap. I, resolution 3.)

Chapter VIII
Adoption of the Report of the Conference

1. At the 6th plenary meeting, on 22 March 2002, the Rapporteur-General introduced the report of the Conference (A/CONF.198/L.1 and Add.1–3).

2. At the same meeting, the Conference adopted the draft report and authorized the Rapporteur-General to finalize the report, in conformity with the practice of the United Nations, with a view to its submission to the General Assembly at its fifty-seventh session.

Chapter IX
Closure of the Conference

1. At the 6th plenary meeting, on 22 March 2002, the representative of Venezuela, on behalf of the States Members of the United Nations that are members of the Group of 77 and China, introduced a draft resolution expressing the Conference's gratitude to the host country (A/CONF.198/L.2).

2. At the same meeting, the Conference adopted the draft resolution (for the text, see chap. I, resolution 2).

3. Also at the same meeting, the Under-Secretary-General for Economic and Social Affairs made a statement.

4. At the same meeting, the Minister of Foreign Affairs of Mexico made a statement and declared the Conference closed.

Annex I
List of documents

Symbol	Title or description
A/CONF.198/1/Rev.1	Provisional agenda
A/CONF.198/2	Provisional rules of procedure
A/CONF.198/3 and Corr.1	Note by the Secretariat transmitting the draft outcome of the Conference
A/CONF.198/4/Rev.1	Note by the Secretariat on organizational and procedural matters
A/CONF.198/5	Report of the Preparatory Committee for the Conference on its fourth session
A/CONF.198/6	Letter dated 5 March 2002 from the Chargé d'affaires of the Permanent Mission of Mexico to the United Nations and the Permanent Representative of Norway to the United Nations addressed to the Secretary-General
A/CONF.198/7	Report of the Credentials Committee
A/CONF.198/8	Note by the Secretariat on summaries of multi-stakeholder round tables
A/CONF.198/8/Add.1	*Addendum*: Ministerial round table A.2
A/CONF.198/8/Add.2	*Addendum*: Ministerial round table A.3
A/CONF.198/8/Add.3	*Addendum*: Ministerial round table A.4
A/CONF.198/8/Add.4	*Addendum*: Ministerial round table A.1
A/CONF.198/8/Add.5	*Addendum*: Ministerial round table B.4
A/CONF.198/8/Add.6	*Addendum*: Ministerial round table B.1
A/CONF.198/8/Add.7	Ministerial round table B.3
A/CONF.198/8/Add.8	*Addendum*: Ministerial round table B.2
A/CONF.198/8/Add.9	*Addendum*: Summit round table C.4
A/CONF.198/8/Add.10	*Addendum*: Summit round table C.3
A/CONF.198/8/Add.11	*Addendum*: Summit round table C.1
A/CONF.198/8/Add.12	*Addendum*: Summit round table C.2
A/CONF.198/9	Letter dated 22 March 2002 from the Permanent Representative of Venezuela to the United Nations addressed to the Secretary-General
A/CONF.198/10	Letter dated 22 March 2002 from the Permanent Representative of Oman to the United Nations addressed to the Secretary-General
A/CONF.198/L.1 and Add.1–3	Draft report of the Conference
A/CONF.198/L.2	Draft resolution submitted by Venezuela (on behalf of the States Members of the United Nations that are members of the Group of 77 and China), entitled "Expression of thanks to the people and Government of Mexico"
A/CONF.198/INF/1	Information for participants
A/CONF.198/INF/2 (Part I and Part II)	Provisional list of delegations to the Conference

Annex II
Opening Statements

Statement by Vicente Fox Quesada, President of Mexico and President of the International Conference on Financing for Development

Distinguished Heads of State and Government;

Mr. Secretary-General of the United Nations;

Distinguished delegates;

Ladies and Gentlemen:

Welcome to Mexico.

Welcome to a nation that seeks to build a bridge from the problems of the past to the opportunities of the future; welcome to a country that, based on a new vision of itself, is seeing the world through new eyes.

Today is a very special day, of great significance to all Mexicans. Today we are celebrating the anniversary of the birth of Benito Juárez, an admirable man who left an indelible mark on our nation. And it is appropriate to recall him here, at this United Nations meeting, because of his belief that respect for the rights of others is equivalent to peace, which is also one of the principles underlying the coexistence among our peoples.

We know from our own experience the suffering and poverty that accompany the lack of development. But we also know the success and prosperity that can be achieved by a country determined to work and to move forward, if it has the necessary resources.

Hence we have enthusiastically supported this meeting between the developing world and the developed countries.

For decades, the nations of the world have endeavoured to come to grips with the problem of development and poverty through international cooperation. So far, however, the results have been meagre, belated and discouraging. We have completed a century where security was identified with the building of walls and barriers. It is our responsibility to pave the way today for a century of bridges, not barriers; a century of encounters, not wars; of shared responsibilities and achievements, not isolated efforts.

Consider yourselves welcome to an historic opportunity to build these bridges by working together. Let us build together, developing and developed countries alike, the bridges between economic growth and human development, between opening up and local development, between an efficient economy and the well-being of all citizens. Let this be the spirit that guides our meeting. Let this be the spirit of Monterrey.

It is time to change; but to change in order to build. This meeting marks the beginning of a new concept of development. Monterrey has become the spark for a new movement designed to combat marginalization and underdevelopment.

Monterrey gives us an opportunity to devote ourselves freely—the developing countries to the implementation of responsible economic policies, and the developed nations to the advancement of the poorest among us. In this new era of shared progress, all of us must assume our responsibilities.

If the twenty-first century is to be a century of development for all, we must be prepared to undertake bold actions. This involves a challenge to our former attitudes and a quest for new ideas and actions. Let this be the spirit of Monterrey.

Distinguished Heads of State and Government;

Ladies and Gentlemen:

This Conference is not an isolated event; it is part of a global movement in pursuit of development. The Millennium Summit marked the beginning of this new effort to eradicate marginalization. At Doha, emphasis was placed on promoting fairer participation by the developing countries in world trade.

In a few months, the Johannesburg summit meeting will focus on the environmental aspects of sustainable development.

We must all contribute to the new world development agenda; we must all help to shape the future of peace, harmony and universal development to which we all aspire, in a new spirit, the spirit of Monterrey.

We can no longer afford a restricted form of well-being, confined to a few nations; we can no longer run the risk of living in a world of exclusion and injustice. The fight against poverty is a fight for justice and for peace in the world.

Let us forge a new future for our nations. Let us adopt the Monterrey Consensus and, beyond that, let us promote the future development of nations in a spirit of responsibility and solidarity.

We hold in our hands a great opportunity; let us also have the determination to use it. Let us not disappoint those who have placed their trust and their hopes in this meeting. We will all benefit from a more humane, more prosperous and more just community.

Future generations will either recognize us for our courage or reproach us for our lack of vision.

Let us be bold enough to make this century one of bridges and encounters, not of walls and barriers.

The time has come to decide, today, here in Monterrey.

Thank you very much.

Statement by Kofi Annan, Secretary-General of the United Nations

We are here to discuss the fate of people. Not people in abstract, but millions upon millions of individual men and women and children—all of them eager to improve their own lives by making their own choices; and all of them able to do so, if only they are given a little chance. At present, they are denied that chance by multiple hardships, each of which makes it harder to escape from the others: poverty, hunger, disease, oppression, conflict, pollution, depletion of natural resources. Development means enabling people to escape from that vicious cycle. And for development, you need resources. Human resources, natural resources and also, crucially, financial resources.

That is why we are here—and it is good to see so many of you here, particularly those of you from developed countries. You have realized, as more and more of your fellow citizens are realizing, that we live in one world, not two; that no one in this world can feel comfortable or safe while so many are suffering and deprived. It is equally good to see so many leaders here from the developing world itself. They are not here asking for handouts. They know that they themselves have much to do to mobilize domestic resources in their own countries, as well as attract and benefit from international private capital. What they are asking for is the chance to make their own voices heard and ensure that their countries' interests are taken into account when the management of the global economy is being discussed.

What they are also asking for is the chance for their countries to trade their way out of poverty, which means that the markets of the developed world must be fully and genuinely open to their products and the unfair subsidies to competing goods must be removed. The promise of Doha must be fulfilled. What many of them are asking for is relief from an unsustainable burden of debt. And many of them are saying that, in order to do without handouts, their countries first need a helping hand up in the form of significant increase in official development aid.

Eighteen months ago, the political leaders of the entire world agreed, at the Millennium Summit, that we must use the first 15 years of this new century to begin a major onslaught on poverty, illiteracy and disease. And they gave us a clear measure of success or failure: the millennium development goals. Achieving those goals by 2015 would not mean the battle for development had been won. But if we fail to achieve them, we shall know we are losing.

And all serious studies concur that we cannot achieve them without at least an additional $50 billion a year of official aid—roughly double current levels—given in an efficient way, which, for instance, leaves recipient countries free to choose the suppliers and contractors that best meet their needs. The clearest and most immediate test of the Monterrey spirit, which the President referred to, is whether the donor countries will provide that aid. The substantial amounts that have been made and the substantial announcements that have been made in the last few days clearly reflect a new spirit and a revival of commitment to aid.

Some donors may still be sceptical, because they are not convinced that "aid works". To them, I say "look at the record". There is abundant evidence that aid does work. Aid brings spectacular improvements in literacy and spectacular declines in infant mortality when it is channelled to countries with enlightened leaders and efficient institutions. Indeed, enlightened leaders can use aid to build efficient institutions.

Aid is vital, but it is not the whole story. Development is a complex process, in which many different actors have to work together and not against each other. To take just one example, it is no good helping dairy farmers in a country if, at the same time, you are exporting subsidized milk powder to it. That is why it is encouraging to see finance ministers and businessmen here, as well as development ministers. And that is why the process of preparing this Conference—with the United Nations, the World Trade Organization and the Bretton Woods institutions working together as never before—has been so extraordinary. At last, we are all tackling the issues together, in a coherent fashion. That is the true spirit of Monterrey, which we must sustain in the months and years ahead. The Monterrey Consensus is not a weak document, as some have claimed. It will be weak if we fail to implement it. But if we live up to the promises it contains and continue working on it together, it can mark a real turning point in the lives of poor people all over the world. Let's make sure that it does!

Statement by Han Seung-soo, President of the General Assembly of the United Nations

I would like to express my profound gratitude to the Government and people of Mexico for hosting this meeting and especially for the warm hospitality extended to all of us. The contributions that Mexico, under the leadership of President Fox, is making to better global governance are a source of inspiration and encouragement for the entire international community. I have no doubt that President Fox's dynamic leadership and keen insight will do much to facilitate a successful conclusion. I would also like to pay tribute to Dr. Ernesto Zedillo for the most valuable contributions he has made as the Chairman of the High-Level Panel on Financing for Development.

Now, more than ever, the challenge of development is the central task confronting humankind. The rapid pace of globalization and the rise of information technologies have given an added urgency to the development agenda. Countries that fail to grasp these unprecedented opportunities in time risk falling permanently behind in the race for development.

In September 2000, world leaders gathered in New York adopted the United Nations Millennium Declaration, which presents a clear vision for the future and, on that basis, sets forth international development targets to be achieved by 2015. Eighteen months have passed since then, and progress towards achieving those targets has been rather slow. Something must be done to galvanize the global political will for an accelerated drive to meet the Millennium Declaration targets. This Conference is our best hope to provide the needed momentum.

In the wake of 11 September, we were forcibly reminded that development, peace and security are inseparable. Underdevelopment and extreme poverty are breeding grounds for violence and despair, thus undermining peace and security for developed and developing countries alike. When the terrorists struck the United States in September 2001, they also dealt a heavy blow to the fragile economies of scores of developing countries. We must find a way to break the vicious cycle of poverty, despair, and violence. And I am convinced that the United Nations Millennium Declaration points the way forward.

I need hardly emphasize that each country should take primary responsibility for its own economic and social progress. In that regard, I also want to stress that no country can achieve sustainable development without meeting at least three preconditions. First, it must have access to financial resources, domestic or external, or most likely a combination of the two. Second, it needs the human capacity to efficiently absorb those resources and the wherewithal to build greater human capacity as more resources are generated. And third, it requires the "appropriate" intangible infrastructure, such as markets to make productive use of available resources.

The core elements of intangible infrastructure include free enterprise, good governance, sound macroeconomic policies, a strong anti-corruption ethic and the transparently applied rule of law. If those are present in large measure, a healthy market economy will, I believe, almost inevitably develop as a result. The preconditions I have broadly described, when met, will not only promote efficient domestic resource allocation but also attract substantial inflows of external financial resources.

Often, developing countries lack an adequate level of domestic savings to finance rapid development. Also, during certain periods and in certain circumstances, inflows of external private capital may fall far short of what is needed. Under such conditions, Official development assistance plays a crucial role in promoting development. The importance of domestic savings, foreign borrowings, FDI and ODA in financing development should not be understated. However, I believe that the most important potential and very self-reliant source of such financing for the developing countries is export earnings. In the post-Second World War period, virtually every country that has completed the transition from underdevelopment to development has relied primarily on income from exports. That pattern of development can be no less apparent at the start of the twenty-first century, the century of globalization.

But for such a strategy to succeed, the developed countries must make their markets more open and accessible to the developing countries and maintain the high levels of growth needed to absorb ever rising imports. And so it is gratifying to note that the United States economy is now showing signs of recovery. I would strongly urge other developed countries to adopt the kind of growth-stimulating policies that would enable them to boost domestic consumer spending, thus benefiting both local consumers and overseas exporters, many from developing countries.

I am pleased to note that the Monterrey Consensus includes the recognition that the United Nations, particularly the General Assembly and the Economic and Social Council, should play a central role in enhancing the coherence, governance and consistency of the international monetary, financial and trading systems. Based on my own experience of the General Assembly, I firmly believe that the General Assembly and its high-level dialogue constitute the most appropriate forum for monitoring and facilitating implementation of the present Conference's outcome, given its universal membership of 189 States and its character as the chief deliberative and policy-making organ in the United Nations system.

It is my profound hope and sincere expectation that through the Monterrey Consensus the global community will be able to achieve the internationally agreed upon goals and objectives, including those contained in the Millennium Declaration. Taken as a whole, they present to us a vision of mankind's future that should inspire our best efforts on behalf of both the six billion human beings alive today and the generations yet unborn.

In his Nobel lecture delivered in 1990, the great Mexican writer Octavio Paz lamented as such: "The advanced democratic societies have reached an enviable level of prosperity; at the same time they are islands of abundance in the ocean of universal misery". I believe that the global community has both the power and the will to cause that ocean to recede and, in time, to build up continents of prosperity where once there were only islands of abundance. Let us commit ourselves heart and soul to this most ambitious of all reclamation projects.

Statement by James D. Wolfensohn, President of the World Bank Group

Please allow me to thank both our host, President Vicente Fox of Mexico, and Secretary-General Kofi Annan for organizing the Conference.

As most of you know, the World Bank has been very closely involved in the financing for development process. We believe this is a great opportunity to reinforce our collective commitment to expand the opportunities and resources necessary to halve world poverty by 2015 and meet the other millennium development goals.

It is apt that we meet here in Monterrey. For Mexico today exemplifies much of what can be achieved from open markets, capacity-building, the creation of an investment climate, good fiscal and monetary policies, an attack on corruption and a commitment to democracy. Mexicans should be proud of their progress. But Mexico also shows how resilient inequality and exclusion can be. Development is a long road. We must not underestimate the challenge ahead.

This Conference brings together heads of State and Government, foreign, finance, development and trade ministers, civil society, business leaders and international institutions for perhaps the first time in an international meeting. And for perhaps the first time in an international meeting there is greater consensus than ever before about what needs to be done.

We must not squander that opportunity. Nor must we forget why we are here. All people have a right to human dignity. All people have a right to control their own lives. Yet for billions poverty snatches that right away. People have a right to opportunity—in education, trade and building a better future for their children. We must not fail them.

I have spoken before of an imaginary wall that separates the rich world from the poor. For too long belief in that wall, and in those separate and separated worlds, has allowed us to view as normal a world where less than 20 per cent of the population—the rich countries—dominates the world's wealth and resources and consumes 80 per cent of its income.

There is no wall. There are not two worlds there is only one. Here at Monterrey, we must rid ourselves of that wall once and for all. We must recognize the link between progress in development and progress in peace so that generations to come will point to Monterrey and say "something new began at Monterrey: a new global partnership was born at Monterrey". And we will remember, and we will tell our children—we were there and we did not fail. For the opportunity is ours to seize.

What is this new partnership? It is an understanding that leaders of the developing and developed world are united by a global responsibility based on ethics, experience and self interest. It is a recognition that opportunity and empowerment—not charity—can benefit us all. It is an acknowledgement that we will not create long-term peace and stability until we acknowledge that we are a common humanity with a common destiny. Our futures are indivisible.

And we have the makings of just such a new partnership before us. A new generation of leaders is taking responsibility in developing countries. Many of those leaders are tackling corruption, putting in place good governance, giving priority to investing in their people, and establishing an investment climate to attract private capital. They are doing it in the private sector, in civil society, in government and in communities. They are doing it not because they have been told to but because they know it is right. We must support more and more countries in taking that path.

And in rich countries, growing numbers of people are beginning to understand that poverty anywhere is poverty everywhere, that imaginary walls will not protect us. And their leaders are listening. I very much welcome—as should we all—the recent decisions by President Bush and the European Union to boost aid spending. There is no debate that our efforts need to be focused and effective. On this we are all agreed. Too much money has been squandered in the past by decisions determined by politics instead of development. I look forward to the forthcoming discussions on increasing the effectiveness of the development community as a whole.

We have come a long way in just a week. But we must not stop there. This is not just about resources. It is about scaling up—moving from individual projects to programmes, building on and then replicating, for example, microcredit for women or community-driven development, in which the poor are at the centre of the solution not the end of a handout. It is about recognizing that any effort to fight poverty must be comprehensive. We know there is no simple formula that alone will defeat poverty, but we know too that there are conditions that foster successful development: education and health programmes to build the human capacity of the country; good and clean government; an effective legal and justice system; and a well-organized and supervised financial system. It is about recognizing that debt reduction for the most highly indebted poor countries is a crucial element in putting countries back on their feet, and that the funds released by debt relief can and must be used effectively for poverty programmes. And we must push ahead with that programme.

We know that, in countries with good governance and strong policies, aid can make an enormous difference. Yet we know too that corruption, bad policies and weak governance will make financial aid ineffective—even counterproductive.

We must support nations to build capacity so that they can create an investment climate and invest in their people, create jobs, increase productivity and boost investment in health and education. This is not about rich countries telling developing countries what to do; it is about creating a chance for developing countries to put in place policies that will enable their economies to grow. Policies that are home grown and home owned. For the surest foundation for long-term change is not development by fiat but social consensus.

But even if developing countries do all this, we estimate that it will take somewhere between $40 to $60 billion in additional resources a year to meet the millennium development goals. We have made a fine start. But we must not stop here. Let us work together for results and build the pressure for additional funds as we succeed in using effectively the funds now promised.

Nor can we shrink from taking action on trade. We must keep urging rich countries to tear down trade barriers that harm the world's poorest workers, depriving them of markets for their products. There will be powerful lobbies ranged against any such action. But it is the task of leaders to remind electorates that the lowering of trade barriers will not cost the rich countries anything in the aggregate; they gain from freer trade in these areas far in excess of any short-term costs of adjustment. There is little sacrifice required and no excuse for failing to take action that would leave all countries better off.

Rich nations must also take action to cut agricultural subsidies—subsidies that rob poor countries of markets for their products; subsidies that are six times what the rich countries provide in foreign aid to the developing world. Trade and agriculture must be a crucial part of the new global deal.

In one week alone, we have seen new commitments on resources, and we have heard new words on interdependence. In recent months, we have seen the launch of a promising new trade Round. We have had a taste of what is possible. But we do not have much time. In 25 years, 2 billion more people will join our planet—the challenge will be greater, the pressure on resources will be more acute and the chances of success may be slimmer. Let us not have come this far to stop now. Let us build on this momentum as we move forward to Johannesburg. Let us tell our children, "We seized the moment; we did not fail".

Statement by Horst Koehler, Managing Director of the International Monetary Fund

I would like to join in giving thanks to President Fox for hosting this Conference, and I would also salute the leadership of Kofi Annan, who has been a constant source of wise advice and friendship. This Conference should become a milestone in the fight against world poverty. I do think it is possible to achieve the millennium development goals. IMF is deeply committed to playing an active part in that effort. It is an honour to share my vision of the IMF role, and to seek your input and support.

I welcome the intensive and critical debate about globalization. We need to work for a better globalization—one that provides opportunities for all and one in which risks are contained. But let us not confuse ourselves—integration into the global economy is good for growth, and growth is essential for fighting poverty. The world needs more integration, not less. But it also needs stronger international cooperation to guide and shape the process of globalization. We must do our utmost to ensure that people at the local level understand the process, are engaged and have the means to take advantage of its opportunities. We need to build bridges through dialogue, cooperation, and inclusion, to create a sense of global ethics. And the interactions between people and nations must respect human rights, while recognizing personal and social responsibility.

I am encouraged that there is an unprecedented degree of agreement about what is required to overcome world poverty. The Monterrey Consensus defines the right priorities. It makes clear that nothing will work without good governance, respect for the rule of law, and policies and institutions which unlock the creative energies of the people and promote investment, including foreign direct investment. It also recognizes that when poor countries are ready to live up to those responsibilities, the international community should provide faster, stronger and more comprehensive support. I see four priorities for that support:

- Trade is the most important avenue for self-help. It generates income and reduces aid dependency in poor countries, and creates a win-win situation for all. We must work ambitiously to open markets and phase out trade-distorting subsidies in the industrial countries, and to reduce barriers to trade among developing countries. I share Mike Moore's appeal that Doha should be the start of a true "development round".

- Second, the international community should stick to the target of 0.7 per cent of GNP for official development assistance. And it should also stick to the principle of channelling support through budget laws because that is the most transparent, accountable and concrete expression of solidarity. The commitment by EU to raise ODA to an average of 0.39 per cent of GNP by 2006 and the recent proposal by President Bush are significant steps forward. I am confident that even stronger support will be possible if the public understands aid even better as an investment in peace, stability and shared prosperity, and—equally important—if poor countries demonstrate that they are putting aid to good use.

- Debt relief is another essential element in a comprehensive effort to fight poverty. The IMF and World Bank are working hard to make the enhanced HIPC initiative a success. But in all our work on debt relief, we should not forget that the ability to lend and borrow is an important element of financing for development, or that trust that contracts will be honoured is essential for a modern economy and a stable international financial system. I would challenge civil society organizations to devote as much energy and attention to a worldwide campaign to increase aid and trading opportunities for poor countries as they have to the successful effort on debt relief.

- Finally, we have to recognize that slow progress in the reforms needed to fight poverty often reflects lack of institutional capacity rather than lack of political will. Our response should be to pay even more attention to capacity-building in our work with poor countries. That is why IMF recently opened regional technical assistance centres in the Pacific and the Caribbean, and why I have proposed to set up regional centres in Africa in the Fund's core areas of responsibility, as part of our support for the New Partnership for Africa's Development (NEPAD).

IMF itself is in a process of reform, learning from experience and driven by our desire to make globalization work for the benefit of all.

- We are making IMF transparent and advocating transparency for our member countries.

- Knowing that financial crises can undo years of economic and social progress, we are concentrating more than ever on crisis prevention.

- We are actively promoting rules of the game for the global economy, through our work on standards and codes.

- We are helping our members to strengthen their domestic financial sectors, and to combat money-laundering and the financing of terrorism.

- In our work on international capital markets, we are looking equally at risks in emerging markets, and risks coming from the advanced countries.

- We are trying to define more clearly the roles of IMF and private creditors in financial crises. I believe it is essential to be able to resolve unsustainable debt situations in a more orderly, faster and less costly manner. I therefore welcome the ongoing debate on IMF management's proposal for a sovereign debt restructuring mechanism.

- We have become more focused on IMF's core responsibility for macroeconomic stability, not as an end in itself but as a precondition for sustained growth, and because the poor suffer most from high inflation, unsound public finance and volatility.

- We are also taking steps to focus IMF conditionality and make room for true national ownership of reform programmes.

- And we are working in close cooperation with other international institutions, especially the World Bank and the broader United Nations family.

We recently completed a thorough review of the poverty reduction strategy paper process, pioneered two years ago by IMF and World Bank, and the IMF Poverty Reduction and Growth Facility. Our worldwide outreach, including the United Nations and civil society, has confirmed that the process is a promising approach for tackling poverty systematically. Why?

- First, because it is a country-led approach.

- Second, because it is a comprehensive, long-term approach, which integrates economic and social perspectives.

- And third, because it aims at broad consultation and engagement with domestic stakeholders and development partners.

Our reviews showed that there is room for improvement. We want to make sure that every paper and Facility-supported programme is tailored to the circumstances of individual countries. We will be working for an open dialogue with stakeholders about the content of reforms and possible alternatives. We need to pay more attention to the sources of sustainable growth, and to poverty and social impact analysis. And donors must better align their assistance with papers, simplify and harmonize their procedures, and work for more predictable aid flows.

It would be right to adopt the proposed "Monterrey Consensus" as an outcome of the present Conference. Beyond Monterrey, we must transform this consensus into concrete action, with a sense of urgency. And we need to develop a comprehensive and transparent system to monitor progress towards the millennium development goals. As part of that process, we should identify more clearly the respective responsibilities of poor countries and their development partners-donor countries, international institutions, the private sector and civil society. On that basis, we can establish better accountability. I would have no hesitation in subjecting IMF to the scrutiny of such a monitoring system, provided that it did not produce bureaucracy and would apply equally to all the parties involved.

With a concerted effort, I am optimistic that we can achieve the goals we have set. The global economy appears to be in a process of recovery. The United States has demonstrated leadership through timely policy action to minimize the risk of a more severe downturn. And I am confident that developing countries will benefit. The resilience of the global economy and financial system shows that the initiatives to strengthen the international financial architecture are beginning to pay off. The implementation of the Monterrey Consensus should be the next chapter in our efforts to create a better world.

Statement by Mike Moore, Director-General, World Trade Organization

I come to you with a clear and simple message: poverty in all its forms is the greatest single threat to peace, democracy, human rights and the environment. It is a time-bomb against the heart of liberty; but it can be conquered, and we have the tools in our hands to do so, if only we have the courage and focus to make proper use of them.

One of those tools is trade liberalization. It can make a huge contribution to the generation of resources for the financing of development. Study after study has shown the enormous impact of trade liberalization. Let me cite but one example. Everyone, globalizer or opponent, NGO or multinational, left or right on the political spectrum, would agree that health and education form the fundamental basis of any development programme. Recent studies have estimated that the cost of achieving the core millennium development goal of universal primary education could be in the region of US$ 10 billion per year. Yet developing countries would gain more than 15 times that amount annually from further trade liberalization, according to one study by the Tinbergen Institute.

Indeed, the staff of IMF and the World Bank estimate that reaching all seven of the millennium development goals would require an additional US$ 54 billion annually—just one third of the Tinbergen estimate of developing country gains from trade liberalization. And the World Bank's *Global Economic Prospects* report estimates that abolishing all trade barriers could boost global income by $2.8 trillion and lift 320 million people out of poverty by 2015.

Of course, those are only estimates and we can quibble about the figures. But the basic message is clear: if Governments put their minds to it, the new trade round launched at Doha can bring huge benefits. It is the immense magnitude of the benefits of trade liberalization, which makes the work your Governments are doing in implementing the Doha Development Agenda so potentially important as a source of finance for development.

Poor countries need to grow their way out of poverty, and trade can serve as a key engine of that growth. But currently, products of developing countries face many obstacles in entering the markets of rich countries. Rich countries need to do more to reduce trade-distorting subsidies and dismantle their existing barriers on competitive exports from developing countries. So a basic priority of the international trade community must be—as the Doha Development Agenda recognized—the creation of conditions in which developing countries can maximize the gains they are able to reap from trade. This requires action in four key areas:

- *Agriculture*: this is the backbone of almost all developing economies. The poorest part of the population—living in the rural areas—depend for their incomes on the development of a sustainable and productive agricultural sector. Nearly 50 developing economies depend on agriculture for over one third of their export earnings. Nearly 40 of them depended on agriculture for over 50 per cent of their export earnings in 1998–2000. Yet massive agricultural support in the OECD countries undercuts the developing countries and forces even the most efficient producers out of markets where they would otherwise be earning foreign exchange. The number one element of a true development agenda will therefore be to reduce substantially such support (and to eliminate the specific export subsidies—but those are only a very small fraction of total agricultural support payments, which reach a billion dollars a day). In addition, the average OECD-bound tariff rate for agricultural products is four times that on industrial products. The return to developing countries in that one area would be eight times all the debt relief granted developing countries thus far. Complete liberalization in all sectors—agriculture, services and manufactures—would amount to about eight times ODA. Rapid action is also needed on this.

- *Textiles and clothing*: this is the greatest export earner for many developing countries, and negotiations must ensure that the sector is cleanly "integrated", as planned for 1 January 2005. Given the back-loading of that agreement, with the bulk of changes substantively improving export prospects of developing countries being left until the final year, there is every reason to be extremely vigilant.

- *Tariff peaks*: study after study has shown how, despite low average non-agricultural tariffs, the products in which developing countries are competitive nevertheless continue to attract relatively high tariffs (in both developed and developing countries); those must imperatively be beaten down in the negotiations if trade is to provide the needed boost to resources for development.

- *Tariff escalation*: even more insidious an issue than tariff peaks is that of tariff escalation, which tilts the tables against the development of indigenous processing/transformation (and thus movement up the value-added chain). If developing countries are ever to diversify their economies away from their dependence on a few primary products for most of their foreign exchange earnings, cutting them off from the most dynamic part of world merchandise trade, such escalation must be rooted out.

How do we pay for our dreams and the vision of this Conference? The restrictions I've outlined are costly to the countries that maintain them. For example, protection costs the European Union, the United States and Japan between US$ 70 and US$ 110 billion each annually. The net losses to the United States associated with its textile and clothing import restrictions alone amount to over $10 billion annually.

This Conference is about financing development in an era when private foreign direct investment outnumbers ODA fourfold, and is 10 times the World Bank's development lending. Knowing that no country has too much invested, we should encourage an international agreement on investment. It's on the Doha Development Agenda, but many countries don't yet feel they have the ability to cope with the complexities of such negotiations.

Other important development and good governance issues, such as transparency in government procurement, competition policy and trade facilitation, need direction from the highest political levels. Trade facilitation, according to APEC and UNCTAD studies, will generate huge returns. An Inter-American Development Bank study showed how in South America, a truck delivering products to markets across two borders took 200 hours, 100 hours of which were bound up in bureaucratic delays at the border. The need for such public service infrastructure improvement is desperately urgent to protect and promote domestic property rights and justice systems. Domestic red-tape and bad governance is costly and corrosive.

The poor's assets need to be legitimized. In Latin America, 80 per cent of all real estate is held outside the law. The extra-legal sectors in developing countries account for 50–70 per cent of all working people. In the poorest nation in Latin America, the assets of the poor are more than 150 times greater than all foreign investment since their independence in 1804. In one African country, it took 77 bureaucratic procedures at 31 public and private agencies to legally acquire land.

And if the United States were to raise its ODA to the United Nations target of 0.7 per cent, it would take the richest country on the planet 150 years to transfer to the world's poor resources equal to those they already possess. Unlocking and securing those investments, talent and skill is the challenge. That is where we can converge with the ambitions of NEPAD and other bold initiatives.

Developing countries need not wait until the conclusion of the Doha development round. South/South trade in the 1990s grew further than world trade, and now accounts for more than one third of developing country exports, or about $650 billion. The World Bank reports that 70 per cent of the burden on developing countries' manufactured exports result from trade barriers of other developing countries. The quicker those walls come down, the quicker the returns to developing countries.

So the way forward is clear: you should resolve at the present Conference to instruct your trade ministers to ensure that their officials cast aside the petty mercantilist methodology, which has pervaded trade negotiations for so many decades, in favour of a grand bargain that would see the barriers I mentioned above (and others which persist in areas I have not mentioned) dismantled. Then trade can play its important role in generating finance for development—a role which, not incidentally, would also reduce significantly the burden on other facets of the finance for development equation.

I have good news to report from Geneva. Donor Governments have kept their word, giving us increased funding in our core budget for additional technical assistance to ensure developing countries can participate fully in the new Round.

In addition, our pledging conference gave us Swiss francs 30 million, double our target. We must redirect ODA and technical assistance to train negotiators, build efficient customs regimes and plug porous tax systems. We must give as much attention to building up the intellectual infrastructures of skilled public servants as we did to filling in potholes and building roads and dams.

The United Nations agencies have been very supportive of WTO and partnerships with sister organizations have been formed, increasing institutional coherence and making better use of your resources. The round is successfully under way, and everything from negotiating structure and time-tabling of meetings to consensus on chairpeople for all committees is on schedule. The Doha development round can be achieved and implemented on time. Conditionality was improved by developing countries at Doha, the condition for success will be improving capacity to provide for good governance to enable them to participate, negotiate, conclude and implement our agenda. This is being done. We must and we can succeed.

Annex III
Parallel and Associated Activities

A. Non-Governmental Organizations Forum

1. In accordance with General Assembly resolution 54/279 and in pursuit of the objective of encouraging multi-stakeholder participation and ownership of the financing for development process, civil society organizations and leadership were involved from the outset in providing inputs, expertise and proposals to the International Conference on Financing for Development. Altogether, representatives of 557 non-governmental organizations attended the Conference (299 were in consultative status with the Economic and Social Council and 258 were accredited to the Conference).

2. Activities involving NGOs on the occasion of the Conference included the Global NGO Forum: Financing the Right to Sustainable and Equitable Development, held in Monterrey from 14 to 16 March 2002, which was organized by a Mexican steering committee, comprising six NGOs, in collaboration with an international support committee, including seven NGO networks. The Forum was held in a large auditorium in the Parque Fundidora (where the Conference venue was also located), and was attended by 2,600 persons, representing 700 organizations worldwide, including a number of government officials and representatives of the United Nations system, the World Bank and the International Monetary Fund. The Forum included eight thematic tents:

Tent No. 1.   Mobilizing domestic resources, structural adjustment.

Tent No. 2.   Foreign direct investment and trade.

Tent No. 3.   Debt and ODA.

Tent No. 4.   Systemic issues and the new international financial architecture.

Tent No. 5.   Cross-cutting issues: gender, human rights, economic, social and cultural rights, environment, and labour issues (those issues were cross-cutting in all the tents; however, in this tent the issues were discussed in a general way).

Tent No. 6.   Popular tent: a place for popular education.

Tent No. 7.   Living together/co-existence, ecumenical space.

Tent No. 8.   Artisan's space and media centre.

3. The Global Forum outcome was presented at the Conference.

4. NGOs held 13 daily issue-based and geographical-based caucus meetings, and participated in seven press conferences.

5. Fifty-seven side events were held during the Conference in the Conference Centre. The events were held in parallel to official meetings and during lunchtime and evening breaks, and were organized/co-sponsored by United Nations Member States (seven), official stakeholders (24) and other stakeholders (17 by NGOs and nine by business). Several other events were held outside the conference centre due to space limitation.

B. International Business Forum

6. Business representation during the Conference focused on developing practical policy proposals to be discussed with Governments and international organizations. An important venue at which those ideas were disseminated and discussed was the International Business Forum, held on Monday, 18 March 2002. In addition, several follow-up dialogues were organized on subsequent days in parallel to the Conference. Business leaders from all over the world attended both the Forum and follow-up dialogues, and exchanged views with representatives of Governments and international organizations.

7. The Forum and follow-up dialogues were organized by a steering committee of business interlocutors, which was chaired by the International Chamber of Commerce and included the Business Council for the United Nations, the World Economic Forum, Money Matters Institute and Samuels Associates. The steering committee was advised and assisted by the financing for development secretariat.

8. A number of policy proposals were made by business representatives during the Forum and follow-up dialogues. All of those proposals were predicated on public/private initiatives and included the following ideas:

- The launching of a global information clearing house, with government-investor networks, independent expert groups and third-party audits.

- Mechanisms to enhance the financing of infrastructure projects in developing countries, particularly through easing access to debt finance.

- Setting up corporate restructuring funds to strengthen small and medium-sized enterprises in developing countries.

- Incubating local sources of venture capital.

- Linking microcredit with connectivity to redevelop Afghanistan.

- Producing investment guides to help least developed countries to attract new investment.

C. Parliamentarians Forum

9. On 14 March 2002, parliamentarians met in Mexico City at the Parliamentarian Forum on the Conference. The aim was to analyse, from the parliamentarian perspective, the main issues of financing for development, and to define a common position and a statement to be presented at the Conference.

Follow-Up to the International Conference on Financing for Development

UN General Assembly Report 58/494

Report of the Second Committee

Rapporteur: Mr. José Alberto **Briz Gutiérrez** (Guatemala)

I. Introduction

1. At its 2nd plenary meeting, on 19 September 2003, the General Assembly, on the recommendation of the General Committee, decided to include in the agenda of its fifty-eighth session the item entitled:

"Follow-up to the International Conference on Financing for Development:

"(a) Follow-up to the International Conference on Financing for Development;

"(b) High-level dialogue for the implementation of the outcome of the International Conference on Financing for Development"

and to allocate it to the Second Committee.

2. The Second Committee considered the item at its 33rd, 34th, 35th and 40th meetings, on 11, 12 and 17 November and 16 December 2003. An account of the Committee's discussion of the item is contained in the relevant summary records (A/C.2/58/SR.33, 34, 35 and 40). Attention is also drawn to the general debate held by the Committee at its 2nd to 6th meetings, from 6 to 9 October 2003 (see A/C.2/58/SR.2-6).

3. For its consideration of the item, the Committee had before it the following documents:

Item 104—Follow-up to the International Conference on Financing for Development

Report of the Secretary-General on the implementation of and follow-up to commitments and agreements made at the International Conference on Financing for Development (A/58/216)

Letter dated 1 October 2003 from the Permanent Representative of Morocco to the United Nations addressed to the Secretary-General, transmitting the ministerial declaration adopted by the Ministers for Foreign Affairs of the Group of 77 and China at their twenty-seventh annual meeting, held at United Nations Headquarters on 25 September 2003 (A/58/413)

Letter dated 3 October 2003 from the Permanent Representative of the Islamic Republic of Iran to the United Nations addressed to the Secretary-General, transmitting the final communiqué of the annual coordination meeting of Ministers for Foreign Affairs of the Member States of the Organization of the Islamic Conference (A/58/415-S/2003/952)

Letter dated 13 October 2003 from the Permanent Representative of Italy to the United Nations addressed to the Secretary-General, transmitting a document entitled "Italy's Contribution to the Enhanced HIPC Initiative" (A/58/437)

Letter dated 20 October 2003 from the Permanent Representative of Italy to the United Nations addressed to the Secretary-General, transmitting a document entitled "Follow-up to the International Conference on Financing for Development (Monterrey, 2002): the EU Barcelona Commitments" (A/58/529)

Summary by the President of the General Assembly of the High-level Dialogue on Financing for Development (A/58/555 and Corr.1)

Summary by the President of the General Assembly of the High-level Dialogue on Financing for Development: summary of the informal hearings of civil society (A/58/555/Add.1)

Summary by the President of the General Assembly of the High-level Dialogue on Financing for Development: summary of the informal hearings of the business sector (A/58/555/Add.2)

(a) Follow-up to the International Conference on Financing for Development

Summary by the President of the Economic and Social Council of the special high-level meetings of the Council with the Bretton Woods institutions and the World Trade Organization (A/58/77-E/2003/62)

Summary of the hearings and dialogue of the Economic and Social Council with members of civil society (A/58/77/Add.1-E/2003/62/Add.2)

Summary of the hearings and dialogue of the Economic and Social Council with business interlocutors (A/58/77/Add.2-E/2003/62/Add.2)

(b) High-level dialogue for the implementation of the outcome of the International Conference on Financing for Development

Note by the Secretary-General on the organizational and procedural matters of the High-level Dialogue on Financing for Development (A/58/436)

Letter dated 29 October 2003 from the Permanent Representative of Denmark to the United Nations addressed to the Secretary-General transmitting Denmark's first report on Millennium Development Goal 8, entitled "Develop a global partnership for development" (A/58/542)

4. At the 33rd meeting, on 11 November, the Acting Head of the Financing for Development Office of the Department of Economic and Social Affairs made an introductory statement (see A/C.2/58/SR.33).

5. At the same meeting, the Under-Secretary-General and High Representative for the Least Developed Countries, Landlocked Developing Countries and Small Island Developing States made a statement (see A/C.2/58/SR.33).

II. Consideration of Proposals

A. Draft resolutions A/C.2/58/L.39, A/C.2/58/L.40 and A/C.2/58/L.83

Draft resolution A/C.2/58/L.39

6. At the 35th meeting, on 17 November, the representative of Saint Lucia introduced a draft resolution entitled "High-level Dialogue on Financing for Development" (A/C.2/58/L.39), to which he made an oral correction. The draft resolution read as follows:

"*The General Assembly*,

"*Recalling* the International Conference on Financing for Development and its resolutions 56/210 B of 9 July 2002 and 57/250, 57/272 and 57/273 of 20 December 2002, as well as Economic and Social Council resolutions 2002/34 of 26 July 2002 and 2003/47 of 24 July 2003,

"*Taking note* of the report of the Secretary-General on the implementation of and follow-up to commitments and agreements made at the International Conference on Financing for Development,

"*Having considered* the summary presented by the President of the General Assembly of the High-level Dialogue on Financing for Development, held on 29 and 30 October 2003,

"*Determined* to continue to build further on and implement the commitments and agreements contained in the Monterrey Consensus of the International Conference on Financing for Development and to strengthen the engagement of all relevant stakeholders in the financing for development process,

"1. *Decides* to consider innovative ways of mobilizing additional resources for development, and in that regard decides to give consideration at its fifty-ninth session to the study on new and innovative sources of financing being completed by the World Institute for Development Economics Research of the United Nations University, at the request of the Department of Economic and Social Affairs of the Secretariat, as a follow-up to paragraph 44 of the Monterrey Consensus as well as other proposals such as that of establishing an "international finance facility";

"2. *Requests* the United Nations Conference on Trade and Development to address the issue of commodities in a focused and comprehensive manner, on an ongoing basis, as well as at its eleventh session in June 2004, and to propose to the General Assembly, at its fifty-ninth session, an appropriate mechanism to address price fluctuations of commodities and declining terms of trade and their impact on the development of developing countries;

"3. *Requests* the Department of Economic and Social Affairs, in collaboration with the United Nations Commission on International Trade Law, to develop, through an informal process, within the Monterrey modalities, a comprehensive, coherent and fair debt workout mechanism to address debt and its development dimensions for consideration by the General Assembly at its fifty-ninth session;

"4. *Calls* for strengthened action and early decisions before the next High-level Dialogue on enhancing the voice and participation of developing countries in the work and decision-making processes of the intergovernmental bodies of the Bretton Woods institutions;

"5. *Invites* the World Trade Organization to strengthen its relationship with the United Nations in ways similar to those which exist between the United Nations and the Bretton Woods institutions, in particular through its active involvement in the meetings of the General Assembly and the Economic and Social Council devoted to financing for development;

"6. *Decides* to convert the United Nations Ad Hoc Group of Experts on International Cooperation in Tax Matters into an intergovernmental subsidiary body of the Economic and Social Council, and to that end requests the Ad Hoc Group of Experts to develop, at its forthcoming eleventh session in December 2003, a concrete proposal for such a conversion, including the composition and definition of functions to be assigned to the new body, for consideration by the Economic and Social Council at its next substantive session and by the General Assembly during its fifty-eighth session;

"7. *Decides* to hold the next High-level Dialogue on Financing for Development in 2005, at the ministerial level, the time and modalities of which will be set by the General Assembly at its fifty-ninth session, taking into account other major events scheduled for 2005 and the need for necessary and adequate provisions for an enhanced dialogue;

"8. *Decides also* that the annual special high-level meeting of the Economic and Social Council with the Bretton Woods institutions should be focused, with the participation of all relevant ministries and increased intergovernmental involvement from the international and finance and trade institutions, and should address one or two topics selected at its previous annual substantive session from the Monterrey Consensus, based on the overall theme of coherence, coordination and cooperation in the implementation of and follow-up to the commitments and agreements made at the International Conference on Financing for Development, bearing in mind that all aspects of the Monterrey Consensus should be adequately addressed in a periodic manner;

"9. *Decides further* to set up a Committee on Financing for Development, as a supporting intergovernmental mechanism of the Economic and Social Council, to be made up of 15 representatives drawn from Member States of the United Nations, on a rotating and geographically-balanced basis, to meet regularly throughout the year, and as necessary, to: assist the President of the General Assembly in the preparation of high-level dialogues; effectively prepare for the special high-level meetings with the Bretton Woods institutions, including the preliminary interactions indicated in paragraph 69(a) of the Monterrey Consensus; provide guidance to the Secretariat on required matters; and deal, on a continuous basis, as they arise, with other related aspects of the follow-up to the International Conference on Financing for Development;

"10. *Recommends* that the regional commissions, in cooperation with regional development banks and with the support of United Nations funds and programmes, make more use of their regular intergovernmental meetings and hold special meetings, as necessary, to address regional and interregional aspects of the follow-up to the Monterrey Conference and thus help bridge any gaps between national, regional and international dimensions of the implementation of the Monterrey Consensus and serve as inputs to the High-level Dialogue as well as to the spring meeting of the Economic and Social Council;

"11. *Decides* to convene informal, multi-stakeholder study groups to examine and make recommendations to the fifty-ninth session of the General Assembly on issues such as the establishment of an information clearing house for the dissemination of information about and the promotion of developing countries in order to enhance the flow of foreign direct investment to developing countries;

"12. *Requests* the Secretary-General to consolidate and strengthen further the structures of the Secretariat set up to support the financing for development follow-up process in order to allow them to perform effectively all the responsibilities and functions indicated in resolution 57/273 and those arising from the implementation of the present resolution in launching a global information campaign and developing a global monitoring framework for the implementation of the commitments and agreements contained in the Monterrey Consensus;

"13. Decides to include in the provisional agenda of its fifty-ninth session an item entitled 'Follow-up to the International Conference on Financing for Development', and requests the Secretary-General to submit a report on the implementation of the present resolution, to be prepared in consultation and cooperation with the major institutional stakeholders."

Draft resolution A/C.2/58/L.40

7. At the 35th meeting, on 17 November, the representative of the United States of America introduced a draft resolution entitled "Follow-up to the International Conference on Financing for Development" (A/C.2/58/L.40), which read:

"*The General Assembly*,

"*Recalling* its resolution 56/210 B of 9 July 2002, by which it endorsed the Monterrey Consensus of the International Conference on Financing for Development, and its resolution 57/273 of 20 December 2002, in which it requests the Secretary-General to establish appropriate arrangements for sustained follow-up within the United Nations to the agreements and commitments reached at the Conference,

"*Bearing in mind* the internationally agreed development goals, including those contained in the United Nations Millennium Declaration, as well as the agreements made at the World Summit on Sustainable Development,

"*Recognizing* that human beings are at the centre of concerns for sustainable development, and that eradicating poverty, achieving the internationally agreed development goals and realizing a sustainable rise in living standards require economic growth supported by rising productivity in national economies,

"*Reaffirming its commitment* to sound economic policies and solid democratic institutions responsive to the needs of the people as the basis for sustained economic growth, poverty eradication and employment creation,

"*Stressing* the need for appropriate policy and regulatory frameworks at their respective national levels and in a manner consistent with national laws to encourage public and private initiatives, including at the local level, to foster a dynamic and well functioning business sector, while improving income growth and distribution, raising productivity, empowering women and protecting labour rights and the environment,

"*Reiterating* the importance of fighting corruption, and in that regard, welcoming the recent agreement on a United Nations Convention against Corruption,

"*Underlining* the importance of increased investment in basic economic and social infrastructure, social services and social protection, including education, health, nutrition, shelter and social security programmes, which are vital for enabling people, especially people living in poverty, to adapt better to and benefit from changing economic conditions and opportunities,

"*Encouraging* the orderly development of capital markets through sound banking systems and other institutional arrangements aimed at addressing development financing needs, including the insurance sector and debt and equity markets, that encourage and channel savings and foster productive investments,

"*Urging* Governments to strengthen their efforts to achieve a transparent, stable and predictable investment climate, with proper contract enforcement and respect for property rights, embedded in sound macroeconomic policies and institutions that allow businesses, both domestic and international, to operate efficiently and profitably and with maximum development impact,

"*Reaffirming its commitment* to trade liberalization and to ensuring that trade plays its full part in promoting economic growth, employment and development for all,

"*Stressing* the importance of enhancing the role of regional and subregional agreements and free trade areas, consistent with the multilateral trading system, in the construction of a better world trading system,

"*Recognizing* the importance for developing countries as well as countries with economies in transition of considering reducing trade barriers among themselves,

"1. *Welcomes* the High-level Dialogue on Financing for Development, held in New York on 29 and 30 October 2003, and reiterates the call for the full implementation of the commitments made in the Monterrey Consensus of the International Conference on Financing for Development;

"2. *Requests* the Secretary-General to strengthen the Financing for Development Office of the Department of Economic and Social Affairs of the Secretariat, through the redeployment of resources, in order to enhance its activities to promote and mobilize support for the Monterrey Consensus, and to include in those activities, *inter alia*:

"(a) Organizing workshops, working parties and multi-stakeholder consultations with experts from the official and private sectors as well as academia and civil society to examine impediments to the mobilization of resources from all available sources for international development and poverty alleviation;

"(b) Convening a public-private process to examine ways to stimulate private investment and financing by mitigating risk at the margin, involving knowledgeable company and financial institution representatives, academic experts and multilateral development bank officials;

"(c) Convening side events during sessions of the General Assembly and other appropriate United Nations forums to showcase success stories in implementing the commitments made in and achieving the goals of the Monterrey Consensus;

"3. *Requests* the Secretary-General to report to the General Assembly at its fifty-ninth session on the implementation of the present resolution, highlighting positive developments at the national and regional levels as well as success stories in an effort to share good practices;

"4. *Decides* to include in the provisional agenda of its fifty-ninth session an item entitled 'Financing for development'."

8. At the same meeting, statements were made by the representatives of Italy (on behalf of the European Union) and Morocco (on behalf of the States Members of the United Nations that are members of the Group of 77 and China).

9. Also at the same meeting, the representative of Malta made a statement on behalf of the Ad Hoc Open-ended Working Group on Informatics.

Action on draft resolutions A/C.2/58/L.39, A/C.2/58/L.40 and A/C.2/58/L.83

10. At the 40th meeting, on 16 December, the Vice-Chairman of the Committee, Henri S. Raubenheimer (South Africa), introduced a draft resolution entitled "Follow-up to and implementation of the outcome of the International Conference on Financing for Development" (A/C.2/58/L.83), which he submitted on the basis of informal consultations held on draft resolutions A/C.2/58/L.39 and A/C.2/58/L.40.

11. At the same meeting the representatives of Cameroon, Morocco, the Russian Federation and the United States of America made oral corrections to the draft resolution.

12. Also at the same meeting, the Secretary of the Committee read out an oral statement on the programme budget implications of draft resolution A/C.2/58/L.83.

13. At the same meeting, the Committee adopted draft resolution A/C.2/58/L.83 as orally corrected (see para. 15).

14. In the light of the adoption of draft resolution A/C.2/58/L.83, draft resolutions A/C.2/58/L.39 and A/C.2/58/L.40 were withdrawn by their sponsors.

III. Recommendation of the Second Committee

15. The Second Committee recommends to the General Assembly the adoption of the following draft resolution:

Follow-up to and implementation of the outcome of the International Conference on Financing for Development

The General Assembly,

Recalling the International Conference on Financing for Development and its resolutions 56/210 B of 9 July 2002, 57/250 and 57/270 B of 23 June 2003, 57/272 and 57/273 of 20 December 2002, as well as Economic and Social Council resolutions 2002/34 of 26 July 2002 and 2003/47 of 24 July 2003,

Taking note of the report of the Secretary-General on the implementation of and follow-up to commitments and agreements made at the International Conference on Financing for Development,[1] prepared in collaboration with the major institutional stakeholders,

---

1   A/58/216.

Having considered the summary presented by the President of the General Assembly of the High-level Dialogue on Financing for Development, held on 29 and 30 October 2003,[2]

Having considered the summary presented by the President of the Economic and Social Council of the special high-level meeting of the Council with the Bretton Woods institutions and the World Trade Organization,[3]

Determined to continue to implement and build further on the commitments made and agreements reached at the International Conference on Financing for Development, and to strengthen the coordinated and coherent engagement of all relevant stakeholders in the financing for development process,

1. *Welcomes* the first High-level Dialogue on Financing for Development, held in New York on 29 and 30 October 2003;

2. *Reiterates* the call to fully implement and to build further on the commitments made and agreements reached at the International Conference on Financing for Development;

3. *Notes* the progress made in the implementation of these commitments and agreements and that much remains to be done in this context;

4. *Emphasizes* the link between financing for development and the achievement of the internationally agreed development goals, including those contained in the United Nations Millennium Declaration;[4]

5. *Stresses*, in order to complement national development efforts, the importance of full implementation of the commitment to enhance further the coherence and consistency of international monetary, financial and trading systems, and in this context requests the Secretary-General to keep actions under review;

6. *Recognizes* initiatives taken to enhance the voice, participation and representation of developing countries and countries with economies in transition in the work and decision-making processes of the intergovernmental bodies of institutional stakeholders, and invites them to continue and strengthen actions aimed at reaching decisions in this regard;

7. *Invites* the World Trade Organization to strengthen its institutional relationship with the United Nations, in particular through its active involvement in the meetings of the General Assembly and the Economic and Social Council devoted to financing for development, and through its participation in the preparation of the annual report on the implementation of and the follow-up to the commitments made and agreements reached at the International Conference on Financing for Development;

8. *Welcomes* the decisions by the major institutional stakeholders of the International Conference on Financing for Development to include in the agendas of

---

2   A/58/555 and Corr.1.

3   A/58/77-E/2003/62.

4   Resolution 55/2.

their intergovernmental bodies relevant items on the implementation of the Monterrey Consensus of the International Conference on Financing for Development,[5] and invites all major institutional stakeholders to consider doing so, in accordance with paragraph 70 of the Monterrey Consensus, and to make a contribution to the assessment of progress made to the High-level Dialogue on Financing for Development of the General Assembly and to the spring meeting of the Economic and Social Council;

9. *Requests* the United Nations Conference on Trade and Development, in cooperation with other relevant stakeholders, to continue to address in a comprehensive way commodities issues and their impact on financing for development;

10. *Requests* the Economic and Social Council, in its examination of the report of the Ad Hoc Group of Experts on International Cooperation in Tax Matters at its next substantive session to give consideration to the institutional framework for international cooperation in tax matters;

11. *Recalls* paragraph 69 of the Monterrey Consensus and building on the experience of the high-level spring meeting of the Economic and Social Council and the High-level Dialogue of the General Assembly in 2003, in the context of the integrated approach to the follow-up to and implementation of the commitments made and agreements reached at the International Conference on Financing for Development, requests:

(a) The President of the General Assembly, in coordination with the President of the Economic and Social Council, to strengthen the preparations with all major institutional and other stakeholders of matters relevant to the organization of the High-level Dialogue, in consultation with all Member States;

(b) The President of the Economic and Social Council, with support from the Vice-Presidents, to enhance the Council's interactions through regular exchanges with the Bretton Woods institutions, the World Trade Organization and the United Nations Conference on Trade and Development on organizational matters related to the follow-up to the International Conference on Financing for Development, within the context of the preparations of the high-level meeting with these institutions, bearing in mind General Assembly resolution 57/270 B and Economic and Social Council resolution 2003/47, and to report thereon to the Council;

(c) The President of the Economic and Social Council, in consultation with all major institutional stakeholders, to focus the annual special high-level meeting on specific issues, within the holistic integrated approach of the Monterrey Consensus, and to report thereon to the Council;

12. *Invites* the regional commissions, with the support of regional development banks, as appropriate, and in cooperation with United Nations funds and programmes, to use the opportunity of their regular intergovernmental sessions

---

5   *Report of the International Conference on Financing for Development, Monterrey, Mexico, 18-22 March 2002* (United Nations publication, Sales No. E.02.II.A.7), chap. I, resolution 1, annex. [Reprinted in this volume.]

to hold special meetings within existing resources, as necessary, to address the regional and interregional aspects of the follow-up to the Monterrey Conference and thus help to bridge any gaps between the national, regional and international dimensions of the implementation of the Monterrey Consensus and serve as inputs to the High-level Dialogue as well as to the spring meeting of the Economic and Social Council;

13. *Welcomes* the establishment of the Financing for Development Office in the Department of Economic and Social Affairs of the Secretariat, and in this regard reiterates the need to fully implement resolution 57/273 of 20 December 2002 to enable the Office to provide effective support to the intergovernmental process entrusted with the follow-up to the International Conference on Financing for Development, and to facilitate the participation of all stakeholders in accordance with the rules of procedure of the United Nations, in particular the accreditation procedures and modalities of participation utilized at the Conference and in its preparatory process, as well as to continue within its mandate:

(a) To organize workshops and multi-stakeholder consultations, including experts from the official and private sectors, as well as academia and civil society, to examine issues related to the mobilization of resources for financing development and poverty eradication;

(b) To convene activities involving various stakeholders, including the private sector and civil society, as appropriate, to promote best practices and exchange information on the implementation of the commitments made and agreements reached at the International Conference for Financing for Development;

14. *Decides* to consider at its fifty-ninth session possible innovative sources of financing for development, and requests the Secretary-General to submit the result of the analysis on this issue as called for in paragraph 44 of the Monterrey Consensus;

15. *Invites* countries to report, *inter alia*, through existing reporting mechanisms, by 2005 on their efforts to implement the Monterrey Consensus, bearing in mind the need to achieve the internationally agreed development goals, including those contained in the Millennium Declaration;

16. *Decides* to hold the 2005 High-level Dialogue on Financing for Development at ministerial level; the time and modalities of this High-level Dialogue will be set by the General Assembly at its fifty-ninth session, taking into account other major events in the same year and the need for adequate provisions for an enhanced dialogue;

17. *Also decides* to include in the provisional agenda of its fifty-ninth session an item entitled "Follow-up to the implementation of the International Conference on Financing for Development", and requests the Secretary-General to submit an annual analytical assessment of the state of the implementation of the Monterrey Consensus, including the implementation of the present resolution, to be prepared in full collaboration with the major institutional stakeholders.

JOHANNESBURG DECLARATION ON SUSTAINABLE DEVELOPMENT
AND
PLAN OF IMPLEMENTATION
OF THE WORLD SUMMIT ON
SUSTAINABLE DEVELOPMENT
(WSSD)

The Johannesburg Declaration on Sustainable Development

4 September 2002

UN Doc. A/CONF. 199/L-6 Rev.2

From our Origins to the Future

1. We, the representatives of the peoples of the world, assembled at the World Summit on Sustainable Development in Johannesburg, South Africa from 2-4 September 2002, reaffirm our commitment to sustainable development.

2. We commit ourselves to build a humane, equitable and caring global society cognizant of the need for human dignity for all.

3. At the beginning of this Summit, the children of the world spoke to us in a simple yet clear voice that the future belongs to them, and accordingly challenged all of us to ensure that through our actions they will inherit a world free of the indignity and indecency occasioned by poverty, environmental degradation and patterns of unsustainable development.

4. As part of our response to these children, who represent our collective future, all of us, coming from every corner of the world, informed by different life experiences, are united and moved by a deeply-felt sense that we urgently need to create a new and brighter world of hope.

5. Accordingly, we assume a collective responsibility to advance and strengthen the interdependent and mutually reinforcing pillars of sustainable development—economic development, social development and environmental protection—at local, national, regional and global levels.

6. From this Continent, the Cradle of Humanity we declare, through the Plan of Implementation and this Declaration, our responsibility to one another, to the greater community of life and to our children.

7. Recognizing that humankind is at a crossroad, we have united in a common resolve to make a determined effort to respond positively to the need to produce a practical and visible plan that should bring about poverty eradication and human development.

From Stockholm to Rio de Janeiro to Johannesburg

8. Thirty years ago, in Stockholm, we agreed on the urgent need to respond to the problem of environmental deterioration. Ten years ago, at the United Nations Conference on Environment and Development, held in Rio de Janeiro, we agreed that the protection of the environment, and social and economic development are fundamental to sustainable development, based on the Rio Principles. To achieve such development, we adopted the global programme, Agenda 21, and the Rio Declaration, to which we reaffirm our commitment. The Rio Summit was a significant milestone that set a new agenda for sustainable development.

9. Between Rio and Johannesburg the world's nations met in several major conferences under the guidance of the United Nations, including the Monterrey Conference on Finance for Development, as well as the Doha Ministerial Conference. These conferences defined for the world a comprehensive vision for the future of humanity.

10. At the Johannesburg Summit we achieved much in bringing together a rich tapestry of peoples and views in a constructive search for a common path, towards a world that respects and implements the vision of sustainable development. Johannesburg also confirmed that significant progress has been made towards achieving a global consensus and partnership amongst all the people of our planet.

The Challenges We Face

11. We recognize that poverty eradication, changing consumption and production patterns, and protecting and managing the natural resource base for economic and social development are overarching objectives of, and essential requirements for sustainable development.

12. The deep fault line that divides human society between the rich and the poor and the ever-increasing gap between the developed and developing worlds pose a major threat to global prosperity, security and stability.

13. The global environment continues to suffer. Loss of biodiversity continues, fish stocks continue to be depleted, desertification claims more and more fertile land, the adverse effects of climate change are already evident, natural disasters are more frequent and more devastating and developing countries more vulnerable, and air, water and marine pollution continue to rob millions of a decent life.

14. Globalization has added a new dimension to these challenges. The rapid integration of markets, mobility of capital and significant increases in investment flows around the world have opened new challenges and opportunities for the pursuit of sustainable development. But the benefits and costs of globalization

are unevenly distributed, with developing countries facing special difficulties in meeting this challenge.

15. We risk the entrenchment of these global disparities and unless we act in a manner that fundamentally changes their lives, the poor of the world may lose confidence in their representatives and the democratic systems to which we remain committed, seeing their representatives as nothing more than sounding brass or tinkling cymbals.

Our Commitment to Sustainable Development

16. We are determined to ensure that our rich diversity, which is our collective strength, will be used for constructive partnership for change and for the achievement of the common goal of sustainable development.

17. Recognizing the importance of building human solidarity, we urge the promotion of dialogue and cooperation among the world's civilizations and peoples, irrespective of race, disabilities, religion, language, culture and tradition.

18. We welcome the Johannesburg Summit focus on the indivisibility of human dignity and are resolved through decisions on targets, timetables and partnerships to speedily increase access to basic requirements such as clean water, sanitation, adequate shelter, energy, health care, food security and the protection of bio-diversity. At the same time, we will work together to assist one another to have access to financial resources, benefit from the opening of markets, ensure capacity building, use modern technology to bring about development, and make sure that there is technology transfer, human resource development, education and training to banish forever underdevelopment.

19. We reaffirm our pledge to place particular focus on, and give priority attention to, the fight against the worldwide conditions that pose severe threats to the sustainable development of our people. Among these conditions are: chronic hunger; malnutrition; foreign occupation; armed conflicts; illicit drug problems; organized crime; corruption; natural disasters; illicit arms trafficking; trafficking in persons; terrorism; intolerance and incitement to racial, ethnic, religious and other hatreds; xenophobia; and endemic, communicable and chronic diseases, in particular HIV/AIDS, malaria and tuberculosis.

20. We are committed to ensure that women's empowerment and emancipation, and gender equality are integrated in all activities encompassed within Agenda 21, the Millennium Development Goals and the Johannesburg Plan of Implementation.

21. We recognize the reality that global society has the means and is endowed with the resources to address the challenges of poverty eradication and sustainable development confronting all humanity. Together we will take extra steps to ensure that these available resources are used to the benefit of humanity.

22. In this regard, to contribute to the achievement of our development goals and targets, we urge developed countries that have not done so to make concrete efforts towards the internationally agreed levels of Official Development Assistance.

23. We welcome and support the emergence of stronger regional groupings and alliances, such as the New Partnership for Africa's Development (NEPAD), to promote regional cooperation, improved international co-operation and promote sustainable development.

24. We shall continue to pay special attention to the developmental needs of Small Island Developing States and the Least Developed Countries.

25. We reaffirm the vital role of the indigenous peoples in sustainable development.

26. We recognize sustainable development requires a long-term perspective and broad-based participation in policy formulation, decision-making and implementation at all levels. As social partners we will continue to work for stable partnerships with all major groups respecting the independent, important roles of each of these.

27. We agree that in pursuit of their legitimate activities the private sector, both large and small companies, have a duty to contribute to the evolution of equitable and sustainable communities and societies.

28. We also agree to provide assistance to increase income generating employment opportunities, taking into account the International Labour Organization (ILO) Declaration of Fundamental Principles and Rights at Work.

29. We agree that there is a need for private sector corporations to enforce corporate accountability. This should take place within a transparent and stable regulatory environment.

30. We undertake to strengthen and improve governance at all levels, for the effective implementation of Agenda 21, the Millennium Development Goals and the Johannesburg Plan of Implementation.

Multilateralism is the Future

31. To achieve our goals of sustainable development, we need more effective, democratic and accountable international and multilateral institutions.

32. We reaffirm our commitment to the principles and purposes of the UN Charter and international law as well as the strengthening of multi-lateralism. We support the leadership role of the United Nations as the most universal and representative organization in the world, which is best placed to promote sustainable development.

33. We further commit ourselves to monitor progress at regular intervals towards the achievement of our sustainable development goals and objectives.

Making it Happen!

34. We are in agreement that this must be an inclusive process, involving all the major groups and governments that participated in the historic Johannesburg Summit.

35. We commit ourselves to act together, united by a common determination to save our planet, promote human development and achieve universal prosperity and peace.

36. We commit ourselves to the Johannesburg Plan of Implementation and to expedite the achievement of the time-bound, socio-economic and environmental targets contained therein.

37. From the African continent, the Cradle of Humankind, we solemnly pledge to the peoples of the world, and the generations that will surely inherit this earth, that we are determined to ensure that our collective hope for sustainable development is realized.

We express our deepest gratitude to the people and the Government of South Africa for their generous hospitality and excellent arrangements made for the World Summit on Sustainable Development.

Plan of Implementation of the World Summit on Sustainable Development

4 September 2002

UN Doc. A/CONF. 199/L-6 Rev.2

I. Introduction

1. The United Nations Conference on Environment and Development, held in Rio de Janeiro in 1992,[1] provided the fundamental principles and the programme of action for achieving sustainable development. We strongly reaffirm our commitment to the Rio principles,[2] the full implementation of Agenda 21[2] and the Programme for the Further Implementation of Agenda 21.[3] We also commit ourselves to achieving the internationally agreed development goals, including those contained in the United Nations Millennium Declaration[4] and in the outcomes of the major United Nations conferences and international agreements since 1992.

2. The present plan of implementation will further build on the achievements made since the United Nations Conference on Environment and Development and expedite the realization of the remaining goals. To this end, we commit ourselves to undertaking concrete actions and measures at all levels and to enhancing international cooperation, taking into account the Rio principles, including, *inter alia*, the principle of common but differentiated responsibilities as set out in principle 7 of the Rio Declaration on Environment and Development.[5] These efforts will also promote the integration of the three components of sustainable development—economic development, social development and environmental

---

1   *Report of the United Nations Conference on Environment and Development, Rio de Janeiro, 3-14 June 1992* (United Nations publication, Sales No. E.93.I.8 and corrigenda).

2   Ibid., vol. I: *Resolutions Adopted by the Conference*, resolution 1, annexes I and II.

3   General Assembly resolution S-19/2, annex.

4   General Assembly resolution 55/2.

5   Report of the *United Nations Conference on Environment and Development, Rio de Janeiro, 3-14 June 1992* (United Nations publication, Sales No. E.93.I.8 and corrigenda), vol. I: *Resolutions Adopted by the Conference*, resolution 1, annex I.

protection—as interdependent and mutually reinforcing pillars. Poverty eradication, changing unsustainable patterns of production and consumption and protecting and man aging the natural resource base of economic and social development are overarching objectives of, and essential requirements for, sustainable development.

3. We recognize that the implementation of the outcomes of the Summit should benefit all, particularly women, youth, children and vulnerable groups. Furthermore, the implementation should involve all relevant actors through partnerships, especially between Governments of the North and South, on the one hand, and between Governments and major groups, on the other, to achieve the widely shared goals of sustainable development. As reflected in the Monterrey Consensus,[6] such partnerships are key to pursuing sustainable development in a globalizing world.

4. Good governance within each country and at the international level is essential for sustainable development. At the domestic level, sound environmental, social and economic policies, democratic institutions responsive to the needs of the people, the rule of law, anti-corruption measures, gender equality and an enabling environment for investment are the basis for sustainable development. As a result of globalization, external factors have become critical in determining the success or failure of developing countries in their national efforts. The gap between developed and developing countries points to the continued need for a dynamic and enabling international economic environment supportive of international cooperation, particularly in the areas of finance, technology transfer, debt and trade and full and effective participation of developing countries in global decision-making, if the momentum for global progress towards sustainable development is to be maintained and increased.

5. Peace, security, stability and respect for human rights and fundamental freedoms, including the right to development, as well as respect for cultural diversity, are essential for achieving sustainable development and ensuring that sustainable development benefits all.

6. We acknowledge the importance of ethics for sustainable development and, therefore, emphasize the need to consider ethics in the implementation of Agenda 21.

II. Poverty Eradication

7. Eradicating poverty is the greatest global challenge facing the world today and an indispensable requirement for sustainable development, particularly for developing countries. Although each country has the primary responsibility for its own sustainable development and poverty eradication and the role of na-

---

6 *Report of the International Conference on Financing for Development, Monterrey, Mexico, 18-22 March 2002* (United Nations publication, Sales No. E.02.II.A.7), chap. I, resolution 1, annex. [Reprinted in this volume.]

tional policies and development strategies cannot be overemphasized, concert ed and concrete measures are required at all levels to enable developing countries to achieve their sustainable development goals as related to the internationally agreed poverty-related targets and goals, including those contained in Agenda 21, the relevant outcomes of other United Nations conferences and the United Nations Millennium Declaration. This would include actions at all levels to:

(a) Halve, by the year 2015, the proportion of the world's people whose income is less than 1 dollar a day and the proportion of people who suffer from hunger and, by the same date, to halve the proportion of people without access to safe drinking water;

(b) Establish a world solidarity fund to eradicate poverty and to promote social and human development in the developing countries pursuant to modalities to be determined by the General Assembly, while stressing the voluntary nature of the contributions and the need to avoid duplication of existing United Nations funds, and encouraging the role of the private sector an d individual citizens relative to Governments in funding the endeavours;

(c) Develop national programmes for sustainable development and local and community development, where appropriate within country-owned poverty reduction strategies, to promote the empowerment of people living in poverty and their organizations. These programmes should reflect their priorities and enable them to increase access to productive resources, public services and institutions, in particular land, water, employment opportunities, credit, education and health;

(d) Promote women's equal access to and full participation in, on the basis of equality with men, decision-making at all levels, mainstreaming gender perspectives in all policies and strategies, eliminating all forms of violence and discrimination against women and improving the status, health and economic welfare of women and girls through full and equal access to economic opportunity, land, credit, education and health-care services;

(e) Develop policies and ways and means to improve access by indigenous people and their communities to economic activities and increase their employment through, where appropriate, measures such as training, technical assistance and credit facilities. Recognize that traditional and direct dependence on renewable resources and ecosystems, including sustainable harvesting, continues to be essential to the cultural, economic and physical well-being of indigenous people and their communities;

(f) Deliver basic health services for all and reduce environmental health threats, taking into account the special needs of children and the linkages between poverty, health and environment, with provision of financial resources, technical assistance and knowledge transfer to developing countries and countries with economies in transition;

(g) Ensure that children everywhere, boys and girls alike, will be able to complete a full course of primary schooling and will have equal access to all levels of education;

(h) Provide access to agricultural resources for people living in poverty, especially women and indigenous communities, and promote, as appropriate, land tenure arrangements that recognize and protect indigenous and common property resource management systems;

(i) Build basic rural infrastructure, diversify the economy and improve transportation and access to markets, market information and credit for the rural poor to support sustainable agriculture and rural development;

(j) Transfer basic sustainable agricultural techniques and knowledge, including natural resource management, to small and medium-scale farmers, fishers and the rural poor, especially in developing countries, including through multi-stakeholder approaches and public-private partnerships aimed at increasing agriculture production and food security;

(k) Increase food availability and affordability, including through harvest and food technology and management, as well as equitable and efficient distribution systems, by promoting, for example, community-based partnerships linking urban and rural people and enterprises;

(l) Combat desertification and mitigate the effects of drought and floods through measures such as improved use of climate and weather information and forecasts, early warning systems, land and natural resource management, agricultural practices and ecosystem conservation in order to reverse current trends and minimize degradation of land and water resources, including through the provision of adequate and predictable financial resources to implement the United Nations Convention to Combat Desertification in Those Countries Experiencing Serious Drought and/or Desertification, particularly in Africa,[7] as one of the tools for poverty eradication;

(m) Increase access to sanitation to improve human health and reduce infant and child mortality, prioritizing water and sanitation in national sustainable development strategies and poverty reduction strategies where they exist.

8. The provision of clean drinking water and adequate sanitation is necessary to protect human health and the environment. In this respect, we agree to halve, by the year 2015, the proportion of people who are unable to reach or to afford safe drinking water (as outlined in the Millennium Declaration) and the proportion of people who do not have access to basic sanitation, which would include actions at all levels to:

(a) Develop and implement efficient household sanitation systems;

(b) Improve sanitation in public institutions, especially schools;

---

7   United Nations, *Treaty Series*, vol. 1954, No. 33480.

(c) Promote safe hygiene practices;

(d) Promote education an d outreach focused on children, as agents of behavioural change;

(e) Promote affordable and socially and culturally acceptable technologies and practices;

(f) Develop innovative financing and partnership mechanisms;

(g) Integrate sanitation into water resources management strategies.

9. Take joint actions and improve efforts to work together at all levels to improve access to reliable and affordable energy services for sustainable development sufficient to facilitate the achievement of the Millennium development goals, including the goal of halving the proportion of people in poverty by 2015, and as a means to generate other important services that mitigate poverty, bearing in mind that access to energy facilitates the eradication of poverty. This would include actions at all levels to:

(a) Improve access to reliable, affordable, economically viable, socially acceptable and environmentally sound energy services and resources, taking into account national specificities and circumstances, through various means, such as enhanced rural electrification and decentralized energy systems, increased use of renewables, cleaner liquid and gaseous fuels and enhanced energy efficiency, by intensifying regional and international cooperation in support of national efforts, including through capacity-building, financial and technological assistance and innovative financing mechanisms, including at the micro-and meso-levels, recognizing the specific factors for providing access to the poor;

(b) Improve access to modern biomass technologies and fuelwood sources and supplies and commercialize biomass operations, including the use of agricultural residues, in rural areas and where such practices are sustainable;

(c) Promote a sustainable use of biomass and, as appropriate, other renewable energies through improvement of current patterns of use, such as management of resources, more efficient use of fuelwood and new or improved products and technologies;

(d) Support the transition to the cleaner use of liquid and gaseous fossil fuels, where considered more environmentally sound, socially acceptable and cost-effective;

(e) Develop national energy policies and regulatory frameworks that will help to create the necessary economic, social and institutional conditions in the energy sector to improve access to reliable, affordable, economically viable, socially acceptable and environmentally sound energy services for sustainable development and poverty eradication in rural, peri-urban and urban areas;

(f) Enhance international and regional cooperation to improve access to reliable, affordable, economically viable, socially acceptable and environmentally sound energy services, as an integral part of poverty reduction programmes, by facilitating the creation of enabling environments and addressing capacity-building needs, with special attention to rural and isolated areas, as appropriate;

(g) Assist and facilitate on an accelerated basis, with the financial and technical assistance of developed countries, including through public-private partnerships, the access of the poor to reliable, affordable, economically viable, socially acceptable and environmentally sound energy services, taking into account the instrumental role of developing national policies on energy for sustainable development, bearing in mind that in developing countries sharp increases in energy services are required to improve the standards of living of their populations and that energy services have positive impacts on poverty eradication and improve standards of living.

10. Strengthen the contribution of industrial development to poverty eradication and sustainable natural resource management. This would include actions at all levels to:

(a) Provide assistance and mobilize resources to enhance industrial productivity and competitiveness as well as industrial development in developing countries, including the transfer of environmentally sound technologies on preferential terms, as mutually agreed;

(b) Provide assistance to increase income-generating employment opportunities, taking into account the Declaration on Fundamental Principles and Rights at Work of the International Labour Organization; [8]

(c) Promote the development of micro, small and medium-sized enterprises, including by means of training, education and skill enhancement, with a special focus on agro-industry as a provider of livelihoods for rural communities;

(d) Provide financial and technological support, as appropriate, to rural communities of developing countries to enable them to benefit from safe and sustainable livelihood opportunities in small-scale mining ventures;

(e) Provide support to developing countries for the development of safe low-cost technologies that provide or conserve fuel for cooking and water heating;

(f) Provide support for natural resource management for creating sustainable livelihoods for the poor.

---

[8] See *ILO Declaration on Fundamental Principles and Rights at Work and its Follow-up Adopted by the International Labour Conference at its Eighty-sixth Session, Geneva, 16 June 1998* (Geneva, International Labour Office, 1998).

11. By 2020, achieve a significant improvement in the lives of at least 100 million slum dwellers, as proposed in the "Cities without slums" initiative. This would include actions at all levels to:

(a) Improve access to land and property, to adequate shelter and to basic services for the urban and rural poor, with special attention to female heads of household;

(b) Use low-cost and sustainable materials and appropriate technologies for the construction of adequate and secure housing for the poor, with financial and technological assistance to developing countries, taking into account their culture, climate, specific social conditions and vulnerability to natural disasters;

(c) Increase decent employment, credit and income for the urban poor, through appropriate national policies, promoting equal opportunities for women and men;

(d) Remove unnecessary regulatory and other obstacles for microenterprises and the informal sector;

(e) Support local authorities in elaborating slum upgrading programmes within the framework of urban development plans and facilitate access, particularly for the poor, to information on housing legislation.

12. Take immediate and effective measures to eliminate the worst forms of child labour as defined in International Labour Organization Convention No. 182, and elaborate and implement strategies for the elimination of child labour that is contrary to accepted international standards.

13. Promote international cooperation to assist developing countries, upon request, in addressing child labour and its root causes, inter alia, through social and economic policies aimed at poverty conditions, while stressing that labour standards should not be used for protectionist trade purposes.

III. Changing Unsustainable Patterns of Consumption and Production

14. Fundamental changes in the way societies produce and consume are indispensable for achieving global sustainable development. All countries should promote sustainable consumption and production patterns, with the developed countries taking the lead and with all countries benefiting from the process, taking into account the Rio principles, including, inter alia, the principle of common but differentiated responsibilities as set out in principle 7 of the Rio Declaration on Environment and Development. Governments, relevant international organizations, the private sector and all major groups should play an active role in changing unsustainable consumption and production patterns. This would include the actions at all levels set out below.

15. Encourage and promote the development of a 10-year framework of pro-grammes in support of regional and national initiatives to accelerate the shift to-wards sustainable consumption and production to promote social and economic development within the carrying capacity of ecosystems by addressing and, where appropriate, delinking economic growth and environmental degradation through improving efficiency and sustainability in the us e of resources and pro-duction processes and reducing resource degradation, pollution and waste. All countries should take action, with developed countries taking the lead, taking into account the development needs and capabilities of developing countries, through mobilization, from all sources, of financial and technical assistance and capacity-building for developing countries. This would require actions at all levels to:

(a) Identify specific activities, tools, policies, measures and monitoring and assessment mechanisms, including, where appropriate, life-cycle analysis and national indicators for measuring progress, bearing in mind that standards applied by some countries may be inappropriate and of unwarranted eco-nomic and social cost to other countries, in particular developing countries;

(b) Adopt and implement policies and measures aimed at promoting sustain-able patterns of production and consumption, applying, inter alia, the pol-luter-pays principle described in principle 16 of the Rio Declaration o n Environment and Development;

(c) Develop production and consumption policies to improve the products and services provided, while reducing environmental and health impacts, us-ing, where appropriate, science-based approaches, such as life-cycle analysis;

(d) Develop awareness-raising programmes on the importance of sustainable production and consumption patterns, particularly among youth and the rel-evant segments in all countries, especially in developed countries, through, inter alia, education, public and consumer information, advertising and other media, taking into account local, national and regional cultural values;

(e) Develop and adopt, where appropriate, on a voluntary basis, effective, transparent, verifiable, non-misleading and non-discriminatory consumer in-formation tools to provide information relating to sustainable consumption and production, including human health and safety aspects. These tools should not be used as disguised trade barriers;

(f) Increase eco-efficiency, with financial support from all sources, where mu-tually agreed, for capacity-building, technology transfer and exchange of technology with developing countries and countries with economies in tran-sition, in cooperation with relevant international organizations.

16. Increase investment in cleaner production and eco-efficiency in all countries through, inter alia, incentives and support schemes and policies directed at es-

tablishing appropriate regulatory, financial and legal frameworks. This would include actions at all levels to:

(a) Establish and support cleaner production programmes and centres and more efficient production methods by providing, inter alia, incentives and capacity-building to assist enterprises, especially small and medium-sized enterprises, particularly in developing countries, in improving productivity and sustainable development;

(b) Provide incentives for investment in cleaner production and eco-efficiency in all countries, such as state-financed loans, venture capital, technical assistance and training programmes for small and medium-sized companies while avoiding trade-distorting measures inconsistent with the rules of the World Trade Organization;

(c) Collect and disseminate information on cost-effective examples in cleaner production, eco-efficiency and environmental management and promote the exchange of best practices and know-how on environmentally sound technologies between public and private institutions;

(d) Provide training programmes to small and medium-sized enterprises on the use of information and communication technologies.

17. Integrate the issue of production and consumption patterns into sustainable development policies, programmes and strategies, including, where applicable, into poverty reduction strategies.

18. Enhance corporate environmental and social responsibility and accountability. This would include actions at all levels to:

(a) Encourage industry to improve social and environmental performance through voluntary initiatives, including environmental management systems, codes of conduct, certification and public reporting on environmental and social issues, taking into account such initiatives as the International Organization for Standardization standards and Global Reporting Initiative guidelines on sustainability reporting, bearing in mind principle 11 of the Rio Declaration on Environment and Development;

(b) Encourage dialogue between enterprises and the communities in which they operate and other stakeholders;

(c) Encourage financial institutions to incorporate sustainable development considerations into their decision-making processes;

(d) Develop workplace-based partnerships and programmes, including training and education programmes.

19. Encourage relevant authorities at all levels to take sustainable development considerations into account in decision-making, including on national and local

development planning, investment in infrastructure, business development and public procurement. This would include actions at all levels to:

(a) Provide support for the development of sustainable development strategies and programmes, including in decision-making on investment in infrastructure and business development;

(b) Continue to promote the internalization of environmental costs and the use of economic instruments, taking into account the approach that the polluter should, in principle, bear the costs of pollution, with due regard to the public interest and without distorting international trade and investment;

(c) Promote public procurement policies that encourage development and diffusion of environmentally sound goods and services;

(d) Provide capacity-building and training to assist relevant authorities with regard to the implementation of the initiatives listed in the present paragraph;

(e) Use environmental impact assessment procedures.

* * *

20. Call upon Governments as well as relevant regional and international organizations and other relevant stakeholders to implement, taking into account national and regional specificities and circumstances, the recommendations and conclusions adopted by the Commission on Sustainable Development concerning energy for sustainable development at its ninth session, including the issues and options set out below, bearing in mind that in view of the different contributions to global environmental degradation, States have common but differentiated responsibilities. This would include actions at all levels to:

(a) Take further action to mobilize the provision of financial resources, technology transfer, capacity-building and the diffusion of environmentally sound technologies according to the recommendations and conclusions of the Commission on Sustainable Development, as contained in section A, paragraph 3, and section D, paragraph 30, of its decision 9/1[9] on energy for sustainable development;

(b) Integrate energy considerations, including energy efficiency, affordability and accessibility, into socio-economic programmes, especially into policies of major energy-consuming sectors, and into the planning, operation and maintenance of long-lived energy consuming infrastructures, such as the public sector, transport, industry, agriculture, urban land use, tourism and construction sectors;

(c) Develop and disseminate alternative energy technologies with the aim of giving a greater share of the energy mix to renewable energies, improving

---

9   *Official Records of the Economic and Social Council, 2001, Supplement No. 9* (E/2001/29), chap. I.B.

energy efficiency and greater reliance on advanced energy technologies, including cleaner fossil fuel technologies;

(d) Combine, as appropriate, the increased use of renewable energy resources, more efficient use of energy, greater reliance on advanced energy technologies, including advanced and cleaner fossil fuel technologies, and the sustainable use of traditional energy resources, which could meet the growing need for energy services in the longer term to achieve sustainable development;

(e) Diversify energy supply by developing advanced, cleaner, more efficient, affordable and cost-effective energy technologies, including fossil fuel technologies and renewable energy technologies, hydro included, and their transfer to developing countries on concessional terms as mutually agreed. With a sense of urgency, substantially increase the global share of renewable energy sources with the objective of increasing its contribution to total energy supply, recognizing the role of national and voluntary regional targets as well as initiatives, where they exist, and ensuring that energy policies are supportive to developing countries' efforts to eradicate poverty, and regularly evaluate available data to review progress to this end;

(f) Support efforts, including through provision of financial and technical assistance to developing countries, with the involvement of the private sector, to reduce flaring and venting of gas associated with crude oil production;

(g) Develop and utilize indigenous energy sources and infrastructures for various local uses and promote rural community participation, including local Agenda 21 groups, with the support of the international community, in developing and utilizing renewable energy technologies to meet their daily energy needs to find simple and local solutions;

(h) Establish domestic programmes for energy efficiency, including, as appropriate, by accelerating the deployment of energy efficiency technologies, with the necessary support of the international community;

(i) Accelerate the development, dissemination and deployment of affordable and cleaner energy efficiency and energy conservation technologies, as well as the transfer of such technologies, in particular to developing countries, on favourable terms, including on concessional and preferential terms, as mutually agreed;

(j) Recommend that international financial institutions and other agencies' policies support developing countries, as well as countries with economies in transition, in their own efforts to establish policy and regulatory frameworks which create a level playing field between the following: renewable energy, energy efficiency, advanced energy technologies, including advanced and cleaner fossil fuel technologies, and centralized, distributed and decentralized energy systems;

(k) Promote increased research and development in the field of various energy technologies, including renewable energy, energy efficiency and advanced energy technologies, including advanced and cleaner fossil fuel technologies, both nationally and through international collaboration; strengthen national and regional research and development institutions/centres on reliable, affordable, economically viable, socially acceptable and environmentally sound energy for sustainable development;

(l) Promote networking between centres of excellence on energy for sustainable development, including regional networks, by linking competent centres on energy technologies for sustainable development that could support and promote efforts at capacity-building and technology transfer activities, particularly of developing countries, as well as serve as information clearing houses;

(m) Promote education to provide information for both men and women about available energy sources and technologies;

(n) Utilize financial instruments and mechanisms, in particular the Global Environment Facility, within its mandate, to provide financial resources to developing countries, in particular least developed countries and small island developing States, to meet their capacity needs for training, technical know-how and strengthening national institutions in reliable, affordable, economically viable, socially acceptable and environmentally sound energy, including promoting energy efficiency and conservation, renewable energy and advanced energy technologies, including advanced and cleaner fossil fuel technologies;

(o) Support efforts to improve the functioning, transparency and information about energy markets with respect to both supply and demand, with the aim of achieving greater stability and predictability, and to ensure consumer access to reliable, affordable, economically viable, socially acceptable and environmentally sound energy services;

(p) Policies to reduce market distortions would promote energy systems compatible with sustainable development through the use of improved market signals and by removing market distortions, including restructuring taxation and phasing out harmful subsidies, where they exist, to reflect their environmental impacts, with such policies taking fully into account the specific needs and conditions of developing countries, with the aim of minimizing the possible adverse impacts on their development;

(q) Take action, where appropriate, to phase out subsidies in this area that inhibit sustainable development, taking fully into account the specific conditions and different levels of development of individual countries and considering their adverse effect, particularly on developing countries;

(r) Governments are encouraged to improve the functioning of national energy markets in such a way that they support sustainable development, overcome market barriers and improve accessibility, taking fully into account that such policies should be decided by each country, and that its own characteristics and capabilities and level of development should be considered, especially as reflected in national sustainable development strategies, where they exist;

(s) Strengthen national and regional energy institutions or arrangements for enhancing regional and international cooperation on energy for sustainable development, in particular to assist developing countries in their domestic efforts to provide reliable, affordable, economically viable, socially acceptable and environmentally sound energy services to all sections of their populations;

(t) Countries are urged to develop and implement actions within the framework of the ninth session of the Commission on Sustainable Development, including through public-private partnerships, taking into account the different circumstances of countries, based on lessons learned by Governments, international institutions and stakeholders, including business and industry, in the field of access to energy, including renewable energy and energy-efficiency and advanced energy technologies, including advanced and cleaner fossil fuel technologies;

(u) Promote cooperation between international and regional institutions and bodies dealing with different aspects of energy for sustainable development within their existing mandate, bearing in mind paragraph 46 (h) of the Programme of Action for the Further Implementation of Agenda 21, strengthening, as appropriate, regional and national activities for the promotion of education and capacity-building regarding energy for sustainable development;

(v) Strengthen and facilitate, as appropriate, regional cooperation arrangements for promoting cross-border energy trade, including the interconnection of electricity grids and oil and natural gas pipelines;

(w) Strengthen and, where appropriate, facilitate dialogue forums among regional, national and international producers and consumers of energy.

* * *

21. Promote an integrated approach to policy-making at the national, regional and local levels for transport services and systems to promote sustainable development, including policies and planning for land use, infrastructure, public transport systems and goods delivery networks, with a view to providing safe, affordable and efficient transportation, increasing energy efficiency, reducing pollution, congestion and adverse health effects and limiting urban sprawl, taking into account national priorities and circumstances. This would include actions at all levels to:

(a) Implement transport strategies for sustainable development, reflecting specific regional, national and local conditions, to improve the affordability, efficiency and convenience of transportation as well as urban air quality and health and reduce greenhouse gas emissions, including through the development of better vehicle technologies that are more environmentally sound, affordable and socially acceptable;

(b) Promote investment and partnerships for the development of sustainable, energy efficient multi-modal transportation systems, including public mass transportation systems and better transportation systems in rural areas, with technical and financial assistance for developing countries and countries with economies in transition.

* * *

22. Prevent and minimize waste and maximize reuse, recycling and use of environmentally friendly alternative materials, with the participation of government authorities and all stakeholders, in order to minimize adverse effects on the environment and improve resource efficiency, with financial, technical and other assistance for developing countries. This would include actions at all levels to:

(a) Develop waste management systems, with the highest priority placed on waste prevention and minimization, reuse and recycling, and environmentally sound disposal facilities, including technology to recapture the energy contained in waste, and encourage small-scale waste-recycling initiatives that support urban and rural waste management and provide income-generating opportunities, with international support for developing countries;

(b) Promote waste prevention and minimization by encouraging production of reusable consumer goods and biodegradable products and developing the infrastructure required.

* * *

23. Renew the commitment, as advanced in Agenda 21, to sound management of chemicals throughout their life cycle and of hazardous wastes for sustainable development as well as for the protection of human health and the environment, inter alia, aiming to achieve, by 2020, that chemicals are used and produced in ways that lead to the minimization of significant adverse effects on human health and the environment, using transparent science-based risk assessment procedures and science-based risk management procedures, taking into account the precautionary approach, as set out in principle 15 of the Rio Declaration on Environment and Development, and support developing countries in strengthening their capacity for the sound management of chemicals and hazardous wastes by providing technical and financial assistance. This would include actions at all levels to:

(a) Promote the ratification and implementation of relevant international instruments on chemicals and hazardous waste, including the Rotterdam Convention on Prior Informed Consent Procedures for Certain Hazardous Chemicals and Pesticides in International Trade[10] so that it can enter into force by 2003 and the Stockholm Convention on Persistent Organic

---

10   UNEP/FAO/PIC/CONF.5, annex III.

Pollutants[11] so that it can enter into force by 2004, and encourage and improve coordination as well as supporting developing countries in their implementation;

(b) Further develop a strategic approach to international chemicals management based on the Bahia Declaration and Priorities for Action beyond 2000 of the Intergovernmental Forum on Chemical Safety[12] by 2005, and urge that the United Nations Environment Programme, the Intergovernmental Forum, other international organizations dealing with chemical management and other relevant international organizations and actors closely cooperate in this regard, as appropriate;

(c) Encourage countries to implement the new globally harmonized system for the classification and labelling of chemicals as soon as possible with a view to having the system fully operational by 2008;

(d) Encourage partnerships to promote activities aimed at enhancing environmentally sound management of chemicals and hazardous wastes, implementing multilateral environmental agreements, raising awareness of issues relating to chemicals and hazardous waste and encouraging the collection and use of additional scientific data;

(e) Promote efforts to prevent international illegal trafficking of hazardous chemicals and hazardous wastes and to prevent damage resulting from the transboundary movement and disposal of hazardous wastes in a manner consistent with obligations under relevant international instruments, such as the Basel Convention on the Control of Transboundary Movements of Hazardous Wastes and Their Disposal; [13]

(f) Encourage development of coherent and integrated information on chemicals, such as through national pollutant release and transfer registers;

(g) Promote reduction of the risks posed by heavy metals that are harmful to human health and the environment, including through a review of relevant studies, such as the United Nations Environment Programme global assessment of mercury and its compounds.

IV. Protecting and Managing the Natural Resource Base of Economic and Social Development

24. Human activities are having an increasing impact on the integrity of ecosystems that provide essential resources and services for human well-being and economic activities. Managing the natural resources base in a sustainable and integrated manner is essential for sustainable development. In this regard, to re-

---

11   www.chem.unep.ch/sc.

12   Intergovernmental Forum on Chemical Safety, third session, Forum III final report (IFCS/Forum III/23w), annex 6.

13   United Nations *Treaty Series*, vol. 1673, No. 28911.

verse the current trend in natural resource degradation as soon as possible, it is necessary to implement strategies which should include targets adopted at the national and, where appropriate, regional levels to protect ecosystems and to achieve integrated management of land, water and living resources, while strengthening regional, national and local capacities. This would include actions at all levels as set out below.

25. Launch a programme of actions, with financial and technical assistance, to achieve the Millennium development goal on safe drinking water. In this respect, we agree to halve, by the year 2015, the proportion of people who are unable to reach or to afford safe drinking water, as outlined in the Millennium Declaration, and the proportion of people without access to basic sanitation, which would include actions at all levels to:

(a) Mobilize international and domestic financial resources at all levels, transfer technology, promote best practice and support capacity-building for water and sanitation infrastructure and services development, ensuring that such infrastructure and services meet the needs of the poor and are gender-sensitive;

(b) Facilitate access to public information and participation, including by women, at all levels in support of policy and decision-making related to water resources management and project implementation;

(c) Promote priority action by Governments, with the support of all stakeholders, in water management and capacity-building at the national level and, where appropriate, at the regional level, and promote and provide new and additional financial resources and innovative technologies to implement chapter 18 of Agenda 21;

(d) Intensify water pollution prevention to reduce health hazards and protect ecosystems by introducing technologies for affordable sanitation and industrial and domestic wastewater treatment, by mitigating the effects of groundwater contamination and by establishing, at the national level, monitoring systems and effective legal frameworks;

(e) Adopt prevent ion and protection measures to promote sustainable water use and to address water shortages.

26. Develop integrated water resources management and water efficiency plans by 2005, with support to developing countries, through actions at all levels to:

(a) Develop and implement national/regional strategies, plans and programmes with regard to integrated river basin, watershed and groundwater management and introduce measures to improve the efficiency of water infrastructure to reduce losses and increase recycling of water;

(b) Employ the full range of policy instruments, including regulation, monitoring, voluntary measures, market and information-based tools, land-use management and cost recovery of water services, without cost recovery objectives becoming a barrier to access to safe water by poor people, and adopt an integrated water basin approach;

(c) Improve the efficient use of water resources and promote their allocation among competing uses in a way that gives priority to the satisfaction of basic human needs and balances the requirement of preserving or restoring eco-systems and their functions, in particular in fragile environments, with human domestic, industrial and agriculture needs, including safeguarding drinking water quality;

(d) Develop programmes for mitigating the effects of extreme water-related events;

(e) Support the diffusion of technology and capacity-building for non-conventional water resources and conservation technologies, to developing countries and regions facing water scarcity conditions or subject to drought and desertification, through technical and financial support and capacity-building;

(f) Support, where appropriate, efforts and programmes for energy-efficient, sustainable and cost-effective desalination of seawater, water recycling and water harvesting from coastal fogs in developing countries, through such measures as technological, technical and financial assistance and other modalities;

(g) Facilitate the establishment of public-private partnerships and other forms of partnership that give priority to the needs of the poor, within stable and transparent national regulatory frameworks provided by Governments, while respecting local conditions, involving all concerned stakeholders, and monitoring the performance and improving accountability of public institutions and private companies.

27. Support developing countries and countries with economies in transition in their efforts to monitor and assess the quantity and quality of water resources, including through the establishment and/or further development of national monitoring networks and water resources databases and the development of relevant national indicators.

28. Improve water resource management and scientific understanding of the water cycle through cooperation in joint observation and research, and for this purpose encourage and promote knowledge-sharing and provide capacity-build-ing and the transfer of technology, as mutually agreed, including remote-sensing and satellite technologies, particularly to developing countries and countries with economies in transition.

29. Promote effective coordination among the various international and inter-governmental bodies and processes working on water-related issues, both within the United Nations system and between the United Nations and interna-tional financial institutions, drawing on the contributions of other international institutions and civil society to inform intergovernmental decision-making;

closer coordination should also be promoted to elaborate and support proposals and undertake activities related to the International Year of Freshwater, 2003
and beyond.

* * *

30. Oceans, seas, islands and coastal areas form an integrated and essential
component of the Earth's ecosystem and are critical for global food security and
for sustaining economic prosperity and the well-being of many national economies, particularly in developing countries. Ensuring the sustainable development of the oceans requires effective coordination and cooperation, including
at the global and regional levels, between relevant bodies, and actions at all
levels to:

(a) Invite States to ratify or accede to and implement the United Nations Convention on the Law of the Sea of 1982,[14] which provides the overall legal
framework for ocean activities;

(b) Promote the implementation of chapter 17 of Agenda 21, which provides
the programme of action for achieving the sustainable development of
oceans, coastal areas and seas through its programme areas of integrated
management and sustainable development of coastal areas, including exclusive economic zones; marine environmental protection; sustainable use and
conservation of marine living resources; addressing critical uncertainties for
the management of the marine environment and climate change; strengthening international, including regional, cooperation and coordination; and
sustainable development of small islands;

(c) Establish an effective, transparent and regular inter-agency coordination
mechanism on ocean and coastal issues within the United Nations system;

(d) Encourage the application by 2010 of the ecosystem approach, noting the
Reykjavik Declaration on Responsible Fisheries in the Marine Ecosystem[15]
and decision V/6 of the Conference of Parties to the Convention on Biological
Diversity; [16]

(e) Promote integrated, multidisciplinary and multisectoral coastal and
ocean management at the national level and encourage and assist coastal
States in developing ocean policies and mechanisms on integrated coastal
management;

(f) Strengthen regional cooperation and coordination between the relevant
regional organizations and programmes, the regional seas programmes of
the United Nations Environment Programme, regional fisheries manage-

---

14   *Official Records of the Third United Nations Conference on the Law of the Sea*, vol. XVII (United Na-
      tions publication, Sa les No. E.84.V.3), document A/CONF.62/122.

15   See Food and Agriculture Organization of the United Nations document C200/INF/25, appen-
      dix I.

16   See UNEP/CBD/COP/5/23, annex III.

ment organizations and other regional science, health and development organizations;

(g) Assist developing countries in coordinating policies and programmes at the regional and subregional levels aimed at the conservation and sustainable management of fishery resources and implement integrated coastal area management plans, including through the promotion of sustainable coastal and small-scale fishing activities and, where appropriate, the development of related infrastructure;

(h) Take note of the work of the open-ended informal consultative process established by the United Nations General Assembly in its resolution 54/33 in order to facilitate the annual review by the Assembly of developments in ocean affairs and the upcoming review of its effectiveness and utility to be held at its fifty-seventh session under the terms of the above-mentioned resolution.

31. To achieve sustainable fisheries, the following actions are required at all levels:

(a) Maintain or restore stocks to levels that can produce the maximum sustainable yield with the aim of achieving these goals for depleted stocks on an urgent basis and where possible not later than 2015;

(b) Ratify or accede to and effectively implement the relevant United Nations and, where appropriate, associated regional fisheries agreements or arrangements, noting in particular the Agreement for the Implementation of the Provisions of the United Nations Convention on the Law of the Sea of 10 December 1982 relating to the Conservation and Management of Straddling Fish Stocks and Highly Migratory Fish Stocks[17] and the 1993 Agreement to Promote Compliance with International Conservation and Management Measures by Fishing Vessels on the High Seas;[18]

(c) Implement the 1995 Code of Conduct for Responsible Fisheries,[19] taking note of the special requirements of developing countries as noted in its article 5, and the relevant international plans of action and technical guidelines of the Food and Agriculture Organization of the United Nations;

(d) Urgently develop and implement national and, where appropriate, regional plans of action, to put into effect the international plans of action of the Food and Agriculture Organization of the United Nations, in particular the International Plan of Action for the Management of Fishing Capacity[20] by 2005 and the International Plan of Action to Prevent, Deter and Eliminate Il-

---

17 See *International Fisheries Instruments* (United Nations publication, Sales No. E.98.V.11), sect. I; see also A/CONF.164/37.

18 Ibid.

19 Ibid., sect. III.

20 Rome, Food and Agriculture Organization of the United Nations, 1999.

legal, Unreported and Unregulated Fishing[21] by 2004. Establish effective monitoring, reporting and enforcement, and control of fishing vessels, including by flag States, to further the International Plan of Action to Prevent, Deter and Eliminate Illegal, Unreported and Unregulated Fishing;

(e) Encourage relevant regional fisheries management organizations and arrangements to give due consideration to the rights, duties and interests of coastal States and the special requirements of developing States when addressing the issue of the allocation of share of fishery resources for straddling stocks and highly migratory fish stocks, mindful of the provisions of the United Nations Convention on the Law of the Sea and the Agreement for the Implementation of the Provisions of the United Nations Convention on the Law of the Sea of 10 December 1982 relating to the Conservation and Management of Straddling Fish Stocks and Highly Migratory Fish Stocks, on the high seas and within exclusive economic zones;

(f) Eliminate subsidies that contribute to illegal, unreported and unregulated fishing and to over-capacity, while completing the efforts undertaken at the World Trade Organization to clarify and improve its disciplines on fisheries subsidies, taking into account the importance of this sector to developing countries;

(g) Strengthen donor coordination and partnerships between international financial institutions, bilateral agencies and other relevant stakeholders to enable developing countries, in particular the least developed countries and small island developing States and countries with economies in transition, to develop their national, regional and subregional capacities for infrastructure and integrated management and the sustainable use of fisheries;

(h) Support the sustainable development of aquaculture, including small-scale aquaculture, given its growing importance for food security and economic development.

32. In accordance with chapter 17 of Agenda 21, promote the conservation and management of the oceans through actions at all levels, giving due regard to the relevant international instruments to:

(a) Maintain the productivity and biodiversity of important and vulnerable marine and coastal areas, including in areas within and beyond national jurisdiction;

(b) Implement the work programme arising from the Jakarta Mandate on the Conservation and Sustainable Use of Marine and Coastal Biological Diversity of the Convention on Biological Diversity,[22] including through the urgent mobilization of financial resources and technological assistance and the de-

---

21 Ibid., 2001.

22 See A/51/312, annex II, decision II/10.

velopment of human and institutional capacity, particularly in developing countries;

(c) Develop and facilitate the use of diverse approaches and tools, including the ecosystem approach, the elimination of destructive fishing practices, the establishment of marine protected areas consistent with international law and based on scientific information, including representative networks by 2012 and time/area closures for the protection of nursery grounds and periods, proper coastal land use and watershed planning and the integration of marine and coastal areas management into key sectors;

(d) Develop national, regional and international programmes for halting the loss of marine biodiversity, including in coral reefs and wetlands;

(e) Implement the Ramsar Convention,[23] including its joint work programme with the Convention on Biological Diversity,[24] and the programme of action called for by the International Coral Reef Initiative to strengthen joint management plans and international networking for wetland ecosystems in coastal zones, including coral reefs, mangroves, seaweed beds and tidal mud flats.

33. Advance implementation of the Global Programme of Action for the Protection of the Marine Environment from Land-based Activities[25] and the Montreal Declaration on the Protection of the Marine Environment from Land-based Activities,[26] with particular emphasis during the period from 2002 to 2006 on municipal wastewater, the physical alteration and destruct ion of habitats, and nutrients, by actions at all levels to:

(a) Facilitate partnerships, scientific research and diffusion of technical knowledge; mobilize domestic, regional and international resources; and promote human and institutional capacity-building, paying particular attention to the needs of developing countries;

(b) Strengthen the capacity of developing countries in the development of their national and regional programmes and mechanisms to mainstream the objectives of the Global Programme of Action and to manage the risks and impacts of ocean pollution;

(c) Elaborate regional programmes of action and improve the links with strategic plans for the sustainable development of coastal and marine resources, noting in particular areas that are subject to accelerated environmental changes and development pressures;

---

23 *Ramsar Convention on Wetlands of International Importance Especially as Waterfowl Habitat* (United Nations, *Treaty Series,* vol. 996, No. 14583).

24 See United Nations Environment Programme, Convention on Biological Diversity (Environmental Law and Institution Programme Activity Centre), June 1992.

25 A/51/116, annex II.

26 See E/CN.17/2002/PC.2/15.

(d) Make every effort to achieve substantial progress by the next Global Programme of Action conference in 2006 to protect the marine environment from land-based activities.

34. Enhance maritime safety and protection of the marine environment from pollution by actions at all levels to:

(a) Invite States to ratify or accede to and implement the conventions and protocols and other relevant instruments of the International Maritime Organization relating to the enhancement of maritime safety and protection of the marine environment from marine pollution and environmental damage caused by ships, including the use of toxic anti-fouling paints, and urge the International Maritime Organization (IMO) to consider stronger mechanisms to secure the implementation of IMO instruments by flag States;

(b) Accelerate the development of measures to address invasive alien species in ballast water. Urge the International Maritime Organization to finalize its draft International Convention on the Control and Management of Ships' Ballast Water and Sediments.

35. Governments, taking into account their national circumstances, are encouraged, recalling paragraph 8 of resolution GC (44)/RES/17 of the General Conference of the International Atomic Energy Agency, and taking into account the very serious potential for environment and human health impacts of radioactive wastes, to make efforts to examine and further improve measures and internationally agreed regulations regarding safety, while stressing the importance of having effective liability mechanisms in place, relevant to international maritime transportation and other transboundary movement of radioactive material, radioactive waste and spent fuel, including, inter alia, arrangements for prior notification and consultations done in accordance with relevant international instruments.

36. Improve the scientific understanding and assessment of marine and coastal ecosystems as a fundamental basis for sound decision-making, through actions at all levels to:

(a) Increase scientific and technical collaboration, including integrated assessment at the global and regional levels, including the appropriate transfer of marine science and marine technologies and techniques for the conservation and management of living and non-living marine resources and expanding ocean-observing capabilities for the timely prediction and assessment of the state of marine environment;

(b) Establish by 2004 a regular process under the United Nations for global reporting and assessment of the state of the marine environment, including socio-economic aspects, both current and foreseeable, building on existing regional assessments;

(c) Build capacity in marine science, information and management, through, inter alia, promoting the use of environmental impact assessments and environmental evaluation and reporting techniques, for projects or activities that are potentially harmful to the coastal and marine environments and their living and non-living resources;

(d) Strengthen the ability of the Intergovernmental Oceanographic Commission of the United Nations Educational, Scientific and Cultural Organization, the Food and Agriculture Organization of the United Nations and other relevant international and regional and subregional organizations to build national and local capacity in marine science and the sustainable management of oceans and their resources.

* * *

37. An integrated, multi-hazard, inclusive approach to address vulnerability, risk assessment and disaster management, including prevention, mitigation, preparedness, response and recovery, is an essential element of a safer world in the twenty-first century. Actions are required at all levels to:

(a) Strengthen the role of the International Strategy for Disaster Reduction and encourage the international community to provide the necessary financial resources to its Trust Fund;

(b) Support the establishment of effective regional, subregional and national strategies and scientific and technical institutional support for disaster management;

(c) Strengthen the institutional capacities of countries and promote international joint observation and research, through improved surface-based monitoring and increased use of satellite data, dissemination of technical and scientific knowledge, and the provision of assistance to vulnerable countries;

(d) Reduce the risks of flooding and drought in vulnerable countries by, inter alia, promoting wetland and watershed protection and restoration, improved land-use planning, improving and applying more widely techniques and methodologies for assessing the potential adverse effects of climate change on wetlands and, as appropriate, assisting countries that are particularly vulnerable to those effects;

(e) Improve techniques and methodologies for assessing the effects of climate change, and encourage the continuing assessment of those adverse effects by the Intergovernmental Panel on Climate Change;

(f) Encourage the dissemination and use of traditional and indigenous knowledge to mitigate the impact of disasters and promote community-based disaster management planning by local authorities, including through training activities and raising public awareness;

(g) Support the ongoing voluntary contribution of, as appropriate, non-governmental organizations, the scientific community and other partners in the management of natural disasters according to agreed, relevant guidelines;

(h) Develop and strengthen early warning systems and information networks in disaster management, consistent with the International Strategy for Disaster Reduction;

(i) Develop and strengthen capacity at all levels to collect and disseminate scientific and technical information, including the improvement of early warning systems for predicting extreme weather events, especially El Niño/La Niña, through the provision of assistance to institutions devoted to addressing such events, including the International Centre for the Study of the El Niño phenomenon;

(j) Promote cooperation for the prevention and mitigation of, preparedness for, response to and recovery from major technological and other disasters with an adverse impact on the environment in order to enhance the capabilities of affected countries to cope with such situations.

* * *

38. Change in the Earth's climate and its adverse effects are a common concern of humankind. We remain deeply concerned that all countries, particularly developing countries, including the least developed countries and small island developing States, face increased risks of negative impacts of climate change and recognize that, in this context, the problems of poverty, land degradation, access to water and food and human health remain at the centre of global attention. The United Nations Framework Convention on Climate Change[27] is the key instrument for addressing climate change, a global concern, and we reaffirm our commitment to achieving its ultimate objective of stabilization of greenhouse gas concentrations in the atmosphere at a level that would prevent dangerous anthropogenic interference with the climate system, within a time frame sufficient to allow ecosystems to adapt naturally to climate change, to ensure that food production is not threatened and to enable economic development to proceed in a sustainable manner, in accordance with our common but differentiated responsibilities and respective capabilities. Recalling the United Nations Millennium Declaration, in which heads of State and Government resolved to make every effort to ensure the en try into force of the Kyoto Protocol to the United Nations Framework Convention on Climate Change,[28] preferably by the tenth anniversary of the United Nations Conference on Environment and Development in 2002, and to embark on the required reduction of emissions of greenhouse gases, States that have ratified the Kyoto Protocol strongly urge States that have not already done so to ratify it in a timely manner. Actions at all levels are required to:

(a) Meet all the commitments and obligations under the United Nations Framework Convention on Climate Change;

(b) Work cooperatively towards achieving the objectives of the Convention;

---

27   A/AC.237/18 (Part II)/Add.1 and Corr.1, annex I.

28   FCCC/CP/1997/7/Add.1, decision 1/CP.3, annex.

(c) Provide technical and financial assistance and capacity-building to developing countries and countries with economies in transition in accordance with commitments under the Convention, including the Marrakesh Accords;[29]

(d) Build and enhance scientific and technological capabilities, inter alia, through continuing support to the Intergovernmental Panel on Climate Change for the exchange of scientific data and information especially in developing countries;

(e) Develop and transfer technological solutions;

(f) Develop and disseminate innovative technologies in regard to key sectors of development, particularly energy, and of investment in this regard, including through private sector involvement, market-oriented approaches, and supportive public policies and international cooperation;

(g) Promote the systematic observation of the Earth's atmosphere, land and oceans by improving monitoring stations, increasing the use of satellites and appropriate integration of these observations to produce high-quality data that could be disseminated for the use of all countries, in particular developing countries;

(h) Enhance the implementation of national, regional and international strategies to monitor the Earth's atmosphere, land and oceans, including, as appropriate, strategies for integrated global observations, inter alia, with the cooperation of relevant international organizations, especially the specialized agencies, in cooperation with the Convention;

(i) Support initiatives to assess the consequences of climate change, such as the Arctic Council initiative, including the environmental, economic and social impacts on local and indigenous communities.

39. Enhance cooperation at the international, regional and national levels to reduce air pollution, including transboundary air pollution, acid deposition and ozone depletion, bearing in mind the Rio principles, including, inter alia, the principle that, in view of the different contributions to global environmental degradation, States have common but differentiated responsibilities, with actions at all levels to:

(a) Strengthen capacities of developing countries and countries with economies in transition to measure, reduce and assess the impacts of air pollution, including health impacts, and provide financial and technical support for these activities;

(b) Facilitate implementation of the Montreal Protocol on Substances that Deplete the Ozone Layer by ensuring adequate replenishment of its fund by 2003/2005;

---

29   FCCC/CP/2001/13 and Add.1 -4.

(c) Further support the effective regime for the protection of the ozone layer established in the Vienna Convention for the Protection of the Ozone Layer and the Montreal Protocol, including its compliance mechanism;

(d) Improve access by developing countries to affordable, accessible, cost-effective, safe and environmentally sound alternatives to ozone-depleting substances by 2010, and assist them in complying with the phase-out schedule under the Montreal Protocol, bearing in mind that ozone depletion and climate change are scientifically and technically interrelated;

(e) Take measures to address illegal traffic in ozone-depleting substances.

* * *

40. Agriculture plays a crucial role in addressing the needs of a growing global population and is inextricably linked to poverty eradication, especially in developing countries. Enhancing the role of women at all levels and in all aspects of rural development, agriculture, nutrition and food security is imperative. Sustainable agriculture and rural development are essential to the implementation of an integrated approach to increasing food production and enhancing food security and food safety in an environmentally sustainable way. This would include actions at all levels to:

(a) Achieve the Millennium Declaration target to halve by the year 2015 the proportion of the world's people who suffer from hunger and realize the right to a standard of living adequate for the health and well-being of themselves and their families, including food, including by promoting food security and fighting hunger in combination with measures which address poverty, consistent with the outcome of the World Food Summit and, for States Parties, with their obligations under article 11 of the International Covenant on Economic, Social and Cultural Rights;[30]

(b) Develop and implement integrated land management and water-use plans that are based on sustainable use of renewable resources and on integrated assessments of socio-economic and environmental potentials and strengthen the capacity of Governments, local authorities and communities to monitor and manage the quantity and quality of land and water resources;

(c) Increase understanding of the sustainable use, protection and management of water resources to advance long-term sustainability of freshwater, coastal and marine environments;

(d) Promote programmes to enhance in a sustainable manner the productivity of land and the efficient use of water resources in agriculture, forestry, wetlands, artisanal fisheries and aquaculture, especially through indigenous and local community-based approaches;

---

30   See General Assembly resolution 2200 A (XXI), annex.

(e) Support the efforts of developing countries to protect oases from silt, land degradation and increasing salinity by providing appropriate technical and financial assistance;

(f) Enhance the participation of women in all aspects and at all levels relating to sustainable agriculture and food security;

(g) Integrate existing information systems on land-use practices by strengthening national research and extension services and farmer organizations to trigger farmer-to-farmer exchange on good practices, such as those related to environmentally sound, low-cost technologies, with the assistance of relevant international organizations;

(h) Enact, as appropriate, measures that protect indigenous resource management systems and support the contribution of all appropriate stakeholders, men and women alike, in rural planning and development;

(i) Adopt policies and implement laws that guarantee well defined and enforceable land and water use rights and promote legal security of tenure, recognizing the existence of different national laws and/or systems of land access and tenure, and provide technical and financial assistance to developing countries as well as countries with economies in transition that are undertaking land tenure reform in order to enhance sustainable livelihoods;

(j) Reverse the declining trend in public sector finance for sustainable agriculture, provide appropriate technical and financial assistance, and promote private sector investment and support efforts in developing countries and countries with economies in transition to strengthen agricultural research and natural resource management capacity and dissemination of research results to the farming communities;

(k) Employ market-based incentives for agricultural enterprises and farmers to monitor and manage water use and quality, inter alia, by applying such methods as small-scale irrigation and wastewater recycling and reuse;

(l) Enhance access to existing markets and develop new markets for value-added agricultural products;

(m) Increase brown-field redevelopment in developed countries and countries with economies in transition, with appropriate technical assistance where contamination is a serious problem;

(n) Enhance international cooperation to combat the illicit cultivation of narcotic plants, taking into account their negative social, economic and environmental impacts;

(o) Promote programmes for the environmentally sound, effective and efficient use of soil fertility improvement practices and agricultural pest control;

(p) Strengthen and improve coordination of existing initiatives to enhance sustainable agricultural production and food security;

(q) Invite countries that have not done so to ratify the International Treaty on Plant Genetic Resources for Food and Agriculture; [31]

(r) Promote the conservation, and sustainable use and management of traditional and indigenous agricultural systems and strengthen indigenous models of agricultural production.

* * *

41. Strengthen the implementation of the United Nations Convention to Combat Desertification in Those Countries Experiencing Serious Drought and/or Desertification, particularly in Africa,[7] to address causes of desertification and land degradation in order to maintain and restore land, and to address poverty resulting from land degradation. This would include actions at all levels to:

(a) Mobilize adequate and predictable financial resources, transfer of technologies and capacity-building at all levels;

(b) Formulate national action programmes to ensure timely and effective implementation of the Convention and its related projects, with the support of the international community, including through decentralized projects at the local level;

(c) Encourage the United Nations Framework Convention on Climate Change, the Convention on Biological Diversity and the Convention to Combat Desertification to continue exploring and enhancing synergies, with due regard to their respective mandates, in the elaboration and implementation of plans and strategies under the respective Conventions;

(d) Integrate measures to prevent and combat desertification as well as to mitigate the effects of drought through relevant policies and programmes, such as land, water and forest management, agriculture, rural development, early warning systems, environment, energy, natural resources, health and education, and poverty eradication and sustainable development strategies;

(e) Provide affordable local access to information to improve monitoring and early warning related to desertification and drought;

(f) Call on the Second Assembly of the Global Environment Facility (GEF) to take action on the recommendations of the GEF Council concerning the designation of land degradation (desertification and deforestation) as a focal area of GEF as a means of GEF support for the successful implementation of the Convention to Combat Desertification; and consequently, consider making GEF a financial mechanism of the Convention, taking into account the prerogatives and decisions of the Conference of the Parties to the Convention, while recognizing the complementary roles of GEF and the Global Mechanism of the Convention in providing and mobilizing resources for the elaboration and implementation of action programmes;

---

31 *Report of the Conference of the Food and Agriculture Organization of the United Nations, Thirty-first Session, Rome, 2 -13 November 2001* (C2001/REP), appendix D.

(g) Improve the sustainability of grassland resources through strengthening management and law enforcement and providing financial and technical support by the international community to developing countries.

* * *

42. Mountain ecosystems support particular livelihoods and include significant watershed resources, biological diversity and unique flora and fauna. Many are particularly fragile and vulnerable to the adverse effects of climate change and need specific protection. Actions at all levels are required to:

(a) Develop and promote programmes, policies and approaches that integrate environmental, economic and social components of sustainable mountain development and strengthen international cooperation for its positive impacts on poverty eradication programmes, especially in developing countries;

(b) Implement programmes to address, where appropriate, deforestation, erosion, land degradation, loss of biodiversity, disruption of water flows and retreat of glaciers;

(c) Develop and implement, where appropriate, gender-sensitive policies and programmes, including public and private investments that help eliminate inequities facing mountain communities;

(d) Implement programmes to promote diversification and traditional mountain economies, sustainable livelihoods and small-scale production systems, including specific training programmes and better access to national and international markets, communications and transport planning, taking into account the particular sensitivity of mountains;

(e) Promote full participation and involvement of mountain communities in decisions that affect them and integrate indigenous knowledge, heritage and values in all development initiatives;

(f) Mobilize national and international support for applied research and capacity-building, provide financial and technical assistance for the effective implementation of the sustainable development of mountain ecosystems in developing countries and countries with economies in transition, and address the poverty among people living in mountains through concrete plans, projects and programmes, with sufficient support from all stakeholders, taking into account the spirit of the International Year of Mountains, 2002.

* * *

43. Promote sustainable tourism development, including non-consumptive and eco-tourism, taking into account the spirit of the International Year of Eco-tourism 2002, the United Nations Year for Cultural Heritage in 2002, the World Eco-tourism Summit 2002 and its Quebec Declaration, and the Global Code of Ethics for Tourism as adopted by the World Tourism Organization in order to increase the benefits from tourism resources for the population in host communi-

ties while maintaining the cultural and environmental integrity of the host communities and enhancing the protection of ecologically sensitive areas and natural heritages. Promote sustainable tourism development and capacity-building in order to contribute to the strengthening of rural and local communities. This would include actions at all levels to:

(a) Enhance international cooperation, foreign direct investment and partnerships with both private and public sectors, at all levels;

(b) Develop programmes, including education and training programmes, that encourage people to participate in eco-tourism, enable indigenous and local communities to develop and benefit from eco-tourism, and enhance stakeholder cooperation in tourism development and heritage preservation, in order to improve the protection of the environment, natural resources and cultural heritage;

(c) Provide technical assistance to developing countries and countries with economies in transition to support sustainable tourism business development and investment and tourism awareness programmes, to improve domestic tourism, and to stimulate entrepreneurial development;

(d) Assist host communities in managing visits to their tourism attractions for their maximum benefit, while ensuring the least negative impacts on and risks for their traditions, culture and environment, with the support of the World Tourism Organization and other relevant organizations;

(e) Promote the diversification of economic activities, including through the facilitation of access to markets and commercial information, and participation of emerging local enterprises, especially small and medium-sized enterprises.

* * *

44. Biodiversity, which plays a critical role in overall sustainable development and poverty eradication, is essential to our planet, human well-being and to the livelihood and cultural integrity of people. However, biodiversity is currently being lost at unprecedented rates due to human activities; this trend can only be reversed if the local people benefit from the conservation and sustainable use of biological diversity, in particular in countries of origin of genetic resources, in accordance with article 15 of the Convention on Biological Diversity. The Convention is the key instrument for the conservation and sustainable use of biological diversity and the fair and equitable sharing of benefits arising from use of genetic resources. A more efficient and coherent implementation of the three objectives of the Convention and the achievement by 2010 of a significant reduction in the current rate of loss of biological diversity will require the provision of new and additional financial and technical resources to developing countries, and includes actions at all levels to:

(a) Integrate the objectives of the Convention into global, regional and national sectoral and cross-sectoral programmes and policies, in particular in the programmes and policies of the economic sectors of countries and international financial institutions;

(b) Promote the ongoing work under the Convention on the sustainable use on biological diversity, including on sustainable tourism, as a cross-cutting issue relevant to different ecosystems, sectors and thematic areas;

(c) Encourage effective synergies between the Convention and other multilateral environmental agreements, inter alia, through the development of joint plans and programmes, with due regard to their respective mandates, regarding common responsibilities and concerns;

(d) Implement the Convention and its provisions, including active follow-up of its work programmes and decisions through national, regional and global action programmes, in particular the national biodiversity strategies and action plans, and strengthen their integration into relevant cross-sectoral strategies, programmes and policies, including those related to sustainable development and poverty eradication, including initiatives which promote community-based sustainable use of biological diversity;

(e) Promote the wide implementation and further development of the ecosystem approach, as being elaborated in the ongoing work of the Convention;

(f) Promote concrete international support and partnership for the conservation and sustainable use of biodiversity, including in ecosystems, at World Heritage sites and for the protection of endangered species, in particular through the appropriate channelling of financial resources and technology to developing countries and countries with economies in transition;

(g) To effectively conserve and sustainably use biodiversity, promote and support initiatives for hot spot areas and other areas essential for biodiversity and promote the development of national and regional ecological networks and corridors;

(h) Provide financial and technical support to developing countries, including capacity-building, in order to enhance indigenous and community-based biodiversity conservation efforts;

(i) Strengthen national, regional and international efforts to control invasive alien species, which are one of the main causes of biodiversity loss, and encourage the development of effective work programme on invasive alien species at all levels;

(j) Subject to national legislation, recognize the rights of local and indigenous communities who are holders of traditional knowledge, innovations and practices, and, with the approval and involvement of the holders of such knowledge, innovations and practices, develop and implement benefit-sharing mechanisms on mutually agreed terms for the use of such knowledge, innovations and practices;

(k) Encourage and enable all stake holders to contribute to the implementation of the objectives of the Convention and, in particular, recognize the specific role of youth, women and indigenous and local communities in conserving and using biodiversity in a sustainable way;

(l) Promote the effective participation of indigenous and local communities in decision and policy-making concerning the use of their traditional knowledge;

(m) Encourage technical and financial support to developing countries and countries with economies in transition in their efforts to develop and implement, as appropriate, inter alia, national suigeneris systems and traditional systems according to national priorities and legislation, with a view to conserving and the sustainable use of biodiversity;

(n) Promote the wide implementation of and continued work on the Bonn Guidelines on Access to Genetic Resources and Fair and Equitable Sharing of Benefits arising out of their Utilization, as an input to assist the Parties when developing and drafting legislative, administrative or policy measures on access and benefit-sharing as well as contract and other arrangements under mutually agreed terms for access and benefit-sharing;

(o) Negotiate within the framework of the Convention on Biological Diversity, bearing in mind the Bonn Guidelines, an international regime to promote and safeguard the fair and equitable sharing of benefits arising out of the utilization of genetic resources;

(p) Encourage successful conclusion of existing processes under the auspices of the Intergovernmental Committee on Intellectual Property and Genetic Resources, Traditional Knowledge and Folklore of the World Intellectual Property Organization, and in the ad hoc open-ended working group on article 8 (j) and related provisions of the Convention;

(q) Promote practicable measures for access to the results and benefits arising from biotechnologies based upon genetic resources, in accordance with articles 15 and 19 of the Convention, including through enhanced scientific and technical cooperation on biotechnology and biosafety, including the exchange of experts, training human resources and developing research-oriented institutional capacities;

(r) With a view to enhancing synergy and mutual supportiveness, taking into account the decisions under the relevant agreements, promote the discussions, without prejudging their outcome, with regard to the relationships between the Convention and agreements related to international trade and intellectual property rights, as outlined in the Doha Ministerial Declaration;[32]

(s) Promote the implementation of the programme of work of the Global Taxonomy Initiative;

---

32   See A/C.2/56/7, annex.

(t) Invite all States that have not already done so to ratify the Convention, the Cartagena Protocol on Biosafety to the Convention[33] and other biodiversity-related agreements, and invite those that have done so to promote their effective implementation at the national, regional and international levels and to support developing countries and countries with economies in transition technically and financially in this regard.

* * *

45. Forests and trees cover nearly one third of the Earth's surface. Sustainable forest management of both natural and planted forests and for timber and non-timber products is essential to achieving sustainable development as well as a critical means to eradicate poverty, significantly reduce deforestation, halt the loss of forest biodiversity and land and resource degradation and improve food security and access to safe drinking water and affordable energy; in addition, it highlights the multiple benefits of both natural and planted forests and trees and contributes to the well-being of the planet and humanity. The achievement of sustainable forest management, nationally and globally, including through partnerships among interested Governments and stakeholders, including the private sector, indigenous and local communities and non-governmental organizations, is an essential goal of sustainable development. This would include actions at all levels to:

(a) Enhance political commitment to achieve sustainable forest management by endorsing it as a priority on the international political agenda, taking full account of the linkages between the forest sector and other sectors through integrated approaches;

(b) Support the United Nations Forum on Forests, with the assistance of the Collaborative Partnership on Forests, as key intergovernmental mechanisms to facilitate and coordinate the implementation of sustainable forest management at the national, regional and global levels, thus contributing, inter alia, to the conservation and sustainable use of forest biodiversity;

(c) Take immediate action on domestic forest law enforcement and illegal international trade in forest products, including in forest biological resources, with the support of the international community, and provide human and institutional capacity-building related to the enforcement of national legislation in those areas;

(d) Take immediate action at the national and international levels to promote and facilitate the means to achieve sustainable timber harvesting and to facilitate the provision of financial resources and the transfer and development of environmentally sound technologies, and thereby address unsustainable timber-harvesting practices;

---

33   Http://www.biodiv.org/biosafety/protocol.asp.

(e) Develop and implement initiatives to address the needs of those parts of the world that currently suffer from poverty and the highest rates of deforestation and where international cooperation would be welcomed by affected Governments;

(f) Create and strengthen partnerships and international cooperation to facilitate the provision of increased financial resources, the transfer of environmentally sound technologies, trade, capacity-building, forest law enforcement and governance at all levels and integrated land and resource management to implement sustainable forest management, including the proposals for action of the Intergovernmental Panel on Forests/Intergovernmental Forum on Forests;

(g) Accelerate implementation of the proposals for action of the Intergovernmental Panel on Forests/Intergovernmental Forum on Forests by countries and by the Collaborative Partnership on Forests and intensify efforts on reporting to the United Nations Forum on Forests to contribute to an assessment of progress in 2005;

(h) Recognize and support indigenous and community-based forest management systems to ensure their full and effective participation in sustainable forest management;

(i) Implement the expanded action-oriented work programme of the Convention on Biological Diversity on all types of forest biological diversity, in close cooperation with the Forum, Partnership members and other forest-related processes and conventions, with the involvement of all relevant stakeholders.

* * *

46. Mining, minerals and metals are important to the economic and social development of many countries. Minerals are essential for modern living. Enhancing the contribution of mining, minerals and metals to sustainable development includes actions at all levels to:

(a) Support efforts to address the environmental, economic, health and social impacts and benefits of mining, minerals and metals throughout their life cycle, including workers' health and safety, and use a range of partnerships, furthering existing activities at the national and international levels among interested Governments, intergovernmental organizations, mining companies and workers and other stakeholders to promote transparency and accountability for sustainable mining and minerals development;

(b) Enhance the participation of stakeholders, including local and indigenous communities and women, to play an active role in minerals, metals and mining development throughout the life cycles of mining operations, including after closure for rehabilitation purposes, in accordance with national regulations and taking into account significant transboundary impacts;

(c) Foster sustainable mining practices through the provision of financial, technical and capacity-building support to developing countries and countries with economies in transition for the mining and processing of minerals, including small-scale mining, and, where possible and appropriate, improve value-added processing, upgrade scientific and technological information and reclaim and rehabilitate degraded sites.

V. Sustainable Development in a Globalizing World

47. Globalization offers opportunities and challenges for sustainable development. We recognize that globalization and interdependence are offering new opportunities for trade, investment and capital flows and advances in technology, including information technology, for the growth of the world economy, development and the improvement of living standards around the world. At the same time, there remain serious challenges, including serious financial crises, insecurity, poverty, exclusion and inequality within and among societies. The developing countries and countries with economies in transition face special difficulties in responding to those challenges and opportunities. Globalization should be fully inclusive and equitable, and there is a strong need for policies and measures at the national and international levels, formulated and implemented with the full and effective participation of developing countries and countries with economies in transition, to help them to respond effectively to those challenges and opportunities. This will require urgent action at all levels to:

(a) Continue to promote open, equitable, rules-based, predictable and non-discriminatory multilateral trading and financial systems that benefit all countries in the pursuit of sustainable development. Support the successful completion of the work programme contained in the Doha Ministerial Declaration and the implementation of the Monterrey Consensus. Welcome the decision contained in the Doha Ministerial Declaration to place the needs and interests of developing countries at the heart of the work programme of the Declaration, including through enhanced market access for products of interest to developing countries;

(b) Encourage ongoing efforts by international financial and trade institutions to ensure that decision-making processes and institutional structures are open and transparent;

(c) Enhance the capacities of developing countries, including the least developed countries, landlocked developing countries and small island developing States, to benefit from liberalized trade opportunities through international cooperation and measures aimed at improving productivity, commodity diversification and competitiveness, community-based entrepreneurial capacity and transportation and communication infrastructure development;

(d) Support the International Labour Organization and encourage its ongoing work on the social dimension of globalization, as stated in paragraph 64 of the Monterrey Consensus;

(e) Enhance the delivery of coordinated, effective and targeted trade-related technical assistance and capacity-building programmes, including taking advantage of existing and future market access opportunities, and examining the relationship between trade, environment and development.

48. Implement the outcomes of the Doha Ministerial Conference by the members of the World Trade Organization, further strengthen trade-related technical assistance and capacity-building and ensure the meaningful, effective and full participation of developing countries in multilateral trade negotiations by placing their needs and interests at the heart of the work programme of the World Trade Organization.

49. Actively promote corporate responsibility and accountability, based on the Rio principles, including through the full development and effective implementation of intergovernmental agreements and measures, international initiatives and public-private partnerships and appropriate national regulations, and support continuous improvement in corporate practices in all countries.

50. Strengthen the capacities of developing countries to encourage public/private initiatives that enhance the ease of access, accuracy, timeliness and coverage of information on countries and financial markets. Multilateral and regional financial institutions could provide further assistance for these purposes.

51. Strengthen regional trade and cooperation agreements, consistent with the multilateral trading system, among developed and developing countries and countries with economies in transition, as well as among developing countries, with the support of international finance institutions and regional development banks, as appropriate, with a view to achieving the objectives of sustainable development.

52. Assist developing countries and countries with economies in transition in narrowing the digital divide, creating digital opportunities and harnessing the potential of information and communication technologies for development through technology transfer on mutually agreed terms and the provision of financial and technical support and, in this context, support the World Summit on the Information Society.

VI. Health and Sustainable Development

53. The Rio Declaration on Environment and Development states that human beings are at the centre of concerns for sustainable development, and that they are entitled to a healthy and productive life, in harmony with nature. The goals of sustainable development can only be achieved in the absence of a high prevalence of debilitating diseases, while obtaining health gains for the whole population requires poverty eradication. There is an urgent need to address the causes of ill health, including environmental causes, and their impact on development, with particular emphasis on women and children, as well as vulnerable groups of society, such as people with disabilities, elderly persons and indigenous people.

54. Strengthen the capacity of health-care systems to deliver basic health services to all in an efficient, accessible and affordable manner aimed at preventing, controlling and treating diseases, and to reduce environmental health threats, in conformity with human rights and fundamental freedoms and consistent with national laws and cultural and religious values, and taking into account the reports of relevant United Nations conferences and summits and of special sessions of the General Assembly. This would include actions at all levels to:

(a) Integrate the health concerns, including those of the most vulnerable populations, into strategies, policies and programmes for poverty eradication and sustainable development;

(b) Promote equitable and improved access to affordable and efficient health-care services, including prevention, at all levels of the health system, essential and safe drugs at affordable prices, immunization services and safe vaccines and medical technology;

(c) Provide technical and financial assistance to developing countries and countries with economies in transition to implement the Health for All Strategy, including health information systems and integrated databases on development hazards;

(d) Improve the development and management of human resources in health-care services;

(e) Promote and develop partnerships to enhance health education with the objective of achieving improved health literacy on a global basis by 2010, with the involvement of United Nations agencies, as appropriate;

(f) Develop programmes and initiatives to reduce, by the year 2015, mortality rates for infants and children under 5 by two thirds, and maternal mortality rates by three quarters, of the prevailing rate in 2000, and reduce disparities between and within developed and developing countries as quickly as possible, with particular attention to eliminating the pattern of disproportionate and preventable mortality among girl infants and children;

(g) Target research efforts and apply research results to priority public health issues, in particular those affecting susceptible and vulnerable populations, through the development of new vaccines, reducing exposures to health risks, building on equal access to health-care services, education, training and medical treatment and technology and addressing the secondary effects of poor health;

(h) Promote the preservation, development and use of effective traditional medicine knowledge and practices, where appropriate, in combination with modern medicine, recognizing indigenous and local communities as custodians of traditional knowledge and practices, while promoting effective protection of traditional knowledge, as appropriate, consistent with international law;

(i) Ensure equal access of women to health-care services, giving particular attention to maternal and emergency obstetric care;

(j) Address effectively, for all individuals of appropriate age, the promotion of healthy living, including their reproductive and sexual health, consistent with the commitments and outcomes of recent United Nations conferences and summits, including the World Summit for Children, the United Nations Conference on Environment and Development, the International Conference on Population and Development, the World Summit for Social Development and the Fourth World Conference on Women, and their respective reviews and reports;

(k) Launch international capacity-building initiatives, as appropriate, that assess health and environment linkages and use the knowledge gained to create more effective national and regional policy responses to environmental threats to human health;

(l) Transfer and disseminate, on mutually agreed terms, including through public-private multisector partnerships, with international financial support, technologies for safe water, sanitation and waste management for rural and urban areas in developing countries and countries with economies in transition, taking into account country-specific conditions and gender equality, including specific technology needs of women;

(m) Strengthen and promote programmes of the International Labour Organization and World Health Organization to reduce occupational deaths, injuries and illnesses, and link occupational health with public health promotion as a means of promoting public health and education;

(n) Improve availability and access for all to sufficient, safe, culturally acceptable and nutritionally adequate food, increase consumer health protection, address issues of micronutrient deficiency and implement existing internationally agreed commitments and relevant standards and guidelines;

(o) Develop or strengthen, where applicable, preventive, promotive and curative programmes to address non-communicable diseases and conditions, such as cardiovascular diseases, cancer, diabetes, chronic respiratory diseases, injuries, violence and mental health disorders and associated risk factors, including alcohol, tobacco, unhealthy diets and lack of physical activity.

55. Implement, within the agreed time frames, all commitments agreed in the Declaration of Commitment on HIV/AIDS[34] adopted by the General Assembly at its twenty-sixth special session, emphasizing in particular the reduction of HIV prevalence among young men and women aged 15 to 24 by 25 per cent in the

---

34   General Assembly resolution S-26/2, annex.

most affected countries by 2005, and globally by 2010, as well as combat malaria, tuberculosis and other diseases by, inter alia:

(a) Implementing national preventive and treatment strategies, regional and international cooperation measures and the development of international initiatives to provide special assistance to children orphaned by HIV/AIDS;

(b) Fulfilling commitments for the provision of sufficient resources to support the Global Fund to Fight AIDS, Tuberculosis and Malaria, while promoting access to the Fund by countries most in need;

(c) Protecting the health of workers and promoting occupational safety, by, inter alia, taking into account, as appropriate, the voluntary Code of Practice on HIV/AIDS and the World of Work of the International Labour Organization, to improve conditions of the workplace;

(d) Mobilizing adequate public, and encouraging private, financial resources for research and development on diseases of the poor, such as HIV/AIDS, malaria, and tuberculosis, directed at biomedical and health research, as well as new vaccine and drug development.

56. Reduce respiratory diseases and other health impacts resulting from air pollution, with particular attention to women and children, by:

(a) Strengthening regional and national programmes, including through public-private partnerships, with technical and financial assistance to developing countries;

(b) Supporting the phasing out of lead in gasoline;

(c) Strengthening and supporting efforts for the reduction of emissions through the use of cleaner fuels and modern pollution control techniques;

(d) Assisting developing countries in providing affordable energy to rural communities, particularly to reduce dependence on traditional fuel sources for cooking and heating, which affect the health of women and children.

57. Phase out lead in lead-based paints and in other sources of human exposure, work to prevent, in particular, children's exposure to lead and strengthen monitoring and surveillance efforts and the treatment of lead poisoning.

VII. Sustainable Development of Small Island Developing States

58. Small island developing States are a special case both for environment and development. Although they continue to take the lead in the path towards sustainable development in their countries, they are increasingly constrained by the interplay of adverse factors clearly underlined in Agenda 21, the Programme of

Action for the Sustainable Development of Small Island Developing States[35] and the decisions adopted at the twenty-second special session of the General Assembly. This would include actions at all levels to:

(a) Accelerate national and regional implementation of the Programme of Action, with adequate financial resources, including through Global Environment Facility focal areas, transfer of environmentally sound technologies and assistance for capacity-building from the international community;

(b) Implement further sustainable fisheries management and improve financial returns from fisheries by supporting and strengthening relevant regional fisheries management organizations, as appropriate, such as the recently established Caribbean Regional Fisheries Mechanism and such agreements as the Convention on the Conservation and Management of Highly Migratory Fish Stocks in the Western and Central Pacific Ocean;

(c) Assist small island developing States, including through the elaboration of specific initiatives, in delimiting and managing in a sustainable manner their coastal areas and exclusive economic zones and the continental shelf, including, where appropriate, the continental shelf areas beyond 200 miles from coastal baselines, as well as relevant regional management initiatives within the context of the United Nations Convention on the Law of the Sea and the regional seas programmes of the United Nations Environment Programme;

(d) Provide support, including for capacity-building, for the development and further implementation of:

(i) Small island developing States-specific components within programmes of work on marine and coastal biological diversity;

(ii) Freshwater programmes for small island developing States, including through the Global Environment Facility focal areas;

(e) Effectively reduce, prevent and control waste and pollution and their health-related impacts by undertaking initiatives by 2004 aimed at implementing the Global Programme of Action for the Protection of the Marine Environment from Land-based Activities in small island developing States;

(f) Work to ensure that, in the ongoing negotiations and elaboration of the World Trade Organization work programme on trade in small economies, due account is taken of small island developing States, which have severe structural handicaps in integrating into the global economy, within the context of the Doha development agenda;

(g) Develop community-based initiatives on sustainable tourism by 2004 and build the capacities necessary to diversify tourism products, while pro-

---

35   *Report of the Global Conference on the Sustainable Development of Small Island Developing States, Bridgetown, Barbados, 25 April-6 May 1994* (United Nations publication, Sales No. E.94.I.18 and corrigenda), chap. I, resolution 1, annex II.

tecting culture and traditions and effectively conserving and managing natural resources;

(h) Extend assistance to small island developing States in support of local communities and appropriate national and regional organizations of small island developing States for comprehensive hazard and risk management, disaster prevention, mitigation and preparedness, and help relieve the consequences of disasters, extreme weather events and other emergencies;

(i) Support the finalization and subsequent early operationalization, on agreed terms, of economic, social and environmental vulnerability indices and related indicators as tools for the achievement of the sustainable development of the small island developing States;

(j) Assist small island developing States in mobilizing adequate resources and partnerships for their adaptation needs relating to the adverse effects of climate change, sea level rise and climate variability, consistent with commitments under the United Nations Framework Convention on Climate Change, where applicable;

(k) Support efforts by small island developing States to build capacities and institutional arrangements to implement intellectual property regimes.

59. Support the availability of adequate, affordable and environmentally sound energy services for the sustainable development of small island developing States by, inter alia:

(a) Strengthening ongoing and supporting new efforts on energy supply and services, by 2004, including through the United Nations system and partnership initiatives;

(b) Developing and promoting efficient use of sources of energy, including indigenous sources and renewable energy, and building the capacities of small island developing States for training, technical know-how and strengthening national institutions in the area of energy management.

60. Provide support to small island developing States to develop capacity and strengthen:

(a) Health-care services for promoting equitable access to health care;

(b) Health systems for making available necessary drugs and technology in a sustainable and affordable manner to fight and control communicable and non-communicable diseases, in particular HIV/AIDS, tuberculosis, diabetes, malaria and dengue fever;

(c) Efforts to reduce and manage waste and pollution and building capacity for maintaining and managing systems to deliver water and sanitation services, in both rural and urban areas;

(d) Efforts to implement initiatives aimed at poverty eradication, which have been outlined in section II of the present document.

61. Undertake a full and comprehensive review of the implementation of the Barbados Programme of Action for the Sustainable Development of Small Island Developing States in 2004, in accordance with the provisions set forth in General Assembly resolution S-22/2, and in this context requests the General Assembly at its fifty-seventh session to consider convening an international meeting for the sustainable development of small island developing States.

VIII. Sustainable Development for Africa

62. Since the United Nations Conference on Environment and Development, sustainable development has remained elusive for many African countries. Poverty remains a major challenge and most countries on the continent have not benefited fully from the opportunities of globalization, further exacerbating the continent's marginalization. Africa's efforts to achieve sustainable development have been hindered by conflicts, insufficient investment, limited market access opportunities and supply side constraints, unsustainable debt burdens, historically declining levels of official development assistance and the impact of HIV/AIDS. The World Summit on Sustainable Development should reinvigorate the commitment of the international community to address these special challenges and give effect to a new vision based on concrete actions for the implementation of Agenda 21 in Africa. The New Partnership for Africa's Development (NEPAD) is a commitment by African leaders to the people of Africa. It recognizes that partnerships among African countries themselves and between them and with the international community are key elements of a shared and common vision to eradicate poverty, and furthermore it aims to place their countries, both individually and collectively, on a path of sustained economic growth and sustainable development, while participating actively in the world economy and body politic. It provides a framework for sustainable development on the continent to be shared by all Africa's people. The international community welcomes NEPAD and pledges its support to the implementation of this vision, including through utilization of the benefits of South-South cooperation supported, inter alia, by the Tokyo International Conference on African Development. It also pledges support for other existing development frameworks that are owned and driven nationally by African countries and that embody poverty reduction strategies, including poverty reduction strategy papers. Achieving sustainable development includes actions at all levels to:

(a) Create an enabling environment at the regional, subregional, national and local levels in order to achieve sustained economic growth and sustainable development and support African efforts for peace, stability and security, the resolution and prevention of conflicts, democracy, good governance, respect for human rights and fundamental freedoms, including the right to development and gender equality;

(b) Support the implementation of the vision of NEPAD and other established regional and subregional efforts, including through financing, technical cooperation and institutional cooperation and human and institutional capacity-building at the regional, subregional and national levels, consistent with national policies, programmes and nationally owned and led strategies for poverty reduction and sustainable development, such as, where applicable, poverty reduction strategy papers;

(c) Promote technology development, transfer and diffusion to Africa and further develop technology and knowledge available in African centres of excellence;

(d) Support African countries in developing effective science and technology institutions and research activities capable of developing and adapting to world class technologies;

(e) Support the development of national programmes and strategies to promote education within the context of nationally owned and led strategies for poverty reduction and strengthen research institutions in education in order to increase the capacity to fully support the achievement of internationally agreed development goals related to education, including those contained in the Millennium Declaration on ensuring that, by 2015, children everywhere, boys and girls alike, will be able to complete a full course of primary schooling and that girls and boys will have equal access to all levels of education relevant to national needs;

(f) Enhance the industrial productivity, diversity and competitiveness of African countries through a combination of financial and technological support for the development of key infrastructure, access to technology, networking of research centres, adding value to export products, skills development and enhancing market access in support of sustainable development;

(g) Enhance the contribution of the industrial sector, in particular mining, minerals and metals, to the sustainable development of Africa by supporting the development of effective and transparent regulatory and management frameworks and value addition, broad-based participation, social and environmental responsibility and increased market access in order to create an attractive and conducive environment for investment;

(h) Provide financial and technical support to strengthen the capacity of African countries to undertake environmental legislative policy and institutional reform for sustainable development and to undertake environmental impact assessments and, as appropriate, to negotiate and implement multilateral environment agreements;

(i) Develop projects, programmes and partnerships with relevant stakeholders and mobilize resources for the effective implementation of the outcome of the African Process for the Protection and Development of the Marine and Coastal Environment;

(j) Deal effectively with energy problems in Africa, including through initiatives to:

(i) Establish and promote programmes, partnerships and initiatives to support Africa's efforts to implement NEPAD objectives on energy, which seek to secure access for at least 35 per cent of the African population within 20 years, especially in rural areas;

(ii) Provide support to implement other initiatives on energy, including the promotion of cleaner and more efficient use of natural gas and increased use of renewable energy, and to improve energy efficiency and access to advanced energy technologies, including cleaner fossil fuel technologies, particularly in rural and peri-urban areas;

(k) Assist African countries in mobilizing adequate resources for their adaptation needs relating to the adverse effects of climate change, extreme weather events, sea level rise and climate variability, and assist in developing national climate change strategies and mitigation programmes, and continue to take actions to mitigate the adverse effects on climate change in Africa, consistent with the United Nations Framework Convention on Climate Change;

(l) Support African efforts to develop affordable transport systems and infrastructure that promote sustainable development and connectivity in Africa;

(m) Further to paragraph 42 above, address the poverty affecting mountain communities in Africa;

(n) Provide financial and technical support for afforestation and reforestation in Africa and to build capacity for sustainable forest management, including combating deforestation and measures to improve the policy and legal framework of the forest sector.

63. Provide financial and technical support for Africa's efforts to implement the Convention to Combat Desertification at the national level and integrate indigenous knowledge systems into land and natural resources management practices, as appropriate, and improve extension services to rural communities and promote better land and watershed management practices, including through improved agricultural practices that address land degradation, in order to develop capacity for the implementation of national programmes.

64. Mobilize financial and other support to develop and strengthen health systems that aim to:

(a) Promote equitable access to health-care services;

(b) Make available necessary drugs and technology in a sustainable and affordable manner to fight and control communicable diseases, including HIV/AIDS, malaria and tuberculosis, and trypanosomiasis, as well as non-communicable diseases, including those caused by poverty;

(c) Build capacity of medical and paramedical personnel;

(d) Promote indigenous medical knowledge, as appropriate, including traditional medicine;

(e) Research and control Ebola disease.

65. Deal effectively with natural disasters and conflicts, including their humanitarian and environmental impacts, recognizing that conflicts in Africa have hindered, and in many cases obliterated, both the gains and efforts aimed at sustainable development, with the most vulnerable members of society, particularly women and children, being the most impacted victims, through efforts and initiatives, at all levels, to:

(a) Provide financial and technical assistance to strengthen the capacities of African countries, including institutional and human capacity, including at the local level, for effective disaster management, including observation and early warning systems, assessments, prevention, preparedness, response and recovery;

(b) Provide support to African countries to enable them to better deal with the displacement of people as a result of natural disasters and conflicts and put in place rapid response mechanisms;

(c) Support Africa's efforts for the prevention and resolution, management and mitigation of conflicts and its early response to emerging conflict situations to avert tragic humanitarian consequences;

(d) Provide support to refugee host countries in rehabilitating infrastructure and environment, including ecosystems and habitats, that were damaged in the process of receiving and settling refugees.

66. Promote integrated water resources development and optimize the upstream and downstream benefits therefrom, the development and effective management of water resources across all uses and the protection of water quality and aquatic ecosystems, including through initiatives at all levels, to:

(a) Provide access to potable domestic water, hygiene education and improved sanitation and waste management at the household level through initiatives to encourage public and private investment in water supply and sanitation that give priority to the needs of the poor within stable and transparent national regulatory frameworks provided by Governments, while respecting local conditions involving all concerned stakeholders and monitoring the performance and improving the accountability of public institutions and private companies; and develop critical water supply, reticulation and treatment infrastructure, and build capacity to maintain and manage systems to deliver water and sanitation services in both rural and urban areas;

(b) Develop and implement integrated river basin and watershed management strategies and plans for all major water bodies, consistent with paragraph 25 above;

(c) Strengthen regional, subregional and national capacities for data collection and processing and for planning, research, monitoring, assessment and enforcement, as well as arrangements for water resource management;

(d) Protect water resources, including groundwater and wetland ecosystems, against pollution, and, in cases of the most acute water scarcity, support efforts for developing non-conventional water resources, including the energy-efficient, cost-effective and sustainable desalination of seawater, rain-water harvesting and recycling of water.

67. Achieve significantly improved sustainable agricultural productivity and food security in furtherance of the agreed Millennium development goals, including those contained in the Millennium Declaration, in particular to halve by 2015 the proportion of people who suffer from hunger, including through initiatives at all levels to:

(a) Support the development and implementation of national policies and programmes, including research programmes and development plans of African countries to regenerate their agricultural sector and sustainably develop their fisheries, and increase investment in infrastructure, technology and extension services, according to country needs. African countries should be in the process of developing and implementing food security strategies, within the context of national poverty eradication programmes, by 2005;

(b) Promote and support efforts and initiatives to secure equitable access to land tenure and clarify resource rights and responsibilities, through land and tenure reform processes that respect the rule of law and are enshrined in national law, and provide access to credit for all, especially women, and that enable economic and social empowerment and poverty eradication as well as efficient and ecologically sound utilization of land and that enable women producers to become decision makers and owners in the sector, including the right to inherit land;

(c) Improve market access for goods, including goods originating from African countries, in particular least developed countries, within the framework of the Doha Ministerial Declaration, without prejudging the outcome of the World Trade Organization negotiations, as well as within the framework of preferential agreements;

(d) Provide support for African countries to improve regional trade and economic integration between African countries. Attract and increase investment in regional market infrastructure;

(e) Support livestock development programmes aimed at progressive and effective control of animal diseases.

68. Achieve sound management of chemicals, with particular focus on hazardous chemicals and wastes, inter alia, through initiatives to assist African countries in elaborating national chemical profiles and regional and national

frameworks and strategies for chemical management and establishing chemical focal points.

69. Bridge the digital divide and create digital opportunity in terms of access infrastructure and technology transfer and application through integrated initiatives for Africa. Create an enabling environment to attract investment, accelerate existing and new programmes and projects to connect essential institutions and stimulate the adoption of information communication technologies in government and commerce programmes and other aspects of national economic and social life.

70. Support Africa's efforts to attain sustainable tourism that contributes to social, economic and infrastructure development through the following measures:

(a) Implementing projects at the local, national and subregional levels, with specific emphasis on marketing African tourism products, such as adventure tourism, ecotourism and cultural tourism;

(b) Establishing and supporting national and cross-border conservation areas to promote ecosystem conservation according to the ecosystem approach, and to promote sustainable tourism;

(c) Respecting local traditions and cultures and promoting the use of indigenous knowledge in natural resource management and ecotourism;

(d) Assisting host communities in managing their tourism projects for maximum benefit, while limiting negative impact on their traditions, culture and environment;

(e) Support the conservation of Africa's biological diversity, the sustainable use of its components and the fair and equitable sharing of the benefits arising out of the utilization of genetic resources, in accordance with commitments that countries have under biodiversity-related agreements to which they are parties, including such agreements as the Convention on Biological Diversity and the Convention on International Trade in Endangered Species of Wild Fauna and Flora, as well as regional biodiversity agreements.

71. Support African countries in their efforts to implement the Habitat Agenda and the Istanbul Declaration through initiatives to strengthen national and local institutional capacities in the areas of sustainable urbanization and human settlements, provide support for adequate shelter and basic services and the development of efficient and effective governance systems in cities and other human settlements and strengthen, *inter alia*, the joint programme on managing water for African cities of the United Nations Human Settlements Programme and the United Nations Environment Programme.

IX. Other Regional Initiatives

72. Important initiatives have been developed within other United Nations regions and regional, subregional and transregional forums to promote sustain-

able development. The international community welcomes these efforts and the results already achieved, calls for actions at all levels for their further development, while encouraging interregional, in traregional and international cooperation in this respect, and expresses its support for their further development and implementation by the countries of the regions.

A. Sustainable Development in Latin America and the Caribbean

73. The Initiative of La tin America and the Caribbean on Sustainable Development is an undertaking by the leaders of that region that, building on the Platform for Action on the Road to Johannesburg, 2002,[36] which was approved in Rio de Janeiro in October 2001, recognizes the importance of regional actions towards sustainable development and takes into account the region's singularities, shared visions and cultural diversity. It is targeted towards the adoption of concrete actions in different areas of sustainable development, such as biodiversity, water resources, vulnerabilities and sustainable cities, social aspects, including health and poverty, economic aspects, including energy, and institutional arrangements, including capacity-building, indicators and participation of civil society, taking into account ethics for sustainable development.

74. The Initiative envisages the development of actions among countries in the region that may foster South-South cooperation and may count with the support of groups of countries, as well as multilateral and regional organizations, including financial institutions. As a framework for cooperation, the Initiative is open to partnerships with governments and all major groups.

B. Sustainable Development in Asia and the Pacific

75. Bearing in mind the target of halving the number of people who live in poverty by the year 2015, as provided in the Millennium Declaration, the Phnom Penh Regional Platform on Sustainable Development for Asia and the Pacific[37] recognized that the region contains over half of the world's population and the largest number of the world's people living in poverty. Hence, sustainable development in the region is critical to achieving sustainable development at the global level.

76. The Regional Platform identified seven initiatives for follow-up action: capacity-building for sustainable development; poverty reduction for sustainable development; cleaner production and sustainable energy; land management and biodiversity conservation; protection and management of and access to freshwater resources; oceans, coastal and marine resources and sustainable development of small island developing States; and action on atmosphere and climate change. Follow-up actions of these initiatives will be taken through national strategies and relevant regional and subregional initiatives, such as the Regional

---

36   E/CN.17/2002/PC.2/5/Add.2.

37   E/CN.17/2002/PC.2/8.

Action Programme for Environmentally Sound and Sustainable Development and the Kitakyushu Initiative for a Clean Environment, adopted at the Fourth Ministerial Conference on Environment and Development in Asia and the Pacific organized by the Economic and Social Commission for Asia and the Pacific.

C. Sustainable Development in the West Asia Region

77. The West Asia region is known for its scarce water and limited fertile land resources. The region has made progress to a more knowledge-based production of higher value-added commodities.

78. The regional preparatory meeting endorsed the following priorities: poverty alleviation, relief of debt burden; and sustainable management of natural re sources, including, inter alia, integrated water resources management, implementation of programmes to combat desertification, integrated coastal zone management and land and water pollution control.

D. Sustainable Development in the Economic Commission for Europe Region

79. The Economic Commission for Europe regional ministerial meeting for the World Summit on Sustainable Development recognized that the region has a major role to play and responsibilities in global efforts to achieve sustainable development by concrete actions. The region recognized that different levels of economic development in countries of the region may require the application of different approaches and mechanisms to implement Agenda 21. In order to address the three pillars of sustainable development in a mutually reinforcing way, the region identified its priority actions for sustainable development for the Economic Commission for Europe region in its Ministerial Statement to the Summit.[38]

80. In furtherance of the region's commitment to sustainable development, there are ongoing efforts at the regional, subregional and transregional levels, including, inter alia, the Environment for Europe process; the fifth Economic Commission for Europe ministerial conference, to be held in Kiev in May 2003; the development of an environmental strategy for the 12 countries of Eastern Europe; the Caucasus and Central Asia; the Central Asian Agenda 21; work of the Organisation for Economic Cooperation and Development on sustainable development, the European Union sustainable development strategy; and regional and subregional conventions and processes relevant to sustainable development, including, inter alia, the Convention on Access to Information, Public Participation in Decision-Making and Access to Justice in Environmental Matters (Aarhus Convention), the Alpine Convention, the North American Commission for Environmental Cooperation, the International Boundary Waters Treaty Act,

---

38   ECE/ACC.22/2001/2, annex I.

the Iqaluit Declaration of the Arctic Council, the Baltic Agenda 21 and the Mediterranean Agenda 21.

X. Means of Implementation

81. The implementation of Agenda 21 and the achievement of the internationally agreed development goals, including those contained in the Millennium Declaration as well as in the present plan of action, require a substantially increased effort, both by countries themselves and by the rest of the international community, based on the recognition that each country has primary responsibility for its own development and that the role of national policies and development strategies cannot be overemphasized, taking fully into account the Rio principles, including, in particular, the principle of common but differentiated responsibilities, which states:

> "States shall cooperate in a spirit of global partnership to conserve, protect and restore the health and integrity of the Earth's ecosystem. In view of the different contributions to global environmental degradation, States have common but differentiated responsibilities. The developed countries acknowledge the responsibility that they bear in the international pursuit of sustainable development in view of the pressures their societies place on the global environment and of the technologies and financial resources they command."

The internationally agreed development goals, including those contained in the Millennium Declaration and Agenda 21, as well as in the present plan of action, will require significant increases in the flow of financial resources as elaborated in the Monterrey Consensus, including through new and additional financial resources, in particular to developing countries, to support the implementation of national policies and programmes developed by them, improved trade opportunities, access to and transfer of environmentally sound technologies on a concessional or preferential basis, as mutually agreed, education and awareness-raising, capacity-building and information for decision-making and scientific capabilities within the agreed time frame required to meet these goals and initiatives. Progress to this end will require that the international community implement the outcomes of major United Nations conferences, such as the programmes of action adopted at the Third United Nations Conference on the Least Developed Countries[39] and the Global Conference on the Sustainable Development of Small Island Developing States, and relevant international agreements since 1992, particularly those of the International Conference on Financing for Development and the Fourth Ministerial Conference of the World Trade Organization, including building on them as part of a process of achieving sustainable development.

82. Mobilizing and increasing the effective use of financial resources and achieving the national and international economic conditions needed to fulfil internationally agreed development goals, including those contained in the Millennium

---

39   A/CONF.192/13.

Declaration, to eliminate poverty, improve social conditions and raise living standards and protect our environment, will be our first step to ensuring that the twenty-first century becomes the century of sustainable development for all.

83. In our common pursuit of growth, poverty eradication and sustainable development, a critical challenge is to ensure the necessary internal conditions for mobilizing domestic savings, both public and private, sustaining adequate levels of productive investment and increasing human capacity. A crucial task is to enhance the efficacy, coherence and consistency of macroeconomic policies. An enabling domestic environment is vital for mobilizing domestic resources, increasing productivity, reducing capital flight, encouraging the private sector and attracting and making effective use of international investment and assistance. Efforts to create such an environment should be supported b y the international community.

84. Facilitate greater flows of foreign direct investment so as to support the sustainable development activities, including the development of infrastructure, of developing countries, and enhance the benefits that developing countries can draw from foreign direct investment, with particular actions to:

(a) Create the necessary domestic and international conditions to facilitate significant increases in the flow of foreign direct investment to developing countries, in particular the least developed countries, which is critical to sustainable development, particularly foreign direct investment flows for infrastructure development and other priority areas in developing countries to supplement the domestic resources mobilized by them;

(b) Encourage foreign direct investment in developing countries and countries with economies in transition through export credits that could be instrumental to sustainable development;

85. Recognize that a substantial increase in official development assistance and other resources will be required if developing countries are to achieve the internationally agreed development goals and objectives, including those contained in the Millennium Declaration. To build support for official development assistance, we will cooperate to further improve policies and development strategies, both nationally and internationally, to enhance aid effectiveness, with actions to:

(a) Make available the increased commitments in official development assistance announced by several developed countries at the International Conference on Financing for Development. Urge the developed countries that have not done so to make concrete efforts towards the target of 0.7 per cent of gross national product as official development assistance to developing countries and effectively implement their commitment on such assistance to the least developed countries as contained in paragraph 83 of the Programme of Action for the Least Developed Countries for the Decade

2001-2010,[40] which was adopted in Brussels on 20 May 2001. We also encourage developing countries to build on progress achieved in ensuring that official development assistance is used effectively to help achieve development goals and targets in accordance with the outcome of the International Conference on Financing for Development. We acknowledge the efforts of all donors, commend those donors whose contributions exceed, reach or are increasing towards the targets, and underline the importance of undertaking to examine the means and time frames for achieving the targets and goals;

(b) Encourage recipient and donor countries, as well as international institutions, to make official development assistance more efficient and effective for poverty eradication, sustained economic growth and sustainable development. In this regard, intensify efforts by the multilateral and bilateral financial and development institutions, in accordance with paragraph 43 of the Monterrey Consensus, in particular to harmonize their operational procedures at the highest standards, so as to reduce transaction costs and make disbursement and delivery of official development assistance more flexible and more responsive to the needs of developing countries, taking into account national development needs and objectives under the ownership of recipient countries, and to use development frameworks that are owned and driven by developing countries and that embody poverty reduction strategies, including poverty reduction strategy papers, as vehicles for aid delivery, upon request.

86. Make full and effective use of existing financial mechanisms and institutions, including through actions at all levels to:

(a) Strengthen ongoing efforts to reform the existing international financial architecture to foster a transparent, equitable and inclusive system that is able to provide for the effective participation of developing countries in the international economic decision-making processes and institutions, as well as for their effective and equitable participation in the formulation of financial standards and codes;

(b) Promote, *inter alia*, measures in source and destination countries to improve transparency and information about financial flows to contribute to stability in the international financial environment. Measures that mitigate the impact of excessive volatility of short-term capital flows are important and must be considered;

(c) Work to ensure that the funds are made available on a timely, more assured and predictable basis to international organizations and agencies, where appropriate, for their sustainable development activities, programmes and projects;

---

40   A/CONF.191/11.

(d) Encourage the private sector, including transnational corporations, private foundations and civil society institutions, to provide financial and technical assistance to developing countries;

(e) Support new and existing public/private sector financing mechanisms for developing countries and countries with economies in transition, to benefit in particular small entrepreneurs and small, medium-sized and community-based enterprises and to improve their infrastructure, while ensuring the transparency and accountability of such mechanisms.

87. Welcome the successful and substantial third replenishment of the Global Environment Facility, which will enable it to address the funding requirements of new focal areas and existing ones and continue to be responsive to the needs and concerns of its recipient countries, in particular developing countries, and further encourage the Global Environment Facility to leverage additional funds from key public and private organizations, improve the management of funds through more speedy and streamlined procedures and simplify its project cycle.

88. Explore ways of generating new public and private innovative sources of finance for development purposes, provided that those sources do not unduly burden developing countries, noting the proposal to use special drawing rights allocations for development purposes, as set forth in paragraph 44 of the Monterrey Consensus.

89. Reduce unsustainable debt burden through such actions as debt relief and, as appropriate, debt cancellation and other innovative mechanisms geared to comprehensively address the debt problems of developing countries, in particular the poorest and most heavily indebted ones. Therefore, debt relief measures should, where appropriate, be pursued vigorously and expeditiously, including within the Paris and London Clubs and other relevant forums, in order to contribute to debt sustainability and facilitate sustainable development, while recognizing that debtors and creditors must share responsibility for preventing and resolving unsustainable debt situations, and that external debt relief can play a key role in liberating resources that can then be directed towards activities consistent with attaining sustainable growth and development. Therefore, we support paragraphs 47 to 51 of the Monterrey Consensus dealing with external debt. Debt relief arrangements should seek to avoid imposing any unfair burdens on other developing countries. There should be an increase in the use of grants for the poorest, debt-vulnerable countries. Countries are encouraged to develop national comprehensive strategies to monitor and manage external liabilities as a key element in reducing national vulnerabilities. In this regard, actions are required to:

(a) Implement speedily, effectively and fully the enhanced heavily indebted poor countries (HIPC) initiative, which should be fully financed through additional resources, taking into consideration, as appropriate, measures to address any fundamental changes in the economic circumstances of those developing countries with unsustainable debt burden caused by natural catastrophes, severe terms-of-trade shocks or affected by conflict, taking into account initiatives which have been undertaken to reduce outstanding indebtedness;

(b) Encourage participation in the HIPC initiative of all creditors that have not yet done so;

(c) Bring international debtors and creditors together in relevant international forums to restructure unsustainable debt in a timely and efficient manner, taking into account the need to involve the private sector in the resolution of crises due to indebtedness, where appropriate;

(d) Acknowledge the problems of the debt sustainability of some non-HIPC low-income countries, in particular those facing exceptional circumstances;

(e) Encourage exploring innovative mechanisms to comprehensively address the debt problems of developing countries, including middle-income countries and countries with economies in transition. Such mechanisms may include debt-for-sustainable-development swaps;

(f) Encourage donor countries to take steps to ensure that resources provided for debt relief do not detract from official development assistance resources intended for developing countries.

90. Recognizing the major role that trade can play in achieving sustainable development and in eradicating poverty, we encourage members of the World Trade Organization (WTO) to pursue the work programme agreed at their Fourth Ministerial Conference. In order for developing countries, especially the least developed among them, to secure their share in the growth of world trade commensurate with the needs of their economic development, we urge WTO members to take the following actions:

(a) Facilitate the accession of all developing countries, particularly the least developed countries, as well as countries with economies in transition, that apply for membership in WTO, in accordance with the Monterrey Consensus;

(b) Support the work programme adopted at the Doha Ministerial Conference as an important commitment on the part of developed and developing countries to mainstream appropriate trade policies in their respective development policies and programmes;

(c) Implement substantial trade-related technical assistance and capacity-building measures and support the Doha Development Agenda Global Trust Fund, established after the Doha Ministerial Conference, as an important step forward in ensuring a sound and predictable basis for WTO-related technical assistance and capacity-building;

(d) Implement the New Strategy for Technical Cooperation for Capacity-Building, Growth and Integration endorsed in the Doha Declaration;

(e) Fully support the implementation of the Integrated Framework for Trade-Related Technical Assistance to Least Developed Countries and urge development partners to significantly increase contributions to the Trust Fund for the Framework, in accordance with the Doha Ministerial Declaration.

91. In accordance with the Doha Declaration as well as with relevant decisions taken at Doha, we are determined to take concrete action to address issues and concerns raised by developing countries regarding the implementation of some WTO agreements and decisions, including the difficulties and resource constraints faced by them in fulfilling those agreements.

92. Call upon members of the World Trade Organization to fulfil the commitments made in the Doha Ministerial Declaration, notably in terms of market access, in particular for products of export interest to developing countries, especially least developed countries, by implementing the following actions, taking into account paragraph 45 of the Doha Ministerial Declaration:

(a) Review all special and differential treatment provisions with a view to strengthening them and making them more precise, effective and operational, in accordance with paragraph 44 of the Doha Ministerial Declaration;

(b) Aim to reduce or, as appropriate, eliminate tariffs on non-agricultural products, including the reduction or elimination of tariff peaks, high tariffs and tariff escalation, as well as non-tariff barriers, in particular on products of export interest to developing countries. Product coverage should be comprehensive and without a priori exclusions. The negotiations shall take fully into account the special needs and interests of developing and least developed countries, including through less than full reciprocity in reduction commitments, in accordance with the Doha Ministerial Declaration;

(c) Fulfil, without prejudging the outcome of the negotiations, the commitment for comprehensive negotiations initiated under article 20 of the Agreement on Agriculture, as referred to in the Doha Ministerial Declaration,[41] aiming at substantial improvements in market access, reductions of with a view to phasing out all forms of export subsidies, and substantial reductions in trade-distorting domestic support, while agreeing that the provisions for special and differential treatment for developing countries shall be an integral part of all elements of the negotiations and shall be embodied in the schedules of concession and commitments and, as appropriate, in the rules and disciplines to be negotiated, so as to be operationally effective and to enable developing countries to effectively take account of their development needs, including food security and rural development. Take note of the non-trade concerns reflected in the negotiating proposals submitted by members of the World Trade Organization and confirm that non-trade concerns will be taken into account in the negotiations as provided for in the Agreement on Agriculture, in accordance with the Doha Ministerial Declaration.

---

41   A/C.2/56/2, annex, paras. 13 and 14.

93. Call on developed countries that have not already done so to work towards the objective of duty-free and quota-free access for all least developed countries' exports, as envisaged in the Programme of Action for the Least Developed Countries for the Decade 2001-2010.

94. Commit to actively pursue the work programme of the World Trade Organization to address the trade-related issues and concerns affecting the fuller integration of small, vulnerable economies into the multilateral trading system in a manner commensurate with their special circumstances and in support of their efforts towards sustainable development, in accordance with paragraph 35 of the Doha Declaration.

95. Build the capacity of commodity-dependent countries to diversify exports through, inter alia, financial and technical assistance, international assistance for economic diversification and sustainable resource management and address the instability of commodity prices and declining terms of trade, as well as strengthen the activities covered by the second account of the Common Fund for Commodities to support sustainable development.

96. Enhance the benefits for developing countries, as well as countries with economies in transition, from trade liberalization, including through public-private partnerships, through, inter alia, action at all levels, including through financial support for technical assistance, the development of technology and capacity-building to developing countries to:

(a) Enhance trade infrastructure and strengthen institutions;

(b) Increase developing country capacity to diversify and increase exports to cope with the instability of commodity prices and declining terms of trade;

(c) Increase the value added of developing country exports.

97. Continue to enhance the mutual supportiveness of trade, environment and development with a view to achieving sustainable development through actions at all levels to:

(a) Encourage the WTO Committee on Trade and Environment and the WTO Committee on Trade and Development, within their respective mandates, to each act as a forum to identify and debate developmental and environmental aspects of the negotiations, in order to help achieve an outcome which benefits sustainable development in accordance with the commitments made under the Doha Ministerial Declaration;

(b) Support the completion of the work programme of the Doha Ministerial Declaration on subsidies so as to promote sustainable development and enhance the environment, and encourage reform of subsidies that have considerable negative effects on the environment and are incompatible with sustainable development;

(c) Encourage efforts to promote cooperation on trade, environment and development, including in the field of providing technical assistance to developing countries, between the secretariats of WTO, UNCTAD, UNDP, UNEP, and other relevant international environmental and development and regional organizations;

(d) Encourage the voluntary use of environmental impact assessments as an important national-level tool to better identify trade, environment and development interlinkages. Further encourage countries and international organizations with experience in this field to provide technical assistance to developing countries for these purposes.

98. Promote mutual supportiveness between the multilateral trading system and the multilateral environmental agreements, consistent with sustainable development goals, in support of the work programme agreed through WTO, while recognizing the importance of maintaining the integrity of both sets of instruments.

99. Complement and support the Doha Ministerial Declaration and the Monterrey Consensus by undertaking further action at the national, regional and international levels, including through public/private partnerships, to enhance the benefits, in particular for developing countries as well as for countries with economies in transition, of trade liberalization, through, *inter alia*, actions at all levels to:

(a) Establish and strengthen existing trade and cooperation agreements, consistent with the multilateral trading system, with a view to achieving sustainable development;

(b) Support voluntary WTO-compatible market-based initiatives for the creation and expansion of domestic and international markets for environmentally friendly goods and services, including organic products, which maximize environmental and developmental benefits through, *inter alia*, capacity-building and technical assistance to developing countries;

(c) Support measures to simplify and make more transparent domestic regulations and procedures that affect trade so as to assist exporters, particularly those from developing countries.

100. Address the public health problems affecting many developing and least developed countries, especially those resulting from HIV/AIDS, tuberculosis, malaria and other epidemics, while noting the importance of the Doha Declaration on the Agreement on Trade-Related Aspects of Intellectual Property Rights (TRIPS Agreement) and public health,[42] in which it was agreed that the TRIPS Agreement does not and should not prevent WTO members from taking measures to protect public health. Accordingly, while reiterating our commitment to the TRIPS Agreement, we reaffirm that the Agreement can and should be interpreted and implemented in a manner supportive of WTO members' right to protect public health and, in particular, to promote access to medicines for all.

---

42   Ibid., paras. 17-19.

101. States should cooperate to promote a supportive and open international economic system that would lead to economic growth and sustainable development in all countries to better address the problems of environmental degradation. Trade policy measures for environmental purposes should not constitute a means of arbitrary or unjustifiable discrimination or a disguised restriction on international trade. Unilateral actions to deal with environmental challenges out side the jurisdiction of the importing country should be avoided. Environmental measures addressing transboundary or global environmental problems should, as far as possible, be based on an international consensus.

102. Take steps with a view to the avoidance of, and refrain from, any unilateral measure not in accordance with international law and the Charter of the United Nations that impedes the full achievement of economic and social development by the population of the affected countries, in particular women and children, that hinders their well-being or that creates obstacles to the full enjoyment of their human rights, including the right of everyone to a standard of living adequate for their health and well-being and their right to food, medical care and the necessary social services. Ensure that food and medicine are not used as tools for political pressure.

103. Take further effective measures to remove obstacles to the realization of the right of peoples to self-determination, in particular peoples living under colonial and foreign occupation, which continue to adversely affect their economic and social development and are incompatible with the dignity and worth of the human person and must be combated and eliminated. People under foreign occupation must be protected in accordance with the provisions of international humanitarian law.

104. In accordance with the Declaration on Principles of International Law concerning Friendly Relations and Cooperation among States in accordance with the Charter of the United Nations,[43] this shall not be construed as authorizing or encouraging any action which would dismember or impair, totally or in part, the territorial integrity or political unity of sovereign and independent States conducting themselves in compliance with the principle of equal rights and self-determination of peoples and thus possessed of a Government representing the whole people belonging to the territory without distinction of any kind.

* * *

105. Promote, facilitate and finance, as appropriate, access to and the development, transfer and diffusion of environmentally sound technologies and corresponding know-how, in particular to developing countries and countries with economies in transition on favourable terms, including on concessional and

---

43   General Assembly resolution 2625 (XXV), annex.

preferential terms, as mutually agreed, as set out in chapter 34 of Agenda 21, including through urgent actions at all levels to:

(a) Provide information more effectively;

(b) Enhance existing national institutional capacity in developing countries to improve access to and the development, transfer and diffusion of environmentally sound technologies and corresponding know-how;

(c) Facilitate country-driven technology needs assessments;

(d) Establish legal and regulatory frameworks in both supplier and recipient countries that expedite the transfer of environmentally sound technologies in a cost-effective manner by both public and private sectors and support their implementation;

(e) Promote the access and transfer of technology related to early warning systems and to mitigation programmes to developing countries affected by natural disasters.

106. Improve the transfer of technologies to developing countries, in particular at the bilateral and regional levels, including through urgent actions at all levels to:

(a) Improve interaction and collaboration, stakeholder relationships and networks between and among universities, research institutions, government agencies and the private sector;

(b) Develop and strengthen networking of related institutional support structures, such as technology and productivity centres, research, training and development institutions, and national and regional cleaner production centres;

(c) Create partnerships conducive to investment and technology transfer, development and diffusion, to assist developing countries, as well as countries with economies in transition, in sharing best practices and promoting programmes of assistance, and encourage collaboration between corporations and research institutes to enhance industrial efficiency, agricultural productivity, environmental management and competitiveness;

(d) Provide assistance to developing countries, as well as countries with economies in transition, in accessing environmentally sound technologies that are publicly owned or in the public domain, as well as available knowledge in the public domain on science and technology, and in accessing the know-how and expertise required in order for them to make independent use of this knowledge in pursuing their development goals;

(e) Support existing mechanisms and, where appropriate, establish new mechanisms for the development, transfer and diffusion of environmentally sound technologies to developing countries and economies in transition.

* * *

107. Assist developing countries in building capacity to access a larger share of multilateral and global research and development programmes. In this regard, strengthen and, where appropriate, create centres for sustainable development in developing countries.

108. Build greater capacity in science and technology for sustainable development, with action to improve collaboration and partnerships on research and development and their widespread application among research institutions, universities, the private sector, governments, non-govern mental organizations and networks, as well as between and among scientists and academics of developing and developed countries, and in this regard encourage networking with and between centres of scientific excellence in developing countries.

109. Improve policy and decision-making at all levels through, inter alia, improved collaboration between natural and social scientists, and between scientists and policy makers, including through urgent actions at all levels to:

(a) Increase the use of scientific knowledge and technology and increase the beneficial use of local and indigenous knowledge in a manner respectful of the holders of that knowledge and consistent with national law;

(b) Make greater use of integrated scientific assessments, risk assessments and interdisciplinary and intersectoral approaches;

(c) Continue to support and collaborate with international scientific assessments supporting decision-making, including the Intergovernmental Panel on Climate Change, with the broad participation of developing country experts;

(d) Assist developing countries in developing and implementing science and technology policies;

(e) Establish partnerships between scientific, public and private institutions, including by integrating the advice of scientists into decision-making bodies to ensure a greater role for science, technology development and engineering sectors;

(f) Promote and improve science-based decision-making and reaffirm the precautionary approach as set out in principle 15 of the Rio Declaration o n Environment and Development, which states:

> "In order to protect the environment, the precautionary approach shall be widely applied by States according to their capabilities. Where there are threats of serious or irreversible damage, lack of full scientific certainty shall not be used as a reason for postponing cost-effective measures to prevent environmental degradation."

110. Assist developing countries, through international cooperation, in enhancing their capacity in their efforts to address issues pertaining to environmental protection, including in their formulation and implementation of policies for en-

vironmental management and protection, including through urgent actions at all levels to:

(a) Improve their use of science and technology for environ mental monitoring, assessment models, accurate databases and integrated information systems;

(b) Promote and, where appropriate, improve their use of satellite technologies for quality data collection, verification and updating, and further improve aerial and ground-based observations, in support of their efforts to collect quality, accurate, long-term, consistent and reliable data;

(c) Set up and, where appropriate, further develop national statistical services capable of providing sound data on science education and research and development activities that are necessary for effective science and technology policy-making.

111. Establish regular channels between policy makers and the scientific community to request and receive science and technology advice for the implementation of Agenda 21 and create and strengthen networks for science and education for sustainable development, at all levels, with the aim of sharing knowledge, experience and best practices and building scientific capacities, particularly in developing countries.

112. Use information and communication technologies, where appropriate, as tools to increase the frequency of communication and the sharing of experience and knowledge and to improve the quality of and access to information and communications technology in all countries, building on the work facilitated by the United Nations Information and Communications Technology Task Force and the efforts of other relevant international and regional forums.

113. Support publicly funded research and development entities to engage in strategic alliances for the purpose of enhancing research and development to achieve cleaner production and product technologies, through, inter alia, the mobilization from all sources of adequate financial and technical resources, including new and additional resources, and encourage the transfer and diffusion of those technologies, in particular to developing countries.

114. Examine issues of global public interest through open, transparent and inclusive workshops to promote a better public understanding of such questions.

115. Further resolve to take concerted action against international terrorism, which causes serious obstacles to sustainable development.

* * *

116. Education is critical for promoting sustainable development. It is therefore essential to mobilize necessary resources, including financial resources at all levels, by bilateral and multilateral donors, including the World Bank and the re-

gional development banks, by civil society and by foundations, to complement the efforts by national governments to pursue the following goals and actions:

(a) Meet the Millennium development goal of achieving universal primary education, ensuring that, by 2015, children everywhere, boys and girls alike, will be able to complete a full course of primary schooling;

(b) Provide all children, particularly those living in rural areas and those living in poverty, especially girls, with the access and opportunity to complete a full course of primary education.

117. Provide financial assistance and support to education, research, public awareness programmes and developmental institutions in developing countries and countries with economies in transition in order to:

(a) Sustain their educational infrastructures and programmes, including those related to environment and public health education;

(b) Consider means of avoiding the frequent, serious financial constraints faced by many institutions of higher learning, including universities around the world, particularly in developing countries and countries in transition.

118. Address the impact of HIV/AIDS on the educational system in those countries seriously affected by the pandemic.

119. Allocate national and international resources for basic education as proposed by the Dakar Framework for Action on Education for All and for improved integration of sustainable development into education and in bilateral and multilateral development programmes, and improve integration between publicly funded research and development and development programmes.

120. Eliminate gender disparity in primary and secondary education by 2005, as provided in the Dakar Framework for Action on Education for All, and at all levels of education no later than 2015, to meet the development goals contained in the Millennium Declaration, with action to ensure, inter alia, equal access to all levels and forms of education, training and capacity-building by gender mainstreaming, and by creating a gender-sensitive educational system.

121. Integrate sustainable development into education systems at all levels of education in order to promote education as a key agent for change.

122. Develop, implement, monitor and review education action plans and programmes at the national, subnational and local levels, as appropriate, that reflect the Dakar Framework for Action on Education for All and that are relevant to local conditions and needs leading to the achievement of community development and make education for sustainable development a part of those plans.

123. Provide all community members with a wide range of formal and non-formal continuing educational opportunities, including volunteer community ser-

vice programmes, in order to end illiteracy and emphasize the importance of lifelong learning and promote sustainable development.

124. Support the use of education to promote sustainable development, including through urgent actions at all levels to:

(a) Integrate information and communications technology in school curriculum development to ensure its access by both rural and urban communities and provide assistance, particularly to developing countries, inter alia, for the establishment of an appropriate enabling environment required for such technology;

(b) Promote, as appropriate, affordable and increased access to programmes for students, researchers and engineers from developing countries in the universities and research institutions of developed countries in order to promote the exchange of experience and capacity that will benefit all partners;

(c) Continue to implement the work programme of the Commission on Sustainable Development on education for sustainable development;

(d) Recommend to the United Nations General Assembly that it consider adopting a decade of education for sustainable development, starting in 2005.

* * *

125. Enhance and accelerate human, institutional and infrastructure capacity-building initiatives and promote partnerships in that regard that respond to the specific needs of developing countries in the context of sustainable development.

126. Support local, national, subregional and regional initiatives with action to develop, use and adapt knowledge and techniques and to enhance local, national, subregional and regional centres of excellence for education, research and training in order to strengthen the knowledge capacity of developing countries and countries with economies in transition through, inter alia, the mobilization from all sources of adequate financial and other resources, including new and additional resources.

127. Provide technical and financial assistance to developing countries, including through the strengthening of capacity-building efforts, such as the United Nations Development Programme Capacity 21 programme, to:

(a) Assess their own capacity development needs and opportunities at the individual, institutional and societal levels;

(b) Design programmes for capacity-building and support for local, national and community-level programmes that focus on meeting the challenges of globalization more effectively and attaining the internationally agreed development goals, including those contained in the Millennium Declaration;

(c) Develop the capacity of civil society, including youth, to participate, as appropriate, in designing, implementing and reviewing sustainable development policies and strategies at all levels;

(d) Build and, where appropriate, strengthen national capacities for carrying out effective implementation of Agenda 21.

* * *

128. Ensure access, at the national level, to environmental information and judicial and administrative proceedings in environmental matters, as well as public participation in decision-making, so as to further principle 10 of the Rio Declaration on Environment and Development, taking into full account principles 5, 7 and 11 of the Declaration.

129. Strengthen national and regional information and statistical and analytical services relevant to sustainable development policies and programmes, including data disaggregated by sex, age and other factors, and encourage donors to provide financial and technical support to developing countries to enhance their capacity to formulate policies and implement programmes for sustainable development.

130. Encourage further work on indicators for sustainable development by countries at the national level, including integration of gender aspects, on a voluntary basis, in line with national conditions and priorities.

131. Promote further work on indicators, in conformity with paragraph 3 of decision 9/4 of the Commission on Sustainable Development.[44]

132. Promote the development and wider use of earth observation technologies, including satellite remote sensing, global mapping and geographic information systems, to collect quality data on environmental impacts, land use and land-use changes, including through urgent actions at all levels to:

(a) Strengthen cooperation and coordination among global observing systems and research programmes for integrated global observations, taking into account the need for building capacity and sharing of data from ground-based observations, satellite remote sensing and other sources among all countries;

(b) Develop information systems that make the sharing of valuable data possible, including the active exchange of Earth observation data;

(c) Encourage initiatives and partnerships for global mapping.

133. Support countries, particularly developing countries, in their national efforts to:

(a) Collect data that are accurate, long-term, consistent and reliable;

---

44   See *Official Records of the Economic and Social Council, 2001, Supplement No. 9* (E/2001/29), chap. I.B.

(b) Use satellite and remote-sensing technologies for data collection and further improvement of ground-based observations;

(c) Access, explore and use geographic information by utilizing the technologies of satellite remote sensing, satellite global positioning, mapping and geographic information systems.

134. Support efforts to prevent and mitigate the impacts of natural disasters, including through urgent actions at all levels to:

(a) Provide affordable access to disaster-related information for early warning purposes;

(b) Translate available data, particularly from global meteorological observation systems, into timely and useful products.

135. Develop and promote the wider application of environmental impact assessments, inter alia, as a national instrument, as appropriate, to provide essential decision-support information on projects that could cause significant adverse effects to the environment.

136. Promote and further develop methodologies at policy, strategy and project levels for sustainable development decision-making at the local and national levels, and where relevant at the regional level. In this regard, emphasize that the choice of the appropriate methodology to be used in countries should be adequate to their country-specific conditions and circumstances, should be on a voluntary basis and should conform to their development priority needs.

XI. Institutional Framework for Sustainable Development

137. An effective institutional framework for sustainable development at all levels is key to the full implementation of Agenda 21, the follow-up to the outcomes of the World Summit on Sustainable Development and meeting emerging sustainable development challenges. Measures aimed at strengthening such a framework should build on the provisions of Agenda 21, as well as the Programme for the Further Implementation of Agenda 21 of 1997, and the principles of the Rio Declaration on Environment and Development and should promote the achievement of the internationally agreed development goals, including those contained in the Millennium Declaration, taking into ac count the Monterrey Consensus and relevant outcomes of other major United Nations conferences and international agreements since 1992. It should be responsive to the needs of all countries, taking into account the specific needs of developing countries including the means of implementation. It should lead to the strengthening of international bodies and organizations dealing with sustainable development, while respecting their existing mandates, as well as to the strengthening of relevant regional, national and local institutions.

138. Good governance is essential for sustainable development. Sound economic policies, solid democratic institutions responsive to the needs of the peo-

ple and improved infrastructure are the basis for sustained economic growth, poverty eradication, and employment creation. Freedom, peace and security, domestic stability, respect for human rights, including the right to development, and the rule of law, gender equality, market-oriented policies, and an overall commitment to just and democratic societies are also essential and mutually reinforcing.

A. Objectives

139. Measures to strengthen institutional arrangements on sustainable development, at all levels, should be taken within the framework of Agenda 21,[45] build on developments since the United Nations Conference on Environment and Development and lead to the achievement of, inter alia, the following objectives:

(a) Strengthening commitments to sustainable development;

(b) Integration of the economic, social and environmental dimensions of sustainable development in a balanced manner;

(c) Strengthening of the implementation of Agenda 21, including through the mobilization of financial and technological resources, as well as capacity-building programmes, particularly for developing countries;

(d) Strengthening coherence, coordination and monitoring;

(e) Promoting the rule of law and strengthening of governmental institutions;

(f) Increasing effectiveness and efficiency through limiting overlap and duplication of activities of international organizations, within and outside the United Nations system, based on their mandates and comparative advantages;

(g) Enhancing participation and effective involvement of civil society and other relevant stakeholders in the implementation of Agenda 21, as well as promoting transparency and broad public participation;

(h) Strengthening capacities for sustainable development at all levels, including the local level, in particular those of developing countries;

(i) Strengthening international cooperation aimed at reinforcing the implementation of Agenda 21 and the outcomes of the Summit.

B. Strengthening the Institutional Framework for Sustainable Development at the International Level

140. The international community should:

(a) Enhance the integration of sustainable development goals as reflected in Agenda 21 and support for implementation of Agenda 21 and the outcomes of the Summit into the policies, work programmes and operational guide-

---

45   References in the present chapter to Agenda 21 are deemed to include Agenda 21, the Programme for the Further Implementation of Agenda 21 and the outcomes of the Summit.

lines of relevant United Nations agencies, programmes and funds, the Global Environment Facility and international financial and trade institutions, within their mandates, while stressing that their activities should take full account of national programmes and priorities, particularly those of developing countries, as well as, where appropriate, countries with economies in transition, to achieve sustainable development;

(b) Strengthen collaboration within and between the United Nations system, international financial institutions, the Global Environment Facility and the World Trade Organization, utilizing the United Nations System Chief Executives Board for Coordination, the United Nations Development Group, the Environment Management Group and other inter-agency coordinating bodies. Strengthened inter-agency collaboration should be pursued in all relevant contexts, with special emphasis on the operational level and involving partnership arrangements on specific issues, to support, in particular, the efforts of developing countries in implementing Agenda 21;

(c) Strengthen and better integrate the three dimensions of sustainable development policies and programmes and promote the full integration of sustainable development objectives into programmes and policies of bodies that have a primary focus on social issues. In particular, the social dimension of sustainable development should be strengthened, inter alia, by emphasizing follow-up to the outcomes of the World Summit for Social Development and its five-year review, and taking into account their reports, and by support to social protection systems;

(d) Fully implement the outcomes of the decision on international environmental governance adopted by the Governing Council of the United Nations Environment Programme at its seventh special session[46] and invite the General Assembly at its fifty-seventh session to consider the important but complex issue of establishing universal membership for the Governing Council/Global Ministerial Environment Forum;

(e) Engage actively and constructively in ensuring the timely completion of the negotiations on a comprehensive United Nations convention against corruption, including the question of repatriation of funds illicitly acquired to countries of origin;

(f) Promote corporate responsibility and accountability and the exchange of best practices in the context of sustainable development, including, as appropriate, through multi-stakeholder dialogue, such as through the Commission on Sustainable Development, and other initiatives;

(g) Take concrete action to implement the Monterrey Consensus at all levels.

141. Good governance at the international level is fundamental for achieving sustainable development. In order to ensure a dynamic and enabling interna-

---

46   UNEP/GCSS.VII/6, annex I.

tional economic environment, it is important to promote global economic governance through addressing the international finance, trade, technology and investment patterns that have an impact on the development prospects of developing countries. To this effect, the international community should take all necessary and appropriate measures, including ensuring support for structural and macroeconomic reform, a comprehensive solution to the external debt problem and increasing market access for developing countries. Efforts to reform the international financial architecture need to be sustained with greater transparency and the effective participation of developing countries in decision-making processes. A universal, rules-based, open, non-discriminatory and equitable multilateral trading system, as well as meaningful trade liberalization, can substantially stimulate development worldwide, benefiting countries at all stages of development.

142. A vibrant and effective United Nations system is fundamental to the promotion of international cooperation for sustainable development and to a global economic system that works for all. To this effect, a firm commitment to the ideals of the United Nations, the principles of international law and those enshrined in the Charter of the United Nations, as well as to strengthening the United Nat ions system and other multilateral institutions and promoting the improvement of their operations, is essential. States should also fulfil their commitment to negotiate and finalize as soon as possible a United Nations convention against corruption in all its aspects, including the question of repatriation of funds illicitly acquired to countries of origin and also to promoting stronger cooperation to eliminate money laundering.

C. Role of the General Assembly

143. The General Assembly of the United Nations should adopt sustainable development as a key element of the overarching framework for United Nations activities, particularly for achieving the internationally agreed development goals, including those contained in the Millennium Declaration, and should give overall political direction to the implementation of Agenda 21 and its review.

D. Role of the Economic and Social Council

144. Pursuant to the relevant provisions of the Charter of the United Nations, the provisions of Agenda 21 regarding the Economic and Social Council and General Assembly resolutions 48/162 and 50/227, which reaffirmed the Council as the central mechanism for the coordination of the United Nations system and its specialized agencies and supervision of subsidiary bodies, in particular its functional commissions, and to promote the implementation of Agenda 21 by strengthening system-wide coordination, the Council should:

(a) Increase its role in overseeing system-wide coordination and the balanced integration of economic, social and environmental aspects of United Nations policies and programmes aimed at promoting sustainable development;

(b) Organize periodic consideration of sustainable development themes in regard to the implementation of Agenda 21, including the means of implementation. Recommendations in regard to such themes could be made by the Commission on Sustainable Development;

(c) Make full use of its high-level, coordination, operational activities and the general segments to effectively take into account all relevant aspects of the work of the United Nations on sustainable development. In this context, the Council should encourage the active participation of major groups in its high-level segment and the work of its relevant functional commissions, in accordance wit h the respective rules of procedure;

(d) Promote greater coordination, complementarity, effectiveness and efficiency of activities of its functional commissions and other subsidiary bodies that are relevant to the implementation of Agenda 21;

(e) Terminate the work of the Committee on Energy and Natural Resources for Development and transfer its work to the Commission on Sustainable Development;

(f) Ensure that there is a close link between the role of the Council in the follow-up to the Summit and its role in the follow-up to the Monterrey Consensus, in a sustained and coordinated manner. To that end, the Council should explore ways to develop arrangements relating to its meetings with the Bretton Woods institutions and the World Trade Organization, as s et out in the Monterrey Consensus;

(g) Intensify its efforts to ensure that gender mainstreaming is an integral part of its activities concerning the coordinated implementation of Agenda 21.

E. Role and Function of the Commission on Sustainable Development

145. The Commission on Sustainable Development should continue to be the high-level commission on sustainable development within the United Nations system and serve as a forum for consideration of issues related to integration of the three dimensions of sustainable development. Although the role, functions and mandate of the Commission as set out in relevant parts of Agenda 21 and adopted in General Assembly resolution 47/191 continue to be relevant, the Commission needs to be strengthened, taking into account the role of relevant institutions and organizations. An enhanced role of the Commission should include reviewing and monitoring progress in the implementation of Agenda 21 and fostering coherence of implementation, initiatives and partnerships.

146. Within that context, the Commission should place more emphasis on actions that enable implementation at all levels, including promoting and facilitating partnerships involving Governments, international organizations and relevant stakeholders for the implementation of Agenda 21.

147. The Commission should:

(a) Review and evaluate progress and promote further implementation of Agenda 21;

(b) Focus on the cross-sectoral aspects of specific sectoral issues and provide a forum for better integration of policies, including through interaction among Ministers dealing with the various dimensions and sectors of sustainable development through the high-level segments;

(c) Address new challenges and opportunities related to the implementation of Agenda 21;

(d) Focus on actions related to implementation of Agenda 21, limiting negotiations in the sessions of the Commission to every two years;

(e) Limit the number of themes addressed in each session.

148. In relation to its role in facilitating implementation, the Commission should emphasize the following:

(a) Review progress and promote the further implementation of Agenda 21. In this context, the Commission should identify constraints on implementation and make recommendations to overcome those constraints;

(b) Serve as a focal point for the discussion of partnerships that promote sustainable development, including sharing lessons learned, progress made and best practices;

(c) Review issues related to financial assistance and transfer of technology for sustain able development, as well as capacity-building, while making full use of existing information. In this regard, the Commission on Sustainable Development could give consideration to more effective use of national reports and regional experience and to this end make appropriate recommendations;

(d) Provide a forum for analysis and exchange of experience on measures that assist sustainable development planning, decision-making and the implementation of sustainable development strategies. In this regard, the Commission could give consideration to more effective use of national and regional reports;

(e) Take into account significant legal developments in the field of sustainable development, with due regard to the role of relevant intergovernmental bodies in promoting the implementation of Agenda 21 relating to international legal instruments and mechanisms.

149. With regard to the practical modalities and programme of work of the Commission, specific decisions on those issues should be taken by the Commission at its next session, when the Commission's thematic work programme will be elaborated. In particular, the following issues should be considered:

(a) Giving a balanced consideration to implementation of all of the mandates of the Commission contained in General Assembly resolution 47/191;

(b) Continuing to provide for more direct and substantive involvement of international organizations and major groups in the work of the Commission;

(c) Give greater consideration to the scientific contributions to sustainable development through, for example, drawing on the scientific community and encouraging national, regional and international scientific networks to be involved in the Commission;

(d) Furthering the contribution of educators to sustainable development, including, where appropriate, in the activities of the Commission;

(e) The scheduling and duration of intersessional meetings.

150. Undertake further measures to promote best practices and lessons learned in sustainable development, and in addition promote the use of contemporary methods of data collection and dissemination, including broader use of information technologies.

F. Role of International Institutions

151. Stress the need for international institutions both within and outside the United Nations system, including international financial institutions, the World Trade Organization and the Global Environment Facility, to enhance, within their mandates, their cooperative efforts to:

(a) Promote effective and collective support to the implementation of Agenda 21 at all levels;

(b) Enhance the effectiveness and coordination of international institutions to implement Agenda 21, the outcomes of the World Summit on Sustainable Development, relevant sustainable development aspects of the Millennium Declaration, the Monterrey Consensus and the outcome of the Fourth Ministerial Meeting of the World Trade Organization, held in Doha in November 2001.

152. Request the Secretary-General of the United Nations, utilizing the United Nations System Chief Executives Board for Coordination, including through informal collaborative efforts, to further promote system-wide inter-agency cooperation and coordination on sustainable development, to take appropriate measures to facilitate exchange of information, and to continue to keep the Economic and Social Council and the Commission informed of actions being taken to implement Agenda 21.

153. Significantly strengthen support for the capacity-building programmes of the United Nations Development Programme for sustainable development, building on the experience gained from the Capacity 21 programme, as important mechanisms for supporting local and national development capacity-building efforts, in particular in developing countries.

154. Strengthen cooperation between the United Nations Environment Programme and other United Nations bodies and specialized agencies, the Bretton Woods institutions and the World Trade Organization, within their mandates.

155. The United Nations Environment Programme, the United Nations Centre for Human Settlements, the United Nations Development Programme and the United Nations Conference on Trade and Development, within their mandates, should strengthen their contribution to sustainable development programmes and the implementation of Agenda 21 at all levels, particularly in the area of promoting capacity-building.

156. To promote effective implementation of Agenda 21 at the international level, the following should also be undertaken:

(a) Streamline the international sustainable development meeting calendar and, as appropriate, reduce the number of meetings, the length of meetings and the amount of time spent on negotiated outcomes in favour of more time spent on practical matters related to implementation;

(b) Encourage partnership initiatives for implementation by all relevant actors to support the outcome of the World Summit on Sustainable Development. In this context, further development of partnerships and partnership follow-up should take note of the preparatory work for the Summit;

(c) Make full use of developments in the field of information and communication technologies.

157. Strengthening of the international institutional framework for sustainable development is an evolutionary process. It is necessary to keep relevant arrangements under review; identify gaps; eliminate duplication of functions; and continue to strive for greater integration, efficiency and coordination of the economic, social and environmental dimensions of sustainable development aiming at the implementation of Agenda 21.

G. Strengthening Institutional Arrangements for Sustainable Development at the Regional Level

158. Implementation of Agenda 21 and the outcomes of the Summit should be effectively pursued at the regional and subregional levels, through the regional commissions and other regional and subregional institutions and bodies.

159. Intraregional coordination and cooperation on sustainable development should be improved among the regional commissions, United Nations Funds, programmes and agencies, regional development banks and other regional and subregional institutions and bodies. This should include, as appropriate, support for development, enhancement and implementation of agreed regional sustainable development strategies and action plans, reflecting national and regional priorities.

160. In particular, taking into account relevant provisions of Agenda 21, the regional commissions, in collaboration with other regional and subregional bodies, should:

(a) Promote the integration of the three dimensions of sustainable development into their work in a balanced way, including through implementation of

Agenda 21. To this end, the regional commissions should enhance their capacity through internal action and be provided, as appropriate, with external support;

(b) Facilitate and promote a balanced integration of the economic, social and environmental dimensions of sustainable development into the work of regional, subregional and other bodies, for example by facilitating and strengthening the exchange of experiences, including national experience, best practices, case studies and partnership experience related to the implementation of Agenda 21;

(c) Assist in the mobilization of technical and financial assistance, and facilitate the provision of adequate financing for the implementation of regionally and subregionally agreed sustainable development programmes and projects, including addressing the objective of poverty eradication;

(d) Continue to promote multi-stakeholder participation and encourage partnerships to support the implementation of Agenda 21 at the regional and subregional levels.

161. Regionally and subregionally agreed sustainable development initiatives and programmes, such as the New Partnership for Africa's Development (NEPAD) and the interregional aspects of the globally agreed Programme of Action for the Sustainable Development of Small Island Developing States, should be supported.

H. Strengthening Institutional Frameworks for Sustainable Development at the National Level

162. States should:

(a) Continue to promote coherent and coordinated approaches to institutional frameworks for sustainable development at all national levels, including through, as appropriate, the establishment or strengthening of existing authorities and mechanisms necessary for policy-making, coordination and implementation and enforcement of laws;

(b) Take immediate steps to make progress in the formulation and elaboration of national strategies for sustainable development and begin their implementation by 2005. To this end, as appropriate, strategies should be supported through international cooperation, taking into account the special needs of developing countries, in particular the least developed countries. Such strategies, which, where applicable, could be formulated as poverty reduction strategies that integrate economic, social and environmental aspects of sustainable development, should be pursued in accordance with each country's national priorities.

163. Each country has the primary responsibility for its own sustainable development, and the role of national policies and development strategies cannot be overemphasized. All countries should promote sustainable development at the national level by, inter alia, enacting and enforcing clear and effective laws that

support sustainable development. All countries should strengthen governmental institutions, including by providing necessary infrastructure and by promoting transparency, accountability and fair administrative and judicial institutions.

164. All countries should also promote public participation, including through measures that provide access to information regarding legislation, regulations, activities, policies and programmes. They should also foster full public participation in sustainable development policy formulation and implementation. Women should be able to participate fully and equally in policy formulation and decision-making.

165. Further promote the establishment or enhancement of sustainable development councils and/or coordination structures at the national level, including at the local level, in order to provide a high-level focus on sustainable development policies. In that context, multi-stakeholder participation should be promoted.

166. Support efforts by all countries, particularly developing countries, as well as countries with economies in transition, to enhance national institutional arrangements for sustainable development, including at the local level. That could include promoting cross-sectoral approaches in the formulation of strategies and plans for sustainable development, such as, where applicable, poverty reduction strategies, aid coordination, encouraging participatory approaches and enhancing policy analysis, management capacity and implementation capacity, including mainstreaming a gender perspective in all those activities.

167. Enhance the role and capacity of local authorities as well as stakeholders in implementing Agenda 21 and the outcomes of the Summit and in strengthening the continuing support for local Agenda 21 programmes and associated initiatives and partnerships and encourage, in particular, partnerships among and between local authorities and other levels of government and stakeholders to advance sustainable development as called for in, inter alia, the Habitat Agenda.[47]

I. Participation of Major Groups

168. Enhance partnerships between governmental and non-governmental actors, including all major groups, as well as volunteer groups, on programmes and activities for the achievement of sustainable development at all levels.

169. Acknowledge the consideration being given to the possible relationship between environment and human rights, including the right to development, with full and transparent participation of Member States of the United Nations and observer States.

170. Promote and support youth participation in programmes and activities relating to sustainable development through, for example, supporting local youth councils or their equivalent, and by encouraging their establishment where they do not exist.

---

47   A/CONF.165/14, chap. I, resolution 1, annex II.

UNITED NATIONS RESOLUTIONS AND IMPLEMENTING MEASURES

General Assembly Resolution 47/190

Report of the United Nations Conference on Environment and Development

93rd Meeting
22 December 1992

The General Assembly

Recalling its resolutions 43/196 of 20 December 1988, 44/172 A and B of 19 December 1989, 44/228 of 22 December 1989, 45/211 of 21 December 1990 and 46/168 of 19 December 1991.

Having considered the report of the United Nations Conference on Environment and Development,[1] which was held at Rio de Janeiro, Brazil, from 3 to 14 June 1992,

Expressing its satisfaction that the Conference and its Preparatory Committee provided for active participation of all States Members of the United Nations and its specialized agencies at the highest level, and of observers and various intergovernmental organizations, as well as non-governmental organizations, representing all the regions of the world,

Reaffirming the need for a balanced and integrated approach to environment and development issues,

Reaffirming also a new global partnership for sustainable development,

Expressing its profound gratitude to the Government and the people of Brazil for the hospitality extended to the participants of the Conference and for facilities, staff and services placed at their disposal,

1. *Takes note with satisfaction* of the report of the United Nations Conference on Environment and Development;[2]

---

1   See *Report of the United Nations Conference on Environment and Development, Rio de Janeiro, 3-14 June 1992* (A/CONF.151/26), vols. I, II and Corr.1, and III.

2   See *Report of the United Nations Conference on Environment and Development, Rio de Janeiro, 3-14 June 1992* (A/CONF.151/26), vols. I, II and Corr.1, and III.

2. *Endorses* the Rio Declaration on Environment and Development, Agenda 21 and the Non-Legally Binding Authoritative Statement of Principles for a Global Consensus on the Management, Conservation and Sustainable Development of All Types of Forests, as adopted at the United Nations Conference on Environment and Development on 14 June 1992;[3]

3. *Notes with satisfaction* that the United Nations Framework Convention on Climate Change[4] and the Convention on Biological Diversity were opened for signature and were signed by a large number of States at the United Nations Conference on Environment and Development, and stresses the need for these Conventions to be brought into force as soon as possible;

4. *Urges* Governments, organs, organizations and programmes of the United Nations system as well as other intergovernmental and non-governmental organizations to take the necessary action to give effective follow-up to the Rio Declaration on Environment and Development, Agenda 21 and the Non-legally Binding Authoritative Statement of Principles for a Global Consensus on the Management, Conservation and Sustainable Development of All Types of Forests;

Calls upon all concerned to implement all commitments, agreements and recommendations reached at the United Nations Conference on Environment and Development, especially by ensuring provision of the means of implementation under section IV of Agenda 21, stressing in particular the importance of financial resources and mechanisms, transfer of environmentally sound technology, cooperation and capacity-building, and international institutional arrangements, in order to achieve sustainable development in all countries;

6. *Takes note with appreciation* of the initial financial commitments made by some developed countries at its forty-seventh session and urges those countries which have not done so to announce their commitments in accordance with paragraph 33.19 of Agenda 21;

7. *Decides* to include in the agenda of its forthcoming sessions a standing item entitled "Implementation of decisions and recommendations of the United Nations Conference on Environment and Development";

Also decides to convene not later than 1997 a special session for the purpose of an overall review and appraisal of Agenda 21 and, in this context, requests the Secretary-General to submit to the General Assembly at its forty-ninth session a report containing recommendations for consideration by the Assembly on the format, scope and organizational aspects of such a special session.

---

3   *Ibid.*
4   A/AC.237/18 (Part II)/Add.1 and Corr.1, annex I.

General Assembly Resolution 47/194

Capacity-Building for Agenda 21

93rd Meeting
22 December 1992

The General Assembly

Welcoming the adoption by the United Nations Conference on Environment and Development of Agenda 21, in particular chapter 37, which contains a set of important recommendations on capacity-building,[1]

Noting with interest the launching by the Administrator of the United Nations Development Programme of the "Capacity 21" initiative,

1. *Invites* the Governing Council of the United Nations Development Programme, taking into account national policies, priorities and plans of recipient countries, to give due consideration to the adoption of concrete programmes and measures to implement Agenda 21 recommendations on capacity-building through, *inter alia*, the "Capacity 21" initiative, with a view to promoting early action in support of developing countries, in particular the least developed countries, in the area of capacity-building;

2. *Invites* all relevant United Nations agencies within their mandates to promote early action to implement chapter 37 of Agenda 21;

3. *Requests* the Commission on Sustainable Development, in execution of its mandate, to give urgent consideration to the implementation of the provisions of Agenda 21 on capacity-building.

---

1   See *Report of the United Nations Conference on Environment and Development, Rio de Janeiro, 3-14 June 1992* (A/CONF.151/26), vol. II.

General Assembly Resolution 47/191

Institutional Arrangements to Follow Up the United Nations Conference on Environment and Development

93rd Meeting
22 December 1992

The General Assembly

Welcoming the adoption by the United Nations Conference on Environment and Development of Agenda 21,[1] in particular chapter 38, entitled "International institutional arrangements", which contains a set of important recommendations on institutional arrangements to follow up the Conference,

Stressing the overall objective of the integration of environment and development issues at the national, subregional, regional and international levels, including the United Nations system institutional arrangements, and the specific objectives recommended by the Conference in paragraph 38.8 of Agenda 21,

Taking note of the report of the Secretary-General,[2] prepared with the assistance of the Secretary-General of the United Nations Conference on Environment and Development, on institutional arrangements to follow up the Conference, as well as the recommendations and proposals contained therein,

1. *Endorses* the recommendations on international institutional arrangements to follow up the United Nations Conference on Environment and Development as contained in chapter 38 of Agenda 21, particularly those on the establishment of a high-level Commission on Sustainable Development;

Commission on Sustainable Development

2. *Requests* the Economic and Social Council, at its organizational session for 1993, to set up a high-level Commission on Sustainable Development as a functional commission of the Council, in accordance with Article 68 of the Charter of the United Nations, in order to ensure effective follow-up to the Conference, as

---

1   *Report of the United Nations Conference on Environment and Development, Rio de Janeiro, 3-14 June 1992* (A/CONF.151/26), chap. I, resolution 1, annex II.

2   A/47/598 and Add.1.

well as to enhance international cooperation and rationalize the intergovernmental decision-making capacity for the integration of environment and development issues and to examine the progress of the implementation of Agenda 21 at the national, regional and international levels, fully guided by the principles of the Rio Declaration on Environment and Development[3] and all other aspects of the Conference, in order to achieve sustainable development in all countries.

3. *Recommends* that the Commission have the following functions, as agreed in paragraphs 38.13, 33.13 and 33.21 of Agenda 21:

(a) To monitor progress in the implementation of Agenda 21 and activities related to the integration of environmental and developmental goals throughout the United Nations system through analysis and evaluation of reports from all relevant organs, organizations, programmes and institutions of the United Nations system dealing with various issues of environment and development, including those related to finance;

(b) To consider information provided by Governments, for example, in the form of periodic communications or national reports regarding the activities they undertake to implement Agenda 21, the problems they face, such as problems related to financial resources and technology transfer, and other environment and development issues they find relevant;

(c) To review the progress in the implementation of the commitments set forth in Agenda 21, including those related to the provision of financial resources and transfer of technology;

(d) To review and monitor regularly progress towards the United Nations target of 0.7 per cent of the gross national product of developed countries for official development assistance; this review process should systematically combine the monitoring of the implementation of Agenda 21 with the review of financial resources available;

(e) To review on a regular basis the adequacy of funding and mechanisms, including efforts to reach the objectives agreed in chapter 33 of Agenda 21, including targets where applicable;

(f) To receive and analyse relevant input from competent non-governmental organizations, including the scientific and the private sector, in the context of the overall implementation of Agenda 21;

(g) To enhance the dialogue, within the framework of the United Nations, with non-governmental organizations and the independent sector, as well as other entities outside the United Nations system;

(h) To consider, where appropriate, information regarding the progress made in the implementation of environmental conventions, which could be made available by the relevant conferences of parties;

---

3   *Report of the United Nations Conference on Environment and Development, Rio de Janeiro, 3-14 June 1992* (A/CONF.151/26), chap. I, resolution 1, annex I.

(i) To provide appropriate recommendations to the General Assembly, through the Economic and Social Council, on the basis of an integrated consideration of the reports and issues related to the implementation of Agenda 21;

(j) To consider, at an appropriate time, the results of the review to be conducted expeditiously by the Secretary-General of all recommendations of the Conference for capacity-building programmes, information networks, task forces and other mechanisms to support the integration of environment and development at regional and subregional levels;

Also recommends that the Commission:

(a) Promote the incorporation of the principles of the Rio Declaration on Environment and Development in the implementation of Agenda 21;

(b) Promote the incorporation of the Non-legally Binding Authoritative Statement of Principles for a Global Consensus on the Management, Conservation and Sustainable Development of All Types of Forests[4] in the implementation of Agenda 21, in particular in the context of the review of the implementation of chapter 11 thereof;

(c) Keep under review the implementation of Agenda 21, recognizing that it is a dynamic programme that could evolve over time, taking into account the agreement to review Agenda 21 in 1997, and make recommendations, as appropriate, on the need for new cooperative arrangements related to sustainable development to the Economic and Social Council and, through it, to the General Assembly;

5. *Decides* that the Commission, in the fulfillment of its functions, will also:

(a) Monitor progress in promoting, facilitating and financing, as appropriate, access to and transfer of environmentally sound technologies and corresponding know-hows, in particular to developing countries, on favourable terms, including on concessional and preferential terms, as mutually agreed, taking into account the need to protect intellectual property rights as well as the special needs of developing countries for the implementation of Agenda 21;

(b) Consider issues related to the provision of financial resources from all available funding sources and mechanisms, as contained in paragraphs 33.13 to 33.16 of Agenda 21;

6. *Recommends* that the Commission consist of representatives of fifty-three States elected by the Economic and Social Council from among the Members of the United Nations and members of its specialized agencies for three-year terms, with due regard to equitable geographical distribution; the regional allocation of seats could be the same as that of the Commission on Science and

---

4   Ibid., annex III.

Technology for Development, as decided by the Economic and Social Council in its decision 1992/222 of 29 May 1992; Representation should be at a high level, including ministerial participation; other Members of the United Nations and members of its specialized agencies, as well as other observers of the United Nations, may participate in the Commission in the capacity of observer, in accordance with established practice;

7. *Also recommends* that the Commission:

(a) Provide for representatives of various parts of the United Nations system and other intergovernmental organizations, including international financial institutions, GATT, regional development banks, subregional financial institutions, relevant regional and subregional economic and technical cooperation organizations and regional economic integration organizations, to assist and advise the Commission in the performance of its functions, within their respective areas of expertise and mandates, and participate actively in its deliberations; and provide for the European Community, within its areas of competence, to participate fully—as will be appropriately defined in the rules of procedure applicable to the Commission—without the right to vote;

(b) Provide for non-governmental organizations, including those related to major groups as well as to industry and the scientific and business communities, to participate effectively in its work and contribute within their areas of competence to its deliberations;

Requests the Secretary-General, in the light of paragraph 7 above, to submit, for the consideration of the Economic and Social Council at its organizational session for 1993, his proposals on the rules of procedure applicable to the Commission, including those related to participation of relevant intergovernmental and non-governmental organizations, as recommended by the Conference, taking into account the following:

(a) The procedures, while ensuring the intergovernmental nature of the Commission, should allow its members to benefit from the expertise and competence of relevant intergovernmental and non-governmental organizations;

(b) The procedures should permit relevant intergovernmental organizations inside and outside the United Nations system, including multilateral financial institutions, to appoint special representatives to the Commission;

(c) The rules of procedure of the Economic and Social Council and those of its functional commissions;

(d) The rules of procedure of the United Nations Conference on Environment and Development;

(e) Decisions 1/1[5] and 2/1[6] of the Preparatory Committee for the United Nations Conference on Environment and Development;

(f) Paragraphs 38.11 and 38.44 of Agenda 21;

9. *Recommends* that the Commission shall meet once a year for a period of two to three weeks; the first substantive session of the Commission will be held in New York in 1993, without prejudice to the venue of future sessions at Geneva and/or in New York;

10. *Requests* the Committee on Conferences to consider the need for readjusting the calendar of meetings in order to take account of the interrelationship between the work of the Commission and the work of other relevant United Nations intergovernmental subsidiary organs, in order to ensure timely reporting to the Economic and Social Council;

11. *Recommends* that in 1993, as a transitional measure, the Commission hold a short organizational session in New York; at that session, the Commission will elect the officers of the Commission, namely, a chairman, three vice-chairmen and a rapporteur, one from each of the regional groups, decide on the agenda of its first substantive session and consider all other organizational issues as may be necessary; the agenda of the organizational session of the organizational session of the Commission shall be decided on by the Economic and Social Council at its organizational session for 1993;

12. *Also recommends* that the Commission, at its first substantive session, adopt a multi-year thematic programme of its work that will provide a framework to assess progress achieved in the implementation of Agenda 21 and ensure an integrated approach to all if its environment and development components as well as linkages between sectoral and cross-sectoral issues; this programme could be of clusters that would integrate in an effective manner related sectoral and cross-sectoral components of Agenda 21 in such a way as to allow the Commission to review the progress of the implementation of the entire Agenda 21 by 1997; the programme of work could be adjusted, as the need arises, at subsequent sessions of the Commission;

13. *Requests* the Secretary-General to submit his proposals for such a programme of work during the organizational session of the Commission;

14. *Recommends* that in order to carry out its functions and implement its programme of work effectively the Commission consider organizing its work on the following lines:

(a) Financial resources, mechanisms, transfer of technology, capacity-building and other cross-sectoral issues;

---

5   See *Official Records of the General Assembly, Forty-fifth Session, Supplement No. 46* (A/45/46), annex I.

6   *Ibid., forty-sixth Session, Supplement No. 48* (A/46/48), vol. I, annex I.

(b) Review of the implementation of Agenda 21 at the international level, as well as at the regional and national levels, including the means of implementation, in accordance with paragraph 12 above and the functions of the Commission, taking into account, where appropriate, information regarding progress in the implementation of relevant environmental conventions;

(c) A high-level meeting, with ministerial participation, to have an integrated overview of the implementation of Agenda 21, to consider emerging policy issues and to provide necessary political impetus to the implementation of the decisions of the Conference and the commitments contained therein;

Review and consideration of the implementation of Agenda 21 should be in an integrated manner;

15. *Requests* the Secretary-General to provide for each session of the Commission, in accordance with the programme of work mentioned in paragraph 12 above and with its organizational modalities, analytical reports containing information on relevant activities to implement Agenda 21, progress achieved and emerging issues to be addressed;

16. *Also requests* the Secretary-General to prepare, for the first substantive session of the Commission, reports containing information and proposals, as appropriate, on the following issues:

(a) Initial financial commitments, financial flows and arrangements to give effect to the decisions of the Conference from all available funding sources and mechanisms;

(b) Progress achieved in facilitating and promoting transfer of environmentally sound technologies, cooperation and capacity-building;

(c) Progress in the incorporation of recommendations of the Conference in the activities of international organizations and measures undertaken by the Administrative Committee on Coordination to ensure that sustainable development principles are incorporated into programmes and processes within the United Nations system;

(d) Ways in which, upon request, the United nations system and bilateral donors are assisting countries, particularly developing countries, in the preparation of national reports and national Agenda 21 action plans;

(e) Urgent and major emerging issues that may be addressed in the course of the high-level meeting;

17. *Decides* that organizational modalities for the Commission should be reviewed in the context of the overall review and appraisal of Agenda 21 during the special session for the General Assembly[7] and adjusted, as may be required, to improve its effectiveness;

---

7   See resolution 47/190, para. 8.

Relationship with other United Nations intergovernmental bodies

18. *Recommends* that the Commission, in discharging its function, submit its consolidated recommendations to the Economic and Social Council and, through it, to the General Assembly, to be considered by the Council and the Assembly in accordance with their respective responsibilities as defined in the charter of the United Nations and with the relevant provisions of paragraphs 38.9 and 38.10 of Agenda 21;

19. *Also recommends* that the Commission actively interact with other intergovernmental United Nations bodies dealing with matters related to environment and development;

20. *Emphasizes* that the ongoing restructuring and revitalization of the United Nations in the economic, social and related fields should take into account the organizational modalities for the Commission, with a view to optimizing its work and the work of other intergovernmental United Nations bodies dealing with matters related to environment and development;

Coordination within the United Nations system

21. *Requests* all specialized agencies and related organizations of the United Nations system to strengthen and adjust their activities, programmes and medium-term plans, as appropriate, in line with Agenda 21, in particular regarding projects for promoting sustainable development, in accordance with paragraph 38.28 of Agenda 21, and make their reports on steps they have taken to give effect to this recommendation available to the Commission and the Economic and Social Council in 1993 or, at the latest, in 1994, in accordance with Article 64 of the Charter;

22. *Invites* all relevant governing bodies to ensure that the tasks assigned to them are carried out effectively, including the elaboration and publication on a regular basis of reports on the activities of the organs, programmes and organizations for which they are responsible, and that continuous reviews are undertaken of their policies, programmes, budgets and activities;

23. *Invites* the World Bank and other international, regional and subregional financial and development institutions, including the Global Environment Facility, to submit regularly to the Commission reports containing information on their experience, activities and plans to implement Agenda 21;

24. *Requests* the Secretary-General to submit to the Commission, at its substantive session of 1993, recommendations and proposals for improving coordination of programmes related to development data that exist within the United Nations system, taking into account the provisions of paragraph 40.13 of Agenda 21, *inter alia* regarding "Development Watch";

United Nations Environment Programme, United Nations Development Programme, United Nations Conference on Trade and Development and United Nations Sudano-Sahelian Office

25. *Requests* the Governing Council of the United Nations Environment Programme, the Governing Council of the United Nations Development Programme and the Trade and Development Board to examine the relevant provisions of chapter 38 of Agenda 21 at their next sessions and to submit to the General Assembly at its forty-eighth session, through the Commission and the Economic and Social Council, reports on their specific plans to implement Agenda 21;

26. *Takes note* of the work of the United Nations Centre for Urgent Environmental Assistance, established by the Governing council of the United Nations Environment Programme on an experimental basis, and invites the Governing Council to report to the General Assembly at its forth-eighth session on the experience gained within the Centre;

Regional Commissions

27. *Requests* United Nations regional commissions to examine the relevant provisions of chapter 38 of Agenda 21 at their next sessions and to submit reports on their specific plans to implement Agenda 21;

28. *Requests* the Economic and Social Council to decide on the arrangements required for the reports of regional commissions with the conclusions related to such a review to be made available to the Commission on Sustainable Development in 1993, or at the latest in 1994;

High-level Advisory Board

29. *Endorses* the view of the Secretary-General that the High-level Advisory Board should consist of eminent persons broadly representative of all regions of the world, with recognized expertise on the broad spectrum of issues to be dealt with by the Commission, drawn from relevant scientific disciplines, industry, finance and other major non-governmental constituencies, as well as various disciplines related to environment and development, and that due account should also be given to gender balance;[8]

30. *Decides* that the main task of the Advisory Board is to give broad consideration to issues related to implementation of Agenda 21, taking into account the thematic multi-year programme of work of the Commission, and provide expert advice in that regard to the Secretary-General and, through him, to the Commission, the Economic and Social Council and the General Assembly;

31. *Takes note* of the views of the Secretary-General regarding the functions of the Advisory Board and of the Committee for Development Planning, and requests him to submit appropriate proposals to the Economic and Social Council

---

8   See A/47/598, para. 59.

at its organizational session for 1993, including the possibility of establishing rosters of experts;

Secretariat support arrangements

32. *Takes note* of the decision of the Secretary-General to establish a new Department for Policy Coordination and Sustainable Development, headed at the Under-Secretary-General level, and in this context calls upon the Secretary-General to establish a clearly identifiable, highly qualified and competent secretariat support structure to provide support for the Commission, the Inter-Agency Committee on Sustainable Development and the High-level Advisory Board, taking into account gender balance at all levels, the paramount importance of securing the highest standards of efficiency, competence and integrity, and the importance of recruiting staff on as wide a geographical basis as possible in accordance with Articles 8 and 101 of the Charter and the following criteria:

(a) It should draw on the expertise gained and the working methods and organizational structures developed during the preparatory process for the Conference;

(b) It should work closely with United Nations and other expert bodies in the field of sustainable development and should cooperate closely and cooperatively with the economic and social entities of the Secretariat and the secretariats of the relevant organs, organizations and bodies of the United Nations system, including the secretariats of international financial institutions, and it should provide for effective liaison with relevant non-governmental organizations, including those related to major groups, in particular non-governmental organizations from developing countries;

(c) The secretariat, which will be located in New York, should ensure to all countries easy access to its services; effective interaction with secretariats of other international organizations, financial institutions and relevant conventions whose secretariats have been established definitively or on an interim basis and should have a relevant office at Geneva to establish close links with activities related to follow-up to legal instruments assigned at or mandated by the Conference and to maintain liaison with agencies in the fields of environment and development; the secretariat should also have a liaison office at Nairobi, on the basis of arrangements made at the Conference;

(d) It should be headed by a high-level official designated by the Secretary-General to work closely and directly with him and with assured access to him, as well as with the heads of relevant organizations of the United Nations system, including the multilateral financial and trade organizations, dealing with the implementation of Agenda 21;

(e) It should be funded from the United Nations regular budget and depend to the maximum extent possible upon existing budgetary resources;

(f) It should be supplemented or reinforced, as appropriate, by secondments from other relevant bodies and agencies of the United Nations system, especially the United Nations Environment Programme, the United Nations Development Programme and the World Bank, taking into account the need to ensure that the work programmes of those organizations are not negatively affected, and from national Governments, as well as by appropriate specialists on limited-term contracts from outside the United Nations in such areas as may be required;

(g) It should take into account relevant resolutions and decisions of the General Assembly and the Economic and Social Council regarding women in the United Nations Secretariat;

(h) Sustainable development should be integrated and coordinated with other economic, social and environmental activities of the Secretariat; organizational decisions should be consistent with consensus resolutions in the context of the restructuring and revitalization of the United Nations in the economic, social and related fields;

33. *Requests* the Secretary-General to make the necessary interim secretariat arrangements to ensure adequate preparations and support for the first session of the Commission and the work of the Inter-Agency Committee;

34. *Also requests* the Secretary-General to report to the General Assembly at its forth-eighth session on the implementation of the present resolution.

General Assembly Resolution 58/218

Implementation of Agenda 21, the Programme for the Further Implementation of Agenda 21 and the Outcomes of the World Summit on Sustainable Development

78th plenary meeting
23 December 2003

Resolution adopted by the General Assembly
[*on the report of the Second Committee (A/58/485)*]

The General Assembly,

Recalling its resolutions 55/199 of 20 December 2000, 56/226 of 24 December 2001, 57/253 of 20 December 2002 and 57/270 A and B of 20 December 2002 and 23 June 2003, respectively,

Recalling also the Rio Declaration on Environment and Development,[1] Agenda 21,[2] the Programme for the Further Implementation of Agenda 21,[3] the Johannesburg Declaration on Sustainable Development[4] and the Plan of Implementation of the World Summit on Sustainable Development ("Johannesburg Plan of Implementation"),[5]

Reaffirming the commitment to implement the Johannesburg Plan of Implementation, including the time-bound goals and targets, and other internationally

---

1   *Report of the United Nations Conference on Environment and Development, Rio de Janeiro, 3-14 June 1992* (United Nations publication, Sales No. E.93.I.8 and corrigenda), vol. I: *Resolutions adopted by the Conference*, resolution 1, annex I.

2   Ibid., annex II.

3   Resolution S-19/2, annex.

4   *Report of the World Summit on Sustainable Development, Johannesburg, South Africa, 26 August-4 September 2002* (United Nations publication, Sales No. E.03.II.A.1 and corrigendum), chap. I, resolution 1, annex.

5   Ibid., resolution 2, annex.

agreed development goals, including those contained in the United Nations Millennium Declaration,[6]

Expressing its satisfaction that the Commission on Sustainable Development, at its eleventh session, agreed on its new organization of work and multi-year programme of work, as well as new methods of work aimed at promoting and supporting implementation and the provision for the Commission to work in a series of two-year action-oriented implementation cycles, alternating review and policy years,[7]

Noting the adoption by the Commission, at its eleventh session, of criteria and guidelines on partnership initiatives voluntarily undertaken by some Governments, international organizations and major groups, announced at the World Summit on Sustainable Development and in the follow-up to the Summit, as endorsed by the Economic and Social Council,[8]

Reaffirming the continuing need to ensure a balance between economic development, social development and environmental protection as interdependent and mutually reinforcing pillars of sustainable development,

Reaffirming also that poverty eradication, changing unsustainable patterns of production and consumption and protecting and managing the natural resource base of economic and social development are overarching objectives of, and essential requirements for, sustainable development,

Noting the convening in Marrakesh, Morocco, from 16 to 19 June 2003, of an international expert meeting on a ten-year framework of programmes for sustainable consumption and production,

Recognizing that good governance within each country and at the international level is essential for sustainable development,

1. *Takes note* of the report of the Secretary-General[9] on the activities undertaken in implementation of Agenda 21,[2] the Programme for the Further Implementation of Agenda 21[3] and the outcomes of the World Summit on Sustainable Development;

2. *Reiterates* that sustainable development is a key element of the overarching framework for United Nations activities, in particular for achieving the internationally agreed development goals, including those contained in the United Nations Millennium Declaration[6] and in the Johannesburg Plan of Implementation;[5]

3. *Calls upon* Governments, all relevant international and regional organizations, the Economic and Social Council, the United Nations funds and programmes, the regional commissions and specialized agencies, the international financial insti-

---

6   See resolution 55/2.

7   See *Official Records of the Economic and Social Council, 2003, Supplement No. 9* (E/2003/29), chap I, sect. A.

8   See Economic and Social Council resolution 2003/61.

9   A/58/210.

tutions, the Global Environment Facility and other intergovernmental organizations, in accordance with their respective mandates, as well as major groups, to take action to ensure the effective implementation of and follow-up to the commitments, programmes and time-bound targets adopted at the Summit, and encourages them to report on concrete progress in that regard;

4. *Calls* for the implementation of the commitments, programmes and time-bound targets adopted at the Summit and, to that end, for the fulfilment of the provisions relating to the means of implementation, as contained in the Johannesburg Plan of Implementation;

5. *Requests* the Secretary-General to strengthen system-wide inter-agency cooperation and coordination for the implementation of Agenda 21, the Programme for the Further Implementation of Agenda 21 and the Johannesburg Plan of Implementation, and in that regard to report on such inter-agency cooperation and coordination activities to the Commission on Sustainable Development and the Economic and Social Council in 2004;

6. *Welcomes* the decision of the Commission at its eleventh session to invite the regional commissions, in collaboration with the secretariat of the Commission, to consider organizing regional implementation meetings in order to contribute to the work of the Commission,[7] and in this regard urges the regional commissions to take into account the relevant thematic clusters contained in the Commission's programme of work and to provide inputs as specified by the Commission at its eleventh session;

7. *Also welcomes* the decision of the Commission at its eleventh session to invite other regional and subregional bodies and institutions within and outside the United Nations system to contribute to the preparations for the Commission's review and policy sessions and the intergovernmental preparatory meeting;[7]

8. *Requests* the Secretary-General, in reporting to the Commission at its twelfth session on the state of implementation of Agenda 21, the Programme for the Further Implementation of Agenda 21 and the Johannesburg Plan of Implementation, on the basis of inputs from all levels, as specified by the Commission at its eleventh session, to submit:

(*a*) One report on each of the issues of water, sanitation and human settlement, to be addressed in an integrated manner during the session, which should contain a detailed review of the progress of implementation relating to those issues, taking into account, as appropriate, their interlinkages, while addressing the cross-cutting issues identified by the Commission at its eleventh session;

(*b*) A report on overall progress in the implementation of Agenda 21, the Programme for the Further Implementation of Agenda 21 and the Johannesburg Plan of Implementation, reflecting:

(i) Cross-cutting issues identified by the Commission at its eleventh session;

(ii) Progress made in the three dimensions of sustainable development and their integration;

(iii) Constraints, challenges, opportunities, best practices, information-sharing and lessons learned;

9. *Invites* the Bureau of the Commission at its twelfth session to continue to recommend to the Commission the specific organizational modalities through open-ended and transparent consultations to be conducted in a timely manner, following the established United Nations rules of procedure, bearing in mind that the activities during Commission meetings should provide for balanced involvement of participants from all regions, as well as for gender balance;

10. *Decides* to allocate the resources previously devoted to the former ad hoc intersessional working groups of the Commission to support the participation of representatives of member States of the Commission in one of their respective regional meetings in each implementation cycle;

11. *Invites* donor countries to consider supporting the participation of experts from developing countries in the areas of water, sanitation and human settlement in the next review and policy sessions of the Commission;

12. *Decides* that resources released by the termination of the work of the Committee on Energy and Natural Resources for Development, whose work has been transferred to the Commission, shall be used to support the work of the Commission;

13. *Encourages* Governments and organizations at all levels, as well as major groups, including the scientific community and educators, to undertake results-oriented initiatives and activities to support the work of the Commission and to promote and facilitate the implementation of Agenda 21, the Programme for the Further Implementation of Agenda 21 and the Johannesburg Plan of Implementation, including through voluntary multi-stakeholder partnership initiatives;

14. *Encourages* Governments to participate, at the appropriate level, through representatives of relevant departments and agencies responsible for water, sanitation and human settlement, in the next review and policy sessions of the Commission,

15. *Requests* the Secretariat to submit a summary report containing synthesized information on partnerships to the Commission at its twelfth session, in accordance with its programme and organization of work, noting the particular relevance of such reports in review years, with a view to sharing lessons learned and best practices and identifying and addressing problems, gaps and constraints in the implementation of Agenda 21, the Programme for the Further Implementation of Agenda 21 and the Johannesburg Plan of Implementation;

16. *Requests* the Commission, in accordance with General Assembly resolution 47/191 of 22 December 1992 and as specified by the Commission at its eleventh session, to examine progress made in the cross-cutting issues in the relevant thematic clusters, utilizing inputs from all levels;

17. *Requests* the Economic and Social Council to implement the provisions of the Johannesburg Plan of Implementation relevant to its mandate, in particular to promote the implementation of Agenda 21 by strengthening system-wide coordination;

18. *Urges* the Secretariat, in the preparation of the reports of the Secretary-General referred to in paragraph 8 above, to take due account of national reports;

19. *Decides* to include in the provisional agenda of its fifty-ninth session the item entitled "Implementation of Agenda 21, the Programme for the Further Implementation of Agenda 21 and the outcomes of the World Summit on Sustainable Development", and requests the Secretary-General, at that session, to submit a report on the implementation of the present resolution.

General Assembly Resolution 58/219

United Nations Decade of Education for Sustainable Development

78th plenary meeting
23 December 2003

Resolution adopted by the General Assembly
[*on the report of the Second Committee (A/58/486)*]

The General Assembly,

Recalling chapter 36 of Agenda 21, on promoting education, public awareness and training, adopted at the United Nations Conference on Environment and Development, held in Rio de Janeiro, Brazil, from 3 to 14 June 1992,[1]

Recalling also the relevant provisions of the Plan of Implementation of the World Summit on Sustainable Development ("Johannesburg Plan of Implementation") on education, in particular its provision 124 (*d*) on the United Nations Decade of Education for Sustainable Development,[2]

Recalling further its resolution 57/254 of 20 December 2002,

Reaffirming the internationally agreed development goal of achieving universal primary education, in particular that by 2015 children everywhere, boys and girls alike, will be able to complete a full course of primary schooling,

Taking note of the report of the Director-General of the United Nations Educational, Scientific and Cultural Organization on the United Nations Decade of Education for Sustainable Development,

---

1   See *Report of the United Nations Conference on Environment and Development, Rio de Janeiro, 3-14 June 1992* (United Nations publication, Sales No. E.93.I.8 and corrigenda), vol. I: *Resolutions adopted by the Conference*, resolution 1, annex II.

2   *Report of the World Summit on Sustainable Development, Johannesburg, South Africa, 26 August-4 September 2002* (United Nations publication, Sales No. E.03.II.A.1 and corrigendum), chap. I, resolution 2, annex.

Welcoming the fact that the Commission on Sustainable Development, at its eleventh session, identified education as one of the cross-cutting issues of its multi-year programme of work,[3]

Emphasizing that education is an indispensable element for achieving sustainable development,

1. *Takes note* of the Framework for a Draft International Implementation Scheme prepared by the United Nations Educational, Scientific and Cultural Organization, requests the United Nations Educational, Scientific and Cultural Organization, as the designated lead agency, to promote the United Nations Decade of Education for Sustainable Development, in coordination with other relevant United Nations agencies and programmes, and further requests it to finalize the international implementation scheme, while clarifying its relationship with the existing educational processes, in particular the Dakar Framework for Action adopted at the World Education Forum[4] and the United Nations Literacy Decade,[5] in consultation with Governments, the United Nations and other relevant international organizations, non-governmental organizations and other stakeholders;

2. *Reaffirms* that education for sustainable development is critical for promoting sustainable development, and in this regard encourages Governments to consider the inclusion of measures to implement the United Nations Decade of Education for Sustainable Development in their respective educational strategies and national development plans by 2005;

3. *Invites* Governments to promote public awareness of and wider participation in the United Nations Decade of Education for Sustainable Development, including through cooperation and initiatives engaging civil society and other relevant stakeholders;

4. *Decides* to include in the provisional agenda of its fifty-ninth session, under the item entitled "Environment and sustainable development", a sub-item entitled "United Nations Decade of Education for Sustainable Development".

---

3 See *Official Records of the Economic and Social Council, 2003, Supplement No. 9* (E/2003/29), chap. I, sect. A.

4 See United Nations Educational, Scientific and Cultural Organization, *Final Report of the World Education Forum, Dakar, Senegal, 26-28 April 2000* (Paris, 2000).

5 See resolution 56/116.

General Assembly Resolution 58/243

Protection of Global Climate for Present and Future Generations of Mankind

79th plenary meeting
23 December 2003

Resolution adopted by the General Assembly
[*on the report of the Second Committee (A/58/484/Add.6)*]

The General Assembly,

Recalling its resolution 54/222 of 22 December 1999, its decision 55/443 of 20 December 2000 and its resolutions 56/199 of 21 December 2001 and 57/257 of 20 December 2002 and other resolutions relating to the protection of the global climate for present and future generations of mankind,

Recalling also the provisions of the United Nations Framework Convention on Climate Change,[1] including the acknowledgement that the global nature of climate change calls for the widest possible cooperation by all countries and their participation in an effective and appropriate international response, in accordance with their common but differentiated responsibilities and respective capabilities and their social and economic conditions,

Recalling further the Johannesburg Declaration on Sustainable Development,[2] the Plan of Implementation of the World Summit on Sustainable Development ("Johannesburg Plan of Implementation")[3] and the Delhi Ministerial Declaration on Climate Change and Sustainable Development, adopted by the Conference of the Parties to the United Nations Framework Convention on Climate Change at its eighth session, held in New Delhi from 23 October to 1 November 2002,[4]

Noting that one hundred and eighty-eight States and one regional economic integration organization have ratified the Convention,

---

1 United Nations, *Treaty Series*, vol. 1771, No. 30822.
2 *Report of the World Summit on Sustainable Development, Johannesburg, South Africa, 26 August-4 September 2002* (United Nations publication, Sales No. E.03.II.A.1 and corrigendum), chap. I, resolution 1, annex.
3 Ibid., resolution 2, annex.
4 FCCC/CP/2002/7/Add.1, decision 1/CP.8.

Remaining deeply concerned that all countries, in particular developing countries, including the least developed countries and small island developing States, face increased risks from the negative impacts of climate change,

Noting the work of the Intergovernmental Panel on Climate Change and the need to build and enhance scientific and technological capabilities, *inter alia*, through continuing support to the Panel for the exchange of scientific data and information, especially in developing countries,

Noting also that, to date, the Kyoto Protocol to the United Nations Framework Convention on Climate Change[5] has attracted one hundred and nineteen ratifications, including from parties mentioned in annex I to the Convention, who account for 44.2 per cent of emissions,

Recalling the United Nations Millennium Declaration,[6] in which heads of State and Government resolved to make every effort to ensure the entry into force of the Kyoto Protocol, preferably by the tenth anniversary of the United Nations Conference on Environment and Development in 2002, and to embark on the required reduction in emissions of greenhouse gases,[7]

Taking note of the report of the Executive Secretary of the United Nations Framework Convention on Climate Change on the work of the Conference of the Parties to the Convention,[8]

1. *Calls upon* States to work cooperatively towards achieving the ultimate objective of the United Nations Framework Convention on Climate Change;[1]

2. *Notes* that States that have ratified the Kyoto Protocol to the United Nations Framework Convention on Climate Change[5] strongly urge States that have not already done so to ratify it in a timely manner;

3. *Notes with interest* the preparations undertaken for the implementation of the flexible mechanisms established by the Kyoto Protocol;

4. *Notes* the ongoing work of the liaison group of the secretariats and officers of the relevant subsidiary bodies of the United Nations Framework Convention on Climate Change, the United Nations Convention to Combat Desertification in Those Countries Experiencing Serious Drought and/or Desertification, Particularly in Africa,[9] and the Convention on Biological Diversity,[10] and encourages cooperation to promote complementarities among the three secretariats while respecting their independent legal status;

---

5   FCCC/CP/1997/7/Add.1, decision 1/CP.3, annex.

6   See resolution 55/2.

7   Ibid., para. 23.

8   A/58/308.

9   United Nations, *Treaty Series*, vol. 1954, No. 33480.

10   Ibid., vol. 1760, No. 30619.

5. *Requests* the Secretary-General to make provisions for the sessions of the Conference of the Parties to the United Nations Framework Convention on Climate Change and its subsidiary bodies in his proposal for the programme budget for the biennium 2004-2005;

6. *Invites* the Executive Secretary of the United Nations Framework Convention on Climate Change to report to the General Assembly at its fifty-ninth session on the work of the Conference of the Parties;

7. *Invites* the conferences of the parties to the multilateral environmental conventions, when setting the dates of their meetings, to take into consideration the schedule of meetings of the General Assembly and the Commission on Sustainable Development so as to ensure the adequate representation of developing countries at those meetings;

8. *Decides* to include in the provisional agenda of its fifty-ninth session the sub-item entitled "Protection of global climate for present and future generations of mankind".

General Assembly Resolution 58/212

Convention on Biological Diversity

78th plenary meeting
23 December 2003

Resolution adopted by the General Assembly
[*on the report of the Second Committee (A/58/484/Add.3)*]

The General Assembly,

Recalling its resolutions 55/201 of 20 December 2000, 56/197 of 21 December 2001 and 57/253 and 57/260 of 20 December 2002,

Reiterating that the Convention on Biological Diversity[1] is the key international instrument for the conservation and sustainable use of biological resources and the fair and equitable sharing of benefits arising from the use of genetic resources,

Recalling the World Summit on Sustainable Development commitments to pursue a more efficient and coherent implementation of the three objectives of the Convention and the achievement by 2010 of a significant reduction in the current rate of loss of biological diversity, which will require action at all levels, including the implementation of national biodiversity strategies and action plans and the provision of new and additional financial and technical resources to developing countries,

Reaffirming the urgency to recognize, subject to national legislation, the rights of local and indigenous communities that are holders of traditional knowledge, innovations and practices, and, with the approval and involvement of the holders of such knowledge, innovations and practices, to develop and implement benefit-sharing mechanisms, on mutually agreed terms, for the use of such knowledge, innovations and practices,

Expressing its deep appreciation for the generous offer of the Government of Malaysia to host the seventh meeting of the Conference of the Parties to the Convention on Biological Diversity and the first meeting of the Conference of the Parties to the Convention serving as the meeting of the Parties to the Cartagena

---

1   United Nations, *Treaty Series*, vol. 1760, No. 30619.

Protocol on Biosafety, to be held at Kuala Lumpur, respectively, from 9 to 20 February and from 23 to 27 February 2004,

1. *Takes note* of the report of the Executive Secretary of the Convention on Biological Diversity, submitted by the Secretary-General to the General Assembly at its fifty-eighth session;[2]

2. *Notes* the outcome of the open-ended intersessional meeting on the multi-year programme of work of the Conference of the Parties to the Convention on Biological Diversity up to 2010, held at Montreal, Canada, from 17 to 20 March 2003;

3. *Notes also* the outcomes of the eighth and ninth meetings of the Subsidiary Body on Scientific, Technical and Technological Advice of the Conference of the Parties to the Convention on Biological Diversity, held at Montreal, Canada, from 10 to 14 March and from 10 to 14 November 2003;

4. *Reiterates* the World Summit on Sustainable Development commitment to negotiate within the framework of the Convention on Biological Diversity, bearing in mind the Bonn Guidelines on Access to Genetic Resources and Fair and Equitable Sharing of the Benefits Arising out of their Utilization, an international regime to promote and safeguard the fair and equitable sharing of benefits arising out of the utilization of genetic resources;

5. *Reiterates also* the World Summit on Sustainable Development commitment to promote the wide implementation of and continued work on the Bonn Guidelines, as an input to assist the parties when developing and drafting legislative, administrative or policy measures on access and benefit-sharing as well as contract and other arrangements under mutually-agreed terms for access and benefit-sharing;

6. *Invites* the countries that have not yet done so to ratify the Convention on Biological Diversity;

7. *Welcomes* the entry into force of the Cartagena Protocol on Biosafety to the Convention on Biological Diversity,[3] on 11 September 2003, and the convening of the first meeting of the Conference of the Parties serving as the meeting of the Parties to the Cartagena Protocol on Biosafety, and invites the parties to the Convention that have not yet ratified or acceded to the Protocol to consider doing so;

8. *Emphasizes* that the effective implementation of the Cartagena Protocol on Biosafety will require full support from parties and relevant international organizations, and further urges parties to facilitate capacity-building in biosafety in developing countries as well as countries with economies in transition, includ-

---

2   A/58/191.

3   See UNEP/CBD/ExCOP/1/3 and Corr.1, part two, annex. in transition, and in this regard welcomes the successful and substantial third replenishment of the Global Environment Facility;

ing to develop and strengthen national capacities for making the required information available to and interacting with the Biosafety Clearing House;

9. *Invites* countries to consider ratifying or acceding to the International Treaty on Plant Genetic Resources for Food and Agriculture;

10. *Encourages* developed countries parties to the Convention to contribute to the relevant trust funds of the Convention, in particular so as to enhance the full participation of the developing countries parties in all its activities;

11. *Urges* parties to the Convention on Biological Diversity to facilitate the transfer of technology for the effective implementation of the Convention in accordance with its provisions;

12. *Underlines* the need for increased financial and technical resources for the implementation of the Convention on Biological Diversity and the Cartagena Protocol on Biosafety by developing countries as well as countries with economies;

13. *Takes note* of the ongoing work of the liaison group of the secretariats and offices of the relevant subsidiary bodies of the United Nations Framework Convention on Climate Change,[4] the United Nations Convention to Combat Desertification in Those Countries Experiencing Serious Drought and/or Desertification, Particularly in Africa,[5] and the Convention on Biological Diversity, and further encourages continuing cooperation in order to promote complementarities among the secretariats, while respecting their independent legal status;

14. *Stresses* the importance of harmonizing the reporting requirements of the biodiversity-related conventions while respecting their independent legal status;

15. *Invites* the Executive Secretary of the Convention on Biological Diversity to continue reporting to the General Assembly on the ongoing work regarding the Convention, including its Cartagena Protocol;

16. *Decides* to include in the provisional agenda of its fifty-ninth session the sub-item entitled "Convention on Biological Diversity".

---

4   United Nations, *Treaty Series*, vol. 1771, No. 30822.
5   Ibid., vol. 1954, No. 33480.

General Assembly Resolution 58/242

Implementation of the United Nations Convention to Combat Desertification in Those Countries Experiencing Serious Drought and/or Desertification, Particularly in Africa

79th plenary meeting
23 December 2003

Resolution adopted by the General Assembly
[*on the report of the Second Committee (A/58/484/Add.2)*]

The General Assembly,

Recalling its resolutions 56/196 of 21 December 2001 and 57/259 of 20 December 2002 and other resolutions relating to the United Nations Convention to Combat Desertification in Those Countries Experiencing Serious Drought and/or Desertification, Particularly in Africa,[1]

Recognizing the strong commitment of the international community, demonstrated at the World Summit on Sustainable Development[2] and the Second Assembly of the Global Environment Facility, to make the Facility available as a financial mechanism of the Convention, pursuant to article 21 of the Convention,

Recognizing also the role of the Conference of the Parties to the Convention, as the highest decision-making body, in providing guidance on matters regarding the implementation of the Convention and in encouraging financial mechanisms to seek to maximize the availability of resources for affected developing countries, while respecting the respective mandates of the mechanisms,

Reaffirming that the Convention is an important tool for poverty eradication, particularly in Africa, and recognizing the importance of the implementation of

---

1   United Nations,*Treaty Series*, vol. 1954, No. 33480.

2   *Report of the World Summit on Sustainable Development, Johannesburg, South Africa, 26 August-4 September 2002* (United Nations publication, Sales No. E.03.II.A.1 and corrigendum), chap. I, resolution 1, annex, and resolution 2, annex.

the Convention for meeting the internationally agreed development goals, including those contained in the United Nations Millennium Declaration,[3]

Reaffirming also the universal membership of the Convention, and acknowledging that desertification and drought are problems of a global dimension, in that they affect all regions of the world,

Expressing its deep appreciation and gratitude to the Government of Cuba for hosting the sixth session of the Conference of the Parties to the Convention in Havana from 25 August to 5 September 2003,

1. *Takes note* of the report of the Secretary-General;[4]

2. *Welcomes* the decision of the Conference of the Parties to the United Nations Convention to Combat Desertification in Those Countries Experiencing Serious Drought and/or Desertification, Particularly in Africa, at its sixth session, to accept the Global Environment Facility as a financial mechanism of the Convention, pursuant to article 21 of the Convention;

3. *Also welcomes* the decision of the Council of the Global Environment Facility at its meeting, held in Washington, D.C., from 14 to 16 May 2003, to establish a new operational programme on sustainable land management, and, in that regard, urges the Executive Secretary, in collaboration with the Managing Director of the Global Mechanism, to consult with the Chief Executive Officer and Chairman of the Global Environment Facility, with a view to preparing and agreeing upon a memorandum of understanding, as mandated by the Conference of the Parties, for the consideration of and adoption by the Conference of Parties and the Council of the Global Environment Facility;

4. *Further welcomes* the outcome of the Second Assembly of the Global Environment Facility, held in Beijing from 16 to 18 October 2002, in particular the decision to designate land degradation as a new focal area of the Facility, which will, inter alia, support the implementation of the Convention;

5. *Notes with appreciation* the increased number of affected developing country parties that have adopted their national, subregional and regional action programmes, and urges affected developing countries that have not yet done so to accelerate the process of elaboration and adoption of their action programmes, with a view to finalizing them as soon as possible;

6. *Invites* affected developing countries to place the implementation of their action programmes to combat desertification high among their priorities in their dialogue with their development partners;

---

3   See resolution 55/2.

4   A/58/158.

7. *Calls upon* affected parties, with the collaboration of relevant multilateral organizations, including the Global Environment Facility implementation agencies, to integrate desertification into their strategies for sustainable development;

8. *Urges* the international community to take effective measures for the implementation of the Convention through bilateral and multilateral cooperation programmes;

9. *Urges* the United Nations funds and programmes, the Bretton Woods institutions, the donor countries and other development agencies to integrate actions in support of the Convention in their strategies to support the achievement of internationally agreed development goals, including those contained in the United Nations Millennium Declaration;[3]

10. *Welcomes* the strengthened cooperation between the secretariat of the Convention and the Global Mechanism through the elaboration and implementation of a joint work plan aimed at maximizing the impact of resources and actions, avoiding duplication and overlap and tapping into the expertise, added value and network of each organization in a collaborative manner as action programmes are implemented;

11. *Invites* all parties to pay promptly and in full the contributions required for the core budget of the Convention for the biennium 2002-2003, and urges all parties that have not yet paid their contributions for the year 1999 and/or the biennium 2000-2001 to do so as soon as possible in order to ensure continuity in the cash flow required to finance the ongoing work of the Conference of the Parties, the secretariat and the Global Mechanism;

12. *Calls upon* Governments, and invites multilateral financial institutions, regional development banks, regional economic integration organizations and all other interested organizations, as well as non-governmental organizations and the private sector, to contribute generously to the General Fund, the Supplementary Fund and the Special Fund, in accordance with the relevant paragraphs of the financial rules of the Conference of the Parties,[5] and welcomes the financial support already provided by some countries;

13. *Takes note* of Conference of the Parties decision 23/COP.6 of 5 September 2003 on the programme and budget for the biennium 2004-2005,[6] as an ongoing process of the Conference of the Parties to undertake a comprehensive review of the activities of the secretariat, as defined in article 23, paragraph 2, of the Convention;

14. *Requests* the Secretary-General to make provision for the sessions of the Conference of the Parties and its subsidiary bodies, including the seventh ordi-

---

5   ICCD/COP (1)/11/Add.1 and Corr.1, decision 2/COP.1, annex, paras. 7-11.
6   See ICCD/COP(6)/11/Add.1.

nary session of the Conference and the meetings of its subsidiary bodies, in his proposal for the programme budget for the biennium 2004-2005;

15. *Also requests* the Secretary-General to report to the General Assembly at its fifty-ninth session on the implementation of the present resolution;

16. *Decides* to include in the provisional agenda of its fifty-ninth session the sub-item entitled "Implementation of the United Nations Convention to Combat Desertification in Those Countries Experiencing Serious Drought and/or Desertification, Particularly in Africa".

General Assembly Resolution 58/226

Implementation of the outcome of the United Nations Conference on Human Settlements (Habitat II) and the strengthening of the United Nations Human Settlements Programme (UN-Habitat)

78th plenary meeting
23 December 2003

Resolution adopted by the General Assembly
[*on the report of the Second Committee (A/58/491)*]

The General Assembly,

Recalling its resolutions 3327 (XXIX) of 16 December 1974, 32/162 of 19 December 1977, 34/115 of 14 December 1979, 56/205 and 56/206 of 21 December 2001 and 57/275 of 20 December 2002,

Taking note of Economic and Social Council resolutions 2002/38 of 26 July 2002 and 2003/62 of 25 July 2003,

Recalling the Habitat Agenda[1] and the Declaration on Cities and Other Human Settlements in the New Millennium,[2]

Recalling also the goal contained in the United Nations Millennium Declaration[3] of achieving a significant improvement in the lives of at least 100 million slum-dwellers by 2020, as proposed in the Cities Without Slums Initiative, and recalling further the goal contained in the Plan of Implementation of the World Summit on Sustainable Development ("Johannesburg Plan of Implementation")[4] to halve, by the year 2015, the proportion of people who are unable to reach or

---

1   *Report of the United Nations Conference on Human Settlements (Habitat II), Istanbul, 3-14 June 1996* (United Nations publication, Sales No. E.97.IV.6), chap. I, resolution 1, annex II.

2   Resolution S-25/2, annex.

3   See resolution 55/2.

4   *Report of the World Summit on Sustainable Development, Johannesburg, South Africa, 26 August-4 September 2002* (United Nations publication, Sales No. E.03.II.A.1 and corrigendum), chap. I, resolution 2, annex.

afford safe drinking water and the proportion of people who do not have access to basic sanitation,

Taking into account the Johannesburg Declaration on Sustainable Development[5] and the Johannesburg Plan of Implementation, as well as the Monterrey Consensus of the International Conference on Financing for Development,[6]

Recognizing that the overall thrust of the new strategic vision of the United Nations Human Settlements Programme (UN-Habitat) and its emphasis on the two global campaigns on secure tenure and urban governance are strategic points of entry for the effective implementation of the Habitat Agenda, especially for guiding international cooperation in respect of adequate shelter for all and sustainable human settlements development,

Conscious of the need to achieve greater coherence and effectiveness in the implementation of the Habitat Agenda, the Declaration on Cities and Other Human Settlements in the New Millennium and the relevant internationally agreed development goals, including those contained in the Millennium Declaration,

Recognizing the need for increased and predictable financial contributions to the United Nations Habitat and Human Settlements Foundation in the new millennium to ensure timely, effective and concrete results in the implementation of the Habitat Agenda, the Declaration on Cities and Other Human Settlements in the New Millennium and the relevant internationally agreed development goals, including those contained in the Millennium Declaration and the Johannesburg Declaration and Plan of Implementation, particularly in developing countries,

Welcoming the establishment by the Executive Director of UN-Habitat of a Water and Sanitation Trust Fund as a financing mechanism to support the creation of enabling environments for pro-poor investment in water and sanitation in developing-country cities,

Commending those countries that have contributed to the United Nations Habitat and Human Settlements Foundation, as indicated in the report of the Secretary-General to the Economic and Social Council,[7]

Reiterating the call to the Executive Director of UN-Habitat to increase her efforts to strengthen the Foundation in order to achieve its primary operative objective, as set out in resolution 3327 (XXIX), of supporting the implementation of the Habitat Agenda, including supporting shelter, related infrastructure-development programmes and housing-finance institutions and mechanisms, particularly in developing countries,

---

5   Ibid., resolution 1, annex.

6   *Report of the International Conference on Financing for Development, Monterrey, Mexico, 18-22 March 2002* (United Nations publication, Sales No. E.02.II.A.7), chap. I, resolution 1, annex. [Reprinted in this volume.]

7   E/2003/76.

Recalling the decision of the Commission on Sustainable Development at its eleventh session to address the themes of water, sanitation and human settlements in its next review and policy sessions,[8]

Noting the efforts by UN-Habitat to forge partnerships with Habitat Agenda partners, other United Nations funds and programmes and international financial institutions, such as the World Bank,

Recognizing that shelter and human settlements planning and administration are important sectors in humanitarian efforts,

Expressing its appreciation to the Government of Spain and the city of Barcelona for their willingness to host the second session of the World Urban Forum in 2004 and to the Government of Canada and the city of Vancouver for their willingness to host the third session of the World Urban Forum in 2006,

1. *Takes note* of the report of the Governing Council of the United Nations Human Settlements Programme (UN-Habitat) on the work of its nineteenth session[9] and the report of the Secretary-General on the special session of the General Assembly for an overall review and appraisal of the implementation of the outcome of the United Nations Conference on Human Settlements (Habitat II) and the strengthening of UN-Habitat;[10]

2. *Recognizes* that Governments have the primary responsibility for the sound and effective implementation of the Habitat Agenda[1] and the Declaration on Cities and Other Human Settlements in the New Millennium,[2] and stresses that the international community should fully implement its commitments to support the Governments of developing countries and countries with economies in transition in their efforts, through the provision of the requisite resources, capacity-building, the transfer of technology and the creation of an international enabling environment;

3. *Encourages* Governments to include issues pertaining to shelter and sustainable human settlements and urban poverty in their national development strategies, including poverty reduction strategy papers, where they exist;

4. *Urges* Governments to promote pro-poor investments in services and infrastructure, in particular water and sanitation, in order to improve living environments, in particular in slums and informal settlements;

5. *Encourages* Governments to establish local, national and regional urban observatories and to provide financial and substantive support to UN-Habitat for the further development of methodologies for data collection, analysis and dissemination;

---

8   See *Official Records of the Economic and Social Council, 2003, Supplement No. 9* (E/2003/29), chap. I, sect. A.

9   *Official Records of the General Assembly, Fifty-eighth Session, Supplement No. 8* (A/58/8).

10   A/58/178.

6. *Also encourages* Governments to support and enable the participation of youth in the implementation of the Habitat Agenda through social, cultural and economic activities at the city level and other national- and local-level activities;

7. *Encourages* Governments and UN-Habitat to continue to promote partnerships with local authorities, non-governmental organizations, the private sector and other Habitat Agenda partners, including women's groups and academic and professional groups, in order to empower them, within the legal framework and conditions of each country, to play a more effective role in the provision of adequate shelter for all and sustainable human settlements development in an urbanizing world;

8. *Encourages* UN-Habitat to continue to work closely with other relevant agencies within the United Nations system, in particular members and observers of the United Nations Development Group and the members of the Inter-Agency Standing Committee;[11]

9. *Requests* UN-Habitat to strengthen further its efforts to make the Cities Alliance initiative an effective means for the implementation of the twin goals of the Habitat Agenda, namely, adequate shelter for all and sustainable human settlements development in an urbanizing world;

10. *Takes note with appreciation* of the efforts by the Cities Alliance partnership between the World Bank and UN-Habitat, and other donor countries, to continue to provide an important forum for policy coordination and development, as well as to provide support for the preparation of pro-poor city development strategies and slum-upgrading programmes within the legal framework and conditions of each country;

11. *Invites* the Secretary-General to incorporate the assessment of the progress towards the target of achieving a significant improvement in the lives of at least 100 million slum-dwellers by 2020 in his report on the review in 2005 of the implementation of the United Nations Millennium Declaration;[3]

12. *Welcomes* the fund-raising efforts of the Executive Director of UN-Habitat, which realized an increase in the general-purpose contributions of the United Nations Habitat and Human Settlements Foundation for the year 2003;

13. *Calls* for continued financial support to UN-Habitat through increased voluntary contributions to the Foundation, and invites Governments to provide multi-year funding to support programme implementation;

14. *Requests* UN-Habitat to collaborate with the Division for Sustainable Development of the Department of Economic and Social Affairs of the Secretariat in the preparations for the twelfth session of the Commission on Sustainable Development to promote a fruitful discussion on the thematic cluster of issues on water, sanitation and human settlements;

---

11   Established pursuant to resolution 46/182 of 19 December 1991.

15. *Requests* the Executive Director of UN-Habitat to inform the Governing Council of the United Nations Human Settlements Programme of the results of the discussions on the topics of water, sanitation and human settlements at the twelfth session of the Commission on Sustainable Development;

16. *Notes* that the upcoming sessions of the World Urban Forum, a non-legislative technical forum, which will be held in Barcelona in 2004 and in Vancouver in 2006, will offer an opportunity to experts to exchange experiences, best practices and lessons learned in the field of human settlements;

17. *Invites* donor countries to support the participation of representatives of the developing countries in the second and future sessions of the World Urban Forum;

18. *Requests* the Secretary-General to keep the resource needs of UN-Habitat and the United Nations Office at Nairobi under review so as to permit the delivery, in an effective manner, of necessary services to UN-Habitat and the other United Nations organs and organizations in Nairobi;

19. *Requests* UN-Habitat, as the focal point for human settlements development and for coordination of human settlements activities within the United Nations system, to work towards coordination of human settlements issues as inputs to the overall coordination of humanitarian efforts, including through its participation in the consideration by the Economic and Social Council, in the near future, of the issue of the transition from relief to development;

20. *Requests* the Secretary-General to submit a report to the General Assembly at its fifty-ninth session on the implementation of the present resolution;

21. *Decides* to include in the provisional agenda of its fifty-ninth session an item entitled "Special session of the General Assembly for an overall review and appraisal of the implementation of the outcome of the United Nations Conference on Human Settlements (Habitat II) and the strengthening of the United Nations Human Settlements Programme (UN-Habitat)".

General Assembly Second Committee Report 58/491

Implementation of the Outcome of the United Nations Conference on Human Settlements (Habitat II) and of the Twenty-Fifth Special Session of the General Assembly

---

Rapporteur: Mr. José Alberto **Briz Gutiérrez** (Guatemala)

I. Introduction

1. At its 2nd plenary meeting, on 19 September 2003, the General Assembly, on the recommendation of the General Committee, decided to include in the agenda of its fifty-eighth session the item entitled "Implementation of the outcome of the United Nations Conference on Human Settlements (Habitat II) and of the twenty-fifth special session of the General Assembly" and to allocate it to the Second Committee.

2. The Second Committee considered the item at its 27th, 34th, 36th and 40th meetings, on 6 and 12 November and 9 and 16 December 2003. An account of the Committee's discussion of the item is contained in the relevant summary records (A/C.2/58/SR.27, 34, 36 and 40). Attention is also drawn to the general debate held by the Committee at its 2nd to 6th meetings, from 6 to 9 October (see A/C.2/58/SR.2-6).

3. For its consideration of the item, the Committee had before it the following documents:

(a) Report of the Governing Council of the United Nations Human Settlements Programme on the work of its nineteenth session;[1]

(b) Report of the Secretary-General on the special session of the General Assembly for an overall review and appraisal of the implementation of the outcome of the United Nations Conference on Human Settlements (Habitat II) and the strengthening of the United Nations Human Settlements Programme (A/58/178);

---

1   *Official Records of the General Assembly, Fifty-eighth Session, Supplement No. 8* (A/58/8).

(c) Letter dated 14 July 2003 from the Permanent Representative of Morocco to the United Nations addressed to the Secretary-General, transmitting the final communiqué adopted by the Chairmen/Coordinators of the Chapters of the Group of 77 at their thirty-fourth meeting, held at Geneva on 26 and 27 June 2003 (A/58/204).

4. At the 27th meeting, on 6 November, the Executive Director of the United Nations Human Settlements Programme (UN-Habitat) made an introductory statement (see A/C.2/58/SR.27).

II. Consideration of proposals

A. Draft resolutions A/C.2/58/L.31 and A/C.2/58/L.64

5. At the 34th meeting, on 12 November, the representative of Morocco, on behalf of the States Members of the United Nations that are members of the Group of 77 and China, introduced a draft resolution entitled "Implementation of the outcome of the United Nations Conference on Human Settlements (Habitat II) and the strengthening of the United Nations Human Settlements Programme (UN-Habitat)" (A/C.2/58/L.31), which read:

"*The General Assembly*,

"*Recalling* its resolutions 3327 (XXIX) of 16 December 1974, 32/162 of 19 December 1977, 34/115 of 14 December 1979, 56/205 and 56/206 of 21 December 2001 and 57/275 of 20 December 2002,

"*Taking note* of Economic and Social Council resolutions 2002/38 of 26 July 2002 and 2003/62 of 25 July 2003,

"*Recalling* the Habitat Agenda and the Declaration on Cities and Other Human Settlements in the New Millennium,

"*Recalling also* the goals contained in the United Nations Millennium Declaration of achieving a significant improvement in the lives of at least 100 million slum dwellers by 2020, as proposed in the Cities Without Slums initiative, and to halve by 2015 the proportion of people who are unable to reach or afford safe drinking water,

"*Taking into account* the Johannesburg Declaration on Sustainable Development and the Plan of Implementation of the World Summit on Sustainable Development ('Johannesburg Plan of Implementation'), as well as the Monterrey Consensus of the International Conference on Financing for Development,

"*Recognizing* the urgent need for increased and predictable financial contributions to the United Nations Habitat and Human Settlements Foundation to ensure timely and effective implementation of the Habitat Agenda, the Declaration on Cities and Other Human Settlements in the New Millennium and the relevant development goals contained in the United Nations Millennium Declaration and the Johannesburg Declaration and Plan of Implementation,

"*Reiterating* the call to the Executive Director of UN-Habitat to strengthen the Foundation in order to achieve its primary operative objective of supporting the implementation of the Habitat Agenda, including supporting shelter, related infrastructure-development programmes and housing-finance institutions and mechanisms, particularly in developing countries,

"*Recalling* the decision of the Commission on Sustainable Development to address the themes of water, sanitation and human settlements in its next review and policy sessions,

"*Noting* the efforts by the United Nations Human Settlements Programme (UN-Habitat) to forge partnerships with Habitat Agenda partners, other United Nations funds and programmes and with international financial institutions, such as the World Bank,

"1. *Takes note* of the report of the Governing Council of the United Nations Human Settlements Programme on the work of its nineteenth session and the report of the Secretary-General on the special session of the General Assembly for an overall review and appraisal of the implementation of the outcome of the United Nations Conference on Human Settlements (Habitat II) and the strengthening of the United Nations Human Settlements Programme (UN-Habitat);

"2. *Calls upon* Governments to integrate sustainable human settlements into their national development strategies;

"3. *Urges* Governments to promote pro-poor investments in water and sanitation in order to improve living environments, in particular in slums and informal settlements;

"4. *Encourages* Governments to establish national urban observatories and to provide financial and substantive support to UN-Habitat for the further development of methodologies for data collection and dissemination;

"5. *Calls upon* the international community and donor countries to support the efforts of developing countries towards achieving the targets and goals on sustainable human settlements through providing assistance in financial resources, technology transfer and capacity-building;

"6. *Encourages* UN-Habitat to continue to promote partnerships with local authorities and other Habitat Agenda partners in order to empower them, within the legal framework and conditions of each country, to play a more effective role in the provision of adequate shelter for all and sustainable human settlements development in an urbanizing world;

"7. *Also encourages* UN-Habitat to continue to work closely with other relevant agencies within the United Nations system, including the United Nations Environment Programme;

"8. *Urges* UN-Habitat to strengthen further its efforts to make the Cities Alliance initiative an effective means for the implementation of the twin goals of the Habitat Agenda, namely, adequate shelter for all and sustainable human settlements development in an urbanizing world;

"9. *Takes note* with appreciation of the efforts by the Cities Alliance partnership between the World Bank and UN-Habitat, and other donor countries, to continue to provide an important forum for policy coordination and development, as well as to provide support for the preparation of pro-poor city development strategies and slum upgrading programmes within the legal framework and conditions of each country;

"10. *Requests* the Secretary-General to incorporate the Cities Without Slums initiative in his report for the 2005 review of the implementation of the United Nations Millennium Declaration;

"11. *Welcomes* the fund-raising efforts of the Executive Director of UN-Habitat, which realized an increase in the general purpose contributions of the Foundation for the year 2003;

"12. *Welcomes also* the establishment by the Executive Director of UN-Habitat of a Water and Sanitation Trust Fund as a financing mechanism to support the creation of enabling environments for pro-poor investment in water and sanitation in developing country cities;

"13. *Calls* for continued financial support to UN-Habitat and its Foundation, including the Water and Sanitation Trust Fund, and invites Governments to increase unearmarked voluntary contributions to the Foundation and to provide multi-year funding to support programme implementation;

"14. *Calls upon* UN-Habitat to work closely with the Division for Sustainable Development of the Department of Economic and Social Affairs of the Secretariat in the preparation for the twelfth session of the Commission on Sustainable Development to ensure fruitful discussion on the thematic cluster of issues on water, sanitation and human settlements;

"15. *Encourages* Governments to participate at the appropriate level with representatives from relevant departments and agencies in water, sanitation and human settlements in the next review and policy sessions of the Commission on Sustainable Development;

"16. *Requests* donor countries to support experts in water, sanitation and human settlements from developing countries to participate in the next review and policy sessions of the Commission on Sustainable Development;

"17. *Invites* donor countries to contribute to the travel and participation of representatives of the developing countries in the second and future sessions of the World Urban Forum;

"18. *Requests* the Secretary-General to ensure that modern conference management and documentation services, systems and technology are made available to the United Nations Office at Nairobi in order to permit the delivery, in an effective manner, of necessary services to the UN-Habitat and the other United Nations organs and organizations in Nairobi;

"19. *Also requests* the Secretary-General to submit a report to the General Assembly at its fifty-ninth session on the implementation of the present resolution;

"20. *Decides* to include in the provisional agenda of its fifty-ninth session an item entitled 'Special session of the General Assembly for an overall review and appraisal of the implementation of the outcome of the United Nations Conference on Human Settlements (Habitat II) and the strengthening of the United Nations Human Settlements Programme (UN-Habitat)'."

6. At the 40th meeting, on 16 December, the Vice-Chairperson of the Committee, Irena Zubčević (Croatia), introduced a draft resolution entitled "Implementation of the outcome of the United Nations Conference on Human Settlements (Habitat II) and the strengthening of the United Nations Human Settlements Programme (UN-Habitat) (A/C.2/58/L.64), which she submitted on the basis of informal consultations held on draft resolution A/C.2/58/L.31.

7. At the same meeting, the representative of Canada orally corrected the text as follows:

(a) At the end of operative paragraph 8, a reference was added to a footnote reading "Established pursuant to General Assembly resolution 46/182 of 19 December 1991";

(b) In operative paragraph 15 the word "(Mexico)" was deleted.

8. At the same meeting, the Committee adopted draft resolution A/C.2/58/L.64, as orally corrected (see para. 15, draft resolution I).

9. In the light of the adoption of draft resolution A/C.2/58/L.64, draft resolution A/C.2/58/L.31 was withdrawn by its sponsors.

B. Draft resolutions A/C.2/58/L.35 and A/C.2/58/L.46

10. At the 34th meeting, on 12 November, the representative of Morocco, on behalf of the States Members of the United Nations that are members of the Group of 77 and China, introduced a draft resolution entitled "Rules of procedure of the Governing Council of the United Nations Human Settlements Programme (UN-Habitat)" (A/C.2/58/L.35), which read:

"*The General Assembly,*

"*Recalling* its resolution 32/162 of 19 December 1977, by which it established the Commission on Human Settlements and the United Nations Centre for Human Settlements (Habitat),

"*Recalling also* its resolution 56/206 of 21 December 2001, by which it transformed the United Nations Centre for Human Settlements (Habitat) into the United Nations Human Settlements Programme (UN-Habitat) and the Commission on Human Settlements into the Governing Council of UN-Habitat as a subsidiary organ of the General Assembly,

"*Recalling further* paragraph 2 of section IA of its resolution 56/206, in which it decided that the Governing Council should propose, for consideration by the General Assembly, the new rules of procedure of the Governing Council, on the basis of the rules of procedure of the Commission on Human Settlements,

"*Bearing in mind* paragraphs 3, 7 and 8 of section IA of its resolution 56/206,

"*Having considered* the recommendations of the Governing Council as contained in its resolution 19/1 of 9 May 2003, including the oral statement by the Chairman of the Working Group on the Rules of Procedure of the Governing Council, as contained in the report of the Governing Council at its nineteenth session,

"*Adopts* the rules of procedure of the Governing Council of the United Nations Human Settlements Programme (UN-Habitat) as annexed to Governing Council resolution 19/1."

11. At the 36th meeting, on 9 December, the Vice-Chairperson of the Committee, Irena Zubčević (Croatia), introduced a draft resolution entitled "Rules of procedure of the Governing Council of the United Nations Human Settlements Programme (UN-Habitat) (A/C.2/58/L.46), which she submitted on the basis of informal consultations held on draft resolution A/C.2/58/L.35.

12. At the same meeting, the Committee adopted draft resolution A/C.2/58/L.46 (see para. 15, draft resolution II).

13. After the adoption of the draft resolution, the representative of Argentina made a statement (see A/C.2/58/SR.36).

14. In the light of the adoption of draft resolution A/C.2/58/L.46, draft resolution A/C.2/58/L.35 was withdrawn by its sponsors.

III. Recommendation of the Second Committee

15. The Second Committee recommends to the General Assembly the adoption of the following draft resolutions:

Draft resolution I
Implementation of the outcome of the United Nations Conference on Human Settlements (Habitat II) and the strengthening of the United Nations Human Settlements Programme (UN-Habitat)

The General Assembly,

Recalling its resolutions 3327 (XXIX) of 16 December 1974, 32/162 of 19 December 1977, 34/115 of 14 December 1979, 56/205 and 56/206 of 21 December 2001 and 57/275 of 20 December 2002,

Taking note of Economic and Social Council resolutions 2002/38 of 26 July 2002 and 2003/62 of 25 July 2003,

Recalling the Habitat Agenda[2] and the Declaration on Cities and Other Human Settlements in the New Millennium,[3]

Recalling also the goal contained in the United Nations Millennium Declaration[4] of achieving a significant improvement in the lives of at least 100 million slum-dwellers by 2020, as proposed in the Cities Without Slums Initiative, and recalling also the goal contained in the Johannesburg Plan of Implementation[5] to halve, by the year 2015, the proportion of people who are unable to reach or afford safe drinking water and the proportion of people who do not have access to basic sanitation,

Taking into account the Johannesburg Declaration on Sustainable Development[6] and the Plan of Implementation of the World Summit on Sustainable Development ("Johannesburg Plan of Implementation"), as well as the Monterrey Consensus of the International Conference on Financing for Development,[7]

Recognizing that the overall thrust of the new strategic vision of the United Nations Human Settlements Programme (UN-Habitat) and its emphasis on the two global campaigns on secure tenure and urban governance are strategic points of entry for the effective implementation of the Habitat Agenda, especially for guid-

---

2   *Report of the United Nations Conference on Human Settlements (Habitat II), Istanbul, 3-14 June 1996* (United Nations publication, Sales No. E.97.IV.6), chap. I, resolution 1, annex II.

3   Resolution S-25/2, annex.

4   See resolution 55/2.

5   *Report of the World Summit on Sustainable Development, Johannesburg, South Africa, 26 August-4 September 2002* (United Nations publication, Sales No. E.03.II.A.1 and corrigendum), chap. I, resolution 2, annex.

6   Ibid., resolution 1, annex.

7   *Report of the International Conference on Financing for Development, Monterrey, Mexico, 18-22 March 2002* (United Nations publication, Sales No. E.02.II.A.7), chap. I, resolution 1, annex.

ing international cooperation in respect of adequate shelter for all and sustainable human settlements development,

Conscious of the need to achieve greater coherence and effectiveness in the implementation of the Habitat Agenda, the Declaration on Cities and Other Human Settlements in the New Millennium and the relevant internationally agreed development goals, including those contained in the United Nations Millennium Declaration,

Recognizing the need for increased and predictable financial contributions to the United Nations Habitat and Human Settlements Foundation in the new millennium to ensure timely, effective and concrete results in the implementation of the Habitat Agenda, the Declaration on Cities and Other Human Settlements in the New Millennium and the relevant internationally agreed development goals, including those contained in the United Nations Millennium Declaration and the Johannesburg Declaration and Plan of Implementation, particularly in developing countries,

Welcoming the establishment by the Executive Director of UN-Habitat of a Water and Sanitation Trust Fund as a financing mechanism to support the creation of enabling environments for pro-poor investment in water and sanitation in developing-country cities,

Commending those countries that have contributed to the United Nations Habitat and Human Settlements Foundation, as indicated in the report of the Secretary-General to the Economic and Social Council,[8]

Reiterating the call to the Executive Director of UN-Habitat to increase her efforts to strengthen the Foundation in order to achieve its primary operative objective, as set out in General Assembly resolution 3327 (XXIX), of 16 December 1974, of supporting the implementation of the Habitat Agenda, including supporting shelter, related infrastructure-development programmes and housing-finance institutions and mechanisms, particularly in developing countries,

Recalling the decision of the Commission on Sustainable Development at its eleventh session to address the themes of water, sanitation and human settlements in its next review and policy sessions,[9]

Noting the efforts by UN-Habitat to forge partnerships with Habitat Agenda partners, other United Nations funds and programmes and international financial institutions, such as the World Bank,

Recognizing that shelter and human settlements planning and administration are important sectors in humanitarian efforts,

Expressing its appreciation to the Government of Spain and the city of Barcelona for their willingness to host the second session of the World Urban Forum in

---

8   E/2003/76.

9   See *Official Records of the Economic and Social Council, 2003, Supplement No. 9* (E/2003/29).

2004 and to the Government of Canada and the city of Vancouver for their willingness to host the third session of the World Urban Forum in 2006,

1. *Takes note* of the report of the Governing Council of the United Nations Human Settlements Programme (UN-Habitat) on the work of its nineteenth session[10] and the report of the Secretary-General on the special session of the General Assembly for an overall review and appraisal of the implementation of the outcome of the United Nations Conference on Human Settlements (Habitat II) and the strengthening of UN-Habitat;[11]

2. *Recognizes* that Governments have the primary responsibility for the sound and effective implementation of the Habitat Agenda[2] and the Declaration on Cities and Other Human Settlements in the New Millennium,[3] and stresses that the international community should fully implement its commitments to support the Governments of developing countries and countries with economies in transition in their efforts, through the provision of the requisite resources, capacity-building, the transfer of technology and the creation of an international enabling environment;

3. *Encourages* Governments to include issues pertaining to shelter and sustainable human settlements and urban poverty in their national development strategies, including poverty reduction strategy papers, where they exist;

4. *Urges* Governments to promote pro-poor investments in services and infrastructure, in particular water and sanitation, in order to improve living environments, in particular in slums and informal settlements;

5. *Encourages* Governments to establish local, national and regional urban observatories and to provide financial and substantive support to UN-Habitat for the further development of methodologies for data collection, analysis and dissemination;

6. *Also encourages* Governments to support and enable the participation of youth in the implementation of the Habitat Agenda through social, cultural and economic activities at the city level and other national-and local-level activities;

7. *Encourages* Governments and UN-Habitat to continue to promote partnerships with local authorities, non-governmental organizations, the private sector and other Habitat Agenda partners, including women's groups and academic and professional groups, in order to empower them, within the legal framework and conditions of each country, to play a more effective role in the provision of adequate shelter for all and sustainable human settlements development in an urbanizing world;

8. *Encourages* UN-Habitat to continue to work closely with other relevant agencies within the United Nations system, in particular members and observers of

---

10   *Official Records of the General Assembly, Fifty-eighth Session, Supplement No. 8* (A/58/8).

11   A/58/178.

the United Nations Development Group and the members of the Inter-Agency Standing Committee;[12]

9. *Requests* UN-Habitat to strengthen further its efforts to make the Cities Alliance initiative an effective means for the implementation of the twin goals of the Habitat Agenda, namely, adequate shelter for all and sustainable human settlements development in an urbanizing world;

10. *Takes note with appreciation* of the efforts by the Cities Alliance partnership between the World Bank and UN-Habitat, and other donor countries, to continue to provide an important forum for policy coordination and development, as well as to provide support for the preparation of pro-poor city development strategies and slum-upgrading programmes within the legal framework and conditions of each country;

11. *Invites* the Secretary-General to incorporate the assessment of the progress towards the target of achieving a significant improvement in the lives of at least 100 million slum-dwellers by 2020 in his report on the review in 2005 of the implementation of the United Nations Millennium Declaration;[4]

12. *Welcomes* the fund-raising efforts of the Executive Director of UN-Habitat, which realized an increase in the general-purpose contributions of the Habitat and Human Settlements Foundation for the year 2003;

13. *Calls* for continued financial support to UN-Habitat through increased voluntary contributions to the Foundation, and invites Governments to provide multi-year funding to support programme implementation;

14. *Requests* UN-Habitat to collaborate with the Division for Sustainable Development of the Department of Economic and Social Affairs of the Secretariat in the preparations for the twelfth session of the Commission on Sustainable Development to promote a fruitful discussion on the thematic cluster of issues on water, sanitation and human settlements;

15. *Requests* the Executive Director of UN-Habitat to inform the Governing Council of the United Nations Human Settlements Programme of the results of the discussions on the topics of water, sanitation and human settlements at the twelfth session of the Commission on Sustainable Development;

16. *Notes* that the upcoming sessions in 2004, to be held in Barcelona, and 2006, to be held in Vancouver, of the World Urban Forum, a non-legislative technical forum, offer an opportunity to experts to exchange experiences, best practices and lessons learned in the field of human settlements;

17. *Invites* donor countries to support the participation of representatives of the developing countries in the second and future sessions of the World Urban Forum;

18. *Requests* the Secretary-General to keep the resource needs of UN-Habitat and the United Nations Office at Nairobi under review so as to permit the delivery, in

---

12   Established pursuant to General Assembly resolution 46/182 of 19 December 1991.

an effective manner, of necessary services to UN-Habitat and the other United Nations organs and organizations in Nairobi;

19. *Requests* UN-Habitat, as the focal point for human settlements development and for coordination of human settlements activities within the United Nations system, to work towards coordination of human settlements issues as inputs to the overall coordination of humanitarian efforts, including through its participation in the consideration of the issue of the transition from relief to development, by the Economic and Social Council in the near future;

20. *Requests* the Secretary-General to submit a report to the General Assembly at its fifty-ninth session on the implementation of the present resolution;

21. *Decides* to include in the provisional agenda of its fifty-ninth session an item entitled "Special session of the General Assembly for an overall review and appraisal of the implementation of the outcome of the United Nations Conference on Human Settlements (Habitat II) and the strengthening of the United Nations Human Settlements Programme (UN-Habitat)".

Draft resolution II
Rules of procedure of the Governing Council of the United Nations Human Settlements Programme

The General Assembly,

Recalling its resolution 32/162 of 19 December 1977, in which it established the Commission on Human Settlements and the United Nations Centre for Human Settlements (Habitat),

Recalling also its resolution 56/206 of 21 December 2001, in which it decided to transform the United Nations Centre for Human Settlements (Habitat) into the secretariat of the United Nations Human Settlements Programme (UN-Habitat), and the Commission on Human Settlements into the Governing Council of UN-Habitat, a subsidiary organ of the General Assembly,

Having considered the recommendation of the Governing Council, in its resolution 19/1 of 9 May 2003,[13] that the General Assembly adopt its draft rules of procedure as contained in the annex to that resolution, and the oral statement by the Chairman of the Working Group on the Rules of Procedure of the Governing Council,[14]

Adopts the draft rules of procedure of the Governing Council of the United Nations Human Settlements Programme (UN-Habitat) as contained in the annex to Governing Council resolution 19/1 of 9 May 2003.[14]

---

13   See *Official Records of the General Assembly, Fifty-eighth Session, Supplement No. 8* (A/58/8), annex I.

14   Ibid., annex II, appendix IV.

General Assembly Resolution 57/261

Promoting an Integrated Management Approach to the Caribbean Sea Area in the Context of Sustainable Development

78th plenary meeting
20 December 2002

Resolution adopted by the General Assembly
[on the report of the Second Committee (A/57/532/Add.6)]

The General Assembly,

Reaffirming the principles and commitments enshrined in the Rio Declaration on Environment and Development[1] and the principles embodied in the Declaration of Barbados[2] and the Programme of Action for the Sustainable Development of Small Island Developing States,[3] as well as other relevant declarations and international instruments,

Recalling the Declaration and review document adopted by the General Assembly at its twenty-second special session,[4]

Taking into account all other relevant General Assembly resolutions, including resolutions 54/225 of 22 December 1999 and 55/203 of 20 December 2000,

---

1   *Report of the United Nations Conference on Environment and Development, Rio de Janeiro, 3–14 June 1992* (United Nations publication, Sales No. E.93.I.8 and corrigenda), vol. I: *Resolutions adopted by the Conference*, resolution 1, annex I.

2   *Report of the Global Conference on the Sustainable Development of Small Island Developing States, Bridgetown, Barbados, 25 April–6 May 1994* (United Nations publication, Sales No. E.94.I.18 and corrigenda), chap. I, resolution 1, annex I.

3   Ibid., annex II.

4   See resolution S-22/2, annex.

Taking into account also the Johannesburg Declaration on Sustainable Development[5] and the Plan of Implementation of the World Summit on Sustainable Development ("Johannesburg Plan of Implementation"),[6]

Noting with interest the respective partnership initiatives voluntarily undertaken by Governments, international organizations and major groups and announced at the Summit,

Reaffirming the United Nations Convention on the Law of the Sea,[7] which provides the overall legal framework for ocean activities, and emphasizing its fundamental character,

Conscious that the problems of ocean space are closely interrelated and need to be considered as a whole through an integrated, interdisciplinary and intersectoral approach,

Emphasizing the importance of national, regional and global action and cooperation in the marine sector as recognized by the United Nations Conference on Environment and Development in chapter 17 of Agenda 21,[8]

Recalling the Convention for the Protection and Development of the Marine Environment of the Wider Caribbean Region, signed at Cartagena de Indias, Colombia, on 24 March 1983,[9] which contains the definition of the wider Caribbean region of which the Caribbean Sea is part,

Welcoming the adoption, on 6 October 1999 in Aruba, of the Protocol Concerning Pollution from Land-based Sources and Activities[10] to the Convention for the Protection and Development of the Marine Environment of the Wider Caribbean Region,

Welcoming also the entry into force, on 18 June 2000, of the Protocol Concerning Specially Protected Areas and Wildlife[10] to the Convention for the Protection and Development of the Marine Environment of the Wider Caribbean Region,

Recalling the relevant work done by the International Maritime Organization,

---

5   *Report of the World Summit on Sustainable Development, Johannesburg, South Africa, 26 August—4 September 2002* (United Nations publication, Sales No. E.03.II.A.1 and corrigendum), chap. I, resolution 1, annex.

6   Ibid., resolution 2, annex.

7   See *The Law of the Sea: Official Texts of the United Nations Convention on the Law of the Sea of 10 December 1982 and of the Agreement relating to the Implementation of Part XI of the United Nations Convention on the Law of the Sea of 10 December 1982 with Index and Excerpts from the Final Act of the Third United Nations Conference on the Law of the Sea* (United Nations publication, Sales No. E.97.V.10).

8   *Report of the United Nations Conference on Environment and Development, Rio de Janeiro, 3–14 June 1992* (United Nations publication, Sales No. E.93.I.8 and corrigenda), vol. I: *Resolutions adopted by the Conference*, resolution 1, annex II.

9   United Nations, *Treaty Series*, vol. 1506, No. 25974.

10   Available on the Internet at www.cep.unep.org/law/sub_law/htm.

Considering that the Caribbean Sea area includes a large number of States, countries and territories, most of which are developing countries and small island developing States that are ecologically fragile, structurally weak and economically vulnerable and are also affected, inter alia, by their limited capacity, narrow resource base, need for financial resources, high levels of poverty and the resulting social problems and the challenges and opportunities of globalization and trade liberalization,

Recognizing that the Caribbean Sea has a unique biodiversity and highly fragile ecosystem,

Emphasizing that the Caribbean countries have a high degree of vulnerability occasioned by climate change and climate variability, associated phenomena, such as the rise in sea level, the El Niño phenomenon and the increase in the frequency and intensity of natural disasters caused by hurricanes, floods and droughts, and that they are also subject to natural disasters, such as those caused by volcanoes, tsunamis and earthquakes,

Underlining the importance of the ongoing work of the working group on climate change and natural disasters established by the Inter-Agency Task Force for Disaster Reduction,

Bearing in mind the heavy reliance of most of the Caribbean economies on their coastal areas, as well as on the marine environment in general, to achieve their sustainable development needs and goals,

Recognizing the Caribbean Environment Outlook process currently being undertaken by the United Nations Environment Programme, and welcoming the support being provided by the Caribbean Environment Programme of the United Nations Environment Programme towards its implementation,

Acknowledging that the intensive use of the Caribbean Sea for maritime transport, as well as the considerable number and interlocking character of the maritime areas under national jurisdiction where Caribbean countries exercise their rights and duties under international law, present a challenge for the effective management of the resources,

Noting the problem of marine pollution caused, inter alia, by land-based sources and the continuing threat of pollution from ship-generated waste and sewage as well as from the accidental release of hazardous and noxious substances in the Caribbean Sea area,

Taking note of resolutions GC(44)/RES/17 of 22 September 2000[11] and GC(46)RES/9 of 20 September 2002[12] of the General Conference of the International Atomic Energy Agency on safety of transport of radioactive materials,

---

11   See International Atomic Energy Agency, *Resolutions and Other Decisions of the General Conference, Forty-fourth Regular Session, 18–22 September 2000* (GC(44)/RES/DEC(2000)).

12   Ibid., *Forty-sixth Regular Session*, 16–20 September 2002 (GC(46)/RES/DEC(2002)).

Mindful of the diversity and dynamic interaction and competition among socio-economic activities for the use of the coastal areas and the marine environment and their resources,

Mindful also of the efforts of the Caribbean countries to address in a more holistic manner the sectoral issues relating to the management of the Caribbean Sea area and, in so doing, to promote an integrated management approach to the Caribbean Sea area in the context of sustainable development, through a regional co-operative effort among Caribbean countries,

Noting the efforts of the Caribbean countries, within the framework of the Association of Caribbean States, to develop further support for their concept of the Caribbean Sea as an area of special importance, in the context of sustainable development and in conformity with the United Nations Convention on the Law of the Sea,

Welcoming the decision by the Association of Caribbean States to establish the Working Group of Experts on the Caribbean Sea Initiative to further advance the implementation of resolution 55/203, inter alia, through the preparation of a technical report,

Cognizant of the importance of the Caribbean Sea to present and future generations and its importance to the heritage and the continuing economic well-being and sustenance of people living in the area, and the urgent need for the countries of the region to take appropriate steps for its preservation and protection, with the support of the international community,

1. *Takes note* of the report of the Secretary-General;[13]

2. *Recognizes* the importance of adopting an integrated management approach to the Caribbean Sea area in the context of sustainable development;

3. *Encourages* the further promotion of an integrated management approach to the Caribbean Sea area in the context of sustainable development, in accordance with the recommendations contained in resolution 54/225, as well as the provisions of Agenda 21,[8] the Programme of Action for the Sustainable Development of Small Island Developing States,[3] the outcome of the twenty-second special session of the General Assembly,[4] the Johannesburg Declaration on Sustainable Development,[5] the Johannesburg Plan of Implementation[6] and the work of the Commission on Sustainable Development, and in conformity with relevant international law, including the United Nations Convention on the Law of the Sea;[7]

4. *Also encourages* the continued efforts of the Caribbean countries to develop further an integrated management approach to the Caribbean Sea area in the context of sustainable development and, in this regard, to continue to develop regional cooperation in the management of their ocean affairs in the context of sustainable development, in order to address such issues as land-based pollution, pollution from ships, physical impacts on coral reefs and the diversity and

---

13   A/57/131.

dynamic interaction of, and competition among, socio-economic activities for the use of the coastal areas and the marine environment and their resources;

5. *Calls upon* States to continue to prioritize action on marine pollution from land-based sources as part of their national sustainable development strategies and programmes, in an integrated and inclusive manner, and also calls upon them to advance the implementation of the Global Programme of Action for the Protection of the Marine Environment from Land-based Activities,[14] and the Montreal Declaration on the Protection of the Marine Environment from Land-based Activities;[15]

6. *Calls upon* the United Nations system and the international community to assist, as appropriate, Caribbean countries and their regional organizations in their efforts to ensure the protection of the Caribbean Sea from degradation as a result of pollution from ships, in particular through the illegal release of oil and other harmful substances, and from illegal dumping or accidental release of hazardous waste, including radioactive materials, nuclear waste and dangerous chemicals, in violation of relevant international rules and standards, as well as pollution from land-based activities;

7. *Calls upon* all relevant States to take the necessary steps to bring into force, and to support the implementation of, the Protocol Concerning Pollution from Land-based Sources and Activities[10] to the Convention for the Protection and Development of the Marine Environment of the Wider Caribbean Region[9] in order to protect the marine environment of the Caribbean Sea from land-based pollution and degradation;

8. *Calls upon* the international community to support the efforts of the Working Group of Experts on the Caribbean Sea Initiative of the Association of Caribbean States to further implement resolution 55/203, and invites the Association to submit a report on its progress to the Secretary-General for consideration during the fifty-ninth session of the General Assembly;

9. *Calls upon* all States to become contracting parties to relevant international agreements to promote the protection of the marine environment of the Caribbean Sea from pollution and degradation from ships;

10. *Supports* the efforts of Caribbean countries to implement sustainable fisheries management programmes by strengthening the recently established Caribbean Regional Fisheries Mechanism;

11. *Calls upon* States, taking into consideration the Convention on Biological Diversity,[16] to develop national, regional and international programmes for halting the loss of marine biodiversity in the Caribbean Sea, in particular fragile ecosystems, such as coral reefs;

---

14   A/51/116, annex II.

15   E/CN.17/2002/PC.2/15, annex, sect. 1.

16   United Nations, Treaty Series, vol. 1760, No. 30619.

12. *Invites* intergovernmental organizations within the United Nations system to continue their efforts to assist Caribbean countries in becoming parties to the relevant conventions and protocols and to implement them effectively;

13. *Calls upon* the international community, the United Nations system and the multilateral financial institutions, and invites the Global Environment Facility, within its mandate, to support actively the above-mentioned approach;

14. *Calls upon* Member States to improve as a matter of priority their emergency response capabilities and the containment of environmental damage, particularly in the Caribbean Sea, in the event of natural disasters or of an accident or incident relating to maritime navigation;

15. *Requests* the Secretary-General to report to it at its fifty-ninth session, under the sub-item entitled "Further implementation of the Programme of Action for the Sustainable Development of Small Island Developing States" of the item entitled "Environment and sustainable development", on the implementation of the present resolution, taking into account the views expressed by relevant regional organizations.

General Assembly Resolution 58/213

Further Implementation of the Programme of Action for the Sustainable Development of Small Island Developing States

78th plenary meeting
23 December 2003

Resolution adopted by the General Assembly
[*on the report of the Second Committee (A/58/484/Add.4)*]

The General Assembly,

Recalling the Declaration of Barbados[1] and the Programme of Action for the Sustainable Development of Small Island Developing States,[2] adopted by the Global Conference on the Sustainable Development of Small Island Developing States, and recalling also its resolution 49/122 of 19 December 1994 on the Global Conference,

Recalling also its resolutions 51/183 of 16 December 1996, 52/202 of 18 December 1997 and 53/189 of 15 December 1998, the review document adopted by the Assembly at its twenty-second special session,[3] and its resolutions 54/224 of 22 December 1999, 55/199 and 55/202 of 20 December 2000, 56/198 of 21 December 2001 and 57/262 of 20 December 2002,

Recalling further the Johannesburg Declaration on Sustainable Development[4] and the Plan of Implementation of the World Summit on Sustainable Development ("Johannesburg Plan of Implementation"),[5] in particular the emphasis given to small island developing States in chapter VII of the Johannesburg Plan of Imple-

---

1   *Report of the Global Conference on the Sustainable Development of Small Island Developing States, Bridgetown, Barbados, 25 April-6 May 1994* (United Nations publication, Sales No. E.94.I.18 and corrigenda), chap. I, resolution 1, annex I.

2   Ibid., annex II.

3   See resolution S-22/2, annex.

4   *Report of the World Summit on Sustainable Development, Johannesburg, South Africa, 26 August-4 September 2002* (United Nations publication, Sales No. E.03.II.A.1 and corrigendum), chap. I, resolution 1, annex.

5   Ibid., resolution 2, annex.

mentation, as well as the references to the specific needs of small island developing States contained in the United Nations Millennium Declaration[6] and the Monterrey Consensus of the International Conference on Financing for Development,[7]

Recalling its decision to convene an international meeting in 2004,[8] including a high-level segment, to undertake a full and comprehensive review of the implementation of the Programme of Action, as called for in the Johannesburg Plan of Implementation,

Welcoming the preparatory activities undertaken at the national and regional levels for the international meeting, and expressing its appreciation to the Governments of Samoa, Cape Verde and Trinidad and Tobago for hosting regional preparatory meetings,

Reaffirming the political importance of the forthcoming ten-year review of the progress achieved since the Global Conference, and stressing that the risk from the vulnerabilities of and challenges to small island developing States has increased and requires the strengthening of cooperation and more effective development assistance towards achieving the goals of sustainable development,

1. *Takes note* of the report of the Secretary-General;[9]

2. *Approves* the provisional rules of procedure of the International Meeting to Review the Implementation of the Programme of Action for the Sustainable Development of Small Island Developing States, as contained in the note by the Secretary-General;[10]

3. *Decides* that the International Meeting shall be open to all States Members of the United Nations and States members of the specialized agencies, with the participation of observers, in accordance with the established practice of the General Assembly and its conferences and with the rules of procedure of the International Meeting;

4. *Welcomes* the efforts made at the national, subregional and regional levels to implement the Programme of Action,[2] and takes note of the reports of the regional preparatory meetings for the Pacific,[11] the Atlantic, Indian Ocean, Medi-

---

6   See resolution 55/2.

7   *Report of the International Conference on Financing for Development, Monterrey, Mexico, 18-22 March 2002* (United Nations publication, Sales No. E.02.II.A.7), chap. I, resolution 1, annex.

8   Resolution 57/262, para. 5.

9   A/58/170.

10   A/58/567 and Corr.1.

11   A/58/303, annex.

terranean and South China Seas[12] and the Caribbean[13] regions of small island developing States;

5. *Reiterates* the urgent need for the full and effective implementation of the Programme of Action, the Declaration of Barbados[1] and the review document adopted by the General Assembly at its twenty-second special session[3] so as to assist small island developing States in their efforts to achieve sustainable development;

6. *Decides* that the International Meeting will be convened from 30 August to 3 September 2004 and will include a high-level segment to undertake a full and comprehensive review of the implementation of the Programme of Action, as called for in the Johannesburg Plan of Implementation,[5] and welcomes the offer of the Government of Mauritius to host the International Meeting;

7. *Also decides* to hold, if deemed necessary by an open-ended preparatory meeting, and if funded from voluntary resources, two days of informal consultations in Mauritius, on 28 and 29 August 2004, to facilitate the effective preparation of the International Meeting;

8. *Urges* that representation and participation at the International Meeting be at the highest possible level;

9. *Decides* that the International Meeting will seek a renewed political commitment by the international community and will focus on practical actions for the further implementation of the Programme of Action, taking into consideration new and emerging issues, challenges and situations since the adoption of the Programme of Action;

10. *Endorses* Economic and Social Council resolution 2003/55 of 24 July 2003, in which it decided, on the recommendation of the Commission on Sustainable Development at its eleventh session, to convene an interregional preparatory meeting for small island developing States in Nassau from 26 to 30 January 2004, expresses its appreciation to the Government of the Bahamas for hosting the meeting, and encourages participation in the meeting at the ministerial level;

11. *Also endorses* the decision of the Economic and Social Council in its resolution 2003/55, on the recommendation of the Commission on Sustainable Development at its eleventh session, to convene during the twelfth session of the Commission a three-day preparatory meeting for the International Meeting, from 14 to 16 April 2004, for an in-depth assessment and appraisal of the implementation of the Programme of Action and to finalize the preparations for the International Meeting, including its agenda;

---

12   A/C.2/58/12, annex.

13   A/C.2/58/14, annex.

12. *Decides* that the preparatory meeting shall be open-ended and shall be held in accordance with the rules of procedure of the functional commissions of the Economic and Social Council and the supplementary arrangements established for the Commission on Sustainable Development by the Council in its decisions 1993/215 of 12 February 1993 and 1995/201 of 8 February 1995, applied to all Member States and other participants, as was the practice in the preparatory committee for the World Summit on Sustainable Development, while maintaining the provisions of the Commission in relation to travel assistance, in accordance with the provisions of Economic and Social Council decision 2003/283 of 24 July 2003;

13. *Encourages* associate members of the regional commissions that are small island developing States to participate in the International Meeting, and decides that their participation shall be in accordance with rule 61 of the provisional rules of procedure of the International Meeting;

14. *Decides* that the participation of major groups, including non-governmental organizations, in the International Meeting shall be in accordance with rule 65 of the provisional rules of procedure of the International Meeting;

15. *Also decides* that non-governmental organizations whose work is relevant to .the subject of the International Meeting, that are not currently accredited by the Economic and Social Council, may submit applications to participate as observers in the International Meeting, as well as its preparatory meeting, subject to the approval of the open-ended preparatory meeting;

16. *Takes note* of the appointment of a Secretary-General of the International Meeting;

17. *Requests* the Secretary-General, in consultation with the relevant United Nations agencies and organizations, and taking into account the submissions he may receive from bilateral, regional and multilateral donor agencies as well as from major groups, including non-governmental organizations, to ensure the timely submission to the Commission on Sustainable Development at its twelfth session of a synthesis report on the basis of the national, regional and interregional preparations and reports by small island developing States and other parties;

18. *Requests* that the necessary resources, from within existing resources, be provided to the Department of Public Information of the Secretariat to ensure that the goals and purposes of the International Meeting receive the widest possible dissemination within Member States, major groups, including non-governmental organizations, and national, regional and international media, including through the Small Island Developing States Information Network, with a view to encouraging contributions to and support for the International Meeting and its preparatory process;

19. *Expresses its appreciation* for the contributions made to the voluntary trust fund established for the purpose of assisting small island developing States to participate fully and effectively in the International Meeting and its preparatory process, as approved by the Economic and Social Council in resolution 2003/55

and decision 2003/283,[14] and urges all Member States and organizations to contribute generously to the fund;

20. *Encourages* the full and effective participation of developing countries in the International Meeting, and invites donor countries and agencies to provide additional extrabudgetary resources, in particular through voluntary contributions to the trust fund, to facilitate their participation;

21. *Welcomes* the coordinating efforts undertaken in the United Nations system through the creation of an inter-agency task force to enable the United Nations system to improve coordination and enhance cooperation on matters pertaining to the preparatory process and to the International Meeting itself;

22. *Calls upon* the Department of Economic and Social Affairs of the Secretariat, through the Division for Sustainable Development and its Small Island Developing States Unit,[15] to undertake activities in both the preparatory processes and the International Meeting to enhance coordination and cooperation within the United Nations system as well as with other relevant multilateral organizations to ensure the effective implementation and monitoring of and follow-up to the outcomes of the ten-year review of the Programme of Action;

23. *Calls upon* the Office of the High Representative for the Least Developed Countries, Landlocked Developing Countries and Small Island Developing States[16] to fulfil its mandate and to advocate strongly, in partnership with the relevant parts of the United Nations as well as with major groups, media, academia and foundations, for the mobilization of international support and resources for the successful outcome of the International Meeting and for the follow-up to the outcomes of the ten-year review of the Programme of Action;

24. *Welcomes* the generous contributions by donors to provide for staffing of the Small Island Developing States Unit, and calls upon the Secretary-General to explore practical options for strengthening the Unit, including by redeployment of resources, on a permanent basis during the biennium 2004-2005, pursuant to resolutions 56/198 and 57/262, with a view to facilitating the full and effective implementation of the Declaration of Barbados and the Programme of Action and the outcomes of the International Meeting;

25. *Decides* to include in the provisional agenda of its fifty-ninth session, under the item entitled "Environment and sustainable development", a sub-item entitled "Further implementation of the outcome of the Global Conference on the Sustainable Development of Small Island Developing States: follow-up to the outcomes of the International Meeting to Review the Implementation of the Barbados Programme of Action", and requests the Secretary-General to submit to the General Assembly at its fifty-ninth session the report of the International Meeting.

---

14   See also A/C.2/58/4.

15   As mandated in the Programme of Action, para. 123, and in para. 15 of resolution 49/122.

16   See resolution 56/227.

General Assembly Resolution 57/142

Large-Scale Pelagic Drift-Net Fishing, Unauthorized Fishing in Zones of National Jurisdiction and on the High Seas/Illegal, Unreported and Unregulated Fishing, Fisheries By-Catch and Discards, and Other Developments

74th plenary meeting
12 December 2002

Resolution adopted by the General Assembly
[*without reference to a Main Committee (A/57/L.49 and Add.1)*]

The General Assembly,

Reaffirming its resolutions 46/215 of 20 December 1991, 49/116 and 49/118 of 19 December 1994, 50/25 of 5 December 1995, 51/36 of 9 December 1996, 52/29 of 26 November 1997, 53/33 of 24 November 1998 and 55/8 of 30 October 2000, as well as other resolutions on large-scale pelagic drift-net fishing, unauthorized fishing in zones of national jurisdiction and on the high seas, fisheries by-catch and discards, and other developments, and bearing in mind resolution 57/143 of 12 December 2002,

Noting that the Code of Conduct for Responsible Fisheries of the Food and Agriculture Organization of the United Nations[1] sets out principles and global standards of behaviour for responsible practices to conserve, manage and develop fisheries, including guidelines for fishing on the high seas and in areas under the national jurisdiction of other States, and on fishing gear selectivity and practices, with the aim of reducing by-catch and discards,

Welcoming the outcomes of the World Summit on Sustainable Development[2] concerning the importance of achieving sustainable fisheries to the maintenance of oceans, seas, islands and coastal areas as an integrated and essential component of the Earth's ecosystem, for global food security and for sustaining economic

---

1   *International Fisheries Instruments with Index* (United Nations publication, Sales No. E.98.V.11), sect. III.

2   See *Report of the World Summit on Sustainable Development, Johannesburg, South Africa, 26 August–4 September 2002* (United Nations publication, Sales No. E.03.II.A.1 and corrigendum), chap. I.

prosperity and the well-being of many national economies, particularly in developing countries,

Noting the importance of the wide application of the precautionary approach to the conservation, management and exploitation of straddling fish stocks and highly migratory fish stocks, in accordance with the Agreement for the Implementation of the Provisions of the United Nations Convention on the Law of the Sea of 10 December 1982 relating to the Conservation and Management of Straddling Fish Stocks and Highly Migratory Fish Stocks ("the Agreement"),[3] and the Code of Conduct for Responsible Fisheries,

Noting also the importance of implementing the principles elaborated in article 5 of the Agreement, including ecosystem considerations, in the conservation and management of straddling fish stocks and highly migratory fish stocks,

Noting further the Reykjavik Declaration on Responsible Fisheries in the Marine Ecosystem[4] and decisions V/6[5] and VI/12[6] of the Conference of the Parties to the Convention on Biological Diversity,

Recognizing the importance of integrated, multidisciplinary and multisectoral coastal and ocean management at the national, subregional and regional levels,

Recognizing also that coordination and cooperation at the global, regional, subregional as well as national levels in the areas, inter alia, of data collection, information-sharing, capacity-building and training are crucial for the conservation, management and sustainable development of marine living resources,

Recognizing further the duty provided as a principle in the Agreement to Promote Compliance with International Conservation and Management Measures by Fishing Vessels on the High Seas ("the Compliance Agreement"),[7] the Agreement and the Code of Conduct for Responsible Fisheries for flag States to exercise effective control over fishing vessels flying their flag and vessels flying their flag which provide support to such vessels, and to ensure that the activities of such vessels do not undermine the effectiveness of conservation and management measures taken in accordance with international law and adopted at the national, subregional, regional or global levels,

Emphasizing the call made in the Plan of Implementation of the World Summit on Sustainable Development ("Johannesburg Plan of Implementation")[8] for States

---

3   *International Fisheries Instruments with Index* (United Nations publication, Sales No. E.98.V.11), sect. I; see also A/CONF.164/37.

4   E/CN.17/2002/PC.2/3, annex.

5   See UNEP/CBD/COP/5/23, annex III.

6   See UNEP/CBD/COP/6/20, annex I.

7   *International Fisheries Instruments with Index* (United Nations publication, Sales No. E.98.V.11), sect. II.

8   See *Report of the World Summit on Sustainable Development, Johannesburg, South Africa, 26 August–4 September 2002* (United Nations publication, Sales No. E.03.II.A.1 and corrigendum), chap. I, resolution 2, annex.

to ratify or accede to and then effectively implement the Agreement and the Compliance Agreement, and noting with concern that the latter agreement has not yet entered into force,

Noting that the Committee on Fisheries of the Food and Agriculture Organization of the United Nations in February 1999 adopted international plans of action for the management of fishing capacity, for reducing the incidental catch of seabirds in longline fisheries and for the conservation and management of sharks, and noting with concern that only a small number of countries have begun implementation of the international plans of action,

Concerned that illegal, unreported and unregulated fishing threatens seriously to deplete populations of certain fish species and significantly damage marine ecosystems and that illegal, unreported and unregulated fishing has a detrimental impact on sustainable fisheries, including the food security and the economies of many States, particularly developing States, and in that regard urging States and entities referred to in the United Nations Convention on the Law of the Sea ("the Convention")[9] and in article 1, paragraph 2 (*b*) of the Agreement to collaborate in efforts to address these types of fishing activities,

Welcoming the adoption by the Food and Agriculture Organization of the United Nations in 2001 of the International Plan of Action to Prevent, Deter and Eliminate Illegal, Unreported and Unregulated Fishing,[10] which focuses on the primary responsibility of the flag State and the use of all available jurisdiction in accordance with international law, including port State measures, coastal State measures, market-related measures and measures to ensure that nationals do not support or engage in illegal, unreported and unregulated fishing,

Noting that the objective of the International Plan of Action is to prevent, deter and eliminate illegal, unreported and unregulated fishing by providing all States with comprehensive, effective and transparent measures by which to act, including through appropriate regional fisheries management organizations in accordance with international law,

Taking note with appreciation of the report of the Secretary-General,[11] and emphasizing the useful role that the report plays in bringing together information relating to the sustainable development of the world's marine living resources provided by States, relevant international organizations, regional and subregional fisheries organizations and non-governmental organizations,

---

9   See *The Law of the Sea: Official Texts of the United Nations Convention on the Law of the Sea of 10 December 1982 and of the Agreement relating to the Implementation of Part XI of the United Nations Convention on the Law of the Sea of 10 December 1982 with Index and Excerpts from the Final Act of the Third United Nations Conference on the Law of the Sea* (United Nations publication, Sales No. E.97.V.10).

10   See Food and Agriculture Organization of the United Nations, *Technical Guidelines for Responsible Fisheries*, no. 9.

11   A/57/459.

Noting with satisfaction that the incidence of reported large-scale pelagic drift-net fishing activities in most regions of the world's oceans and seas has continued to be low,

Concerned that the practice of large-scale pelagic drift-net fishing remains a threat to marine living resources,

Expressing its continuing concern that efforts should be made to ensure that the implementation of resolution 46/215 in some parts of the world does not result in the transfer to other parts of the world of drift nets that contravene the resolution,

Expressing concern at the significant level of by-catch, including of juvenile fish, and discards in several of the world's fisheries, recognizing that the development and use of selective, environmentally safe and cost-effective fishing gear and techniques will be important for reducing or eliminating by-catch and discards, and calling attention to the impact this activity can have on efforts to conserve and manage fish stocks, including restoring some stocks to sustainable levels,

Expressing concern also at the reports of continued loss of seabirds, particularly albatrosses, as a result of incidental mortality from longline fishing operations, and the loss of other marine species, including sharks and fin-fish species, as a result of incidental mortality, noting with satisfaction the successful conclusion of negotiations on the Agreement for the Conservation of Albatrosses and Petrels under the Convention on the Conservation of Migratory Species of Wild Animals, and encouraging States to give due consideration to participation in this Agreement,

Noting with satisfaction the recent entry into force of the Inter-American Convention for the Protection and Conservation of Sea Turtles and Their Habitats, which contains provisions to minimize the incidental catch of sea turtles in fishing operations,

Noting with satisfaction also the recent adoption of regional sea turtle conservation instruments in the West African and Indian Ocean-South East Asia regions,

Recognizing the continuing need for the International Maritime Organization, the Food and Agriculture Organization of the United Nations, the United Nations Environment Programme, in particular its Regional Seas programme, and regional and subregional fisheries management organizations and arrangements to address the issue of marine debris derived from land-based and ship-generated sources of pollution, including derelict fishing gear, which can cause mortality and habitat destruction of marine living resources,

1. *Reaffirms* the importance it attaches to the long-term conservation, management and sustainable use of the marine living resources of the world's oceans and seas and the obligations of States to cooperate to this end, in accordance with international law, as reflected in the relevant provisions of the Convention,[9] in particular the provisions on cooperation set out in part V and part VII, section 2, of the Convention regarding straddling stocks, highly migratory species, ma-

rine mammals, anadromous stocks and marine living resources of the high seas, and where applicable, the Agreement;[3]

2. *Also reaffirms* the commitment made at the World Summit on Sustainable Development to restore depleted fish stocks on an urgent basis and where possible not later than 2015;[2]

3. *Urges* all States to apply the precautionary approach widely to the conservation, management and exploitation of straddling fish stocks and highly migratory fish stocks, and calls upon States parties to the Agreement to implement fully the provisions of article 6 of the Agreement as a matter of priority;

4. *Encourages* States to apply by 2010 the ecosystem approach, notes the Reykjavik Declaration on Responsible Fisheries in the Marine Ecosystem[4] and decisions V/6[5] and VI/12[6] of the Conference of the Parties to the Convention on Biological Diversity, supports continuing work under way in the Food and Agriculture Organization of the United Nations to develop guidelines for the implementation of ecosystem considerations in fisheries management, and notes the importance of relevant provisions of the Agreement and the Code of Conduct for Responsible Fisheries[1] to this approach;

5. *Reaffirms* the importance it attaches to compliance with its resolutions 46/215, 49/116, 49/118, 50/25, 52/29, 53/33 and 55/8, and urges States and entities referred to in the Convention and in article 1, paragraph 2 (*b*), of the Agreement to enforce fully the measures recommended in those resolutions;

6. *Reiterates* the importance of efforts by States directly or, as appropriate, through the relevant regional and subregional organizations, and by other international organizations, including through financial and/or technical assistance, to increase the capacity of developing States to achieve the goals and implement the actions called for in the present resolution;

7. *Appeals* to States and regional fisheries organizations, including regional fisheries management bodies and regional fisheries arrangements, to promote the application of the Code of Conduct for Responsible Fisheries within their areas of competence;

8. *Encourages* coastal States to develop ocean policies and mechanisms on integrated management, including at the subregional and regional levels, and also including assistance to developing States in accomplishing these objectives;

9. *Calls upon* States and other entities referred to in article 10, paragraph 1, of the Compliance Agreement[7] that have not deposited instruments of acceptance of the Compliance Agreement to do so as a matter of priority;

10. *Calls upon* States not to permit vessels flying their flag to engage in fishing on the high seas or in areas under the national jurisdiction of other States, unless duly authorized by the authorities of the States concerned and in accordance with the conditions set out in the authorization, without having effective control over their activities, and to take specific measures, in accordance with the rele-

vant provisions of the Convention, the Agreement and the Compliance Agreement, to control fishing operations by vessels flying their flag;

11. *Also calls upon* States, in accordance with Agenda 21, adopted at the United Nations Conference on Environment and Development,[12] to take effective action, consistent with international law, to deter reflagging of vessels by their nationals as a means of avoiding compliance with applicable conservation and management measures for fishing vessels on the high seas;

12. *Notes with satisfaction* the continuing activities of the Food and Agriculture Organization of the United Nations through its Interregional Programme of Assistance to Developing Countries for the Implementation of the Code of Conduct for Responsible Fisheries, including the Global Partnerships for Responsible Fisheries, as a special programme funded through donor trust fund contributions aimed at, inter alia, promoting the implementation of the Code of Conduct and its associated international plans of action;

13. *Encourages* States to implement directly or, as appropriate, through the relevant international, regional and subregional organizations and arrangements, the international plans of action of the Food and Agriculture Organization of the United Nations for reducing the incidental catch of seabirds in longline fisheries, for the conservation and management of sharks and for the management of fishing capacity, since, according to the timetables contained within the international plans of action, progress on implementation, in particular through the development of national plans of action, should be either completed or at an advanced stage;

14. *Urges* States to develop and implement national and, where appropriate, regional plans of action, to put into effect by 2004 the International Plan of Action to Prevent, Deter and Eliminate Illegal, Unreported and Unregulated Fishing of the Food and Agriculture Organization of the United Nations[10] and to establish effective monitoring, reporting and enforcement and control of fishing vessels, including by flag States, to further the International Plan of Action;

15. *Also urges* States, as a matter of priority, to coordinate their activities and cooperate directly and, as appropriate, through relevant regional fisheries management organizations, in the implementation of the International Plan of Action, to promote information-sharing, to encourage the full participation of all stakeholders, and in all efforts to coordinate all the work of the Food and Agriculture Organization of the United Nations with other international organizations, including the International Maritime Organization;

16. *Invites* the Food and Agriculture Organization of the United Nations to continue its cooperative arrangements with United Nations agencies on the implementation of the International Plan of Action and to report to the Secretary-General, for inclusion in his annual report on oceans and the law of the sea, on priorities for cooperation and coordination in this work;

---

12   *Report of the United Nations Conference on Environment and Development, Rio de Janiero, 3–14 June 1992* (United Nations publication, Sales No. E.93.I.8 and corrigenda), vol. I: *Resolutions adopted by the Conference*, resolution 1, annex II.

17. *Affirms* the need to strengthen, where necessary, the international legal framework for intergovernmental cooperation in the management of fish stocks and in combating illegal, unreported and unregulated fishing, in a manner consistent with international law;

18. *Notes with satisfaction* the continuing activities of the Food and Agriculture Organization of the United Nations aimed at providing assistance to developing countries in upgrading their capabilities in monitoring, control and surveillance, including through its Global Partnerships for Responsible Fisheries project, "Management for Responsible Fisheries, Phase I", which provides assistance to developing countries in upgrading their capabilities in monitoring, control and surveillance, and improving the provision of scientific advice for fisheries management;

19. *Also notes with satisfaction* the establishment of the International Monitoring, Control, and Surveillance Network for Fisheries-Related Activities, a voluntary network of monitoring, control and surveillance professionals designed to facilitate exchange of information and to support countries in satisfying their obligations pursuant to international agreements, in particular the Compliance Agreement, and encourages States to consider becoming members of the Network;

20. *Urges* States to eliminate subsidies that contribute to illegal, unreported and unregulated fishing and to over-capacity, while completing the efforts undertaken at the World Trade Organization to clarify and improve its disciplines on fisheries subsidies, taking into account the importance of this sector to developing countries;

21. *Urges* States, relevant international organizations and regional and subregional fisheries management organizations and arrangements that have not done so to take action to reduce or eliminate by-catch, fish discards and post-harvest losses, including juvenile fish, consistent with international law and relevant international instruments, including the Code of Conduct for Responsible Fisheries, and in particular to consider measures including, as appropriate, technical measures related to fish size, mesh size or gear, discards, closed seasons and areas and zones reserved for selected fisheries, particularly artisanal fisheries, the establishment of mechanisms for communicating information on areas of high concentration of juvenile fish, taking into account the importance of ensuring confidentiality of such information, and support for studies and research that will minimize by-catch of juvenile fish;

22. *Notes with satisfaction* the activities of the Food and Agriculture Organization of the United Nations, in cooperation with relevant United Nations agencies, in particular the United Nations Environment Programme and the Global Environment Facility, aimed at promoting the reduction of by-catch and discards in fisheries activities;

23. *Calls upon* the Food and Agriculture Organization of the United Nations, the United Nations Environment Programme, in particular its Regional Seas programme, the International Maritime Organization, regional and subregional fisheries management organizations and arrangements and other appropriate intergovernmental organizations to take up, as a matter of priority, the issue of ma-

rine debris as it relates to fisheries and, where appropriate, to promote better coordination and help States to implement fully relevant international agreements, including annex V to the Guidelines of the International Convention for the Prevention of Pollution from Ships, 1973, as modified by the Protocol of 1978 relating thereto;

24. *Invites* States entitled to become parties to the Inter-American Convention for the Protection and Conservation of Sea Turtles and their Habitats to consider doing so, and to participate in its work;

25. *Invites* States entitled to become parties to the Memorandum of Understanding concerning Conservation Measures for Marine Turtles of the Atlantic Coast of Africa and the Memorandum of Understanding on the Conservation and Management of Marine Turtles and Their Habitats of the Indian Ocean and South-East Asia to consider doing so, and to participate in their work;

26. *Invites* regional and subregional fisheries management organizations and arrangements to ensure that all States having a real interest in the fisheries concerned may become members of such organizations or participate in such arrangements, in accordance with the Convention and the Agreement;

27. *Requests* the Secretary-General to bring the present resolution to the attention of all members of the international community, relevant intergovernmental organizations, the organizations and bodies of the United Nations system, regional and subregional fisheries management organizations and relevant non-governmental organizations, and to invite them to provide the Secretary-General with information relevant to the implementation of the present resolution;

28. *Also requests* the Secretary-General to submit to the General Assembly at its fifty-ninth session a report on "Sustainable fisheries, including through the 1995 Agreement for the Implementation of the Provisions of the United Nations Convention on the Law of the Sea of 10 December 1982 relating to the Conservation and Management of Straddling Fish Stocks and Highly Migratory Fish Stocks, and related instruments", taking into account information provided by States, relevant specialized agencies, in particular the Food and Agriculture Organization of the United Nations, and other appropriate organs, organizations and programmes of the United Nations system, regional and subregional organizations and arrangements for the conservation and management of straddling fish stocks and highly migratory fish stocks, as well as other relevant intergovernmental bodies and non-governmental organizations, and consisting of elements to be provided by the General Assembly in its resolution on fisheries to be adopted at its fifty-eighth session;

29. *Decides* to include in the provisional agenda of its fifty-eighth session, under the item entitled "Oceans and the law of the sea", a sub-item entitled "Sustainable fisheries, including through the 1995 Agreement for the Implementation of the Provisions of the United Nations Convention on the Law of the Sea of 10 December 1982 relating to the Conservation and Management of Straddling Fish Stocks and Highly Migratory Fish Stocks, and related instruments".

General Assembly Resolution 57/143

Agreement for the Implementation of the Provisions of the United Nations Convention on the Law of the Sea of 10 December 1982 Relating to the Conservation and Management of Straddling Fish Stocks and Highly Migratory Fish Stocks

74th plenary meeting
12 December 2002

Resolution adopted by the General Assembly
[*without reference to a Main Committee (A/57/L.50 and Add.1)*]

The General Assembly,

Recalling the relevant provisions of the United Nations Convention on the Law of the Sea ("the Convention"),[1] and bearing in mind the relationship between the Convention and the Agreement for the Implementation of the Provisions of the United Nations Convention on the Law of the Sea of 10 December 1982 relating to the Conservation and Management of Straddling Fish Stocks and Highly Migratory Fish Stocks ("the Agreement"),[2]

Recalling also its resolution 56/13 of 28 November 2001, and bearing in mind its resolution 57/142 of 12 December 2002,

Recognizing that, in accordance with the Convention, the Agreement sets forth provisions concerning the conservation and management of straddling fish stocks and highly migratory fish stocks, including provisions on subregional and regional cooperation in enforcement, binding dispute settlement and the rights

---

1   See *The Law of the Sea: Official Texts of the United Nations Convention on the Law of the Sea of 10 December 1982 and of the Agreement relating to the Implementation of Part XI of the United Nations Convention on the Law of the Sea of 10 December 1982 with Index and Excerpts from the Final Act of the Third United Nations Conference on the Law of the Sea* (United Nations publication, Sales No. E.97.V.10).

2   *International Fisheries Instruments with Index* (United Nations publication, Sales No. E.98.V.11), sect. I; see also A/CONF.164/37.

and obligations of States in authorizing the use of vessels flying their flags for fishing on the high seas,

Welcoming the entry into force of the Agreement, and noting that the entry into force of the Agreement entails responsibilities for States parties and other important considerations as outlined in the Agreement,

Welcoming also the outcomes of the World Summit on Sustainable Development,[3] in particular those relating to the conservation and management of straddling fish stocks and highly migratory fish stocks,

Deploring the fact that the straddling fish stocks and highly migratory fish stocks in many parts of the world are overfished or subject to sparsely regulated and heavy fishing efforts, mainly as a result of, *inter alia*, unauthorized fishing, inadequate regulatory measures and excess fishing capacity,

Recognizing that insufficient monitoring, control and surveillance measures and inadequate flag State control over vessels fishing for straddling fish stocks and highly migratory fish stocks in many parts of the world exacerbate the problem of overfishing, and recognizing also the urgent need for capacity-building in monitoring, control and surveillance measures and addressing inadequate flag State control for developing States, in particular the least developed among them and small island developing States,

Noting the obligation of all States, pursuant to the provisions of the Convention, to cooperate in the conservation and management of straddling fish stocks and highly migratory fish stocks,

Conscious that the Agreement requires States, and entities referred to in the Convention and in article 1, paragraph 2 (*b*), of the Agreement, to pursue cooperation in relation to straddling fish stocks and highly migratory fish stocks either directly or through appropriate subregional or regional fisheries management organizations or arrangements, taking into account the specific characteristics of the subregion or region, to ensure the effective conservation, management and long-term sustainability of such stocks, and to establish such organizations or arrangements where none exist,

Recognizing the obligation of States to cooperate, either directly or through subregional, regional or global organizations, to enhance the ability of developing States, in particular the least developed among them and small island developing States, to conserve and manage straddling fish stocks and highly migratory fish stocks and to develop their own fisheries for such stocks,

Calling attention to the circumstances affecting fisheries in many developing States, in particular African States and small island developing States,

---

3   See *Report of the World Summit on Sustainable Development, Johannesburg, South Africa, 26 August—4 September 2002* (United Nations publication, Sales No. E.03.II.A.1 and corrigendum), chap. I.

Taking into account that, in accordance with the Convention, the Agreement and the Code of Conduct for Responsible Fisheries of the Food and Agriculture Organization of the United Nations,[4] States fishing for straddling fish stocks or highly migratory fish stocks on the high seas, and relevant coastal States, shall give effect to their duty to cooperate either directly or by becoming members of the subregional or regional fisheries management organizations or participants in arrangements of that nature, or by agreeing to apply the conservation and management measures established by such organizations or arrangements, and that States having a real interest in the fisheries concerned may become members of such organizations or participants in such arrangements,

Recognizing the importance of the Agreement for the conservation and management of straddling fish stocks and highly migratory fish stocks and the need for the regular consideration by the General Assembly of developments relating thereto,

Noting the outcomes of the first informal consultations of States parties to the Agreement, and taking into account the recommendations to the General Assembly by the States parties that participated in that meeting,[5]

Emphasizing that, as recognized during the first informal consultations of States parties to the Agreement, implementation of the provisions in Part VII of the Agreement is fundamental to the successful implementation of the Agreement and, in particular, to assisting developing States, in particular the least developed among them and small island developing States, in meeting their obligations and realizing their rights under the Agreement,

Welcoming the conclusion of negotiations, and the ongoing preparatory work, to establish new regional instruments, arrangements and organizations in several heretofore unmanaged fisheries, and noting the role of the Convention and the Agreement, while taking into account the Code of Conduct for Responsible Fisheries, in the elaboration of these instruments, arrangements and organizations,

Welcoming also the fact that a growing number of States, and entities referred to in the Convention and in article 1, paragraph 2 (*b*), of the Agreement, as well as regional and subregional fisheries management organizations and arrangements, have enacted legislation, established regulations, adopted conventions or taken other measures as steps towards implementation of the provisions of the Agreement,

1. *Expresses its deep satisfaction* at the entry into force of the Agreement;[2]

2. *Calls upon* all States, and entities referred to in the Convention[1] and in article 1, paragraph 2 (*b*), of the Agreement, that have not done so to ratify or accede to it and to consider applying it provisionally;

---

4   *International Fisheries Instruments with Index* (United Nations publication, Sales No. E. 98.V.11), sect. III.

5   See A/57/57/Add.1.

3. *Calls upon* all States that have not done so, in order to achieve the goal of universal participation, to become parties to the Convention, which sets out the legal framework within which all activities in the oceans and seas must be carried out, taking into account the relationship between the Convention and the Agreement;

4. *Reaffirms* the outcomes of the World Summit on Sustainable Development,[3] in particular those relating to the conservation and management of straddling fish stocks and highly migratory fish stocks;

5. *Emphasizes* the importance of the effective implementation of the provisions of the Agreement, including those provisions relating to bilateral, regional and subregional cooperation in enforcement, and urges continued efforts in this regard;

6. *Urges* all States, and entities referred to in the Convention and in article 1, paragraph 2 (*b*), of the Agreement, to pursue cooperation in relation to straddling fish stocks and highly migratory fish stocks, either directly or through appropriate subregional or regional fisheries management organizations or arrangements, to ensure the effective conservation, management and long-term sustainability of such stocks, to agree upon measures necessary to coordinate and, where there are no subregional or regional fisheries management organizations or arrangements in respect of particular straddling or highly migratory fish stocks, to cooperate to establish such organizations or enter into other appropriate arrangements;

7. *Welcomes* the initiation of negotiations and ongoing preparatory work to establish regional and subregional fisheries management organizations or arrangements in several fisheries, and urges participants in those negotiations to apply provisions of the Convention and the Agreement to their work;

8. *Calls upon* all States to ensure that their vessels comply with the conservation and management measures that have been adopted by subregional and regional fisheries management organizations and arrangements in accordance with relevant provisions of the Convention and of the Agreement;

9. *Invites* States and international financial institutions and organizations of the United Nations system to provide assistance according to Part VII of the Agreement, including, if appropriate, the development of special financial mechanisms or instruments to assist developing States, in particular the least developed among them and small island developing States, to enable them to develop their national capacity to exploit fishery resources, including developing their domestically flagged fishing fleet, value-added processing and the expansion of their economic base in the fishing industry, consistent with the duty to ensure the proper conservation and management of those fisheries resources;

10. *Invites* States and relevant intergovernmental organizations to develop projects, programmes and partnerships with relevant stakeholders and mobilize re-

sources for the effective implementation of the outcome of the African Process for the Protection and Development of the Marine and Coastal Environment, and to consider the inclusion of fisheries components in this work;

11. *Also invites* States and relevant intergovernmental organizations to further implement sustainable fisheries management and improve financial returns from fisheries by supporting and strengthening relevant regional fisheries management organizations, as appropriate, such as the recently established Caribbean Regional Fisheries Mechanism and such agreements as the Convention on the Conservation and Management of Highly Migratory Fish Stocks in the Western and Central Pacific;

12. *Recognizes* the benefits of developing a programme of assistance with multiple components in accordance with Part VII of the Agreement, to complement programmes at the bilateral, subregional, regional and global levels;

13. *Requests* the Secretary-General to include in his next report on the status and implementation of the Agreement a background study on current activities under Part VII of the Agreement, and emphasizes the importance of this request to the successful development of terms of reference for a Part VII fund, calls for the study to include a survey of current assistance programmes under way in support of Part VII principles and an analysis of such programmes, and requests that the study be completed before the next round of informal consultations of the Secretary-General with States parties to the Agreement;

14. *Considers* that one component of a programme of assistance to be developed in accordance with Part VII of the Agreement should be the establishment of a voluntary trust fund (Part VII fund) within the United Nations system, to support developing States parties, in particular the least developed among them and small island developing States, dedicated to Part VII implementation, notes the role of the Food and Agriculture Organization of the United Nations as the specialized agency responsible for fisheries, and that of the Division for Ocean Affairs and the Law of the Sea of the Office of Legal Affairs of the Secretariat as the secretariat for the Agreement, and requests the Committee on Fisheries of the Food and Agriculture Organization at its next meeting to consider its participation in the development and management of the Part VII fund;

15. *Urges* States parties to the Agreement to develop detailed terms of reference for the Part VII fund, and requests that the following activities be considered for early implementation through the Part VII fund:

(*a*) Facilitating the participation of developing States parties in relevant regional and subregional fisheries management organizations and arrangements;

(*b*) Assisting with travel costs associated with the participation of developing States parties in meetings of relevant global organizations;

(*c*) Supporting ongoing and future negotiations to establish new regional or subregional fisheries management organizations and arrangements in areas where such bodies are not currently in place, and to strengthen existing sub-regional and regional fisheries management organizations and arrangements;

(*d*) Building capacity for activities in key areas such as monitoring, control and surveillance, data collection and scientific research;

(*e*) Exchanging information and experience on the implementation of the Agreement;

(*f*) Assisting with human resources development and technical assistance;

16. *Emphasizes* the importance of outreach to potential donor organizations to contribute to the programme of assistance;

17. *Recalls* paragraph 6 of its resolution 56/13, and requests the Secretary-General to convene a second round of informal consultations with States that have either ratified or acceded to the Agreement, for the purposes and objectives of considering the national, regional, subregional and global implementation of the Agreement, and making any appropriate recommendation to the General Assembly;

18. *Requests* the Secretary-General to invite States, and entities referred to in the Convention and in article 1, paragraph 2 (*b*), of the Agreement, not party to the Agreement, as well as the United Nations Development Programme, the Food and Agriculture Organization of the United Nations and other specialized agencies, the Commission on Sustainable Development, the World Bank, the Global Environment Facility and other relevant international financial institutions, regional fishery bodies and arrangements and relevant non-governmental organizations to attend the second round of informal consultations with States parties to the Agreement as observers;

19. *Also requests*, the Secretary-General to develop, in consultation with the Food and Agriculture Organization of the United Nations, a voluntary survey to solicit information from States parties and other States that may wish to participate, as well as regional and subregional fisheries management organizations and arrangements, on activities related to the implementation of provisions of the Agreement, similar to the survey currently in use by the Food and Agriculture Organization concerning implementation of the Code of Conduct for Responsible Fisheries,[4] with a view to encouraging through this mechanism a greater exchange of information with regard to implementation of the Agreement, and to include the results of the survey in the report of the Secretary-General to the General Assembly at its fifty-eighth session, on the understanding that such a report will also be available to the second round of informal consultations of States parties for their consideration;

20. *Further requests* the Secretary-General to submit to the General Assembly at its fifty-ninth session a report on "Sustainable fisheries, including through the 1995 Agreement for the Implementation of the Provisions of the United Nations Convention on the Law of the Sea of 10 December 1982 relating to the Conservation and Management of Straddling Fish Stocks and Highly Migratory Fish Stocks, and related instruments", taking into account information provided by

States, relevant specialized agencies, in particular the Food and Agriculture Organization of the United Nations, and other appropriate organs, organizations and programmes of the United Nations system, regional and subregional organizations and arrangements for the conservation and management of straddling fish stocks and highly migratory fish stocks, as well as other relevant intergovernmental bodies and non-governmental organizations, and consisting of elements to be provided by the General Assembly in its resolution on fisheries to be adopted at the fifty-eighth session;

21. *Decides* to include in the provisional agenda of its fifty-eighth session, under the item entitled "Oceans and the law of the sea", a sub-item entitled "Sustainable fisheries, including through the 1995 Agreement for the Implementation of the Provisions of the United Nations Convention on the Law of the Sea of 10 December 1982 relating to the Conservation and Management of Straddling Fish Stocks and Highly Migratory Fish Stocks, and related instruments".

General Assembly Resolution 58/14

Sustainable Fisheries, Including Through the 1995 Agreement for the Implementation of the Provisions of the United Nations Convention on the Law of the Sea of 10 December 1982 Relating to the Conservation and Management of Straddling Fish Stocks and Highly Migratory Fish Stocks, and Related Instruments

64th plenary meeting
24 November 2003

Resolution adopted by the General Assembly
[*without reference to a Main Committee (A/58/L.18 and Add.1)*]

The General Assembly,

Reaffirming its resolutions 46/215 of 20 December 1991, 49/116 and 49/118 of 19 December 1994, 50/25 of 5 December 1995 and 57/142 of 12 December 2002, as well as other resolutions on large-scale pelagic drift-net fishing, unauthorized fishing in zones of national jurisdiction and on the high seas, fisheries by-catch and discards, and other developments, and its resolutions 56/13 of 28 November 2001 and 57/143 of 12 December 2002 on the Agreement for the Implementation of the Provisions of the United Nations Convention on the Law of the Sea of 10 December 1982 relating to the Conservation and Management of Straddling Fish Stocks and Highly Migratory Fish Stocks ("the Agreement"),[1]

Recalling the relevant provisions of the United Nations Convention on the Law of the Sea ("the Convention"),[2] and bearing in mind the relationship between the Convention and the Agreement,

---

1   *International Fisheries Instruments with Index* (United Nations publication, Sales No. E.98.V.11), sect. I; see also A/CONF.164/37.

2   See *The Law of the Sea: Official Texts of the United Nations Convention on the Law of the Sea of 10 December 1982 and of the Agreement relating to the Implementation of Part XI of the United Nations Convention on the Law of the Sea of 10 December 1982 with Index and Excerpts from the Final Act of*

Recognizing that, in accordance with the Convention, the Agreement sets forth provisions concerning the conservation and management of straddling fish stocks and highly migratory fish stocks, including provisions on subregional and regional cooperation in enforcement, binding dispute settlement and the rights and obligations of States in authorizing the use of vessels flying their flags for fishing on the high seas,

Noting that the Code of Conduct for Responsible Fisheries of the Food and Agriculture Organization of the United Nations ("the Code")[3] and its associated international plans of action set out principles and global standards of behaviour for responsible practices to conserve, manage and develop fisheries, including guidelines for fishing on the high seas and in areas under the national jurisdiction of other States, and on fishing gear selectivity and practices, with the aim of reducing by-catch and discards,

Noting with satisfaction the Strategy for Improving Information on Status and Trends of Capture Fisheries recently adopted by the Food and Agriculture Organization of the United Nations,[4] and recognizing that the long-term improvement of the knowledge and understanding of fishery status and trends is a fundamental basis for fisheries policy and management for implementing the Code,

Recognizing the need to implement, as a matter of priority, the Plan of Implementation of the World Summit on Sustainable Development ("Johannesburg Plan of Implementation"),[5] in relation to achieving sustainable fisheries,

Deploring the fact that fish stocks, including straddling fish stocks and highly migratory fish stocks, in many parts of the world are overfished or subject to sparsely regulated and heavy fishing efforts, mainly as a result of, *inter alia*, unauthorized fishing, inadequate regulatory measures and excess fishing capacity,

Concerned that illegal, unreported and unregulated fishing threatens seriously to deplete populations of certain fish species and to significantly damage marine ecosystems, to the detriment of sustainable fisheries as well as the food security and the economies of many States, particularly developing States,

Recognizing that inadequate flag State control over fishing vessels, including those fishing for straddling fish stocks and highly migratory fish stocks, and in-

---

the Third United Nations Conference on the Law of the Sea (United Nations publication, Sales No. E.97.V.10).

3   *International Fisheries Instruments with Index* (United Nations publication, Sales No. E.98.V.11), sect. III.

4   Food and Agriculture Organization of the United Nations, *Report of the twenty-fifth session of the Committee on Fisheries, Rome, 24–28 February 2003*, appendix H.

5   *Report of the World Summit on Sustainable Development, Johannesburg, South Africa, 26 August– 4 September 2002* (United Nations publication, Sales No. E.03.II.A.1 and corrigendum), chap. I, resolution 2, annex.

sufficient monitoring, control and surveillance measures exacerbate the problem of overfishing,

Recognizing also that the interrelationship between ocean activities, such as shipping and fishing, and environmental issues needs further consideration,

Calling attention to the circumstances affecting fisheries in many developing States, in particular African States and small island developing States, and recognizing the urgent need for capacity-building to assist such States in meeting their obligations under international instruments and realizing the benefits from fisheries resources,

Noting the obligation of all States, pursuant to the provisions of the Convention, to cooperate in the conservation and management of straddling fish stocks and highly migratory fish stocks, and recognizing the importance of coordination and cooperation at the global, regional, subregional as well as national levels in the areas, *inter alia*, of data collection, information-sharing, capacity-building and training for the conservation, management and sustainable development of marine living resources,

Recognizing the duty provided in the Convention, the Agreement to Promote Compliance with International Conservation and Management Measures by Fishing Vessels on the High Seas ("the Compliance Agreement"),[6] the Agreement and the Code for flag States to exercise effective control over fishing vessels flying their flag and vessels flying their flag which provide support to such vessels, and to ensure that the activities of such vessels do not undermine the effectiveness of conservation and management measures taken in accordance with international law and adopted at the national, subregional, regional or global levels,

Recognizing also the urgent need for action at all levels to ensure the long-term sustainable use and management of fisheries resources,

Recognizing further the economic and cultural importance of sharks in many countries, the biological importance of sharks in the marine ecosystem, the vulnerability of some shark species to over-exploitation and the need for measures to promote the long-term sustainability of shark populations and fisheries,

Reaffirming its support for the initiative of the Food and Agriculture Organization of the United Nations and relevant regional and subregional fisheries management organizations and arrangements on the conservation and management of sharks, while noting with concern that only a small number of countries have implemented the International Plan of Action for the Conservation and Management of Sharks, adopted by the Food and Agriculture Organization in 1999,

Noting with satisfaction the outcomes of the second round of informal consultations of States parties to the Agreement, held in New York from 23 to 25 July 2003,

---

6   *International Fisheries Instruments with Index* (United Nations publication, Sales No. E.98.V.11), sect. II.

Taking note with appreciation of the report of the Secretary-General,[7] and emphasizing the useful role that the report plays in bringing together information relating to the sustainable development of the world's marine living resources provided by States, relevant international organizations, regional and subregional fisheries organizations and non-governmental organizations,

Noting with satisfaction that the incidence of reported large-scale pelagic drift-net fishing activities in most regions of the world's oceans and seas has continued to be low,

Expressing concern that the practice of large-scale pelagic drift-net fishing remains a threat to marine living resources,

Emphasizing that efforts should be made to ensure that the implementation of resolution 46/215 in some parts of the world does not result in the transfer to other parts of the world of drift nets that contravene the resolution,

Expressing concern at the reports of continued loss of seabirds, particularly albatrosses, as a result of incidental mortality from longline fishing operations, and the loss of other marine species, including sharks and fin-fish species, as a result of incidental mortality, and noting with satisfaction the imminent entry into force of the Agreement for the Conservation of Albatrosses and Petrels under the Convention on the Conservation of Migratory Species of Wild Animals,

Welcoming the fact that a growing number of States, and entities referred to in the Convention and in article 1, paragraph 2 (*b*), of the Agreement, as well as regional and subregional fisheries management organizations and arrangements, have enacted legislation, established regulations, adopted conventions or taken other measures as steps towards implementation of the provisions of the Agreement,

Recognizing the significant contribution of sustainable fisheries to food security, income and wealth for present and future generations,

I
Achieving sustainable fisheries

1. *Reaffirms* the importance it attaches to the long-term conservation, management and sustainable use of the marine living resources of the world's oceans and seas and the obligations of States to cooperate to this end, in accordance with international law, as reflected in the relevant provisions of the Convention,[2] in particular the provisions on cooperation set out in Part V and Part VII, section 2, of the Convention regarding straddling stocks, highly migratory species, marine mammals, anadromous stocks and marine living resources of the high seas, and where applicable, the Agreement;[1]

---

7   A/58/215.

2. *Calls upon* all States that have not done so, in order to achieve the goal of universal participation, to become parties to the Convention, which sets out the legal framework within which all activities in the oceans and seas must be carried out, taking into account the relationship between the Convention and the Agreement;

3. *Reaffirms* the importance of the Johannesburg Plan of Implementation in relation to fisheries, in particular the commitment made therein to restore depleted fish stocks on an urgent basis and, where possible, not later than 2015;[8]

4. *Urges* all States to apply the precautionary approach widely to the conservation, management and exploitation of fish stocks, including straddling fish stocks and highly migratory fish stocks, and calls upon States parties to the Agreement to implement fully the provisions of article 6 of the Agreement as a matter of priority;

II
Implementation of the 1995 Agreement for the Implementation of the Provisions of the United Nations Convention on the Law of the Sea of 10 December 1982 relating to the Conservation and Management of Straddling Fish Stocks and Highly Migratory Fish Stocks

5. *Calls upon* all States, and entities referred to in the Convention and in article 1, paragraph 2 (*b*), of the Agreement, that have not done so to ratify or accede to the Agreement and to consider applying it provisionally;

6. *Emphasizes* the importance of the effective implementation of the provisions of the Agreement, including those provisions relating to bilateral, regional and subregional cooperation in enforcement, and urges continued efforts in this regard;

7. *Welcomes* the entry into force of the Convention on the Conservation and Management of Fishery Resources in the South-East Atlantic Ocean on 13 April 2003, and invites signatory States and other States with real interest whose vessels fish in the Convention area for fishery resources covered by that Convention to ratify or to accede to the Convention;

8. *Calls upon* all States to ensure that their vessels comply with the conservation and management measures that have been adopted by subregional and regional fisheries management organizations and arrangements in accordance with relevant provisions of the Convention and of the Agreement;

9. *Invites* States and international financial institutions and organizations of the United Nations system to provide assistance according to Part VII of the

---

8   See *Report of the World Summit on Sustainable Development, Johannesburg, South Africa, 26 August–4 September 2002* (United Nations publication, Sales No. E.03.II.A.1 and corrigendum), chap. I, resolution 2, annex, para. 31 (*a*).

Agreement, including, if appropriate, the development of special financial mechanisms or instruments to assist developing States, in particular the least developed among them and small island developing States, to enable them to develop their national capacity to exploit fishery resources, including developing their domestically flagged fishing fleet, value-added processing and the expansion of their economic base in the fishing industry, consistent with the duty to ensure the proper conservation and management of those fisheries resources;

10. *Decides* to establish an Assistance Fund under Part VII of the Agreement to assist developing States parties in the implementation of the Agreement, to be administered by the Food and Agriculture Organization of the United Nations, which should act as the implementing office for the Fund, in collaboration with the United Nations, in accordance with the terms of reference as agreed at the second round of informal consultations of the States parties to the Agreement and appropriate arrangements made between them;

11. *Emphasizes* the importance of outreach to potential donor organizations to contribute to the programme of assistance, including the Assistance Fund newly established under Part VII of the Agreement;

12. *Recalls* paragraph 6 of its resolution 56/13, and requests the Secretary-General to convene a third round of informal consultations of States parties to the Agreement, for the purposes and objectives of considering the national, regional, subregional and global implementation of the Agreement, in particular by conducting an evaluation of the implementation of the Agreement by regional fisheries management organizations as well as considering initial preparatory steps for the review conference to be convened by the Secretary-General pursuant to article 36 of the Agreement, and making any appropriate recommendation to the General Assembly;

13. *Requests* the Secretary-General to invite States, and entities referred to in the Convention and in article 1, paragraph 2 (*b*), of the Agreement, not party to the Agreement, as well as the United Nations Development Programme, the Food and Agriculture Organization of the United Nations and other specialized agencies, the Commission on Sustainable Development, the World Bank, the Global Environment Facility and other relevant international financial institutions, regional fishery bodies and arrangements and relevant non-governmental organizations to attend the third round of informal consultations of States parties to the Agreement as observers;

III
Related fisheries instruments

14. *Welcomes* the entry into force of the Compliance Agreement,[6] and calls upon all States and other entities referred to in article 10, paragraph 1, of the Compliance Agreement that have not yet deposited instruments of acceptance to do so as a matter of priority;

15. *Urges* parties to the Compliance Agreement to exchange information in the implementation of that Agreement;

16. *Urges* States and subregional and regional fisheries management organizations and arrangements to promote the application of the Code within their areas of competence;

17. *Invites* States to support implementation of the Strategy for Improving Information on Status and Trends of Capture Fisheries[4] at the national and regional levels, giving particular emphasis to capacity-building in developing countries;

18. *Urges* States to develop and implement national and, as appropriate, regional plans of action to put into effect the international plans of action of the Food and Agriculture Organization of the United Nations, namely the International Plan of Action for the Management of Fishing Capacity, the International Plan of Action for Reducing Incidental Catch of Seabirds in Longline Fisheries, the International Plan of Action for the Conservation and Management of Sharks and the International Plan of Action to Prevent, Deter and Eliminate Illegal, Unreported and Unregulated Fishing;

IV
Illegal, unreported and unregulated fishing

19. *Calls upon* States not to permit vessels flying their flag to engage in fishing on the high seas or in areas under the national jurisdiction of other States, unless duly authorized by the authorities of the States concerned and in accordance with the conditions set out in the authorization, without having effective control over their activities, and to take specific measures, including deterring the reflagging of vessels by their nationals, in accordance with the relevant provisions of the Convention, the Agreement and the Compliance Agreement, to control fishing operations by vessels flying their flag;

20. *Affirms* the need to strengthen, where necessary, the international legal framework for intergovernmental cooperation, in particular at the regional and subregional levels, in the management of fish stocks and in combating illegal, unreported and unregulated fishing, in a manner consistent with international law, and for States and entities referred to in the Convention and in article 1, paragraph 2 (*b*), of the Agreement to collaborate in efforts to address these types of fishing activities;

21. *Encourages* States to consider becoming members of the International Monitoring, Control, and Surveillance Network for Fisheries-Related Activities, a voluntary network of monitoring, control and surveillance professionals designed to facilitate exchange of information and to support countries in discharging their obligations pursuant to international agreements, in particular the Compliance Agreement;

22. *Invites* the International Maritime Organization and other relevant competent international organizations to study, examine and clarify the role of the

"genuine link" in relation to the duty of flag States to exercise effective control over ships flying their flag, including fishing vessels;

23. *Calls upon* flag and port States to take all measures consistent with international law necessary to prevent the operation of sub-standard vessels and illegal, unreported and unregulated fishing activities;

24. *Encourages* States in their work with regional and subregional fisheries management organizations and arrangements to develop and implement vessel monitoring systems and, where appropriate and consistent with international law, trade monitoring schemes;

25. *Urges* States to develop and implement national and, where appropriate, regional plans of action, to put into effect by 2004 the International Plan of Action to Prevent, Deter and Eliminate Illegal, Unreported and Unregulated Fishing and to establish effective monitoring, reporting and enforcement and control of fishing vessels, including by flag States, to further the International Plan of Action;

26. *Urges* relevant regional and subregional fisheries management organizations and arrangements to implement effective measures against illegal, unreported and unregulated fishing, *inter alia*, by compiling a record of vessels authorized to fish in their area of competence, in accordance with the Code;

27. *Urges* States to eliminate subsidies that contribute to illegal, unreported and unregulated fishing and to overcapacity, while completing the efforts undertaken at the World Trade Organization to clarify and improve its disciplines on fisheries subsidies, taking into account the importance of this sector to developing countries;

28. *Commends* the Food and Agriculture Organization of the United Nations for its activities in combating illegal, unreported and unregulated fishing, including its initiative to organize the intergovernmental technical consultation on illegal, unreported and unregulated fishing and fleet overcapacity, to be held in June 2004, and the intergovernmental technical consultation on the role of the port State in combating illegal, unreported and unregulated fishing, to be held in September 2004;

29. *Recognizes* the need for enhanced port State controls to combat illegal, unreported and unregulated fishing, urges States to cooperate, in particular at the regional level, and through regional and subregional fisheries management organizations and arrangements, as well as through participation, where appropriate, in the efforts of the Food and Agriculture Organization of the United Nations in cooperation with the International Maritime Organization to address substantive issues relating to the role of the port State, noting that such efforts include the elaboration of principles and guidelines for the establishment of regional memorandums of understanding on port State measures to prevent, deter and eliminate illegal, unreported and unregulated fishing;

V
Fishing overcapacity

30. *Calls upon* States and relevant regional fisheries management organizations, as a matter of priority, to take effective measures to improve the management of fishing capacity and to put into effect by 2005 the International Plan of Action for the Management of Fishing Capacity, taking into account the need, through these actions, to avoid the transfer of fishing capacity to other fisheries or areas including, but not limited to, those areas where fisheries are overexploited or in a depleted condition;

31. *Urges* those States and other entities referred to in article X, paragraph 1, of the Compliance Agreement that have become parties to it to establish a record of fishing vessels authorized to fish on the high seas and, pursuant to articles IV and VI thereof, to make such a record available to the Food and Agriculture Organization of the United Nations as a matter of priority, and urges the Food and Agriculture Organization to quickly establish the record of fishing vessels as called for in the Compliance Agreement;

32. *Calls upon* all States to assist this work of the Food and Agriculture Organization of the United Nations, to take measures to halt the increase of large-scale fishing vessels in accordance with the International Plan of Action for the Management of Fishing Capacity and to participate in the intergovernmental technical consultation on illegal, unreported and unregulated fishing and fleet overcapacity to be organized by the Food and Agriculture Organization in 2004;

VI
Large-scale pelagic drift-net fishing

33. *Reaffirms* the importance it attaches to continued compliance with its resolution 46/215 and other subsequent resolutions on large-scale pelagic drift-net fishing, and urges States and entities referred to in the Convention and in article 1, paragraph 2 (*b*), of the Agreement to enforce fully the measures recommended in those resolutions;

VII
Fisheries by-catch and discards

34. *Urges* States, relevant international organizations and regional and subregional fisheries management organizations and arrangements that have not done so to take action to reduce or eliminate by-catch, catch by lost or abandoned gear, fish discards and post-harvest losses, including juvenile fish, consistent with international law and relevant international instruments, including the Code, and in particular to consider measures including, as appropriate, technical measures related to fish size, mesh size or gear, discards, closed seasons and areas and zones reserved for selected fisheries, particularly artisanal fisheries, the establishment of mechanisms for communicating information on areas of high

concentration of juvenile fish, taking into account the importance of ensuring confidentiality of such information, and support for studies and research that will reduce or eliminate by-catch of juvenile fish;

35. *Encourages* States and entities referred to in the Convention and in article 1, paragraph 2 (*b*), of the Agreement to give due consideration to participation, as appropriate, in regional and subregional organizations with mandates to conserve non-target species taken incidentally in fishing operations, and notes in particular the Inter-American Convention for the Protection and Conservation of Sea Turtles and Their Habitats, regional sea turtle conservation instruments in the West African, the wider Caribbean, and the Indian Ocean/South-East Asia regions, the work of the Southeast Asian Fisheries Development Centre on turtle conservation and management, the Agreement on the Conservation of Small Cetaceans of the Baltic and North Seas[9] and the Agreement on the Conservation of Albatrosses and Petrels under the Convention on the Conservation of Migratory Species of Wild Animals in this regard;

36. *Notes with satisfaction* the activities of the Food and Agriculture Organization of the United Nations, in cooperation with relevant United Nations agencies, in particular the United Nations Environment Programme and the Global Environment Facility, aimed at promoting the reduction of by-catch and discards in fisheries activities;

VIII
Subregional and regional cooperation

37. *Urges* coastal States and States fishing on the high seas, in accordance with the Convention and the Agreement, to pursue cooperation in relation to straddling fish stocks and highly migratory fish stocks, either directly or through appropriate subregional or regional fisheries management organizations or arrangements, to ensure the effective conservation and management of such stocks;

38. *Encourages* States fishing for straddling fish stocks and highly migratory fish stocks on the high seas, and relevant coastal States, where a subregional or regional fisheries management organization or arrangement has the competence to establish conservation and management measures for such stocks, to give effect to their duty to cooperate by becoming members of such an organization or participants in such an arrangement, or by agreeing to apply the conservation and management measures established by such an organization or arrangement;

39. *Invites*, in this regard, subregional and regional fisheries management organizations and arrangements to ensure that all States having a real interest in the fisheries concerned may become members of such organizations or participants in such arrangements, in accordance with the Convention and the Agreement;

---

9   United Nations, *Treaty Series*, vol. 1772, No. 30865.

40. *Encourages* relevant coastal States and States fishing on the high seas for a straddling fish stock or a highly migratory fish stock, where there is no subregional or regional fisheries management organization or arrangement to establish conservation and management measures for such stock, to cooperate to establish such an organization or enter into another appropriate arrangement to ensure the conservation and management of such stocks, and to participate in the work of the organization or arrangement;

41. *Welcomes* the initiation of negotiations and ongoing preparatory work to establish regional and subregional fisheries management organizations or arrangements in several fisheries, and urges participants in those negotiations to apply provisions of the Convention and the Agreement to their work;

42. *Encourages* States to develop ocean policies and mechanisms on integrated management, including at the subregional and regional levels, and also including assistance to developing States in accomplishing these objectives, as well as by promoting improved cooperation between regional fisheries management organizations and other regional entities, such as the United Nations Environment Programme regional seas programmes and conventions;

IX
Responsible fisheries in the marine ecosystem

43. *Encourages* States to apply by 2010 the ecosystem approach, notes the Reykjavik Declaration on Responsible Fisheries in the Marine Ecosystem[10] and decisions V/6[11] and VI/12[12] of the Conference of the Parties to the Convention on Biological Diversity, encourages States to consider the guidelines of the Food and Agriculture Organization of the United Nations for the implementation of ecosystem considerations in fisheries management, and notes the importance to this approach of relevant provisions of the Agreement and the Code;

44. *Calls upon* the Food and Agriculture Organization of the United Nations, the United Nations Environment Programme, in particular its Regional Seas programme, the International Maritime Organization, regional and subregional fisheries management organizations and arrangements and other appropriate intergovernmental organizations to take up, as a matter of priority, the issue of marine debris as it relates to fisheries and, where appropriate, to promote better coordination and help States to implement fully relevant international agreements, including annex V to the International Convention for the Prevention of Pollution from Ships, 1973, as modified by the Protocol of 1978 relating thereto;

---

10   E/CN.17/2002/PC.2/3, annex.

11   See UNEP/CBD/COP/5/23, annex III.

12   See UNEP/CBD/COP/6/20, annex I.

45. *Urges* all States to implement the Global Programme of Action for the Protection of the Marine Environment from Land-based Activities[13] and to accelerate activity to safeguard the marine environment against pollution and physical degradation;

46. *Requests* the Secretary-General, in close cooperation with the Food and Agriculture Organization of the United Nations, and in consultation with States, regional and subregional fisheries management organizations and arrangements and other relevant organizations, in his next report concerning fisheries to include a section outlining current risks to the marine biodiversity of vulnerable marine ecosystems including, but not limited to, seamounts, coral reefs, including cold water reefs and certain other sensitive underwater features, related to fishing activities, as well as detailing any conservation and management measures in place at the global, regional, subregional or national levels addressing these issues;

47. *Calls upon* States, the Food and Agriculture Organization of the United Nations and subregional or regional fisheries management organizations and arrangements to implement fully the International Plan of Action for the Conservation and Management of Sharks as a matter of priority, *inter alia*, by conducting assessments of shark stocks and developing and implementing national plans of action, recognizing the need of some States, in particular developing States, for assistance in this regard;

48. *Urges* States, including those working through subregional or regional fisheries management organizations and arrangements in implementing the International Plan of Action for the Conservation and Management of Sharks, to collect scientific data regarding shark catches and to consider adopting conservation and management measures, particularly where shark catches from directed and non-directed fisheries have a significant impact on vulnerable or threatened shark stocks, in order to ensure the conservation and management of sharks and their long-term sustainable use, including by banning directed shark fisheries conducted solely for the purpose of harvesting shark fins and by taking measures for other fisheries to minimize waste and discards from shark catches, and to encourage the full use of dead sharks;

49. *Urges* all States to cooperate with the Food and Agriculture Organization of the United Nations in order to assist developing States in implementing the International Plan of Action for the Conservation and Management of Sharks, including through voluntary contributions to work of the organization, such as its FishCODE programme;

50. *Invites* the Food and Agriculture Organization of the United Nations, in consultation with relevant subregional or regional fisheries management organizations or arrangements, to prepare a study relating to the impact on shark populations of shark catches from directed and non-directed fisheries and their

---

13   A/51/116, annex II.

impact on ecologically related species, taking into account the nutritional and socio-economic considerations as reflected in the International Plan of Action for the Conservation and Management of Sharks, particularly as they relate to small-scale, subsistence and artisanal fisheries and communities, as well as up-dating Technical Paper 389 of the Food and Agriculture Organization, entitled "Shark utilization, marketing and trade", in order to facilitate improved shark conservation, management and utilization, and to report to the Secretary-General for inclusion in a fisheries-related report as soon as practicable;

X
Capacity-building

51. *Reiterates* the crucial importance of cooperation by States directly or, as appropriate, through the relevant regional and subregional organizations, and by other international organizations, including through financial and/or technical assistance, in accordance with the Agreement, the Compliance Agreement, the Code and the International Plan of Action to Prevent, Deter and Eliminate Illegal, Unreported and Unregulated Fishing, to increase the capacity of developing States to achieve the goals and implement the actions called for in the present resolution;

52. *Invites* States and relevant intergovernmental organizations to develop projects, programmes and partnerships with relevant stakeholders and mobilize resources for the effective implementation of the outcome of the African Process for the Protection and Development of the Marine and Coastal Environment, and to consider the inclusion of fisheries components in this work;

53. *Also invites* States and relevant intergovernmental organizations to further implement sustainable fisheries management and improve financial returns from fisheries by supporting and strengthening relevant regional fisheries management organizations, as appropriate, such as the Caribbean Regional Fisheries Mechanism and such agreements as the Convention on the Conservation and Management of Highly Migratory Fish Stocks in the Western and Central Pacific;

XI
Cooperation within the United Nations system

54. *Requests* the relevant parts of the United Nations system, international financial institutions and donor agencies to support increased enforcement and compliance capabilities for regional fisheries management organizations and their member States;

55. *Invites* the Food and Agriculture Organization of the United Nations to continue its cooperative arrangements with United Nations agencies on the implementation of the international plans of action and to report to the Secretary-General, for inclusion in his annual report on oceans and the law of the sea, on priorities for cooperation and coordination in this work;

XII
Fifty-ninth session of the General Assembly

56. *Requests* the Secretary-General to bring the present resolution to the attention of all members of the international community, relevant intergovernmental organizations, the organizations and bodies of the United Nations system, regional and subregional fisheries management organizations and relevant non-governmental organizations, and to invite them to provide the Secretary-General with information relevant to the implementation of the present resolution;

57. *Also requests* the Secretary-General to submit to the General Assembly at its fifty-ninth session a report on "Sustainable fisheries, including through the 1995 Agreement for the Implementation of the Provisions of the United Nations Convention on the Law of the Sea of 10 December 1982 relating to the Conservation and Management of Straddling Fish Stocks and Highly Migratory Fish Stocks, and related instruments", taking into account information provided by States, relevant specialized agencies, in particular the Food and Agriculture Organization of the United Nations, and other appropriate organs, organizations and programmes of the United Nations system, regional and subregional organizations and arrangements for the conservation and management of straddling fish stocks and highly migratory fish stocks, as well as other relevant intergovernmental bodies and non-governmental organizations, and consisting, *inter alia*, of elements provided in relevant paragraphs in the present resolution;

58. *Decides* to include in the provisional agenda of its fifty-ninth session, under the item entitled "Oceans and the law of the sea", a sub-item entitled "Sustainable fisheries, including through the 1995 Agreement for the Implementation of the Provisions of the United Nations Convention on the Law of the Sea of 10 December 1982 relating to the Conservation and Management of Straddling Fish Stocks and Highly Migratory Fish Stocks, and related instruments".

DOCUMENT INDEX

DOCUMENT INDEX

Page

Agenda 21
Capacity building, UNGA Res. 47/194 . 843
Endorsement of, UNGA Res. 47/190 . . 841
Follow up concerning institutional
arrangements, UNGA Res. 47/191 845

Armed Conflicts
Millennium Declaration, Sec. II 575
Millennium Report, Sec. IV 618

Atmosphere, Protection of
Agenda 21, Sec. II, Ch. 9 157
UNGA Res. 58/243 863

Biological Diversity
Agenda 21, Sec. II, Ch. 15 263
UNGA Res. 58/212 867

Biotechnology
Agenda 21, Sec. II, Ch. 16 273

Consumption Patterns
Agenda 21, Sec. I, Ch. 4 73
WSSD Implementation Plan, Sec. III . . 771

Data Gap, Bridging
Agenda 21, Sec. IV, Ch. 40 563

Deforestation
Agenda 21, Sec. II, Ch. 11 177

**Demographic Dynamics and
Sustainability**
Agenda 21, Sec. I, Ch. 5 81

Page

Desertification
Agenda 21, Sec. II, Ch. 12 197
UNGA Res. 58/242 871

Ecosystem Protection
Millennium Report, Sec. V 630

Energy
Johannesburg Declaration on
Sustainable Development 759

Environmental Awareness
Agenda 21, Sec. IV, Ch. 36 523
Introduction, Secs. A-B 4-10
Millennium Declaration, Sec. IV 578
UNGA Res. 58/219 861

Environmental Governance
Introduction, Secs. C-H 10-44

Environmental Problems
Urgency of, Introduction, Sec. D 12

Environmentally Sound Technology
Agenda 21, Sec. IV, Ch. 34 499

Financial Resources and Mechanisms
Agenda 21, Sec. IV, Ch. 33 493

Financing for Development
See Monterrey Consensus and Report

Freshwater Resources
Agenda 21, Sec. II, Ch. 18 335

Page

Globalization
Millennium Report, Sec. II 586
WSSD Implementation Plan, Sec. V . . 799

Habitat
See Sustainable Human Settlements

Hazardous Waste Management
Agenda 21, Sec. II, Ch. 20 401

Health
Agenda 21, Sec. I, Ch. 6 93
WSSD Implementation Plan, Sec. VI . . 800

International Conference on Financing for Development, Report of
See Monterrey Consensus and Report

International Legal Instruments and Mechanisms
Agenda 21, Sec. IV, Ch. 39 557

Johannesburg Declaration on Sustainable Development
See also Sustainable Development
Challenges, Arts. 11-15, ... 760-61
Commitment to the Declaration,
Arts. 34-37 763
From human origins to the future,
Arts. 1-7 759
From Stockholm to Rio de Janeiro
to Johannesburg, Arts. 8-10 760
Multilateralism, Arts. 31-33 762
Sustainable Development,
commitment to, Arts. 16-30 761-62

Land-Resource Use
Agenda 21, Sec. II, Ch. 10 169

**Millennium Declaration
(UNGA Res. 55/2)**
Africa, special needs, Sec. VII 580
Development and poverty
eradication, Sec. III 576
Environmental protection, Sec. IV . . . 578
Human rights, Sec. V 579

Page

Peace, security and disarmament,
Sec. II 575
Protection of the vulnerable,
Sec. VI. 580
UN, strengthening of, Sec. VIII 581
Values and principles, Sec. I 573

Millennium Report (We the Peoples: The Role of the United Nations in the Twenty-First Century, UNGA Report 54/2000)
Armed Conflicts, Sec. IV 618
Ecosystem Protection, Sec. V 630
Globalization, Sec. II. 586
Poverty, Sec. III. 595
UN challenges for the 21st Century,
Sec. I. 583
UN future goals, Sec. VI 642

Monterrey Consensus and Report (Report of the International Conference on Financing for Development)
Adoption of the Monterrey
Consensus, Ch. VI 725
Adoption of the report of the
Conference, Ch. VIII 727
Closure of the Conference, Ch. IX . . . 727
Follow-up report, UNGA
Report 58/494. 747
Opening Statements, Annex II 729
    Annan. 731
    Koehler 737
    Moore 740
    Quesada. 729
    Seung-soo 732
    Wolfensohn 734
Organization, Ch. II. 676
Report of high-level officials, Ch. III . . 684
Report of the Credentials
Committee, Ch. VII 725
Report of the ministerial segment,
Ch. IV 685
Report of the summit segment, Ch. V . 709
Resolutions, Ch. I 657

Page

Monterrey Follow-up Report (UNGA Report 58/494)
Introduction, Sec. I 747
Consideration of proposals, Sec. II . . . 749
Recommendation of the Second
Committee, Sec. III 753

Mountain Ecosystems
Agenda 21, Sec. II, Ch. 13 219

Ocean Resources
Agenda 21, Sec. II, Ch. 17 295
UNGA Res. 57/142 903
UNGA Res. 57/143 911
UNGA Res. 57/261 891
UNGA Res. 58/14 919

Poverty
Agenda 21, Sec. I, Ch. 3 67
Millennium Declaration, Sec. III 576
Millennium Report, Sec. III 595
Monterrey Consensus and Report . . . 657
UNGA Report 58/494 (Monterrey
Follow-Up) 747
WSSD Implementation Plan, Sec. II . . 766

Radioactive Waste Management
Agenda 21, Sec. II, Ch. 22 439

Small Island Developing States
UNGA Res. 58/213 897
WSSD Implementation Plan, Sec. VII . 803

Solid Waste Problems
Agenda 21, Sec. II, Ch. 21 419

Sustainable Agriculture and Rural Development
Agenda 21, Sec. II, Ch. 14 229

Sustainable Development
See also World Summit on Sustainable
Development Implementation Plan

  Building National Capacity
  Agenda 21, Sec. IV, Ch. 37 535

Page

Developing Countries
Agenda 21, Sec. I, Ch. 2 51
Monterrey Consensus and
Report 657-758

Global Action for Women
Agenda 21, Sec. III, Ch. 24 (Note:
Ch. 23 consists of a preamble to
Sec. III which emphasizes the
importance of the involvement
of all social groups in achieving
sustainable development.) 445

Johannesburg Declaration on Sustainable Development
See entries under Johannesburg
Declaration

Policy-Making
Agenda 21, Sec. I, Ch. 8 139
UNGA Res. 58/218 855

Social Partners
Agenda 21, Sec. III, Ch. 25-32 . . 451-491

Science
Agenda 21, Sec. IV, Ch. 35 509

Strengthening Institutions
Agenda 21, Sec. IV, Ch. 38 543

World Summit on Sustainable Development (WSSD) Implementation Plan
Africa, Sec. VIII 806
Consumption and production
patterns, Sec. III 771
Globalization aspects, Sec. V 799
Health aspects, Sec. VI 800
Implementation, Sec. X 814
Institutional framework, Sec. XI . . . 829
Poverty eradication, Sec. II 766
Protection of natural resource
base, Sec. IV 779
Regional initiatives, Sec. IX 811
Small island developing states,
Sec. VII 803

Page

Sustainable Human Settlements
Agenda 21, Sec. I, Ch. 7 113
UNGA Res. 58/226. 875
UNGA Report 58/491 881

Toxic Chemicals, Safe Use of
Agenda 21, Sec. II, Ch. 19 379

United Nations
Challenges for the 21st century,
Millennium Report, Sec. I 583
Future goals, Millennium Report,
Sec. VI 642
Strengthening of, Millennium
Declaration, Sec. VIII 581

UN General Assembly Reports
54/2000 (Millennium Rept) 583
58/491. 881
58/494 (Monterrey Follow-Up) 747
A/CONF. 198/11 (Monterrey
Consensus) 657
A/CONF. 199/L-6 Rev. 2
(Johannesburg Declaration &
Implementation Plan) 759

UN General Assembly Resolutions
47/190. 841
47/191. 845
47/194. 843
55/2 (Millennium Declaration) 573
57/142. 903

Page

57/143. 911
57/261. 891
58/14. 919
58/212. 867
58/213. 897
58/218. 855
58/219. 861
58/226. 875
58/242. 871
58/243. 863

Water
Agenda 21, Sec. II, Ch. 18 335
Introduction 3
Millennium Declaration, Sec. IV 578
UNGA Res. 58/226. 875
World Summit on Sustainable
Development (WSSD)
Implementation Plan,
Secs. II, IV, VI-IX. 766, 779, 800-814

**We the Peoples: the Role of the United
Nations in the Twenty-first Century**
See entries under Millennium Report

**World Summit on Sustainable
Development (WSSD) Implementation
Plan**
See entries under Sustainable
Development